An Index
to Book Reviews
in the Humanities

Volume 26
1985

Phillip Thomson
Williamston, Michigan

This volume of the Index contains data collected up to 31 December 1985.

This is an index to book reviews in humanities periodicals. Beginning with volume 12 of this Index (dated 1971), the former policy of selectively indexing reviews of books in certain subject categories only was dropped on favor of a policy of indexing all reviews in the periodicals indexed, with the one exception of children's books — the reviews of which will not be indexed.

The form of the entries used is as follows:

Author. Title.
Reviewer. Identifying Legend.

The author's name used is the name that appears on the title-page of the book being reviewed, as well as we are able to determine, even though this name is known to be a pseudonym. The title only is shown; subtitles are included only where they are necessary to identify a book in a series. The identifying legend consists of the periodical, each of which has a code number, and the date and page number of the periodical where the review is to be found. PMLA abbreviations are also shown (when a periodical has such an abbreviation, but such abbreviations are limited to four letters) immediately following the code number of the periodical. To learn the name of the periodical in which the review appears, it is necessary to refer the code number to the numerically-arranged list of periodicals beginning on page iii. This list also shows the volume and number of the periodical issues indexed in this volume.

Reviews are indexed as they appear and no attempt is made to hold the title until all the reviews are published. For this reason it is necessary to refer to previous and subsequent volumes of this Index to be sure that the complete roster of reviews of any title is seen. As an aid to the user, an asterisk (*) has been added immediately following any title that was also indexed in Volume 25 (1984) of this Index.

Authors with hyphenated surnames are indexed under the name before the hyphen, and the name following the hyphen is not cross-indexed. Authors with more than one surname, but where the names are not hyphenated, are indexed under the first of the names and the last name is cross-indexed. When alphabetizing surnames containing umlauts, the umlauts are ignored. Editors are always shown in the author-title entry, and they are cross-indexed (except where the editor's surname is the same as that of the author). Translators are shown only when they are necessary to identify the book being reviewed (as in the classics), and they are not cross-indexed unless the book being reviewed has no author or editor. Certain reference works and anonymous works that are known primarily by their title are indexed under that title and their editors are cross-indexed.

A list of abbreviations used is shown on page ii.

* * * * * *

Mr. Victor G. Wiebe, Reference Librarian at the University of Saskatchewan Library, has written to point out that the classification number of this Index (like most other books) is now commonly typed on a paper label which is then affixed to the spine, obscuring either the title or the date. In this volume we have moved the title up a little, reduced its size, and moved the date down a little, clearing as much space as possible given our unwieldy title.

We have not seen the result as this is written, but hope it will help. Our thanks to Mr. Wiebe.

ABBREVIATIONS

```
Anon.........Anonymous
Apr..........April
Aug..........August
Bk...........Book
Comp(s)......Compiler(s)
Cont.........Continued
Dec..........December
Ed(s)........Editor(s) [or] Edition(s)
Fasc.........Fascicule
Feb..........February
Jan..........January
Jul..........July
Jun..........June
Mar..........March
No...........Number
Nov..........November
Oct..........October
Prev.........Previous volume of this Index
Pt...........Part
Rev..........Revised
Sep..........September
Ser..........Series
Supp.........Supplement
Trans........Translator(s)
Vol..........Volume
* (asterisk)....This title was also shown
                in the volume of this Index
                immediately preceding this
                one
```

The periodicals in which the reviews appear are identified in this Index by a number. To supplement this number, and to promote ready identification, PMLA abbreviations are also given following this number. Every attempt will be made to index those issues shown here as "missing" in a later volume of this Index.

The following is a list of the periodicals indexed in volume 26:

2(AfrA) - African Arts. Los Angeles.
    Nov83 thru Aug84 (vol 17 complete)
9(AlaR) - Alabama Review. University.
    Jan84 thru Oct84 (vol 37 complete)
16 - American Art Journal. New York.
    Winter84 thru Autumn84 (vol 16 complete)
18 - American Film. Washington.
    Oct84 thru Sep85 (vol 10 complete)
24 - American Journal of Philology. Baltimore.
    Spring84 thru Winter84 (vol 105 complete)
26(ALR) - American Literary Realism, 1870-1910. Arlington.
    Spring84 and Autumn84 (vol 17 complete)
27(AL) - American Literature. Durham.
    Mar84 thru Dec84 (vol 56 complete)
29(APR) - The American Poetry Review. Philadelphia.
    Jan-Feb85 thru Nov-Dec85 (vol 14 complete)
30 - American Poetry. Jefferson.
    Fall83 thru Spring85 (vols 1 and 2 complete)
31(ASch) - American Scholar. Washington.
    Winter83/84 thru Autumn84 (vol 53 complete)
35(AS) - American Speech. University.
    Spring84 thru Winter84 (vol 59 complete)
37 - The Américas. Washington.
    Jan-Feb84 thru Nov-Dec84 (vol 36 complete)
38 - Anglia. Tübingen.
    Band 102 complete
39 - Apollo. London.
    Jan84 thru Dec84 (vols 119 and 120 complete)
40 - Analytical and Enumerative Bibliography. De Kalb.
    Vol 8 No 1
42(AR) - Antioch Review. Yellow Springs.
    Winter84 thru Fall84 (vol 42 complete)
43 - Architectura. München.
    Band 14 complete
44 - Architectural History. London.
    Vol 27 [no reviews indexed]
45 - Architectural Record. New York.
    Jan84 thru Mar84 and May84 thru Dec84 (vol 172 no 1-3 and 6-14)
    [Apr84 and Mid-May84 issues missing]
46 - Architectural Review. London.
    Jan84 thru Dec84 (vols 175 and 176 complete)
48 - Archivo Español de Arte. Madrid.
    Jan-Mar83 thru Oct-Dec84 (vols 56 and 57 complete)

49 - Ariel. Calgary.
    Jan84 thru Oct84 (vol 15 complete)
50(ArQ) - Arizona Quarterly. Tucson.
    Spring84 thru Winter84 (vol 40 complete)
52 - Arcadia. Berlin.
    Band 19 complete
53(AGP) - Archiv für Geschichte der Philosophie. Berlin.
    Band 66 complete
54 - Art Bulletin. New York.
    Mar84 thru Dec84 (vol 66 complete)
55 - Art News. New York.
    Jan84 thru Dec84 (vol 83 complete)
57 - Artibus Asiae. Ascona.
    Vol 45 complete
59 - Art History. London.
    Mar84 thru Dec84 (vol 7 complete)
60 - Arts of Asia. Hong Kong.
    Jan-Feb84 thru Nov-Dec84 (vol 14 complete)
61 - Atlantic Monthly. Boston.
    Jan85 thru Dec85 (vols 255 and 256 complete)
62 - Artforum. New York.
    Sep84 thru Summer85 (vol 23 complete)
63 - Australasian Journal of Philosophy. Bundoora.
    Mar84 thru Dec84 (vol 62 complete)
64(Arv) - ARV: Scandinavian Yearbook of Folklore. Uppsala.
    Vol 38
67 - AUMLA [Journal of the Australasian Universities Language and Literature Assn.]. Hobart.
    May84 and Nov84 (no 61 and 62)
70 - American Notes and Queries. Owingsville.
    Sep-Oct83 thru May-Jun84 (vol 22 complete)
71(ALS) - Australian Literary Studies. St. Lucia.
    May84 and Oct84 (vol 11 no 3 and 4)
72 - Archiv für das Studium der neueren Sprachen und Literaturen. Berlin.
    Band 221 complete
73 - Art Magazine. Toronto.
    Winter83 (vol 15 no 66) [no reviews indexed]
77 - Biography. Honolulu.
    Winter84 thru Fall84 (vol 7 complete)
78(BC) - Book Collector. London.
    Spring84 thru Winter84 (vol 33 complete)
81 - Boundary 2. Binghamton.
    Winter82 thru Winter84 (vol 10 no 2 and 3, vol 11 complete, vol 12 no 1 and 2)
83 - The British Journal for Eighteenth-Century Studies. Oxford.
    Spring84 and Autumn84 (vol 7 complete)
84 - The British Journal for the Philosophy of Science. Aberdeen.
    Mar84 thru Dec84 (vol 35 complete)
85(SBHC) - Studies in Browning and His Circle. Waco.
    Spring-Fall84 (vol 12 complete)
86(BHS) - Bulletin of Hispanic Studies. Liverpool.
    Jan84 thru Oct84 (vol 61 complete)

257(IRAL) - IRAL: International Review of
Applied Linguistics in Language Teaching. Heidelberg.
Feb84 thru Nov84 (vol 22 complete)
258 - International Philosophical Quarterly. New York and Namur.
Mar84 thru Dec84 (vol 24 complete)
259(IIJ) - Indo-Iranian Journal. Dordrecht.
Jan84 thru Oct84 (vol 27 complete)
260(IF) - Indogermanische Forschungen.
Berlin.
Band 89
261 - Indian Linguistics. Pune.
Mar/Jun82 thru Mar/Dec83 (vols 43
and 44 complete)
262 - Inquiry. Oslo.
Mar84 thru Dec84 (vol 27 complete)
263(RIB) - Revista Interamericana de Bib-
liografía/Inter-American Review of
Bibliography. Washington.
Vol 34 complete
268(IFR) - The International Fiction Review. Fredericton.
Winter85 and Summer85 (vol 12 complete)
269(IJAL) - International Journal of American Linguistics. Chicago.
Jan84 thru Oct84 (vol 50 complete)
271 - The Iowa Review. Iowa City.
Winter84 thru Fall84 (vol 14 complete)
272(IUR) - Irish University Review. Dublin.
Spring84 and Autumn84 (vol 14 complete)
275(IQ) - Italian Quarterly. New Brunswick.
Winter84 and Spring84 (vol 25
no 95 and 96)
276 - Italica. New York.
Spring84 thru Winter84 (vol 61 complete)
278(IS) - Italian Studies. Hull.
Vol 39
283 - Jabberwocky - The Journal of the
Lewis Carroll Society. Burton-on-
Trent.
Summer83 and Autumn83 (vol 12 no
3 and 4) [no reviews indexed]
284 - The Henry James Review. Baton Rouge.
Spring84 and Fall84 (vol 5 no 3,
vol 6 no 1)
285(JapQ) - Japan Quarterly. Tokyo.
Jan-Mar84 thru Oct-Dec84 (vol 31
complete)
287 - Jewish Frontier. New York.
Jan84 thru Nov-Dec84 (vol 51 complete)
289 - The Journal of Aesthetic Education.
Urbana.
Spring84 thru Winter84 (vol 18 complete)
290(JAAC) - Journal of Aesthetics and Art
Criticism. Greenvale.
Fall84 thru Summer85 (vol 43 complete)
292(JAF) - Journal of American Folklore.
Washington.
Jan/Mar84 thru Oct/Dec84 (vol 97
complete)
293(JASt) - Journal of Asian Studies. Ann
Arbor.
Nov83 thru Aug84 (vol 43 complete)

294 - Journal of Arabic Literature. Leiden.
Vol 15
295(JML) - Journal of Modern Literature.
Philadelphia.
Mar84 thru Nov84 (vol 11 complete)
297(JL) - Journal of Linguistics. Cambridge.
Mar84 and Sep84 (vol 20 complete)
298 - Journal of Canadian Studies/Revue
d'études canadiennes. Peterborough.
Spring84 thru Winter84/85 (vol 19
complete)
299 - Journal of Beckett Studies. London.
Autumn82 (no 8) and No 9
300 - Journal of English Linguistics. Bellingham.
Vol 17
301(JEGP) - Journal of English and Germanic Philology. Champaign.
Jan84 thru Oct84 (vol 83 complete)
302 - Journal of Oriental Studies. Hong
Kong.
Vol 20 complete [entries wholly
in Chinese are not indexed]
303(JoHS) - Journal of Hellenic Studies.
London.
Vol 104
304(JHP) - Journal of Hispanic Philology.
Tallahassee.
Winter84 thru Fall84 (vol 8 no 2
and 3, vol 9 no 1)
305(JIL) - The Journal of Irish Literature.
Newark.
Jan-May84 and Sep84 (vol 13 complete)
307 - Journal of Literary Semantics.
Heidelberg.
Apr84 thru Nov84 (vol 13 complete)
308 - Journal of Music Theory. New Haven.
Spring84 and Fall84 (vol 28 complete)
309 - Journal of Musicological Research.
London.
Vol 5 complete
311(JP) - Journal of Philosophy. New York.
Jan84 thru Dec84 (vol 81 complete)
313 - Journal of Roman Studies. London.
Vol 74
314 - Journal of South Asian Literature.
East Lansing.
Winter-Spring84 and Summer-Fall84
(vol 19 complete)
316 - Journal of Symbolic Logic. Pasadena.
Mar84 thru Dec84 (vol 49 complete)
317 - Journal of the American Musicological Society. Philadelphia.
Spring84 thru Fall84 (vol 37 complete)
318(JAOS) - Journal of the American Oriental Society. New Haven.
Jan-Mar83 thru Oct-Dec83 (vol 103
complete)
319 - Journal of the History of Philosophy.
San Diego.
Jan85 thru Oct85 (vol 23 complete)
320(CJL) - Canadian Journal of Linguistics.
Ottawa.
Spring84 and Fall84 (vol 29 complete)
321 - The Journal of Value Inquiry. The
Hague.
Vol 18 complete

322(JHI) - Journal of the History of Ideas.
Philadelphia.
Jan-Mar84 thru Oct-Dec84 (vol 45
complete)
323 - The Journal of the British Society
for Phenomenology. Manchester.
Jan84 thru Oct84 (vol 15 complete)
324 - Journal of the Royal Society of Arts.
London.
Dec84 thru Nov85 (vol 133 complete)
326 - Journal of the William Morris Society. London.
Summer84 and Winter84/85 (vol 6
complete)
329(JJQ) - James Joyce Quarterly. Tulsa.
Fall84 thru Summer85 (vol 22 complete)
339(KSMB) - The Keats-Shelley Memorial
Assn. Bulletin. Heslington.
No 35
340(KSJ) - Keats-Shelley Journal. New York.
Vol 33
341 - Konsthistorisk Tidskrift. Stockholm.
Vol 53 complete
342 - Kant-Studien. Berlin.
Band 75 complete
343 - Komparatistische Hefte. Bayreuth.
Heft 9/10
344 - The Kenyon Review. Gambier.
Winter85 thru Fall85 (vol 7 complete)
345(KRQ) - Kentucky Romance Quarterly.
Lexington.
Vol 31 complete
349 - Language and Style. Flushing.
Winter84 thru Fall84 (vol 17 complete) [no reviews indexed]
350 - Language. Baltimore.
Mar85 thru Dec85 (vol 61 complete)
351(LL) - Language Learning. Ann Arbor.
Mar84 thru Dec84 (vol 34 complete)
352(LATR) - Latin American Theatre Review.
Lawrence.
Fall84 and Spring85 (vol 18 complete)
353 - Linguistics. Amsterdam.
Vols 21 and 22 complete
354 - The Library. London.
Mar84 thru Dec84 (vol 6 complete)
355(LSoc) - Language in Society. New York.
Mar84 thru Dec84 (vol 13 complete)
356(LR) - Les Lettres Romanes. Korbeek-lo.
Feb/May84 thru Nov84 (vol 38 complete)
357 - Legacy. Amherst.
Spring84 thru Fall85 (vols 1 and 2
complete)
361 - Lingua. Amsterdam.
Jan/Feb84 thru Dec84 (vols 62-64
complete)
362 - The Listener. London.
3Jan85 thru 19/26Dec85 (vols 113
and 114 complete)
363(LitR) - The Literary Review. Madison.
Fall84 thru Summer85 (vol 28 complete)
364 - London Magazine. London.
Apr/May84 thru Mar85 (vol 24 complete)
365 - Literary Research Newsletter. Brock-
port.
Winter84 thru Fall84 (vol 9 complete)

366 - Literature and History. London.
Spring84 and Autumn84 (vol 10 complete)
376 - Malahat Review. Victoria.
Feb84 thru Oct84 (no 67-69)
377 - Manuscripta. St. Louis.
Mar84 (vol 28 no 1)
379(MedR) - Medioevo romanzo. Bologna.
Apr84 thru Dec84 (vol 9 complete)
380 - Master Drawings. New York.
Spring84 thru Autumn84 (vol 22 no
1-3)
381 - Meanjin Quarterly. Parkville.
Mar84 thru Dec84 (vol 43 complete)
382(MAE) - Medium Aevum. Oxford.
1984/1 and 1984/2 (vol 53 complete)
384 - Merkur. Stuttgart.
Jan84 thru Dec84 (Band 38 complete)
385(MQR) - Michigan Quarterly Review. Ann
Arbor.
Winter85 thru Fall85 (vol 24 complete)
389(MQ) - The Midwest Quarterly. Pitts-
burg.
Autumn84 thru Summer85 (vol 26 complete)
390 - Midstream. New York.
Jan84 thru Dec84 (vol 30 complete)
391 - Milton Quarterly. Athens.
Mar84 thru Dec84 (vol 18 complete)
392 - The Mississippi Quarterly. Mississippi State.
Winter83/84 thru Fall84 (vol 37
complete)
393(Mind) - Mind. Oxford.
Jan84 thru Oct84 (vol 93 complete)
394 - Mnemosyne. Leiden.
Vol 37 complete
395(MFS) - Modern Fiction Studies. West
Lafayette.
Spring84 thru Winter84 (vol 30
complete)
396(ModA) - Modern Age. Bryn Mawr.
Winter84 thru Fall84 (vol 28 complete)
397(MD) - Modern Drama. Downsview.
Mar84 thru Dec84 (vol 27 complete)
399(MLJ) - Modern Language Journal. Madison.
Spring84 thru Winter84 (vol 68
complete)
400(MLN) - MLN (Modern Language Notes).
Baltimore.
Jan84 thru Dec84 (vol 99 complete)
401(MLQ) - Modern Language Quarterly.
Seattle.
Sep83 thru Mar84 (vol 44 no 3 and
4, vol 45 no 1)
402(MLR) - Modern Language Review. London.
Jan84 thru Oct84 (vol 79 complete)
403(MLS) - Modern Language Studies. New
York.
Winter84 thru Fall84 (vol 14 complete)
404 - Modern Haiku. Madison.
Winter-Spring84 thru Autumn84 (vol
15 complete)
405(MP) - Modern Philology. Chicago.
Aug84 thru May85 (vol 82 complete)
406 - Monatshefte. Madison.
Spring84 thru Winter84 (vol 76
complete)

407(MN) - Monumenta Nipponica. Tokyo.
Spring84 thru Winter84 (vol 39 complete)

410(M&L) - Music and Letters. London.
Jan84 thru Oct84 (vol 65 complete)

414(MusQ) - Musical Quarterly. New York.
Winter84 thru Fall84 (vol 70 complete)

415 - Musical Times. London.
Jan84 thru Dec84 (vol 125 complete)

418(MR) - Massachusetts Review. Amherst.
Spring84 thru Winter84 (vol 25 complete)

424 - Names. New York.
Mar84 thru Dec84 (vol 32 complete)

432(NEQ) - New England Quarterly. Boston.
Mar84 thru Dec84 (vol 57 complete)

435 - New Orleans Review. New Orleans.
Spring84 thru Fall/Winter84 (vol 11 complete)

436(NewL) - New Letters. Kansas City.
Fall84 thru Summer85 (vol 51 complete)

439(NM) - Neuphilologische Mitteilungen. Helsinki.
1984/1 thru 1984/4 (vol 85 complete)

440 - New York Folklore. Saranac Lake.
Winter-Spring84 and Summer-Fall84 (vol 10 complete)

441 - New York Times Book Review. New York.
6Jan85 thru 29Dec85 (vol 90 complete)

442(NY) - New Yorker. New York.
7Jan85 thru 30Dec85 (vol 60 no 47-53, vol 61 no 1-45) (vol 61 begins with 25Feb85 issue)

445(NCF) - Nineteenth-Century Fiction. Berkeley.
Jun84 thru Mar85 (vol 39 complete)

446(NCFS) - Nineteenth-Century French Studies. Fredonia.
Summer-Fall84 thru Summer85 (vol 12 no 4/vol 13 no 1 thru vol 13 no 4)

447(N&Q) - Notes and Queries. London.
Feb83 thru Dec83 (vol 30 complete)

448 - Northwest Review. Eugene.
Vol 22 complete

449 - Noûs. Bloomington.
Mar84 thru Nov84 (vol 18 complete)

450(NRF) - La Nouvelle Revue Française. Paris.
Jan84 thru Dec84 (vols 63 and 64 complete)

451 - 19th Century Music. Berkeley.
Summer84 thru Spring85 (vol 8 complete)

452(NJL) - Nordic Journal of Linguistics. Oslo.
Vol 7 complete

453(NYRB) - The New York Review of Books.
17Jan85 thru 19Dec85 (vol 31 no 21/22, vol 32 no 1-20)

454 - Novel. Providence.
Fall84 thru Spring85 (vol 18 complete)

457(NRFH) - Nueva Revista de Filología Hispánica. Mexico City.
Tomo 32 núm 1

459 - Obsidian. Detroit.
Vol 8 complete

460(OhR) - The Ohio Review. Athens.
No 33 thru no 35

461 - The Ontario Review. Princeton.
Spring-Summer84 and Fall-Winter 84/85 (no 20 and 21) [no reviews indexed]

462(OL) - Orbis Litterarum. Copenhagen.
Vol 39 complete

463 - Oriental Art. Richmond.
Spring84 thru Winter84/85 (vol 30 complete)

464 - Orbis. Louvain.
Vol 30 fasc 1/2

468 - Paideuma. Orono.
Spring84 (vol 13 no 1)

469 - Parabola. New York.
Vol 10 complete

470 - Papers of the Bibliographical Society of Canada/Cahiers de la Société bibliographique du Canada. Toronto.
Vol 22

471 - Pantheon. München.
Jan/Feb/Mar84 thru Oct/Nov/Dec84 (vol 42 complete)

472 - Parnassus: Poetry in Review. New York.
Fall/Winter84 (vol 12 no 1)

473(PR) - Partisan Review. Boston.
1/1984 thru 4/1984 and 1/1985 (vol 51 complete)

474(PIL) - Papers in Linguistics. Edmonton.
Vol 16 complete [no reviews indexed]

475 - Papers on French Seventeenth Century Literature. Seattle and Tübingen.
Vol 11 no 20 and 21

477(PLL) - Papers on Language and Literature. Edwardsville.
Winter84 thru Fall84 (vol 20 complete)

478 - Philosophy and Literature. Baltimore.
Apr84 and Oct84 (vol 8 complete)

479(PhQ) - Philosophical Quarterly. Oxford.
Jan84 thru Oct84 (vol 34 complete)

480(P&R) - Philosophy and Rhetoric. University Park.
Vol 17 complete

481(PQ) - Philological Quarterly. Iowa City.
Winter84 thru Fall84 (vol 63 complete)

482(PhR) - Philosophical Review. Ithaca.
Jan84 thru Oct84 (vol 93 complete)

483 - Philosophy. Cambridge.
Jan84 thru Oct84 (vol 59 complete)

484(PPR) - Philosophy and Phenomenological Research. Providence.
Sep84 thru Jun85 (vol 45 complete)

485(PE&W) - Philosophy East and West. Honolulu.
Jan84 thru Oct84 (vol 34 complete)

486 - Philosophy of Science. East Lansing.
Mar84 and Jun84 (vol 51 no 1 and 2)

487 - Phoenix. Toronto.
Spring84 thru Winter84 (vol 38 complete)

488 - Philosophy of the Social Sciences. Waterloo.
Mar84 thru Dec84 (vol 14 complete)

489(PJGG) - Philosophisches Jahrbuch. Freiburg.
  Band 91 complete
490 - Poetica. Amsterdam.
  Band 15 and 16 complete
491 - Poetry. Chicago.
  Apr84 thru Mar85 (vols 144 and 145 complete)
493 - Poetry Review. London.
  Jan84 thru Sep84 (vol 73 no 4, vol 74 no 1-3)
494 - Poetics Today. Jerusalem.
  Summer82 and Autumn82 (vol 3 no 3 and 4), Vol 4 no 1 and Vol 5 complete
495(PoeS) - Poe Studies. Pullman.
  Jun84 and Dec84 (vol 17 complete)
496 - Poet Lore. Washington.
  Spring84 thru Winter85 (vol 79 complete)
497(PolR) - Polish Review. New York.
  Vol 29 complete
500 - Post Script. Jacksonville.
  Fall84 thru Spring-Summer85 (vol 4 complete)
502(PrS) - Prairie Schooner. Lincoln.
  Spring84 thru Winter84 (vol 58 complete)
505 - Progressive Architecture. New York.
  Jan84 thru Dec84 (vol 65 complete)
506(PSt) - Prose Studies. London.
  May84 thru Dec84 (vol 7 complete)
507 - Print. New York.
  Jan/Feb84 thru Nov/Dec84 (vol 38 complete)
513 - Perspectives of New Music. Seattle.
  Fall-Winter83/Spring-Summer84 (vol 22 complete)
517(PBSA) - Papers of the Bibliographical Society of America. New York.
  Vol 78 complete
518 - Philosophical Books. Oxford.
  Jan84 thru Oct84 (vol 25 complete)
519(PhS) - Philosophical Studies. Dordrecht.
  Jan84 thru Nov84 (vols 45 and 46 complete)
520 - Phronesis. Assen.
  Vol 29 complete
526 - Quarry. Kingston.
  Winter84 thru Autumn84 (vol 33 complete)
529(QQ) - Queen's Quarterly. Kingston.
  Spring84 thru Winter84 (vol 91 complete)
533 - Raritan. New Brunswick.
  Summer84 thru Spring85 (vol 4 complete)
534(RALS) - Resources for American Literary Study. College Park.
  Spring82 and Autumn82 (vol 12 complete)
535(RHL) - Revue d'Histoire Littéraire de la France. Paris.
  Jan-Feb84 thru Nov-Dec84 (vol 84 complete)
536 - Review. Charlottesville.
  Vols 5 and 6
537 - Revue de Musicologie. Paris.
  Vol 70 no 1

538(RAL) - Research in African Literatures. Austin.
  Spring84 thru Winter84 (vol 15 complete)
539 - Renaissance and Reformation/Renaissance et Réforme. Mississauga.
  Nov84 thru Aug85 (vol 8 no 4, vol 9 no 1-3)
540(RIPh) - Revue Internationale de Philosophie. Wetteren.
  Vol 38 complete
541(RES) - Review of English Studies. London.
  Feb84 thru Nov84 (vol 35 complete)
542 - Revue Philosophique de la France et de l'Étranger. Paris.
  Jan-Mar84 thru Oct-Dec84 (vol 174 complete)
543 - Review of Metaphysics. Washington.
  Sep83 thru Jun84 (vol 37 complete)
545(RPh) - Romance Philology. Berkeley.
  Aug83 thru May84 (vol 37 complete)
546(RR) - Romanic Review. New York.
  Jan84 thru Nov84 (vol 75 complete)
547(RF) - Romanische Forschungen. Frankfurt am Main.
  Band 96 complete
549(RLC) - Revue de Littérature Comparée. Paris.
  Jan-Mar84 thru Oct-Dec84 (vol 58 complete)
550(RusR) - Russian Review. Stanford.
  Jan84 thru Oct84 (vol 43 complete)
551(RenQ) - Renaissance Quarterly. New York.
  Spring84 thru Winter84 (vol 37 complete)
552(REH) - Revista de estudios hispánicos. University.
  Jan84 thru Oct84 (vol 18 complete)
553(RLiR) - Revue de Linguistique Romane. Strasbourg.
  Jan-Jun84 and Jul-Dec84 (vol 48 complete)
554 - Romania. Paris.
  Vol 104 complete
555 - Revue de Philologie. Paris.
  Vol 58 complete
556 - Russell. Hamilton.
  Summer84 and Winter84/85 (vol 4 complete)
558(RLJ) - Russian Language Journal. East Lansing.
  Winter-Spring84 (vol 38 no 129/130)
559 - Russian Linguistics. Dordrecht.
  Vol 8 complete
560 - Salmagundi. Saratoga Springs.
  Winter84 thru Fall84 (no 62-65)
561(SFS) - Science-Fiction Studies. Montréal.
  Mar84 thru Nov84 (vol 11 complete)
562(Scan) - Scandinavica. Norwich.
  May84 and Nov84 (vol 23 complete)
563(SS) - Scandinavian Studies. Lawrence.
  Winter84 thru Autumn84 (vol 56 complete)
564 - Seminar. Toronto.
  Feb84 thru Nov84 (vol 20 complete)
565 - Stand Magazine. Newcastle upon Tyne.
  Winter83/84 thru Autumn84 (vol 25 complete)

566 - The Scriblerian. Philadelphia.
  Autumn84 and Spring85 (vol 17 complete)
567 - Semiotica. Amsterdam.
  Vols 46-52 complete
568(SCN) - Seventeenth-Century News. University Park.
  Spring-Summer84 thru Winter84 (vol 42 complete)
569(SR) - Sewanee Review. Sewanee.
  Winter84 thru Fall84 (vol 92 complete)
570(SQ) - Shakespeare Quarterly. Washington.
  Spring84 thru Winter84 (vol 35 complete)
571(ScLJ) - Scottish Literary Journal. Aberdeen.
  May84 thru Winter84 (vol 11 complete and supp 20 and 21)
572 - Shaw: The Annual of Bernard Shaw Studies. University Park.
  Vol 5
573(SSF) - Studies in Short Fiction. Newberry.
  Winter84 thru Fall84 (vol 21 complete)
574(SEEJ) - Slavic and East European Journal. Tucson.
  Spring84 thru Winter84 (vol 28 complete)
575(SEER) - Slavonic and East European Review. London.
  Jan84 thru Oct84 (vol 62 complete)
576 - Journal of the Society of Architectural Historians. Philadelphia.
  Mar84 thru Dec84 (vol 43 complete)
577(SHR) - Southern Humanities Review. Auburn.
  Winter84 thru Fall84 (vol 18 complete)
578 - Southern Literary Journal. Chapel Hill.
  Spring85 and Fall85 (vol 17 no 2, vol 18 no 1)
579(SAQ) - South Atlantic Quarterly. Durham.
  Winter84 thru Autumn84 (vol 83 complete)
580(SCR) - The South Carolina Review. Clemson.
  Fall84 and Spring85 (vol 17 complete)
581 - Southerly. Marrickville.
  Mar84 thru Dec84 (vol 44 complete)
583 - Southern Speech Communication Journal. Tampa.
  Fall84 thru Summer85 (vol 50 complete)
584(SWR) - Southwest Review. Dallas.
  Winter84 thru Autumn84 (vol 69 complete)
585(SoQ) - The Southern Quarterly. Hattiesburg.
  Fall83 thru Summer85 (vols 22 and 23 complete)
587(SAF) - Studies in American Fiction. Boston.
  Spring84 and Autumn84 (vol 12 complete)
588(SSL) - Studies in Scottish Literature. Columbia.
  Vol 19

589 - Speculum. Cambridge.
  Jan84 thru Oct84 (vol 59 complete)
590 - Studies in the Humanities. Indiana.
  Dec84 and Jun85 (vol 11 no 2, vol 12 no 1)
591(SIR) - Studies in Romanticism. Boston.
  Spring84 thru Winter84 (vol 23 complete)
592 - Studio International. London.
  Vol 196 no 1004, vol 197 no 1005-1007
593 - Symposium. Washington.
  Spring84 thru Winter84/85 (vol 38 complete)
594 - Studies in the Novel. Denton.
  Spring84 thru Winter84 (vol 16 complete)
595(ScS) - Scottish Studies. Edinburgh.
  Vol 27
596(SL) - Studia Linguistica. Lund.
  Vol 38 complete
597(SN) - Studia Neophilologica. Stockholm.
  Vol 56 complete
598(SoR) - The Southern Review. Baton Rouge.
  Winter85 thru Autumn85 (vol 21 complete)
599 - Style. De Kalb.
  Winter84 thru Fall84 (vol 18 complete)
600 - Simiolus. Utrecht.
  Vol 14 complete
601(SuF) - Sinn und Form. Berlin.
  Jan-Feb84 thru Nov-Dec84 (Band 36 complete)
602 - Sprachkunst. Vienna.
  Band 15 complete
603 - Studies in Language. Amsterdam.
  Vol 8 complete
604 - Spenser Newsletter. Albany.
  Winter84 thru Fall84 (vol 15 complete)
605(SC) - Stendhal Club. Grenoble.
  15Oct84 thru 15Jul85 (vol 27 complete)
606 - Synthese. Dordrecht.
  Jan84 thru Dec84 (vols 58-61 complete)
607 - Tempo. London.
  Mar84 thru Dec84 (no 148-151)
608 - TESOL Quarterly. Washington.
  Mar85 thru Dec85 (vol 19 complete)
609 - Theater. New Haven.
  Fall/Winter84 thru Summer/Fall85 (vol 16 complete)
610 - Theatre Research International. Oxford.
  Spring84 thru Autumn84 (vol 9 complete)
611(TN) - Theatre Notebook. London.
  Vol 38 complete
612(ThS) - Theatre Survey. Albany.
  May84 and Nov84 (vol 25 complete)
613 - Thought. Bronx.
  Mar84 thru Dec84 (vol 59 complete)
614 - The Textile Booklist. Arcata.
  Winter85 thru Summer85 (vol 10 no 1-3)
615(TJ) - Theatre Journal. Baltimore.
  Mar82 and Dec82, Mar84 thru Dec84 (vol 34 no 1 and 4, vol 36 complete)

616 – Thalia. Ottawa.
   Spring/Summer84 and Fall/Winter84
   (vol 7 complete)
617(TLS) – Times Literary Supplement. London.
   4Jan85 thru 27Dec85 (no 4266-4317)
619 – Transactions of the Charles S.
   Peirce Society.
   Winter84 thru Fall84 (vol 20 complete)
627(UTQ) – University of Toronto Quarterly.
   Fall83 thru Summer84 (vol 53 complete) [in Summer issue, only the
   "Humanities" section is indexed]
628(UWR) – University of Windsor Review.
   Windsor.
   Fall-Winter84 and Spring-Summer85
   (vol 18 complete)
636(VP) – Victorian Poetry. Morgantown.
   Spring84 thru Winter84 (vol 22 complete)
637(VS) – Victorian Studies. Bloomington.
   Autumn83 thru Summer84 (vol 27 complete)
639(VQR) – Virginia Quarterly Review.
   Charlottesville.
   Winter84 thru Autumn84 (vol 60
   complete)
646 – Walt Whitman Quarterly Review. Iowa
   City.
   Summer84 thru Spring85 (vol 2 complete)
648(WCR) – West Coast Review. Burnaby.
   Jun84 thru Apr85 (vol 19 complete)
649(WAL) – Western American Literature.
   Logan.
   May84 thru Feb85 (vol 19 complete)
650(WF) – Western Folklore. Glendale.
   Jan84 thru Oct84 (vol 43 complete)
651(WHR) – Western Humanities Review.
   Salt Lake City.
   Spring84 thru Winter84 (vol 38
   complete)
654(WB) – Weimarer Beiträge. Berlin.
   1/1984 thru 12/1984 (vol 30 complete)
656(WMQ) – William and Mary Quarterly.
   Williamsburg.
   Jan84 thru Oct84 (vol 41 complete)
658 – Winterthur Portfolio. Chicago.
   Spring84 thru Winter84 (vol 19
   complete)
659(ConL) – Contemporary Literature.
   Madison.
   Spring85 thru Winter85 (vol 26 complete)
660(Word) – Word. Elmont.
   Apr84 thru Dec84 (vol 35 complete)
661(WC) – The Wordsworth Circle. Philadelphia.
   Winter84 thru Autumn84 (vol 15
   complete)
676(YR) – Yale Review. New Haven.
   Autumn84 thru Spring85 (vol 74 no
   1-3)
677(YES) – The Yearbook of English Studies.
   London.
   Vol 14
678(YCGL) – Yearbook of Comparative and
   General Literature. Bloomington.
   No 32 and no 33

679 – Zeitschrift für allgemeine Wissen-
   schaftstheorie. Wiesbaden.
   Band 15 complete
680(ZDP) – Zeitschrift für deutsche Philologie. Berlin.
   Band 103 complete
682(ZPSK) – Zeitschrift für Phonetik,
   Sprachwissenschaft und Kommunikations-
   forschung. Berlin.
   Band 37 complete
683 – Zeitschrift für Kunstgeschichte.
   München.
   Band 47 complete
684(ZDA) – Zeitschrift für deutsches
   Altertum und deutsche Literatur
   [Anzeiger section]. Wiesbaden.
   Band 113 complete
685(ZDL) – Zeitschrift für Dialektologie
   und Linguistik. Wiesbaden.
   1/1984 thru 3/1984 (Band 51 complete)
687 – Zeitschrift für Philosophische Forschung. Meisenheim/Glan.
   Jan-Mar84 thru Nov-Dec84 (Band 38
   complete)
688(ZSP) – Zeitschrift für slavische
   Philologie. Heidelberg.
   Band 44 Heft 1 and 2
700 – Shenandoah. Lexington.
   Vols 34 and 35 complete
701(SinN) – Sin Nombre. San Juan.
   Oct-Dec83 thru Jul-Sep84 (vol
   14 complete)
703 – Sulfur. Los Angeles.
   No 10 thru No 12 (vol 4 complete)
705 – The Wallace Stevens Journal. Pots-
   dam.
   Spring84 and Fall84 (vol 8 complete)
706 – Studia Leibnitiana. Wiesbaden.
   Band 16 complete
707 – Sight and Sound. London.
   Winter83/84 thru Autumn84 (vol 53
   complete)

   Each year we are unable (for one reason
or another) to index the reviews appearing
in all of the periodicals scanned. The
following is a list of the periodicals
whose reviews were not included in this
volume of the Index. Every attempt will
be made to index these reviews in the next
volume of the Index:

112 – Celtica. Dublin.
113 – Centrum. Minneapolis.
115 – The Centennial Review. East Lansing.
126(CCC) – College Composition and Communication. Urbana.
138 – Conjunctions. New York.
140(CH) – Crítica Hispánica. Miami.
180(ESA) – English Studies in Africa.
   Johannesburg.
239 – Hispanic Linguistics. Pittsburgh.
255(HAB) – Humanities Association Review/
   La Revue de l'Association des Human-
   ités. Kingston.
264(I&L) – Ideologies and Literature.
   Minneapolis/Valencia.

273(IC) – Islamic Culture. Hyderabad.
277(ITL) – ITL, a Review of Applied Linguistics. Leuven.
279 – International Journal of Slavic
   Linguistics and Poetics. Columbus.
296(JCF) – Journal of Canadian Fiction.
   Guelph.
360(LP) – Lingua Posnaniensis. Poznań.
367(L&P) – Literature and Psychology.
   Oyster Bay.
398(MPS) – Modern Poetry Studies. Buffalo.
412 – Music Review. Cambridge.
434 – New England Review and Bread Loaf
   Quarterly. Hanover.
438 – The New Scholasticism. Washington.
455 – The North American Review. Cedar
   Falls.
476 – Performing Arts Review. Washington.
492 – Poetics. Amsterdam.
498 – Popular Music and Society. Bowling
   Green.
503 – The Private Library. Pinner.
504 – Praxis. Los Angeles.
582(SFQ) – Southern Folklore Quarterly.
   Gainesville.
586(SoRA) – Southern Review. Adelaide.
618 – Trivia. North Amherst.
635(VPR) – Victorian Periodicals Review.
   Edwardsville.
675(YER) – Yeats Eliot Review. Edmonton.
702 – Shakespeare Studies. New York.
704(SFR) – Stanford French Review. Saratoga.

Aalders, G.J.D. Plutarch's Political Thought.
  O.D. Watkins, 303(JoHS):Vol 104-219
Aaron, D. - see Inman, A.C.
Aarsleff, H. From Locke to Saussure.*
  R. Mankin, 184(EIC):Apr84-164
  M. Sprinker, 125:Winter84-190
Abasqulijev, T. Ingilis atalar sözläri vä onlaryn azärbajǧanǧa, rusǧa qaršylyqlary.
  G.F. Meier, 682(ZPSK):Band37Heft4-525
Abbas, F. L'Indépendance confisquée 1962-1978.
  F. Ghilès, 617(TLS):19Apr85-428
Abbey, L. Destroyer and Preserver.*
  S. Hall, 577(SHR):Winter84-65
Abbot, J. Insects of Georgia.
  70:Jan-Feb84-90
Abbot, W.W. and others - see Washington, G.
Abbott, H.P. Diary Fiction.
  J. Bayley, 617(TLS):21Jun85-697
Abbott, J.L. John Hawkesworth.*
  P. Rogers, 83:Spring84-122
  W.A. Speck, 366:Autumn84-271
Abbott, S. Womenfolks.
  A.F. Scott, 579(SAQ):Autumn84-486
Abdeen, A. English-Arabic Dictionary of Accounting and Finance.
  J.R. Constantine, 399(MLJ):Spring84-68
Abdul-Hai, M. Tradition and English and American Influence in Arabic Romantic Poetry.
  R. Allen, 294:Vol 15-143
Abe, J. Saṅkhepatthajotanī Visuddhimaggacullaṭīka Sīla-dhutaṅga.
  J.W. de Jong, 259(IIJ):Jul84-219
Abeel, E. The Last Romance.
  D. Finkle, 441:26May85-10
Abegg-Mengold, C. Die Bezeichnungsgeschichte von Mais, Kartoffel und Ananas im Italienischen.*
  R. Kahane, 545(RPh):Nov83-245
Abegglen, J.C. and G. Stalk, Jr. Kaisha.
  N.D. Kristof, 441:20Oct85-51
Abel, A. Die Zwölftontechnik Weberns und Goethes Methodik der Farbenlehre.
  D. Jarman, 410(M&L):Oct84-366
Abel, E., ed. Writing and Sexual Difference.*
  P.M. Cohen, 403(MLS):Winter84-89
  T. Eagleton, 402(MLR):Oct84-879
  A. Vink, 204(FdL):Sep84-223
Abel, E., M. Hirsch and E. Langland, eds. The Voyage In.
  L. Goldensohn, 594:Fall84-339
  E.B. Jordan, 395(MFS):Summer84-429
Abel, R. French Cinema: The First Wave, 1915-1929.
  N. King, 617(TLS):15Mar85-290
  D. Polan, 500:Winter85-63
Abel, V.L.S. Prokrisis.
  D.M. Lewis, 123:Vol34No2-344
Abella, I. and H. Troper. None Is Too Many.
  G. Tulchinsky, 529(QQ):Winter84-1024
Abellán, J.L. Historia crítica del pensamiento español. (Vol 3)
  H. Sonneville, 356(LR):Aug84-247
Abellio, R. Visages immobiles.
  F. de Martinoir, 450(NRF):Feb84-96
Abercrombie, N. Class Structure and Knowledge.
  K. Dixon, 488:Jun84-263

Abernethy, F.E., ed. T for Texas.
  D.C. Grover, 649(WAL):Aug84-172
Aberth, O. Computable Analysis.
  C.W. Henson, 316:Sep84-988
Abidi, A.H.H. China, Iran, and the Persian Gulf.
  M. Gurtov, 293(JASt):Feb84-303
Abirached, R. - see de Laclos, P-A.C.
Aboulafia, M. The Self-Winding Circle.
  R.P. Horstmann, 53(AGP):Band66Heft3-333
  C. Shapiro, 543:Jun84-837
About, P-J. and M. Boy - see Pascal, B. and P. de Fermat
  P. Pellegrin, 542:Oct-Dec84-447
Abraham, C. On the Structure of Molière's "Comédies-Ballets."
  R.W. Tobin, 207(FR):May85-888
Abraham, C. Tristan L'Hermite.
  H.G. Hall, 208(FS):Apr84-198
Abraham, D. The Collapse of the Weimar Republic.
  D. Barnouw, 221(GQ):Winter84-119
  J. Joll, 453(NYRB):26Sep85-5
  A. Orde, 161(DUJ):Dec83-128
Abraham, G., ed. The Age of Beethoven.
  L. Botstein, 414(MusQ):Winter84-146
  J. Rushton, 410(M&L):Jan84-51
Abraham, P. and D. MacKey. Contact USA.
  J. Ross, 399(MLJ):Summer84-196
Abrahams, P. The View From Coyaba.
  J. Wilson, 441:26May85-14
  D. Wright, 617(TLS):22Mar85-326
Abrahams, R.D., ed. African Folktales.
  L. Haring, 440:Winter-Spring84-116
Abrahams, R.D., ed. Afro-American Folktales.
  P-L. Adams, 61:May85-104
  J. Berry, 441:25Aug85-16
  W. Lambrecht, 469:Vol 10No2-114
Abrahams, R.D. The Man-of-Words in the West Indies.
  J.C. Beck, 292(JAF):Oct-Dec84-472
Abrahams, W., ed. Prize Stories 1985: The O. Henry Awards.
  H. Benedict, 441:14Apr85-26
Abrahamsen, D. Confessions of Son of Sam.
  S. Roberts, 441:28Apr85-34
Abramov, F. Two Winters and Three Summers.*
  R. Elman, 441:3Feb85-22
  639(VQR):Autumn84-132
Abrams, M.H. The Correspondent Breeze.
  C. Baldick, 617(TLS):27Dec85-1484
Abrams, N. and M.D. Buckner, eds. Medical Ethics.
  R. Baker, 185:Jan85-370
Abse, D. Doctors and Patients.
  S. Soupel, 189(EA):Oct-Dec85-490
Abse, D. One-Legged on Ice.
  P. Breslin, 491:Dec84-166
Abt, S. Breakaway.
  S. Tesich, 441:28Jul85-9
Accad, E. Veil of Shame.
  S. Ghaly, 107(CRCL):Jun84-346
Aceña, P.M. and L. Prados de la Escosura - see under Martín Aceña, P. and L. Prados de la Escosura
Acevedo, R.L. La novela centroamericana.*
  J.E. Ciruti, 240(HR):Winter84-107

Achard, G. Pratique, rhétorique et idéologie politique dans les discours "optimates" de Cicéron.
E. Rawson, 122:Jan84-69
Achberger, K. Literatur als Libretto.
A. Fehn, 221(GQ):Spring84-339
Achebe, C. and C.L. Innes, eds. African Short Stories.
A. Appiah, 441:11Aug85-22
Achinstein, P. The Nature of Explanation.
J. Woodward, 185:Jan85-359
Ackerley, C. and L.J. Clipper. A Companion to "Under the Volcano."
M. Hofmann, 617(TLS):18Oct85-1159
Ackerman, D. On Extended Wings.
P.R. Ehrlich, 441:22Dec85-19
Ackermann, H.C. and J-R. Gisler, eds. Lexicon iconographicum mythologiae classicae. (Vol 1)
M. Robertson, 303(JoHS):Vol 104-266
Ackermann, P.K. - see Brecht, B.
Ackery, P.R. and R.I. Vane-Wright. Milkweed Butterflies.
M. Ridley, 617(TLS):23Aug85-935
Ackland, V. For Sylvia.
A. Duchêne, 617(TLS):25Jan85-94
P.N. Furbank, 362:21Feb85-25
J. Neville, 364:Feb85-109
E. Perényi, 453(NYRB):18Jul85-27
Ackley, C.S. Printmaking in the Age of Rembrandt.*
J.P. Filedt Kok, 600:Vol 14No1-45
Ackroyd, P. T.S. Eliot.*
J. Bayley, 364:Dec84/Jan85-130
M. Lebowitz, 344:Summer85-118
J. Updike, 442(NY):25Mar85-120
D. Von Drehle, 152(UDQ):Winter85-115
Ackroyd, P. Hawksmoor.
A. Hollinghurst, 617(TLS):27Sep85-1049
B. Maddox, 362:5Dec85-30
Ackroyd, P. The Last Testament of Oscar Wilde.*
M. Montaut, 272(IUR):Spring84-136
639(VQR):Spring84-55
Ackroyd, P., ed. PEN New Fiction 1.*
J. Mellors, 362:10Jan85-24
Acorn, M. Captain Neal MacDougal And The Naked Goddess.
A. Brooks, 102(CanL):Autumn84-115
Acuff, R. Roy Acuff's Nashville.
J.L. Tharpe, 585(SoQ):Spring84-145
de Acuña, H. Varias poesías. (L.F. Díaz Larios, ed)
D.G. Walters, 86(BHS):Oct84-524
Ådahl, K. A Khamsa of Nizami of 1439.
B.W. Robinson, 39:Jul84-32
Adair, G. Alice Through the Needle's Eye.
A. Bell, 617(TLS):4Jan85-18
J. Fuller, 441:5May85-42
442(NY):13May85-147
Adam, J.H. Longman Concise Dictionary of Business English.
J.H.C. Leach, 617(TLS):28Jun85-717
Adam, J-P. L'architecture militaire grecque.
R.A. Tomlinson, 303(JoHS):Vol 104-252
Adam, R. - see Livy
Adamec, P. Obrazovanie predloženij iz propozicij v sovremennom russkom jazyke.
M. Guiraud-Weber, 559:Vol18No3-559
"Adami: Peintures récentes."
T. Murray, 153:Fall84-100
Adamo, M.G. - see du Camp, M.

Adams, A. Examples.
T. Reese, 507:May/Jun84-112
Adams, A. Brother Fox and Other Relatives.* An Island Chapter.
A. Stevenson, 493:Jun84-66
Adams, A. Return Trips.
B. Lowry, 441:1Sep85-5
Adams, A., ed and trans. The Romance of "Yder."
B. Schmolke-Hasselmann, 547(RF): Band96Heft1/2-170
Adams, A. Superior Women.*
J. Mellors, 364:Feb85-102
Adams, A., with M.S. Alinder. Ansel Adams.
A. Grundberg, 441:8Dec85-22
442(NY):23Dec85-91
Adams, B. London Illustrated 1604-1851.*
A. Griffiths, 354:Sep84-297
J.M. Robinson, 39:Jun84-467
Adams, B.S. Traditional Bhutanese Textiles.
S.H. Safrani, 60:Jul-Aug84-126
Adams, C. American Lithographers 1900-1960.*
J.L., 90:Aug84-510
Adams, D. North Into Love.
D. Anderson, 236:Fall-Winter84-44
Adams, D. So Long, and Thanks for All the Fish.
B. Tritel, 441:10Feb85-25
Adams, D.W., with R.W. Lester - see Jefferson, T.
Adams, G. Falls Memories.
J. Lordson, 174(Éire):Spring84-156
Adams, G. Games of the Strong.
P. Lewis, 565:Spring84-64
Adams, H. Joyce Cary's Trilogies.*
M. Freehan, 223:Winter84-429
B. Murray, 395(MFS):Winter84-770
Y. Tosser, 189(EA):Jul-Sep85-345
295(JML):Nov84-416
Adams, H. The Letters of Henry Adams.* (J.C. Levenson and others, eds)
J. Clive, 31(ASch):Winter83/84-116
J. Jacobson, 481(PQ):Fall84-533
Adams, H. Philosophy of the Literary Symbolic.*
M. Bickman, 478:Apr84-143
M. Cusin, 189(EA):Jul-Sep85-296
M. Freehan, 223:Winter84-429
H. Kellner, 400(MLN):Dec84-1220
295(JML):Nov84-373
Adams, J. Good Intentions.
J. McCorkle, 441:30Jun85-20
Adams, J. Papers of John Adams. (Vols 5 and 6) (R.J. Taylor, G.J. Lint and C. Walker, eds)
P.C. Nagel, 432(NEQ):Jun84-264
Adams, J.D. and J.L. Sharpe 3d. A Leaf from the Letters of St. Jerome. (B. Gilbert, ed)
N. Barker, 78(BC):Summer84-239
Adams, J.N. The Latin Sexual Vocabulary.*
P. Flobert, 555:Vol58fasc1-127
A. Richlin, 24:Winter84-491
Adams, J.Q. Diary of John Quincy Adams.* (Vols 1 and 2) (D.G. Allen and others, eds)
R.A. Becker, 656(WMQ):Jan84-167
Adams, J.W. Decorative Folding Screens.
90:Jan84-50
Adams, M. Private Visions.
M.B. Joseph, 2(AfrA):Feb84-85

Adams, N. and C. Donahue, Jr., eds.
Select Cases from the Ecclesiastical
Courts of the Province of Canterbury,
c. 1200-1301.
M.M. Sheehan, 589:Jan84-106
Adams, P.G. Travel Literature and the
Evolution of the Novel.*
M. Blondel, 189(EA):Jul-Sep85-301
T.M. Curley, 566:Spring85-193
L.W. Lynch, 207(FR):Mar85-573
R.D. Spector, 173(ECS):Spring85-410
639(VQR):Summer84-86
Adams, R. Maia.
B. Tritel, 441:13Jan85-28
442(NY):11Feb85-126
Adams, R. Our Lives and Our Children.
G. Marcus, 62:Mar85-87
Adams, R. and others. Minor White.
C. Reid, 617(TLS):6Dec85-1385
Adams, S. R. Murray Schafer.*
G.A. Proctor, 627(UTQ):Summer84-513
Adams, T.R. The American Controversy.*
J.L. Bullion, 517(PBSA):Vol78No1-95
Adams, W.H. Jefferson's Monticello.*
D. Wiebenson, 576:Dec84-372
"Adam's Luxury and Eve's Cookery."
W. and C. Cowen, 639(VQR):Spring84-68
Adamson, D. Balzac: "Illusions perdues."
A. Finch, 208(FS):Jan84-73
Adamson, E., with J. Timlin. Art as Heal-
ing.
P. Cotes, 324:Apr85-370
Adamson, G. Le Procédé de Raymond Roussel.
L. Hill, 208(FS):Oct84-486
Adcock, F., ed. The Oxford Book of Con-
temporary New Zealand Poetry.*
P. Bland, 364:Apr/May84-99
R. Pybus, 565:Summer84-56
Adcock, F. Selected Poems.*
T. Eagleton, 565:Summer84-76
B. Ruddick, 148:Winter84-61
Adcock, F. The Virgin and The Nightingale.
B. Ruddick, 148:Winter84-61
Adcock, F. - see "Medieval Latin Poems"
Addams, C. Addams and Evil.
P.N. Furbank, 362:3Oct85-27
Addington, L.H. The Patterns of War since
the Eighteenth Century.
B. Bond, 617(TLS):19Jul85-804
Addiss, S., ed. Japanese Ghosts and
Demons.
P-L. Adams, 61:Sep85-116
Adel, K. Aufbruch und Tradition.
R.E. Lorbe, 221(GQ):Fall84-681
Adelman, A. and R. Reading, eds. Confron-
tation in the Caribbean Basin.
L. Schoultz, 263(RIB):Vol34No3/4-424
Adelson, L. and A. Tracht. Aymara Weav-
ings.*
A.L. Mayer, 614:Summer85-18
Adereth, M. The French Communist Party.
J.E.S. Hayward, 617(TLS):10May85-516
Aderman, R.M., H.L. Kleinfield and J.
Banks - see Irving, W.
Ades, D. Posters. (M. Friedman, ed)
S. Heller, 507:Nov/Dec84-138
Adkins, G. A Difficult Peace.
J. Saunders, 565:Spring84-55
Adler, B. and T. Chastain. Who Killed the
Robins Family?
639(VQR):Winter84-26
Adler, J. Face à la persécution.
M.R. Marrus, 617(TLS):24May85-586

Adler, J.S. War in Melville's Imagination.
H. Beaver, 402(MLR):Jul84-679
Adler, M.J. A Pragmatic Logic for Com-
mands.
M. Pool de Madrigal, 457(NRFH):Tomo32
núm1-232
Adler, M.J. Ten Philosophical Mistakes.
L. Hafrey, 441:28Apr85-25
Adler, R. Pitch Dark.*
S. Bray, 390:Aug/Sep84-59
W. Lesser, 249(HudR):Autumn84-476
Adler, W. Corpus Rubenianum Ludwig Burch-
ard.* (Pt 18, Vol 1)
J. Ferguson, 324:Dec84-68
Adomeit, H. Soviet Risk-Taking and Crisis
Behavior.
M. McCauley, 575(SEER):Apr84-311
Adorni, S. and K. Primorac. English Gram-
mar for Students of Italian.*
D. Marx-Scouras, 399(MLJ):Spring84-82
Adorno, R., ed. From Oral to Written
Expression.
L.A. Daniel, 238:Sep84-477
J. Higgins, 86(BHS):Oct84-518
Adorno, T. Aesthetic Theory.
D. Kuspit, 62:Dec84-72
Adorno, T. Minima Moralia.
D. Kuspit, 62:Dec84-71
Adrian, A.A. Dickens and the Parent-
Child Relationship.
R.J. Dunn, 155:Autumn84-165
R.J. Dunn, 594:Winter84-458
G.B. Tennyson, 445(NCF):Sep84-236
Adrian-Nilsson, G. den gudomliga geomet-
rien 1922.
Å. Fant, 341:Vol53No3-136
Adriani, G. Cézanne Watercolors.*
S.S., 376:Feb84-143
Adriani, G. Degas: Pastels, Oil Sketches,
Drawings.
J. House, 617(TLS):22Nov85-1316
Advani, R. E.M. Forster as Critic.
G. Cavaliero, 617(TLS):5Apr85-390
"Adventure Book II."
V.G. Stoddart, 37:Nov-Dec84-63
Aélion, R. Euripide héritier d'Eschyle.
(Vol 1)
M. Lloyd, 123:Vol34No1-18
Aélion, R. Euripide héritier d'Eschyle.
(Vol 2)
M. Lloyd, 123:Vol34No2-309
Aers, D., J. Cook and D. Punter. Roman-
ticism and Ideology.*
M. Roberts, 541(RES):Aug84-385
C. Siskin, 149(CLS):Summer84-228
Aeschliman, M.D. The Restitution of Man.
B. Murray, 395(MFS):Winter84-770
Aeschylus. Aeschylus I: The Oresteia.
(R. Lattimore, trans) Aeschylus: The
Oresteia. (R. Fagles, trans; W.B.
Stanford, ed)
R. Bushnell, 403(MLS):Fall84-76
Aeschylus. L'"Agamemnon" d'Eschyle.*
(Vols 1 and 2) (J. Bollack and P. Judet
de La Combe, eds)
A. Neschke, 490:Band16Heft3/4-356
"African Literature Today." (Vol 12)
J.E.O. Apronti, 538(RAL):Spring84-116
Agarwal, A., R. Chopra and K. Sharma, eds.
The State of India's Environment 1982.
M., 176:Apr85-38

3

Ager, W. Sons of the Old Country.
    J.E. Rasmussen, 563(SS):Autumn84-399
    M. Sandbach, 617(TLS):15Feb85-178
Ageyev, M. Novel with Cocaine.*
    J. Lasdun, 176:Jul/Aug85-48
    F. Williams, 617(TLS):5Jul85-756
Agius, P. and S. Jones. Ackermann's
    Regency Furniture and Interiors.
    J.M. Crook, 617(TLS):10May85-519
Agnellus of Ravenna. Lectures on Galen's
    "De sectis."
    Y.V. O'Neill, 589:Jan84-226
Agnon, S.Y. A Simple Story.
    R. Alter, 441:22Dec85-8
Agosin, M. Las desterradas del paraíso.
    N. Lindstrom, 263(RIB):Vol34No1-89
Agostiniani, L. and L. Giannelli, eds.
    Fonologia etrusca, fonetica toscana.
    N. Vincent, 350:Sep85-688
Agud Aparicio, A. and M.P. Fernandez.
    Manual de lengua gotica.
    E.A. Ebbinghaus, 215(GL):Vol24No2-129
Águeda, M. and X. de Salas - see de Goya,
    F.
Agüera Ros, J.C. Un ciclo pictório del
    600 murciano.
    A.F. Pérez Sánchez, 48:Jul-Sep83-304
de Aguiar e Silva, V.M. Competência lin-
    guística e competência literária.
    A. Brakel, 494:Autumn82-179
Aguilar Piñal, F. Bibliografía de autores
    españoles del siglo XVIII.*
    R.P. Sebold, 240(HR):Summer84-407
Agulhon, M. and others. Histoire et lan-
    gage dans "L'Éducation Sentimentale" de
    Flaubert.
    P. Feyler, 535(RHL):Mar/Apr84-293
    T. Unwin, 208(FS):Jul84-357
Agursky, M. The Ideology of National
    Bolshevism.
    M. Heller, 390:Feb84-52
Aharoni, Y., with others. Arad Inscrip-
    tions.
    P.E. Dion, 318(JAOS):Apr-Jun83-470
von der Ahé, K-R. Rezeption schwedischer
    Literatur in Deutschland 1933-1945.
    W. Butt, 562(Scan):Nov84-190
Ahearn, B. Zukofsky's "A."*
    A. Golding, 30:Winter85-92
    M. Perloff, 27(AL):May84-296
Ahearn, E.J. Rimbaud.*
    R. Chambers, 446(NCFS):Winter-Spring85-
    160
    K. Ross, 223:Fall84-325
    639(VQR):Autumn84-126
Ahern, T. - see Joyce, J.
Ahmad, K. and Z.I. Ansari, eds. Islamic
    Perspectives.
    A. Schimmel, 318(JAOS):Oct-Dec83-762
Ahmad, N. University Library Practices in
    Developing Countries.
    J. Feather, 617(TLS):12Jul85-784
Ahrbom, N. Arkitektur och samhälle.
    J. Sjöström, 341:Vol53No1-44
Ahye, M. Cradle of Caribbean Dance.
    P.A. Bialor, 37:Mar-Apr84-61
Ai Qing. Selected Poems of Ai Qing. (E.C.
    Eoyang, P. Wenlan and M. Chin, eds and
    trans)
    J.R. Allen, 116:Jul83-129
Aichinger, I. Ilse Aichinger: Selected
    Poetry and Prose.* (A.H. Chappel, ed
        [continued]

[continuing]
    and trans)
    J. Newman, 448:Vol22No3-129
Aickman, R. Night Voices.
    C. Greenland, 617(TLS):6Dec85-1407
Aiken, J. Mansfield Revisited.*
    P. Beer, 441:21Jul85-12
Aiken, S.R. and others. Development and
    Environment in Peninsular Malaysia.
    W.L. Thomas, 293(JASt):May84-592
"Aimer en France, 1760-1860."
    J. Roussel, 535(RHL):Jan/Feb84-118
Aitken, R. The Mind of Clover.
    T. Buckley, 469:Vol 10No2-90
Aitken, W.R. Scottish Literature in
    English and Scots.
    E. Hulse, 470:Vol22-128
    G.R.R., 588(SSL):Vol 19-299
    H. Schnelling, 568(SCN):Spring-
    Summer84-20
Aiyar, K.N. Thirty Minor Upanishads.
    H. Alper, 318(JAOS):Oct-Dec83-813
Ajami, F. The Arab Predicament.
    T.Y. Ismael, 529(QQ):Spring84-219
Ajayi, J.F.A. and M. Crowder, eds. Histor-
    ical Atlas of Africa.
    C. Fyfe, 617(TLS):25Oct85-1200
    J. Keay, 362:18Jul85-28
Ajdukiewicz, K. The Scientific World Per-
    spective and Other Essays. Problems and
    Theories in Philosophy. Pragmatic Logic.
    P. Engel, 98:Jan-Feb84-42
Ajuwon, B. Funeral Dirges of Yoruba
    Hunters.
    O. Olajubu, 538(RAL):Winter84-592
Akbar, M.J. India.
    B.D. Nossiter, 441:29Sep85-47
Akenson, D. The Lazar House Notebooks.
    A.J. Harding, 102(CanL):Winter83-89
Akhmatova, A. Poems.* (L. Coffin, trans)
    E. Grosholz, 249(HudR):Spring84-137
    D. McDuff, 565:Spring84-72
Akhmatova, A., M. Tsvetayeva and B. Akhma-
    dulina. Three Russian Women Poets.
    J.F. Cotter, 249(HudR):Autumn84-498
Akiner, S. Islamic Peoples of the Soviet
    Union.
    S. Shuiskii, 574(SEEJ):Winter84-560
    D.S.M. Williams, 575(SEER):Jul84-476
Akrigg, G.P.V. - see King James VI and I
Aksenov, V. Ostrov krym.
    M. Feofis, 558(RLJ):Winter-Spring84-
    318
Aksyonov, V. The Burn.*
    F. Eberstadt, 129:Jul85-39
Aksyonov, V. The Island of Crimea.*
    F. Eberstadt, 129:Jul85-39
    R.E. Peterson, 574(SEEJ):Fall84-410
    J. Updike, 442(NY):15Apr85-122
    639(VQR):Summer84-96
Aksyonov, V. Surplussed Barrelware. (J.
    Wilkinson and S. Yastremski, eds and
    trans)
    S. Jacoby, 441:28Apr85-28
Aksyonov, V. and others - see "Metropol"
"Akten zur deutschen auswärtigen Politik,
    1918-1945." (Ser A, Vol 1; Ser B, Vol
    18)
    F.L. Carsten, 575(SEER):Apr84-301
"Akten zur deutschen auswärtigen Politik,
    1918-1945." (Ser B, Vol 19)
    F.L. Carsten, 575(SEER):Oct84-615

4

Al, B.P.F. and others. Van Dale, Groot woordenboek Frans-Nederlands.
　H. Nuiten, 204(FdL):Jun84-148
Alain-Fournier. Le Grand Meaulnes. (C. Herzfeld, ed)
　J. Cruickshank, 402(MLR):Apr84-465
　C. Dédéyan, 535(RHL):May/Jun84-467
de Alarcón, P.A. El sombrero de tres picos.* (L. Bonet, ed)
　E. García Sarriá, 86(BHS):Jan84-51
Alarcos Llorach, E. Anatomía de "La lucha por la vida."*
　L. Hickey, 86(BHS):Oct84-527
Alarcos Llorach, E. Estudis de lingüística catalana.
　J. Gulsoy, 240(HR):Autumn84-523
Alas, L. La Regenta.* (J. Rutherford, trans)
　B.J. Vance, 238:Dec84-672
Alas, L. La Regenta.* (G. Sobejano, ed)
　N.G. Round, 402(MLR):Jan84-217
Alas, L. Su único hijo.* (C. Richmond, ed)
　R. Eberenz, 547(RF):Band96Heft1/2-216
　J. Rutherford, 86(BHS):Oct84-526
Alas, L. Treinta relatos. (C. Richmond, ed)
　C.R. Thompson, Jr., 238:Sep84-474
Alazraki, J. En busca del unicorno.
　C. Delacre Capestany, 37:Sep-Oct84-60
Albarracín-Sarmiento, C. Estructura del "Martín Fierro."
　P.R. Beardsell, 86(BHS):Apr84-211
　M.I. Lichtblau, 240(HR):Spring84-252
Alberoni, F. Movement and Institution.
　G. Poggi, 617(TLS):21Jun85-701
Albers, D.J. and G.L. Alexanderson, eds. Mathematical People.
　M.A. Guillen, 441:30Jun85-26
Albert, C. Der melancholische Bürger.
　C. Zelle, 680(ZDP):Band103Heft2-278
Albert, H. Treatise on Critical Reason.
　A. Grieder, 617(TLS):5Jul85-754
Albert, S. As Is.
　W. Zander, 363(LitR):Fall84-145
Albery, N. The House of Kanzë.
　S. Altinel, 617(TLS):13Dec85-1434
de Albornoz, A. José Hierro.
　E.E. De Torre, 240(HR):Winter84-104
Albouy, P. - see Hugo, V.
Albrecht, C., ed. Zehn Jahre: John Neumeier und das Hamburger Ballett, 1973-1983.
　A. Barzel, 151:Jun84-55
Albrecht, K. and R. Zemke. Service America!
　P. Baida, 441:20Oct85-50
Albrecht, M. Kants Antinomie der praktischen Vernunft.*
　H. Hoppe, 53(AGP):Band66Heft3-319
Alcalde, M.M. - see under Moreno Alcalde, M.
Alcock, J.B. - see Durkheim, É.
Alcorn, A. The Pull of the Earth.
　R. Houston, 441:19May85-22
Alcover, M. Poullain de la Barre.*
　R. Büff-Konrad, 72:Band221Heft2-443
　H-J. Lüsebrink, 547(RF):Band96Heft1/2-186
Alden, J. and D.C. Landis, eds. European Americana.* (Vols 1 and 2)
　E. Wolf 2nd, 517(PBSA):Vol78No1-91

Alder, G. Beyond Bokhara.
　M. Yapp, 617(TLS):20Sep85-1041
Alderink, L.J. Creation and Salvation in Ancient Orphism.
　D.R. Jordan, 487:Spring84-105
Alderson, A.D. and F. İz. The Oxford Turkish-English Dictionary. (3rd ed)
　A. Mango, 617(TLS):26Apr85-473
Alderson, C. and A. Hughes, eds. Issues in Language Testing.
　P.M. Rea, 351(LL):Sep84-175
Aldington, R. Death of a Hero.
　C. Buck, 617(TLS):25Jan85-102
Aldiss, B. Seasons in Flight.*
　J. Mellors, 362:10Jan85-24
　J. Melmoth, 364:Nov84-109
Aldiss, B.W. Helliconia Winter.
　C. Greenland, 617(TLS):17May85-561
　G. Jonas, 441:28Apr85-20
Aldrich, W. Metric Pattern Cutting for Children's Wear from 2-14 Years.
　S. Sherrer, 614:Spring85-25
Aldridge, A.O. Early American Literature.*
　W. Göbel, 52:Band19Heft1-84
　R.S. Levine, 405(MP):May85-429
Aldridge, J.W. The American Novel and the Way We Live Now.*
　J.C. Rowe, 659(ConL):Summer85-212
Aleichem, S. From the Fair. (C. Leviant, ed and trans)
　C. Potok, 441:14Jul85-12
　442(NY):22Jul85-90
Aleichem, S. The Nightingale.
　442(NY):9Dec85-160
Alekseev, M.P. Russko-angliiskie literaturnye sviazi (XVIII vek — pervaia polovina XIX veka).*
　V. Boss, 550(RusR):Oct84-393
Alekseev, M.P. Sravnitel'noe literaturovedenie.
　V. Boss, 550(RusR):Oct84-393
Alekseev, M.P., B.B. Tomashevskii and V.V. Zakharov, comps. Angliiskaia poeziia v russkikh perevodakh (XIV-XIX veka).
　V. Boss, 550(RusR):Oct84-425
Aleksova, B. and J. Wiseman, eds. Studies in the Antiquities of Stobi. (Vol 3)
　C. Foss, 122:Apr84-178
Alexander, C. A Bibliography of the Manuscripts of Charlotte Brontë.
　S. Hanson, 87(BB):Mar84-47
Alexander, C. The Early Writings of Charlotte Brontë.
　J.K. Gezari, 184(EIC):Oct84-349
　W. Holtz, 445(NCF):Mar85-471
Alexander, C. - see Brontë, C.
Alexander, C.C. Ty Cobb.*
　R.B. Heilman, 31(ASch):Autumn84-541
　D. Hotaling, 42(AR):Fall84-504
　639(VQR):Summer84-89
Alexander, G.M. The Prelude to the Truman Doctrine.*
　S. Wichert, 575(SEER):Jul84-464
Alexander, H. Fans.
　R.L. Shep, 614:Spring85-19
Alexander, J. Theoretical Logic in Sociology.* (Vols 1-4)
　K. Soltan, 185:Jul85-951
Alexander, J.H. and D. Hewitt, eds. Scott and his Influence.
　G. McMaster, 571(ScLJ):Autumn84-30

Alexander, L. Safe Houses.
  L. Graeber, 441:22Dec85-18
  D. Steiner, 617(TLS):5Jul85-747
Alexander, M. Old English Literature.
  N.F. Blake, 179(ES):Apr84-172
  B. Windeatt, 184(EIC):Oct84-339
Alexander, P. Roy Campbell.*
  R. Smith, 538(RAL):Spring84-140
  639(VQR):Winter84-14
Alexander, P. Ideas, Qualities and Cor-
  puscles.
  J.G. Cottingham, 617(TLS):13Dec85-1430
Alexander, P. Navigable Waterways.
  J.D. McClatchy, 441:26May85-16
Alexander, P. - see Campbell, R.
Alexander, P. and R. Gill, eds. Utopias.*
  483:Jul84-419
Alexander, S. Nicodemus.
  S. Altinel, 617(TLS):12Jul85-776
  S. Laschever, 441:27Jan85-22
Alexander, S. Nutcracker.
  J.A. Lukas, 441:16Jun85-3
Alexeyeva, L. Soviet Dissent.
  A. Puddington, 129:Dec85-66
  P. Reddaway, 453(NYRB):10Oct85-5
  J. Woll, 441:14Jul85-42
Alfonso XI. Libro de la montería. (D.P.
  Seniff, ed)
  L. Winget, 238:Mar84-141
Alfonso el Sabio. Setenario. (K.H. Van-
  derford, ed)
  A.V., 379(MedR):Dec84-475
Algar, H. - see Imam Khomeini
Algarin, J.P. Japanese Folk Literature.
  C.I. Mulhern, 407(MN):Summer84-201
Algren, N. The Devil's Stocking.
  639(VQR):Winter84-27
Ali, T. An Indian Dynasty. (British
  title: The Nehrus and the Gandhis.)
  W. Borders, 441:21Apr85-25
  J. Grigg, 362:31Jan85-24
Alifano, R. Twenty-Four Conversations
  with Borges, including a Selection of
  Poems.
  295(JML):Nov84-412
Alighieri, D. - see under Dante Alighieri
Alissandratos, J. Medieval Slavic and
  Patristic Eulogies.
  R.D. Bosley, 550(RusR):Jan84-83
  R. Mathiesen, 574(SEEJ):Spring84-108
"All-American: A Sportswear Tradition."
  R.L. Shep, 614:Spring85-16
Allain, M-F. The Other Man.
  A.A. De Vitis, 395(MFS):Winter84-773
Allan, J.W. Islamic Metalwork.
  L. Komaroff, 318(JAOS):Oct-Dec83-775
Allan, S. The Heir and the Sage.
  S.L. Mickel, 293(JASt):Nov83-129
Allanbrook, W.J. Rhythmic Gesture in
  Mozart.
  M.S. Cole, 173(ECS):Spring85-459
Allard, G.H. and S. Lusignan, eds. Les
  arts mécanique au moyen âge.
  J. Jolivet, 542:Jan-Mar84-68
  J.G. Ruelland, 154:Sep84-536
Allard, L. Le Goéland Blessé.
  R. Ewing, 102(CanL):Autumn84-160
Allbeury, T. Children of Tender Years.
  M. Laski, 362:14Nov85-35
Allegra, G. - see de Torquemada, A.
Allemand, A. L'oeuvre romanesque de
  Nathalie Sarraute.*
  J. Baetens, 462(OL):Vol39No1-89

Allen, B. Mad White Giant.
  J. Keay, 362:18Jul85-28
  J. Ure, 617(TLS):2Aug85-847
Allen, B. and W.L. Montell. From Memory
  to History.*
  D.J. Russo, 106:Winter84-397
Allen, C. and S. Dwivedi. Lives of the
  Indian Princes.
  B. Fothergill, 617(TLS):2Aug85-849
Allen, D. Bibliography of Discographies.
  (Vol 2)
  E. Southern, 91:Spring84-137
Allen, D. Overnight in the Guest House of
  the Mystic.
  R. Phillips, 491:Mar85-348
  L. Russ, 469:Vol 10No4-100
Allen, D.G. and others - see Adams, J.Q.
Allen, D.R. - see Arlott, J.
Allen, E. A Woman's Place in the Novels
  of Henry James.
  N. Bradbury, 617(TLS):8Mar85-264
Allen, G.W. Waldo Emerson.*
  W.E. Williams, 27(AL):Mar84-102
Allen, G.W. The Solitary Singer.
  617(TLS):9Aug85-887
Allen, H.W. Poindexter of Washington.
  A. Desbiens, 106:Summer84-211
Allen, J.B. The Ethical Poetic of the
  Later Middle Ages.*
  P. Gradon, 447(N&Q):Aug83-352
  A.J. Minnis, 589:Apr84-363
  G. Morgan, 382(MAE):1984/1-110
Allen, J.B. and T.A. Moritz. A Distinc-
  tion of Stories.*
  H. Cooper, 541(RES):May84-219
  J.C. Hirsh, 382(MAE):1984/1-123
  B. Rowland, 178:Jun84-221
Allen, J.J. Don Quixote: Hero or Fool?
  (Pt 2)
  J.S. Herrero, 345(KRQ):Vol31No3-348
Allen, J.J. The Reconstruction of a
  Spanish Golden Age Playhouse.
  F.P. Casa, 651(WHR):Winter84-382
  J. Orrell, 304(JHP):Fall84-92
  V.G. Williamsen, 238:Dec84-669
Allen, J.L. Yeats's Epitaph.*
  D. Kiberd, 272(IUR):Autumn84-301
Allen, J.S. and I. Ševčenko, eds. Dumbar-
  ton Oaks Bibliographies. (Ser 2, Vol 1)
  M. Harrison, 303(JoHS):Vol 104-271
Allen, J.W.T. - see Bakari, M.M.
Allen, L. Burma.
  R. Callahan, 617(TLS):8Mar85-248
  J. Keay, 362:31Jan85-25
Allen, L. Liberty.
  R.F. Shepard, 441:15Dec85-20
Allen, M.J.B. The Platonism of Marsilio
  Ficino.
  C.B. Schmitt, 617(TLS):21Jun85-688
Allen, M.J.B. and K. Muir - see Shake-
  speare, W.
Allen, M.S. We Are Called Human.*
  F. Garber, 651(WHR):Spring84-80
  H. Ostrom, 30:Fall83-91
Allen, P.G., ed. Studies in American
  Indian Literature.
  T. King, 649(WAL):Aug84-170
Allen, R. The Arabic Novel.*
  I.J. Boullata, 318(JAOS):Oct-Dec83-770
Allen, R.E. The Attalid Kingdom.
  J. Briscoe, 123:Vol34No2-266
  A.M. Ward, 124:Sep-Oct84-50
  É. Will, 555:Vol58fasc2-307

Allen, R.E. Plato's "Parmenides."*
  A. Barker, 123:Vol34No2-205
  L.P. Gerson, 487:Winter84-377
Allén, S. - see Engwall, G.
Allen, T.F.H. and T.B. Starr. Hierarchy.
  S. Sarkar, 486:Jun84-359
Allen, V.F. Techniques in Teaching Vocabu-
lary.
  J.F. Lalande 2d, 399(MLJ):Winter84-382
Allen, W. The Short Story in English.*
  D. Hewitt, 541(RES):May84-275
Allen, W.B. - see Ames, F.
Allende, I. The House of the Spirits.
  P-L. Adams, 61:Jun85-104
  R.M. Adams, 453(NYRB):18Jul85-20
  A. Beevor, 617(TLS):5Jul85-747
  V. Bogdanor, 362:4Jul85-31
  A. Coleman, 441:12May85-1
Allerton, D.J. Valency and the English
Verb.*
  K. Brown, 297(JL):Sep84-378
Alleyne, M.C. Comparative Afro-American.*
  D.K. Nylander, 603:Vol8No3-397
Allingham, M. The Beckoning Lady. Hide
My Eyes.
  R. Hill, 617(TLS):5Apr85-394
Allingham, W. A Diary, 1824-1889.
  617(TLS):27Sep85-1071
Allione, T. Women of Wisdom.
  A.C. Klein, 469:Vol 10No1-153
Allison, G.T., A. Carnesale and J.S. Nye,
Jr., eds. Hawks, Doves, and Owls.
  C.A. Kojm, 441:14Jul85-23
  Lord Zuckerman, 453(NYRB):15Aug85-21
Allison, H.E. Kant's Transcendental Ideal-
ism.
  P. Kitcher, 319:Jul85-439
  W.H. Walsh, 518:Oct84-207
Allison, R. Finland's Relations with the
Soviet Union, 1944-84.
  N. Bruce, 617(TLS):7Jun85-630
Allison, S. The English Biscuit and
Cookie Book.
  W. and C. Cowen, 639(VQR):Spring84-67
Allman, E.J. Player-King and Adversary.
  L. Salingar, 570(SQ):Autumn84-361
Allott, M., ed. Essays on Shelley.*
  R.C. Casto, 541(RES):Nov84-566
  J. Hall, 591(SIR):Spring84-147
  S. Hall, 577(SHR):Spring84-180
  P. Hamilton, 447(N&Q):Dec83-539
  M. O'Neill, 161(DUJ):Dec83-143
  M. O'Neill, 339(KSMB):No35-107
Alloway, L. Roy Lichtenstein.
  J. Bell, 55:Apr84-29
  J. Russell, 441:2Jun85-16
Allwood, M., ed. Modern Scandinavian
Poetry 1900-1975.
  D. McDuff, 565:Spring84-72
  I. Scobie, 562(Scan):Nov84-189
Almansi, G. and S. Henderson. Harold Pin-
ter.*
  L. Powlick, 615(TJ):Mar84-138
  M. Prunet, 189(EA):Jan-Mar85-99
Almeida, A. Nasalitätsdetektion und Voka-
lerkennung.
  G.F. Meier, 682(ZPSK):Band37Heft4-530
de Almeida, H. Byron and Joyce through
Homer.*
  F. Garber, 661(WC):Summer84-125
  P.W. Martin, 339(KSMB):No35-97
Almendros, N. A Man with a Camera.*
  C.H., 62:Summer85-97

Aloni, A. Le Muse di Archiloco.
  S.R. Slings, 394:Vol37fasc1/2-169
Alonzo, A-M. Veille.
  K.W. Meadwell, 102(CanL):Autumn84-95
Alperovitz, G. Atomic Diplomacy. (rev)
  G. Smith, 441:18Aug85-16
Alpers, A. - see Mansfield, K.
Alpers, S. The Art of Describing.*
  C. Ashwin, 592:Vol 196No1004-55
  J. Glynne, 59:Jun84-247
  E. de Jongh, 600:Vol 14No1-51
  D. Mannings, 89(BJA):Summer84-271
  J. Stumpel, 90:Sep84-580
Alphant, M. L'Histoire enterrée.
  A. Clerval, 450(NRF):Feb84-100
Alphéus, K. Kant und Scheler. (B.
Wolandt, ed)
  H. Oberer, 342:Band75Heft1-128
Alquié, F. Le rationalisme de Spinoza.*
  F. Duchesneau, 154:Dec84-711
Alsberg, J. Modern Art and its Enigma.
  D. Carrier, 290(JAAC):Fall84-106
de Alta Silva, J. Dolopathos or The King
and the Seven Wise Men. (B.B. Gilleland,
trans)
  W. Maaz, 196:Band25Heft3/4-345
Altenberg, B. The Genitive vs. the
"of-"Construction.
  W. Elmer, 38:Band102Heft1/2-153
  S. Jacobson, 597(SN):Vol56No2-235
Alter, R. The Art of Biblical Narrative.*
  J. Barton, 447(N&Q):Oct83-452
Alter, R. The Art of Biblical Poetry.
  P. Levi, 441:20Oct85-36
Alter, R. Motives for Fiction.
  295(JML):Nov84-374
"Alternativas de educación para grupos cul-
turalmente diferenciados."
  I. Chamorro, 263(RIB):Vol34No1-101
Alther, L. Other Women.*
  442(NY):21Jan85-94
Altieri, C. Act and Quality.*
  B. Bashford, 536:Vol6-303
  D. Gorman, 494:Vol5No1-159
  E. Watkins, 81:Fall83-235
Altieri, C. Self and Sensibility in Con-
temporary American Poetry.
  D.T. O'Hara, 659(ConL):Fall85-335
  295(JML):Nov84-392
Altman, J.B. The Tudor Play of Mind.
  W. Weiss, 38:Band102Heft1/2-227
Altman, J.G. Epistolarity.*
  J.T. Matthews, 223:Spring83-108
  G. Prince, 494:Vol4No1-199
Altmann, A. Die trostvolle Aufklärung.
  D. Breazeale, 543:Dec83-387
  S. Zac, 192(EP):Jul-Sep84-403
Altner, M. Die deutsche Kinder- und
Jugendliteratur zwischen Gründerzeit und
Novemberrevolution.
  C. Emmrich, 654(WB):4/1984-694
Álvarez, M. and M. Flórez, eds. Estudios
sobre Kant y Hegel.
  M.P.M. Caimi, 342:Band75Heft4-512
Alvarez Alvarez, C. El condado de Luna en
la baja edad media.
  W.D. Phillips, Jr., 589:Oct84-885
Álvarez-Borland, I. Discontinuidad y
ruptura en Guillermo Cabrera Infante.
  J. Sánchez-Boudy, 238:May84-312

Alvarez-Detrell, T. and M.G. Paulson, eds.
The Gambling Mania On and Off the Stage
in Pre-Revolutionary France.
  F. Assaf, 475:Vol 11No20-205
Alzati, G.C. - see under Cantoni Alzati, G.
Amabile, G. Ideas of Shelter.*
  J. Rodriguez, 102(CanL):Autumn84-145
Amacher, R.E. Edward Albee. (rev)
  A. Paolucci, 397(MD):Sep84-453
Amadi, E. Ethics in Nigerian Culture.
  P.O. Iheakaram, 538(RAL):Summer84-309
Amado, J. Pen, Sword, Camisole.
  N. Ramsey, 441:19May85-22
  442(NY):19Aug85-89
Amann, E. Cicada Voices. (G. Swede, ed)
  404:Winter-Spring84-40
Amann, K. Adalbert Stifters "Nachsommer."
  G.F. Folkers, 221(GQ):Winter84-156
Amanuddin, S. World Poetry in English.
  T.R. Knipp, 538(RAL):Spring84-134
Amastae, J. and L. Elías-Olivares, eds.
Spanish in the United States.*
  F. Nuessel, 361:Mar84-247
Amato, A., ed. Analisi contrastiva e
analisi degli errori.
  W. Schweickard, 72:Band221Heft2-326
Amato, J.A. Ethics, Living or Dead?
  S.G.P., 185:Apr85-767
Ambirajan, S. Classical Political Economy
and British Policy in India.
  J. Masselos, 302:Vol20No2-252
Ambler, E. Here Lies.
  J. Bayley, 617(TLS):2Aug85-839
  G. Millar, 362:20Jun85-25
Ambler, E. The Levanter. Doctor Frigo.
  J. Bayley, 617(TLS):2Aug85-839
Ambrière, M. - see de Balzac, H.
Ambrose, S.E. Eisenhower. (Vol 1)
  M. Howard, 617(TLS):8Feb85-135
Ambrose, S.E. Eisenhower.* (Vol 2)
  N. Bliven, 442(NY):1Jul85-95
  A. Hartley, 176:Apr85-61
  M. Howard, 617(TLS):8Feb85-135
  S. Warren, 129:Apr85-81
Ambrose, S.E. Pegasus Bridge.
  D. Middleton, 441:28Apr85-25
Ameling, W. Herodes Atticus. (Vol 1)
  A.J.S. Spawforth, 313:Vol74-214
  M.B. Trapp, 123:Vol34No2-346
Ameling, W. Herodes Atticus. (Vol 2)
  M.B. Trapp, 123:Vol34No2-346
"The American Heritage Dictionary."* (2nd
College ed)
  C. Eble, 35(AS):Spring84-72
"American Literary Scholarship, 1978."
  (J.A. Robbins, ed) "American Literary
Scholarship, 1979." (J. Woodress, ed)
  A. Hook, 447(N&Q):Jun83-285
Ameriks, K. Kant's Theory of Mind.*
  P. Guyer, 543:Sep83-97
  C. Janaway, 393(Mind):Oct84-632
  A. Stanguennec, 542:Jan-Mar84-77
  L. Stevenson, 479(PhQ):Oct84-514
van Amerongen, M. Wagner.
  R. Anderson, 415:Feb84-96
  R. Hollinrake, 410(M&L):Oct84-390
Ames, F. Works of Fisher Ames. (S. Ames,
ed; rev by W.B. Allen)
  D.R. Hickey, 656(WMQ):Oct84-678
Ames, R.T. The Art of Rulership.*
  J. Ching, 322(JHI):Jul-Sep84-476

Ames-Lewis, F. Drawing in Early Renais-
sance Italy.*
  K. Oberhuber, 551(RenQ):Summer84-258
  N. Rash, 589:Jul84-606
  H. Wohl, 54:Jun84-335
  380:Autumn84-329
Ames-Lewis, F. and J. Wright. Drawing in
the Italian Renaissance Workshop.*
  380:Autumn84-329
"Ami and Amile."* (S. Danon and S.N.
Rosenberg, trans)
  S. Maddux, 589:Jan84-231
Amichai, Y. Great Tranquility.*
  W. Logan, 491:Nov84-109
  D. McDuff, 565:Summer84-68
  N. Stiller, 287:Apr84-26
Amichai, Y. The World is a Room.
  R. Alter, 617(TLS):3May85-498
Amiel, J. Birthright.
  K. Olson, 441:12May85-18
Amiet, P. and others. Art in the Ancient
World.
  L. Morgan, 303(JoHS):Vol 104-264
Amirthanayagam, G., ed. Asian and Western
Writers in Dialogue.*
  L.A. Flemming, 293(JASt):May84-505
Amirthanayagam, G., ed. Writers in East-
West Encounter.
  J. Gibbs, 538(RAL):Fall84-431
Amis, J. Amiscellany.
  H. Cole, 362:13Jun85-27
Amis, K. How's Your Glass?
  H. Stevens, 364:Dec84/Jan85-155
Amis, K. Stanley and the Women.*
  P-L. Adams, 61:Nov85-143
  S.F. Schaeffer, 441:22Sep85-9
  442(NY):21Oct85-149
Amis, M. Money.*
  W. Balliett, 442(NY):10Jun85-136
  V. Geng, 441:24Mar85-36
  C. Hawtree, 364:Oct84-85
  J. Lasdun, 176:Feb85-46
Amor, A.C. Mrs. Oscar Wilde.
  B. Bashford, 177(ELT):Vol27No3-254
Amore, R.C. and L.D. Shinn. Lustful Maid-
ens and Ascetic Kings.
  S.H. Blackburn, 293(JASt):Nov83-173
Amory, M. - see Fleming, A.
Amos, A.C. Linguistic Means of Determin-
ing the Dates of Old English Literary
Texts.*
  M.R. Godden, 541(RES):Aug84-346
  H. Sauer, 260(IF):Band89-368
Amos, H.D. and G.P. Lang. These Were the
Greeks.
  S. Fineberg, 124:Jan-Feb85-225
Amos, W. The Originals.
  A. Burgess, 617(TLS):29Nov85-1349
Amossy, R. Les Jeux de l'allusion littér-
aire dans "Un Beau Ténébreux" de Julien
Gracq.*
  J. Alter, 494:Vol4No1-191
Amossy, R. Parcours symbolique chez
Julien Gracq.*
  Y. de la Quérière, 207(FR):Oct84-138
  J. Roach, 208(FS):Jan84-98
Amossy, R. and E. Rosen. Les Discours du
cliché.*
  E. Cardonne-Arlyck, 546(RR):Mar84-263
  A. Herschberg-Pierrot, 535(RHL):
    Sep/Oct84-819
  A. Jefferson, 208(FS):Jan84-109

Amprimoz, A.L. Germain Nouveau dit Humi-
lis. La Poésie érotique de Germain
Nouveau.
   B.L. Knapp, 446(NCFS):Summer85-290
Amster, G. and B. Asbell. Transit Point
Moscow.
   C.R. Whitney, 441:17Feb85-21
"An einem Ort muss man anfangen."
   I. Siegel, 654(WB):8/1984-1382
Anahory Librowicz, O., ed. Florilegio de
romances sefardíes de la Diáspora (una
colección malagueña).
   J.G. Cummins, 86(BHS):Jan84-65
Anastaplo, G. The Artist as Thinker.
   295(JML):Nov84-374
Anaxagoras. The Fragments.* (D. Sider,
ed)
   C. Emlyn-Jones, 303(JoHS):Vol 104-196
Ancelet, B.J. and E. Morgan, Jr. The
Makers of Cajun Music/Musiciens Cadiens
et Creoles.
   J. Berry, 441:20Jan85-19
Andaya, L.Y. The Heritage of Arung Pal-
akka.
   H. Sutherland, 293(JASt):May84-593
Andereggen, A. Les Verbes français.
   T.J. Cox, 207(FR):May85-901
Andersen, A-C. and others. Fra barn til
kvinne.
   J.E. Rasmussen, 563(SS):Spring84-178
Andersen, F.G., O. Holzapfel and T. Pettit.
The Ballad as Narrative.*
   C.A. Cartwright, 292(JAF):Apr-Jun84-
225
   E.R. Long, 650(WF):Apr84-141
   S.H. Rossel, 301(JEGP):Oct84-590
Andersen, H. and F. Lasson, eds. Blix-
eniana 1982.
   M.J. Blackwell, 563(SS):Autumn84-386
Andersen, H.C. Hans Andersen's Fairy
Tales. (L.W. Kingsland, trans) Hans
Andersen: His Classic Fairy Tales. (E.
Haugaard, trans)
   B. Alderson, 617(TLS):5Jul85-758
Andersen, R., ed. Pidginization and Creol-
ization as Language Acquisition.
   J. Vizmuller-Zocco, 257(IRAL):Nov84-
321
Anderson, A. and C. Saltus, eds. Jean
Cocteau and the French Scene.
   S. Morgan, 62:Dec84-78
Anderson, C.L. - see Roos, R.
Anderson, D. - see Cavalcanti, G.
Anderson, D.D., ed. Critical Essays on
Sherwood Anderson.
   G.O. Carey, 573(SSF):Winter84-84
Anderson, D.G. Abraham Lincoln.
   R.W. Johannsen, 579(SAQ):Summer84-348
Anderson, D.K. The Works of Charles T.
Griffes.
   A. Berger, 453(NYRB):13Jun85-26
Anderson, F. A People's Army.
   T.H. Breen, 453(NYRB):5Dec85-48
   R.A. Rosenstone, 441:17Mar85-27
Anderson, G. Ancient Fiction.
   S. Soupel, 189(EA):Oct-Dec85-490
Anderson, G. Eros Sophistes.*
   H. Bacon, 124:Jul-Aug85-616
Anderson, G.K. - see "The Saga of the
Völsungs Together with Excerpts from the
Nornageststhåttr and Three Chapters from
the Prose Edda"

Anderson, J. Cypresses.
   E. Pankey, 389(MQ):Autumn84-110
Anderson, J. Guns in American Life.
   P.V. Murphy, 441:24Feb85-9
Anderson, J., ed. Language Form and Lin-
guistic Variation.*
   R.I. McDavid, Jr., 35(AS):Fall84-249
Anderson, J. The Milky Way.*
   R. McDowell, 249(HudR):Spring84-117
   F. Muratori, 448:Vol122No3-139
   D. Wojahn, 502(PrS):Winter84-93
Anderson, J. The Only Daughter.
   J. Neville, 617(TLS):4Oct85-1097
   H. Wolitzer, 441:24Mar85-12
Anderson, J. Sir Walter Scott and History,
with Other Papers.*
   C. Dédéyan, 189(EA):Oct-Dec85-469
Anderson, J. Tirra Lirra by the River.*
   C.R., 376:Jun84-143
Anderson, J. - see Wind, E.
Anderson, J.H. Biographical Truth.*
   A.B. Ferguson, 551(RenQ):Winter84-649
   J. Goldberg, 570(SQ):Winter84-499
   F.J. Levy, 250(HLQ):Summer84-233
Anderson, J.J., ed. Records of Early
English Drama: Newcastle-upon-Tyne.*
   D. Pearsall, 179(ES):Dec84-572
   D.S. Vinter, 130:Spring84-87
Anderson, L. About John Ford.
   J.P. Telotte, 500:Fall84-64
Anderson, L. Charles Bonnet and the Order
of the Known.
   J-M. Gabaude, 542:Oct-Dec84-476
Anderson, L. We Can't All Be Heroes, You
Know.
   C. Colman, 441:24Feb85-22
   442(NY):11Mar85-136
Anderson, O.B. An Investigation into the
Present State of Standard Chinese Pronun-
ciation. (Pt 1a)
   G.F. Meier, 682(ZPSK):Band37Heft1-122
Anderson, P. Arguments within English
Marxism.
   W. Stafford, 366:Spring84-105
Anderson, P. Children's Hospital.
   N. Cardozo, 441:23Jun85-21
Anderson, P. In the Tracks of Historical
Materialism.*
   J.S., 185:Jul85-972
Anderson, S. Sherwood Anderson: Selected
Letters.* (C.E. Modlin, ed)
   D. Stouck, 395(MFS):Winter84-800
Anderson, S. Letters to Bab. (W.A.
Sutton, ed)
   D. Aaron, 441:8Sep85-41
Anderson, S. The Teller's Tales. (F.
Gado, ed)
   G.O. Carey, 573(SSF):Spring84-161
de Andrade, C.D. - see under Drummond de
Andrade, C.
Andrade, C.V. - see under Valderrama
Andrade, C.
de Andrade, M. Macunaíma.
   A. Coleman, 441:3Mar85-13
   J. Gledson, 617(TLS):20Dec85-1462
André, J. Caraïbales.
   W. Bader, 343:Heft9/10-135
André, J., ed and trans. Traité de physi-
ognomonie.
   P. Flobert, 555:Vol58fasc1-137
Andre, M. The Gates.
   P.K. Smith, 99:Jun/Jul84-40

André, R. L'Éducation inachevée.
P. Olivier, 450(NRF):Jul/Aug84-158
Andreas Capellanus - see under Capellanus
Andreasen, N.C. The Broken Brain.
I. Rosenfield, 453(NYRB):14Mar85-34
H.M. Schmeck, Jr., 441:10Mar85-25
Andreeva, I., ed. Pis'ma V.F. Khoda-
sevicha B.A. Sadovskomu.
J.A. Miller, 550(RusR):Jan84-92
Andreini, A. - see Gadda, C.E.
Andreu, A.G. Galdós y la literatura pop-
ular.
F. Romero Pérez, 345(KRQ):Vol31No2-235
Andreu, P.A.G. - see under Galera Andreu,
P.A.
Andréucci, C. and M. Green - see Jacob, M.
Andrew, C. Secret Service.
D. Hunt, 362:17Oct85-32
Andrew, D. Concepts in Film Theory.
J. Hoberman, 18:Dec84-69
A.G. Robson, 399(MLJ):Winter84-391
S. Scobie, 376:Oct84-108
Andrewartha, H.G. and L.C. Birch. The
Ecological Web.
W. George, 617(TLS):29Nov85-1368
Andrews, B. Praxis.
J. Retallack, 472:Fall/Winter84-213
Andrews, B. and C. Bernstein, eds. The
L=A=N=G=U=A=G=E Book.*
J. Retallack, 472:Fall/Winter84-213
Andrews, J., ed. The Dancing Sun.
M.J. Evans, 102(CanL):Summer84-124
Andrews, J. and J. Taylor. John Andrews.
J. Parker, 529(QQ):Summer84-429
Andrews, K.R. Trade, Plunder and Settle-
ment.
N. Canny, 617(TLS):8Mar85-251
Andrews, W.L., ed. Literary Romanticism
in America.*
W. Branch, 447(N&Q):Jun83-283
Andreyev, Y., comp. Soviet Russian Litera-
ture 1917-1977.
V. Babenko-Woodbury, 399(MLJ):Spring84-
88
Anfousse, G. Fabien 1. Fabien 2.
D. Thaler, 102(CanL):Summer84-161
Anfousse, G. Le Savon. L'Hiver, ou le
Bonhomme Sept Heures.
C.R. La Bossiere, 102(CanL):Winter83-
125
Angadi, P. The Governess.
J. Mellors, 362:21Mar85-25
Angelet, C. Symbolisme et invention for-
melle dans les premiers écrits d'André
Gide (Le Traité du Narcisse, Le Voyage
d'Urien, Paludes).*
E. Apter, 546(RR):Jan84-116
D. Moutote, 535(RHL):Sep/Oct84-817
R. Theis, 547(RF):Band96Heft1/2-193
Angelou, M. Gather Together in My Name.
J. Neville, 617(TLS):14Jun85-674
Angenot, M. La Parole Pamphlétaire.*
D. Polan, 494:Vol5No4-878
Anger, K. Hollywood Babylon II.
J. Waters, 18:Jan/Feb85-53
Angier, C. Jean Rhys.
A. Huth, 362:5Dec85-27
Anglade, J. Le Pays oublié.
C. Mackey, 207(FR):Oct84-150
Anglès, A. and P. de Gaulmyn - see Claudel,
P. and J. Rivière

Angold, M. The Byzantine Empire 1025-1204.
J.D. Howard-Johnston, 617(TLS):31May85-
616
Angulo Íñiguez, D. and A.E. Pérez Sánchez.
Pintura madrileña del segundo tercio del
siglo XVII.
E. Bermejo, 48:Oct-Dec84-389
Anhalt, I. Alternative Voices.
P. Standford, 415:Oct84-574
Anisfeld, M. Language Development from
Birth to Three.
S.H. Foster, 353:Vol22No5-757
Anna, T.E. Spain and the Loss of America.*
W.G. Lovell, 529(QQ):Autumn84-715
"Annales Benjamin Constant, 2."
P. Delbouille, 535(RHL):Mar/Apr84-286
"Annales Benjamin Constant, 3."
C.P. Courtney, 208(FS):Oct84-468
Annan, N. Leslie Stephen.*
J. Clive, 453(NYRB):31Jan85-19
442(NY):1Apr85-113
Annas, J. An Introduction to Plato's
"Republic."*
T.C. Brickhouse, 482(PhR):Jan84-147
W. Charlton, 393(Mind):Jan84-125
S. Umphrey, 543:Sep83-100
Annas, J., ed. Oxford Studies in Ancient
Philosophy. (Vol 1)
A.W. Price, 518:Apr84-75
Annas, J. and J. Barnes. The Modes of
Scepticism.
D. Sedley, 617(TLS):13Sep85-1005
"Annual Bibliography of Victorian Studies"
(1976-1980) [and] "Cumulated Bibliogra-
phy of Victorian Studies 1976-1980." (B.
Chaudhuri, ed)
S. Monod, 189(EA):Oct-Dec85-470
"Annual Review of Applied Linguistics:
1981." (R.B. Kaplan, general ed)
A. Cumming, 320(CJL):Fall84-188
Anscombe, G.E.M. and G.H. von Wright - see
Wittgenstein, L.
Anscombe, I. A Woman's Touch.
C. Ellis, 46:Dec84-81
S. Pollak, 324:Aug85-671
J. Rutherford, 617(TLS):1Feb85-129
Anscombre, J-C. and O. Ducrot. L'argumen-
tation dans la langue.
G. Kleiber, 553(RLiR):Jul-Dec84-464
M. Seymour, 154:Sep84-514
G. Stahl, 542:Jan-Mar84-111
Anstett, J-J., with U. Behler - see
Schlegel, F.
Anten, H. Van realisme naar zakelijkheid.
J. Goedegebuure, 204(FdL):Mar84-70
Antès, S. - see Corippus
Anthony, E. Voices on the Wind.
M. Laski, 362:14Nov85-35
Anthony, P.D. John Ruskin's Labour.*
R. Watkinson, 326:Winter84/85-28
Antin, M. The Promised Land.
617(TLS):22Nov85-1339
Antoine, G. Vis-à-vis ou le double regard
critique.*
J. Cruickshank, 208(FS):Jul84-372
Antokoletz, E. The Music of Béla Bartók.
A. Whittall, 617(TLS):16Aug85-904
Anton, J.P. and A. Preus, eds. Essays in
Ancient Greek Philosophy. (Vol 2)
R.M., 185:Apr85-780
E. Thury, 124:Jul-Aug85-618
Antonelli, R. - see da Lentini, G.

Antonijević, D. Obredi i običaji balkan-
skih stočara.
  A. Lopasic, 575(SEER):Apr84-313
de Antonio, E. and M. Tuchman. Painters
Painting.
  E. Turner, 55:Nov84-36
Antonioni, M. That Bowling Alley on the
Tiber.
  S. Schiff, 441:15Dec85-15
Anttila, R. Analogy.
  C.V.J. Russ, 685(ZDL):1/1984-120
Anz, T., ed. Phantasien über den Wahnsinn.
  W. Paulsen, 133:Band17Heft1/2-157
Anz, T. and M. Stark, eds. Expressionis-
mus.
  D. Barnouw, 221(GQ):Winter84-119
Anzelewsky, F. Dürer.*
  J.M. Massing, 90:Dec84-788
Aparicio, A.A. and M.P. Fernandez - see
under Agud Aparicio, A. and M.P. Fernan-
dez
Apel, K-O. Charles S. Peirce.*
  C. Chauvire, 98:Oct84-797
van Apeldoorn, J. Pratiques de la descrip-
tion.
  J.H. Duffy, 402(MLR):Jul84-720
Apfel, R.J. and S.M. Fisher. To Do No
Harm.
  A. Knopf, 441:20Jan85-19
Apollinaire, G. Le Poète Assassiné.*
  (British title: The Poet Assassinated
and Other Stories.) (R. Padgett, trans)
  D. Coward, 617(TLS):19Apr85-451
Appadurai, A. Worship and Conflict under
Colonial Rule.*
  P. Kolenda, 318(JAOS):Jul-Sep83-666
Appel, A., Jr. Signs of Life.
  J.P. Sisk, 31(ASch):Autumn84-568
Appel, J., J. Schumann and D. Rösler. Pro-
gression im Fremdsprachenunterricht.
  R.W. Walker, 399(MLJ):Autumn84-268
Appel, L. Mask Characterization.
  K. Conlin, 615(TJ):Mar84-122
Appelfeld, A. The Retreat.*
  R. Alter, 617(TLS):3May85-498
Appignanesi, R. Italia Perversa. (Pt 1)
  A. Beevor, 617(TLS):2Aug85-855
  J. Mellors, 362:25Jul85-32
Appignanesi, R. Italia Perversa. (Pt 2)
  A. Beevor, 617(TLS):22Nov85-1310
Appleby, D.P. The Music of Brazil.
  E.D. Curtis, 37:Jan-Feb84-58
  E. Garmendia, 263(RIB):Vol34No1-89
  A. Seeger, 187:Winter85-124
Appleby, J. Capitalism and a New Social
Order.
  639(VQR):Summer84-80
Applewhite, J. Foreseeing the Journey.*
  L. Goldensohn, 491:Apr84-40
Apresjan, J.D. Tipy informacii dlja
poverxnostno-sematičeskogo komponenta
modeli Smysl ↔ Tekst. (T. Reuther, ed)
  C.V. Chvany, 574(SEEJ):Fall84-383
Apte, M.L. Humor and Laughter.
  V. Crapanzano, 617(TLS):12Jul85-782
Apter, D.F. and N. Sawa. Against the
State.*
  Sakai Takeshi, 285(JapQ):Oct-Dec84-455
Apter, R. Digging for the Treasure.
  M. Korn, 617(TLS):8Nov85-1258
  B. Raffel, 363(LitR):Summer85-634
Aptheker, H. - see Du Bois, W.E.B.

Aquila, R.E. Representational Mind.
  G. Franzwa, 319:Oct85-593
Aquinas, T. Opera omnia iussu Leonis XIII
P.M. edita, 23.
  B.H. Zedler, 589:Jul84-704
Aquinas, T. St. Thomas Aquinas, Quodlib-
etal Questions 1 and 2. (S. Edwards, ed
and trans)
  J.F. Wippel, 319:Oct85-585
Aquinas, T. Sancti Thomae Aquinatis opera
omnia. (R. Busa, ed)
  D.M. Burton, 589:Oct84-891
Ara Gil, C.J. and J.M. Parrado del Olmo.
Antiguo Partido Judicial de Tordesillas.
  M. Estella, 48:Jan-Mar84-120
Arab, A. Politics and the Novel in Africa.
  R. Mane, 189(EA):Jan-Mar85-108
Arac, J., W. Godzich and W. Martin, eds.
The Yale Critics.*
  W. Kendrick, 613:Dec84-519
  J. Mowitt, 141:Summer84-290
  S.F.R., 131(CL):Summer84-263
Aradi, N., ed. Mednyánszky.
  J.B. Smith, 39:Jul84-75
"Arakawa: Padiglione d'arte contemporanea."
  T. Murray, 153:Fall84-100
Arata, L.O. The Festive Play of Fernando
Arrabal.*
  F.H. Londré, 130:Spring84-94
  J. Lyon, 86(BHS):Apr84-209
Arato, A. and E. Gebhardt, eds. The Essen-
tial Frankfurt School Reader.
  P.U. Hohendahl, 221(GQ):Spring84-295
Arbuckle, E.S. - see Martineau, H.
"Diane Arbus: Magazine Work."* (D. Arbus
and M. Israel, eds)
  L. Liebmann, 62:Dec84-3
Arbuzov, A. Selected Plays of Aleksei
Arbuzov.
  S. Golub, 615(TJ):Mar84-135
Arce, J. El último siglo de la España
romana: 284-409.
  N. Mackie, 123:Vol34No1-96
Arce, M.M. - see under Maples Arce, M.
Archambault, G. One for the Road.
  E. Dansereau, 526:Summer84-88
Archambault, G. and others. Fuites et
poursuites.
  M. Benson, 102(CanL):Summer84-102
  L. Martineau, 207(FR):Oct84-151
Archer, J.H.G., ed. Art and Architecture
in Victorian Manchester.
  M. Girouard, 617(TLS):1Nov85-1225
Archer, M. - see Lipski, L.L.
Archer, S.M. American Actors and
Actresses.
  R.K. Bank, 615(TJ):Mar84-124
Archibald, D. Yeats.
  E. Bartlett, 628(UWR):Spring-Summer85-
101
  B. Dolan, 305(JIL):Jan-May84-143
  E. Engelberg, 177(ELT):Vol27No2-176
  S. Poger, 174(Éire):Summer84-152
"Archives de philosophie du droit." (Vol
25)
  A. Reix, 192(EP):Apr-Jun84-265
"Arco Guide to Knitting Stitches."
  K. Buffington, 614:Summer85-17
Ardagh, J. France in the 1980s.*
  W. Wrage, 399(MLJ):Summer84-158
Ardery, J.S. - see Garland, J.
Ardizzone, E. Indian Diary 1952-53.*
  A. Ross, 364:Jul84-107

11

Ardman, H. Normandie.
S. Mantell, 441:19May85-23
Ardouin, P. La "Délie" de Maurice Scève
et ses cinquante emblèmes, ou les noces
secrètes de la poésie et du signe.
D. Fenoaltea, 551(RenQ):Autumn84-482
de Arellano, R.R. - see under Ramírez de
Arellano, R.
Arenas, R. Farewell to the Sea.
J. Cantor, 441:24Nov85-31
Arenda, J. and A. Kling, eds. Der Dichter
ist kein verlorener Stein.
H-O. Dill, 654(WB):6/1984-1048
Arendt, E. Das zweifingrige Lachen. Star-
rend von Zeit und Helle.
H-T. Lehmann, 384:Oct84-827
Arendt, H. Lectures on Kant's Political
Philosophy.* (R. Beiner, ed)
M.J. Gregor, 543:Sep83-102
K. Hartmann, 323:Oct84-317
E.M. Pybus, 518:Apr84-113
R. Schürmann, 342:Band75Heft1-123
Arendt, H. La vie de l'esprit. (Vol 2)
M. Adam, 542:Apr-Jun84-246
Arens, W. and R. Schöwerling, eds. Mittel-
englische Lyrik, englisch/deutsch.*
H. Käsmann, 38:Band102Heft1/2-205
Argetsinger, G.S. Ludvig Holberg's Come-
dies.
R. Kejzlar, 562(Scan):Nov84-173
E. Sprinchorn, 563(SS):Spring84-185
Ariosto, L. Orlando Furioso. (E. Bigi,
ed)
D. Javitch, 400(MLN):Jan84-171
Aris, M. Views of Medieval Bhutan.*
J. Lowry, 463:Summer84-195
Aris, S. Going Bust.
J.H.C. Leach, 617(TLS):6Dec85-1392
Aristides. Aristides Quintilianus on
Music. (T.J. Mathiesen, ed and trans)
D.D. Feaver, 124:Sep-Oct84-61
L. Rowell, 308:Fall84-302
Aristophanes. Commedie di Aristofane.
(Vol 1) (G. Mastromarco, ed and trans)
A.H. Sommerstein, 123:Vol34No2-177
Aristotle. Aristote, "Météorologiques."*
(Vols 1 and 2) (P. Louis, ed and trans)
R. Brague, 192(EP):Jan-Mar84-107
Aristotle. Aristotle's "De Generatione et
Corruptione."* (C.J.F. Williams, ed and
trans) Aristotle's "Eudemian Ethics."*
(Bks 1, 2 and 8) (M.J. Woods, ed and
trans)
M. Schofield, 483:Jul84-392
Aristotle. Aristotle's "Physics" Books
III and IV. (E. Hussey, ed and trans)
W.H. Hay, 319:Jan85-100
M. Schofield, 483:Jul84-392
S. Waterlow, 84:Dec84-404
Aristotle. Aristotle's "Poetics." (J.
Hutton, trans)
I. Rutherford, 123:Vol34No2-210
Aristotle. Les attributions (Catégories).
(Y. Pelletier, with others, eds and
trans)
P. Bellemare, 154:Sep84-548
Aristotle. Complete Works. (J. Barnes,
ed)
C. Rowe, 617(TLS):8Feb85-150
Aristotle. The Politics.* (T.A. Sinclair,
trans; rev by T.J. Saunders)
H. de Ley, 394:Vol37fascl/2-190

Ariyoshi, S. The Twilight Years.
A. Cheuse, 441:20Jan85-18
Arksey, L., N. Pries and M. Reed. Ameri-
can Diaries. (Vol 1)
M.L. Ford, 517(PBSA):Vol78No4-530
S.E. Kagle, 165(EAL):Fall85-174
Arlen, M.J. Say Goodbye to Sam.*
A. Kavounas, 617(TLS):29Mar85-340
Arlott, J. Arlott on Cricket. (D.R.
Allen, ed)
T.D. Smith, 617(TLS):12Apr85-419
Armand, O., ed. Toward an Image of Latin
American Poetry.*
G. Simon, 448:Vol22No3-135
de Armas, F.A., D.M. Gitlitz and J.A.
Madrigal, eds. Critical Perspectives on
Calderón de la Barca.*
W.F. Hunter, 402(MLR):Jan84-216
Armes, R. French Cinema.
C. Redpath, 617(TLS):19Jul85-793
Armistead, S.G., with others. El Roman-
cero Judeo-Español en el Archivo
Menéndez Pidal.*
B.R. Jonsson, 64(Arv):Vol38-180
Armistead, S.G. and J.H. Silverman. En
torno al romancero sefardí (Hispanismo
y balcanismo de la tradición judeo-
española).
B.A. Beatie, 292(JAF):Jul-Sep84-364
Armistead, S.G. and J.H. Silverman - see
Benardete, M.J.
Armitage, G.E. A Season of Peace.
N. Shack, 617(TLS):4Oct85-1096
Armour, L. The Idea of Canada and the
Crisis of Community.*
J.T. Stevenson, 154:Dec84-701
Armstrong, D.M. What Is a Law of Nature?
J. Woodward, 185:Jul85-949
Armstrong, I. Language as Living Form in
Nineteenth-Century Poetry.*
P. Barry, 175:Summer84-152
Armstrong, J.A. Nations before National-
ism.
G. Schöpflin, 575(SEER):Jan84-124
Armstrong, J.D. Revolutionary Diplomacy.
J.Y.S. Cheng, 302:Vol20No2-189
Armstrong, L. Renaissance Miniature
Painters and Classical Imagery.*
I. Ragusa, 589:Jan84-110
W.S. Sheard, 54:Mar84-157
Armstrong, P.B. The Phenomenology of
Henry James.*
M. Deakin, 395(MFS):Winter84-791
J.W. Tuttleton, 445(NCF):Sep84-228
295(JML):Nov84-458
639(VQR):Autumn84-126
Armstrong, R. The Painted Stream.
A. Atha, 617(TLS):20Dec85-1466
Armstrong, R. Structure and Change.
E.J. Talbot, 207(FR):Apr85-743
Armstrong, R.D. Nevada Printing History.*
R.C. Fyffe, 354:Jun84-197
P.A. Metzger, 517(PBSA):Vol78No2-251
Arnáez, E. Orfebrería religiosa en la
provincia de Segovia hasta 1700.
I. Mateo Gómez, 48:Apr-Jun84-190
Arnaiz, J.M. Eugenio Lucas.
P.E. Muller, 90:Mar84-169
Arnason, D. 50 Stories and a Piece of
Advice.
R. Hatch, 102(CanL):Summer84-140

Ashbee, A., ed. Lists of Payments to the
King's Musick in the Reign of Charles II
(1660-1685).
  W. Shaw, 410(M&L):Jan84-81
Ashbery, J. Selected Poems.
  J. Fenton, 441:29Dec85-10
Ashbery, J. A Wave.*
  J. Hollander, 676(YR):Autumn84-xxiii
  J.D. McClatchy, 491:Feb85-291
  R. McDowell, 364:Dec84/Jan85-126
  T. Paulin, 493:Sep84-32
  P. Stitt, 219(GaR):Fall84-628
  D. Walker, 199:Spring85-63
Ashbrook, J. The Astronomical Scrapbook.
  (L.J. Robinson, ed)
  S. Boxer, 441:21Apr85-39
Ashbrook, W. Donizetti and his Operas.*
  R. Swift, 451:Fall84-164
Ashe, G. The Discovery of King Arthur.
  P-L. Adams, 61:Mar85-124
Ashelford, J. A Visual History of Cos-
tume: The Sixteenth Century.*
  B. Scott, 39:Aug84-148
Ashford, O.M. Prophet or Professor?
  J. Mason, 617(TLS):29Mar85-366
Ashkenazy, V. and J. Parrott. Ashkenazy.
  J. Methuen-Campbell, 415:Dec84-705
Ashley, M. Dancing for Balanchine.
  R. Craft, 453(NYRB):7Nov85-42
  N. Goldner, 441:14Apr85-27
Ashley, M. The People of England.
  639(VQR):Winter84-16
Ashton, D. About Rothko.*
  639(VQR):Spring84-63
Ashton, D. Rosa Bonheur.
  E. Tufts, 584(SWR):Autumn84-473
Ashton, R. The German Idea.*
  J. Boening, 149(CLS):Summer84-227
  P. Hamilton, 541(RES):Aug84-397
Ashtor, E. The Jews of Moslem Spain.
  (Vol 3)
  R. Fletcher, 617(TLS):18Oct85-1190
Ashworth, M. and P. Wakefield. Teaching
the Non-English-Speaking Child: Grades
K-2.
  F. Stevens, 399(MLJ):Autumn84-269
Asimov, I. The Exploding Suns.
  I. Poliski, 441:21Apr85-39
Asimov, I. Robots and Empire.
  G. Jonas, 441:20Oct85-20
Asimov, I. and K.A. Frenkel. Robots.
  R. Draper, 453(NYRB):24Oct85-46
Asín Palacios, M. The Mystical Philosophy
of Ibn Masarra and His Followers.
  P.E. Walker, 318(JAOS):Oct-Dec83-761
Asín Palacios, M. Saint John of the Cross
and Islam.
  W. Gray, 485(PE&W):Apr84-232
Aslet, C. The Last Country Houses.*
  S. Meacham, 637(VS):Spring84-382
Aslet, C. and A. Powers. The National
Trust Book of the English House.
  H.G. Slade, 617(TLS):8Nov85-1273
Aspaturian, V.V., J. Valenta and D.P.
Burke, eds. Eurocommunism Between East
and West.
  J. De Bardeleben, 104(CASS):Fall84-363
Aspital, A.W., comp. Catalogue of the
Pepys Library at Magdalene College,
Cambridge. (Vol 3, Pt 1)
  J. van der Waals, 600:Vol 14No2-143

Aspley, K., D. Bellos and P. Sharratt, eds.
Myth and Legend in French Literature.*
  W.D. Howarth, 402(MLR):Apr84-448
Asplund, A. and M. Hako, eds. Kansan-
musiikki.
  P. Anttonen, 64(Arv):Vol138-191
Asquith, M. The Autobiography of Margot
Asquith. (M. Bonham Carter, ed)
  617(TLS):27Sep85-1071
"Assays: Critical Approaches to Medieval
and Renaissance Texts." (Vol 1) (P.A.
Knapp and M.A. Stugrin, eds)
  V. Edden, 541(RES):Aug84-351
Assezat, C. and J-B. Martin. Le Velay.
  J-P. Chambon, 553(RLiR):Jul-Dec84-446
Assouline, P. Gaston Gallimard.
  P. Fawcett, 617(TLS):12Apr85-412
Astaf'ev, V. Car'-ryba.
  D. Milivojević, 558(RLJ):Winter-
  Spring84-330
Astley, T. An Item from the Late News.
Beachmasters.
  S. Dawson, 617(TLS):15Nov85-1295
Aston, M. Lollards and Reformers.
  R.M., 617(TLS):5Apr85-395
Åström, P. and S.A. Eriksson. Finger-
prints and Archaeology.*
  Y. Calvet, 555:Vol58fascl-108
Aswad, B. Family Passions.
  R.D. MacDougall, 441:4Aug85-16
Athanassiadi-Fowden, P. Julian and Hellen-
ism.*
  E.D. Hunt, 303(JoHS):Vol 104-221
  W.E. Kaegi, Jr., 122:Oct84-349
Atkins, G.D. The Faith of John Dryden.*
  J.D. Canfield, 677(YES):Vol 14-316
  P. Hammond, 541(RES):Feb84-85
Atkins, G.D. Reading Deconstruction/Decon-
structive Reading.*
  W.E. Cain, 128(CE):Dec84-811
  R.H. Dammers, 536:Vol6-321
  E.F. Mengel, 566:Spring85-176
Atkins, H. and P. Cotes. The Barbirollis.
  R. Anderson, 415:Apr84-212
Atkins, S. and B. Hoggett. Women and the
Law.
  M. Cremona, 617(TLS):8Feb85-143
Atkins, W. The Elgar-Atkins Friendship.
  R. Anderson, 415:Aug84-442
Atkinson, D. The End of the Russian Land
Commune 1905-1930.
  B. Eklof, 104(CASS):Winter84-480
  D.A.J. Macey, 550(RusR):Apr84-197
  M. Perrie, 575(SEER):Jul84-460
Atkinson, M. Explanations in the Study of
Child Language Development.
  S.H. Foster, 350:Mar85-206
Atkinson, M. Plotinus, "Ennead V. 1."
  É. des Places, 555:Vol58fasc2-309
Atkinson, M., D. Kilby and I. Roca. Foun-
dations of General Linguistics.*
  T.E. Kiffer, 399(MLJ):Summer84-184
Attanasio, A.A. In Other Worlds.
  G. Jonas, 441:20Jan85-21
Attebery, B. The Fantasy Tradition in
American Literature.*
  R. Gray, 447(N&Q):Apr83-184
Atten, A. Le wallon frontalier de Doncols-
Sonlez/Grenzwallonisch aus Doncols-
Soller.
  J. Kramer, 547(RF):Band96Heft1/2-133

Attridge, D. The Rhythms of English
  Poetry.*
  N.S. Laff, 128(CE):Sep84-493
  A. Rodway, 89(BJA):Winter84-83
  J. Shapiro, 405(MP):Feb85-345
  E. Standop, 38:Band102Heft1/2-187
Atwood, M. Bluebeard's Egg.*
  C.R., 376:Feb84-138
Atwood, M. Interlunar.
  R.B. Hatch, 648(WCR):Apr85-47
Atwood, M. Murder in the Dark.*
  K. Irie, 526:Winter84-85
Atwood, M. Second Words.*
  C. Gerson, 102(CanL):Winter83-176
Atwood, M. True Stories.*
  R. Pybus, 565:Winter83/84-68
Aubenas, J., ed. Chantal Akerman.
  J. Van Baelen, 207(FR):Dec84-343
Aubert, J. Baker's Dozen.
  J. Carter, 219(GaR):Winter84-881
Aubrun, M-M. Léon Benouville, 1821-1859.
  J.J.L. Whiteley, 90:May84-302
Aubrun, M-M. Supplément au catalogue
  raisonné de l'oeuvre de Jules Dupré.
  N. Green, 90:Feb84-94
Auchincloss, L. Honorable Men.
  T.R. Edwards, 453(NYRB):19Dec85-54
  A.R. Gurney, Jr., 441:13Oct85-3
Auden, W.H. Secondary Worlds.
  617(TLS):8Mar85-271
Auden, W.H. and P.B. Taylor. Norse Poems.*
  U. Dronke, 541(RES):Aug84-417
Audley, P. Canada's Cultural Industries.
  G. Woodcock, 102(CanL):Summer84-86
Audry, C. L'Héritage.
  R. Millet, 450(NRF):Sep84-99
Audureau, J. Félicité.
  B.L. Knapp, 207(FR):Apr85-751
Auel, J.M. The Mammoth Hunters.
  C. Cambas, 441:24Nov85-24
Auerbach, N. Woman and the Demon.*
  C.S.C., 636(VP):Winter84-456
  S. Hudson, 577(SHR):Spring84-185
  L. Pannill, 70:Mar-Apr84-121
  P. Thomson, 637(VS):Winter84-237
  M. Tippett, 529(QQ):Summer84-479
Augarde, T. The Oxford Guide to Word
  Games.
  D.A.N. Jones, 362:3Jan85-28
Augros, R.M. and G.N. Stanciu. The New
  Story of Science.
  S. Montgomery, 469:Vol 10No3-108
Aulotte, R., ed. Le pamphlet en France au
  XVIe siècle.
  J.J. Supple, 208(FS):Jul84-333
Aulotte, R. Mathurin Régnier: Les Satires.
  C. Abraham, 475:Vol 11No20-210
  J.D. Lyons, 210(FrF):Sep84-366
  D.L. Rubin, 551(RenQ):Winter84-646
Auroux, S. La sémiotique des encyclo-
  pédistes.
  J. Andresen, 567:Vol149No3/4-361
Ausband, S.C. Myth and Meaning, Myth and
  Order.
  H.W. Fulmer, 583:Fall84-94
Austen, J. Jane Austen's "Sir Charles
  Grandison."* (B. Southam, ed)
  P. Honan, 447(N&Q):Apr83-173
Austen, J. Selected Letters. (R.W. Chap-
  man, ed)
  617(TLS):8Mar85-271
Auster, A. Actresses and Suffragists.
  R.K. Bank, 615(TJ):Oct84-433

Auster, P. City of Glass.
  T. Olson, 441:3Nov85-31
  442(NY):30Dec85-79
Auster, P., ed. The Random House Book of
  Twentieth-Century French Poetry.*
  G.W. Ireland, 529(QQ):Spring84-204
  D. Schier, 569(SR):Fall84-xc
Auster, P. - see Joubert, J.
Austin, A. Matthew Lyon.
  R.C. Stuart, 106:Summer84-159
Austin, D. The Portable City.
  J. Acheson, 102(CanL):Autumn84-162
Austin, M. A Woman of Genius.
  B.L. Clark, 441:1Sep85-14
"Authors and Philosophers."
  H. Godin, 208(FS):Oct84-496
Autin, J. Prosper Mérimée.
  B.T. Cooper, 446(NCFS):Summer-Fall84-
  209
van der Auwera, J. and W. Vandeweghe, eds.
  Studies over Nederlandse partikels.
  B.J. Hoff, 204(FdL):Dec84-316
Auxter, T. Kant's Moral Teleology.
  A. Broadie, 342:Band75Heft4-500
Auzas, P-M., ed. Actes du Colloque Inter-
  national Viollet-le-Duc, Paris 1980.
  B. Bergdoll, 90:Jun84-363
"The Available Press/PEN Short Story Col-
  lection."
  R. Atwan, 441:29Dec85-7
Avalle-Arce, J.B. - see de Cervantes
  Saavedra, M.
Avanesova, R.I. and V.V. Ivanova, eds.
  Istoričeskaja grammatika russkogo jazyka.
  (Vol 3)
  F.Y. Gladney, 574(SEEJ):Winter84-565
  R. Marti, 559:Vol8No1-59
Avedon, R. In the American West: 1979-
  1984.
  A. Grundberg, 441:8Dec85-22
Aveleyra-Sadowska, T. Cartas de Polonia.
  E.S. Urbański, 497(PolR):Vol29No1/2-
  170
Avellaneda, A. El habla de la ideología.*
  T. Running, 238:Sep84-479
Averill, J. - see Wordsworth, W.
Avilés Farré, J. La Izquierda burguesa en
  la II República.
  R. Carr, 617(TLS):4Oct85-1105
Avineri, S. The Making of Modern Zionism.*
  J. Agassi, 262:Jul84-311
Avins, C. Border Crossings.
  B. Jones, 104(CASS):Winter84-444
  M. Raskin, 395(MFS):Winter84-730
Avishai, B. The Tragedy of Zionism.
  A. Hertzberg, 441:13Oct85-7
Avison, M. Winter Sun/The Dumbfounding.
  R. Berry, 102(CanL):Autumn84-136
Avonto, L. Mercurino Arborio di Gattinara
  e l'America.
  R. Bireley, 551(RenQ):Autumn84-449
Avonto, L. and others, eds. Mercurino
  Arborio di Gattinara, Gran Cancelliere
  di Carlo V.
  R. Bireley, 551(RenQ):Autumn84-449
Avril, F. and others. Manuscrits enlum-
  inés de la Bibliothèque Nationale:
  Manuscrits de la Peninsule Iberique.
  M.C. Muñoz-Delgado, 48:Jul-Sep83-307
Awasthi, S. and I., eds. Chambers English-
  Hindi Dictionary.
  M.C. Shapiro, 318(JAOS):Oct-Dec83-749

Axelrod, A. Charles Brockden Brown.*
    B. Rosenthal, 587(SAF):Spring84-114
    J.R. Russo, 594:Fall84-341
Axelrod, S.G. and H. Deese. Robert Lowell.
    S. Moore, 534(RALS):Autumn82-251
Axelrod, T.M. Collecting Historical Docu-
    ments.
    K.W. Rendell, 517(PBSA):Vol78No4-529
Axsom, R.H. The Prints of Frank Stella.
    G. van Hensbergen, 90:Feb84-100
Axtell, J. The Invasion Within.
    W. Cronon, 441:3Nov85-15
Ayal, E.B., ed. The Study of Thailand.
    R. Basham, 293(JASt):May84-594
de Ayala, P.L. - see under López de Ayala,
    P.
Ayckbourn, A. Way Upstream.
    D. Devlin, 157:No153-46
Ayer, A.J. Freedom and Morality and Other
    Essays.*
    483:Oct84-558
Ayer, A.J. Philosophy in the Twentieth
    Century.*
    J. Teichman, 483:Jul84-415
    D.D. Todd, 154:Mar84-169
Ayer, A.J. Wittgenstein.
    C. McGinn, 617(TLS):7Jun85-626
    A. Quinton, 362:13Jun85-28
    A. Ryan, 176:Nov85-63
    442(NY):30Dec85-79
Ayers, J. The Catalogue of the Baur Col-
    lection, Geneva: Japanese Ceramics.*
    "Skipjack," 463:Summer84-196
Ayerst, D. Garvin of the Observer.
    P. Clarke, 617(TLS):12Apr85-400
    A. Hetherington, 362:7Feb85-24
Ayim, M. Peirce's View of the Roles of
    Reason and Instinct in Scientific
    Inquiry.
    J.J. Fitzgerald, 619:Summer84-343
Ayling, S. A Portrait of Sheridan.
    D. Profumo, 617(TLS):20Sep85-1034
Ayme, A. Seize et une variations.
    C. Limousin, 98:Oct84-844
Azar, I. Discurso retórico y mundo pas-
    toral en "Égloga segunda" de Garcilaso.*
    I.A. Corfis, 547(RF):Band96Heft1/2-212
    D. Fernández-Morera, 240(HR):Spring84-
    235
Azarya, V. The Armenian Quarter of Jerusa-
    lem.
    D. Pryce-Jones, 617(TLS):21Jun85-691
Azéma, J-P. From Munich to the Liberation,
    1938-1944.
    M. Larkin, 617(TLS):28Jun85-731
Aziz, M. - see James, H.
Aziza, C. and others. Dictionnaire des
    figures et des personnages.
    J. Laroche, 207(FR):Feb85-468
Aznar, J.C. - see under Camón Aznar, J.
Azoy, G.W. Buzkashi.*
    R.L. Canfield, 293(JASt):Nov83-174
Azuela, A. Shadows of Silence.
    J. Kandell, 441:21Jul85-7

Baader, G. and G. Keil, eds. Medizin im
    mittelalterlichen Abendland.
    B.D. Haage, 684(ZDA):Band113Heft4-163
Babbitt, I. Representative Writings.
    (G.A. Panichas, ed)
    A. Netboy, 149(CLS):Summer84-253

Babcock, A.E. Portraits of Artists.
    J.C. McLaren, 207(FR):May85-898
Babington-Smith, C. John Masefield.
    617(TLS):27Dec85-1491
Bablet, D., ed. Les voies de la création
    théâtrale XI.
    D. Gerould, 615(TJ):Dec84-549
Bacarisse, S., ed. Contemporary Latin-
    American Fiction.*
    J. Labanyi, 402(MLR):Jan84-221
Baccheschi, E., ed. Il Museo dell'
    Accademia Ligustica di Belle Arti: La
    Pinacoteca.
    E. Waterhouse, 90:Oct84-646
Bacchi, C.L. Liberation Deferred?
    S. Jackel, 102(CanL):Autumn84-90
Bacchus, W.I. Staffing for Foreign
    Affairs.
    639(VQR):Spring84-59
Bach, H.I. The German Jew.
    G. Craig, 453(NYRB):13Jun85-3
    A. Knopf, 441:24Mar85-25
    A.J. Sherman, 617(TLS):28Jun85-730
Bach, S. Final Cut.
    W. Murray, 441:28Jul85-7
Bachelard, G. The New Scientific Spirit.
    J. Schmidt, 441:24Mar85-19
Bachem, M. Heimito von Doderer.*
    A.C. Ulmer, 406:Summer84-236
Bachman, B. Upstream.
    C. Verderese, 441:17Mar85-27
Bachman, R. Thinner.
    J. Eidus, 441:14Apr85-27
Bachmann, C., J. Lindenfeld and J. Simonin.
    Langage et comunications sociales.*
    D. Birdsong, 207(FR):Oct84-178
Bachmann, I. Bilder aus ihrem Leben. (A.
    Hapkemeyer, ed)
    R. Pichl, 602:Band15Heft1-165
Bachmann, I. Wir müssen wahre Sätze
    finden. (C. Koschel and I. von Weiden-
    baum, eds)
    R. Pichl, 602:Band15Heft1-168
Bachmann-Geiser, B. Die Volksmusikinstru-
    mente der Schweiz.*
    T. Vennum, Jr., 187:Fall85-517
Bachrach, A.G.H. and R.G. Collmer - see
    Huygens, L.
Bacigalupo, M. The Formèd Trace.*
    R. Casillo, 536:Vol6-275
    D. Davie, 107(CRCL):Mar84-144
Backes, H. Die Hochzeit Merkurs und der
    Philologie.
    J.C. King, 589:Apr84-366
    R.H. Lawson, 301(JEGP):Apr84-265
Backès, J-L. Le mythe d'Hélène.
    R. Pouilliart, 356(LR):Nov84-320
Backès, J-L. Racine.
    R. Parish, 208(FS):Jul84-338
Backus, C. The Nan-chao Kingdom and T'ang
    China's Southwestern Frontier.
    H.J. Wechsler, 293(JASt):Nov83-130
Bacon, F. La nouvelle Atlantide [suivi
    de] le Doeuff, M. and M. Llasera.
    Voyage dans la pensée baroque.
    J. Bernhardt, 154:Mar84-167
    G. Rees, 189(EA):Jan-Mar85-80
Bacon, R. Roger Bacon's Philosophy of
    Nature. (D.C. Lindberg, ed and trans)
    G. Marcil, 589:Oct84-921
    K.H. Tachau, 319:Oct85-586
Baczko, B. Les imaginaires sociaux.
    R. Gervais, 154:Sep84-551

Badash, L. Kapitza, Rutherford, and the Kremlin.
  L. Graham, 441:12May85-11
  D. Joravsky, 453(NYRB):5Dec85-26
  J. Ziman, 617(TLS):12Jul85-765
Badash, L., J. Hirschfelder and H. Broida, eds. Reminiscences of Los Alamos, 1943-1945.
  J.W. Grove, 529(QQ):Spring84-73
Badcock, C.R. Madness and Modernity.
  S.G.P., 185:Jul85-974
Bader, W. and J. Riesz, eds. Literatur und Kolonialismus I.
  B. Sändig, 654(WB):9/1984-1564
Badhab, I.M. Un Tratado Sefardi de Moral. (A.M. Riaño Lopez, trans)
  E. Koditi, 390:Jan84-50
Badi, B. and P. Birnbaum. The Sociology of the State.
  J.K., 185:Jan85-390
Badinter, E. Émilie, Émilie.*
  J.L. Epstein, 188(ECr):Winter84-84
Badura-Skoda, E. and P. Branscombe, eds. Schubert Studies.
  L.M. Griffel, 414(MusQ):Spring84-278
  J. Reed, 410(M&L):Jan84-74
"Baebii Italici, 'Ilias Latina.'" (M. Scaffai, ed)
  P. Flobert, 555:Vol58fasc1-136
Baehr, R. - see Marie de France
Baender, P. - see Twain, M.
Baer, F.E. Sources and Analogues of the Uncle Remus Tales.*
  R.D. Abrahams, 538(RAL):Summer84-293
  R. Hemenway, 650(WF):Apr84-150
Baer, J.A. Equality under the Constitution.
  C.R. Sunstein, 185:Oct84-153
de Baere, G. - see van Ruusbroec, J.
Baerentzen, L. - see Stevens, J.M., C.M. Woodhouse and D.J. Wallace
Bagdikian, B.H. The Media Monopoly.*
  D. Henry, 583:Fall84-96
Bagger, H. and B. Nørretranders. Politikens Ruslandshistorie. (Vol 2)
  D. Kirby, 575(SEER):Oct84-594
Bagley, J.J. The Earls of Derby 1485-1985.
  D. Cannadine, 617(TLS):31May85-600
Bagnall, N. A Defence of Clichés.
  D.J. Enright, 617(TLS):28Jun85-717
Bagni, P. Guercino a Piacenza.
  N. Turner, 90:Oct84-641
Bahdanovič, M., A. Harun and Ž. Biadula. The Images Swarm Free. (V. Rich, trans; A. McMillin, ed)
  S. Akiner, 575(SEER):Jul84-473
  M. Pursglove, 402(MLR):Jan84-254
Bahl, K.C. Studies in the Semantic Structure of Hindi. (Vol 1)
  V. Gambhir, 318(JAOS):Oct-Dec83-814
Bahner, W. Formen, Ideen, Prozesse in den Literaturen der romanischen Völker. (Vol 1)
  A. Scaglione, 545(RPh):May84-526
Bahner, W. Kontinuität und Diskontinuität in der Herausbildung der romanischen Sprachwissenschaft.
  H. Meier, 547(RF):Band96Heft4-436
Bahr, E., E.P. Harris and L.G. Lyon, eds. Humanität und Dialog.*
  G.L. Fink, 133:Band17Heft1/2-137

Bahri, H. Learners' Hindi-English Dictionary.*
  M.C. Shapiro, 318(JAOS):Oct-Dec83-749
Bahro, R. From Red to Green.
  T.G. Ash, 453(NYRB):31Jan85-33
Baier, L. Die grosse Ketzerei.
  C. Neubaur, 384:Oct84-823
Bail, M. Ian Fairweather.*
  U. Hoff, 39:Mar84-225
Bail, M. Homesickness.
  P. Lewis, 565:Spring84-64
Bailey, A. Along the Edge of the Forest.*
  639(VQR):Winter84-19
Bailey, A. England, First and Last.
  N.A. Basbanes, 441:1Sep85-15
  442(NY):7Oct85-142
Bailey, B. The English Village Green.
  S. Jenkins, 362:5Sep85-25
Bailey, C.J. A Guide to Reference and Bibliography for Theatre Research. (2nd ed)
  R.H. Hethmon, 610:Autumn84-260
Bailey, C-J.N. On the Yin and Yang Nature of Language.
  D.H., 355(LSoc):Mar84-127
  J.P. Stemberger, 350:Mar85-241
Bailey, D.R.S. - see under Shackleton Bailey, D.R.
Bailey, H. Hannie Richards.
  V. Bogdanor, 362:23May85-32
  N. Lawson, 617(TLS):19Jul85-800
Bailey, J. Selected Essays.
  R. Asselineau, 189(EA):Jul-Sep85-302
Bailey, L.R., ed. The Word of God.
  W. Allen, 577(SHR):Fall84-351
Bailey, R.W. - see Pike, K.L.
Bailey, R.W. and M. Görlach, eds. English as a World Language.*
  D. Nehls, 257(IRAL):Nov84-325
  U. Oomen, 38:Band102Heft1/2-171
Bailly-Herzberg, J. - see Pissarro, C.
Bain, D.M. - see Menander
Bainbridge, B. Mum and Mr. Armitage.
  D.J. Enright, 362:5Dec85-32
  P. Kemp, 617(TLS):20Dec85-1463
Bainbridge, B. Watson's Apology.*
  J. Lasdun, 176:Feb85-42
  M. Stasio, 441:20Oct85-7
  442(NY):25Nov85-163
Bainbridge, C., ed. 100 Years of Journalism.
  A. Hetherington, 362:24Jan85-25
Baines, E. The Birth Machine.
  L. Marcus, 617(TLS):27Sep85-1070
Bak, J.M. and B.K. Király, eds. From Hunyadi to Rákóczi.
  R.J.W. Evans, 575(SEER):Apr84-277
Bakalla, M.H. Arabic Linguistics.
  R. Allen, 355(LSoc):Mar84-127
  G.F. Meier, 682(ZPSK):Band37Heft5-639
Bakari, M.M. The Customs of the Swahili People. (J.W.T. Allen, ed and trans)
  J.D. Rollins, 538(RAL):Winter84-619
Baker, C. Baby Doll.
  J. Nangle, 200:Feb84-113
Baker, C. The Echoing Green.*
  L. Wagner, 659(ConL):Winter85-482
Baker, C. - see Hemingway, E.
Baker, C.A. Practical Law for Arts Administrators.
  J. Pick, 157:No153-53
Baker, D. Laws of the Land.
  B. Weller, 502(PrS):Spring84-87

17

Baker, D.C., J.L. Murphy and L.B. Hall,
Jr., eds. The Late Medieval Religious
Plays of Bodleian MSS Digby 133 and E
Museo 160.*
S. Carpenter, 541(RES):Aug84-352
Baker, G.P. and P.M.S. Hacker. Frege.
M. Dummett, 479(PhQ):Jul84-377
Baker, G.P. and P.M.S. Hacker. Language,
Sense and Nonsense.
C. Wright, 617(TLS):11Jan85-46
Baker, G.P. and P.M.S. Hacker. Scepticism,
Rules and Language.
A. Margalit, 617(TLS):24May85-587
Baker, G.P. and P.M.S. Hacker. Wittgen-
stein.* (Vol 1)
P. Carruthers, 606:Mar84-451
483:Jan84-140
Baker, H.A., Jr. Blues, Ideology, and
Afro-American Literature.
R.E.F., 30:Spring85-93
R.G. O'Meally, 441:17Mar85-18
Baker, H.R., Jr., ed. Three American
Literatures.
T. King, 649(WAL):Aug84-170
Baker, J. and R. Cardinal, eds. Conserva-
tion, Réhabilitation, Recyclage.
H. Kalman, 576:Mar84-77
Baker, L. Brandeis and Frankfurter.*
J. Rury, 42(AR):Summer84-376
639(VQR):Autumn84-120
Baker, L. The Percys of Mississippi.
J.E. Hardy, 578:Spring85-127
R.S. Moore, 27(AL):Oct84-438
J.B. Wittenberg, 395(MFS):Winter84-796
639(VQR):Spring84-54
Baker, M. Cops: Their Lives in Their Own
Words.
442(NY):14Oct85-144
Baker, M. Our Three Selves.
T. Mallon, 441:8Sep85-3
Baker, P. and C. Corne. Isle de France
Creole.*
J. Holm, 355(LSoc):Mar84-99
S.G. Thomason, 355(LSoc):Mar84-94
A. Valdman, 399(MLJ):Winter84-396
Baker, P.G. A Reassessment of D.H.
Lawrence's "Aaron's Rod."
295(JML):Nov84-471
Baker, R. Growing Up.*
M. Ellmann, 569(SR):Fall84-661
Baker, R.S. The Dark Historic Page.
A. Dommergues, 189(EA):Jul-Sep85-344
C.M. Holmes, 594:Winter84-460
D. Watt, 301(JEGP):Jul84-457
Baker, T.L. A Field Guide to American
Windmills.
A. Pollack, 441:11Aug85-14
Baker, W. The Libraries of George Eliot
and G.H. Lewes.
R. Ashton, 541(RES):Nov84-594
Baker, W.A. The Mayflower and Other Colo-
nial Vessels.
J.O. Sands, 658:Winter84-302
Bakhash, S. The Reign of the Ayatollahs.*
B. Lewis, 453(NYRB):17Jan85-10
P. Mansfield, 362:7Feb85-22
D. Spanier, 176:Apr85-73
Bakhtin, M.M. The Dialogic Imagination.*
(M. Holquist, ed)
M. Ehre, 494:Vol5No1-172
B. Kochis and W.G. Regier, 223:
Winter81-530
K. Pomorska, 567:Vol48No1/2-169

Bakker, B.H. - see Zola, É.
Bakker, B.H., with C. Becker - see Zola, É.
Bakker, J. Fiction as Survival Strategy.
G. Hily-Mane, 189(EA):Jan-Mar85-102
J. Tavernier-Courbin, 395(MFS):
Winter84-810
Balaban, J. Coming Down Again.
442(NY):26Aug85-87
Balakian, A., ed. The Symbolist Movement
in the Literature of European Languages.*
J-L. Backès, 549(RLC):Jan-Mar84-105
Etiemble, 149(CLS):Spring84-76
H. Peyre, 107(CRCL):Jun84-313
Balakian, P. Sad Days of Light.
J. Elledge, 491:May84-111
Balan, J., ed. Identifications.
E. Orenstein, 627(UTQ):Summer84-496
Balazard, S. Le Château des tortues.
E. Sellin, 207(FR):Feb85-488
Balbert, P. and P.L. Marcus, eds. D.H.
Lawrence.
K. Brown, 617(TLS):18Oct85-1171
Balbir, N., ed and trans. Dānāṣṭakakathā.
J.W. de Jong, 259(IIJ):Jul84-215
Baldi, P. An Introduction to the Indo-
European Languages.
A.M. Davies, 353:Vol22No4-559
H.M. Hoenigswald, 215(GL):Vol24No1-71
Baldi, P., ed. Papers from the XIIth Lin-
guistic Symposium on Romance Languages.
R. Posner, 353:Vol22No6-913
Baldick, C. The Social Mission of English
Criticism, 1848-1932.*
M. Roberts, 506(PSt):Dec84-269
Baldinger, F. Vom Faktum zur Fiktion.
P. Goetsch, 72:Band221Heft2-378
Baldinger, K. Complément bibliographique
au "Provenzalisches Supplementwörterbuch"
d'Emil Levy.
G. Straka, 553(RLiR):Jul-Dec84-484
Baldinger, K. Dictionnaire étymologique
de l'ancien français.* (fasc C4)
K.A. Goddard, 208(FS):Apr84-193
Baldinger, K. Dictionnaire onomasiolo-
gique de l'ancien gascon. (fasc 1 and
2/3)
P. Swiggers, 464:Vol30fasc1/2-269
Baldinger, K. Dictionnaire onomasiolo-
gique de l'ancien occitan.* (fasc 1)
(rev by I. Popelar)
K.A. Goddard, 208(FS):Oct84-451
P. Swiggers, 464:Vol30fasc1/2-269
Baldinger, K. Dictionnaire onomasiolo-
gique de l'ancien occitan. (fasc 2)
(rev by I. Popelar)
P. Swiggers, 464:Vol30fasc1/2-269
Baldwin, A. The Theme of Government in
"Piers Plowman."*
P.M. Kean, 541(RES):Feb84-113
D. Mehl, 72:Band221Heft2-478
Baldwin, B. Suetonius.
A.R. Birley, 313:Vol74-245
Baldwin, B., with M. Gardine. Billy Bald-
win.
D. Guimaraes, 441:20Oct85-41
Baldwin, C. Nigerian Literature.
C.T. Maduka, 538(RAL):Spring84-128
Baldwin, D.A. Economic Statecraft.
M. Olson, 617(TLS):6Dec85-1391
Baldwin, H.L. Samuel Beckett's Real
Silence.
K. Morrison, 299:Number9-142

Baldwin, J. The Evidence of Things Not
Seen.
  J. Fleming, 441:24Nov85-25
Baldwin, J. Jimmy's Blues.
  R. Pybus, 565:Summer84-56
Baldwin, J. The Price of the Ticket.
  S. Muwakkil, 441:20Oct85-35
  T. Teachout, 129:Dec85-76
Baldwin, M. King Horn.
  D. O'Driscoll, 493:Jan84-70
Baldwin, T.D., ed. Teaching Materials for
Italian.
  G. King, 278(IS):Vol39-152
Balfour, D. - see Symeon of Thessalonica
Ball, J. Paul and Thomas Sandby, Royal
Academicians.
  E. Adams, 617(TLS):25Oct85-1216
Ball, M.S. The Promise of American Law.
  T.D. Eisele, 396(ModA):Spring/Summer84-
  273
Ball, R.J. - see Highet, G.
Ballagh, R. Dublin.
  R. Tracy, 174(Éire):Fall84-157
Ballanche, P-S. "La Ville des expiations"
et autres textes. (J-R. Derré, ed)
  F.P. Bowman, 535(RHL):Jul/Aug84-632
Ballantine, C. Twentieth Century Symphony.
  L. Foreman, 607:Mar84-51
  S. Walsh, 415:Jan84-28
Ballard, G. Memoirs of Several Ladies of
Great Britain. (R. Perry, ed)
  B. Brophy, 617(TLS):26Jul85-814
Ballard, J.G. Empire of the Sun.*
  A. Higgins, 364:Oct84-88
Ballesteros, J.B. - see under Bernales
Ballesteros, J.
Ballmer, T. and W. Brennenstuhl. Speech
Act Classification.*
  S.R. Sharma, 261:Mar/Jun82-38
Ballweg, O. and T-M. Seibert, eds. Rhetor-
ische Rechtslehre.
  J-L. Gardies, 542:Apr-Jun84-244
Balmas, E. Saggi e studi sul Rinascimento
francese.
  Y. Bellenger, 535(RHL):May/Jun84-450
Balmer, H.P. Philosophie der menschlichen
Dinge.
  P. Probst, 687:Apr-Jun84-332
Balmori, D., S.F. Voss and M. Wortman.
Notable Family Networks in Latin America.
  R. Carr, 617(TLS):10May85-515
Balsamo, L. Produzione e circolazione
libraria in Emilia (XV-XVIII sec.).
  C. Fahy, 78(BC):Autumn84-385
  D.E. Rhodes, 354:Sep84-292
Baltrušaitis, J. Aberrations.
  J-L. Gautier, 450(NRF):Apr84-126
Balys, J.P., comp. Lithuanian Periodicals
in American Libraries.
  J.I. Press, 575(SEER):Jul84-477
de Balzac, H. Louis Lambert; Les Pro-
scrits; Jésus-Christ en Flandre. (S.S.
de Sacy, ed)
  C. Smethurst, 208(FS):Jul84-353
de Balzac, H. La Peau de chagrin. (M.
Ambrière, ed)
  M. Ménard, 535(RHL):May/Jun84-459
de Balzac, H. La Vieille Fille. (R. Kopp,
ed)
  C. Smethurst, 208(FS):Jul84-353
de Balzac, J-L.G. Épîtres Latines. (J.
Jehasse and B. Yon, eds and trans)
  A.H.T. Levi, 208(FS):Jan84-54

Bambara, T.C. Gorilla, My Love. The Sea
Birds Are Still Alive.
  L. Marcus, 617(TLS):27Sep85-1070
Bamber, L. Comic Women, Tragic Men.*
  L.E. Boose, 405(MP):Aug84-91
  M.B. Rose, 570(SQ):Spring84-123
Bamborschke, U. and others. Die Erzählung
über Petr Ordynskij.
  C. Goehrke, 688(ZSP):Band44Heft2-438
Bambrough, R. Moral Scepticism and Moral
Knowledge.
  D.C. Long, 449:Mar84-132
Bamford, C. - see Milosz, O.V.D.
Bamford, F. A Dictionary of Edinburgh
Wrights and Furniture Makers, 1660-1840.
  S.J., 90:Nov84-713
  G. Wills, 39:Jul84-76
Bammesberger, A., ed. Das etymologische
Wörterbuch.
  L. Zgusta, 350:Mar85-215
Bammesberger, A. A Handbook of Irish: An
Outline of Modern Irish Grammar.
  J.E. McElwain, 215(GL):Vol24No4-258
Bammesberger, A. A Handbook of Irish:
Essentials of Modern Irish.*
  Toshio Doi, 215(GL):Vol24No4-254
Banac, I., ed. The Effects of World War I.
  G. Schöpflin, 575(SEER):Oct84-635
Banac, I. The National Question in Yugo-
slavia.
  I. Deak, 453(NYRB):7Nov85-49
Banac, I. and P. Bushkovitch, eds. The
Nobility in Russia and Eastern Europe.
  M. Confino, 104(CASS):Winter84-457
  O. Subtelny, 550(RusR):Oct84-438
Bance, A. Theodor Fontane.
  M.S. Fries, 395(MFS):Summer84-387
Bance, A., ed. Weimar Germany.
  O. Durrani, 402(MLR):Oct84-990
  H. Siefken, 220(GL&L):Jan85-184
Bancroft, A. The Luminous Vision.
  R. Bradley, 589:Jul84-715
Bandelier, A. and others. Table de con-
cordances rythmique et syntaxique des
"Poésies" d'Arthur Rimbaud.* (Vol 2)
[shown in prev under Eigeldinger, F. and
others]
  A.L. Amprimoz, 446(NCFS):Summer85-298
Bandem, I.M. and F.E. de Boer. Kaja and
Kelod.
  B. Parr, 60:Sep-Oct84-121
Bandera Viani, M.C. Musei d'Italia,
Meraviglie d'Italia. (Vol 8)
  U. Middeldorf, 90:May84-291
Bandini, G. Die Erörterung der Wirksam-
keit.
  R. Rocher, 318(JAOS):Oct-Dec83-778
Bandle, O., W. Baumgartner and J. Glauser,
eds. Strindbergs Dramen im Lichte
neuerer Methodendiskussionen.*
  B. Lide, 301(JEGP):Jul84-428
Bandy, M.L., ed. Rediscovering French
Film.
  E.B. Turk, 207(FR):Apr85-747
Banfield, A. Unspeakable Sentences.*
  C. Lyas, 290(JAAC):Fall84-101
  H.F. Mosher, Jr., 599:Spring84-229
  G. Prince, 131(CL):Winter84-81
  H. Rinehart, 529(QQ):Summer84-450
Banfield, E.C. The Democratic Muse.*
  R.A. Smith, 290(JAAC):Winter84-221

Banham, J. and J. Harris, eds. William
Morris and the Middle Ages.
T. Hilton, 453(NYRB):25Apr85-22
Banks, I. Walking on Glass.
J. Mellors, 364:Mar85-100
Banks, I. The Wasp Factory.*
M. Hulse, 364:Jun84-111
Banks, O. The Caravaggio Obsession.*
M. Laski, 362:18Apr85-26
Banks, R. Continental Drift.
J. Atlas, 61:Feb85-94
C. Hitchens, 617(TLS):25Oct85-1203
J. Mellors, 362:10Oct85-29
J. Strouse, 441:24Mar85-11
R. Towers, 453(NYRB):11Apr85-36
442(NY):15Apr85-126
Bannister, M. Privileged Mortals.
H.T. Barnwell, 208(FS):Oct84-462
Bannour, W. Eugénie de Guérin ou une
chasteté ardente.
F-E. Dorenlot, 207(FR):Apr85-733
Banu, G. Bertolt Brecht ou le petit
contre le grand.
F. Pastorello, 549(RLC):Jul-Sep84-374
Baptist-Hlawatsch, G. Das katechetische
Werk Ulrichs von Pottenstein.
R. Hinderling, 684(ZDA):Band113Heft3-
124
R.E. Walker, 221(GQ):Winter84-141
Bar-Zohar, M. Arrows of the Almighty.
J. Coleman, 441:29Dec85-22
Barabasch, J. Fragen der Ästhetik und
Poetik.
A. Trebess, 654(WB):12/1984-2089
Barac-Kostrenčić, V. and others. Let's
Learn Croatian, Stage One.
T.F. Magner, 574(SEEJ):Summer84-279
Baraka, A. - see under Jones, L./A. Baraka
Baraka, A. and A., eds. Confirmation.
C. St. Peter, 376:Feb84-142
Barański, Z. and J. Litwinow, eds. Rosyj-
skie kierunki literackie.
H. Stephan, 574(SEEJ):Summer84-277
Barasch, M. Theories of Art.
D. Carrier, 617(TLS):2Aug85-842
Barash, D. Aging.
42(AR):Summer84-380
Barbagallo, A. Omaggio e Silone.
G. Pandini, 275(IQ):Winter84-113
Barbagallo, F. - see Fortunato, G.
Barbalet, J.M. Marx's Construction of
Social Theory.
D.I., 185:Jul85-983
Barber, B. The Logic and Limits of Trust.
R.E.G., 185:Oct84-177
Barber, B.R. Strong Democracy.*
S.A. Hadari, 185:Jul85-940
Barber, C. Mysterious Wales.
L.V. Grinsell, 203:Vol95No1-134
Barber, R. - see "Arthurian Literature"
Barbera, J. and W. McBrien. Stevie.
C. Reid, 617(TLS):29Nov85-1369
Barbera, J. and W. McBrien - see Smith, S.
Barberi, F. Tipografi romani del Cinque-
cento.
D.E. Rhodes, 354:Jun84-181
Barbier, C.P. and C.G. Millan - see
Mallarmé, S.
Barbier, J.P. Tobaland.
E.N. Quarcoopome, 2(AfrA):Feb84-80
Barbour, B.M., ed. Benjamin Franklin.
S. Neumann, 106:Winter84-421

Barbour, D. Visible Visions. (S. Kam-
boureli and R. Kroetsch, eds)
M. Fee, 376:Oct84-122
Barbour, D. - see Harris, B., G. Sawai and
F. Stenson
Barbour, D. and S. Scobie. The Pirates
of Pen's Chance.
M. Fiamengo, 102(CanL):Summer84-145
Barbour, D. and M.L. Stanley, eds. Writ-
ing Right.
P. Monk, 102(CanL):Winter83-85
Barbour, R. Greek Literary Hands (A.D.
400-1600).*
P.E. Easterling, 123:Vol34No2-297
R.S. Nelson, 122:Oct84-351
Barchilon, J. and P. Flinders. Charles
Perrault.*
J-L. Gautier, 535(RHL):Jul/Aug84-608
Barck, K., D. Schlenstedt and W. Thierse,
eds. Künstlerische Avantgarde.
M. Eifler, 221(GQ):Fall84-632
Bardazzi, S. and E. Castellani. La Villa
Medicea di Poggio a Caiano.
J.S. Ackerman, 551(RenQ):Spring84-107
Barendregt, H.P. The Lambda Calculus.
E. Engeler, 316:Mar84-301
Barentsen, A.A., R. Sprenger and M.G.M.
Tielmans, eds. South Slavic and Balkan
Linguistics.*
V.M. Du Feu, 575(SEER):Jul84-429
P. Herrity, 402(MLR):Jul84-761
Barfoot, J. Dancing in the Dark.
W. Keitner, 102(CanL):Winter83-116
L. Marcus, 617(TLS):27Sep85-1070
Barguillet, F. Le Roman au XVIIIe siècle.
G. Bremner, 208(FS):Jul84-346
Barickman, R., S. MacDonald and M. Stark.
Corrupt Relations.*
N. Auerbach, 301(JEGP):Oct84-570
J. Halperin, 579(SAQ):Winter84-123
M. Myers, 637(VS):Spring84-379
Baring, M. Flying Corps Headquarters 1914-
1918.
617(TLS):27Dec85-1491
Barish, J. The Antitheatrical Prejudice.*
J.R. Heller, 615(TJ):Mar82-130
C. Koelb, 131(CL):Summer84-260
Barkan, L. - see "Renaissance Drama"
Lady Barker. Station Life in New Zealand.
P. Bland, 364:Mar85-108
Barker, A.L. No Word of Love.
A. Duchêne, 617(TLS):21Jun85-702
J. Mellors, 362:30May85-32
Barker, E. The Making of a Moonie.*
S. Kemperman, 441:10Feb85-25
Barker, G. Anno Domini.*
R. Pybus, 565:Autumn84-73
Barker, J. The Superhistorians.*
A.P. Fell, 529(QQ):Summer84-438
Barker, J. - see Davies, W.H.
Barker, N. and J. Collins. A Sequel to
"An Enquiry into the Nature of Certain
Nineteenth Century Pamphlets" by John
Carter and Graham Pollard.*
A. Freeman, 354:Dec84-415
D. Gallup, 517(PBSA):Vol78No4-447
D. McKitterick, 78(BC):Spring84-105
C. Ricks, 453(NYRB):28Feb85-34
Barker, N. and J. Collins - see Carter, J.
and G. Pollard
Barker, P. Union Street.*
M. Gorra, 249(HudR):Spring84-154

20

Bass, T.A. The Eudaemonic Pie.
    F. Hapgood, 441:19May85-12
Bassanese, F. Gaspara Stampa.
    L. Tenenbaum, 276:Autumn84-261
Bassein, B.A. Women and Death.
    295(JML):Nov84-341
Bassnett-McGuire, S. Luigi Pirandello.
    R.W. Oliver, 397(MD):Dec84-646
    A. Paolucci, 130:Winter84/85-377
Basso, A., ed. Dizionario enciclopedico
    universale. (Vols 1 and 2)
    F. Lesure, 537:Vol70No1-121
Basson, M., R. Lipson and D. Ganos, eds.
    Troubling Problems in Medical Ethics.
    R. Baker, 185:Jan85-370
Basta Donzelli, G. Studio sull'Elettra di
    Euripide.
    E.M. Craik, 303(JoHS):Vol 104-203
Bastian, F. Defoe's Early Life.*
    J. Sutherland, 447(N&Q):Oct83-475
Bastian, K. Joyce Carol Oates's Short
    Stories Between Tradition and Innovation.
    W.N., 102(CanL):Winter83-189
Bastien, P. Le monnayage de l'atelier de
    Lyon de la réforme monétaire de Dioclé-
    tien à la fermeture temporaire de
    l'atelier en 316 (294-316). Le monnay-
    age de l'atelier de Lyon de la réouver-
    ture de l'atelier en 318 à la mort de
    Constantin (318-337).
    C.E. King, 313:Vol74-223
Bataille, G.M. and K.M. Sands. American
    Indian Women.
    C. Hunter, 223:Winter84-434
    R.D. Ortiz, 649(WAL):Nov84-244
Batchelor, J. The Edwardian Novelists.*
    N. Bradbury, 541(RES):Nov84-575
    P. Swinden, 148:Winter84-88
Batchelor, J. H.G. Wells.
    B. Bergonzi, 176:Jul/Aug85-31
    P. Kemp, 617(TLS):27Dec85-1479
Batchelor, J.C. American Falls.
    R. Smoodin, 441:13Oct85-32
Bates, D. Normandy before 1066.
    E.Z. Tabuteau, 589:Jul84-610
Bates, M.J. Wallace Stevens.
    D. Gioia, 441:27Oct85-13
Bateson, G. Geist und Natur.
    G. Vollmer, 687:Jul-Oct84-489
Bateson, V. Woven Fashion.
    P. Bach, 614:Summer85-38
Batkay, W.H. Authoritarian Politics in a
    Transitional State.
    A.C. Janos, 104(CASS):Spring-Summer84-
    221
Batman, R. American Ecclesiastes.
    A.M. Josephy, Jr., 441:17Mar85-46
    442(NY):11Feb85-127
Bätschmann, O. Dialektik der Malerei von
    Nicolas Poussin.*
    G. Boehm, 683:Band47Heft2-284
Bätschmann, O. and B. Schubiger - see
    Maurer, E.
Battesti-Pelegrin, J. Lope de Stúñiga.
    M. Ciceri, 547(RF):Band96Heft1/2-207
Battesti-Pelegrin, J. - see de Stúñiga, L.
Baude, M. P.H. Azaïs, témoin de son temps.
    A.J.L. Busst, 208(FS):Jul84-354
Baudelaire, C. Baudelaire's Flowers of
    Evil and Other Poems. (F. Duke, ed and
    trans)
    W.T. Bandy, 207(FR):Oct84-131

Baudelaire, C. Les Fleurs du Mal.* (R.
    Howard, trans)
    E. Grosholz, 249(HudR):Spring84-132
"Baudelaire: poeta e critico."
    G. Van Slyke, 535(RHL):Jul/Aug84-639
Baudot, A. and T. Lior. Basic Rules for
    Typesetting in French — Where They
    Differ from Rules in English.
    R.W. Tobin, 207(FR):Dec84-329
Baudrillard, J. Les stratégies fatales.
    M. Guillaume, 98:Mar84-198
Bauer, E. Deutsche Entlehnungen im tsche-
    chischen Wortschatz des J.A. Comenius.
    D. Short, 575(SEER):Jan84-575
Bauer, G., ed. Der Hochaltar der Schwab-
    acher Stadtkirche.
    E. König, 683:Band47Heft4-552
Bauer, L. English Word-Formation.
    G. Bourcier, 189(EA):Jan-Mar85-78
    J.T. Jensen, 320(CJL):Fall84-197
    J. Vizmuller-Zocco, 361:Mar84-255
Bauer, R. Didaktik der Barockpoetik.
    P. Hess, 221(GQ):Summer84-466
Bauer, R. and J. Wertheimer, eds. Das
    Ende des Stegreifspiels — Die Geburt
    des Nationaltheaters.
    M. Carlson, 678(YCGL):No33-93
Bauerle, R., ed. The James Joyce Song-
    book.*
    Z. Bowen, 329(JJQ):Spring85-327
    J. Hurt, 301(JEGP):Jan84-140
Baugh, J. Black Street Speech.
    R. Burling, 350:Mar85-204
Baugh, J. and J. Sherzer, eds. Language
    in Use.
    R. King, 350:Sep85-730
"Bauhaus Photography."
    A. Fern, 441:22Sep85-22
Baum, G. and D. Cameron. Ethics and Eco-
    nomics.
    V. di Norcia, 99:Oct84-34
Baum, M.T. - see under Tanguy Baum, M.
Bauman, R. Let Your Words Be Few.*
    A.L. Becker, 350:Dec85-916
    R.L. Schmalstieg, 215(GL):Vol24No4-250
Bauman, R. and R. Abrahams, eds. "And
    Other Neighborly Names."
    W.A. Owens, 187:Winter85-123
Bauman, Z. Memories of Class.
    P.L.M., 185:Jan85-388
Baumann, G. Robert Musil: Ein Entwurf.*
    M.A.E. Aue, 221(GQ):Spring84-327
    E. Boa, 402(MLR):Jan84-242
Baumann, W. Erinnerung und Erinnertes in
    Gor'kijs "Kindheit."
    P. Henry, 575(SEER):Jan84-111
Baumann, W. Die Faszination des Heiligen
    bei Kliment Ochridski.
    C.M. MacRobert, 575(SEER):Jan84-106
Baumgarten, A.G. Philosophische Betracht-
    ungen über einige Bedingungen des
    Gedichts. Texte zur Grundlegung der
    Ästhetik. Theoretische Ästhetik.
    M. Damnjanović, 687:Nov-Dec84-687
Baumgartner, A.J. Untersuchungen zur
    Anthologie des Codex Salmasianus.
    G.J.M. Bartelink, 394:Vol137fasc1/2-220
    D.R. Shackleton Bailey, 122:Jul84-252
Baumgartner, H. Bairische Sagen.
    G. Petschel, 196:Band25Heft3/4-326
Baumgärtner, K. - see de Mauro, T.

Baurmeister, U. and others, eds. Biblio-
thèque Nationale: Catalogue des incun-
ables. (Vol 2, fasc 3)
    B.M. Rosenthal, 517(PBSA):Vol78No4-526
Bausch, K-H. Modalität und Konjunktivge-
brauch in der gesprochenen deutschen
Standardsprache. (Pt 1)
    G. Koller, 685(ZDL):3/1984-386
Bauschatz, P.C. The Well and the Tree.*
    E.S. Dick, 589:Jul84-616
    J. Lindow, 301(JEGP):Apr84-264
Bawden, C.R. Shamans, Lamas and Evangeli-
cals.
    D.J. Enright, 362:4Apr85-27
    M. Raeff, 617(TLS):5Apr85-381
Baxandall, M. Die Kunst der Bildschnitz-
ler.
    E. König, 683:Band47Heft4-542
Baxandall, M. The Limewood Sculptors of
Renaissance Germany.*
    E. König, 683:Band47Heft4-535
Baxandall, M. Pattern of Intention.
    A. Harrison, 617(TLS):6Dec85-1384
Baxi, U. The Crisis of the Indian Legal
System.
    R.L. Kidder, 293(JASt):Nov83-177
Baxter, A. In Search of Your British and
Irish Roots.
    L.R.N. Ashley, 424:Mar84-82
Baxter, C. Harmony of the World.
    F. Camoin, 651(WHR):Winter84-354
    F. Kuffel, 181:Vol34No1-82
Baxter, C. Through the Safety Net.
    R. Hansen, 441:25Aug85-18
"Glen Baxter His Life."
    F. Tuten, 62:Dec84-76
Baxter, J. Shakespeare's Poetic Styles.*
    R.J.A. Weis, 179(ES):Dec84-574
Baxter, S.B., ed. England's Rise to Great-
ness, 1660-1763.* (Vol 7)
    H. Horwitz, 566:Autumn84-72
Bay, A. The Coyote Cried Twice.
    N. Callendar, 441:10Nov85-22
Bayard, S.P., ed. Dance to the Fiddle,
March to the Fife.
    A. Jabbour, 292(JAF):Jul-Sep84-345
"The Bayeux Tapestry."
    D.J.R. Bruckner, 441:15Dec85-22
Bayles, M. Reproductive Ethics.
    R.T., 185:Apr85-785
Bayley, J. An Essay on Hardy.
    R.P. Draper, 447(N&Q):Aug83-365
Bayley, J. Selected Essays.*
    K. Fitzlyon, 364:Jun84-96
    E. Griffiths, 175:Summer84-177
    W.H. Pritchard, 249(HudR):Winter84/85-
    639
Bayley, J. Shakespeare and Tragedy.*
    T.W. Craik, 541(RES):Feb84-82
    P. Edwards, 402(MLR):Apr84-417
    D. Mehl, 72:Band221Heft1-178
Bayley, P., ed. Selected Sermons of the
French Baroque (1600-1650).
    T.C. Cave, 208(FS):Oct84-456
    V. Kapp, 475:Vol 11No20-213
    W.C. Marceau, 207(FR):Apr85-726
Bayley, P. and D.G. Coleman, eds. The
Equilibrium of Wit.*
    B. Beugnot, 546(RR):Jan84-104
    M.M. McGowan, 402(MLR):Apr84-451
    A. Steele, 208(FS):Jan84-51

Bayley, S. The Albert Memorial.
    J.C., 90:May84-304
    T.J. Edelstein, 637(VS):Winter84-242
    A. Yarrington, 59:Mar84-110
Bayley, S. Harley Earl and the Dream
Machine.*
    J. Glancey, 46:Jul84-68
    A. Nahume, 592:Vol 196No1004-56
Baylon, C. and P. Fabre. Les noms de
lieux et de personnes.*
    H.J. Wolf, 547(RF):Band96Heft1/2-114
Bayly, C.A. Rulers, Townsmen, and Bazaars.
    M.H. Fisher, 293(JASt):May84-561
Baym, N. Novels, Readers, and Reviewers.
    A.T. Margolis, 357:Spring84-17
Bazanov, V. Sergei Esenin i krest'ian-
skaia Rossiia.
    D.M. Bethea, 550(RusR):Oct84-421
Bazire, J. and J.E. Cross, eds. Eleven
Old English Rogationtide Homilies.
    D. Yerkes, 589:Apr84-368
Bazzoli, L. and R. Renzi. Il Miracolo
Mattei.
    M. Clark, 617(TLS):31May85-604
Beach, D., ed. Aspects of Schenkerian
Theory.
    C. Ayrey, 410(M&L):Jan84-83
    R. Swift, 451:Fall84-164
Beadle, R., ed. The York Plays.*
    N.F. Blake, 179(ES):Jun84-274
    C. Davidson, 130:Summer84-179
Beale, P. - see Partridge, E.
Bealer, G. Quality and Concept.*
    I.G. McFetridge, 393(Mind):Jul84-455
    M. Wilson, 482(PhR):Oct84-636
Beales, P. Classic Roses.
    J.L. Faust, 441:8Dec85-30
Bear, G. Blood Music.
    G. Jonas, 441:28Apr85-20
Beard, G. Craftsmen and Interior Decora-
tion in England 1660-1820.
    D. Sutton, 39:Jun84-394
Beard, G. Stucco and Decorative Plaster-
work in Europe.*
    G.W., 90:Nov84-713
Beard, J.F., L. Schachterle and K.M. Ander-
sen, Jr. - see Cooper, J.F.
Beard, M. and M. Crawford. Rome in the
Late Republic.
    E. Rawson, 617(TLS):15Nov85-1302
Beard, R.R. Creating the World of Tomor-
row.
    P. Missac, 98:Dec84-1014
Beardsley, J. Earthworks and Beyond.
    A. Anderson, 62:May85-2
Beardsley, M.C. The Aesthetic Point of
View.* (M.J. Wreen and D.M. Callen,
eds)
    F.N. Sibley, 518:Jan84-31
    F. Sparshott, 311(JP):Apr84-230
    M. Steinmann, Jr., 478:Apr84-119
    D.D. Todd, 154:Dec84-745
Beardsley, M.C. Aesthetics. (2nd ed)
    J. Fisher, 289:Spring84-93
Beardsley, P.L. Redefining Rigor.
    J. Kassiola, 488:Mar84-73
Beardsmore, H.B., ed. Language and Tele-
vision.
    B. Johnstone, 350:Dec85-932
Beare, G.C. The Illustrations of W. Heath
Robinson.
    V. Powell, 39:Mar84-223

24

Beasley, J.C. Novels of the 1740s.*
  M.A. Doody, 405(MP):Feb85-326
  P.J. Korshin, 301(JEGP):Apr84-243
Beattie, A. Love Always.
  A. Hoffman, 441:2Jun85-7
  D. Ketcham, 617(TLS):25Oct85-1203
  J. Mellors, 362:7Nov85-28
  J. Rubins, 453(NYRB):18Jul85-40
  J. Updike, 442(NY):5Aug85-80
Beattie, G. Talk.
  S.H. Elgin, 350:Jun85-508
Beattie, J. The Life and Career of Klaus
  Barbie.
  H.R. Kedward, 617(TLS):15Nov85-1282
Beattie, S. The New Sculpture.*
  P. Skipwith, 90:Oct84-645
  A. Yarrington, 59:Mar84-110
Beauchamp, S. and P. Bouchard. Le Fran-
  çais et les medias.
  A. Lipou, 355(LSoc):Dec84-565
Beauchamp, T. and L. Walters, eds. Con-
  temporary Issues in Bioethics.
  R. Baker, 185:Jan85-370
Beauchamp, T.L. Case Studies in Business,
  Society, and Ethics.
  H.C.K., 185:Jan85-405
Beauchamp, T.L. and L.B. McCullough. Med-
  ical Ethics.
  R.M.M., 185:Jul85-989
Beauchemin, N., P. Martel and M. Théorêt.
  Concordance du corpus de l'Estrie (Forme,
  fréquence, contexte).
  G. Dulong, 320(CJL):Spring84-80
Beauchesne, Y. Nuit battante.
  E. Hamblet, 207(FR):Mar85-591
Beaufret, J. Entretiens avec Frédéric de
  Towarnicki.
  J-P. Guinle, 450(NRF):Nov84-89
  M. Haar, 192(EP):Jul-Sep84-404
Beaufret, J. - see Parmenides
de Beaugrande, R. Text, Discourse, and
  Process.*
  L. Lipka, 38:Band102Heft3/4-461
  M.F. McTear, 257(IRAL):Feb84-77
de Beaugrande, R. - see Schmidt, S.J.
de Beaugrande, R-A. and W.U. Dressler.
  Introduction to Text Linguistics.*
  (German title: Einführung in die Textlin-
  guistik.)
  P.L. Carrell, 351(LL):Mar84-111
  C. Gellinek, 205(ForL):Aug82-92
  D. Justice, 545(RPh):Nov83-236
  U. Oomen, 72:Band221Heft1-148
  S. Romaine, 597(SN):Vol56No2-233
  S. Stojanova-Jovčeva, 260(IF):Band89-
  292
Beaujeu, J. - see Cicero
Beaujour, M. Miroirs d'encre.
  J-C. Margolin, 192(EP):Apr-Jun84-266
de Beaujoyeulx, B. Le Balet comique,
  1581.*
  M. Franko, 546(RR):Nov84-504
Beaulieu, M. Robert Le Lorrain (1666-
  1743).
  T. Hodgkinson, 90:Nov84-704
Beauman, S. The Royal Shakespeare Com-
  pany.*
  J.M.B., 179(ES):Aug84-382
Beaumont, A. Busoni the Composer.
  R. Stevenson, 617(TLS):6Dec85-1398
Beaumont, F. and J. Fletcher. The Dramat-
  ic Works in the Beaumont and Fletcher
  [continued]

[continuing]
Canon. (Vol 6) (F. Bowers, general ed)
  K. Duncan-Jones, 617(TLS):20Sep85-1034
Beaumont, K. Alfred Jarry.
  J. Weightman, 617(TLS):21Jun85-687
Beaune, J-C. Le vagabond et la machine.
  F. Dagognet, 192(EP):Oct-Dec84-553
  P. Guenancia, 98:Apr84-276
Beausoleil, C. Concrete City.
  S.S., 376:Jun84-145
  P. Stratford, 102(CanL):Autumn84-159
Beausoleil, C. Dans la matière rêvant
  comme d'une émeute.
  S. Lawall, 207(FR):Mar85-592
Beauverd, J. and others. La Petite Mus-
  ique de Verlaine.
  Y A. Favre, 535(RHL):Sep/Oct84-811
de Beauvoir, S. - see Sartre, J-P.
Beaver, H. The Great American Masquerade.
  S. Fender, 617(TLS):13Dec85-1438
Beccaria, G.L. and M.L. Porzio Gernia -
  see Terracini, B.
Bech, G. Studium über das deutsche Verbum
  infinitum. (2nd ed)
  A. von Stechow, 353:Vol22No2-225
Bechert, H., ed. Die Sprache der ältesten
  buddhistischen Überlieferung/The Lan-
  guage of the Earliest Buddhist Tradi-
  tion.*
  D.S. Ruegg, 318(JAOS):Jul-Sep83-652
Bechert, H. and R. Gombrich, eds. The
  World of Buddhism.
  A. Grimshaw, 617(TLS):15Feb85-181
Beck, A. Hölderlins Weg zu Deutschland.
  C.A. Juengling, 67:May84-96
Beck, H. Der Begriff "Silly Fool" im
  Slang einer englischen Schule.
  H. Ulherr, 38:Band102Heft3/4-498
Beck, J. Italian Renaissance Painting.
  90:Jul84-449
Beck, J.C., ed. Always in Season.
  D.D. Fanelli, 292(JAF):Apr-Jun84-244
Beck, J.M. Joseph Howe.* (Vol 1)
  G.W., 102(CanL):Summer84-187
Beck, J.M. Joseph Howe. (Vol 2)
  G.W., 102(CanL):Autumn84-194
Beck, M. Secret Contenders.
  J. Brinkley, 441:4Aug85-17
Beck, M. and J. Veselý, eds. Exil und
  Asyl.
  I. Seehase, 654(WB):3/1984-517
Becker, C. and others - see Hegel, G.F.W.
Becker, G.J. Master European Realists of
  the Nineteenth Century.
  W.K. Buckley, 594:Spring84-118
Becker, H. and C. Nedelmann. Psycho-
  analyse und Politik.
  F. Dieckmann, 384:Oct84-816
Becker, M.B. Medieval Italy.
  P.D. Partner, 589:Jan84-113
Becker, P. The Pathfinders.
  L. Charlton, 441:22Sep85-23
Becker, R.O. and G. Selden. The Body
  Electric.
  C. West, 441:21Apr85-39
Becker, R.P., ed. German Humanism and
  Reformation.*
  T.W. Best, 221(GQ):Fall84-643
  T.C. Hanlin, 399(MLJ):Summer84-168
Becker, S.D. The Origins of the Equal
  Rights Amendment.
  F.H. Early, 106:Summer84-199

25

Becker-Cantarino, B., ed. Martin Opitz.
G.R. Hoyt, 221(GQ):Fall84-645
Beckett, B.A. The Reception of Pablo
Neruda's Works in the German Democratic
Republic.*
A. Dessau, 107(CRCL):Jun84-334
Beckett, S. Collected Shorter Prose 1945-
1980.
M. Gee, 617(TLS):21Jun85-698
Beckett, S. Disjecta.* (R. Cohn, ed)
272(IUR):Spring84-153
Beckwith, C. and M. van Offelen. Nomads
of Niger.*
P.J. Imperato, 2(AfrA):May84-88
Bédard, E. and J. Maurais, eds. La Norme
linguistique.
R. Martin, 553(RLiR):Jan-Jun84-207
Beddow, M. The Fiction of Humanity.*
T.C. Hanlin, 221(GQ):Summer84-493
M.W. Jennings, 221(GQ):Summer84-495
D. Roberts, 67:May84-101
W. Witte, 402(MLR):Apr84-489
Bédé, J-A. and W.B. Edgerton, eds. Colum-
bia Dictionary of Modern European Litera-
ture.* (2nd ed)
L. Kibler, 276:Summer84-180
Bedeski, R.E. The Fragile Entente.
Nakajima Mineo, 285(JapQ):Jan-Mar84-87
The Duke of Bedford, with G. Mikes. How
To Run a Stately Home.
M. Drabble, 362:25Apr85-23
Beechcroft, W. Image of Evil.
N. Callendar, 441:21Jul85-18
Beeh, V. Sprache und Spracherlernung.
W. Hogrebe, 679:Band15Heft1-170
Beekman, E.M. - see Rumphius, G.E.
de Beer, E.S. - see Locke, J.
Beer, G. Darwin's Plots.*
J.L. Bradley, 184(EIC):Oct84-356
G.B. Tennyson, 445(NCF):Jun84-112
Beer, J. William Blake.
J. Bogan, 88:Winter84/85-151
Beer, J. Sämtliche Werke. (Vol 1) (F.
van Ingen and H-G. Roloff, eds)
J. Fletcher, 67:Nov84-256
Beer, J. Der Simplicianische Welt-Kucker
oder Abentheuerliche Jan Rebhu.
J. Fletcher, 67:Nov84-256
Beer, J.M.A. Narrative Conventions of
Truth in the Middle Ages.*
J.C. Laidlaw, 402(MLR):Oct84-928
Beer, L.W. Freedom of Expression in Japan.
D. Wessels, 407(MN):Winter84-472
Beer, P. The Lie of the Land.*
J. Saunders, 565:Autumn84-66
Beerbohm, M. The Illustrated Zuleika Dob-
son. (N.J. Hall, ed)
A. Bell, 617(TLS):30Aug85-959
442(NY):16Sep85-122
Beg, M.A.J. Arabic Loan Words in Malay.*
G. Hudson, 660(Word):Dec84-278
Begiebing, R.J. Acts of Regeneration.
K. Probert, 106:Spring84-93
Begum, H. Moore's Ethics.
R. Kearney, 63:Sep84-311
Behl, C.F.W. Aufsätze, Briefe und Tage-
buchnotizen. (K. Hildebrandt, ed)
S. Hoefert, 564:May84-143
Behlmer, R. America's Favorite Movies.
G. Evans, 106:Winter84-481
Behlmer, R., ed. Inside Warner Bros.
(1935-1951).
A. Harmetz, 441:24Nov85-24

Behn, A. The Lucky Chance.
D. Devlin, 157:No154-49
Behrendt, S.C. The Moment of Explosion.
S.D. Cox, 173(ECS):Spring85-391
R. Lister, 324:Sep85-739
A.K. Mellor, 661(WC):Summer84-110
J. Wittreich, 391:Oct84-92
Behrens, R.R. Art and Camouflage.
J.A. Richardson, 289:Spring84-93
Behrmann, A. and J. Wohlleben. Büchner:
"Dantons Tod."
W.B. Armstrong, 406:Spring84-101
Beidler, P.D. American Literature and the
Experience of Vietnam.
J. Hellmann, 125:Winter84-188
T. Ludington, 577(SHR):Fall84-339
T. Myers, 395(MFS):Spring84-165
Beierwaltes, W. Regio Beatitudinis.
G. Bonner, 123:Vol34No1-138
Beierwaltes, W. - see Schelling, F.W.J.
Beik, W. Absolutism and Society in
Seventeenth-Century France.
R. Bonney, 617(TLS):16Aug85-897
Beile, W. and A. Sprechsituationen aus
dem Alltag, II. Teil (Modelle 5).
Themen und Meinungen im Für und Wider
(Modelle 6).
P.J. Campana, 399(MLJ):Winter84-402
Beilharz, R., ed. Balzac.
B. Münzer, 224(GRM):Band34Heft3-362
Beiner, R. Political Judgment.*
S.A.H., 185:Jan85-388
Beiner, R. - see Arendt, H.
Beissel, H. and F. Lach. Cantos North.*
A. Morton, 526:Summer84-72
"Beiträge zur Indienforschung."
D.S. Ruegg, 318(JAOS):Jul-Sep83-649
Beja, M., S.E. Gontarski and P. Astier,
eds. Samuel Beckett.
B. Mitchell, 395(MFS):Winter84-779
Bekker-Nielsen, H., P. Foote and O. Olsen,
eds. Proceedings of the Eighth Viking
Congress, Århus 24-31 August 1977.
R.W. McTurk, 382(MAE):1984/1-146
Lady Bell. At the Works.
617(TLS):8Mar85-271
Bell, A. The Cherry Tree.
617(TLS):25Oct85-1219
Bell, A.O., with A. McNeillie - see Woolf,
V.
Bell, C. Saint.
S. Vogan, 441:17Nov85-30
Bell, D. Frege's Theory of Judgement.*
T.G. Ricketts, 482(PhR):Apr84-313
Bell, D.S. and B. Criddle. The French
Socialist Party.
P. McCarthy, 617(TLS):29Mar85-362
Bell, E.S. - see Boyle, K.
Bell, I. The Dominican Republic.
E.M. Thomas-Hope, 86(BHS):Jan84-59
Bell, I.F.A. Critic as Scientist.*
A. Woodward, 541(RES):Aug84-416
Bell, I.F.A., ed. Henry James.
M. Seymour, 617(TLS):13Dec85-1438
Bell, L.A., ed. Visions of Women.
R.M. McCleary, 185:Oct84-165
Bell, M. Drawn by Stones, by Earth, by
Things that Have Been in the Fire.*
F. Garber, 29(APR):Sep/Oct85-14
R. Phillips, 491:Mar85-349
639(VQR):Autumn84-137

Bell, M.   The Sentiment of Reality.*
    J.J. Burke, Jr., 594:Fall84-343
    I.C. Ross, 189(EA):Jul-Sep85-299
Bell, M. 3d.   Morgantina Studies.* (Vol 1)
    R. Higgins, 303(JoHS):Vol 104-262
Bell, M.D.   The Development of American
  Romance.*
    M. Kramer, 536:Vol5-3i
Bell, M.J.   The World from Brown's Lounge.
    J. Baugh, 355(LSoc):Jun84-249
    W.M. Clements, 292(JAF):Jul-Sep84-346
    E. Wachs, 650(WF):Apr84-154
Bell, M.S.   Waiting for the End of the
  World.
    D. Montrose, 617(TLS):22Nov85-1310
    M. Wolitzer, 441:18Aug85-18
    442(NY):11Nov85-154
Bell, M.S.   The Washington Square Ensem-
  ble.*
    M.R. Winchell, 569(SR):Spring84-xliii
Bell, Q.   The Brandon Papers.
    R. Fuller, 362:28Feb85-27
    A. Goreau, 441:13Oct85-14
    J. Symons, 364:Feb85-98
    E.S. Turner, 617(TLS):1Mar85-227
    442(NY):18Nov85-174
Bell, Q.   A New and Noble School.
    M. Warner, 90:Jan84-48
Bell, S.G. and K.M. Offen, eds.   Women,
  the Family and Freedom.
    K.J. Crecelius, 446(NCFS):Winter-
      Spring85-184
Bell, S.M.   Nathalie Sarraute.
    V. Minogue, 208(FS):Apr84-231
Bell-Metereau, R.   Hollywood Androgyny.
    M. Haskell, 441:31Mar85-10
    A. Mars-Jones, 617(TLS):24May85-582
Bellah, R.N. and others.   Habits of the
  Heart.
    W. Kristol, 129:Jul85-76
    D. Martin, 617(TLS):20Sep85-1022
    P. Steinfels, 441:14Apr85-1
Bellamy, J.   Robin Hood.
    R.B. Dobson, 617(TLS):22Feb85-191
    M. Keen, 453(NYRB):9May85-27
Bellefroid, J.   Les Étoiles filantes.
    C. Coustou, 450(NRF):Jul/Aug84-165
Bellemin-Noël, J.   Gradiva au pied de la
  lettre.
    J. Le Hardi, 450(NRF):Feb84-113
Bellenger, Y.   Dix études sur le XVIe et
  le XVIIe siècles.*
    J. Bailbé, 535(RHL):Jul/Aug84-592
Bellenger, Y. - see Du Bellay, J.
Bellina, A.L., B. Brizi and M. Grazia
  Pensa.   I libretti vivaldiani.
    E. Cross, 410(M&L):Jan84-62
    M. Talbot, 415:Feb84-98
Bellingham, S.   Twenty-five Fine Books at
  the University of Waterloo.
    D.B. Kotin, 470:Vol122-132
Bellman, C.M.   Epistles and Songs III.
    J. Lutz, 563(SS):Spring84-198
Bellos, D. - see Spitzer, L.
Bellour, R.   L'Analyse du film.
    M. Turim, 567:Vol50No1/2-181
Bellow, G., J.S. Robbins and R.J. Tabak,
  comps.   Documentation Concerning Serious
  Factual Errors in Forthcoming Book by
  Richard Cummings Purportedly about
  Allard K. Lowenstein.
    H. Hertzberg, 453(NYRB):10Oct85-34

Bellow, S.   Au jour le jour.
    L. Kovacs, 450(NRF):Mar84-141
Bellow, S.   The Dean's December.*
    S. Epstein, 152(UDQ):Spring85-139
Bellow, S.   Him with His Foot in His Mouth
  and Other Stories.*
    A. Bloom, 249(HudR):Winter84/85-622
    S. Epstein, 152(UDQ):Spring85-139
    L. Lemon, 502(PrS):Winter84-110
    S. Pinsker, 573(SSF):Fall84-404
    639(VQR):Autumn84-132
Bellringer, A.W.   "The Ambassadors."
    P. Horne, 175:Autumn84-263
Bellush, J. and B.   Union Power and New
  York.
    D. Stetson, 441:10Feb85-25
Belluzzi, A. and others.   Mantova nel
  settecento.
    R. Middleton, 90:Dec84-790
Bellwinkel, M.   Die Kasten-Klassenproblema-
  tik im städtisch-industriellen Bereich.
    J. Newborn, 293(JASt):Aug84-775
Beloff, N.   Tito's Flawed Legacy.
    R. Fox, 362:22Aug85-29
    M. Wheeler, 617(TLS):11Oct85-1150
Belsey, C.   Critical Practice.
    R. Markley, 223:Fall81-411
Belsky, D.   One for the Money.
    N. Callendar, 441:22Dec85-30
Belting, H.   Das Bild und sein Publikum im
  Mittelalter.*
    H.W. van Os, 600:Vol 14No3/4-225
Belting, H.   Das Ende der Kunstgeschichte?
    M. Warnke, 384:Jul84-565
Bem, J.   Désir et savoir dans l'oeuvre de
  Flaubert.
    J. Neefs, 535(RHL):May/Jun84-460
Bemelmans, L.   Tell Them It Was Wonderful.
  (M. Bemelmans, ed)
    P.L. Adams, 61:Dec85-118
    442(NY):23Dec85-91
Ben-Ami, S.   Fascism from Above.*
    R. Carr, 453(NYRB):17Jan85-39
    639(VQR):Summer84-79
Ben-Arieh, Y.   Jerusalem in the 19th Cen-
  tury: The Old City.
    D. Pryce-Jones, 617(TLS):8Nov85-1272
Benardete, M.J., comp.   Judeo-Spanish Bal-
  lads from New York.* (S.G. Armistead
  and J.H. Silverman, eds)
    H. Goldberg, 545(RPh):Nov83-230
    L.P. Harvey, 86(BHS):Apr84-192
Benardete, S. - see Plato
Benario, H.   A Commentary on the "Vita
  Hadriani" in the "Historia Augusta."*
    E. Champlin, 122:Jan84-76
Bénassy-Berling, M.C.   Humanisme et reli-
  gion chez Sor Juan Inés de la Cruz.
    A. Márquez, 240(HR):Summer84-420
Benatar, S.   Such Men are Dangerous.
    T. Sattin, 617(TLS):15Nov85-1296
Bence-Jones, M.   The National Trust Ances-
  tral Houses.
    T. Russell-Cobb, 324:Mar85-303
Bence-Jones, M.   The Viceroys of India.
    E. Hirschmann, 637(VS):Spring84-388
Benchley, N.   The Benchley Roundup.
    P.K. Bell, 617(TLS):14Jun85-666
Bender, M.L., ed.   Nilo-Saharan Language
  Studies.
    P. Unseth, 350:Dec85-926
Benditt, T.M.   Rights.*
    S. Wein, 154:Dec84-732

Bene, E., ed. Les Lumières en Hongrie, en
Europe centrale et en Europe orientale.*
  L. Versini, 535(RHL):Sep/Oct84-804
Benecke, G. Maximilian I, 1459-1519.
  J.A. Vann, 551(RenQ):Spring84-69
Benedict, B., ed. The Anthropology of
World's Fairs.*
  J. Maass, 658:Spring84-93
  T. Russell-Cobb, 324:Apr85-371
Benedict, E. Slow Dancing.
  A. Barnet, 441:3Mar85-9
Benedikt, M. Bestimmende und reflektier-
ende Urteilskraft.*
  W. Steinbeck, 342:Band75Heft1-113
Benelli, G. La necessità della parola.
  I. Vivan, 538(RAL):Winter84-606
Benet, J. Return to Region.
  W. Herrick, 441:15Sep85-24
Benfey, C.E.G. Emily Dickinson and the
Problem of Others.
  D. Porter, 344:Fall85-116
Benigni, C. and H.B. Hempel. C'est ça.*
  E.W. Munley, 399(MLJ):Summer84-159
Benigni, C. and H.B. Hempel. Chacun son
goût.
  R.E. Hiedemann, 399(MLJ):Autumn84-284
Benito, F. La arquitectura del Colegio
del Patriarca y sus artífices.
  F. Marías, 48:Apr-Jun84-192
Benjamin, A. - see Mandela, W.
Benjamin, W. Charles Baudelaire.*
  P. Somville, 542:Jan-Mar84-136
Benjamin, W. Essais. (Vols 1 and 2)
  C. Dis, 450(NRF):Apr84-117
Benjamin, W. Das Passagen-Werk.* (R.
Tiedemann, ed)
  S. Buck-Morss, 221(GQ):Summer84-456
  M. Kesting, 547(RF):Band96Heft1/2-157
Benko, S. Pagan Rome and the Early Chris-
tians.
  W.H.C. Frend, 617(TLS):5Jul85-755
Benkovitz, M.J. A Bibliography of Ronald
Firbank.* (2nd ed)
  J.G. Watson, 447(N&Q):Dec83-556
Benn, T. The (Almost) Compleat Angler.
  A. Atha, 617(TLS):20Dec85-1466
Bennet, P. Sky-Riding.
  S. O'Brien, 617(TLS):1Feb85-128
  G. Szirtes, 493:Sep84-76
Bennett, B. Modern Drama and German Clas-
sicism.*
  J. Lyons, 214:Vol 11No41-127
Bennett, B., J. Hay and S. Ashford, comps.
Western Australian Literature.
  L. Hergenhan, 71(ALS):Oct84-565
Bennett, B.T. - see Shelley, M.W.
Bennett, D. and others. Horizons.
  C.R. McRae, 207(FR):Dec84-334
Bennett, J. Handling White Oak.
  K.S. Hofweber, 614:Spring85-22
Bennett, J. A Study of Spinoza's Ethics.*
  D. Garber, 185:Jul85-961
Bennett, J.A. The Mathematical Science of
Christopher Wren.
  H. Dorn, 576:Mar84-83
Bennett, J.A.W. Essays on Gibbon.
  P. Rogers, 541(RES):Feb84-91
Bennett, J.T. and T.J. Di Lorenzo.
Destroying Democracy.
  E. Van den Haag, 441:22Dec85-23
Bennett, M.J. Community, Class and Career-
ism.
  J.T. Rosenthal, 589:Jul84-619

Bennett, T. Formalism and Marxism.*
  M. Ryan, 223:Summer81-276
Bennett, W.L. and M.S. Feldman. Recon-
structing Reality in the Courtroom.*
  R.D. Rieke, 480(P&R):Vol 17No4-249
Bennigsen, A. and M. Broxup. The Islamic
Threat to the Soviet State.
  M. McCauley, 575(SEER):Apr84-314
Benoît de Canfield. La Règle de Perfec-
tion/The Rule of Perfection. (J. Orci-
bal, ed)
  H. Sonneville, 356(LR):Nov84-324
Benrekassa, G. Le concentrique et
l'excentrique.*
  R. Sasso, 192(EP):Oct-Dec84-557
Benrekassa, G. La Politique et sa Mémoire.
  P. Roger, 208(FS):Jul84-347
Bens, J. OuLiPo: 1960-1963.
  C. Shorley, 208(FS):Apr84-242
Bensa, A. and J-C. Rivierre. Les chemins
de l'alliance.
  B. Juillerat, 98:Nov84-925
Bense, E., P. Eisenberg and H. Haberland,
eds. Beschreibungsmethoden des amerikan-
ischen Strukturalismus.
  B. Henn, 685(ZDL):1/1984-122
Benseler, F. - see Lukács, G.
Bensley, C. Moving In.*
  H. Davies, 617(TLS):1Feb85-128
  W. Scammell, 364:Mar85-90
  G. Szirtes, 493:Sep84-76
Benson, C.D. The History of Troy in Mid-
dle English Literature.*
  F.N.M. Diekstra, 179(ES):Dec84-567
Benson, E. J.M. Synge.
  N. Grene, 610:Summer84-150
Benson, J., ed. The Working Class in
England 1875-1914.
  M. Dupree, 617(TLS):6Sep85-983
Benson, J.J. The True Adventures of John
Steinbeck, Writer.*
  J. Ditsky, 628(UWR):Spring-Summer85-90
  T.A. Gullason, 573(SSF):Fall84-415
  J.R. Millichap, 395(MFS):Winter84-826
  R.E. Morsberger, 649(WAL):Nov84-231
  295(JML):Nov84-507
  639(VQR):Summer84-87
Benson, M. - see Fugard, A.
Benson, R. German Expressionist Drama,
Ernst Toller and Georg Kaiser.
  H. Rorrison, 157:No153-50
Benstock, B., ed. The Seventh of Joyce.*
  272(IUR):Spring84-154
van Benthem, J.F.A.K. The Logic of Time.
  J. Butterfield, 518:Jan84-53
Bentini, J. Quaderni della Soprintendenza
per i Beni Artistici e Storici per le
Provincie di Bologna, Ferrara, Forlì e
Ravenna. (No 4)
  R. Gibbs, 90:Jul84-438
Bentley, E. The Brecht Commentaries, 1943-
1980.*
  G. Steel, 214:Vol 11No41-120
Bentley, E. The Kleist Variations.
  D. Rubin, 108:Spring84-127
Bentley, G.E., Jr. Blake Books.
  M. Gassenmeier, 38:Band102Heft1/2-248
Bentley, G.E., Jr. - see Blake, W.
Bentley, J. Guide to the Dordogne.
  R. Fox, 362:24Jan85-27
Bentley, J. The Importance of Being Con-
stance.
  442(NY):25Feb85-104

Bentley, J. Martin Niemoller.
  N.K. Gottwald, 441:13Jan85-17
Bentley, J.H. Humanists and Holy Writ.
  D. Bornstein, 539:Aug85-220
Bentley, R. The Way into Town.
  J. Carter, 219(GaR):Winter84-881
Benton, R.A. The Flight of the Amokura.
  T. Huebner, 355(LSoc):Sep84-382
Benvenuti, A.T. and M.P. Mussini Sacchi -
  see under Tissoni Benvenuti, A. and M.P.
  Mussini Sacchi
Benzie, W. Dr. F.J. Furnivall.^
  R.D. Fulton, 389(MQ):Autumn84-122
  G.W., 102(CanL):Summer84-187
"Beowulf" - see also "A Readable 'Beowulf'"
de Berceo, G. A New Berceo Manuscript.
  (B. Dutton, ed)
  P. Such, 402(MLR):Jul84-726
de Berceo, G. Poema de Santa Oria. (I.
  Uría Maqua, ed)
  I. MacPherson, 86(BHS):Jan84-45
  R. Pellen, 553(RLiR):Jul-Dec84-475
de Berceo, G. Signos que aparecerán antes
  del juico final, Duelo de la Virgen,
  Martirio de San Lorenzo. (A.M. Ramoneda,
  ed)
  I. MacPherson, 86(BHS):Jan84-45
Berchet, J-C. - see Gautier, T.
Bercuson, D.J., R. Bothwell and J.L.
  Granatstein. The Great Brain Robbery.
  P. Marchak, 99:Dec84-35
Beregovski, M. Old Jewish Folk Music.*
  (M. Slobin, ed and trans)
  H. Sapoznik, 292(JAF):Jan-Mar84-85
Berenson, E. Populist Religion and Left-
  Wing Politics in France, 1830-1852.
  T. Judt, 617(TLS):1Mar85-234
  639(VQR):Autumn84-117
Berenson, M. Mary Berenson, a Self-
  Portrait from her Letters and Diaries.*
  (B. Strachey and J. Samuels, eds)
  A. Brink, 556:Winter84/85-313
  639(VQR):Autumn84-124
Berg, C. Jean de Boschère ou le mouvement
  de l'attente.*
  P. Cola, 356(LR):Feb/May84-131
Berg, J. and others. Sozialgeschichte der
  deutschen Literatur von 1918 bis zur
  Gegenwart.*
  J. Strutz, 602:Band15Heft1-170
Berg, M. The Age of Manufactures.
  J.R. Harris, 617(TLS):23Aug85-922
Berg, M-A. Aspects of Time.
  R. Asselineau, 189(EA):Jul-Sep85-351
Berg, S., ed. In Praise of What Persists.
  D. Carlson, 219(GaR):Spring84-196
  295(JML):Nov84-375
Berg, S., ed. Singular Voices.
  L.B., 30:Spring85-93
Berg, W.J., M. Grimaud and G. Moskos.
  Saint/Oedipus.*
  L.M. Porter, 593:Fall84-258
  B. Schlossman, 400(MLN):Dec84-1267
Bergad, L.W. Coffee and the Growth of
  Agrarian Capitalism in Nineteenth-
  Century Puerto Rico.*
  639(VQR):Winter84-18
Bergé, C. - see Crews, J.
Bergé, M. Pour un humanisme vécu.
  J.A. Bellamy, 318(JAOS):Oct-Dec83-768

Bergen, J.J. and C.D. Bills, eds. Spanish
  and Portuguese in Social Context.
  C. Baker, 399(MLJ):Winter84-414
  S.N. Gynan, 238:Sep84-484
  H. Meier, 547(RF):Band96Heft4-459
Bergenholtz, H. and J. Mugdan. Einführung
  in die Morphologie.
  G. Koller, 685(ZDL):2/1984-269
  U. Schröter, 682(ZPSK):Band37Heft4-516
Berger, B.M. The Survival of a Counter-
  culture.
  J-L. Fabiani, 98:Jun/Jul84-449
Berger, C. Science, God, and Nature in
  Victorian Canada.
  T.D. MacLulich, 102(CanL):Autumn84-84
Berger, C.R. and J.J. Bradac. Language
  and Social Knowledge.*
  J. Bilmes, 355(LSoc):Mar84-87
Berger, D., ed. The Legacy of Jewish Immi-
  gration: 1881 and Its Impact.
  A. Levin, 104(CASS):Winter84-467
Berger, F.R. Happiness, Justice and Free-
  dom.
  R. Arneson, 185:Jul85-954
Berger, G.M. - see Mutsu Munemitsu
Berger, J. And Our Faces, My Heart, Brief
  as Photos.*
  M. Ignatieff, 617(TLS):4Jan85-7
  D. Kuspit, 62:Dec84-78
Berger, T. Nowhere.
  F. Busch, 441:5May85-17
  442(NY):8Jul85-73
de Bergerac, S.D. - see under de Cyrano de
  Bergerac, S.
Berggren, W.A. and J.A. Van Couvering, eds.
  Catastrophes and Earth History.
  M. Sweeting, 617(TLS):1Mar85-242
Berghahn, V.R. Modern Germany.*
  P. Milbouer, 221(GQ):Fall84-688
Bergin, J. Cardinal Richelieu.
  P. Johnson, 362:5Dec85-31
Berginz-Plank, G. Literaturrezeption in
  einer Kleinstadt.
  C.J. Wickham, 406:Summer84-204
Bergman, J. Vera Zasulich.^
  B.A. Engel, 550(RusR):Apr84-208
  R. Freeborn, 575(SEER):Oct84-605
Bergman, M. Karin.
  J-A. Goodwin, 617(TLS):13Dec85-1433
Bergmann, R., P. Pauly and M. Schlaefer.
  Einführung in die deutsche Sprachwissen-
  schaft.*
  B.J. Koekkoek, 406:Fall84-347
Bergold, W. Der Zweikampf des Paris und
  Menelaos.
  A.H.M. Kessels, 394:Vol37fasc1/2-166
Bergquist, M.F. Ibero-Romance.*
  G. Colón, 553(RLiR):Jul-Dec84-474
  T. Riiho, 439(NM):1984/1-125
Bergreen, L. James Agee.
  R. Spears, 676(YR):Winter85-296
Berio, L., R. Delmonte and B.A. Varga.
  Luciano Berio: Two Interviews. (D.
  Osmond-Smith, ed and trans)
  P. Griffiths, 617(TLS):15Feb85-161
  J. Peyser, 441:19May85-23
Berka, K. Measurement.
  P. Février, 542:Apr-Jun84-221
  P. Jaenecke, 679:Band15Heft2-354
Berke, B. Tragic Thought and the Grammar
  of Tragic Myth.*
  T.J. Reiss, 107(CRCL):Mar84-108
Berkey, J.C. and others - see Dreiser, T.

Berkhout, C.T. and M.M. Gatch, eds. Anglo-Saxon Scholarship: The First Three Centuries.*
R.I. Page, 447(N&Q):Oct83-443

Berkhout, C.T. and J.B. Russell. Medieval Heresies.
A. Hudson, 382(MAE):1984/1-149

Berkowitz, D.S., ed. Humanist Scholarship and Public Order.
M.L. Robertson, 250(HLQ):Spring84-133

Berkowitz, G.M. New Broadways.*
G. Anthony, 106:Fall84-361

Berkowitz, G.M. Sir John Vanbrugh and the End of Restoration Comedy.*
E. Burns, 541(RES):May84-236
J.P. Vander Motten, 179(ES):Jun84-281

Berkowitz, L. and T.F. Brunner - see Sophocles

Berkson, C. Elephanta, the Cave of Shiva. (text by W.D. O'Flaherty, G. Michell and C. Berkson)
C.D. Collins, 463:Winter84/85-379

Berkvam, D.D. Enfance et maternité dans la littérature française des XIIe et XIIIe siècles.*
B.N. Sargent-Baur, 589:Jan84-117

Berland, A. Culture and Conduct in the Novels of Henry James.*
P. Buitenhuis, 178:Mar84-111
V. Jones, 541(RES):Feb84-102
W.R. Macnaughton, 106:Fall84-323

Berlanstein, L.R. The Working People of Paris, 1871-1914.
J.F. McMillan, 617(TLS):9Aug85-883

Berle, W. Heinrich Mann und die Weimarer Republik.
K. Geissler, 654(WB):12/1984-2097
K. Petersen, 564:Sep84-224

Berlin, I. and R. Hoffman, eds. Slavery and Freedom in the Age of the American Revolution.
C. Levy, 173(ECS):Winter84/85-275

Berlin, N. Eugene O'Neill.*
M. Manheim, 397(MD):Mar84-140

"Berlin und seine Bauten." (3rd ed) (Vols 1-13)
P. Güttler, 46:Sep84-120

Berliner, P.F. The Soul of Mbira.
G. Fortune, 538(RAL):Summer84-303

Berliner, R. and G. Egger. Ornamentale Vorlageblätter des 15. bis 19. Jahrhunderts.*
G. Irmscher, 683:Band47Heft1-137

Berlitz, C. Native Tongues.
B.K. Mudge, 35(AS):Fall84-244

Berman, A. L'Épreuve de l'étranger.
M.F. Meurice, 450(NRF):Jul/Aug84-171

Berman, E. Art and Artists of South Africa. (new ed)
D. Goddard, 324:Jun85-501

Bermant, C. Dancing Bear.*
B. Tritel, 441:31Mar85-22

Bermejo Martínez, E. La Pintura de los primitivos flamencos en España. (Vol 2)
D. Angulo Íñiguez, 48:Apr-Jun83-166

Bernales Ballesteros, J. Francisco Antonio Gijón.
D. Angulo Íñiguez, 48:Apr-Jun83-167

Bernand, É. Inscriptions grecques d'Égypte et de Nubie.
P-L. Gatier, 555:Vol58fasc1-108
J. Marcillet-Jaubert, 555:Vol58fasc2-302

Bernard, A. and C. Floquet. Album Sacha Guitry.
D. Desanti, 207(FR):May85-925

Bernard, B. The Bible and its Painters.*
N. Powell, 39:Jul84-77

Bernard, G. The Power of the Early Tudor Nobility.
M. James, 617(TLS):12Apr85-404

Bernard, J-P. Les Rébellions de 1837-1838.
A.B. Chartier, 207(FR):Apr85-745

Bernard, P. and H. Dubief. The Decline of the Third Republic, 1914-1938.
M. Larkin, 617(TLS):28Jun85-731

Bernard, R.M. and B.R. Rice, eds. Sunbelt Cities.
L. Milazzo, 584(SWR):Summer84-336

Bernard, T.J. The Consensus-Conflict Debate.
K.S., 185:Apr85-773

Bernardelli, G. La Poesia a rovescio.
J. Pierrot, 535(RHL):Jul/Aug84-642

Bernays, A. The Address Book.
W. Lesser, 249(HudR):Autumn84-472

Berndtson, A. Power, Form, and Mind.
J. Benardete, 543:Dec83-392

Bernet, C. Le Vocabulaire des tragédies de Jean Racine.
R.W. Tobin, 207(FR):Mar85-579

Bernhard, H.J., ed. Geschichte der deutschen Literatur: Literatur der BRD.
D. Ulle, 654(WB):11/1984-1931

Bernhard, T. Concrete.*
D.J. Enright, 453(NYRB):28Mar85-31
J. Updike, 442(NY):4Feb85-97

Bernhard, T. Der Untergeher.
H. Graf, 384:Jan84-86

Bernhardt, R. Odysseus' Tod — Prometheus' Leben.
V. Riedel, 654(WB):3/1984-511

Bernheimer, C. Flaubert and Kafka.*
E. Engelberg, 678(YCGL):No33-94
E. Hollahan, 594:Spring84-120
J. Rolleston, 301(JEGP):Apr84-292

Berni Canani, U. and others. L'analisi delle frequenze.*
R. Sasso, 192(EP):Oct-Dec84-558

Bernier, O. Louis the Beloved.
J. Rogister, 617(TLS):22Feb85-204
W. Smith, 441:20Jan85-10
442(NY):8Apr85-129

Berning, S. - see von Droste-Hülshoff, A.

Bernstein, C. Resistance.*
B. Hollander, 703:No12-139
J. Retallack, 472:Fall/Winter84-213

Bernstein, C. Le Rival invincible.
R.J. Golsan, 207(FR):May85-909

Bernstein, G.L. Haruko's World.
A. Waswo, 407(MN):Summer84-221

Bernstein, I. A Caring Society.
R.J. Margolis, 441:16Jun85-41

Bernstein, M.A. The Tale of the Tribe.
P. Makin, 402(MLR):Apr85-441

Bernstein, R. From the Center of the Earth.
J-H.L. Upshur, 293(JASt):Feb84-304

Bernstein, R.J. Beyond Objectivism and Relativism.*
R. Eldridge, 478:Oct84-292
S.A. Hadari, 185:Oct84-164

Bernstein, S.J. The Strands Entwined.
A.F. Sponberg, 615(TJ):Mar82-131

Berquet, G. and J-P. Collinet - see Conrart, V.

Binney, M., M. Hamm and A. Foehl. Great
Railway Stations of Europe.
   D. Luckhurst, 324:Sep85-738
   N. Ramsey, 441:28Apr85-24
Binni, W. Monti poeta del consenso. Ugo
Foscolo.
   M. Mari, 228(GSLI):Vol 161fasc514-300
Binns, R. Malcolm Lowry.
   M. Hofmann, 617(TLS):18Oct85-1159
Binswanger, H.P. and others, eds. Rural
Household Studies in Asia.
   N. Dannhaeuser, 293(JASt):May84-506
Binyan, L. - see under Liu Binyan
Binyon, H. Eric Ravilious.*
   R. Berthoud, 39:Feb84-144
Binyon, M. Life in Russia.*
   A. Friendly, Jr., 550(RusR):Oct84-413
   639(VQR):Summer84-95
Biondi, C. Ces esclaves sont des hommes.
   N. Suckling, 208(FS):Jan84-69
Birch, C. and J.B. Cobb, Jr. The Libera-
tion of Life.*
   M.E. Zimmerman, 258:Mar84-99
Birch-Jones, S. A First Class Funeral.
   C.R., 376:Feb84-139
Birckbichler, D.W. Creative Activities
for the Second Language Classroom.
   W.F. Smith, 399(MLJ):Spring84-65
Bird, I.L. This Grand Beyond. (C.P.
Havely, ed) Unbeaten Tracks in Japan.
   C. Blacker, 617(TLS):15Feb85-163
Birdsall, E. and P.M. Zall - see Words-
worth, W.
Birgander, P. Boris Vian romancier.
   C. La Fontaine, 546(RR):May84-396
   C. Shorley, 208(FS):Jan84-99
Birkenhauer, R. Reimpoetik am Beispiel
Stefan Georges.
   B. Bjorklund, 133:Band17Heft1/2-165
Birkett, J., ed and trans. The Body and
the Dream.
   D. Coward, 208(FS):Jul84-373
Birkett, M.E. Lamartine and the Poetics
of Landscape.*
   W. Greenberg, 207(FR):Mar85-583
   J.C. Ireson, 402(MLR):Apr84-459
   E. Lillie, 446(NCFS):Winter-Spring85-
   144
   J. Schulze, 547(RF):Band96Heft1/2-189
Birley, A.R. The "Fasti" of Roman Brit-
ain.*
   K.R. Bradley, 122:Jan84-88
Birley, A.R. - see Syme, R.
Birnbaum, H. Essays in Early Slavic
Civilization/Studien zur Frühkultur der
Slaven.*
   J.V.A. Fine, Jr., 104(CASS):Spring-
   Summer84-182
Birnbaum, H. Lord Novgorod the Great.
(Pt 1)
   J.R. Howlett, 575(SEER):Jan84-120
Birnbaum, H. and T. Eekman, eds. Fiction
and Drama in Eastern and Southeastern
Europe.
   J.W. Connolly, 558(RLJ):Winter-
   Spring84-293
Birnbaum, P., ed and trans. Rabbits,
Crabs, Etc.* [shown in prev under title]
   V.V. Nakagawa, 293(JASt):Nov83-155
Birnbaum, S. Walt Disney World.
   P. Missac, 98:Dec84-1014
Birnbaum, S.A. Yiddish.*
   W. Weinberg, 685(ZDL):3/1984-377

Birringer, J.H. Marlowe's "Dr. Faustus"
and "Tamburlaine."
   S. Billington, 610:Autumn84-263
Bisanz, A.J. and R. Trousson, eds. Ele-
mente der Literatur.*
   O.F. Best, 406:Winter84-458
Biscardi, A. Diritto greco antico.
   D.M. MacDowell, 123:Vol34No1-62
Bischoff, B. Mittelalterliche Studien
III.*
   M.W. Wierschin, 221(GQ):Spring84-304
Bishop, E. The Collected Prose.* (R.
Giroux, ed)
   A. Hollinghurst, 493:Jun84-69
   H. Moss, 442(NY):1Apr85-104
   M.J. Rosen, 219(GaR):Fall84-651
Bishop, E. The Complete Poems 1927-1979.*
   R. Pybus, 565:Summer84-56
Bishop, I. Chaucer's "Troilus and
Criseyde."*
   G.C. Britton, 447(N&Q):Feb83-71
   J.D. Burnley, 541(RES):May84-218
   A.A. MacDonald, 179(ES):Jun84-279
Bishop, J.P. and A. Tate. The Republic of
Letters in America.* (T.D. Young and
J.J. Hindle, eds)
   J.E. Brown, 534(RALS):Spring82-101
   M.R. Winchell, 106:Summer84-229
Bishop, L. In Search of Style.
   L.H. Bourke, 446(NCFS):Winter-Spring85-
   142
Bishop, M., ed. The Language of Poetry.
   M. Sheringham, 208(FS):Apr84-241
Bishop, R. American Folk Art.
   M.S. Young, 39:Sep84-218
Bishop, R. and P. Coblentz. American
Decorative Arts.*
   T. Reese, 507:Sep/Oct84-110
Biskind, P. Seeing is Believing.*
   T. De Pietro, 219(GaR):Summer84-434
   R. Durgnat, 707:Autumn84-303
   C. MacCabe, 617(TLS):22Feb85-199
   639(VQR):Summer84-99
Bissell, R.W. Orazio Gentileschi and the
Poetic Tradition in Caravaggesque Paint-
ing.*
   J.T. Spike, 54:Dec84-696
Bissett, B. Northern Birds in Color.
   A. Mandel, 102(CanL):Summer84-149
Bissett, B. Seagull on Yonge Street.
   S.S., 376:Jun84-146
Bitsakis, E. Physique et matérialisme.
   A. Reix, 542:Jan-Mar84-112
Bittner, R. Moralisches Gebot oder Auton-
omie.
   D.M.R., 185:Jan85-381
Björk, L.A. - see Hardy, T.
Björkenlid, B. Kvinnokrav i manssamhälle.
   C. Register, 563(SS):Spring84-181
Björkvall, G., G. Iversen and R. Jonsson,
eds. Corpus troporum, III.*
   J. Caldwell, 410(M&L):Jan84-80
Bjørnflaten, J.I. Marr og språkvitenska-
pen i Sovjetunionen.*
   A. Liberman, 355(LSoc):Sep84-409
Bjornson, R., ed. Approaches to Teaching
Cervantes' "Don Quixote."
   E.C. Riley, 304(JHP):Spring84-248
Bjürström, P. Drawings in Swedish Public
Collections. (Vol 4)
   P. Rosenberg, 380:Spring84-64
Black, E. The Transfer Agreement.*
   639(VQR):Autumn84-116

Black, J., ed. Britain in the Age of
  Walpole.
    J. Cannon, 617(TLS):20Sep85-1035
Black, J. The British and the Grand Tour.
    B. Fothergill, 617(TLS):11Oct85-1141
Black, J. British Foreign Policy in the
  Age of Walpole.
    H.T. Dickinson, 617(TLS):27Sep85-1058
Black, K.L. - see Matejic, M. and others
Black, M. The Prevalence of Humbug and
  Other Essays.*
    A.G.N. Flew, 518:Jan84-59
    639(VQR):Winter84-29
Black, M. and J.S. Reed, eds. Perspec-
  tives on the American South. (Vol 2)
    639(VQR):Autumn84-134
Black, M.H. Cambridge University Press:
  1584-1984.*
    H. Schmoller, 324:Feb85-238
Black, P.R. Ernst Kaltenbrunner.
    639(VQR):Autumn84-124
Black, R. Benedetto Accolti and the
  Florentine Renaissance.
    L. Martines, 617(TLS):20Dec85-1465
Blackall, E.A. The Novels of the German
  Romantics.*
    H. Eichner, 301(JEGP):Oct84-602
    C.A.M. Noble, 529(QQ):Winter84-1019
    549(RLC):Oct-Dec84-471
Blackbourn, D. and G. Eley. The Peculiar-
  ities of German History.
    J. Joll, 617(TLS):2Aug85-861
Blackburn, P. The Collected Poems of Paul
  Blackburn. (E. Jarolim, ed)
    P. Schjeldahl, 441:10Nov85-30
Blackburn, S. Spreading the Word.*
    R.M. Martin, 150(DR):Fall84-629
Blackett-Ord, M. Hell-Fire Duke.
    J.A. Downie, 83:Autumn84-258
Blackman, M.B. During My Time.
    G.W., 102(CanL):Winter83-189
Blackmur, R.P. Studies in Henry James.*
  (V.A. Makowsky, ed)
    C. Camper, 219(GaR):Winter84-893
Blackwelder, J.K. Women of the Depression.
    L. Milazzo, 584(SWR):Summer84-336
Blackwell, K. and others - see Russell, B.
Blackwell, M.J. C.J.L. Almqvist and Roman-
  tic Irony.
    E.O. Johannesson, 563(SS):Summer84-292
Blackwood, C. Corrigan.*
    C. Gaiser, 441:14Jul85-19
    D. Taylor, 364:Oct84-90
Blackwood, C. On the Perimeter.*
    M. Robinson, 441:1Dec85-11
Blair, B.G. Strategic Command and Control.
    M.R. Gordon, 441:14Jul85-9
Blair, C., general ed. Pollard's History
  of Firearms.*
    A.V.B. Norman, 39:May84-388
Blair, C. Ridgway's Paratroopers.
    R. Bailey, 441:1Sep85-15
Blair, D.S. African Literature in French.*
    C. Wake, 208(FS):Jan84-106
Blair, R. Robert Blair's "The Grave,"
  Illustrated by William Blake. (R.N.
  Essick and M.D. Paley, eds)
    A. Wilton, 88:Summer84-54
    J. Wordsworth, 541(RES):Nov84-547
Blair, W. and R.I. McDavid, Jr., eds. The
  Mirth of a Nation.
    G.W. Boswell, 650(WF):Oct84-280
                              [continued]

[continuing]
    L. Pederson, 300:Vol 17-97
    R.B. Shuman, 35(AS):Winter84-365
Blaisdell, A. Felony Report.
    T.J. Binyon, 617(TLS):7Jun85-644
Blaise, C. Lusts.
    L. Hutcheon, 102(CanL):Autumn84-56
Blake, B., J. McNeish and D. Simmons. Art
  of the Pacific.
    D.C. Starzecka, 39:Nov84-360
Blake, J. La falsa prospettiva in Italian
  Renaissance Architecture.
    S.Y. Edgerton, Jr., 551(RenQ):Autumn84-
    464
Blake, K. Love and the Woman Question in
  Victorian Literature.*
    V. Colby, 445(NCF):Dec84-344
Blake, N.F. Shakespeare's Language.
    D. Birch, 610:Summer84-140
    M. Grivelet, 189(EA):Jul-Sep85-319
    M. Scheler, 38:Band102Heft3/4-480
Blake, N.F. - see Chaucer, G.
Blake, P. - see Hayward, M.
Blake, R. The Conservative Party from
  Peel to Thatcher.
    R. Foster, 362:19Sep85-25
    A. Howard, 617(TLS):14Jun85-657
Blake, R. The Decline of Power 1915-1964.
    R. Foster, 362:19Sep85-25
    A. Sykes, 617(TLS):18Oct85-1164
Blake, R. Forbidden Dreams.
    G.M., 62:May85-5
Blake, W. William Blake: Selected Poems.*
  (P.H. Butter, ed)
    B. Beatty, 83:Spring84-130
Blake, W. William Blake's Writings. (G.E.
  Bentley, Jr., ed)
    M. Gassenmeier, 38:Band102Heft1/2-248
Blake, W. The Complete Poetry and Prose
  of William Blake.* (rev) (D.V. Erdman,
  ed)
    P.A. Taylor, 529(QQ):Autumn84-719
    88:Summer84-4
Blake, W. The Letters of William Blake,
  with Related Documents. (3rd ed) (G.
  Keynes, ed)
    J. Beer, 402(MLR):Apr84-425
Blake, W. Oeuvres, IV. (J. Blondel, ed
  and trans)
    P. Marshall, 189(EA):Apr-Jun85-235
    F. Morvan, 450(NRF):Apr84-134
Blamires, H., ed. A Guide to Twentieth
  Century Literature in English.*
    295(JML):Nov84-327
Blanc, O. La Dernière Lettre.
    E. Weber, 617(TLS):1Mar85-235
Blanch, J.M.L. - see under Lope Blanch,
  J.M.
Blanch, L. Pierre Loti.*
    R. Stanley, 446(NCFS):Winter-Spring85-
    167
Blanchard, J., ed. Le Pastoralet.
    G. Roques, 553(RLiR):Jan-Jun84-252
Blanchard, M.E. Description.*
    D.H., 355(LSoc):Sep84-417
    J. MacCannell, 223:Fall81-418
    G.C. Spivak, 567:Vol149No3/4-347
Blanchet, C. and B. Dard. Statue of
  Liberty.
    R.F. Shepard, 441:15Dec85-20
Blanchot, M. The Sirens' Song. (G.
  Josipovici, ed)
    295(JML):Nov84-375

34

Blanck, J. Bibliography of American Literature.* (Vol 7) (V.L. Smyers and M. Winship, eds)
P.A. Baker, 70:Mar-Apr84-122
J. Myerson, 517(PBSA):Vol78No1-45
Blanco, J.J.R. - see under Rivera Blanco, J.J.
Blancpain, M., Y. Brunsvick and P. Ginestier. Les Français à travers leurs romans.
H. Godin, 208(FS):Jul84-370
Bland, P. The Crusoe Factor.
S. Rae, 617(TLS):20Sep85-1039
Blank, D.L. Ancient Philosophy and Grammar.
A.C. Lloyd, 303(JoHS):Vol 104-219
Blank, L. and J. Bogan, eds. Burden of Dreams.
K. Scott, 441:20Jan85-23
Blank, R.H. Redefining Human Life.
R.T., 185:Apr85-785
Blanpied, J.W. Time and the Artist in Shakespeare's English Histories.
R. Ornstein, 401(MLQ):Mar84-85
Blanshard, B. Four Reasonable Men.*
G. Warnock, 617(TLS):5Apr85-389
483:Oct84-558
Blasco Pascual, F.J. La poética de Juan Ramón Jiménez.
R.A. Cardwell, 86(BHS):Apr84-202
J.C. Wilcox, 400(MLN):Mar84-403
Blasi, A. Un novelista argentino del 80: Manuel T. Podestá.
M.I. Lichtblau, 238:Sep84-481
Blasier, C. The Giant's Rival.
J.N. Goodsell, 263(RIB):Vol34No3/4-426
Blasing, R. To Continue.
J. Elledge, 491:May84-110
Blassingame, J.W. - see Douglass, F.
Blau, H. Take Up the Bodies. Blooded Thought.
A. Aronson, 615(TJ):Oct84-438
W.D. King, 609:Fall/Winter84-80
Blau, J. The Renaissance of Modern Hebrew and Modern Standard Arabic.
A.S. Kaye, 318(JAOS):Oct-Dec83-793
Blaug, M. The Methodology of Economics.*
D.W. Hands, 488:Mar84-115
Blaukopf, H. - see Mahler, G. and R. Strauss
Blayney, P.W.M. The Texts of "King Lear" and their Origins. (Vol 1)
P. Bertram, 551(RenQ):Winter84-658
G.B. Evans, 402(MLR):Oct84-901
A. Hammond, 354:Mar84-89
S.W. Reid, 517(PBSA):Vol78No4-489
M. Spevack, 156(JDSh):Jahrbuch1984-225
78(BC):Spring84-7
Blech, M. Studien zum Kranz bei den Griechen.
J. Boardman, 123:Vol34No2-337
Blecua, A. Manual de crítica textual.
E.L. Rivers, 304(JHP):Spring84-241
Bleikasten, A. Parcours de Faulkner.
N. Polk, 395(MFS):Summer84-324
Bleser, C., ed. The Hammonds of Redcliffe.*
L.T. McDonnell, 106:Summer84-167
Blessing, R. Poems and Stories.
L.L. Lee, 649(WAL):Aug84-137
R. McDowell, 249(HudR):Spring84-130
Blewett, D. - see Defoe, D.

Bleznick, D.W. A Sourcebook for Hispanic Literature and Language. (2nd ed)
J.R. Chatham, 552(REH):Oct84-457
J.R. Jones, 238:Sep84-476
J.L. Laurenti, 399(MLJ):Autumn84-301
Blickle, P. Deutsche Untertanen.
P. Beicken, 221(GQ):Summer84-514
Blindheim, C. Moster Sigrid.
A. Saether, 562(Scan):May84-53
Blinn, H., ed. Shakespeare-Rezeption.* (Vol 1)
D. Feldmann, 156(JDSh):Jahrbuch1984-264
Blishen, E. A Second Skin.
A. Ross, 617(TLS):18Jan85-68
Bliss, A., ed. Spoken English in Ireland, 1600-1740.*
J. Monaghan, 38:Band102Heft3/4-483
Bliss, A. Weeds.
D. Miller, 614:Summer85-37
Bliss, C.D. Daffodils or the Death of Love.
W. Sanders, 573(SSF):Winter84-76
Bliss, L. The World's Perspective.
M.C. Bradbrook, 570(SQ):Summer84-250
H. Diehl, 223:Summer83-191
R. Ornstein, 301(JEGP):Jul84-437
Bliss, M. The Discovery of Insulin.*
M. Borell, 529(QQ):Autumn84-724
Blissett, W. The Long Conversation.
R. Luckett, 97(CQ):Vol 13No3-266
Blittersdorf, T. and others, comps. Die mittelalterlichen Grabmäler in Rom und Latium vom 13. bis zum 15. Jahrhundert. (Vol 1)
G.M. Radke, 589:Jan84-120
Bloch, D. The Modern Common Wind.
J. Crace, 617(TLS):7Jun85-627
Bloch, E. Briefe 1903-1975. (U. Opolka and others, eds) Essays on the Philosophy of Music.
G. Steiner, 617(TLS):4Oct85-1087
Bloch, R.H. Etymologies and Genealogies.*
T. Hunt, 208(FS):Jul84-319
R. Pensom, 402(MLR):Oct84-925
Bloch, S. and P. Reddaway. Soviet Psychiatric Abuse.*
A. Puddington, 129:Dec85-66
Block, A.A. and F.R. Scarpitti. Poisoning for Profit.
R. Blumenthal, 441:10Mar85-25
442(NY):4Mar85-119
Block, I., ed. Perspectives on the Philosophy of Wittgenstein.*
O.R. Jones, 393(Mind):Jan84-131
I. McFetridge, 479(PhQ):Jan84-69
B. Stroud, 482(PhR):Jan84-140
J. Zwicky, 154:Jun84-357
Block, J.F. The Uses of Gothic.*
M. Pearson, 658:Winter84-319
Blockley, R.C., ed. The Fragmentary Classicising Historians of the Later Roman Empire.*
A.B. Breebaart, 394:Vol37fasc1/2-232
R.D. Scott, 303(JoHS):Vol 104-244
Blodgett, E.D. Arché/Elegies.
L. Ricou, 102(CanL):Autumn84-192
Blodgett, E.D. Beast Gate.*
T. Goldie, 102(CanL):Autumn84-64
Blodgett, E.D. Configuration.
H. Hoy, 102(CanL):Winter83-107
P. Merivale, 107(CRCL):Mar84-149
M. Redekop, 678(YCGL):No33-103

Bloesch, H. - see Isler, H.P. and others
Blois, M.S. Information and Medicine.
  C. Lawrence, 617(TLS):19Apr85-442
Blom, Å.G. Norske mellomalderballadar 1.
  M.P. Barnes, 64(Arv):Vol38-181
Blom, L.A. and L.T. Chaplin. The Intimate
Act of Choreography.
  S.J. Cohen, 615(TJ):Oct84-442
  J.L. Hanna, 567:Vol52No1/2-141
Blom, M. Charlotte Brontë.
  G. Kelly, 178:Dec84-488
Blomberg, M. Observations on the Dodwell
Painter.
  E.J. Holmberg, 341:Vol53No1-32
Blond, A. The Book Book.
  N. Cross, 617(TLS):3May85-493
Blöndal, L.H. Um uppruna Sverrissögu.
  T.M. Andersson, 301(JEGP):Jul84-425
  P. Schach, 563(SS):Autumn84-393
Blondel, J. - see Blake, W.
Bloom, C. Limelight and After.
  K. Conlin, 615(TJ):Mar84-126
Bloom, F.E., A. Lazerson and L. Hofstadter.
Brain, Mind, and Behavior.
  I. Rosenfield, 453(NYRB):14Mar85-34
Bloom, H. Agon.*
  T.R. Frosch, 661(WC):Summer84-87
  F. McCombie, 447(N&Q):Dec83-567
  C. Molesworth, 473(PR):1/1984-155
  T. Redman, 543:Sep83-105
Bloom, H. The Breaking of the Vessels.*
  T.R. Frosch, 661(WC):Summer84-87
  C. Molesworth, 473(PR):1/1984-155
  P. van Rutten, 107(CRCL):Mar84-91
Bloomfield, F. and Leong Mo-ling, eds.
The 7th Festival of Asian Arts.
  K. Benitez, 187:Winter85-121
Bloomfield, L. An Introduction to the
Study of Language. (new ed)
  F. Chevillet, 189(EA):Jul-Sep85-303
  D.H., 355(LSoc):Jun84-275
  W.G. Moulton, 320(CJL):Fall84-201
Bloomfield, M.W., ed. Allegory, Myth, and
Symbol.*
  J.D. Black, 494:Vol4No1-109
Blotner, J. Faulkner.
  M. Grimwood, 578:Fall85-101
  639(VQR):Autumn84-118
Blotnick, S. Otherwise Engaged.
  D. Mason, 441:9Jun85-23
Blount, R., Jr. Not Exactly What I Had in
Mind.
  P.F. McManus, 441:17Nov85-14
Bluche, F. and J-F. Solnon. La véritable
hiérarchie sociale de l'ancienne France.
  J. Rogister, 617(TLS):20Sep85-1036
Blue, L. A Backdoor to Heaven.
  H. Maccoby, 362:14Nov85-30
Blühm, E., J. Garber and K. Garber, eds.
Hof, Staat und Gesellschaft in der Lit-
eratur des 17. Jahrhunderts.
  G.R. Hoyt, 221(GQ):Fall84-647
Bluhm, W.T. Force or Freedom?
  J.N. Gray, 617(TLS):8Mar85-253
Blum, H. Wishful Thinking.
  D. Stern, 441:28Jul85-8
Blum, J., ed. Our Forgotten Past.
  N. Philip, 203:Vol95No2-263
Blum, J.M. - see Lippmann, W.
Blüm, W., H-P. Dürr and H. Rechenberg -
see Heisenberg, W.

Blumenberg, H. Arbeit am Mythos.* The Le-
gitimacy of the Modern Age. Wirklichkei-
ten in denen wir leben.
  H. Hrachovec, 533:Summer84-109
Blumenberg, H. Die Lesbarkeit der Welt.
  G. Mattenklott, 384:Jan84-75
Blumenson, M. Mark Clark.*
  D. Hunt, 617(TLS):29Mar85-363
Blumenson, M. Patton.
  E.M. Coffman, 441:29Dec85-8
Blumenthal, A.R. Theater Art of the
Medici.
  A. Hughes, 59:Sep84-378
Blumenthal, E. Joseph Chaikin.
  R. Bryden, 441:10Feb85-18
Blumenthal, H.J. and A.C. Lloyd, eds.
Soul and the Structure of Being in Late
Neoplatonism.*
  A. Meredith, 123:Vol34No1-135
Blumenthal, M. Days We Would Rather Know.*
  J.F. Cotter, 249(HudR):Autumn84-504
  P. Stitt, 219(GaR):Winter84-857
  639(VQR):Autumn84-139
Blumenthal, M. Laps.
  S. Birkerts, 472:Fall/Winter84-78
  P. Stitt, 219(GaR):Winter84-857
Blumenthal, P. Semantische Dichte.
  W. Pöckl, 547(RF):Band96Heft3-293
Blumenthal, P. La Syntaxe du message.*
  W.J. Ashby, 545(RPh):Aug83-81
Blunck, J. Mars and its Satellites. (2nd
ed)
  K.B. Harder, 424:Sep84-326
Blunck, R. Friedrich Nietzsche.
  J. Kjaer, 462(OL):Vol39No2-169
Blunden, C. and M. Elvin. Cultural Atlas
of China.*
  70:Jan-Feb84-91
Blunt, A. Guide to Baroque Rome.*
  J. Gash, 89(BJA):Winter84-89
Bly, C. Backbone.
  T. Gallagher, 441:27Jan85-19
Bly, C. Letters from the Country.
  P.M. Paton, 271:Fall84-191
Bly, P.A. Galdós's Novel of the Histori-
cal Imagination.
  L.B. Barr, 345(KRQ):Vol31No2-238
  R. Benítez, 240(HR):Summer84-411
  R. Kirsner, 238:Mar84-144
Bly, R. The Eight Stages of Translation.
  D. McDuff, 565:Summer84-68
Bly, R. Loving a Woman in Two Worlds.
  F. Chappell, 441:13Oct85-15
Blyth, A., ed. Opera on Record, 2.*
  E. Forbes, 415:May84-275
Blythe, R. Characters and Their Land-
scapes.*
  295(JML):Nov84-375
Blythe, R. The Stories of Ronald Blythe.
  V. Cunningham, 617(TLS):9Aug85-874
Blythe, R. The Visitors.
  E. Spencer, 441:8Dec85-68
Boahen, A.A., ed. General History of
Africa. (Vol 7)
  R. Oliver, 617(TLS):9Aug85-867
Boaistuau, P. Bref discours de l'excel-
lence et dignité de l'homme (1558).*
(M. Simonin, ed)
  R.A. Carr, 207(FR):Dec84-284
  J-C. Margolin, 535(RHL):Sep/Oct84-802

Boaistuau, P. Le Théâtre du monde (1558).*
(M. Simonin, ed)
R.A. Carr, 207(FR):Dec84-284
P.A. Chilton, 402(MLR):Jan84-184
C. Clark, 208(FS):Jul84-327
Boardman, J. and N.G.L. Hammond, eds. The
Cambridge Ancient History.* (Vol 3, Pt
3) (2nd ed)
R. Sealey, 122:Jul84-235
Boardman, M.E. Defoe and the Uses of Nar-
rative.*
T.K. Meier, 173(ECS):Fall84-144
M. Schonhorn, 401(MLQ):Dec83-410
Boas, J. Boulevard des Misères.
H.L. Mason, 441:20Oct85-30
Boccaccio, G. Chaucer's Boccaccio.*
(N.R. Havely, ed and trans)
F.N.M. Diekstra, 179(ES):Dec84-558
Bock, I. Die Analyse der Handlungsstruk-
turen von Erzählwerken am Beispiel von
N.V. Gogol's "Die Nase" und "Der Mantel."
A. McMillin, 575(SEER):Apr84-260
Böckerstette, H. Aporien der Freiheit
und ihre Aufklärung durch Kant.
W. Steinbeck, 342:Band75Heft1-108
Bode, E. This Favored Place.
L. Clayton, 649(WAL):Nov84-254
Bodea, C. and V. Cândea. Transylvania in
the History of the Romanians.
V.F. Bowen, 104(CASS):Spring-Summer84-
224
Bödefeld, H. Untersuchungen zur Datierung
der Alexandergeschichte des Q. Curtius
Rufus.
E.D. Carney, 124:Jan-Feb85-227
Bodel, J.P. Roman Brick Stamps in the
Kelsey Museum.
G.E. Rickman, 123:Vol34No1-151
Bodéüs, R. Le Philosophie et la cité.*
C.J. Rowe, 123:Vol34No2-209
Bodey, D. F.N.G.
C. Salzberg, 441:29Dec85-18
Bodo, M. The Way of St. Francis.
H. Lomas, 249(HudR):Summer84-325
Body, J. and others - see Giraudoux, J.
Boeck, W., ed. Kommunikativ-funktionale
Sprachbetrachtung als theoretische Grund-
lage für den Fremdsprachenunterricht.
L. Wilske, 682(ZPSK):Band37Heft6-733
Boehm, R. Vom Gesichtspunkt der Phänomen-
ologie II.
J.J. Drummond, 543:Sep83-106
P. Simpson, 323:May84-203
Boehm, R.G. Vigiliae Tullianae, Emenda-
tionen zu den Texten vorwiegend der
Briefe von und an M. Tullius Cicero.
(Vol 1)
J. Beaujeu, 555:Vol58fasc1-139
Boehne, P.J. J.V. Foix.
J. Piqué i Angordans, 552(REH):Jan84-
157
Boekraad, C., F. Bool and H. Henkels, eds.
De Stijl.
S. Frank, 505:Feb84-162
Boelhower, W.Q. - see Goldmann, L.
Boening, J., ed. The Reception of Class-
ical German Literature in England, 1760-
1860.
P. Boerner, 173(ECS):Fall84-134
de Boer, S.P., E.J. Driessen and H.L. Ver-
haar, eds. Biographical Dictionary of
Dissidents in the Soviet Union, 1956-
[continued]

[continuing]
1975.*
I. Elliot, 575(SEER):Jan84-157
Boerhaave, H. Boerhaave's Orations. (E.
Kegel-Brinkgreve and A.M. Luyendijk-
Elshout, trans)
L.V.R., 568(SCN):Winter84-79
Boesche, R. - see de Tocqueville, A.
Boettcher, T.D. Vietnam.
R. Bailey, 441:2Jun85-46
Boff, L. Church: Charism and Power.
P. Hebblethwaite, 617(TLS):6Sep85-986
Bogan, J. and F. Goss, eds. Sparks of
Fire.*
J. La Belle, 88:Summer84-48
Bogardus, R.F. and F. Hobson, eds. Litera-
ture at the Barricades.*
W. French, 395(MFS):Summer84-330
T. Hayashi, 577(SHR):Spring84-191
Bogdanovich, P. The Killing of the Uni-
corn.*
B. Ehrenreich, 18:Nov84-75
Bogel, F.V. Literature and Insubstantial-
ity in Later Eighteenth-Century England.
S. Soupel, 189(EA):Oct-Dec85-465
639(VQR):Autumn84-127
Boghardt, C., M. Boghardt and R. Schmidt.
Die zeitgenössischen Drucke von Klop-
stocks Werken.*
N. Oellers, 52:Band19Heft3-307
Bogin, R. Abraham Clark and the Quest for
Equality in the Revolutionary Era, 1774-
1794.
P.D. Chase, 656(WMQ):Jan84-162
Bohachevsky-Chomiak, M. and B.G. Rosenthal,
eds. A Revolution of the Spirit.
J. Brooks, 550(RusR):Jul84-297
Bohlmann, O. Yeats and Nietzsche.
J. Olney, 569(SR):Summer84-451
Böhme, T. Mit der Sanduhr am Gürtel.
J. Engler, 654(WB):4/1984-643
Bohnen, K. Brandes und die "Deutsche
Rundschau."
H. Uecker, 52:Band19Heft2-193
Bohnen, K., ed. Brechts Gewehre der Frau
Carrar.
G. Michels, 221(GQ):Fall84-674
Bohnen, K., ed. Der Essay als kritischer
Spiegel.
H. Uecker, 52:Band19Heft2-193
Bohnen, K. and S-A. Jorgensen, eds. Kul-
tur und Gesellschaft in Deutschland von
der Reformation bis zur Gegenwart.
J.K. Swaffar, 399(MLJ):Spring84-78
Bohner, C.H. Robert Penn Warren.* (rev)
N. Nakadate, 392:Winter83/84-115
Böhr, E. Der Schaukelmaler.
D.C. Kurtz, 123:Vol34No1-106
Bohrer, K.H. Plötzlichkeit.
R. Rochlitz, 98:Nov84-864
Bohstedt, J. Riots and Community Politics
in England and Wales 1790-1810.
J. Stevenson, 617(TLS):19Apr85-443
Boie, B. L'homme et ses simulacres.
H. Jechova, 549(RLC):Jul-Sep84-361
du Bois, P. History, Rhetorical Descrip-
tion and the Epic from Homer to Spenser.*
[shown in prev under Du Bois]
T. Comito, 589:Apr84-396
Boisserée, S. Tagebücher. (Vols 1 and 2)
(H-J. Weitz, ed)
H. Eichner, 301(JEGP):Apr84-284

37

de la Boissière, R. Rum and Coca-Cola.
    D. Montrose, 617(TLS):15Feb85-179
Boisvert, L., M. Juneau and C. Poirier,
    eds. Travaux de Linguistique Québécoise
    2.
    H.J. Wolf, 547(RF):Band96Heft4-452
Boitani, P. English Medieval Narrative in
    the Thirteenth and Fourteenth Centuries.*
    H. Cooper, 382(MAE):1984/1-121
    V.B. Richmond, 589:Jul84-623
Bokarev, E.A. Sravnitel'no-istoričeskaja
    fonetika vostočnokavkazkich jazykov.
    K. Müller, 682(ZPSK):Band37Heft6-716
Bold, A., ed. Byron.
    C. Bergerolle, 189(EA):Jan-Mar85-87
    E. Frykman, 571(ScLJ):Autumn84-19
Bold, A. The Edge of the Wood.
    D. Montrose, 617(TLS):4Jan85-9
Bold, A. In This Corner — Selected Poems
    1963-1983.
    D. McDuff, 565:Spring84-72
Bold, A. MacDiarmid.
    F.R. Hart, 659(ConL):Winter85-508
Bold, A. Modern Scottish Literature.
    W.R. Aitken, 588(SSL):Vol 19-288
    L. Paterson, 571(ScLJ):Autumn84-28
Bold, A., ed. Harold Pinter.
    J. Melmoth, 617(TLS):30Aug85-953
Bold, A., ed. Sir Walter Scott.
    G. McMaster, 571(ScLJ):Autumn84-15
Bold, A., ed. Smollett.*
    M. Irwin, 541(RES):Nov84-552
Bold, A., ed. Muriel Spark.
    Y. Tosser, 189(EA):Oct-Dec85-481
Boldman, R. Wind in the Chimes.
    R. Spiess, 404:Summer84-44
Boléo, M.D. A língua portuguesa do Conti-
    nente, dos Açores e do Brasil.
    A. Gier, 553(RLiR):Jul-Dec84-478
Boles, J.B. Black Southerners, 1619-1869.
    R. Blackett, 392:Fall84-500
    42(AR):Summer84-384
    639(VQR):Spring84-48
Boles, J.B., ed. Dixie Dateline.
    639(VQR):Spring84-57
"Boletin de la Academia Norteamericana de
    la Lengua Española." (No 4-5) (E. Chang-
    Rodríguez, ed)
    C. Gariano, 238:Mar84-161
"Lord Bolingbroke: Contributions to the
    'Craftsman.'"* (S. Varey, ed)
    J. Black, 566:Autumn84-61
    W.B. Coley, 677(YES):Vol 14-324
    G. Laprevotte, 189(EA):Jul-Sep85-327
Böll, H. A Soldier's Legacy.
    P-L. Adams, 61:Jul85-100
    J. Agee, 441:23Jun85-9
Böll, H. What's to Become of the Boy?*
    M. Butler, 617(TLS):26Jul85-813
    J. Rae, 362:21Feb85-26
Bollack, J. and P. Judet de La Combe - see
    Aeschylus
Bollack, M. - see Szondi, P.
Bollée, A. and G. Lionnet - see Young, R.
Bölling, K. Die Fernen Nachbarn.
    T.G. Ash, 453(NYRB):31Jan85-33
Bollow, L. One Acts and Monologues for
    Women.
    T.G. Dunn, 615(TJ):Dec84-551
Bolls, I.L. Glass Walker.
    J. Carter, 219(GaR):Summer84-415
Bolnick, J.P. Winnie.
    L. Thomas, 441:1Dec85-24

Bolsterli, M.J. - see Jackson, N.S.
Bolt, C. Escape Entertainment.
    R. Plant, 102(CanL):Summer84-155
    J. Wasserman, 102(CanL):Summer84-91
Bolter, J.D. Turing's Man.*
    J. Marsh, 129:Feb85-66
Bolton, K. Talking to You.
    J. Forbes, 381:Sep84-453
Bolton, W.F. The Language of 1984.*
    N. Berry, 175:Autumn84-271
Bombal, M-L. New Islands.* (French title:
    Les Îles nouvelles.)
    J-M. le Sidaner, 450(NRF):Nov84-102
Bömer, F. P. Ovidius Naso, "Metamor-
    phosen": Kommentar, Buch XII-XIII.
    E.J. Kenney, 123:Vol34No1-33
    W.R. Nethercut, 124:Jul-Aug85-620
Bomhard, A.R. Toward Proto-Nostratic.
    A.S. Kaye, 350:Dec85-887
Bonafoux, P. Portraits of the Artist.
    J.D. McClatchy, 441:25Aug85-16
Bonansea, B.M. Man and His Approach to
    God in John Duns Scotus.
    R.P. Desharnais, 543:Jun84-842
Bonar, A. The Macmillan Treasury of Herbs.
    L. Yang, 441:2Jun85-14
Bonavia, D. Verdict in Peking.
    G. Walden, 617(TLS):11Jan85-47
Bond, D.J. The Fiction of André Pieyre de
    Mandiargues.*
    H.K. Charney, 207(FR):Feb85-462
Bond, D.J. The Temptation of Despair.*
    J-A. Elder, 102(CanL):Summer84-121
Bond, E.J. Reason and Value.*
    N.J.H. Dent, 483:Jul84-411
    H.C.K., 185:Jan85-380
    J. Narveson, 154:Jun84-327
Bond, G.A. - see William VII
Bond, G.W. Euripides: "Heracles."*
    E.M. Craik, 303(JoHS):Vol 104-199
Bondanella, J.C. Petrarch's Visions and
    Their Renaissance Analogues.
    A. de Colombí-Monguió, 545(RPh):May84-
    501
Bondanella, P. Italian Cinema.
    A.G. Robson, 399(MLJ):Spring84-70
Bondanella, P. and J.C. The Macmillan Dic-
    tionary of Italian Literature.
    P. Cola, 356(LR):Aug84-261
Bonderup, J. The Saint Martial Polyphony.
    D. Hiley, 410(M&L):Jan84-60
Bondeson, W.B. and others, eds. Philos-
    ophy and Medicine. (Vol 13)
    J.C., 185:Oct84-195
Bondesson, P. Karen Blixens bogsamling på
    Rungstedlund.
    P.M. Mitchell, 563(SS):Winter84-68
Bonesteel, G. More Lap Quilting with
    Georgia Bonesteel.
    P.J. Christenson, 614:Spring85-25
Bonet, L. Literatura, regionalismo y
    lucha de clases (Galdós, Pereda, Narcís
    Oller y Ramón de Perés).
    M. Montes-Huidobro, 238:Dec84-670
Bonet, L. - see de Alarcón, P.A.
Bonet Correa, A. and others, eds. Biblio-
    grafía de arquitectura, ingeniería y
    urbanismo en España (1498-1880).*
    C. Wilkinson, 576:May84-178
Bonfante, G. and L. The Etruscan Lan-
    guage.*
    R.A. Fowkes, 660(Word):Aug84-189
                                    [continued]

[continuing]
H.M. Hoenigswald, 123:Vol34No2-340
N. Vincent, 350:Sep85-688
Bonfatti, E. La "Civil Conversazione" in
Germania.
P. Riesz-Musumeci, 343:Heft9/10-159
Bonfield, L. Marriage Settlements,
1601-1740.*
J.A. Priest, 83:Spring84-103
Bonfioli, M. Tre arcate marmoree protobiz-
antine a Lison di Portogruaro.
C. Mango, 123:Vol34No1-152
Bonghi Jovino, M. La necropoli preromana
di Vico Equense.
D. Ridgway, 123:Vol34No2-353
Donham Cartor, M. - see Asquith, M.
Bonheim, H. The Narrative Modes.*
M.D. Rapisarda, 395(MFS):Summer84-403
Böni, F. Die Alpen. Alle Züge fahren
nach Salem.
M. Hofmann, 617(TLS):4Jan85-17
Saint Boniface. Bonifatius: "Ars grammat-
ica" (G.J. Gebauer and B. Löfstedt, eds)
"Ars metrica." (B. Löfstedt, ed)
T. Lawler, 589:Jan84-227
Bonifaz Nuño, R. - see Maples Arce, M.
Bonino, J.M. - see under Míguez Bonino, J.
Bonito Oliva, A. Transavant-garde inter-
national.
E. Darragon, 98:Aug/Sep84-693
Bonitzer, P. Le Champ aveugle.
A. Thiher, 207(FR):Mar85-610
Bonnell, V.E. Roots of Rebellion.
R.C. Elwood, 104(CASS):Winter84-476
Bonnell, V.E., ed. The Russian Worker.
F.C. Giffin, 104(CASS):Winter84-475
Bonner, A. - see Llull, R.
Bonner, T., Jr., comp. William Faulkner.
(G. Nanez Falcon, ed)
E. Gallafent, 677(YES):Vol 14-353
Bonney, R. The King's Debts.*
D. Bitton, 551(RenQ):Spring84-84
Bonnie, F. Displaced Persons.
J. Acheson, 102(CanL):Autumn84-162
A. Brennan, 198:Autumn84-90
Bono, B.J. Literary Transvaluation.
G. Taylor, 617(TLS):16Aug85-905
de Bono, E. Tactics.
C. Brown, 617(TLS):9Aug85-886
Bonoma, T.V. The Marketing Edge.
C.L. Harris, 441:20Oct85-50
Bonss, W. and A. Honneth, eds. Sozialfor-
schung als Kritik.
D. Misgeld, 488:Mar84-97
Bony, J. The English Decorated Style.
P. Kidson, 90:Sep84-570
Bony, J. French Gothic Architecture of
the Twelfth and Thirteenth Centuries.*
F. Bucher, 576:Dec84-367
L. Grant, 90:Sep84-570
"Bookman's Price Index." (Vol 23) (D.F.
McGrath, ed)
H. Schnelling, 568(SCN):Fall84-45
Boon, J.A. Other Tribes, Other Scribes.
R.D. Abrahams, 292(JAF):Oct-Dec84-487
Boone, E.H. - see "The Codex Magliabechi-
ano"
Boone, L.P. From A to Z in Latah County,
Idaho.
L.W. Otness, 424:Dec84-450
Boorman, J. Money into Light.
M. Le Fanu, 617(TLS):15Nov85-1287

Boorman, S., ed. Studies in the Perfor-
mance of Late Medieval Music.
J. Stevens, 617(TLS):25Jan85-101
Boorstin, D.J. The Discoverers.*
R. Porter, 617(TLS):26Apr85-463
Boos, F.S. - see Morris, W.
Booth, A. and P. McCawley, eds. The Indo-
nesian Economy During the Soeharto Era.
G. Hart, 293(JASt):Feb84-366
Booth, J. Writers and Politics in Nige-
ria.*
R.N. Egudu, 538(RAL):Fall84-423
Booth, M. Looking for the Rainbow Sign.
A. Stevenson, 493:Jun84-66
Booth, M. Meeting the Snowy North Again.
R. Pybus, 565:Winter83/84-68
Booth, M., ed. What I Believe. Christian
Short Stories.
O. Bowcock, 617(TLS):20Dec85-1444
Booth, M.R. Victorian Spectacular Theatre
1850-1910.*
L.W. Conolly, 615(TJ):Dec82-547
Booth, M.R., ed. Victorian Theatrical
Trades.*
J. Donohue, 637(VS):Autumn83-91
Booth, M.W. The Experience of Song.*
D. Lindley, 447(N&Q):Oct83-455
Booth, S. "King Lear," "Macbeth," Indefi-
nition, and Tragedy.*
L.S. Champion, 179(ES):Dec84-576
W.H. Matchett, 401(MLQ):Mar84-87
C. Pye, 615(TJ):Oct84-429
639(VQR):Winter84-8
Booth, S. The True Adventures of the
Rolling Stones.
A. Cockburn, 617(TLS):29Mar85-338
Booth, W.C. Critical Understanding.*
J. Phelan, 128(CE):Jan84-63
Booty, J.E. - see Hooker, R.
Borch, O. Olai Borrichii Itinerarium 1660-
1665. (H.D. Schepelern, ed)
J.R. Christianson, 551(RenQ):Winter84-
627
Borck, J.S. - see "The Eighteenth Century:
A Current Bibliography"
von Borcke, A. and G. Simon. Neue Wege
der Sowjetunion-Forschung.
W.A. Welsh, 104(CASS):Fall84-334
Bordes, J. Politeia dans la pensée
grecque jusqu'à Aristote.
P. Demont, 555:Vol58fasc1-117
P.J. Rhodes, 487:Summer84-179
T.J. Saunders, 123:Vol34No1-83
Bordinat, P. and S.B. Blaydes. Sir Wil-
liam Davenant.*
K. Robinson, 447(N&Q):Oct83-472
Bordman, G. American Musical Revue.
J.S. Wilson, 441:22Sep85-23
Bordman, G. The Oxford Companion to
American Theatre.
J. Simon, 617(TLS):26Apr85-477
Bordwell, D., J. Staiger and K. Thompson.
The Classical Hollywood Cinema.
T. Elsaesser, 18:May85-52
R. Grenier, 617(TLS):13Dec85-1423
Borgatti, J. Cloth as Metaphor.
K.P. Kent, 2(AfrA):Feb84-17
Borgeaud, W. Fasti Umbrici.
J.W. Poultney, 124:Sep-Oct84-51
Borges, J.L. Ficciones.
M.B., 62:May85-4

Boudinot, E. Cherokee Editor. (T. Perdue, ed)
  M.Z. Searcy, 9(AlaR):Jul84-231
Boudon, R. - see Tarde, G.
Boudon, R. and F. Bourricaud. Diction-
  naire critique de la sociologie.
  J-C. Chamboredon, 98:Jun/Jul84-460
Boudou, J-R. Une Heure de ta vie.
  J-A. Elder, 102(CanL):Autumn84-61
Bouhdiba, A. Sexuality in Islam.
  R. Irwin, 617(TLS):4Oct85-1112
Boulanger, D. Hôtel de l'image.
  P.J.T. Gormally, 207(FR):Oct84-153
Boulanger, D. Les Noces du merle.
  R. Buss, 617(TLS):4Oct85-1113
du Boulay, A. Christie's Pictorial His-
  tory of Chinese Ceramics.
  R.E. Scott, 617(TLS):6Sep85-987
Boulet, R. The Canadian Earth.
  S. and J. Wasserman, 102(CanL):
  Winter83-166
Boulin, R-H. Médaillons d'infini.
  N.S. Hellerstein, 207(FR):May85-910
Boulle, P. Pour l'Amour de l'art.
  D. Johnson, 617(TLS):11Oct85-1155
Boulle, P. Trouble in Paradise.
  442(NY):16Sep85-122
Boult, A. Boult on Music.*
  M. Kennedy, 410(M&L):Oct84-384
  D. Matthews, 607:Mar84-48
Boulton, J. and A. Robertson - see Law-
  rence, D.H.
Boulton-Smith, J. Frederick Delius and
  Edvard Munch.
  J.P. Hodin, 562(Scan):Nov84-182
Boumelha, P. Thomas Hardy and Women.*
  E.J. Higgins, 95(CLAJ):Jun85-477
  J. Simons, 541(RES):Nov84-573
Bouquiaux, L. and J.M.C. Thomas, eds.
  Enquête et Description des Langues
  à Tradition Orale.
  H.E.M. Klein, 269(IJAL):Apr84-243
Bouraoui, H., ed. The Canadian Alterna-
  tive.
  K.P. Stich, 102(CanL):Winter83-91
de Bourbon Busset, J. Le Berger des
  nuages.
  D. O'Connell, 207(FR):Feb85-490
Bourcier, G. An Introduction to the His-
  tory of the English Language.*
  A. Fill, 38:Band102Heft1/2-145
  B.D.H. Miller, 541(RES):May84-216
  B.M.H. Strang, 402(MLR):Apr84-410
Bourdieu, P. Homo academicus.
  D. Johnson, 617(TLS):26Apr85-461
Bourgeade, P. La Fin du monde.
  A. Clerval, 450(NRF):Dec84-96
Bourgeade, P. Les Serpents.
  P.A. Mankin, 207(FR):May85-911
Bourgeois, P.L. and S.B. Rosenthal. The-
  matic Studies in Phenomenology and Prag-
  matism.
  C.R. Hausman, 619:Fall84-473
Bourhis, R.Y., ed. Conflict and Language
  Planning in Quebec.
  W. Grabe, 350:Dec85-937
Bourne, K. Palmerston: The Early Years
  1784-1841.
  J.E. Cookson, 637(VS):Winter84-239
Bousquet, J. La Connaissance du Soir.
  I. Higgins, 208(FS):Oct84-491

Boussel, P. Beaumarchais, le Parisien
  universel.
  D.C. Spinelli, 207(FR):Feb85-454
Boutier, J., A. Dewerpe and D. Nordman,
  eds. Un Tour de France royal.
  P. Burke, 617(TLS):25Jan85-81
Boutilier, J.A., ed. The RCN in Retro-
  spect, 1910-1968.*
  D.M. Schurman, 529(QQ):Spring84-180
Boutry, P. and J. Nassif. Martin L'Arch-
  ange.
  E. Weber, 617(TLS):15Nov85-1281
Bouveresse, J. Le philosophe chez les
  autophages.
  M. Jarrety, 450(NRF):Jun84-108
  F. Regnault, 98:May84-362
Bouwsma, O.K. Without Proof or Evidence.
  (J.L. Craft and R.E. Hustwit, eds)
  J.I.C., 185:Apr85-767
  483:Oct84-559
Bova, B. Assured Survival.
  S. Zuckerman, 441:20Jan85-6
Bove, E. Meine Freunde. Armand.
  W. van Rossum, 384:Mar84-215
Bové, P.A. Destructive Poetics.*
  M.T. Beehler, 223:Summer81-284
  S. Cresap, 125:Winter84-197
Bow, E.L. Spanish Through Proverbs. (Vol
  1) 808 Spanish Verbs. 700 Spanish Pro-
  verbs.
  L. Martin, 238:Sep84-484
Bowden, B. Performed Literature.
  L. Bartlett, 30:Winter84-93
  M. Booth, 577(SHR):Winter84-78
  B. Hinton, 203:Vol95No1-134
Bowen, B.C. Words and the Man in French
  Renaissance Literature.*
  H.H. Glidden, 210(FrF):Sep84-358
  A. Moss, 208(FS):Oct84-455
  F. Rigolot, 546(RR):May84-386
Bowen, D. Paul Cardinal Cullen and the
  Shaping of Modern Irish Catholicism.*
  M.E. Daly, 272(IUR):Autumn84-285
Bowen, J. The McGuffin.*
  J. Mellors, 364:Dec84/Jan85-145
Bowen, Z.R. and J.R. Carens, eds. A Com-
  panion to Joyce Studies.
  E.R. Steinberg, 329(JJQ):Summer85-429
  295(JML):Nov84-462
Bower, T. Klaus Barbie.
  H.R. Kedward, 617(TLS):15Nov85-1282
Bower, T. Blind Eye to Murder.
  R. Jeffreys-Jones, 529(QQ):Winter84-
  1025
Bowering, G. Kerrisdale Elegies.
  S.S., 376:Jun84-146
Bowering, G. The Mask in Place.
  R. Billings, 102(CanL):Autumn84-109
Bowering, G. A Place to Die.*
  A. Brennan, 198:Autumn84-90
Bowering, G. Smoking Mirror.
  C. Tapping, 102(CanL):Summer84-158
  T. Whalen, 198:Summer84-101
Bowering, G. A Way With Words.* West Win-
  dow.*
  T. Whalen, 198:Summer84-101
Bowering, M. Giving Back Diamonds.*
  P. Stuewe, 529(QQ):Spring84-206
Bowerman, G.E., Jr. The Compensations of
  War.
  639(VQR):Winter84-14
Bowers, F. - see Beaumont, F. and J. Flet-
  cher

Bowers, F. - see Nabokov, V.
Bowersock, G.W. Roman Arabia.
  T.R.S. Broughton, 487:Autumn84-286
Bowie, M., A. Fairlie and A. Finch, eds.
  Baudelaire, Mallarmé, Valéry.*
  U. Franklin, 446(NCFS):Summer-Fall84-187
  L.M. Porter, 210(FrF):Jan84-124
Bowker, G., ed. Malcolm Lowry Remembered.
  M. Hofmann, 617(TLS):18Oct85-1159
  P. Kemp, 362:15Aug85-28
Bowle, J. John Evelyn and his World.
  R.D. Hume, 402(MLR):Jul84-666
Bowle, J. - see Evelyn, J.
Bowler, P.J. Evolution.
  R. Porter, 617(TLS):2Aug85-853
Bowles, E.A. La Pratique musicale au
  moyen âge/Musical Performance in the
  Late Middle Ages.
  J. Caldwell, 410(M&L):Jul84-306
Bowles, J. Out in the World. (M. Dillon,
  ed)
  H. Marten, 441:28Jul85-10
Bowles, J. Plain Pleasures and Other Stor-
  ies.
  P. Craig, 617(TLS):26Apr85-479
Bowlt, J.E. Russian Stage Design — Scenic
  Innovation, 1900-1930.
  L. Hecht, 574(SEEJ):Summer84-275
Bowlt, J.E., ed. Zapiski Russkoi Akade-
  micheskoi Gruppy v S. Sh. A. (Vol 15)
  S.C. Feinstein, 104(CASS):Spring-
    Summer84-173
Bowring, R. - see "Murasaki Shikibu: Her
  Diary and Poetic Memoirs"
Boxill, A. V.S. Naipaul's Fiction.*
  W.J. Howard, 627(UTQ):Summer84-438
  S.F.D. Hughes, 395(MFS):Autumn84-573
Boyarsky, A. Shreiber.
  C. McLay, 102(CanL):Autumn84-87
Boyd, J. - see McFadden, R.
Boyd, J.P. and R.W. Lester - see Jefferson,
  T.
Boyd, M. Bach.*
  A. Bond, 415:Mar84-152
  P. Williams, 410(M&L):Oct84-391
Boyd, M. The Reflexive Novel.
  H. Hawkins, 136:Vol 17No2-153
  J.A. Varsava, 395(MFS):Summer84-409
  295(JML):Nov84-384
Boyd, W. Stars and Bars.*
  C. Hawtree, 364:Oct84-85
  C. Seebohm, 441:14Apr85-17
  442(NY):20May85-125
Boyde, P. Dante, Philomythes and Philos-
  opher.*
  V. Cioffari, 276:Autumn84-263
Boydston, J.A. - see Dewey, J.
Boyer, E.L. High School.*
  P. Rothman, 42(AR):Winter84-115
Boyer, M.C. Dreaming the Rational City.
  J. Albrecht, 576:Oct84-271
Boyer, P. By the Bomb's Early Light.
  M. Silk, 441:10Nov85-27
Boylan, M. Method and Practice in Aris-
  totle's Biology.
  J. Barnes, 123:Vol34No1-55
  P. Pellegrin, 542:Jan-Mar84-65
  J.A. Richmond, 303(JoHS):Vol 104-215
Boyle, K. Words That Must Somehow Be
  Said. (E.S. Bell, ed)
  A. Chisholm, 617(TLS):27Sep85-1076
  H. Ford, 441:25Aug85-20

Boyle, K. and T. Hadden. Ireland.
  C. Townshend, 617(TLS):1Nov85-1231
Boyle, L. Medieval Latin Palaeography.
  R. McKitterick, 617(TLS):21Jun85-707
Boyle, M.O. Rhetoric and Reform.
  J.C. Olin, 551(RenQ):Winter84-618
Boyle, R. Acid Rain.
  639(VQR):Winter84-19
Boyle, T.C. Greasy Lake.
  L. McCaffery, 441:9Jun85-15
Boynard-Frot, J. Un Matriarcat en procès.
  E.D. Blodgett, 168(ECW):Winter84/85-146
  P. Hébert, 627(UTQ):Summer84-471
Boytinck, P. C.P. Snow.
  J.G. Watson, 447(N&Q):Jun83-266
Boyum, J.G. Double Exposure.
  W. Paul, 441:17Nov85-24
Bozzi, A. Note di lessicografia ippocra-
  tica.
  J. Vallance, 123:Vol34No2-313
Braccesi, A. Soneti e canzone. (F. Mag-
  nani, ed)
  A. Tissoni Benvenuti, 228(GSLI):
    Vol 161fasc514-290
Bracken, P. The Command and Control of
  Nuclear Forces.*
  R.H., 185:Jan85-403
  T. Powers, 453(NYRB):17Jan85-33
Brackenbury, A. Breaking Ground.
  D. Davis, 362:6Jun85-31
Brackenbury, R. Sense and Sensuality.
  J. Mellors, 362:21Mar85-25
  M. Seymour, 617(TLS):1Mar85-226
Braconnier, C. Le système tonal du dioula
  d'Odienné. (Vol 1)
  L.M. Hyman, 350:Jun85-474
Bradbrook, M. Aspects of Dramatic Form in
  the English and Irish Renaissance.
  639(VQR):Spring84-44
Bradbury, E. Is That You This Is Me.
  B. Pirie, 102(CanL):Autumn84-121
Bradbury, M. The Modern American Novel.*
  M. Couturier, 189(EA):Jan-Mar85-116
  M. Rohrberger, 395(MFS):Summer84-335
  C. Werner, 27(AL):Mar84-132
Bradbury, M. Rates of Exchange.*
  J.L. Halio, 598(SoR):Winter85-204
  P. Lewis, 565:Autumn84-55
  M. Théry, 189(EA):Jul-Sep85-349
  639(VQR):Spring84-57
Bradbury, M. and D. Palmer, eds. Shake-
  spearian Tragedy.
  J. Kerrigan, 617(TLS):22Feb85-208
Bradbury, R. Death is a Lonely Business.
  G. O'Brien, 441:3Nov85-26
Bradby, D., L. James and B. Sharratt, eds.
  Performance and Politics in Popular
  Drama.*
  G.K. Hunter, 677(YES):Vol 14-362
Braddon, R. and others. River Journeys.
  W.L. Heat-Moon, 441:8Dec85-16
Bradford, B.T. Hold the Dream.
  K. Olson, 441:9Jun85-22
Bradford, D.E. The Concept of Existence.
  L. Addis, 321:Vol 18No3-247
Bradford, E. Julius Caesar.
  442(NY):4Feb85-102
Bradford, M.E. Generations of the Faith-
  ful Heart.
  M.R. Winchell, 585(SoQ):Winter85-123
Bradford, S. Disraeli.
  J. Halperin, 637(VS):Autumn83-104

Bradley, B.L.   Zu Rilkes Malte Laurids
Brigge.
   T. Fiedler, 133:Band17Heft1/2-169
Bradley, I.   The Strange Rebirth of
Liberal Britain.
   S. Jenkins, 617(TLS):20Sep85-1024
Bradley, I. - see Gilbert, W.S. and A.S.
Sullivan
Bradley, J. - see Curzon, M.
Bradley, J.L., ed.   Ruskin: The Critical
Heritage.
   P. Conner, 59:Dec84-499
   M.W., 90:Dec84-796
Bradshaw, J.   Dreams That Money Can Buy.
   M. Seldes, 441:5May85-28
Bradshaw, P.F.   Daily Prayer in the Early
Church.
   R.E. Reynolds, 589:Oct84-970
Brady, A.M. and B. Cleeve, eds.   A Bio-
graphical Dictionary of Irish Writers.
   D. Kiberd, 617(TLS):1Nov85-1240
Brady, F.   James Boswell: The Later Years
1769-1795.*
   I. Ehrenpreis, 453(NYRB):28Mar85-3
   J. Melmoth, 364:Dec84/Jan85-139
   C. Rawson, 441:13Jan85-37
   J.C. Ward, 344:Fall85-125
Brady, F. and W.K. Wimsatt - see Johnson,
S.
Brady, K.   The Short Stories of Thomas
Hardy.*
   S. Gatrell, 541(RES):Nov84-572
   K. Wilson, 150(DR):Spring84-177
Bragance, A.   Une Valse noire.
   L. Vines, 207(FR):May85-912
Bragger, J. and D. Rice.   Allons-y!
   J.H. Manley, 207(FR):Mar85-605
Bragger, J.D. and R. Ariew.   Chère Fran-
çoise.   (2nd ed)
   M N. Little, 207(FR):May85-903
   L.K. Martin, 399(MLJ):Winter84-397
Brague, R.   Du temps chez Platon et Aris-
tote.*
   P. Louis, 555:Vol58fasc1-120
Braham, J.   A Sort of Columbus.
   K.M. Opdahl, 395(MFS):Winter84-834
   L. Simon, 27(AL):Oct84-446
Braida, D.D., comp.   Na Pua'oli Puke'
ekolu (Joyous Blossoms).
   R. Spiess, 404:Summer84-43
Braine, J.   These Golden Days.
   C. Hawtree, 617(TLS):15Nov85-1296
Brainerd, B., ed.   Historical Linguistics.*
   E.S. Wheeler, 660(Word):Dec84-290
Brakel, A.   Phonological Markedness and
Distinctive Features.
   J-L. Nespoulous, 320(CJL):Spring84-85
Brams, S.J.   Superior Beings.
   H. Nurmi, 262:Mar84-159
Branca, V.   Poliziano e l'umanesimo della
parola.
   E. Bigi, 228(GSLI):Vol 161fasc516-587
Brand, C.   Buffet for Unwelcome Guests.
(F.M. Nevins, Jr. and M.H. Greenberg,
eds)
   J.M. Purcell, 573(SSF):Spring84-163
Brand, M.   Intending and Acting.
   D.W.D. Owen, 617(TLS):19Apr85-432
Brandão, I.D.   And Still the Earth.
   L. Rohter, 441:29Sep85-38
Brandes, G.   Levned.   (T. Kaarsted, ed)
   H. Uecker, 52:Band19Heft2-193

Brandes, M.A.   Siegelabrollungen aus den
archaischen Bauschichten in Uruk-Warka.
   E. Porada, 318(JAOS):Apr-Jun83-476
Brandes, S.   Forty.
   B.F. Williamson, 441:8Sep85-25
Brandes, U.   Zitat und Montage in der
neueren DDR-Prosa.
   C. Cosentino, 222(GR):Fall84-163
Brandon, J.R., ed.   Chūshingura.*
   S. Matisoff, 293(JASt):May84-541
Brandon, R.   The Spiritualists.
   42(AR):Summer84-382
Brandon, R.N. and R.M. Burian, eds.   Genes,
Organisms, Populations.
   L. Shaffer, 617(TLS):18Jan85-74
Brandon, S.   Buttonhooks and Shoehorns.
   C. Campbell, 614:Summer85-20
Brandreth, G.   Cockburn's A-Z of After-
Dinner Entertainment.
   H. Jacobson, 617(TLS):20Dec85-1453
   J. Lyon, 86(BHS):Oct84-512
Brandreth, G.   John Gielgud.*
   A.E. Kalson, 615(TJ):Dec84-559
   G. Playfair, 157:No153-49
Brands, H.   "Cogito ergo sum."
   H. Schmitz, 489(PJGG):Band91Heft2-382
Brandstätter, C. and others, eds.   Arthur
Schnitzler.
   J.B. Berlin, 406:Spring84-105
Brandt, A.M.   No Magic Bullet.
   E. Chesler, 441:14Jul85-23
Brandt, B.   London in the Thirties.*
   N. Moufarrege, 62:Dec84-78
Brandt, G.W., ed.   British Television
Drama.*
   M. Erdmenger, 38:Band102Heft3/4-564
Brandys, K.   A Warsaw Diary 1978-1981.*
   G.T. Kapolka, 497(PolR):Vol129No3-105
Branfoot, G.   Men Have All The Fun.
   L. Duguid, 617(TLS):19Jul85-800
Branford, W.   Structure, Style, and Com-
munication.
   T.J. Taylor, 541(RES):Aug84-342
Brang, P. and M. Züllig, with K. Brang.
Kommentierte Bibliographie zur Slav-
ischen Soziolinguistik.
   T.F. Magner, 574(SEEJ):Fall84-417
Bransford, S.   Riders of the Long Road.
   S. Mantell, 441:27Jan85-22
Brantlinger, P.   Bread and Circuses.
   A.J., 185:Apr85-775
   M. Vicinus, 141:Fall84-390
Brantôme.   Les Dames galantes.   (P. Pia,
ed)
   D. Maskell, 208(FS):Jan84-50
Brasch, C.   Collected Poems.   (A. Roddick,
ed)
   F. Adcock, 617(TLS):12Apr85-403
Brasch, W.M.   Black English and the Mass
Media.*
   J.P. Brewer, 355(LSoc):Dec84-537
   C. Eble, 35(AS):Fall84-232
Brasch, W.M.   Columbia County Place Names.*
   E.P. Hamp, 269(IJAL):Apr84-253
Brashear, W.M.   Ptolemäische Urkunden aus
Mumienkartonage (GBU XIV).
   J.D. Thomas, 123:Vol34No2-357
Brasil, E. and W.J. Smith, eds.   Brazilian
Poetry (1950-1980).*
   M-O.L. McBride, 238:Sep84-482
Brask, P.   Om "En landsbydegns dagbog,"
1-2.
   P.M. Mitchell, 563(SS):Autumn84-392

Braswell, L.N. Western Manuscripts from Classical Antiquity to the Renaissance.*
    J.G. Plante, 589:Jan84-122
Braswell, M.F. The Medieval Sinner.*
    C. Clark, 179(ES):Dec84-570
Brathwaite, E.K. History of the Voice.
    J. Martini, 343:Heft9/10-130
Brathwaite, E.K. Sun Poem.
    N. Mackey, 703:No11-200
Brătulescu, M. Colinda Românească.
    Y.R. Lockwood, 292(JAF):Apr-Jun84-222
Braude, L.Y. Skandinavskaya literaturnaya skazka.
    G. Orton, 562(Scan):Nov84-170
Braudy, S. What the Movies Made Me Do.
    M. Cantwell, 441:13Oct85-32
Brauer, O.D. Dialektik der Zeit.
    J. Burbidge, 543:Mar84-615
Braun, C. Kritische Theorie versus Kritizismus.
    A. Stanguennec, 542:Jan-Mar84-92
Braun, D. Der Indische Ozean.
    T.P. Thornton, 293(JASt):Feb84-350
Braun, G. Norm und Geschichtlichkeit der Dichtung.
    J.H. Petersen, 52:Band19Heft3-314
Braun, H. Joseph Gregor Wink.
    P. Königfeld, 471:Oct/Nov/Dec84-403
Braun, O. A Comintern Agent in China, 1932-1939.
    J. Ch'en, 104(CASS):Fall84-318
Braun, T. Disraeli the Novelist.*
    L. Gordon, 447(N&Q):Aug83-357
    E.A. Horsman, 541(RES):Aug84-401
Braun, W. Der Stilwandel in der Musik um 1600.
    D. Arnold, 410(M&L):Oct84-397
Braun, W. - see Shakespeare, W.
Braune, W. Gotische Grammatik. (19th ed rev by E.A. Ebbinghaus)
    E. Seebold, 685(ZDL):3/1984-375
Braunmuller, A.R., ed. A Seventeenth-Century Letter-Book.*
    G. Bourcier, 189(EA):Jul-Sep85-321
Bravmann, R.A. African Islam.
    L. Siroto, 2(AfrA):May84-23
Bravmann, R.A. The Poetry of Form.
    S. Patton, 2(AfrA):Aug84-88
Bray, B. and I. Landy-Houillon, eds. Lettres Portugaises, Lettres d'une Péruvienne et autres romans d'amour par lettres.
    G.M. Fondi, 475:Vol 11No20-201
Bray, N. Dress Fitting, Basic Principles and Practice. (2nd ed)
    S. Sherrer, 614:Spring85-20
Bray, R. Rediscoveries.
    P. Franklin, 26(ALR):Spring84-149
Braybrooke, D. Ethics in the World of Business.
    T. Donaldson, 185:Oct84-167
Brazeau, P. Parts of a World.*
    M. Beehler, 598(SoR):Winter85-231
    J. Carroll, 152(UDQ):Winter85-94
    D. Emerson and F. Doggett, 705:Spring84-57
    D. Gioia, 249(HudR):Summer84-343
    M. Strom, 432(NEQ):Dec84-583
    295(JML):Nov84-508
Brearley, M. The Art of Captaincy.
    A. Hislop, 617(TLS):28Jun85-734

Brecht, B. Briefe 1913-1956.* (G. Glaeser, ed)
    S. Mews, 301(JEGP):Jan84-95
    K. Schuhmann, 601(SuF):May-Jun84-646
Brecht, B. Die Dreigroschenoper — The Threepenny Opera. (P.K. Ackermann, ed)
    R.C. Helt, 399(MLJ):Summer84-173
Brecht, B. Short Stories, 1921-1946.* (J. Willett and R. Manheim, eds)
    A. Masters, 157:No151-50
    G. Weales, 569(SR):Summer84-lxv
Bredero, G.A. The Spanish Brabanter.
    G.C. Schoolfield, 568(SCN):Fall84-38
Bredin, J.D. L'Affaire.*
    M. Alcover, 207(FR):Dec84-322
Bredsdorff, E. Revolutionaer humanisme.
    P. Houe, 562(Scan):May84-68
    N. Ingwersen, 563(SS):Spring84-174
Bredsdorff, T. Tristans børn.
    P. Buvik, 172(Edda):1984/4-244
Brée, G. Twentieth-Century French Literature 1920-1970.
    639(VQR):Winter84-7
Breech, J. The Silence of Jesus.
    B.R. Bater, 529(QQ):Spring84-223
Breeze, D., ed. Studies in Scottish Antiquity presented to Stewart Cruden.
    C. Thomas, 176:Jan85-50
Breger, L. Freud's Unfinished Journey.
    R. Oxlade, 529(QQ):Summer84-330
Bregman, J. Synesius of Cyrene.
    A. Cameron, 487:Autumn84-294
    J.H.W.G. Liebeschuetz, 303(JoHS):Vol 104-222
Brehmer, K. Rawls' "Original Position" oder Kants "Ursprünglicher Kontrakt."
    V. Gerhardt, 342:Band75Heft4-504
Breit, H. and M.B. Lowry - see Lowry, M.
Breitinger, E., ed. Black Literature.
    R.W. Sander, 538(RAL):Spring84-123
Breivik, L.E. Existential "There."*
    P. Erdmann, 257(IRAL):Nov84-317
    C. Platzack, 452(NJL):Vol7No1-73
    E.W. Schneider, 685(ZDL):3/1984-402
Bremmer, J. The Early Greek Concept of the Soul.
    T. Fleming, 121(CJ):Dec84/Jan85-165
Bremner, G. Order and Chance.*
    M. Hobson, 208(FS):Jul84-343
Brémond, C., J. Le Goff and J-C. Schmitt. L'"exemplum."
    C.B. Faulhaber, 589:Oct84-887
Brenkert, G.G. Marx's Ethics of Freedom.
    W.L.M., 185:Oct84-187
Brenman-Gibson, M. Clifford Odets.*
    M.W. Estrin, 534(RALS):Autumn82-244
    K. King, 577(SHR):Fall84-356
Brennan, P. Zarkeen.*
    T. Bishop, 102(CanL):Autumn84-118
Brenner, G. Concealments in Hemingway's Works.
    L. Butts, 594:Winter84-448
    K. McSweeney, 529(QQ):Winter84-877
    S. Pinsker, 395(MFS):Summer84-310
    295(JML):Nov84-453
Brenner, G. and H.J. Kolvenbach. Praxishandbuch Kinder- und Jugendliteratur.
    L. Petzoldt, 196:Band25Heft3/4-327
Brenner, P.J. Die Krise der Selbstbehauptung.
    B.B. Cantarino, 301(JEGP):Apr84-277
Brenner, R. History — the Human Gamble.
    K.S., 185:Apr85-773

Brenni, V.J. Bookbinding.
   S. Ellenport, 517(PBSA):Vol78No1-106
   M.M. Foot, 354:Dec84-419
Brenni, V.J. Book Printing in Britain and
America.
   87(BB):Sep84-172
Brentano, F. Deskriptive Psychologie.
   (R.M. Chisholm and W. Baumgartner, eds)
   K. Mulligan and B. Smith, 484(PPR):
   Jun85-627
Brenzel, B.M. Daughters of the State.
   N.H. Rafter, 432(NEQ):Jun84-307
Brereton, G.E. and J.M. Ferrier - see "Le
Menagier de Paris"
Bresc-Bautier, G. Artistes, Patriciens et
Confréries.
   J. Cardnor, 90:Mar84-160
Breslauer, G.W. Khrushchev and Brezhnev
as Leaders.
   M. McCauley, 575(SEER):Jan84-146
Breslin, J.E.B. From Modern to Contempor-
ary.
   L. Wagner, 659(ConL):Winter85-482
Bresnan, J., ed. The Mental Representa-
tion of Grammatical Relations.
   M. Baltin, 350:Dec85-863
Breton, A. Poems of André Breton.* (J-P.
   Cauvin and M.A. Caws, eds and trans)
   R. Cardinal, 529(QQ):Winter84-1029
Breton, S. Unicité et monthéisme.
   A. Reix, 192(EP):Jan-Mar84-109
de la Bretonne, R. - see under Restif de
la Bretonne
Brett, B. This Here's a Good'un.
   L. Milazzo, 584(SWR):Winter84-89
Brett, L. Our Selves Unknown.
   M. Lutyens, 617(TLS):25Jan85-94
Brett, P., ed. Benjamin Britten: "Peter
Grimes."
   M. Cooper, 415:Oct84-573
   P. Evans, 410(M&L):Jul84-279
Brett, S. A Box of Tricks.
   T.J. Binyon, 617(TLS):5Apr85-394
Brett, S. Murder in the Title.
   639(VQR):Winter84-27
Brett, S. Not Dead, Only Resting.*
   N. Callendar, 441:3Feb85-37
Brett, S. A Shock to the System.
   T.J. Binyon, 617(TLS):15Feb85-179
   N. Callendar, 441:18Aug85-15
   442(NY):2Sep85-88
Brettell, R. and C. Lloyd. A Catalogue of
the Drawings by Camille Pissarro in the
Ashmolean Museum, Oxford.
   R. Schiff, 54:Dec84-681
Brettell, R.R. and C.B. Painters and
Peasants in the Nineteenth Century.
   G. Pollock, 59:Sep84-359
Breuer, D. Deutsche Metrik und Versge-
schichte.
   E.S. Dick, 133:Band17Heft1/2-115
Breuer, D. Oberdeutsche Literatur 1565-
1650.
   F.M. Eybl, 224(GRM):Band34Heft1/2-228
Brévart, F.B. - see von Sacrobosco, J.
Brewer, D. Chaucer. An Introduction to
Chaucer.
   B. O'Donoghue, 617(TLS):12Apr85-416
Brewer, J. and J. Styles, eds. An Ungov-
ernable People.*
   P. Borsay, 83:Spring84-101

"Brewer's Dictionary of Phrase and Fable."
   (rev) (I.H. Evans, ed)
   J.R. Gaskin, 569(SR):Winter84-114
Brewington, D.E.R. Dictionary of Marine
Artists.
   D.C., 90:Sep84-583
Brewster, E. Digging In.*
   L. Rogers, 102(CanL):Winter83-153
Brewster, E. A House Full of Women.
   D. Martens, 526:Summer84-81
Brewster, E. Junction.*
   B. Godard, 198:Autumn84-83
   B. MacLaine, 102(CanL):Winter83-127
Brewster, E. The Way Home.*
   B. MacLaine, 102(CanL):Winter83-127
Breyer, B.J. - see Trollope, A.
Breytenbach, B. The True Confessions of
an Albino Terrorist.*
   N. Ascherson, 453(NYRB):18Jul85-3
   J. Lelyveld, 441:10Feb85-1
   A. Maja-Pearce, 364:Feb85-93
   S. Schwartz, 129:Oct85-71
Bridenthal, R., A. Grossmann and M. Kaplan,
   eds. When Biology Became Destiny.
   A.K. Kuhn, 441:12May85-19
Bridge, A. One Man's Advent.
   A. Webster, 617(TLS):20Dec85-1444
Bridges, R. The Selected Letters of
Robert Bridges, With the Correspondence
of Robert Bridges and Lionel Muirhead.*
   (Vols 1 and 2) (D.E. Stanford, ed)
   P.N. Burbank, 617(TLS):1Feb85-107
   R. Fuller, 364:Dec84/Jan85-133
Bridgman, R. Dark Thoreau.*
   R. Du Pree, 577(SHR):Winter84-93
   D.M. Holman, 569(SR):Winter84-144
Bridgwater, P. The German Poets of the
First World War.
   E. Timms, 617(TLS):11Oct85-1146
Brier, P.A. and A. Arthur. American Prose
and Criticism, 1900-1950.
   M. Lopez, 506(PSt):Sep84-199
Brierley, D. Czechmate.
   J. Hone, 364:Oct84-105
Brierley, D. Skorpion's Death.
   T.J. Binyon, 617(TLS):5Jul85-757
   M. Laski, 362:18Jul85-29
Briggs, A. The BBC: The First Fifty Years.
   J. Symons, 617(TLS):3May85-485
Briggs, A. Collected Essays.
   R. Shannon, 617(TLS):13Sep85-1007
Briggs, A. - see Morris, W.
Briggs, A. and A. Macartney. Toynbee Hall.
   P. Willmott, 617(TLS):15Feb85-164
Briggs, A.D.P. Alexander Pushkin.*
   T.A. Greenan, 402(MLR):Oct84-1002
   A. McMillin, 575(SEER):Apr84-258
Briggs, J. This Stage-Play World.
   W.B. Patterson, 569(SR):Spring84-xxiv
   J.A. Quitslund, 570(SQ):Winter84-502
Briggs, R. When the Wind Blows.
   D. Devlin, 157:No154-49
Brigstocke, H. - see Buchanan, W.
Brillante, C., M. Cantilena and C.O.
Pavese, eds. I Poemi epici rapsodici
non omerici e la tradizione orale.*
   J.S. Clay, 24:Spring84-101
Brin, D. The Postman.
   G. Jonas, 441:24Nov85-33
Brincard, M-T., ed. The Art of Metal in
Africa.
   R. Sieber, 2(AfrA):Nov83-12

45

Brind'amour, L. and E. Vance, eds.
L'Archéologie du signe.
L.S. Crist, 210(FrF):Sep84-356
S.G. Nichols, 400(MLN):Dec84-1185
Brind'Amour, P., R. Kilpatrick and P.
Senay, eds. Mélanges Étienne Gareau.
E.F. D'Arms, 487:Spring84-108
Brindel, J.R. Phaedra.
F. Randall, 441:15Sep85-24
Bringéus, N-A. Bildlore.
E. Danielson, 64(Arv):Vol38-175
Bringéus, N-A. Sydsvenska bonadsmålningar.
M. Lindgren, 341:Vol53No1-35
Bringhurst, R. The Beauty of the Weapons.*
R. Berry, 102(CanL):Autumn84-136
Bringhurst, R. and others, eds. Visions.
R.J. Belton, 627(UTQ):Summer84-507
Bringmann, M. Friedrich Pecht (1814-1903).
M. Koch, 683:Band47Heft1-141
Brink, A. Mapmakers.*
C. Hope, 364:Jun84-99
Brink, A. The Wall of the Plague.*
N. Ascherson, 453(NYRB):25Apr85-55
A. Hulbert, 441:17Mar85-35
J. Mellors, 364:Oct84-81
442(NY):1Apr85-112
Brink, C.O. Horace on Poetry.*
R.B. Rutherford, 313:Vol74-239
Brinker-Gabler, G. Poetisch-Wissenschaft-
liche Mittelalter-Rezeption.
R.W. Fisher, 67:May84-91
Brinkley, A. Voices of Protest.
O.L. Graham, Jr., 579(SAQ):Summer84-
345
W.M. McClay, 396(ModA):Winter84-87
Brinkmann, H. Mittelalterliche Hermeneu-
tik.*
F. Rädle, 684(ZDA):Band113Heft2-55
Brinner, W.M. - see Nissim ben Jacob ibn
Shāhīn
Brisebarre, J. Li Restor du Paon. (E.
Donkin, ed)
M. Bambeck, 547(RF):Band96Heft1/2-171
W. Rothwell, 208(FS):Jan84-47
Briskin, J. Too Much Too Soon.
B. Sherman, 441:15Sep85-25
Brisson, L. Platon: les mots et les
mythes.*
C. Gill, 303(JoHS):Vol 104-207
Brisson, L. and others. Porphyre, "La vie
de Plotin." (Vol 1)
A.H. Armstrong, 123:Vol34No1-57
H.J. Blumenthal, 303(JoHS):Vol 104-220
Brisson, L., with H. Ioannidi. Platon
(1975-1980).
Y. Lafrance, 154:Jun84-347
Bristol, E., ed. East European Literature.
R.C. Porter, 402(MLR):Oct84-1008
Bristol, E., ed. Russian Literature and
Criticism.
N. Cornwell, 402(MLR):Jul84-767
Brisville, J-C. La Révélation d'une voix
et d'un nom.
R. Knee, 207(FR):Dec84-305
Britain, I. Fabianism and Culture.*
C. Waters, 637(VS):Autumn83-96
Brito, E. La christologie de Hegel.
L-P. Luc, 154:Mar84-163
Brittain, V. and W. Holtby. Testament of
a Generation. (P. Berry and A. Bishop,
eds)
S. Williams, 362:21Nov85-33

Brittin, N.A. Edna St. Vincent Millay.
(rev)
L. Mizejewski, 70:Nov-Dec83-56
Britton, C. Paybacks.
M. Buck, 441:9Jun85-22
Brixhe, C. Essai sur le grec anatolien au
début de notre ère.
L. Zgusta, 350:Mar85-217
Broad, W.J. Star Warriors.
J. Bernstein, 441:20Oct85-7
Broadhurst, R.J.C. - see al-Maqrīzī, T.D.
Broch, H. Hugo von Hofmannsthal and His
Time. (M.P. Steinberg, ed and trans)
S.S. Prawer, 617(TLS):8Mar85-254
G. Steiner, 442(NY):28Jan85-92
Broch, H. The Sleepwalkers.
T. Ziolkowski, 441:3Nov85-14
Broch, I. and E.H. Jahr. Russenorsk — et
pidginspråk i Norge.*
A. Liberman, 563(SS):Winter84-75
Brochu, A. and G. Marcotte. Le Littéra-
ture et le reste.
B. Godard, 102(CanL):Winter83-97
Brock, D.H. A Ben Jonson Companion.
C. Spivack, 365:Winter84-24
Brock, W.H. From Protyle to Proton.
J. Polkinghorne, 617(TLS):13Sep85-992
Brockhaus, H.A. Europäische Musik-
geschichte. (Vol 1)
G. Abraham, 415:Jun84-334
Brockington, J.L. The Sacred Thread.
J.M. Koller, 485(PE&W):Apr84-234
Brockway, G.P. Economics.
E. Cowan, 441:24Mar85-25
Broderick, J. The Rose Tree.
T. Fitton, 617(TLS):10May85-528
Broderick, J. The Trial of Father Dilling-
ham.
M. Montaut, 272(IUR):Spring84-136
Broderick, J.C. and others - see Thoreau,
H.D.
Brodeur, P. Outrageous Misconduct.
E. Eckholm, 441:24Nov85-22
Brodeur, P. Restitution.
F. Jennings, 441:22Sep85-25
Brodkey, H. Women and Angels.
D.J. Enright, 453(NYRB):26Sep85-19
Brödner, E. Die römischen Thermen und das
antike Badewesen.*
D.B. Small, 313:Vol74-225
Brodribb, G. Next Man In.
A.L. Le Quesne, 617(TLS):15Nov85-1303
Brodsky, L.D. and R.W. Hamblin, eds.
Faulkner. (Vol 2)
J.G. Watson, 395(MFS):Summer84-319
295(JML):Nov84-434
Brody, J. Lectures de Montaigne.*
R.D. Cottrell, 551(RenQ):Spring84-125
M.M. McGowan, 402(MLR):Jul84-702
F. Paré, 539:May85-144
Brody, R. and C. Rossman, eds. Carlos
Fuentes.*
A. Josephs, 395(MFS):Summer84-344
Brogan, H. The Life of Arthur Ransome.*
W. Scammell, 364:Apr/May84-120
Brogan, H. Longman History of the United
States of America.
A. Brinkley, 617(TLS):24May85-567
P. Whitehead, 362:4Apr85-25
Brogan, T.V.F. English Versification,
1570-1980.*
A. Elliott, 541(RES):Aug84-419

Brogyanyi, B., ed. Studies in Diachronic, Synchronic, and Typological Linguistics.
J. Udolph, 260(IF):Band89-270
Broinowski, A., ed. Understanding ASEAN.
E. Young, 293(JASt):May84-596
Brombert, V. Victor Hugo and the Visionary Novel.*
F. Brown, 453(NYRB):17Jan85-41
R.B. Grant, 446(NCFS):Summer85-287
D. Kelley, 617(TLS):11Oct85-1123
Brome, R. The English Moore. (S.J. Steen, ed)
A.H. Andreadis, 568(SCN):Fall84-39
Bromke, A. Poland: The Last Decade.*
S.R. Burant, 497(PolR):Vol29No3-114
Brommer, F. Theseus.*
E.D. Francis and M. Vickers, 303(JoHS): Vol 104-267
Bromwich, D. Hazlitt.*
A. Phillips, 364:Jul84-95
639(VQR):Summer84-82
Bronk, W. Vectors and Smoothable Curves.*
B. Raffel, 363(LitR):Fall84-154
Bronstein, A. The Triple Struggle.
A.R. Williams, 37:Jul-Aug84-62
Brontë, C. The Poems. (T. Winnifrith, ed)
G. Lindop, 617(TLS):9Aug85-872
Brontë, C. Something About Arthur. (C. Alexander, ed)
J.D. Ghnassia, 517(PBSA):Vol78No2-261
P. Thomson, 541(RES):Nov84-571
Brontë, P.B. The Poems of Patrick Branwell Brontë. (T. Winnifrith, ed)
639(VQR):Summer84-91
Brook, S. Honkytonk Gelato.
P-L. Adams, 61:Oct85-106
E. Fawcett, 617(TLS):20Sep85-1023
A. Lacy, 441:29Sep85-16
442(NY):9Dec85-161
Brook, S., ed. The Oxford Book of Dreams.
J. Mitcham, 219(GaR):Summer84-430
639(VQR):Spring84-64
Brooke, C.N.L. and R.A.B. Mynors - see Map, W.
Brooke, J. - see Walpole, H.
Brooke-Rose, C. Amalgamemnon.*
I. Hassan, 441:8Sep85-20
K.C. O'Brien, 362:14Mar85-27
Brooke-Rose, C. A Rhetoric of the Unreal.*
C. Britton, 494:Summer82-233
B. McHale, 494:Summer82-211
M. Rose, 131(CL):Spring84-169
A.L. Smith, 183(ESQ):Vol30No4-260
Brookner, A. Family and Friends.
P-L. Adams, 61:Nov85-144
D.J. Enright, 453(NYRB):5Dec85-35
C. James, 441:10Nov85-15
D. May, 362:5Sep85-26
A.N. Wilson, 617(TLS):6Sep85-973
Brookner, A. Hotel du Lac.*
P-L. Adams, 61:Mar85-124
J. Lasdun, 176:Feb85-42
A. Mars-Jones, 453(NYRB):31Jan85-17
J. Mellors, 364:Nov84-105
A. Tyler, 441:3Feb85-1
442(NY):18Feb85-121
Brookner, A. Look At Me.
P. Craig, 617(TLS):26Apr85-479
Brookner, A. Providence.*
W. Lesser, 249(HudR):Autumn84-478

Brooks, C. William Faulkner: First Encounters.*
C.S. Brown, 569(SR):Summer84-474
J.L. Capps, 27(AL):May84-289
J.V. Creighton, 395(MFS):Summer84-327
42(AR):Summer84-382
295(JML):Nov84-435
639(VQR):Spring84-43
Brooks, C. Signs for the Times.
D. Bowen, 324:Jul85-576
M. Bright, 445(NCF):Mar85-463
L. Ormond, 90:Nov84-707
A. Sanders, 155:Autumn84-167
Brooks, D. - see Lord Rochester
Brooks, J. Quicksand and Cactus.
W. Mulder, 649(WAL):Aug84-167
Brooks, M. Heavenly Deception.
L. Taylor, 617(TLS):15Nov85-1294
Brooks, M. Loose Connections.*
442(NY):18Mar85-130
Brooks, N., ed. Latin and the Vernacular Languages in Early Medieval Britain.*
T.M. Charles-Edwards, 313:Vol74-252
Brooks, P. Reading for the Plot.*
T. Cave, 617(TLS):4Jan85-14
G.M. Crump, 344:Summer85-114
D. Lodge, 176:Jul/Aug85-27
27(AL):Dec84-631
42(AR):Fall84-507
Brooks, R. and S. - see "Haiku Review '84"
Brooks, T. America's Black Musical Heritage.
S.W. Oliver, 187:Spring/Summer85-380
Brooks-Davies, D. The Mercurian Monarch.*
J. Black, 566:Autumn84-60
Broome, J.H. Molière: "L'Ecole des femmes" and "Le Misanthrope."
W.D. Howarth, 208(FS):Jan84-55
L.W. Riggs, 207(FR):Oct84-126
Brophy, C. The Liberation of Margaret McCabe.
A. Haverty, 617(TLS):20Sep85-1029
Brosman, C.S. Jean-Paul Sartre.
A.D. Ranwez, 207(FR):Mar85-586
D. Schier, 569(SR):Spring84-xlv
Broude, N. and M.D. Garrard, eds. Feminism and Art History.
R. Greenberg, 529(QQ):Summer84-481
Brouillette, A. and others. Pecos to Rio Grande.
G.E. Lich, 585(SoQ):Winter85-125
Broun, H. Inner Tube.
A. Roiphe, 441:25Aug85-6
442(NY):7Oct85-138
Brouwer, L.E.J. Brouwer's Cambridge Lectures on Intuitionism.* (D. van Dalen, ed)
J. Weiner, 84:Mar84-90
Brown, A. Locatives. This Strange Wood.
B. Hilderley, 526:Winter84-94
Brown, A. and M. Kaser, éds. Soviet Policy for the 1980s.
Z.M. Fallenbuchl, 104(CASS):Fall84-348
P. Frank, 575(SEER):Jan84-147
Brown, B.C. The Marsh Marlowe Letters. (Vol 1)
C. Hawtree, 617(TLS):3May85-493
Brown, C. Days Without Weather.
J. Helbert, 649(WAL):Aug84-151
Brown, C. Images of a Golden Past.
J. Flam, 62:Dec84-2
Brown, C. A Promising Career.
M. Montaut, 272(IUR):Spring84-137

Brown, C. Scenes of Everyday Life.
  D. Freedberg, 617(TLS):22Mar85-313
Brown, C. Van Dyck.*
  R. Wendorf, 31(ASch):Winter83/84-136
Brown, C.H. Language and Living Things.
  R. Blust, 350:Dec85-891
Brown, C.M., with A.M. Lorenzoni. Isa-
  bella d'Este and Lorenzo da Pavia.*
  G. Durosoir, 537:Vol70No1-135
Brown, D. Choices.
  R.J. Regan, 258:Dec84-447
Brown, D. The Divine Trinity.
  D.M. MacKinnon, 617(TLS):5Apr85-392
Brown, D. Hawaii Recalls.
  D. Hibbard, 658:Spring84-104
Brown, D. Tchaikovsky.* (Vol 2)
  R. Swift, 451:Fall84-164
Brown, D.A. Raphael and America.*
  P. Joannides, 278(IS):Vol39-109
Brown, D.B. Ashmolean Museum, Oxford:
  Catalogue of the Collection of Drawings.*
  (Vol 4)
  A. Wilton, 380:Summer84-214
Brown, D.C., ed. Ars Orientalis XII.
  R.S. Wicks, 318(JAOS):Oct-Dec83-803
Brown, D.M. and I. Ishida, eds and trans.
  The Future and the Past.
  G.C. Hurst 3d, 318(JAOS):Jul-Sep83-645
Brown, E.J. Russian Literature Since the
  Revolution.* (rev)
  R.L. Chapple, 104(CASS):Spring-
    Summer84-166
  J. Graffy, 575(SEER):Apr84-271
  N.N. Shneidman, 558(RLJ):Winter-
    Spring84-304
Brown, F., ed. Marthe, a Woman and Her
  Family.
  A. Brookner, 617(TLS):28Jun85-718
  M. Drabble, 362:11Jul85-27
Brown, F.M. The Diary of Ford Madox
  Brown.* (V. Surtees, ed)
  M. Case, 637(VS):Autumn83-125
Brown, G. and G. Yule. Discourse Analysis.
  F. Chevillet, 189(EA):Jul-Sep85-302
  G.L. Dillon and others, 350:Jun85-446
Brown, G.M. Voyages.*
  S.J. Boyd, 493:Jan84-69
  D. McDuff, 565:Spring84-72
Brown, H.M., ed. A Florentine Chansonnier
  from the Time of Lorenzo the Magnifi-
  cent.*
  C.V. Palisca, 551(RenQ):Autumn84-479
Brown, J. Hot Wire.
  A. Becker, 441:23Jun85-20
  442(NY):8Jul85-73
Brown, J. Vita's Other World.
  D. Saville, 617(TLS):1Nov85-1244
Brown, J.M. Dickens.*
  R. Mason, 447(N&Q):Dec83-541
Brown, J.M. Modern India.
  D.A. Low, 617(TLS):2Aug85-849
Brown, J.R. Discovering Shakespeare.*
  C. Hoy, 569(SR):Spring84-256
  D.M. Zesmer, 570(SQ):Autumn84-368
Brown, J.R., ed. Focus on "Macbeth."
  M. Charney, 405(MP):May85-419
  J.L. Halio, 570(SQ):Summer84-251
Brown, J.R. Marlowe: A Selection of Crit-
  ical Essays.
  G. Bas, 189(EA):Jan-Mar85-79
Brown, J.R., ed. Modern British Drama-
  tists.
  J. Melmoth, 617(TLS):30Aug85-953

Brown, J.S., Jr., ed. Up Before Daylight.*
  M. Boynton, 292(JAF):Apr-Jun84-237
Brown, K. Linguistics Today.
  F.R. Palmer, 353:Vol22No3-421
Brown, K.D. The English Labour Movement:
  1700-1951.*
  S. Meacham, 637(VS):Autumn83-100
Brown, L. English Dramatic Form, 1660-
  1760.
  G.D. Atkins, 615(TJ):Dec82-546
  P.T. Dircks, 612(ThS):May84-108
  V. Liesenfeld, 223:Fall82-337
Brown, L. Alexander Pope.
  L. Mackinnon, 617(TLS):5Jul85-752
Brown, L.W. Amiri Baraka.
  M. Fabre, 402(MLR):Apr84-444
Brown, M. Cane and Rush Seating.
  L. Stearns, 614:Summer85-20
Brown, M. The Shape of German Romanticism.
  K. Richter, 53(AGP):Band66Heft1-106
Brown, M.H., ed. Musorgsky.
  M. Cooper, 575(SEER):Apr84-283
  H. Robinson, 550(RusR):Jan84-90
  R. Swift, 451:Fall84-164
Brown, M.H. Tracings.
  P. Klovan, 102(CanL):Winter83-119
Brown, N.D. Hood, Bonnet, and Little
  Brown Jug.*
  L. Milazzo, 584(SWR):Spring84-211
Brown, O.J. Natural Rectitude and Divine
  Law in Aquinas.
  B.H. Zedler, 589:Jan84-228
Brown, P. Genèse de l'Antiquité tardive.
  J-P. Guinle, 450(NRF):Jul/Aug84-174
Brown, P. Society and the Holy in Late
  Antiquity.*
  J.D. Adams, 589:Apr84-373
Brown, R.M. Elie Wiesel.*
  L. Field, 395(MFS):Winter84-837
Brown, S. Leibniz.
  H. Ishiguro, 617(TLS):15Nov85-1300
Brown, S.C., ed. Philosophical Disputes
  in the Social Sciences.
  R. Brown, 488:Sep84-418
Brown, T.H. Thèmes et Discussions.
  J.C. Evans, 399(MLJ):Autumn84-285
Brown, T.S. Gentlemen and Officers.
  A. Cameron, 617(TLS):14Jun85-665
Browne, A., D. Collins and M. Goodwin. I,
  Koch.
  J. Kornbluth, 441:25Aug85-17
Browne, J. The Secular Ark.
  P.R. Evans, 83:Autumn84-275
Browne, M.E. and H. Two in One.
  J. Stokes, 402(MLR):Oct84-922
Browne, N. The Rhetoric of Filmic Narra-
  tion.*
  H. Charney, 207(FR):Mar85-611
Browne, R., ed. Music Theory.
  R. Chrisman, 308:Fall84-313
Browne, T. Pseudodoxia Epidemica.* (R.
  Robbins, ed)
  D.F. Bratchell, 447(N&Q):Apr83-167
  J. Carey, 541(RES):Aug84-378
  R. Dunlap, 481(PQ):Summer84-413
Browning, E.B. The Letters of Elizabeth
  Barrett Browning to Mary Russell Mitford
  1836-1854. (M.B. Raymond and M.R.
  Sullivan, eds)
  W.S. Peterson, 441:3Feb85-13
Browning, J.D., ed. Satire in the 18th
  Century.
  P. Brückmann, 173(ECS):Winter84/85-295

Browning, J.D., ed. The Stage in the 18th
Century.
 B. Mittman, 615(TJ):Dec82-553
Browning, R. Robert Browning: The Poems.*
(J. Pettigrew, ed; completed by T.J.
Collins)
 D. Karlin, 541(RES):Aug84-406
 J. Korg, 536:Vol5-41
Browning, R., ed. The Greek World.
 A.A. Rhodes, 441:15Dec85-21
Browning, R. The Poetical Works of Robert
Browning.* (Vol 1) (I. Jack and M.
Smith, eds)
 C. Baldick, 617(TLS):12Jul85-770
 M. Hicks, 148:Autumn84-85
Browning, R. The Poetical Works of Robert
Browning. (Vol 2) (I. Jack and M. Smith,
eds)
 C. Baldick, 617(TLS):12Jul85-770
Browning, R. Political and Constitutional
Ideas of the Court Whigs.*
 H.T. Dickinson, 83:Spring84-98
Browning, R. and E.B. The Brownings' Cor-
respondence. (Vols 1 and 2) (P. Kelley
and R. Hudson, eds)
 W. Barnes, 85(SBHC):Spring-Fall84-181
 S. Hanson, 87(BB):Dec84-239
 M. Mason, 617(TLS):8Mar85-262
 W.S. Peterson, 441:3Feb85-13
"Browning Institute Studies." (Vol 8)
(W.S. Peterson, ed)
 P. Drew, 541(RES):May84-281
 K. McSweeney, 677(YES):Vol 14-342
Brownjohn, A. Collected Poems 1952-83.*
 C. Rawson, 493:Apr84-56
Brownlee, D.B. The Law Courts.
 M. Girouard, 617(TLS):5Apr85-371
Brownlee, J.S., ed. History in the
Service of the Japanese Nation.
 G.K. Goodman, 407(MN):Winter84-463
Brownlee, M.S. The Poetics of Literary
Theory.*
 B.W. Ife, 402(MLR):Oct84-956
Brownlow, K. "Napoleon:" Abel Gance's
Classic Film.*
 W.K. Everson, 200:Jan84-58
 K. Reader, 707:Autumn84-305
Brownlow, T. John Clare and Picturesque
Landscape.
 G. Crossan, 591(SIR):Winter84-581
 S. Soupel, 189(EA):Apr-Jun85-239
 W. Walling, 661(WC):Summer84-108
Brownmiller, S. Femininity.*
 G. Finn, 99:Aug/Sep84-45
Brownstein, R.M. Becoming a Heroine.*
 R.A. Colby, 445(NCF):Dec84-339
 V. Middleton, 577(SHR):Spring84-183
Bruaire, C. L'être et l'esprit.
 M. Adam, 542:Apr-Jun84-247
Bruccoli, M. Some Sort of Epic Grandeur.
 L.R. Broer, 577(SHR):Spring84-165
Bruccoli, M.J. James Gould Cozzens.*
 J.W. Crowley, 432(NEQ):Mar84-151
 G. Garrett, 569(SR):Summer84-495
 I. Malin, 651(WHR):Summer84-176
 D.W. Petrie, 395(MFS):Winter84-814
 295(JML):Nov84-423
Bruccoli, M.J. Ross Macdonald/Kenneth
Millar.*
 D.H. Keller, 87(BB):Dec84-241
Bruce, D. Pure Daughter.
 B. Galvin, 389(MQ):Winter85-249

Bruce, H. and C. Harris. A Basket of
Apples.
 E-M. Kroller, 102(CanL):Summer84-148
Bruce-Gardyne, J. Mrs. Thatcher's First
Administration.*
 S. Brittan, 176:Apr85-51
Bruce-Novoa, J.D. Chicano Authors.
 G.H. Bell-Villada, 447(N&Q):Apr83-186
Bruchac, J., ed. Breaking Silence.
 J.D. Houston, 649(WAL):Feb85-322
Bruchac, J., ed. Songs from This Earth
on Turtle's Back.
 J. Gleason, 472:Fall/Winter84-21
 S. Hamill, 649(WAL):Nov84-243
Bruchis, M. One Step Back, Two Steps For-
ward.*
 D. Deletant, 575(SEER):Jan84-105
Brucker, E. Die spätvedische Kulturepoche
nach den Quellen der Śrauta-, Grhya- und
Dharmasūtras.
 H.W. Bodewitz, 259(IIJ):Jul84-207
 L. Rocher, 318(JAOS):Oct-Dec83-777
Bruckner, A. and R. Marichal, eds. Char-
tae Latinae antiquiores. (Vol 14)
 D. Ganz, 589:Oct84-889
Bruckner, A. and R. Marichal, eds. Char-
tae Latinae antiquiores. (Vol 20)
 B. Ross, 589:Jul84-625
Bruckner, D.J.R. Van der Steen's Cats.
 M. Piercy, 441:3Feb85-36
Bruckner, M.T. Narrative Invention in
Twelfth-Century French Romance.*
 A.H. Diverres, 208(FS):Oct84-445
Brueckner, H-D., ed. Fabeln, Märchen,
Anekdoten und Anderes.
 W. Blomster, 399(MLJ):Winter84-404
Bruemmer, F. and others. The Arctic World.
 P-L. Adams, 61:Dec85-118
 E.R. Lipson, 441:15Dec85-22
Bruézière, M. L'Alliance Française.
 E. Morot-Sir, 207(FR):Oct84-170
Bruffee, K.A. Elegiac Romance.
 W. Buchanan, 573(SSF):Summer84-286
 R.C. Murfin, 136:Vol 17No1-63
 P. Stevick, 395(MFS):Winter84-857
Bruhn, P. and H. Glade. Heinrich Böll in
der Sowjetunion 1952-1979.*
 K.E. Kuhn-Osius, 406:Summer84-241
Brulotte, G. Le Surveillant.*
 J-A. Elder, 102(CanL):Autumn84-61
Brumfield, W.C. Gold in Azure.
 S. Southworth, 505:May84-186
Brummack, J., ed. Heinrich Heine: Epoche —
Werk — Wirkung.*
 P. Branscombe, 402(MLR):Oct84-981
Brummels, J.V. 614 Pearl.
 R.E. Knoll, 502(PrS):Summer84-106
Brummels, J.V. and M. Sanders - see Kloef-
korn, W. and others
Brun, J. Les masques du désir.
 E. Joós, 154:Mar84-157
Brunel, J. - see Rapin, N.
Brunel, P. Théâtre et cruauté ou Dionysos
profané.
 M. Regnaut, 535(RHL):Sep/Oct84-820
Brunetta, G.P. Storia del cinema italiano.
 G. Angeli, 98:Aug/Sep84-655
Brüning, E., H. Förster and E. Manske.
Studien zum amerikanischen Roman der
Gegenwart.
 F. Hajek, 654(WB):8/1984-1400

Brunkhorst, M. Tradition und Transformation.*
  W. Pache, 107(CRCL):Mar84-124
  I. Simon, 179(ES):Jun84-282
Brunner, E.J. Splendid Failure.
  L. Mackinnon, 617(TLS):13Dec85-1438
Brunner, H. and J. Helbig - see Scherer, W.
  and E. von Steinmeyer
Bruno, G. Cabala del cavallo Pegaseo. (C.
  Sini, ed)
  N. Ordine, 228(GSLI):Vol 161fasc513-
  116
Brunot, F. Histoire de la Langue Fran-
  çaise. (Vol 11, Pt 2)
  P. Gomis, 202(FMod):No68/70-379
Bruns, G.L. Inventions.*
  J. Guillory, 125:Winter84-173
  H. Lindenberger, 405(MP):Feb85-349
Brunt, P.A. - see Arrian
Bruscagli, R. Stagioni della civiltà
  estense.
  R. Fedi, 228(GSLI):Vol 161fasc515-
  457
Brushwood, J.S. Genteel Barbarism.*
  M.S. Arrington, Jr., 345(KRQ):Vol31No3-
  346
  E. Busto Ogden, 240(HR):Winter84-111
de Bruyn, G. Neue Herrlichkeit.
  J.J. White, 617(TLS):22Feb85-210
Bryan, J. 3d. Merry Gentlemen (and One
  Lady).
  P.T. O'Conner, 441:29Dec85-19
Bryan, S. Salt Air.*
  L. Goldensohn, 491:Apr84-40
Bryan, T.A. Censorship and Social Con-
  flict in the Spanish Theatre.
  J. Spencer, 552(REH):Oct84-460
Bryant, J. Melville Dissertations, 1924-
  1980.
  S.E. Marovitz, 87(BB):Jun84-104
Bryant, S.M. - see Pérez de Hita, G.
Bryce, J. Cosimo Bartoli (1503-1572).
  E. Cochrane, 551(RenQ):Autumn84-422
Bryce, J.C. - see Smith, A.
Bryer, J.R. The Critical Reputation of F.
  Scott Fitzgerald. (Supp)
  J.M. Flora, 573(SSF):Fall84-424
Bryer, J.R., ed. The Short Stories of F.
  Scott Fitzgerald.*
  V.A. Makowsky, 536:Vol6-139
Brynhildsvoll, K. Hans Henny Jahnn und
  Henrik Ibsen.
  S. Brantly, 563(SS):Autumn84-374
Bryson, K.A. Death Can Be Beautiful.
  L. Westra, 154:Mar84-161
Bryson, N. Tradition and Desire.
  L. Eitner, 617(TLS):12Apr85-413
Bryson, N. Vision and Painting.*
  P.N. Humble, 290(JAAC):Winter84-219
  M. Podro, 59:Jun84-243
  639(VQR):Winter84-29
Bryson, N. Word and Image.*
  K. Garlick, 447(N&Q):Dec83-549
  N. Llewelyn, 402(MLR):Oct84-937
  B. Norman, 207(FR):Dec84-328
Brzezinski, Z. Power and Principle.*
  W.S. Burke, 396(ModA):Spring/Summer84-
  264
Bubacz, B. St. Augustine's Theory of Know-
  ledge.
  P. Corrigan, 543:Mar84-616

Bubeník, V. The Phonological Interpreta-
  tion of Ancient Greek.
  B. Newton, 320(CJL):Fall84-208
  A.H. Sommerstein, 353:Vol22No3-417
Buber, M. Gog et Magog.
  M.F. Meurice, 450(NRF):May84-121
Bubser, R.K. and W. Koepke. Deutsch im
  Sprachgebrauch.
  B. Lewis, 399(MLJ):Autumn84-291
Buchan, D., ed. A Book of Scottish Bal-
  lads.
  617(TLS):12Jul85-783
Buchan, D., ed. Scottish Tradition.
  W.F.H. Nicolaisen, 571(ScLJ):Autumn84-
  34
Buchan, J. A Parish of Rich Women.*
  R.B. Cramer, 441:21Jul85-22
Buchan, J. Under The Moon.
  M. Stobie, 102(CanL):Autumn84-175
Buchanan, A. Marx and Justice.
  D.P.H. Allen, 154:Jun84-343
Buchanan, G. Tragedies. (P. Sharratt and
  P.G. Walsh, eds)
  J.H. McGregor, 208(FS):Jul84-326
Buchanan, J.M. and R.D. Tollison, eds.
  The Theory of Public Choice. (Vol 2)
  J.R., 185:Jul85-986
Buchanan, T. Photographing Historic Build-
  ings.*
  M. Charles, 46:Feb84-76
Buchanan, W. William Buchanan and the
  19th Century Art Trade.* (H. Brig-
  stocke, ed)
  D. Sutton, 39:Jun84-397
Buchholz, H-G. and E. Althaus. Nisyros-
  Giali-Kos.
  R.W.V. Catling, 123:Vol34No1-147
Büchner, G. Woyzeck and Other Writings.
  (H.J. Schmidt, ed)
  M. Tussing, 399(MLJ):Winter84-407
"Georg Büchner I." "Georg Büchner II."
  "Georg Büchner III." (H.L. Arnold, ed
  of all)
  H.J. Schmidt, 564:May84-134
"Georg Büchner Jahrbuch 2/1982." (H.
  Gersch, T.M. Mayer and G. Oesterle, eds)
  R. Thieberger, 564:May84-137
Buchner, H., W.G. Jacobs and A. Pieper -
  see Schelling, F.W.J.
Buchner, H. and J. Jantzen, with others -
  see Schelling, F.W.J.
Buchwald, A. "You Can Fool All of the
  People All the Time."
  F. Lamport, 441:13Oct85-13
Buchwald, W., A. Hohlweg and O. Prinz, eds.
  Tusculum-Lexikon griechischer und latein-
  ischer Autoren des Altertums und des
  Mittelalters. (3rd ed)
  P. Flobert, 555:Vol58fasc2-358
Buck, A. Studia humanitatis. (B. Guth-
  müller, K. Kohut and O. Roth, eds)
  W. Hirdt, 547(RF):Band96Heft1/2-152
Buck, A. Victorian Costume. (2nd ed)
  P. Bach, 614:Spring85-31
Buckdahl, E.M. Diderot, critique d'art.
  (Vol 2)
  J. Chouillet, 535(RHL):Jul/Aug84-624
Buckle, R. In the Wake of Diaghilev.
  N. Macdonald, 151:Jul84-82
Buckler, W.E. On the Poetry of Matthew
  Arnold.
  W.A. Madden, 637(VS):Summer84-515

Burke, D.B. American Painting in the
Metropolitan Museum of Art. (Vol 3)
(K. Luhrs, ed)
A. Wilton, 90:Feb84-99
Burke, D.B. J. Alden Weir.
A. Wilton, 90:Nov84-708
Burke, H.L. and others. Seven Deadly Sins.
C. Hawtree, 617(TLS):26Ju185-833
Burke, J. Joy Hester.
G. Catalano, 381:Sep84-429
Burke, J.G., ed. The Uses of Science in
the Age of Newton.
P. Harman, 617(TLS):25Jan85-89
Burke, J.J., Jr. and D. Kay, eds. The
Unknown Samuel Johnson.*
R.H. Bell, 401(MLQ):Sep83-322
B. Boyce, 579(SAQ):Autumn84-479
H.T. Dickinson, 366:Autumn84 269
M. McGovern, 569(SR):Fall84-xcvii
I. Rivers, 83:Autumn84-251
J.A. Vance, 173(ECS):Winter84/85-279
Burke, K. Attitudes Toward History. (3rd
ed) Permanence and Change. (3rd ed)
D. Donoghue, 453(NYRB):26Sep85-39
Burke, T.E. The Philosophy of Popper.
R. Fellows, 518:Oct84-250
K.S., 185:Oct84-185
Burkert, W. Greek Religion.
J. Griffin, 453(NYRB):27Jun85-30
J. Macquarrie, 441:22Sep85-30
Burkert, W. Homo Necans.*
W.F. Hansen, 124:Jan-Feb85-222
Burkert, W. Structure and History in
Greek Mythology and Ritual.*
M.L. West, 303(JoHS):Vol 104-232
Burkhardt, F. - see James, W.
Burkhardt, F. and S. Smith - see Darwin, C.
Burkhardt, H. Logik und Semiotik in der
Philosophie von Leibniz.*
G. Hunter, 543:Jun84-843
Burkholz, H. The Snow Gods.
P. Patton, 441:16Jun85-24
Burks, A.W. Japan.
K.J. Fukuda, 302:Vol20No2-224
Burleigh, M. Prussian Society and the
German Order.
K. Leyser, 617(TLS):22Feb85-206
Burleson, D.R. H.P. Lovecraft.
M.E. Barth, 395(MFS):Winter84-867
Bürli-Storz, C. Deliberate Ambiguity in
Advertising.
B. Hansen, 682(ZPSK):Band37Heft3-382
Burling, R. Sounding Right.
D. Pearson, 355(LSoc):Sep84-417
J. Yalden, 320(CJL):Spring84-105
Burman, E. The Inquisition.
A. Hamilton, 617(TLS):28Jun85-729
Burn, G. "... somebody's husband, some-
body's son."*
S. Rae, 364:Jul84-109
Burne-Jones, E.C. Burne-Jones Talking,
His Conversations 1895-1898.* (M. Lago,
ed)
G.L. Aho, 536:Vol5-73
M. Case, 637(VS):Autumn83-125
Burnett, A. Milton's Style.*
G.M. Ridden, 366:Spring84-123
M. Toolan, 599:Winter84-111
Burnett, A.P. Three Archaic Poets.*
M. Davies, 123:Vol34No2-169
Burnett, C. - see Hermann of Carinthia
Burnett, D. Colville.
R.J. Belton, 627(UTQ):Summer84-507

Burnett, D. and M. Schiff. Contemporary
Canadian Art.
R.J. Belton, 627(UTQ):Summer84-507
E. Milroy, 99:May84-29
Burnett, J., D. Vincent and D. Mayall, eds.
The Autobiography of the Working Class.
(Vol 1)
J.F.C. Harrison, 617(TLS):22Feb85-207
Burnett, V. Towers at the Edge of a World.
J. Farnsworth, 526:Autumn84-89
Burney, F. A Busy Day. (T.G. Wallace, ed)
P. Rogers, 617(TLS):7Jun85-642
Burney, F. The Journals and Letters of
Fanny Burney (Madame d'Arblay).* (Vol
8) (P. Hughes, with J. Hemlow, eds)
J.N. Waddell, 179(ES):Jun84-284
Burney, F. The Journals and Letters of
Fanny Burney (Madame d'Arblay). (Vols 9
and 10) (W. Derry, ed)
R.L. Brett, 541(RES):Nov84-555
Burney, F. The Journals and Letters of
Fanny Burney (Madame d'Arblay). (Vols
11 and 12) (J. Hemlow, with A. Douglas
and P. Hawkins, eds)
P. Rogers, 617(TLS):4Jan85-8
Burnham, D. The Rise of the Computer
State.
639(VQR):Winter84-20
Burnier, M-A. Le Testament de Sartre.
F. Fejtö, 176:Apr85-49
Burnley, D. A Guide to Chaucer's Lan-
guage.*
A. Crépin, 189(EA):Jan-Mar85-110
Burns, C.A. Henry Céard et le natural-
isme.*
C. Lloyd, 402(MLR):Jan84-200
Burns, J. Internal Memorandum.
J. Saunders, 565:Spring84-55
Burns, J.M. The Power to Lead.*
639(VQR):Autumn84-134
Burns, J.M. The Workshop of Democracy.
P. Conn, 441:29Sep85-22
442(NY):7Oct85-140
Burns, M. Rural Society and French Pol-
itics.
S. Englund, 617(TLS):1Mar85-234
Burns, R. Us.
L. Runciman, 389(MQ):Spring85-382
Burns, R.D., ed. Guide to American
Foreign Relations since 1700.
F.M. Carroll, 106:Summer84-221
Burns, R.M. The Great Debate on Miracles,
from Joseph Glanvil to David Hume.*
E.R. Briggs, 83:Autumn84-261
Burns, W. Journey Through the Dark Woods.*
W.K. Buckley, 50(ArQ):Autumn84-282
Burnyeat, M., ed. The Skeptical Tradition.
G.H. Bird, 617(TLS):22Feb85-192
R. McKim, 124:Sep-Oct84-60
B. Mates, 185:Apr85-749
Buroker, J.V. Space and Incongruence.*
M.A. Hammond, 518:Apr84-120
J.M. Young, 342:Band75Heft3-352
Burr, A. I Am Not My Body.
A.D. Jones, 617(TLS):8Mar85-267
Burr, A. Political Correspondence and
Public Papers of Aaron Burr.* (M-J.
Kline and others, eds)
G.J. Saladino, 656(WMQ):Oct84-675
Burr, E.E. The Journal of Esther Edwards
Burr 1744-1757.* (C.F. Karlsen and L.
Crumpacker, eds)
S.E. Kagle, 165(EAL):Fall85-174

53

Burra, E. Well, Dearie! (W. Chappell, ed)
  F. Spalding, 617(TLS):30Aug85-951
Burrell, D. Aquinas: God and Action.
  J.R. Catan, 449:Mar84-125
Burrison, J.A. Brothers in Clay.
  P. Grootkerk, 585(SoQ):Summer85-99
  J.M. Vlach, 658:Winter84-321
Burroughs, W.S. The Place of Dead Roads.*
  639(VQR):Summer84-97
Burroughs, W.S. Queer.
  H. Marten, 441:3Nov85-22
Burrow, J.A. Essays on Medieval Litera-
  ture.*
  M-M. Dubois, 189(EA):Jul-Sep85-314
Burrow, J.A. Medieval Writers and Their
  Work.*
  M. Markus, 38:Band102Heft1/2-201
  J. Simpson, 382(MAE):1984/2-307
Burrow, J.W. Gibbon.
  D. Womersley, 617(TLS):27Sep85-1058
Burrow, J.W. A Liberal Descent.*
  D.R. Woolf, 529(QQ):Autumn84-524
Burrow, T. and M.B. Emeneau. A Dravidian
  Etymological Dictionary. (2nd ed)
  S.B. Steever, 350:Jun85-477
Burroway, J. Opening Nights.
  J. Dunning, 441:23Jun85-20
  442(NY):1Jul85-97
Burroway, J. Writing Fiction.
  D. Kirby, 128(CE):Mar84-248
Bursill-Hall, G.L. A Census of Medieval
  Latin Grammatical Manuscripts.*
  M.C. Woods, 589:Jan84-123
Bursk, C. Making Wings.
  J. Carter, 219(GaR):Summer84-415
Burstyn, V., ed. Women Against Censorship.
  B. Ehrenreich, 441:29Sep85-50
Burton, J., comp. The New Latin American
  Cinema. (new ed)
  R. Okey, 37:Jul-Aug84-63
Burton, O.V. In My Father's House Are
  Many Mansions.
  C.V. Woodward, 453(NYRB):10Oct85-30
Burton, R. Bird Behavior.
  G. Gold, 441:18Aug85-21
Burton, T.G., ed. Tom Ashley, Sam McGee,
  Bukka White.
  L.C. Burman-Hall, 187:Fall85-507
Buruma, I. Behind the Mask.*
  M. Sayle, 453(NYRB):28Mar85-33
Burunat, S. and J. Nuevas voces hispanas.
  D.R. McKay, 399(MLJ):Winter84-412
  S.E. Torres, 238:Dec84-687
Burunat, S. and E. Starčević. El español
  y su estructura.
  M.E. Barker, 238:May84-319
  H. Ruiz-Morales, 399(MLJ):Summer84-187
Busa, R. Index Thomisticus.
  D.M. Burton, 589:Oct84-891
Busa, R. - see Aquinas, T.
Busby, K. Gauvain in Old French Litera-
  ture.
  A.H. Diverres, 208(FS):Jan84-45
  A.J. Holden, 554:Vol 104No1-125
Busby, K., ed and trans. Raoul de Hodenc,
  "Le Roman des Eles," the Anonymous
  "Ordene de Chevalierie."
  J. Beston, 589:Oct84-970
  L. Löfstedt, 439(NM):1984/2-255
Busch, M. - see Schumann, E.

Buschhausen, H. Die südіtalienische Bau-
  plastik im Königreich Jerusalem von
  König Wilhelm II. bis Kaiser Friedrich
  II.
  Z. Jacoby, 683:Band47Heft3-400
Buschinger, D., ed. La Légende de Tristan
  au Moyen Age.
  F. Shaw, 402(MLR):Oct84-971
Buschkuhl, M. Great Britain and the Holy
  See, 1746-1870.*
  M.E. Daly, 272(IUR):Autumn84-285
Bush, G. Left, Right and Centre.
  G. Poole, 415:Aug84-445
Bush, M.L. The English Aristocracy.
  J. Habakkuk, 617(TLS):22Feb85-205
Bush, R. T.S. Eliot.*
  D. Donoghue, 598(SoR):Winter85-178
  L. Menand, 676(YR):Autumn84-119
  639(VQR):Summer84-86
Bush, R. Grace King.*
  M.A. Wimsatt, 27(AL):Dec84-606
  J.B. Wittenberg, 395(MFS):Winter84-796
Bush, S. and H-Y. Shih, eds. Early Chi-
  nese Texts on Painting.
  M. Sullivan, 617(TLS):13Dec85-1425
Bush-Brown, A. SOM: Skidmore Owings &
  Merrill; Architecture and Urbanism 1973-
  1983.
  J. Winter, 46:Aug84-64
Bushaway, B. By Rite.
  V. Neuburg, 203:Vol95No2-263
Bushman, R.L. Joseph Smith and the Begin-
  nings of Mormonism.
  D.B. Davis, 453(NYRB):15Aug85-15
  R.L. Moore, 441:21Jul85-11
Busi, F. The Transformations of Godot.*
  A. Karátson, 549(RLC):Jul-Sep84-376
Buss, C., M. Molinelli and G. Butazzi.
  Tessuti Serici Italiani: 1450-1530.*
  B. Scott, 39:Mar84-226
Busset, J.D. - see under de Bourbon Busset,
  J.
de Bustamante, J.M.D. - see under Díaz de
  Bustamante, J.M.
Bustin, D. If You Don't Outdie Me.
  M. Boynton, 292(JAF):Apr-Jun84-237
Butala, S., B. Burnard and S. Sparling.
  Coming Attractions.
  D. Martens, 526:Summer84-81
Butchart, D.S. I madrigali di Marco da
  Gagliano.
  T. Carter, 410(M&L):Jan84-82
Buthlay, K. Hugh MacDiarmid.*
  B. Ruddick, 148:Winter84-91
Butler, C. After the Wake.
  B. McHale, 494:Summer82-211
Butler, C. Interpretation, Deconstruction
  and Ideology.*
  S. Scobie, 376:Oct84-107
Butler, D. The Fall of Saigon.
  F. Butterfield, 441:12May85-11
Butler, D. and P. Jowett. Party Strat-
  egies in Britain.
  P. Johnson, 617(TLS):11Oct85-1128
Butler, E. Milton Friedman.
  P. Jay, 617(TLS):6Dec85-1393
Butler, F. - see "Children's Literature"
Butler, F. and R. Rotert, eds. Reflec-
  tions on Literature for Children.
  S. Wintle, 617(TLS):21Jun85-703
Butler, H. Escape from the Anthill.
  R. Foster, 617(TLS):6Sep85-980

54

Butler, L.S. Samuel Beckett and the Meaning of Being.
M. Gee, 617(TLS):21Jun85-698
Butler, M. Romantics, Rebels and Reactionaries.*
L.R. Leavis, 396(ModA):Winter84-95
F.W. Shilstone, 577(SHR):Spring84-178
Butler, M. Theatre and Crisis 1632-1642.
D. Norbrook, 617(TLS):16Aug85-906
Butler, R. Balzac and the French Revolution.
D. Bellos, 402(MLR):Oct84-944
J.P. Gilroy, 446(NCFS):Winter-Spring85-177
Butler, R. Choiseul.* (Vol 1)
R. Hatton, 161(DUJ):Dec83-118
Butler, R.O. On Distant Ground.
J. Klein, 441:21Apr85-26
Butlin, M. The Paintings and Drawings of William Blake.*
J. Wordsworth, 541(RES):Feb84-92
Butlin, M. and E. Joll. The Paintings of J.M.W. Turner.
J. Hayes, 617(TLS):26Apr85-465
Butlin, R.A. The Transformation of Rural England c. 1580-1800.
A.J. Budd, 83:Autumn84-254
Butor, M. and M. Launay. Résistances.
D. Coste, 207(FR):May85-900
Butson, T.G. Gorbachev.
M. Uhlig, 441:24Feb85-8
Butson, T.G. The Tsar's Lieutenant.*
H. Bering-Jensen, 129:Apr85-77
Butt, J. Miguel de Unamuno: "San Manuel Bueno, mártir."*
M. Nozick, 240(HR):Spring84-248
N. Orringer, 403(MLS):Summer84-88
I. Soto, 402(MLR):Jan84-219
Butt, W. Hj. Söderberg: "Martin Bircks ungdom." (2nd ed)
D.M. Mennie, 562(Scan):Nov84-196
Butter, P.H. - see Blake, W.
Butterfield, F. China Alive in the Bitter Sea.
J-H.L. Upshur, 293(JASt):Feb84-305
Butterfield, H. The Origins of History.
D.R. Woolf, 529(QQ):Autumn84-524
Butterfield, R.W., ed. Modern American Poetry.
D. Davis, 617(TLS):15Mar85-293
Butterfield, S. Amway.
J. Eidus, 441:29Sep85-47
Butterick, G.F. - see Olson, C.
Butters, H.C. Governors and Government in Early Sixteenth-Century Florence 1502-1519.
L. Martines, 617(TLS):20Dec85-1465
Butterworth, B., ed. Language Production. (Vol 1)
R. Thiele, 682(ZPSK):Band37Heft3-383
Butterworth, B., ed. Language Production. (Vol 2)
A. Cutler, 353:Vol122No3-418
J.P. Stemberger, 350:Dec85-929
Buttitta, T. and B. Witham. Uncle Sam Presents.
D.B. Heard, 615(TJ):Mar84-144
A. Todras, 397(MD):Jun84-274
J.A. Williams, 536:Vol5-131
Büttner, G. Samuel Becketts Roman "Watt."
K. Schoell, 299:Number9-152

Butz, B. Morphosyntax der Mundart von Vermes (Val Terbi).
A. Schwegler, 545(RPh):Feb84-374
van Buuren, C., ed. The Buke of the Sevyne Sagis.
D. Fox, 589:Oct84-962
Buxbaum, M.H. Benjamin Franklin 1721-1906.*
J.A.L. Lemay, 365:Fall84-85
Buxton, D.R. The Wooden Churches of Eastern Europe.*
R. Lucas, 575(SEER):Jan84-119
Buyssens, E. Épiotémologie de la phonématique.*
H. van den Bussche, 553(RLiR): Jan-Jun84-210
G.F. Meier, 682(ZPSK)·Band37Heft3-386
Buzón, M.R. - see under Rodríguez Buzón, M.
Byatt, A.S. Still Life.
A. Mars-Jones, 617(TLS):28Jun85-720
J. Naughton, 362:8Aug85-31
P. West, 441:24Nov85-15
Byers, M. and M. McBurney. The Governor's Road.
J.M. Zezulka, 102(CanL):Summer84-94
Bynon, J., ed. Current Progress in Afro-Asiatic Linguistics.
A.S. Kaye, 350:Dec85-887
Bynum, C.W. Jesus as Mother.
R. Bradley, 481(PQ):Winter84-141
Byock, J. Feud in the Icelandic Saga.
D. Conquergood, 292(JAF):Jul-Sep84-347
K. Grimstad, 563(SS):Spring84-192
H. Kratz, 133:Band17Heft1/2-132
W.I. Miller, 589:Apr84-376
H. Pálsson, 301(JEGP):Oct84-588
Byrd, M. Finders Weepers.
T.J. Binyon, 617(TLS):27Dec85-1478
Byrd, M. "Tristram Shandy."
D. Profumo, 617(TLS):29Nov85-1352
Byrne, F.L. and J.P. Soman - see Spiegel, M.
Byrnes, H., ed. Georgetown University Round Table on Languages and Linguistics 1982.
P. Stoller, 355(LSoc):Dec84-532
Byrnes, R.F., ed. After Brezhnev.
V. Mastny, 550(RusR):Apr84-186
R. Walker, 575(SEER):Oct84-625
Byrom, M. Punch in the Italian Puppet Theatre.
G. Speaight, 610:Summer84-145
Lord Byron. The Complete Poetical Works.* (Vols 1-3) (J.J. McGann, ed)
A. Rutherford, 447(N&Q):Jun83-255
Lord Byron. Selected Letters and Journals.* (L.A. Marchand, ed)
D.D. Fischer, 340(KSJ):Vol133-214
506(PSt):Sep84-202
Byron, H.J. Plays by H.J. Byron.* (J. Davis, ed)
D. Devlin, 157:No152-50
Bytwerk, R.L. Julius Streicher.
C.A. Smith, 583:Winter85-182

Cabanis, J. Lacordaire et quelques autres.
L. Le Guillou, 535(RHL):Sep/Oct84-809
Cabezas, O. Fire from the Mountain.
R. Gott, 617(TLS):25Oct85-1201
S. Kinzer, 441:30Jun85-17
Cabibbo, P., ed. Melvilliana.
R. Asselineau, 189(EA):Jul-Sep85-365

Cable, J. Diplomacy at Sea.
  B. Ranft, 617(TLS):8Nov85-1268
Cabrera, R. and P.F. Meyers. Classic
  Tailoring Techniques.*
  E. Hoffman, 614:Spring85-18
Cabrera, V. Juan Benet.
  M.V. Tibbits, 552(REH):May84-318
Cabrera Infante, G. Infante's Inferno.*
  G. Kearns, 249(HudR):Winter84/85-616
  P. Lewis, 364:Oct84-93
Cachin, F., C. Moffett and J.W. Bareau.
  Manet, 1832-1883.
  R. Thomson, 59:Jun84-259
Cadart-Ricard, O. and others. Les Gammas!
  R.J. Melpignano, 399(MLJ):Spring84-71
de Cadenas y Vicent, V. Entrevistas con
  el Emperador Carlos V.
  D.R. Gerling, 238:May84-303
Cadima, W.O.M. - see under Muñoz Cadima,
  W.O.
Cadsby, H. and M. Jacobs, eds. The Third
  Taboo.
  G. Hill, 137:May84-43
Cady, E.H. Stephen Crane.
  J. Osborne, 677(YES):Vol 14-348
Cady, E.H. and N.W., eds. Critical Essays
  on W.D. Howells.
  A. Delbanco, 587(SAF):Autumn84-236
  C.L. Eichelberger, 26(ALR):Spring84-
  136
Caesar, M. and P. Hainsworth, eds. Writ-
  ers and Society in Contemporary Italy.*
  J.A. Cannon, 395(MFS):Winter84-740
Cage, J. Journal. Le Livre des champig-
  nons.
  M.F. Meurice, 450(NRF):Feb84-124
Cage, R.A. The Scots Abroad.
  A. Hook, 617(TLS):22Mar85-308
Caglioti, L. The Two Faces of Chemistry.
  S. Bernstein, 42(AR):Spring84-257
  J.D. McCowan, 529(QQ):Summer84-468
Cahalan, J.M. Great Hatred, Little Room.
  P. Craig, 617(TLS):11Jan85-39
  K.E. Marre, 395(MFS):Summer84-361
  272(IUR):Autumn84-308
"Cahiers Debussy." (No 4 and 5) (F.
  Lesure, ed)
  R. Nichols, 415:Feb84-97
"Cahiers Henri Bosco, 21."
  F.P. Bowman, 535(RHL):Jul/Aug84-651
"Cahiers Saint-John Perse."* (Vols 1-6)
  (J-L. Lalanne, ed)
  G. Straka, 553(RLiR):Jan-Jun84-203
Cahill, J. The Distant Mountains. The
  Compelling Image.
  W. Watson, 90:Jan84-48
Cahill, J. Sakaki Hyakusen and Early
  Nanga Painting.
  L. Ledderose, 407(MN):Autumn84-365
  M. Takeuchi, 293(JASt):May84-544
Cahm, E. and V. Fišera, eds. Socialism
  and Nationalism in Contemporary Europe
  (1848-1945). (Vol 2)
  B. Rigby, 208(FS):Jan84-111
Cain, T.G.S., ed. Jacobean and Caroline
  Poetry.*
  J.A.V. Chapple, 447(N&Q):Oct83-469
Cain, W.E. The Crisis in Criticism.
  F. Day, 580(SCR):Spring85-116
  W.H. Pritchard, 249(HudR):Winter84/85-
  637

Cain, W.E., ed. Philosophical Approaches
  to Literature.
  J. Annas, 617(TLS):18Jan85-55
Caine, L. What Did I Do Wrong?
  M. Scarf, 441:7Jul85-6
Cairncross, A. Years of Recovery.
  P. Clarke, 617(TLS):21Jun85-683
Cairns, F. Tibullus.
  J.H. Brouwers, 394:Vol37fasc1/2-214
Caizergues, P. Apollinaire journaliste.
  (Vol 1)
  C. Debon, 535(RHL):Jul/Aug84-646
Caizzi, F.D. - see under Decleva Caizzi, F.
Calandra, D. New German Dramatists.
  A.J. Meech, 610:Autumn84-257
Caldarini, E. - see Du Bellay, J.
Calder, D.G. Cynewulf.*
  D.W. Frese, 405(MP):Aug84-87
  J. Roberts, 447(N&Q):Feb83-68
  C. Schaar, 382(MAE):1984/2-313
  H.L.C. Tristram, 38:Band102Heft1/2-193
Calder, W.M. 3d - see von Wilamowitz-
  Moellendorff, U.
Calderón Quijano, J.A. Las espadañas de
  Sevilla.
  D. Angulo Íñiguez, 48:Jul-Sep83-305
Calderwood, J.L. Metadrama in Shake-
  speare's Henriad.*
  P. Saccio, 570(SQ):Autumn84-360
Calderwood, J.L. To Be and Not To Be.
  L.S. Champion, 179(ES):Dec84-576
  M. Charney, 551(RenQ):Summer84-306
  J. Church, 615(TJ):May84-279
  C.H. Clifton, 478:Oct84-300
  S. Homan, 301(JEGP):Oct84-560
  M. Rose, 570(SQ):Summer84-232
  639(VQR):Winter84-7
Caldwell, J. Editing Early Music.
  D. Fallows, 617(TLS):12Apr85-415
Caldwell, L.K. International Environmen-
  tal Policy.
  D. Poore, 324:Aug85-667
Caldwell, P. The Puritan Conversion Narra-
  tive.*
  N.S. Grabo, 27(AL):Dec84-593
  B. Greenfield, 150(DR):Spring84-179
  N. Pettit, 432(NEQ):Sep84-421
Calefato, P. Tempo e segno.
  M.A. Bonfantini, 567:Vol52No1/2-119
Calhoun, T.O. Henry Vaughan.*
  E.R. Cunnar, 111:Fall85-8
  A. Rudrum, 541(RES):Aug84-381
  S.C. Seelig, 402(MLR):Oct84-904
Calice, N. Ernesto e Giustino Fortunato
  L'azienda di Gaudiano e il collegio di
  Melfi.
  L. Mascilli Migliorini, 98:Aug/Sep84-
  717
Calin, W. A Muse for Heroes.
  W.A. Guentner, 446(NCFS):Winter-
  Spring85-140
Calisher, H. Mysteries of Motion.
  J.L. Halio, 598(SoR):Winter85-204
  639(VQR):Spring84-55
Calisher, H. Saratoga, Hot.
  R. Brown, 441:26May85-10
Calkins, R.G. Illuminated Books of the
  Middle Ages.
  M. Camille, 59:Dec84-508
  J.F. Cotter, 249(HudR):Summer84-295
  C. De Hamel, 39:Jul84-73
  R.S. Wieck, 517(PBSA):Vol78No4-501

Callaghan, B. As Close as We Came.
  G.P. Greenwood, 102(CanL):Summer84-135
Callaghan, B. The Black Queen Stories.*
  A. Hicks, 102(CanL):Summer84-143
Callaghan, M. A Time for Judas.*
  G. Carr, 168(ECW):Winter84/85-309
  E. Thompson, 198:Summer84-97
  P.S. Wilson, 529(QQ):Winter84-1011
Callaghan, M.R. Confessions of a Prodigal
  Daughter.
  A. Haverty, 617(TLS):20Sep85-1029
Callahan, W.J. Church, Politics, and Soci-
  ety in Spain 1750-1874.
  F. Lannon, 617(TLS):8Feb85-152
Callan, E. Auden.*
  D. Bromwich, 569(SR):Summer84-492
  T. Eagleton, 493:Jan84-60
  M. Lebowitz, 344:Summer85-118
  S. Smith, 366:Autumn84-255
Callan, E. Alan Paton.
  B.E. McCarthy, 268(IFR):Summer85-124
Callard, D.A. Pretty Good for a Woman.
  R. Blythe, 362:4Jul85-28
  E. Langer, 617(TLS):29Nov85-1349
Callen, A. Techniques of the Impression-
  ists.
  J. Burr, 39:Apr84-305
  90:Feb84-102
Callender, R. and E. Cohen. Unfinished
  Dream.
  B. Case, 617(TLS):15Nov85-1288
de Callières, F. The Art of Diplomacy by
  François de Callières. (H.M.A. Keens-
  Soper and K.W. Schweizer, eds)
  J. Black, 83:Autumn84-257
Callow, P. New York Insomnia and Other
  Poems.
  S. O'Brien, 617(TLS):1Feb85-128
Callow, S. Being an Actor.*
  R. Kift, 157:No153-48
Callu, J-P. - see Symmachus
Calonne, D.S. William Saroyan.
  J. Lang, 27(AL):Oct84-444
  G. Scharnhorst, 395(MFS):Winter84-803
  W. Shear, 649(WAL):Feb85-331
  295(JML):Nov84-502
Calvet, L-J. La Chanson dans la classe de
  français langue étrangère.
  J. Abrate, 207(FR):Dec84-336
Calvetti, C.G. - see under Gallicet Cal-
  vetti, C.
Calvino, I. Collezione di sabbia.
  J. Keates, 617(TLS):12Jul85-769
Calvino, I. Difficult Loves.*
  M. Taylor, 99:Aug/Sep84-41
Calvino, I. La Machine Littérature.
  G. Cesbron, 356(LR):Nov84-319
Calvino, I. Marcovaldo.*
  D. Flower, 249(HudR):Summer84-308
Calvino, I. Mr. Palomar.*
  S. Heaney, 441:29Sep85-1
  G. Millar, 362:5Dec85-26
  J. Updike, 442(NY):18Nov85-167
Calvino, I. Wenn ein Reisender in einer
  Winternacht.
  M.R. Becher, 384:Apr84-339
Camden, W. Remains concerning Britain.
  (R.D. Dunn, ed)
  H. Trevor-Roper, 617(TLS):14Jun85-671
Camenzind-Herzog, E. Robert Walser —
  "eine Art verlorener Sohn."*
  F. Schäublin, 680(ZDP):Band103Heft4-
  625

Cameron, A. Continuity and Change in
  Sixth-Century Byzantium.
  R.D. Scott, 313:Vol74-221
Cameron, A. Earth Witch.
  B. Pirie, 102(CanL):Winter83-146
Cameron, A. Procopius.
  C. Mango, 617(TLS):13Dec85-1422
Cameron, D.K. The Cornkister Days.
  W. Donaldson, 571(ScLJ):Winter84-33
Cameron, E., ed. Hugh MacLennan: 1982.
  H. Hoy, 102(CanL):Winter83-107
Cameron, E. The Reformation of the Here-
  tics.
  H.A. Oberman, 617(TLS):8Feb85-152
Cameron, K.N. Marxism.
  B. Berger, 441:31Mar85-18
Cameron, S. Lyric Time.*
  B. Duffey, 131(CL):Winter84-90
  C.R. Steele, 106:Spring84-63
Camilleri, J.A. The State and Nuclear
  Power.
  J.C. Sawhill, 441:17Feb85-23
Cammarata, J. Mythological Themes in the
  Works of Garcilaso de la Vega.
  A. Rey, 238:Sep84-471
Camon, F. La Maladie humaine.
  F. de Martinoir, 450(NRF):Sep84-116
Camon, F. The Story of Sirio.
  J. Marcus, 441:22Dec85-18
Camón Aznar, J. Goya.
  N. Glendinning, 90:Nov84-706
du Camp, M. Expédition des Deux-Siciles.
  (M.G. Adamo, ed)
  G. Dédéyan, 535(RHL):Jul/Aug84-639
du Camp, M. Souvenirs littéraires.
  D. Coward, 617(TLS):1Feb85-126
Campagna, A.M.P.C., ed. Testi lucani del
  Quattro e Cinquecento. (Vol 1)
  S. Lazard, 553(RLiR):Jul-Dec84-483
Campanella, T. La città del sole: dialogo
  poetico/The City of the Sun: A Poetical
  Dialogue.* (D.J. Donno, ed and trans)
  B.M. Bonansea, 543:Jun84-845
Campbell, A. No Memory of a Move.
  J. Bayly, 526:Winter84-88
  C. Hlus, 137:May84-17
  P. Stuewe, 529(QQ):Winter84-1013
Campbell, B.C. Representative Democracy.
  A. Desbiens, 106:Summer84-211
Campbell, D. A Brighter Sunshine.
  F. Urquhart, 157:No152-54
Campbell, D. The Unsinkable Aircraft
  Carrier.
  L. Freedman, 617(TLS):30Aug85-944
Campbell, D. Women at War with America.
  N. Lefkowitz, 617(TLS):5Jul85-746
Campbell, D.A. The Golden Lyre.*
  A.P. Burnett, 487:Summer84-184
Campbell, D.A. - see "Greek Lyric"
Campbell, J.L. Canna.
  T.C. Smout, 617(TLS):5Apr85-386
Campbell, M. Studies in the Third Book of
  Apollonius Rhodius' "Argonautica."
  N. Hopkinson, 123:Vol34No2-311
Campbell, R. The Selected Poems of Roy
  Campbell.* (P. Alexander, ed) Roy Camp-
  bell, Selected Poems. (M. Leveson, ed)
  R. Smith, 538(RAL):Spring84-140
Campbell, R.H. and A.S. Skinner, eds. The
  Origins and Nature of the Scottish
  Enlightenment.
  L. Hartveit, 179(ES):Apr84-185
  R.B. Sher, 518:Jul84-149

Campbell, T. The Left and Rights.*
R. Young, 63:Mar84-88
Campbell-Harding, V. Textures in Embroidery.
C. Campbell, 614:Summer85-37
Campbell-Johnson, A. Mission with Mountbatten.
617(TLS):27Sep85-1072
Campoamor González, A. Bibliografía general de Juan Ramón Jiménez.
G. Gullón, 240(HR):Autumn84-551
Campus, L. Ceramica attica a figure mere.
E.A. Moignard, 303(JoHS):Vol 104-260
Camus, A. and J. Grenier. Correspondance 1932-1960. (M. Dobrenn, ed)
J.S.T. Garfitt, 208(FS):Apr84-236
"Canada on Stage." (1980-81)
J. Wasserman, 102(CanL):Summer84-91
"Canadian Book Review Annual 1980."
(D. Tudor, N. Tudor and B. Struthers, eds)
T. Goldie, 102(CanL):Winter83-177
Canani, U.B. and others - see under Berni Canani, U. and others
Canary, R.H. T.S. Eliot.
J. Olney, 569(SR):Summer84-451
Canavaggio, J. - see de Cervantes Saavedra, M.
Canavan, F., ed. The Ethical Dimension of Political Life.
C.W.G., 185:Apr85-769
P. Gottfried, 396(ModA): Spring/Summer84-261
Candaux, J-D. and others - see de Charrière, I. [Belle de Zuylen]
Candaux, J-D. and B. Lescaze, eds. Cinq siècles d'imprimerie genevoise.
J. Renwick, 402(MLR):Oct84-925
de Candé, R. Historia universal de la música.
R. Pouilliart, 356(LR):Nov84-337
Candelaria, N. Not by the Sword.
R. Lint, 649(WAL):May84-62
Cane, A. Mario Praz critico e scrittore.
M. Bacigalupo, 402(MLR):Oct84-954
F. Donini, 617(TLS):29Mar85-337
Canellas López, A., ed. Diplomatario de Francisco de Goya.
N. Glendinning, 90:Nov84-706
Canetti, E. Das Augenspiel.
I. Parry, 617(TLS):26Jul85-813
Canetti, E. La Conscience des mots.
J. Blot, 450(NRF):Dec84-107
Canetti, E. The Human Province.*
J.T. Brewer, 399(MLJ):Spring84-76
D.J. Enright, 362:24Oct85-35
Canetti, E. The Numbered.
D.A.N. Jones, 362:14Feb85-24
Canetti, E. The Tongue Set Free.* Auto-da-Fé. The Conscience of Words. Crowds and Power. Earwitness.
J.T. Brewer, 399(MLJ):Spring84-76
de Canfield, B. - see under Benoît de Canfield
Canfield, J.V. Wittgenstein.*
R. Coburn, 482(PhR):Apr84-271
I. McFetridge, 479(PhQ):Jan84-69
Canfora, L. Studi sull'"Athenaion politeia" pseudosenofontea.*
G.J.D. Aalders H. Wzn., 394: Vol37fasc1/2-176

von Canitz, F.R.L. Friedrich Rudolph Ludwig Freiherr von Canitz: Gedichte. (J. Stenzel, ed)
P.M. Mitchell, 301(JEGP):Jul84-408
Cannadine, D. and D. Reeder - see Dyos, H.J.
Canning, P. British Policy Towards Ireland 1921-1941.
C. Townshend, 617(TLS):27Sep85-1051
Cannon, J. Aristocratic Century.
J. Habakkuk, 617(TLS):22Feb85-205
Cano, C.I. - see under Iniesta Cano, C.
Cano, J.L., ed. Antología de los poetas del 27.
J. Cano Ballesta, 240(HR):Summer84-413
G. Connell, 86(BHS):Apr84-202
Canoui, B. Plume de plomb.
J-M. Guieu, 207(FR):Apr85-753
"Cantar de mio Cid (Chanson de mon Cid)."*
(J. Horrent, ed and trans)
M.S. Brownlee, 589:Oct84-916
B. Powell, 402(MLR):Jul84-724
Cantelli, G. Repertorio della pittura Fiorentina del Seicento.
M. Wynne, 39:Oct84-291
Canter, K. and D. Swann. Entertaining with Cranks.
A.T. Ellis, 617(TLS):20Dec85-1467
Cantilena, M. Enjambement e poesia esametrica orale.
G.P. Edwards, 123:Vol34No1-125
Cantoni Alzati, G. La Biblioteca di S. Giustina di Padova.
M. Chiesa, 228(GSLI):Vol 161fasc516-601
Cantor, J. The Death of Che Guevara.
D. Flower, 249(HudR):Summer84-314
Cantor, L., ed. The English Medieval Landscape.
F.L. Cheyette, 589:Oct84-956
Cantwell, R. Bluegrass Breakdown.
F.W. Childrey, Jr., 585(SoQ):Summer85-103
Canziani, G. and G. Paganini, eds. Theophrastus Redivivus.
R.H. Popkin, 551(RenQ):Winter84-630
"Robert Capa Photographs." (C. Capa and R. Whelan, eds)
H. Simons, 441:22Sep85-13
Capaldi, N. Out of Order.
E.B. Fiske, 441:8Sep85-25
Capasso, M. - see Epicurus
Capecchi, G. and others. Palazzo Peruzzi, Palazzo Rinuccini (Collezioni florentine di antichità, 2 = Archeologica, 12).
R. Adam, 555:Vol58fasc2-352
Capek, M. Bergson and Modern Physics.
P.T. Sagal, 323:Jan84-103
Capellanus, A. On Love. (P.G. Walsh, ed and trans)
D. Carlson, 589:Jul84-608
P. Cherchi, 405(MP):Feb85-315
Capelle, G. and F. Grellet. C'est facile à dire.
Y.R. Ozzello, 207(FR):Oct84-141
Caplan, H.H. The Classified Directory of Artists' Signatures, Symbols and Monograms. (rev)
90:Mar84-170
Caplan, P.J. The Myth of Women's Masochism.
J. Johnston, 441:22Dec85-19

Caplan, U. Like One That Dreamed.*
L. Rubinoff, 298:Summer84-163
Caplow, T. and others. Middletown Fami-
lies.
D.A. Pyron, 639(VQR):Spring84-365
Capote, T. One Christmas.
639(VQR):Spring84-52
Cappriolo, E. - see Castri, M.
Capra, F. and C. Spretnak. Green Pol-
itics.*
B. Johnson, 617(TLS):4Jan85-4
Caputi, A. Storms and Son.
A. Krystal, 441:7Jul85-16
442(NY):2Sep85-86
Caputo, P. Del Corso's Gallery.
639(VQR):Winter84-26
Carafiol, P. Transcendent Reason.*
E. Elliott, 27(AL):Mar84-105
W.G. Heath, 106:Fall84-311
Caramello, C. Silverless Mirrors.
R.M. Davis, 223:Fall84-330
S. Jeffords, 651(WHR):Winter84-380
T. Le Clair, 27(AL):Dec84-627
L. McCaffery, 659(ConL):Winter85-487
R.A. Morace, 363(LitR):Summer85-617
Caras, S. and P. Martins. Balanchine.
D. Hurford, 441:24Nov85-26
Carasso-Kok, M., ed. Repertorium van
verhalende historische bronnen uit de
middeleeuwen.
B. Lyon, 589:Jan84-229
Cárcel Orti, V. Iglesia y revolución en
España (1868-1874).
D.W. Lomax, 86(BHS):Jan84-52
Carchedi, G. Problems in Class Analysis.
M.F., 185:Oct84-183
Card, C. and others, eds. Discourse in
Ethnomusicology II.
J.C. Dje Dje, 187:Winter85-118
I.V. Jackson, 91:Spring84-131
R. Joseph, 410(M&L):Oct84-398
Card, O.S. Ender's Game.
G. Jonas, 441:16Jun85-18
Cardinal, A. The Figure of Paradox in the
Work of Robert Walser.
M. Pender, 402(MLR):Oct84-982
Cardinal, M. Le Passé empiété.
J. Labat, 207(FR):May85-912
Cardinal, R. Expressionism.
S.S. Prawer, 617(TLS):7Jun85-640
Cardinal, R. Figures of Reality.*
G. Chesters, 494:Vol5No1-208
Cardona, R. - see Pérez Galdós, B.
Carduner, J., ed. Pratiques culturelles.
J.M. Laroche, 207(FR):Oct84-169
Cardus, N. A Cardus for All Seasons. (M.
Hughes, ed)
T.D. Smith, 617(TLS):28Jun85-734
Cardwell, M. - see Dickens, C.
Cardy, L. and A. Dart. Maternity Clothes.
S. Sherrer, 614:Summer85-29
Cardy, M. The Literary Doctrines of Jean-
François Marmontel.
A. Cismaru, 207(FR):Oct84-129
V. Mylne, 402(MLR):Oct84-940
Carey, G. Marlon Brando.
J. Eidus, 441:12May85-19
Carey, P. Exotic Pleasures. Bliss.
P. Lewis, 565:Spring84-64
Carey, P. Illywhacker.
A. Hislop, 617(TLS):3May85-492
H. Jacobson, 441:17Nov85-15
[continued]

[continuing]
J. Mellors, 362:25Apr85-27
D.J. Taylor, 176:Sep-Oct85-52
442(NY):11Nov85-154
Carey Evans, O., with M. Garner. Lloyd
George Was My Father.
P. Clarke, 617(TLS):26Jul85-819
Cargill, J. The Second Athenian League.*
T.R. Martin, 122:Jul84-243
"Caribbean Databook." (1984 ed)
A.R. Williams, 37:Jan-Feb84-60
Carkeet, D. Double Negative.
R. Hill, 617(TLS):5Apr85-394
M. Laski, 362:18Apr85-26
Carle, R. and others, eds. Gava'.
F. Lichtenberk, 361:Jan/Feb84-162
Carlen, A. Theatergeschichte des deut-
schen Wallis.
W.F. Michael, 221(GQ):Spring84-350
Carleton, D. The Prince's of Park Row.
F. Urquhart, 157:No152-54
Carleton, D.E. Red Scare!
R. Dugger, 441:12May85-19
Carleton, D.E. Who Shot the Bear?
L. Milazzo, 584(SWR):Autumn84-462
Carley, E.A-L. Classics from a French
Kitchen.
W. and C. Cowen, 639(VQR):Spring84-65
Carley, L. - see Delius, F.
Carlin, P., ed. Criminal Women.
J. Fairleigh, 617(TLS):12Jul85-782
Carlisle, E.F. Loren Eiseley.*
B. Howard, 502(PrS):Fall84-97
Carlisle, H. The Jonah Man.*
M. Howard, 676(YR):Winter85-ix
de Carlo, A. Treno di panna. Ucceli da
gabbia e da voliera.
J-M. Gardair, 98:Aug/Sep84-750
Carlson, H.G. Strindberg and the Poetry
of Myth.*
E.O. Johannesson, 563(SS):Autumn84-401
Carlson, L.H. Martin Marprelate, Gentle-
man.*
P. Collinson, 354:Mar84-86
R.A. McCabe, 677(YES):Vol 14-308
Carlson, M. Theories of the Theatre.
J.H. Mason, 617(TLS):25Jan85-100
Carlton, D. and C. Schaerf, eds. Reassess-
ing Arms Control.
J. Luxmoore, 617(TLS):19Jul85-804
Carlut, C. and W. Meiden. French for Oral
and Written Review.* (3rd ed)
M. Donaldson-Evans, 399(MLJ):Autumn84-
286
Carlyle, T. A Carlyle Reader.* (G.B.
Tennyson, ed)
S. Monod, 189(EA):Jul-Sep85-362
Carlyle, T. Carlyle's Latter-Day Pamph-
lets. (M.K. Goldberg and J.P. Siegel,
eds)
P. Morgan, 627(UTQ):Summer84-428
Carlyle, T. and J.W. The Collected Let-
ters of Thomas and Jane Welsh Carlyle.*
(Vols 8 and 9) (C.R. Sanders and K.J.
Fielding, eds)
G. Storey, 541(RES):May84-251
Carlyle, T. and J. Ruskin. The Correspon-
dence of Thomas Carlyle and John Ruskin.*
(G.A. Cate, ed)
P. Morgan, 179(ES):Aug84-380
B. Richards, 637(VS):Winter84-274
Carmen, A. and H. Moody. Working Women.
E.L. Sturz, 441:27Oct85-30

Carmi, T. At the Stone of Losses.*
  D. McDuff, 565:Spring84-72
Carne-Ross, D.S. Pindar.
  D.J.R. Bruckner, 441:21Jul85-23
  B. Knox, 453(NYRB):24Oct85-42
Carner, M. Alban Berg. (2nd ed)
  A. Clements, 415:Jan84-28
Carner, M. Puccini.
  A. Suied, 450(NRF):May84-143
Carner, M. Giacomo Puccini: "Tosca."
  J. Budden, 617(TLS):25Oct85-1205
Carney, J.G. To Be a Revolutionary.
  A. Schmitz, 441:18Aug85-21
Carney, R. American Dreaming.
  N. Gabler, 441:25Aug85-6
Caro, M.A. Escritos sobre don Andrés
  Bello. (C. Valderrama Andrade, ed)
  O.T. Myers, 545(RPh):May84-528
Caro, R. The Years of Lyndon Johnson: The
  Path to Power.*
  P.F. Kress, 577(SHR):Summer84-245
Caron, C., B. Haentjens and S. Trudel.
  Strip.
  J. Moss, 102(CanL):Autumn84-171
Caron, L. Les Fils de la liberté II.
  P.G. Lewis, 207(FR):Feb85-491
Carotenuto, A., ed. A Secret Symmetry.
  D.J. Fisher, 473(PR):3/1984-473
Carozzi, M. Voltaire's Attitude Toward
  Geology.
  R. Porter, 208(FS):Apr84-207
Carp, E.W. To Starve the Army at Pleasure.
  T.H. Breen, 453(NYRB):5Dec85-48
Carpenter, B. The Poetic Avant-Garde in
  Poland, 1918-1939.*
  S. Barańczak, 497(PolR):Vol129No3-103
  M.G. Levine, 574(SEEJ):Winter84-562
Carpenter, C.H., Jr. Gorham Silver, 1831-
  1981.*
  G.W.R. Ward, 658:Spring84-92
Carpenter, D. The Class of '49.
  G. Krist, 441:3Nov85-26
Carpenter, E. Edward Carpenter: Selected
  Writings. (Vol 1) (N. Grieg and D. Fern-
  bach, eds)
  P. Parker, 364:Dec84/Jan85-158
  J. Ryle, 617(TLS):25Jan85-95
Carpenter, H. O.U.D.S.
  M. Sanderson, 617(TLS):15Mar85-290
Carpenter, H. Secret Gardens.
  J. Cott, 441:21Jul85-9
  R. Lewis, 176:Sep-Oct85-54
  I. Quigly, 617(TLS):21Jun85-703
  A. Ryan, 362:18Apr85-24
  J.A. Smith, 453(NYRB):27Jun85-20
  442(NY):1Jul85-97
Carpenter, K.E., ed. Books and Society in
  History.
  T.A. Birrell, 354:Dec84-397
  M. Harris, 78(BC):Winter84-528
Carpenter, R.H. The Eloquence of Fred-
  erick Jackson Turner.
  W.W. Braden, 583:Winter85-180
Carpio, L.D. - see under de Vega Carpio, L.
Carr, E.H. The Comintern and the Spanish
  Civil War.* (T. Deutscher, ed)
  S.G. Payne, 617(TLS):17May85-553
Carr, J. Helmut Schmidt.
  R. Jenkins, 617(TLS):15Mar85-278
  R.G. Livingston, 441:14Jul85-18
  E. Pearce, 129:Apr85-84

Carr, J.L. The Battle of Pollock's Cross-
  ing.
  A. Huth, 362:24Oct85-33
  E. Korn, 617(TLS):9Aug85-874
Carr, J.L. A Month in the Country.*
  639(VQR):Winter84-26
Carr, W. Poland to Pearl Harbor.
  D. Carlton, 617(TLS):9Aug85-870
Carrasco, D. Quetzalcoatl and the Irony
  of Empire.*
  P. Mark, 2(AfrA):Feb84-84
Carrega, A. and P. Navone, eds. Le
  proprietà degli animali.
  C. Rebuffi, 379(MedR):Dec84-467
Carrell, S.L. Le Soliloque de la passion
  féminine ou le dialogue illusoire.*
  F. Sturzer, 173(ECS):Summer85-587
Carreño, A. La dialéctica de la identidad
  en la poesía contemporanea.*
  D. Cañas, 240(HR):Winter84-100
  D. Harris, 402(MLR):Jul84-735
  J. Parker, 86(BHS):Apr84-203
Carreño, A. El romancero lírico de Lope
  de Vega.
  M. Swislocki, 400(MLN):Mar84-394
Carrère d'Encausse, H. Confiscated Power.*
  A History of the Soviet Union, 1917-
  1953.* (Vols 1 and 2)
  R.M. Slusser, 550(RusR):Jan84-99
Carretta, V. The Snarling Muse.*
  C. Bruneteau, 189(EA):Jul-Sep85-326
  J. Gray, 150(DR):Spring84-172
  R. Paulson, 141:Summer84-273
  S. Shesgreen, 566:Autumn84-50
  639(VQR):Summer84-84
Carrier, L.S. Experience and the Objects
  of Perception.
  B. Maund, 63:Mar84-95
Carringer, R.L. The Making of "Citizen
  Kane."
  A. Quindlen, 441:15Sep85-9
Carrington, L.D., ed. Studies in Carib-
  bean Language.
  S.M. Embleton, 350:Dec85-927
Carrington, S.M. - see Jamyn, A.
Carrington, T. The Year They Sold Wall
  Street.
  J. Train, 441:8Dec85-36
Carrión, A.M. - see under Morales Carrión,
  A.
Carroll, A. Scotland Yard Photo Crimes
  from the Files of Inspector Black.
  639(VQR):Spring84-64
Carroll, D. The Subject in Question.*
  M. Bal, 494:Vol5No4-857
  J.M. Mellard, 599:Spring84-218
  K. Racevskis, 153:Winter84-37
  M.G. Sokolyansky, 402(MLR):Apr84-390
  M.B. Wiseman, 478:Apr84-130
Carroll, J. The Cultural Theory of Mat-
  thew Arnold.
  S.L. Chell, 125:Spring84-286
  W.A. Madden, 637(VS):Summer84-515
Carroll, J.M. Toward a Structural Psychol-
  ogy of Cinema.
  J.K. Chambers, 320(CJL):Fall84-157
Carroll, K.K. The Parthenon Inscription.
  A.G. Woodhead, 303(JoHS):Vol 104-269
Carroll, L. Alice's Adventures in Wonder-
  land. (B. Moser, illustrations)
  A.G., 636(VP):Spring84-92

Carroll, L. Alice's Adventures in Wonderland. (J. Todd, illustrator)
A. Bell, 617(TLS):4Jan85-18
Carruth, H. Asphalt Georgics.
R.W. Flint, 441:14Jul85-15
Carruth, H. The Mythology of Dark and Light.
J. Carter, 219(GaR):Summer84-415
Carruth, H. Working Papers.* (J. Weissman, ed)
B. Raffel, 363(LitR):Fall84-154
Carson, R.A.G. Principal Coins of the Romans. (Vol 3)
C.E. King, 313:Vol74-223
Carter, A. Black Venus. Come Unto These Yellow Sands.
L. Sage, 617(TLS):18Oct85-1169
Carter, A. Nights at the Circus.*
C. See, 441:24Feb85-7
Carter, B. Yesterday's Harvest.
J.W. Blench, 161(DUJ):Dec83-151
Carter, E.C. 2d, J.C. Van Horne and C.E. Brownell - see Latrobe, B.H.
Carter, J. The Blood of Abraham.
B. Lewis, 441:28Apr85-10
C.C. O'Brien, 362:1Aug85-26
D. Pipes, 129:Jun85-78
442(NY):20May85-126
Carter, J. Keeping Faith.*
W.S. Burke, 396(ModA):Spring/Summer84-264
Carter, J. and P.H. Muir, eds. Printing and the Mind of Man.* (2nd ed)
D. McKitterick, 78(BC):Autumn84-386
Carter, J. and G. Pollard. An Enquiry into the Nature of Certain Nineteenth Century Pamphlets.* (2nd ed) (N. Barker and J. Collins, eds)
A. Freeman, 354:Dec84-415
D. Gallup, 517(PBSA):Vol78No4-447
D. McKitterick, 78(BC):Spring84-105
C. Ricks, 453(NYRB):28Feb85-34
Carter, J.C. The Sculpture of the Sanctuary of Athena Polias at Priene.*
G.B. Waywell, 90:Nov84-712
Carter, J.L. The Paper Makers.*
J. Walker, 568(SCN):Spring-Summer84-18
Carter, M.B. - see under Bonham Carter, M.
Carter, M.G. Arabic Linguistics.
K.I. Semaan, 318(JAOS):Oct-Dec83-812
Carter, R. and D. Burton, eds. Literary Text and Language Study.
C.S. Brown, 355(LSoc):Dec84-552
Carter, R.E. Dimensions of Moral Education.
S.G.P., 185:Apr85-788
Carter, W.C. and R.F. Vines. A Concordance to the "Oeuvres Complètes" of Arthur Rimbaud.
A.L. Amprimoz, 446(NCFS):Summer85-297
Cartier-Bresson, H. Photoportraits.
442(NY):9Dec85-163
Carton, F. and others. Les accents des Français.
R. Jolivet, 209(FM):Oct84-244
J.C. Walz, 207(FR):Apr85-767
Cartwright, N. How the Laws of Physics Lie.*
Y. Gauthier, 154:Sep84-522
P. Gibbins, 84:Dec84-390
J. Katz, 150(DR):Fall84-637
M.L.G. Redhead, 479(PhQ):Oct84-513

Carty, R. and V. Smith. Perpetuating Poverty.
J. Stephens, 298:Winter84/85-132
Lord Carver. The Seven Ages of the British Army.*
R.F. Weigley, 441:24Feb85-12
Carver, R. Cathedral.*
M. Gorra, 249(HudR):Spring84-155
J.W. Grinnell, 573(SSF):Winter84-71
Carver, R. Fires. The Stories of Raymond Carver.
J. Clute, 617(TLS):24May85-572
P. Kemp, 362:1Aug85-30
Carver, R. - see Kittredge, W.
Carver, T. Marx and Engels.*
S,W., 185:Jan85-393
Carville, G. The Occupation of Celtic Sites in Medieval Ireland by the Canons Regular of St. Augustine and the Cistercians.
G.W. Dunleavy, 589:Apr84-468
Cary, C.W. and H.S. Limouze, eds. Shakespeare and the Arts.
D. Barrett, 615(TJ):Dec84-556
Cary, M.B., Jr. A Bibliography of the Village Press, 1903-1938.
D. Pankow, 517(PBSA):Vol78No2-259
Casagrande, J. The Sound System of French.
J.T. Chamberlain, 207(FR):May85-932
Casagrande, P.J. Unity in Hardy's Novels.*
D. Kramer, 579(SAQ):Spring84-234
Casal, G. and others. The People and Art of the Philippines.
T.M. Kiefer, 293(JASt):Nov83-195
Casale, O. - see Pino, G.B.
Casale, O.M. - see Leopardi, G.
Casanova, J. Anarquismo y revolución en la sociedad rural aragonesa.
R. Carr, 617(TLS):4Oct85-1105
Cascardi, A.J. The Limits of Illusion.
N.D. Shergold, 617(TLS):22Feb85-208
Casciato, A.D. and J.L.W. West 3d, eds. Critical Essays on William Styron.*
S. Fogel, 106:Winter84-487
D.B. Kesterson, 392:Fall84-483
Case, J. Digital Future.
L. Winner, 441:19May85-33
Casement, P. On Learning from the Patient.
P. Lomas, 617(TLS):19Jul85-788
Casella, M.T. Tra Boccaccio e Petrarca.
M. Pozzi, 228(GSLI):Vol 161fasc515-451
Casertano, G., ed. Democrito, Dall'atomo alla città.
É. des Places, 555:Vol58fasc2-290
Cash, J. Man in Black.
J.L. Tharpe, 585(SoQ):Spring84-145
Casimir, H.B.G. Haphazard Reality.
B. Castel, 529(QQ):Winter84-1050
de Caso, J. and P.B. Sanders. Rodin's Sculpture.
J.M. Hunisak, 54:Jun84-348
Caso González, J.M. and S. Cerra Suárez - see Feijoo, B.J.
Caspar, G. - see Uhse, B.
Cassar, G.H. The Tragedy of Sir John French.
K. Jeffery, 617(TLS):13Dec85-1417
Cassidy, F.G. - see "Dictionary of American Regional English"
Cassill, R.V. After Goliath.
R.P. Brickner, 441:16Jun85-27
Cassin, B., ed and trans. Si Parménide.*
G.B. Kerferd, 53(AGP):Band66Heft1-89

Cassirer, E. Individu et cosmos dans la
philosophie de la Renaissance.
  M. Jarrety, 450(NRF):Mar84-128
Cassou-Yager, H. La Polyvalence du thème
de la mort dans "Les Fleurs du mal" de
Baudelaire.
  G. Chesters, 208(FS):Jan84-77
  W. Greenberg, 546(RR):Jan84-113
Castañeda, S.G. - see under García Casta-
ñeda, S.
Castelein de la Lande, A. Pièces en un
acte.
  J. Moss, 102(CanL):Autumn84-171
Casteleyn, M. A History of Literacy and
Libraries in Ireland.* [shown in prev
under Casteltyn]
  M. Pollard, 354:Dec84-399
Castellani, A. La prosa italiana delle
origini, I.
  S. Lazard, 553(RLiR):Jan-Jun84-220
Castellet, J.M. Josep Pla o la razón nar-
rativa.
  A. Terry, 86(BHS):Oct84-515
Castells, M. The City and the Grassroots.
  K.S., 185:Apr85-790
Castex, P-G. Horizons romantiques.
  J. Gaulmier, 535(RHL):Nov/Dec84-974
  B. Juden, 208(FS):Jul84-363
Castille, P. and W. Osborne, eds. South-
ern Literature in Transition.
  P. Lentz, 392:Spring84-187
  A. Rampersad, 578:Fall85-110
del Castillo, A.H. - see under Hernández
del Castillo, A.
Castillo-Feliú, G.I., ed. The Creative
Process in the Works of José Donoso.
  R.L. Acevedo, 238:May84-313
Castle, T. Clarissa's Ciphers.*
  L.J. Davis, 536:Vol6-237
  C. Kay, 81:Winter84-197
  R. Perry, 481(PQ):Spring84-284
Castleman, A.S. Das Lautsystem der Mun-
dart von Zweibrücken-Niederauerbach.
  H. Moser, 685(ZDL):1/1984-99
Castor, G. and T. Cave, eds. Neo-Latin
and the Vernacular in Renaissance
France.*
  P. Ford, 208(FS):Oct84-455
Castoriadis, C. Devant la guerre. (Vol 1)
  F. Trémolières, 450(NRF):Jun84-118
Castri, M. Pirandello Ottanta. (E. Cap-
priolo, ed)
  G. Banu, 98:Aug/Sep84-671
Castro, M. Interpreting the Indian.
  P. Pavich, 649(WAL):Feb85-323
Castronovo, D. Edmund Wilson.
  J. Atlas, 441:28Jul85-6
Casway, J.I. Owen Roe O'Neill and the
Struggle for Catholic Ireland.
  T. Barnard, 617(TLS):5Jul85-742
Catalán, D., ed. Gran crónica de Alfonso
XI.*
  R. MacDonald, 589:Jan84-230
"Catalog of the Inter-American Review of
Bibliography, 1951-1982."
  C. Rodríguez, 37:Jan-Feb84-60
Catan, J.R. - see Owens, J.
Cate, C. The War of the Two Emperors.
  P-L. Adams, 61:Nov85-143
Cate, G.A. - see Carlyle, T. and J. Ruskin
Cathcart, R. The Most Contrary Region.
  M. O'Brien, 362:24Jan85-24

Cathcart, R. and M. Strong. Beyond the
Classroom.
  J. Ross, 399(MLJ):Autumn84-308
Cather, W. The Troll Garden. (J. Wood-
ress, ed)
  M.R. Bennett, 649(WAL):Aug84-141
  27(AL):Mar84-134
"Catholic Social Teaching and the US
Economy."
  A. Hacker, 453(NYRB):28Feb85-37
Caticchio, T., ed. La Poesia Italiana
Nel Quebec.
  R. Furgiuele, 627(UTQ):Summer84-498
Cattin, G. Music of the Middle Ages I.
  D. Leech-Wilkinson, 617(TLS):1Mar85-
229
Cau, J. Croquis de mémoire.
  D. Johnson, 617(TLS):2Aug85-856
Cauchies, J-M. La législation princière
pour le conté de Hainaut.
  E.L. Cox, 589:Jan84-125
Caudwell, S. The Shortest Way to Hades.
  T.J. Binyon, 617(TLS):15Feb85-179
  M. Laski, 362:18Jul85-29
Caufield, C. In the Rainforest.
  E.W. Chu, 441:24Mar85-25
Cauman, L.S. and others, eds. How Many
Questions?
  R.M.M., 185:Jan85-385
Causey, A. Edward Burra Complete Cata-
logue.
  F. Spalding, 617(TLS):30Aug85-951
Causley, C. Secret Destinations.
  J. Mole, 176:Jul/Aug85-53
  S. Rae, 617(TLS):26Apr85-470
Cauvin, J-P. and M.A. Caws - see Breton, A.
Cavaglion, A. Otto Weininger in Italia.
  M. Anderson, 400(MLN):Jan84-172
Cavalca Schiroli, M.G. - see Seneca
Cavalcanti, G. Pound's Cavalcanti. (D.
Anderson, ed)
  G. Bornstein, 534(RALS):Autumn82-241
  C.F. Terrell, 30:Fall83-81
Cavallari, H.M. Leopoldo Marechal.*
  M. Agosin, 263(RIB):Vol34No1-91
Cavalli-Björkman, G. and B. Lindwall. The
World of Carl Larsson.
  J.B. Smith, 39:Aug84-148
Cave, K. - see Farington, J.
Cave, M., A. McAuley and J. Thornton, eds.
New Trends in Soviet Economics.*
  Z.M. Fallenbuchl, 104(CASS):Fall84-350
Cave, O. and J. Hodges. Smocking.
  A.L. Mayer, 614:Summer85-35
Cavendish, G. Metrical Visions.* (A.S.G.
Edwards, ed)
  G. Kipling, 541(RES):Feb84-80
Cavendish, J.M. A Handbook of Copyright
in British Publishing Practice.
  M. Field, 617(TLS):26Apr85-475
Cavendish, R., ed. Legends of the World.
  A.C. Percival, 203:Vol95No1-132
Caviness, M.H. The Windows of Christ
Church Cathedral, Canterbury.
  G. Gilmore-House, 589:Jul84-627
Caviró, B.M. - see under Martínez Caviró,
B.
Cawley, A.C. and others. The Revels His-
tory of Drama in English. (Vol 1)
  P. Storfer, 157:No154-52

Caws, M.A. The Eye in the Text.*
  W. Bohn, 131(CL):Spring84-167
  P. Florence, 208(FS):Jul84-372
  A. Hughes, 90:Jun84-368
Caws, M.A. A Metapoetics of the Passage.*
  M. Warehime, 188(ECr):Summer84-107
Caws, M.A. Reading Frames in Modern Fic-
tion.
  R. Brown, 617(TLS):27Sep85-1075
Caws, M.A., ed. Writing in a Modern Tem-
per.
  R.D. Cottrell, 207(FR):May85-895
Caws, M.A. and H. Riffaterre, eds. The
Prose Poem in France, Theory and Prac-
tice.
  D. Scott, 208(FS):Apr84-245
  N. Watson, 546(RR):Nov84-516
Cayrol, J. Un mot d'auteur.
  P.H. Solomon, 207(FR):May85-913
Cazaux, Y. - see Palma-Cayet, P-V.
Cazden, N., H. Haufrecht and N. Studer,
eds. Folk Songs of the Catskills.*
  P. Dickinson, 410(M&L):Oct84-376
  D.W. Steel, 309:Vol5No1/3-260
Cazelles, B. Le Corps de sainteté d'après
Jehan Bouche d'Or, Jehan Paulus et quel-
ques vies des XIIe et XIIIe siècles.
  G.T. Diller, 207(FR):Oct84-118
Cazelles, R. Société politique, noblesse
et couronne sous Jean le Bon et Charles
V.
  J.B. Henneman, 589:Jan84-127
Cazemajou, J. and J-P. Martin. La Crise
du melting-pot.
  N. Glazer, 189(EA):Jan-Mar85-106
Cazort, J.E. and C.T. Hobson. Born To
Play.
  D.E. McGinty, 91:Spring84-133
Ceauşescu, I., ed. War, Revolution, and
Society in Romania.
  J.C. Campbell, 104(CASS):Winter84-502
  D. Deletant, 575(SEER):Oct84-598
Cèbe, J-P. - see Varro
de Ceccatty, R. L'Extrémité du Monde.
  J. Kirkup, 617(TLS):14Jun85-678
Cecchetti, D. Petrarca, Pietramala e
Clamanges.*
  P. Trivero, 547(RF):Band96Heft1/2-228
Cecchetti, G. - see Leopardi, G.
Cccil, D. A Portrait of Charles Lamb.
  J. Aaron, 339(KSMB):No35-90
Cecil, D. - see MacCarthy, D.
Cela, C.J. El juego de los tres madroños.
  U.J. De Winter, 238:May84-308
"Celebration: A World of Art and Ritual."
  E.A. Early, 650(WF):Oct84-265
"Céline: Actes du colloque international
d'Oxford."
  I. Noble, 208(FS):Jan84-89
Célis, R., ed. Littérature et musique.*
  C.S. Brown, 678(YCGL):No32-145
  E. Lorenz, 547(RF):Band96Heft3-327
Celletti, R. Storia del belcanto.
  C. Gianturco, 410(M&L):Oct84-371
Cellini, B. The Autobiography of Benven-
uto Cellini. (C. Hope and A. Nova, eds)
  C. Gould, 39:May84-389
  B. Moloney, 278(IS):Vol39-136
Celsus. La préface du "De Medicina" de
Celse. (P. Mudry, ed and trans)
  H. King, 313:Vol74-244
  J. Vallance, 123:Vol34No2-319

Cencellotti, D. and C. Zanoni. Fabbricato
in Italia.
  A.G. Cioffari, 399(MLJ):Autumn84-297
Cendrars, M. Blaise Cendrars.
  P. Adam, 98:Apr84-339
Censer, J.T. North Carolina Planters and
Their Children, 1800-1860.
  639(VQR):Autumn84-117
Cercignani, F. Shakespeare's Works and
Elizabethan Pronunciation.*
  C. Barber, 541(RES):May84-224
  N.F. Blake, 72:Band221Heft1-174
  A. Ward, 447(N&Q):Feb83-95
Cérésa, F. Le Cimetière des grands
enfants.
  F.J. Greene, 207(FR):May85-914
Cernuda, L. La Realidad y el Deseo.
  (M.J. Flys, ed)
  D. Harris, 402(MLR):Oct84-960
Cerny, P.G. and M.A. Schain, eds. Social-
ism, the State and Public Policy in
France.
  J.E.S. Hayward, 617(TLS):10May85-516
Ceronetti, G. Le Silence du corps.
  T. Cordellier, 450(NRF):Oct84-97
Cerullo, J.J. The Secularization of the
Soul.
  G. Mariz, 637(VS):Summer84-512
de Cervantes Saavedra, M. Entremeses. (J.
Canavaggio, ed)
  R.J. Oakley, 86(BHS):Jan84-65
de Cervantes Saavedra, M. Novelas
ejemplares. (J.B. Avalle-Arce, ed)
  R. El Saffar, 304(JHP):Winter84-147
Cervera Vera, L. Arquitectura del Colegio
Mayor de Santa Cruz en Valladolid.
  F. Marías, 48:Jan-Mar84-120
Césaire, A. Aimé Césaire: The Collected
Poetry.* (C. Eshleman and A. Smith, eds
and trans)
  E. Snyder, 538(RAL):Winter84-602
  C. Wake, 617(TLS):19Jul85-792
  639(VQR):Spring84-62
Césaire, A. Aimé Césaire: Some African
Poems in English.
  T.A. Hale, 538(RAL):Spring84-83
Césaire, A. Moi, laminaire...
  C. Michael, 207(FR):Dec84-307
Césaire, A. Non-vicious Circle.
  C. Wake, 617(TLS):19Jul85-792
de Césarée, B. - see under Basile de
Césarée
Cesarini, D. Giuseppe Piermarini, archi-
tetto neoclassico.
  R. Middleton, 90:Dec84-790
de Cessolis, J. Konrad von Ammenhausen:
"Das Schachzabelbuch." (K. von Ammen-
hausen, trans; C. Bosch-Schairer, ed)
  R.F.M. Byrn, 402(MLR):Jan84-227
Cetron, M., with A. Pagano and O. Port.
The Future of American Business.
  H.D. Shapiro, 441:20Oct85-54
"Da Cézanne a Morandi e oltre."
  V. Nicolson, 39:May84-388
Chabot, C.B. Freud on Schreber.*
  E. Slater, 447(N&Q):Dec83-571
Chabot, J. L'Autre Moi.
  P.W.M. Cogman, 208(FS):Oct84-471
Chabot, M. and A. Vidricaire, eds. Objet
pour la philosophie.
  P. Bellemare, 154:Sep84-538
Chace, W.M. Lionel Trilling.
  I. Clarke, 506(PSt):May84-89

Chadwick, H. Boethius: The Consolations
of Music, Logic, Theology, and Philos-
ophy.*
   A.M. Peden, 382(MAE):1984/1-99
   J. Procopé, 541(RES):Nov84-519
   J.A. Weisheipl, 319:Jan85-101
Chafe, W.H. The Unfinished Journey.
   J.C. Furnas, 441:3Nov85-35
   442(NY):30Dec85-79
"Chagall Lithographs, 1974-1979."
   R. Bass, 55:Nov84-41
Chaika, E. Language — The Social Mirror.
   R.M. Barasch, 399(MLJ):Winter84-411
   E. Finegan, 350:Sep85-729
Chailley, J., P. Imbs and D. Poirion, eds.
   Guillaume de Machaut.
   A. Dzelzainis, 208(FS):Jul84-324
Chaillou, M. Domestique chez Montaigne.*
   R.H. Simon, 207(FR):Feb85-492
Chainey, G. A Literary History of Cam-
bridge.
   G. Hough, 617(TLS):25Oct85-1217
Chajkowsky, W.E. Royal Flying Corps.
   S.E. Read, 102(CanL):Winter83-83
Chakoo, B.L. Aldous Huxley and Eastern
Wisdom.
   J. Meckier, 268(IFR):Winter85-42
Chakravarti, A. The Sdok Kak Thom Inscrip-
tion. (Pts 1 and 2)
   P.N. Jenner, 293(JASt):Nov83-197
Chalfant, E. Both Sides of the Ocean.*
   J.W. Tuttleton, 534(RALS):Autumn82-215
Chaliand, G. and J-P. Rageau. Atlas stra-
tégique.
   H. Cronel, 450(NRF):Nov84-95
Challe, R. Difficultés sur la religion
proposées au Père Malebranche. (F.
Deloffre and M. Menemencioglu, eds)
   C.J. Betts, 402(MLR):Oct84-935
   G. Menant-Artigas, 535(RHL):Jul/Aug84-
614
   H. Sonneville, 356(LR):Aug84-253
Chalmers, M. Paying for Defence.
   L. Freedman, 617(TLS):30Aug85-944
Chalon, J. Le Lumineux Destin d'Alexandra
David-Néel.
   C. von Fürer-Haimendorf, 617(TLS):
4Oct85-1111
Chamard, H. - see under Du Bellay, J.
Chamberlain, J. A Life with the Printed
Word.
   P.F. Lawler, 396(ModA):Winter84-90
Chamberlain, J.S. Ibsen.*
   S.G. McLellan, 130:Summer84-182
   E. Sprinchorn, 301(JEGP):Apr84-309
Chamberlin, J.E. and S.L. Gilman, eds.
   Degeneration.
   D. Pick, 617(TLS):4Oct85-1109
Chambers, A. Booktalk.
   L. Mackinnon, 617(TLS):16Aug85-910
Chambers, B.T. Bibliography of French
Bibles.
   F.D. Desroussilles, 354:Sep84-294
   R.M. Kingdon, 551(RenQ):Winter84-614
Chambers, B.W. Art and Artists of the
South.
   J.H. Bonner, 585(SoQ):Summer85-94
Chambers, D., ed. Private Press Books
1978.
   B.R. Johnson, 517(PBSA):Vol78No3-378
Chambers, J. Milestones 1.
   P. Stevens, 99:May84-34

Chambers, J. Milestones 2.
   F. Davis, 441:3Nov85-26
Chambers, J.K. and P. Trudgill. Dialectol-
ogy.*
   Y. Malkiel, 355(LSoc):Mar84-29
Chambers, R. Story and Situation.
   J.J. Sosnoski, 395(MFS):Winter84-849
Champigny, R. Sartre and Drama.
   K. Gore, 208(FS):Apr84-238
   C. Howells, 402(MLR):Jul84-718
   J. Labat, 207(FR):Feb85-460
   R.C. Lamont, 397(MD):Jun84-267
   G. Prince, 478:Apr84-133
   295(JML):Nov84-502
Champion, T. and others. Prehistoric
Europe.
   C. Thomas, 176:Jan85-49
Chan, A. The Glory and Fall of the Ming
Dynasty.
   P. Huang, 293(JASt):May84-510
Chan, A.B. Arming the Chinese.
   J. Sheridan, 293(JASt):Feb84-306
Chan, H-L. and W.T. de Bary, eds. Yüan
Thought.
   L. Struve, 293(JASt):Aug84-737
Chan, M. Music in the Theatre of Ben
Johnson.*
   D. Lindley, 447(N&Q):Oct83-467
   J. Michon, 189(EA):Jan-Mar85-81
Chan, V. Leader of My Angels.
   380:Autumn84-330
Chandler, R. Raymond Chandler's Unknown
Thriller. (J. Pepper, ed)
   P-L. Adams, 61:Sep85-114
Chandos, J. Boys Together.*
   E. Claridge, 364:Aug/Sep84-110
Chaney, E. and N. Ritchie, eds. Oxford,
China and Italy.*
   D. Sutton, 39:Oct84-224
Chang, H.C. Chinese Literature 3.*
   R.J. Cutter, 268(IFR):Winter85-63
Chang, K.C. Art, Myth, and Ritual.
   M. Loewe, 617(TLS):11Jan85-47
   M. Sullivan, 39:Nov84-357
Chang, K.C., ed. Food in Chinese Culture.
   T. Whittaker, 529(QQ):Winter84-785
Chang, K-I.S. - see under Sun Chang, K-I.
Chang, R.T. The Justice of the Western
Consular Courts in Nineteenth Century
Japan.
   J.E. Hoare, 407(MN):Winter84-464
Chang Yü-fa. Chung-kuo hsien-tai-hua te
ch'ü-yü yen-chiu.
   D.D. Buck, 293(JASt):Feb84-308
Chang-ming, H. - see under Hua Chang-ming
Chang-Rodríguez, E. Latinoamérica.
   J. Otero, 238:Dec84-688
   E. Spinelli, 399(MLJ):Autumn84-301
Chang-Rodríguez, E. Poética e ideología
en José Carlos Mariátegui.
   H.L. Johnson, 238:Sep84-478
   S. Lipp, 263(RIB):Vol34No1-92
Chang-Rodríguez, E. - see "Boletín de la
Academia Norteamericana de la Lengua
Española"
Chang-Rodríguez, R. Violencia y subver-
sión en la prosa colonial hispanoamer-
icana, siglos XVI y XVII.*
   B. Boling, 345(KRQ):Vol31No4-457
"The Changelings." (R.F. Willig, trans)
   A. Gatten, 244(HJAS):Jun84-257
   T.J. Harper, 407(MN):Winter84-455
   H.M. Horton, 293(JASt):Aug84-773

Changeux, J-P. Neuronal Man. (French
title: L'Homme Neuronal.)
  R.C. Lewontin, 453(NYRB):10Oct85-18
  F. Lurçat, 450(NRF):Dec84-104
Channer, C.C. Lacemaking. (rev by M.
Waller)
  C. Campbell, 614:Spring85-24
Chant, C. and I. Hogg, comps. Nuclear War
in the 1980's?
  639(VQR):Spring84-59
Chapel, J. Victorian Taste.*
  J. Maas, 90:Nov84-707
Chapin, B. Criminal Justice in Colonial
America, 1606-1660.
  B.H. Mann, 656(WMQ):Apr84-305
Chapin, K. Dogwood Afternoons.
  J. Leggett, 441:24Nov85 23
Chaplais, P. English Medieval Diplomatic
Practice. (Pt 1)
  G.P. Cuttino, 589:Jul84-630
Chapman, J.W.M. and others. Japan's Quest
for Comprehensive Security.
  Shindō Eiichi, 285(JapQ):Jan-Mar84-89
Chapman, L.H. Instant Art Instant Culture.
  J.U. Gray, 289:Spring84-117
Chapman, R. The Duchess's Diary.
  O. Conant, 441:17Mar85-23
Chapman, R. The Treatment of Sounds in
Language and Literature.*
  B. Vine, 350:Dec85-934
Chapman, R.W. - see Austen, J.
Chapman, S. The Rise of Merchant Banking.
  S.G. Checkland, 617(TLS):3May85-486
Chapman, T. Time.
  R.M. Gale, 154:Mar84-153
  I. Hinckfuss, 63:Jun84-208
Chapon, F. Mystères et splendeurs de
Jacques Doucet 1853-1929.
  J. Aeply, 450(NRF):Jun84-113
Chappel, A.H. - see Aichinger, I.
Chappell, F. I Am One of You Forever.
  D. Guy, 441:15Sep85-21
Chappell, W. - see Burra, E.
Chapple, F. Sparks Fly!*
  H. Bering-Jensen, 129:Nov85-118
Chapple, J.A.V., with G. Sharps - see
Gaskell, E.
Chappuzeau, S. Le Cercle des Femmes et
L'Academie des Femmes. (J. Crow, ed)
  I. Maclean, 208(FS):Apr84-200
Char, R. Oeuvres complètes.
  H. Peyre, 207(FR):Oct84-137
  M.J. Worton, 208(FS):Apr84-232
Charbonneau, P. La Baie heureuse.
  J.M. Paterson, 102(CanL):Winter83-142
du Chardin, P. Le roman de la conscience
malheureuse.*
  J. Cruickshank, 402(MLR):Apr84-464
  J. Hervier, 549(RLC):Jul-Sep84-368
Chardonne, J. and R. Nimier. Correspon-
dance 1950-1962.
  A. Clerval, 450(NRF):Nov84-78
Lord Charlemont. The Travels of Lord
Charlemont in Greece and Turkey, 1749.
(W.B. Stanford and E.J. Finopoulos, eds)
  P. Johnson, 362:11Apr85-24
Charles, D. Aristotle's Philosophy of
Action.
  N. Denyer, 617(TLS):18Oct85-1189
Charles, M. Rhétorique de la lecture.
  M.D. Picazo, 202(FMod):No65/67-313
Charles, S.C. and E. Kennedy. Defendant.
  M. Pines, 441:11Aug85-15

Charles-Saget, A. L'architecture du
divin.*
  H.J. Blumenthal, 542:Oct-Dec84-455
  C. Guérard, 192(EP):Jul-Sep84-406
  A. Sheppard, 123:Vol134No1-136
  J. Whittaker, 303(JoHS):Vol 104-230
Charleston, R.J. English Glass and the
Glass Used in England, circa 400-1940.
  J. Poole, 617(TLS):1Feb85-129
Charlesworth, N. Peasants and Imperial
Rule.
  D. Washbrook, 617(TLS):20Sep85-1042
Charlet, J-L. Le Création poétique dans
le "Cathemerinon" de Prudence.
  A-M. Palmer, 123:Vol134No2-328
  M. Reydellet, 555:Vol555:Vol58fasc2-
    341
Charlton, D.G., ed. The French Romantics.
  V. Brombert, 617(TLS):4Jan85-15
  549(RLC):Oct-Dec84-473
Charlton, D.G. New Images of the Natural
in France.
  P. France, 617(TLS):1Feb85-126
Charlton, M. The Eagle and the Small
Birds.*
  A. Brown, 617(TLS):4Oct85-1104
Charlton, P. John Stainer and the Musical
Life of Victorian Britain.*
  W. Hillsman, 415:Sep84-501
Charney, G. A Long Journey.
  T. Draper, 453(NYRB):9May85-32
Charney, M. Joe Orton.
  J. Melmoth, 617(TLS):30Aug85-953
Charney, M. Sexual Fiction.*
  S.M. Gilbert, 223:Winter82-488
Charney, M., ed. Shakespearean Comedy.
  I. Donaldson, 402(MLR):Jan84-144
Charny, I. How Can We Commit the Unthink-
able?
  E. Grosholz, 584(SWR):Spring84-219
Charpentier, F. - see Labé, L.
de Charrière, I. [Belle de Zuylen]
Oeuvres complètes. (Vol 6) (J-D. Can-
daux and others, eds)
  P. and M. Higonnet, 617(TLS):17May85-
    535
Charry, E., G. Koefoed and P. Muysken, eds.
De talen van Suriname.
  A. Kramp, 204(FdL):Mar84-73
Charters, A., ed. The Beats.*
  J. Lititz, 87(BB):Jun84-97
  L.S.T., 70:Mar-Apr84-120
Chartier, R., ed. Figures de la gueuserie.
  L. Andries, 535(RHL):Nov/Dec84-960
Charyn, J. War Cries Over Avenue C.
  J. Cantor, 441:16Jun85-24
Chase, C., ed. The Dating of "Beowulf."*
  N. Jacobs, 382(MAE):1984/1-117
  J.B. Trahern, Jr., 301(JEGP):Jan84-107
Chase, J. During the Reign of the Queen
of Persia.*
  C. Rooke, 376:Oct84-118
Chastagnol, A. L'évolution politique,
sociale et économique du monde romain
(284-363).
  J.P. Callu, 555:Vol58fasc2-346
Chastain, K. Relatos simbólicos.
  T.V. Higgs, 399(MLJ):Summer84-188
  M. Prado, 238:Mar84-159
Chastel, A., ed. Le Palais Farnèse.
(Vols 1 and 2)
  J.S. Ackerman, 576:Mar84-75

Chastel, A. The Sack of Rome, 1527.*
(French title: Le Sac de Rome, 1527.)
D.S. Chambers, 90:May84-296
J.R. Hale, 617(TLS):22Mar85-314
D. Hay, 551(RenQ):Summer84-247
Chastel, A. and others. The Renaissance.*
R. Catani, 278(IS):Vol139-137
de Chateaubriand, F.R. Correspondance
générale.* (Vol 4) (P. Riberette, ed)
F. Bassan, 446(NCFS):Summer85-299
R. Lebègue, 535(RHL):Nov/Dec84-973
Chatfield-Taylor, J. Backstage at the
Opera.
C.J. Gianakaris, 615(TJ):May84-286
Chatillon, P. Poèmes.
K.W. Meadwell, 102(CanL):Autumn84-95
Chatterjee, V. Mysticism in English
Poetry.
S. Wyler, 447(N&Q):Dec83-534
Chaucer, G. "The Canterbury Tales" by
Geoffrey Chaucer.* (N.F. Blake, ed)
D.C. Baker, 191(ELN):Mar85-72
Chaucer, G. Geoffrey Chaucer: "Troilus
and Criseyde." (B.A. Windeatt, ed) The
Prologue to The Canterbury Tales by
Geoffrey Chaucer in the Original Text
from Caxton's First Edition with a Trans-
lation into Modern English by Nevill
Coghill.
B. O'Donoghue, 617(TLS):12Apr85-416
Chaucer, G. A Variorum Edition of the
Works of Geoffrey Chaucer. (Pt 3, Vol 2:
The Miller's Tale.) (T.W. Ross, ed)
N.F. Blake, 179(ES):Apr84-177
C.K. Zacher, 536:Vol6-49
Chaucer, G. A Variorum Edition of the
Works of Geoffrey Chaucer. (Vol 5: The
Minor Poems, Pt 1) (G.B. Pace and A.
David, eds)
N.F. Blake, 179(ES):Apr84-175
R.T. Lenaghan, 589:Apr84-379
Chaudenson, R. Textes créoles anciens (La
Réunion et Ile Maurice).*
J. Chaurand, 209(FM):Oct84-247
Chaudhuri, B. - see "Annual Bibliography
of Victorian Studies" (1976-1980) [and]
"Cumulated Bibliography of Victorian
Studies 1976-1980"
Chaudhuri, B. - see "Indian Book Review
Digest"
Chaudhuri, S. Infirm Glory.*
T.W. Craik, 541(RES):Feb84-82
R. Lengeler, 156(JDSh):Jahrbuch1984-
250
Chaurette, N. La Société de Métis.
J. Moss, 207(FR):May85-915
J.B. Moss, 102(CanL):Autumn84-98
Chaussinand-Nogaret, G. The French Nobil-
ity in the Eighteenth Century.
J. Rogister, 617(TLS):20Sep85-1036
Chazal, R. Gérard Depardieu, l'autodi-
dacte inspiré.
R. Hammond, 207(FR):Feb85-464
Chaze, E. Little David.
N. Callendar, 441:13Oct85-29
442(NY):19Aug85-90
Chaze, E. Mr. Yesterday.
N. Callendar, 441:27Jan85-33
Cheatwood, K.T-H. Psalms of Redemption.
B. Brown, 95(CLAJ):Sep84-102
Chęcinski, M. Poland.*
H. Nordon, 390:Oct84-58

Cheever, S. Home Before Dark.*
Z. Leader, 617(TLS):22Feb85-189
M. Wood, 362:14Feb85-25
Chekhov, A. Oncle Vania. (M. Tremblay,
trans)
J. Moss, 102(CanL):Autumn84-171
Chekhov, A. The Selected Letters of Anton
Chekhov. (L. Hellman, ed)
V.L. Smith, 617(TLS):11Jan85-43
Chellis, M. The Joan Kennedy Story.
E. Fawcett, 617(TLS):22Nov85-1338
Chénetier, M. Richard Brautigan.
T. Hunt, 649(WAL):Aug84-166
D. Seed, 189(EA):Jul-Sep85-363
Cheng, V.J. Shakespeare and Joyce.*
M.P. Gillespie, 329(JJQ):Winter85-233
M. Magalaner, 395(MFS):Winter84-760
J. Mays, 272(IUR):Autumn84-304
295(JML):Nov84-462
Ch'eng-ta, F. - see under Fan Ch'eng-ta
Chepesiuk, R. and A. Shankman, comps.
American Indian Archival Material.
J.W. Geary, 87(BB):Dec84-243
Cherchari, A. Réception de la littéra-
ture africaine d'expression française
jusqu'en 1970.
J. Riesz, 52:Band19Heft3-324
Cherfas, J. and J. Gribbin. The Redundant
Male.
L. Tiger, 441:23Jun85-10
Chernaik, W.L. The Poet's Time.*
M. Dzelzainis, 175:Summer84-139
R. Howell, Jr., 366:Spring84-119
M. Stocker, 184(EIC):Jul84-248
J.H. Summers, 401(MLQ):Sep83-319
Chernin, K. The Hungry Self.
P-L. Adams, 61:Jul85-101
P. Chesler, 441:21Jul85-10
Chernin, K. In My Mother's House.
A.S. Grossman, 617(TLS):3May85-502
Cherniss, M.D. Ingeld and Christ.
K. Reichl, 72:Band221Heft2-366
Chertkov, L. - see Vaginoy, K.
Cherubim, D., ed. Fehlerlinguistik.*
E. Bauer, 685(ZDL):1/1984-102
Chéry-Aynesworth, J. Approche rhétorique
de la dialectique des sens chez Bernanos.
(Vol 1)
G.R. Montbertrand, 207(FR):Oct84-134
Cheshire, J. Variation in an English
Dialect.*
B.M. Horvath, 355(LSoc):Jun84-259
L. Milroy, 297(JL):Mar84-177
Cheshire, L. The Light of Many Suns.
M. Howard, 617(TLS):9Aug85-869
Chesney, E.A. The Countervoyage of Rabe-
lais and Ariosto.*
M.U. Sowell, 539:May85-119
Chesnut, M. Mary Chesnut's Civil War.
(C.V. Woodward, ed)
L.T. McDonnell, 106:Summer84-167
Chesnut, M. The Private Mary Chesnut.*
(C.V. Woodward and E. Muhlenfeld, eds)
P-L. Adams, 61:Mar85-125
Chesterton, G.K. The Bodley Head G.K.
Chesterton. (P.J. Kavanagh, ed)
R. Hattersley, 617(TLS):12Jul85-770
Chetwode, P. Two Middle-Aged Ladies in
Andalusia.
617(TLS):8Mar85-271
Chevalier, J-C. and M. Gross, eds. Méth-
odes en grammaire française.*
H. Weinrich, 547(RF):Band96Heft1/2-113

Chevallier, R. Provincia.
H. Lavagne, 555:Vol58fasc2-353
Chevallier, R. La romanisation de la Celtique du Pô. (Vol 1)
J-C. Richard, 555:Vol58fasc1-164
Chevrel, Y. Le naturalisme.*
D. Baguley, 678(YCGL):No32-138
E. Ibsch, 549(RLC):Jan-Mar84-122
M. Kanes, 131(CL):Fall84-373
B. Nelson, 208(FS):Oct84-480
U. Schulz-Buschhaus, 52:Band19Heft1-98
H.H. Weinberg, 446(NCFS):Summer85-292
Chevrel, Y., ed. Le Naturalisme dans le littératures de langues européennes.
B. Nelson, 208(FS):Oct84-480
Chevrier, J-F. Proust et la Photographie.*
R.A. Kingcaid, 188(ECr):Summer84-106
Cheyfitz, E. The Trans-Parent.
R.A. Yoder, 591(SIR):Summer84-268
Chi Pang-Yuan and others, eds. An Anthology of Contemporary Chinese Literature, Taiwan: 1949-1974.
C. Tung, 318(JAOS):Apr-Jun83-463
Chiampi, J.T. Shadowy Prefaces.*
J.M. Ferrante, 589:Jan84-129
Chiappini di Sorio, I. Palazzo Pisani Moretta.
M. Levey, 90:Aug84-509
Chiarini, P. and W. Dietze, eds. Deutsche Klassik und Revolution.*
N. Oellers, 52:Band19Heft3-307
Chiaromonte, N. The Paradox of History.
H. White, 441:22Sep85-7
Chibnall, M., ed. Charters and Custumals of the Abbey of Holy Trinity Caen.
E.Z. Tabuteau, 589:Jul84-631
Chibnall, M. The World of Orderic Vitalis.
R.H.C. Davis, 617(TLS):8Feb85-152
Chicago, J. The Birth Project.
J. Stein, 441:15Sep85-31
"Chicago Architects Design."
J.F. Block, 658:Summer/Autumn84-219
"The Chicago Manual of Style." (13th ed)
N.A. Blumenstock, 293(JASt):May84-509
G. Trett, 536:Vol6-201
Chiclet, F. and S.D. La Tour. Les Français des Français.
J.C. Walz, 207(FR):Apr85-767
Chieger, B. and P. Sullivan. Inside Golf.
P-L. Adams, 61:Sep85-115
Chiellino, C. Italien. (Vol 1)
C. Dipper, 72:Band221Heft1-234
Ch'ien Mu. Traditional Government in Imperial China.
S. Gray, 293(JASt):May84-511
dalla Chiesa, N. Delitto imperfetto.
C. Duggan, 617(TLS):2Aug85-846
Child, L.M. Lydia Maria Child: Selected Letters, 1817-1880.* (M. Meltzer, P.G. Holland and F. Krasno, eds) The Collected Correspondence of Lydia Maria Child, 1817-1880. (P.G. Holland, M. Meltzer and F. Krasno, eds)
C.L. Karcher, 357:Spring85-19
"Children's Literature."* (Vols 8 and 9) (F. Butler, ed)
W. Keutsch, 38:Band102Heft1/2-273
Childress, J.F. Moral Responsibility in Conflicts.*
N. Dower, 518:Jul84-186
Childs, B.S. The New Testament as Canon.
E.P. Sanders, 617(TLS):13Dec85-1431

Childs, D. The GDR.*
R. Smith, 575(SEER):Apr84-310
Childs, J. Armies and Warfare in Europe, 1648-1789.*
R.A. Doughty, 173(ECS):Fall84-81
Chilton, C.W. Early Hull Printers and Booksellers.
E.A. Swaim, 517(PBSA):Vol78No2-245
Chilver, G.E.F., with G.B. Townend, eds. A Historical Commentary on Tacitus' Histories IV and V.
M. Crawford, 617(TLS):30Aug85-957
"China: Facts and Figures Annual, Vol 4." (J.L. Scherer, ed)
G.A. Hoston, 293(JASt):Nov83-148
"The Chinese Bronzes of Yunnan."
M. Sullivan, 39:Nov84-357
Ching, J. Confucianism and Christianity.
C.D. Orzech, 318(JAOS):Jul-Sep83-640
Chisholm, A. Faces of Hiroshima.
M. Howard, 617(TLS):9Aug85-869
Chisholm, D. and S.P. Sondrup, comps. Konkordanz zu den gedichten Conrad Ferdinand Meyers mit einem Versmass- und Reimschemaregister.
M. Burkhard, 301(JEGP):Jul84-414
Chisholm, R.M. The Foundations of Knowing.*
J. Levine, 482(PhR):Jul84-462
Chisholm, R.M. and W. Baumgartner - see Brentano, F.
Chisick, H. The Limits of Reform in the Enlightenment.
T.E. Kaiser, 173(ECS):Fall84-128
Chislett, A. Quiet in the Land.
P.K. Smith, 99:Jun/Jul84-40
Chissell, J. Clara Schumann.*
E. Brody, 415:Apr84-209
R. Taylor, 410(M&L):Oct84-378
Chittenden, J., ed. Donatus Ortigraphus, Ars grammatica.
M. Irvine, 589:Oct84-971
Chitty, S. Now to My Mother.
A. Chisholm, 617(TLS):14Jun85-662
V. Glendinning, 362:25Jul85-31
Chocheyras, J. Le Théâtre religieux en Savoie au XVIe siècle, avec des fragments inédits. Le Théâtre religieux en Dauphiné du Moyen Age au XVIIIe siècle (domaine français et provençal).
J. Beck, 545(RPh):Nov83-224
Chodorow, S. and C. Duggan - see Holtzmann, W.
Chojecka, E. Bayerische Bild-Enzyklopädie.
H. Boockmann, 683:Band47Heft4-559
Cholakian, R.C. The Moi in the Middle Distance.
G. Defaux, 210(FrF):Sep84-359
T. Thomson, 402(MLR):Oct84-932
Chollet, R. Balzac journaliste.
J.P. Gilroy, 446(NCFS):Winter-Spring85-158
B.L. Knapp, 207(FR):Apr85-732
Chomsky, N. Reflexiones sobre el lenguaje.
S. Saporta, 552(REH):Jan84-155
Chŏngju, S. - see under Sŏ Chŏngju.
Chopra, M.K. India and the Indian Ocean.
M. Shyam, 293(JASt):Aug84-778
"Choreography by George Balanchine."
M. Gurewitsch, 617(TLS):21Jun85-686
Chou, E. Mao Tse-tung.
B. Crozier, 176:Apr85-46

Choudhury, G.W. China in World Affairs.
  S.I. Levine, 293(JASt):May84-513
Chouillet, A-M. - see de Condillac, É.B.
Chouillet, A-M. and F. Moureau. Diction-
  naire des journalistes (1600-1789).
  (Supp 1)
  J. Voisine, 549(RLC):Jan-Mar84-112
Chouillet, J. and A-M. - see Diderot, D.
Chowder, K. Jadis.
  M. Engel, 441:21Apr85-13
  442(NY):13May85-146
Choyce, L. Fast Living.
  M. Fee, 102(CanL):Summer84-98
Chraibi, D. La Mère du printemps.
  K.Q. Warner, 207(FR):Oct84-154
Chraibi, D. Mother Comes of Age.
  S. El-Gabalawy, 268(IFR):Summer85-121
Chrétien de Troyes. Lancelot, or The
  Knight of the Cart (Le Chevalier de la
  Charrete).* (W.W. Kibler, ed and trans)
  H. Klüppelholz, 72:Band22lHeft2-425
Chrisman, M.U. Bibliography of Strasbourg
  Imprints, 1480-1599.
  L.V. Gerulaitis, 589:Jul84-634
Chrisman, M.U. Lay Culture, Learned Cul-
  ture.*
  H.J. Cohn, 366:Autumn84-265
  L.V. Gerulaitis, 589:Jul84-634
  M. Pegg, 354:Mar84-85
Christ, C.T. Victorian and Modern Poetics.
  C. Baldick, 617(TLS):25Jan85-80
Christensen, A.E. and others - see Feld-
  baek, O.
Christensen, A.S. Lactantius the His-
  torian.*
  O. Nicholson, 123:Vol34No2-322
Christensen, J. Coleridge's Blessed
  Machine of Language.*
  G. Dekker, 405(MP):Aug84-106
Christensen, S.A. and K. Rasmussen. Poli-
  tikens Ruslandshistorie. (Vol 1)
  D. Kirby, 575(SEER):Oct84-594
Christian, B. Black Feminist Criticism.
  P. Giddings, 441:30Jun85-21
Christian, S. Nicaragua.
  T.G. Ash, 441:28Jul85-1
Christian, W.A., Jr. Local Religion in
  Sixteenth-Century Spain.*
  D. Gifford, 86(BHS):Jan84-48
Christians, C.G. and J.M. Van Hook, eds.
  Jacques Ellul.
  D. Janicaud, 192(EP):Jan-Mar84-111
Christiansen, K. Gentile da Fabriano.*
  C. Eisler, 551(RenQ):Spring84-92
  D. Ekserdjian, 683:Band47Heft3-405
  H. Wohl, 54:Sep84-522
Christiansen, R. Prima Donna.*
  G. Walker, 441:9Jun85-13
Christianson, G.E. In the Presence of the
  Creator.
  B. Pippard, 617(TLS):13Sep85-992
Christie, A. Chinese Mythology. (new ed)
  M. Loewe, 617(TLS):11Jan85-47
Christie, A. First Act.
  A.M. Davidon, 441:13Jan85-22
Christie, G. Samplers and Stitches.
  C. Campbell, 614:Summer85-35
Christie, I.R. Stress and Stability in
  Late Eighteenth-Century Britain.
  W. Thomas, 617(TLS):19Apr85-443
Christie, I.R. Wars and Revolutions:
  Britain, 1760-1815.*
  M. Fitzpatrick, 83:Spring84-91

Christine de Pisan. The Book of the City
  of Ladies.* (E.J. Richards, trans)
  V. Callies, 77:Summer84-266
Christison, M.A. and S. Bassano. Look
  Who's Talking. (2nd ed)
  K.A. Mullen, 399(MLJ):Spring84-101
Christopher, G.B. Milton and the Science
  of the Saints.*
  G.M. Ridden, 366:Autumn84-266
  J. Wittreich, 401(MLQ):Dec83-425
Christopher, W. and others. American
  Hostages in Iran.
  H. Goodman, 441:14Jul85-23
Christy, J. The Price of Power.
  D. Traxel, 441:2Jun85-18
Christy, T.C. Uniformitarianism in Lin-
  guistics.
  R. Lass, 297(JL):Sep84-409
  I. Rauch, 350:Mar85-212
  R.H. Robins, 353:Vol22No4-561
Chu, C.C-H. A Reference Grammar of Man-
  darin Chinese for English Speakers.
  C-R. Huang, 350:Sep85-723
Chu Szu-te. Chung-kuo nung-ts'un ching-
  chi wen-t'i: Min-kuo erh-shih-nien chih
  san-shih nien-tai.
  R. Myers, 293(JASt):Nov83-149
Chu-Chang, M., ed. Asian- and Pacific-
  American Perspectives in Bilingual Educa-
  tion.
  W.K. Sergent, Jr., 399(MLJ):Winter84-
  388
Chuang, W. - see under Wei Chuang
"Chuang-tzu: The Seven Inner Chapters and
  Other Writings from the Book Chuang-
  tzu."* (A.C. Graham, trans)
  D.L. Hall, 485(PE&W):Jul84-329
Chuaqui, R.B. Axiomatic Set Theory.
  F.R. Drake, 316:Dec84-1422
Chubb, J. Patronage, Power and Poverty in
  Southern Italy.
  P. Allum, 278(IS):Vol139-152
Chudakov, A.P. Chekhov's Poetics.
  S.J. Rabinowitz, 574(SEEJ):Summer84-
  267
Chueca Goitia, F. Casas reales en monas-
  terios y conventos españoles.
  A. Bustamante García, 48:Jan-Mar84-123
Chukovsky, K.I. The Art of Translation.*
  (L.G. Leighton, ed and trans)
  M. Sendich, 558(RLJ):Winter-Spring84-
  321
Church, M. Structure and Theme.
  M. Magalaner, 395(MFS):Summer84-415
  295(JML):Nov84-386
Churcher, B. Molvig.
  G. Catalano, 381:Sep84-429
Churchill, K. Italy and English Litera-
  ture 1764-1930.*
  S. Albertazzi, 541(RES):May84-270
Churchill, W.S. and F.D. Roosevelt.
  Churchill and Roosevelt, The Complete
  Correspondence.* (W.F. Kimball, ed)
  J.K. Galbraith, 617(TLS):8Feb85-137
  M. Gilbert, 453(NYRB):14Feb85-33
  J. Lukacs, 442(NY):16Sep85-114
Churchland, P.M. Matter and Consciousness.
  P. Snowdon, 617(TLS):11Jan85-45
Chusid, M. - see Verdi, G.
Chute, C. The Beans of Egypt, Maine.
  (British title: The Beans.)
  B. Harris, 441:13Jan85-7
  V. Miner, 617(TLS):6Dec85-1406

Chvany, C.V. and R.D. Brecht, eds. Morpho-
syntax in Slavic.*
R. Schupbach, 104(CASS):Spring-
Summer84-155
Chwast, S. and S. Heller, eds. The Art of
New York.
T. Reese, 507:May/Jun84-110
Chylińska, T. - see Szymanowski, K.
Ciardi Dupre dal Poggetto, M.G. Il
Maestro del codice di San Giorgio e il
Cardinale Jacopo Stefaneschi.
R. Gibbs, 90:Oct84-640
Cibulka, H. Swantow.
K. Höpcke, 601(SuF):Jan-Feb84-165
Ciccone, A.A. The Comedy of Language.
C.N. Smith, 208(FS):Oct84-458
P.A. Wadsworth, 475:Vol 11No20-215
Cicero. Cicéron, "Correspondance." (Vol
8) (J. Beaujeu, ed)
E. Rawson, 123:Vol34No1-132
R.W., 555:Vol58fasc2-322
Cicero. M. Tulli Ciceronis Epistulae:
"Epistulae ad Familares."* (W.S. Watt,
ed)
P. Flobert, 555:Vol58fasc1-130
Cicero. M. Tulli Ciceronis Scripta Quae
Manserunt Omnia. (fasc 28) (P. Fedeli,
ed)
H.M. Hine, 123:Vol34No1-36
Cikovsky, N., Jr. - see Morse, S.F.B.
Cinotti, M. Michelangelo Merisi detto il
Caravaggio.
R.E. Spear, 90:Mar84-162
Cinzio, G.G. - see under Giraldi Cinzio, G.
Cioranescu, A. Le Masque et le visage.
J. Alter, 240(HR):Autumn84-537
P.A. Wadsworth, 207(FR):Feb85-449
Cipolla, C.M. The Monetary Policy of Four-
teenth-Century Florence.
M.M. Bullard, 551(RenQ):Autumn84-421
Cirici Narváez, J.R. Arquitectura isabel-
ina en Cádiz.
A. Bustamante García, 48:Jul-Sep84-332
Cirincione, J., ed. Central America and
the Western Alliance.
F. Lewis, 441:19May85-13
Ciucci, G. and others. The American City.
R.J. Findley, 505:Jul84-117
Cizek, E. Néron.
J.P. Sullivan, 124:Sep-Oct84-47
Clampitt, A. The Kingfisher.*
H. Lomas, 364:Aug/Sep84-141
Clampitt, A. What the Light Was Like.
A. Corn, 441:19May85-30
M. Kinzie, 29(APR):Nov/Dec85-7
Clanchy, M.T. England and Its Rulers,
1066-1272.
382(MAE):1984/2-338
Clancy, L. The Novels of Vladimir Nabokov.
D. Sexton, 617(TLS):14Jun85-675
Clancy, T. The Hunt for Red October.
T.J. Binyon, 617(TLS):15Nov85-1294
A. Krystal, 441:21Apr85-24
Clapham, A.R., T.G. Tutin and E.F. Warburg,
eds. Flora of the British Isles. (2nd
ed)
617(TLS):12Jul85-783
Clare, J. John Clare's Birds.* Clare's
Countryside. John Clare's Autobiograph-
ical Writings. (E. Robinson, ed of all)
G. Crossan, 591(SIR):Winter84-581

Clare, J. The Rural Muse.* (R.K.R. Thorn-
ton, ed) The Midsummer Cushion. (A.
Tibble and R.K.R. Thornton, eds) Birds
Nest. (A. Tibble, ed) John Clare:
Selected Poems. (E. Feinstein, ed)
G. Crossan, 591(SIR):Winter84-581
Clareson, T.D. Robert Silverberg.
M.E. Barth, 395(MFS):Summer84-346
G.K. Wolfe, 561(SFS):Jul84-211
Clareson, T.D. Robert Silverberg: A Prim-
ary and Secondary Bibliography.
G.K. Wolfe, 561(SFS):Jul84-211
Clarfield, G.H. and W.M. Wiecek. Nuclear
America.
J. Purcell, 441:21Jul85-23
"Clorin" - see under Alus, L.
Clark, A. Echoes of the Great War. (J.
Munson, ed)
E.S. Turner, 617(TLS):29Nov85-1346
Clark, A.M. Murder under Trust.*
T.H. Howard-Hill, 588(SSL):Vol 19-262
C. Hoy, 569(SR):Spring84-256
G.W. Williams, 579(SAQ):Summer84-361
Clark, D. Between Pulpit and Pew.
M.J. Lovelace, 292(JAF):Jan-Mar84-90
Clark, D. Dead Letter.
T.J.B., 617(TLS):1Mar85-227
Clark, D. Victor Grayson.
K.O. Morgan, 617(TLS):18Oct85-1165
Clark, E. Tamrart.
J. McCulloch, 441:5May85-25
Clark, I. Christ Revealed.*
M. Elsky, 301(JEGP):Jan84-117
M.L. Kessel, 568(SCN):Fall84-36
Clark, I. Limited Nuclear War.
L. Groarke, 529(QQ):Summer84-457
Clark, J. From a High Thin Wire.*
H. Barratt, 198:Spring84-116
R. Hatch, 102(CanL):Summer84-140
Clark, J.C.D. The Dynamics of Change.*
J. Black, 161(DUJ):Dec83-120
Clark, K. The Art of Humanism.
J. Pope-Hennessy, 39:Feb84-145
Clark, K. The Soviet Novel.*
V. Terras, 268(IFR):Summer85-116
Clark, K. and M. Holquist. Mikhail
Bakhtin.
G.S. Morson, 441:10Feb85-32
T. Todorov, 617(TLS):14Jun85-675
Clark, M. Modern Italy 1871-1982.
P.A. Ginsborg, 617(TLS):10May85-514
Clark, P., ed. The Transformation of
English Provincial Towns, 1600-1800.
F.M.L. Thompson, 617(TLS):15Mar85-297
Clark, R. The Japanese Company.
Shunichiro Umetani, 302:Vol20No2-225
Clark, R.L. From Athens to Jerusalem.
483:Oct84-560
Clark, R.P. The Basque Insurgents.
P. Preston, 617(TLS):27Dec85-1471
Clark, R.W. Einstein. (rev)
N. Ramsey, 441:13Jan85-22
Clark, R.W. Benjamin Franklin.*
R.A. Bosco, 27(AL):Mar84-107
Clark, R.W. The Survival of Charles Dar-
win.
G. Beer, 617(TLS):2Aug85-853
S. Boxer, 441:27Jan85-23
J. Howard, 362:30May85-29
R.C. Lewontin, 453(NYRB):10Oct85-18
442(NY):8Jul85-73
Clark, R.W. Works of Man.
D. Murray, 441:27Oct85-41

Clark, S. The Elizabethan Pamphleteers.*
V. Thomas, 506(PSt):Sep84-187
Clark, S.R.L. Aristotle's Man.
S.A.H., 185:Jan85-396
Clark, S.R.L. From Athens to Jerusalem.
D.Z. Phillips, 617(TLS):25Jan85-98
Clark, S.R.L. The Nature of the Beast.*
M-C. Geach, 483:Apr84-275
Clark, T.J. The Painting of Modern Life.
M. Berger, 62:May85-2
F. Cachin, 453(NYRB):30May85-24
R. Shiff, 441:3Mar85-16
E. Weber, 617(TLS):9Aug85-882
Clark, V.A., M. Hodson and C. Neiman, eds.
The Legend of Maya Deren.
E. Stein, 441:29Sep85-47
Clark, W.W., with R. King. Courtauld
Institute Illustration Archives. (Com-
panion Text I: Laon Cathedral; Architec-
ture, I.)
N.C., 90:Sep84-584
Clarke, D.M. Descartes' Philosophy of
Science.
H.A.S. Schankula, 518:Oct84-197
Clarke, D.V., T.G. Gowie and A. Foxon.
Symbols of Power at the Time of Stone-
henge.
C. Chippindale, 617(TLS):25Oct85-1215
Clarke, F. Hospital at Home.
D. Widgery, 362:24Jan85-26
Clarke, F.R.C. Healey Willan.
C. Morey, 627(UTQ):Summer84-511
Clarke, G. Letter from a Far Country.*
J. Saunders, 565:Spring84-55
Clarke, H. The Archaeology of Medieval
England.
C. Thomas, 176:Jan85-50
Clarke, H. Homer's Readers.
O. Taplin, 123:Vol34No2-307
Clarke, J.W. American Assassins.
G.S. Smith, 529(QQ):Autumn84-728
Clarke, M.A. and J. Handscombe, eds. On
TESOL '82.
D.P. Harris, 399(MLJ):Spring84-100
Clarke, P. and J.S. Gregory, eds. Western
Reports on the Taiping.
R.N. Weiss, 293(JASt):Feb84-311
Clarke, R. and R. Swift, eds. Ties that
Bind.
D. Powell, 298:Winter84/85-130
Clarke, R.A. and D.J.I. Matko. Soviet
Economic Facts, 1917-81. (2nd ed)
A.H. Smith, 575(SEER):Apr84-317
Clarke, S. North-West River (Sheshātshīt)
Montagnais.
W. Cowan, 269(IJAL):Apr84-247
D.H. Pentland, 320(CJL):Spring84-88
Clarkson, S. Canada and the Reagan Chal-
lenge.
J.J. Sokolsky, 529(QQ):Spring84-182
Clarson-Leach, R. Berlioz.
J. Methuen-Campbell, 415:Apr84-211
Claster, J.N. The Medieval Experience,
300-1400.
W. Goffart, 589:Apr84-470
Claudel, P. and J. Rivière. Correspon-
dance 1907-1924. (A. Anglès and P.
de Gaulmyn, eds)
P. McCarthy, 617(TLS):4Jan85-16
Claus, D.B. Toward the Soul.*
T. Fleming, 121(CJ):Dec84/Jan85-165
R. Renehan, 122:Oct84-327

Clauss, M. Sparta.
P. Cartledge, 123:Vol34No2-344
Clay, C.G.A. Economic Expansion and
Social Change.
K. Wrightson, 617(TLS):19Apr85-444
Clay, D. Lucretius and Epicurus.
E. Asmis, 319:Jul85-424
Clay, H. The Papers of Henry Clay. (Vol
7) (R. Seager 2d, ed)
639(VQR):Winter84-12
Clay, J. Culbertson.
A. Massie, 362:19/26Dec85-54
P. Swinnerton-Dyer, 617(TLS):20Dec85-
1406
Clay, J.S. The Wrath of Athena.*
N. Austin, 124:Nov-Dec84-127
Clayre, A. The Heart of the Dragon.*
J.S. Major, 441:26May85-14
Clayton, B. Forgotten Prophet.
R.W. Fox, 441:13Jan85-12
Cleary, T.R. Henry Fielding, Political
Writer.
W.A. Speck, 566:Spring85-184
Cleaves, F.W., ed and trans. The Secret
History of the Mongols. (Vol 1)
W. Heissig, 244(HJAS):Dec84-587
J.R. Krueger, 293(JASt):May84-514
Clecak, P. America's Quest for the Ideal
Self.*
M.D. Clark, 396(ModA):Spring/Summer84-
291
S. Pinsker, 219(GaR):Spring84-189
Cleere, H., ed. Approaches to the Archae-
ological Heritage.
C. Thomas, 176:Jan85-48
Clegg, H.A. A History of British Trade
Unions Since 1889. (Vol 2)
R. McKibbin, 617(TLS):18Oct85-1164
Clegg, J. John Ruskin.
D. Gervais, 97(CQ):Vol 13No2-178
Clegg, J. Ruskin and Venice.
P. Conner, 59:Dec84-498
K.O. Garrigan, 637(VS):Spring84-365
Cleland, J. Memoirs of a Woman of Plea-
sure. (P. Sabor, ed) Fanny Hill. (P.
Wagner, ed)
P. Rogers, 617(TLS):27Sep85-1066
Clément, C. The Lives and Legends of
Jacques Lacan.
R. Jackson, 219(GaR):Fall84-645
Clements, G.N. and S.J. Keyser. CV Phon-
olgy.
J.T. Jensen, 320(CJL):Fall84-194
Clements, K. Henry Lamb.
J. Darracott, 617(TLS):15Nov85-1284
D. Wright, 362:11Apr85-24
Clements, P. and I. Grundy, eds. Virginia
Woolf.*
J. Guiguet, 189(EA):Jan-Mar85-95
Clémessy, N. Emilia Pardo Bazán como nov-
elista (de la teoría a la práctica).
C. De Coster, 240(HR):Winter84-99
M. Lentzen, 547(RF):Band96Heft1/2-217
Clemoes, P., ed. Anglo-Saxon England.
(Vols 4 and 5)
G. Kotzor, 38:Band102Heft3/4-511
Clemoes, P., ed. Anglo-Saxon England.*
(Vols 6-8)
J.E. Cross, 447(N&Q):Dec83-529
G. Kotzor, 38:Band102Heft3/4-511

Clemoes, P., ed. Anglo-Saxon England.*
(Vol 9)
  J.E. Cross, 447(N&Q):Dec83-529
  G. Kotzor, 38:Band102Heft3/4-511
  J.D. Pheifer, 541(RES):Aug84-343
  P.E. Szarmach, 402(MLR):Oct84-891
Clemoes, P., ed. Anglo-Saxon England.*
(Vol 10)
  J.E. Cross, 447(N&Q):Dec83-529
  T.F. Hoad, 541(RES):Aug84-345
  G. Kotzor, 38:Band102Heft3/4-511
  E.G. Stanley, 72:Band221Heft1-163
  B. Yorke, 366:Spring84-117
Clemoes, P., ed. Anglo-Saxon England.*
(Vol 11)
  J.E. Cross, 447(N&Q):Dec83-529
  C. Gauvin, 189(EA):Jul-Sep85-313
  G. Kotzor, 38:Band102Heft3/4-511
  E.G. Stanley, 72:Band221Heft2-363
Clerc, C., ed. Approaches to "Gravity's
Rainbow."*
  S. Fogel, 106:Winter84-487
Cleveland, H. The Knowledge Executive.
  L.S. Ritter, 441:8Sep85-25
Clifford, D.K., Jr. and R.E. Cavanagh.
The Winning Performance.
  A. Sloan, 441:20Oct85-50
Clifford, J.L. - see Smollett, T.
Clifford, P. Marie de France: "Lais."
  G.S. Burgess, 208(FS):Oct84-443
  N.J. Lacy, 207(FR):Feb85-443
Clifton, T. Music as Heard.*
  F. Sparshott, 415:Mar84-153
  R. Swift, 451:Fall84-164
Clifton, T. and C. Leroy. God Cried.
  R. Jean and E. Isaac, 390:Aug/Sep84-45
Clifton-Taylor, A. and A.S. Ireson. Eng-
lish Stone Building.*
  P. Gibson, 46:Mar84-57
Clinard, M.B. Corporate Ethics and Crime.
  T.D., 185:Apr85-789
Clinton, C. The Plantation Mistress.*
  J. Lewis, 656(WMQ):Apr84-327
Clinton, D., T. Montag and C.W. Truesdale,
eds. A Geopoetics Landmark.
  J. Matthias, 598(SoR):Winter85-183
Clissold, S. Djilas.
  E. Barker, 575(SEER):Jul84-462
Clitheroe, F. - see Nouveau, G.
Clive, N. A Greek Experience 1943-1948.
  R. Clogg, 617(TLS):31May85-610
  D. Hunt, 362:27Jun85-29
Cloake, J. Templer.
  J. Grigg, 362:27Jun85-28
  H. Toye, 617(TLS):20Sep85-1042
Clogg, R., ed. Greece in the 1980s.
  R.J. Crampton, 575(SEER):Oct84-627
Clopper, L.M., ed. Records of Early
English Drama: Chester.*
  W. Weiss, 38:Band102Heft3/4-535
Clouscard, M. La bête sauvage.
  J-M. Gabaude, 542:Apr-Jun84-243
Clover, C.J. The Medieval Saga.*
  G. Clark, 222(GR):Fall84-157
  M.E. Kalinke, 402(MLR):Oct84-996
  P. Skårup, 301(JEGP):Jan84-103
  382(MAE):1984/2-341
Clubb, L.G. - see Della Porta, G.
Clubb, O. KAL Flight 007.
  P. Taubman, 441:21Apr85-7
Clubbe, J. Byron's Natural Man.
  E. Frykman, 571(ScLJ):Autumn84-19

Clubbe, J. and E. Giddey. Byron et la
Suisse.
  F.L. Beaty, 340(KSJ):Vol33-210
Clubbe, J. and E.J. Lovell, Jr. English
Romanticism.
  P. Magnuson, 661(WC):Summer84-134
Clutterbuck, R. Conflict and Violence in
Singapore and Malaysia.
  H. Toye, 617(TLS):20Sep85-1042
Clüver, C. Thornton Wilder und André
Obey.*
  W.D. Howarth, 208(FS):Oct84-492
Cluysenaar, A. and S. Hewat. Double
Helix.*
  R. Pybus, 565:Winter83/84-68
Clyne, M. Multilingual Australia.
  J. Williams, 355(LSoc):Jun84-275
Coad, J. Historic Architecture of the
Royal Navy.
  J.M. Richards, 46:May84-86
Coakley, J.F. - see Robinson, J.A.T.
Coates, J. The Semantics of the Modal Aux-
iliaries.
  L. Hermerén, 596(SL):Vol38No2-170
  A. Houston, 355(LSoc):Jun84-276
  M.R. Perkins, 297(JL):Sep84-384
  P. Westney, 257(IRAL):Aug84-229
Coates, J. and M. Kilian. Heavy Losses.
  H.G. Summers, Jr., 441:15Sep85-11
Coates, P. The Realist Fantasy.
  295(JML):Nov84-386
Coates, P. The Story of the Lost Reflec-
tion.
  P. Brunette, 441:20Oct85-27
Coates, W.H., A.S. Young and V.F. Snow,
eds. The Private Journals of the Long
Parliament 3 January to 5 March 1642.
  P. Christianson, 529(QQ):Autumn84-635
Cobarrubias, J. and J.A. Fishman, eds.
Progress in Language Planning.
  A. Cumming, 320(CJL):Fall84-188
Cobb, C.W. Lorca's "Romancero Gitano."
  P.H. Dust, 238:May84-307
Cobb, E.L. No Ceasefires.
  R.J. Margolis, 441:3Feb85-14
Cobb, R. A Classical Education.
  B. Bainbridge, 617(TLS):26Apr85-458
  P.N. Furbank, 362:25Apr85-20
Cobb, R. French and Germans, Germans and
French.
  M. Burns, 31(ASch):Summer84-425
  B.T. Cooper, 207(FR):Dec84-324
Cobb, R. People and Places.
  A. Watkins, 362:14Nov85-34
Cobb, R. Promenades.
  L. Wylie, 131(CL):Spring84-188
Cobb, R. Les Tours de France de Monsieur
Cobb.
  J-F. Fourny, 207(FR):Feb85-480
Cobbett, W. Cobbett's Tour in Scotland.
  (D. Green, ed)
  J. Grimond, 364:Aug/Sep84-104
  P.H. Scott, 571(ScLJ):Autumn84-14
Cobbett, W. A Grammar of the English Lan-
guage.
  617(TLS):8Mar85-271
Cobbett, W. A Grammar of the English Lan-
guage. (C.C. Nickerson and J.W. Osborne,
eds)
  J. Lavédrine, 189(EA):Jul-Sep85-306
Coben, L.A. and D.C. Ferster. Japanese
Cloisonné.*
  D. Waterhouse, 293(JASt):Nov83-158

71

Coburn, A. Sweetheart.
N. Callendar, 441:24Nov85-43
Cochran, B. Welfare Capitalism — And
After.
639(VQR):Summer84-95
Cochrane, E. Historians and Historio-
graphy in the Italian Renaissance.*
J.K. Hyde, 366:Spring84-118
D.R. Woolf, 529(QQ):Autumn84-524
Cochrane, J. The One-Room School in
Canada.
J.M. Zezulka, 102(CanL):Summer84-94
Cock, V. Dressmaking Simplified.
E. Hoffman, 614:Summer85-23
Cockburn, C. Beat the Devil. Ballan-
tyne's Folly.
J.K.L. Walker, 617(TLS):29Nov85-1371
Cockburn, P. Figure of Eight.
D. Murphy, 617(TLS):30Aug85-943
A. Quinton, 362:15Aug85-27
Cocke, R. Veronese's Drawings.
F. Ames-Lewis, 617(TLS):22Mar85-314
Cocking, J.M. Proust.*
V.E. Graham, 627(UTQ):Fall83-124
L.B. Price, 207(FR):Feb85-458
Cocks, A.S. - see "The V and A Album 3"
Cocks, A.S. and C. Truman. The Thyssen-
Bornemisza Collection.*
K. Snowman, 39:Sep84-216
Cocks, G. Psychotherapy in the Third
Reich.
S. Bloch, 617(TLS):4Oct85-1109
R.J. Lifton, 441:27Jan85-1
F. Stern, 453(NYRB):19Dec85-48
Cockshut, A.O.J. The Art of Autobiography
in 19th and 20th Century England.*
A. Broyard, 441:27Jan85-25
442(NY):11Mar85-137
"Jean Cocteau and the French Scene."
H. Peyre, 441:13Jan85-13
"The Codex Magliabechiano."* (Vol 1 ed by
Z. Nuttall; Vol 2 ed and trans by E.H.
Boone)
G. Brotherston, 617(TLS):29Mar85-361
Cody, L. Stalker.*
T.J. Binyon, 617(TLS):11Jan85-42
N. Callendar, 441:24Mar85-29
Coe, B. Jacques-Henri Lartigue.
A.J. Stirling, 324:Jul85-578
Coe, R.N. When the Grass Was Taller.
R. Dinnage, 617(TLS):2Aug85-844
Coetzee, J.M. Life and Times of Michael
K.*
D. Flower, 249(HudR):Summer84-313
C. Rooke, 376:Oct84-119
Coffee, J.M. Faulkner's Un-Christlike
Christians.
295(JML):Nov84-435
Coffey, M.P. Fitting In.
L.A. Kupetzky, 399(MLJ):Spring84-102
Cogan, M. The Human Thing.*
V. Hunter, 125:Fall83-90
Cogan, R. New Images of Musical Sound.
B. Pippard, 617(TLS):23Aug85-931
Coggeshall, R. Traffic, With Ghosts.
J. Graham, 441:10Feb85-30
D.C. Hill, 110:Winter85-103
Cogswell, F. Pearls.
G.V. Downes, 102(CanL):Autumn84-153
Cogswell, F. - see Nelligan, E.
Cohen, A. Jewish Life under Islam.*
L. Rosen, 617(TLS):7Jun85-648

Cohen, A.A. An Admirable Woman.
L. Elkin, 287:Jan84-24
D. Steiner, 617(TLS):15Mar85-283
Cohen, B.L. Before It's Too Late.
T.C. Holyoke, 42(AR):Summer84-378
Cohen, D. Theft in Athenian Law.
D.M. MacDowell, 123:Vol34No2-229
Cohen, D.S. The Folklore and Folklife of
New Jersey.
G. Carey, 650(WF):Oct84-276
Cohen, G.A., ed. The Learning Traveler.
(Vols 1 and 2)
R. Neff, 399(MLJ):Spring84-61
Cohen, G.L. Origin of the Term "Shyster."
S.M. Embleton, 350:Dec85-924
S. Steinmetz, 35(AS):Winter84-367
Cohen, H.R. Les Gravures musicales dans
"L'Illustration."
H. Macdonald, 617(TLS):8Feb85-141
Cohen, I.B. Revolution in Science.
J. Lederberg, 441:21Apr85-29
D. Papineau, 617(TLS):13Sep85-991
Cohen, J. and J. Rogers. On Democracy.
G. Dworkin, 482(PhR):Oct84-623
Cohen, J.R. Charles Dickens and His
Original Illustrators.
N. Pickwoad, 541(RES):May84-272
Cohen, L. Book of Mercy.
S.S., 376:Jun84-147
Cohen, M., ed. Ronald Dworkin and Con-
temporary Jurisprudence.*
C. Silver, 185:Jan85-356
Cohen, M. Sensible Words.
K. Reich, 38:Band102Heft1/2-158
Cohen, M. The Spanish Doctor.
F. Davey, 99:Jan85-36
D. Levenberg, 441:12May85-18
Cohen, M. and R. Copeland, eds. What is
Dance?
W.J. Earle, 290(JAAC):Fall84-104
Cohen, N. Long Steel Rail.*
C.A. La Londe, 440:Winter-Spring84-113
Cohen, N.W. Encounter with Emancipation.
J.D. Sarna, 129:Sep85-72
Cohen, P.C. A Calculating People.
R.N. Lokken, 656(WMQ):Jan84-158
Cohen, R. Theatre.
P.A. Davis, 615(TJ):Dec82-562
Cohen, R. - see Lambert, R-R.
Cohen, S. English Zionists and British
Jews.
P. Williamson, 161(DUJ):Dec83-125
Cohen, S.B., ed. From Hester Street to
Hollywood.
L.D. Friedman, 651(WHR):Summer84-172
M. Shapiro, 130:Winter84/85-380
R. Sklott, 615(TJ):May84-284
Cohen, S.F., ed. An End to Silence.*
S.L. Wolchik, 104(CASS):Fall84-326
Cohen, S.F. Rethinking the Soviet Exper-
ience.
R. Lowenthal, 441:3Feb85-10
H. Shukman, 617(TLS):13Sep85-1010
Cohen, S.F. Sovieticus.
J. Haslam, 441:29Sep85-28
442(NY):21Oct85-150
Cohen, W.S. and G. Hart. The Double Man.
F.X. Clines, 441:5May85-24
442(NY):12Aug85-86
Cohn, A. Recorded Classical Music.
O. Luening, 414(MusQ):Winter84-152

Cohn, A.M. and K.K. Collins. The Cumu-
lated Dickens Checklist 1970-1979.
L. Hartveit, 179(ES):Jun84-225
S. Monod, 189(EA):Oct-Dec85-470
Cohn, H. Human Rights in Jewish Law.
J.G.H., 185:Jul85-986
Cohn, N. Démonolâtrie et sorcellerie au
Moyen Age.
F. Azouvi, 192(EP):Jan-Mar84-109
Cohn, R. Just Play.*
E. Brater, 299:Autumn82-147
Cohn, R. - see Beckett, S.
Coirault, Y. - see Duc de Saint-Simon
Coke, G. In Search of James Giles.
J. Mallet, 90:Nov84-705
Coke, T. Vice Chamberlain Coke's Theatri-
cal Papers, 1706-1715.* (J. Milhous and
R.D. Hume, eds)
K.A. Burnim, 566:Spring85-194
B.S. Hammond, 541(RES):Nov84-545
Coke-Enguídanos, M. Word and Work in the
Poetry of Juan Ramón Jiménez.
T.J. Rogers, 238:Mar84-145
Coker, A. The Craft of Straw Decoration.
L. Stearns, 614:Summer85-22
Coker, C. The Other David.
N. Callendar, 441:17Mar85-39
Colace, P.R. Choerili Samii Reliquiae.
A.H.M. Kessels, 394:Vol37fascl/2-173
Colacurcio, M.J. The Province of Piety.
A. Delbanco, 676(YR):Winter85-276
D. Levin, 165(EAL):Fall85-164
M. Seymour, 617(TLS):15Feb85-177
Colaiaco, J.A. James Fitzjames Stephen
and the Crisis of Victorian Thought.
R.J. Halliday, 637(VS):Summer84-514
Colander, P. Hugh Hefner's First Funeral
and Other True Tales of Love and Death
in Chicago.
J. Austin, 441:4Aug85-17
Colbert, F. Le Marché québécois du thé-
âtre.
L.E. Doucette, 627(UTQ):Summer84-483
Colburn, D. and G.E. Pozzetta, eds.
Reform and Reformers in the Progressive
Era.
A. Finkel, 106:Winter84-465
Colburn, S.E. - see Sexton, A.
Colby, A. Samplers.
C. Campbell, 614:Summer85-34
Cole, B. The Renaissance Artist at Work.*
C. Gould, 39:May84-389
Cole, D. Captured Heritage.
S. Mantell, 441:3Nov85-27
Cole, D. Eleanor Raymond, Architect.
L.M. Soo, 576:Mar84-89
Cole, D.B. Martin Van Buren and the Ameri-
can Political System.
P. Marshall, 617(TLS):24May85-568
Cole, H.C. The "All's Well" Story from
Boccaccio to Shakespeare.*
J.C. Bondanella, 131(CL):Summer84-271
M. Charney, 301(JEGP):Jan84-115
Colegate, I. A Glimpse of Sion's Glory.
A. Bernays, 441:17Nov85-33
T. Fitton, 617(TLS):21Jun85-702
J. Mellors, 362:30May85-32
442(NY):16Dec85-168
Colegate, I. The Shooting Party.
P. Craig, 617(TLS):26Apr85-479
Colegate, I. Three Novels.
W. Lesser, 249(HudR):Autumn84-471

Coleiro, E. An Introduction to Vergil's
"Bucolics" with a Critical Edition of
the Text.*
R. Coleman, 123:Vol34No1-28
Coleman, A. Eça de Queirós and European
Realism.
E.M. Dias, 131(CL):Winter84-92
Coleman, A. and A. Hammond, eds. Poetry
and Drama, 1570-1700.*
W. Habicht, 570(SQ):Autumn84-364
E.A.J. Honigmann, 161(DUJ):Dec83-130
Coleman, B. The Later Adventures of Tom
Jones.
J. Seelye, 441:8Dec85-42
Coleman, D.G. An Illustrated Love "Can-
zoniere."
F. Lecercle, 535(RHL):Jan/Feb84-95
Coleman, E.H. Varieties of Aesthetic
Experience.
K. Jones, 89(BJA):Autumn84-361
Coleman, J. At Mother's Request.
J.A. Lukas, 441:16Jun85-3
Coleman, J. "Piers Plowman" and the "Mod-
erni."
J. Simpson, 382(MAE):1984/1-125
Coleman, P. Rousseau's Political Imagina-
tion.
J.H. Mason, 617(TLS):29Mar85-365
Coleman, S. Family Planning in Japanese
Society.
Kitō Hiroshi, 285(JapQ):Jul-Sep84-336
T.S. Lebra, 293(JASt):Aug84-755
Coleno, N. and U. Hucke - see Dejean, P.
Coleridge, N. Around the World in 78
Days.*
J. Austin, 441:5May85-25
Coleridge, S.T. The Collected Works of
Samuel Taylor Coleridge.* (Vol 7:
Biographia Literaria, or Biographical
Sketches of My Literary Life and
Opinions.) (J. Engell and W.J. Bate,
eds)
R.L. Brett, 148:Autumn84-83
L. Buell, 191(ELN):Dec84-74
E. Marks, 661(WC):Summer84-99
J.R. Watson, 506(PSt):Dec84-264
K.M. Wheeler, 184(EIC):Jan84-87
Coleridge, S.T. The Collected Works of
Samuel Taylor Coleridge.* (Vol 12:
Marginalia, Pt 1) (G. Whalley, ed)
G. Dekker, 402(MLR):Apr84-432
Coleridge, S.T. The Collected Works of
Samuel Taylor Coleridge.* (Vol 13:
Logic) (J.R.D. Jackson, ed)
R.S. Downie, 506(PSt):May84-72
P. Hamilton, 541(RES):May84-246
Colette. The Collected Stories of
Colette.* (R. Phelps, ed)
D. Rifkind, 31(ASch):Autumn84-549
639(VQR):Spring84-56
Colette. Oeuvres. (Vol 1) (C. Pichois,
ed)
R. Pouilliart, 356(LR):Nov84-331
Coli, D. Croce, Laterza e la cultura
europea.*
S. Woolf, 617(TLS):1Feb85-113
Coll, A.R. and A.C. Arend, eds. The Falk-
lands War.
M. Deas, 617(TLS):27Sep85-1050
Collazos, O. García Márquez: La soledad
y la gloria.
G.H. Bell-Villada, 454:Spring85-281

Conrad, B. Referring and Non-Referring
Phrases.
  B. Hlebec, 361:Oct/Nov84-234
  J. Lavêdrine, 189(EA):Oct-Dec85-452
Conrad, C. Strategic Organizational Com-
munication.
  C.L. Waagen, 583:Spring85-303
Conrad, J. The Collected Letters of
Joseph Conrad.* (Vol 1) (F.R. Karl
and L. Davies, eds)
  W.S. Dowden, 177(ELT):Vol27No4-335
  J. Halperin, 395(MFS):Summer84-352
  D.L. Higdon, 536:Vol6-157
  J. Kertzer, 49:Jul84-101
  D. Kramer, 301(JEGP):Oct84-573
  S. Monod, 189(EA):Jan-Mar85-94
  D.W. Rude, 136:Vol 17No1-37
  J.M. Szczypień, 497(PolR):Vol29No3-89
  N. Taylor, 575(SEER):Jul84-443
  C. Watts, 136:Vol 17No1-68
Conrad, J. Oeuvres. (Vol 1) (S. Monod,
ed)
  J.H. Stape, 136:Vol 17No2-156
Conrad, J. Under Western Eyes.* (J. Haw-
thorn, ed)
  D.L. Higdon, 136:Vol 17No2-151
Conrad, P. The Art of the City.*
  A. Corn, 249(HudR):Autumn84-525
  J. Morris, 176:Mar85-60
  A.B. Sandback, 62:Dec84-76
Conrad, P. The Everyman History of
English Literature.
  P. Rogers, 617(TLS):15Nov85-1279
Conrart, V. Lettres à Lorenzo Magalotti.*
(G. Berquet and J-P. Collinet, eds)
  F. Waquet, 535(RHL):Jul/Aug84-596
Conron, J. and C.A. Denne - see Cooper,
J.F.
Conroy, F. Midair.
  W.H. Pritchard, 441:22Sep85-12
Conry, Y., ed. De Darwin au darwinisme.
  P. Pellegrin, 542:Jan-Mar84-85
Consett, T. For God and Peter the Great.
(J. Cracraft, ed)
  M.J. Okenfuss, 104(CASS):Spring-
    Summer84-188
  W.F. Ryan, 575(SEER):Apr84-315
Constable, J. Constable with his Friends
in 1806. (G. Reynolds, ed)
  C.S. Rhyne, 380:Spring84-70
Constantine, D. Watching for Dolphins.*
  R. Pybus, 565:Autumn84-73
Constantine, K.C. Always a Body to Trade.
  T.J. Binyon, 617(TLS):11Oct85-1125
Constantine, K.C. Upon Some Midnights
Clear.
  N. Callendar, 441:27Oct85-24
Constantine, S. The Making of British
Colonial Development Policy 1914-1940.
  M. Crowder, 617(TLS):12Jul85-780
"Contemporary Artists." (2nd ed)
  J. Burr, 39:Mar84-223
Conti, A. La Miniatura Bolognese.
  R. Gibbs, 90:Oct84-638
Contreras, J.M.S. - see under Serrera
Contreras, J.M.
Conway, A. The Principles of the Most
Ancient and Modern Philosophy.* (P.
Lopston, ed)
  R.H. Popkin, 319:Apr85-260
Conway, J.F. The West.
  D. Gruending, 99:Jun/Jul84-40

Conway, R.E. Townswomen and Other Poems.
  M. Harry, 198:Summer84-117
  L. Rogers, 102(CanL):Winter83-153
Conyngham, W.J. The Modernization of
Soviet Industrial Management.*
  G. Gorelik, 104(CASS):Fall84-339
Cook, A. French Tragedy.*
  R. Parish, 208(FS):Jan84-58
Cook, A.J. The Privileged Playgoers of
Shakespeare's London, 1576-1642.*
  W. Habicht, 156(JDSh):Jahrbuch1984-254
  C. Hoy, 569(SR):Spring84-256
Cook, A.S. Myth and Language.*
  D. Halliburton, 131(CL):Spring84-165
Cook, B. Brecht in Exile.
  S.J. Whitfield, 385(MQR):Fall85-634
"Beryl Cook's New York."
  S.M. Halpern, 441:27Oct85-40
Cook, C. Joyce Cary.
  A. Maack, 447(N&Q):Jun83-265
Cook, C. - see "Pears Cyclopaedia"
Cook, D. Charles de Gaulle.*
  D. O'Connell, 207(FR):Mar85-617
Cook, D. Sunrising.*
  J. Mellors, 364:Apr/May84-135
Cook, D. Walter.
  V. Miner, 441:17Feb85-20
Cook, D. Winter Doves.
  W. Herbert, 441:23Jun85-20
Cook, E. and others, eds. Centre and Laby-
rinth.*
  G. Forst, 102(CanL):Autumn84-69
  S. Kane, 627(UTQ):Summer84-411
  D. O'Hara, 141:Winter84-91
Cook, G.M. Love En Route.
  L. Rogers, 102(CanL):Winter83-153
Cook, J. The Price of Freedom.
  B. Williams, 617(TLS):4Oct85-1083
Cook, M., ed. Contes révolutionnaires.*
  M. Delon, 535(RHL):Nov/Dec84-967
  P. Jimack, 402(MLR):Apr84-458
Cook, M.L. Monthly Murders.*
  J. Ballinger, 517(PBSA):Vol78No1-107
Cook, M.L. Mystery Fanfare.
  E.S. Lauterbach, 395(MFS):Summer84-379
Cook, R. Mindbend.
  D. Barry, 441:3Mar85-22
Cook, R.M. Clazomenian Sarcophagi.
  E.A. Moignard, 303(JoHS):Vol 104-256
Cook, R.T. The City Lights Pocket Poets
Series.
  T.A. Goldwasser, 517(PBSA):Vol78No2-
    257
Cook, S. Upperdown.
  T.J. Binyon, 617(TLS):12Jul85-777
Cooke, C. Russian Avant-Garde Art and
Architecture.
  639(VQR):Summer84-98
Cooke, D. Vindications.*
  S.M. Filler, 309:Vol5No4-374
Cooke, J.B. The Snowblind Moon.
  H. Benedict, 441:24Mar85-24
Cooke, J.E. Georges Bernanos.
  J.C. McLaren, 207(FR):Oct84-136
Cooke, M. Acts of Inclusion.
  M. Brown, 107(CRCL):Mar84-132
Cooke, M.G. Afro-American Literature in
the Twentieth Century.
  R.G. O'Meally, 441:7Apr85-15
  A. Rampersad, 617(TLS):14Jun85-674

76

Cooke, T.D., ed. The Present State of
Scholarship in Fourteenth-Century Lit-
erature.*
E.D. Blodgett, 589:Jul84-636
Cookson, C. The Bannaman Legacy.
A.P. Harris, 441:30Jun85-20
Cool Root, M. The King and Kingship in
Achaemenid Art.
H. Koch, 260(IF):Band89-318
Cooley, D., ed. Draft.*
R. Thacker, 649(WAL):May84-41
Cooley, D. Leaving. Fielding.
K. Gunnars, 137:Sep84-28
Cooley, D., ed. RePlacing.
G. Boire, 102(CanL):Summer84-111
R. Thacker, 649(WAL):May84-41
Coomer, J. Kentucky Love.
P-L. Adams, 61:Sep85-114
C. Ames, 441:21Jul85-22
Cooney, S. - see Bukowski, C. and A. Purdy
Cooney, S. and others, eds. Blast 3.
J. Symons, 441:10Feb85-29
Cooney, T.J. Telling Right From Wrong.
S. Hook, 441:30Jun85-13
Cooper, A., ed. D.H. Lawrence 1885-1930.
K. Brown, 617(TLS):18Oct85-1171
Cooper, B. Michel Foucault.
J. Rajchman, 529(QQ):Autumn84-623
Cooper, D. Theatre Year 1983.
P. Storfer, 157:No152-53
Cooper, D. and G. Tinterow. The Essential
Cubism 1907-1920.
J. Adamson, 59:Mar84-124
Cooper, H.R., Jr. Francè Prešeren.*
J.L. Conrad, 574(SEEJ):Spring84-132
Cooper, J. Dealing with Dealers.
C. Fox, 617(TLS):29Mar85-343
Cooper, J. Scaffolding.*
D. Davis, 362:3Jan85-26
Cooper, J. and others, eds. Extended Out-
looks.
J. Barnes, 639(VQR):Spring84-343
Cooper, J.F. Gleanings in Europe: England.
(J.P. Elliott, K.W. Staggs and R.D. Madi-
son, with others, eds) Wyandotté, or
The Hutted Knoll. (T. and M. Philbrick,
eds) The Last of the Mohicans. (J.A.
Sappenfield and E.N. Feltskog, eds)
E.S. Fussell, 165(EAL):Spring85-67
T. Martin, 534(RALS):Spring82-78
Cooper, J.F. Gleanings in Europe: France.
(T. Philbrick and C.A. Denne, eds)
Lionel Lincoln. (D.A. and L.B. Ringe,
eds)
E.S. Fussell, 165(EAL):Spring85-67
Cooper, J.F. The Pioneers, or The Sources
of the Susquehanna. (J.F. Beard, L.
Schachterle and K.M. Andersen, Jr., eds)
The Pathfinder, or The Inland Sea. (R.D.
Rust, ed) Gleanings in Europe: Switzer-
land. (R.F. Spiller and others, eds)
Gleanings in Europe: Italy. (J. Conron
and C.A. Denne, eds)
E.S. Fussell, 165(EAL):Spring85-67
B. Lawson-Peebles, 541(RES):May84-248
T. Martin, 534(RALS):Spring82-78
Cooper, J.M., Jr. The Warrior and the
Priest.*
N. Bliven, 442(NY):26Aug85-85
639(VQR):Spring84-50
Cooper, L., ed. La gran conquista de
Ultramar.
C.B. Fitch, 345(KRQ):Vol31No3-347

Cooper, M.H. To Ride a Tiger.
N. Callendar, 441:22Dec85-30
Cooper, N. The Diversity of Moral Think-
ing.
J.M. Day, 393(Mind):Jul84-440
Cooper, P.L. Signs and Symptoms.*
S. Weisenburger, 395(MFS):Summer84-331
Cooper, R.L., ed. Language Spread.*
J.H. Hill, 355(LSoc):Mar84-81
Cooper, R.M. The Literary Guide and Com-
panion to Southern England.
P. Ward-Green, 617(TLS):25Oct85-1217
Cooper-Clark, D., ed. Designs of Darkness.
T. Steele, 395(MFS):Summer84-423
Coote, S., ed. The Penguin Book of Homo-
sexual Verse.*
R.K. Martin, 491:Jun84-166
Coover, J. Musical Instrument Collections.
H. Schott, 410(M&L):Oct84-370
Coover, R. Gerald's Party.
C. Newman, 441:29Dec85-1
Cope, J. The Adversary Within.*
S. Roberts, 538(RAL):Fall84-471
Cope, J.I. Dramaturgy of the Daemonic.
J.L. Styan, 130:Winter84/85-373
Copeland, J.E., ed. New Directions in
Linguistics and Semiotics.
P.H. Salus, 350:Sep85-705
Copeland, R. and M. Cohen, eds. What Is
Dance?
J.R. Acocella, 151:Nov83-90
S.J. Cohen, 615(TJ):Oct84-442
Copetas, A.C. Metal Men.
D. Fong, 441:20Oct85-50
Copland, A. and V. Perlis. Copland: 1900
Through 1942.*
A. Berger, 453(NYRB):28Feb85-21
Copp, D. and S. Wendell, eds. Pornography
and Censorship.
B.B., 185:Oct84-195
Coppel, A. The Marburg Chronicles.
W. Smith, 441:7Jul85-16
Coppens, P. Passe.
P.G. Lewis, 207(FR):Oct84-155
Copper, J.F., F. Michael and Y-L. Wu.
Human Rights in Post-Mao China.
D. Fong, 441:23Jun85-21
de Coppet, L. and A. Jones. The Art
Dealers.
N. Moufarrege, 62:Dec84-78
Copplestone, T. The Macmillan Art
Informer.
N. Powell, 39:Jul84-77
Corbett, G.G. Hierarchies, Targets and
Controllers.
B. Comrie, 297(JL):Sep84-413
G. Gazdar, 350:Jun85-503
P. Sgall, 353:Vol22No5-756
Corbin, H. Face de Dieu, face de l'homme.
L'Homme et son ange.
A. Reix, 542:Apr-Jun84-254
Corbineau-Hoffmann, A. Marcel Proust.
H.W. Eirich, 343:Heft9/10-163
A. Henry, 72:Band221Heft2-459
Corbineau-Hoffmann, A. and A. Gier, eds.
Aspekte der Literatur des fin-de-siècle
in der Romania.
M. Schmeling, 547(RF):Band96Heft4-463
Corbo, V.C. Il Santo Sepolcro di Gerusa-
lemme.
R. Ousterhout, 576:Oct84-266
Cordelier, J. Chez l'Espérance.
R.J. Hartwig, 207(FR):Oct84-156

Cott, J., ed. Victorian Color Picture Books.
C. James, 441:15Sep85-24
Cotterill, R. The Cambridge Guide to the Material World.
G. Krist, 441:21Apr85-38
Cottingham, J. Rationalism.
S. Clark, 617(TLS):29Mar85-365
Cottino-Jones, M. Order from Chaos.
V. Kirkham, 276:Winter84-353
P.M. Price, 589:Apr84-387
Cotton, H. Documentary Letters of Recommendation in Latin from the Roman Empire.*
A.N. Sherwin-White, 313:Vol74-238
Cotton, J. The Storyville Portraits.*
S. O'Brien, 617(TLS):6Sep85-979
Cottrell, R.D. Sexuality/Textuality.*
C. Dickson, 207(FR):Dec84-283
S.J. Holyoake, 402(MLR):Jan84-188
Couch, J.A. and others. Una vez más.
L.A. Swisher, 238:May84-319
Coudrette. Le Roman de Mélusine ou Histoire de Lusignan.* (E. Roach, ed)
M.W. Morris, 589:Jul84-639
Couffignal, R. Le drame de l'Eden, le récit de la Genèse et sa fortune littéraire.
A. Dabezies, 549(RLC):Jul-Sep84-354
E.S. Shaffer, 208(FS):Jan84-108
Coughtry, J. The Notorious Triangle.
H.A. Gemery, 656(WMQ):Oct84-662
Coulanges, C. and F. Daniel. Un Coup d'oeil sur la France.
N. Aronson, 399(MLJ):Spring84-73
Coulet, H. and M. Gilot. Marivaux, Le Prince travesti et Le Triomphe de l'Amour.
C. Jordens, 356(LR):Feb/May84-130
Coulet du Gard, R. Dictionary of Spanish Place Names in the U.S.A.
K.B. Harder, 424:Dec84-459
Coulmas, F., ed. Conversational Routine.
D. Haggo and K. Kuiper, 353:Vol21No3-531
Coulmas, F., ed. A Festschrift for Native Speaker.
D. Kilby, 361:Oct/Nov84-245
Coulson, A. Tanzania.*
C. Leys, 529(QQ):Spring84-217
Coult, T. and B. Kershaw, eds. Engineers of the Imagination.
R.F. Gross, 615(TJ):Dec84-550
Coulter, H.L. and B.L. Fisher. DPT.
H. Schwartz, 441:3Feb85-19
Coulthard, M. and M. Montgomery, eds. Studies in Discourse Analysis.*
T.J. Taylor, 541(RES):Aug84-342
Countryman, E. A People in Revolution.*
A.G. Condon, 106:Fall84-287
Courdy, J-C. The Japanese.*
639(VQR):Autumn84-136
Coursen, H.R. The Leasing Out of England.
H.A. Kelly, 405(MP):Nov84-204
Court, A. Puck of the Droms.
D.H. Greene, 441:17Nov85-32
Courtney, C.P. A Bibliography of Editions of the Writings of Benjamin Constant to 1833.*
A. Anninger, 517(PBSA):Vol78No4-512
J-D. Candaux, 535(RIIL):Jul/Aug84-629
N. King, 402(MLR):Oct84-941

Courtney, C.P. Isabelle de Charrière [Belle de Zuylen].
J-D. Candaux, 547(RF):Band96Heft4-476
J. Vercruysse, 535(RHL):Sep/Oct84-806
Courtney, R. Longman Dictionary of Phrasal Verbs.
F. Chevillet, 189(EA):Jan-Mar85-77
Courtney, W.F. Young Charles Lamb, 1775-1802.*
J. Aaron, 339(KSMB):No35-90
J.R. Nabholtz, 340(KSJ):Vol33-234
F.V. Randel, 591(SIR):Fall84-413
Cousins, M. and A. Hussain. Michel Foucault.
A. Sheridan, 617(TLS):5Apr85-389
Coussy, D. and others, eds. Anthologie Critique de la Littérature Africaine Anglophone.
J. Conteh-Morgan, 268(IFR):Winter85-53
Couturier, M., ed. Representation and Performance in Postmodern Fiction.
P.S. Nichols, 395(MFS):Winter84-854
Couzyn, J., ed. The Bloodaxe Book of Contemporary Women Poets.
M. Hofmann, 617(TLS):29Nov85-1370
Couzyn, J. Life by Drowning.
M. Hofmann, 617(TLS):29Nov85-1370
H. Kirkwood, 526:Autumn84-82
P. Stuewe, 529(QQ):Winter84-1013
R. Sullivan, 99:Jan85-34
Coverdale, J.F. The Basque Phase of Spain's First Carlist War.
F. Lannon, 617(TLS):6Sep85-985
Covino, M. The Off-Season.
K. Nunn, 441:27Oct85-40
Cowan, B. Exiled Waters.*
J.R. Reaver, 577(SHR):Summer84-264
Cowan, D.A. Language and Negation.
J.K. Swindler, 449:May84-355
Cowan, I.B. and D. Shaw, eds. The Renaissance and Reformation in Scotland.
T.F. Mayer, 539:May85-154
Cowan, J.C., ed. D.H. Lawrence.* (Vol 1)
J.B. Humma, 594:Spring84-111
Coward, D. Marivaux: "La Vie de Marianne and Le Paysan parvenu."
L.W. Lynch, 207(FR):Mar85-581
H. Mason, 208(FS):Jul84-341
Coward, N. The Collected Stories of Noel Coward.
J.R. Moore, 573(SSF):Fall84-409
Coward, R. Patriarchal Precedents.
I.S., 185:Oct84-181
Coward, R. and J. Ellis. Language and Materialism.
N. Bruss, 355(LSoc):Dec84-553
Cowart, D. Arches and Light.
L. Butts, 573(SSF):Spring84-165
L. Butts, 594:Fall84-347
R. Merrill, 27(AL):Oct84-450
R.A. Morace, 395(MFS):Winter84-845
R.A. Morace, 363(LitR):Summer85-617
295(JML):Nov84-445
Cowasjee, S. Suffer Little Children.
S. Gingell, 102(CanL):Summer84-129
Cowdrey, A.E. This Land, This South.
V.A. Kramer, 392:Fall84-497
Cowdrey, H.E.J. The Age of Abbot Desiderius.*
382(MAE):1984/2-338
Cowell, P. Women Poets in Pre-Revolutionary America 1650-1775.
J. Spencer, 447(N&Q):Jun83-276

Cowen, R.C., ed. Dramen des deutschen
Naturalismus.
  H-P. Bayerdörfer, 133:Band17Heft1/2-
  150
Cowhey, P.F. The Problems of Plenty.
  P. McDonald, 617(TLS):6Dec85-1392
Cowie, A.P. and R. Mackin. Oxford Diction-
ary of Current Idiomatic English. (Vol
1)
  W. Paprotté, 257(IRAL):Nov84-322
Cowie, A.P., R. Mackin and I.R. McCaig.
Oxford Dictionary of Current Idiomatic
English. (Vol 2)
  W. Paprotté, 257(IRAL):Nov84-322
Cowley, M. The Flower and the Leaf. (D.W.
Faulkner, ed)
  R.M. Adams, 441:10Feb85-16
Cowley, R.L.S. Marriage à-la-mode.*
  V. Carretta, 173(ECS):Spring85-456
Cowper, R. The Custodians.
  G. Jonas, 441:20Oct85-20
Cowper, W. William Cowper: Selected Poems.
(N. Rhodes, ed)
  J.H. Pittock, 83:Autumn84-249
Cowper, W. The Letters and Prose Writings
of William Cowper.* (Vol 2) (J. King
and C. Ryskamp, eds)
  P. Danchin, 179(ES):Feb84-80
Cowper, W. The Letters and Prose Writings
of William Cowper.* (Vol 3) (J. King
and C. Ryskamp, eds)
  D.H. Reiman, 88:Winter84/85-146
Cox, A. and A. Rockingham Pottery and
Porcelain 1745-1842.*
  G. Wills, 39:Apr84-306
Cox, B.J. and D.J. Anderson. Miguel Cov-
arrubias Caricatures.
  442(NY):11Mar85-137
Cox, D.R., ed. Sexuality and Victorian
Literature.
  G.B. Tennyson, 445(NCF):Dec84-363
Cox, E. Familiar Ground.
  B. Lowry, 441:10Mar85-33
Cox, M. M.R. James.
  J.C.T. Oates, 354:Jun84-179
  B.L. St. Armand, 573(SSF):Spring84-167
Cox, P. Biography in Late Antiquity.*
  D. Glew, 124:Sep-Oct84-57
Cox, R.G., ed. Thomas Hardy: The Critical
Heritage.
  S. Monod, 549(RLC):Jul-Sep84-357
Cox, S.D. "The Stranger Within Thee."*
  D. Worrall, 88:Summer84-31
Cox-Rearick, J. Dynasty and Destiny in
Medici Art.
  J. Russell, 441:2Jun85-15
Coyle, B. A Thought to be Rehearsed.
  F.C. Hoerner, Jr., 705:Fall84-114
Crabtree, L.V. Sweet Hollow.*
  T.D. Adams, 585(SoQ):Summer85-90
Cracraft, J. - see Consett, T.
Craddock, P.B. Young Edward Gibbon.*
  M. Baridon, 173(ECS):Fall84-141
  F. Doherty, 161(DUJ):Dec83-139
  J. Smitten, 125:Winter84-194
Craft, J.L. and R.E. Hustwit - see Bouwsma,
O.K.
Craft, R. Present Perspectives.
  H. Saal, 441:13Jan85-24
Craft, R. - see Stravinsky, I.
Crafts, N.F.R. British Economic Growth
during the Industrial Revolution.
  R. Floud, 617(TLS):19Jul85-794

Craig, C. Yeats, Eliot, Pound and the
Politics of Poetry.*
  H.M. Block, 651(WHR):Summer84-186
  F. Moramarco, 30:Winter84-86
  J. Olney, 569(SR):Summer84-451
  A. Rodway, 447(N&Q):Dec83-558
Craig, E.G. Craig on Theatre.* (J.M. Wal-
ton, ed)
  G. Playfair, 157:No152-52
  A. Rood, 615(TJ):Oct84-443
Craig, E.Q. Black Drama of the Federal
Theatre Era.*
  P. Sporn, 459:Vol8No2/3-193
  J.A. Williams, 536:Vol5-131
Craige, B.J., ed. Relativism in the Arts.
  F. Berenson, 89(BJA):Summer84-259
Craik, E.M., ed. Marriage and Property.
  M. Crawford, 617(TLS):26Jul85-814
Cramp, H.S. A Yeoman Farmer's Son.
  P. Horn, 617(TLS):16Aug85-909
Cramp, R. Corpus of Anglo-Saxon Stone
Sculpture in England. (Vol 1)
  R. Bruce-Mitford, 617(TLS):4Jan85-21
  R.J.B. Morris, 324:Sep85-735
Crampton, C. Canework. (24th ed)
  L. Stearns, 614:Spring85-18
Crampton, R.J. Bulgaria 1878-1918.
  J.D. Bell, 104(CASS):Winter84-504
Crane, H. Complete Poems. (B. Weber, ed)
  D. Dunn, 617(TLS):1Mar85-239
Crane, L. African Names. (J.E. Mohraz,
ed)
  R.M. Rennick, 424:Mar84-78
Crane, M. and M. Stofflet, eds. Corre-
spondence Art.
  G.M., 62:May85-5
Crane, R. and A. Running the Himalayas.
  J. Keay, 362:31Jan85-25
Crane, R.I. and N.G. Barrier, eds. Brit-
ish Imperial Policy in India and Sri
Lanka.
  R.J. Moore, 293(JASt):Nov83-179
Crane, S. Stephen Crane: Prose and Poetry.
(J.C. Levenson, ed)
  D.A.N. Jones, 362:4Apr85-26
Crane, S. The Red Badge of Courage.* (H.
Binder, ed)
  J. Katz, 27(AL):May84-280
  E. Solomon, 301(JEGP):Jan84-153
Cranston, M. Jean-Jacques.*
  P. Coleman, 207(FR):Apr85-730
  M. Jack, 173(ECS):Winter84/85-267
  M. Mudrick, 249(HudR):Spring84-105
  A. Rosenberg, 627(UTQ):Winter83/84-217
Cranston, M. and P. Mair, eds. Langage et
politique/Language and Politics.
  A. Boyer, 542:Jan-Mar84-99
Cranz, F.E. A Bibliography of Aristotle
Editions 1501-1600. (2nd ed) (C.B.
Schmitt, ed)
  P.F. Grendler, 539:Aug85-219
Crapanzano, V. Tuhami.
  R. Joseph, 567:Vol48No1/2-175
Crapanzano, V. Waiting.
  N. Ascherson, 453(NYRB):18Jul85-3
  J.M. Coetzee, 441:14Apr85-3
  C.C. O'Brien, 61:May85-100
  S. Watson, 617(TLS):16Aug85-895
Crase, D. The Revisionist.*
  F. Garber, 29(APR):Jan/Feb85-18

Craven, W.G. Giovanni Pico della Miran-
dola, "Symbol of His Age."*
  P.J.W. Miller, 551(RenQ):Summer84-233
  C. Trinkaus, 589:Jan84-133
Cravens, H., ed. Ideas in America's Cul-
tures.
  J. Tagg, 106:Winter84-451
Craw, H.A. - see Dussek, J.L.
Crawford, A. C.R. Ashbee.
  S. Gardiner, 362:21Nov85-31
  P. Thompson, 617(TLS):15Nov85-1283
Crawford, F.D. Mixing Memory and Desire.*
  W. Harmon, 577(SHR):Summer84-274
Crawford, F.D. H.M. Tomlinson.
  J. Tyler, 447(N&Q):Aug83-376
Crawford, J.M. Cocopa Texts.
  D.H., 355(LSoc):Jun84-279
Crawford, L. Ghost of a Chance.
  E. Pall, 441:28Jul85-18
Crawford, M. Lords of the Plain.
  M.S. Kaplan, 441:20Jan85-18
  442(NY):15Apr85-129
Crawford, M., ed. Sources for Ancient His-
tory.*
  S. Hornblower, 123:Vol34No2-241
Crawford, R.W., comp. In Art We Trust.
  D. Buck, 108:Fall84-119
Crawford, S.C. The Evolution of Hindu
Ethical Ideals. (2nd ed)
  A.B. Creel, 485(PE&W):Apr84-229
Crawford, T. Walter Scott.*
  B. Ruddick, 148:Winter84-91
Crawley, E. A House Divided.
  D. Rock, 617(TLS):2Aug85-847
Crawshaw, R.H. - see Dancourt, F.C.
Creamer, R.W. Stengel.*
  639(VQR):Autumn84-122
de Crébillon, P.J. Électre.* (J. Dunkley,
ed)
  H.G. Hall, 208(FS):Oct84-463
Creel, B.L. The Religious Poetry of Jorge
de Montemayor.*
  G. Sabat de Rivers, 547(RF):Band96
  Heft1/2-214
  C. Thompson, 86(BHS):Oct84-506
Creeley, R. The Collected Poems of Robert
Creeley 1945-1975.*
  S.I. Bellman, 649(WAL):Aug84-142
  R. Feld, 472:Fall/Winter84-95
  S.S., 376:Jun84-147
Creeley, R. Hello. Later.
  R. Feld, 472:Fall/Winter84-95
Creeley, R. Mirrors.*
  B. Bawer, 491:Sep84-345
  R. Feld, 472:Fall/Winter84-95
  S.S., 376:Jun84-147
  639(VQR):Spring84-62
Creighton, D.G. Jacques-François De Luc
of Geneva and His Friendship with Jean-
Jacques Rousseau.
  G. Adams, 173(ECS):Spring85-431
Cremona, I. Il tempo dell'art nouveau.
  N. Powell, 39:Dec84-440
Cremona, V. La poesia civile di Orazio.
  J. Perret, 555:Vol58fasc1-142
Crespo, A. - see Duque de Rivas
Cress, L.D. Citizens in Arms.*
  L. Kennett, 173(ECS):Spring85-440
  R.C. Stuart, 106:Summer84-159
Crevel, R. Babylon.
  C. Eshleman, 441:22Sep85-31

Crewe, J.V. Unredeemed Rhetoric.*
  D.A. Carroll, 125:Spring84-311
  M.W. Ferguson, 551(RenQ):Summer84-300
  P. Ramsey, 539:Aug85-223
Crews, J. The Clock of Moss. (C. Bergé,
ed)
  J.W. Clark, 649(WAL):Nov84-240
Crick, B. - see Orwell, G.
Crick, M. Scargill and the Miners.
  D. Macintyre, 617(TLS):1Mar85-220
Criscuolo, L. Bolli d'anfora greci e
romani.
  R.S. Bagnall, 24:Winter84-500
Crisp, J., comp. Jessie Fothergill 1851-
1891.
  J. Shattock, 402(MLR):Jul84-682
Critchley, J. Westminster Blues.
  R. Hattersley, 617(TLS):31May85-600
  A. Sherman, 362:23May85-28
Croft, P.J. - see Sidney, R.
Croiset Van Uchelen, A.R.A. Hellinga
Festschrift/Feestbundel/Mélanges.
  A.I. Doyle, 354:Mar84-76
de la Croix, F.P. - see under Pétis de la
Croix, F.
de la Croix, J. - see under Jean de la
Croix
Crompton, L. Byron and Greek Love.
  R. Jenkyns, 617(TLS):6Sep85-964
  B. Knox, 453(NYRB):19Dec85-3
Crone, A. Bridie Steen.
  P. Craig, 617(TLS):22Mar85-326
Croney, J. Drawing Figure Movement.
  90:Mar84-170
Cronin, A. Heritage Now.
  J.L. Schneider, 395(MFS):Summer84-359
Cronin, R. Shelley's Poetic Thoughts.*
  S. Hall, 577(SHR):Spring84-181
Cronon, W. Changes in the Land.*
  G.W. La Fantasie, 432(NEQ):Mar84-120
Crook, J.M. and C.A. Lennox-Boyd. Axel
Haig.
  J.S. Curl, 324:Dec84-71
  A. McIntyre, 46:Mar84-57
Cropper, E. The Ideal of Painting.
  H. Brigstocke, 617(TLS):1Mar85-228
Cros, E. Ideología y genética textual.
  T. Bubnova, 457(NRFH):Tomo32núm1-224
Crosland, M. Piaf.
  L. Haney, 441:24Nov85-9
Cross, A. Sweet Death, Kind Death.*
  T.J. Binyon, 617(TLS):15Feb85-179
Cross, A.G. The Tale of the Russian
Daughter and her Suffocated Lover.
  J. Sullivan, 402(MLR):Apr84-506
Cross, J.E. and T.D. Hill, eds. The
"Prose Solomon and Saturn" and "Adrian
and Ritheus."
  G. Russom, 589:Apr84-388
Cross, N. The Royal Literary Fund 1790-
1918.
  P-G. Boucé, 189(EA):Oct-Dec85-494
Cross, R.K. and J.T. McMillan - see
Stribling, T.S.
Cross, T. Painting the Warmth of the Sun.
  F. Spalding, 617(TLS):1Mar85-232
Crossley, C. Edgar Quinet (1803-1875).
  O.A. Haac, 446(NCFS):Summer-Fall84-227
  K. Wren, 402(MLR):Oct84-946
  B. Wright, 208(FS):Oct84-470
Crossley-Holland, K., ed and trans. The
Anglo-Saxon World.
  P.J. Lucas, 447(N&Q):Oct83-447

Crossley-Holland, K. Axe-Age, Wolf-Age.
A. Wawn, 617(TLS):10May85-530
Crossley-Holland, K. Time's Oriel.*
M. O'Neill, 493:Jan84-65
Crotty, K. Song and Action.
F.J. Nisetich, 24:Fall84-358
Crouan, K., ed. John Linnell.*
W. Vaughan, 59:Sep84-368
Croucher, T., comp. Early Music Discography.
J.R. Haefer, 589:Jan84-137
Crouwel, J.H. Chariots and Other Means of
Land Transport in Bronze Age Greece.
V. Hankey, 303(JoHS):Vol 104-246
Crouzet, F. The First Industrialists.
S. Pollard, 617(TLS):19Jul85-794
Crouzet, M. La Poétique de Stendhal.
C.J. Stivale, 446(NCFS):Summer-Fall84-
178
Crouzet, M. La "Vie de Henry Brulard" ou
l'Enfance de la révolte.
V. Brombert, 535(RHL):Jul/Aug84-634
Crow, C.M. Paul Valéry and the Poetry of
Voice.*
B. Ajac, 535(RHL):Sep/Oct84-814
K.R. Dutton, 67:May84-89
S. Winspur, 546(RR):May84-395
Crow, J. - see Chappuzeau, S.
Crow, J.A. and E. Dudley. El cuento.
(2nd ed)
J.A. Castañeda, 399(MLJ):Winter84-413
Crow, T.E. Painters and Public Life in
Eighteenth-Century Paris.
A. Brookner, 617(TLS):29Nov85-1348
Crowder, M., ed. The Cambridge History of
Africa. (Vol 8)
R. Robinson, 617(TLS):16Aug85-895
Crowley, E.T., ed. Acronyms, Initialisms
and Abbreviations Dictionary, 1983-84.
(8th ed)
K.B. Harder, 424:Mar84-90
Crown, P. Drawings by E.F. Burney in the
Huntington Collection.
380:Autumn84-331
Crowther, M.A. The Workhouse System 1834-
1929.
P. Dunkley, 637(VS):Autumn83-118
Crozier, B., D. Middleton and J. Murray-
Brown. This War Called Peace.
F. Barnes, 441:23Jun85-16
Crozier, L. The Weather.
S.S., 376:Jun84-147
Crozier, M. The Trouble with America.
J.B. Hehir, 441:27Jan85-26
I. Kristol, 617(TLS):6Dec85-1381
Cruickshank, D. A Guide to the Georgian
Buildings of Britain and Ireland.
E. McParland, 617(TLS):13Dec85-1424
Cruickshank, J. Pascal: "Pensées."
A.J. Krailsheimer, 208(FS):Oct84-459
Cruickshank, J. Variations on Catastro-
phe.*
T. Myers, 395(MFS):Spring84-165
Cruise, B. and M. Harton. Signor Far-
anta's Iron Theatre.
A. Demling, 585(SoQ):Summer84-86
Crum, M., comp. Catalogue of the Mendels-
sohn Papers in the Bodleian Library,
Oxford. (Vol 2)
R.L. Todd, 410(M&L):Oct84-363
Crumbach, K-H. Thelogie in kritischer
Öffentlichkeit.
A.J. Bucher, 342:Band75Heft1-122

Crummey, R.G. Aristocrats and Servitors.*
C.M. Foust, 104(CASS):Winter84-454
Crump, J. The Origins of Socialist
Thought in Japan.
F.G. Notehelfer, 293(JASt):Feb84-323
Crump, M. and M. Harris, eds. Searching
the Eighteenth Century.*
G. Barber, 354:Dec84-410
P.J. Korshin, 566:Autumn84-73
W.A. Speck, 83:Autumn84-272
Crumpacker, E. Seasonal Gifts from the
Kitchen.
W. and C. Cowen, 639(VQR):Spring84-68
Crunden, R.M. Ministers of Reform.*
A. Finkel, 106:Winter84-465
Crutch, D. - see Williams, S.H.
de la Cruz, R. Sainetes, I.* (J. Dowling,
ed)
G. Paolini, 238:Mar84-143
Cryle, P.M. The Thematics of Commitment.
J. Cruickshank, 617(TLS):20Sep85-1040
Csáth, G. The Magician's Garden and Other
Stories.
C. Gyorgyey, 390:Oct84-60
Cua, A.S. The Unity of Knowledge and
Action.*
L.A. Barth, 293(JASt):May84-515
J. Ching, 322(JHI):Jul-Sep84-476
D. Dahlstrom, 258:Dec84-442
Cubero, J.D. - see under Domínguez Cubero,
J.
"Cuckolds, Clerics and Countrymen."* · (J.
Du Val, trans; R. Eichmann, ed)
R.J. Pearcy, 589:Oct84-895
Cudjoe, S.R. Resistance and Caribbean Lit-
erature.*
J.J. Figueroa, 538(RAL):Spring84-118
A. Shucard, 125:Fall83-97
K. Williamson, 447(N&Q):Jun83-280
Cuénin, M. Le Duel sous l'Ancien Régime.
M-O. Sweetser, 475:Vol 11No20-225
Cuevas, C., ed. Fray Luis de León y la
escuela salmantina.
M. Durán, 240(HR):Autumn84-533
Culbertson, J.T. Consciousness.
P. Cam and C. Mortensen, 63:Dec84-420
Culhane, J. Walt Disney's "Fantasia."
J. Canemaker, 507:Mar/Apr84-104
Culhane, T. Russian.
A.K. Donchenko, 558(RLJ):Winter-
Spring84-282
Cullen, P. and T.P. Roche, Jr. - see
"Spenser Studies"
Culler, J. Barthes.*
P. Collier, 402(MLR):Apr84-467
D. Knight, 494:Vol5No4-831
G. Strickland, 97(CQ):Vol 13No2-164
Culler, J. Flaubert. Structuralist
Poetics. Saussure.
G. Strickland, 97(CQ):Vol 13No2-164
Culler, J. On Deconstruction.*
D. Boak, 67:May84-104
M. Boyd and L. Brodkey, 355(LSoc):
Dec84-555
M. Brown, 401(MLQ):Sep83-327
G.L. Bruns, 153:Spring84-12
J.A. Buttigieg, 405(MP):May85-448
W.E. Cain, 128(CE):Dec84-811
A. Easthope, 366:Spring84-109
M. Hobson, 208(FS):Apr84-246
W. Kendrick, 613:Dec84-515
A. Megill, 478:Oct84-285
[continued]

Dallek, R. Ronald Reagan.*
 D. Henry, 583:Summer85-386
Dallin, A. Black Box.
 P. Johnson, 617(TLS):23Aug85-917
 M. Sayle, 453(NYRB):25Apr85-44
 P. Taubman, 441:21Apr85-7
Dallmayr, F. Twilight of Subjectivity.
 T. McCarthy, 142:Fall84-115
 D.M. Rasmussen, 142:Fall84-111
Dalos, G. 1985. (S. Hood and E. Schmid,
 eds)
 T.G. Ash, 617(TLS):8Feb85-147
d'Alpuget, B. Robert J. Hawke.
 K. Tsokhas, 381:Jun84-266
Dalsimer, A. - see Nally, T.H.
Dalton, D. and R. Cayen. James Dean.*
 G. Marcus, 62:May85-2
Damas, D., ed. Handbook of North American
 Indians. (Vol 5)
 H. Brody, 617(TLS):7Jun85-631
Damborenea, R.G. - see under García Dam-
 borenea, R.
Damian, P. Book of Gomorrah.
 R.J. Hexter, 589:Jul84-642
Damiani, B.M. "La Diana" of Montemayor as
 Social and Religious Teaching.*
 F.A. de Armas, 238:Dec84-667
Damiani, B.M. Montemayor's "Diana," Music,
 and the Visual Arts.*
 F.P. Casa, 345(KRQ):Vol31No3-342
 T.L. Kassier, 238:Mar84-142
Damiani, B.M. - see López de Ubeda, F.
D'Amico, J.F. Renaissance Humanism in
 Papal Rome.
 E. Lee, 551(RenQ):Winter84-601
 L.V.R., 568(SCN):Spring-Summer84-26
Dammers, R. Richard Steele.
 C. Winton, 536:Vol6-129
Damrosch, L., Jr. God's Plot and Man's
 Stories.
 G.M. Crump, 344:Summer85-114
Damrosch, L., Jr. Symbol and Truth in
 Blake's Myth.*
 J. Beer, 402(MLR):Apr84-425
Danchin, P., ed. The Prologues and
 Epilogues of the Restoration 1660-1700.*
 (Pt 1)
 J.P. Vander Motten, 179(ES):Feb84-77
Danchin, P., ed. The Prologues and Epi-
 logues of the Restoration 1660-1700.
 (Pt 2)
 A.H. Scouten, 189(EA):Oct-Dec85-460
D'Ancona, M.L. - see under Levi D'Ancona,
 M.
Dancourt, F.C. Le Chevalier à la mode.
 (R.H. Crawshaw, ed)
 G.J. Mallinson, 208(FS):Jan84-57
D'Andrea, A. Il nome della storia.
 C. Di Girolamo, 379(MedR):Apr84-137
Danesi, M., ed. Issues in Language.*
 D.J. Napoli, 205(ForL):Dec82-182
Danforth, L.M. The Death Rituals of Rural
 Greece.*
 J. Dubisch, 292(JAF):Jan-Mar84-88
Dangel, J. La phrase oratoire chez Tite-
 Live.
 A. Hus, 555:Vol58fasc2-319
D'Angeli, C. - see Pasolini, P.P.
D'Angiolini, P. and C. Pavone, eds. Guida
 generale degli archivi di stato italiani.
 (Vol 1)
 J.M. Najemy, 589:Jan84-153
Daniel, A. - see under Arnaut Daniel

Daniel, E.V. Fluid Signs.
 D. Mosse, 617(TLS):19Jul85-805
Daniel, F. Una mirada a España.
 M.E. Beeson, 399(MLJ):Spring84-93
Daniel, K.W. Francis Poulenc.
 H. Meltzer, 143:Issue 35-65
Daniel, S.H. John Toland.
 J. Drury, 617(TLS):23Aug85-930
Daniell, R. Sleeping With Soldiers.
 J. O'Reilly, 441:24Mar85-16
Daniels, B.C. Dissent and Conformity on
 Narragansett Bay.
 A.T. Klyberg, 432(NEQ):Sep84-445
Daniels, H.A. Famous Last Words.
 D.E. Baron, 35(AS):Fall84-226
 L. Moskovit, 191(ELN):Jun85-65
Daniels, K. The White Wave.
 E. Grosholz, 249(HudR):Winter84/85-654
Daniels, R.V. Russia.
 M. McAuley, 617(TLS):4Oct85-1104
Danielson, D.R. Milton's Good God.*
 J.S. Bennett, 301(JEGP):Jan84-120
 M. Fixler, 405(MP):Feb85-310
Danielsson, B., E. Gomer and M. Morris-
 Nygren, eds. Prisma's Modern Swedish-
 English, English-Swedish Dictionary.
 (3rd ed)
 M.J. Blackwell, 399(MLJ):Winter84-420
Daninos, G. Aspects de la nouvelle poésie
 algérienne de langue française.
 L. Tremaine, 538(RAL):Spring84-94
Danjou-Flaux, N. and others. Lexique 1.
 K. Connors, 320(CJL):Spring84-74
Danjou-Flaux, N. and G. Gary-Prieur, eds.
 Adverbes en -ment, manière, discours.
 F.M. Jenkins, 207(FR):Dec84-330
Danky, J.P., ed. Women's Periodicals and
 Newspapers from the 18th Century to 1981.
 (M.E. Hady, B.C. Noonan and N.E. Strache,
 comps)
 J.A. Tracy, 517(PBSA):Vol78No2-262
Danly, R.L. In the Shade of Spring
 Leaves.*
 G.B. Petersen, 529(QQ):Autumn84-707
Dannhaeuser, N. Contemporary Trade Strat-
 egies in the Philippines.
 J. Warren, 293(JASt):Aug84-797
Danon, S. and S.N. Rosenberg - see "Ami
 and Amile"
Dansereau, L-M. Chez Paul-ette bière, vin,
 liqueur et nouveautés.* Ma maudite main
 gauche veut pus suivre.*
 C.F. Coates, 207(FR):Mar85-594
Danset, A. Eléments de psychologie du
 développement (Introduction et aspects
 cognitifs).
 J-M. Gabaude, 542:Jan-Mar84-134
Danson, L., ed. On "King Lear."*
 C. Hoy, 569(SR):Spring84-256
 R.J.A. Weis, 179(ES):Dec84-574
Danson, L. Tragic Alphabet.
 R. Stamm, 179(ES):Apr84-162
Dante Alighieri. Dante's Inferno. (T.
 Phillips, trans and illustrator)
 C. Grayson, 617(TLS):26Jul85-816
Dante Alighieri. The Divine Comedy.*
 (Vol 1: Inferno, and Vol 3: Paradiso).
 (A. Mandelbaum, trans)
 J. Ahern, 441:21Apr85-12

Dante Alighieri. The Divine Comedy.*
  (Vol 2: Purgatorio) (A. Mandelbaum,
  trans)
    J. Ahern, 441:21Apr85-12
    R.H. Lansing, 589:Apr84-390
D'Antuono, N.L. Boccaccio's "Novelle" in
  the Theatre of Lope de Vega.
    C.G. Peale, 238:May84-304
Dany, M. and others. Le Français des
  relations internationales.
    W. Greenberg, 399(MLJ):Summer84-161
Daoust, J-P. Poèmes de Babylone.
    S. Lawall, 207(FR):Dec84-306
Daphinoff, D. - see Echlin, E.
Da Pozzo, G. - see Foscolo, U.
Darby, E. and N. Smith. The Cult of the
  Prince Consort.*
    R. Treble, 90:Jan84-47
Darby, T. The Feast.*
    M. Husain, 154:Dec84-740
d'Arcais, G.B.F. and R.J. Jarvella, eds.
  The Process of Language Understanding.
    C.A. Jackson, 350:Dec85-929
Dargis, D. Scénario grammatical.
    S. Lawall, 207(FR):Apr85-753
Darius, J. Beyond Vision.
    442(NY):4Mar85-119
Darling, S. Chicago Furniture.
    C. Wilk, 617(TLS):6Sep85-987
Darlington, B. - see Wordsworth, W. and M.
Darmon, P. Trial by Impotence.
    P. Laslett, 617(TLS):28Jan85-728
D'Arms, J.H. Commerce and Social Standing
  in Ancient Rome.*
    P. Garnsey, 122:Jan84-85
Darnton, R. The Great Cat Massacre.*
    M. Kraus, 42(AR):Fall84-504
    F. Tuten, 62:Dec84-70
Darnton, R. The Literary Underground of
  the Old Regime.*
    G. Barber, 354:Sep84-302
    N. Barker, 78(BC):Spring84-101
    M. Hutt, 402(MLR):Jan84-192
    J. Proust, 535(RHL):Nov/Dec84-966
    R.C. Rosbottom, 173(ECS):Fall84-76
    D.L. Wick, 517(PBSA):Vol78No2-242
Darragh, T. Pi in the Skye.
    J. Retallack, 472:Fall/Winter84-213
Dart, A.K. ESL Grammar Workbook 1 and 2.
  ESL Grammar Handbook. ESL Grammar Quiz
  Book.
    C.W. Kreidler, 399(MLJ):Summer84-198
Daruwalla, K. Sword and Abyss.
    B. Padhi, 268(IFR):Summer85-125
Daruwalla, K.N. The Keeper of the Dead.
    A. Stevenson, 617(TLS):19Apr85-449
Daruwalla, K.N., ed. Two Decades of
  Indian Poetry, 1960-1980.*
    A. Hashmi, 314:Winter-Spring84-219
Darwin, C. The Correspondence of Charles
  Darwin. (Vol 1) (F. Burkhardt and S.
  Smith, eds)
    S. Collini, 617(TLS):10May85-511
    S.J. Gould, 441:21Apr85-27
    J. Howard, 362:30May85-29
    R.C. Lewontin, 453(NYRB):10Oct85-18
Dary, D.A. The Buffalo Book.
    T. Nipper, 649(WAL):Aug84-165
Das, H.C. Tantricism.
    A. Bharati, 293(JASt):Aug84-777
Dash, I.G. Wooing, Wedding, and Power.*
    E.H. Hageman, 570(SQ):Spring84-126
    C. Hoy, 569(SR):Spring84-256

Da Silva, Z.S. Beginning Spanish. (5th
  ed)
    C.M. Cherry, 399(MLJ):Summer84-189
Daspre, A. - see du Gard, R.M.
Datlof, N. and others, eds. George Sand
  Papers.
    R. Feigenbaum-Knox, 446(NCFS):Summer-
      Fall84-183
Datta, B. A Linguistic Study of Personal
  Names and Surnames in Bengali.
    M.L. Apte, 350:Mar85-227
d'Aubigné, A. Histoire universelle.*
  (Vol 1) (A. Thierry, ed)
    F. Gray, 207(FR):Feb85-446
d'Aubigné, A. Histoire universelle. (Vol
  2) (A. Thierry, ed)
    F. Gray, 207(FR):Feb85-446
    R. Zuber, 535(RHL):Jul/Aug84-590
Dauby, J. and M. Durieux. Les Sentences
  du Coq, de Séraphin Jurion.
    F. Carlton, 553(RLiR):Jul-Dec84-501
Daudet, A. Lettres de mon moulin. (J-H.
  Bornecque, ed)
    G. Hare, 208(FS):Apr84-215
Daugherty, S.B. The Literary Criticism of
  Henry James.
    R. Gard, 447(N&Q):Apr83-176
    V. Jones, 541(RES):May84-259
Madame d'Aulnoy. The Peacock King and
  Other Stories. (A. Macdonnell and Miss
  Lee, trans)
    A. Duchêne, 617(TLS):29Nov85-1362
Daunton, M.J. Royal Mail.
    B. Supple, 617(TLS):29Nov85-1347
Dauphiné, J. Le Cosmos de Dante.
    S. Maser, 539:Aug85-226
Dauphiné, J. Guillaume de Saluste Du
  Bartas.
    C.M. Hill, 551(RenQ):Winter84-642
Dauster, F. and L.F. Lyday, eds. En un
  acto.* (2nd ed)
    J. Ortega, 399(MLJ):Spring84-94
Dave, K.N. Birds in Sanskrit Literature.
    J.A.C. Greppin, 617(TLS):27Dec85-1486
Davenport, G. Apples and Pears and Other
  Stories.
    442(NY):28Jan85-97
Davenport, G. Cities on Hills.
    30:Fall84-96
    295(JML):Nov84-493
Davenport, G. Eclogues. The Geography of
  the Imagination.
    A. Mars-Jones, 617(TLS):8Mar85-263
Davenport, W.A. Fifteenth Century English
  Drama.*
    S. Carpenter, 382(MAE):1984/2-321
    D. Mills, 541(RES):Nov84-524
Davenport-Hines, R.P.T. Dudley-Docker.
    J. Turner, 617(TLS):17May85-537
Davey, F. Capitalistic Affection!*
    T. Whalen, 198:Summer84-101
Davey, F. Edward and Patricia.
    S.S., 376:Jun84-148
Davey, F. Surviving the Paraphrase.
    W.J. Keith, 627(UTQ):Summer84-459
Davey, F. and B.P. Nichols - see Kroetsch,
  R.
David, E. An Omelette and a Glass of
  Wine.*
    C. Rosen, 441:14Jul85-3
David, J. and G. Kleiber, eds. La notion
  sémantico-logique de modalité.
    J.C. Pellat, 553(RLiR):Jul-Dec84-456

Davidson, A.E. Mordecai Richler.*
  M. Greenstein, 102(CanL):Autumn84-74
  M. Levene, 627(UTQ):Summer84-457
Davidson, C., ed. A Middle English Trea-
tise of the Playing of Miracles.
  G.H.V. Bunt, 179(ES):Apr84-180
  A.C. Cawley, 541(RES):May84-280
Davidson, C., C.J. Gianakaris and J.H.
Stroupe, eds. The Drama of the Middle
Ages.*
  D. Mills, 541(RES):Nov84-524
Davidson, D. Inquiries into Truth and
Interpretation.*
  G. Helman, 215(GL):Vol24No4-240
Davidson, D.L. Nuclear Weapons and the
American Churches.
  S.G.P., 185:Apr85-782
Davidson, G. Origami.
  C. Campbell, 614:Summer85-31
Davidson, H.M. Blaise Pascal.
  A.J. Krailsheimer, 208(FS):Jul84-338
Davidson, M. Beef Wellington Blue.
  T. Fitton, 617(TLS):12Apr85-406
Davidson, M.B. The Drawing of America.
  D. Tatham, 658:Summer/Autumn84-213
Davie, D. Collected Poems 1970-1983.*
  D. McDuff, 565:Spring84-72
  W.H. Pritchard, 249(HudR):Summer84-341
Davie, E. A Traveller's Room.
  T. Fitton, 617(TLS):19Apr85-434
  A. Hulbert, 441:8Sep85-24
Davies, B. An Introduction to the Philos-
ophy of Religion.*
  S.T. Davis, 258:Jun84-201
Davies, J.A. John Forster.
  E.D. Engel, 445(NCF):Jun84-99
  S. Monod, 189(EA):Jan-Mar85-91
Davies, J.G. Everyday Conversations in
Spanish.
  G.A. Olivier, 399(MLJ):Spring84-92
Davies, M-H. Laughter in a Genevan Gown.
  H.H. Watts, 395(MFS):Winter85-861
Davies, N. God's Playground.* (Vols 1
and 2)
  S.A. Blejwas, 104(CASS):Spring-
    Summer84-204
  W. McClellan, 639(VQR):Winter84-177
Davies, P. The St. Ives Years.
  F. Spalding, 617(TLS):1Mar85-232
Davies, P. Superforce.*
  M. Gardner, 453(NYRB):13Jun85-31
  C.A. Ronan, 617(TLS):21Jun85-693
Davies, R. The Mirror of Nature.
  J.S. Grant, 627(UTQ):Summer84-433
Davies, R. The Rebel Angels.*
  S. Stone-Blackburn, 168(ECW):Spring84-
    93
Davies, R. What's Bred in the Bone.
  L. McCaffery, 441:15Dec85-6
Davies, S. Emily Brontë.*
  K.C. Odom, 594:Summer84-244
Davies, S. Images of Kingship in "Para-
dise Lost."*
  J. Di Salvo, 391:Oct84-97
  J. Egan, 568(SCN):Winter84-57
Davies, S. Paris and the Provinces in
Eighteenth-Century Prose Fiction.
  A. Cismaru, 207(FR):Dec84-290
Davies, T. The Electric Harvest.
  C. Salzberg, 441:18Aug85-20
Davies, W.H. Selected Poems. (J. Barker,
ed) Later Days.
  J. Bayley, 617(TLS):25Jan85-79

Davis, B. The Long Surrender.
  P-L. Adams, 61:May85-104
  H. Mitgang, 441:19May85-23
Davis, B.C., M. Scriven and S. Thomas.
The Evaluation of Composition Instruc-
tion.
  B.J. Wagner, 128(CE):Feb84-133
Davis, B.H. Thomas Percy.
  J.R. Watson, 161(DUJ):Dec83-145
Davis, C.T. and H.L. Gates, Jr. The
Slave's Narrative.
  F.S. Foster, 441:7Jul85-17
Davis, D. The Covenant.
  T. Dooley, 617(TLS):28Jun85-732
Davis, D. Stars.
  J. Nangle, 200:Apr84-245
Davis, D. Wisdom and Wilderness.*
  R. Asselineau, 189(EA):Jan-Mar85-104
Davis, D.B. Slavery and Human Progress.
  M.I. Finley, 441:3Feb85-26
  J.M. Kousser, 617(TLS):1Feb85-123
  J.H. Plumb, 453(NYRB):17Jan85-26
Davis, E.W. and H.E. Gerber, eds. Thomas
Hardy. (Vol 2)
  D.J. Winslow, 40(AEB):Vol8No1-45
Davis, G. and M. Senior, eds. South
Africa.
  N. Masilela, 538(RAL):Fall84-474
Davis, H.L. Robert Desnos, une voix, un
chant, un cri.
  M-C. Dumas, 535(RHL):Nov/Dec84-986
  J. Gratton, 208(FS):Apr84-231
Davis, J. - see Byron, H.J.
Davis, J.H., Jr. Fénelon.*
  P.J. Bayley, 208(FS):Jan84-57
Davis, K.C. Two-Bit Culture.*
  J. Carter, 219(GaR):Fall84-654
Davis, K.S. F.D.R.: The New York Years,
1928-1933.
  442(NY):23Dec85-90
Davis, L.G., comp. A Paul Robeson
Research Guide.
  E.H. Freydberg, 615(TJ):May84-277
  T.E. Miller, 87(BB):Mar84-47
Davis, L.J. Factual Fictions.*
  J.J. Burke, Jr., 594:Fall84-343
  J. Dussinger, 173(ECS):Spring85-453
  B. Foley, 223:Winter84-422
  W. Kendrick, 613:Dec84-525
  M. McKeon, 405(MP):Aug84-76
  J. Mezciems, 83:Spring84-131
  566:Spring85-192
Davis, L.M. English Dialectology.*
  W.N. Francis, 355(LSoc):Dec84-561
  R.I. McDavid, Jr., 300:Vol 17-91
Davis, M. Twenty-Eight Days.
  T. O'Brien, 236:Spring-Summer84-40
Davis, M. and D. Wallbridge. Eine Einfüh-
rung in das Werk von D.W. Winnicott.
  C. Neubaur, 384:Sep84-704
Davis, M.T. Light and Dark.
  S. Altinel, 617(TLS):18Jan85-67
Davis, N. The Last Two Years of Salvador
Allende. (British title: The Last Years
of Salvador Allende.)
  S. Collier, 617(TLS):25Oct85-1201
  T. Szulc, 441:30Jun85-27
Davis, N., ed. Non-Cycle Plays and The
Winchester Dialogues.*
  S. Carpenter, 541(RES):Feb84-79
Davis, N.Z. The Return of Martin Guerre.*
  D.R. Kelley, 551(RenQ):Summer84-252

Davis, R. A History of Music in American Life.
  T. Riis, 309:Vol5No1/3-256
Davis, R.J., comp. Samuel Beckett.*
  B. Mitchell, 299:Autumn82-152
Davis, R.M. Evelyn Waugh, Writer.*
  A. Blayac, 189(EA):Jan-Mar85-98
  W. Sullivan, 569(SR):Summer84-442
Davis, S. Bob Marley.
  R.F. Grass, 441:31Mar85-23
Davis, S.D. and P.D. Beidler, eds. The Mythologizing of Mark Twain.
  T. Wortham, 445(NCF):Mar85-487
Davis, S.T. Logic and the Nature of God.
  P. Sherry, 518:Oct84-255
Davis, T.J. A Rumor of Revolt.
  442(NY):14Oct85-144
Davis, T.M. Faulkner's "Negro."*
  C.S. Brown, 569(SR):Summer84-474
  T.L. McHaney, 585(SoQ):Summer84-88
  J.T. Matthews, 27(AL):Mar84-122
  N. Polk, 536:Vol6-1
  L.W. Wagner, 587(SAF):Spring84-111
  J.G. Watson, 395(MFS):Summer84-319
Davis, W.C., ed. The Image of War, 1861-1865.* (Vol 6)
  T. Wicker, 441:6Jan85-18
Davison, P. Barn Fever and Other Poems.*
  J. Saunders, 565:Autumn84-66
Davison, P. Contemporary Drama and the Popular Dramatic Tradition in England.*
  G. Bas, 189(EA):Oct-Dec85-482
  J. Harrop, 397(MD):Mar84-148
Davison, P. Praying Wrong.
  R.W. Flint, 441:27Jan85-18
Davison, P. - see Orwell, G.
Davison, R.A. Charles G. Norris.
  M.J. Fertig, 26(ALR):Autumn84-293
d'Avray, D. The Preaching of the Friars.
  B. Stock, 617(TLS):31May85-616
Davydov, A. Vospominaniia.
  D.C.B. Lieven, 575(SEER):Jan84-132
  S.C. Ramer, 550(RusR):Jul84-313
Davydov, S. "Teksty — Matryoshki" Vladimira Nabokova.*
  J. Grayson, 575(SEER):Jan84-118
Dawe, G. and E. Longley, eds. Across a Roaring Hill.
  P. Craig, 617(TLS):1Nov85-1238
Dawe, R.D. - see Sophocles
Dawe, R.D. and J. Diggle - see Page, D.L.
Dawidowicz, L.S. The Holocaust and the Historians.
  N.J. Kressel, 390:Apr84-57
Dawisha, K. The Kremlin and the Prague Spring.
  A. Brown, 617(TLS):4Oct85-1104
Dawkins, C. Charleyhorse.
  P. Reedy, 441:22Sep85-22
Dawkins, L. Natives and Strangers.
  E. Langer, 441:22Dec85-11
Dawkins, R. The Extended Phenotype.*
  R.C. Richardson, 486:Jun84-357
Dawson, F. Virginia Dare.
  T. Olson, 441:26May85-14
Dawson, J. The Ha-Ha.
  P. Craig, 617(TLS):26Apr85-479
Dawson, J.G. 3d. Army Generals and Reconstruction Louisiana, 1862-1877.
  A.P. McDonald, 9(AlaR):Jan84-68
Dawson, P.M.S. The Unacknowledged Legislator.*
  R. Cronin, 339(KSMB):No35-76

Day, F. Sir William Empson.*
  R.M. Adams, 453(NYRB):11Apr85-32
Day, J.W. The Glory of Athens.*
  N. Robertson, 487:Winter84-381
Day, M. Modern Art in English Churches.
  E. Esdaile, 324:Aug85-668
Day, R. and G.C. Weaver, eds. Creative Writing in the Classroom.
  D. Kirby, 128(CE):Mar84-248
Day, R.B. - see Bukharin, N.I.
Day, T.P. The Conception of Punishment in Early Indian Literature.*
  R.W. Lariviere, 293(JASt):May84-565
Day, W.P. In the Circles of Fear and Desire.
  S.S. Prawer, 617(TLS):20Dec85-1461
Dayan, Y. My Father, His Daughter.
  A. Knopf, 441:3Nov85-18
Daydí-Tolson, S. The Post-Civil War Spanish Social Poets.
  B. Ciplijauskaité, 238:May84-308
Daymond, D. and L. Monkman, eds. Canadian Novelists and the Novel.*
  M.P. Loverso, 178:Jun84-240
Dazai, O. Return to Tsugaru.
  A. Tyler, 441:2Jun85-13
Dazai Osamu. Selected Stories and Sketches.
  D. Brudnoy, 407(MN):Winter84-457
Deacon, G. John Clare and the Folk Tradition.*
  G. Crossan, 591(SIR):Winter84-581
Deacon, R. "C."
  N. Clive, 617(TLS):5Apr85-374
  P. Hennessy, 362:21Feb85-28
Deakin, M.F. Rebecca West.
  C. Cook, 447(N&Q):Aug83-378
Dean, I. Memory and Desire.
  G. Johnson, 441:28Jul185-18
Dean, S.F.X. It Can't Be My Grave.
  N. Callendar, 441:27Jan85-33
Deane, S. Celtic Revivals.
  D. Donoghue, 617(TLS):1Nov85-1239
Deane, S. Civilians and Barbarians.
  M. Harmon, 272(IUR):Spring84-126
Deane, S. History Lessons.
  M. Riordan, 617(TLS):15Mar85-294
Deane, S. Talking Drums.
  N. Barley, 617(TLS):1Nov85-1243
Dearlove, J. and P. Saunders. Introduction to British Politics.*
  I. Davidson, 176:Apr85-72
Deathridge, J. and C. Dahlhaus. The New Grove Wagner.
  G. Abraham, 617(TLS):1Feb85-115
Debicki, A.P. Poetry of Discovery.*
  A.A. Anderson, 402(MLR):Oct84-961
  D. Cañas, 400(MLN):Mar84-406
  J. Pérez, 238:Mar84-147
De Boer, J., ed. Dyeing for Fibres and Fabrics.
  P.B., 614:Winter85-21
Debon, C. Guillaume Apollinaire après "Alcools." (Vol 1)
  P. Caizergues, 535(RHL):May/Jun84-465
Debon, G. Grundbegriffe der chinesischen Schrifttheorie und ihre Verbindung zu Dichtung und Malerei.
  D. Holzman, 318(JAOS):Apr-Jun83-456
Debray, R. Les Empires contre l'Europe.
  P. McCarthy, 617(TLS):13Dec85-1418

Debreczeny, P., ed. American Contributions to the Ninth International Congress of Slavists, Kiev, September 1983. (Vol 2)
  A. McMillin, 575(SEER):Oct84-583
Debreczeny, P. The Other Pushkin.*
  D. Bethea, 574(SEEJ):Fall84-400
  J.D. Clayton, 104(CASS):Winter84-432
  S. Davydov, 550(RusR):Oct84-405
  I.P. Foote, 617(TLS):11Jan85-43
Debussy, C. Claude Debussy: Letters 1884-1918. (F. Lesure, ed)
  R. Nichols, 410(M&L):Apr84-194
De Carlo, A. Macno.
  P. Hainsworth, 617(TLS):26Jul85-832
Décaudin, M. - see Verlaine, P.
Decaux, A. Victor Hugo.
  D. Kelley, 617(TLS):11Oct85-1123
Decavalles, A. Ransoms to Time.
  R. Hadas, 441:28Apr85-33
De Cesare, R. Songs for the French Class.
  J. Abrate, 207(FR):Mar85-605
Dechert, H.W. and M. Raupach, eds. Towards a Crosslinguistic Assessment of Speech Production.
  M. Eisenstein, 351(LL):Jun84-139
Decker, K. Backyard Gene Pool.
  D. Ingham, 102(CanL):Winter83-109
Decleva Caizzi, F. Pirrone, Testimonianze.
  A.A. Long, 123:Vol34No2-219
Decourt, J. Un sentier dans le siècle.
  J. Théodoridès, 605(SC):15Jul85-380
Decrosse, A. and others. Sociosémiotique.
  J. Lindenfeld, 350:Sep85-733
Décsy, G., ed. Global Linguistic Connections.
  S. Levin, 215(GL):Vol24No4-260
Décsy, G. Sprachherkunftsforschung. (Vol 2)
  R.W. Wescott, 567:Vol48No1/2-181
Dedijer, V. Novi Prilozi za Biografiju Josipa Broza Tita, Treči Tom.
  E. Barker, 617(TLS):18Jan85-61
Deely, J. Introducing Semiotic.*
  C.J. Swearingen, 480(P&R):Vol 17No3-171
Deen, L.W. Conversing in Paradise.
  S.D. Cox, 173(ECS):Spring85-391
  E.J. Rose, 661(WC):Summer84-111
  C. Werner, 391:Mar84-35
Deeney, J.J., ed. Chinese-Western Comparative Literature.
  J.T. Wixted, 293(JASt):Feb84-312
Dees, A. Atlas des formes et des constructions des chartes françaises du 13e siècle.*
  W. Rothwell, 208(FS):Apr84-189
Deese, J. Thought Into Speech.
  T.C. Christy, 350:Mar85-234
Defaux, G. Le Curieux, le glorieux et la sagesse du monde dans la prémière moitié du XVIe siècle.*
  T. Cave, 402(MLR):Apr84-449
  E.M. Duval, 210(FrF):Jan84-110
  G. de Rocher, 207(FR):Dec84-281
Defaux, G. Molière, ou les métamorphoses du comique.*
  J. Grimm, 72:Band221Heft2-440
Defaux, G., ed. Montaigne.*
  I.D. McFarlane, 551(RenQ):Summer84-293
  I. Maclean, 208(FS):Jul84-328

Defoe, D. Moll Flanders.* (introduction by P. Rogers)
  566:Autumn84-62
Defoe, D. Roxana, The Fortunate Mistress. (D. Blewett, ed)
  R.H. Carnie, 627(UTQ):Summer84-422
  566:Autumn84-62
Deford, F. Everybody's All-American.
  D. Johnson, 577(SHR):Fall84-368
Degenhart, B. and A. Schmitt. Jacopo Bellini.
  B. Boucher, 617(TLS):27Dec85-1488
Degenhart, B. and A. Schmitt, with H-J. Eberhardt. Corpus der Italienischen Zeichnungen, 1300-1450. (Pt 2, Vol 4)
  F. Ames-Lewis, 380:Spring84-78
  J. Beck, 90:Dec84-789
De George, R.T., ed. Semiotic Themes.*
  W.C. Watt, 567:Vol50No1/2-97
Degering, T. Das Elend der Entsagung.
  M.W. Jennings, 221(GQ):Summer84-476
Deggau, H-G. Die Aporien der Rechtslehre Kants.
  H. Williams, 83:Spring84-135
Degrada, F. - see Planelli, A.
De Grazia, V. The Culture of Consent.
  C.F. Delzell, 275(IQ):Winter84-117
Deguise, A. Trois femmes.*
  K. Bieber, 149(CLS):Summer84-237
  P. and M. Higonnet, 617(TLS):17May85-535
  A. Miller, 406:Fall84-361
  D. Wood, 208(FS):Jul84-344
Deguy, M. Gisants.
  M. Edwards, 617(TLS):4Oct85-1092
De Haven, T. Funny Papers.
  M. Peters, 441:17Mar85-21
  442(NY):18Mar85-129
Deichgräber, K. Die Patienten des Hippokrates.
  J. Vallance, 123:Vol34No2-314
Deighton, L. London Match.
  J. Lester, 441:1Dec85-22
Deighton, L. Mexico Set.*
  A. Krystal, 441:10Mar85-16
  M. Laski, 362:10Jan85-25
  442(NY):11Mar85-138
De Jean, J. Libertine Strategies.*
  C. Gaudiani, 188(ECr):Fall84-88
  C. Reichler, 535(RHL):Nov/Dec84-961
Dejean, P. Carlo, Rembrandt, Ettore, Jean Bugatti. (N. Coleno and U. Hucke, eds)
  R. Banham, 453(NYRB):7Nov85-35
Dejeux, J. Littérature maghrébine de langue française.
  N. Kattan, 107(CRCL):Jun84-344
Dekker, R. and L. van de Pol. Daar was laatse een meisje loos.
  E. Moser-Rath, 196:Band25Heft1/2-123
De Koven, M. A Different Language.*
  M.J. Hoffman, 395(MFS):Summer83-318
  R. Merrill, 27(AL):May84-292
  S.S., 376:Feb84-144
  L. Simon, 454:Fall84-89
Delacorta. Lola.
  K. Tucker, 441:21Apr85-24
  442(NY):29Apr85-132
Delacorta. Vida.
  R.D. Rosen, 441:13Oct85-24
Delafield, E.M. The Diary of a Provincial Lady.
  P. Craig, 617(TLS):26Apr85-479

Delano, S.F. "The Harbinger" and New England Transcendentalism.
  D.S. Reynolds, 27(AL):Oct84-430
  J.A. Sokolow, 432(NEQ):Sep84-467
De-la-Noy, M. Elgar the Man.*
  M. Kennedy, 410(M&L):Jul84-270
De-la-Noy, M. The Honours System.
  A. Bell, 617(TLS):9Aug85-886
  P. Hennessy, 362:13Jun85-26
De-la-Noy, M. Denton Welch.*
  R. Dinnage, 453(NYRB):21Nov85-47
  P. Parker, 364:Nov84-96
De-la-Noy, M. - see Welch, D.
Delany, S.R. Stars in My Pocket Like Grains of Sand.
  G. Jonas, 441:10Feb85-15
Delaunay, C. Rose ou la Confidente.
  J-J. Varoujean, 450(NRF):May84-141
Delay, C. Le Hammam.
  D. Gunn, 617(TLS):4Oct85-1113
Delbanco, A. William Ellery Channing.
  K. Versluys, 179(ES):Feb84-85
Delbanco, N. About My Table and Other Stories.*
  G. Morris, 502(PrS):Spring84-91
Delbanco, N. The Beaux Arts Trio.
  B. Holland, 441:27Jan85-23
  442(NY):28Jan85-98
Delbanco, N. Group Portrait.*
  T.K. Bender, 577(SHR):Summer84-268
Delbourg, P. Génériques.
  N.S. Hellerstein, 207(FR):Oct84-157
Delebecque, É., ed and trans. Les Actes des Apôtres.
  É. des Places, 555:Vol58fasc1-125
Deledda, G. After the Divorce.
  J. Landry, 617(TLS):26Jul85-832
Deletant, D. Colloquial Romanian.
  C.M. Carlton, 399(MLJ):Autumn84-300
  E. Close, 67:Nov84-262
  E. Tappe, 575(SEER):Jul84-433
Deleuze, G. Nietzsche and Philosophy.
  A. Nehamas, 482(PhR):Oct84-641
  C.S. Taylor, 518:Oct84-212
  E. Wright, 494:Vol5No4-882
van Delft, L. Le Moraliste classique.*
  L.K. Horowitz, 207(FR):Dec84-288
  P. Zoberman, 546(RR):Mar84-264
Delgado, J.L.G. - see under García Delgado, J.L.
Delgado, J.P., A. Enríquez Gómez and M. de Barrios - see under Pinto Delgado, J., A. Enríquez Gómez and M. de Barrios
Delibes, M. Cinco horas con Mario (Versión teatral). (G. Sobejano, ed)
  H.L. Boudreau, 240(HR):Summer84-416
Delière, J. and R.C. Lafayette. Connaître la France.*
  R.E. Hiedemann, 399(MLJ):Autumn84-284
De Lillo, D. White Noise.
  P-L. Adams, 61:Feb85-100
  D. Johnson, 453(NYRB):14Mar85-6
  J.A. Phillips, 441:13Jan85-1
De Lio, T. Circumscribing the Open Universe.
  P. Jones, 607:Dec84-43
Delius, F. Delius: a Life in Letters.* (Vol 1) (L. Carley, ed)
  R. Anderson, 415:Jun84-329
Delius, H. Self-Awareness.
  D. Wandschneider, 687:Jan-Mar84-152

Dell, D.J. and others, eds. Guide to Hindu Religion.
  P. Mundschenk, 485(PE&W):Jul84-321
Della Neva, J.A. Song and Counter-Song.
  W.J. Beck, 207(FR):Apr85-723
Della Porta, G. Gli duoi fratelli rivaldi. (L.G. Clubb, ed and trans)
  G. Guarino, 551(RenQ):Summer84-288
dell'Arco, M.F., ed. The Vatican and its Treasures.
  C. Gould, 39:Sep84-216
Dellheim, C. The Face of the Past.*
  M. Bright, 637(VS):Summer84-513
Del Litto, V. and K. Ringger, with others, eds. Stendhal et le romantisme.
  S. Bokobza, 605(SC):15Apr85-286
Delman, D. Murder in the Family.
  N. Callendar, 441:30Jun85-29
Delmas, H. and A. Julian. Le rayon SF.
  S. Beaulé, 561(SFS):Jul84-217
Deloffre, F. and M. Menemencioglu - see Challe, R.
Deloffre, F. and J. Van den Heuvel - see de Voltaire, F.M.A.
De Lorean, J.Z., with T. Schwartz. De Lorean.
  R. Rosenbaum, 441:20Oct85-56
Deloria, V., Jr. and C.M. Lytle. American Indians, American Justice.
  J.L.H., 185:Jan85-398
Delplace, C. Le griffon de l'archaïsme à l'époque impériale.
  A. Hus, 555:Vol58fasc1-169
De Luca, V.A. Thomas De Quincey.*
  R.M. Maniquis, 591(SIR):Spring84-139
  S.M. Tave, 677(YES):Vol 14-333
De Lutiis, G. Storia dei servizi segreti in Italia.
  G. Reid, 617(TLS):4Oct85-1116
Delz, J. - see Tacitus
Demand, N.H. Thebes in the Fifth Century.*
  S.M. Burstein, 487:Winter84-372
De Mauro, T. Idee e ricerche linguistiche nella cultura italiana.
  M.D. Barrado, 202(FMod):No68/70-388
Dembkowski, H.E. The Union of Lublin.
  D. Stone, 104(CASS):Spring-Summer84-210
Dembo, L.S., ed. Interviews with Contemporary Writers. (2nd Ser)
  C. Wright, 219(GaR):Fall84-639
Demers, R.F. Modernization in a New England Town.
  P. Tedesco, 432(NEQ):Sep84-470
Demerson, G. and C. Lauvergnat-Gagnière - see Rabelais, F.
Demetrakopoulos, S. Listening to Our Bodies.
  J. Grumman, 395(MFS):Summer84-425
Demetz, P. - see Fontane, T.
D'Emilio, J. Sexual Politics, Sexual Communities.*
  E.Z. Friedenberg, 529(QQ):Spring84-227
De Mille, N. Word of Honor.
  R. Nalley, 441:1Dec85-24
"Demographic and Socioeconomic Aspects of Aging in the United States."
  A. Hacker, 453(NYRB):28Feb85-37
De Mott, R. Steinbeck's Reading.
  J. Ditsky, 628(UWR):Spring-Summer85-90
  J.R. Millichap, 395(MFS):Winter84-826
  R. Simmonds, 649(WAL):Feb85-331

De Mouy, J.K.   Katherine Anne Porter's
   Women.*
      585(SoQ):Summer84-90
      639(VQR):Winter84-8
Dempsey, C.   Annibale Carracci and the
   Beginnings of Baroque Style.
      D.S. Pepper, 54:Sep84-531
Dempster, B.   Fables for Isolated Men.*
      R. Billings, 102(CanL):Summer84-109
Dempster, B.   Globe Doubts.
      J. Fitzgerald, 102(CanL):Autumn84-154
Demus, O., with R.M. Kloss and K. Weitz-
   mann.   The Mosaics of San Marco in
   Venice.*
      C. Mango, 617(TLS):22Mar85-309
d'Encausse, H.C. - see under Carrère
   d'Encausse, H.
Denecke, L., ed.   Brüder Grimm Gedenken.*
   (Vol 3)
      C.L. Gottzmann, 684(ZDA):Band113Heft2-
      94
De Neef, A.L.   Spenser and the Motives of
   Metaphor.*
      D. Cheney, 551(RenQ):Summer84-298
      L.E. Orange, 568(SCN):Spring-Summer84-
      3
Denholm, A.   Lord Ripon 1827-1909.
      R.K. Huch, 637(VS):Winter84-277
Denisoff, R.S.   Waylon.
      M. Kirby, 441:19May85-31
Denman, H.   Steen Steensen Blicher-litter-
   aturen 1834-1982.
      A. Jørgensen, 172(Edda):1984/3-185
Dennett, D.C.   Elbow Room.
      G. Strawson, 617(TLS):19Apr85-431
Dennis, C.   The Near World.
      T. Sleigh, 441:21Jul85-24
Dennison, G.   Luisa Domic.
      T.R. Edwards, 453(NYRB):19Dec85-54
      H.F. Mosher, 441:22Sep85-22
Dennys, J.   Henrietta's War.
      E.S. Turner, 617(TLS):29Nov85-1346
De Nonno, M., ed.   La Grammatica dell'-
   "Anonymus Bobiensis" (GL I 533-565 Kiel).
      A.C. Dionisotti, 313:Vol74-202
      M. Gibson, 123:Vol34No2-324
Dent, P., ed.   The Full Note.
      J. Penberthy, 617(TLS):6Sep85-979
      J. Penberthy, 703:No12-150
Dentan, M.   Le Texte et son lecteur.
      C.J. Stivale, 207(FR):May85-894
Dentinger, J.   Murder on Cue.
      T.J. Binyon, 617(TLS):5Jul85-757
Denton, M.   Evolution.
      L. Shaffer, 617(TLS):26Apr85-464
Dentoni, F.   Il Giappone nel dilemma fra
   tradizione e modernità.
      G. Bartoli, 407(MN):Autumn84-364
Den Uyl, D.J. and D.B. Rasmussen, eds.
   The Philosophic Thought of Ayn Rand.
      M.C., 185:Apr85-775
Denvir, B.   A Documentary History of Taste
   in Britain: The Eighteenth Century.*
      P. Jones, 89(BJA):Summer84-273
      566:Autumn84-67
Denyer, N.   Time, Action and Necessity.*
      P. Fitzgerald, 543:Mar84-621
      T. Kapitan, 449:Sep84-526
      N. Kretzmann, 482(PhR):Apr84-285
Déon, M.   Je vous écris d'Italie.
      P. Bourgeade, 450(NRF):Dec84-95

De Piaggi, G.   La Sposa perfetta.
      J. Geffriaud-Rosso, 535(RHL):Jan/Feb84-
      98
Deppermann, M.   Andrej Belyj's ästhetische
   Theorie des schöpferischen Bewusstseins.*
      T.R. Beyer, Jr., 574(SEEJ):Fall84-404
Deppert, K.   Corpus Vasorum Antiquorum.
   (Deutschland, Vol 50)
      B.A. Sparkes, 303(JoHS):Vol 104-257
De Quincey, T.   Klosterheim; or: The
   Masque.
      E.M. Eigner, 445(NCF):Dec84-351
Derbolav, J., C. Menze and F. Nicolin, eds.
   Sinn und Geschichtlichkeit.
      R. Lüthe, 687:Jan-Mar84-158
Deregowski, J.B.   Distortion in Art.
      D. Carrier, 290(JAAC):Fall84-112
Derleth, A. and S.T. Joshi - see Lovecraft,
   H.P.
De Rosa, G.   Vescovi popolo e magia nel
   Sud.
      L. Mascilli Migliorini, 98:Aug/Sep84-
      717
De Rose, P.L. and S.W. McGuire.   A Concor-
   dance to the Works of Jane Austen.
      D. Gilson, 354:Jun84-195
Deroux, C., ed.   Studies in Latin Litera-
   ture and Roman History.   (Vol 3)
      P. Jal, 555:Vol58fasc2-332
Derré, J-R. - see Ballanche, P-S.
Derré, J-R. and C. Giesen - see Heine, H.
Derrida, J.   Signéponge/Signsponge.
      S. Scobie, 376:Oct84-107
      42(AR):Summer84-381
Derriman, P.   Bodyline.
      A.L. Le Quesne, 617(TLS):28Jun85-734
Derry, W. - see Burney, F.
Der Stricker - see under Stricker
De Ruyt, F.   Alba Fucens III.
      A-M. Adam, 555:Vol58fasc2-350
Déry, T.   Kein Urteil, Memoiren.
      M. Lange, 601(SuF):Jul-Aug84-860
Desai, A.   In Custody.*
      J. Mellors, 364:Dec84/Jan85-145
      A.C. Mojtabai, 441:3Mar85-7
De Salvo, L. and M.A. Leaska - see Sack-
   ville-West, V.
Desanti, D.   Sacha Guitry.
      J. Decock, 207(FR):May85-923
De Santis, H.   The Diplomacy of Silence.
      H. Hanak, 575(SEER):Apr84-304
Desautels, D.   L'Ecran.
      K.W. Meadwell, 102(CanL):Autumn84-95
Descartes, R.   Gespräch mit Burman.*   (H.W.
   Arndt, ed and trans)
      A. Robinet, 192(EP):Apr-Jun84-267
      R. Specht, 687:Jan-Mar84-144
Descartes, R.   Principles of Philosophy.
   (V.R. and R.P. Miller, eds and trans)
      D.M. Clarke, 518:Jan84-17
      T. Lennon, 154:Jun84-368
Deschaux, R., ed.   Les Oeuvres de Pierre
   Chastellain et de Vaillant, poètes du
   XVe siècle.*
      J.C. Laidlaw, 402(MLR):Oct84-931
Deschodt, E.   La Gloire au Liban.
      R. Holzberg-Namad, 207(FR):Dec84-309
Descombes, V.   Grammaire d'objets en tous
   genres.
      P. Engel, 98:Dec84-954
Descotes, M.   Histoire de la critique dram-
   atique en France.*
      W. Henning, 547(RF):Band96Heft4-465

Díaz, J. and L. Díaz Viana. Romances tra-
dicionales de Castilla y León.
  M-A. Börger-Reese, 240(HR):Winter84-77
Díaz, J.S. Bibliografía de la literatura
hispánica. (Vol 12)
  J.L. Laurenti, 552(REH):Oct84-455
Díaz, J.S. - see under Simón Díaz, J.
Díaz, S.J. - see under Julia Díaz, S.
Díaz de Bustamante, J.M. Draconcio y sus
"Carmina Profana."
  J.B. Hall, 123:Vol34No2-331
Díaz Larios, L.F. - see under de Acuña, H.
Di Cicco, P.G. Dark to Light.
  M.S. Madoff, 628(UWR):Spring-Summer84-
  84
Dick, J. Conceptions.
  P. Monk, 102(CanL):Winter83-85
Dick, P.K. Puttering About in a Small
Land.
  B. Tritel, 441:1Dec85-24
Dick, P.K. Robots, Androids, and Mechani-
cal Oddities. (P.S. Warwick and M.H.
Greenberg) Lies, Inc.
  T.M. Disch, 617(TLS):18Jan85-67
Dick, S. - see Woolf, V.
Dickens, C. The Letters of Charles
Dickens. (Vol 4) (K. Tillotson, ed)
  S.M. Tave, 402(MLR):Apr84-434
Dickens, C. The Letters of Charles Dick-
ens.* (Vol 5) (G. Storey and K.J. Field-
ing, eds)
  T.J. Cribb, 541(RES):Feb84-99
Dickens, C. Martin Chuzzlewit.* (M. Card-
well, ed)
  L. Hartveit, 179(ES):Feb84-83
  S. Monod, 402(MLR):Jan84-159
  A. Sanders, 155:Spring84-46
  A. Shelston, 148:Autumn84-87
"Dickens Studies Annual."* (Vol 8) (M.
Timko, F. Kaplan and E. Guiliano, eds)
  R. Bennett, 541(RES):May84-252
  A. Sadrin, 402(MLR):Apr84-435
"Dickens Studies Annual."* (Vol 10) (M.
Timko, F. Kaplan and E. Guiliano, eds)
  J. Beaty, 155:Spring84-49
Dickey, J. Night Hurdling.*
  R. Baughman, 580(SCR):Spring85-113
  P. Rice, 219(GaR):Fall84-647
Dickey, J. Puella.*
  J. Applewhite, 598(SoR):Winter85-214
Dickinson, A. and M.L. Todd. Austin and
Mabel.* (P. Longsworth, ed)
  G. Johnson, 219(GaR):Summer84-436
  R.E. Spiller, 27(AL):Dec84-599
  42(AR):Summer84-384
Dickinson, C. Crows.
  F. Eberstadt, 617(TLS):22Nov85-1310
  D. Unger, 441:30Jun85-9
Dickinson, C. Waltz in Marathon.
  42(AR):Spring84-259
Dickinson, E. The Manuscript Books of
Emily Dickinson.* (R.W. Franklin, ed)
  J. Loving, 536:Vol5-195
Dickinson, P. Death of a Unicorn.
  M. Stasio, 441:14Apr85-26
  442(NY):4Feb85-103
Dickinson, P. Hindsight.
  639(VQR):Summer84-96
Dickinson, P. A Rift in Time.
  J. Saunders, 565:Spring84-55
Dickson, E., ed. The Englishwoman's Bed-
room.
  P. Bach, 614:Summer85-23

Dickson, M. Maddy's Song.
  A. Shapiro, 441:10Mar85-24
Dickson, P. Words.
  R.B. Shuman, 35(AS):Fall84-251
"Dictionary of American Regional English."
(Vol 1) (chief ed, F.G. Cassidy)
  S.B. Flexner, 441:15Dec85-1
  442(NY):16Dec85-168
"A Dictionary of Buddhist Terms and Con-
cepts."
  G.J. Tanabe, Jr., 407(MN):Winter84-484
"Dictionary of Canadian Biography/Diction-
naire Biographique du Canada."* (Vol 11)
(F.G. Halpenny and J. Hamelin, eds)
  S. Neuman, 102(CanL):Summer84-82
"Dictionary of Literary Biography." (Vol
7) (J. MacNicholas, ed)
  C.M. Mazer, 402(MLR):Jul84-694
"Dictionary of Literary Biography." (Vols
19 and 20) (D.E. Stanford, ed)
  J.H.J., 636(VP):Winter84-455
Diderot, D. Le Neveu de Rameau.* (J. and
A-M. Chouillet, eds)
  G. Bremner, 402(MLR):Apr84-455
"Diderot Studies XX."* (O. Fellows and
D.G. Carr, eds)
  A. Becq, 535(RHL):Jul/Aug84-621
  A. Strugnell, 208(FS):Jul84-343
"Diderot Studies XXI." (O. Fellows and
D.G. Carr, eds)
  P.H. Meyer, 546(RR):May84-386
Didier, B. - see Stendhal
Didion, J. Democracy.*
  M. Howard, 676(YR):Winter85-xiii
  W. Lesser, 249(HudR):Autumn84-475
  J. Mellors, 364:Oct84-81
  639(VQR):Autumn84-133
Diebold, J. Making the Future Work.*
  H. Wheldon, 324:Aug85-666
Diederichsen, D. and B. Rudin, eds. Less-
ing im Spiegel der Theaterkritik 1945-
1979.*
  L.F. Helbig, 221(GQ):Spring84-316
Diefendorf, B.B. Paris City Councillors
in the Sixteenth Century.
  J.H.M. Salmon, 551(RenQ):Summer84-250
Diehl, J.F. Dickinson and the Romantic
Imagination.*
  S. Juhasz, 536:Vol6-35
  V.M. Kouidis, 577(SHR):Winter84-85
Diehl, L.B. The Late, Great Pennsylvania
Station.
  P-L. Adams, 61:Dec85-119
Diehl, R.A. Tula.*
  F.L. Phelps, 37:Sep-Oct84-61
Dien, T.V. Once in Vietnam: A Magic Cross-
bow and Other Stories.
  N-D.T. Nguyen, 399(MLJ):Winter84-429
Dien, T.V. and W. Gritter, eds. Folk
Tales for Children: The Story of the
Bird Named Bim Bip and Other Stories.
Folk Tales for Children: The Raven and
the Star Fruit Tree and Other Stories.
Folk Tales for Children: The North Wind
and the Sun and Other Stories.
  N-D.T. Nguyen, 399(MLJ):Winter84-429
Dien, T.V. and L.T. Thong. Once in Viet-
nam: The Bridge of Reunion and Other
Stories.
  N-D.T. Nguyen, 399(MLJ):Winter84-429
Dien, T.V. and T.C. Xuan. Once in Vietnam.
(Vol 3)
  N-D.T. Nguyen, 399(MLJ):Winter84-429

Dienes, L. Bibliographie des oeuvres de Gaito Gazdanov.* (T.A. Ossorguine, ed)
A. McMillin, 575(SEER):Jul84-474

Dienstag, J.I., ed. Eschatology in Maimonidean Thought.
I. Robinson, 589:Jan84-232

Dierkes, H. Literaturgeschichte als Kritik.
M.T. Jones, 221(GQ):Summer84-482
H. Slessarev, 406:Spring84-97

Dierks, M. Autor — Text — Leser.
E.W. Herd, 564:May84-150

de Diesbach, G. Madame de Staël.
D. Johnson-Cousin, 446(NCFS):Summer-Fal184-208

Dieter, W. Beyond the Mountain.
442(NY):11Feb85-126

Dieterich, T.G. and C. Freeman. A Linguistic Guide to English Proficiency Testing in Schools.
C. Stansfield, 399(MLJ):Summer84-157

Dietrich, M. Marlène D.*
G. Annan, 453(NYRB):14Feb85-5

Dietrich, M., ed. Max Mell als Theaterkritiker.
K. Heydemann, 602:Band15Heft2-343
W.E. Yates, 402(MLR):Oct84-988

Dietrich, M. and H. Kindermann - see von Hofmannsthal, H. and M. Mell

"Marlene Dietrich's ABC."* (rev) "Marlene Dietrich: Portraits 1926-1960."
G. Annan, 453(NYRB):14Feb85-5

Dietrich, R.A. Sprache und Wirklichkeit in Wittgensteins "Tractatus."
S. Kanngiesser, 260(IF):Band89-273

Dietrich von Freiberg. Opera omnia. (B. Mojsisch and others, eds)
J. Jolivet, 542:Jan-Mar84-69

Dietz, L. Franz Kafka: Die Veröffentlichungen zu seinen Lebzeiten (1908-1924).*
E. Middell, 654(WB):6/1984-1039
R.R. Nicolai, 564:May84-145
J.J. White, 402(MLR):Oct84-989

Dietz, S. and others. Asine. (Vol 2)
O.T.P.K. Dickinson, 303(JoHS):Vol 104-248

Dietze, G. Kant und der Rechtsstaat.
P. Burg, 342:Band75Heft4-509

Dietze, W. and A. Oprea, eds. Dialoge/Dialoguri.
G. Heinrich, 654(WB):9/1984-1581

Diffey, N.R. Jakob Michael Reinhold Lenz and Jean-Jacques Rousseau.
F.A. Brown, 406:Summer84-218
W.A. O'Brien, 221(GQ):Spring84-317

Digby, A. and P. Searby. Children, School and Society in Nineteenth-Century England.
V.A. McClelland, 637(VS):Autumn83-106

Digges, A. Letters of Thomas Attwood Digges (1742-1821). (R.H. Elias and E.D. Finch, eds)
C.H. Hay, 656(WMQ):Jan84-165

Diggins, J.P. The Lost Soul of American Politics.
B.R. Barber, 441:13Jan85-9
G.S. Wood, 453(NYRB):28Feb85-29

Diggins, J.P. and M.E. Kann, eds. The Problem of Authority in America.
J. Tagg, 106:Winter84-451

Diggle, J. Studies on the Text of Euripides.
C. Collard, 123:Vol34No1-9
D. Kovacs, 24:Summer84-236
P. Mason, 303(JoHS):Vol 104-201

Diggle, J. - see Euripides

Diggory, T. Yeats and American Poetry.*
H.J. Levine, 639(VQR):Winter84-174
V. Mercier, 617(TLS):25Jan85-80
J. Olney, 569(SR):Summer84-451
W. Spiegelman, 560:Fal184-146
L. Woodman, 27(AL):May84-295

Digo, R. De l'Ennui à la Mélancolie.
L. Millet, 192(EP):Jan-Mar84-110

Dihle, A. The Theory of Will in Classical Antiquity.*
C. Kirwan, 123:Vol34No2-335
R. Sokolowski, 543:Mar84-624

van Dijk, T.A. Studies in the Pragmatics of Discourse.*
S.H. Foster, 355(LSoc):Sep84-369

van Dijk, T.A. Text and Context.
G. Rauh, 260(IF):Band89-294

Dik, S.C., ed. Advances in Functional Grammar.
R. Gebruers, 361:Apr84-349
M.B. Harris, 297(JL):Sep84-403

Dil, A.S. - see McDavid, R.I., Jr.

Dil, A.S. - see McQuown, N.A.

Dilks, D. Neville Chamberlain.* (Vol 1)
D. Cannadine, 453(NYRB):28Mar85-29
K. Harris, 441:17Feb85-10
S. Jenkins, 362:10Jan85-21

Dillard, A. Teaching a Stone to Talk.
D.S. Miller, 569(SR):Winter84-160

Dillard, H. Daughters of the Reconquest.
J. Edwards, 617(TLS):19Jul85-807

Dillard, R.H.W. The First Man on the Sun.
639(VQR):Spring84-54

Diller, K.C., ed. Individual Differences and Universals in Language Learning Aptitude.*
B. Saint-Jacques, 350:Mar85-239

Dillon, E. The Head of the Family.
M. Montaut, 272(IUR):Spring84-137

Dillon, J. Shakespeare and the Solitary Man.*
R. Lengeler, 156(JDSh):Jahrbuch1984-250
F.O. Waage, 570(SQ):Spring84-114

Dillon, M. - see Bowles, J.

"Dilthey-Jahrbuch für Philosophie und Geschichte der Geisteswissenschaften." (Vol 1) (F. Rodi, ed)
T.D. Nordenhaug, 319:Oct85-599

Dima, N. Bessarabia and Bukovina.*
D. Deletant, 575(SEER):Oct84-619
L.K.D. Kristof, 104(CASS):Fal184-360
G. Ursal, 550(RusR):Apr84-216

Di Maio, I.S. The Multiple Perspective.*
N.A. Kaiser, 221(GQ):Summer84-491

Dimitrowa, B. Die Lawine.
E. Nährlich-Slatewa, 654(WB):3/1984-476

Dimler, G.R. - see Spee, F.

Dinekov, P. - see Parpulova, L.

Diner, H.R. Erin's Daughters in America.
S. Thernstrom, 432(NEQ):Jun84-298

Diner, S.J. A City and Its Universities.
W. Bruneau, 106:Spring84-73

Dinesen, I. Letters from Africa, 1914-1931. (F. Lasson, ed)
D.W. Hannah, 538(RAL):Fal184-482

"Isak Dinesen's Africa."
  W.L. Heat-Moon, 441:8Dec85-14
Dini, P. Silvestro Lega gli anni di Pia-
gentina.
  N. Powell, 39:Dec84-440
Dinnerstein, L. America and the Survivors
of the Holocaust.
  J.M. Wachs, 287:Jan84-25
Di Noto, A. Art Plastic.
  A. Anderson, 62:Dec84-79
Dinzelbacher, P. Vision und Visionsliter-
atur im Mittelalter.*
  L. Intorp, 224(GRM):Band34Heft1/2-197
  B. McGinn, 589:Jan84-138
Diogenes of Apollonia. Diogène d'Appollo-
nie: la dernière cosmologie présocra-
tique. (A. Laks, ed and trans)
  É. des Places, 555:Vol58fasc1-112
Dion, S. Ecarts.
  L. Ferrara, 207(FR):Apr85-754
Di Piero, W.S. Early Light.
  T. Sleigh, 441:21Jul85-24
Di Piero, W.S. The Only Dangerous Thing.
  E. Grosholz, 249(HudR):Winter84/85-647
Dippie, B.W. The Vanishing American.*
  B.M. Smith, 106:Summer84-185
Dirven, R. and others. The Scene of Lin-
guistic Action and its Perspectivization
by "Speak," "Talk," "Say" and "Tell."
  S.H. Elgin, 350:Jun85-507
Di Salvo, J. War of Titans.
  A. Ferry, 551(RenQ):Winter84-671
  J. Wittreich, 391:Oct84-92
Disandro, C.A. La Poesia Physica de
Homero.
  A. Bonnafé, 555:Vol58fasc1-111
Diskin, M., ed. Trouble in Our Backyard.*
  639(VQR):Summer84-94
Disney, M. The Hidden Universe.
  C.A. Ronan, 617(TLS):26Apr85-464
Disraeli, B. Benjamin Disraeli: Letters.*
(Vols 1 and 2) (J.A.W. Gunn, D.M. Schur-
man and M.G. Wiebe, eds)
  W. Cragg, 178:Sep84-370
Disraeli, B. and S. A Year at Hartlebury;
or, The Election.
  P. Allen, 627(UTQ):Summer84-426
  A. Brown, 445(NCF):Jun84-102
Dittmann, R. Eros and Psyche.
  P. Vinten-Johansen, 563(SS):Spring84-
179
Dittrich, K. and H. Würzner, eds. Die Nie-
derlande und das deutsche Exil 1933-1940.
  C. ter Haar, 72:Band221Heft2-324
Dixon, R.M.W. Where Have All the Adjec-
tives Gone? and Other Essays in Seman-
tics and Syntax.
  K. Allan, 350:Jun85-461
  P.H. Matthews, 297(JL):Mar84-165
Dixon, S. Fall and Rise.
  J. House, 441:7Jul85-16
Dixon, S. Movies.*
  M. Kreyling, 573(SSF):Summer84-275
  M. Moyle, 580(SCR):Fall84-113
Dixon, S. Time to Go.*
  P. La Salle, 573(SSF):Fall84-403
  J. Mellors, 362:10Jan85-24
  M. Moyle, 580(SCR):Fall84-113
"Dizionario degli istituti di perfezione."
(Vols 1-6) (G. Pelliccia and G. Rocca,
eds)
  P. Meyvaert, 589:Apr84-391

"Dizionario inglese-italiano italiano-
inglese." (4th ed)
  R.C. Melzi, 275(IQ):Winter84-99
Dje Dje, J.C. Distribution of the One-
String Fiddle in West Africa.
  F.E. Besmer, 187:Fall85-528
Djilas, M. Rise and Fall.
  N. Beloff, 453(NYRB):11Apr85-12
  R. Conquest, 441:24Feb85-6
  S. McConnell, 129:May85-71
  J. Simpson, 362:12Sep85-27
Djilas, M. Vlast.
  E. Barker, 617(TLS):18Jan85-61
Djwa, S. and R.S. Macdonald, eds. On F.R.
Scott.*
  D.M.R. Bentley, 627(UTQ):Summer84-452
  G. Carr, 168(ECW):Winter84/85-131
  T. Ware, 105:Fall/Winter84-99
Dmytryshyn, B. and E.A.P. Crownhart-
Vaughan - see Golovin, P.N.
Döblin, A. A People Betrayed.
  L. Kahn, 390:Feb84-59
Döblin, A. Tales of a Long Night.*
  442(NY):11Mar85-136
Dobrée, B. - see Pope, A.
Dobrenn, M. - see Camus, A. and J. Grenier
Dobroszycki, L., ed. The Chronicle of the
Lodz Ghetto, 1941-1944.*
  M. Friedberg, 129:Feb85-64
Dobson, E.J. and F.L. Harrison. Medieval
English Songs.
  J.A. Dutka, 597(SN):Vol56No2-233
Dobyns, H.F. Their Number Become Thinned.
  D.K. Richter, 656(WMQ):Oct84-649
Dobyns, S. Black Dog, Red Dog.*
  E. Grosholz, 249(HudR):Winter84/85-655
  P. Stitt, 219(GaR):Winter84-857
Dobyns, S. Cold Dog Soup.
  R.P. Brickner, 441:24Nov85-24
Dobyns, S. Saratoga Headhunter.
  N. Callendar, 441:29Sep85-21
  442(NY):29Jul85-78
Docherty, T. Reading (Absent) Character.*
  E. van Alphen, 204(FdL):Sep84-236
  S. Cohan, 454:Spring85-267
  R. Pearce, 659(ConL):Fall85-331
Docker, J. In a Critical Condition.
  G. Manning, 381:Sep84-414
Doctorow, E.L. Lives of the Poets.*
  A. Mars-Jones, 617(TLS):5Apr85-376
Doctorow, E.L. World's Fair.
  P-L. Adams, 61:Dec85-119
  W. Balliett, 442(NY):9Dec85-153
  D. Leavitt, 441:10Nov85-3
  R. Towers, 453(NYRB):19Dec85-23
Dodd, A. The Core Model.
  W. Mitchell, 316:Jun84-661
Dodd, P., ed. Walter Pater.
  D.T. O'Hara, 637(VS):Autumn83-110
Dodd, S.M. Old Wives' Tales.*
  E. Schwamm, 441:3Mar85-36
Doderer, K., ed. Ästhetik der Kinderlit-
eratur.
  L. Petzoldt, 196:Band25Heft3/4-327
Dodgson, J.M. The Place-Names of Cheshire.
(Pt 5, Vols 1 and 2)
  G. Kristensson, 179(ES):Jun84-285
Dodsley, R. The Toy-Shop (1735) [and] The
King and the Miller of Mansfield (1737).
  P-G. Boucé, 189(EA):Oct-Dec85-492
  566:Autumn84-65
Dodsworth, M. Hamlet Closely Observed.
  D.J. Enright, 362:1Aug85-29

Doyle, M. A Steady Hand.
  R.W. Harvey, 168(ECW):Winter84/85-344
Doyle, M.E. The Sympathetic Response.*
  C. Viera, 577(SHR):Spring84-184
Dozier, R.R. For King, Constitution and
  Country.
  F. O'Gorman, 173(ECS):Spring85-415
Drabble, M. Arnold Bennett.
  617(TLS):12Jul85-783
Drabble, M., ed. The Oxford Companion to
  English Literature. (5th ed)
  R. Davies, 362:9May85-24
  J.R. Kincaid, 441:14Jul85-1
  I. McGilchrist, 617(TLS):26Apr85-455
Drache, S. The Mikveh Man and Other
  Stories.
  D. Pope, 376:Oct84-119
Dragland, S., ed. Approaches to the Work
  of James Reaney.
  W.J. Keith, 627(UTQ):Summer84-459
Dragnich, A.N. and S. Todorovich. The
  Saga of Kosovo.
  D. Binder, 441:17Mar85-27
Drago, E.L. Black Politicians and Recon-
  struction in Georgia.
  R.M. Willingham, Jr., 392:Winter83/84-
  123
Dragonas, P.J. The High School Goes
  Abroad.
  M.W. Conner, 399(MLJ):Autumn84-270
Draine, B. Substance under Pressure.
  M.M. Rowe, 395(MFS):Summer84-377
Drakard, D. and P. Holdway. Spode Printed
  Ware.
  G. Wills, 39:Jan84-69
Drake, B. Writing Poetry.
  D. Kirby, 128(CE):Mar84-248
Drake, J. - see Milhaud, D.
Drakondaidis, P.D. To spiti tis thias.
  P. Mackridge, 617(TLS):4Oct85-1117
Draper, R.P., ed. Tragedy.*
  R.J. Dingley, 447(N&Q):Feb83-93
Draper, T. Present History.
  639(VQR):Winter84-20
Dreher, D. From the Neck Up.
  R. Ingham, 615(TJ):May84-288
Dreiser, T. An Amateur Laborer. (R.W.
  Dowell, ed)
  R.S. Kennedy, 395(MFS):Summer84-303
  J. Wallace, 26(ALR):Spring84-142
Dreiser, T. Theodore Dreiser: The Amer-
  ican Diaries 1902-1926.* (T.P. Riggio,
  J.L.W. West 3d and N.M. Westlake, eds)
  J. Griffin, 106:Fall84-349
  J. Stronks, 405(MP):Aug84-110
Dreiser, T. Sister Carrie. (J.C. Berkey
  and others, eds)
  J. Griffin, 106:Fall84-349
Drell, S.D. Facing the Threat of Nuclear
  Weapons.
  A.R. De Luca, 550(RusR):Oct84-433
Drescher, H.W., ed. Thomas Carlyle 1981.*
  R.L. Tarr, 588(SSL):Vol 19-296
Dressler, W.U. and others, eds. Discus-
  sion Papers, Fifth International Phonol-
  ogy Meeting.
  H. Penzl, 350:Sep85-706
Drew, E. Campaign Journal.
  N. Lemann, 441:17Mar85-20
Drew, E. Politics and Money.
  639(VQR):Winter84-19

Drew, P. The Architecture of Arata Iso-
  zaki.*
  M. Treib, 592:Vol 197No1005-57
Drewal, H.J. and M.T. Gẹlẹdẹ.
  J. Pemberton 3d, 2(AfrA):May84-10
  D.B. Welch, 187:Winter85-116
Drewitz, I. Die zerstörte Kontinuität.
  T.S. Hansen, 406:Summer84-235
Drewry, G., ed. The New Select Committees.
  F. Field, 362:5Sep85-23
Drews, P. Die slawische Avantgarde und
  der Westen.
  B.G. Rosenthal, 104(CASS):Winter84-442
Drews, R. Basileus.*
  P.J. Rhodes, 487:Summer84-179
Dreyfus, H.L. and P. Rabinow. Michel
  Foucault.* (2nd ed)
  J. Rajchman, 529(QQ):Autumn84-623
  M. Seltzer, 153:Spring84-78
  M. Sprinker, 141:Fall84-383
Driggs, F. and H. Levine. Black Beauty,
  White Heat.
  G.L. Starks, Jr., 91:Fall84-269
Drinkwater, J.F. Roman Gaul.
  E.M. Wightman, 124:Jul-Aug85-617
Driscoll, J.P. Identity in Shakespearean
  Drama.
  J.L. Calderwood, 551(RenQ):Summer84-
  308
  J.T. Shawcross, 570(SQ):Summer84-239
  C.J. Summers, 130:Fall84-287
Droescher, H-M. Grundlagenstudium zur Lin-
  guistik.
  K.H. Schmidt, 685(ZDL):3/1984-370
Lord Drogheda, K. Davison and A. Wheat-
  croft, eds. The Covent Garden Album.
  B.N., 636(VP):Spring84-93
Drogin, M. Anathema!
  517(PBSA):Vol78No3-382
Dronke, P. Women Writers of the Middle
  Ages.*
  M. Kraus, 42(AR):Fall84-503
Dronke, U. and others, eds. Speculum
  Norroenum.*
  R.J. Glendinning, 589:Jan84-140
  R.W. McTurk, 382(MAE):1984/1-144
Drosnin, M. Citizen Hughes.
  A. Howard, 617(TLS):3May85-490
  W. Turner, 441:17Feb85-14
von Droste-Hülshoff, A. Historisch-
  Kritische Ausgabe. (Vol 3, Pt 1 ed by L.
  Jordan; Vol 5, Pt 1 ed by W. Huge; Vol 6,
  Pt 1 ed by S. Berning)
  B. Peucker, 301(JEGP):Oct84-608
Drower, M.S. Flinders Petrie.
  S. Piggott, 617(TLS):20Sep85-1021
Drucker, P.F. Innovation and Entrepreneur-
  ship.
  J. Cohn, 129:Aug85-66
  H. Stein, 441:9Jun85-15
Drudy, P.J. - see "Irish Studies"
Druick, D. and M. Hoog. Fantin-Latour.
  E.A. Reid, 627(UTQ):Summer84-518
  R. Thomson, 59:Jun84-258
Drumbl, J. Quem quaeritis.
  U. Hennig, 684(ZDA):Band113Heft2-60
Drummond de Andrade, C. The Minus Sign.
  J. Gledson, 86(BHS):Oct84-520
Druon, M. The Iron King. The Strangled
  Queen.
  S. Altinel, 617(TLS):13Dec85-1434
Druskin, M. Igor Stravinsky.*
  A. Whittall, 410(M&L):Jan84-55

Dryfhout, J.H. The Work of Augustus Saint-
Gaudens.*
    A. Yarrington, 59:Mar84-110
Drzemczewski, A.Z. European Human Rights
Convention in Domestic Law.
    C.B.J., 185:Jan85-397
D'Sa, F.X. Śabdaprāmāṇyam in Śabara and
Kumārila.*
    M. Hattori, 259(IIJ):Apr84-153
Duban, J. Melville's Major Fiction.
    M. Bickman, 27(AL):Dec84-595
    L. Mackinnon, 617(TLS):22Nov85-1328
    H. Parker, 445(NCF):Dec84-358
    M.R. Stern, 432(NEQ):Sep84-458
Duban, J.M. Ancient and Modern Images of
Sappho.
    R. Martin, 124:Nov-Dec84-133
Dube, W-D. Expressionists and Expression-
ism.*
    J.B. Smith, 39:Dec84-437
Du Bellay, J. La Monomachie de David et
de Goliath. (E. Caldarini, ed)
    M.C. Smith, 208(FS):Jul84-331
Du Bellay, J. Oeuvres poétiques I. (H.
Chamard, ed; newly ed by Y. Bellenger)
    H.W. Wittschier, 547(RF):Band96Heft1/2-
    174
Dubie, N. Selected and New Poems.*
    W. Logan, 491:Nov84-105
    R. Peters, 30:Fall84-90
    P. Stitt, 219(GaR):Summer84-402
    D. Wojahn, 651(WHR):Autumn84-261
    V. Young, 472:Fall/Winter84-307
Dubnick, R.K. The Structure of Obscurity.
    C. Zinn, 27(AL):Dec84-611
Dubois, J. and others. Diccionario de
Lingüística.
    L. López Jiménez, 202(FMod):No68/70-
    377
Du Bois, P. - see under du Bois, P.
Dubois, R-D. 26 bis, impasse du Colonel
Foisy.
    J. Moss, 102(CanL):Autumn84-171
Du Bois, W.E.B. Against Racism. (H.
Aptheker, ed)
    N.I. Huggins, 441:29Sep85-25
Dubuc, R. and J-C. Boulanger. Régional-
ismes québécois usuels.
    M. Piron, 209(FM):Oct84-246
Dubus, A. The Times Are Never So Bad.*
    P. La Salle, 573(SSF):Winter84-73
Dubus, A. Voices from the Moon.*
    J. Updike, 442(NY):4Feb85-94
Dubus, A. We Don't Live Here Anymore.
    P. Kemp, 617(TLS):22Feb85-196
    J. Mellors, 362:10Jan85-24
Duchêne, R. L'imposture littéraire dans
les "Provinciales" de Pascal.
    A.J. Krailsheimer, 208(FS):Oct84-459
    L.A. MacKenzie, Jr., 207(FR):May85-889
Duchêne, R. Ninon de Lenclos.*
    M-O. Sweetser, 207(FR):Mar85-621
Duchesneau, F. La physiologie des
lumières.*
    P.R. Sloan, 319:Jan85-109
Ducrot, O. Les Échelles Argumentatives.
    M. Whitford, 208(FS):Jan84-111
Ducrot, O. and T. Todorov, eds. Encyclo-
pedic Dictionary of the Sciences of Lan-
guage.
    P. Mühlhäusler, 541(RES):May84-214
"Duden Français."
    P. Wagner, 257(IRAL):Feb84-81

Dudley, J. Gott und "Theoria" bei Aristo-
teles.
    S. Benardete, 543:Sep83-112
Duerr, H.P. Dreamtime.
    W.D. O'Flaherty, 441:8Sep85-12
    P. Winch, 617(TLS):4Oct85-1119
Duff, S.G. - see under Grant Duff, S.
Duffy, C. The Fortress in the Age of
Vauban and Frederick the Great 1660-
1789.
    S. Pepper, 617(TLS):1Nov85-1226
Duffy, D. Gardens, Covenants, Exiles.*
    M. Fowler, 178:Mar84-115
Duffy, F.H. and N. Geschwind, eds. Dys-
lexia.
    T. Rosenfield, 453(NYRB):21Nov85-49
Duffy, H. and F.K. Smith. The Brave New
World of Fritz Brandtner/Le Meilleur des
Mondes de Fritz Brandtner.
    E. Trépanier, 627(UTQ):Summer84-505
Duffy, K. Children of the Forest.
    A. Shoumatoff, 441:12May85-19
Dugan, A. New and Collected Poems, 1961-
1983.*
    J.D. McClatchy, 491:Feb85-291
    P. Stitt, 219(GaR):Summer84-402
    D. Wojahn, 651(WHR):Autumn84-261
    639(VQR):Summer84-92
Dugdale, N. Running Repairs.
    N. Jenkins, 493:Jan84-71
Duggan, W. The Great Thirst.
    M. Bowden, 441:17Nov85-30
Dugger, R. On Reagan.*
    639(VQR):Spring84-58
Dugger, R. The Politician.
    P.F. Kress, 577(SHR):Summer84-245
Dühnfort, E. Am Rande von Atlantis.
    K.H. Schmidt, 196:Band25Heft1/2-126
Duhoux, Y. L'Étéocrétois.
    A.M. Davies, 123:Vol34No2-339
Duinhoven, A.M. Bijdragen tot reconstruc-
tie van de "Karel ende Elegast." (Vol 2)
    C.B. Hieatt, 589:Jan84-142
Duis, P.R. The Saloon.
    J.T. O'Toole, 432(NEQ):Jun84-301
    639(VQR):Summer84-80
Dujčev, I., A. Kirmagova and A. Paunova,
eds. Kirilometodievska bibliografija,
1940-1980.
    H. Leeming, 575(SEER):Oct84-632
Duke, C.R. and S.A. Jacobson, eds. Read-
ing and Writing Poetry.
    D. Kirby, 128(CE):Mar84-248
Duke, D.C. Distant Obligations.*
    D. Berthold, 27(AL):Mar84-130
    D. Wyatt, 569(SR):Fall84-lxxxvi
Duke, F. - see Baudelaire, C.
Duke, M., J.R. Bryer and M.T. Inge, eds.
American Women Writers.*
    G.L. Nagel, 26(ALR):Autumn84-287
Duke, M. and D.P. Jordan, eds. A Richmond
Reader: 1733-1983.
    B.J. Griffin, 585(SoQ):Summer84-87
Dukore, B.F. Harold Pinter.*
    L. Powlick, 615(TJ):Mar84-138
Dulay, H., M. Burt and S. Krashen. Lan-
guage Two.*
    S. Takala, 351(LL):Sep84-157
Dull, J.L. - see Hou, C-Y.
Dumas, A. Le Corricolo. (preface by J-N.
Schifano)
    V.D.L., 605(SC):15Apr85-296

Dumenil, L. Freemasonry and American Cul-
ture, 1880-1930.
  L.L. Gould, 617(TLS):15Mar85-296
Dumézil, G. La Courtisane et les seig-
neurs colorés. ... Le Moyne noir en
gris dedans Varennes.
  M. Jarrety, 450(NRF):May84-127
Dumézil, G. The Stakes of the Warrior.
  (J. Puhvel, ed)
  C.S. Littleton, 650(WF):Oct84-283
Duminil, M-P. Le sang, les vaisseaux, le
coeur dans la Collection hippocratique.
  P. Pellegrin, 542:Jul-Sep84-383
Dumitrescu-Buşulenga, D. and M. Bucur, eds.
Literatur Rumäniens 1944 bis 1980.
  K. Bochmann, 654(WB):12/1984-2108
Dümling, A. Die fremden Klänge der hängen-
der Gärten.
  A. Clayton, 410(M&L):Oct84-387
Dummett, M. The Interpretation of Frege's
Philosophy.*
  D.R. Bell, 393(Mind):Apr84-276
  T. Burge, 482(PhR):Jul84-454
  J.N. Mohanty, 323:Jan84-79
  J. Skorupski, 479(PhQ):Jul84-402
Dumont, J-C. and others. Insula Sacra.
  (C. Nicolet, ed)
  A. Lintott, 313:Vol74-224
Dumonteil, J. and B. Cheronnet, eds. Le
For d'Oloron.
  W. Rothwell, 208(FS):Oct84-450
Dumoulin, B. Recherches sur le premier
Aristote.*
  D.A. Rees, 123:Vol34No2-334
Dunar, A.J. The Truman Scandals and the
Politics of Morality.
  C. Trueheart, 441:24Feb85-23
Dunbabin, J. France in the Making 843-
1180.
  E. James, 617(TLS):20Sep85-1036
Dunbar, P. William Blake's Illustrations
to the Poetry of Milton.*
  B.C. Werner, 88:Summer84-33
  J. Wittreich, 677(YES):Vol 14-329
Dunbar-Nelson, A. Give Us Each Day. (G.T.
Hull, ed)
  B. Staples, 441:14Apr85-20
  442(NY):13May85-147
Duncan, E. Unless Soul Clap Its Hands.
  S. Maloff, 441:10Mar85-21
Duncan, E.H., ed. Thomas Reid's Lectures
on Natural Theology (1780).
  P.B. Wood, 518:Oct84-205
Duncan, G., ed. Democratic Theory and
Practice.
  A.J. Simmons, 185:Oct84-151
Duncan, J.A. Les Romans de Paul Adam.
  Y. Vadé, 535(RHL):Sep/Oct84-812
Duncan, R. Ground Work.
  M. Davidson, 703:No12-133
  M. Rudman, 441:4Aug85-13
Duncan, R. and M. Weston-Smith, eds. The
Encyclopaedia of Medical Ignorance.
  J. Le Fanu, 441:12May85-33
Duncan, S.J. The Pool in the Desert.
  C. Rooke, 376:Oct84-120
Dundes, A., ed. Cinderella.
  T.C. Humphrey, 292(JAF):Jan-Mar84-77
  S.S. Jones, 650(WF):Apr84-148
  N. Philip, 203:Vol195No2-265
Dundes, A. Life is Like a Chicken Coop
Ladder.
  J. Zipes, 222(GR):Fall84-162

Dundes, A., ed. Sacred Narrative.
  E.T. Lawson, 469:Vol 10No1-149
Dundy, E. Elvis and Gladys.
  T. Russell, 617(TLS):24May85-583
Duneton, C. and F. Pagès. A hurler le
soir au fond des collèges.
  A. Valdman, 207(FR):Feb85-485
Dunkerley, J. Rebellion in the Veins.
  P. Cammack, 617(TLS):8Feb85-142
Dunkley, C. Television Today and Tomorrow.
  J. Aitken, 362:24Oct85-27
Dunkley, J. - see de Crébillon, P.J.
Dunleavy, J.E., ed. George Moore in Per-
spective.
  A. Gandolfo, 395(MFS):Winter84-747
Dunleavy, P. and C.T. Husbands. British
Democracy at the Crossroads.
  P. Johnson, 617(TLS):11Oct85-1128
Dunlop, J.B. The Faces of Contemporary
Russian Nationalism.*
  M. Pomar, 574(SEEJ):Winter84-556
  639(VQR):Summer84-93
Dunmore, H. The Apple Fall.
  P. Didsbury, 493:Jan84-71
  R. Pybus, 565:Autumn84-73
Dunn, D. Elegies.
  D. Davis, 362:6Jun85-31
  J. Mole, 176:Jul/Aug85-51
  B. Morrison, 617(TLS):5Apr85-377
Dunn, D. Europa's Lover.*
  J. Saunders, 565:Spring84-55
Dunn, D. St. Kilda's Parliament.*
  R. Watson, 588(SSL):Vol 19-194
Dunn, D. Secret Villages.
  M. O'Neill, 617(TLS):31May85-597
Dunn, H.T. Recollections of Dante Gabriel
Rossetti and his Circle, or Cheyne Walk
Life.
  M. Warner, 90:Dec84-792
Dunn, J. The Politics of Socialism.*
  D. Miller, 617(TLS):8Feb85-142
Dunn, J. Rethinking Modern Political
Theory.
  A. Wright, 362:24Oct85-31
Dunn, J. Sisters and Brothers.
  C. Chanteau, 362:10Jan85-22
Dunn, M. Australia and the Empire.
  K. Tsokhas, 381:Dec84-531
Dunn, P.M. The First Vietnam War.
  R.B. Smith, 617(TLS):13Sep85-1011
Dunn, P.N. The Spanish Picaresque Novel.
  P.J. Donnelly, 402(MLR):Jul84-726
Dunn, R.D. - see Camden, W.
Dunn, S. Not Dancing.
  E. Grosholz, 249(HudR):Winter84/85-657
Dunn, S. and J. Gennard. The Closed Shop
in British Industry.
  D. Macintyre, 617(TLS):11Jan85-35
Dunn, S.P. - see Klibanov, A.I.
Dunn, T.P. and R.D. Erlich, eds. The
Mechanical God.
  P.A. McCarthy, 561(SFS):Nov84-337
Dunne, D. The Two Mrs. Grenvilles.
  J. Cohen, 441:8Sep85-25
Dünnhaupt, G. Bibliographisches Handbuch
der Barockliteratur.* (Pts 1-3)
  K.F. Otto, Jr., 406:Fall84-332
  H. Rüdiger, 52:Band19Heft2-175
  B.L. Spahr, 222(GR):Summer84-118
Dunning, J. "But First a School."
  R. Craft, 453(NYRB):7Nov85-42
  D. Hurford, 441:24Nov85-26

Ebbinghaus, J. – see Kant, I.
Eberhard, W. China's Minorities.
  J.T. Dreyer, 293(JASt):Feb84-314
Eberhart, R. The Long Reach.
  J.F. Cotter, 249(HudR):Autumn84-500
Eberstadt, F. Low Tide.
  L. Taylor, 617(TLS):28Jun85-733
  L.S. de Teran, 441:26May85-13
Ebert, K.H. Sprache und Tradition der
  Kera (Tschad). (Pts 1 and 2)
  G.F. Meier, 682(ZPSK):Band37Heft5-641
Eberwein, R.T. Film and the Dream Screen.
  C. Gébler, 617(TLS):13Dec85-1423
Eccles, J.C. The Human Psyche.
  F. Jackson, 488:Sep84-397
Eccles, M. Brief Lives.
  R.J. Schoeck, 570(SQ):Winter84-498
Eccles, M. – see Shakespeare, W.
Echavarría, A. Lengua y literatura de
  Borges.
  E. Barradas, 701(SinN):Oct-Dec83-76
Echevarría, R.G. and K. Müller-Bergh – see
  under González Echevarría, R. and K.
  Müller-Bergh
Echeverria, E.J. Criticism and Commitment.
  J-M. Gabaude, 542:Apr-Jun84-251
Echlin, E., ed. An Alternative Ending to
  Richardson's "Clarissa."* (D. Daphinoff,
  ed)
  M. Philp, 83:Spring84-129
Eck, D.L. Banaras.*
  L.A. Babb, 293(JASt):Nov83-180
Eck, J. De sacrificio missae, libri tres
  (1536). (E. Iserloh, V. Pfnür and P.
  Fabisch, eds)
  W.L. Moore, Jr., 551(RenQ):Summer84-
  240
Eckhardt, C.M. Fanny Wright.*
  B. Sicherman, 617(TLS):15Mar85-296
Eckhardt, K.A. and A., eds and trans. Lex
  Frisionum.
  K.F. Drew, 589:Jan84-232
Meister Eckhart. Maître Eckhart, L'oeuvre
  latine. (Vol 1) (A. de Libera, E. Weber
  and E.Z. Brunn, eds and trans)
  M. Adam, 542:Oct-Dec84-461
Eckley, G. Children's Lore in "Finnegans
  Wake."
  H.B. Staples, 329(JJQ):Summer85-435
Eckstein, J. The Deathday of Socrates.
  R. Burger, 543:Sep83-113
Eco, U. The Name of the Rose.* (Italian
  title: Il nome della rosa; French title:
  Le nom de la rose.)
  V. Flieger, 219(GaR):Spring84-178
  P. Renard, 98:Aug/Sep84-579
  F. Schiavoni, 381:Dec84-573
Eco, U. Postscript to "The Name of the
  Rose."* (British title: Reflections on
  "The Name of the Rose.")
  P-L. Adams, 61:Jan85-100
  P. Hainsworth, 617(TLS):29Nov85-1373
  B. Woolley, 362:11Apr85-25
Eco, U. The Role of the Reader.
  T.G. Pavel, 107(CRCL):Mar84-95
Eco, U. Semiotics and the Philosophy of
  Language.*
  S. Scobie, 376:Oct84-107
  P. Swiggers, 350:Dec85-919
Eco, U., V.V. Ivanov and M. Rector.
  Carnival!
  P. Burke, 617(TLS):28Jun85-728
Ecole, J. – see Wolff, C.

Ede, J. A Way of Life: Kettle's Yard.*
  J.R.B., 148:Autumn84-93
  D. Farr, 39:Jul84-77
Edel, A. Aristotle and His Philosophy.*
  A.R. Lacey, 393(Mind):Oct84-606
  G.A. Press, 518:Jan84-11
  M. Schofield, 483:Jul84-392
  R.W. Sharples, 303(JoHS):Vol 104-211
Edel, L. Henry James: A Life.
  M. Bell, 441:24Nov85-12
  442(NY):9Dec85-161
Edel, L. Stuff of Sleep and Dreams.*
  W. Harmon, 577(SHR):Fall84-370
Edel, L. Writing Lives.*
  442(NY):21Jan85-94
Edel, L. – see James, H.
Edel, L. – see Wilson, E.
Edel, L. and D.H. Laurence. A Bibliog-
  raphy of Henry James.* (3rd ed rev
  with J. Rambeau)
  D. Seed, 40(AEB):Vol8No1-49
Edel, L., with M. Wilson – see James, H.
Edelson, M. Hypothesis and Evidence in
  Psychoanalysis.
  J.C.R., 185:Jul85-973
Edey, W. French Clocks in North American
  Collections.
  R.G., 90:Jan84-50
Edgerton, C. Raney.
  C. Verderese, 441:23Jun85-20
Edmond, L. Catching It.
  B. O'Donoghue, 617(TLS):5Jul85-753
Edmond, M. End Wall.*
  R. Pybus, 565:Summer84-56
Edmonds, J. and J.M. Reilly. Global
  Energy.
  S. Diamond, 441:21Apr85-38
Edmonds, M. Lytton Strachey.
  J.H. Stape, 87(BB):Jun84-102
Edmonds, W.D. The South African Quirt.
  D. Quammen, 441:14Apr85-31
Edmondson, J.A. Einführung in die Trans-
  formationssyntax des Deutschen.*
  M. Kohrt, 603:Vol8No2-287
Edmondson, L.H. Feminism in Russia, 1900-
  1917.
  639(VQR):Summer84-81
Saint Edmund of Abingdon. Mirour de
  Seinte Eglise. (A.D. Wilshere, ed)
  L. Morini, 379(MedR):Dec84-455
Edmunds, L. The Sphinx in the Oedipus
  Legend.
  R. Parker, 123:Vol34No2-336
Edmunds, L. and A. Dundes, eds. Oedipus.
  J. Glenn, 121(CJ):Dec84/Jan85-168
Edmunds, R.D. The Shawnee Prophet.
  C. Callender, 656(WMQ):Jul84-526
Edric, R. Winter Garden.
  N. Shack, 617(TLS):4Oct85-1096
Edsall, T.B. The New Politics of Inequal-
  ity.*
  M. Kempton, 453(NYRB):28Feb85-3
"Education for All."
  D.J. O'Keeffe, 176:Dec85-70
Edwards, A. A Remarkable Woman.
  H. Pakula, 441:3Nov85-25
Edwards, A. The Road to Tara.*
  L.Z. Smith, 395(MFS):Summer84-313
Edwards, A.S.G., ed. Skelton: The Criti-
  cal Heritage.*
  I. Lancashire, 536:Vol5-137
Edwards, A.S.G. – see Cavendish, G.

Edwards, A.S.G. and D. Pearsall, eds.
Middle English Prose.*
O.S. Pickering, 72:Band221Heft1-165
Edwards, C. The Lion's Mouth.
T. Bishop, 102(CanL):Autumn84-118
I. Huggan, 526:Winter84-82
Edwards, F. The Jesuits in England.
E. Norman, 617(TLS):9Aug85-885
Edwards, G.J. The International Film
Poster.
P. Brunette, 441:29Dec85-19
Edwards, J. Christian Córdoba.
G. McKendrick, 382(MAE):1984/2-333
J.F. Powers, 589:Jul84-645
Edwards, J.C. Ethics Without Philosophy.
M.U. Coyne, 258:Jun84-198
A. Janik, 319:Oct85-602
A. Taylor, 543:Mar84-626
Edwards, M. Towards a Christian Poetics.*
R.L. McCarron, 590:Jun85-45
D. O'Connell, 207(FR):May85-880
Edwards, O.D. The Quest for Sherlock
Holmes.
R.F. Fleissner, 95(CLAJ):Dec84-238
Edwards, P. - see Lewis, W.
Edwards, P. and others. The Revels His-
tory of Drama in English.* (Vol 4)
G. Bas, 189(EA):Jan-Mar85-73
K.E. Maus, 612(ThS):May84-107
J.J. Peereboom, 179(ES):Oct84-468
Edwards, P., I-S. Ewbank and G.K. Hunter,
eds. Shakespeare's Styles.*
J. Schäfer, 156(JDSh):Jahrbuch1984-260
Edwards, P.D. Anthony Trollope's Son in
Australia.*
M. Harris, 581:Jun84-247
Edwards, P.D., comp. Edmund Yates 1831-
1894.
J. Shattock, 402(MLR):Jul84-682
Edwards, R.B., ed. Psychiatry and Ethics.
J.D., 185:Oct84-194
Edwards, R.B. A Return to Moral and Reli-
gious Philosophy in Early America.*
A.J. Reck, 543:Jun84-846
Edwards, R.D. The Saint Valentine's Day
Murders.*
N. Callendar, 441:29Sep85-21
Edwards, S. - see Aquinas, T.
Edwards, T. Beyond the Last Oasis.
J. Keay, 362:18Jul85-28
Edwards, T.R.N. Three Russian Writers and
the Irrational.*
E.L. Frost, 558(RLJ):Winter-Spring84-
302
P. Petro, 104(CASS):Spring-Summer84-
167
ver Eecke, J., ed and trans. Le Sihalavat-
thuppakaraṇa.
J.P. McDermott, 318(JAOS):Apr-Jun83-
442
Eekman, T. and D.S. Worth, eds. Russian
Poetics.
B.P. Scherr, 550(RusR):Jan84-93
Eells, E. Rational Decision and Causal-
ity.*
R. Campbell, 150(DR):Fall84-608
J. Cargile, 311(JP):Mar84-163
P.J. Kett, 63:Sep84-299
van Eemeren, F.H., R. Grootendorst and T.
Kruiger. Het analyseren van een betoog.
W.K.B. Koning, 204(FdL):Sep84-227
Egan, C.L. Neither Peace Nor War.
A.H. Bowman, 656(WMQ):Jul84-522

Egan, D. Seeing Double.*
M. Harmon, 272(IUR):Spring84-126
Egan, D.R. and M. V.I. Lenin.
L.E. Holmes, 125:Spring84-307
Egan, E. Such a Vision of the Street.
D. Manuel, 441:19May85-23
Egan, M. - see "The Vidas of the Trouba-
dours"
Eggert, G.G. Steelmasters and Labor
Reform, 1886-1923.
A. Finkel, 106:Winter84-465
Eggum, A. Edvard Munch.
R. Cardinal, 617(TLS):22Mar85-320
S. Gardiner, 362:17Jan85-23
J.P. Hodin, 324:Nov85-888
P. Vinten-Johansen, 563(SS):Summer84-
272
Egleton, C. A Conflict of Interests.*
639(VQR):Summer84-96
Ehrard, J., ed. Études sur le XVIIIe
siècle.
J.H. Brumfitt, 208(FS):Jan84-70
Ehrenpreis, I. Acts of Implication.
J. Mezciems, 541(RES):Aug84-384
Ehrenpreis, I. Swift.* (Vols 1 and 2)
M. Mudrick, 249(HudR):Winter84/85-595
Ehrenpreis, I. Swift.* (Vol 3)
A. Carpenter, 272(IUR):Autumn84-277
C. Fabricant, 566:Spring85-167
P. Harth, 173(ECS):Spring85-406
M. Mudrick, 249(HudR):Winter84/85-595
639(VQR):Summer84-87
Ehrenreich, B. The Hearts of Men.
P.S.M., 185:Apr85-783
Ehret, C. and M. Posnansky, eds. The Ar-
chaeological and Linguistic Reconstruc-
tion of African History.
M.L. Bender, 350:Sep85-694
Ehrhardt, R. Canadian Development Assis-
tance to Bangladesh.
D. Glover, 298:Winter84/85-133
Ehrhart, W.D. Vietnam-Perkasie.
639(VQR):Summer84-87
Ehrlich, E. and others - see "Oxford Amer-
ican Dictionary"
Ehrlich, G. The Solace of Open Spaces.
J. Moore, 441:1Dec85-41
Ehrman, J. The Younger Pitt.
P.D.G. Thomas, 83:Spring84-92
Eichenbaum, L. and S. Orbach. Understand-
ing Women.
P. Roazen, 529(QQ):Autumn84-734
Eichler, E. - see Kühnel, P.
Eichmann, R. - see "Cuckolds, Clerics and
Countrymen"
Eidevall, G. Amerika i svensk 1900-tals-
litteratur.
R. Wright, 563(SS):Autumn84-375
Eigeldinger, F. and others - see under
Bandelier, A. and others
Eigeldinger, F. and G. Schaeffer. Table
de concordances rythmique et syntaxique
des "Poésies" d'Arthur Rimbaud.* (Vol 1)
A.L. Amprimoz, 446(NCFS):Summer85-297
Eigeldinger, F.S. Table de concordances
rythmique et syntaxiuqe de "Une Saison
en Enfer" d'Arthur Rimbaud.
A.L. Amprimoz, 446(NCFS):Summer85-298
"The Eighteenth Century: A Current Bibli-
ography." (Vol 6) (J.S. Borck, ed)
566:Spring85-186

Eikmeyer, H-J. and H. Rieser, eds. Words,
Worlds, and Contexts.
  I.L. Humberstone, 63:Jun84-197
  D. Justice, 393(Mind):Jul84-470
Eikoh Hosoe. Barakei.
  I. Buruma, 453(NYRB):10Oct85-15
  J. Eidus, 441:3Nov85-27
Einhoff, E. Emanzipatorische Aspekte im
Frauenbild von "The Review," "The Spec-
tator" und "The Female Spectator."
  F. Rau, 38:Band102Heft1/2-243
"Einstein: A Portrait."
  N. Ramsey, 441:13Jan85-22
Eisenberg, D. Romances of Chivalry in the
Spanish Golden Age.*
  J.R. Jones, 240(HR):Autumn84-529
  E. Williamson, 86(BHS):Apr84-194
Eisenberg, D., with T.L. Wright. Encoun-
ters with Qi.
  B. Gastel, 441:13Oct85-16
Eisenhower, D.D. Ike's Letters to a
Friend. (R. Griffith, ed)
  J. Palmer, 617(TLS):23Aug85-920
Eisenman, P. House X.
  A. Betsky, 505:Mar84-100
Eisenstadt, S.N. and O. Ahimer, eds. The
Welfare State and its Aftermath.
  R. Klein, 617(TLS):16Aug85-899
Eisenstein, M.R. Language Variation and
the ESL Curriculum.
  M.R. Miller, 399(MLJ):Autumn84-270
Eisenstein, S. Immoral Memories.
  G. Millar, 362:11Jul85-30
Eisenzweig, U., ed. Autopsies du roman
policier.
  A. Calame, 450(NRF):Apr84-124
Eisler, H. Musik und Politik. (Vols 2
and 3) (G. Mayer, ed)
  S. Hinton, 410(M&L):Oct84-382
Eisner, E.W. Cognition and Curriculum.
  L. Chiarelott, 289:Spring84-120
Eissler, K.R. Goethe. (Vol 1)
  M. Schneider, 384:Apr84-323
Eitel, W., ed. Lateinamerikanische Lit-
eratur der Gegenwart in Einzeldarstel-
lungen.*
  A. Dessau, 107(CRCL):Mar84-159
Eitner, L.E.A. Géricault.*
  N. Bryson, 208(FS):Oct84-469
  B. Weller, 344:Winter85-114
  H. Zerner, 453(NYRB):17Jan85-36
Eiximenis, F. Lo libre de les dones.*
  (F. Naccarato, ed)
  J. Dagenais, 240(HR):Winter84-78
  B. Schmid, 553(RLiR):Jan-Jun84-225
Ekdahl, S. Die Schlacht bei Tannenberg
1410.* (Vol 1)
  R.C. Hoffmann, 104(CASS):Spring-
    Summer84-209
Ekeland, I. Le calcul, l'imprévu.
  J. Largeault, 542:Apr-Jun84-222
Ekelöf, G. Songs of Something Else.*
  J. Lutz, 563(SS):Spring84-197
Ekman, P. Telling Lies.
  C.Z. Malatesta, 441:31Mar85-9
Elagin, J. Temnyj genij.
  J. Freedman, 574(SEEJ):Winter84-551
Elamrani-Jamal, A. Logique aristotéli-
cienne et grammaire arabe.
  G. Stahl, 542:Jul-Sep84-392
Elbaz, A.E. Folktales of the Canadian
Sephardim.
  G. Thomas, 102(CanL):Winter83-160

El Beheiry, K.A.S. L'Influence de la
littérature française sur le roman arabe.
  T. le Gassik, 107(CRCL):Jun84-341
Elbert, S. A Hunger for Home.
  N. Baym, 432(NEQ):Sep84-472
Elderfield, J. The Drawings of Henri
Matisse.*
  M. Middleton, 324:May85-428
Elderfield, J. The Modern Drawing.
  J. Burr, 39:Apr84-305
Elderfield, J. Kurt Schwitters.
  R. Cardinal, 617(TLS):22Nov85-1325
Eldershaw, M.B. Tomorrow and Tomorrow and
Tomorrow.
  J. Roe, 381:Jun84-241
Eldredge, N. Time Frames.
  A. Prochaintz, 441:21Apr85-38
Eldridge, M. Walking the Dog and Other
Stories.
  J.L. Crain, 441:3Mar85-22
Eleen, L. The Illustrations of the Paul-
ine Epistles in French and English
Bibles of the Twelfth and Thirteenth
Centuries.
  E.P. McLachlan, 627(UTQ):Summer84-516
Elert, C-C. and others, eds. Nordic
Prosody III.
  C.A. Creider, 350:Sep85-715
Eleuteri, P. Storia della tradizione mano-
scritta di Museo.
  R. Browning, 123:Vol34No1-22
Elgin, S.H. Native Tongue.
  E.T. Johnson, 350:Sep85-739
Elia, P., ed. Coplas hechas sobre la
batalla de Olmedo que llaman las de la
panadera.
  C. De Nigris, 379(MedR):Apr84-154
  D.W. Lomax, 86(BHS):Jan84-64
Eliach, Y. Hasidic Tales of the Holocaust.
  S. Taitz, 390:Apr84-56
Eliade, M. A History of Religious Ideas.
  (Vol 2)
  J.P. McDermott, 318(JAOS):Jul-Sep83-
    659
  P. Slater, 529(QQ):Winter84-1042
Elias, A.C., Jr. Swift at Moor Park.*
  P. Danchin, 179(ES):Aug84-374
  P. Rogers, 402(MLR):Jul84-667
Elias, R.H. and E.D. Finch - see Digges,
A.
Eliav-Feldon, M. Realistic Utopias.
  P.F. Grendler, 551(RenQ):Summer84-245
Eliot, G. A George Eliot Miscellany.*
  (F.B. Pinion, ed) [shown in prev under
ed]
  J. Herron, 637(VS):Autumn83-102
Eliot, G. Selections from George Eliot's
Letters. (G.S. Haight, ed)
  G. Beer, 441:16Jun85-10
  H. Bloom, 453(NYRB):26Sep85-43
  A. Leighton, 617(TLS):28Jun85-713
Elisabeth Charlotte, Duchesse d'Orléans -
see under von der Pfalz, L.
Elkin, S. Stanley Elkin's The Magic
Kingdom.
  R.M. Adams, 453(NYRB):18Jul85-20
  M. Apple, 441:24Mar85-34
  442(NY):8Apr85-128
Elkington, J. The Gene Factory.
  B. Dixon, 617(TLS):19Apr85-442
Elledge, S. E.B. White.*
  P.K. Bell, 617(TLS):1Mar85-238

Elwert, W.T., ed. Rätoromanisches Collo-
quium Mainz (am 13. und 14. Dezember
1974).
　R. Liver, 685(ZDL):1/1984-109
Emad, P. Heidegger and the Phenomenology
of Values.
　B.P. Dauenhauer, 543:Sep83-115
Emanuel, J.A. The Broken Bowl.
　B. Brown, 95(CLAJ):Sep84-102
"Embroidered Samplers."
　C. Campbell, 614:Spring85-21
Emecheta, B. The Rape of Shavi.*
　C. Martin, 441:5May85-24
　442(NY):22Apr85-142
Emeljanow, V., ed. Chekhov: The Critical
Heritage.
　S.M. Carnicke, 615(TJ):Dec82 559
Emeneau, M.B. Language and Linguistic
Area.
　P. Dasgupta, 261:Sep/Dec82-37
Emeneau, M.B. Toda Grammar and Texts.
　S.B. Steever, 350:Jun85-477
Emerson, E. The Authentic Mark Twain.
　H. Hill, 26(ALR):Autumn84-278
　W.R. Macnaughton, 27(AL):Dec84-602
　T.A. Shippey, 617(TLS):1Feb85-111
　T. Wortham, 445(NCF):Mar85-486
Emerson, E.T. The Letters of Ellen Tucker
Emerson.* (E.E.W. Gregg, ed)
　W.G. Heath, 106:Fall84-311
Emerson, G. Some American Men.
　J. Fallows, 441:1Dec85-9
Emerson, R.L., G. Girard and R. Runte, eds.
Man and Nature/L'Homme et la Nature.*
(Vol 1)
　D. Williams, 83:Autumn84-279
Emerson, R.W. The Collected Works of
Ralph Waldo Emerson. (Vol 3) (A.R. Fer-
guson and J.F. Carr, eds)
　L.J. Budd, 579(SAQ):Autumn84-486
Emerson, R.W. Emerson in His Journals.*
(J. Porte, ed)
　J. Loving, 534(RALS):Spring82-81
Emerson, R.W. Die Natur. (M. Pütz, ed)
　L. Cerny, 72:Band221Heft1-194
　J. Manthey, 384:Jan84-83
Emerson, R.W. Natur [und] Essays.
　J. Manthey, 384:Jan84-83
Emerson, S. The American House of Saud.
　S. McCracken, 129:Sep85-68
　H. Purvis, 441:23Jun85-14
"Emigrés français en Allemagne/Emigrés
allemands en France (1685-1945)."
　W. Jost, 343:Heft9/10-161
Emmanuel, P. Le Grand Oeuvre.
　M. Edwards, 617(TLS):15Feb85-160
Emme, E.M., ed. Science Fiction and Space
Futures Past and Present.
　R. Dwyer, 561(SFS):Jul84-214
Emmel, H. Kritische Intelligenz als
Methode. (C.Z. Romero, ed)
　I. Solbrig, 133:Band17Heft1/2-119
　M. Winkler, 406:Winter84-457
Emmerich, W. Kleine Literaturgeschichte
der DDR.*
　J. Rosellini, 406:Winter84-482
Emmerich, W. Heinrich Mann: "Der Unter-
tan."*
　R.N. Linn, 406:Winter84-464
Emmert, R. and others, eds. Dance and
Music in South Asian Drama.
　J. Katz, 410(M&L):Oct84-408

Emmet, D. The Effectiveness of Causes.
　K. Lennon, 617(TLS):24May85-588
Emmons, T. The Formation of Political
Parties and the First National Elections
in Russia.
　T. Fallows, 550(RusR):Apr84-199
　J. Zimmerman, 104(CASS):Winter84-471
Empedocles. Empedocles: The Extant
Fragments. (M.R. Wright, ed and trans)
　S. Umphrey, 543:Sep83-162
Empson, W. Collected Poems.*
　R.M. Adams, 453(NYRB):11Apr85-32
Empson, W. Using Biography.*
　R.M. Adams, 453(NYRB):11Apr85-32
　J. Lucas, 493:Sep84-64
　442(NY):8Apr85-129
Emrich, E. Macht und Geist im Werk Hein-
rich Manns.*
　R.N. Linn, 406:Winter84-464
Emrich, W. Deutsche Literatur der Barock-
zeit.
　P. Hess, 406:Fall84-357
　U. Maché, 221(GQ):Spring84-310
　V. Meid, 301(JEGP):Jul84-407
von Ems, R. - see under Rudolf von Ems
Enchi, F. Masks.*
　J. Burnham, 617(TLS):14Jun85-678
Ende, M. Momo.
　F. Levy, 441:17Feb85-34
Endo, S. Stained Glass Elegies.*
　J. Mellors, 362:10Jan85-24
　A.N. Wilson, 441:21Jul85-21
Engberg, R. and D. Wesling. John Muir to
Yosemite and Beyond.
　D. Wyatt, 569(SR):Winter84-149
Engberg, S. A Stay by the River.
　T. Gallagher, 441:3Nov85-20
Engberg-Pedersen, T. Aristotle's Theory
of Moral Insight.
　A.W.H. Adkins, 319:Oct85-581
　A. Madigan, 258:Sep84-327
　N. Sherman, 185:Oct84-175
Engdahl, E. and E. Ejerhed, eds. Readings
on Unbounded Dependencies in Scandina-
vian Languages.
　S. Hellberg, 452(NJL):Vol7No2-185
Engel, B.A. Mothers and Daughters.*
　L. Edmondson, 575(SEER):Oct84-603
　N.G.O. Pereira, 104(CASS):Winter84-465
Engel, H. Murder on Location.
　D.R. Bartlett, 102(CanL):Autumn84-134
　N. Callendar, 441:23Jun85-33
Engel, H. Murder Sees the Light.
　T.J. Binyon, 617(TLS):30Aug85-946
　N. Callendar, 441:10Nov85-22
Engel, H. The Ransom Game.
　N. Callendar, 441:24Mar85-29
Engel, J-M. - see Livy
Engelberg, K., ed. The Romantic Heritage.
　J. Raimond, 189(EA):Oct-Dec85-468
Engelbrecht, T. and R. Herring. Sophus
Claussen.
　L. Isaacson, 563(SS):Spring84-199
von Engelhardt, W. and J. Zimmermann.
Theorie der Geowissenschaft.
　W. Schröder, 679:Band15Heft2-363
Engelkamp, J. and H.D. Zimmer. Dynamic
Aspects of Language Processing.
　S. Garrod, 353:Vol22No6-928
Engell, J. The Creative Imagination.
　D.P. Haase, 406:Summer84-212
　A. Krystal, 31(ASch):Spring84-283

Engell, J., ed. Johnson and His Age.
    D. Nokes, 617(TLS):29Nov85-1351
Engell, J. and W.J. Bate - see Coleridge,
S.T.
Engelmann, B. Germany Without Jews.
    C.M. Kimmich, 441:6Jan85-10
Engelmayer, S. and R. Wagman. Lord's
Justice.
    R. Cherry, 441:22Sep85-37
Engelstad, I. Amalie Skram om seg selv.
    J.E. Rasmussen, 563(SS):Spring84-184
Engelstein, L. Moscow, 1905.*
    M. Perrie, 575(SEER):Apr84-296
    R.G. Suny, 104(CASS):Spring-Summer84-
    200
England, A.B. Energy and Order in the
Poetry of Swift.*
    J. Mezciems, 541(RES):Feb84-88
    P.J. Schakel, 301(JEGP):Jan84-123
England, N.C. A Grammar of Mam.
    W.F. Hanks, 350:Jun85-484
Englebretsen, G. Three Logicians.* Logi-
cal Negation.*
    P. Loptson, 154:Dec84-716
Engler, E. Shelleys imaginative Dichter-
theorie und ihre lyrische Praxis.
    R.P. Lessenich, 72:Band221Heft2-375
Englert, R.W. Scattering and Oneing.
    R. Bradley, 589:Oct84-972
English, E.P. Canadian Development Assis-
tance to Haiti.
    D. Glover, 298:Winter84/85-133
Engman, M. St. Petersburg och Finland.
    M. Metcalf, 550(RusR):Oct84-429
Engwall, G. Vocabulaire du roman français
(1962-1968). (S. Allén, ed)
    C. Muller, 553(RLiR):Jul-Dec84-488
Ennius. The Annals of Q. Ennius. (O.
Skutsch, ed)
    E.J. Kenney, 617(TLS):12Jul85-768
Enquist, P.O. The March of the Musicians.
    D. Steiner, 617(TLS):13Dec85-1433
Enright, D.J. Academic Year.
    B. Morrison, 617(TLS):29Nov85-1371
Enright, D.J., ed. Fair of Speech.
    A. Burgess, 617(TLS):12Apr85-399
    W. Deedes, 362:18Apr85-23
    G. Ewart, 176:May85-52
Enright, D.J. Instant Chronicles.
    J.W. Aldridge, 441:3Nov85-28
    G. Ewart, 176:May85-51
    D. May, 362:2May85-26
    P. Reading, 617(TLS):7Jun85-649
Enright, D.J. A Mania for Sentences.
    J.W. Aldridge, 441:3Nov85-28
Enriquez, A.R. - see under Reyes Enriquez,
A.
"The Entry of Henri II into Paris, 16 June
1549."* (I.D. McFarlane, ed)
    N.G. Brooks, 539:May85-139
Enzensberger, H.M. Critical Essays. (R.
Grimm and B. Armstrong, eds)
    T.C. Hanlin, 399(MLJ):Summer84-168
Eogan, G. Excavations at Knowth I.
    M. Harmon, 272(IUR):Autumn84-283
Eösze, L. Wenn Wagner ein Tagebuch
geführt hätte.
    S. Gut, 537:Vol70No1-140
Eoyang, E.C., P. Wenlan and M. Chin - see
Ai Qing
Ephron, N. Heartburn.
    J.L. Halio, 598(SoR):Winter85-204

Epicurus. Trattato etico epicureo (P.
Herc. 346). (M. Capasso, ed and trans)
    D.P. Fowler, 123:Vol134No2-216
    H.M. Hine, 303(JoHS):Vol 104-216
"La época de Fernando VI."*
    D.T. Gies, 240(HR):Winter84-87
Eppard, P.B. and G. Monteiro, eds. A
Guide to the Atlantic Monthly Contrib-
utors' Club.*
    K. Vanderbilt, 26(ALR):Spring84-148
Epps, G. The Floating Island.
    R. Plunket, 441:14Jul85-16
Epstein, D.F. The Political Theory of
"The Federalist."
    J.R. Pole, 617(TLS):24May85-584
    T.S., 185:Jul85-985
Epstein, E.L., ed. A Starchamber Quiry.
    W. Harmon, 569(SR):Summer84-466
    R.D. Newman, 577(SHR):Summer84-279
Epstein, J. The Middle of My Tether.*
    J. Parini, 249(HudR):Spring84-172
Epstein, J. Plausible Prejudices.
    S. Fender, 617(TLS):2Aug85-857
    W.H. Pritchard, 441:24Feb85-8
Epstein, J. and D. Thompson, eds. The
Chartist Experience.
    D. Nicholls, 637(VS):Spring84-397
Epstein, L. Goldkorn Tales.
    D. Evanier, 441:7Apr85-8
Epstein, L. The Steinway Quintet: Plus
Four.
    F. Busch, 219(GaR):Fall84-525
Epstein, S. Wills and Wealth in Medieval
Genoa, 1150-1250.
    D. Abulafia, 617(TLS):23Aug85-921
"Equality Now."
    K.A. Moodley, 529(QQ):Winter84-795
Erasmus. Collected Works of Erasmus.*
(Vol 6) (P.G. Bietenholz, ed)
    J.F. McDiarmid, 539:Feb85-68
    L.V.R., 568(SCN):Winter84-77
Erasmus. Collected Works of Erasmus.*
(Vol 31) (R.A.B. Mynors, ed)
    L.V.R., 568(SCN):Winter84-77
Erasmus. Desiderius Erasmus, "Opera
omnia." (Vol 2, No 5 and 6) (F. Heini-
mann and E. Kienzle, with S. Seidel-
Menchi, eds)
    J.K. Sowards, 551(RenQ):Spring84-71
Erb, G. Zu Komposition und Aufbau im
ersten Buch Martials.*
    W. Hottentot, 394:Vol37fasc1/2-217
Erdman, D.V. - see Blake, W.
Erdman, P. Paul Erdman's Money Book.*
(British title: Paul Erdman's Money
Guide.)
    J. Hardie, 617(TLS):22Mar85-328
Erdoes, R. and A. Ortiz, eds. American
Indian Myths and Legends.
    J. Bruchac, 469:Vol 10No1-126
    J. Gleason, 472:Fall/Winter84-21
    J. Highwater, 441:3Feb85-11
Erdrich, L. Jacklight.
    P. Stitt, 219(GaR):Winter84-857
Erdrich, L. Love Medicine.*
    G. Davenport, 344:Fall85-122
    E. Jahner, 469:Vol 10No2-96
    L. Taylor, 617(TLS):22Feb85-196
    R. Towers, 453(NYRB):11Apr85-36
    442(NY):7Jan85-76
Erhart, A. Struktura indoíránských jazyků.
    V. Bubeník, 260(IF):Band89-335

Ericksen, R.P. Theologians Under Hitler.
  M. Silk, 441:28Jul85-19
Erickson, C. Anne Boleyn.
  C. Haigh, 617(TLS):22Feb85-204
Erickson, F. and J. Shultz. The Counselor
  as Gatekeeper.
  H. Mehan, 355(LSoc):Jun84-251
Erickson, J. The Road to Berlin.*
  W.C. Fuller, Jr., 550(RusR):Oct84-434
Erickson, S. Days Between Stations.
  F. Randall, 441:12May85-18
Ericson, L. Fabrics ... Reconstructed.
  A.L. Mayer, 614:Spring85-22
Erikson, E. The Life Cycle Completed.
  E.S. Person, 473(PR):3/1984-458
Eriksson, O. L'attribut de localisation
  et les nexus locatifs en français
  moderne.*
  G. Gross, 209(FM):Apr84-81
Erisman, F. and R.W. Etulain, eds. Fifty
  Western Writers.*
  J.G. Cawelti, 26(ALR):Autumn84-284
  R.H. Cracroft, 651(WHR):Spring84-90
  S.E. Marovitz, 87(BB):Mar84-42
"Erkundungen: 16 palästinensische Erzäh-
  ler."
  D. Erpenbeck, 654(WB):12/1984-2057
Erlich, J. Schabbat.
  C. Daxelmüller, 196:Band25Heft1/2-127
Erlich, V. Russian Formalism. (3rd ed)
  M. Makin, 447(N&Q):Dec83-570
Ermarth, E.D. Realism and Consensus in
  the English Novel.*
  W.K. Buckley, 594:Summer84-248
  M. Childers, 141:Fall84-394
  J. Preston, 402(MLR):Oct84-881
  D.D. Stone, 637(VS):Summer84-524
  J. Wallen, 400(MLN):Dec84-1260
  639(VQR):Winter84-8
Ermengaud, M. - see under Matfre Ermengaud
Ermolaev, H. Mikhail Sholokhov and His
  Art.*
  J.S. Durrant, 104(CASS):Spring-
  Summer84-170
Ermolin, A.P. Revoliutsiia i kazachestvo
  (1917-1920).
  O. Andriewsky, 550(RusR):Apr84-202
Ernaux, A. La Place.
  F. de Martinoir, 450(NRF):Apr84-111
Ernst, J. A Not-So-Still Life.*
  J. Bell, 55:Dec84-29
  A. Korner, 62:Dec84-70
  M.S. Young, 39:Aug84-148
Errington, F.K. Manners and Meaning in
  West Sumatra.
  P. Carey, 617(TLS):4Oct85-1112
Erskine-Hill, H. The Augustan Idea in
  English Literature.*
  J.M. Aden, 569(SR):Spring84-xxxii
  J. Maule, 175:Spring84-61
  A. Morvan, 189(EA):Jul-Sep85-300
  R.G. Peterson, 173(ECS):Summer85-568
Ertz, K. Jan Brueghel der Ältere (1568-
  1625).
  D. Freedberg, 90:Sep84-575
Eruli, B. Jarry.
  K.S. Beaumont, 208(FS):Apr84-224
Ervin, S. Humor of a Country Lawyer.
  639(VQR):Winter84-29
Erzgräber, W., ed. Europäisches Spätmit-
  telalter.
  R. Bergmann, 684(ZDA):Band113Heft1-22
  K. Reichl, 382(MAE):1984/1-105

von Eschenbach, W. - see under Wolfram von
  Eschenbach
Escobedo, T.H., ed. Early Childhood Bilin-
  gual Education.
  M.I. Duke dos Santos, 238:Sep84-483
  M. Saville-Troike, 399(MLJ):Winter84-
  389
Escribano, J.G. and T. Lambert. Por aquí.*
  K.E. Breiner-Sanders, 238:Mar84-158
Eshleman, C. and A. Smith - see Césaire, A.
Espinosa Ruiz, U. Debate Agrippa-Mecenas
  en Dión Cassio.
  J.M. Alonso-Núñez, 123:Vol34No1-94
Espinosa Soriano, W. Los cayambes y caran-
  gues; siglos XV-XVI.
  J. Villamarin, 263(RIB):Vol34No1-93
Esposito, J.L. Evolutionary Metaphysics.
  P. Skagestad, 567:Vol148No1/2-133
"Essays in Honor of James Edward Walsh on
  his Sixty-Fifth Birthday."
  S. Parks, 517(PBSA):Vol78No3-380
van Essen, A.J. E. Kruisinga.*
  B. Rigter, 204(FdL):Mar84-63
Essick, R.N. The Separate Plates of Wil-
  liam Blake.
  S.D. Cox, 173(ECS):Spring85-391
  D. Fuller, 161(DUJ):Dec83-141
Essick, R.N. and M.D. Paley - see Blair, R.
Estang, L. Corps à coeur.*
  M. Guiney, 207(FR):Mar85-595
Estaver, P. Salisbury Beach, 1954.
  D. Chorlton, 496:Winter85-248
de Esteban, J. Las constituciones de
  España.
  R.M. Pepiol, 86(BHS):Oct84-511
Esteban Lorente, J.F., F. Galtier Martí
  and M. García Guatas. El nacimiento del
  arte románico en Aragón.
  J. Williams, 589:Jan84-233
Estève, M. Bernanos et Bresson.
  [together with] Jurt, J. Bernanos et
  Jouve.
  M. Watthee-Delmotte, 356(LR):Feb/May84-
  135
Estleman, L.D. Roses Are Dead.
  N. Callendar, 441:24Nov85-43
Estleman, L.D. Sugartown.
  N. Callendar, 441:24Mar85-29
Estrada, F.L. - see under López Estrada, F.
"Estudios en Homenaje a Don Claudio
  Sánchez Albornoz en sus 90 años."
  P. Linehan, 617(TLS):11Oct85-1144
"Estudios históricos sobre la Iglesia
  española contemporánea."
  D.W. Lomax, 86(BHS):Apr84-208
Etchepareborda, R. Zeballos.
  J. Finan, 263(RIB):Vol34No2-303
Etherege, G. The Plays of Sir George
  Etherege. (M. Cordner, ed)
  B.S.H., 83:Autumn84-281
Etherton, M. The Development of African
  Drama.*
  D. Bradby, 610:Autumn84-254
  E. Savory, 538(RAL):Fall84-448
Ethier-Blais, J. Les Pays étrangers.
  L. Mailhot, 102(CanL):Winter83-130
"Ethnic Recordings in America."
  J.P. Leary, 292(JAF):Jan-Mar84-81
Étiemble. Quelques essais de littérature
  universelle.
  G.M. Vajda, 149(CLS):Fall84-352

Ewing, K.M.H. A. Aubrey Bodine.
  A. Grundberg, 441:8Dec85-24
Eyerman, R. False Consciousness and Ideology in Marxist Theory.
  R. Gilbert, 488:Dec84-575
Eygun, F-X. L'Écharpe d'Iris.
  M-N. Little, 207(FR):Oct84-158
Eylat, M. Analyse anthroponymique des noms de famille des Juifs, en Alsace, au dix-huitième siècle.
  A. Lapierre, 424:Sep84-330
Eysenck, H. Decline and Fall of the Freudian Empire.
  A. Clare, 362:29Aug85-24
Ezawa, K. and K.H. Rensch, eds. Sprache und Sprechen.
  J. Göschel, 260(IF)·Band89-291
Ezekiel, N. Latter-Day Psalms.
  D. McDuff, 565:Spring84-72
  A. Stevenson, 617(TLS):19Apr85-449
Ezergailis, I. Women Writers.
  S.L. Cocalis, 221(GQ):Summer84-504

Faas, E. Young Robert Duncan.
  30:Fall84-95
  295(JML):Nov84-429
von Faber, H., ed. Lesen in der Fremdsprache.
  M.P. Alter, 399(MLJ):Autumn84-271
Faber, R. The Brave Courtier.
  J. Halden, 568(SCN):Winter84-66
  C. Probyn, 566:Autumn84-59
Fabian, B. Buch, Bibliothek und geisteswissenschaftliche Forschung.
  D. Paisey, 354:Sep84-299
"Fables from Old French." (N.R. Shapiro, trans)
  M.J. Ward, 207(FR):Oct84-119
Fabre, G. Drumbeats, Masks, and Metaphor.
  R.A. Adubato, 615(TJ):Oct84-436
  L.E. Scott, 95(CLAJ):Jun85-473
Fabre, G. Libertus.*
  J.H. D'Arms, 122:Apr84-170
Fabre, J. Enquête sur un enquêteur: Maigret.
  C. Gothot-Mersch, 535(RHL):Jul/Aug84-652
Fabre, J. Lumières et romantisme. (new ed)
  T.E.D. Braun, 207(FR):Oct84-128
Fabre, M. La Rive noire.
  R. Asselineau, 189(EA):Jul-Sep85-366
Fabricant, C. Swift's Landscape.*
  S. Donnelly, 174(Éire):Fall84-153
  A.B. England, 173(ECS):Fall84-92
  D. Oakleaf, 49:Jan84-90
  R. Quintana, 402(MLR):Oct84-906
  L. Speirs, 179(ES):Apr84-183
de Fabry, A.S. Jeux de Miroirs.*
  R.J. Howells, 208(FS):Apr84-207
Faccenna, D. Butkara I (Swat, Pakistan) 1956-1962.
  M. Baistrocchi, 60:May-Jun84-118
Faderman, L. Scotch Verdict.
  V.S. Carr, 639(VQR):Summer84-514
Faderman, L. Surpassing the Love of Men.
  E. Marks, 81:Winter84-99
Fagen, R.R. and O. Pellicer, eds. The Future of Central America.
  L. Cardenas, Jr., 263(RIB):Vol34No1-95

Fagiolo, M. and M.L. Madonna. Il Teatro del Sole.
  D. Garstang, 90:Apr84-239
Fagiolo, M. and G. Spagnesi, eds. Immagini del Barocco.
  H. Tratz, 471:Jul/Aug/Sep84-303
Fagundo, A.M. Desde chanatel, el canto.
  I.R.M. Galbis, 552(REH):May84-317
Fahmy, J.M. Voltaire et Paris.*
  J. Balcou, 535(RHL):Jul/Aug84-616
Fai-hsi, W. - see under Wang Fai-hsi
Faigan, J. Paul Sandby Drawings.
  D.B., 90:Aug84-510
Fainlight, R. Climates.*
  R. Pybus, 565:Autumn84-73
  A. Stevenson, 493:Jun84-66
Fainlight, R. Fifteenth to Infinity.*
  R. Pybus, 565:Autumn84-73
Fairbairns, Z. Here Today.*
  P. Craig, 617(TLS):29Nov85-1372
Fairbank, J.K. and K-C. Liu. Cambridge History of China.* (Vol 11, Pt 2)
  A.Y.C. Lui, 302:Vol20No2-195
Fairbank, W. - see under Liang Ssu-ch'eng
Fairbanks, C. and S.B. Sundberg. Farm Women on the Prairie Frontier.
  L.R., 102(CanL):Autumn84-152
Fairbanks, J.L. and R.L. Trent. New England Begins.
  R.M. Candee, 658:Summer/Autumn84-207
Fairclough, O. and E. Leary. Textiles by William Morris and Company, 1861-1940.
  G.L. Aho, 536:Vol5-73
Fairer, D. Pope's Imagination.
  D. Donoghue, 617(TLS):8Feb85-139
Fairweather, J. Seneca the Elder.*
  H.C. Gotoff, 122:Apr84-166
"Faith in the City."
  F. Cairncross, 617(TLS):20Dec85-1445
Falco, E. Concert in the Park of Culture.
  S.M. Gibson, 219(GaR):Winter84-903
Falcon, G.N. - see under Nanez Falcon, G.
Falconer, R. and others. Four Scottish Poets.
  D. McDuff, 565:Spring84-72
Faletti, H.F. Die Jahreszeiten des Fin de siècle.
  M. Winkler, 133:Band17Heft1/2-166
Falivene, M.R., comp. Historical Catalogue of the Manuscripts of Bible House Library. (A.F. Jesson, ed)
  S. Brock, 354:Mar84-72
Falk, J. "Ser" y "estar" con atributos adjetivales.
  S.N. Dworkin, 545(RPh):Aug83-97
Falk, Q. Travels in Greeneland.
  A. Young, 617(TLS):22Feb85-199
Falk, T. Katalog der Zeichnungen des 15. und 16. Jahrhunderts im Kupferstichkabinett Basel. (Pt 1)
  J. Rowlands, 90:May84-295
Falkenberg, G. Lügen.
  A.F.J. Pauwels, 67:Nov84-260
Fallada, H. Erzählungen.
  M. Lynch, 399(MLJ):Winter84-403
Fallaize, E. Malraux: "La Voie royale."
  J. Dale, 208(FS):Jan84-92
Fallani, G. Dante moderno.
  G. Costa, 545(RPh):Nov83-251
Fallon, D. The German University.
  J. Herbst, 406:Fall84-343

Fallon, P. Winter Work.
  M. Harmon, 272(IUR):Spring84-126
  N. Jenkins, 493:Jan84-71
  M. Riordan, 617(TLS):15Mar85-294
Fallon, R.T. Captain or Colonel.
  J. Pitcher, 617(TLS):23Aug85-932
Fallows, D. A Mother's Work.
  E. Crow, 441:27Oct85-12
Faludy, G. Learn This Poem of Mine by
  Heart. (J.R. Colombo, ed)
  C. Matyas, 168(ECW):Winter84/85-352
Fan Ch'eng-ta. Five Seasons of a Golden
  Year, A Chinese Pastoral. (G. Bullett,
  trans)
  J.M. Hargett, 116:Jul83-196
Fanning, R. Independent Ireland.
  272(IUR):Spring84-152
Fanselow, G. Zur Syntax und Semantik der
  Nominalkomposition.
  S. Wolff, 660(Word):Aug84-197
Fantham, E. Seneca's "Troades."*
  M. Billerbeck, 487:Autumn84-289
  H. Zehnacker, 555:Vol58fasc2-324
Fanthorpe, U.A. Standing To.
  J. Saunders, 565:Spring84-55
Fanthorpe, U.A. Voices Off.
  T. Dooley, 617(TLS):6Dec85-1405
  J. Mole, 176:Jul/Aug85-56
al-Fārābī. Al-Fārābī's Commentary and
  Short Treatise on Aristotle's "De
  Interpretatione."* (F.W. Zimmermann,
  ed and trans)
  M.E. Marmura, 318(JAOS):Oct-Dec83-763
Farber, J. A Field Guide to the Aesthetic
  Experience.*
  W. Charlton, 89(BJA):Spring84-173
Fardoulis-Lagrange, M. Théodicée.
  T. Cordellier, 450(NRF):Nov84-93
Faret, N. Projet de l'Académie pour
  servir de Préface à ses Statuts. (J.
  Rousselet, ed)
  F. Higman, 208(FS):Jul84-335
Farge, A., ed. Le Miroir des femmes.
  L. Andries, 535(RHL):Nov/Dec84-960
Farge, A. and C. Klapisch-Zuber, eds.
  Madame ou Mademoiselle?
  B.T. Cooper, 207(FR):May85-929
Farington, J. The Diary of Joseph Faring-
  ton.* (Vols 1-6 ed by K. Garlick and A.
  MacIntyre; Vols 7-10 ed by K. Cave)
  A. Tennant, 59:Sep84-375
Farington, J. The Diary of Joseph Faring-
  ton. (Vols 11 and 12) (K. Cave, ed)
  L. Herrmann, 90:Apr84-240
Farington, J. The Diary of Joseph Faring-
  ton. (Vols 13 and 14) (K. Cave, ed)
  L.H., 90:Dec84-796
  M. Pointon, 617(TLS):17May85-539
Farington, J. The Diary of Joseph Faring-
  ton. (Vols 15 and 16) (K. Cave, ed)
  M. Pointon, 617(TLS):17May85-539
Farley, J., ed. Women Workers in Fifteen
  Countries.
  A. Kessler-Harris, 441:4Aug85-12
Farley-Hills, D. The Comic in Renaissance
  Comedy.*
  K. Robinson, 447(N&Q):Apr83-169
Farmakides, A. Advanced Modern Greek.
  J.E. Rexine, 399(MLJ):Autumn84-295
Farmer, J. Dayworld.
  G. Jonas, 441:28Apr85-21

Farmer, J. Lay Bare the Heart.
  C. Sitton, 441:24Mar85-20
  442(NY):25Feb85-103
Farmer, P. Eve, Her Story.
  J. Winterson, 617(TLS):21Jun85-702
Farmer, P.J. The Classic Philip José
  Farmer, 1952-1964. (M.H. Greenberg, ed)
  D. Barbour, 561(SFS):Jul84-200
Farnan, D.J. Auden in Love.*
  P. Kemp, 362:21Mar85-25
  J. Symons, 617(TLS):22Mar85-305
Farnsworth, R.M. Melvin B. Tolson, 1898-
  1966.
  W.C. Daniel, 95(CLAJ):Mar85-361
Farr, D.M. John Ford and the Caroline
  Theatre.
  L.G. Black, 447(N&Q):Feb83-78
Farr, J. The Life and Art of Elinor Wylie.
  H. McNeil, 617(TLS):5Apr85-378
  G. Scharnhorst, 395(MFS):Winter84-803
  639(VQR):Summer84-89
Farrar, L.L., Jr. Arrogance and Anxiety.
  I.V. Hull, 221(GQ):Spring84-351
Farré, J.A. - see under Avilés Farré, J.
Farrell, B.A. The Standing of Psycho-
  analysis.*
  M. Lavin, 486:Mar84-177
  R. Oxlade, 529(QQ):Summer84-330
  R.S. Wallerstein, 449:Sep84-534
Farrell, J.T. Hearing Out James T. Far-
  rell. (D. Phelps, ed)
  S. Krim, 441:28Jul85-19
Farrell, J.T. On Irish Themes.* (D.
  Flynn, ed)
  J.L. Schneider, 395(MFS):Summer84-359
Farrell, M.J. Devoted Ladies.* The Ris-
  ing Tide.*
  M. Gordon, 441:29Sep85-43
Farwell, B. Eminent Victorian Soldiers.
  E. Weber, 441:16Jun84-13
Fast, H. The Immigrant's Daughter.
  D. Gess, 441:15Sep85-24
Fattori, M. and M. Bianchi, eds. I° Collo-
  quio Internazionale del Lessico Intel-
  lettuale Europeo. II° Colloquio Inter-
  nazionale del Lessico Intellettuale
  Europeo. III° Colloquio Internazionale
  del Lessico Intellettuale Europeo.
  R. Sasso, 192(EP):Oct-Dec84-558
Faulkes, A. - see Snorri Sturluson
Faulkner, D.W. - see Cowley, M.
Faulkner, P. Against the Age.* Wilfrid
  Scawen Blunt and the Morrises.
  G.L. Aho, 536:Vol5-73
Faulkner, W. Father Abraham. (J.B. Meri-
  wether, ed)
  442(NY):4Feb85-101
Faulkner, W. Faulkner's MGM Screenplays.
  (B.F. Kawin, ed)
  R. Fadiman, 534(RALS):Spring82-97
  J.G. Watson, 395(MFS):Summer84-319
Faulkner, W. Sanctuary, the Original
  Text.* (N. Polk, ed)
  J.L. Capps, 534(RALS):Spring82-95
Faulkner, W. Visions in Spring.
  M. Grimwood, 578:Fall85-101
Faulks, S. A Trick of the Light.*
  P. Lewis, 364:Jul84-99
Faure, A., Y. Flesch and A. Nivelle - see
  Thieberger, R.
Faust, I. The Year of the Hot Jock.
  H. Gold, 441:14Jul85-13

Faust, M., R. Hartweg and W. Lehfeldt, eds.
Allgemeine Sprachwissenschaft, Sprach-
typologie und Textlinguistik.
E. Albrecht, 682(ZPSK):Band37Heft4-513
K.P. Lange, 361:May84-97
Fausto-Sterling, A. Myths of Gender.
D.J. Kevles, 441:29Dec85-12
de Faveri, F. and R. Wagenknecht, eds and
trans. Italienische Lyrik der Gegenwart.
E. Leube, 72:Band22lHeft2-473
Favre, Y-A., ed. Le Colloque André Suarès.
H. Godin, 208(FS):Apr84-223
Fawcett, R.P. and others, eds. The Semi-
otics of Culture and Language.
T. Moore, 617(TLS):8Feb85-155
Fawkner, H.W. The Timescapes of John
Fowles.
P. Smelt, 617(TLS):22Feb85-198
Faxon, A.C. Jean-Louis Forain.
R. Thomson, 90:Feb84-96
Fay-Hallé, A. and B. Mundt. Nineteenth-
Century European Porcelain.
G. Wills, 39:Sep84-217
Feather, J. The English Provincial Book
Trade before 1850.
A.D. Sterenberg, 447(N&Q):Dec83-550
Fedeli, P. Sesto Properzio.
J. den Boeft, 394:Vol37fascl/2-212
Fedeli, P. - see Cicero
Feder, G., with W. Rehm and M. Ruhnke, eds.
Quellenforschung in der Musikwissen-
schaft.
B. Cooper, 410(M&L):Jan84-103
Feder, L. Madness in Literature.
J.C. Voelker, 577(SHR):Winter84-90
Federman, R. Smiles on Washington Square.
A. Cheuse, 441:24Nov85-24
Federspiel, J.F. The Ballad of Typhoid
Mary.*
M. Howard, 676(YR):Winter85-x
Fedorov, V.I. Istorija russkoj literatury
XVIII veka.
I. Radezky, 574(SEEJ):Winter84-539
Fedorowicz, J.K., ed and trans. A Repub-
lic of Nobles.*
P. Brock, 104(CASS):Spring-Summer84-
211
Feeley, K. Flannery O'Connor.
M. Morton, 392:Winter83/84-89
Feely, T. Limelight.
F. Llorente, 441:9Jun85-22
Feeny, D. The Political Economy of Pro-
ductivity.
L. Small, 293(JASt):Aug84-798
Fegert, H. and G. Rodekuhr. Die Morphonol-
ogie der Neutra auf "-stv-" im Polnis-
chen und Russischen.
H.D. Pohl, 260(IF):Band89-382
Feher, M. Conjurations de la violence.
R. Sasso, 192(EP):Apr-Jun84-268
Fehr, K. Conrad Ferdinand Meyer.
M. Burkhard, 301(JEGP):Oct84-609
Fei Hsiao Tung. Toward a People's Anthro-
pology.
R.D. Arkush, 293(JASt):Feb84-315
Feigon, L. Chen Duxiu.
639(VQR):Summer84-87
Feijoo, B.J. Obras completas.* (Vol 1)
(J.M. Caso González and S. Cerra Suárez,
eds)
R.M. Cox, 240(HR):Winter84-91
I.L. McClelland, 86(BHS):Oct84-525

Feijoo, L.I. La trayectoria dramática de
Antonio Buero Vallejo.
D. Gagen, 402(MLR):Oct84-964
M.T. Halsey, 238:Mar84-145
W. Newberry, 593:Spring84-84
Feilchenfeldt, K., U. Schweikert and R.E.
Steiner - see Varnhagen, R.
Fein, D.A. Charles d'Orléans.
A.T. Harrison, 207(FR):Apr85-722
Feinberg, G. Solid Clues.
H.F. Judson, 441:21Apr85-32
M.F. Perutz, 453(NYRB):26Sep85-14
Feinberg, J. The Moral Limits of the Crim-
inal Law. (Vol 1)
J. Bell, 617(TLS):8Feb85-143
Feingold, M. The Mathematicians' Appren-
ticeship.*
S. Soupel, 189(EA):Oct-Dec85-458
Feinstein, E. The Border.*
G. Steiner, 442(NY):29Apr85-130
Feinstein, E. Bessie Smith.
A. Huth, 362:5Dec85-27
Feinstein, E. - see Clare, J.
Feissel, D. Recueil des inscriptions
chrétiennes de Macédoine du IIIe au VIe
siècle.
C. Mango, 123:Vol34No1-119
Feist, R.E. Magician.
C. Fein, 441:3Mar85-22
Feld, S. Sound and Sentiment.*
R. Wagner, 355(LSoc):Mar84-108
Feldbaek, O. Tiden 1730-1814. (A.E.
Christensen and others, eds)
H.A. Barton, 563(SS):Spring84-191
Feldges, U. Landschaft als topograph-
isches Porträt.
J. White, 90:Mar84-160
Feldman, I. Teach Me, Dear Sister.*
R. Asselineau, 189(EA):Jul-Sep85-364
Felgar, R. Richard Wright.
M. Fabre, 402(MLR):Apr84-444
Felice, C. Downtime.
G. Jonas, 441:8Sep85-28
de Felice, T. Le Patois de la zone
d'implantation protestante du nord-est
de la Haute-Loire.
J-P. Chambon, 553(RLiR):Jul-Dec84-439
Fell, A. Kisses for Mayakovsky.
M. Shaw, 493:Sep84-67
Fell, A.L. Origins of Legislative Sover-
eignty and the Legislative State. (Vols
1 and 2)
J. Kirshner, 551(RenQ):Autumn84-425
Fell, C., with C. Clark and E. Williams.
Women in Anglo-Saxon England.
W. Smith, 441:11Aug85-15
Fell, M. The Persistence of Memory.*
639(VQR):Autumn84-137
"Fellini par Fellini."
C. Thomas, 98:Aug/Sep84-662
Fellmann, F. Phänomenologie und Expres-
sionismus.
W. Paulsen, 133:Band17Heft1/2-157
Fellows, J. Ruskin's Maze.*
P. Fontaney, 189(EA):Oct-Dec85-473
K.O. Garrigan, 637(VS):Spring84-365
Fellows, O. and D.G. Carr - see "Diderot
Studies"
Fellows, R.A. Sir Reginald Blomfield.
A. Saint, 617(TLS):22Feb85-195
Felman, S. The Literary Speech Act.
D. Gorman, 478:Apr84-140

Felperin, H. Beyond Deconstruction.
  C. Craig, 617(TLS):22Nov85-1314
Fels, L. Ein Unding der Liebe.
  E. Henscheid, 384:Sep84-691
Femia, J.V. Gramsci's Political Thought.
  M.A. Finocchiaro, 262:Jul84-291
Fender, S. Plotting the Golden West.*
  D. Seed, 541(RES):Aug84-423
Feng Jicai. Chrysanthemums.
  H. Cooke, 441:28Jul85-12
Fenlon, I., ed. Cambridge Music Manu-
  scripts 900-1700.*
  A. Wathey, 410(M&L):Jan84-61
Fenlon, I., ed. Early Music History.*
  (Vol 1)
  N. Sevestre, 537:Vol70No1-129
Fenlon, I., ed. Early Music History.
  (Vol 2)
  D. Fallows, 410(M&L):Jul84-285
Fenlon, I. Music and Patronage in Six-
  teenth-Century Mantua.* (Vol 2)
  D. Arnold, 410(M&L):Jan84-98
Fennell, F.L. Dante Gabriel Rossetti.*
  M. Warner, 90:Dec84-792
Fennell, J. The Crisis of Medieval Russia,
  1200-1304.
  M. Dimnik, 589:Oct84-898
Fenoaltea, D. "Si haulte Architecture."*
  I.D. McFarlane, 208(FS):Jan84-50
  J.C. Nash, 210(FrF):Jan84-112
Fenton, J. Children in Exile.*
  E. Grosholz, 249(HudR):Winter84/85-652
  W. Logan, 491:Nov84-111
  E. Longley, 493:Apr84-59
  P. Stitt, 219(GaR):Spring84-166
  639(VQR):Autumn84-139
Fenton, J. The Memory of War.*
  E. Longley, 493:Apr84-59
Fergus, J. Jane Austen and the Didactic
  Novel.
  M.A. Doody, 445(NCF):Mar85-465
Ferguson, A.R. and J.F. Carr - see Emerson,
  R.W.
Ferguson, C.A. and S.B. Heath, eds. Lan-
  guage in the USA.*
  K.E. Müller, 399(MLJ):Spring84-63
Ferguson, J.M., Jr. The Summerfield
  Stories.
  H. Benedict, 441:25Aug85-16
Ferguson, M.W. Trials of Desire.
  M.J. Bugeja, 568(SCN):Fall84-33
  R.L. Levao, 551(RenQ):Spring84-118
  J.L. Smarr, 301(JEGP):Oct84-559
  J.C. Tylus, 400(MLN):Dec84-1234
Ferguson, P. Family Myths and Legends.
  E. Fisher, 617(TLS):1Feb85-110
  J. Mellors, 362:21Mar85-25
Ferguson, R.A. Law and Letters in Amer-
  ican Culture.
  L. Auchincloss, 165(EAL):Spring85-75
  M. Peters, 441:27Jan85-23
  B. Thomas, 454:Spring85-274
Ferguson, S., ed. Critical Essays on Ran-
  dall Jarrell.
  D.B. Kesterson, 392:Fall84-483
  S. Wright, 569(SR):Summer84-lxviii
Ferland, M. Les Batteux.
  J.B. Moss, 102(CanL):Autumn84-98
Fermor, P.L. The Violins of Saint-Jacques.
  M. Seymour, 617(TLS):4Oct85-1097
Fernald, D. The Hans Legacy.
  T.A. Sebeok, 617(TLS):8Mar85-268

Fernández, A.L. - see under Labandeira
  Fernández, A.
Fernandez, J.W. Bwiti.
  L. Siroto, 2(AfrA):Feb84-86
Fernandez, M.B. - see under Borrero Fernan-
  dez, M.
Fernández, M.T.D. - see under de Garay Fer-
  nández, M.T.
Fernández, R.G. La vida es un special
  $1/30.75.
  J. Febles, 238:May84-315
Fernández-Armesto, F. The Canary Islands
  after the Conquest.
  P.E.H. Hair, 86(BHS):Oct84-504
Fernández-Lopez, D. The Lyre and the
  Oaten Flute.
  P. Waley, 86(BHS):Apr84-193
Fernandez Santos, J. Extramuros.*
  639(VQR):Autumn84-133
Fernea, E.W., ed. Women and the Family in
  the Middle East.
  A. Rassam, 441:29Sep85-61
Fernie, E. The Architecture of the Anglo-
  Saxons.*
  A. Borg, 90:Jan84-41
  J. Glancey, 46:May84-84
  I. Wood, 59:Jun84-253
Ferns, H.S. Reading from Left to Right.
  M. Beloff, 176:Apr85-43
  A. Mills, 99:Apr84-33
  G. Woodcock, 617(TLS):9Aug85-881
Ferrante, J. and C.W. Rackoff. The Compu-
  tational Complexity of Logical Theories.
  D. Siefkes, 316:Jun84-670
Ferrari, A. Formazione e struttura del
  canzoniere portoghese della Biblioteca
  Nazionale di Lisbona (cod. 10991:
  Colocci-Brancuti).
  E. Gonçalves, 554:Vol 104No3-403
Ferrari, F. Ricerche sul testo di
  Sofocle.
  N.G. Wilson, 123:Vol34No1-128
Ferrari, J. Les Philosophes salariés.
  G.L., 185:Oct84-183
Ferraro, G.A., with L.B. Francke. Ferraro.
  M. Dowd, 441:3Nov85-7
Ferrars, E. The Crime and the Crystal.
  T.J. Binyon, 617(TLS):18Oct85-1173
Ferrars, E.X. Root of All Evil.
  442(NY):28Jan85-100
Ferreira, M.J. Doubt and Religious Commit-
  ment.
  J. Donnelly, 543:Dec83-398
Ferrell, A. Where She Was.
  D. Cole, 441:24Nov85-24
  R. Towers, 453(NYRB):19Dec85-23
Ferrell, K. H.G. Wells.
  R.H. Costa, 395(MFS):Summer84-362
Ferrell, R.H. Woodrow Wilson and World
  War I: 1917-1921.
  C.R. Herron, 441:14Jul85-23
  D.M. Kennedy, 61:Apr85-136
Ferrer, J. and P.W. De Poleo. Bridge the
  Gap.
  K.A. Mullen, 399(MLJ):Spring84-101
Ferretti, M. Rapporti della Soprinten-
  denza per i Beni Artistici e Storici per
  le provincie di Bologna, Ferrara, Forli
  e Ravenna. (No 32)
  R. Gibbs, 90:Jul84-438
Ferretti, V. Il Giappone e la politica
  estera italiana 1935-41.
  G. Krebs, 407(MN):Autumn84-361

Ferrier, S. Marriage. The Inheritance.
  B. Hardy, 617(TLS):7Jun85-641
Ferrill, A. The Origins of War.
  R. Rogers, 617(TLS):2Aug85-860
Ferris, I. William Makepeace Thackeray.
  E. Wright, 627(UTQ):Summer84-429
Ferris, P. - see Thomas, D.
Ferris, T. Spaceshots.
  S. Boxer, 441:3Mar85-22
Ferris, W. Blues from the Delta.
  A. Prévos, 91:Fall84-270
Ferris, W. Local Color. (B. McCallum, ed)
  K.G. Congdon, 292(JAF):Jan-Mar84-86
Ferris, W. and M.L. Hart, eds. Folk Music
  and Modern Sound.*
  N.V. Rosenberg, 292(JAF):Jul-Sep84-365
Ferriss, L. Philip's Girl.
  C. Bancroft, 441:18Aug85-20
Ferro, M. The Use and Abuse of History.*
  V. Bogdanor, 176:Jan85-42
Ferro, R. The Blue Star.
  W.J. Harding, 441:14Apr85-26
Ferry, A. The "Inward Language."
  B.G. Lyons, 533:Fall84-109
Ferry, D. Strangers.*
  W.H. Pritchard, 249(HudR):Summer84-328
Ferry, J. and A. Renaut - see Fichte, J.G.
Ferry, L. Philosophie politique.
  T. Cordellier, 450(NRF):Dec84-98
Fertig, M. Releasing the Spirit.
  B. Pirie, 102(CanL):Winter83-146
Festa-McCormick, D. Proustian Optics of
  Clothes.
  L.M. Porter, 395(MFS):Winter84-724
"Festschrift Richard Milesi: Beiträge aus
  den Geisteswissenschaften."
  D. von Naredi-Rainer, 471:
  Jul/Aug/Sep84-302
Fet, A. I have come to you to greet you.
  E. Klenin, 574(SEEJ):Summer84-262
Fetzer, L., ed and trans. Pre-Revolution-
  ary Russian Science Fiction.
  H. Stephan, 574(SEEJ):Fall84-413
Feuchtwanger, E.J. Democracy and Empire.
  C. Matthew, 617(TLS):13Sep85-1008
Feuchtwanger, L. Simone. Die Füchse im
  Weinberg.
  K. Modick, 384:Mar84-223
Feuchtwanger, L. Der Teufel in Frankreich.
  K. Modick, 384:Mar84-220
Feuchtwanger, M. Nur eine Frau.
  K. Modick, 384:Mar84-223
Feudel, G., ed. Zur Ausbildung der Norm
  der deutschen Literatursprache (1470-
  1730).
  B.J. Koekkoek, 350:Dec85-884
Feuer, L.S. The Case of the Revolution-
  ist's Daughter.
  N. Weyl, 390:Mar84-58
  639(VQR):Winter84-25
Feuerwerker, Y-T.M. Ding Ling's Fiction.*
  T.E. Barlow, 116:Jul83-125
Feyerabend, P.K. Philosophical Papers.*
  S.R.L. Clark, 479(PhQ):Apr84-172
  J.A. Martin, 482(PhR):Apr84-277
Feynman, R.P., with R. Leighton. "Surely
  You're Joking, Mr. Feynman!" (E. Hutch-
  ings, ed)
  K.C. Cole, 441:27Jan85-13
  442(NY):25Feb85-104

Fiała, E. and B. Pietrasiewicz. Polish
  Literature in the Culture of Christian
  Europe.
  A. Jaroszyński, 497(PolR):Vol29No4-103
Fichte, J.G. Gesamtausgabe der Bayer-
  ischen Akademie der Wissenschaften.
  (Vol 1, Pt 6) (R. Lauth and H. Gliwitzky,
  with others, eds)
  J. Widmann, 489(PJGG):Band91Heft1-208
Fichte, J.G. Machiavel et autres écrits
  philosophiques et politiques de 1806-
  1807.* (L. Ferry and A. Renaut, eds
  and trans)
  J-F. Courtine, 192(EP):Jan-Mar84-111
Fichte, J.G. Wissenschaftslehre nova
  methodo. (E. Fuchs, ed) Über das Ver-
  hältnis der Logik zur Philosophie oder
  Transzendentale Logik. (R. Lauth and
  P.K. Schneider, eds)
  J. Widmann, 489(PJGG):Band91Heft1-209
Fichte, J.O. Alt- und Mittelenglische
  Literatur.*
  K. Dietz, 260(IF):Band89-373
Fichter, A. Poets Historical.*
  J.J. Conlon, 275(IQ):Winter84-105
  A.K. Hieatt, 301(JEGP):Oct84-557
  E. McCutcheon, 125:Winter84-175
  H. Morris, 569(SR):Spring84-290
Fickert, K.J. Hermann Hesse's Quest.
  H.A. Pausch, 107(CRCL):Jun84-322
Fidjestøl, B. Det norrøne fyrstediktet.
  M.C. Ross, 301(JEGP):Jul84-424
Fidjestøl, B. and others - see Fidjestøl, B.
Fiedler, L. What Was Literature?*
  S. Tatum, 649(WAL):May84-57
  M.R. Winchell, 585(SoQ):Winter85-123
Fiedler, L.A. Olaf Stapledon.
  S.A. Cowan, 150(DR):Spring84-187
  D.M. Hassler, 395(MFS):Summer84-383
  R.M. Philmus, 561(SFS):Mar84-71
Field, A. Djuna. (British title: The
  Formidable Miss Barnes.)
  G. Garrett, 569(SR):Summer84-495
  R. Merrill, 27(AL):May84-292
  H.C. Ricks, 659(ConL):Spring85-114
  D. Seed, 189(EA):Jan-Mar85-105
  L.Z. Smith, 395(MFS):Summer84-313
  295(JML):Nov84-405
Field, H.H. Science Without Numbers.*
  K.L. Manders, 316:Mar84-303
Field, L. - see Wolfe, T.
Fielding, H. Jonathan Wild.* (D. Nokes,
  ed)
  566:Autumn84-63
Fields, G. From Bonsai to Levi's.
  G.B. Petersen, 529(QQ):Autumn84-709
Fields, G.S. and O.S. Mitchell. Retire-
  ment, Pensions, and Social Security.
  F. Cairncross, 617(TLS):20Sep85-1025
Fields, R. How the Swans Came to the Lake.
  K.P. Pedersen, 485(PE&W):Jan84-95
Fields, V.M. and others. The Hover Collec-
  tion of Karuk Baskets.
  K.S. Hofweber, 614:Spring85-23
Fiengo, R. Surface Structure.*
  H. Kardela, 215(GL):Vol24No4-263
Fiering, N. Moral Philosophy of Seven-
  teenth-Century Harvard.*
  H.C. Mansfield, Jr., 543:Sep83-116
"The Fifties: Photographs of America."
  N. Ramsey, 441:21Jul85-22
  442(NY):2Sep85-87

Figes, E. Light.*
639(VQR):Winter84-27
Figes, E. Sex and Subterfuge.
J.H. Murray, 637(VS):Winter84-257
Figueira, T.J. Aegina.
S.M. Burstein, 487:Winter84-372
Filion, J-P. A mes ordres, mon colonel!
J. Moss, 207(FR):Dec84-311
Filippova, B. and È. Rajsa - see Vološin,
M.
Filloux, J-C. Durkheim et le socialisme.
J-C. Chamboredon, 98:Jun/Jul84-460
della Fina, G.M. Le antichità a Chiusi.
L. Bonfante, 124:Jan-Feb85-219
R. Rebuffat, 555:Vol58fasc2-351
Finch, A. Stendhal: La Chartreuse de
Parme.*
I.H. Smith, 67:Nov84-248
Fincke, M., ed. Handbuch der Sowjetver-
fassung.
W.E. Butler, 575(SEER):Oct84-623
Finder, J. Red Carpet.
R.C. Williams, 550(RusR):Apr84-189
639(VQR):Winter84-20
Findlater, R. These Our Actors.
G. Playfair, 157:No152-52
Findlay, J.A. Modern Latin American Art.
V.G. Stoddart, 37:Sep-Oct84-62
Findlay, J.N. Kant and the Transcendental
Object.*
P. Moran, 484(PPR):Mar85-473
R.J. Pinkerton, 63:Sep84-305
Findlay, J.N. Wittgenstein.
G. Baker, 617(TLS):5Jul85-754
Findley, P. They Dare to Speak Out.
A. Clymer, 441:14Jul85-23
Findley, T. Dinner Along the Amazon.
C. Rooke, 376:Oct84-120
Findley, T. Not Wanted on the Voyage.
J. Fitzgerald, 99:Feb85-36
R.A. Fothergill, 617(TLS):1Nov85-1228
J. McCorkle, 441:10Nov85-14
Fine, B. and R. Millar, eds. Policing the
Miners' Strike.
B. Supple, 617(TLS):15Mar85-279
Fine, J. and R.O. Freedle, eds. Develop-
mental Issues in Discourse.
C.T. Adger, 350:Dec85-931
Fine, J.V.A. The Ancient Greeks.*
S. Hornblower, 123:Vol34No2-243
R.L. Pounder, 124:Jul-Aug85-605
Fine, J.V.A., Jr. The Early Medieval
Balkans.
D. Abulafia, 575(SEER):Apr84-275
W.S. Vucinich, 589:Oct84-900
Fine, R.E. Gemini G.E.L.
D. Salle, 62:May85-3
Fineberg, J. - see "Les Tendances Nou-
velles"
Fingerhut, E.R. Survivor.
R.J. Champagne, 656(WMQ):Apr84-318
Fink, A. I — Mary.*
R.G. Ballard, 649(WAL):May84-71
B.H. Gelfant, 454:Fall84-64
Fink, L. Social Graces.
A. Korner, 62:Dec84-72
Fink, M. Pindarfragmente.
D. Constantine, 402(MLR):Oct84-980
H. Gaskill, 133:Band17Heft1/2-143
Finkelman, P. An Imperfect Union.
W.R. Brock, 161(DUJ):Dec83-124

Finkelstein, M.J. The American Academic
Profession.
R.A. McCaughey, 441:31Mar85-23
Finkenstaedt, T. and G. Scholtes, eds.
Towards a History of English Studies in
Europe.
N.E. Enkvist, 439(NM):1984/3-375
Finlay, J. The Wide Porch and Other Poems.
D. Middleton, 598(SoR):Spring85-558
Finlayson, I. The Moth and the Candle.*
N. Berry, 364:Jul84-92
Finley, G. George Heriot.
I.S. Maclaren, 627(UTQ):Summer84-502
G.W., 102(CanL):Summer84-186
M.S. Young, 39:Jan84-70
Finley, M.I. The Ancient Economy.
617(TLS):12Jul85-783
Finley, M.I. Democracy Ancient and Modern.
617(TLS):22Nov85-1339
Finn, J., ed. Global Economics and Reli-
gion.
639(VQR):Spring84-60
Finneran, R.J. Editing Yeats's Poems.*
D. Albright, 453(NYRB):31Jan85-29
272(IUR):Spring84-153
Finneran, R.J., ed. Recent Research on
Anglo-Irish Writers.
J.W. Weaver, 177(ELT):Vol27No2-168
Finneran, R.J. - see Yeats, W.B.
Finney, B. - see Lawrence, D.H.
Finnis, J. Fundamentals of Ethics.*
J. Donnelly, 518:Oct84-227
D. Gordon, 258:Sep84-329
Finocchiaro, M. and C. Brumfit. The Func-
tional-Notional Approach.*
C.K. Knop, 399(MLJ):Autumn84-272
Finocchiaro, M.A. Galileo and the Art of
Reasoning.*
H.I. Brown, 488:Jun84-280
E. McMullin, 551(RenQ):Winter84-624
Finson, J.W. and L. Todd, eds. Mendels-
sohn and Schumann.
J. Warrack, 617(TLS):26Jul85-825
Fiorenza, E.S. Bread Not Stone.
E.H. Pagels, 441:7Apr85-3
"Fire Insurance Maps in the Library of Con-
gress."
R. Bruegmann, 576:May84-174
Firla, M. Untersuchungen zum Verhältnis
von Anthropologie und Moralphilosophie
bei Kant.
H. Jansohn, 342:Band75Heft3-359
Firmage, G.J. and R. Kennedy - see Cum-
mings, E.E.
Firmat, G.P. - see under Pérez Firmat, G.
Firmianus, L. - see under Lactantius Firm-
ianus
Firth, K.R. The Apocalyptic Tradition in
Reformation Britain 1530-1645.
R. Pineas, 125:Fall83-82
Fisch, M.H. - see Peirce, C.S.
Fischer, C. Italian Drawings in the J.F.
Willumsen Collection.
M. Royalton-Kisch, 39:Nov84-361
Fischer, C., I. Hijiya-Kirschnereit and R.
Schneider - see Lewin, B.
Fischer, D. Preventing War in the Nuclear
Age.
A. Dowty, 617(TLS):25Jan85-83
Fischer, E. Zur Problematik der Opern-
struktur.
S. Hinton, 410(M&L):Jul84-272
[continued]

[continuing]
    S. Strasser-Vill, 490:Band16Heft3/4-
      360
Fischer, E. and H. Himmelheber. The Arts
   of the Dan in West Africa.
    M. Adams, 2(AfrA):Aug84-20
Fischer, J.I. and D.C. Mell, Jr., with D.M.
   Vieth, eds. Contemporary Studies of
   Swift's Poetry.*
    W.B. Carnochan, 677(YES):Vol 14-322
    C.J. Rawson, 541(RES):May84-238
Fischer, K-H. Wertform und Dichtung.
    K. Weissenberger, 221(GQ):Summer84-480
Fischer, M. Does Deconstruction Make Any
   Difference?
    M. Sprinker, 617(TLS):20Sep85-1040
Fischer, M., comp. Katalog der Architek-
   tur- und Ornamentstichsammlung. (Pt 1)
    E. Harris, 78(BC):Winter84-529
Fischer, M.S. Nationale Images als
   Gegenstand Vergleichender Literatur-
   geschichte.*
    W. Hoffmeister, 133:Band17Heft1/2-190
Fischer, S.R. The Complete Medieval Dream-
   book.
    A.M. Peden, 382(MAE):1984/1-104
Fischer, W.C. and C.K. Lohmann - see
   Howells, W.D.
Fischer-Galati, S., R. Florescu and G.R.
   Ursul, eds. Romania between East and
   West.
    J.C. Campbell, 104(CASS):Spring-
     Summer84-222
    D. Deletant, 575(SEER):Jul84-475
Fischer-Lichte, E. Semiotik des Theaters.
    D.E. Wellbery, 400(MLN):Dec84-1225
Fischler, B-Z., ed. Hebrew Books, Arti-
   cles and Doctoral Theses on Contemporary
   Hebrew Published in Israel (1948-1980).
    J.A. Reif, 399(MLJ):Autumn84-296
Fish, S. Is There a Text in This Class?*
    J.T. Bagwell, 494:Vol14No1-127
Fishburn, A. The Batsford Book of Lamp-
   shades.
    C. Campbell, 614:Summer85-19
Fisher, A. Africa Adorned.*
    R.L.S., 614:Winter85-16
    A. Stewart, 324:Sep85-735
Fisher, A. The Terioki Crossing.
    S. Altinel, 617(TLS):18Jan85-67
Fisher, C. and D. Richardson. August
   Strindberg: "Hemsöborna."
    D.M. Mennie, 562(Scan):Nov84-196
Fisher, J., ed. Essays on Aesthetics.*
    P.N. Humble, 89(BJA):Autumn84-362
    C.A. Lyas, 518:Jan84-34
    S.L.R., 185:Oct84-184
    D.D. Todd, 154:Dec84-745
    G. Wihl, 150(DR):Spring84-164
Fisher, L. Constitutional Conflicts
   Between Congress and the President.
    G. Marshall, 617(TLS):24May85-577
Fisher, M.F.K. Two Towns in Provence.
    617(TLS):12Jul85-783
Fisher, P. Hard Facts.
    C. Baldick, 617(TLS):22Nov85-1328
Fisher, P. Los Alamos Experience.
    K. Hacker, 441:24Nov85-25
Fisher, P. Making Up Society.
    J. Herron, 637(VS):Autumn83-102
Fisher, R. and J.M. Bumsted - see Walker,
   A.

Fisher, S. and A.D. Todd, eds. The Social
   Organization of Doctor-Patient Communica-
   tion.
    J.E. Frader, 355(LSoc):Dec84-520
Fishkin, J.S. Justice, Equal Opportunity,
   and the Family.*
    B.R. Boxill, 482(PhR):Oct84-618
Fishkin, J.S. The Limits of Obligation.*
    L.A. Kornhauser, 449:May84-374
    M.C. Overvold, 518:Jul84-188
    A.J. Simmons, 482(PhR):Apr84-300
Fishman, J.A., ed. Never Say Die!
    D. Katz, 287:Feb84-25
Fisiak, J., ed. A Bibliography of Writ-
   ings for the History of the English Lan-
   guage.
    R. Nagucka, 300:Vol 17-116
Fisiak, J., ed. Theoretical Issues in
   Contrastive Linguistics.
    R. Cattell, 307:Apr84-149
Fisk, E.J. Parrots' Wood.
    N.B. Cardozo, 441:13Oct85-14
Fiske, R. Scotland in Music.
    J. Warrack, 415:Mar84-151
Fitch, B.T. Monde à l'envers, texte réver-
   sible.*
    P. Collier, 402(MLR):Apr84-466
    V. Conley, 207(FR):Dec84-302
    M.B. Holland, 208(FS):Jan84-91
Fitch, N.R. Sylvia Beach and the Lost
   Generation.*
    R. Merrill, 27(AL):May84-292
    295(JML):Nov84-333
Fitch, R.E. The Poison Sky.*
    P. Conner, 59:Dec84-499
    K.O. Garrigan, 637(VS):Spring84-365
    C.D. Ryals, 579(SAQ):Winter84-122
    A. Whittick, 89(BJA):Spring84-179
Fitz Gerald, E. The Letters of Edward
   Fitz Gerald.* (A.M. and A.B. Terhune,
   eds)
    A. Bell, 677(YES):Vol 14-336
Fitzgerald, J. Beneath the Skin of Para-
   dise.
    R.B. Hatch, 648(WCR):Apr85-47
Fitzgerald, J. Split/Levels.
    C. Hlus, 137:May84-17
    S.S., 376:Feb84-140
Fitzgerald, L.S. and E.I. Kearney. The
   Continental Novel.
    D.P. Deneau, 573(SSF):Winter84-83
    P.H. Dubé, 446(NCFS):Summer-Fall84-205
    C. Rigolot, 207(FR):Apr85-719
Fitzgerald, P. At Freddie's.
    R. Robinson, 441:8Sep85-24
Fitzgerald, P. - see Morris, W.
Fitzgerald, R. Enlarging the Change.
    M. Duberman, 441:13Jan85-39
    G. Josipovici, 617(TLS):17May85-560
    442(NY):10Jun85-140
Fitz Gibbon, T. Love Lies at a Loss.
    R. Scott, 362:21Feb85-28
Fitzhenry, R.L., ed. The Fitzhenry and
   Whiteside Book of Quotations.
    T. Goldie, 102(CanL):Winter83-177
Fitzpatrick, B. Catholic Royalism in the
   Department of the Gard: 1814-1852.
    R.J. Sealy, 446(NCFS):Summer-Fall84-
     226
Fitzpatrick, G. Wollongong Poems.
    B. Roberts, 381:Sep84-408
Fitzpatrick, S. The Russian Revolution.*
    J. Keep, 575(SEER):Apr84-294

Flores, R. The Rhetoric of Doubtful
Authority.
   S. Scobie, 376:Oct84-107
Flores, R.M. Sancho Panza through Three
Hundred Seventy-five Years of Continua-
tions, Imitations, and Criticism, 1605-
1980.*
   D. Eisenberg, 86(BHS):Oct84-507
   J.A. Engelbert, 238:Mar84-143
Flori, J. L'idéology du glaive, préhis-
toire de la chevalerie.
   G. Roques, 553(RLiR):Jul-Dec84-503
Flory, W.S. Ezra Pound and "The Cantos."*
   R. Casillo, 536:Vol6-275
   E. Hesse, 38:Band102Heft3/4-550
Flower, J.E. Literature and the Left in
France.*
   B. Stoltzfus, 395(MFS):Winter84-727
Floyd, S.A., Jr. and M.J. Reisser. Black
Music in the United States.
   E. Southern, 91:Spring84-137
Floyd, V. - see O'Neill, E.
Fluck, W., J. Peper and W.P. Adams, eds.
Forms and Functions of History in Amer-
ican Literature.
   M.T. Marsden, 125:Winter84-180
Fluegelman, A. and J.J. Hewes. Writing in
the Computer Age.
   F.A. Hubbard, 128(CE):Feb84-128
Flügge, M. Verweigerung oder Neue Ordnung.
   W.D. Howarth, 208(FS):Apr84-234
Flynn, C.H. Samuel Richardson.*
   D. Nokes, 83:Autumn84-246
   L. Speirs, 179(ES):Aug84-376
   T. Wright, 161(DUJ):Dec83-137
Flynn, C.L., Jr. White Land, Black Labor.*
   639(VQR):Spring84-46
Flynn, D. Murder on the Hudson.
   N. Callendar, 441:2Jun85-38
Flynn, D. - see Farrell, J.T.
Flynn, N., S. Leach and C. Vielba. Aboli-
tion or Reform?
   G. Stamp, 617(TLS):13Sep85-1009
Flynt, C. Sins Of Omission.*
   R. Kaveney, 617(TLS):20Sep85-1028
Flys, M.J. - see Cernuda, L.
Foat, G., with L. Foreman. Never Guilty,
Never Free.
   J. Howard, 441:29Sep85-11
Fodor, I. and C. Hagège, eds. Language
Reform.
   R.B. Le Page, 353:Vol22No6-919
Fogel, D.M. Henry James and the Structure
of the Romantic Imagination.*
   A.W. Bellringer, 402(MLR):Oct84-917
   V. Jones, 541(RES):Feb84-102
Fogel, J.A. Politics and Sinology.
   S.H. Nolte, 407(MN):Winter84-468
Fogelin, R.J. Hume's Skepticism in the
"Treatise of Human Nature."
   B. Stroud, 617(TLS):30Aug85-942
Foix, J.V. Diari 1918.
   D. Keown, 86(BHS):Jan84-67
Folch-Ribas, J. Une Aurore Boréale.
   P. Collet, 102(CanL):Winter83-171
Foley, H.P., ed. Reflections of Women in
Antiquity.*
   N.R.E. Fisher, 123:Vol34No2-247
   J. Garland, 24:Summer84-235
Foley, J.M., ed. Oral Traditional Litera-
ture.*
   D. Ward, 187:Fall85-504

Foley, J.M. and others. Approaches to
Beowulfian Scansion.* (A. Renoir and A.
Hernández, eds)
   J.C. Pope, 589:Apr84-433
"Folio: Essays on Foreign Languages and
Literatures." (No 14) (M. O'Nan, ed)
   J. Gale, 446(NCFS):Winter-Spring85-171
Folkenflik, R., ed. The English Hero,
1660-1800.
   J.M. Armistead, 579(SAQ):Spring84-236
   D. Wheeler, 83:Autumn84-250
Follet, S. Athènes au IIe et au IIIe
siècle.
   A.J.S. Spawforth, 313:Vol74-214
Follett, K. The Modigliani Scandal.
   D.E. Westlake, 441:30Jun85-16
   442(NY):8Jul85-75
Fónagy, I. La métaphore en phonétique.
   P. Wunderli, 547(RF):Band96Heft3-296
Fónagy, I. Situation et signification.*
   N.E. Enkvist, 596(SL):Vol38No1-88
Fónagy, I. and P.R. Léon, eds. L'accent
en Français Contemporain.
   J. Klare, 682(ZPSK):Band37Heft8-717
Fonda, J., with M. McCarthy. Women Coming
of Age.
   F. Randall, 441:13Jan85-16
Foner, P.S. - see Martí, J.
Fontaine, J. Grammaire du texte et aspect
du verbe en russe contemporain.
   E. Klenin, 104(CASS):Winter84-425
Fontane, T. Short Novels and Other Writ-
ings. (P. Demetz, ed)
   T.C. Hanlin, 399(MLJ):Summer84-168
Fontanella de Weinberg, M.B. Dinámica
social de un cambio lingüístico.*
   C. Silva-Corvalán, 545(RPh):Nov83-219
de Fontenay, E. Diderot ou le matérial-
isme enchanté.
   H. Cohen, 207(FR):May85-892
   P. Kamuf, 188(ECr):Spring84-124
de Fontenelle, B.L. Fontenelles "Histoire
des Ajaoiens."
   P. Kuon, 547(RF):Band96Heft3-346
Fontenrose, J. Orion.*
   R.G.A. Buxton, 303(JoHS):Vol 104-233
Fontes, M.D. - see under da Costa Fontes,
M.
Foot, D. Cricket's Unholy Trinity.
   S. Collini, 617(TLS):23Aug85-919
Foot, M.M. The Henry Davis Gift. (Vol 2)
   R.G. Halwas, 517(PBSA):Vol78No2-236
   A. Hobson, 90:Jun84-358
   P. Morgan, 354:Mar84-96
Foot, P. Red Shelley.
   R. Cronin, 339(KSMB):No35-76
Foot, P. Virtues and Vices, and Other
Essays in Moral Philosophy.* Moral
Relativism.
   N.L. Sturgeon, 311(JP):Jun84-326
Foot, R. The Phenomenon of Speechlessness
in the Poetry of Marie Luise Kaschnitz,
Günter Eich, Nelly Sachs and Paul Celan.
   J. Glenn, 221(GQ):Fall84-684
   K. Weissenberger, 133:Band17Heft1/2-
181
Foote, G. The Labour Party's Political
Thought.
   J. Campbell, 617(TLS):13Sep85-1009
Forbes, B. The Rewrite Man.
   N. Peck, 441:3Feb85-22

Forbes, D. August Autumn.
  L. Mackinnon, 617(TLS):7Jun85-649
  J. Mole, 176:Jul/Aug85-57
Forbes, E. Mario and Grisi.
  R. Christiansen, 617(TLS):26Jul85-825
Forbes, P. Abolishing the Dark.*
  G. Szirtes, 493:Sep84-76
Forbes, P. and M.H. Smith, eds. Harrap's
  Concise French and English Dictionary.
  (rev and ed by H. Knox)
  G. Craig, 617(TLS):26Apr85-475
Force, J.E. William Whiston.
  B. Pippard, 617(TLS):13Sep85-992
Forché, C. El Salvador. (H. Mattison, S.
  Meiselas and F. Rubinstein, eds)
  J. Guimond, 219(GaR):Summer84-424
Forcione, A.K. Cervantes and the Humanist
  Vision.
  J.J. Allen, 240(HR):Spring84-237
  R. El Saffar, 551(RenQ):Spring84-129
Forcione, A.K. Cervantes and the Mystery
  of Lawlessness.
  E.C. Riley, 617(TLS):31May85-605
Ford, A. Men.
  J. Aitken, 362:28Mar85-27
  P.P. Read, 617(TLS):29Mar85-364
Ford, B., ed. The New Pelican Guide to
  English Literature. (Vol 1, Pt 1)
  D. Mehl, 447(N&Q):Aug83-351
  J. Simpson, 382(MAE):1984/2-307
Ford, B., ed. The New Pelican Guide to
  English Literature. (Vols 7 and 8)
  295(JML):Nov84-329
Ford, C. By Violent Means.
  S. Morrissey, 137:Feb85-42
  S.S., 376:Feb84-140
Ford, C. The Womb Rattles Its Pod Poems.
  M. Fiamengo, 102(CanL):Summer84-145
Ford, D. The Button.
  B. Brophy, 617(TLS):29Nov85-1345
  M.R. Gordon, 441:14Jul85-9
  Lord Zuckerman, 453(NYRB):15Aug85-21
Ford, E.B. and J.S. Haywood. Church Trea-
  sures in the Oxford District.
  617(TLS):1Feb85-131
Ford, F.L. Political Murder.
  E. Weber, 441:17Nov85-13
Ford, F.M. The Fifth Queen. A Call.
  H. Carpenter, 617(TLS):14Jun85-673
Ford, F.M. The Rash Act.
  C. Cook, 175:Summer84-159
Ford, J. The Broken Heart. (T.J.B.
  Spencer, ed)
  M. Hattaway, 541(RES):Aug84-375
Ford, J.A. The Brave White Flag.
  G. Mangan, 617(TLS):29Nov85-1371
Ford, P.J. George Buchanan.*
  G. Demerson, 535(RHL):Jul/Aug84-588
  A.A. MacDonald, 179(ES):Aug84-312
Ford, P.K., ed. Celtic Folklore and Chris-
  tianity.
  K.H. Schmidt, 196:Band25Heft3/4-332
Fordyn, P., ed. The "Experimentes of
  Cophon, the Leche of Salerne."
  A.S.G. Edwards, 589:Jul84-717
"Foreign Relations of the United States,
  1952-1954." (Vol 4)
  T.J. Dodd, 263(RIB):Vol34No2-316
Foreman, L. Bax.
  J. Canarina, 607:Mar84-46
Forester, B. Signs and Omens.
  N. Callendar, 441:3Mar85-35

Forester, T., ed. The Information Technol-
  ogy Revolution.
  S.M. Halpern, 441:21Apr85-38
des Forêts, L-R. Les mendiants. Le
  bavard. Les mégères de la mer. La
  chambre des enfants.
  S. Canadas, 98:Mar84-229
Forgie, G.B. Patricide in the House
  Divided.
  C.J.G. Griffin, 583:Fall84-93
Forke, A. Chinesische Dramen der Yüan-
  Dynastie. (M. Gimm, ed)
  W. Schlepp, 318(JAOS):Jul-Sep83-638
Forlani Tempesti, A. Raffaello: Disegni.
  J. Beck, 380:Autumn84-328
Formel, G. Bibliographie des "Mémoires"
  du duc de Saint-Simon.
  Y. Coirault, 535(RHL):Jan/Feb84-102
Formisano, R.P. The Transformation of
  Political Culture.*
  J.M. Banner, Jr., 656(WMQ):Apr84-298
Formosa, G. The Pleasure of Seeing.
  M. Segger, 648(WCR):Oct84-68
Fornaro, P. Flavio Giuseppe, Tacito e
  l'impero.
  J-M. André, 555:Vol58fasc1-146
Fornaro, P. La voce fuori scena.
  É. des Places, 555:Vol58fasc1-126
Forrer, M., ed. Essays on Japanese Art
  Presented to Jack Hillier.
  Susumu Takiguchi, 463:Spring84-100
Forrest, J.F. and R.L. Greaves. John
  Bunyan.
  J.B.H. Alblas, 179(ES):Dec84-578
Forrester, A., S. Lansley and R. Pauley.
  Beyond our Ken.
  G. Stamp, 617(TLS):13Sep85-1009
Forrester, H. Lime Street at Two.
  P. Willmott, 617(TLS):29Nov85-1350
"Forschungen zur osteuropäischen Ge-
  schichte." (Vol 29)
  S.R. Thompstone, 575(SEER):Apr84-281
Forster, E. - see von der Pfalz, L.
Forster, E.M. "Arctic Summer" and Other
  Fiction. (E. Heine and O. Stallybrass,
  eds)
  J. Colmer, 677(YES):Vol 14-349
  E. Hanquart, 189(EA):Jul-Sep85-289
Forster, E.M. "The Hill of Devi" and
  Other Indian Writings. (E. Heine, ed)
  E. Hanquart, 189(EA):Jul-Sep85-289
  F.P.W. McDowell, 177(ELT):Vol27No2-163
  R.J. Voorhees, 395(MFS):Summer84-367
Forster, E.M. The Longest Journey. (E.
  Heine, ed)
  C. Hawtree, 617(TLS):5Apr85-390
Forster, E.M. The New Collected Short
  Stories of E.M. Forster. (P.N. Furbank,
  ed)
  J. Drummond, 362:25Apr85-19
Forster, E.M. Selected Letters of E.M.
  Forster.* (Vol 1) (M.M. Lago and P.N.
  Furbank, eds)
  K.W. Gransden, 176:Sep-Oct85-43
  E. Hanquart, 189(EA):Jul-Sep85-289
Forster, E.M. Selected Letters of E.M.
  Forster. (Vol 2) (M. Lago and P.N. Fur-
  bank, eds)
  J. Bayley, 453(NYRB):15Aug85-19
  J. Beer, 617(TLS):24May85-569
  J. Drummond, 362:25Apr85-19
  J. Epstein, 129:Sep85-48
                              [continued]

[continuing]
P. Fussell, 61:Jan85-94
K.W. Gransden, 176:Sep-Oct85-43
L. Graver, 441:5May85-12
P. Parker, 364:Jun84-92
442(NY):14Oct85-143
Forster, G. Im Anblick des grossen Rades.
(R.R. Wuthenow, ed)
T.P. Saine, 221(GQ):Spring84-321
Forster, J.R. The "Resolution" Journal of
Johann Reinhold Forster 1772-1775. (M.E.
Hoare, ed)
O.H.K. Spate, 677(YES):Vol 14-327
Forster, K. A Pronouncing Dictionary of
English Place-Names.*
B. Diensberg, 72:Band221Heft2-353
H. Ulherr, 38:Band102Heft3/4-493
Forster, M. Significant Sisters.*
C. Klein, 441:17Feb85-12
442(NY):22Apr85-143
Forster, M.H. Historia de la poesía his-
panoamericana.*
I.A. Schulman, 240(HR):Winter84-109
Forster, P.G. The Esperanto Movement.
G.F. Meier, 682(ZPSK):Band37Heft3-387
Forsyth, K. "Ariadne auf Naxos" by Hugo
von Hofmannsthal and Richard Strauss.*
D.G. Daviau, 222(GR):Summer84-122
S.P. Sondrup, 301(JEGP):Apr84-291
U. Weisstein, 131(CL):Summer84-278
W.E. Yates, 402(MLR):Jan84-244
Forsyth, M. Buildings for Music.
P.S. Byard, 441:13Oct85-20
Forte, A. and S.E. Gilbert. Introduction
to Schenkerian Analysis.
J. Dubiel, 414(MusQ):Spring84-269
R. Kamien, 308:Spring84-113
R. Swift, 451:Fall84-164
Fortescue, W. Alphonse de Lamartine.
P.A. Ouston, 402(MLR):Jul84-710
Forth, G.L. Rindi.
N.M. Lutz, 293(JASt):May84-597
Forti, F. Incontri e letture del Nove-
cento (1940-1980).
A. Cottignoli, 228(GSLI):Vol 161
fasc515-464
Fortunato, G. Scritti politici. (F. Bar-
bagallo, ed)
L. Mascilli Migliorini, 98:Aug/Sep84-
717
Fortune, R. Alexander Sukhovo-Kobylin.*
P. Doyle, 402(MLR):Jul84-762
A. McMillin, 575(SEER):Jul84-436
L. Senelick, 550(RusR):Apr84-190
Foscolo, U. Studi su Dante. (Pt 1) (G.
Da Pozzo, ed)
M. Picone, 545(RPh):Aug83-110
Foscue, V.O. The Place Names of Sumter
County, Alabama.
W. Viereck, 685(ZDL):1/1984-108
Foshay, T. - see Lewis, W.
Foss, C. Ephesus after Antiquity.
M. Harrison, 123:Vol134No1-103
Fossier, F. La bibliothèque Farnèse.
J. Hankins, 551(RenQ):Spring84-63
Foster, D.W., comp. Argentine Literature.*
(2nd ed)
J.M. Flint, 86(BHS):Oct84-530
Foster, D.W. Mexican Literature.*
J. Labanyi, 86(BHS):Jan84-68

Foster, D.W. and R. Reis, comps. A Dic-
tionary of Contemporary Brazilian
Authors.*
J. Gledson, 86(BHS):Jan84-70
Foster, H., ed. The Anti-Aesthetic.
J.A. Richardson, 289:Spring84-93
Foster, J. The Case for Idealism.*
R.A. Fumerton, 484(PPR):Mar85-459
F. Jackson, 262:Dec84-463
H. Kincaid, 482(PhR):Jul84-465
Foster, J.B., Jr. Heirs to Dionysus.*
E. Kern, 301(JEGP):Apr84-295
V. Mahon, 541(RES):Nov84-591
Foster, J.L., ed. A Very First Poetry
Book.
W. Cope, 617(TLS):8Feb85-154
Foster, K. and P. Boyde, eds. Cambridge
Readings in Dante's "Comedy."*
T. Barolini, 589:Jan84-233
Foster, K.P. Minoan Ceramic Relief.
P. Warren, 303(JoHS):Vol 104-255
Foster, S. Victorian Women's Fiction.
E. Letley, 617(TLS):7Jun85-642
Foster, V. A Visual History of Costume:
The Nineteenth Century.
R.L.S., 614:Winter85-32
B. Scott, 39:Aug84-148
Foucart, B. and others. Normandie.
J. Maxtone-Graham, 441:15Dec85-20
Foucault, M. The Foucault Reader. (P.
Rabinow, ed)
J. Daynard, 441:6Jan85-21
442(NY):27May85-100
Foucault, M. Histoire de la sexualité.
(Vol 1) (German title: Sexualität und
Wahrheit.)
R. Schlesier, 384:Oct84-817
Foucault, M. This Is Not A Pipe.* (J.
Harkness, ed and trans)
D. Craven, 59:Dec84-477
J. Margolis, 290(JAAC):Winter84-224
J. Wolff, 89(BJA):Autumn84-368
Foucault, M. The Use of Pleasure.*
(French title: Histoire de la Sexualité.
(Vol 2))
M.C. Nussbaum, 441:10Nov85-13
de Fougères, É. - see under Étienne de
Fougères
Foulkes, A.P. Literature and Propaganda.
A. Boué, 189(EA):Oct-Dec85-448
H. Siefken, 220(GL&L):Jan85-190
Foulkes, D. Dreaming.
S. Sutherland, 617(TLS):22Nov85-1318
Fountain, L.G., with J.R. Maxim. Dark
Star.
B. Gelb, 441:21Apr85-14
Fourcade, D. Rose-déclic. Rose-déclic 2.
Rose-déclic 3. Rose-déclic 4. Rose-
déclic 5. Rose-déclic 6. Le ciel pas
d'angle.
Y. Michaud, 98:Mar84-224
de Fournival, R. - see under Richard de
Fournival
Fourtouni, E., ed and trans. Four Greek
Women.
E. Grosholz, 249(HudR):Spring84-140
Fowke, E. Folktales of French Canada.
G. Thomas, 102(CanL):Winter83-160
Fowke, E., ed. Sea Songs and Ballads from
Nineteenth Century Nova Scotia.*
M.E. Cohane, 292(JAF):Jan-Mar84-95
Fowke, E. - see Kane, A.

Frank, A. The Science Fiction and Fantasy
Film Handbook.
  A. Gordon, 561(SFS):Mar84-97
Frank, A.P. Das englische und amerikan-
ische Härspiel.
  M. Erdmenger, 38:Band102Heft3/4-564
Frank, E. Louise Bogan.
  P-L. Adams, 61:Feb85-100
  W. Maxwell, 442(NY):29Jul85-73
  A. Ostriker, 441:3Mar85-1
Frank, E. Jackson Pollock.
  J. Bell, 55:Apr84-29
Frank, E.E. Literary Architecture.
  J-G. Ritz, 189(EA):Oct-Dec85-448
Frank, F. and F. Anshen. Language and the
Sexes.
  S.M. Embleton, 350:Dec85-935
Frank, F.S., ed. Guide to the Gothic.
  G.L. Green, 223:Fall84-322
Frank, J. Dostoevsky: The Years of Ordeal,
1850-1859.*
  P. Debreczeny, 573(SSF):Fall84-418
  D. Fanger, 550(RusR):Oct84-417
Frank, L. Charles Dickens and the Roman-
tic Self.
  N. Auerbach, 441:17Mar85-43
Frank, M. Der kommende Gott.
  G. Mattenklott, 384:Jan84-77
Frank, M. Was ist Neostrukturalismus?
  J. Fohrmann and H. Müller, 384:Dec84-
  940
Frank, M., A.P. Frank and K.P.S. Jochum.
T.S. Eliot Criticism in English, 1916-
1965.
  A.M. Cohn, 365:Winter84-37
Frank, R.H. Choosing the Right Pond.
  L.C. Thurow, 453(NYRB):21Nov85-34
Frankel, E.R. Novy Mir.*
  L. Loseff, 104(CASS):Fall84-322
Frankel, J., ed. Studies in Contemporary
Jewry.
  A.J. Sherman, 617(TLS):28Jun85-730
Frankel, P. Pretoria's Praetorians.
  S. Jenkins, 617(TLS):19Apr85-426
Frankenthal, K. Der dreifache Fluch.
  R-E.B. Joeres, 221(GQ):Spring84-329
Frankenthaler, M.R., ed. Skills for Bi-
lingual Legal Personell/Técnicas para
el personal bilingüe al área legal.
  V.R. Foster, 238:Mar84-161
Frankland, M. The Mother-of-Pearl Men.
  S. Dalby, 617(TLS):8Nov85-1266
Franklin, B. The Autobiography of Benja-
min Franklin.* (J.A.L. Lemay and P.M.
Zall, eds)
  O.M. Brack, Jr., 447(N&Q):Feb83-84
  P. Gaskell, 402(MLR):Oct84-908
  S. Neumann, 106:Winter84-421
Franklin, J. The Gentleman's Country
House and its Plan, 1835-1914.
  J.D. Forbes, 637(VS):Autumn83-108
Franklin, J.H. George Washington Williams.
  I. Berlin, 441:17Nov85-12
Franklin, M. All That Swagger.
  S. Altinel, 617(TLS):12Jul85-776
Franklin, R.W. - see Dickinson, E.
Franklin, W. The New World of James Fen-
imore Cooper.*
  J. Rubin-Dorsky, 405(MP):Feb85-330
Franolić, B. A Short History of Literary
Croatian.
  K.E. Naylor, 574(SEEJ):Spring84-133

Franqui, C. Family Portrait with Fidel.*
  G.K. Lewis, 617(TLS):4Jan85-5
Frantz, J.B. The Forty Acre Follies.
  L. Milazzo, 584(SWR):Summer84-336
Frantzen, A.J. The Literature of Penance
in Anglo-Saxon England.
  C.A. Regan, 301(JEGP):Oct84-553
Franzén, G. Ortnamn i Östergötland.
  J.E. Cathey, 563(SS):Summer84-303
Franzen, W. Die Bedeutung von "wahr" und
"Wahrheit."
  F. Rapp, 679:Band15Heft2-365
Frappier, J. Chrétien de Troyes.
  X. Baron, 125:Spring84-291
Frascina, F. and C. Harrison, eds. Modern
Art and Modernism.
  S. Watney, 59:Mar84-102
Fraser, A. Oxford Blood.
  T.J.B., 617(TLS):22Nov85-1310
  B.L. Clark, 441:13Oct85-24
Fraser, A. The Weaker Vessel.*
  R. Browning, 344:Spring85-130
  R. Flannagan, 391:Dec84-132
  L. Stone, 453(NYRB):11Apr85-21
Fraser, A.M. - see Borrow, G.
Fraser, C. and K.R. Scherer, eds. Ad-
vances in the Social Psychology of Lan-
guage.*
  M. Crawford, 355(LSoc):Dec84-525
Fraser, D. And We Shall Shock Them.
  R.F. Weigley, 441:24Feb85-12
Fraser, D., ed. Municipal Reform and the
Industrial City.
  D.J. Olsen, 637(VS):Winter84-245
Fraser, D.M. The Voice of Emma Sachs.
  E. Popham, 102(CanL):Autumn84-106
Fraser, G. PQ.
  E. Dumas, 99:Dec84-31
Fraser, G.M. Flashman and the Dragon.
  E.S. Turner, 617(TLS):11Oct85-1125
Fraser, G.S. Poems of G.S. Fraser. (I.
Fletcher and J. Lucas, eds)
  R. Watson, 588(SSL):Vol 19-194
Fraser, H. and R. Hughes. Historic Houses
of Barbados.
  A.R. Williams, 37:Mar-Apr84-60
Fraser, J. America and the Patterns of
Chivalry.*
  B. Curtis, 579(SAQ):Spring84-231
  K. Moreland, 577(SHR):Fall84-374
  A. Rowe, 392:Winter83/84-109
  S.J. Sniegoski, 396(ModA):
  Spring/Summer84-259
Fraser, J. The Name of Action.
  R. Asselineau, 189(EA):Jul-Sep85-367
  P. Kemp, 362:7Feb85-26
Fraser, O. The Pure Account. (H.M. Shire,
ed)
  R. Watson, 588(SSL):Vol 19-194
Fraser, R. In Search of a Past.*
  E. Mendelson, 441:17Feb85-12
Fraser, R. A Mingled Yarn.
  G. Garrett, 569(SR):Summer84-495
  F. Kermode, 473(PR):1/1984-138
Fraser, R. The Novels of Ayi Kwei Armah.
  M.B. Cham, 538(RAL):Fall84-444
Fraser, R. The Three Romes.
  E. Welborn, 441:16Jun85-25
Frasso, G. Studi su i "Rerum vulgarium
fragmenta" e i "Triumphi." (Vol 1)
  C. Fahy, 402(MLR):Jul84-721
Fraticelli, M. Night Coach.
  H.R. Runte, 102(CanL):Autumn84-124

Fratus, D. The Riverman's Wedding and Other Poems.
 W. Zander, 363(LitR):Fall84-145
Frauenlob (Heinrich von Meissen). Leichs, Sangsprüche, Lieder. (K. Stackmann and K. Bertau, eds)
 P. Kern, 680(ZDP):Band103Heft1-136
 N.F. Palmer, 402(MLR):Jan84-224
Frauwallner, E. Kleine Schriften. (G. Oberhammer and E. Steinkellner, eds)
 J.W. de Jong, 259(IIJ):Jul84-222
Freadman, R., ed. Literature, Criticism and the Universities.
 A.P. Riemer, 581:Jun84-236
Fréchet, A. John Galsworthy.*
 J. Coudriou, 177(ELT):Vol27No1-76
Freddi, C. The Elder.
 P. Davis, 441:17Nov85-36
Fredén, G. Östan om solen nordan om jorden.
 T. Lundell, 563(SS):Summer84-279
Frederic, H. The Market-Place. (S. Garner and C. Dodge, eds)
 C.S. McClure, 534(RALS):Autumn82-227
 H. Springer, 26(ALR):Spring84-141
Frederickson, T.L. and P.F. Wedel. English by Newspaper.
 M.E. Call, 399(MLJ):Winter84-427
Frederiksen, A. Red Roe Run.
 G. Davenport, 569(SR):Winter84-128
Fredman, S. Poet's Prose.
 R. Kern, 659(ConL):Summer85-221
 J. McGarry, 703:No11-205
 W. Sharpe, 189(EA):Jul-Sep85-357
Fredson, J. John Fredson Edward Sapir Hàa Googwandak. (J. McGary, ed)
 J. Ramsey, 292(JAF):Apr-Jun84-219
Freeborn, R. The Russian Revolutionary Novel.*
 M. Futrell, 104(CASS):Spring-Summer84-160
 D.G.B. Piper, 575(SEER):Jan84-108
 B.P. Scherr, 574(SEEJ):Spring84-115
 A. Woronzoff, 550(RusR):Jul84-287
Freed, L. T.S. Eliot.
 J.S. Cunningham, 506(PSt):May84-82
Freedberg, D. Dutch Landscape Prints of the Seventeenth Century.
 A. Hughes, 90:Sep84-578
Freedberg, S.J. Circa 1600.*
 C. Gould, 39:Apr84-304
 P. Sohm, 529(QQ):Winter84-1002
 C. van Tuyll, 90:Mar84-161
von Freeden, J. "Oikia Kyrrēstoy."
 G.V. Lalonde, 124:Sep-Oct84-48
 J. Pouilloux, 555:Vol58fasc2-313
 A.J.S. Spawforth, 313:Vol74-214
Freedland, M. The Warner Brothers.
 P. French, 707:Winter83/84-69
Freedman, L.Z., ed. By Reason of Insanity.
 J.D., 185:Apr85-789
Freedman, W. The Study of Chinese Society. (W. Skinner, ed)
 N. Diamond, 318(JAOS):Jul-Sep83-639
Freedman, P. Glad to be Grey.
 H. Jacobson, 617(TLS):20Dec85-1453
Freedman, P.H. The Diocese of Vic.*
 B.F. Reilly, 589:Oct84-973
Freedman, R.O., ed. Soviet Jewry in the Decisive Decade, 1971-80.
 M. Gilbert, 453(NYRB):30May85-37

Freedman, R.O. Soviet Policy Toward the Middle East Since 1970. (3rd ed)
 S.N. MacFarlane, 104(CASS):Fall84-328
Freehling, A.G. Drift Toward Dissolution.*
 C.N. Degler, 639(VQR):Spring84-330
Freely, M. The Life of the Party.
 P-L. Adams, 61:Feb85-100
 S. Altinel, 617(TLS):29Mar85-341
 J. Mellors, 362:30May85-32
 B. Thompson, 441:17Feb85-22
Freeman, C. Illusions of Love.
 A.P. Harris, 441:13Jan85-23
Freeman, D. The Last Days of Alfred Hitchcock.*
 P. Dunne, 18:Jan/Feb85-51
Freeman, D. Liebe ohne Aggression.
 J. Clifford, 384:Mar84-208
Freeman, D.B. Speaking of Survival.
 L.A. Kupetzky, 399(MLJ):Spring84-102
Freeman, D.C., ed. Essays in Modern Stylistics.*
 T.J. Taylor, 541(RES):Aug84-342
Freeman, J.A. Milton and the Martial Muse.*
 D. Fuller, 161(DUJ):Dec83-136
Freeman, M.E.W. Selected Stories of Mary E. Wilkins Freeman. (M. Pryse, ed)
 P. Craig, 617(TLS):5Jul85-757
 G.L. Nagel, 26(ALR):Autumn84-287
Freeman, M.H. - see Patterson, R.
Freeman, P. and others, eds. New Art.
 A. Anderson, 62:Dec84-3
Freemantle, B. Charlie Muffin and Russian Rose.
 M. Laski, 362:18Apr85-26
Freer, C. The Poetics of Jacobean Drama.*
 A.R. Braunmuller, 539:Feb85-58
 S. Colley, 405(MP):May85-422
 H. Diehl, 223:Summer83-191
 S.B. Garner, Jr., 568(SCN):Spring-Summer84-11
Freese, W., ed. Philologie und Kritik.
 M. Swales, 402(MLR):Jul84-757
Freeze, G.L. The Parish Clergy in Nineteenth-Century Russia.
 L. Gerstein, 104(CASS):Winter84-462
 639(VQR):Winter84-18
von Freiberg, D. - see under Dietrich von Freiberg
Freiberg, M., ed. Journals of the House of Representatives of Massachusetts, 1775-1776. (Vol 51, Pt 2)
 J.A. Schutz, 432(NEQ):Mar84-140
Freiwald-Korth, G. San Isidro Labrador und Santa María de la Cabeza.
 S. Sebastián, 48:Jul-Sep83-306
Frénaud, A. Haeres.*
 M. McCluney, 207(FR):Dec84-313
French, M. Beyond Power.
 L. Stone, 441:23Jun85-3
French, P.A. Ethics in Government.
 W.J. Waluchow, 154:Jun84-364
French, P.A., T.E. Uehling, Jr. and H.K. Wettstein, eds. Midwest Studies in Philosophy V.
 J.E. Adler, 606:Nov84-261
French, W.P. and others. Afro-American Poetry and Drama 1760-1975.
 A. Rampersad, 402(MLR):Jan84-155
Frend, W.H.C. The Rise of Christianity.
 P. Garnsey, 617(TLS):5Apr85-380

Friis-Jensen, K., ed. Saxo Grammaticus.
   H. O'Donoghue, 382(MAE):1984/1-147
Frings, M.S. - see Scheler, M.
Frisch, M. Sketchbook 1946-1949. Sketch-
   book 1966-1971.
   W.C. Reeve, 529(QQ):Winter84-1018
Frisch, W. Brahms and the Principle of
   Developing Variation.
   R. Pascall, 617(TLS):15Mar85-291
Frischer, B. The Sculpted Word.
   D. Clay, 24:Winter84-484
   J.J. Pollitt, 54:Jun84-332
Frith, D. England versus Australia.
   A.L. Le Quesne, 617(TLS):12Apr85-420
Fritsch, C. and L. Winckler, eds. Faschis-
   muskritik und Deutschlandbild im Exil-
   roman.
   K. Kändler, 654(WB):1/1984-156
Fritz, G. Kohärenz.
   K. Meng, 682(ZPSK):Band37Heft6-737
Fritz, R. Die Gefässe aus Kokosnuss in
   Mitteleuropa, 1250-1800.
   A.S. Cocks, 90:Jun84-355
Fritze, W.H., ed. Germania Slavica.
   (Vols 1 and 2)
   J.M. Bak, 104(CASS):Spring-Summer84-
   203
Fröberg, I. Une "histoirè secrète" à
   matiére nordique.*
   Å. Grafström, 72:Band221Heft2-444
Frobesius, J.N. Christiani Wolffii Philos-
   ophia rationalis sive Logica in compen-
   dium et luculentas tabulas redacta cum
   observationibus atque indice.
   J. Ecole, 192(EP):Jan-Mar84-113
Froeschle, H. - see "Deutschkanadisches
   Jahrbuch/German-Canadian Yearbook"
Fröhlich, K. The Emergence of Russian
   Constitutionalism, 1900-1904.
   T. Emmons, 104(CASS):Spring-Summer84-
   198
   D.C.B. Lieven, 575(SEER):Jan84-130
Frohock, F.M. Abortion.
   J.W. De Cew, 185:Jan85-375
Froidevaux, G. L'Art et la vie.
   M. Dentan, 535(RHL):Nov/Dec84-985
"From the Heart: Folk Art in Canada."
   C. Thomas, 102(CanL):Autumn84-106
Fromkin, V. and R. Rodman. An Introduc-
   tion to Language.* (3rd ed)
   J. Algeo, 300:Vol 17-75
Fromkin, V.A., ed. Errors in Linguistic
   Performance.
   R. Schreyer, 38:Band102Heft1/2-138
Fromm, H., P. Ganz and M. Reis, eds.
   Beiträge zur Geschichte der deutschen
   Sprache und Literatur.
   K.R. Jankowsky, 205(ForL):Apr83-239
Fromm, W-D. Häufigkeitswörterbuch der
   modernen arabischen Zeitungssprache,
   Arabisch-Deutsch-Englisch.
   S. Wittich, 682(ZPSK):Band37Heft5-637
Froning, H. Essen, Museum Folkwang: Kata-
   log der griechischen und italischen
   Vasen.
   B.A. Sparkes, 303(JoHS):Vol 104-258
Froula, C. To Write Paradise.
   M. Korn, 617(TLS):8Nov85-1258
Frow, G. "Oh, Yes It Is!"
   A. Marshall, 617(TLS):20Dec85-1458

Frucht, R.C. Dunărea Noastră.
   D. Deletant, 575(SEER):Jan84-134
   D.B. Lungu, 104(CASS):Spring-Summer84-
   225
Frühwald, W., F. Heiduk and H. Koopmann,
   eds. Aurora 42.
   O. Seidlin, 221(GQ):Fall84-660
Frühwald, W. and W. Schieder, with W.
   Hinck, eds. Leben im Exil.*
   A. Stephan, 406:Summer84-234
Fruzzetti, L.M. The Gift of a Virgin.
   C. Prindle, 293(JASt):Feb84-352
Fry, G.K. The Changing Civil Service.
   H. Young, 617(TLS):3May85-486
Fry, P.H. The Poet's Calling in the
   English Ode.*
   F.W. Bradbrook, 447(N&Q):Feb83-94
Fry, P.H. The Reach of Criticism.*
   C. Altieri, 153:Winter84-58
   639(VQR):Winter84-9
Frye, J. and H. North to Thule.
   S. Altinel, 617(TLS):13Dec85-1434
Frye, N. Divisions on a Ground.* (J.
   Polk, ed)
   B. Cameron, 102(CanL):Summer84-113
Frye, N. The Myth of Deliverance.*
   J. Baxter, 627(UTQ):Summer84-419
   G. Forst, 102(CanL):Autumn84-69
   D. O'Hara, 141:Winter84-92
   P.N. Siegel, 191(ELN):Sep84-70
   R.P. Wheeler, 570(SQ):Autumn84-365
Frye, N. Spiritus Mundi.
   H.A. Pausch, 107(CRCL):Jun84-283
Frye, N., S. Baker and G. Perkins. The
   Harper Handbook to Literature.
   I. McGilchrist, 617(TLS):26Apr85-455
Frye, R.M. The Renaissance "Hamlet."
   J. Kerrigan, 617(TLS):22Feb85-208
Fuchs, D. Saul Bellow.*
   K.M. Opdahl, 395(MFS):Winter84-834
   L. Simon, 27(AL):Oct84-446
Fuchs, E. - see Fichte, J.G.
Fuchs, E., with R. Lauth and W. Schieche,
   eds. J.G. Fichte im Gespräch.* (Vol 2)
   J. Widmann, 489(PJGG):Band91Heft1-212
Fuchs, E., with R. Lauth and W. Schieche,
   eds. J.G. Fichte im Gespräch.* (Vol 3)
   A. Renaut, 192(EP):Apr-Jun84-269
   J. Widmann, 489(PJGG):Band91Heft1-212
Fuentes, C. The Old Gringo.
   P-L. Adams, 61:Dec85-118
   T.R. Edwards, 453(NYRB):19Dec85-54
   E. Shorris, 441:27Oct85-1
Fugard, A. Notebooks 1960-1977.* (M. Ben-
   son, ed)
   C. Hope, 364:Jun84-99
Fugard, S. A Revolutionary Woman.*
   P. Bonnell, 441:6Oct85-28
   J.M. Coetzee, 453(NYRB):24Oct85-12
   D. Wright, 617(TLS):15Feb85-179
Fugate, B.I. Operation Barbarossa.
   M.S. Kaplan, 441:3Mar85-23
Fugère, J-P. En quatre journées.*
   J.D. Wilson, 207(FR):Mar85-597
Fugger, B. Ausbreitungswege und Irradia-
   tionszentren der französischen Gemein-
   sprache in der Franche-Comté.
   D. Evans, 208(FS):Oct84-503
Fühmann, F. and D. Simon - see Freud, S.
Fuhrmann, M., H.R. Jauss and W. Pannenberg,
   eds. Text und Applikation.*
   H.G. Haile, 221(GQ):Spring84-293

Gablik, S. Has Modernism Failed?*
F. Tuten, 62:Dec84-78
Gabriel, N. Peter Handke und Österreich.
A. Obermayer, 564:May84-151
Gabriel, R.A. Military Incompetence.
P.A. Odeen, 441:20Oct85-31
Gabrieli, I.M. Rilettura di Ibsen.
J.A. Parente, Jr., 563(SS):Summer84-281
Gabrielsen, V. Remuneration of State
Officials in Fourth Century B.C. Athens.*
H.W. Pleket, 394:Vol37fasc1/2-244
Gadamer, H-G. Philosophical Apprentice-
ships.
S.S. Wolin, 441:28Jul85-12
Gadamer, H-G. Reason in the Age of
Science.*
R. Holmes, 154:Mar84-175
Gadd, M. Lost Language. (D. Marlatt and
I. Klassen, eds)
R. Donovan, 137:Feb85-10
A. Mandel, 102(CanL):Summer84-149
Gadda, C.E. Lettere a una gentile signora.
(G. Marcenaro, ed)
E. Bonora, 228(GSLI):Vol 161fasc514-304
Gadda, C.E. Il palazzo degli ori. (A.
Andreini, ed)
E. Saccone, 400(MLN):Jan84-176
Gaddis, W. Carpenter's Gothic.
P-L. Adams, 61:Aug85-92
C. Iannone, 129:Dec85-62
C. Ozick, 441:7Jul85-1
Gado, F. - see Anderson, S.
Gaeng, P.A. Collapse and Reorganization
of the Latin Nominal Inflection.
D.C. Walker, 350:Dec85-923
Gage, J.T. In the Arresting Eye.*
V.M. Kouidis, 577(SHR):Summer84-285
A. Robinson, 541(RES):May84-266
Gagne, C. and T. Caras. Soundpieces.
P. Dickinson, 410(M&L):Oct84-369
P. Dickinson, 415:Jan84-28
Gagnon, A. Il n'y a pas d'hiver à King-
ston.
M.E. Kidd, 102(CanL):Autumn84-92
Gagnon, C. Pourquoi les moutons frisent.
D. Thaler, 102(CanL):Autumn84-168
Gaines, E.J. A Gathering of Old Men.*
G.D. Kendrick, 95(CLAJ):Mar85-354
Gaínza, M.C.G. and others - see under
García Gaínza, M.C. and others
Gair, R. The Children of Paul's.*
R.A. Foakes, 551(RenQ):Spring84-138
R. Foulkes, 611(TN):Vol38No3-148
W. Habicht, 156(JDSh):Jahrbuch1984-254
E.J. Jensen, 130:Spring84-82
Gaite, C.M. - see under Martín Gaite, C.
Gajda, P.A. Postscript to Victory.
P.S. Wandycz, 575(SEER):Jan84-136
Gal, G. and R. Wood - see Ockham, William
of
Gal-Or, B. Cosmology, Physics, and Philos-
ophy.
A. Loose, 679:Band15Heft1-173
Galasso, G. L'altra Europa.
L. Mascilli Migliorini, 98:Aug/Sep84-717
Galay, J-L. Philosophie et invention tex-
tuelle.
J.J. Wunenberger, 342:Band75Heft2-250
Galbán, E.S. - see under Suárez Galbán, E.
Galdós, B.P. - see under Pérez Galdós, B.

Galeano, E. Memory of Fire. (Vol 1)
R. Christ, 441:27Oct85-22
Galen. Galen's Commentary on the Hippo-
cratic Treatise "Airs, Waters, Places"
in the Hebrew Translation of Solomon ha-
Me'ati.* (A. Wasserstein, ed and trans)
C.S.F. Burnett, 123:Vol34No2-315
Galera Andreu, P.A. Arquitectura y arqui-
tectos en Jaén a fines del siglo XVI.
F. Marías, 48:Jan-Mar83-83
Galgan, G.J. The Logic of Modernity.*
E. Fontinell, 543:Sep83-118
J.W. Yolton, 518:Jan84-63
Galgut, D. A Sinless Season.
K. Nunn, 441:31Mar85-7
Galisson, R. Lexicologie et enseignement
des langues.
F. Mazière, 209(FM):Apr84-96
Galisson, R. Des mots pour communiquer.
D.B. Perramond, 207(FR):Dec84-338
Galisson, R. La Suggestion dans l'en-
seignement.
D.B. Perramond, 207(FR):Dec84-339
Gall, S.M. Ramon Guthrie's "Maximum
Security Ward."
R. Asselineau, 189(EA):Jul-Sep85-365
295(JML):Nov84-449
Gall, S.M. - see Guthrie, R.
Gallagher, D. - see Waugh, E.
Gallagher, E.J., J.A. Mistichelli and J.A.
van Eerde. Jules Verne.
J. Newton, 208(FS):Apr84-214
Gallagher, J. Companions of the Dead.
H. von Winning, 2(AfrA):May84-46
Gallagher, S.F., ed. Woman in Irish
Legend, Life and Literature.
C.A. Carlon, 272(IUR):Spring84-148
B. Dolan, 305(JIL):Jan-May84-145
B. John, 627(UTQ):Summer84-414
Gallagher, T. Willingly.*
E. Grosholz, 249(HudR):Winter84/85-656
P. Stitt, 219(GaR):Fall84-628
Gallais, P. Dialectique du récit médiéval
(Chrétien de Troyes et l'hexagone
logique).*
M-C. Struyf, 356(LR):Aug84-248
Gallant, M. Home Truths.*
M. Howard, 441:5May85-1
Gallavotti, C. Metri e ritmi nelle iscriz-
ioni greche.
P.A. Hansen, 123:Vol34No2-286
Galley, E. and A. Estermann, eds. Hein-
rich Heines Werk im Urteil seiner Zeit-
genossen. (Vol 1)
R.C. Holub, 221(GQ):Spring84-324
Galli-Pahlari, A. - see Waugh, A.
Galliani, R. and F. Loirette. Études sur
Montesquieu (1981).
J.G. Rosso, 535(RHL):Jul/Aug84-616
Galliazzo, V. Sculture greche e romane
del Museo Civico di Treviso.
S. Lattimore, 124:Sep-Oct84-64
Gallicet Calvetti, C. Benedetto Spinoza
di fronte a Leone Ebreo (Jehudah
Abarbanel).
J-P. Osier, 192(EP):Oct-Dec84-567
Gallie, W.B. Philosophers of Peace and
War.* (Spanish title: Filósofos de la
Paz y de la Guerra.)
M. Caimi, 342:Band75Heft4-516
Galliher, J.F. and J.L. De Gregory. Vio-
lence in Northern Ireland.
G. Townshend, 617(TLS):1Nov85-1231

Gallix, F. - see White, T.H.

Gallo, F.A. Music of the Middle Ages II.
  D. Fallows, 617(TLS):1Nov85-1227

Gallop, J. The Daughter's Seduction.*
  K. Ross, 188(ECr):Fall84-91

Galloway, P.K., ed. La Salle and His
  Legacy.
  R. Fabel, 9(AlaR):Oct84-304

Gallup, D. Ezra Pound.* (2nd ed)
  G. Bornstein, 534(RALS):Autumn82-241
  C.F. Terrell, 30:Fall83-81

Gallup, D. - see Wilder, T.

Galsworthy, J. Strife. (N. Worrall, ed)
  Galsworthy: Five Plays.
  D. Devlin, 157:No152-50

Galt, G. Trailing Pythagoras.*
  J.A. Wainwright, 198:Summer84-94

Galtung, J. There Are Alternatives!
  A.J. Pierre, 441:3Feb85-23

Galvin, J. God's Mistress.
  F. Garber, 29(APR):Sep/Oct85-14

Gambelli, D. and A.M. Scaiola. Littérature française et critique italienne
  (1950-1980).
  A. Levi and J. Baldran, 535(RHL):
  May/Jun84-475

Gandhi, J.S. Lawyers and Touts.
  P.G. Price, 293(JASt):May84-566

Gandossy, R.P. Bad Business.
  M. Singer, 441:20Oct85-50

Ganim, J.M. Style and Consciousness in
  Middle English Narrative.
  639(VQR):Spring84-45

Gans-Ruedin, E. Indian Carpets.
  R.L.S., 614:Winter85-26
  J. Thompson, 617(TLS):17May85-563

Gant, R. - see Thomas, E.

Ganzel, B. Dust Bowl Descent.*
  L. Milazzo, 584(SWR):Autumn84-462
  442(NY):14Jan85-119

Ganzel, D. Fortune and Men's Eyes.*
  A. Bell, 354:Dec84-413
  S. Bennett, 637(VS):Winter84-260
  K. Muir, 569(SR):Spring84-270

Garapon, R. Le premier Corneille.*
  W. Henning, 547(RF):Band96Heft1/2-181

Garavaglia, L.A. and C.G. Worman. Firearms of the American West, 1803-1865.
  L. Milazzo, 584(SWR):Summer84-336

Garavini, F. - see de Montaigne, M.E.

de Garay Fernández, M.T. Introducción a
  la obra poética de Francisco López de
  Zárate.
  R.M. Price, 86(BHS):Apr84-198

Garbagnati, L., ed. Claudel aux États-
  Unis, 1927-1933.
  M. Malicet, 535(RHL):Sep/Oct84-816

Garber, E. and L. Paleo. Uranian Worlds.
  K.L. Spencer, 561(SFS):Mar84-98

Garber, F. The Autonomy of the Self from
  Richardson to Huysmans.*
  G. Gillespie, 52:Band19Heft1-86
  V. Nemoianu, 107(CRCL):Mar84-128
  D. Nokes, 83:Autumn84-252
  P. Parrinder, 402(MLR):Apr84-403

Garber, K., ed. Europäische Bukolik und
  Georgik.
  J. Amsler, 549(RLC):Jul-Sep84-356

Garber, M. Coming of Age in Shakespeare.*
  D. Bevington, 405(MP):Aug84-95
  C. Hoy, 569(SR):Spring84-256
                                [continued]

[continuing]
  C. Kahn, 301(JEGP):Jul84-434
  R. Lengeler, 156(JDSh):Jahrbuch1984-
  250

Garcia, J. The Alchemy of the Body and
  Other Poems.
  P. Stratford, 102(CanL):Autumn84-159

García Castañeda, S. Miguel de los Santos
  Álvarez (1818-1892).
  J. Escobar, 345(KRQ):Vol31No1-106

García Damborenea, R. La Encrucijada
  Vasca.
  R. Carr, 453(NYRB):17Jan85-39

García de la Concha, V. - see de Jesús, T.

García Delgado, J.L., ed. La España de la
  Restauración.
  R. Carr, 617(TLS):4Oct85-1105

García Gaínza, M.C. and others. Catálogo
  monumental de Navarra. (vol unknown)
  D. Angulo Íñiguez, 48:Jan-Mar84-124

García Lorenzo, L. - see Pérez Galdós, B.

García Márquez, G. Collected Stories.
  J. Updike, 442(NY):20May85-118

García Márquez, G. El coronel no tiene
  quien le escriba.* (G. Pontiero, ed)
  E. Williamson, 402(MLR):Apr84-480

García Riera, G. Guillermo Meneses.
  J. Wilson, 86(BHS):Jan84-70

García Sebastián, J.L. Fernando Gallego
  y su taller en Salamanca.
  I. Mateo Gómez, 48:Jul-Sep83-308

García y García, A. and others - see
  Suarez, F.

García Yebra, V. Teoría y Práctica de la
  Traducción.*
  E. Barjau, 202(FMod):No74/76-313

García Yebra, V. En torno a la traducción.
  A. Gullón, 240(HR):Summer84-418

Garcilaso de la Vega. Obras completas.
  (A. Labandeira Fernández, ed)
  J. Gornall, 402(MLR):Apr84-473

du Gard, R.C. - see under Coulet du Gard,
  R.

du Gard, R.M. Le Lieutenant-colonel de
  Maumort.* (A. Daspre, ed)
  M. Jarrety, 450(NRF):Jan84-120

Gardam, J. Bilgewater.
  P. Craig, 617(TLS):5Jul85-757

Gardam, J. Crusoe's Daughter.
  V. Bogdanor, 362:23May85-32
  B. Hardy, 617(TLS):31May85-599

Garde, P., ed. IIIe Colloque de Linguistique Russe ...
  E. Klenin, 350:Mar85-228

Gardella, P. Innocent Ecstasy.
  D.D. Hall, 441:18Aug85-12

Gärdenfors, P., B. Hansson and N-E. Sahlin,
  eds. Evidentiary Value.
  D.V. Lindley, 84:Sep84-293
  L.J. O'Neill, 63:Sep84-302

Gardiner, D.B. Intonation and Music.
  F. Daneš, 355(LSoc):Mar84-113
  P. Trost, 215(GL):Vol124No4-261

Gardiner, M. The Deadly Innocents.
  P. Highsmith, 617(TLS):6Sep85-967

Gardner, G.W. and P. Carr. Gun People.
  S. Laschever, 441:10Nov85-29

Gardner, H. Art, Mind, and Brain.
  F. Smolucha, 289:Summer84-108

Gardner, H. Gribouillages et dessins
  d'enfants.
  P. Somville, 542:Jan-Mar84-136

129

Gardner, H. In Defence of the Imagination.*
R.J. Dingley, 447(N&Q):Dec83-568
Gardner, H. The Mind's New Science.
S. Sutherland, 441:13Oct85-12
Gardner, J. The Art of Fiction.
639(VQR):Summer84-84
Gardner, J. On Becoming a Novelist.
D. Weiser, 436(NewL):Fall84-107
Gardner, J. The Secret Generations.
M. Laski, 362:14Nov85-35
E. Zuckerman, 441:1Dec85-24
Gardner, J., with S. Ravenel, eds. The Best American Short Stories 1982.*
T.A. Gullason, 573(SSF):Spring84-156
Gardner, J. and N. Tsukui - see Itaya, K.
Gardner, J.B. and G.R. Adams, eds. Ordinary People and Everyday Life.
L.G. Carr, 656(WMQ):Jul84-499
Gardner, M. The Magic Numbers of Dr. Matrix.
G. Krist, 441:26May85-15
Gardner, M. Mathematical Magic Show.
H. Mellar, 617(TLS):8Mar85-268
Gardner, M., ed. The Sacred Beetle and Other Great Essays in Science.
617(TLS):27Dec85-1491
Gardner, P. Kingsley Amis.
J. Tyler, 447(N&Q):Jun83-268
Garebian, K. Hugh Hood.
W.J. Keith, 99:Apr84-32
W.B. Stone, 573(SSF):Summer84-284
Garfield, B. Western Films.
R.W. Etulain, 649(WAL):May84-73
Garfield, J.L. and P. Hennessey, eds. Abortion.
W. Kaminer, 441:28Apr85-25
Garfinkel, A., ed. ESL and the Foreign Language Teacher.
E.K. Horwitz, 399(MLJ):Spring84-64
Garfinkel, A., ed. The Foreign Language Classroom.
T.V. Higgs, 399(MLJ):Autumn84-383
C.K. Knop, 207(FR):May85-904
Garfinkel, A. Forms of Explanation.
R. Hudelson, 482(PhR):Jan84-116
S. Turner, 488:Sep84-416
Garfinkel, A. and G. Latorre. Trabajo y vida.
F. Nuessel, 399(MLJ):Spring84-94
W. Woodhouse, 238:Dec84-685
Garfitt, J.S.T. The Work and Thought of Jean Grenier (1898-1971).
J. Llewelyn, 402(MLR):Jul84-716
R.M. McLure, 208(FS):Apr84-235
H. Peyre, 207(FR):Apr85-737
Garfitt, R. The Broken Road.
D. McDuff, 565:Spring84-72
Gargano, A. - see de Flores, J.
Garin, E. Astrology in the Renaissance.*
D. Pingree, 589:Jul84-650
Garitano, R. Rainy Day Man.
A.M. Davidon, 441:26May85-14
Garlan, Y. Les esclaves en Grèce ancienne.*
R. Seager, 303(JoHS):Vol 104-239
Garland, J. Welcome the Traveler Home.
(J.S. Ardery, ed)
585(SoQ):Summer84-90
Garland, J.E. Down to the Sea.
A.W. German, 432(NEQ):Jun84-310

Garland, R. The Greek Way of Death.
J. Griffin, 362:8Aug85-29
H. King, 617(TLS):16Aug85-893
Garlick, K. and A. MacIntyre - see Farington, J.
Garmadi, J. La Sociolinguistique.
F. Helgorsky, 209(FM):Oct84-225
Garmey, S. Gramercy Park.
S.M. Halpern, 441:14Jul85-22
Garner, J.S. The Model Company Town.
R. Bailey, 441:23Jun85-21
Garner, P. Emile Gallé.*
A. Anderson, 62:Dec84-72
Garner, S. and C. Dodge - see Frederic, H.
Garner, W. Think Big, Think Dirty.
639(VQR):Winter84-26
Garnett, A. Deceived With Kindness.*
J. Malcolm, 453(NYRB):24Oct85-17
N. Sayre, 441:24Mar85-26
442(NY):22Apr85-142
Garnsey, P., K. Hopkins and C.R. Whittaker, eds. Trade in the Ancient Economy.
G.E. Rickman, 123:Vol34No1-78
Garnsey, P. and C.R. Whittaker, eds. Trade and Famine in Classical Antiquity.
É. Will, 555:Vol58fasc2-303
Garrard, J. Cold Comfort.
I. Gaskell, 198:Spring84-97
J. Ripley, 168(ECW):Winter84/85-304
Garrard, J. Mikhail Lermontov.*
C. Marsh, 575(SEER):Jan84-107
R. Reid, 402(MLR):Apr84-508
Garrard, J., ed. The Russian Novel from Pushkin to Pasternak.*
M.R. Katz, 104(CASS):Winter84-431
Garrels, E. Mariátegui y la Argentina.
M.S. Stabb, 238:Mar84-153
Garrett, G. The Collected Poems of George Garrett.
B. Galvin, 389(MQ):Winter85-249
D.E. Richardson, 598(SoR):Spring85-547
Garrett, G. An Evening Performance.
G. Johnson, 441:6Oct85-28
Garrett, G. James Jones.*
A. Boyer, 395(MFS):Winter84-843
Garrett, G. The Succession.*
R.A. Cosgrove, 50(ArQ):Autumn84-287
G.L. Geckle, 588(SSL):Vol 19-301
R.T. Sorrells, 580(SCR):Fall84-111
W. Sullivan, 569(SR):Spring84-xx
Garrett, W. Charles Wentworth Dilke.
J.C. Grigely, 339(KSMB):No35-113
Garrick, D. David Garrick: Selected Verse.
(J.D. Hainsworth, ed)
I. Donaldson, 541(RES):Nov84-548
Garrick, D. The Plays of David Garrick.*
(Vols 1 and 2) (H.W. Pedicord and F.L. Bergmann, eds)
J.A. Vance, 477(PLL):Summer84-339
Garrick, D. The Plays of David Garrick.*
(Vols 3 and 4) (H.W. Pedicord and F.L. Bergmann, eds)
I. Donaldson, 541(RES):Nov84-548
R.D. Hume, 301(JEGP):Jan84-130
J.A. Vance, 477(PLL):Summer84-339
Garrick, D. The Plays of David Garrick.*
(Vols 5-7) (H.W. Pedicord and F.L. Bergmann, eds)
R.D. Hume, 301(JEGP):Jan84-130
J.A. Vance, 477(PLL):Summer84-339
Garrison, J. and P. Shivpuri. The Russian Threat.
D. Holloway, 617(TLS):11Jan85-34

Garrison, M. and A. Gleason, eds. Shared Destiny.
  A. Austin, 441:27Oct85-18
Garrison, W.L. The Letters of William Lloyd Garrison. (Vol 6) (W.M. Merrill and L. Ruchames, eds)
  L.T. McDonnell, 106:Summer84-167
Garside, P. - see Scott, W.
Garsoïan, N.G., T.F. Mathews and R.W. Thomson, eds. East of Byzantium.
  W.E. Kaegi, Jr., 589:Apr84-473
Garstang, D. Giacomo Serpotta and the Stuccatori of Palermo 1560-1790.
  B. Boucher, 39:Nov84-356
  A. Laing, 617(TLS):4Jan85-21
Garthoff, R.L. Detente and Confrontation.
  W. Taubman, 441:30Jun85-7
Garver, J. China's Decision for Rapprochement with the United States, 1968-1971.
  M. Baron, 293(JASt):May84-517
Garvey, M. The Marcus Garvey and Universal Negro Improvement Association Papers. (Vol 4) (R.A. Hill, with E.J. Tolbert and D. Forczek, eds)
  C.E. Walker, 441:22Dec85-12
Garvi, P.A. Zapiski Sotsial Demokrata (1906-1921).
  V. Brovkin, 550(RusR):Jul84-296
Garvin, H.R., ed. Literature, Arts, and Religion.
  U. Weisstein, 107(CRCL):Mar84-102
Garvin, H.R., with P.C. Carafiol, eds. The American Renaissance.
  L. Buell, 432(NEQ):Sep84-435
Garvin, H.R. and J.M. Heath, eds. Literature and Ideology.
  J. Carson, 478:Apr84-146
Garvin, H.R., with J.M. Heath, eds. Science and Literature.
  D.A. White, 125:Spring84-301
Garvin, T. The Evolution of Irish Nationalist Politics.
  T.E. Hachey, 637(VS):Autumn83-112
Gascar, P. Buffon.
  J. Aeply, 450(NRF):Mar84-117
Gascar, P. Le Fortin.
  C. Dis, 450(NRF):Jan84-122
Gash, J. Caravaggio.
  R.E. Spear, 90:Mar84-162
Gash, J. Pearlhanger.
  T.J. Binyon, 617(TLS):5Apr85-394
  N. Callendar, 441:23Jun85-33
Gash, N. Mr. Secretary Peel.
  617(TLS):27Dec85-1491
Gaskell, E. Elizabeth Gaskell: A Portrait in Letters. (J.A.V. Chapple, with G. Sharps, eds)
  W.A. Craik, 447(N&Q):Apr83-174
Gaskell, P. From Writer to Reader.
  J.K. Walton, 447(N&Q):Feb83-75
Gaskin, J.C.A. The Quest for Eternity.
  M. Wiles, 617(TLS):25Jan85-98
Gasparini, L. The Climate of The Heart.
  L. Rogers, 102(CanL):Winter83-153
Gass, W.H. Habitations of the Word.
  F. Kermode, 441:10Mar85-12
Gassendi, P. Institutio Logica.* (H. Jones, ed and trans)
  T.M. Lennon, 535(RHL):Nov/Dec84-953
  G.A.J. Rogers, 518:Apr84-88
Gassier, P. Léopold Robert.
  D. Wakefield, 39:May84-386
  J.J.L. Whiteley, 90:Jun84-364

Gasster, M. China's Struggle to Modernize. (2nd ed)
  C. Lynch, 293(JASt):Aug84-740
Gateau, J-C. Paul Éluard et la peinture surréaliste (1910-1939).*
  C.H. Winn, 547(RF):Band96Heft3-362
Gatenby, G., ed. Whales.*
  C. Rooke, 376:Oct84-126
Gates, C. From Cremation to Inhumation.
  J. Boardman, 123:Vol34No1-149
  R. Higgins, 303(JoHS):Vol 104-248
Gates, H.L., Jr., ed. Black Literature and Literary Theory.*
  Chinweizu, 617(TLS):17May85-560
Gathercole, P., A.L. Kaeppler and D. Newton. The Art of the Pacific Islands.
  D.C. Starzecka, 39:Nov84-360
Gathorne-Hardy, J. The Centre of the Universe is 18 Baedekerstrasse.
  C. Benfey, 441:11Aug85-14
  J.K.L. Walker, 617(TLS):22Mar85-327
Gauchat, L., J. Jeanjaquet and E. Tappolet. Glossaire des patois de la Suisse romande. (fasc 74-75)
  P. Swiggers, 353:Vol22No6-933
Gaudreault-Labrecque, M. Le mystère du grenier.
  C. Gerson, 102(CanL):Summer84-127
Gauger, H-M., W. Oesterreicher and R. Windisch. Einführung in die romanische Sprachwissenschaft.*
  P. Swiggers, 353:Vol22No6-935
Gaugh, H.F. Willem de Kooning.
  J. Bell, 55:Apr84-29
Gauguin, P. Paul Gauguin: 45 Lettres à Vincent, Théo et Jo van Gogh.
  B. Welsh-Ovcharov, 90:Feb84-96
Gaukroger, S., ed. Descartes: Philosophy, Mathematics and Physics.*
  P. Kraus, 543:Mar84-627
Gaulmier, J., with J. Boissel - see de Gobineau, A-J.
Gaunt, D. Familjeliv i Norden.
  S.P. Oakley, 562(Scan):Nov84-172
Gauquelin, M. Birthtimes.
  A. Doueihi, 469:Vol 10No1-140
Gaur, A. A History of Writing.
  N. Gray, 617(TLS):20Sep85-1043
Gaus, G. Wo Deutschland Liegt.
  T.G. Ash, 453(NYRB):31Jan85-33
Gaus, G.F. The Modern Liberal Theory of Man.
  P. Franco, 185:Jan85-364
Gauthier, G. and Y. Lacroix - see Perrault, P.
Gauthier, H. L'Image de l'homme intérieur chez Balzac.
  D. Festa-McCormick, 446(NCFS): Summer85-282
Gauthier, N. L'évangélisation des pays de la Moselle.
  J. Harries, 313:Vol74-219
Gautier, T. Voyage en Espagne. (J-C. Berchet, ed)
  J. Newton, 208(FS):Jan84-74
  J. Newton, 208(FS):Jul84-355
Gautier, T. Voyage en Espagne [suivi de] España. (P. Berthier, ed)
  J. Newton, 208(FS):Jul84-355
"Théophile Gautier: l'art et l'artiste."
  A.B. Smith, 446(NCFS):Winter-Spring85-145

Gautreau, E. Tale Spinners in a Spruce
Tipi.
M. Whitaker, 102(CanL):Winter83-79
Gavronsky, S. Culture Ecriture.
J. Adamson, 188(ECr):Fall84-87
Gay, J. John Gay: Dramatic Works. (J.
Fuller, ed)
J. Hamard, 189(EA):Jul-Sep85-332
B.S. Hammond, 83:Autumn84-244
P. Lewis, 566:Spring85-182
Gay, J. L'Opéra du gueux/The Beggar's
Opera. (J. Michon, ed and trans)
R.A. Day, 189(EA):Jul-Sep85-330
Gay, M. Eclaboussures.*
J.L. Pallister, 207(FR):Feb85-493
Gay, P. Freud for Historians.
A.A. Rogow, 441:8Sep85-26
442(NY):14Oct85-142
Gay, V.P. Reading Jung.
S.E.H., 185:Jul85-982
Gay-Crosier, R., ed. Albert Camus 9.
I.H. Walker, 208(FS):Jan84-95
Gaylin, W. The Rage Within.
B. Harvey, 441:10Feb85-25
Gaylnor, E. and K. Haavisto. Finland:
Living Design.
R.L.S., 614:Winter85-23
Gayraud, M. Narbonne antique des origines
à la fin du IIIe siècle.
H. Lavagne, 555:Vol58fasc2-353
al-Gazālī. Ihyā' 'Ulūm ad-Dīn. (Bk 14)
(R. Morelon, ed and trans)
R.M. Frank, 318(JAOS):Oct-Dec83-811
Gazdar, G., E. Klein and G.K. Pullum, eds.
Order, Concord and Constituency.
J. Hoeksema, 361:Jul-Aug84-335
Gazzaniga, M.S. The Social Brain.
D.C. Dennett, 441:17Nov85-53
Geach, P.T. Reference and Generality.*
(3rd ed)
Z. Vendler, 316:Jun84-655
Gealt, A.M. Looking at Art.
J. Povey, 2(AfrA):Aug84-90
Gearhart, S. The Open Boundary of History
and Fiction.
S. Bann, 617(TLS):8Feb85-153
J.W. Brown, 150(DR):Spring84-184
Geary, C. Things of the Palace.
T. Northern, 2(AfrA):Aug84-15
Geary, J.S. Formulaic Diction in the
"Poema de Fernán González" and the
"Mocedades de Rodrigo."*
G.W. Du Bois, 545(RPh):Feb84-347
Gebauer, G. Der Einzelne und sein gesell-
schaftliches Wissen.
F. Jacques, 540(RIPh):Vol38fasc3-315
Gebauer, G.J. and B. Löfstedt - see Saint
Boniface
Gébler, C. The Eleventh Summer.
C. Hawtree, 617(TLS):1Feb85-110
J. Mellors, 364:Feb85-102
R. O'Meally, 441:6Oct85-28
442(NY):16Dec85-168
Geddes, G. and others. Chinada.
A. Appenzell, 102(CanL):Winter83-167
Geddes, P. A State of Corruption.
M. Laski, 362:18Jul85-29
Geddes, T. Hj. Söderberg: "Doktor Glas."
(2nd ed)
D.M. Mennie, 562(Scan):Nov84-196
Gee, M. The Burning Book.*
P. Craig, 617(TLS):5Jul85-757

Gee, M. Light Years.
R. Kaveney, 617(TLS):4Oct85-1097
J. Mellors, 362:7Nov85-28
Geertz, C. Local Knowledge.*
42(AR):Winter84-121
Geertz, C.C. Bali, Interprétation d'une
culture.
H. Cronel, 450(NRF):Jul/Aug84-176
Geeslin, C. The Bonner Boys.
G. Haslam, 649(WAL):May84-66
Géfin, L.K. Ideogram.*
G.F. Butterick, 30:Fall83-85
M. Heller, 460(OhR):No33-145
S. Paul, 301(JEGP):Jan84-104
Gehm, J. Bringing it Home.
P. Delaney, 441:24Feb85-13
Gehman, C. Beloved Gravely.
E. Schwamm, 441:3Mar85-36
Geier, R., H. Huth and U. Wittich. Ver-
ständlich und wirksam schreiben.
J. Scharnhorst, 682(ZPSK):Band37Heft6-
739
Geis, D. The Gilbert and Sullivan Operas.
F.J. Cullinan, 615(TJ):May84-290
Geisen, H. and D. Wessels - see Shake-
speare, W.
Geiser, C. Wüstenfahrt.
M. Hofmann, 617(TLS):4Jan85-17
Geisler, E. Geld bei Quevedo.*
W.B. Berg, 72:Band221Heft1-230
Geisler, H. Studien zur typologischen
Entwicklung.*
K. Hunnius, 547(RF):Band96Heft4-438
E. Pulgram, 205(ForL):Apr83-260
Gelb, N. Scramble.
H. Goodman, 441:29Dec85-19
Gelber, H.G. - see Holcot, R.
Gelfand, E.D. Imagination in Confinement.
R. Goldberg, 208(FS):Oct84-499
S. Tarrow, 446(NCFS):Winter-Spring85-
186
Gélinas, G. Les Fridolinades, 1941 et
1942, 1943 et 1944.
J.E. Pavelich, 102(CanL):Winter83-103
Geller, M. Andrej Platonov v poiskax
sčast'ja.
T. Seifrid, 574(SEEJ):Winter84-569
Gellinek, C. Elementare Linguistik.
B.J. Koekkoek, 406:Fall84-347
Gellman, B. Contending With Kennan.
D. Fromkin, 441:12May85-31
Gellner, E., ed. Soviet and Western
Anthropology.
E. Dunn, 104(CASS):Fall84-344
Gellner, E. Nations and Nationalism.
B.B., 185:Oct84-182
Gély, C. - see de Guérin, M.
Gelzer, M. Die Nobilität der römischen
Republik. (new ed) (J. von Ungern-
Sternberg, ed)
J-C. Richard, 555:Vol58fasc2-343
Gendron, B. Technology and the Human
Condition.
T. Settle, 488:Dec84-515
Gendron, M. Les Espaces glissants.
P.S. Rogers, 207(FR):Mar85-598
Genet, J. Le Balcon.* (D.H. Walker, ed)
A. Callen, 402(MLR):Jan84-203
Genet, J., ed. William Butler Yeats.
N. Grene, 189(EA):Apr-Jun85-240

132

Genette, G. Figures of Literary Dis-
course.*
    J. Fletcher, 366:Spring84-112
    D. Kelly, 446(NCFS):Summer-Fall84-216
Genette, G. Nouveau discours du récit.
    J. Catesson, 98:Nov84-920
    P. Dulac, 450(NRF):Apr84-122
    G. Prince, 494:Vol5No4-867
    C.J. Stivale, 207(FR):Apr85-742
Genette, G. Palimpsestes.*
    P. Carrard, 494:Vol5No1-205
    H. Mitterand, 627(UTQ):Fall83-119
Genève, M. Ordo.
    R. Robe, 207(FR):May85-916
Geng, V. Partners.*
    G. Marcus, 62:Dec84-77
Genoud, C. and Takao Inoue. Buddhist Wall
Painting of Ladakh.
    D. Klimburg-Salter, 293(JASt):Feb84-
359
"Le Genre pastoral en Europe du XVe au
XVIIe siècle."
    R.F. Hardin, 107(CRCL):Jun84-294
Gensei. Grass Hill. (B. Watson, trans)
    M. Collcutt, 407(MN):Autumn84-351
Gent, L. Picture and Poetry 1560-1620.
    J. Doebler, 570(SQ):Autumn84-372
    A.M., 125:Fall83-95
Gent, P. The Franchise.*
    639(VQR):Spring84-56
Gentile, G. Rousseau filosofo della crisi.
    J-L. Lecercle, 535(RHL):Jan/Feb84-117
Gentili, B. and G. Cerri. Storia e bio-
grafia nel pensiero antico.
    J.M. Alonso-Núñez, 123:Vol34No2-332
Gentsch, G. Faulkner zwischen Schwarz und
Weiss.
    M.N. Love, 395(MFS):Winter84-824
Genuist, M. Languirand et l'absurde.*
    L.E. Doucette, 627(UTQ):Summer84-483
    J-A. Elder, 102(CanL):Summer84-121
Geoghegan, C. Louis Aragon.* (Vol 1)
    M. Sheringham, 208(FS):Oct84-488
George, D. - see Smith, I.
George, E., ed. Contemporary East Euro-
pean Poetry.*
    T. Eagleton, 565:Summer84-76
Georgel, P. and A-M. Lecoq. La Peinture
dans la Peinture.
    90:Mar84-170
Georges, R.A. and S. Stern. American and
Canadian Immigrant and Ethnic Folklore.
    R.W. Brednich, 196:Band25Heft1/2-128
    E. Wachs, 292(JAF):Apr-Jun84-245
Georgescu, V. Istoria românilor de la
origini pînă în zilele noastre.
    V. Nemoianu, 617(TLS):4Oct85-1106
Georgiades, T. Music and Language.
    J. Caldwell, 410(M&L):Jul84-287
    D. Fallows, 415:Mar84-154
Georgiev, V.I. Introduction to the His-
tory of the Indo-European Languages.
    B.G. Hewitt, 361:Jul-Aug84-327
Geraets, T.F., ed. L'esprit absolu/The
Absolute Spirit.
    L-P. Luc, 154:Dec84-715
Geraghty, P.A. The History of the Fijian
Languages.
    N. Besnier, 350:Mar85-231
    F. Lichtenberk, 361:Dec84-386
Geraghty, T. Freefall Factor.
    T.J. Binyon, 617(TLS):29Nov85-1353

Gérard, A.S. African Language Litera-
tures.*
    W. Glinga, 343:Heft9/10-141
    D.P. Kunene, 107(CRCL):Mar84-163
    C. Moore, 268(IFR):Winter85-51
Gérard, A.S. Comparative Literature and
African Literatures.
    S.D. Ngcongwane, 538(RAL):Fall84-426
Gerard, K. American Survivors.
    K. Auletta, 441:27Jan85-10
Gerber, D.E. Pindar's "Olympian One."*
    M.C. Howatson, 123:Vol34No2-173
    F.J. Nisetich, 24:Winter84-480
Gerber, L.E. and M. McFadden. Loren
Eiseley.
    B. Howard, 502(PrS):Fall84-97
    P. Wild, 651(WHR):Summer84-191
Gerber, M. and others, eds. Studies in
GDR Culture and Society.*
    D. Sevin, 406:Fall84-341
Gerber, M.J. Honeymoon.
    A. Becker, 441:15Dec85-28
Gerdts, W.H. American Impressionism.
    A. Washton, 55:Dec84-27
    J. Yau, 62:Dec84-77
Gere, J. and N. Turner. Drawings by
Raphael from English Collections.
    P. Joannides, 278(IS):Vol39-109
Gere, J.A. and P. Pouncey, with R. Wood.
Italian Drawings in the Department of
Prints and Drawings in the British
Museum: Artists Working in Rome c. 1550
to c. 1640.*
    K. Andrews, 380:Summer84-212
Gerhard, S.F. "Don Quixote" and the
Shelton Translation.*
    G. Martínez Lacalle, 86(BHS):Apr84-196
Gérin, P. and P.M. Marichette, Lettres
acadiennes, 1895-1898.
    F. Des Roches, 627(UTQ):Summer84-490
Gérin, W. Anne Thackeray Ritchie.*
    R.B. Martin, 541(RES):May84-257
    J. Shattock, 155:Summer84-119
Gerl, H-B. Philosophie und Philologie.
    C.B. Schmitt, 123:Vol34No2-363
Gerlach, U.H., comp. Hebbel-Museum Wessel-
buren.
    R. Salter, 301(JEGP):Apr84-285
Gerlaud, B. - see Triphiodorus
Gerli, E.M., ed. Triste deleytación.
    E.H. Friedman, 238:Mar84-141
Germain, G-H. Un Minou fait comme un rat.
    D. Thaler, 102(CanL):Summer84-161
German, T. Tom Penny.
    P.L. Hart, 102(CanL):Autumn84-167
German, T.J. Hamann on Language and Reli-
gion.
    J.C. O'Flaherty, 221(GQ):Summer84-469
    J.C. O'Flaherty, 222(GR):Summer84-121
Germino, D. Political Philosophy and the
Open Society.*
    P. Salstrom, 396(ModA):Winter84-91
    E. Webb, 125:Spring84-284
Germond, J.W. and J. Witcover. Wake Us
When It's Over.
    K. Auletta, 441:28Jul85-3
Gernet, J. Chine et christianisme.*
    J-F. Billeter, 98:Apr84-255
Gernet, L. The Anthropology of Ancient
Greece.*
    J.A.S. Evans, 529(QQ):Summer84-324

133

Gerould, D. Witkacy.*
 S.E. Croft, 615(TJ):Dec82-561
 N. Taylor, 575(SEER):Apr84-273
Gerrard, J. Cold Comfort.
 S. Stone-Blackburn, 102(CanL):Autumn84-
 140
Gerrard, J., ed. The Russian Novel from
 Pushkin to Pasternak.
 A.R. Durkin, 395(MFS):Summer84-391
Gersch, H., T.M. Mayer and G. Oesterle -
 see "Georg Büchner Jahrbuch 2/1982"
Gershator, D. - see Lorca, F.G.
Gershon, K. The Bread of Exile.
 M. Haltrecht, 617(TLS):10May85-529
Gerson, C. and K. Mezei, eds. The Prose
 of Life.
 E. Waterston, 102(CanL):Summer84-165
Gerson, L.P., ed. Graceful Reason.
 A. Reix, 542:Oct-Dec84-462
Gerstenberg, R. Zur Erzähltechnik von
 Günter Grass.
 A.L. Cobbs, 221(GQ):Spring84-335
 J.W. Rohlfs, 402(MLR):Apr84-505
Gervais, C.H. The Fighting Parson.
 N. Carson, 102(CanL):Autumn84-189
Gervais, C.H. Into a Blue Morning.
 E. Trethewey, 102(CanL):Summer84-84
Gervais; D. Flaubert and Henry James.
 M. Bell, 473(PR):3/1984-462
Gervers, M. The Hospitaller Cartulary in
 the British Library (Cotton MS Nero E
 VI).
 W.T. Reedy, 589:Jan84-144
"Geschichte als demokratischer Auftrag."
 D. Kirby, 575(SEER):Oct84-637
Geschwind, N. Selected Papers on Language
 and the Brain.
 I. Rosenfield, 453(NYRB):21Nov85-49
Geschwind, N. and A.M. Galaburda, eds.
 Cerebral Dominance.
 I. Rosenfield, 453(NYRB):21Nov85-49
Gethin, D. Point of Honor.
 N. Callendar, 441:15Sep85-33
Gethner, P. and E.J. Campion - see du Ryer,
 P.
Getz, L.M. Nature and Grace in Flannery
 O'Connor's Fiction.
 W.J. Stuckey, 395(MFS):Winter84-832
Getzler, I. Kronstadt 1917-1921.*
 P. Kenez, 550(RusR):Jan84-80
 L. Schapiro, 575(SEER):Apr84-298
Geuss, R. The Idea of a Critical Theory.
 D. Misgeld, 488:Jun84-284
 H.N. Tuttle, 543:Jun84-848
Geuter, U. Die Professionalisierung der
 deutschen Psychologie im Nationalsozial-
 ismus.
 F. Stern, 453(NYRB):19Dec85-48
Gewecke, F. Die Karibik.
 U. Fleischmann, 343:Heft9/10-134
Gewirth, A. Human Rights.*
 E.M. Adams, 543:Jun84-849
Ghalem, A. A Wife for My Son.
 V. Bogdanor, 362:4Jul85-31
Ghersi, G. La città e la selva.
 C. Di Biase, 275(IQ):Spring84-71
Ghoshal, B. Indonesian Politics, 1955-
 1959.
 D. Hindley, 293(JASt):Aug84-799
Giamatti, A.B. Exile and Change in Renais-
 sance Literature.
 M. Evans, 191(ELN):Jun85-63
 [continued]

[continuing]
 R.H. Wells, 179(ES):Dec84-571
 639(VQR):Spring84-43
Giamatti, A.B. The University and the
 Public Interest.*
 I.B. Holley, Jr., 579(SAQ):Spring84-
 228
Giancana, A. and T.C. Renner. Mafia Prin-
 cess.*
 639(VQR):Autumn84-122
Giangrande, C. The Nuclear North.
 R.W. Reford, 529(QQ):Winter84-1005
Giannakes, G.N. Orpheōs Lithika.* [shown
 in prev under Giannakis]
 N. Hopkinson, 123:Vol34No1-19
Giannantonio, P. Endiadi.
 V. Cioffari, 276:Autumn84-266
Giannetto, N., ed. Vittorino da Feltre e
 la sua scuola.
 A. Buck, 72:Band221Heft1-236
Gianturco, C. Mozart's Early Operas.
 M.F. Robinson, 410(M&L):Jan84-65
Giantvalley, S. Walt Whitman, 1838-1939.*
 J. Loving, 534(RALS):Spring82-81
Gibaldi, J., ed. Approaches to Teaching
 Chaucer's "Canterbury Tales."*
 J.M. Fyler, 677(YES):Vol 14-305
Gibaldi, J., ed. Introduction to Scholar-
 ship in Modern Languages and Literatures.
 J. Culler, 223:Winter81-521
Gibaldi, J. and W.S. Achtert. MLA Hand-
 book for Writers of Research Papers,
 Theses, and Dissertations.
 G. Trett, 536:Vol6-201
Gibaud, H. Un Inédit d'Érasme.*
 A.J. Brown, 617(TLS):5Jul85-760
Gibbon, E. Histoire du déclin et de la
 chute de l'empire romain.
 A. Reix, 542:Jan-Mar84-78
Gibbon, J. Textile Design Strategies.
 E. Hoffman, 614:Summer85-36
Gibbons, B. - see Shakespeare, W.
Gibbons, R. and S. Hahn, eds. TQ 20.
 J. Leggett, 441:6Oct85-22
Gibbs, A.M. The Art and Mind of Shaw.*
 R. Simard, 615(TJ):Dec84-548
Gibian, G. and S.J. Parker, eds. The
 Achievements of Vladimir Nabokov.
 C.S. Ross, 395(MFS):Winter84-829
Gibson, A. Growing Up with Cricket.
 T.D. Smith, 617(TLS):28Jun85-734
Gibson, F.W. Queen's University. (Vol 2)
 P. Axelrod, 529(QQ):Winter84-765
 M. Ross, 150(DR):Spring84-200
Gibson, G. Perpetual Motion.*
 A.E. Davidson, 102(CanL):Autumn84-80
Gibson, M., ed. Boethius.*
 R.A. Peck, 589:Oct84-903
Gibson, M. Dancing with Mermaids.
 D. Montrose, 617(TLS):10May85-528
Gibson, M. Workers' Rights.
 M.L., 185:Jan85-399
Gibson, M. - see Hunt, R.W.
Gibson, M.I. The Roots of Russian Through
 Chekhov.*
 M.I. Levin, 558(RLJ):Winter-Spring84-
 280
Gibson, R.F., Jr. The Philosophy of W.V.
 Quine.*
 H.A. Lewis, 518:Jan84-51
 P.A. Roth, 606:Nov84-205
Gibson, W. Neuromancer.*
 G. Jonas, 441:24Nov85-33

Giddens, A. The Constitution of Society.
  S. Lukes, 617(TLS):18Oct85-1163
Giddens, A. Contemporary Critique of His-
torical Materialism. (Vol 1)
  J.B. Thompson, 488:Dec84-543
Giddings, R., ed. The Changing World of
Charles Dickens.
  S. Connor, 155:Spring84-48
  S. Monod, 189(EA):Jul-Sep85-341
Giddings, R., ed. J.R.R. Tolkien.
  L. Basney, 395(MFS):Winter84-768
  S. Medcalf, 617(TLS):19Jul85-802
Giddins, G. Rhythm-a-ning.
  F. Davis, 441:7Apr85-9
  C. Fox, 617(TLS):15Nov85-1288
Cide, A. and D. Bussy. Selected Letters
of André Cide and Dorothy Bussy.* (R.
Tedeschi, ed and trans)
  P.H. Solomon, 395(MFS):Summer84-393
  295(JML):Nov84-447
Gidel, H. Le Théâtre de Feydeau.
  W.D. Howarth, 208(FS):Jan84-79
Gidley, C. The Raging of the Sea.
  J. Haskins, 441:27Jan85-22
Gier, N.F. Wittgenstein and Phenomenol-
ogy.*
  D. Rubinstein, 488:Dec84-582
Gies, D.T. Nicolás Fernández de Moratín.
  P.B. Goldman, 345(KRQ):Vol31No1-107
Gies, F. The Knight in History.*
  442(NY):14Jan85-119
Giesbert, F-O. Monsieur Adrien.
  P.H. Solomon, 207(FR):Dec84-314
Giffhorn, J. Studien am Survey of English
Dialects.
  W. Viereck, 685(ZDL):1/1984-107
Gifford, H. Tolstoy.*
  N.O. Warner, 550(RusR):Apr84-190
Gifford, J. and others. The Buildings of
Scotland.* (Vol 2: Edinburgh.)
  J.S. Curl, 324:Nov85-885
  I. Gow, 617(TLS):22Feb85-195
Gifford, N.L. When in Rome.
  R. Phillips, 63:Jun84-192
Gigante, M., ed. Contributi alla storia
della Officina dei Papiri Ercolanesi.
  W.E.H. Cockle, 123:Vol34No1-153
Gikandi, S. Notes on Camara Laye's "The
African Child."
  K. Dramé, 538(RAL):Spring84-89
Gil, C.J.A. and J.M. Parrado del Olmo -
see under Ara Gil, C.J. and J.M. Parrado
del Olmo
Gilbert, B. Westering Man.
  H.L. Carter, 649(WAL):Aug84-162
Gilbert, B. - see Adams, J.D. and J.L.
Sharpe 3d
Gilbert, C. Across the Mutual Landscape.
  A. Williamson, 441:23Jun85-26
Gilbert, C. Bonfire.
  L. Gregerson, 491:Oct84-39
Gilbert, J.B. Clear Speech.
  A-L. Sheikh-Ibrahim, 608:Sep85-585
Gilbert, M. Jerusalem.
  W. Kaminer, 441:25Aug85-17
  D. Pryce-Jones, 617(TLS):21Jun85-691
Gilbert, M. The Jews of Hope.*
  P. Hallie, 441:13Jan85-11
  A. Puddington, 129:Jun85-71
Gilbert, M. The Long Journey Home.
  T.J. Binyon, 617(TLS):29Nov85-1353
  M. Laski, 362:18Jul85-29
  442(NY):20May85-127

Gilbert, N. Capitalism and the Welfare
State.*
  A. Hacker, 453(NYRB):28Feb85-37
Gilbert, S.M. and S. Gubar. The Madwoman
in the Attic.
  D. Porter, 432(NEQ):Mar84-106
  A.J. Wiemer, 107(CRCL):Jun84-319
Gilbert, S.M. and S. Gubar, eds. The
Norton Anthology of Literature by Women.
  G. Godwin, 441:28Apr85-13
  P. Rose, 61:Aug85-88
Gilbert, S.M. and S. Gubar, eds. Shake-
speare's Sisters.
  D. Porter, 432(NEQ):Mar84-106
Gilbert, W.S. Plays by W.S. Gilbert.* (G.
Rowell, ed)
  J. Donohue, 637(VS):Autumn83-91
Gilbert, W.S. and A.S. Sullivan. The Anno-
tated Gilbert and Sullivan.* (I. Brad-
ley, ed)
  R.K. Higgins, 637(VS):Summer84-520
Gilbert, W.S. and A.S. Sullivan. The Anno-
tated Gilbert and Sullivan, 2. (I. Tay-
lor, ed)
  A. Lamb, 415:Dec84-704
Gilchrist, E. The Annunciation.*
  C. Stubblefield, 502(PrS):Summer84-107
Gilchrist, E. In the Land of Dreamy
Dreams.
  442(NY):5Aug85-82
Gilchrist, E. Victory Over Japan.*
  D. Sexton, 617(TLS):24May85-573
Gildea, J., ed. L'Hystoire Job. (Vol 2)
  S. Kay, 545(RPh):May84-521
Gilder, G. The Spirit of Enterprise.*
  R. Hattersley, 617(TLS):13Sep85-993
  T. Lindberg, 129:Apr85-63
Gildin, H. Rousseau's Social Contract.
  R. Grimsley, 173(ECS):Winter84/85-257
Cildner, C. The Crush.
  S. Watson, 219(GaR):Fall84-666
Gilead, Z. and D. Krook. Gideon's Spring.
  R.F. Shepard, 441:22Sep85-23
Giles, M. Rough Translations.
  R. Grant, 441:12May85-18
Gilkes, M. The West Indian Novel.
  R.W. Sander, 343:Heft9/10-129
Gill, B. McGarr and the Method of Des-
cartes.*
  N. Callendar, 441:14Apr85-16
Gill, B. McGarr and the P.M. of Belgrave
Square.
  639(VQR):Spring84-56
Gill, F. I Could Not Interpret the Spring.
  G. Szirtes, 493:Sep84-76
Gill, J.H. Wittgenstein and Metaphor.
  L.M. Hinman, 484(PPR):Mar85-465
Gill, S. - see Lawrence, D.H.
Gillespie, R.B. Heads You Lose.
  N. Callendar, 441:30Jun85-29
Gilliatt, P. They Sleep Without Dreaming.
  R. Kaveney, 617(TLS):29Nov85-1353
  L. Zeidner, 441:27Oct85-40
Gillies, D.A. Frege, Dedekind and Peano
on the Foundations of Arithmetic.
  J.P. Mayberry, 479(PhQ):Jul84-424
Gillies, V. Bed of Stone.
  T. Dooley, 617(TLS):10May85-527
Gillilan, P. Minima.
  J. Saunders, 565:Spring84-55
Gillis, C.M. The Paradox of Privacy.
  S. Soupel, 189(EA):Jul-Sep85-336

Gillispie, C.C. The Montgolfier Brothers and the Invention of Aviation, 1783-1784.*
  D.M. Knight, 83:Autumn84-276
  G. McNamee, 31(ASch):Autumn84-566
Gilman, S.L. On Blackness without Blacks.
  S. Bauschinger, 564:Feb84-77
  M.K. Flavell, 402(MLR):Oct84-970
  M. Steins, 52:Band19Heft1-89
Gilman, S.L., with I. Reichenbach, eds. Begegnungen mit Nietzsche.*
  E. Behler, 221(GQ):Fall84-685
  P. Heller, 301(JEGP):Jan84-93
Gilmont, J-F. Bibliographie des éditions de Jean Crespin, 1550-1572.*
  R.M. Kingdon, 551(RenQ):Spring84-89
Gilmore, M.T. The Middle Way.
  F. Martín Gutiérrez, 202(FMod):No65/67-338
Gilmour, D. The Transformation of Spain.
  R. Fox, 362:18Apr85-25
  K. Maxwell, 441:29Dec85-30
  D. Smyth, 617(TLS):7Jun85-629
Gilmour, R. The Idea of the Gentleman in the Victorian Novel.*
  W.A. Craik, 541(RES):Aug84-400
  V. Sanders, 447(N&Q):Dec83-553
  B.R. Westburg, 67:May84-85
Gilmour-Bryson, A. The Trial of the Templars in the Papal State and the Abruzzi.
  F.L. Cheyette, 589:Oct84-937
Giloy-Hirtz, P. Deformation des Minnesangs.
  O. Ehrismann, 680(ZDP):Band103Heft3-467
Gilroy, J.P., ed. Francophone Literatures of the New World.*
  G. Warner, 102(CanL):Summer84-164
Gilson, D. A Bibliography of Jane Austen.*
  J. Wiesenfarth, 365:Winter84-21
  A. Wright, 445(NCF):Jun84-95
Gilson, E. Constantes philosophiques de l'être.
  M. Adam, 542:Apr-Jun84-252
  B. Dumoulin, 192(EP):Jul-Sep84-408
Giménez Ruiz, P., C. Nachón González and M. Díaz Cuétara. La iglesia de San Fernando, de Torrero.
  F. Marías, 48:Jul-Sep84-330
Gimm, M. - see Forke, A.
Gindin, L.A. Drevnejšaja onomastika vostočnych Balkan (Frako-chetto-luvijskie i frako-maloazijskie izoglossy).
  W.P. Schmid, 260(IF):Band89-362
Ginet, C. and S. Shoemaker, eds. Knowledge and Mind.
  S.P. Stich, 185:Jan85-357
Gingell, S. - see Pratt, E.J.
Gingerich, M.E. Contemporary Poetry in America and England, 1950-1975.
  295(JML):Nov84-329
Gingrich, N. Window of Opportunity.
  G.A. Fossedal, 129:Jan85-27
Ginsberg, A. Collected Poems 1947-1980.*
  G. Ewart, 362:25Apr85-25
  L. Mackinnon, 617(TLS):24May85-574
  M. Perloff, 29(APR):Mar/Apr85-35
  R. Richman, 129:Jul85-50
Ginsberg, W. The Cast of Character.
  E.T. Hansen, 401(MLQ):Sep83-311
Ginsburg, M. Victorian Dress in Photographs.
  G. Cavaliero, 324:Jan85-159

Ginzberg, E. and G. Vojta. Beyond Human Scale.
  R. Krulwich, 441:14Jul85-26
Ginzburg, C. The Night Battles.*
  P. Burke, 453(NYRB):28Feb85-32
Ginzburg, M. Style and Epoch.
  M. Green, 574(SEEJ):Winter84-559
Ginzburg, N. All Our Yesterdays.
  G. Annan, 453(NYRB):7Nov85-29
  W. Weaver, 441:5May85-39
Ginzburg, N. La città e la casa.
  D. Davis, 617(TLS):4Oct85-1115
Ginzburg, N. Family Sayings.
  G. Annan, 453(NYRB):7Nov85-29
Ginzburg, N. The Little Virtues.
  G. Annan, 453(NYRB):7Nov85-29
  P.N. Furbank, 362:25Jul85-31
  J. McCulloch, 441:13Oct85-25
Ginzburg, N. Le voci della sera.* (A. Bullock, ed)
  M. Caesar, 402(MLR):Jul84-723
Gioia, D. Daily Horoscope.
  J. Carter, 219(GaR):Summer84-415
Gioia, D. - see Kees, W.
Giono, J. Oeuvres romanesques complètes. (Vol 5) (R. Ricatte and others, eds)
  W.D. Redfern, 208(FS):Jan84-90
Giono, J. Oeuvres romanesques complètes.* (Vol 6) (R. Ricatte, with others, eds)
  W.D. Redfern, 208(FS):Jul84-366
"Jean Giono, 3."
  H. Godard, 535(RHL):May/Jun84-469
Giordan, H. Démocratie culturelle et droit à la différence.
  J. Paulhan, 207(FR):Oct84-176
Giordano, M. and J.L. Pallister. Béroalde de Verville: "Le Moyen de Parvenir."*
  G. Breuer, 547(RF):Band96Heft1/2-176
Giordano Rampioni, A. Sulpiciae conquestio (Ep. Bob. 37).
  J. Soubiran, 555:Vol58fasc1-136
Giovanni, N. Those Who Ride the Night Winds.
  J.F. Cotter, 249(HudR):Autumn84-499
Giraldi Cinzio, G. - see under Speroni, S.
Girard, L. Les Libéraux français.
  J-F. Revel, 176:May85-36
Girard, R. Des choses cachées depuis la fondation du monde.
  R. Dupree, 543:Dec83-400
Girardet, K.M. Die Ordnung der Welt.
  M. Ducos, 555:Vol58fasc2-329
  J.G.F. Powell, 123:Vol134No2-318
Girardot, N.J. Myth and Meaning in Early Taoism.*
  R.L. Janelli, 292(JAF):Oct-Dec84-475
Giraud, Y., ed. L'Emblème à la Renaissance.
  D. Russell, 551(RenQ):Summer84-282
Giraudoux, J. Théâtre complet.* (J. Body and others, eds)
  R. Pouilliart, 356(LR):Nov84-333
Girgus, S.B. The New Covenant.*
  L. Field, 395(MFS):Winter84-837
  I. Saposnik, 659(ConL):Winter85-492
Girke, W. and H. Jachnow, eds. Theoretische Linguistik in Osteuropa.
  K. Reichl, 38:Band102Heft3/4-456
Girling, R., ed. The Sunday Times Travel Book.
  J. Campbell, 617(TLS):27Dec85-1477

Girnus, W. Aus den Papieren des Germain Tawordschus.
  I. Hiebel, 654(WB):7/1984-1187
Girouard, M. Cities and People.
  D. Cannadine, 617(TLS):20Sep85-1019
  P. Johnson, 362:26Sep85-25
  P. Partner, 453(NYRB):5Dec85-38
  442(NY):18Nov85-175
Girouard, M. Robert Smythson and the Elizabethan Country House.*
  H. Colvin, 46:Mar84-56
  A.T. Friedman, 576:Oct84-268
  W.T. MacCaffrey, 551(RenQ):Autumn84-497
Giroud, F. Le Bon Plaisir.
  L. Vinço, 207(FR):Apr85-755
Giroux, R. The Book Known as Q.*
  R. Jacobs, 541(RES):Aug84-372
  R. Kimbrough, 579(SAQ):Autumn84-468
Giroux, R. - see Bishop, E.
Gish, N.K. Hugh MacDiarmid.
  F.R. Hart, 659(ConL):Winter85-508
Gish, N.K. Time in the Poetry of T.S. Eliot.
  R. Marsack, 447(N&Q):Aug83-374
Gish, R. Paul Horgan.
  F. Erisman, 651(WHR):Autumn84-291
Gitler, I. Swing to Bop.
  N. Tesser, 441:22Dec85-20
Gitlin, T. Inside Prime Time.
  D. Henry, 583:Fall84-96
Gittelson, C. Saving Grace.
  J. O'Faolain, 617(TLS):15Mar85-284
Gittings, R. and J. Manton. Dorothy Wordsworth.
  N. Fruman, 617(TLS):28Jun85-711
Gittleman, Z. Becoming Israelis.
  G. Nahshon, 390:Apr84-53
Giuffrida Ientile, M. La pirateria tirrenica, momenti e fortuna.
  D. Briquel, 555:Vol58fasc2-267
Giusberti, F. Materials for a Study of Twelfth-Century Scholasticism.
  E.J. Ashworth, 589:Oct84-974
Giusti, P. and P. Leone de Castris. Medioevo e produzione artistica di serie.
  M. Campbell, 90:Jun84-353
Giustiniani, V.R. Neulateinische Dichtung in Italien 1850-1950.
  G. Costa, 545(RPh):Feb84-377
Givner, J. Katherine Anne Porter.*
  G. Garrett, 569(SR):Summer84-495
  B.H. Gelfant, 454:Fall84-64
Givner, J. Tentacles of Unreason.
  A. Becker, 441:15Dec85-28
Gjelten, B.H. H.C. Andersen som teaterconnaisseur.
  F. Brun, 563(SS):Spring84-190
Gjerstad, E. Ages and Days in Cyprus.*
  M. Fortin, 487:Autumn84-267
Gladkij, A.V. and I.A. Mel'čuk. Elements of Mathematical Linguistics. (J. Lehrberger, ed)
  B. Brainerd, 320(CJL):Fall84-177
  W. Frawley, 350:Mar85-246
Gladkova, T. and L. Mnukhin, eds. Bibliographie des oeuvres de Marina Tsvetaeva.* (T.A. Ossorguine, ed)
  G.S. Smith, 575(SEER):Jan84-115
  J.A. Taubman, 104(CASS):Spring-Summer84-168
Glaeser, G. - see Brecht, B.

Glage, L. and J. Rublack. Die gestörte Identität.*
  P. Zenzinger, 588(SSL):Vol 19-283
Glanville, B. Kissing America.
  P. Smelt, 617(TLS):22Mar85-327
Glanville, B. Love Is Not Love.
  P. Lewis, 364:Mar85-105
  P. Smelt, 617(TLS):22Mar85-327
Glare, P.G.W. - see "Oxford Latin Dictionary"
Glaser, F. Antike Brunnenbauten (Krēnai) in Griechenland.
  R.A. Tomlinson, 303(JoHS):Vol 104-254
Glaser, H.A., ed. Zwischen Absolutismus und Aufklärung.
  R. Dumont, 549(RLC):Jan-Mar84-112
Glass, D.F. Italian Romanesque Sculpture.
  P.W., 90:Oct84-647
Glass, F.W. The Fertilizing Seed.
  R. Anderson, 415:Feb84-96
  A. Whittall, 410(M&L):Jul84-278
Glass, J.M. Woman Wanted.
  P-L. Adams, 61:Aug85-91
  C. See, 441:25Aug85-10
Glass, N. - see de Nerval, G.
Glasser, R.J. Another War, Another Peace.
  J. Klein, 441:21Apr85-26
Glassie, H., ed. Irish Folktales.
  D.H. Greene, 441:17Nov85-32
Glassie, H. Passing the Time in Ballymenone.* Irish Folk History: Texts from the North.*
  D.K. Wilgus, 292(JAF):Apr-Jun84-238
Glatthaar, J.T. The March to the Sea and Beyond.
  H. Mitgang, 441:1Sep85-15
Glauser, A. Fonctions du nombre chez Rabelais.
  E.M. Duval, 551(RenQ):Spring84-121
  T. Thomson, 402(MLR):Jan84-183
Glauser, J. Isländische Märchensagas.
  F. Hugus, 589:Oct84-905
Glazebrook, P. Journey to Kars.
  R. Fox, 362:24Jan85-26
  N. Miller, 441:27Jan85-23
  442(NY):4Feb85-101
Glazer, D. Three Women.
  L. Taylor, 617(TLS):4Jan85-9
Glazer, M., ed. Flour from Another Sack, and Other Proverbs, Folk Beliefs, Tales, Riddles and Recipes.
  B. Allen, 650(WF):Oct84-285
Glazer, N., ed. Clamor at the Gates.
  M. Novak, 129:Dec85-71
  R. Pear, 441:28Jul85-19
Glazer, N. and K. Young, eds. Ethnic Pluralism and Public Policy.
  R.E.G., 185:Jan85-398
Gleason, W. Alexander Guchkov and the End of the Russian Empire.
  B.T. Norton, 104(CASS):Winter84-473
Gleckner, R.F. Blake's Prelude.*
  S.D. Cox, 173(ECS):Spring85-391
  P. Dunbar, 536:Vol6-187
  N. Hilton, 591(SIR):Fall84-409
  S. Peterfreund, 403(MLS):Summer84-82
  F. Piquet, 189(EA):Apr-Jun85-237
  J. Wittreich, 661(WC):Summer84-113
Gledson, J. The Deceptive Realism of Machado de Assis.
  J.G. Merquior, 617(TLS):1Feb85-127

Glen, H. Vision and Disenchantment.
S. Matthews, 175:Spring84-66
F. Piquet, 189(EA):Oct-Dec85-465
D. Simpson, 88:Spring85-227
J. Williams, 366:Autumn84-272
Glendinning, R.J. and H. Bessasson, eds.
Edda.
J.E. Cathey, 589:Oct84-974
M.E. Kalinke, 402(MLR):Oct84-995
H. Roe, 564:Sep84-219
Glendinning, V. Vita.*
639(VQR):Spring84-50
Glenn, C.W. Jim Dine: Drawings.
C. Ratcliff, 617(TLS):6Sep85-970
Glenn, E.S., with C.G. Glenn. Man and Man-
kind.*
J. Verschueren, 355(LSoc):Dec84-489
Glennerster, H. Paying for Welfare.
R. Klein, 617(TLS):16Aug85-899
Glick, A. Winters Coming, Winters Gone.
R. Elman, 441:11Aug85-14
Glickman, N. Uno de sus Juanes y otros
cuentos.
N. Lindstrom, 238:Dec84-680
Glickman, S. Complicity.
J. Seim, 99:May84-34
Glimm, J.Y. Flatlanders and Ridgerunners.
B. Allen, 650(WF):Oct84-285
Gloag, J. Blood for Blood.
C. Hawtree, 617(TLS):10May85-529
M. Laski, 362:18Jul85-29
Globerman, S. Cultural Regulation in
Canada.
B. Trotter, 529(QQ):Winter84-1004
Glorieux, J-P. Novalis dans les lettres
françaises à l'époque et au lendemain
du symbolisme (1885-1914).
P. Gorceix, 52:Band19Heft3-321
R. Lloyd, 678(YCGL):No32-150
Glover, D. The Love Island.
J. Crace, 617(TLS):26Jul85-833
Glover, D.E. C.S. Lewis.
C. Manlove, 447(N&Q):Jun83-282
Glover, J. The Wall and the Candle.
D. McDuff, 565:Spring84-72
Gloversmith, F., ed. The Theory of Read-
ing.
C. Baldick, 617(TLS):14Jun85-676
Glowacki, J. Give Us This Day.
M.T. Kaufman, 441:6Jan85-12
Glück, L. The Triumph of Achilles.
L. Rosenberg, 441:22Dec85-22
Glucksmann, A. La force du vertige.*
G-H. de Radkowski, 98:Oct84-814
Glynn, P. Skin to Skin.
A.M. Tomcik, 529(QQ):Spring84-186
"Glyph 8." (W.B. Michaels, ed)
T. Hawkes, 447(N&Q):Apr83-191
Gō, S. Requiem.
C. Ames, 441:27Oct85-40
J. Kirkup, 617(TLS):9Aug85-875
Gobiet, R. - see Hainhofer, P.
de Gobineau, A-J. Oeuvres.* (Vol 1)
(J. Gaulmier, with J. Boissel, eds)
M.D. Biddiss, 208(FS):Jan84-75
A. Smith, 446(NCFS):Winter-Spring85-
151
Gochet, P. Outline of a Nominalist Theory
of Propositions.*
P. Swiggers, 567:Vol50No3/4-283
Gockel, H. Mythos und Poesie.*
C. Jamme, 489(PJGG):Band91Heft2-435

Godard de Donville, L. La Mythologie au
XVIIe siècle.*
C. Rouben, 535(RHL):Nov/Dec84-954
Goddard, L. and B. Judge. The Metaphysics
of Wittgenstein's "Tractatus."*
I. Block, 154:Jun84-361
Goddard, L. and R. Routley. The Logic of
Significance and Context. (Vol 1)
N.B. Cocchiarella, 316:Dec84-1413
Godden, G. Chamberlain-Worcester Porce-
lain, 1788-1852.
J.V.G. Mallet, 90:Feb84-93
Godenne, R. Les Romans de Mlle. de
Scudéry.
N. Aronson, 475:Vol 11No20-228
H.T. Barnwell, 208(FS):Apr84-199
B. Beugnot, 546(RR):Jan84-107
J. De Jean, 210(FrF):Jan84-114
G. Verdier, 207(FR):Apr85-728
Godey, J. Fatal Beauty.*
M. Laski, 362:18Jul85-29
Godfrey, W.G. Pursuit of Profit and Pre-
ferment in Colonial North America.
S.W. Jackman, 432(NEQ):Mar84-124
I.K. Steele, 656(WMQ):Apr84-310
Godin, A. Erasme: lecteur d'Origène.
J.D. Tracy, 551(RenQ):Autumn84-441
Godley, M.R. The Mandarin-Capitalists
from Nanyang.
W.E. Cheong, 302:Vol20No2-239
Godman, D., ed. Be As You Are.
M. Barrett, 469:Vol 10No4-94
Godman, P., ed. Poetry of the Carolingian
Renaissance.
J. Griffin, 362:23May85-29
J. Marenbon, 617(TLS):23Aug85-936
Godwin, D. "Les Nouvelles françaises ou
les divertissements de la princesse
Aurélie" de Segrais.
P.A. Wadsworth, 207(FR):May85-891
Godwin, G. The Finishing School.
J. Mellors, 362:21Mar85-25
M. Seymour, 617(TLS):29Mar85-340
F. Taliaferro, 441:27Jan85-7
442(NY):18Feb85-121
Godwin, G., with S. Ravenel, eds. The
Best American Short Stories 1985.
A. Krystal, 441:29Sep85-46
Godwin, J. Athanasius Kircher.
F. Brauen, 90:May84-298
Godwin, W. Caleb Williams. (D. McCracken,
ed) The Castle of Otranto. (W.S. Lewis,
ed)
B.S.H., 83:Autumn84-282
Goebl, H., ed. Dialectology.
M.E. Schaffer, 350:Sep85-709
Goede, W. Quantrill.
A.J. Harding, 102(CanL):Winter83-89
L.K. MacKendrick, 198:Spring84-110
Goertzen, R. Juergen Habermas.
D. Misgeld, 488:Mar84-97
von Goethe, J.W. Faust. (A. Stapfer,
trans)
J. Voisine, 549(RLC):Jan-Mar84-121
von Goethe, J.W. Goethe: Ecrits sur l'art.
(J-M. Schaeffer and T. Todorov, eds and
trans)
P. Dubrunquez, 450(NRF):Jan84-136
P. Schnyder, 602:Band15Heft1-147
von Goethe, J.W. Goethe: Selected Poems.
(C. Middleton, ed)
E. Grosholz, 249(HudR):Spring84-135

"Goethe Yearbook." (Vol 1) (T.P. Saine, ed)
  H. Froeschle, 221(GQ):Summer84-474
  I.H. Solbrig, 173(ECS):Summer85-583
Goetinck, J.F. Essai sur le rôle des Allemands dans le Dictionnaire Historique et Critique (1697) de Pierre Bayle.
  P-E. Knabe, 475:Vol 11No20-232
Goetschel, R. Meir Ibn Gabbay.*
  J.H.A. Wijnhoven, 318(JAOS):Apr-Jun83-453
Goetzmann, W.H. and K. Sloan. Looking Far North.
  A. Ronald, 649(WAL):Nov84-256
Goffman, E. Forms of Talk.
  W.K. Rawlins, 480(P&R):Vol 17No3-181
Gogan, B. The Common Corps of Christendom.
  E. McCutcheon, 568(SCN):Spring-Summer84-28
  T.I. White, 551(RenQ):Spring84-78
Gohdes, C. and S.E. Marovitz, eds. Bibliographical Guide to the Study of Literature of the U.S.A. (5th ed)
  K.M. Roemer, 26(ALR):Autumn84-296
Goitein, S.D. A Mediterranean Society. (Vol 4)
  L. Rosen, 617(TLS):7Jun85-648
Goitia, F.C. - see under Chueca Goitia, F.
Golb, N. and O. Pritsak, eds and trans. Khazarian Hebrew Documents of the Tenth Century.
  S. Bowman, 589:Apr84-474
  S. Ettinger, 550(RusR):Oct84-436
Gold, E. Owl.
  M. Galvin, 496:Fall84-177
Goldbarth, A. Original Light.*
  V. Contoski, 502(PrS):Fall84-114
  W. Logan, 491:Nov84-103
  R. McDowell, 249(HudR):Spring84-118
  M. Simms, 584(SWR):Summer84-344
Goldberg, A. Ilya Ehrenburg.* (E. de Mauny, ed)
  L. Kochan, 129:Jan85-70
  M. Scammell, 453(NYRB):28Feb85-26
Goldberg, E.L. Patterns in Late Medici Art Patronage.
  E. Chaney, 617(TLS):1Mar85-228
  A. Hughes, 59:Sep84-378
Goldberg, J. Endlesse Worke.*
  J.D. Guillory, 405(MP):Aug84-89
  D.L. Miller, 577(SHR):Winter84-75
  G.L. Teskey, 539:May85-121
Goldberg, J. James I and the Politics of Literature.*
  J. Dollimore, 141:Winter84-83
  J.E. Howard, 570(SQ):Summer84-234
  K.E. Maus, 400(MLN):Dec84-1239
  D. Norbrook, 175:Autumn84-251
  D. Palomo, 290(JAAC):Summer85-411
Goldberg, M.K. and J.P. Siegel - see Carlyle, T.
Goldberg, R., ed. Tonos a lo divino y a lo humano.
  C. Lee, 86(BHS):Apr84-199
Goldberger, P. On the Rise.
  E. Gibson, 648(WCR):Oct84-65
Goldemberg, I. Play by Play.
  A. Dorfman, 441:4Aug85-12
Golden, M. The Friendship Quilt Book.
  P.J. Christenson, 614:Spring85-22
Golden, M. Migrations of the Heart.
  J. Beerman, 42(AR):Winter84-117

Goldenberg, S. The Thomson Empire.
  T. Traves, 99:Oct84-32
Goldensohn, L. The Tether.
  W.H. Pritchard, 249(HudR):Summer84-330
Goldfrank, D.M. - see Volotsky, I.
Goldhaber, G.M. Organizational Communication. (3rd ed)
  K.J. Krayer, 583:Spring85-298
Goldhill, S. Language, Sexuality, Narrative.
  O. Taplin, 617(TLS):15Mar85-292
Golding, W. An Egyptian Journal.
  P. Beer, 362:29Aug85-25
  J. Ray, 617(TLS):1Nov85-1243
  442(NY):11Nov85-157
Golding, W. A Moving Target.*
  I. McGilchrist, 402(MLR):Jan84-176
Golding, W. The Paper Men.*
  P. Craig, 617(TLS):5Jul85-757
  G. Klaus, 189(EA):Jan-Mar85-116
  W. Lesser, 249(HudR):Autumn84-469
  P. Lewis, 565:Autumn84-55
Goldman, M. Acting and Action in Shakespearean Tragedy.
  G. Taylor, 617(TLS):16Aug85-905
Goldman, M. High Hopes.
  M. Banham, 576:Oct84-273
Goldman, P. and T. Fuller, with others. The Quest for the Presidency 1984.
  A. Day, 441:18Aug85-25
  N. Lemann, 61:Oct85-102
Goldman, R. and J. Children's Sexual Thinking.
  W.W. Watters, 529(QQ):Spring84-230
Goldman, W. Heat.
  D. Mamet, 441:19May85-15
  442(NY):29Jul85-78
Goldmann, L. Method in the Sociology of Literature. (W.Q. Boelhower, ed)
  R. Poole, 447(N&Q):Aug83-382
Goldner, G.R. Master Drawings from the Woodner Collection.
  M. Royalton-Kish, 39:Aug84-147
Goldring, E.O. Laser Treatment.
  D. Jaffe, 436(NewL):Fall84-103
Goldsborough, J.F. with others. Silver in Maryland.
  D.D. Waters, 658:Winter84-297
Goldscheider, C. and A. Zuckerman. The Transformation of the Jews.
  D. Singer, 129:Jul85-71
Goldsmith, J. - see Hinks, R.
Goldsmith, M.E. The Figure of Piers Plowman.*
  J.A. Alford, 589:Jan84-146
  H. Gillmeister, 38:Band102Heft3/4-532
  D. Mehl, 72:Band221Heft2-478
  A.V.C.S., 382(MAE):1984/2-314
Goldsmith, U.K., with T. Schneider and S.S. Coleman, eds. Rainer Maria Rilke: A Verse Concordance to His Complete Lyrical Poetry.*
  T. Fiedler, 133:Band17Heft1/2-171
Goldsmith, W. and D. Clutterbuck. The Winning Streak.
  F. Cairncross, 617(TLS):31May85-613
Goldstein, D., ed. The Ashkenazi Haggadah.
  R.A. May, 617(TLS):21Jun85-705
Goldstein, D.I. Dostoyevsky and the Jews.*
  D. Bilik, 149(CLS):Summer84-240
Goldstein, L. The Dream Years.
  G. Jonas, 441:20Oct85-20

Goldstein, R. The Mind-Body Problem.
  G. Strawson, 617(TLS):1Mar85-227
Goldstein, S.M., L.S. Rakow and J.K. Rakow.
  Cameo Glass.
  G. Wills, 39:Jan84-69
Goldstein, T. The News at any Cost.
  J.D. Atwater, 441:1Sep85-16
Goldstone, H. Coping with Vulnerability.
  S.H. Gale, 397(MD):Sep84-457
Goldsworthy, P. Readings from Ecclesi-
  astes.
  R. Pybus, 565:Summer84-56
Goldthwaite, R.A. The Building of Renais-
  sance Florence.*
  A. Tönnesmann, 683:Band47Heft2-263
Goldziher, I. Introduction to Islamic
  Theology and Law.*
  P.E. Walker, 318(JAOS):Oct-Dec83-761
Goleman, D. Vital Lies, Simple Truths.
  Z. Rubin, 441:16Jun85-9
Golitsyn, A. New Lies for Old.*
  639(VQR):Autumn84-134
Göller, K.H., ed. The Alliterative "Morte
  Arthure."*
  J. Finlayson, 382(MAE):1984/1-127
  M. Hamel, 536:Vol5-155
  O.D. Macrae-Gibson, 541(RES):Aug84-359
Göller, K.H. and H.W. Wurster. Das Regens-
  burger Dollingerlied.
  F. Schanze, 684(ZDA):Band113Heft1-25
Golovin, P.N. Civil and Savage Encounters.
  (B. Dmytryshyn and E.A.P. Crownhart-
  Vaughan, eds and trans)
  A. Schrier, 550(RusR):Jul84-295
Golubkova, E. - see Messerer, A.
Gom, L. Northbound.
  S.S., 376:Jun84-149
  S. Shreve, 648(WCR):Jun84-62
Gombrich, E.H. The Image and the Eye.*
  M. Kemp, 59:Jun84-228
Gombrich, E.H. Tributes.*
  S.S. Prawer, 384:Sep84-692
Gombrowicz, W. Journal. (Vols 1-3) Test-
  ament. Trans-Atlantique. Les envoûtés.
  La pornographie. Cosmos. Yvonne,
  princesse de Bourgogne. Ferdydurke.
  M-A. Lescourret, 98:Jan-Feb84-29
Gómez, I.M. - see under Mateo Gómez, I.
Gómez, J.M.G. and M.J. Carrasco Terriza -
  see under González Gómez, J.M. and M.J.
  Carrasco Terriza
Gomez, L. and H.W. Woodward, Jr., eds.
  Barabuḍar.*
  J.P. McDermott, 318(JAOS):Apr-Jun83-
  442
Gomez-Arcos, A. The Carnivorous Lamb.
  J. McCulloch, 441:17Mar85-26
Gómez de la Serna, R. La Quinta de Pal-
  myra. (C. Richmond, ed)
  R. Cardona, 240(HR):Spring84-250
  A. Hoyle, 86(BHS):Apr84-205
  E.D. Myers, 238:Mar84-144
  A. Sinclair, 402(MLR):Jul84-734
Gómez-Martínez, J.L. Teoría del ensayo.*
  T. Mermall, 240(HR):Winter84-75
Gomme, A.W., A. Andrewes and K.J. Dover.
  A Historical Commentary on Thucydides.
  (Vol 5)
  G.J.D. Aalders H. Wzn., 394:
  Vol37fasc1/2-177
  W.R. Connor, 122:Jul84-230
  P.J. Rhodes, 303(JoHS):Vol 104-204

Gonda, J. The Haviryajñāḥ Somāḥ.
  K. Mylius, 259(IIJ):Jul84-210
Gonda, J., ed. A History of Indian Litera-
  ture. (Vol 9, fasc 3)
  R.P. Das, 259(IIJ):Jan84-51
Gondos, V., Jr. J. Franklin Jameson and
  the Birth of The National Archives 1906-
  1926.
  J.R. Pole, 161(DUJ):Dec83-127
de Góngora, L. Letrillas. (R. Jammes, ed)
  D. McGrady, 240(HR):Summer84-401
de Góngora, L. Romances. (J.M. de Cossío,
  ed)
  R. Ruiz, 552(REH):May84-314
de Góngora, L., with P. Picasso. Góngora.
  (A.S. Trueblood, trans)
  A. Barnet, 441:15Dec85-21
  J. Golding, 453(NYRB):21Nov85-11
Gonzales, L. El vago.
  Bruce-Novoa, 37:May-Jun84-60
  D.L. Zelman, 649(WAL):May84-64
Gonzáles-Montes, Y. Pasión y forma en
  "Cal y canto" de Rafael Alberti.*
  F. Colecchia, 403(MLS):Fall84-83
González, A.C. - see under Campoamor Gon-
  zález, A.
González, C. El Cavallero Zifar y el
  reino lejano.
  M.A. Diz, 304(JHP):Fall84-76
González, J.M.C. and S. Cerra Suárez - see
  under Caso González, J.M. and S. Cerra
  Suárez
Gonzalez, M.D.M. - see under Martinez
  Gonzalez, M.D.
Gonzalez-Crussi, F. Notes of an Anatomist.
  D.J. Enright, 441:7Jul85-9
  442(NY):29Jul85-78
González Echevarría, R. and K. Müller-
  Bergh, comps. Alejo Carpentier.
  N. Luna, 238:Sep84-481
  E.P. Mocega-Gonzalez, 263(RIB):Vol34
  No1-97
González Gómez, J.M. and M.J. Carrasco
  Terriza. Escultura mariana onubense.
  D. Angulo Iñiguez, 48:Jul-Sep83-309
González Núñez, J.A. and P. Alcázar López -
  see de Flores, J.
González Ollé, F. Lengua y literatura
  española medievales.
  A.B. Lasry, 545(RPh):Feb84-351
Gonzalo Rubio, C. La Angelología en la
  Literatura Rabínica Sefardí.
  E. Roditi, 390:Jan84-50
Gooch, B.N.S. and D.S. Thatcher, comps.
  Musical Settings of British Romantic
  Literature.*
  A. Levine, 340(KSJ):Vol33-239
Gooch, S. All Together Now.
  C. Tighe, 157:No153-52
Good, D.F. The Economic Rise of the Habs-
  burg Empire, 1750-1914.
  M. Hurst, 617(TLS):2Aug85-861
Good, E.M. Giraffes, Black Dragons, and
  other Pianos.
  H. Schott, 410(M&L):Apr84-195
Good, M. Every Inch a Lear.*
  R. Ellis, 615(TJ):Oct84-430
Goodall, H.L., Jr. and G.M. Phillips. Mak-
  ing It In Any Organization.
  G.L. Wilson, 583:Spring85-302
Goodell, G. Independent Feature Film Pro-
  duction.
  J. Gallagher, 200:Jan84-61

Goodheart, E. The Skeptic Disposition in Contemporary Criticism.
M. Dickstein, 441:14Jul85-34
Goodin, R.E. Political Theory and Public Policy.
A.M. Macleod, 185:Oct84-157
A. Taylor, 543:Mar84-630
Goodis, D. Four Novels.
L. Sante, 453(NYRB):28Mar85-18
Goodman, C. - see Koestler, M.
Goodman, E.J., comp. The Exploration of South America.
M.H. Sable, 263(RIB):Vol34No1-98
Goodman, I. Heart Failure.*
F. Camoin, 651(WHR):Winter84-354
Goodman, M. Hurrah for the Next Man Who Dies.
P-L. Adams, 61:Apr85-140
R. Smith, 441:19May85-22
Goodman, N. Of Mind and Other Matters.
A. Nehamas, 290(JAAC):Winter84-209
J.S., 185:Jul85-975
Goodman, P. Parents' Day.
D. Guy, 441:29Sep85-46
Goodrich, L. Thomas Eakins.*
T. Fairbrother, 90:Jun84-366
Goodwin, J. Brotherhood of Arms.
A. Sloan, 441:22Sep85-23
Goodwin, J. Cry Amandla!
V. Crapanzano, 441:6Jan85-36
Goodwin, J. - see Hall, P.
Goodwin, K.L. Understanding African Poetry.
R. Fraser, 538(RAL):Spring84-136
Goody, J. The Development of the Family and Marriage in Europe.
S. Treggiari, 123:Vol34No1-144
Goody, J., ed. Literalität in traditionalen Gesellschaften.
H. Schlaffer, 490:Band15Heft1/2-179
Goodyear, F.H., Jr. Welliver.
A.A., 62:Summer85-96
Goodyear, F.R.D. - see Tacitus
Goossens, J. Die Reynaert-Ikonographie.
354:Sep84-318
Goossens, J. Reynaerts historie.
S. Krause, 196:Band25Heft3/4-334
Goossens, J. and T. Sodmann, eds. Reynaert-Reynard-Reynke.*
H. Heinen, 406:Summer84-206
Goossens, J. and T. Sodmann, eds. Third International Beast Epic, Fable and Fabliau Colloquium.*
J. Ziolkowski, 589:Oct84-975
Gopal, S. Jawaharlal Nehru.* (Vol 3)
J. Vijayatunga, 364:Mar85-95
na Gopaleen, M. (F. O'Brien). Myles Away from Dublin. (M. Green, ed)
E. Korn, 617(TLS):30Aug85-959
Goran, L. Mrs. Beautiful.
442(NY):14Oct85-142
Gorceix, P. Le symbolisme en Belgique.
H-J. Lope, 547(RF):Band96Heft1/2-195
Gordimer, N. Something Out There.*
G. Kearns, 249(HudR):Winter84/85-619
J. Mellors, 364:Jun84-101
Gordon, A. Foul Ball!
L. Mifflin, 441:21Jul85-23
Gordon, A.E. Illustrated Introduction to Latin Epigraphy.
G.W. Houston, 124:Sep-Oct84-58

Gordon, C. The Southern Mandarins. (S. Wood, ed)
W.J. Stuckey, 395(MFS):Winter84-832
Gordon, G., ed. Modern Short Stories 2.
G. Bas, 189(EA):Jan-Mar85-96
Gordon, J. James Joyce's Metamorphoses.
J.P. Riquelme, 329(JJQ):Winter85-238
Gordon, J. The Myth of the Monstrous Male and Other Feminist Fables.
D. Duncalfe, 529(QQ):Winter84-1045
Gordon, K.E. The Well-Tempered Sentence.*
42(AR):Winter84-118
Gordon, L. Robert Coover.*
R.A. Morace, 363(LitR):Summer85-617
J. Voelker, 573(SSF):Winter84-77
Gordon, L. Virginia Woolf.*
C. Heilbrun, 441:10Feb85-12
M. Meyer, 364:Nov84-100
442(NY):15Apr85-130
Gordon, M. Head of the Harbour.
S. Ruddell, 102(CanL):Winter83-87
A.R. Young, 198:Spring84-93
A.R. Young, 198:Summer84-121
Gordon, M. Men and Angels.
P. Craig, 617(TLS):25Oct85-1202
M. Drabble, 441:31Mar85-1
C. Iannone, 129:Jun85-62
J. Mellors, 362:7Nov85-28
442(NY):29Apr85-132
Gordon, M. and A.C. Swinburne. The Children of the Chapel. (R.E. Lougy, ed)
E.M. Eigner, 445(NCF):Dec84-351
Gordon, R. Doctor on the Ball.
B. Hepburn, 617(TLS):19Apr85-442
Gordon, S. Hitler, Germans, and the "Jewish Question."*
639(VQR):Autumn84-118
Gordon, V. The English Cookbook.
C. Reid, 617(TLS):20Dec85-1467
Gordon, W.T. A History of Semantics.*
P. Pupier, 320(CJL):Fall84-215
Goreau, A. Reconstructing Aphra.*
D. Hirst, 541(RES):Feb84-87
Goreau, A. The Whole Duty of a Woman.
C. Erickson, 441:31Mar85-16
Gorecki, J. Capital Punishment.
J.D., 185:Jan85-401
Gorelov, A.A. - see "Russkaja literatura i fol'klor"
Goren, A.A. - see Magnes, J.L.
Gorham, D. The Victorian Girl and the Feminine Ideal.
S.G. Bell, 637(VS):Winter84-249
M. Tippett, 529(QQ):Summer84-479
Görisch, R. Matthias Claudius und der Sturm und Drang.
H. Rowland, 406:Fall84-361
Görland, I. - see Heidegger, M.
Gorman, J.L. The Expression of Historical Knowledge.*
W.H. Dray, 529(QQ):Summer84-440
Gornick, V. The Romance of American Communism.
T. Draper, 453(NYRB):30May85-44
Gorodetsky, G. Stafford Cripps' Mission to Moscow, 1940-42.
S.M.M. Lawlor, 617(TLS):8Mar85-248
de Gorog, R. Dictionnaire inverse de l'ancien français.*
D.A. Kibbee, 207(FR):Apr85-769
Görög-Karady, V., ed. Genres, Forms, Meanings.
L. Haring, 538(RAL):Summer84-298

Görög–Karady, V. Littérature orale
d'Afrique Noire.* [shown in prev under
Görög, V.]
    D. Ben-Amos, 538(RAL):Summer84-319
Gorre, R. Die Ketzer im 11. Jahrhundert.
    R.E. Lerner, 589:Jul84-718
Gorškov, A.I. Teoretičeskie osnovy
istorii rysskogo literatyrnogo jazyka.
    H. Keipert, 559:Vol8No2-159
Goruppi, T., ed. L'Instrumentation
verbale.
    T.M.P. Lima, 535(RHL):Jul/Aug84-643
Goscilo, H. - see Lermontov, M.
Gose, E.B., Jr. The World of the Irish
Wonder Tale.
    T.A. Shippey, 617(TLS):5Jul85-758
Gosling, J.C.B. and C.C.W. Taylor. The
Greeks on Pleasure.*
    J. Boulogne, 555:Vol58fasc2-295
    W. Charlton, 393(Mind):Oct84-603
    C.A. Huffman, 121(CJ):Feb-Mar85-267
    H. Ruttenberg, 185:Jul85-963
Gosling, P. Monkey Puzzle.
    T.J. Binyon, 617(TLS):10May85-528
Gossen, C.T. - see von Wartburg, W.
Gossett, P. Anna Bolena and the Artistic
Maturity of Gaetano Donizetti.
    W. Ashbrook, 617(TLS):10May85-526
Gossett, P. and others. Masters of Ital-
ian Opera.
    L. Salter, 415:Apr84-211
Gossett, T.F. "Uncle Tom's Cabin" and
American Culture.
    D.H. Donald, 441:8Sep85-16
Gossip, C.J. - see de Cyrano de Bergerac,
S.
Gossman, L. The Empire Unpossess'd.*
    M. Baridon, 173(ECS):Fall84-141
    P. Rogers, 541(RES):Feb84-91
Gostelow, M. Blackwork.
    C. Campbell, 614:Summer85-19
Goswami, A., with M. Goswami. The Cosmic
Dancers.
    C.E., 561(SFS):Nov84-338
Goth, M. Rilke and Valéry.*
    A. Nivelle, 549(RLC):Jul-Sep84-372
    J. Ryan, 678(YCGL):No32-154
    D.A. Scrase, 131(CL):Summer84-280
    I.H. Solbrig, 406:Summer84-223
Gotlieb, Y. Self-Determination in the
Middle East.
    Z. Frazer, 287:Feb84-27
Gottfried, M. In Person.
    J.L. Mankiewicz, 441:8Dec85-17
Gottfried, R.K. The Art of Joyce's Syntax
in "Ulysses."*
    R. Mason, 447(N&Q):Aug83-372
Gottlieb, D. Ontological Economy.*
    H. Field, 449:Mar84-160
Gottlieb, R. and P. Wiley. America's
Saints.
    K.G. Barnhurst, 129:Mar85-75
    D.B. Davis, 453(NYRB):15Aug85-15
Gottlieb, V. Chekhov and the Vaudeville.*
    J.D. Clayton, 104(CASS):Spring-
    Summer84-161
    I. Kirk, 397(MD):Mar84-153
Gottschald, M. Deutsche Namenkunde.
    J. Göschel, 685(ZDL):1/1984-92
Götz, M. Türkische Handschriften. (Pts
2 and 4)
    E. Birnbaum, 318(JAOS):Apr-Jun83-413

Götze, K-H. and K.R. Scherpe, eds. Die
Ästhetik des Widerstands lesen.
    K. Kändler, 654(WB):1/1984-156
Götze, L. Valenzstrukturen deutscher Ver-
ben und Adjektive.*
    H. Meier, 682(ZPSK):Band37Heft3-388
Goudriaan, T. and S. Gupta. Hindu Tantric
and Šākta Literature.*
    H. Alper, 318(JAOS):Jul-Sep83-662
Gough, K. Rural Society in Southeast
India.
    A. Appadurai, 293(JASt):May84-481
Gough, R. The History of Myddle. (D. Hey,
ed)
    L.K.J. Glassey, 566:Spring85-193
Gough, W. Maud's House.
    L. Spalding, 99:Mar85-37
Gouhier, H. Rousseau et Voltaire.
    E.R. Anderson, 83:Autumn84-270
    J. Brun, 192(EP):Jul-Sep84-418
    D. Leduc-Fayette, 542:Jan-Mar84-79
    R. Pomeau, 535(RHL):Jan/Feb84-77
    J. Starobinski, 98:Oct84-757
Goukowsky, P. Essai sur les origines du
mythe d'Alexandre (336-270 B.C.). (Vol
2)
    P.M. Fraser, 123:Vol34No2-345
Goulart, R. A Graveyard of My Own.
    N. Callendar, 441:30Jun85-29
Gould, C. Bernini in France.*
    H. Tratz, 471:Jul/Aug/Sep84-303
Gould, C. Marx's Social Ontology.
    R. Brockhaus, 142:Summer84-91
Gould, E. Mythical Intentions in Modern
Literature.*
    I. Buchler, 567:Vol148No3/4-319
    P. Murphy, 541(RES):Nov84-592
    M. Perloff, 402(MLR):Jul84-688
Gould, E. - see Jabès, E.
Gould, G. The Glenn Gould Reader.* (T.
Page, ed)
    D. Reubart, 648(WCR):Apr85-61
    442(NY):4Feb85-102
Gould, H. Cocktail.
    M. Buck, 441:13Jan85-22
Gould, J. No Other Place.*
    P-L. Adams, 61:Mar85-124
Gould, J.L. Ethology.
    P. Colgan, 529(QQ):Spring84-202
Gould, R.A., ed. Shipwreck Anthropology.
    J.O. Sands, 658:Winter84-295
Gould, S.J. The Flamingo's Smile.
    D. Quammen, 441:22Sep85-24
    J. Updike, 442(NY):30Dec85-76
Gould, S.J. Hen's Teeth and Horse's Toes.*
    639(VQR):Winter84-28
Gould, S.J. Ontogeny and Phylogeny.
    617(TLS):25Oct85-1219
Gould, T. - see Bell, A.
Goulden, J.C., with A.W. Raffio. The
Death Merchant.*
    E. Fawcett, 617(TLS):19Jul85-804
Gouldner, A.W. Against Fragmentation.
    A. Giddens, 617(TLS):6Sep85-981
    A. Walicki, 453(NYRB):25Apr85-41
Goulet, A. Le Parcours moebien de l'écri-
ture: "Le Voyeur."*
    M. Ball, 208(FS):Apr84-240
Gourdon, A-M., ed. Les voies de la créa-
tion théâtrale: La formation du comédien.
(Vol 9)
    A. Neuschäfer, 72:Band221Heft2-465

Gournay, J-F. L'Appel du Proche-Orient.
P. Marshall, 189(EA):Oct-Dec85-473
Gowda, H.H.A., ed. The Colonial and the
Neo-Colonial Encounters in Commonwealth
Literature.
A.L. McLeod, 49:Apr84-118
P.I. Okeh, 538(RAL):Fall84-427
Gowing, L., general ed. A Biographical
Dictionary of Artists.
C. Ashwin, 592:Vol 196No1004-55
M. Royalton-Kish, 39:Aug84-147
Gowing, L. Lucian Freud.*
F. Spalding, 90:Feb84-101
de Goya, F. Cartas a Martín Zapater. (M.
Águeda and X. de Salas, eds)
D. Angulo Íñiguez, 48:Jul-Sep83-304
N. Glendinning, 90:Nov84-706
Goyen, W. Had I a Hundred Mouths.
V. Bourjaily, 441:9Jun85-28
Goytisolo, J. Coto Vedado.
J.W. Butt, 617(TLS):31May85-605
Grab, H. Der Stadtpark.
J. Adler, 617(TLS):11Oct85-1146
Grabbe, A. The Private World of the Last
Czar. (P. and B. Grabbe, eds)
J. Daynard, 441:10Feb85-24
Grabes, H. The Mutable Glass.
C. Clark, 179(ES):Aug84-370
M. Leslie, 354:Jun84-181
M-M. Martinet, 189(EA):Jul-Sep85-315
Grabher, G. Emily Dickinson.
L. Hönnighausen, 72:Band221Heft2-390
Grabo, N.S. The Coincidental Art of
Charles Brockenden Brown.*
D. Seed, 447(N&Q):Aug83-380
Grabowicz, G.G. The Poet as Mythmaker.*
M.M. Naydan, 591(SIR):Summer84-285
Grace, S.E. The Voyage that Never Ends.*
R.K. Cross, 395(MFS):Winter84-774
K. Harrison, 268(IFR):Summer85-111
P. Tiessen, 102(CanL):Winter83-163
Grace, S.E. and L. Weir, eds. Margaret
Atwood.*
B.H. Gelfant, 102(CanL):Autumn84-71
R. Lecker, 627(UTQ):Summer84-462
T.D. MacLulich, 168(ECW):Winter84/85-
115
Gracia, J.A.F. - see under Frago Gracia,
J.A.
Gracia, J.J.E. - see Suarez, F.
Gracq, J. La Forme d'une ville.
P. Thody, 617(TLS):30Aug85-955
"Julien Gracq."
C. Delmas, 535(RHL):May/Jun84-470
Grad, B.L. and T.A. Riggs. Visions of
City and Country.*
M.E. Birkett, 210(FrF):Jan84-121
Grade, C. Rabbis and Wives.*
K. Cushman, 573(SSF):Summer84-279
Gradidge, R. Edwin Lutyens, Architect
Laureate.*
R.G. Wilson, 505:Apr84-149
Gradman, B. Metamorphosis in Keats.*
M. Allott, 402(MLR):Jul84-677
Graebner, W. A History of Retirement.
J. Tagg, 106:Winter84-451
Graeser, A. Die Philosophie der Antike 2.
A.W. Müller, 319:Jul85-422
Graf, O.A. Die Kunst des Quadrats zum
Werk von Frank Lloyd Wright.
P.B. Jones, 46:Aug84-64
A.W., 90:May84-304

Grafe, F. Rene Gruau.
R.L. Shep, 614:Spring85-29
Grafteaux, S. Mémé Santerre.
E. O'Shaughnessy, 441:3Nov85-27
Grafton, A. Joseph Scaliger — A Study in
the History of Classical Scholarship.
(Vol 1)
W.M. Calder 3d, 124:Jul-Aug85-606
W. Gundersheimer, 589:Oct84-907
R.J. Schoeck, 121(CJ):Apr-May85-358
Graham, A.C. Chuang-tzu: Textual Notes to
a Partial Translation.*
D.L. Hall, 485(PE&W):Jul84-329
Graham, A.C. - see "Chuang-tzu: The Seven
Inner Chapters and Other Writings from
the Book Chuang-tzu"
Graham, C. The Envy of the Stranger.
T.J. Binyon, 617(TLS):22Feb85-197
Graham, D., ed. Critical Essays on Frank
Norris.*
R.E. Spiller, 677(YES):Vol 14-347
Graham, D. - see Douglas, K.
Graham, D., J.W. Lee and W.T. Pilkington,
eds. The Texas Literary Tradition.
S.A. Grider, 649(WAL):Feb85-318
Graham, H.F. - see Skrynnikov, R.G.
Graham, J. Erosion.*
D. St. John, 42(AR):Summer84-371
Graham, M. New World Architecture.
P. Hampl, 441:17Nov85-22
Graham, M.H. Tightening the Reins of
Justice in America.
G. Hughes, 453(NYRB):14Mar85-17
Graham, O.L., Jr. and M.R. Wander, eds.
Franklin D. Roosevelt.
R.J. Margolis, 441:16Jun85-41
Graham, P. The Art of the Knock.
N. Rachlin, 441:3Feb85-27
Graham, P.W. - see Hobhouse, J.C.
Graham, R. Spain.*
H. Giniger, 441:6Jan85-21
Graham, R.B.C. - see under Cunninghame
Graham, R.B.
Graham, W. The Loving Cup.
S. Altinel, 617(TLS):18Jan85-67
Graham, W.T., Jr. "The Lament for the
South."*
J.R. Allen, 318(JAOS):Jul-Sep83-637
K.P.H. Ho, 302:Vol20No2-215
Grahame, K. Il vento nei salici. (J.
Meddemmen, ed; B. Fenoglio, trans)
E. Saccone, 450(MLN):Jan84-180
Gran, T. The Norwegian with Scott. (G.
Hattersley-Smith, ed)
S. Mills, 617(TLS):8Mar85-250
Granarolo, J. Catulle, ce vivant.
J. Chomarat, 555:Vol58fasc1-141
K. Quinn, 67:May84-82
Granatstein, J.L. and D. Morton. Bloody
Victory.
R. Hall, 99:Oct84-33
Grandi, R. I Monumenti dei Dottori e la
Scultura a Bologna.
R. Gibbs, 90:Jul84-438
Grand'maison, J. Tel un coup d'archet.
P. Merivale, 102(CanL):Autumn84-130
de Grandsaigne, J. L'Espace combraysien.
B. Brun, 535(RHL):Jul/Aug84-647
R. Gibson, 208(FS):Apr84-225
Granger, B.H. Arizona's Names.
M.F. Burrill, 424:Dec84-453

Gray, P.   T.S. Eliot's Intellectual and
     Poetic Development 1909-1922.*
     L. Gordon, 541(RES):Nov84-583
     J. Olney, 569(SR):Summer84-451
     M. Perloff, 402(MLR):Jul84-688
Gray, R., ed.   American Fiction.*
     W.C. Hamlin, 395(MFS):Winter84-787
Gray, R.   Cardinal Manning.
     J. Bossy, 362:5Sep85-24
Gray, R., ed.   Robert Penn Warren.
     M.R. Winchell, 106:Summer84-229
Gray, S., ed.   Athol Fugard.
     D. Walder, 538(RAL):Fall84-461
Gray, S.   An Unnatural Pursuit and Other
     Pieces.
     P. Oakes, 617(TLS):6Sep85-978
Gray, S.K.   English South African Litera-
     ture in the Last Ten Years.
     A. Gérard, 538(RAL):Fall84-468
Grayson, C., ed.   The World of Dante.*
     T. Barolini, 545(RPh):May84-519
Grazia, A.   Catalogo delle cinquecentine
     conservate nella Biblioteca Comunale
     dell'Archiginnasio di Bologna.
     354:Sep84-320
Graziano, F., ed.   Georg Trakl.*
     C. Hagen, 448:Vol22No3-126
     A. Landor, 364:Aug/Sep84-157
     P. Wild, 219(GaR):Spring84-191
"Great Drawings from the Art Institute of
     Chicago."
     D.J.R. Bruckner, 441:20Oct85-34
Greaves, R.L. - see Bunyan, J.
Greaves, R.L. and R. Zaller, eds.   Bio-
     graphical Dictionary of British Radicals
     in the Seventeenth Century. (Vol 3)
     C. Hill, 617(TLS):15Feb85-182
Gréban, A.   Le Mystère de la Passion.
     (Vol 2) (O. Jodogne, ed)
     G. Roques, 553(RLiR):Jul-Dec84-511
"Greek Lyric."* (Vol 1) (D.A. Campbell,
     trans)
     D.E. Gerber, 487:Summer84-194
Greeley, A.M.   Happy Are the Meek.
     M. Stasio, 441:29Sep85-46
Greeley, A.M.   Virgin and Martyr.
     J. Cooney, 441:10Mar85-13
Greeley, A.M. and M.G. Durkin.   How to
     Save the Catholic Church.
     R.A. Schroth, 441:6Jan85-18
Green, A.   Tormented Master.
     H. Schwartz, 390:Oct84-62
Green, B.   Selma Lagerlöf: "Herr Arnes
     penningar."
     D.M. Mennie, 562(Scan):Nov84-196
Green, D.   Bunter Sahib.
     D. Sexton, 617(TLS):20Sep85-1028
Green, D. - see Cobbett, W.
Green, D.H.   The Art of Recognition in
     Wolfram's "Parzival."
     W.T.H. Jackson, 222(GR):Spring84-80
Green, D.H., L.P. Johnson and D. Wuttke,
     eds.   From Wolfram and Petrarch to
     Goethe and Grass.
     W. Bies, 52:Band19Heft1-78
Green, E. and W. Sachse.   Names of the
     Land.
     F.G. Cassidy, 424:Mar84-97
Green, G.   Literary Criticism and the
     Structures of History.
     T. Eagleton, 402(MLR):Apr84-385
     A.J. Kuhn, 579(SAQ):Autumn84-467
     H. Peyre, 678(YCGL):No33-99

Green, G.   Pardon Me For Living.
     A. Ross, 617(TLS):12Apr85-419
Green, G.N.   The Establishment in Texas
     Politics.
     L. Milazzo, 584(SWR):Summer84-336
Green, H., with M-E. Perry.   The Light of
     the Home.*
     L.L. Stevenson, 658:Winter84-312
     639(VQR):Winter84-16
Green, J.   Beyond Here.
     A. Brooks, 102(CanL):Autumn84-115
     P. Stevens, 649(WAL):Aug84-143
Green, J.   God's Fool.
     R. Billington, 441:29Sep85-14
Green, J.   Histoires de vertige.
     J. Aeply, 450(NRF):Apr84-105
Green, J.   L'Autre Sommeil.
     R. Millet, 450(NRF):Jun84-94
Green, J.A. - see Schwob, M.
Green, M.   The English Novel in the Twenti-
     eth Century.
     P. Kemp, 362:7Feb85-26
     J. Symons, 617(TLS):22Feb85-198
Green, M.   Tolstoy and Gandhi.*
     A. Denman, 42(AR):Spring84-256
     M. Juergensmeyer, 293(JASt):Feb84-293
Green, M. - see na Gopaleen, M.
Green, M. and J.F. Berry.   The Challenge
     of Hidden Profits.
     H. Goodman, 441:15Sep85-25
Green, M. and J. Katsell - see Olesha, Y.
Green, M.D.   The Politics of Indian
     Removal.*
     G.A. Schultz, 106:Winter84-433
Green, P.   Retrieving Democracy.
     G. Tyler, 441:24Feb85-31
Green, R.   Ford Madox Ford.*
     M. Stannard, 402(MLR):Jul84-684
Green, R. and others - see Herrad of Hohen-
     bourg
Green, R.F.   Poets and Princepleasers.*
     H.S. Houghton, 131(CL):Winter84-85
Green, R.L. and J.M. Gibson.   A Bibliog-
     raphy of A. Conan Doyle.*
     E. James, 354:Sep84-315
     E. Lauterbach, 177(ELT):Vol27No3-251
     E.S. Lauterbach, 395(MFS):Summer84-379
     P. Nordon, 189(EA):Jan-Mar85-94
Green, S.   The Great Clowns of Broadway.*
     J. Lahr, 617(TLS):24May85-582
Green, W.M.   The Romanov Connection.
     K. Fitz Lyon, 617(TLS):2Aug85-855
     H. Jackson, 441:27Jan85-22
Greenawalt, K.   Discrimination and Reverse
     Discrimination.
     R.K. Fullinwider, 185:Oct84-154
Greenbaum, S., ed.   The English Language
     Today.
     J.M. Sinclair, 617(TLS):28Jun85-715
Greenbaum, S., G. Leech and J. Svartvik,
     eds.   Studies in English Linguistics for
     Randolph Quirk.*
     L. Lipka, 38:Band102Heft3/4-472
Greenberg, A.   The Man in the Cardboard
     Mask.
     S. Tanenhaus, 441:4Aug85-16
Greenberg, J.   Theatre Careers.
     A.B. Harris, 615(TJ):Mar84-146
Greenberg, M.H. - see Farmer, P.J.
Greenberg, M.H. and J.D. Olander, eds.
     Philip K. Dick.
     J. Fekete, 561(SFS):Mar84-78

145

Greenberg, V.D. Literature and Sensibilities in the Weimar Era.*
  A. Kaes, 680(ZDP):Band103Heft4-627
Greenblatt, S., ed. The Power of Forms in the English Renaissance.*
  J.N. King, 570(SQ):Summer84-237
Greenblatt, S. Renaissance Self-Fashioning.*
  B.L. Harman, 153:Spring84-52
  R. Strier, 81:Spring82-383
Greenblatt, S.J., ed. Allegory and Representation.
  J.D. Black, 494:Vol4No1-109
Greenburg, D. True Adventures.
  J. Kaufman, 441:31Mar85-23
Greene, A. Bright River Trilogy.
  D. Merkin, 441:20Jan85-7
Greene, A.C. Dallas USA.*
  L. Milazzo, 584(SWR):Autumn84-462
Greene, C.C. Other Plans.
  M. Bell, 441:7Apr85-14
Greene, D. - see Johnson, S.
Greene, D.B. Temporal Processes in Beethoven's Music.*
  B. Cooper, 410(M&L):Jan84-70
  W. Drabkin, 415:Feb84-97
Greene, G. Getting to Know the General.*
  G.K. Lewis, 617(TLS):4Jan85-5
  D. Pryce-Jones, 176:Feb85-35
Greene, G. The Tenth Man.
  P-L. Adams, 61:May85-104
  W.F. Buckley, Jr., 441:10Mar85-11
  P. French, 176:Jul/Aug85-37
  C. Hitchens, 617(TLS):15Mar85-283
  D.A.N. Jones, 362:14Mar85-23
  442(NY):22Apr85-142
Greene, T. Dire.
  N.S. Hellerstein, 207(FR):Oct84-157
Greene, T.M. The Light in Troy.*
  S.K. Heninger, Jr., 551(RenQ):Spring84-113
  J.H. McGregor, 191(ELN):Sep84-68
  H. Morris, 569(SR):Spring84-290
  A.L. Prescott, 210(FrF):Jan84-112
  L.V.R., 568(SCN):Fall84-51
  R.A. Rebholz, 405(MP):May85-414
Greenfield, S.B. - see "A Readable 'Beowulf'"
Greenfield, S.B. and F.C. Robinson. A Bibliography of Publications on Old English Literature to the End of 1972.*
  R.H. Bremmer, Jr., 179(ES):Feb84-38
  J.E. Cross, 402(MLR):Apr84-412
Greenfield, T.N. The Eye of Judgment.*
  B. King, 569(SR):Spring84-284
Greenhalgh, M. Donatello and his Sources.*
  J. Anderson, 313:Vol74-231
  V. Herzner, 471:Apr/May/Jun84-208
  R. Jones, 278(IS):Vol39-123
  M. Robertson, 123:Vol134No1-123
Greenhalgh, P. Pompey.
  A.M. Ward, 122:Apr84-167
Greenhalgh, P. and E. Eliopoulos. Deep into Mani.
  P.L. Fermor, 617(TLS):30Aug85-947
Greenhill, R. Engineer's Witness.
  D.W. Dunlap, 441:14Apr85-26
Greenhowe, J. Cuddly Toys and Dolls.
  M.C., 614:Winter85-20
Greenhowe, J. Making Miniature Toys and Dolls.
  C. Campbell, 614:Summer85-28

Greening, J. Winter Journeys.
  A. Stevenson, 493:Jun84-66
Greenland, C. The Entropy Exhibition.*
  D.M. Hassler, 395(MFS):Summer84-383
Greenleaf, S. The Ditto List.
  L. Moore, 441:16Jun85-11
  442(NY):3Jun85-124
Greenleaf, S. Fatal Obsession.
  T.J. Binyon, 617(TLS):22Feb85-197
Greenough, P.R. Prosperity and Misery in Modern Bengal.*
  A. Appadurai, 293(JASt):May84-481
Greenspan, E. The Schlemiel Comes to America.
  L. Field, 395(MFS):Winter84-837
Greenspan, L. The Incompatible Prophecies.
  L. Pineau, 529(QQ):Summer84-464
Greenstein, F.I., ed. The Reagan Presidency.
  639(VQR):Winter84-21
Greenwald, R. - see "WRIT 14"
Greer, G. Sex and Destiny.*
  N. Baym, 271:Fall84-165
Greger, M. Kites for Everyone.
  E. Hoffman, 614:Summer85-27
Gregerson, L. Fire in the Conservatory.
  P. Stitt, 344:Summer85-123
Gregg, E.E.W. - see Emerson, E.T.
Gregg, P. King Charles I.*
  P. Christianson, 529(QQ):Autumn84-635
Gregor, B. Genuszuordnung.
  D. Stark, 350:Mar85-223
Gregor, T. Anxious Pleasures.
  R.A. Paul, 441:12May85-15
Gregor-Dellin, M. Richard Wagner.*
  R. Anderson, 415:Feb84-96
di Gregorio, M.A. T.H. Huxley's Place in Natural Science.
  S.J. Gould, 617(TLS):18Jan85-70
Gregory, T. and others. Ricerche su letteratura libertina e letteratura clandestina nel Seicento.
  É. Labrousse, 535(RHL):Jul/Aug84-597
  R.H. Popkin, 551(RenQ):Winter84-630
Gregotti, V. Il disegno del prodotto industriale.
  V. Ugo, 98:Aug/Sep84-725
Gregson, J.M. Public and Private Man in Shakespeare.
  M. Knapp, 615(TJ):May84-281
Greif, H.K. Historia de Nacimientos.
  R. Warner, 86(BHS):Apr84-204
Greig, A. Surviving Passages.*
  J. Saunders, 565:Spring84-55
Greimas, A.J. Structural Semantics.
  R.C. Davis, 400(MLN):Dec84-1211
Greimas, A.J. and J. Courtés. Semiotics and Language.*
  R.A. Champagne, 399(MLJ):Autumn84-299
  C. Segre, 567:Vol50No3/4-269
Greiner, N. Studien zu "Much Ado About Nothing."
  D. Mehl, 72:Band221Heft2-479
Greisch, J., ed. La Vérité.
  M. Adam, 542:Apr-Jun84-254
Greisenegger, W. Die Realität im religiösen Theater des Mittelalters.
  H. Linke, 224(GRM):Band34Heft1/2-191
Grekova, I. Russian Women.
  J. Updike, 442(NY):15Apr85-118
  639(VQR):Summer84-97
Grekova, I. The Ship of Widows.
  E. Winter, 617(TLS):5Jul85-756

146

Gruber, A. Gebrauchssilber des 16. bis
19. Jahrhunderts.
   M. Stürmer, 683:Band47Heft2-289
Gruber, J. Die Dialektik des Trobar.
   G. Gouiran, 553(RLiR):Jan-Jun84-232
   L.M. Paterson, 208(FS):Oct84-446
Gruber, M. Pandora's Pride.
   K. Buffington, 614:Spring85-27
Gruber, M.I. Aspects of Nonverbal Communi-
cation in the Ancient Near East.
   D.R. Hillers, 318(JAOS):Jul-Sep83-672
Gruen, E.S. The Hellenistic World and the
Coming of Rome.*
   P. Green, 617(TLS):16Aug85-891
Gruending, D. Gringo.
   L. Ricou, 102(CanL):Autumn84-192
Gruenfelder, J.K. Influence in Early
Stuart Elections 1604-1640.
   P. Christianson, 529(QQ):Autumn84-635
Grumach, R., ed. Goethe: Begegnungen und
Gespräche. (Vol 4)
   R. Spaethling, 406:Spring84-94
Grumbach, D. The Ladies.*
   S. Altinel, 617(TLS):12Jul85-776
   M. Howard, 676(YR):Winter85-viii
de Grummond, N.T., ed. A Guide to Etrus-
can Mirrors.
   F.R.S. Ridgway, 123:Vol134No1-151
Grünbaum, A. The Foundations of Psycho-
analysis.
   J. Lieberson, 453(NYRB):31Jan85-24
Grundfest, J. George Clymer.
   R.M. Baumann, 656(WMQ):Jul84-513
Grundlehner, P. Sprich Deutsch! (2nd ed)
   R.J. Rundell, 399(MLJ):Spring84-78
Grundmann, H., ed. Friedrich Hebbel.
   H.F. Weiss, 301(JEGP):Apr84-286
Grundstrom, A.W. L'Analyse du français.
   B.K. Barnes, 399(MLJ):Winter84-398
   J. Casagrande, 207(FR):Apr85-768
Grundy, I., ed. Samuel Johnson.
   D. Nokes, 617(TLS):29Nov85-1351
Grundy, P. - see Tsaloumas, D.
de Grunne, B. La Poterie ancienne du Mali.
   R.J. McIntosh, 2(AfrA):Feb84-20
Grunwell, P. The Nature of Phonological
Disability in Children.
   E.D. Malissa, 355(LSoc):Dec84-566
Grushow, I. The Imaginary Reminiscences
of Sir Max Beerbohm.
   M. Stimpson, 617(TLS):5Apr85-390
Gruzalski, B. and C. Nelson, eds. Value
Conflicts in Health Care Delivery.
   A.W., 185:Oct84-194
Gryson, R., ed. Scripta Arriana Latina.
(Vol 1) Le recueil arien de Vérone (MS.
LI de la Bibliothèque capitulaire et
feuillets inédits de la collection
Giustiniani Recanati).
   S. Fanning, 589:Oct84-977
Gschnitzer, F. Griechische Sozialge-
schichte.*
   N.R.E. Fisher, 303(JoHS):Vol 104-236
   H.W. Pleket, 394:Vol137fasc1/2-235
Gschossmann-Hendershot, E.F. German Gram-
mar. (2nd ed)
   P.J. Campana, 399(MLJ):Summer84-173
Gualtieri, M., M. Salvatore and A. Small,
eds. Lo scavo di S. Giovanni di Ruoti
ed il periodo tardoantico in Basilicata.
   J.E.B. Lloyd, 487:Winter84-395

Guarducci, M. La cosiddetta Fibula Prenes-
tina: elementi nuovi.
   D. Ridgway, 617(TLS):8Feb85-149
Guarducci, M. Scritti scelti sulla relig-
ione greca e romana e sul cristianesimo.
   É. des Places, 555:Vol58fasc2-314
Guariglia, O.N. Quellenkritische und log-
ische Untersuchungen zur Gegensatzlehre
des Aristoteles.
   M. Isnardi Parente, 53(AGP):Band66
   Heft1-91
Guback, D. Français commercial.
   D.E. Rivas, 399(MLJ):Winter84-399
Gudnason, B., ed. Danakonunga sogur.
   T.M. Andersson, 563(SS):Winter84-78
Guého, R. Mobilité, rupture, vitesse.
   S. Ettinger, 209(FM):Oct84-262
Guenancia, P. Descartes et l'ordre poli-
tique.
   J-M. Gabaude, 542:Oct-Dec84-468
Guénon, R. Multiple States of Being.
   P. Jordan-Smith, 469:Vol 10No1-120
Guenther, R.J. - see Orlova, A.
Guérif, F. Le Cinéma policier français.
   E.B. Turk, 207(FR):Feb85-465
de Guérin, M. Le Cahier vert. (C. Gély,
ed)
   C.E. Bernard, 446(NCFS):Winter-
   Spring85-149
Guérin, M. La Politique de Stendhal.
   K.G. McWatters, 402(MLR):Apr84-460
Guérin, R. Parmi tant d'autres feux.
   F. de Martinoir, 450(NRF):Mar84-119
Guérin Dalle Mese, J. Una cronica vicen-
tina del Cinquecento.
   M. Guglielminetti, 228(GSLI):Vol 161
   fasc514-292
Guerlac, R. - see Hutton, J.
Guerra, R. Boris Zaitsev.
   S.A. Zenkovsky, 574(SEEJ):Spring84-123
Guest, B. Herself Defined.*
   R. Blythe, 362:4Jul85-28
   G.F. Butterick, 703:No12-144
   S.S. Friedman, 659(ConL):Spring85-107
   639(VQR):Summer84-89
Guest, L. Yedo.
   S. Altinel, 617(TLS):12Jul85-776
Gugelberger, G.M. Ezra Pound's Medieval-
ism.
   P. Makin, 402(MLR):Apr84-438
Guha, R., ed. Subaltern Studies I.
   S.B. Freitag, 293(JASt):Aug84-779
Guibert de Nogent. Autobiographie. (E-R.
Labande, ed and trans)
   J.F. Benton, 589:Jan84-151
Guichemerre, R. La Tragi-comédie.*
   J. Morel, 549(RLC):Oct-Dec84-489
"Guide to British Historical Manuscripts
in the Huntington Library."
   L.J. Daly, 377:Mar84-61
Guidubaldi, E. Dal "De Luce" di R. Gros-
satesta all'islamico "Libro della Scala."
   M. Picone, 545(RPh):May84-514
Guieu, J-M. Le Théâtre lyrique d'Emile
Zola.
   L. Kamm, 207(FR):Feb85-457
   R.S. Mall, 446(NCFS):Summer85-304
Guignonnat, H. Daemon in Lithuania.
   L. Graeber, 441:23Jun85-20
Guilbaut, S. How New York Stole the Idea
of Modern Art.*
   M. Amaya, 39:Jul84-76

[continued]

Gurevich, A.J. Categories of Medieval Culture.
 A. Murray, 617(TLS):22Mar85-303
 B. Woolley, 362:17Jan85-24
Gurney, A.R., Jr. The Snow Ball.
 N.W. Aldrich, Jr., 441:10Feb85-14
Guro, E. The Little Camels of the Sky.
 N. Kolchevska, 574(SEEJ):Summer84-269
Guroff, G. and F.V. Carstensen, eds. Entrepreneurship in Imperial Russia and the Soviet Union.
 R.M. Haywood, 104(CASS):Winter84-460
Gurr, A. The Shakespearean Stage, 1574-1642.* (2nd ed)
 D. Bevington, 570(SQ):Winter84-487
Gürttler, K.R. and H. Scheer, eds. Kontakte, Konflikte, Konzepte.
 W.E. Riedel, 107(CRCL):Mar84-157
Gusdorf, G. Fondements du savoir romantique.
 A. Montandon, 535(RHL):Jul/Aug84-626
Gusdorf, G. L'Homme romantique.
 A.K. Thorlby, 617(TLS):11Oct85-1124
Gussenhoven, C. On the Grammar and Semantics of Sentence Accents.
 J. House, 353:Vol122No6-899
Gustafson, R. At the Ocean's Verge.
 R. Hadas, 441:28Apr85-33
Gustafson, R. The Moment is All. Gradations of Grandeur.
 A. Brown, 526:Winter84-97
Gustafsson, L. Litteraturhistorikern Schück.
 S.P. Sondrup, 563(SS):Summer84-274
Gustafsson, L. The Tennis Players.*
 C.S. McKnight, 563(SS):Spring84-196
 639(VQR):Winter84-25
"Gutenberg-Jahrbuch 1984." (H-J. Koppitz, ed)
 J.L. Flood, 617(TLS):4Jan85-23
Guthke, K.S. Das Abenteuer der Literatur.*
 M.K. Flavell, 402(MLR):Jan84-231
Guthke, K.S. Der Mythos der Neuzeit.
 R. Baasner, 52:Band19Heft2-204
 J. Osborne, 402(MLR):Oct84-886
Guthmüller, B. Ovidio metamorphoseos vulgare.*
 R.W. Hanning, 551(RenQ):Spring84-56
Guthmüller, B., K. Kohut and O. Roth - see Buck, A.
Guthrie, A.B., Jr. Playing Catch-Up.
 N. Callendar, 441:17Nov85-46
Guthrie, W.K.C. A History of Greek Philosophy.* (Vol 6)
 M. Schofield, 483:Jul84-392
 R.K. Sprague, 122:Jan84-67
Guthrie, R. Maximum Security Ward and Other Poems. (S.M. Gall, ed)
 R. Hadas, 472:Fall/Winter84-133
 R. Phillips, 491:Mar85-350
Gutman, J.M. Through Indian Eyes.
 F.G. Hutchins, 293(JASt):Nov83-183
Gutman, Y. The Jews of Warsaw, 1939-1943.*
 M. Stanislawski, 104(CASS):Spring-Summer84-215
Gutsche, G.J. and L.G. Leighton, eds. New Perspectives on Nineteenth-Century Russian Prose.*
 B. Heldt, 104(CASS):Spring-Summer84-158
 D.J. Richards, 402(MLR):Apr84-507

Guttentag, M. and P.F. Secord. Too Many Women?
 R.M. McCleary, 185:Oct84-165
Gutteridge, D. God's Geography.*
 L. Welch, 198:Summer84-112
Gutting, G. Religious Belief and Religious Skepticism.
 B.L. Hebblethwaite, 483:Oct84-544
Guy, A.J. Oeconomy and Discipline.
 W.A. Speck, 617(TLS):17May85-552
Guy, D. Second Brother.
 W. Kittredge, 441:3Nov85-26
Guy, R. My Love, My Love.
 A. Goreau, 441:1Dec85-24
Madame Guyon and Fénelon. La correspondance secrète.
 A. Keix, 547:Oct-Dec84-470
Guzmán, J. Una constante didáctico-moral del "Libro de buen amor."
 I.A. Corfis, 547(RF):Band96Heft1/2-204
Gwei-djen, L. and J. Needham - see under Lu Gwei-djen and J. Needham
Gwynn, R.D. Huguenot Heritage.
 B. Godlee, 617(TLS):11Oct85-1127
Gysin, F. Model as Motif in "Tristram Shandy."
 S. Soupel, 189(EA):Jul-Sep85-337
Gysseling, M., with W. Pijnenburg. Corpus van Middelnederlandse teksten (tot en met het jaar 1300).* (Ser 1)
 P. Swiggers, 353:Vol122No3-432

H.D. Collected Poems 1912-1944.* (L.L. Martz, ed)
 W.H. Pritchard, 249(HudR):Summer84-336
 M. Shaw, 493:Apr84-65
 639(VQR):Autumn84-136
H.D. Her. Bid Me to Live. (H. McNeil, ed of both) The Gift. (G. Ohanessian, ed)
 C. Buck, 617(TLS):25Jan85-102
H.D. Tribute to Freud. Helen in Egypt.
 D. Hudson, 617(TLS):27Sep85-1068
Haac, O.A. Jules Michelet.*
 C. Crossley, 402(MLR):Jan84-196
van den Haag, E. and J.P. Conrad. The Death Penalty.*
 J.D., 185:Jan85-401
Haag, K.H. Der Fortschritt in der Philosophie.
 H.G. Holl, 384:Jan84-93
Haak, B. The Golden Age.
 J. Flam, 62:Dec84-2
 D. Freedberg, 617(TLS):22Mar85-313
 J. Hayes, 324:Nov85-887
Haakonssen, K. The Science of a Legislator.*
 R.F. Teichgraeber 3d, 173(ECS):Winter84/85-242
Haarmann, H. Grundzüge der Sprachtypologie.
 T.T. Büttner, 685(ZDL):1/1984-89
Haarmann, H. Multilinguale Kommunikationsstructuren. (Vols 1-4)
 G. Doerfer, 260(IF):Band89-322
Haas, R. Die mittelenglische Totenklage.*
 G. Schmitz, 38:Band102Heft3/4-522
Haas, W., ed. Standard Languages, Spoken and Written.*
 H. Käsmann, 38:Band102Heft3/4-478

Haas, W. and G.B. Mathieu. Deutsch für alle. (2nd ed)
  M.H. Gupta, 399(MLJ):Winter84-405
Habegger, A. Gender, Fantasy and Realism in American Literature.*
  A. Kaplan, 676(YR):Autumn84-126
  H.H. Kolb, Jr., 27(AL):Mar84-111
  D.J. Nordloh, 587(SAF):Spring84-109
  D. Pizer, 183(ESQ):Vol30No3-193
Haberkamp, G. and M. Münster. Die ehemaligen Musikhandschriftensammlungen der Königlichen Hofkapelle und der Kurfürstin Maria Anna in München.
  F. Smart, 410(M&L):Jul84-293
Haberly, D.T. Three Sad Races.*
  R.J. Oakley, 402(MLR):Jul84-738
Habermann, S. Bayreuther Gartenkunst.
  B. Matsche-von Wicht, 683:Band47Heft4-567
Habermas, J. Habermas: Critical Debates. (J.B. Thompson and D. Held, eds)
  Theorie des kommunikativen Handelns.
  D. Misgeld, 488:Mar84-97
Habermas, J. Lectures on the Discourse of Modernity.
  R. Rorty, 98:Mar84-181
Habermas, J., ed. Observations on "The Spiritual Situation of the Age."*
  S.B.S., 185:Jan85-387
Habermas, J. Philosophical-Political Profiles.*
  F.H. Adler, 42(AR):Summer84-375
  J.J., 185:Oct84-178
Habib, I. An Atlas of the Mughal Empire.
  J.E. Schwartzberg, 293(JASt):May84-567
Habiby, E. The Secret Life of Saeed the Pessoptimist.
  V. Bogdanor, 362:4Jul85-31
Habicht, C. Studien zur Geschichte Athens in hellenistischer Zeit.
  M.J. Osborne, 123:Vol34No2-264
  L.A. Tritle, 24:Winter84-490
Habicht, W., E. Leisi and R. Stamm, eds. Englisch-deutsche Studienausgabe der Dramen Shakespeares.
  H.F. Plett, 156(JDSh):Jahrbuch1984-245
"The Hachette Guide to France."
  A. Tyler, 441:2Jun85-13
Hachten, W.A. and C.A. Giffard, eds. The Press and Apartheid.
  S. Uys, 617(TLS):19Apr85-426
Hacker, M. Assumptions.
  J.D. McClatchy, 441:26May85-16
Hackett, J.W. The Zen Haiku and Other Zen Poems of J.W. Hackett.
  404:Winter-Spring84-38
Hacking, I., ed. Exercises in Analysis.
  H. Robinson, 617(TLS):1Nov85-1246
Hacking, I. Representing and Intervening.*
  A. Franklin, 84:Dec84-381
  T. Vinci, 150(DR):Fall84-617
Hackl, U. Senat und Magistratur in Rom von der Mitte des 2. Jahrhunderts v. Chr. bis zur Diktatur Sullas.
  J. Briscoe, 123:Vol34No1-89
Hackmann, W. Seek and Strike.
  G. Till, 617(TLS):8Feb85-136
Hadas, R. Slow Transparency.*
  W. Logan, 491:Nov84-107
  P. Stitt, 219(GaR):Summer84-402
Haddad, W. Hard Driving.
  R. Rosenbaum, 441:20Oct85-56

Haddinga, J. and T. Schuster. Das Buch vom ostfriesischen Humor. (Vols 1 and 2)
  U. von der Nahmer, 196:Band25Heft3/4-336
Hadfield, A.M. Charles Williams.*
  H.H. Watts, 395(MFS):Winter84-861
  295(JML):Nov84-519
Hadfield, J., ed. Modern Short Stories to 1940.
  G. Bas, 189(EA):Jan-Mar85-96
Hadingham, E. Early Man and the Cosmos.*
  J.V. Oldham, 42(AR):Summer84-375
Hadjinicolau, N. Histoire de l'art et lutte des classes.
  J.A. Richardson, 289:Spring84-93
Hady, M.E., B.C. Noonan and N.E. Strache - see Danky, J.P.
Haeffner, G. Heideggers Begriff der Metaphysik.
  J. Stambaugh, 543:Dec83-401
Haegeman, L.M.V. The Semantics of "Will" in Present-Day British English.
  L. Hermerén, 596(SL):Vol38No2-170
  F.R. Palmer, 353:Vol22No4-551
  M.R. Perkins, 297(JL):Sep84-384
Haffenden, J., ed. W.H. Auden: The Critical Heritage.*
  T. Eagleton, 493:Jan84-60
  M. Lebowitz, 344:Summer85-118
  S. Smith, 366:Autumn84-255
Haffenden, J. The Life of John Berryman.*
  H. Beaver, 472:Fall/Winter84-123
  G. Garrett, 569(SR):Summer84-495
  G. Hill, 184(EIC):Jul84-262
  F. Kermode, 473(PR):1/1984-138
Haffenden, J. Novelists in Interview.
  J. Melmoth, 617(TLS):18Oct85-1178
Hafner, H. Prolegomena zu einer linguistisch-literaturwissenschaftlichen Zeichentheorie.
  M. Andreotti, 602:Band15Heft1-174
Hagan, D.V. Félicien David 1810-1876.
  H. Macdonald, 617(TLS):26Jul85-825
Hagan, K.J., ed. In Peace and War.
  F.C. Drake, 106:Winter84-407
Hagège, C. La structure des langues.
  C. Lehmann, 603:Vol8No1-97
Hageman, E.H. Robert Herrick.
  R.B. Rollin, 568(SCN):Fall84-35
Hagen, M. Die Entfaltung politischer Öffentlichkeit in Russland, 1906-1914.
  W.E. Mosse, 575(SEER):Apr84-297
Hagen, U. Sources.
  K. Conlin, 615(TJ):Mar84-126
Hagenberg, R. Untitled '84.
  N. Moufarrege, 62:Dec84-74
Hager, S. Hip Hop.
  G. Marcus, 62:Dec84-71
Hägg, T. The Novel in Antiquity.*
  S. West, 123:Vol34No2-201
  J.J. Winkler, 124:Sep-Oct84-65
Haggard, M. Sing Me Back Home.
  J.L. Tharpe, 585(SoQ):Spring84-145
Hagstrum, J.H. Sex and Sensibility.*
  A. Ostriker, 88:Summer84-52
Hahl-Koch, J. - see Schoenberg, A. and W. Kandinsky
Hahn, H.G. Henry Fielding.
  C.J. Rawson, 402(MLR):Apr84-421
Hahn, R. Die Theorie der Erfahrung bei Popper und Kant.
  H. Fischer, 342:Band75Heft2-245

Hall, K.L. The Politics of Justice.
 J.R. Sharp, 106:Spring84-49
Hall, M.B. All Scientists Now.
 R. Porter, 617(TLS):25Jan85-89
Hall, M.L. Music Lesson.*
 M. Hallissy, 573(SSF):Fall84-410
 B. Jarrett, 598(SoR):Spring85-554
Hall, N.J. - see Beerbohm, M.
Hall, N.J. - see Trollope, A.
Hall, P. Peter Hall's Diaries.* (J. Good-
 win, ed)
 C. Williams, 157:No151-51
Hall, P. A Minor Operation.
 S. Morrissey, 137:Feb85-42
Hall, P. The World Cities.
 J. Morris, 176:Mar85-61
Hall, R. The Viking Dig.
 C. Thomas, 176:Jan85-50
Hall, R. and R. Woolhouse, eds. Eighty
 Years of Locke Scholarship.
 R.H., 185:Oct84-188
 G. Kemerling, 40(AEB):Vol8No1-42
 J.S. Yolton, 518:Apr84-99
Hall, R.A., Jr. The Kensington Rune-Stone
 is Genuine.*
 H. Beck, 260(IF):Band89-367
 S.M. Embleton, 660(Word):Apr84-113
 W.J. Sullivan, 205(ForL):Apr83-276
 J. Wilson, 563(SS):Summer84-289
Hall, R.A., Jr. Proto-Romance Morphology.
 P.M. Lloyd, 350:Dec85-881
Hallam, A.H. The Letters of Arthur Henry
 Hallam.* (J. Kolb, ed)
 C. Ricks, 541(RES):Aug84-402
 S. Shatto, 447(N&Q):Dec83-544
Hallaråker, P. Norwegian-Nynorsk.
 D. Buttry, 399(MLJ):Winter84-409
Hallberg, G., S. Isaksson and B. Pamp, eds.
 Personnamnsterminologi.
 J.E. Cathey, 563(SS):Summer84-303
von Hallberg, R. American Poetry and Cul-
 ture, 1945-1980.
 H. Vendler, 453(NYRB):7Nov85-53
Hallé, A. La Vallée des blés d'or.
 P. Merivale, 102(CanL):Autumn84-130
Halleran, M.R. Stagecraft in Euripides.
 D. Bain, 617(TLS):22Feb85-209
Halleran, T. A Cool, Clear Death.
 N. Callendar, 441:14Apr85-16
Halleran, T. Sudden Death Finish.
 N. Callendar, 441:15Sep85-33
Hallett, C.A. and E.S. The Revenger's Mad-
 ness.*
 J.J. Peereboom, 179(ES):Oct84-468
Hallett, G. Reason and Right.
 W.T., 185:Jul85-971
Hallett, J.P. Fathers and Daughters in
 Roman Society.
 M. Beard, 617(TLS):1Mar85-222
Halleux, R. Le problème des métaux dans
 la science antique.
 G. Serbat, 555:Vol58fasc1-170
Hallewell, L. Books in Brazil.
 R.A. Preto-Rodas, 238:Mar84-154
Halliburton, D. Poetic Thinking.*
 J.A. Buttigieg, 149(CLS):Summer84-248
 J. Conway, 258:Mar84-102
 D. O'Hara, 131(CL):Winter84-78
Halliday, D. The Black Bird.*
 R.W. Harvey, 168(ECW):Winter84/85-344
 J. Orange, 102(CanL):Autumn84-112
Halliday, D. Making Movies.
 R. Seamon, 102(CanL):Autumn84-151

Hallin-Bertin, D. La Fantastique dans
 l'oeuvre en prose de Marcel Thiry.
 A. Guyaux, 535(RHL):Mar/Apr84-298
Hallinan, B. Le Présent et le passé
 composé des verbes réguliers et
 irréguliers.
 T.J. Cox, 207(FR):May85-904
Hallo, R. Schriften zur Kunstgeschichte
 in Kassel, Sammlungen — Denkmäler —
 Judaica.
 I. Weber, 471:Apr/May/Jun84-209
Halpenny, F.G. and J. Hamelin - see "Dic-
 tionary of Canadian Biography/Diction-
 naire Biographique du Canada"
Halperin, J. Gissing.*
 M. Collie, 637(VS):Spring84-389
 D. Kramer, 579(SAQ):Winter84-121
 R.L. Selig, 536:Vol5-203
Halperin, J. The Life of Jane Austen.*
 J. Bayley, 453(NYRB):9May85-3
 M. Butler, 441:24Feb85-25
 H. Lee, 617(TLS):2Aug85-859
Halperin, J., ed. Trollope Centenary
 Essays.*
 R.C. Burke, 301(JEGP):Apr84-248
 S.P. MacDonald, 579(SAQ):Autumn84-480
 R.C. Terry, 637(VS):Winter84-271
Halpern, B. The American Jew.
 D. Polish, 287:Jan84-20
Halpert, H., ed. A Folklore Sampler from
 the Maritimes.
 B. Allen, 650(WF):Oct84-285
 G. Boyes, 203:Vol95No1-129
 R. Wehse, 196:Band25Heft1/2-130
Halttunen, K. Confidence Men and Painted
 Women.*
 H. Green, 658:Winter84-308
 R.F. Sayre, 271:Fall84-205
 E.J. Sundquist, 141:Summer84-277
Hamalian, L. D.H. Lawrence in Italy.*
 D. Edwards, 363(LitR):Fall84-165
Hambrick-Stowe, C.E. The Practice of
 Piety.*
 J. Blondel, 189(EA):Jan-Mar85-111
 J.F. Cooper, Jr., 539:May85-134
 J.W.T. Youngs, 656(WMQ):Jan84-141
Hamburger, J. Le Journal d'Harvey.
 J. Aeply, 450(NRF):Sep84-109
Hamburger, L. and J. Troubled Lives.
 W. Thomas, 617(TLS):8Nov85-1253
Hamburger, M. - see Rilke, R.M.
de Hamel, C. Glossed Books of the Bible
 and the Origins of the Paris Booktrade.
 R.W. Pfaff, 617(TLS):16Aug85-911
Hamerow, T.S. The Birth of a New Europe.
 639(VQR):Spring84-46
Hamers, J.F. and M. Blanc. Bilingualité
 et bilinguisme.
 J. Lindenfeld, 350:Sep85-725
Hamill, D. Pig in the Middle.
 C. Townshend, 617(TLS):1Nov85-1231
Hamilton, A. The Family of Love.
 I.B. Horst, 551(RenQ):Spring84-80
Hamilton, A. Textiles Home Care and Con-
 servation.
 P.B., 614:Winter85-31
Hamilton, A.G. Numbers, Sets and Axioms.
 J. Henle, 316:Dec84-1421
Hamilton, C. American Autographs: Signers
 of the Declaration of Independence,
 Revolutionary War Leaders, Presidents.*
 T. Alford, 432(NEQ):Jun84-282

Hamilton, H.W.   The Aftermath of War.
   M.B. Biskupski, 550(RusR):Jul84-314
Hamilton, I.   Koestler.*
   R. Merrill, 536:Vol6-311
Hamilton, I.   Robert Lowell.*
   H. Beaver, 472:Fall/Winter84-123
   G. Garrett, 569(SR):Summer84-495
   F. Kermode, 473(PR):1/1984-138
   S. Moore, 534(RALS):Autumn82-251
   N. Procopiow, 77:Summer84-276
   R. Richman, 31(ASch):Spring84-266
Hamilton, I., ed.   The New Review Anthol-
   ogy.
   N. Berry, 617(TLS):22Nov85-1312
Hamilton, J.   A Holiday History of France.
   617(TLS):7Jun85-651
Hamilton, V.   The Cognitive Structures and
   Processes of Human Motivation and Person-
   ality.
   J.W. de Felix, 351(LL):Dec84-107
Hamilton, W.   The Charlatan.
   R.P. Mills, 441:14Jul85-22
   442(NY):2Sep85-86
Hamlin, D.   The Nazi/Skokie Conflict.
   D.G. Dalin, 390:Aug/Sep84-61
Hamlin, F.R., with A. Cabrol.   Les noms de
   lieux du département de l'Hérault.
   F.M. Chambers, 589:Jul84-719
   G. Rohlfs, 424:Sep84-336
Hamm, C.   Music in the New World.
   W. Mellers, 415:Apr84-207
Hamm, J.   Action Replay.
   J.W. Blench, 161(DUJ):Dec83-111
Hamm, J-J., ed.   Lectures de Gérard Bes-
   sette.
   A. Belleau, 627(UTQ):Summer84-481
Hamm, M. and H. Ulmschneider, eds.   Die
   "Rechtssumme" Bruder Bertholds.
   R. Hildebrandt, 685(ZDL):3/1984-396
Hammacher, K., ed.   Der transzendentale
   Gedanke.
   A. Renaut, 192(EP):Apr-Jun84-269
Hammel, E.   The Root.
   J. Brinkley, 441:11Aug85-10
Hammer, L. and S. Schyfter, eds and trans.
   Recent Poetry of Spain.
   W.D. Barnette, 399(MLJ):Winter84-416
   S.J. Fajardo, 238:Sep84-475
Hammer, R.D., ed.   Critical Perspectives
   on V.S. Naipaul.
   L.W. Brown, 459:Vol8No2/3-181
Hammer-Tugendhat, D.   Hieronymus Bosch.*
   W.S. Gibson, 54:Mar84-160
Hammerschmidt, H.   Die Importgüter der
   Handelsstadt London als Sprach- und Bild-
   bereich des elisabethanischen Dramas.
   G. Rohmann, 38:Band102Heft1/2-230
Hammond, A. - see Shakespeare, W.
Hammond, B.S.   Pope and Bolingbroke.
   D. Donoghue, 617(TLS):8Feb85-139
   J. Sitter, 191(ELN):Jun85-69
   S. Varey, 566:Spring85-174
Hammond, F.   Girolamo Frescobaldi.*
   A. Newcomb, 551(RenQ):Autumn84-475
   A. Silbiger, 317:Fall84-593
Hammond, G.   The Making of the English
   Bible.
   W. Allen, 569(SR):Spring84-xxviii
Hammond, G.   Pursuit of Arms.
   T.J. Binyon, 617(TLS):27Dec85-1478
Hammond, J.R.   An Edgar Allan Poe Compan-
   ion.
   A. Massa, 447(N&Q):Dec83-540

Hammond, N.G.L.   Three Historians of Alex-
   ander the Great.*
   S. Hornblower, 123:Vol34No2-261
Hammond, P.   John Oldham and the Renewal
   of Classical Culture.*
   C. Koralek, 175:Summer84-145
Hammond, R.   The Writer and the Word
   Processor.*
   P. Whitehead, 362:17Jan85-22
Hammond, T.T.   Red Flag Over Afghanistan.
   639(VQR):Autumn84-135
Hammond, T.T., ed.   Witnesses to the
   Origins of the Cold War.
   A.A. Offner, 550(RusR):Jul84-300
Hamon, P.   Introduction à l'analyse du des-
   criptif.
   R. Chambers, 549(RLC):Jul-Sep84-351
   H.F. Mosher, Jr., 546(RR):Jan84-101
   R. Zeller, 490:Band15Heft3/4-355
Hamon, P.   Le personnel du roman.
   M. Bal, 204(FdL):Jun84-155
   R. Chambers, 446(NCFS):Summer-Fall84-
   197
   B. Nelson, 208(FS):Apr84-217
Hampe, R. and E. Simon.   The Birth of
   Greek Art from the Mycenaean to the
   Archaic Period.
   L. Morgan, 303(JoHS):Vol 104-264
Hampl, P.   A Romantic Education.
   P.M. Paton, 271:Fall84-191
Hampshire, G., ed.   The Bodleian Library
   Account Book 1613-1646.
   D. McKitterick, 354:Mar84-93
Hampshire, S.   Morality and Conflict.*
   R. Dworkin, 453(NYRB):24Oct85-37
   W.K. Frankena, 185:Apr85-740
   483:Apr84-279
Hampsten, E.   Read This Only to Yourself.*
   L.Z. Bloom, 534(RALS):Autumn82-232
Han-ch'ing, M. - see under Meng Han-ch'ing
Hanan, P.   The Chinese Vernacular Story.*
   T.C. Wong, 302:Vol20No2-211
Hanbury-Tenison, R.   Worlds Apart.*
   R.D. Martin, 617(TLS):17May85-562
Hancock, G., ed.   Illusion one.   Illusion
   two.
   A.J. Harding, 102(CanL):Autumn84-66
Hancock, J. and J. Kushlan.   The Herons
   Handbook.
   E. Dunn, 617(TLS):18Jan85-72
Handke, P.   Der Chinese des Schmerzes.*
   Phantasien der Wiederholung.*
   J. Manthey, 384:Jan84-80
Handke, P.   Histoire d'enfant.
   L. Kovacs, 450(NRF):Feb84-123
Handke, P.   Slow Homecoming.
   M. Bradbury, 441:4Aug85-11
   A. Fothergill, 617(TLS):15Nov85-1297
Handke, P.   The Weight of the World.*
   A. Fothergill, 617(TLS):15Nov85-1297
Handschuh, D. and others.   Sprachatlas der
   deutschen Schweiz.   (Vol 3 and Vol 5,
   Pt 2)
   R.E. Keller, 402(MLR):Oct84-967
Handy, C.   The Future of Work.
   P. Gorb, 324:Apr85-369
Handy, D.A.   The International Sweethearts
   of Rhythm.
   D.E. McGinty, 91:Spring84-133
Hanff, H.   Q's Legacy.
   H. Benedict, 441:11Aug85-15
   E.S. Turner, 617(TLS):13Sep85-996
   R. Twisk, 362:3Oct85-29

Hanke, A.M. Spatiotemporal Consciousness in English and German Romanticism.
    E. Bernhardt-Kabisch, 678(YCGL):No32-143
    J.D. Simons, 221(GQ):Winter84-156
Hankin, C.A. Katherine Mansfield and Her Confessional Stories.*
    M. Magalaner, 395(MFS):Winter84-765
Hankins, T.L. Science and the Enlightenment.
    S. Schaffer, 617(TLS):18Oct85-1166
Hanks, J.M. Ronsard and Biblical Tradition.*
    F. Gray, 207(FR):Dec84-282
    J. Pineaux, 535(RHL):Jul/Aug84-588
    T. Thomson, 539:May85-137
Hanley, A. Hart Crane's Holy Vision.*
    P. Nicholls, 447(N&Q):Dec83-565
Hanley, J. What Farrar Saw and Other Stories.*
    J. Mellors, 364:Jun84-101
Hanley, S. The "Lit de Justice" of the Kings of France.*
    C. Stocker, 551(RenQ):Winter84-610
Hanley, T.O. Revolutionary Statesman.
    D.C. Skaggs, 656(WMQ):Jul84-511
Hannah, B. Captain Maximus.
    G. Stade, 441:9Jun85-14
    J. Wolcott, 453(NYRB):27Jun85-33
Hannay, A. Kierkegaard.*
    D.Z. Phillips, 393(Mind):Oct84-610
    L.P. Pojman, 518:Apr84-127
    42(AR):Spring84-258
Hanning, R.W. and D. Rosand, eds. Castiglione, the Ideal and the Real in Renaissance Culture.*
    C.H. Clough, 551(RenQ):Summer84-241
    T.A. Goeglein, 568(SCN):Spring-Summer84-14
    C. Salvadori Lonergan, 278(IS):Vol139-130
Hanrahan, B. Annie Magdalene.
    J. Motion, 617(TLS):18Oct85-1173
Hanrahan, B. Dove.
    P. Lewis, 565:Spring84-64
Hänsch, I. Heinrich Steinhöwels Übersetzungskommentare in "De claris mulieribus" und "Äsop."
    J.L. Flood, 402(MLR):Jan84-228
Hanscombe, G.E. The Art of Life.
    P. Boumelha, 541(RES):Nov84-577
    G.G. Fromm, 177(ELT):Vol127No2-158
Hansen, C. Language and Logic in Ancient China.
    A.S. Cua, 543:Mar84-634
Hansen, F.E. The Grammar of Gregorian Tonality.
    M. Huglo, 317:Summer84-416
Hansén, I. Les adverbes prédicatifs français en "-ment."
    F.J. Hausmann, 547(RF):Band96Heft1/2-131
Hansen, P.A., ed. Carmina epigraphica Graeca saeculorum VIII-V a.Chr.n.
    A. Johnston, 123:Vol134No2-284
    A.G. Woodhead, 303(JoHS):Vol 104-269
Hansen, R. The Assassination of Jesse James by the Coward Robert Ford.*
    M. Gorra, 249(HudR):Spring84-160
    R.E. Morsberger, 649(WAL):Feb85-343
Hansen, R. Autumn Begins.
    R. Spiess, 404:Winter-Spring84-43

Hansen, R. Fox and Geese and Fences.
    K.B., 614:Winter85-23
Hansen, V. and G. Heine, eds. Frage und Antwort.
    D.W. Adolphs and E. Schwarz, 133:Band17Heft1/2-175
    H. Lehnert, 462(OL):Vol39No1-79
Hansen, W.F. Saxo Grammaticus and the Life of "Hamlet."*
    K.R. Dungey, 563(SS):Summer84-294
    J. Martinez-Pizarro, 589:Apr84-475
    K. Muir, 570(SQ):Autumn84-370
    J.J. O'Connor, 551(RenQ):Spring84-140
    J.M. Stitt, 121(CJ):Oct-Nov84-65
Hansen-Love, O. Emmanuel Kant, Analytique du beau.
    P. Somville, 542:Jan-Mar84-80
Hanson, A.M. Musical Life in Biedermeier Vienna.
    H.C. Robbins Landon, 617(TLS):6Dec85-1398
Hanson, C. and A. Gurr. Katherine Mansfield.
    P. Boumelha, 541(RES):May84-282
Hanson, K., ed. An Everyday Story.
    N. Ramsey, 441:10Mar85-24
Hanson, R.P.C. The Life and Writings of the Historical Saint Patrick.
    J.F.T. Kelly, 589:Jul84-652
Hantula, R. - see Soloviev, S.M.
Hapkemeyer, A. - see Bachmann, I.
Harasymiw, B. Political Elite Recruitment in the Soviet Union.
    A. Pravda, 617(TLS):8Feb85-142
Haraszti-Takács, M. Spanish Genre Painting in the Seventeenth Century.*
    N. Glendinning, 39:Nov84-359
    E. Harris, 90:Jun84-357
Haraszti-Takács, M. Spanish Painting from the Primitives to Ribera.
    J. Rogelio Buendía, 48:Jan-Mar83-85
Harbert, E.N. and R.A. Rees, eds. Fifteen American Authors Before 1900. (rev)
    K.M. Roemer, 26(ALR):Autumn84-296
Harder, H. Le président de Brosses et le voyage en Italie au XVIIIe siècle.
    E. Chevallier, 549(RLC):Jul-Sep84-359
Hardie, A. Statius and the "Silvae."
    K.M. Coleman, 123:Vol134No2-190
Hardie, D. Hollyhocks, Lambs and Other Passions.
    C. Verderese, 441:27Oct85-41
Hardin, G. Filters Against Folly.
    R.B. Swain, 441:4Aug85-14
Hardin, G. Naked Emperors.
    B.B., 185:Oct84-192
Harding, D.W. Experience into Words.
    E.D. Mackerness, 447(N&Q):Dec83-554
Harding, H. Organizing China.
    S.L. Greenblatt, 293(JASt):Feb84-317
    K. Morrison, 318(JAOS):Oct-Dec83-806
Harding, N., ed. Marxism in Russia.
    D. Pearl, 550(RusR):Jul84-303
Harding, N., ed. The State in Socialist Society.
    A. Nove, 617(TLS):18Jan85-60
Harding, R.E.M. The Metronome and its Precursors.
    D. Fallows, 415:Aug84-445
Harding, S. and M.B. Hintikka, eds. Discovering Reality.
    A. Seller, 518:Oct84-253

Harding, S.F. Remaking Ibieca.*
    J. MacClancy, 617(TLS):7Jun85-633
Harding, W.H. Mill Song.
    M. Bell, 441:17Feb85-20
Hardinge, G., ed. Winter's Crimes 17.
    T.J. Binyon, 617(TLS):27Dec85-1478
Hardt, U.H. - see Wollstonecraft, M.
Hardwick, E. Bartleby in Manhattan and
    Other Essays.* A View of My Own.
    S. Brown, 569(SR):Fall84-649
Hardwick, E. - see Sontag, S.
Hardy, B. Forms of Feeling in Victorian
    Fiction.
    P. Kemp, 362:7Feb85-26
    S. Wall, 617(TLS):6Dec85-1408
Hardy, B. Particularities.*
    J. Herron, 637(VS):Autumn83-102
    I. Murray, 161(DUJ):Dec83-147
Hardy, F. Viraha-Bhakti.
    N. Cutler, 293(JASt):Aug84-781
Hardy, J. Jane Austen's Heroines.
    P. Kemp, 362:7Feb85-26
Hardy, P. The Western.
    T. Milne, 707:Spring84-157
    J. Nangle, 200:Oct84-504
Hardy, T. The Collected Letters of Thomas
    Hardy.* (Vol 4) (R.L. Purdy and M. Mill-
    gate, eds)
    D. Kramer, 177(ELT):Vol27No4-331
    N. Page, 150(DR):Spring84-174
Hardy, T. The Collected Letters of Thomas
    Hardy. (Vol 5) (R.L. Purdy and M. Mill-
    gate, eds)
    H. Jacobson, 617(TLS):7Jun85-625
Hardy, T. The Complete Poetical Works of
    Thomas Hardy.* (Vol 1) (S. Hynes, ed)
    W.E. Davis, 177(ELT):Vol27No4-325
    R.C. Schweik, 536:Vol16-171
    R.C. Schweik, 636(VP):Autumn84-341
    J. Stillinger, 301(JEGP):Jul84-454
    639(VQR):Winter84-22
Hardy, T. The Complete Poetical Works of
    Thomas Hardy. (Vol 2) (S. Hynes, ed)
    R.C. Schweik, 638(VP):Autumn84-341
Hardy, T. The Life and Work of Thomas
    Hardy by Thomas Hardy. (M. Millgate, ed)
    H. Jacobson, 617(TLS):7Jun85-625
Hardy, T. The Literary Notebooks of
    Thomas Hardy.* (L.A. Björk, ed)
    H. Jacobson, 617(TLS):7Jun85-625
Hardy, T. Remèdes désespérés.
    C. Jordis, 450(NRF):Sep84-114
Hardy, T. Tess of the d'Urbervilles.* (J.
    Grindle and S. Gatrell, eds)
    T. Davis, 354:Dec84-386
    J. Goode, 402(MLR):Jul84-680
    D. Kramer, 517(PBSA):Vol78No3-363
    A.L. Manford, 301(JEGP):Apr84-250
    N. Page, 177(ELT):Vol27No2-156
    F.B. Pinion, 541(RES):May84-258
    M. Thorpe, 179(ES):Oct84-474
Hardy, T. The Woodlanders.* (D. Kramer,
    ed)
    T. Davis, 354:Dec84-386
    R.P. Draper, 447(N&Q)Feb83-88
    F.B. Pinion, 541(RES):Feb84-101
"Thomas Hardy Annual."* (No 1) (N. Page,
    ed)
    L. Horne, 49:Jul84-104
    D. Kramer, 637(VS):Spring84-393
    J.B. Wittenberg, 594:Spring84-126
Hare, A. George Frederick Cooke.*
    S.M. Archer, 615(TJ):Dec82-549

Hare, D. The History Plays.
    D. Devlin, 157:No153-46
Hare, J.E. and C.B. Joynt. Ethics and
    International Affairs.*
    M. Hughes, 483:Oct84-547
Hare, P. Aeroplanes in Childhood.*
    G. Szirtes, 493:Sep84-76
Hare, P.H. A Woman's Quest for Science.
    M. Gardiner, 617(TLS):7Jun85-634
Hare, R.M. Moral Thinking.*
    F. Feldman, 519(PhS):Mar84-269
    D.W. Haslett, 321:Vol 18No1-69
    K. Lennon, 393(Mind):Oct84-617
    G. Sher, 449:Mar84-179
    D. Zimmerman, 482(PhR):Apr84-293
Hare, R.M. Plato.*
    D. Gallop, 154:Jun84-349
    P. Thom, 63:Sep84-310
Haren, M. Medieval Thought.
    J. Marenbon, 617(TLS):6Dec85-1410
Hargrove, R.J., Jr. General John Bur-
    goyne.*
    T. Hayter, 83:Autumn84-255
Harkness, D. Northern Ireland since
    1920.
    272(IUR):Spring84-152
Harkness, J. - see Foucault, M.
Harkness, M. The Aesthetics of Dedalus
    and Bloom.
    R. Brown, 617(TLS):11Jan85-40
Harlan, L.R. Booker T. Washington.
    D.E. Alsobrook, 9(AlaR):Oct84-300
    639(VQR):Winter84-14
Harlan, L.R. and R.W. Smock - see Washing-
    ton, B.T.
Harlap, A. New Israeli Architecture.
    G. Herbert, 576:Dec84-376
Harleston, H., Jr. The Keystone. (Bk 1)
    J. George, 469:Vol 10No3-118
Harlfinger, D., ed. Griechische Kodikol-
    ogie und Textüberlieferung.*
    K. Snipes, 121(CJ):Dec84/Jan85-160
Härmä, E.S. Les Structures Narratives
    dans le "Roman de Renart."
    E. Strietman, 208(FS):Apr84-188
Härmä, J. Recherches sur les construc-
    tions imbriquées relatives et interroga-
    tives en français.
    F.J. Hausmann, 547(RF):Band96Heft1/2-
    132
Harman, B.L. Costly Monuments.*
    S. Gottlieb, 551(RenQ):Spring84-144
    B. King, 569(SR):Spring84-284
    R. Strier, 141:Winter84-86
Harman, G. Das Wesen der Moral.
    D. Birnbacher, 687:Jan-Mar84-148
Harman, P.M. Energy, Force, and Matter.
    S. French, 84:Sep84-297
Harman, P.M. Metaphysics and Natural Phi-
    losophy.*
    G.A.J. Rogers, 518:Apr84-106
Harmetz, A. Rolling Breaks and Other
    Movie Business.
    J. Nangle, 200:Apr84-244
Harmon, F.G. and G. Jacobs. The Vital Dif-
    ference.
    S.E. Prokesch, 441:20Oct85-51
Harmon, M. Seán O'Faoláin.
    J. Montague, 617(TLS):6Sep85-980
Harmon, R.B. Elements of Bibliography.
    D.D. Mann, 365:Winter84-34

Hartmann, E. The Nightmare.
  J. McCulloch, 441:13Jan85-23
  C. Rycroft, 453(NYRB):28Mar85-9
Hartmann, J. Subsistenzproduktion und
  Agrarentwicklung in Java/Indonesien.
  M. Schweizer, 293(JASt):May84-601
Hartmann, K. Politische Philosophie.
  K. Homann, 687:Jan-Mar84-146
  W.L.M., 185:Oct84-178
Hartmann, K-H. Wiederholungen im Erzählen.
  G. Marahrens, 107(CRCL):Mar84-94
Hartnoll, P., ed. The Oxford Companion to
  the Theatre.
  R. Findlater, 157:No151-52
Hartshorne, C. Insights and Oversights of
  Great Thinkers.
  J. Collins, 319:Apr85-273
Hartshorne, C. Omnipotence and Other Theo-
  logical Mistakes.
  B. Langtry, 63:Sep84-316
  M. Marsh, 543:Jun84-851
Hartsock, N.C.M. Money, Sex and Power.
  I.M. Young, 185:Oct84-162
Hartung, W. Die Spielleute.
  M. Dobozy, 589:Jan84-156
Hartwell, D. Age of Wonders.
  G. Jonas, 441:10Mar85-31
Hartwell, D.G. and others. Reflections on
  Fantasy and Science Fiction.
  L. Leith, 561(SFS):Mar84-99
Hartwig, J. Shakespeare's Analogical
  Scene.
  M. Rose, 551(RenQ):Winter84-664
Hartwig, R.E. Roads to Reason.
  J.M. Rausch, 263(RIB):Vol34No2-305
Hartz, P.F. Merger.
  B. Harvey, 441:18Aug85-21
Haruf, K. The Tie That Binds.
  P. Glasser, 441:6Jan85-16
Harvey, A. No Diamonds, No Hat, No Honey.*
  D. Davis, 362:6Jun85-31
Harvey, A. One Last Mirror.
  D. Sexton, 617(TLS):22Feb85-196
  J. van de Wetering, 441:28Jul85-14
Harvey, A.D. English Literature and the
  Great War with France.
  B. Gasser, 447(N&Q):Apr83-185
Harvey, A.D. English Poetry in a Changing
  Society, 1780-1825.*
  E.B. Murray, 541(RES):Feb84-96
Harvey, J. Coup d'Etat.
  C. Hawtree, 617(TLS):18Jan85-67
  R. Jones, 362:24Jan85-28
  442(NY):30Dec85-79
Harvey, N. Patterns for Tapestry Weaving.
  P. Bach, 614:Spring85-72
Harvey, P. La Ville aux gueux.
  M.A. Fitzpatrick, 207(FR):Oct84-159
  J.R. Waelti-Walters, 102(CanL):
  Summer84-90
Harvey, P.D.A., ed. The Peasant Land
  Market in Medieval England.
  J.R. Maddicott, 617(TLS):4Jan85-19
Harvey, R. Kamouraska d'Anne Hébert.*
  G. Merler, 102(CanL):Winter83-132
Harvey, S. and others, eds. Reappraisals
  of Rousseau.*
  P. Coleman, 173(ECS):Fall84-96
Harwood, J.T. Critics, Values, and Restor-
  ation Comedy.*
  A. Kaufman, 301(JEGP):Jul84-441
  J. Milhous, 615(TJ):Mar84-133

Harwood, R., ed. The Ages of Gielgud.*
  A.E. Kalson, 615(TJ):Dec84-559
Hasan, I. Robert Bridges.
  J-G. Ritz, 189(EA):Oct-Dec85-475
Hasan, N. Thomas Hardy.*
  J.B. Wittenberg, 594:Spring84-126
Hasenberg, P. "By What You See Them Act."
  M. Beyer, 156(JDSh):Jahrbuch1984-262
Haskell, D. Listening at Night.
  A. Urquhart, 581:Dec84-480
Haskell, F. and N. Penny. Taste and the
  Antique.
  L.D. Ettlinger, 54:Sep84-527
Haskins, J. Richard Pryor.
  J. Stokes, 617(TLS):24May85-583
Haslam, G. Hawk Flights.*
  D.C. Grover, 649(WAL):May84-62
Haslam, M. and others. The Amazing Bugat-
  tis.
  R. Banham, 453(NYRB):7Nov85-35
Haslinger, J. Die Ästhetik des Novalis.*
  G. Rommel, 654(WB):7/1984-1228
Hasluck, N. The Bellarmine Jug.
  J. Crace, 617(TLS):8Mar85-266
Hass, R. Twentieth Century Pleasures.
  D. Davis, 617(TLS):15Mar85-293
  T. Gardner, 30:Spring85-91
  E. Hirsch, 491:Mar85-345
  A. Libby, 441:3Mar85-37
  H. Vendler, 453(NYRB):7Nov85-53
Hassan, I. and S., eds. Innovation/Reno-
  vation.*
  W.B. Bache, 395(MFS):Summer84-406
  42(AR):Summer84-383
  639(VQR):Spring84-45
Hasse, J.E., ed. Ragtime.
  J. Litweiler, 441:16Jun85-25
Hasselbeck, O. Illusion und Funktion.
  H.H.F. Henning, 406:Spring84-92
Hassler, D.M. Hal Clement.
  P. Fitting, 561(SFS):Mar84-88
Hassler, D.M., ed. Patterns of the Fantas-
  tic.
  M.E. Barth, 395(MFS):Winter84-867
Hassler, J. A Green Journey.
  J. Eidus, 441:24Mar85-24
Hast, A. Loyalism in Revolutionary Vir-
  ginia: The Norfolk Area and the Eastern
  Shore.*
  A.G. Condon, 106:Fall84-287
Hastings, M. Overlord.*
  639(VQR):Autumn84-116
Hastings, M., ed. The Oxford Book of Mil-
  itary Anecdotes.
  M. Carver, 362:10Oct85-25
  K. Jeffery, 617(TLS):29Nov85-1346
Hastings, M. A Spy in Winter.*
  639(VQR):Autumn84-131
Hastings, M. and G. Stevens. Victory in
  Europe.
  K. Jeffery, 617(TLS):17May85-555
  442(NY):3Jun85-125
Hastings, S. Nancy Mitford.
  A. Chisholm, 617(TLS):25Oct85-1210
  S. Spender, 362:21Nov85-27
Hastrup, K. Culture and History in Medie-
  val Iceland.
  H. Davidson, 617(TLS):6Dec85-1410
Hatch, E. and H. Farhady. Research Design
  and Statistics for Applied Linguistics.*
  A.R. Baggaley, 355(LSoc):Sep84-421
  S.M. Embleton, 660(Word):Dec84-283
  S. Flynn, 608:Mar85-155

Hatcher, W.S. and J.D. Martin. The Baha'i
Faith.
  M. Ruthven, 617(TLS):25Oct85-1214
Hathaway, W. The Gymnast of Inertia.*
  P. Stitt, 491:Jul84-231
Hattaway, M. Elizabethan Popular Theatre.*
  M.C. Bradbrook, 570(SQ):Summer84-250
  T.R. Griffiths, 611(TN):Vol38No3-153
Hattersley-Smith, G. - see Gran, T.
Hatto, A.T., ed. Traditions of Heroic and
Epic Poetry.* (Vol 1)
  D. Ben-Amos, 292(JAF):Apr-Jun84-227
  M A. Börger-Reese, 240(HR):Spring84-
  233
Hatzenbuehler, R.L. and R.L. Ivie. Con-
gress Declares War.
  R.M. Bell, 656(WMQ):Jul84 524
Häublein, E. The Stanza.
  W. Weiss, 38:Band102Heft1/2-278
Haudry, J. Préhistoire de la flexion
nominale indo-européenne.
  G.R. Hart, 123:Vol34No1-140
Hauerwas, S. The Peaceable Kingdom.
  J.B. Benestad, 543:Jun84-852
  R.A.H., 185:Apr85-770
Hauerwas, S. Should War Be Eliminated?
  T.N., 185:Apr85-780
Hauge, H-E. Masai Religion and Folklore.
  R. Grambo, 64(Arv):Vol38-175
Haugen, E. Ole Edvart Rölvaag.
  G. Thorson, 26(ALR):Autumn84-291
Haugen, E. Scandinavian Language Struc-
tures.
  B. Hagström, 301(JEGP):Apr84-302
  B.J.P. Lundahl, 67:May84-118
Haugen, E., J.D. McClure and D.S. Thomson,
eds. Minority Languages Today.*
  S. Romaine, 597(SN):Vol56No1-114
Haule, J.M. and P.H. Smith, Jr., eds. A
Concordance to "The Waves."
  E. Heine, 395(MFS):Winter84-756
Haumann, H. Kapitalismus im zaristischen
Staat 1906-1917.
  A. Ascher, 550(RusR):Jan84-83
Haupt, R., with M. Grattan. 31 Days to
Power.
  K. Tsokhas, 381:Jun84-266
Häuptli, B.W. - see Seneca
Hauptman, R. The Pathological Vision.
  B. Stoltzfus, 395(MFS):Winter84-727
Hauptmann, G. Notiz-Kalender 1889 bis
1891.* (M. Machatzke, ed)
  W.A. Reichart, 301(JEGP):Apr84-288
Hauschild, B. Geselligkeitsformen und
Erzählstruktur.*
  W. Paulsen, 133:Band17Heft1/2-149
Hauser, A. The Sociology of Art.*
  O.K. Werckmeister, 59:Sep84-345
Hauser, G. Gophers and Swans.
  L. Rogers, 102(CanL):Winter83-153
Hauser, L. Religion als Prinzip und Fak-
tum.
  W. Steinbeck, 342:Band57Heft2-241
Hauser, M. Essai sur la poétique de la
Négritude.
  V.Y. Mudimbe, 538(RAL):Winter84-606
Hauser, T. The Beethoven Conspiracy.
  N. Callendar, 441:17Mar85-39
  442(NY):11Feb85-129
Hausmann, F.J., ed. Die französische
Sprache von heute.
  G. Kleiber, 553(RLiR):Jul-Dec84-461
  P. Swiggers, 353:Vol22No4-555

de Hauteville, P. La confession et testa-
ment de l'amant trespassé de deuil de
Pierre de Hauteville.* (R.M. Bidler, ed)
  L. Löfstedt, 439(NM):1984/4-520
  T. Scully, 589:Jul84-688
Havard, W.C. and W. Sullivan, eds. A Band
of Prophets.*
  M. Hudson, 577(SHR):Winter84-87
Havelock, E.A. The Literate Revolution in
Greece and its Cultural Consequences.*
  C. Gill, 123:Vol34No2-341
  E.L. Rivers, 131(CL):Spring84-162
  R.W., 555:Vol58fasc1-111
Havely, C.P. - see Bird, I.L.
Havely, N.R. - see Boccaccio, G.
Haverkamp-Begemann, E. Rembrandt: The
Nightwatch.
  S. Alpers, 90:Mar84-168
  W.L. Strauss, 471:Apr/May/Jun84-210
Haverson, W.W. and J.L. Haynes. ESL/Lit-
eracy for Adult Learners.
  M.R. Webb, 399(MLJ):Summer84-200
Haward, A. - see Vergil
Haward, B. Nineteenth-Century Norfolk
Stained Glass.
  P. Cormack, 46:Oct84-83
Hawdon, D., ed. The Changing Structure of
the World Oil Industry.
  P. McDonald, 617(TLS):6Dec85-1392
Hawes, L. Presences of Nature.*
  L. Herrmann, 90:May84-301
  W. Vaughan, 59:Sep84-368
Hawkes, J. Adventures in the Alaskan Skin
Trade. Innocence in Extremis.
  J. Beatty, 441:29Sep85-9
Hawkesworth, C. Ivo Andrić.
  F. Rosslyn, 617(TLS):13Dec85-1437
Hawkins, E.A. Hawaiian Sentence Struc-
tures.
  P. Munro, 350:Mar85-231
Hawkins, J.A. Word Order Universals.
  D.L. Payne, 350:Jun85-462
Hawkins, P.S. The Language of Grace.*
  D. Crane, 617(TLS):5Apr85-393
  J.M. Mellard, 395(MFS):Summer84-417
Hawley, J.S., with S. Goswami. At Play
With Krishna.*
  R.K. Barz, 259(IIJ):Jan84-71
  S. Sandahl, 318(JAOS):Apr-Jun83-437
Hawley, J.S. and D.M. Wulff, eds. The
Divine Consort.
  I.V. Peterson, 293(JASt):May84-570
Hawthorn, J. - see Conrad, J.
Hawthorne, N. Nathaniel Hawthorne: Tales
and Sketches.* (R.H. Pearce, ed)
  D.A.N. Jones, 362:4Apr85-26
Hawtree, C., ed. Night and Day.
  V. Cunningham, 617(TLS):22Nov85-1312
Hawtrey, R.S.W. Commentary on Plato's
"Euthydemus."
  D.B. Robinson, 303(JoHS):Vol 104-206
Hay, E.K. T.S. Eliot's Negative Way.*
  J. Olney, 569(SR):Summer84-451
  G. Smith, 27(AL):Mar84-116
Hay, M. The Life of Robert Sidney.
  S. Freedman, 617(TLS):27Sep85-1057
Hay, S.H. Story Hour.
  B. Galvin, 389(MQ):Winter85-249
Hayashi, T., ed. William Faulkner.
  H.H. McAlexander, 27(AL):May84-291
Hayden, A.L. All-American Bears to Cross
Stitch.
  P.J. Christenson, 614:Summer85-16

Hayden, D.E. Wordsworth's Walking Tour of 1790.
  E. Birdsall, 661(WC):Summer84-136
Hayden, R. American Journal.
  J. Saunders, 565:Spring84-55
Hayek, F.A. New Studies in Philosophy, Politics, Economics and the History of Ideas.
  617(TLS):9Aug85-887
Hayes, A.W. Roberto Arlt.*
  R. Olea Franco, 457(NRFH):Tomo32núm1-228
  D.C. Scroggins, 240(HR):Winter84-113
Hayes, J. The Landscape Paintings of Thomas Gainsborough.*
  E.J. Nygren, 173(ECS):Winter84/85-239
  D. Sutton, 39:Jun84-395
Hayes, J. and L. Stainton. Gainsborough Drawings.
  P. Noon, 380:Autumn84-328
Hayim, G.J. The Existential Sociology of Jean-Paul Sartre.*
  J.A. Schumacher, 488:Dec84-559
Hayles, N.K. The Cosmic Web.
  H. Eiland, 344:Spring85-123
Hayley, B. Carleton's Traits and Stories and the Nineteenth Century Anglo-Irish Tradition.
  J. Dunne, 272(IUR):Spring84-135
Hayman, J. - see Ruskin, J.
Hayman, R. Brecht.*
  A. Masters, 157:No151-50
Hayman, R. Kafka.*
  A. Northey, 564:Sep84-222
Hayman, R. Secrets.
  M. Jones, 362:29Aug85-25
  P. Oakes, 617(TLS):2Aug85-844
Haymon, S.T. Stately Homicide.*
  T.J. Binyon, 617(TLS):11Jan85-42
Haynes, B. and J. Lucas. The Trent Bridge Battery.
  S. Collini, 617(TLS):23Aug85-919
Haynes, J. Thanks for Coming!*
  J. Neville, 364:Apr/May84-122
Haynes, R.D. H.G. Wells.*
  D.Y. Hughes, 561(SFS):Mar84-61
Hays, D. The Dixie Association.
  639(VQR):Autumn84-130
Hayward, J.W. Perceiving Ordinary Magic.
  M. Heyneman, 469:Vol 10No2-105
Hayward, M. Writers in Russia: 1917-1978.* (P. Blake, ed)
  B.P. Scherr, 574(SEEJ):Fall84-408
Haywood, H. Black Bolshevik.
  T. Draper, 453(NYRB):9May85-32
Hazard, J.N. Recollections of a Pioneering Sovietologist.
  D. Galton, 575(SEER):Oct84-611
Hazen, H. Endless Rapture.
  C.R., 376:Jun84-150
Hazledine, T. Full Employment Without Inflation.
  W. Eltis, 617(TLS):22Mar85-328
Hazlehurst, F.H. Gardens of Illusion.*
  C. Tadgell, 576:Dec84-370
Head, C. Imperial Byzantine Portraits.
  A.W. Epstein, 589:Jan84-235
Headings, P.R. T.S. Eliot. (rev)
  J. Olney, 569(SR):Summer84-451
Headley, J.M. The Emperor and His Chancellor.
  R. Bireley, 551(RenQ):Autumn84-449

Healy, D. Fighting with Shadows.
  B. Morton, 617(TLS):11Jan85-41
Healy, J.F. Blunt Darts.*
  442(NY):7Jan85-79
Healy, P. - see Gray, J.
Heaney, S. An Open Letter.
  M. Harmon, 272(IUR):Spring84-126
Heaney, S. Station Island.*
  N. Christopher, 441:10Mar85-9
  D. Dunn, 364:Nov84-92
  R. Ellmann, 453(NYRB):14Mar85-19
  J. Mole, 176:Feb85-47
  H. Vendler, 442(NY):23Sep85-108
Heaney, S. Sweeney Astray.*
  J.F. Cotter, 249(HudR):Autumn84-496
  D. Dunn, 364:Nov84-92
  M. Harmon, 272(IUR):Spring84-126
  J. Mole, 176:Feb85-48
  B. O'Donoghue, 493:Apr84-62
  L. Russ, 469:Vol 10No4-100
Hearn, L. Writings from Japan. (F. King, ed)
  A. Thwaite, 617(TLS):11Jan85-32
Hearn, M.F. Romanesque Sculpture.
  W. Sauerländer, 54:Sep84-520
Hearon, S. Group Therapy.*
  J. Brans, 584(SWR):Autumn84-470
  639(VQR):Autumn84-130
Hearon, S. A Small Town.
  E. Tallent, 441:20Oct85-22
Heartz, D. and B. Wade, eds. International Musicological Society, Report of the Twelfth Congress: Berkeley 1977.
  J. Porter, 187:Fall85-524
Heath, C. Behaving Badly.*
  B.F. Williamson, 441:28Apr85-24
Heath, C.D. The Pronunciation of English in Cannock, Staffordshire.
  G. Melchers, 597(SN):Vol56No2-237
Heath, J., ed. The Moths and Butterflies of Great Britain and Ireland. (Vols 1, 2, 9 and 10)
  M. Ridley, 617(TLS):27Dec85-1487
Heath, J. The Picturesque Prison.*
  R.M. Davis, 577(SHR):Summer84-283
  G. Donaldson, 178:Jun84-238
Heath, J., ed. Profiles in Canadian Literature. (Vols 3 and 4)
  W.J. Keith, 627(UTQ):Summer84-442
Heath, J., E. Pollard and J. Thomas. Atlas of Butterflies in Britain and Ireland.
  E. Korn, 617(TLS):18Jan85-74
Heath, S. The Sexual Fix.*
  E. Griffiths, 184(EIC):Apr84-176
Heath, S.B. Ways With Words.
  C. Feagin, 350:Jun85-489
  K. Walters, 355(LSoc):Dec84-515
Heath, T. The Last Hiding Place.
  R. Harvey, 102(CanL):Autumn84-86
Heath-Stubbs, J. The Immolation of Aleph.
  D. Davis, 362:5Dec85-33
Hebblethwaite, B. and S. Sutherland, eds. The Philosophical Frontiers of Christian Theology.
  T. McPherson, 393(Mind):Apr84-311
Hebblethwaite, P. Pope John XXIII.*
  X. Rynne, 441:24Mar85-9
Hebel, J.P. Der Rheinländische Hausfreund.* (L. Rohner, ed)
  F.H. Voit, 406:Summer84-221
Hébert, A. Les fous de Bassan.*
  G. Merler, 102(CanL):Winter83-132

Hébert, A. Héloïse.*
    B. Godard, 198:Autumn84-83
Hébert, F. Le Rendez-vous.
    J. Cowan, 102(CanL):Summer84-117
Hébert, P. Le Temps et la forme.
    P.G. Lewis, 207(FR):Mar85-574
Hecht, K. Der St. Galler Klosterplan.
    W. Haas, 43:Band14Heft1-86
Hecht, L. The USSR Today. (2nd ed)
    G. Holliday, 558(RLJ):Winter-Spring84-
    288
Hechter, M., ed. The Microfoundations of
Macrosociology.
    K-D. Opp, 185:Jan85-360
Hector, L.C. and B.F. Harvey, eds and
    trans. The Westminster Chronicle, 1381-
    1394.
    J.R. Lander, 589:Jan84-157
Hedges, I. Languages of Revolt.*
    K. Aspley, 402(MLR):Jul84-715
Hedges, J.W. Tomb of the Eagles.
    S. Piggott, 617(TLS):25Jan85-97
Hedin, T. The Sculpture of Gaspard and
Balthazard Marsy.*
    B. Scott, 39:Sep84-217
    F.J.B. Watson, 324:Feb85-235
Heed, S.Å. Le Coco du Dada.
    C.N. Smith, 610:Autumn84-259
Heesterman, J.C. The Inner Conflict of
Tradition.
    C.J. Fuller, 617(TLS):13Dec85-1432
Heffernan, J.A.W. The Re-Creation of Land-
scape.
    R. Williams, 617(TLS):20Sep85-1038
Hefner, R.W. Hindu Javanese.
    R.H. Barnes, 617(TLS):13Dec85-1432
Hegel, G.W.F. Lectures on the Philosophy
of Religion. (Vol 1) (P.C. Hodgson, ed)
    M.A.G., 185:Jul85-979
Hegel, G.W.F. The Letters. (C. Butler
and C. Seiler, trans)
    H.S. Harris, 617(TLS):2Aug85-841
Hegel, G.W.F. La philosophie de l'esprit
de la Realphilosophie (1805).* (G.
Planty-Bonjour, trans)
    D. Janicaud, 192(EP):Jan-Mar84-114
Hegel, G.W.F. Die Philosophie des Rechts.
(K.H. Ilting, ed) Vorlesungen. (Vol 1)
(C. Becker and others, eds) Philosophie
des Rechts.
    R. Bubner, 384:Jun84-433
Hegel, G.W.F. La positivité de la reli-
gion chrétienne. (G. Planty-Bonjour,
ed)
    A. Reix, 542:Oct-Dec84-490
Hegel, G.W.F. Science de la Logique.
(P-J. Labarrière and G. Jarczyk, eds and
trans)
    J. Bernhardt, 542:Oct-Dec84-492
Hegel, R.E. The Novel in Seventeenth-
Century China.*
    J.S. Lin, 107(CRCL):Mar84-120
"Hegel-Studien." (Vol 18)
    H. Faes, 542:Oct-Dec84-485
Hegyi, O., ed. Cinco Leyendas y otros
relatos moriscos.*
    R. Kontzi, 547(RF):Band96Heft3-375
    L. López-Baralt, 457(NRFH):Tomo32núm1-
    220
von Hehn, J. Die Umsiedlung der balt-
ischen Deutschen — das letzte Kapitel
baltisch-deutscher Geschichte.
    J. Hiden, 575(SEER):Apr84-307

Heidegger, M. The Basic Problems of Phe-
nomenology.
    J. Llewelyn, 323:May84-202
    C.M. Sherover, 543:Sep83-120
Heidegger, M. Interprétation phénomélo-
gique de la "Critique de la Raison pure"
de Kant.* (I. Görland, ed)
    M. Haar, 192(EP):Jul-Sep84-412
Heidegger, M. Kant e il problema della
metafisica.
    G.V. Di Tommaso, 342:Band75Heft4-515
Heidegger, M. The Metaphysical Founda-
tions of Logic.
    T.B.S., 185:Jul85-977
Heidegger, M. Nietzsche.* (Vol 4) (D.F.
Krell, ed)
    M. Platt, 543:Mar84-637
Heidegger, M. La "Phénoménologie de
l'esprit" de Hegel.
    M.F. Meurice, 450(NRF):Jun84-102
Heidegger, M. Le Principe de raison.
    T. Cordellier, 450(NRF):Jan84-127
Heidegger, M. Die Selbstbehauptung der
deutschen Universität. (H. Heidegger,
ed)
    D. Sternberger, 176:Sep-Oct85-61
Heidenreich, R. and H., eds. Daniel
Defoe.*
    W. Theiss, 196:Band25Heft1/2-131
Heidner, J. - see Scheffer, C.F.
Heidtmann, H. Utopisch-phantastische
Literatur in der DDR.
    F. Jameson, 561(SFS):Jul84-194
    M. Nagl, 196:Band25Heft1/2-133
    O.R. Spittel, 654(WB):4/1984-700
Heigeldinger, M. Poésie et métamorphose.
    J.A. Millán, 202(FMod):No65/67-331
Heikal, M. Autumn of Fury.*
    I. Alteras, 390:Apr84-55
Heil, J. Perception and Cognition.
    P.K. Moser, 258:Sep84-332
Heilbron, J.L. Electricity in the 17th
and 18th Centuries.
    H. Stein, 486:Mar84-172
Heilbron, J.L. Physics at the Royal Soci-
ety during Newton's Presidency.
    I.B. Cohen, 617(TLS):25Jan85-89
Heilbroner, R.L. The Nature and Logic of
Capitalism.
    K.E. Boulding, 441:20Oct85-43
Heilbrun, C.G. and M.T. Higonnet, eds.
The Representation of Women in Fiction.
    J. Grumman, 395(MFS):Summer84-425
    S. Hudson, 577(SHR):Spring84-185
    M.B. Pringle, 268(IFR):Winter85-64
Heilbut, A. Exiled in Paradise.*
    S.J. Whitfield, 385(MQR):Fall85-634
Heilfurth, G. Der Bergbau und seine Kul-
tur.
    W.D. Hand, 292(JAF):Oct-Dec84-478
Heilman, S. The Gate Behind the Wall.
    A. Hertzberg, 441:3Feb85-7
Heim, M. Contemporary Czech.
    M. Fryščák, 399(MLJ):Autumn84-283
    P. Herrity, 402(MLR):Oct84-1007
    D. Short, 575(SEER):Apr84-253
Heimberg, U. Das Kabirenheiligtum bei
Theben. (Vol 3)
    A. Schachter, 303(JoHS):Vol 104-259
Heimberg, U. Die Keramik des Kabirions.
    J. Boardman, 123:Vol134No1-149

Heimert, A. and A. Delbanco, eds. The
Puritans in America.
P.F. Gura, 165(EAL):Fall85-156
Heine, E. and O. Stallybrass - see Forster,
E.M.
Heine, H. The Complete Poems of Heinrich
Heine.* (H. Draper, trans)
R.C. Holub, 221(GQ):Summer84-485
Heine, H. Historisch-kritische Gesamtaus-
gabe der Werke. (Vol 8, Pts 1 and 2)
(M. Windfuhr, ed)
W. Grab, 224(GRM):Band34Heft1/2-237
Heine, H. Historisch-Kritische Gesamtaus-
gabe der Werke. (Vol 12, Pts 1 and 2)
(J-R. Derré and C. Giesen, eds)
S.S. Prawer, 617(TLS):11Oct85-1137
Heine, H. Poetry and Prose. (J. Hermand
and R.C. Holub, eds)
T.C. Hanlin, 399(MLJ):Summer84-168
Heine-Harabasz, I. - see Shakespeare, W.
Heinekamp, A. Leibniz-Bibliographie.
J. Ecole, 192(EP):Jul-Sep84-514
Heinekamp, A., ed. Leibniz et la Renais-
sance.
J-L. Gardies, 542:Oct-Dec84-471
Heineman, H. Mrs. Trollope.
C. Havely, 447(N&Q):Jun83-259
Heineman, H. Restless Angels.
N. Auerbach, 344:Winter85-120
Heinemann, M. Puritanism and Theatre.*
A. Brissenden, 541(RES):Feb84-84
A.J. Cook, 402(MLR):Jan84-146
Heinesen, W. Faroese Art.
J. Boulton-Smith, 39:Nov84-361
Heinesen, W. The Wingéd Darkness and
Other Stories.
W.G. Jones, 562(Scan):May84-74
D.R. Margolin, 563(SS):Autumn84-404
Heinimann, F. and E. Kienzle, with S.
Seidel-Menchi - see Erasmus
Heinisch, K.J. Der Wassermensch.
C. Daxelmüller, 196:Band25Heft3/4-337
Heinlein, R.A. The Cat Who Walks Through
Walls.
D. Bradley, 441:22Dec85-6
Heinrich, A.V. Fragments of Rainbows.
J. Beichman, 407(MN):Spring84-91
R. Epp, 293(JASt):Feb84-329
Heinrich, G. Geschichte Preussens.
H-U. Wehler, 384:Jul84-571
Heinrich, P. A Patch of Grass.
404:Autumn84-59
Heinrichs, A. and others, eds and trans.
Óláfs saga hins helga.
P. Schach, 563(SS):Autumn84-388
Heinrichs, J. Sprachtheorie.
S.R. Dunde, 687:Nov-Dec84-674
Heintel, P. and L. Nagl, eds. Zur Kant-
forschung der Gegenwart.
V. Gerhardt, 342:Band75Heft4-510
Heinz, S. Determination und Re-präsenta-
tion im Altfranzösischen.
K. Brademann, 72:Band221Heft2-413
Heinzle, J. Mittelhochdeutsche Dietrich-
epik.
F.V. Spechtler, 224(GRM):Band34Heft1/2-
211
Heiple, D.L. Mechanical Imagery in Span-
ish Golden Age Poetry.
I.P. Rothberg, 238:Dec84-669
E.F. Stanton, 304(JHP):Spring84-250

Heisenberg, W. Gesammelte Werke. (Band 1)
(W. Blüm, H-P. Dürr and H. Rechenberg,
eds)
B. Pippard, 617(TLS):1Feb85-112
Heitmann, A. Noras Schwestern.*
S. Brantly, 563(SS):Summer84-293
B. Gentikow, 562(Scan):May84-65
Heitmann, K., ed. Europäische Romantik
II.*
J. Voisine, 549(RLC):Oct-Dec84-473
Hekman, S. Weber, the Ideal Type, and Con-
temporary Social Theory.
J.K., 185:Jan85-393
Helander, H. The Noun "Victoria" as Sub-
ject.*
C. Guiraud, 555:Vol58fasc1-127
Helbling, R.E. and others. Aspekte.
W.E. Petig, 399(MLJ):Winter84-406
Helbling, R.E. and others. First-Year
German. (3rd ed)
R.W. Walker, 399(MLJ):Spring84-79
Helbo, A. Sémiologie des Messages Sociaux.
N. Wing, 494:Vol5No4-880
Helck, W. Die Beziehungen Ägyptens und
Vorderasiens zur Ägäis bis ins 7. Jahr-
hundert v. Chr.
D.B. Redford, 318(JAOS):Apr-Jun83-481
Held, D. Introduction to Critical Theory.*
M.G. Kalin, 543:Mar84-639
Held, J. The Collections of the Detroit
Institute of Arts: Flemish and German
Paintings of the 17th Century.
C. Brown, 90:Dec84-789
Held, J.S. Rubens and His Circle.* (A.W.
Lowenthal, D. Rosand and J. Walsh, Jr.,
eds)
J.M. Muller, 600:Vol 14No3/4-227
Heldmann, K. Die Niederlage Homers im
Dichterwettstreit mit Hesiod.
N.J. Richardson, 123:Vol34No2-308
Helgerson, R. The Elizabethan Prodigals.
W. Weiss, 38:Band102Heft1/2-229
Helgerson, R. Self-Crowned Laureates.*
D.C., 604:Spring-Summer84-34
A. Ferry, 551(RenQ):Spring84-133
D.L. Miller, 577(SHR):Summer84-257
G.W. Pigman 3d, 250(HLQ):Summer84-240
W. Sypher, 569(SR):Spring84-300
S.G. Wong, 568(SCN):Spring-Summer84-1
Helimski, E. The Language of the First
Selkup Books.
B. Comrie, 350:Sep85-722
Hellegouarc'h, J. - see Velleius Pater-
culus
Heller, A., ed. Lukács Reappraised.
J.S., 185:Jan85-392
M. Winkler, 478:Oct84-294
639(VQR):Spring84-44
Heller, A. A Theory of History.
C.B. McCullagh, 63:Jun84-202
Heller, J. God Knows.*
A. Alvarez, 453(NYRB):11Apr85-15
R. Kaplan, 129:Feb85-59
P. Lewis, 364:Dec84/Jan85-148
D.R. Slavitt, 385(MQR):Winter85-134
Heller, R. Munch.
A. Anderson, 62:Dec84-75
R. Cardinal, 617(TLS):22Mar85-320
S. Gardiner, 362:17Jan85-23
J.P. Hodin, 324:Nov85-888
Heller, R. The Naked Manager.
F. Norris, 441:20Oct85-51

Heller, S. The Man Who Drank a Thousand Beers.*
   F. Camoin, 651(WHR):Winter84-354
Hellgardt, E. Die exegetischen Quellen von Otfrids Evangelienbuch.*
   W. Schröder, 684(ZDA):Band113Heft1-10
Hellie, R. Slavery in Russia, 1450-1725.*
   D.B. Miller, 589:Jul84-653
Hellman, J. Simone Weil.*
   S. Rava, 207(FR):Feb85-459
Hellman, L. - see Chekhov, A.
Hellmann, J. Fables of Fact.*
   C.L. Saffioti, 125:Spring84-310
Hellmundt, C. and K. Meyer - see Shostakovich, D.
Hellström, P. and T. Thieme. Labraunda: Swedish Excavations and Researches. (Vol 1, Pt 3)
   J.M. Cook, 303(JoHS):Vol 104-250
Helm, A. The English Mummers' Play.*
   J.W. Saunders, 541(RES):Aug84-420
Helmers, H., ed. Verfremdung in der Literatur.
   A. Berger, 602:Band15Heft2-341
Helmholz, R.H. and T.A. Green. Juries, Libel and Justice.
   G. Lamoine, 189(EA):Oct-Dec85-492
Helprin, M. Winter's Tale.*
   J.L. Halio, 598(SoR):Winter85-204
   42(AR):Spring84-259
Helsinger, E.K. Ruskin and the Art of the Beholder.*
   P. Conner, 59:Dec84-499
   K.O. Garrigan, 637(VS):Spring84-365
   P. Morgan, 179(ES):Aug84-381
   D.G. Riede, 591(SIR):Fall84-416
Helterman, J. Symbolic Action in the Plays of the Wakefield Master.
   K.J. Harty, 615(TJ):Dec82-545
Helvétius, C-A. Correspondance générale d'Helvétius.* (Vol 1) (D. Smith, ed-in-chief)
   M. Cardy, 83:Autumn84-267
Helwig, D. The Only Son.
   J. Mills, 648(WCR):Jun84-59
Helwig, D. A Sound Like Laughter.*
   G. Spender, 648(WCR):Oct84-54
Hemenway, R.E. - see Hurston, Z.N.
Hemingway, E. The Dangerous Summer.
   P-L. Adams, 61:Jul85-100
   W. Kennedy, 441:9Jun85-1
   F. Raphael, 617(TLS):16Aug85-894
Hemingway, E. Ernest Hemingway on Writing. (L.W. Phillips, ed)
   F. Raphael, 617(TLS):16Aug85-894
Hemingway, E. Ernest Hemingway: Selected Letters 1917-1961.* (C. Baker, ed)
   K. McSweeney, 529(QQ):Winter84-877
Hemingway, M. Emilia Pardo Bazán.
   M. Bieder, 395(MFS):Winter84-738
   R.E. Lott, 238:May84-306
Hemlow, J., with A. Douglas and P. Hawkins - see Burney, F.
Hemming, J., ed. Change in the Amazon Basin.
   A. Hurrell, 617(TLS):30Aug85-956
Hemmings, F.W.J. Baudelaire the Damned.*
   J.A. Hiddleston, 402(MLR):Apr84-463
   639(VQR):Spring84-53
Hempel, A. Reasons to Live.
   S. Ballantyne, 441:28Apr85-9

Hempel, W., ed. Französische Literatur im Zeitalter der Aufklärung.
   P.H. Meyer, 546(RR):Jan84-108
Hempel, W. and D. Briesemeister, eds. Actas del Coloquio hispano-alemán Ramón Menéndez Pidal.
   M. Lentzen, 72:Band221Heft2-475
   R. Wright, 86(BHS):Apr84-189
Hempfer, K.W. and G. Regn, eds. Interpretation.
   P. Boyde, 402(MLR):Apr84-468
Hemphill, P. The Sixkiller Chronicles.
   R. Goodman, 441:5May85-24
Henbest, N., ed. Observing the Universe.
   C.A. Ronan, 617(TLS):26Apr85-464
Henderson, A.A.R. - see Ovid
Henderson, A.G. - see Congreve, W.
Henderson, B., with others, eds. The Pushcart Prize, X.
   W. Kendrick, 441:24Nov85-15
Henderson, N. The Private Office.
   A. Watson, 617(TLS):31May85-611
Hendry, J.F. A World Alien.
   R. Watson, 588(SSL):Vol 19-194
Heng, L. and J. Shapiro - see under Liang Heng and J. Shapiro
Hengel, M. Between Jesus and Paul.
   C.R. Phillips 3d, 124:Sep-Oct84-46
Henig, M., ed. A Handbook of Roman Art.*
   A.T. Hodge, 529(QQ):Spring84-167
   R. Ling, 123:Vol34No1-111
Henig, M. Religion in Roman Britain.
   C. Thomas, 617(TLS):25Jan85-97
Henige, D. Oral Historiography.
   B. Allen, 292(JAF):Apr-Jun84-241
Henighan, T. Natural Space in Literature.
   J. Clare, 627(UTQ):Summer84-413
Henke, R. Studien zum Romanushymnus des Prudentius.
   A-M. Palmer, 123:Vol34No2-327
Henkel, H. Clavichorde.
   H. Schott, 410(M&L):Oct84-397
Henne, H. Herrschaftsstruktur, historischer Prozess und epische Handlung.
   D.H. Green, 402(MLR):Oct84-975
Henne, H. and G. Objartel, eds. Bibliothek zur historischen deutschen Studenten- und Schülersprache.
   A. Kirkness, 680(ZDP):Band103Heft3-474
Hennequin, É. La Critique scientifique. (D. Hoeges, ed)
   C. Evans, 208(FS):Apr84-219
Hennig, B. "Maere" und "werc."*
   W.H. Jackson, 402(MLR):Jun84-222
Henningsen, G. The Witches' Advocate.
   D. Gifford, 86(BHS):Jan84-49
Henri, A., R. McGough and B. Patten. New Volume. The Mersey Sound. (rev)
   S. Ellis, 493:Jan84-70
Henri, C. and A. Henry - see Vico, G.
Henrich, D., ed. Stuttgarten Hegel-Kongress 1981: Kant oder Hegel?
   R. Bubner, 384:Jun84-435
Henrich, D. and W. Iser, eds. Theorien der Kunst.
   U. Schulz-Buschhaus, 490:Band16Heft1/2-162
Henriksson, A. The Tsar's Loyal Germans.*
   R.P. Bartlett, 575(SEER):Oct84-602
Henry, A. "Amers" de Saint-John Perse: une poésie du mouvement.*
   R. Little, 208(FS):Jan84-88

Henry, A. Marcel Proust.
  J.M. Cocking, 208(FS):Apr84-226
Henry, A. - see Perse, S.
Henry, A.S. Honours and Privileges in
  Athenian Decrees.
  D.M. Lewis, 123:Vol34No2-357
Henry, D.P. The Most Subtle Question
  ("Quaestio Subtilissima").
  P. Clarke, 617(TLS):24May85-588
Henry, M. Marx.*
  Q. Lauer, 258:Jun84-197
  W.L. McBride, 323:Oct84-319
Henry, P. A Hamlet of His Time — Vse-
  volod Garshin.*
  G. Donchin, 575(SEER):Jul84-441
  C.J.G. Turner, 104(CASS):Winter84-439
Henry, P. and H-R. Schwyzer - see Plotinus
Henry, P. Private Justice.
  K.S., 185:Apr85-790
Henry, W.A., 3d. Visions of America.
  K. Auletta, 441:28Jul85-3
  442(NY):23Sep85-117
Hentoff, N. The Man From Internal Affairs.
  N. Callendar, 441:22Dec85-30
Heny, F. and B. Richards, eds. Linguistic
  Categories. (Vol 1)
  J.D. McCawley, 350:Dec85-849
Henze, H.W. Music and Politics.*
  E.C. McIrvine, 513:Fall-Winter83/
    Spring-Summer84-545
Hepburn, R.W. "Wonder" and Other Essays.
  J.H. Gill, 290(JAAC):Spring85-329
Hepokoski, J.A. Giuseppe Verdi: "Fal-
  staff."*
  R. Anderson, 415:May84-273
Heppenstall, R. Raymond Roussel.
  L. Sante, 453(NYRB):31Jan85-14
Herail, R.J. and E.A. Lovatt, eds. Dic-
  tionary of Modern Colloquial French.
  G. Craig, 617(TLS):26Apr85-475
  H. Wackett, 362:28Mar85-26
Herbert, B. German Expressionism.
  90:Feb84-102
Herbert, F. Chapterhouse: Dune.
  G. Jonas, 441:16Jun85-18
Herbert, G. The Dream of the Factory-Made
  House.
  A. Saint, 617(TLS):21Jun85-690
Herbert, M.C. and B. McNeil. Biography
  and Genealogy Master Index 1981-82
  Supplement.
  K.B. Harder, 424:Mar84-90
Herbert, P.D. The Sincerest Form of Flat-
  tery.
  E. Lauterbach, 177(ELT):Vol27No3-251
Herbert, R.L., E.S. Apter and E.K. Kenney,
  eds. The Société Anonyme and the Dreier
  Bequest at Yale University.
  A. Grieve, 90:Dec84-793
  R.S. Short, 617(TLS):22Mar85-312
  M. Yorke, 324:Jun85-498
Herbert, Z. Barbarian in the Garden.
  A. Alvarez, 453(NYRB):18Jul85-7
  J. Bayley, 362:11Jul85-28
Herbert, Z. Report from the Besieged City
  and Other Poems. Selected Poems.
  A. Alvarez, 453(NYRB):18Jul85-7
Herbst, T., D. Heath and H-M. Dederding.
  Grimm's Grandchildren.*
  H. Schmidt, 682(ZPSK):Band37Heft6-719

Herd, E.W. and A. Obermayer, eds. Glos-
  sary of German Literary Terms.
  H. Lehnert, 67:Nov84-263
  R. Samuel, 402(MLR):Oct84-968
  R. Samuel, 564:Feb84-67
Herdeg, K. The Decorated Diagram.*
  R. Campbell, 432(NEQ):Mar84-149
  W. Segal, 46:Jul84-69
  S. Williams, 45:May84-117
  M.N. Woods, 505:Nov84-149
Herdman, J. Voice Without Restraint.
  P. Schlicke, 571(ScLJ):Autumn84-25
Herdmann, U. Die Südliche Poeme A.S.
  Puškins.
  A. McMillin, 575(SEER):Apr84-258
Heren, L. The Power of the Press?
  M. Davie, 617(TLS):29Mar85-364
Herf, J. Reactionary Modernism.
  J. Joll, 617(TLS):5Jul85-744
Hergenhan, L. Unnatural Lives.
  A.J. Hassall, 71(ALS):May84-422
Herken, G. Counsels of War.
  D. Blair, 129:Jul85-74
  M. Mandelbaum, 441:16Jun85-31
  L. Zuckerman, 453(NYRB):18Jul85-11
Herken, G. The Winning Weapon.
  R. Bothwell, 106:Spring84-99
Herlihy, D. and C. Klapisch-Zuber. Tus-
  cans and their Families.
  J.K. Hyde, 617(TLS):23Aug85-921
Herlin, H. The Last Spring in Paris.
  N. Ramsey, 441:20Jan85-18
Herman, N. My Kleinian Home.
  N. Isbister, 617(TLS):11Oct85-1130
Hermand, J., ed. Zu Ernst Toller.
  E.W. Herd, 564:Feb84-74
Hermand, J. and R.C. Holub - see Heine, H.
Hermand, J., H. Pietsch and K.R. Scherpe,
  eds. Nachkriegsliteratur in Westdeutsch-
  land 1945-49.
  K. Kändler, 654(WB):1/1984-156
  R.W. Williams, 402(MLR):Oct84-991
Hermann, J.P. and J.J. Burke, eds. Signs
  and Symbols in Chaucer's Poetry.*
  I. Bishop, 541(RES):Aug84-357
  R.T. Davies, 447(N&Q):Feb83-73
  D. Mehl, 38:Band102Heft1/2-214
Hermann of Carinthia. De essentiis. (C.
  Burnett, ed and trans)
  B. Eastwood, 589:Oct84-911
Hermann von Sachsenheim. The "Schleier-
  tüchlein" of Hermann von Sachsenheim.
  (D.K. Rosenberg, ed)
  T. Kerth, 221(GQ):Spring84-303
Hermans, T. The Structure of Modernist
  Poetry.
  J.J. White, 402(MLR):Apr84-406
Hermansen, G. Ostia.*
  B.M. Boyle, 576:May84-173
  G.P.R. Métraux, 487:Summer84-198
Hermansen, H.P. Fra krigstilstand til
  allianse.
  T.I. Leiren, 563(SS):Spring84-183
Hermary-Vieille, C. L'Epiphanie des dieux.
  I.M. Kohn, 207(FR):Apr85-756
Hermerén, G. Aspects of Aesthetics.
  M. Budd, 89(BJA):Autumn84-364
Hernadi, P., ed. The Horizon of Litera-
  ture.*
  S. Vander Closter, 480(P&R):Vol 17No4-
    247

Hey, G. Die slavischen Siedlungen im Kön-
igreich Sachsen mit Erklärung ihrer
Namen.
H. Leeming, 575(SEER):Jul84-472
Heyd, D. Supererogation.*
J. Cottingham, 393(Mind):Oct84-619
C.L. Ten, 63:Mar84-86
Heyd, M. Between Orthodoxy and the En-
lightenment.
R.A. Watson, 319:Apr85-259
Heyen, W. Along This Water.
J. Carter, 219(GaR):Winter84-881
Heyen, W. Erika.
J. Graham, 441:10Feb85-30
Heym, S. Schwarzenberg.
T.G. Ash, 453(NYRB):31Jan85-33
Heymann, C.D. Poor Little Rich Girl.
V. Glendinning, 362:4Apr85-27
E.S. Turner, 617(TLS):19Apr85-440
Heyndels, R., ed. Littérature, Enseigne-
ment, Société.
M. Richman, 494:Vol5No1-177
Heywood, T. Englands Elizabeth. (P.R.
Rider, ed)
H.D. Janzen, 40(AEB):Vol8No1-38
S. Manoogian-Pearce, 568(SCN):Winter84-
69
Heyworth, P. Otto Klemperer.* (Vol 1)
S. Sadie, 415:Jun84-330
Heyworth, P.L., ed. Medieval Studies for
J.A.W. Bennett, Aetatis suae LXX.*
J. Frankis, 541(RES):Aug84-349
D. Pearsall, 447(N&Q):Jun83-246
Hibbard, G.R., ed. The Elizabethan Thea-
tre VII.
J. Gasper, 447(N&Q):Feb83-76
Hibbard, G.R., ed. The Elizabethan The-
atre, VIII.
A. Leggatt, 627(UTQ):Summer84-417
Hibbard, H. Caravaggio.*
R.E. Spear, 90:Mar84-162
C. Whitfield, 39:Apr84-305
Hibbert, C. Rome, the Biography of a City.
M. Fitz Herbert, 617(TLS):12Jul85-769
442(NY):21Oct85-150
Hibbert, C. - see Queen Victoria
Hicken, K.L. Aspects of Harmony.
H. Keller, 607:Dec84-37
Hickey, D. and G. Smith. Operation Ava-
lanche.
D. Middleton, 441:3Mar85-23
Hickey, J. Religion and the Northern Ire-
land Problem.
T. Garvin, 272(IUR):Autumn84-306
Hickmann, R. Indische Albumblätter.
B.D.H. Miller, 463:Summer84-195
Hickok, K. Representations of Women.
C.S.C., 636(VP):Winter84-456
Hicks, J.V. Silence Like the Sun.
A. Amprimoz, 526:Winter84-92
P. Stevens, 649(WAL):Aug84-143
Hidalgo Ogayar, J. Miniatura del Renaci-
miento en la Alta Andalucía: Provincia
de Jaén.
C. Muñoz-Delgado, 48:Jan-Mar84-117
Hiddleston, J.A. Essai sur Laforgue et
les "Derniers vers" suivi de Laforgue
et Baudelaire.
B.C. Swift, 208(FS):Jan84-79
Hierocles. Hieroklès, "Kommentar zum
pythagorischen goldenen Gedicht." (W.
Kohler, trans)
É. des Places, 555:Vol58fasc2-310

Hierro Pescador, J. La teoría de las
ideas innatas en Chomsky.
R. Barriga Villanueva, 457(NRFH):
Tomo32núm1-207
Hiersche, A. and E. Kowalski, eds. Was
kann denn ein Dichter auf Erden.
W. Reiss, 654(WB):6/1984-1051
Higdon, D.L. and T.K. Bender. A Concor-
dance to Conrad's "Under Western Eyes."
H.H. Kollmeier, 136:Vol 17No1-75
Higgins, D.S. Rider Haggard.*
K. McCormack, 561(SFS):Mar84-93
Higgins, G.V. Penance for Jerry Kennedy.
P-L. Adams, 61:May85-104
S. Epstein, 441:24Feb85-27
442(NY):18Mar85-130
Higgins, H. Vietnam. (2nd ed)
T.B. Lam, 293(JASt):May84-607
Higgins, J. Confessional.
D.G. Myers, 441:21Jul85-23
Higgins, J. The Poet in Peru.*
F. Dauster, 240(HR):Spring84-254
Higgins, J. and T. Johns. Computers in
Language Learning.
J.P. Lantolf, 399(MLJ):Winter84-392
Higgs, R.J. Laurel and Thorn.*
D. Johnson, 577(SHR):Winter84-95
C.K. Messenger, 536:Vol5-119
Higgs, T.V., ed. Teaching for Proficiency.
J.D. Bragger, 207(FR):May85-906
F.W. Medley, Jr., 399(MLJ):Winter84-
384
High, E.C. Past Titan Rock.
T.D. Adams, 585(SoQ):Fall84-90
Higham, C. American Swastika.
H. Goodman, 441:23Jun85-21
Higham, C. Orson Welles.
A. Quindlen, 441:15Sep85-9
Higham, C. and R. Moseley. Princess Merle.
J. Nangle, 200:May84-311
Highet, G. The Classical Papers of Gil-
bert Highet.* (R.J. Ball, ed)
J.E. Phillips, 124:Nov-Dec84-134
Highfield, A. and A. Valdman, eds. Histor-
icity and Variation in Creole Studies.*
S. Jones, 355(LSoc):Mar84-129
Highsmith, P. Mermaids on the Golf Course
and Other Stories.
C. Brown, 617(TLS):27Sep85-1048
Highsmith, P. People Who Knock on the
Door.
M. Stasio, 441:24Nov85-24
Highwater, J. Ritual of the Wind.
J. Gleason, 472:Fall/Winter84-21
Hignett, S. Brett.
A.S. Grossman, 441:9Jun85-23
C.K. Stead, 617(TLS):25Jan85-94
Higuchi, T. The Visual and Spatial Struc-
ture of Landscapes.
C. Fawcett, 46:Feb84-78
Higurashi, Y. The Accent of Extended Word
Structures in Tokyo Standard Japanese.
L.M. Hyman, 350:Sep85-724
Hijiya-Kirschnereit, I. Selbstentblös-
sungsrituale.
B. Yoshida-Krafft, 407(MN):Spring84-94
Hikmet, N. Human Landscapes.*
E. Grosholz, 249(HudR):Spring84-138
Hilberg, R. The Destruction of the Euro-
pean Jews. (2nd ed)
M.R. Marrus, 617(TLS):8Mar85-247
D.S. Wyman, 441:11Aug85-3

Hild, F. Das byzantinische Strassensystem
in Kappadokien.
C. Foss, 589:Jul84-656
Hild, F. and M. Restle. Kappadokien.
C. Foss, 589:Jul84-656
Hildebidle, J. Thoreau.*
D.M. Holman, 569(SR):Winter84-144
S. Paul, 301(JEGP):Jul84-460
Hildebrand, K. The Third Reich.
C.M. Kimmich, 441:6Jan85-10
Hildebrandt, K. - see Behl, C.F.W.
Hildesheimer, W. Marbot.
U. Reinhold, 654(WB):11/1984-1908
H. Urbahn de Jauregui, 601(SuF):
Mar-Apr84-422
Hildesheimer, W. Mozart.*
J. Adas, 143:Issue 35-69
Hildner, D.J. Reason and the Passions in
the "Comedias" of Calderón.
S.H. Lipmann, 304(JHP):Fall84-89
Hiley, J. Theatre at Work.
C.R. Mueller, 615(TJ):Mar82-128
Hilfer, A.C. The Ethics of Intensity in
American Fiction.
K. Probert, 106:Spring84-93
Hilfiker, D. Healing the Wounds.
J.G. Deaton, 441:3Nov85-24
Hill, A.G. - see Wordsworth, D.
Hill, A.G. - see Wordsworth, W. and D.
Hill, B. Eighteenth-Century Women.
D.C. Payne, 566:Spring85-188
Hill, B.W. British Parliamentary Parties
1742-1832.
F. O'Gorman, 617(TLS):27Sep85-1058
Hill, C. The Eleven Million Mile High
Dancer.
E. Prager, 441:31Mar85-11
Hill, C. The Experience of Defeat.*
D. Underdown, 453(NYRB):28Mar85-41
Hill, C., B. Reay and W. Lamont. The
World of the Muggletonians.*
T.W. Hayes, 568(SCN):Fall84-37
Hill, C.M. - see Héroët, A.
Hill, D. In Turner's Footsteps.
G. Cavaliero, 324:Aug85-669
Hill, D. Klinger's Novels.
H. Kaiser, 680(ZDP):Band103Heft2-280
Hill, D.L. - see Pater, W.
Hill, F. Out of Bounds.
L. Duguid, 617(TLS):8Mar85-266
Hill, G. The Lords of Limit.*
J. Lucas, 493:Sep84-64
A. Phillips, 364:Jun84-109
P. Robinson, 175:Summer84-167
Hill, G. The Mystery of the Charity of
Charles Péguy.*
J. Hollander, 676(YR):Autumn84-xiii
Hill, J.W., ed. Studies in Musicology in
Honor of Otto E. Albrecht.
I. Fenlon, 410(M&L):Jul84-268
Hill, L. Secrets of Plant Propagation.
L. Yang, 441:2Jun85-14
Hill, P. The Bombay Marines.
S. Altinel, 617(TLS):12Jul85-776
Hill, R. Blue Rise.
639(VQR):Winter84-28
Hill, R.A., with E.J. Tolbert and D.
Forczek - see Garvey, M.
Hill, S. A Bit of Singing and Dancing.
M. Simpson, 441:17Mar85-26

Hill, S. Saying Hello at the Station.*
D. Davis, 362:3Jan85-26
B. O'Donoghue, 493:Jun84-61
W. Scammell, 364:Mar85-90
Hillen, W. Raymond Queneau.
J. Langenbacher-Liebgott, 547(RF):
Band96Heft1/2-200
Hillerman, T. Dance Hall of the Dead.
T.J. Binyon, 617(TLS):5Apr85-394
Hillerman, T. The Ghostway.
T.J. Binyon, 617(TLS):27Dec85-1478
N. Callendar, 441:2Jun85-38
442(NY):25Feb85-106
Hillesum, E. An Interrupted Life.*
(British title: Etty.)
L.L. Langer, 385(MQR):Winter85-125
639(VQR):Summer84-89
Hillgarth, J.N. and G. Silano. The Regis-
ter "Notule communium" 14 of the Diocese
of Barcelona (1345-1348).
P. Freedman, 589:Jul84-720
Hilliard, N. Art of Limning.* (A.F.
Kinney and L.B. Salamon, eds)
F. Cossa, 570(SQ):Winter84-491
L. Gent, 551(RenQ):Winter84-637
Hillier, B. John Betjeman.
V.S. Pritchett, 442(NY):24Jun85-94
Hillier, B. The Style of the Century 1900-
1980.
J. Daniels, 39:Jun84-468
Hillier, J. The Art of Hokusai in Book
Illustration.
J.E., 90:Apr84-244
C.J. Shankel, 318(JAOS):Jul-Sep83-646
S.E. Thompson, 70:Sep-Oct83-27
Hillier, J., ed. Cahiers du cinéma. (Vol
1)
P. Brunette, 18:Jul/Aug85-53
D. Kehr, 441:4Aug85-1
T. Rafferty, 442(NY):30Sep85-113
C. Redpath, 617(TLS):19Jul85-793
Hillman, B. Coffee, 3 A.M.
D. St. John, 42(AR):Summer84-368
Hillman, B. White Dress.
F. Garber, 29(APR):Sep/Oct85-14
Hillman, J. and C. Boer, eds. Freud's Own
Cookbook.
F. Ferretti, 441:26May85-15
Hills, P., ed. Alice Neel.
L. Alloway, 127:Summer84-191
R. Bass, 55:Mar84-37
Hilpert, H-E. Kaiser- und Papstbriefe in
den Chronica majora des Matthaeus Paris.
K. Pennington, 589:Jan84-159
Hilton, J.B. Passion in the Peak.
T.J. Binyon, 617(TLS):27Dec85-1478
Hilton, N. Literal Imagination.
M. Bracher, 478:Apr84-136
S.D. Cox, 173(ECS):Spring85-391
P. Dunbar, 536:Vol6-187
M. Ferber, 141:Fall84-397
B. Wilkie, 301(JEGP):Oct84-566
Hilton, O. Scientific Examination of
Questioned Documents. (rev)
P.S. Koda, 517(PBSA):Vol78No4-507
Hilton, T. John Ruskin: The Early Years
1819-1859.
J. Bayley, 453(NYRB):24Oct85-10
P.N. Furbank, 362:30May85-30
P. Gay, 617(TLS):14Jun85-655
Hily-Mane, G. Le Style de Ernest Heming-
way.*
J. Templeton, 189(EA):Jan-Mar85-100

169

Himmelsbach, S. Un fidèle reflet de son
époque.
    J. Emelina, 535(RHL):Jul/Aug84-635
Hinchliffe, A.P. Harold Pinter. (rev)
    T. Postlewait, 615(TJ):Dec82-552
    R.W. Strang, 447(N&Q):Jun83-283
Hinchliffe, I. Per Olof Sundman: "Ingen-
jör Andrées luftfard."
    D.M. Mennie, 562(Scan):Nov84-196
Hinck, W., ed. Handbuch des deutschen
Dramas.
    J. Guthrie, 220(GL&L):Oct84-57
Hinckley, J. and J.A., with E. Sherrill.
Breaking Points.
    D. Kagan, 441:18Aug85-23
Hinde, T. Forests of Britain.
    S. Leathart, 617(TLS):22Mar85-331
Hinderer, W., ed. Goethes Dramen.*
    H. Hamm, 654(WB):3/1984-521
Hinderer, W., ed. Kleists Dramen.*
    M. Gelus, 406:Fall84-363
Hinderer, W. Der Mensch in der Geschichte.
    J.F. Hyde, Jr., 406:Fall84-363
Hinderer, W. Über deutsche Literatur und
Rede.*
    M.K. Flavell, 402(MLR):Jan84-231
    H.D. Osterle, 221(GQ):Spring84-296
Hinderer, W. - see von Kleist, H.
Hindley, A. and B.J. Levy. The Old French
Epic.*
    W.W. Kibler, 207(FR):May85-883
    K. Pratt, 208(FS):Oct84-444
Hindman, S., ed. The Early Illustrated
Book.*
    M. Camille, 59:Dec84-509
Hindmarsh, P. Frank Bridge.
    P. Dickinson, 415:Jun84-329
Hine, H.M. An Edition with Commentary of
Seneca, "Natural Questions," Book Two.
    F.R.D. Goodyear, 123:Vol34No1-44
Hines, B. Unfinished Business.
    P. Craig, 617(TLS):5Jul85-757
Hines, G. Stephen Gill and His Works.
    U. Parameswaran, 102(CanL):Winter83-
144
Hines, T.S. Richard Neutra and the Search
for Modern Architecture.*
    P. Smithson, 46:Apr84-85
    M.N. Woods, 45:Mar84-73
Hingley, R. Nightingale Fever.*
    E. Bristol, 574(SEEJ):Spring84-127
Hingley, R. Pasternak.
    R.B. Anderson, 395(MFS):Winter84-734
    G.S. Smith, 402(MLR):Oct84-1005
    639(VQR):Spring84-53
Hingley, R. Russian Writers and Soviet
Society 1917-1978.
    A.V. Knowles, 447(N&Q):Jun83-288
Hinks, R. The Gymnasium of the Mind.* (J.
Goldsmith, ed)
    C. Gould, 324:Dec84-70
    B. Gray, 39:Sep84-214
Hinojosa, R. Dear Rafe.
    R. Houston, 441:18Aug85-20
Hinojoso, G.M. A Borderlands Town in
Transition.
    L. Milazzo, 584(SWR):Winter84-88
Hinske, N., ed. Alexandrien.
    C.E. Vafopoulou-Richardson, 123:
Vol34No2-347
Hintikka, J., D. Gruender and E. Agazzi,
eds. Proceedings of the 1978 Pisa Con-
                   [continued]

[continuing]
ference on the History and Philosophy of
Science.
    M.A. Finocchiaro, 488:Dec84-572
Hinz, E.J., ed. Beyond Nationalism.*
    M.P. Loverso, 178:Jun84-240
Hinz, E.J. and J.J. Teunissen - see Miller,
H.
Hinze, C. and U. Diederichs, eds. Ost-
preussische Sagen.
    W. Wunderlich, 196:Band25Heft1/2-134
Hipkiss, R.A. The American Absurd.
    P.B. McElwain, 590:Jun85-47
Hiro, D. Iran Under the Ayatollahs.
    P. Mansfield, 362:7Feb85-22
    D. Spanier, 176:Apr85-73
von Hirsch, A. Past or Future Crimes.
    D.C. Anderson, 441:15Dec85-16
Hirsch, E. The Concept of Identity.*
    A. Brennan, 449:Sep84-541
    W.R. Carter, 482(PhR):Jul84-468
    R. Kennedy, 484(PPR):Mar85-467
    H.W. Noonan, 479(PhQ):Apr84-175
Hirsch, M. Beyond the Single Vision.
    P.S. Nichols, 395(MFS):Winter84-854
Hirsch, R., ed. A Catalogue of the Manu-
scripts and Archives of the Library of
The College of Physicians of Philadel-
phia.
    V. Steele, 517(PBSA):Vol78No2-263
Hirschhorn, C. The Universal Story.
    J. Nangle, 200:Mar84-182
Hirsh, J.E. The Structure of Shakespear-
ean Scenes.*
    C. Hoy, 569(SR):Spring84-256
    E. Jones, 541(RES):Aug84-365
Hirsh, S.L. Ferdinand Hodler.*
    P. Vignau-Wilberg, 471:Jan/Feb/Mar84-
96
Hirst, D. Intonative Features.
    G.F. Meier, 682(ZPSK):Band37Heft1-109
Hirst, W.Z. John Keats.*
    S.M. Sperry, 591(SIR):Summer84-259
Hirt, H. The Heat of Winter.
    T.J. Binyon, 617(TLS):15Mar85-284
"História do mui nobre Vespasiano Impera-
dor de Roma."
    T.F. Earle, 382(MAE):1984/2-330
"Historical Morphology."
    G.F. Meier, 682(ZPSK):Band37Heft3-390
de Hita, G.P. - see under Pérez de Hita, G.
Hitch, N.S. Passport to America.
    S. Plann, 399(MLJ):Winter84-424
Hitchcock, B., ed. Sightseeing.
    W.L. Heat-Moon, 441:8Dec85-16
Hitchcock, G. The Wounded Alphabet.
    R. McDowell, 249(HudR):Spring84-115
Hitchcock, H-R. German Renaissance Archi-
tecture.*
    J. Bialostocki, 90:Oct84-636
Hitchcock, H.W. Les Oeuvres de/The Works
of/Marc-Antoine Charpentier.*
    B. Gustafson, 317:Spring84-170
Hitchens, M.G. Germany, Russia, and the
Balkans.
    R.K. Debo, 104(CASS):Winter84-484
    639(VQR):Spring84-49
Hite, M. Ideas of Order in the Novels of
Thomas Pynchon.
    D.L. Cook, 27(AL):Dec84-625
    S. Weisenburger, 395(MFS):Summer84-331
Hiż, H. - see Harris, Z.S.

170

Hoffmann, W. Untersuchungen zur frühneu-
hochdeutschen Verbflexion am Beispiel
ripuarischer Texte.
N.R. Wolf, 685(ZDL):1/1984-94
Hoffmeister, G. Byron und der europäische
Byronismus.
E. Frykman, 571(ScLJ):Autumn84-19
L.R. Furst, 107(CRCL):Jun84-308
Hoffmeister, G., ed. German Baroque Lit-
erature.
H.B. Segel, 107(CRCL):Jun84-299
F.J. Warnke, 678(YCGL):No33-105
Höfler, M., ed. La lexicographie fran-
çaise du XVIe au XVIIIe siècle.
D. Messner, 547(RF):Band96Heft1/2-123
Hofmann, É., ed. Benjamin Constant,
Madame de Staël et le Groupe de Coppet.*
H. Grange, 535(RHL):Nov/Dec84-968
A.C. Ritchie, 546(RR):May84-388
D. Wood, 402(MLR):Jan84-193
Hofmann, G. Our Conquest.
J.A. Snead, 441:14Apr85-26
442(NY):20May85-125
Hofmann, M. Nights in the Iron Hotel.*
A. Hollinghurst, 493:Jan84-62
W. Logan, 491:Nov84-100
von Hofmannsthal, H. and M. Mell. Hugo
von Hofmannsthal — Max Mell: Brief-
wechsel. (M. Dietrich and H. Kindermann,
eds)
W.E. Yates, 402(MLR):Jul84-755
von Hofmannsthal, H. and P. Zifferer.
Briefwechsel. (H. Burger, ed)
W.E. Yates, 402(MLR):Oct84-987
Höfner, E. Literarität und Realität.
A.W. Raitt, 208(FS):Jan84-82
Hofstadter, D.R. Metamagical Themas.
J. Maddox, 441:21Apr85-37
Hofstadter, D.R. and D.C. Dennett, eds.
The Mind's I.*
A. Hamilton, 479(PhQ):Jan84-80
Hogan, J.F. Fabric into Flowers.
C. Campbell, 614:Summer84-24
Hogan, R. "Since O'Casey" and Other
Essays on Irish Drama.*
N. Grene, 610:Summer84-150
C. Murray, 272(IUR):Spring84-139
Högemann, B. Die Idee der Freiheit und
das Subjekt.
V. Gerhardt, 342:Band75Heft4-498
Höger, A. Frank Wedekind.
A.B. Willeke, 406:Summer84-228
Hogg, J. Anecdotes of Sir Walter Scott.*
(D.S. Mack, ed)
G.H. Hughes, 571(ScLJ):Winter84-52
Hogg, J. and M. Sargent, eds. The
"Chartae" of the Carthusian General
Chapter; Cava MS. 61; and Aula Dei: The
Louber "Manuale" from the Charterhouse
of Buxheim.
R.B. Marks, 589:Jan84-236
Hogue, J. Aube.
C-L. Rogers, 102(CanL):Autumn84-147
Hogwood, C. Handel.
W. Dean, 453(NYRB):19Dec85-44
J. Keates, 617(TLS):11Jan85-31
J. Rockwell, 441:23Jun85-26
R. Savage, 362:3Jan85-24
Hogwood, C. and R. Luckett, eds. Music in
Eighteenth-Century England.*
W. Shaw, 410(M&L):Jan84-48

Hohler, T.P. Imagination and Reflection.*
D. Breazeale, 543:Jun84-854
G. Satty, 258:Jun84-210
Hohlfelder, R., ed. City, Town, and
Countryside in the Early Byzantine Era.
M.A. Alexander, 124:Sep-Oct84-55
Höke, H. - see Meng Han-ch'ing
Holbro, P.S. Tarnished Expansion.
639(VQR):Winter84-17
Holbrook, M. Print Production Highlights.
T. Reese, 507:Nov/Dec84-140
Holcombe, R.G. Public Finance and the
Political Process.
M.W., 185:Oct84-192
Holcot, R. Exploring the Boundaries of
Reason. (H.G. Gelber, ed)
A. Reix, 542:Oct-Dec84-463
Holden, J. Falling from Stardom.
J.F. Cotter, 249(HudR):Autumn84-501
Holden, J. Leverage.
B. Weigl, 496:Summer84-113
Holden, J. The Rhetoric of the Contempor-
ary Lyric.*
R. Belflower, 541(RES):Feb84-106
S. Fender, 677(YES):Vol 14-363
Holden, U. Eric's Choice.*
J. Melmoth, 364:Nov84-109
Holderness, G. D.H. Lawrence.*
R.S. Baker, 125:Fall83-86
C. Holmes, 366:Spring84-133
M. Montaut, 272(IUR):Spring84-137
Holdheim, W.W. The Hermeneutic Mode.
C. Baldick, 617(TLS):15Mar85-295
Holdstock, R. Mythago Wood.
C. Greenland, 617(TLS):15Mar85-284
G. Jonas, 441:24Nov85-34
Holiday, G. People of Illusion.
A. Beevor, 617(TLS):10May85-528
Holinger, W. The Fence Walker.
R.O. Butler, 441:20Oct85-39
van Holk, A.G.F., ed. Dutch Contributions
to the Ninth International Congress of
Slavists, Kiev, September 6-14, 1983:
Linguistics.
V.M. Du Feu, 575(SEER):Apr84-250
van Holk, A.G.F., ed. Dutch Contributions
to the Ninth International Congress of
Slavists, Kiev, September 6-14, 1983:
Literature.
L. Burnett, 402(MLR):Oct84-1000
J. Graffy, 575(SEER):Apr84-257
Holladay, C.R. Fragments from Hellenistic
Jewish Authors. (Vol 1)
S.J.D. Cohen, 124:Jan-Feb85-227
Holland, C. Pillar of the Sky.
S. Altinel, 617(TLS):13Dec85-1434
M. Buck, 441:21Jul85-22
Holland, L.B. The Expense of Vision.
E. Carton, 284:Fall84-60
Holland, N.N. Laughing.*
R.B. Henkle, 569(SR):Winter84-121
B.O. States, 249(HudR):Spring84-165
Holland, P. - see Wycherley, W.
Holland, P.G., M. Meltzer and F. Krasno -
see Child, L.M.
Hollander, J. Blue Wine and Other Poems.
Spectral Emanations. In Place.
D. Lehman, 472:Fall/Winter84-190
Hollander, J. The Figure of Echo.*
D. Chambers, 541(RES):Aug84-379
D. Lehman, 472:Fall/Winter84-190
J. Wittreich, 301(JEGP):Apr84-237

Hollander, J. Powers of Thirteen.*
P. Breslin, 491:Dec84-171
D. Lehman, 472:Fall/Winter84-190
639(VQR):Spring84-62
Hollander, J. Rhyme's Reason.*
M. English, 536:Vol5-125
D. Lehman, 472:Fall/Winter84-190
Hollander, P. Political Pilgrims.*
N. Weyl, 390:Jan84-55
Hollier, D. Politique de la prose.*
S. Kofman, 153:Winter84-9
A. Leupin, 188(ECr):Spring84-126
G. Prince, 153:Winter84-2
Hollingshead, G. Famous Players.
E. Johnston, 102(CanL):Winter83-114
Hollingsworth, M. Operators and Bushed.
Ever Loving.
R. Plant, 102(CanL):Summer84-155
Hollington, M. Günter Grass.
J. Wieczorek, 299:Autumn82-154
Hollingworth, B., ed. Songs of the People.
C.S.C., 636(VP):Spring84-93
Hollingworth, C. Mao and the Men Against
Him.
D. Wilson, 617(TLS):21Jun85-692
Hollinrake, R. Nietzsche, Wagner and the
Philosophy of Pessimism.*
F.R. Love, 221(GQ):Summer84-511
F.R. Love, 410(M&L):Jan84-106
C.S. Taylor, 518:Oct84-214
Hollins, T. Beyond Broadcasting?
B. Winston, 707:Summer84-228
Hollis, C.C. Language and Style in
"Leaves of Grass."*
H. Levine, 223:Summer83-194
J.P. Warren, 599:Winter84-113
639(VQR):Winter84-10
Hollis, D.W. 3d. An Alabama Newspaper
Tradition.
J.M. Thornton 3d, 9(AlaR):Jul84-227
Hollis, M. Invitation to Philosophy.
D.W.D. Owen, 617(TLS):4Oct85-1095
Hollis, M. and S. Lukes, eds. Rational-
ity and Relativism.*
J. Benardete, 543:Sep83-122
D. Macintosh, 529(QQ):Summer84-461
Hollos, M. and B.C. Maday, eds. New Hun-
garian Peasants.
G. Schöpflin, 575(SEER):Oct84-638
Hollow, J., ed. The After-Summer Seed.
P. Thompson, 59:Dec84-496
Hollow, J. Against the Night, the Stars.
D.M. Hassler, 395(MFS):Summer84-383
E.S. Rabkin, 561(SFS):Jul84-210
Holloway, D. The Soviet Union and the
Arms Race.*
A.R. De Luca, 550(RusR):Oct84-432
639(VQR):Winter84-21
Holloway, J. Narrative and Structure.*
A. Finch, 208(FS):Apr84-247
Holloway, J.B. - see Latini, B.
Holly, M.A. Panofsky and the Foundations
of Art History.
A.C. Danto, 617(TLS):2Aug85-842
Holm, B. The Box of Daylight.
L.R., 102(CanL):Autumn84-5
42(AR):Summer84-381
Holm, J., ed. Central American English.
J.L. Dillard, 350:Jun85-487
S. Jones, 355(LSoc):Jun84-281
L. Todd, 660(Word):Dec84-288
Holman, A. White River, Brown Water.
J. Keay, 362:18Jul85-28

Holman, D. Noone of the Ulu.
617(TLS):5Apr85-395
Holman, M. Breaking and The New York City
Breakers.
J. Yau, 62:Dec84-73
Holme, T. The Assisi Murders.
T.J. Binyon, 617(TLS):5Apr85-394
Holmes, F.L. Lavoisier and the Chemistry
of Life.
M. Crosland, 617(TLS):18Oct85-1166
Holmes, G. Augustan England.*
H.T. Dickinson, 566:Autumn84-71
Holmes, M. The Labour Government, 1974-79.
B. Pimlott, 617(TLS):15Nov85-1285
Holmes, P. Vilhelm Moberg: "Utvandrarna."
(2nd ed)
D.M. Mennie, 562(Scan):Nov84-196
Holmes, R. Firing Line.
C. Townshend, 617(TLS):23Aug85-920
Holmes, R. Footsteps.
L. Hafrey, 441:20Oct85-23
P. Quennell, 617(TLS):19Jul85-795
Holmes, S. Benjamin Constant and the Mak-
ing of Modern Liberalism.
N. Hampson, 617(TLS):31May85-617
Holmes, W.C. La Statira.
M. Boyd, 415:Mar84-152
Holmquist, I. and E. Witt-Brattström, eds.
Kvinnornas litteraturhistoria. (Vol 2)
I. Clareus, 563(SS):Summer84-296
Holoman, D.K. and C.V. Palisca, eds. Musi-
cology in the 1980s.
D. Crawford, 309:Vol5No1/3-251
Holquist, M. - see Bakhtin, M.M.
Holroyd, M. - see Peterley, D.
Holt, H. and H. Pym - see Pym, B.
Holt, J.C. Discipline.*
C.S. Prebish, 318(JAOS):Apr-Jun83-441
Holt, J.C. Robin Hood.*
I.M. Benecke, 161(DUJ):Dec83-129
B.A. Hanawalt, 589:Jan84-237
Holt, T. Lucia in Wartime.
C. Hawtree, 617(TLS):13Sep85-1000
Holton, M. and H. Kuhner, eds and trans.
Austrian Poetry Today.
P. Demetz, 441:18Aug85-18
Holton, S.W. Down Home and Uptown.
J. Benson, 573(SSF):Fall84-427
A. Rampersad, 578:Fall85-110
Holtsmark, E.B. Tarzan and Tradition.
D. Damrosch, 149(CLS):Summer84-246
J. Solomon, 121(CJ):Oct-Nov84-63
Holtus, G. and E. Radtke, eds. Varietäten-
linguistik des Italienischen.
P. Koch, 547(RF):Band96Heft4-454
G. Roques, 553(RLiR):Jan-Jun84-203
Holtz, B.W., ed. Back to the Sources.
R. Alter, 129:Mar85-69
Holtzmann, S.H. and C.M. Leich, eds. Witt-
genstein.
I. McFetridge, 479(PhQ):Jan84-69
Holtzmann, W. Decretales ineditae saeculi
XII. (S. Chodorow and C. Duggan, eds)
J. Gilchrist, 589:Jan84-163
Holub, R.C. Heinrich Heine's Reception of
German Grecophilia.
J. Kolb, 221(GQ):Fall84-662
Holub, R.C. Reception Theory.
S. Scobie, 376:Oct84-107
J.J. Sosnoski, 395(MFS):Winter84-849

Hope, C. Kruger's Alp.*
   R. Loewinsohn, 441:5May85-9
   J. Mellors, 364:Oct84-81
Hope, C. and A. Nova - see Cellini, B.
Hopkin, A. A Joke Goes a Long Way in the
   Country.
   M. Montaut, 272(IUR):Spring84-137
Hopkin, A. The Out-Haul.
   J. Mellors, 362:28Feb85-27
   S. Posesorski, 441:22Dec85-18
Hopkins, A. Pathway to Music.
   P. Standford, 415:Jun84-331
Hopkins, J. Nicholas of Cusa's Meta-
   physics of Contraction.*
   C.L. Miller, 319:Jan85-103
Hopkins, K. Death and Renewal.*
   R.P. Duncan-Jones, 123:Vol34No2-270
Hopkinson, D. Edward Penrose Arnold.
   D. Birch, 447(N&Q):Aug83-359
Hopkinson, N., ed. Callimachus: Hymn to
   Demeter.
   J.H.C. Leach, 617(TLS):1Nov85-1245
Hopkirk, P. Setting the East Ablaze.
   S. Ferrell, 441:1Sep85-15
   E. de Mauny, 617(TLS):1Mar85-224
Hoppe, A. Grundzüge der Kommunikativen
   Grammatik. (Pt 1)
   G.F. Meier, 682(ZPSK):Band37Heft1-111
Hoppe, A. The Marital Arts.
   M.K. Blakely, 441:22Sep85-20
Hoppe, D. Aussprache und sozialer Status.
   R. Jolivet, 209(FM):Oct84-245
Hopper, P.J., ed. Tense Aspect.*
   P. Friedrich, 350:Mar85-182
   F. Lichtenberk, 361:Jul-Aug84-330
   C. Vet, 603:Vol8No2-296
Hopper, R. The Ceramic Spectrum.
   T.A. Lockett, 324:Sep85-737
Horace. The Complete Works of Horace.*
   (C.E. Passage, trans)
   M.S. Santirocco, 124:Sep-Oct84-45
Horecký, J., ed. COLING 82.
   W. Frawley, 350:Mar85-247
Hörisch, J. Gott, Geld und Glück.
   J. Jacobs, 680(ZDP):Band103Heft4-606
Horkheimer, M. and T.W. Adorno. La Dialec-
   tique de la raison.
   M.F. Meurice, 450(NRF):Mar84-125
Hörmann, H. Psycholinguistics. (2nd ed)
   G.F. Meier, 682(ZPSK):Band37Heft5-641
Horn, G.M. Lexical-Functional Grammar.
   T. Hoekstra, 353:Vol22No2-243
   D.J. Napoli, 350:Mar85-180
Horn, K. Der aktive und per passive
   Märchenheld.
   E. Moser-Rath, 196:Band25Heft3/4-339
Horn, P. The Changing Countryside in Vic-
   torian and Edwardian England and Wales.
   Rural Life in England in the First World
   War.
   G.E. Mingay, 617(TLS):25Jan85-96
Hornback, B.G. "The Hero of My Life."*
   T. Braun, 447(N&Q):Dec83-542
   R. Gilmour, 301(JEGP):Oct84-568
Hornblower, S. Mausolus.*
   R. Lonis, 555:Vol58fasc2-305
   S.M. Sherwin-White, 123:Vol34No2-254
Hornblower, S. and M.C. Greenstock, eds.
   The Athenian Empire. (3rd ed)
   D.L. Stockton, 123:Vol34No2-343
Horne, D. The Great Museum.
   S. Bann, 617(TLS):19Apr85-445
Horne, P.R. - see Pascoli, G.

Hornig, D. Aspekte des französischen
   Desillusionsromans.
   T.M. Scheerer, 72:Band221Heft2-449
Hornig, D. Foul Shot.
   N. Callendar, 441:3Feb85-37
Hornsby, J. Actions.
   C. Ginet, 482(PhR):Jan84-120
Hornsby, P.R.G. Pewter of the Western
   World, 1600-1850.
   G. Wills, 39:Apr84-306
Hornstein, N. and D. Lightfoot, eds. Ex-
   planation in Linguistics.
   F.W. Gester, 38:Band102Heft1/2-132
Hornung, M. - see Kranzmayer, E.
Horowitz, D.L. Ethnic Groups in Conflict.
   A. Lijphart, 441:10Nov85-31
Horowitz, I.L., C. Wright Mills.
   J. Rury, 42(AR):Winter84-116
Horowitz, L.K. Honoré d'Urfé.
   K. Wine, 207(FR):Apr85-725
Horrent, J. Les Versions françaises et
   étrangères des enfances de Charlemagne.
   W.G. van Emden, 208(FS):Jan84-41
Horrent, J. - see "Cantar de mio Cid ... "
Horridge, A. The Prahu.
   R.J. Young, 318(JAOS):Oct-Dec83-816
ter Horst, R. Calderón: The Secular
   Plays.*
   D. Fox, 131(CL):Fall84-364
   E.H. Friedman, 551(RenQ):Spring84-127
   C. González, 240(HR):Winter84-85
   M.J. Treacy, 403(MLS):Summer84-90
Hortie, C. Strike at Eldorado.
   T. Goldie, 102(CanL):Summer84-131
Horton, J. and S. Mendus, eds. Aspects of
   Toleration.
   M. Warnock, 617(TLS):27Dec85-1485
Horton, J.J., comp. Iceland.
   R.F. Tomasson, 563(SS):Autumn84-381
von Horváth, Ö. The Age of the Fish.
   l. Huish, 617(TLS):17May85-540
Horvath-Peterson, S. Victor Duruy and
   French Education.
   S.S. Bryson, 207(FR):May85-928
Horwich, P. Probability and Evidence.*
   M.R.F., 185:Jul85-977
   I.J. Good, 84:Jun84-161
   T. Seidenfeld, 482(PhR):Jul84-474
   S. Spielman, 311(JP):Mar84-168
Horwood, W. Adolphe Sax 1814-1894.
   N. O'Loughlin, 415:Jun84-333
Hosford, H. German Teacher's Companion.
   H.F. Taylor, 399(MLJ):Summer84-176
Hosking, G. A History of the Soviet Union.
   A.B. Ulam, 617(TLS):13Sep85-1010
Hoskings, G. Beyond Socialist Realism.
   O. Hayward, 125:Fall83-93
Hösle, J. Die katalanische Literatur von
   der Renaixença bis zur Gegenwart.
   T. Barrass, 86(BHS):Oct84-529
   A.G. Hauf, 402(MLR):Jan84-221
   K. Süss, 52:Band19Heft1-93
Hösle, J., D. Janik and W. Theile - see
   Wais, K.
Hosoe, E. - see under Eikoh Hosoe
Hospers, J. Understanding the Arts.
   G. Geahigan, 289:Fall84-119
Hospital, J.T. Borderline.
   C. Fein, 441:1Sep85-8
Hospital, J.T. The Ivory Swing.
   M. Taylor, 198:Winter84-93

Howell, M.J. Byron Tonight.
  F.L. Beaty, 340(KSJ):Vol33-210
  G.B. Cross, 637(VS):Winter84-244
  W. Ruddick, 611(TN):Vol38No1-43
Howell, P. A Commentary on Book One of
the Epigrams of Martial.
  P. White, 121(CJ):Feb-Mar85-263
Howells, R.J. Pierre Jurieu.
  C.N. Smith, 208(FS):Apr84-202
Howells, W.D. Selected Letters of W.D.
Howells. (Vol 5) (W.C. Fischer and C.K.
Lohmann, eds)
  J. Katz, 579(SAQ):Spring84-240
Howker, J. The Nature of the Beast.
  J. Mellors, 362:28Feb85-27
Howkins, A. Poor Labouring Men.
  J.F.C. Harrison, 617(TLS):12Jul85-779
Hoxie, F. A Final Promise.
  42(AR):Fall84-506
Hoy, D.C. The Critical Circle.*
  P.L. Bourgeois, 543:Sep83-124
  R. Holmes, 154:Mar84-159
Hoy, H., ed. Modern English-Canadian
Prose.
  W.J. Keith, 168(ECW):Winter84/85-136
  D.W. McLeod, 470:Vol22-116
  L. Ricou, 627(UTQ):Summer84-445
Hoy, P.C., ed. Les Carnets bibliogra-
phiques de la Revue des Lettres Modernes:
Paul Valéry.
  W.N. Ince, 208(FS):Oct84-485
Hoyle, F. The Intelligent Universe.*
  639(VQR):Summer84-99
Hoyle, P. The Man in the Iron Mask.
  P. Lewis, 565:Autumn84-55
de Hoyos, L. Klaus Barbie.
  F.D. Gray, 453(NYRB):27Jun85-12
  H.R. Kedward, 617(TLS):15Nov85-1282
  A. Knopf, 441:27Oct85-41
Hoyt, E.P. On to the Yalu.
  H.G. Summers, Jr., 441:17Feb85-21
Hoyt, R. Fish Story.
  N. Callendar, 441:9Jun85-37
  442(NY):26Aug85-88
Hsiao, H-H.M. Government Agricultural
Strategies in Taiwan and South Korea.
  R.E. Barrett, 293(JASt):May84-518
Hsiao Tseng. Hsiao Tseng hui-i-lu:
t'u-ti kai-ke wu-shih-nien.
  R. Myers, 293(JASt):Nov83-149
Hsu, C-Y. Bibliographic Notes on Studies
of Early China.
  S.W. Durrant, 318(JAOS):Jul-Sep83-639
  L.E. Hubbard, 293(JASt):May84-519
Hsu, C-Y. Han Agriculture. (J.L. Dull,
ed)
  C.S. Goodrich, 318(JAOS):Oct-Dec83-804
Hsu, R.C. Food for One Billion.
  M.A. Weininger, 293(JASt):May84-521
Hsu, T.H. Chansons populaires de Fulao à
Taïwan.
  Cheng Shui-Cheng, 537:Vol70No1-124
Hsu, V.L., ed. Born of the Same Roots.*
  T.E. Barlow, 116:Jul83-193
Hsüan-chih, Y. - see under Yang Hsüan-chih
Hu-De Hart, E. Yaqui Resistance and Sur-
vival.
  J.H. Kelley, 263(RIB):Vol34No3/4-429
Hua Chang-ming. La Condition féminine et
les communistes Chinois en action:
Yan'an, 1935-1946.
  P. Stranahan, 293(JASt):Aug84-741

Hubala, E. Johann Michael Rottmayr.
  A. Laing, 90:Jun84-359
Hubala, E., ed. Rubens: Kunstgeschicht-
liche Beiträge.
  J.M. Muller, 54:Mar84-163
Hubback, D. No Ordinary Press Baron.
  P. Clarke, 617(TLS):12Apr85-400
  A. Hetherington, 362:7Feb85-24
Hubenova, M., A. Dzhumadanova and M. Mar-
inova. A Course in Modern Bulgarian.
(Pt 1)
  M.J. Elson, 574(SEEJ):Summer84-280
  E. Scatton, 399(MLJ):Autumn84-281
Hubenova, M., A. Dzhumadanova and M. Mari-
nova. A Course in Modern Bulgarian.
(Pt 2)
  M.J. Elson, 574(SEEJ):Summer84-280
  E. Scatton, 399(MLJ):Autumn84-281
Huber, H.M. Licht und Schönheit in Wol-
frams "Parzival."
  D.H. Green, 402(MLR):Apr84-485
Huber, L. and J.J. White, eds. Musil in
Focus.
  W. Hoffmeister, 301(JEGP):Apr84-301
Huber, L.V. Clasped Hands.
  R.E. Meyer, 577(SHR):Fall84-368
Hubert, A. Le Pain et l'olive.
  A. Davidson, 617(TLS):26Jul85-835
Hübner, I. Kulturelle Opposition.
  R. Dolz, 654(WB):8/1984-1394
Hubrich-Messow, G. Personennamen in
schleswig-holsteinischen Volksmärchen
(AT 300-AT 960).
  E. Moser-Rath, 196:Band25Heft1/2-137
Hucker, C.O. A Dictionary of Official
Titles in Imperial China.
  W.J.F. Jenner, 617(TLS):31May85-618
Huddleston, E.L. Thomas Jefferson.
  J.A.L. Lemay, 365:Fall84-85
Hudson, A., ed. English Wycliffite
Sermons. (Vol 1)
  N.F. Blake, 402(MLR):Jul84-664
  C. Clark, 179(ES):Oct84-467
Hudson, C., ed. Black Drink.
  B.M. Smith, 106:Summer84-185
Hudson, H. Criminal Trespass.
  R. Hoffman, 441:21Jul85-22
Hudson, L. Bodies of Knowledge.
  G.M. Mayes, 89(BJA):Winter84-91
Hudson, L. Night Life.
  S. Sutherland, 617(TLS):22Nov85-1318
Hudson, M. Afterlight.*
  B. Bawer, 491:Sep84-348
Hudson, R. Word Grammar.
  P.H. Matthews, 617(TLS):4Jan85-22
Hudson, R.A. Sociolinguistics.
  F. Anshen, 660(Word):Aug84-200
  J.J. Berthout, 596(SL):Vol38No1-92
Hudson, W.D. Modern Moral Philosophy.
  B. Baxter, 479(PhQ):Oct84-509
Hudspeth, R.N. - see Fuller, M.
Huenen, R. and P. Perron. Balzac.
  D. Bellos, 208(FS):Jul84-351
Huerta, J.A. Chicano Theater.*
  A. McDermott, 86(BHS):Jan84-61
  D. McDermott, 612(ThS):May84-124
Huet, H-H. Rehearsing the Revolution.*
  S. Petrey, 173(ECS):Spring85-435
Huf, L. A Portrait of the Artist as a
Young Woman.
  A. Habegger, 27(AL):Oct84-451
  S. Morgan, 594:Summer84-252

Hufbauer, K. The Formation of the German
Chemical Community.
    H. Lowood, 173(ECS):Fall84-108
Huffman, C.D. Montale and the Occasions
of Poetry.*
    C. Asselin, 276:Autumn84-269
    J. Davies, 402(MLR):Apr84-470
    F.J. Jones, 278(IS):Vol39-143
Hufford, D.J. The Terror That Comes in
the Night.
    G.A. Fine, 292(JAF):Apr-Jun84-229
    D. Ward, 650(WF):Oct84-274
Hufschmidt, J. and others. Sprachver-
halten in ländlichen Gemeinden.
    B.J. Koekkoek, 350:Sep85-714
Huge, W. - see von Droste-Hülshoff, A.
Hughes, A. Henry Irving, Shakespearean.*
    J. Ellis, 402(MLR):Apr84-436
Hughes, A. Medieval Manuscripts for Mass
and Office.*
    D.G. Hughes, 317:Summer84-412
Hughes, D. But for Bunter.
    J. Mellors, 362:10Oct84-29
    D. Sexton, 617(TLS):20Sep85-1028
Hughes, D. The Pork Butcher.*
    P. Craig, 617(TLS):29Nov85-1372
    M. Hulse, 364:Jun84-110
    G.A. Schirmer, 441:19May85-15
Hughes, E.J. Marcel Proust.*
    P. Brady, 268(IFR):Winter85-60
    R. Gibson, 402(MLR):Jul84-713
    J. Murray, 207(FR):Dec84-299
    A.H. Pasco, 446(NCFS):Winter-Spring85-
    169
    S.L. Wolitz, 395(MFS):Winter84-717
Hughes, G. Barns of Rural Britain.
    A. Gomme, 617(TLS):23Aug85-934
    S. Jenkins, 362:5Sep85-25
Hughes, G.E. - see Buridan, J.
Hughes, G.R. Emerson's Demanding Optimism.
    T.D. Armstrong, 617(TLS):13Sep85-1012
Hughes, H.S. Prisoners of Hope.*
    E. Roditi, 390:Nov84-53
Hughes, J.M. Emotion and High Politics.*
    K.A.P. Sandiford, 637(VS):Summer84-529
Hughes, K., ed and trans. Franz Kafka.*
    R.C. Davis, 579(SAQ):Summer84-357
Hughes, M. Hunter in the Dark.
    M.J. Evans, 102(CanL):Autumn84-63
Hughes, M. - see Cardus, N.
Hughes, P. Behind the Rainbow.
    J. Burr, 39:Mar84-223
Hughes, P., with J. Hemlow - see Burney, F.
Hughes, R. Fiction as Truth. (R. Poole,
ed)
    J. Hamard, 189(EA):Oct-Dec85-480
Hughes, T. River.*
    R.B. Hatch, 648(WCR):Apr84-47
    E. Longley, 493:Jan84-58
    639(VQR):Autumn84-138
Hughes, T. Gabrielle Roy et Margaret
Laurence.
    M. Chabot, 628(UWR):Spring-Summer85-
    104
    B. Godard, 627(UTQ):Summer84-479
Hughes, T. - see Plath, S.
Hughey, M.W. Civil Religion and Moral
Order.
    J.I.C., 185:Jul85-986
Hugo, R. Making Certain it Goes On.*
    M.S. Allen, 649(WAL):Nov84-236
    J.D. McClatchy, 491:Feb85-291
                                [continued]

[continuing]
    W.H. Pritchard, 249(HudR):Summer84-337
    D. Wojahn, 651(WHR):Autumn84-261
    639(VQR):Summer84-91
Hugo, R. Sea Lanes Out.
    S.C., 219(GaR):Summer84-441
    L. Runciman, 649(WAL):May84-51
Hugo, V. The Distance, The Shadows. (H.
Guest, trans)
    N. Rinsler, 208(FS):Jul84-354
Hugo, V. Odes et Ballades. (P. Albouy,
ed)
    W.J.S. Kirton, 208(FS):Jan84-74
Huizenga, J. Looking at American Signs.
Looking at American Recreation. Looking
at American Food.
    B. Powell, 399(MLJ):Autumn84-310
Huizinga, J. Men and Ideas.
    617(TLS):5Apr85-395
Hulin, M., ed and trans. Mrgendrāgama.
    J. Borelli, 318(JAOS):Apr-Jun83-435
Hull, C. and J. Murrell. Techniques of
Pewtersmithing.
    D. Hayward, 324:Jul85-580
Hull, G.T. - see Dunbar-Nelson, A.
Hull, S.W. Chaste, Silent and Obedient.*
    N. Linnell, 354:Mar84-98
    J. Tormey, 322(JHI):Oct-Dec84-619
Hulliung, M. Citizen Machiavelli.*
    T.A.S., 185:Jan85-396
Hulme, K. The Bone People.
    A. Beevor, 617(TLS):25Oct85-1202
    A. Huth, 362:24Oct85-33
    C. Tate, 441:17Nov85-11
Hulse, C. Metamorphic Verse.*
    H. Morris, 569(SR):Spring84-290
    F. Mouret, 549(RLC):Oct-Dec84-487
    R.S. White, 541(RES):Aug84-363
Hulse, M. Propaganda.
    S. Romer, 617(TLS):29Nov85-1370
van Hulsen, E. and M. Merian. Repraesenta-
tio der fvrstlichen Avfzvg vnd Ritter-
spil.
    R. Hildebrandt, 685(ZDL):1/1984-123
van der Hulst, H. and N. Smith, eds. The
Structure of Phonological Representa-
tions.
    D. Goyvaerts, 297(JL):Sep84-365
Hult, G. Hala Sultan Tekke, 7.
    Y. Calvet, 555:Vol58fasc1-107
Hulton, P., ed. America 1585.*
    E. Emerson, 578:Fall85-125
"Human Procreation."
    S.G.P., 185:Jul85-990
"Human Rights in Latin America, 1964-1980."
    D. Padilla, 263(RIB):Vol34No3/4-429
Hume, A. Edmund Spenser.*
    B. Tannier, 189(EA):Apr-Jun85-232
Hume, A., ed. A Birdwatcher's Miscellany.
    S. Mills, 617(TLS):18Jan85-73
Hume, R.D. The Rakish Stage.
    B. Corman, 566:Autumn84-57
    C. Spencer, 130:Fall84-274
    H. Weber, 401(MLQ):Dec83-429
    J.A. Winn, 615(TJ):Mar84-132
Humes, H. Winter Weeds.*
    639(VQR):Summer84-91
Humes, W.M. and H.M. Paterson, eds. Scot-
tish Culture and Scottish Education 1800-
1980.
    L. Hartveit, 179(ES):Apr84-185
Hume, A. and N. ABC et Cetera.
    S.K. Sperling, 441:15Dec85-23

179

Husserl, E. Ideas Pertaining to A Pure
Phenomenology and to A Phenomenological
Philosophy. (Vol 1)
R. Sokolowski, 543:Mar84-640
Husserl, E. Logique formelle et logique
transcendentale.
T. Cordellier, 450(NRF):Sep84-103
Hussey, E. - see Aristotle
Hussey, S.S. The Literary Language of
Shakespeare.*
A. Ward, 447(N&Q):Oct83-451
Hussey, W. Patron of Art.
C. Reid, 617(TLS):7Jun85-640
Hussman, L.E., Jr. Dreiser and His Fic-
tion.
W. Baker, 42(AR):Fall84-503
R.W. Dowell, 395(MFS):Summer84-304
D. Pizer, 587(SAF):Autumn84-235
J.A. Robinson, 27(AL):May84-284
295(JML):Nov84-429
Hustad, A-M. Rekrutskie plachi — Recruit-
ing Laments.
E. Warner, 575(SEER):Oct84-633
Huston, J.D. Shakespeare's Comedies of
Play.
C. Hoy, 569(SR):Spring84-256
M. Novy, 405(MP):Aug84-98
R.Y. Turner, 570(SQ):Summer84-254
Hutcheon, L. Narcissistic Narrative.*
J. Levine, 102(CanL):Winter83-121
Hutcheon, L. A Theory of Parody.
T. Hawkes, 617(TLS):27Sep85-1075
Hutchings, A. Purcell.*
N.F., 410(M&L):Oct84-362
Hutchings, B. The Poetry of William Cow-
per.
V. Newey, 83:Autumn84-247
Hutchings, E. - see Feynman, R.P., with R.
Leighton
Hutchings, R. The Soviet Budget.
M.D. Dietrich, 575(SEER):Oct84-620
C.W. Lewis, 550(RusR):Oct84-441
Hutchinson, E.P. Legislative History of
American Immigration Policy 1798-1965.
P.A.M. Taylor, 161(DUJ):Dec83-123
Hutchinson, J. Letters.
W. Gardner, 324:Dec84-71
Hutchinson, P. Games Authors Play.*
J.J. Sosnoski, 395(MFS):Winter84-849
Hutchinson, S. Henry James.*
A.W. Bellringer, 402(MLR):Oct84-917
S. Perosa, 395(MFS):Summer84-295
Huters, T. Qian Zhongshu.*
E.M. Gunn, 116:Jul83-119
Huth, A. Wanting.*
S. Laschever, 441:25Aug85-16
Hutt, M. Chouannerie and Counter-Revolu-
tion.*
N. Ravitch, 173(ECS):Spring85-448
Hüttl-Folter, G. Die trat/torot-Lexeme in
den altrussischen Chroniken.
D. Freydank, 559:Vol8No3-313
Hutton, J. Themes of Peace in Renaissance
Poetry. (R. Guerlac, ed)
J. Bate, 617(TLS):13Dec85-1436
Hutton, R. The Restoration.
J. Miller, 617(TLS):26Jul85-830
Hutton, R. The Royalist War Effort 1642-
1646.
P. Christianson, 529(QQ):Autumn84-635
R.R. Rea, 577(SHR):Winter84-83

Huussen, A.H., Jr. Grillen des Verlicht-
ing.
W.R. Augustine, 104(CASS):Spring-
Summer84-190
Huxley, A. Green Inheritance.
M. Jebb, 617(TLS):3May85-507
Huxtable, A.L. The Tall Building Artisti-
cally Reconsidered.
M. Filler, 453(NYRB):5Dec85-11
C.W. Moore, 441:23Jun85-22
Huygens, L. The English Journal, 1651-
1652.* (A.G.H. Bachrach and R.G. Coll-
mer, eds and trans)
J.D. Bangs, 551(RenQ):Summer84-277
P.R. Sellin, 405(MP):May85-424
Huygens, R.B.C. De constructione castri
Saphet.
D. Pringle, 589:Jan84-165
Huỳnh Sanh Thông, ed and trans. The Her-
itage of Vietnamese Poetry.
D-H. Nguyen, 318(JAOS):Jul-Sep83-648
Huyssen, A. and others, eds. The Techno-
logical Imagination.
M. Silberman, 406:Fall84-344
Hyde, A. The Red Fox.
T.J. Binyon, 617(TLS):27Dec85-1478
J. Skvorecky, 441:1Sep85-8
442(NY):23Sep85-118
Hyde, G.M. D.H. Lawrence and the Art of
Translation.
J. Worthen, 447(N&Q):Jun83-262
Hyde, H.M. Lord Alfred Douglas.
S. Marcus, 441:17Nov85-7
J. Stokes, 617(TLS):12Jul85-778
Hyde, H.M. - see Wilde, O.
Hyde, L. The Gift.*
S.C., 219(GaR):Fall84-663
S. Paul, 271:Fall84-200
Hyde, L., ed. On the Poetry of Allen Gins-
berg.
L. Mackinnon, 617(TLS):24May85-574
Hyde, M. - see Shaw, G.B. and A. Douglas
Hyde-Chambers, F.R. Lama.
K. Ray, 441:14Jul85-22
Hyginus. Hygin, "L'Astronomie." (A.
Le Boeuffle, ed and trans)
P. Flobert, 555:Vol58fasc2-328
Hyland, G. Just Off Main.*
I. Sowton, 102(CanL):Autumn84-125
Hyland, P. Poems of Z.
R. Pybus, 565:Winter83/84-68
Hyland, P. Wight.
P. Cox, 617(TLS):15Mar85-299
Hyman, A. Charles Babbage, Pioneer of the
Computer.
617(TLS):10May85-531
Hyman, B.D. My Mother's Keeper.
P. Chaplin, 617(TLS):22Nov85-1338
J. Eidus, 441:9Jun85-23
Hyman, H.M. and W.M. Wiecek. Equal
Justice Under Law.
J.E. Semonche, 579(SAQ):Spring84-238
Hyman, V.D. and W.C.C. Hu. Carpets of
China and its Border Regions.
U. Roberts, 60:Jan-Feb84-120
Hymes, D., ed. Studies in the History of
Linguistics.
J. Nichols, 545(RPh):Aug83-72
Hyneman, C.S. and D.S. Lutz, eds. Ameri-
can Political Writing During the Found-
ing Era, 1760-1805.*
A.R.L. Cayton, 173(ECS):Summer85-565
Hynes, S. - see Hardy, T.

180

Hyvönen, H. Russian Porcelain.
C.T., 90:May84-303

Iacocca, L., with W. Novak. Iacocca.*
M. Dowie, 617(TLS):29Mar85-343
M.S. Krossel, 129:May85-74
Iakovidis, S.E. Late Hellenic Citadels on
Mainland Greece.
D. Field, 303(JoHS):Vol 104-245
Ibargüengoitia, J. Two Crimes.*
P. Lewis, 364:Oct84-93
"Iberiul-k'avk'asiuri enactmecnierebis
c'elic'deuli." (Vol 5)
G.F. Meier, 682(ZPSK):Band37Heft3-391
Ibn al-'Arīf. Maḥāsin al-Majālis. (W.
Elliot and A.K. Abdalla, trans)
A. Schimmel, 318(JAOS):Oct-Dec83-809
Ibn Gabirol, S. Selección de Perlas. (D.
Gonzalo Maeso, trans)
E. Roditi, 390:Jan84-50
Ibuse, M. Black Rain.
F.M. Halloran, 441:8Sep85-14
Idema, W. and S.H. West. Chinese Theater
1100-1450.
W.O. Hennessey, 293(JASt):Aug84-743
V.H. Mair, 244(HJAS):Jun84-266
Ientile, M.G. - see under Giuffrida
Ientile, M.
Iffland, J. Quevedo and the Grotesque.
(Vol 2)
C.B. Johnson, 304(JHP):Winter84-171
Iffland, J., ed. Quevedo in Perspective.
L.S. Lerner, 240(HR):Summer84-403
P.J. Smith, 402(MLR):Jul84-730
Ifrah, G. From One to Zero.
J.A. Paulos, 441:29Sep85-13
Ifri, P.A. Proust et son narrataire dans
"A la Recherche du temps perdu."*
R. Gibson, 208(FS):Oct84-483
P. Rogers, 546(RR):May84-393
de la Iglesia, M.R.S. - see under Saurín
de la Iglesia, M.R.
Ignatieff, G. The Making of a Peacemonger.
H.S. Ferns, 617(TLS):8Nov85-1268
Ignatieff, M. The Needs of Strangers.*
A. Tonelson, 441:5May85-20
Ignatow, D. Leaving the Door Open.
J.F. Cotter, 249(HudR):Autumn84-502
G. Kuzma, 219(GaR):Winter84-901
639(VQR):Autumn84-137
Ignatow, D. Open Between Us. (R.J. Mills,
Jr., ed)
B. Raffel, 363(LitR):Fall84-154
Ignatow, Y. The Flaw.*
639(VQR):Winter84-23
Ihle, S.N. Malory's Grail Quest.
A.H. Diverres, 208(FS):Apr84-192
J.R. Goodman, 589:Jul84-721
J. Jesmok, 401(MLQ):Dec83-419
C. Lee, 379(MedR):Apr84-135
G.R. Mermier, 207(FR):May85-884
Ihrie, M. Skepticism in Cervantes.*
D. Finello, 238:Mar84-142
M.D. McGaha, 593:Spring84-85
Ikko, T. and K. Kazuko, eds. Japan Design.
R.L.S., 614:Winter85-26
Ilari, V. Guerra e diritto nel mondo
antico. (Vol 1)
D.J. Mosley, 303(JoHS):Vol 104-238
Ilie, P. Literature and Inner Exile.*
M.L. Bretz, 345(KRQ):Vol31No1-105

"I'll Take My Stand."
M. Hudson, 577(SHR):Winter84-87
Illyés, E. National Minorities in Romania.
D. Deletant, 575(SEER):Oct84-612
L.K.D. Kristof, 104(CASS):Fall84-360
Ilting, K.H. - see Hegel, G.W.F.
Imbert, P. Roman québécois contemporain
et cliché.
P. Hébert, 627(UTQ):Summer84-471
Imdahl, M. Arbeiter diskutieren moderne
Kunst.
M. Warnke, 384:Jul84-567
Imdahl, M. Giotto: Arenafresken.
R. Salvini, 683:Band47Heft1-126
Imfeld, A. Verlernen, was mich stumm
macht.
F. Schulze, 538(RAL):Fall84-485
Imfeld, A. Vision und Waffe.
F. Schulze, 538(RAL):Fall84-486
Imhof, H. Rilkes "Gott."
B.L. Bradley, 301(JEGP):Oct84-612
Im Hof, U. Das gesellige Jahrhundert.
P.F. Veit, 221(GQ):Winter84-166
Imo, W. Wirklichkeitsauffassung und Wick-
lichkeitsdarstellung im Erzählwerk Julio
Cortázars.
K. Kohut, 72:Band221Heft1-232
Imperato, P.J. Buffoons, Queens and
Wooden Horsemen.
D. Zahan, 2(AfrA):Aug84-90
Imperato, P.J. and G. Mitchell. Accept-
able Risks.
G. Bylinsky, 441:10Mar85-14
Imrie, J. and J.G. Dunbar, eds. Accounts
of the Masters of Works. (Vol 2)
H. Colvin, 46:Feb84-76
Inbar, E.M. Shakespeare in Deutschland:
Der Fall Lenz.*
B. Duncan, 301(JEGP):Apr84-280
"Incipit."
D.W. Lomax, 86(BHS):Jan84-64
"Index of Manuscripts in the British Lib-
rary." (Vol 1)
D. Vaisey, 617(TLS):25Jan85-103
"Index to Selected Bibliographical Jour-
nals 1933-1970."
B.J. McMullin, 517(PBSA):Vol78No1-57
"Indian Book Review Digest." (Vol 1) (B.
Chaudhuri, ed)
J. Masselos, 302:Vol20No2-253
Ineichen, G., ed. Romanische Bibliogra-
phie 1975-1976.
W. Kowalk, 547(RF):Band96Heft1/2-101
Ineichen, G. - see Renzi, L.
Infante, G.C. - see under Cabrera Infante,
G.
Ingalls, R. Three of a Kind.
C. Greenland, 617(TLS):25Oct85-1202
Ingamells, J. The English Episcopal Por-
trait 1559-1835.
M. Rogers, 90:Apr84-239
Inge, M.T. and E.E. MacDonald, eds. James
Branch Cabell.
W.J. Stuckey, 395(MFS):Summer84-316
van Ingen, F. and H-G. Roloff - see Beer,
J.
Ingenschay-Goch, D. Richard Wangers neu
erfundener Mythos.
H.R. Vaget, 221(GQ):Summer84-509
Ingham, M. Men.
P.P. Read, 617(TLS):29Mar85-364

Islam, N. Foreign Trade and Economic Controls in Development.
  P. Streeten, 293(JASt):Nov83-184
Isler, H.P. and others. Greek Vases from the Hirschmann Collection. (H. Bloesch, ed)
  B.A. Sparkes, 303(JoHS):Vol 104-258
Israel, J.I. The Dutch Republic and the Hispanic World, 1606-1661.
  B.L. Parker, 568(SCN):Fall84-45
Israel, L. Estée Lauder.
  M. Bender, 441:17Nov85-16
Israeli, R. Muslims in China.
  A.E. Dien, 302:Vol20No2-203
  J.N. Lipman, 293(JASt):Nov83-152
Issacharoff, M. and J-C. Vilquin, eds. Sartre et la mise en signe.*
  C. Howells, 208(FS):Oct84-489
  C. Krance, 494:Vol4No1-195
Issel, W. Social Change in the United States 1945-83.
  S.E. Ambrose, 617(TLS):14Jun85-658
Isserman, M. Which Side Were You On?
  T. Draper, 453(NYRB):9May85-32
  T. Draper, 453(NYRB):30May85-44
Issorel, J., ed. Edición facsímil de Papel de Aleluyas.
  R.A. Cardwell, 86(BHS):Jan84-54
Itaya, K. Tengu Child.* (J. Gardner and N. Tsukui, eds and trans)
  Y.K. Dykstra, 407(MN):Spring84-97
Ito, H. The Language of "The Spectator."
  F. Rau, 224(GRM):Band34Heft3-366
Itwaru, A. Shattered Songs.*
  I. Sowton, 102(CanL):Winter83-154
de Iuliis, C. Love's Sinning Song and Other Poems.
  U. Parameswaran, 102(CanL):Winter83-144
Ivanov, V.I. and M.O. Gershenzon. Correspondence Across a Room.
  J. Daynard, 441:21Apr85-25
Ivens, D. Main-Course Soups and Stews.
  W. and C. Cowen, 639(VQR):Spring84-67
Ives, S., ed. The Parkman Dexter Howe Library. (Pt 1)
  E. Emerson, 432(NEQ):Sep84-442
Iwaichi, F. - see under Fujiwara Iwaichi
Iwaniuk, W. Evenings on Lake Ontario.*
  U. Parameswaran, 102(CanL):Winter83-144
Izutsu, T. and T. The Theory of Beauty in the Classical Aesthetics of Japan.
  S. Heine, 485(PE&W):Apr84-227

Jabès, E. The Sin of the Book. (E. Gould, ed)
  B. Harlow, 441:14Apr85-27
Jaccottet, P. Pensées sous les nuages.*
  D. Leuwers, 450(NRF):Apr84-99
Jaccottet, P. La Semaison: 1954-1979.*
  C. Dis, 450(NRF):Jul/Aug84-153
Jack, I. - see Sterne, L.
Jack, I. and M. Smith - see Browning, R.
Jack, R.D.S. and R.J. Lyall - see Urquhart, T.
Jack, R.D.S. and A. Noble, eds. The Art of Robert Burns.*
  T. Crawford, 571(ScLJ):Autumn84-1
  D.A. Low, 541(RES):Nov84-556
Jäckel, E. Hitler in History.
  F. Stern, 441:12May85-7

Jackel, S., ed. A Flannel Shirt and Liberty.*
  L.K. Smedick, 649(WAL):Aug84-150
Jackman, J.C. and C.M. Borden, eds. The Muses Flee Hitler.
  M. Webber, 564:Sep84-229
  S.J. Whitfield, 385(MQR):Fall85-634
Jackowska, N. Earthwalks.*
  J. Saunders, 565:Spring84-55
Jackson, A.M. Illustration and the Novels of Thomas Hardy.*
  N. Pickwoad, 541(RES):May84-272
Jackson, B. Law and Disorder.
  A.M. Dershowitz, 441:17Mar85-30
Jackson, C. Who Will Take Our Children?
  B. Bainbridge, 617(TLS):17May85-554
Jackson, C.T. The Oriental Religions and American Thought.*
  K.P. Pedersen, 485(PE&W):Jan84-95
Jackson, D. Voyages of the Steamboat Yellow Stone.
  J. Daynard, 441:27Oct85-41
Jackson, H.J., ed. Editing Polymaths.
  C. Spadoni, 470:Vol22-130
Jackson, J.E. La Mort Baudelaire.
  G. Chesters, 402(MLR):Jan84-198
  R. Lloyd, 208(FS):Oct84-474
Jackson, J.R.D. - see Coleridge, S.T.
Jackson, M. Allegories of the Wilderness.*
  P.M. Peek, 650(WF):Oct84-281
  P. Seitel, 292(JAF):Jul-Sep84-352
Jackson, M.P. and V. O'Sullivan. The Oxford Book of New Zealand Writing Since 1945.
  R.L. Buckland, 573(SSF):Spring84-164
Jackson, N.S. Vinegar Pie and Chicken Bread.* (M.J. Bolsterli, ed)
  L.E. Harding, 585(SoQ):Winter84-94
Jackson, R., ed. Acts of Mind.*
  C. Wright, 219(GaR):Fall84-639
Jackson, R. Fantasy.*
  J. Birkett, 208(FS):Jan84-107
  E.S. Rabkin, 223:Winter81-523
  A.L. Smith, 183(ESQ):Vol30No4-260
Jackson, R. - see Jones, H.A.
Jackson, R.A. Vive le Roi!
  P. Burke, 617(TLS):25Jan85-81
Jackson, S. Childhood and Sexuality.
  W.W. Watters, 529(QQ):Spring84-230
Jackson, W. Vision and Re-vision in Alexander Pope.*
  M.R. Brownell, 301(JEGP):Apr84-241
  J. King, 173(ECS):Summer85-574
Jackson, W., W. Berry and B. Colman, eds. Meeting the Expectations of the Land.
  F. Graham, Jr., 441:7Apr85-23
Jackson, W.E. Reinmar's Women.*
  I. Glier, 221(GQ):Fall84-640
  H-H.S. Räkel, 564:May84-130
  382(MAE):1984/2-339
Jackson, W.H., ed. Knighthood in Medieval Literature.
  C. Lee, 379(MedR):Aug84-315
Jackson, W.T.H. The Hero and the King.*
  M. Curschmann, 221(GQ):Summer84-463
  W.R. Johnson, 405(MP):Nov84-226
  382(MAE):1984/2-338
Jackson-Stops, G., ed. The Treasure Houses of Britain.
  D. Cannadine, 453(NYRB):19Dec85-17
  L. Colley, 617(TLS):15Nov85-1293

Jakobson, R. and L. Waugh. Le charpente phonique du langage.
R. Sasso, 192(EP):Jan-Mar84-115
Jallat, J. Introduction aux figures valéryennes.
M-F.E. Baer, 446(NCFS):Winter-Spring85-165
U. Franklin, 207(FR):May85-897
Jamālzādeh, S.M.A. Isfahan is Half the World.*
G.M. Wickens, 529(QQ):Autumn84-751
JamaspAsa, K.M., ed and trans. Aogəmadaēcā.
F.M. Kotwal, 259(IIJ):Apr84-163
D.N. MacKenzie, 260(IF):Band89-320
Jambet, C. La logique des Orientaux.
A. Reix, 542:Apr-Jun84-254
James I of Scotland. The Kingis Quair.*
(J. Norton-Smith, ed)
A. Hudson, 541(RES):Aug84-434
King James VI and I. Letters of James VI and I.* (G.P.V. Akrigg, ed)
J. Kenyon, 617(TLS):3May85-488
James, A. and P. Westney, eds. New Linguistic Impulses in Foreign Language Teaching.
R.J. Alexander, 257(IRAL):Feb84-79
James, B. The Bill James Historical Baseball Abstract.
L.S. Ritter, 441:8Dec85-20
James, B. The Music of Jean Sibelius.*
S. Johnson, 415:Dec84-705
James, C. Falling Towards England.
R. Davies, 362:12Sep85-26
E. Korn, 617(TLS):13Sep85-995
James, C. Flying Visits.*
W. Scammell, 364:Dec84/Jan85-154
James, C.J., ed. Practical Applications of Research in Foreign Language Teaching.
E.G. Joiner, 399(MLJ):Summer84-156
James, D. Georg Büchner's "Dantons Tod."
J. Guthrie, 402(MLR):Apr84-498
D.G. Richards, 221(GQ):Fall84-666
James, D.C. The Years of MacArthur. (Vol 3)
D. Middleton, 441:25Aug85-8
James, H. All the Forgotten Places.
D.E. Alsobrook, 9(AlaR):Jan84-69
James, H. Carnets. (F.O. Matthiessen and K.B. Murdock, eds; L. Servicen, trans)
C. Jordis, 450(NRF):Jul/Aug84-184
James, H. Henry James: Autobiography. (F.W. Dupee, ed)
F. Wegener, 676(YR):Winter85-269
James, H. Henry James: Letters. (Vols 1-3) (L. Edel, ed)
D. Flower, 249(HudR):Autumn84-461
James, H. Henry James: Letters.* (Vol 4) (L. Edel, ed)
D. Flower, 249(HudR):Autumn84-461
R.W.B. Lewis, 676(YR):Winter85-261
A.R. Tintner, 26(ALR):Autumn84-264
James, H. Henry James: Literary Criticism. (L. Edel, with M. Wilson, eds)
H. Beaver, 617(TLS):22Nov85-1327
L. Bersani, 61:Mar85-120
K.S. Lynn, 129:Jun85-73
S. Perosa, 441:17Feb85-7
James, H. Henry James: Novels 1871-1880. (W.T. Stafford, ed)
M. Deakin, 395(MFS):Winter84-791

James, H. Henry James: Selected Tales.* (P. Messent and T. Paulin, eds)
J. Tyler, 447(N&Q):Aug83-364
James, H. The Tales. (Vol 3) (M. Aziz, ed)
N. Bradbury, 617(TLS):8Mar85-264
James, M.R. - see Map, W.
James, R.R. Prince Albert.* (British title: Albert, Prince Consort.)
R.K. Webb, 441:3Mar85-17
James, S. The Content of Social Explanation.
Z. Bauman, 617(TLS):22Feb85-211
James, W. The Works of William James. (Vols 7 and 9) (F. Burkhardt, ed)
M. Vetö, 192(EP):Jan-Mar84-116
James, W.C. - see Twomey, A.C.
Jameson, F. The Political Unconscious.*
M. Clark, 435:Spring84-67
D.S. Gross, 223:Summer81-271
J. Howard, 435:Spring84-52
J. Iffland, 435:Spring84-36
C.P. James, 435:Spring84-59
J.H. Kavanagh, 435:Spring84-20
J-F. Lyotard, 435:Spring84-73
L. Mykyta, 435:Spring84-46
M. Ryan, 435:Spring84-29
Jamieson, K.H. Packaging the Presidency.*
G. Peele, 617(TLS):24May85-577
Jamme, C. and O. Pöggeler, eds. Homburg von der Höhe in der deutschen Geistesgeschichte.
N. Waszek, 402(MLR):Apr84-495
Jammer, M. Das Problem des Raumes.
M. Heller, 543:Dec83-402
Jammes, A. and E.P. Janis. The Art of French Calotype.
C. East, 219(GaR):Spring84-193
R. Pickvance, 90:Jun84-365
Jammes, F. Clairières dans le Ciel.
D. Steel, 208(FS):Jan84-84
Jammes, R. - see de Góngora, L.
Jamyn, A. Les Oeuvres poétiques. (Bks 2-4) (S.M. Carrington, ed)
I.D. McFarlane, 208(FS):Jul84-330
Jancey, M., ed. St. Thomas Cantilupe, Bishop of Hereford.
H.S. Offler, 161(DUJ):Dec83-115
Janelli, R.L. and D.Y. Ancestor Worship and Korean Society.
B.S. Hoe, 292(JAF):Oct-Dec84-476
Janert, K.L. and N.N. Poti, eds. Yākka Sālēre Kathe.
I.V. Peterson, 318(JAOS):Oct-Dec83-780
Janes, R. Gabriel García Márquez.*
G.H. Bell-Villada, 454:Spring85-281
Janeway, E. Cross Sections from a Decade of Change.
S. Brown, 569(SR):Fall84-649
Jangfeldt, B., ed. V.V. Maiakovskii i L. Iu. Brik: Perepiska 1915-1930.
Z. Folejewski, 104(CASS):Spring-Summer84-165
J. Graffy, 575(SEER):Apr84-269
Janicaud, D. and J-F. Mattéi. La métaphysique à la limite.*
M. Haar, 192(EP):Jan-Mar84-116
T. Rockmore, 258:Mar84-98
Janicki, K. The Foreigner's Language in a Sociolinguistic Perspective.
S. Wojnicki, 355(LSoc):Dec84-548

Janics, K. Czechoslovak Policy and the
Hungarian Minority, 1945-1948.
F.L. Kaplan, 104(CASS):Fall84-358
Janik, D.I. The Curve of Return.
W.C. Latta, Jr., 49:Jul84-107
Jankel, A. and R. Morton. Creative Com-
puter Graphics.
M. Asnes, 441:21Apr85-38
Janko, R. Homer, Hesiod and the Hymns.*
N. Postlethwaite, 303(JoHS):Vol 104-
192
Jan Mohamed, A.R. Manichean Aesthetics.
M. Fabre, 189(EA):Oct-Dec85-494
C.L. Innes, 538(RAL):Fall84-420
C. Sarvan, 395(MFS):Summer84-431
Janney, F. Alejo Carpentier and his Early
Works.
J. Labanyi, 402(MLR):Apr84-479
Janning, J. and others, eds. Gott im
Märchen.
H. Rölleke, 196:Band25Heft3/4-344
Janos, A.C. The Politics of Backwardness
in Hungary, 1825-1945.
R. Okey, 575(SEER):Jan84-128
S.Z. Pech, 104(CASS):Spring-Summer84-
220
Janowitz, M. The Reconstruction of Patri-
otism.*
N. Bliven, 442(NY):11Feb85-120
J.D. Moon, 185:Apr85-765
Janowitz, P. Visiting Rites.
A. Fulton, 385(MQR):Summer85-492
Jansen, E., ed. Ernst Barlach.
J. Lloyd, 90:Feb84-98
Jansen, M. A Show Trial Under Lenin.*
J. Burbank, 550(RusR):Jan84-85
R.A. Wade, 104(CASS):Fall84-314
Janson, H.W. 19th-Century Sculpture.
C.B. McGee, 441:30Jun85-20
Janssen, A. Francis Godwin's "The Man in
the Moone."
A. Grün-Oesterreich, 72:Band221Heft1-
182
W. von Koppenfels, 38:Band102Heft3/4-
539
Janssen, H. Das sogenannte "Genre objek-
tif."
J. Goheen, 406:Summer84-205
Jansson, B. Trolösheten.
P. Buvik, 172(Edda):1984/5-305
Jansson, E. India, Pakistan or Pakhtun-
istan?
D. Gilmartin, 293(JASt):Feb84-358
Janvier, L. Naissance.
D. Gunn, 617(TLS):2Aug85-856
F. de Martinoir, 450(NRF):Oct84-87
Janz, C.P. Nietzsche. (Vol 1)
T. Cordellier, 450(NRF):Jul/Aug84-166
Janz, C.P. Friedrich Nietzsche Biographie.
J. Kjaer, 462(OL):Vol139No2-174
Janzen, J.M. Lemba, 1650-1930.
P. Riesman, 538(RAL):Winter84-624
P. Stevens, Jr., 2(AfrA):May84-29
Jarczyk, G. Système et liberté dans la
logique de Hegel.
A. Renaut, 192(EP):Jan-Mar84-119
Jardin, A. Histoire du libéralisme poli-
tique.
J-F. Revel, 176:May85-36
Jardin, A. and A-J. Tudesq. Restoration
and Reaction, 1815-1848.
T. Judt, 617(TLS):1Mar85-234

Jardine, L. Still Harping on Daughters.
T. Helton, 568(SCN):Fall84-40
C. Kahn, 570(SQ):Winter84-489
M. Knapp, 615(TJ):May84-281
Jarka, H. - see Soyfer, J.
Jarman, D. Kurt Weill.
J. Fuegi, 221(GQ):Fall84-689
D.J. Jung, 615(TJ):Oct84-444
Jarman, M. The Rote Walker.
R. McDowell, 364:Feb85-42
Jarolim, E. - see Blackburn, P.
Jarrell, R. Randall Jarrell's Letters.
(M. Jarrell, with S. Wright, eds)
C. Benfey, 453(NYRB):9May85-29
A. Broyard, 441:19May85-11
B. Quinn, 578:Fall85-121
Jarvis, A.C., R. Lebredo and F. Mena.
Basic Spanish Grammar. (2nd ed)
J.S. Bailey, 399(MLJ):Winter84-416
Jarvis, A.C., R. Lebredo and F. Mena.
¡Continuemos! (2nd ed)
E. Spinelli, 399(MLJ):Summer84-192
Jarzębski, J. Gra w Gombrowicza.
N. Taylor, 575(SEER):Oct84-590
de Jasay, A. The State.
M. Rosen, 617(TLS):26Jul85-812
Jasmin, C. Les Contes du Sommet-Bleu.
C.R. La Bossiere, 102(CanL):Winter83-
125
Jasmin, C. Maman-Paris Maman-la-France.
J. Cotnam, 102(CanL):Autumn84-58
Jasper, D. Coleridge as Poet and Reli-
gious Thinker.
P. Hamilton, 617(TLS):27Dec85-1484
Jastrow, R. How to Make Nuclear Weapons
Obsolete.
W.J. Broad, 441:7Jul85-10
Jauralde Pou, P. Manual de investigación
literaria.*
H. Sonneville, 356(LR):Feb/May84-119
Jauss, H.R. Aesthetic Experience and Lit-
erary Hermeneutics.* (German title:
Ästhetische Erfahrung und literarische
Hermeneutik.)
H.R. Brittnacher, 224(GRM):Band34
Heft1/2-245
W. Kendrick, 613:Dec84-516
D. Kremers, 547(RF):Band96Heft3-322
W. Raible, 490:Band16Heft3/4-371
R. Rochlitz, 98:Nov84-864
Jauss, H.R. Toward an Aesthetic of Recep-
tion.*
W. Kendrick, 613:Dec84-516
R. Machin, 89(BJA):Spring84-184
Javor, P. Far From You.
U. Parameswaran, 102(CanL):Winter83-
144
Jay, D. Sterling.
W.A.P. Manser, 617(TLS):24May85-585
Jay, E., ed. The Evangelical and Oxford
Movements.*
J.M. le Bour'his, 189(EA):Jan-Mar85-
88
506(PSt):Sep84-203
Jay, G.S. T.S. Eliot and the Poetics of
Literary History.*
C. Baxter, 141:Spring84-206
M. Dickie, 301(JEGP):Oct84-583
W.V. Harris, 651(WHR):Spring84-93
G.G. Leithauser, 478:Oct84-296
L. Woodman, 27(AL):Dec84-613
295(JML):Nov84-431
639(VQR):Spring84-45

Jay, P. Being in the Text.
   A. Reed, 661(WC):Summer84-138
   S. Scobie, 376:Oct84-107
   639(VQR):Autumn84-126
Jaye, M.C. and A.C. Watts, eds. Litera-
   ture and the Urban Experience.*
   R. Lehan, 405(MP):Nov84-230
Jeal, T. Livingstone.
   617(TLS):7Jun85-651
Jean, G. Paroles d'Acadie et d'après.
   E. Hamblet, 207(FR):Oct84-160
Jean de la Croix. Poésies complètes. (B.
   Sesé, trans)
   G. Quinsat, 450(NRF):Feb84-89
Jeannotte, M. Le vent n'a pas d'écho.*
   I. Joubert, 298:Fall84-164
   L. Martineau, 207(FR):Mar85-600
Jeanson, F. Sartre and the Problem of
   Morality.
   M. Warnock, 482(PhR):Apr84-303
Jedruch, J. Constitutions, Elections and
   Legislatures of Poland, 1493-1977.*
   M. Siekierski, 550(RusR):Apr84-220
Jeffares, A.N. A New Commentary on the
   Poems of W.B. Yeats.*
   D. Albright, 453(NYRB):31Jan85-29
Jeffares, A.N., ed. Yeats, Sligo and Ire-
   land.*
   C.F. Totten, 174(Éire):Spring84-153
Jefferies, A. High Jinx.
   J. Forbes, 381:Sep84-453
Jeffers, H.P. Murder on Mike.
   N. Callendar, 441:14Apr85-16
Jefferson, A. The Complete Gilbert and
   Sullivan Opera Guide.
   A. Lamb, 415:Dec84-704
Jefferson, A. The Nouveau Roman and the
   Poetics of Fiction.*
   B. McHale, 494:Summer82-211
Jefferson, A. and D. Robey, eds. Modern
   Literary Theory.*
   R. Cardinal, 494:Vol5No1-156
Jefferson, G. Edward Garnett.
   D. Gray, 637(VS):Summer84-509
   295(JML):Nov84-446
Jefferson, T. Thomas Jefferson: Collected
   Works. (M.D. Peterson, ed)
   D.A.N. Jones, 362:4Apr85-26
Jefferson, T. Jefferson's Extracts from
   the Gospels. (D.W. Adams, with R.W.
   Lester, eds)
   F. Shuffelton, 165(EAL):Winter84/85-
   304
   C. Wright, 656(WMQ):Apr84-319
Jefferson, T. The Papers of Thomas Jeff-
   erson. (Vol 20) (J.P. Boyd and R.W.
   Lester, eds)
   N.E. Cunningham, Jr., 579(SAQ):
   Summer84-340
"Thomas Jefferson: Writings." (M.D. Peter-
   son, ed)
   H.S. Commager, 441:7Jul85-19
Jeffery, K. The British Army and the
   Crisis of Empire 1918-22.
   J. Gooch, 617(TLS):15Feb85-166
Jeffrey, R. Formal Logic. (2nd ed)
   T. McCarthy, 316:Dec84-1408
Jeffreys, E.M. and M.J. Popular Litera-
   ture in Late Byzantium.
   E.A. Hanawalt, 589:Jul84-721
Jeffri, J. The Emerging Arts.*
   D. Cardinal, 108:Fall84-120

Jehasse, J. and B. Yon - see de Balzac,
   J-L.G.
Jelavich, B. History of the Balkans.*
   S.D. Spector, 104(CASS):Winter84-501
Jelinek, E.C., ed. Women's Autobiography.*
   S. Neumann, 106:Winter84-421
Jelinek, J.A. The Lust for Power.
   O. Ulč, 104(CASS):Winter84-496
Jellema, R. The Eighth Day.
   S.T. Layesman, 496:Summer84-123
Jellison, C.A. Besieged.
   K. Jeffery, 617(TLS):17May85-555
Jember, G.K. and F. Kemmler. A Basic
   Vocabulary of Old English Prose/Grund-
   wortschatz altenglische Prosa.
   A. Bammesberger, 260(IF):Band89-371
   B. Diensberg, 72:Band221Heft2-355
Jen-kai, L. - see under Liu Jen-kai
Jenkins, H. - see Shakespeare, W.
Jenkins, I. Social Order and the Limits
   of Law.*
   J.P. Dougherty, 543:Sep83-126
Jenkins, J.H. Basic Texas Books.
   L. Milazzo, 584(SWR):Winter84-88
Jenkins, L. Faulkner and Black-White
   Relations.
   E. Gallafent, 677(YES):Vol 14-353
Jenkins, M.F.O. Artful Eloquence.
   M. Quainton, 208(FS):Jan84-48
Jenkins, S. and A. Sloman. With Respect,
   Ambassador.
   A. Watkins, 362:11Apr85-23
   A. Watson, 617(TLS):8Nov85-1268
Jenkyns, R. Three Classical Poets.
   W.S. Anderson, 149(CLS):Fall84-345
   S.H. Braund, 313:Vol74-236
   R. Mayer, 123:Vol34No1-133
Jenkyns, R. The Victorians and Ancient
   Greece.
   S. Monod, 549(RLC):Jul-Sep84-363
Jenner, P.N. and S. Pou. A Lexicon of
   Khmer Morphology.
   F.E. Huffman, 293(JASt):Aug84-803
   G.F. Meier, 682(ZPSK):Band37Heft6-728
Jennings, G. World of Words.
   P-L. Adams, 61:Feb85-101
Jennings, H. Pandaemonium. (M-L. Jen-
   nings and C. Madge, eds)
   R. Porter, 617(TLS):25Oct85-1199
Jennings, L.B. Justinus Kerners Weg nach
   Weinsberg (1809-1819).*
   D.P. Haase, 301(JEGP):Jul84-410
Jensen, E.J., ed. The Future of "Nineteen
   Eighty-Four."
   D. Patai, 385(MQR):Winter85-110
   R.J. Voorhees, 395(MFS):Winter84-769
Jensen, J.F. and others. Dansk litteratur-
   historie, 4.
   A. Aarseth, 172(Edda):1984/1-59
Jensen, J.M. and S. Davidson, eds. A
   Needle, a Bobbin, a Strike.
   K. Wilson, 614:Summer85-30
Jensen, L. Shelter.
   C. Kizer, 441:3Nov85-13
Jensen, M.S. The Homeric Question and the
   Oral-Formulaic Theory.*
   A.H.M. Kessels, 394:Vol37fasc1/2-165
Jensen, R. and P. Conway. Ornamentalism.*
   D.D. Keyes, 127:Summer84-193
Jensen, T. and C. Nicolaisen, eds. Udvik-
   lingsromanen — en genres historie.*
   N.L. Jensen, 562(Scan):Nov84-176
   P.M. Mitchell, 678(YCGL):No32-153

Jensen, U.J. and R. Harré, eds. The Philosophy of Evolution.
  V. Pratt, 84:Mar84-81
  M. Ruse, 154:Mar84-171
Jenson, J. and G. Ross. The View from Inside.
  T. Draper, 453(NYRB):30May85-44
  P. McCarthy, 617(TLS):16Aug85-898
  R. Paxton, 441:10Feb85-28
Jentoft, C.W. Sir Thomas Wyatt and Henry Howard, Earl of Surrey.*
  D.C. Kay, 447(N&Q):Oct83-457
Jeřábek, D. Václav Vladivoj Tomek a Karel Havlíček v letech bachovské reakce.
  R.B. Pynsent, 575(SEER):Jan84-155
Jernakoff, N., ed. Transactions of the Association of Russian-American Scholars in the USA, Inc. (Vol 16)
  D. Lowe, 104(CASS):Winter84-436
Jerram, C.S. - see Lucian
Jervis, R. The Illogic of American Nuclear Strategy.*
  A. Dowty, 617(TLS):25Jan85-83
Jervis, S. The Penguin Dictionary of Design and Designers.
  R.W. Grant, 324:Feb85-237
Jesson, A.F. - see Falivene, M.R.
de Jesús, T. Libro de las Fundaciones. (V. García de la Concha, ed)
  J.A. Jones, 86(BHS):Oct84-522
Jeter, K.W. The Glass Hammer.
  G. Jonas, 441:4Aug85-20
Jevons, M. The Fatal Equilibrium.
  R. Krulwich, 441:20Oct85-55
Jewett, I.B.H. Alexander W. Kinglake.
  R. Mason, 447(N&Q):Aug83-356
Jewtuschenko, J. Beerenreiche Gegenden.
  K. Kasper, 654(WB):12/1984-2048
Jhingran, S. The Roots of World Religions.
  K.N. Upadhyaya, 485(PE&W):Oct84-465
Jicai, F. - see under Feng Jicai
Jimack, P. Rousseau: "Emile."
  L.W. Lynch, 207(FR):Mar85-581
  P. Robinson, 208(FS):Oct84-465
Jiménez, A. and others. La arquitectura de nuestra ciudad.
  F. Marías, 48:Apr-Jun84-194
Jiménez, J. El ángel caído. La estética como utopía antropológica.
  H. Osborne, 89(BJA):Spring84-180
Jiménez, J.O. La presencia de Antonio Machado en la poesía española de posguerra.
  E. Oyola, 238:Sep84-474
Jimenez, M. Vers une esthétique négative (Adorno et la modernité).
  T. Cordellier, 450(NRF):Jun84-105
Jiménez-Fajardo, S. and J.C. Wilcox, eds. At Home and Beyond.
  A.P. Debicki, 240(HR):Spring84-246
Joannides, P. The Drawings of Raphael.*
  J. Beck, 551(RenQ):Winter84-638
  C.M. Goguel, 90:Jul84-438
  T. Puttfarken, 59:Dec84-504
Jodogne, O. - see Gréban, A.
Johanides, J. František Martin Pelcl.
  J-P. Danès, 549(RLC):Jan-Mar84-114
Johannsen, R.W. To the Halls of the Montezumas.
  F. Freidel, 441:14Apr85-37
  442(NY):16Sep85-123

Johansen, J.D. and M. Nøjgaard, eds. Danish Semiotics.
  U. Musarra-Schrøder, 307:Apr84-92
Johansen, K.G. Guds lys og mannens mørke.
  A. Saether, 562(Scan):May84-53
Johanson, R. All about Sewing Machines.
  K.S.H., 614:Winter85-16
John, E. Persönlichkeit — Kunst — Lebensweise.
  E. Brüshafer, 654(WB):4/1984-676
John, N., ed. English National Opera Guides. (Vol 21)
  R. Anderson, 415:May84-273
  J. Kerman, 453(NYRB):15Aug85-36
John, N., ed. English National Opera Guides. (Vols 23 and 24)
  R. Anderson, 415:May84-273
John, N., ed. English National Opera Guides. (Vols 25-27)
  R. Anderson, 415:Dec84-706
John, N., ed. English National Opera Guides. (Vol 28)
  R. Anderson, 415:Dec84-706
  J. Kerman, 453(NYRB):15Aug85-36
John, N., ed. English National Opera Guides. (Vol 31)
  J. Kerman, 453(NYRB):15Aug85-36
Johns, E. Thomas Eakins.*
  A. Berman, 55:Nov84-35
  639(VQR):Summer84-88
Johnson, A.H. Whitehead and His Philosophy.
  B. Hendley, 154:Jun84-345
Johnson, B. The Critical Difference.*
  R.A. Barney, 223:Fall81-413
Johnson, B., ed. The Pedagogical Imperative.
  P.W. Willis, 446(NCFS):Summer-Fall84-229
Johnson, B. True Correspondence.
  K. Brady, 177(ELT):Vol27No3-248
  A. Gandolfo, 395(MFS):Winter84-747
  R.C. Murfin, 445(NCF):Mar85-481
  295(JML):Nov84-451
Johnson, B.S. Christie Malry's Own Double-Entry.
  J. House, 441:29Sep85-46
Johnson, B.S. House Mother Normal.
  P. Lewis, 565:Autumn84-55
Johnson, C.B. Inside "Guzmán de Alfarache."
  B.W. Ife, 86(BHS):Jan84-50
Johnson, C.B. Madness and Lust.
  J.G. Weiger, 238:May84-304
  639(VQR):Winter84-9
Johnson, C.D. The Productive Tension of Hawthorne's Art.
  R. Miles, 447(N&Q):Dec83-563
Johnson, C.D. and V.E., comps. Nineteenth-Century Theatrical Memoirs.
  R.K. Bank, 615(TJ):Mar84-124
  J.W. Robinson, 610:Summer84-146
Johnson, D. Angels.*
  42(AR):Winter84-123
Johnson, D. Fiskadoro.
  E. Hoffman, 441:26May85-7
  S. Lardner, 442(NY):15Jul85-83
  J. Neville, 617(TLS):24May85-573
Johnson, D. Dashiell Hammett.*
  639(VQR):Spring84-52
Johnson, D. Terrorists and Novelists.
  S. Brown, 569(SR):Fall84-649

Jonson, B. Volpone or, the Fox. (R.B. Parker, ed)
P. Hyland, 67:Nov84-246
Jonsson, B.R., M. Jersild and S-B. Jansson, eds. Sveriges Medeltida Ballader. (Vol 1)
L. Huldén, 64(Arv):Vol38-187
L. Isaacson, 563(SS):Summer84-278
Jónsson, J.H. Das Partizip Perfekt der schwachen "ja-"Verben.
R. Schrodt, 685(ZDL):3/1984-375
Joppa, F.A. L'Engagement des écrivains africains noirs de langue française.
C.L. Dehon, 207(FR):Oct84-116
A.O. Umeh, 538(RAL):Spring84-99
Joppien, R. and B. Smith. The Art of Captain Cook's Voyages.
G. Dening, 441:11Aug85-1
Jordan, B. The Athenian Navy in the Classical Period.
H.T. Wallinga, 394:Vol37fasc1/2-239
Jordan, B. The State.
M. Rosen, 617(TLS):26Jul85-812
A. Ryan, 362:15Aug85-29
Jordan, D.P. Political Leadership in Jefferson's Virginia.*
R.E. Shalhope, 656(WMQ):Jul84-518
Jordan, D.P. The Revolutionary Career of Maximilien Robespierre.
L. Hunt, 441:8Sep85-42
Jordan, H. Crisis.
W.S. Burke, 396(ModA):Spring/Summer84-264
Jordan, J.M. Paul Klee and Cubism.*
R. Verdi, 90:Nov84-711
Jordan, L. - see von Droste-Hülshoff, A.
Jordan, L., B. Kortländer and F. Nies, eds. Interferenzen — Deutschland und Frankreich.
F. Baasner, 52:Band19Heft3-303
Jordan, M.P. Rhetoric of Everyday English Texts.
W. Grabe, 350:Dec85-931
Jordan, T.G. Texas Graveyards.*
J.J. Edgette, 292(JAF):Jul-Sep84-359
Jordanova, L.J. Lamarck.
R.C. Lewontin, 453(NYRB):10Oct85-18
J.A. Secord, 617(TLS):18Jan85-70
Jorden, W.J. Panama Odyssey.
W.L. Furlong, 263(RIB):Vol34No3/4-431
Jordens, C. Pierre Emmanuel: Introduction générale à l'oeuvre.
J. Decreus, 208(FS):Apr84-239
Jörg, C.J.A. Porcelain and the Dutch China Trade.*
C. Sheaf, 60:Sep-Oct84-118
Jorgens, E.B. The Well-Tun'd Word.*
B.M. Horner, 568(SCN):Spring-Summer84-10
Jørgensen, A., ed. Gruppeteater i Norden.
J. Aarkrog, 562(Scan):Nov84-192
Jose, N. Ideas of the Restoration in English Literature, 1660-71.
C.D. Reverand 2d, 566:Spring85-189
639(VQR):Summer84-84
Josefson, E-K. La vision citadine et sociale dans l'oeuvre d'Émile Verhaeren.*
H-J. Lope, 547(RF):Band96Heft4-477
S. Taylor-Horrex, 402(MLR):Apr84-465
Joseph, B.D. The Synchrony and Diachrony of the Balkan Infinitive.
G. Mallinson, 350:Sep85-691

Joseph, J. Beyond Descartes.*
J. Saunders, 565:Autumn84-66
Joseph, L. Shouting at No One.*
J. Elledge, 491:May84-109
Joseph, T. George Grossmith.*
J. Donohue, 637(VS):Autumn83-91
Josephs, A. White Wall of Spain.
M. Jato Macías, 238:Sep84-475
639(VQR):Spring84-62
Josephus. Flavius Josèphe, "Guerre des Juifs." (Vol 3, Bks 4 and 5) (A. Pelletier, ed and trans)
D.A. Bertrand, 555:Vol58fasc2-308
Joshi, S.D., ed. CASS Studies. (No 4)
H. Scharfe, 260(IF):Band89-309
Joshi, S.D., ed. Proceedings of the Winter Institute on Ancient Indian Theories on Sentence-Meaning.
H. Scharfe, 260(IF):Band89-307
Joshi, S.D. - see Kiparsky, P.
Joshi, S.T. H.P. Lovecraft.
M.E. Barth, 395(MFS):Summer84-346
Josipovici, G. Writing and the Body.*
B. Harrison, 89(BJA):Winter84-87
I. McGilchrist, 402(MLR):Oct84-878
P. Swinden, 148:Autumn84-82
Josipovici, G. - see Blanchot, M.
Jost, R. "Er war unser Lehrer."
G. Müller-Waldeck, 654(WB):10/1984-1751
Jost, U. Die französischen Lehnwörter im Englischen von 1750-1759.
H. Käsmann, 38:Band102Heft1/2-162
Jouary, J-P. and A. Spire. Invitation à la philosophie marxiste.
A. Reix, 542:Jan-Mar84-88
Joubert, J. The Notebooks of Joseph Joubert.* (P. Auster, ed and trans)
T.J. Jamieson, 396(ModA):Fall84-384
Jouhandeau, M. Les Pincengrain.
C. Dis, 450(NRF):Sep84-96
Joukovsky, F. Le regard intérieur.*
W.J. Kennedy, 551(RenQ):Winter84-640
F. Lecercle, 535(RHL):Jul/Aug84-586
Joukovsky, F. - see d'Alcripe, P.
"Le Journalisme d'Ancien Régime."
H-J. Lüsebrink, 547(RF):Band96Heft3-352
Jouve, M. L'âge d'or de la caricature anglaise.
C.J. Hynes-Higman, 89(BJA):Summer84-274
Jouve, P.J. La scène capitale.* Folie et génie. L'aventure de Catherine Crachat.
M. Canto, 98:Nov84-888
de Jouvenel, B. Un voyageur dans le siècle. (Vol 1)
R. Nelson, 628(UWR):Spring-Summer85-93
Jouvenet, L-P. Horizon politique des pédagogies non directives.
J-M. Gabaude, 542:Apr-Jun84-241
Jovino, M.B. - see under Bonghi Jovino, M.
Jowell, J.L. and J.P.W.B. McAuslan, eds. Lord Denning.*
S.R. Letwin, 362:3Jan85-25
Jowitt, D. The Dance in Mind.
M. Bernheimer, 441:24Feb85-23
Joyce, D. and E. Tihanyi. Stone Wear/A Sequence of the Blood.
L. Rogers, 102(CanL):Winter83-153
Joyce, D.F. Gatekeepers of Black Culture.
E.N. Kaplan, 517(PBSA):Vol78No2-253

Joyce, J. Finnegans Wake. (P. Lavergne, trans)
  S. and B. Benstock, 329(JJQ):Winter85-231
Joyce, J. James Joyce, "Finnegans Wake" Chapter One.* (T. Ahern, ed)
  L.V. Harrod, 174(Éire):Spring84-157
Joyce, J. Ulysses.* (H.W. Gabler, with W. Steppe and C. Melchior, eds)
  C. Froula, 676(YR):Spring85-454
Joyce, R.B. Samuel Walker Griffith.
  J.B. Paul, 617(TLS):12Jul85-780
Joyce, W.L. and others, eds. Printing and Society in Early America.*
  W.H. Bond, 432(NEQ):Jun84-279
Joyner, P. Samuel Hieronymus Grimm: Views in Wales.
  380:Autumn84-330
Jrade, C.L. Rubén Darío and the Romantic Search for Unity.*
  O. Rivera-Rodas, 238:Sep84-478
Judd, A. Short of Glory.*
  R. Jones, 362:24Jan85-28
  J. Mellors, 364:Nov84-105
  442(NY):15Jul85-85
Judge, A. and F.G. Healey. A Reference Grammar of Modern French.*
  M.S. Howden, 399(MLJ):Autumn84-287
  H. Wise, 208(FS):Jul84-375
Judge, E.H. Plehve.
  R. Pearson, 575(SEER):Oct84-606
  T. Taranovski, 104(CASS):Winter84-469
Judge, H. A Generation of Schooling.
  J. Mackay, 617(TLS):25Jan85-85
Judson, J.R. and C. van de Velde. Corpus Rubenianum Ludwig Burchard. (Pt 21)
  C. Brown, 90:Jun84-353
Juergensen, H. The Record of a Green Planet.
  M. Andrews, 496:Fall84-185
Juergensmeyer, M. Religion as Social Vision.
  E. Zelliot, 293(JASt):Nov83-187
Juhasz, S., ed. Feminist Critics Read Emily Dickinson.
  D. Porter, 432(NEQ):Mar84-106
  295(JML):Nov84-425
  639(VQR):Spring84-43
Juhasz, S. The Undiscovered Continent.*
  E. Ammons, 27(AL):Oct84-431
  G. Monteiro, 432(NEQ):Sep84-449
  295(JML):Nov84-425
Juhl, P.D. Interpretation.*
  P. O'Donnell, 223:Summer81-281
Juin, H. Victor Hugo. (Vol 2)
  D. Kelley, 617(TLS):11Oct85-1123
Juin, H. - see de Maupassant, G.
Julià, P. Explanatory Models in Linguistics.
  F. D'Agostino, 84:Dec84-408
  D.H., 355(LSoc):Mar84-131
Julía Díaz, S. Madrid 1931-1934.
  R. Carr, 617(TLS):4Oct85-1105
Julier, J. Studien zur spätgotischen Baukunst am Oberrhein.
  B. Schock-Werner, 683(Band47Heft1-131
Jully, J.J. Labraunda: Swedish Excavations and Researches.* (Vol 2, Pt 3)
  J.M. Cook, 303(JoHS):Vol 104-250
Juneau, M. Problèmes de lexicologie québécoise.
  H.J. Wolf, 547(RF):Band96Heft1/2-136

Jung, C.G. The Essential Jung. (A. Storr, ed)
  J.D. O'Hara, 639(VQR):Winter84-160
Jung, C.G. and C. Kerényi. Science of Mythology.
  617(TLS):7Jun85-651
Jung, W. Theorie und Praxis des Typischen bei Honoré de Balzac.
  U. Schulz-Buschhaus, 52:Band19Heft3-317
Junger, E. Soixante-dix s'efface.*
  L. Kovacs, 450(NRF):Oct84-112
Junger, E. Soixante-dix s'efface, II.
  J. Théodoridès, 605(SC):15Jul85-379
Junghanns, K. Der Deutsche Werkbund — Sein erstes Jahrzehnt.
  M. Hofmann, 654(WB):3/1984-497
Junghare, I.Y. Topics in Pāli Historical Phonology.
  C. Caillat, 259(IIJ):Apr84-138
Jungius, J. Praelectiones Physicae. (C. Meinel, ed)
  H-J. Hess, 706:Band16Heft1-119
Jurgensen, M., ed. Thomas Bernhard.*
  G.P. Knapp, 564:Feb84-75
Jurgensen, M., ed. Frauenliteratur.
  A. Obermayer, 564:Nov84-307
Jurt, J. - see under Estève, M.
Justus, J.H. The Achievement of Robert Penn Warren.*
  B. Quinn, 585(SoQ):Winter84-96
  M.R. Winchell, 106:Summer84-229
Juszczakowska, H. La fortune de la "Nouvelle Héloïse" de J-J. Rousseau dans la Pologne du XVIIIe siècle.
  M. de Rougemont and J. Voisine, 549(RLC):Oct-Dec84-490
Juxon, J. Lewis and Lewis.*
  639(VQR):Autumn84-122

Kaarsted, T. - see Brandes, G.
Kadaré, I. La Niche de la honte.
  L. Kovacs, 450(NRF):Dec84-109
Kade, O. Die sprachmittlung als gesellschaftliche Erscheinung und Gegenstand wissenschaftlicher Untersuchung.
  M. Doherty, 682(ZPSK):Band37Heft3-394
Kadima-Nzuji, M. Jacques Rabemananjara.
  M.E. Mudimbe-Boyi, 538(RAL):Spring84-87
Kael, P. State of the Art.
  N. Gabler, 441:8Dec85-48
Kael, P. Taking It All In.*
  J. Nangle, 200:Oct84-504
Kaelble, B. Untersuchungen zur grossfigurigen Plastik des Samsonmeisters.*
  D. Gillerman, 589:Jan84-167
Kaelin, E.F. The Unhappy Consciousness.*
  A. Easthope, 323:Jan84-94
  R.P. Harrison, 543:Sep83-127
Kafitz, D. Grundzüge einer Geschichte des deutschen Dramas von Lessing bis zum Naturalismus.
  L. Ehrlich, 654(WB):7/1984-1219
Kafker, F.A., ed. Notable Encyclopedias of the Seventeenth and Eighteenth Centuries.*
  O. Kenshur, 173(ECS):Fall84-124
  A. Rey, 535(RHL):Jan/Feb84-105
  A. Strugnell, 402(MLR):Apr84-453

Kagan, A. Paul Klee: Art and Music.*
  C. Butler, 410(M&L):Oct84-407
  R.V., 90:Nov84-714
Kagan, L. and K. Westerfield. Meet the US.
  D.S. Rood, 399(MLJ):Winter84-425
Kahan, G. George Alexander Stevens and
  "The Lecture on Heads."
  R. Savage, 617(TLS):15Mar85-290
Kahane, H. and R. Abendland und Byzanz:
  Sprache.
  J. Knobloch, 545(RPh):Aug83-77
Kahane, H. and R. Graeca et romanica.
  G.M. Messing, 350:Jun85-470
Kahler, H. Von Hofmannsthal bis Benjamin.
  T. Rietzschel, 654(WB):6/1984-1045
Kahn, C. Beyond the Helix.
  T. Monmaney, 441:1Dec85-25
Kahn, D. - see Lorain, P.
Kahn, E.J., Jr. The Staffs of Life.
  J. Fleming, 441:14Apr85-29
Kahn, J-F. L'Extraordinaire Métamorphose.
  D. Kelley, 617(TLS):11Oct85-1123
Kahn, J.Y. Modes of Medical Instruction.
  D.C. Andrews, 350:Sep85-736
Kahn, L. Hermès passe ou les ambiguïtés
  de la communication.
  J.N. Bremmer, 394:Vol37fasc3/4-461
Kahn, L., ed. In Her Mother's Tongue.
  H.S. Madland, 399(MLJ):Summer84-177
Kahn, R. Good Enough to Dream.
  B. Ryan, 441:8Sep85-14
Kahrl, G.M., with D. Anderson. The Gar-
  rick Collection of Old English Plays.*
  M.R. Mahard, 517(PBSA):Vol78No4-515
  H.W. Pedicord, 611(TN):Vol38No3-156
Kahsnitz, R., U. Mende and E. Rücker. Das
  Goldene Evangelienbuch von Echternach.
  R. Deshman, 589:Apr84-478
Kaimio, J. The Romans and the Greek Lan-
  guage.
  H.J. Mason, 487:Summer84-191
Kain, R.J.P. and H.C. Prince. The Tithe
  Surveys of England and Wales.
  J. Thirsk, 617(TLS):13Sep85-1008
Kaiser, D.H. The Growth of the Law in
  Medieval Russia.*
  N.S. Kollman, 550(RusR):Jan84-81
Kaiser, E. Strukturen der Frage im Franzö-
  sischen.
  G. Ernst, 547(RF):Band96Heft4-441
Kaiser, G.R. Einführung in die vergleich-
  ende Literaturwissenschaft.* (M. Schmel-
  ing, ed)
  J. Hervier, 549(RLC):Jul-Sep84-347
Kaiser, H.H. Great Camps of the Adiron-
  dacks.
  E.C. Cromley, 658:Winter84-317
Kaiser, L.M., ed. Early American Latin
  Verse, 1625-1825.
  H. Jantz, 27(AL):Dec84-591
  G.A. Kennedy, 656(WMQ):Oct84-660
  L.V.R., 568(SCN):Fall84-55
  J.E. Ziolkowski, 124:Jul-Aug85-607
Kakar, S. The Inner World.
  A. Padoux, 98:Apr84-300
Kakar, S. Shamans, Mystics, and Doctors.
  P. Claus, 293(JASt):May84-573
  A. Padoux, 98:Apr84-300
  K.G. Zysk, 318(JAOS):Oct-Dec83-786
Kaletski, A. Metro.
  V. Bogdanor, 362:26Sep85-31
  G. Kovarsky, 441:30Jun85-20
  F. Williams, 617(TLS):13Dec85-1433

Kalinke, M.E. King Arthur North-by-North-
  west.
  R. Frank, 301(JEGP):Jul84-420
  C.B. Hieatt, 563(SS):Spring84-188
  I.J. Kirby, 402(MLR):Oct84-997
Kalinnikova, E.J. Indian-English Litera-
  ture.*
  S.K. Aithal, 268(IFR):Winter85-66
  J.P. Gemmill, 314:Winter-Spring84-201
Kalinowski, G. L'impossible métaphysique.*
  P-M. Hombert, 192(EP):Apr-Jun84-272
Kalme, E. In the Shadow of Freedom.
  B.T. Lupack, 497(PolR):Vol29No1/2-166
Kalnins, M. - see Lawrence, D.H.
Kalpakian, L. These Latter Days.
  R. Byard, 441:5May85-24
  442(NY):?7May85-99
Kaluzny, A.E. La philosophie du coeur de
  Grégoire Skovoroda.
  P. Bellemare, 154:Sep84-525
Kalverkämper, H. Orientierung zur Text-
  linguistik.*
  H-W. Eroms, 685(ZDL):3/1984-373
Kamata, S. Japan in the Passing Lane.
  W.H. Newell, 293(JASt):Feb84-344
  M. Sayle, 453(NYRB):28Mar85-33
Kamboureli, S. and R. Kroetsch - see
  Barbour, D.
Kamen, H. European Society 1500-1700.
  G. Parker, 617(TLS):19Apr85-444
Kamen, H. Inquisition and Society in
  Spain in the Sixteenth and Seventeenth
  Centuries.
  J. Bossy, 617(TLS):6Sep85-985
Kamen, M.D. Radiant Science, Dark Pol-
  itics.
  M. Berkley, 441:21Apr85-39
Kamenszain, T. El texto silencioso.
  D.T. Jaén, 238:Sep84-480
Kamerman, J.B. and R. Martorella. Perform-
  ers and Performances.
  G.L. Ratliff, 615(TJ):Oct84-432
Kamhi, D.J. Modern Hebrew.
  D.M. Golomb, 399(MLJ):Spring84-81
Kamińska, A. Brandenburg-Prussia and
  Poland.
  R.I. Frost, 575(SEER):Jul84-454
Kaminsky, H. Simon de Cramaud and the
  Great Schism.
  E.K. Burger, 377:Mar84-57
Kampen, N. Image and Status.
  D.C. Bellingham, 313:Vol74-227
Kamper, D. Das gefangene Einhorn.
  H-J. Ortheil, 384:Jan84-89
Kampf, A. Jewish Experience in the Art of
  the Twentieth Century.
  D. Kuspit, 62:Dec84-78
von Kamptz, H. Homerische Personennamen.
  J. Chadwick, 303(JoHS):Vol 104-192
  R. Janko, 123:Vol34No2-305
Kamuf, P. Fictions of Feminine Desire.*
  L. Gasbarrone, 188(ECr):Fall84-90
  R. Goldberg, 208(FS):Oct84-499
  H. Josephs, 210(FrF):Jan84-117
  G. May, 400(MLN):Dec84-1210
Kandel, B. Taiping Jing.
  R.G. Henricks, 318(JAOS):Oct-Dec83-800
Kandell, J. Passage Through El Dorado.*
  P. Bennett, 37:Nov-Dec84-62
  A. Hurrell, 617(TLS):4Jan85-6
  J. Keay, 362:31Jan85-25

193

Kane, A. Songs and Sayings of an Ulster
Childhood. (E. Fowke, ed)
   P.L. Hart, 102(CanL):Autumn84-167
Kane, G. Chaucer.
   B. O'Donoghue, 617(TLS):12Apr85-416
Kane, J.E. - see François ler
Kane, P. and P. Short. Entretiens avec
les mots.
   L. Schryver, 207(FR):Apr85-772
Kanet, R.E., ed. Soviet Foreign Policy in
the 1980's.
   S.N. MacFarlane, 104(CASS):Fall84-347
Kanfer, S. The International Garage Sale.
   S. Lawson, 441:2Jun85-20
   442(NY):19Aug85-89
Kanger, S. and S. Öhman, eds. Philosophy
and Grammar.
   M. Davies, 393(Mind):Jan84-149
Kanin, P.C., ed. Shakespeare in the South.
   S.J. Teller, 389(MQ):Autumn84-115
Kant, I. Critique of Pure Reason. (W.
Schwarz, ed and trans)
   P. Foulkes, 483:Oct84-555
   C.M. Sherover, 319:Jan85-115
Kant, I. Kant's "Critique of Pure Reason."
(H. Palmer, ed and trans)
   T.E. Wilkerson, 518:Apr84-117
Kant, I. La religion dans les limites de
la simple raison. (M. Naar, ed)
   A. Stanguennec, 542:Oct-Dec84-479
Kant, I. Transición de los Principios
Metafísicos de la Ciencia Natural a la
física. (F. Duque, ed)
   H. Widmer, 342:Band75Heft3-350
Kant, I. Über den Gemeinspruch. (4th ed)
(J. Ebbinghaus, ed)
   R. Malter, 342:Band75Heft1-133
Kantakuzenos, J. Geschichte. (Pt 1, Bk 1)
   D.M. Nicol, 575(SEER):Jan84-122
Kantor, M. Medieval Slavic Lives of
Saints and Princes.
   F. Wigzell, 575(SEER):Oct84-582
Kantowsky, D. Sarvodaya.*
   M. Juergensmeyer, 293(JASt):Feb84-293
Kaplan, E.K. - see Michelet, J.
Kaplan, F. Thomas Carlyle.*
   S. Monod, 189(EA):Jul-Sep85-340
Kaplan, F. - see Pascal, B.
Kaplan, H. Power and Order.*
   D. Pizer, 183(ESQ):Vol30No3-193
Kaplan, J. - see Whitman, W.
Kaplan, R.B. - see "Annual Review of
Applied Linguistics: 1981"
Kaplan, S.L. Provisioning Paris.
   O. Hufton, 617(TLS):9Aug85-883
Kaplan, S.L., ed. Understanding Popular
Culture.
   P. Burke, 617(TLS):28Jun85-728
Kapp, V. "Télémaque" de Fénelon.*
   H. Hillenaar, 535(RHL):Jul/Aug84-609
Kappel-Smith, D. Wintering.
   H. Middleton, 441:6Jan85-21
Kappeler, S. Writing and Reading in Henry
James.*
   V. Jones, 447(N&Q):Feb83-89
Kappeler, S. and N. Bryson, eds. Teaching
the Text.
   M. Grivelet, 189(EA):Jan-Mar85-75
Kapschutschenko, L. El labertino en la
narrativa hispanoamericana contempor-
ánea.*
   S. Boldy, 86(BHS):Jan84-69

Kapuściński, R. The Emperor.
   G.T. Kapolka, 497(PolR):Vol29No1/2-155
   W. Osiatynski, 42(AR):Fall84-495
Kapuscinski, R. Shah of Shahs.
   M. Kennedy, 441:7Apr85-7
Karady, V. - see Durkheim, E.
Karady, V. - see Mauss, M.
Karageorghis, V. and others. Excavations
at Kition.* (Vol 4)
   V. Tatton-Brown, 303(JoHS):Vol 104-259
Karamanski, T.J. Fur Trade and Explora-
tion.
   G.W., 102(CanL):Summer84-189
Karanikas, A. Hellenes and Hellions.
   C. Leach, 447(N&Q):Jun83-285
Karas, J. Music in Terezin 1941-1945.
   S. Taitz, 441:28Apr85-14
Karas, T. The New High Ground.
   D. Paul, 529(QQ):Summer84-460
Karátson, A. and J. Bessière. Déracine-
ment et littérature.
   M.W. Blades, 207(FR):Feb85-441
   J. Riesz, 52:Band19Heft1-101
Karavites, P. Capitulations and Greek
Interstate Relations.
   J.F. Lazenby, 303(JoHS):Vol 104-238
Karen, R., ed. Toward the Year 2000.
   G. Daugherty, 441:200ct85-51
Karl, B.D. The Uneasy State.*
   639(VQR):Summer84-79
Karl, F.R. American Fictions, 1940-1980.*
   R.M. Davis, 223:Fall84-330
   S. Fender, 617(TLS):2Aug85-857
   S. Pinsker, 219(GaR):Winter84-891
   P. Wolfe, 395(MFS):Winter84-841
   295(JML):Nov84-387
Karl, F.R. and L. Davies - see Conrad, J.
Karlekar, M. Poverty and Women's Work.
   J. Kirkpatrick, 293(JASt):Aug84-782
Karlinger, F. Grundzüge einer Geschichte
des Märchens im deutschen Sprachraum.
   E. Moser-Rath, 196:Band25Heft3/4-350
Karlinsky, S. and A. Olcott - see Poplav-
skij, B.
Karlsen, C.F. and L. Crumpacker - see Burr,
E.E.
Karnapp, W. Die Stadtmauer von Resafa in
Syrien.
   M. Harrison, 123:Vol34No1-105
Karnick, M. Rollenspiel und Welttheater.*
   J.P. Aikin, 107(CRCL):Jun84-302
   A.J. Niesz, 406:Summer84-211
Karp, A.J. Haven and Home.
   A.L. Goldman, 441:4Aug85-17
Karpinski, J., ed. Capital of Happiness.
   S. Mills, 617(TLS):18Jan85-73
Kars, H. Le portrait chez Marivaux.*
   W. Henning, 72:Band22lHeft1-209
   H. Mason, 208(FS):Jul84-341
Karsh, Y. Karsh.
   J. Kaufmann, 31(ASch):Autumn84-559
Kasack, W. Die russische Literatur 1945-
82.
   M. Dalton, 104(CASS):Winter84-450
Kasell, W. Marcel Proust and the Strategy
of Reading.*
   A. Corbineau-Hoffmann, 547(RF):
      Band96Heft1/2-197
   S. Neuman, 107(CRCL):Mar84-141
Kaser, K. Handbuch der Regierungen Süd-
osteuropas (1833-1980). (Pt 1)
   R.J. Crampton, 575(SEER):Jan84-154

Keller, E.F.   Reflections on Gender and
  Science.
    E. Shaw, 441:21Apr85-36
Keller, G.   Stories.   (F.G. Ryder, ed)
    T.C. Hanlin, 399(MLJ):Summer84-168
Keller, K.   The Only Kangaroo Among the
  Beauty.
    C.R. Steele, 106:Spring84-63
Kelley, D.R.   The Solzhenitsyn-Sakharov
  Dialogue.
    J.B. Dunlop, 550(RusR):Oct84-439
Kelley, F.E. and G.I. Etzkorn - see Ockham,
  William of
Kelley, M.   Private Woman, Public Stage.*
    W-C. Dimock, 219(GaR):Winter84-869
    A.G. Jones, 357:Fall85-74
Kelley, P. and R.A. Coley, comps.   The
  Browning Collections.
    C. Coover, 517(PBSA):Vol78No4-517
    A.C. Dooley, 87(BB):Jun84-99
Kelley, P. and R. Hudson - see Browning, R.
  and E.B.
Kelliher, W.H. - see Wordsworth, W.
Kelly, B. and M. London.   Amazon.*
    J. Keay, 362:31Jan85-25
Kelly, L.D.   The Life and Works of Eliza-
  beth Stuart Phelps.
    K.O. Garrigan, 395(MFS):Summer84-373
Kelly, M.   Modern French Marxism.*
    T. Eagleton, 208(FS):Jan84-112
    R. Elliot, 63:Mar84-101
Kelly, M.   Necessary Treasons.
    A. Haverty, 617(TLS):19Jul85-800
    K.C. O'Brien, 362:11Jul85-32
Kelly, M. - see Milton, J.
Kelly, M.T.   The Ruined Season.
    R. Harvey, 102(CanL):Autumn84-86
Kelly, N.   In the Shadow of King's.
    T.J. Binyon, 617(TLS):11Jan85-42
Kelly, P.   Fighting for Hope.*
    T.G. Ash, 453(NYRB):31Jan85-33
Kelly, P.   The Hawke Ascendancy.
    K. Tsokhas, 381:Jun84-266
Kelly, R.   A Transparent Tree.
    L. McCaffery, 441:15Sep85-18
Kelman, J.   A Chancer.
    N. Shack, 617(TLS):6Dec85-1407
Kelman, J., A. Owens and A. Gray.   Lean
  Tales.
    J. Campbell, 617(TLS):10May85-529
Kelsall, M.   Christopher Marlowe.*
    J.J. Peereboom, 179(ES):Oct84-468
Kelvin, N. - see Morris, W.
Kelz, R.K.   Conversational Spanish for
  Medical Personnel.   (2nd ed)
    J.S. Conde, 238:Mar84-160
    J. Shreve, 399(MLJ):Spring84-95
Kemal, Y.   The Sea-Crossed Fisherman.
    S. Altinel, 617(TLS):31May85-598
    N.S. Ludington, 441:6Oct85-18
Kemelman, H.   Someday the Rabbi Will
  Leave.
    T.J. Binyon, 617(TLS):27Dec85-1478
    N. Callendar, 441:5May85-35
Kemp, J.   The American Idea.
    G.A. Fossedal, 129:Jan85-27
Kemp, P.   binding twine.
    P. Young, 376:Oct84-123
Kemp, P.   H.G. Wells and the Culminating
  Ape.*
    D.Y. Hughes, 561(SFS):Mar84-61
    J.R. Reed, 637(VS):Winter84-241

Kemp, T.J., ed.   Connecticut Researcher's
  Handbook.
    K.B. Harder, 424:Mar84-90
Kemp, W.   John Ruskin.
    M. Warnke, 384:Jul84-567
Kemper, H-G.   Gottebenbildlichkeit und
  Naturnachahmung im Säkularisierungs-
  prozess.
    G. Sutton, 402(MLR):Apr84-488
Kempton, W.   The Folk Classification of
  Ceramics.
    C.L. Briggs, 355(LSoc):Dec84-534
Kendrigan, M.L.   Political Equality in a
  Democratic Society.
    J.H., 185:Apr85-782
Keneally, T.   A Family Madness.
    J. Mellors, 362:10Oct85-29
    M. Wood, 617(TLS):18Oct85-1169
Keneally, T.   Schindler's Ark.
    P. Lewis, 565:Spring84-64
Kenec'hdu, T.   Avatars du français.
    P. Rickard, 189(EA):Oct-Dec85-453
Kengen, J.H.L., ed.   Memoriale Credencium.
    D. Pearsall, 72:Band221Heft1-168
Kennan, K. and D. Grantham.   The Technique
  of Orchestration.   (3rd ed)
    P. Standford, 415:Oct84-574
Kennedy, A.   Dramatic Dialogue.
    B. Johnston, 130:Fall84-280
Kennedy, E., ed.   "Lancelot do Lac."*
    E. Baumgartner, 554:Vol 104No1-127
    B. Schmolke-Hesselmann, 547(RF):
      Band96Heft1/2-168
Kennedy, G.A.   Greek Rhetoric under Chris-
  tian Emperors.*
    J.D. Frendo, 123:Vol34No2-204
    A. Kazhdan, 589:Jul84-662
Kennedy, L.   The Airman and the Carpenter.
    H. Brogan, 617(TLS):10May85-513
    R. Goldfarb, 441:16Jun85-11
    C. Sigal, 362:25Apr85-21
Kennedy, M. - see "The Concise Oxford
  Dictionary of Music"
Kennedy, M. - see "The Oxford Dictionary
  of Music"
Kennedy, R.S., ed.   Thomas Wolfe: A Har-
  vard Perspective.
    L. Field, 395(MFS):Summer84-306
Kennedy, R.S. - see Wolfe, T.
Kennedy, R.S. - see Wolfe, T. and E.
  Nowell
Kennedy, X.J.   Cross Ties.
    L. Mackinnon, 617(TLS):20Sep85-1039
    D. Ray, 441:24Nov85-28
Kenner, H.   A Colder Eye.*
    R. Bush, 141:Summer84-288
    D.L. Eder, 639(VQR):Autumn84-729
    F. Kersnowski, 573(SSF):Spring84-169
    G.A. Schirmer, 569(SR):Summer84-lviii
    295(JML):Nov84-359
Kenner, H.   A Homemade World.
    S. Fender, 677(YES):Vol 14-363
Kenney, E.J. and W.V. Clausen, eds.   The
  Cambridge History of Classical Litera-
  ture.*   (Vol 2)
    W.S. Anderson, 131(CL):Fall84-362
Kenney, R.   The Evolution of the Flight-
  less Bird.*
    J.F. Cotter, 249(HudR):Autumn84-505
    J.D. McClatchy, 491:Feb85-291
    P. Stitt, 219(GaR):Fall84-628
Kenny, A.   Aquinas.
    J. Owens, 154:Jun84-352

Kiernan, R.F. Gore Vidal.*
  S. Fogel, 106:Winter84-487
Kiesel, H. Erich Kästner.
  M.S. Fries, 221(GQ):Summer84-496
Kieser, R. Erzwungene Symbiose.*
  B.L. Bradley, 222(GR):Summer84-119
Kihlman, G. All My Sons.
  J. Mellors, 364:Dec84/Jan85-145
Kihlman, C. Sweet Prince.
  I. Scobbie, 562(Scan):Nov84-193
Kilbridge, J. Heaton Farm Haiku.
  A. Vakar, 404:Winter-Spring84-41
Kile, M.M. - see "The Quilt Digest 3"
Killen, G. Ancient Egyptian Furniture.
  (Vol 1)
  P. Der Manuelian, 318(JAOS):Oct-Dec83-792
Killen, L. The Russian Bureau.
  639(VQR):Summer84-81
Killy, W., ed. 18. Jahrhundert. (Vol 4)
  W. Grossmann, 173(ECS):Spring85-437
Kilmartin, T. A Reader's Guide to "Remembrance of Things Past."* (British title:
  A Guide to Proust: "Remembrance of Things Past.")
  L.M. Porter, 395(MFS):Winter84-724
Kilmister, C.W. Russell.
  R.M. Sainsbury, 617(TLS):16Aug85-908
Kimball, W.F. - see Churchill, W.S. and F.D. Roosevelt
Kimbell, D.R.B. Verdi in the Age of Italian Romanticism.*
  R. Swift, 451:Fall84-164
Kincaid, J. Annie John.
  P-L. Adams, 61:May85-104
  S. Kenney, 441:7Apr85-6
  I. Onwordi, 617(TLS):29Nov85-1374
Kincaid, J. At the Bottom of the River.*
  J. Mellors, 362:10Jan85-24
  I. Onwordi, 617(TLS):29Nov85-1374
Kincaid, J.R. and A.J. Kuhn, eds. Victorian Literature and Society.
  R.B. Martin, 617(TLS):8Mar85-262
  G.B. Tennyson, 445(NCF):Dec84-362
Kinder, A.G. Spanish Protestants and Reformers in the Sixteenth Century.
  A. Márquez, 304(JHP):Winter84-166
Kindermann, W. Analyse and Synthese im Werk William Faulkners.
  M.N. Love, 395(MFS):Winter84-824
Kindleberger, C.P. Keynesianism vs. Monetarism and Other Essays in Financial History.
  S. Strange, 617(TLS):27Dec85-1475
Kindrick, R.L. Robert Henryson.
  D.D. Evans, 588(SSL):Vol 19-286
Kindstrand, J.F. Anacharsis.*
  G. Anderson, 303(JoHS):Vol 104-194
  D.M. Schenkeveld, 394:Vol137fasc1/2-202
Kindstrand, J.F. The Stylistic Evaluation of Aeschines in Antiquity.*
  M.J. Edwards, 303(JoHS):Vol 104-210
  L. Pernot, 555:Vol58fasc2-300
King, A. The Writings of Camara Laye.
  K. Dramé, 538(RAL):Spring84-89
King, A. and M. Sheraton. Is Salami and Eggs Better Than Sex?
  J. Greenfeld, 441:6Oct85-20
King, A.H. A Mozart Legacy.
  H.C.R. Landon, 617(TLS):15Mar85-291

King, A.H. A Wealth of Music in the Collections of the British Library (Reference Division) and the British Museum.
  P.W. Jones, 410(M&L):Oct84-365
  J. Sachs, 415:Sep84-501
King, B., ed. West Indian Literature.
  L.W. Brown, 459:Vol18No2/3-181
King, B. Women of the Future.
  L. Leith, 561(SFS):Nov84-341
King, D. and C. Porter. Images of Revolution.
  639(VQR):Spring84-64
King, D.J.C. Castellarium Anglicanum.
  F.L. Cheyette, 589:Oct84-943
King, F. Act of Darkness.*
  P. Craig, 617(TLS):5Jul85-757
  D. Flower, 249(HudR):Summer84-304
King, F. Confessions of a Failed Southern Lady.
  B. Creaturo, 441:10Feb85-27
  J. Neville, 617(TLS):18Oct85-1191
King, F. One is a Wanderer.
  J. Symons, 617(TLS):13Sep85-1001
King, F., ed. Twenty Stories.
  C. Hawtree, 617(TLS):26Jul85-833
King, F. Voices in an Empty Room.*
  442(NY):25Feb85-103
King, F. - see Hearn, L.
King, J. Troubled Water.
  W. Biddle, 441:29Sep85-42
King, J. and C. Ryskamp - see Cowper, W.
King, J.N. English Reformation Literature.*
  H. Davies, 570(SQ):Spring84-113
  F.J. Levy, 401(MLQ):Dec83-422
  J.M. Mueller, 405(MP):Nov84-195
  W.B. Patterson, 569(SR):Spring84-xxiv
  H.M. Richmond, 301(JEGP):Apr84-233
  A.D. Weiner, 125:Spring84-278
King, J.R. The Literary Moment as a Lens on Reality.
  295(JML):Nov84-344
King, M., ed. Parsing Natural Language.
  E.J. Briscoe, 297(JL):Sep84-390
King, M., L. Novik and C. Citrenbaum. Irresistible Communication.
  S. Auyash, 583:Summer85-382
King, N. Abel Gance.*
  K. Reader, 707:Autumn84-305
King, P. Snares of the Enemy.
  T.J. Binyon, 617(TLS):10May85-528
King, S. Skeleton Crew.
  S. Bolotin, 441:9Jun85-11
King, T.M. and J.F. Salmon, eds. Teilhard and the Unity of Knowledge.
  R.J. O'Connell, 258:Jun84-213
King, W.N. Hamlet's Search for Meaning.
  C. Hoy, 569(SR):Spring84-256
King-Farlow, J. Self-Knowledge and Social Relations.
  E.J. Kremer, 154:Jun84-341
Kingston, P.J. Anti-Semitism in France During the 1930's.
  D. Stephens, 207(FR):Mar85-615
Kingston-Mann, E. Lenin and the Problem of Marxist Peasant Revolution.
  W.L.M., 185:Oct84-186
Kington, M. Moreover, Too.
  H. Jacobson, 617(TLS):20Dec85-1453
Kinnaird, J. Olaf Stapledon.
  R.M. Philmus, 561(SFS):Mar84-71
Kinnell, G. Mortal Acts, Mortal Words.
  L. Goldensohn, 418(MR):Summer84-303

[continued]

[continuing]
H. Reinhold, 549(RLC):Jul-Sep84-365
H.H. Rudnick, 52:Band19Heft1-97
van der Klift-Tellegen, H. Knitting from
the Netherlands.
K. Buffington, 614:Summer85-28
Kligman, G. Căluş.
Y.R. Lockwood, 292(JAF):Apr-Jun84-222
Klíma, I. My Merry Mornings.
G. Annan, 441:28Jul85-8
M. Glenny, 617(TLS):5Jul85-756
Klimenko, M., ed and trans. The "Vita" of
St. Sergii of Radonezh.
N.W. Ingham, 574(SEEJ):Summer84-257
Kline, G.C. The Last Courtly Lover.
T. Parkinson, 177(ELT):Vol27No2-171
Kline, M. Mathematics and the Search for
Knowledge.
E. Nagel, 453(NYRB):24Oct85-40
Kline, M-J. and others - see Burr, A.
Klinefelter, W. Origins of Sherlock
Holmes.
E. Lauterbach, 177(ELT):Vol27No3-251
E.S. Lauterbach, 395(MFS):Summer84-379
Klinkott, M. Islamische Baukunst in
Afghanisch-Sīstān.
C. Ewert, 43:Band14Heft2-175
Klinkowitz, J. The Self-Apparent Word.
R.M. Davis, 223:Fall84-330
R.A. Morace, 363(LitR):Summer85-617
Klinkowitz, J. Kurt Vonnegut.
D. Seed, 447(N&Q):Aug83-381
Klinkowitz, J. and J. Knowlton. Peter
Handke and the Postmodern Transforma-
tion.
C. Bedwell, 395(MFS):Winter84-735
Klinzing, D. and D. Communication for
Allied Health Professionals.
S. Auyash, 583:Summer85-382
Klitgaard, R. Choosing Elites.
D. Nyberg, 441:5May85-7
Klockow, R. Linguistik der Gänsefüsschen.
N. Nail, 685(ZDL):1/1984-118
Kloefkorn, W. and others. On Common
Ground. (J.V. Brummels and M. Sanders,
eds)
R. Jackson, 502(PrS):Winter84-105
J.R. Saucerman, 649(WAL):Feb85-326
Kloocke, K. Benjamin Constant.
M.A. Wégimont, 446(NCFS):Summer85-297
D. Wood, 208(FS):Oct84-468
Klopfenstein, E. Tausend Kirschbäume,
Yoshitsune.
D. Schauwecker, 407(MN):Spring84-111
Klopstock, F.G. Werke und Briefe.
(Briefe, Vol 1, Pt 1) (H. Riege, ed)
H.T. Betteridge, 402(MLR):Jul84-743
P.M. Mitchell, 301(JEGP):Apr84-279
N. Oellers, 52:Band19Heft3-307
Klopstock, F.G. Werke und Briefe.
(Briefe, Vol 7, Pts 2 and 3) (H.
Riege, ed)
H.T. Betteridge, 402(MLR):Jul84-743
P.M. Mitchell, 301(JEGP):Jul84-409
N. Oellers, 52:Band19Heft3-307
Klopstock, F.G. Werke und Briefe.*
(Werke, Vol 2) (K. Hurlebusch, ed)
[shown in prev under sub-title]
H.T. Betteridge, 402(MLR):Jan84-234
N. Oellers, 52:Band19Heft3-307
Klose, K. Russia and the Russians.*
A. Friendly, Jr., 550(RusR):Oct84-413
639(VQR):Autumn84-134

Kluback, W. Hermann Cohen.
D. Novak, 390:Nov84-57
Kluge, E-H.W. The Ethics of Deliberate
Death.
L.W. Sumner, 154:Sep84-503
Klychkov, S. Sakharnyi nemets. (2nd ed)
H. Ermolaev, 550(RusR):Jul84-325
Knab, E., E. Mitsch and K. Oberhuber, with
S. Ferino-Pagden. Raphael: Die Zeichnun-
gen.
C.M. Goguel, 90:Jul84-438
Knack, M.C. and O.C. Stewart. As Long As
the River Shall Run.
M. Peters, 441:26May85-15
Knapp, B. Andrée Chedid.
E. Sellin, 593:Fall84-262
Knapp, B. Sacha Guitry.
J. Decock, 207(FR):May85-923
Knapp, B.L. Archetype, Dance and the
Writer.
T. Hadar, 446(NCFS):Summer-Fall84-218
Knapp, B.L. Paul Claudel.
M.M. Nagy, 397(MD):Mar84-149
Knapp, B.L. Dream and Image.
P.J. Whyte, 208(FS):Jul84-362
Knapp, B.L. Theatre and Alchemy.*
M.G. Hamilton, 107(CRCL):Mar84-111
Knapp, G.P., ed. Max Frisch: Aspekte des
Bühnenwerks.
M.E. Musgrave, 406:Winter84-474
Knapp, G.P. and M. Gabriele Wohmann.*
R-E.B. Joeres, 221(GQ):Spring84-338
C. Poore, 406:Winter84-471
Knapp, L.M. - see Smollett, T.
Knapp, P.A. and M.A. Stugrin - see "Assays:
Critical Approaches to Medieval and
Renaissance Texts"
Knapp, R.C. Roman Córdoba.
R. Brilliant, 124:Nov-Dec84-131
S.L. Spaar, 121(CJ):Dec84/Jan85-169
Knapp, R.G., ed. China's Island Frontier.
J. Huber, 293(JASt):Nov83-134
Knapp-Potthoff, A. and K. Knapp. Fremd-
sprachenlernen und -lehren.
F.W. Gester, 38:Band102Heft3/4-505
Knapp-Tepperberg, E-M. Literatur und
Unbewusstes.*
D. Bellos, 208(FS):Jan84-110
H.P. Lund, 535(RHL):Mar/Apr84-299
Knappert, J. Epic Poetry in Swahili and
Other African Languages.
J.L. Mbele, 538(RAL):Winter84-589
Knappert, J. Malay Myths and Legends.
C.W. Watson, 293(JASt):May84-610
Knechtges, D.R. - see Xiao Tong
Kneen, P. Soviet Scientists and the State.
A. Brown, 617(TLS):27Sep85-1078
Knepler, M. Let's Talk About It.
D.S. Rood, 399(MLJ):Winter84-425
Knibiehler, Y. and others. De la pucelle
à la minette.
B.T. Cooper, 207(FR):May85-929
Knight, A.E. Aspects of Genre in Late
Medieval French Drama.
G.A. Runnalls, 402(MLR):Oct84-930
H.F. Williams, 207(FR):May85-885
Knight, D. Flaubert's Characters.
C. Prendergast, 617(TLS):13Dec85-1416
Knight, D. The Man in the Tree.
C. Greenland, 617(TLS):30Aug85-946
Knight, G.W. Klinton Top.
P. Redgrove, 617(TLS):14Jun85-677

Knight, K.L. Atlantic Circle.
  C. Buckley, 441:10Feb85-15
Knight, R. Edwin Muir.*
  E. Longley, 447(N&Q):Jun83-264
  J.R. Watson, 402(MLR):Jul84-686
Knight, S. Form and Ideology in Crime
  Fiction.*
  J.S. Whitley, 447(N&Q):Dec83-537
Knight, S. Historical Scripts.
  W. Gardner, 324:Jul85-578
Knight, S. The Killing of Justice Godfrey.
  J. Miller, 617(TLS):18Jan85-57
Knights, L.C. Selected Essays in Criti-
  cism.
  A. Davis, 447(N&Q):Apr83-171
Knilli, F. and S. Zielinski. Holocaust
  zur Unterhaltung. Betrifft "Holocaust."
  M. Silberman, 221(GQ):Fall84-693
Knister, R. Windfalls for Cider. (J.
  Kuropatwa, ed)
  B. Pell, 628(UWR):Spring-Summer85-108
"Knizhnoe iskusstvo SSSR." (Vol 1)
  354:Mar84-103
Knobel, L. The Faber Guide to Twentieth-
  Century Architecture.
  H. Winterbotham, 617(TLS):8Nov85-1273
Knopf, J. Alltages-Ordnung.
  H. Sührig, 196:Band25Heft3/4-351
Knopf, J. Brecht-Handbuch: Theater.
  K-H. Schoeps, 406:Summer84-231
Knorr-Cetina, K.D. The Manufacture of
  Knowledge.
  J. Agassi, 262:Mar84-166
Knorr-Cetina, K.D. and A.V. Cicourel, eds.
  Advances in Social Theory and Methodol-
  ogy.
  S. Fuller, 167:Nov84-439
Knott, B. Becos.*
  F. Garber, 29(APR):Sep/Oct85-14
Knowler, D. The Falconer of Central Park.*
  S. Mills, 617(TLS):18Jan85-73
Knowles, A.V. - see Turgenev, I.S.
Knowles, C. Les enseignements de Théodore
  Paléologue.
  A.E. Laiou, 589:Oct84-917
  R. Morse, 402(MLR):Oct84-929
Knowles, F.E. and J.I. Press, eds. Papers
  in Slavonic Linguistics. (Vol 1)
  V.M. Du Feu, 575(SEER):Apr84-251
Knowles, T.D. Ideology, Art and Commerce.
  I. Campbell, 571(ScLJ):Autumn84-22
  L. Hartveit, 179(ES):Aug84-371
  P. Morere, 189(EA):Jul-Sep85-342
Knowlson, J., ed. Theatre Workbook 1: Sam-
  uel Beckett, "Krapp's Last Tape."
  K. O'Malley, 299:Number9-145
Knowlson, J. and J. Pilling. Frescoes of
  the Skull.
  J. Acheson, 299:Autumn82-149
Knox, B. - see Sophocles
Knox, C. The House Party.
  P. Stitt, 219(GaR):Spring84-166
Knox, E.C. Patterns of Person.
  D. Brewer, 210(FrF):Jan84-118
  R. Galle, 547(RF):Band96Heft4-469
  M-F. Hilgar, 207(FR):Oct84-127
Knox, G. Piazzetta.
  J. Steer, 324:May85-427
Knox, G. - see Forbes, P. and M.H. Smith
Knust, H. Bertolt Brecht: Leben des
  Galilei.
  S. Mews, 221(GQ):Summer84-502

Koblitz, A.H. A Convergence of Lives.
  B.E. Clements, 104(CASS):Winter84-466
Koch, C.J. The Doubleman.
  R. Jones, 362:2May85-27
  P. Smelt, 617(TLS):7Jun85-644
  D.J. Taylor, 176:Sep-Oct85-52
Koch, E.I., with W. Rauch. Politics.
  K. Auletta, 441:22Dec85-7
Koch, H. and others. Zur Theorie der soz-
  ialistischen Kultur.
  W. Kahle, 654(WB):4/1984-679
Koch, P. Verb — Valenz — Verfügung.
  C. Schmitt, 72:Band221Heft2-400
Koch, W.A. Poetizität.
  G. Michel, 682(ZPSK):Band37Heft6-720
Kochan, L. and R. Abraham. The Making of
  Modern Russia. (rev)
  J. Keep, 575(SEER):Apr84-294
Kochman, T. Black and White Styles in Con-
  flict.*
  J. Verschueren, 355(LSoc):Dec84-489
Kockel, V. Die Grabbauten vor dem Herkul-
  aner Tor in Pompeji.
  R. Ling, 123:Vol34No2-280
Kocourek, R. La langue française de la
  technique et de la science.
  H. Kalverkämper, 547(RF):Band96Heft1/2-
  125
Koebner, T., ed. Weimars Ende.
  D. Barnouw, 221(GQ):Winter84-119
Koehler, L. N.F. Fedorov.
  E. Koutaissoff, 575(SEER):Jan84-98
Koehn, L. The Eyes of the Wind. Forest
  Full of Rain.
  J. Rodriguez, 102(CanL):Autumn84-145
Koelb, C. The Incredulous Reader.
  C. Baldick, 617(TLS):14Jun85-676
  E.W. White, 395(MFS):Winter84-851
Koelb, C. - see Mann, T.
Koenker, D. Moscow Workers and the 1917
  Revolution.*
  R.C. Elwood, 104(CASS):Spring-Summer84-
  201
Koentjaraningrat. Javanese Culture.
  R.H. Barnes, 617(TLS):13Dec85-1432
Koepke, W., with S.B. Knoll, eds. Johann
  Gottfried Herder.
  J.K. Fugate, 221(GQ):Fall84-652
Koepke, W. and M. Winkler, eds. Deutsch-
  sprachige Exilliteratur.
  S.S. Prawer, 617(TLS):11Oct85-1137
Koerner, E.F.K. Ferdinand de Saussure.
  P. Swiggers, 353:Vol22No3-423
Koerner, K. - see Pedersen, H.
Koestler, M. Living with Koestler. (C.
  Goodman, ed)
  A. Huth, 362:7Feb85-23
  E. Pearce, 129:Aug85-67
  P. Thody, 617(TLS):10May85-524
Koethe, J. The Late Wisconsin Spring.*
  M. Kinzie, 29(APR):Nov/Dec85-7
Kofman, S. Le respect des femmes.
  C. Chalier, 192(EP):Oct-Dec84-565
Kogan, V. The Flowers of Fiction.*
  J. Langenbacher-Liebgott, 547(RF):
  Band96Heft1/2-201
  W.D. Redfern, 402(MLR):Jan84-205
  J. Sareil, 207(FR):May85-899
Kohak, E. The Embers and the Stars.
  L.G., 185:Apr85-768

Kohfeldt, M.L. Lady Gregory.
R. Foster, 617(TLS):12Jul85-778
D. Rushe, 441:3Mar85-12
D. Shawe-Taylor, 442(NY):13May85-146
Kohl, H. Growing Minds.
L. King, 42(AR):Summer84-376
639(VQR):Summer84-93
Köhler, I. Baudelaire et Hoffmann.*
G.R. Kaiser, 224(GRM):Band34Heft3-356
Kohut, Z.E., ed. The American Bibliog-
raphy of Slavic and East European
Studies for 1981.
C. Kern-Simirenko, 550(RusR):Oct84-435
Kōjirō, Y. - see under Yoshikawa Kōjirō
"Kokinshū." (L.R. Rodd and M.C. Henkenius,
trans)
C. Dunn, 617(TLS):29Mar85-360
Kokott, H. "Reynke de Vos."
H. Heinen, 406:Summer84-207
Kolakowski, L. Main Currents of Marxism.*
W.G. Regier, 152(UDQ):Spring84-119
Kolb, F. Agora und Theater, Volks- und
Festversammlung.*
R.A. Tomlinson, 303(JoHS):Vol 104-253
Kolb, J. - see Hallam, A.H.
Kolb, P. - see Proust, M.
Kolde, G. Sprachkontakte in gemischt-
sprachigen Städten.*
W. Lenschen, 209(FM):Oct84-254
Kolenbrock-Netz, J. Fabrikation — Experi-
ment — Schöpfung.*
K. Zieger, 535(RHL):Jul/Aug84-641
Kolenda, K. Philosophy in Literature.*
T.D. Howells, 478:Apr84-128
Kolesnikoff, N. Bruno Jasieński.
J.T. Baer, 497(PolR):Vol29No1/2-160
N. Taylor, 575(SEER):Jul84-446
Kolin, P.C., ed. Shakespeare in the South.
K. King, 392:Spring84-205
Kolitz, Z. The Teacher.
J. Riemer, 390:May84-62
Koljević, S. The Epic in the Making.*
I. Markoff, 187:Fall85-520
Koller, A.M. The Theater Duke.*
H. Henderson, 609:Summer/Fall85-92
Kolln, M. Understanding English Grammar.
P.R. Randall, 35(AS):Summer84-182
Kolmer, L. Ad capiendas vulpes.
J.H. Mundy, 589:Apr84-401
Kolodny, A. The Land Before Her.*
N. Baym, 27(AL):Oct84-427
M. Breitwieser, 141:Fall84-392
J. Eis, 219(GaR):Winter84-896
M. Pryse, 357:Fall84-13
Kolodny, A. The Lay of the Land.
295(JML):Nov84-344
Kolve, V.A. Chaucer and the Imagery of
Narrative.*
K.J. Harty, 573(SSF):Fall84-419
P. Neuss, 175:Autumn84-247
Kom, A., ed. Dictionnaire des oeuvres
littéraires négro-africaines de langue
française des origines à 1978.
V. Coulon, 538(RAL):Fall84-490
S. Crosta, 627(UTQ):Summer84-524
Komarovsky, M. Women in College.
A. Simmons, 441:6Oct85-34
Kome, P. The Taking of Twenty-Eight.
M. Cohen, 99:Apr84-28
Komlos, J., ed. Economic Development in
the Habsburg Monarchy in the Nineteenth
Century.
S.Z. Pech, 104(CASS):Winter84-493

Komparu, K. The Noh Theater.
M. Bethe, 407(MN):Summer84-224
J.K. Gillespie, 293(JASt):Aug84-765
Kondylis, P. Die Aufklärung im Rahmen des
neuzeitlichen Rationalismus.*
B. Wirkus, 687:Apr-Jun84-329
Konefsky, A.S. and A.J. King - see Webster,
D.
König-Nordhoff, U. Ignatius von Loyola.
B.R. Brinkman, 90:Nov84-701
Konigsberg, I., ed. American Criticism in
the Poststructuralist Age.
J. Phelan, 567:Vol148No3/4-345
Kono, T. Strategy and Structure of Japan-
ese Enterprises.
F. Cairncross, 617(TLS):31May85-613
Konolige, K. The Richest Women in the
World.
M. Dowd, 441:25Aug85-17
Konrad, H. and W. Neugebauer, eds. Ar-
beiterbewegung — Faschismus — National-
bewusstsein.
F.L. Carsten, 575(SEER):Jul84-461
Konstan, D. Roman Comedy.
E. Fantham, 529(QQ):Summer84-434
S.M. Goldberg, 130:Summer84-175
Konstantinović, Z., W. Anderson and W.
Dietze, eds. Klassische Modelle in der
Literatur.
M. Brunkhorst, 52:Band19Heft1-75
Konstantinović, Z., M. Naumann and H.R.
Jauss, eds. Literarische Kommunikation
und Rezeption.
M. Brunkhorst, 52:Band19Heft1-75
Kontzi, R., ed. Substrate und Superstrate
in den romanischen Sprachen.
D. Nehls, 257(IRAL):Aug84-235
P. Swiggers, 353:Vol22No2-249
Konwicki, T. A Minor Apocalypse.*
G.T. Kapolka, 497(PolR):Vol29No3-107
639(VQR):Winter84-25
Konyves, T. Poetry in Performance.
A. Mandel, 102(CanL):Summer84-149
Koon, H. and R. Switzer. Eugène Scribe.
H.G. Hall, 208(FS):Jan84-71
Kopečný, F. Základní všeslovanská slovní
zásoba.
H. Leeming, 575(SEER):Oct84-631
Köpeczi, B., G.M. Vajda and J. Kovács, eds.
Actes du VIIIe Congrès de l'Association
Internationale de Littérature Comparée/
Proceedings of the 8th Congress of the
International Comparative Literature
Association.*
D.W. Fokkema, 494:Autumn82-176
Kopelman, L. and J.C. Moskop, eds. Ethics
and Mental Retardation.
S.G.P., 185:Jul85-990
Köpf, G., ed. Rezeptionspragmatik.
Y. Chevrel, 549(RLC):Oct-Dec84-478
Kopff, E.C. - see Euripides
Kopff, E.C. - see Otis, B.
Köpke, W. Lion Feuchtwanger.
K. Modick, 384:Mar84-219
Kopp, R. - see de Balzac, H.
Köppel, S. and others. Englisch.
D. Nehls, 257(IRAL):Feb84-82
Koppelman, S., comp. Old Maids.
B. Lyons, 573(SSF):Fall84-411
Koppenberg, P. Hagiographische Studien zu
den Biskupa Sögur, unter besonderer
Berücksichtigung der "Jóns saga helga."
M. Cormack, 563(SS):Autumn84-380

205

Koppenhaver, J. and L. Winget. Essential Spanish Grammar in Review.
   R.B. Klein, 399(MLJ):Summer84-194
Koppensteiner, J. Österreich.
   R. Jurasek, 399(MLJ):Autumn84-293
Koppitz, H-J. - see "Gutenberg-Jahrbuch 1984"
Köppl, S. and others, eds. Englisch.
   M.I.M., 300:Vol 17-123
Korda, M. Queenie.
   M. Thiébaux, 441:28Apr85-24
Koren, R. L'Anti-récit.
   B.L. Knapp, 207(FR):Apr85-740
Korman, G. "I Want to Go Home!"
   M.J. Evans, 102(CanL):Autumn84-63
Korn, M. Ezra Pound.
   295(JML):Nov84-494
Korn, R. Generations.
   M. Harry, 198:Summer84-117
Kornai, J. Growth, Shortage and Efficiency.
   H. Neary, 104(CASS):Fall84-368
Kornaros, V. Erotokritos.
   R. Beaton, 617(TLS):11Oct85-1149
Kornblatt, J.R. White Water.
   K. Morton, 441:7Jul85-12
Kornelius, J., E. Otto and G. Stratmann, eds. Einführung in die zeitgenössische irische Literatur.
   E. Kreutzer, 72:Band221Heft2-385
Kornheiser, T. The Baby Chase.
   639(VQR):Spring84-63
Kornilov, V. Building a Prison.
   F. Eberstadt, 129:Jul85-42
   R. Lourie, 441:14Apr85-21
   R. Milner-Gulland, 617(TLS):5Jul85-756
Kornilov, V. Girls to the Front.
   R. Milner-Gulland, 617(TLS):5Jul85-756
Korshin, P.J., ed. The Eighteenth Century. (Vol 5)
   J. Freehafer, 566:Autumn84-68
Korshin, P.J. Typologies in England, 1650-1820.*
   G.P. Landow, 536:Vol6-21
   J.S. Ryan, 67:May84-83
   M. Smith, 83:Spring84-119
Korsten, F.J.M. Roger North (1651-1734), Virtuoso and Essayist.
   P. Millard, 447(N&Q):Feb83-80
   J. Morrill, 541(RES):Aug84-436
Kortian, G. Metacritique.
   D. Misgeld, 488:Jun84-284
Koschel, C. and I. von Weidenbaum - see Bachmann, I.
Koschorreck, W. and W. Werner, eds. Codex Manesse.*
   I. Glier, 589:Jan84-169
   L.E. Stamm, 471:Jan/Feb/Mar84-96
Koshal, S. Ladakhi Grammar.* (B.G. Misra, ed)
   S.R. Sharma, 261:Mar/Jun82-35
Kosinski, J. The Devil Tree. (rev)
   B.T. Lupack, 497(PolR):Vol29No1/2-147
Koslowski, P. Ethik des Kapitalismus.* Gesellschaft und Staat.
   K. Hartmann, 489(PJGG):Band91Heft2-411
Kosok, H., ed. Drama und Theater im England des 20. Jahrhunderts.*
   H. Rorrison, 447(N&Q):Dec83-535
Kosok, H., ed. Das englische Drama im 18. Jahrhundert.
   W. Riehle, 224(GRM):Band34Heft1/2-253

Kosok, H., ed. Studies in Anglo-Irish Literature.
   E. Kreutzer, 72:Band221Heft2-385
   C. Ward, 174(Éire):Summer84-156
Koss, S. Asquith.
   617(TLS):12Jul85-783
Kosta, P. Eine russische Kosmographie aus dem 17. Jahrhundert.
   U. Schweier, 559:Vol8No2-180
Kostelanetz, R. - see Stein, G.
Köster-Bunselmeyer, D. Literarischer Sozialismus.
   G. Tiemann-Kaplan, 67:May84-98
Kostof, S. A History of Architecture.
   W. Alonso, 441:28Apr85-1
Kostrovitskaya, V. One Hundred Lessons in Classical Dance.
   M. Horosko, 151:Jan84-98
Koszarski, R. The Astoria Studio and its Fabulous Films.
   W.K. Everson, 200:Jan84-59
Koszarski, R. The Man You Loved to Hate.*
   W.K. Everson, 200:Jan84-59
   J. Rosenbaum, 707:Winter83/84-68
   639(VQR):Spring84-52
Kott, J. The Theater of Essence.
   R. Brustein, 453(NYRB):14Mar85-3
   R. Bryden, 441:10Feb85-18
   K. Elam, 617(TLS):20Dec85-1458
   442(NY):8Jul85-74
Kotzor, G., ed. Das altenglische Martyrologium.*
   M. Clayton, 541(RES):Aug84-347
   J.E. Cross, 38:Band102Heft3/4-518
   T.H. Leinbaugh, 589:Jan84-172
   C. Sisam, 447(N&Q):Feb83-67
Kotzwinkle, W. E.T.: The Book of the Green Planet.
   J. Grossman, 441:5May85-24
Kotzwinkle, W. Jewel of the Moon.
   R. Cohen, 441:29Dec85-18
Kousser, J.M. and J.M. McPherson, eds. Region, Race, and Reconstruction.*
   C.N. Degler, 579(SAQ):Spring84-216
   M. Kreyling, 392:Winter83/84-97
Kouwenhoven, J.A. Half a Truth is Better Than None.*
   M.S. Young, 39:Jan84-70
Kouwenhoven, J.K. Apparent Narrative as Thematic Metaphor.*
   B. Tannier, 189(EA):Apr-Jun85-231
Kovàcs, K.S. "Le Rêve et la vie."
   E.F. Gray, 207(FR):Dec84-294
   P.M. Wetherill, 535(RHL):Nov/Dec84-975
Kovacs, P.D. The "Andromache" of Euripides.
   D.J. Conacher, 122:Jan84-53
   E.M. Craik, 303(JoHS):Vol 104-202
   S.E. Scully, 487:Spring84-93
Kovic, R. Around the World in Eight Days.
   J. Eidus, 441:17Feb85-20
Kowalk, W. Alexander Pope.*
   J. McLaverty, 447(N&Q):Feb83-81
Kowet, D. A Matter of Honor.*
   639(VQR):Autumn84-134
Kowinski, W.S. The Malling of America.
   G. Clay, 441:17Feb85-11
Kozloff, M. The Restless Decade. (L. Thomas, ed)
   J. Yau, 62:Dec84-79

Kozol, J. Illiterate America.
  R. Meisler, 385(MQR):Fall85-650
  J.S. Murphy, 441:14Apr85-36
  442(NY):1Apr85-113
Kozovoï, V. Hors de la colline.
  G. Quinsat, 450(NRF):Oct84-86
Kraft, E. The Personal History, Adventures, Experiences and Observations of Peter Leroy.
  R. Plunket, 441:29Sep85-38
Kraggerud, E. Der Namensatz der taciteischen Germania.*
  C. Guiraud, 555:Vol58fasc1-147
Kramer, B., C. Römer and D. Hagedorn, eds. Kölner Papyri 4.
  J. Rusten, 487:Summer84-186
Kramer, D. - see Hardy, T.
Kramer, H. The Age of the Avant Garde.
  J.A. Richardson, 289:Spring84-93
Krämer, H. Platone e i fondamenti della metafisica.
  P. Louis, 555:Vol58fasc2-295
  P. Pellegrin, 542:Oct-Dec84-451
Kramer, H. The Revenge of the Philistines.
  R. Wollheim, 441:17Nov85-11
Kramer, K. A Handbook for Visitors from Outer Space.*
  A. Kavounas, 617(TLS):20Sep85-1028
Kramer, L. A Lifelong House.
  H. Davies, 617(TLS):1Feb85-128
Kramer, L. Music and Poetry.
  L. Beckett, 617(TLS):18Oct85-1162
Kramer, V. Thomas Merton.
  G. Reynolds, 30:Spring85-90
Kramer, V.A. and others. Andrew Lytle, Walker Percy, Peter Taylor.
  E. Sarcone, 392:Spring84-201
Krampen, M. Meaning in the Urban Environment.
  D. Preziosi, 567:Vol49No1/2-175
Kramrisch, S. Exploring India's Sacred Art.* (B.S. Miller, ed)
  D.M. Stadtner, 293(JASt):May84-580
Kramrisch, S. The Presence of Śiva.*
  K. Vatsyayan, 318(JAOS):Apr-Jun83-431
Kranes, D. The Hunting Years.
  M. Berkley, 441:20Jan85-18
Kranzberg, M., ed. Ethics in an Age of Pervasive Technology.
  T. Settle, 488:Dec84-515
Kranzmayer, E. Laut- und Flexionslehre der deutschen zimbrischen Mundart.* (M. Hornung, ed)
  G.A. Henrotte, 350:Mar85-222
Krasa, J. The "Travels" of Sir John Mandeville.
  J.F. Cotter, 249(HudR):Summer84-299
Krashen, S.D., R.C. Scarcella and M.H. Long, eds. Child-Adult Differences in Second Language Acquisition.*
  E.B. Bernhardt, 399(MLJ):Autumn84-274
Krashen, S.D. and T.D. Terrell. The Natural Approach.
  K.J. Krahnke, 608:Sep85-591
  S.S. Magnan, 399(MLJ):Autumn84-277
  G. Taylor, 351(LL):Dec84-97
Krasikov, A. From Dictatorship to Democracy.
  P. Preston, 617(TLS):27Dec85-1471
Krasner, W. Resort to Murder.
  N. Callendar, 441:6Oct85-35
Kratins, O. The Dream of Chivalry.
  W.H. Jackson, 402(MLR):Jul84-740

Krätzer, A. Studien zum Amerikabild in der neueren deutschen Literatur.
  M. Knapp, 222(GR):Spring84-78
Kratzmann, G., ed. "Colkelbie Sow" and "The Talis of the Fyve Bestes."
  F. Riddy, 571(ScLJ):Autumn84-10
Kraulis, J.A., ed. Canada.
  529(QQ):Summer84-488
Kraus, K. In These Great Times.* (H. Zohn, ed)
  J.P. Stern, 441:14Jul85-20
Krause, D. The Profane Book of Irish Comedy.*
  R.B. Henkle, 569(SR):Winter84-121
  F. Kinahan, 405(MP):Nov84-222
  S. Watt, 301(JEGP):Jan84-137
Krause, M. Das Trivialdrama der Goethezeit, 1780-1805.
  S.D. Martinson, 221(GQ):Summer84-473
Krauss, A. Das Vergnügen.
  U. Heukenkamp, 654(WB):9/1984-1540
Krauss, H. Atemtherapie.
  G.F. Meier, 682(ZPSK):Band37Heft6-728
Krauss, H. Epica feudale e pubblico borghese.
  T.D. Hemming, 208(FS):Jan84-42
Krauss, H., ed. Europäisches Hochmittelalter.*
  D.H. Green, 402(MLR):Apr84-397
  J.A. Schultz, 221(GQ):Winter84-138
Krauss, H. and R. Wolff, eds. Psychoanalytische Literaturwissenschaft und Literatursoziologie.
  B. Burmeister, 654(WB):1/1984-166
Krauss, M.E., ed. In Honor of Eyak.*
  J.A. Shulimson, 292(JAF):Jul-Sep84-363
Krauss, R. and J. Livingston. L'Amour Fou.
  A. Grundberg, 441:8Dec85-24
Krauthammer, C. Cutting Edges.
  M. Kramer, 441:10Nov85-18
Kreft, W. Ikonographische Studien zur altčechischen Alexandreis.
  A. Mĕšťan, 688(ZSP):Band44Heft1-225
Kreimendahl, L. Humes verborgener Rationalismus.
  H. Beck, 319:Apr85-263
  M. Kuehn, 518:Apr84-110
  R. Lüthe, 687:Nov-Dec84-679
Kreindler, I., ed. The Changing Status of Russian in the Soviet Union.*
  J.I. Press, 575(SEER):Jan84-103
Kreiner, P. People Like Us in a Place Like This.
  J. Acheson, 102(CanL):Autumn84-162
Kreiswirth, M. William Faulkner.
  A. Bleikasten, 189(EA):Jul-Sep85-358
  M. Grimwood, 578:Fall85-101
  D. Krause, 395(MFS):Winter84-819
  C.E. Rollyson, Jr., 627(UTQ):Summer84-434
  295(JML):Nov84-436
Kreitman, E.S. Deborah.*
  442(NY):14Jan85-117
Krell, D.F. - see Heidegger, M.
Kremer, D. and R. Lorenzo, eds. Tradición, actualidade e futuro do galego.
  D. Messner, 547(RF):Band96Heft3-319
Kreml, W.P. Relativism and the Natural Left.
  M.W.H., 185:Jul85-974
Kremnitz, G. Français et créole — ce qu'en pensent les enseignants.
  A. Hull, 207(FR):Dec84-333

207

Kremnitz, G. Das Okzitanische.*
    G.F. Meier, 682(ZPSK):Band37Heft3-396
Kren, T., ed. Renaissance Painting in
Manuscripts.*
    J.F. Cotter, 249(HudR):Summer84-297
    C. de Hamel, 354:Sep84-288
    J.M. Massing, 78(BC):Autumn84-377
Krentz, P. The Thirty at Athens.
    D.M. Lewis, 487:Autumn84-293
    C. Tuplin, 303(JoHS):Vol 104-242
Krepon, M. Strategic Stalemate.
    C.A. Kojm, 441:17Feb85-21
    P. Windsor, 617(TLS):17May85-557
Kreps, G. and B. Thornton. Health Communi-
cation.
    S. Auyash, 583:Summer85-382
Kress, G. Learning to Write.
    G.A. Edwards, 355(LSoc):Mar84-133
Kretschmer, B. Höfische und altwest-
nordische Erzähltradition in den Riddara-
sögur.
    J. Glauser, 562(Scan):Nov84-165
Kretzmann, N., ed. Infinity and Continu-
ity in Ancient and Medieval Thought.
    J.A. Benardete, 449:May84-367
Kretzmann, N., A. Kenny and J. Pinborg,
eds. The Cambridge History of Later
Medieval Philosophy.*
    F.C. Copleston, 123:Vol34No2-223
    A.J. Freddoso, 311(JP):Mar84-150
    J.R. Milton, 518:Jan84-15
    C. Panaccio, 482(PhR):Jan84-155
    S. Read, 479(PhQ):Apr84-170
Kretzschmar, W.A., Jr., with others - see
McDavid, R.I., Jr.
Kreutzer, H.J. - see "Kleist-Jahrbuch"
Kreuzer, H. and G. Helmes, eds. Expres-
sionismus — Aktivismus — Exotismus.
    G. Benda, 406:Spring84-114
Krick, H. Das Ritual der Feuergründung
(Agnyādheya). (G. Oberhammer, ed)
    K. Mylius, 259(IIJ):Jul84-211
Krieger, M. Arts on the Level.
    A. Montefiore, 447(N&Q):Jun83-273
Krimm, B.G. W.B. Yeats and the Emergence
of the Irish Free State, 1818-1939.*
    R.J. Finneran, 536:Vol5-59
    H. Pyle, 541(RES):Aug84-411
Krinsky, C.H. Synagogues of Europe.
    A. Hertzberg, 441:18Aug85-13
Kripke, S. La logique des noms propres.
    J-M. Salanskis, 98:Apr84-289
Kripke, S.A. Wittgenstein on Rules and
Private Language.*
    G.E.M. Anscombe, 185:Jan85-342
    R. Eldridge, 543:Jun84-859
    E. Gellner, 31(ASch):Spring84-243
    P. Horwich, 486:Mar84-163
    A. Hyslop, 63:Jun84-193
    C. Peacocke, 482(PhR):Apr84-263
    R. Scruton, 393(Mind):Oct84-592
Krishna Rao, M.V.N. Indus Script Deci-
phered.
    K.R. Norman, 361:Jul-Aug84-313
Krishnamoorthy, K. - see Kuntaka
Kristeller, P.O. and H. Maier. Thomas
Morus als Humanist.
    W. von Koppenfels, 52:Band19Heft1-81
Kristensen, E.T. and P. Olsen. Gamle
kildevaeld.
    C. Daxelmüller, 196:Band25Heft1/2-140
Kristensen, S.M. Georg Brandes.
    H. Uecker, 52:Band19Heft2-193

Kristeva, J. Desire in Language.
    C.M. Bové, 81:Winter84-217
    C. Chase, 141:Spring84-193
    J. Fletcher, 366:Spring84-112
Kristeva, J. Powers of Horror.
    C. Chase, 141:Spring84-193
Kritseli-Providi, I. Toichographies tou
Thrēskeutikou kentrou tōn Mykēnōn.
    L. Nixon, 303(JoHS):Vol 104-256
Kritzman, L.D. Destruction/Découverte.*
    F.S. Brown, 494:Vol4No1-200
Krivatsy, N. Bibliography of the Works of
Gregorio Leti.
    C. Fahy, 354:Mar84-100
    U.L., 278(IS):Vol139-138
Kroeber, K. Traditional Literatures of
the American Indian.*
    A. Krupat, 447(N&Q):Jun83-286
Kroetsch, R. Alibi.*
    L. Hutcheon, 102(CanL):Autumn84-76
    T. York, 376:Feb84-132
Kroetsch, R. Essays. (F. Davey and B.P.
Nichol, eds)
    R. Billings, 102(CanL):Autumn84-109
    D. Cooley, 137:Sep84-19
    R. Lecker, 627(UTQ):Summer84-466
Kröhnke, F. Jungen in schlechter Gesell-
schaft.*
    D. Dethlefsen, 564:Feb84-72
Kroker, A. Technology and the Canadian
Mind.
    L. Dubinsky, 150(DR):Spring84-197
Kroll, B.M. and G. Wells, eds. Explora-
tions in the Development of Writing.
    W. Frawley, 350:Mar85-236
Kroll, L. Composants.
    P.B. Jones, 46:Apr84-85
Kroll, P.W. Meng Hao-jan.
    D. Bryant, 244(HJAS):Dec84-563
    V.B. Cass, 116:Jul83-111
Krömer, W. Dichtung und Weltsicht des 19.
Jahrhunderts.
    W. Jung, 52:Band19Heft2-214
Krömer, W. Flaubert.
    A. Green, 208(FS):Jan84-77
Kronauer, B. Rita Münster.
    E. Henscheid, 384:Sep84-691
Kronman, A.T. Max Weber.
    J. Knight, 185:Apr85-756
Kross, J. The Evolution of an American
Town.
    G.H. Nobles, 656(WMQ):Jul84-506
Kruberg, G. A Handbook for Translating
from English into Russian.
    M.I. Levin, 558(RLJ):Winter-Spring84-
286
Krückeberg, E. Der Begriff des Erzählens
im 20. Jahrhundert.
    U. Rainer, 406:Summer84-222
Krull, W. Politische Prosa des Expression-
ismus.
    W. Paulsen, 133:Band17Heft1/2-160
Kruman, M.W. Parties and Politics in
North Carolina, 1836-1865.
    639(VQR):Winter84-15
Krummacher, H-H., ed. Beiträge zur biblio-
graphischen Lage in der germanistischen
Literaturwissenschaft.*
    B. Melzwig, 654(WB):1/1984-172
Krupa, V. The Polynesian Languages.
    E.A. Hawkins, 399(MLJ):Spring84-87

Krupnick, M., ed. Displacement.*
  W.V. Harris, 478:Oct84-297
  S. Scobie, 376:Oct84-107
Kruse, H.H. Mark Twain and "Life on the
  Mississippi."*
  G. Cardwell, 536:Vol6-95
  J. Seelye, 534(RALS):Autumn82-224
  T.A. Tenney, 579(SAQ):Autumn84-478
Kryger, E. La notion de liberté chez
  Rousseau et ses répercussions sur Kant.
  J. Ferrari, 342:Band75Heft3-356
Krynen, J. Idéal du prince et pouvoir
  royal en France à la fin du moyen âge
  (1380-1440).
  S. Gaumond, 539:May85-129
Krysl, M. Mozart, Westmoreland, and Me.
  T. Le Clair, 441:29Dec85-18
Krzyzanow, L. and I. Nayerski - see Zimmer,
  S.K.
Kubota, H. China.
  W.L. Heat-Moon, 441:8Dec85-14
Kucich, J. Excess and Restraint in the
  Novels of Charles Dickens.*
  K.J. Fielding, 541(RES):Nov84-568
Kuczaj, S.A. 2d. Crib Speech and Language
  Play.
  M. Heller, 350:Jun85-509
Kuehl, J. and S. Moore, eds. In Recogni-
  tion of William Gaddis.
  B. Stonehill, 659(ConL):Fall85-362
Kuehn, T. Emancipation in Late Medieval
  Florence.*
  R.F.E. Weissman, 551(RenQ):Summer84-
  230
Kugel, J.L. The Idea of Biblical Poetry.*
  M. O'Connor, 318(JAOS):Apr-Jun83-478
Kühlmann, W. Gelehrtenrepublik und Für-
  stenstaat.
  C.L. Brancaforte, 301(JEGP):Oct84-599
  F. Gaede, 564:Nov84-299
  M.K. Kremer, 221(GQ):Spring84-352
Kuhn, H. Entwürfe zu einer Literatursys-
  tematik des Spätmittelalters.*
  D. Rocher, 224(GRM):Band34Heft1/2-220
Kuhn, H. Minnelieder Walthers von der
  Vogelweide. (C. Cormeau, ed)
  T. Kerth, 221(GQ):Fall84-641
Kuhn, H. - see Neckel, G.
Kuhn, R., ed. The Politics of Broadcast-
  ing.
  J. Symons, 617(TLS):3May85-485
Kühnel, P. Die slavischen Orts- und Flur-
  namen im Lüneburgischen. (E. Eichler,
  ed)
  H. Leeming, 575(SEER):Jul84-472
Kühnhold, I. and others, comps. Deutsche
  Wortbildung. (Pt 3)
  W. Seibicke, 685(ZDL):3/1984-381
Kuhns, R. Psychoanalytic Theory of Art.
  M.H. Bornstein, 290(JAAC):Fall84-98
  G. McFee, 89(BJA):Summer84-261
Kuhs, E. Buchstabendichtung.
  D. Ziegler, 475:Vol 11No20-251
Kuhweide, P. and C-G. Hilgenstock. Über-
  setzungen in eine tote Sprache.
  N. Feinäugle, 685(ZDL):2/1984-267
Kuisel, R.F. Capitalism and the State in
  Modern France.* (French title: Le Cap-
  italisme de l'État en France.)
  J-P. Guinle, 450(NRF):Oct84-103

Kuist, J.M. The Nichols File of "The Gen-
  tleman's Magazine," Attributions of
  Authorship and Other Documentation in
  Editorial Papers at the Folger Library.*
  W.B. Todd, 517(PBSA):Vol78No1-98
Kuklick, B. The Rise of American Philos-
  ophy.
  D. Henrich, 384:Dec84-929
Kully, E., ed. Codex Weimar Q 565.*
  M.W. Wierschin, 221(GQ):Summer84-465
Kully, R.M. Hanns Wagner.
  M. Peters, 72:Band22Heft1-151
Kumar, A. The Night of the Seven Dawns.
  A.L. Weir, 314:Winter-Spring84-209
Kümmel, P. Formalization of Natural Lan-
  guages.*
  A. Lötscher, 685(ZDL):1/1984-121
Kümmell, J. Bäuerliche Gesellschaft und
  städtische Herrschaft im Spätmittelalter.
  B.M. Kaczynski, 589:Oct84-979
Kundera, M. The Book of Laughter and For-
  getting.* (French title: Le Livre du
  rire et de l'oubli.)
  J. Mills, 648(WCR):Oct84-43
Kundera, M. L'insoutenable légèreté de
  l'être.
  Y. Hersant, 98:Nov84-878
  L. Kovacs, 450(NRF):May84-137
Kundera, M. The Unbearable Lightness of
  Being.*
  P. Buitenhuis, 648(WCR):Oct84-41
  M. Howard, 676(YR):Winter85-xxi
  W. Lesser, 249(HudR):Autumn84-480
  P. Lewis, 364:Aug/Sep84-151
  639(VQR):Autumn84-131
Kunio, K. The Noh Theater.
  P. Arnott, 157:No153-51
Kunne, W. and others. Parts and Moments.
  J-M. Salanskis, 98:Apr84-289
Kunstler, J.H. An Embarrassment of Riches.
  P-L. Adams, 61:Aug85-91
Kunt, M.I. The Sultan's Servants.
  J.L. Bacharach, 104(CASS):Winter84-506
Kuntaka. Vakrokti-jīvita of Kuntaka. (K.
  Krishnamoorthy, ed)
  A. Aklujkar, 259(IIJ):Apr84-140
Kunze, E. Finnische Literatur in deut-
  scher Übersetzung 1675-1975.
  H.P. Neureuter, 52:Band19Heft2-208
Kunze, E. Friedrich Rückert und Finn-
  land.*
  U. Groenke, 52:Band19Heft2-213
Kunze, K., ed. Die "Elsässische Legenda
  aurea." (Vol 2)
  M. Görlach, 67:Nov84-253
Kunze, M., ed. Pompeji 79 — 1979.
  G. Schwarz, 52:Band19Heft2-201
Kunze-Götte, E. Corpus Vasorum Antiquorum.
  (Deutschland, Vol 48)
  B.A. Sparkes, 303(JoHS):Vol 104-257
Kuperberg, M. and C. Beitz, eds. Law,
  Economics, and Philosophy.
  C.S., 185:Oct84-180
Kupfer, J.H. Experience as Art.*
  J.A. Hobbs, 289:Summer84-120
Kupper, J-L. Liège et l'église impériale
  XIe-XIIe siècles.*
  L. Löfstedt, 439(NM):1984/1-122
Kupperman, J.J. The Foundations of Moral-
  ity.*
  R. Young, 63:Mar84-89

Lalonde, R. Le Dernier Été des Indiens.
P. Collet, 102(CanL):Winter83-171
Lamar, H.R. - see Perlot, J-N.
Lamarque, H. and G. Soubeille, eds. Ovide
en France dans le Renaissance.
R.W. Hanning, 551(RenQ):Spring84-56
Lamarque, P., ed. Philosophy and Fiction.
A. Ellis, 89(BJA):Spring84-174
D. Novitz, 478:Apr84-144
Lamb, W.K. - see Vancouver, G.
Lambardi, N. Il "Timaeus," Ciceroniano.*
P. Flobert, 555:Vol58fasc2-330
Lambert, A.J. Victorian and Edwardian
Country-House Life from Old Photographs.
J.D. Forbes, 637(VS):Autumn83-108
Lambert, C. Music Ho!
617(TLS):27Sep85-1072
Lambert, F. - see Guilloux, L.
Lambert, J-C. Cobra, un art libre.*
L. Cooke, 90:Sep84-583
Lambert, M. Dickens and the Suspended
Quotation.*
P. Ingham, 541(RES):May84-253
K. Tetzeli von Rosador, 38:Band102
Heft3/4-548
Lambert, P.F. and K.A. Franks, eds.
Voices from the Oil Fields.
L. Milazzo, 584(SWR):Autumn84-462
Lambert, R.D. and B.F. Freed, eds. The
Loss of Language Skills.*
R. King, 660(Word):Dec84-285
J. Walz, 207(FR):Oct84-180
J. Williams, 355(LSoc):Jun84-281
Lambert, R-R. Carnet d'un témoin, 1940-
1943. (R. Cohen, ed)
M.R. Marrus, 617(TLS):24May85-586
Lambi, I.N. The Navy and German Power
Politics 1862-1914.
B. Ranft, 617(TLS):5Apr85-388
Lambrecht, K. Topic, Antitopic and Verb
Agreement in Non-Standard French.*
M.B. Harris, 545(RPh):Aug83-85
R. Martin, 553(RLiR):Jul-Dec84-490
Lambrick, G. The Rollright Stones.
L. Grinsell, 203:Vol195No2-267
Lambton, A. Elizabeth and Alexandra.
K. Fitz Lyon, 617(TLS):2Aug85-855
J. Mellors, 362:25Jul85-32
de Lamirande, C. L'Occulteur.
J.M. Paterson, 102(CanL):Winter83-142
Lamirande, E. Paulin de Milan et la "Vita
Ambrosii."
C.E. Straw, 589:Oct84-919
Lamiroy, B. Les verbes de mouvement en
français et en espagnol.
S. Norwood, 350:Sep85-716
Lamis, A.P. The Two-Party South.
J.M. Kousser, 617(TLS):30Aug85-940
Lamm, R.D. Megatraumas.
M. Tolchin, 441:3Nov85-27
Lamming, R.M. In the Dark.
E. Fisher, 617(TLS):28Jun85-721
Lamming, R.M. The Notebook of Gismondo
Cavalletti.*
K. Ray, 441:6Jan85-20
Lamonde, Y. Je me souviens.
G. Frémont, 193(ELit):Autumn84-417
P. Hébert, 627(UTQ):Summer84-477
Lamonde, Y., ed. L'Imprimé au Québec.
D.M. Hayne, 627(UTQ):Summer84-475
Lamont, C. - see Scott, W.
Lamontagne, M. Business Cycles in Canada.
L. Robinson, 99:Dec84-33

Lamott, A. Joe Jones.
442(NY):30Dec85-79
L'Amour, L. Ride the River.
R.L. Gale, 649(WAL):May84-66
L'Amour, L. Jubal Sackett.
L. Erdrich, 441:2Jun85-7
Lampe, J.R. and M.R. Jackson. Balkan
Economic History, 1500-1950.
D. Deletant, 575(SEER):Oct84-599
D.F. Good, 104(CASS):Spring-Summer84-
233
Lamport, F.J. Lessing and the Drama.*
J.T. Malloy, 221(GQ):Spring84-314
S.D. Martinson, 173(ECS):Winter84/85-
300
Lamy, B. De l'art de parler (1675). (E.
Ruhe, ed)
G. Le Coat, 475:Vol 11No20-266
Lancashire, I., ed. Two Tudor Interludes.
D.C. Kay, 447(N&Q):Oct83-458
Lancaster, L.R. The Korean Buddhist Canon.
V.H. Mair, 318(JAOS):Apr-Jun83-468
"Lancelot, roman en prose du XIIIe siècle."
(Vol 9) (A. Micha, ed)
F. Bogdanow, 208(FS):Jul84-322
F. Lecoy, 554:Vol 104No4-558
Lanchester, E. Elsa Lanchester, Herself.*
G. Playfair, 157:No151-50
Lanciani, G. and G. Bellini, eds. Studi
Latinoamericani 81.
D. Janik, 547(RF):Band96Heft3-379
L. Pollmann, 72:Band221Heft2-467
Landa, L.A. Essays in Eighteenth-Century
English Literature.*
C.J. Rawson, 677(YES):Vol 14-320
Landau, N. The Justices of the Peace 1679-
1760.
G. Holmes, 617(TLS):7Jun85-628
Landau, S.B. P.B. Wight.
J.F. Block, 658:Summer/Autumn84-219
Landau, S.I. Dictionaries.
H. Lindquist, 350:Sep85-709
C.R. Sleeth, 617(TLS):22Mar85-306
Landau, Y. Le désir de la matière pour la
forme dans la pensée d'Aristote. [in
Hebrew]
R. Brague, 192(EP):Apr-Jun84-274
Landau, Z. and J. Tomaszewski. The Polish
Economy in the Twentieth Century.
L. Sirc, 617(TLS):12Jul85-766
de la Lande, A.C. - see under Castelein de
la Lande, A.
Landgrebe, L. Faktizität und Individua-
tion.*
J-F. Courtine, 192(EP):Jul-Sep84-415
Landi, A. Antroponimia siceliota, strut-
tura e funzione.
O. Masson, 555:Vol58fasc1-103
Landi, L. L'Inghilterra e il pensiero
politico di Montesquieu.
C. Rosso, 535(RHL):Jan/Feb84-104
Landon, H.C.R. Handel and His World.
W. Dean, 453(NYRB):19Dec85-44
J. Keates, 617(TLS):11Jan85-31
Landon, H.C.R. Mozart and the Masons.*
A.H. King, 410(M&L):Jan84-69
Landow, G.P. Images of Crisis.*
W.H. McClain, 221(GQ):Spring84-291
Landow, G.P. Ruskin.
P. Gay, 617(TLS):14Jun85-655
Landow, G.P. Victorian Types, Victorian
Shadows.*
S.M. Smith, 677(YES):Vol 14-339

Landrum, L.N. American Popular Culture.
  L.J. Budd, 365:Winter84-22
Landry, F. L'imaginaire chez Stendhal.
  V.D.L., 605(SC):15Apr85-293
Lane, C.W. Evelyn Waugh.*
  F. McCombie, 447(N&Q):Jun83-281
Lane, D. The End of Social Inequality?
  B. Kerblay, 575(SEER):Jul84-466
  V. Tomović, 104(CASS):Fall84-333
Lane, E. Dante Alighieri's Publishing
  Company.
  P. Smelt, 617(TLS):16Aug85-907
Lane, E.W. Arabic-English Lexicon.
  R. Irwin, 617(TLS):26Apr85-474
Lane, P. Old Mother.*
  D. Livesay, 102(CanL):Winter83-124
  P. Stuewe, 529(QQ):Spring84-206
Lane, P. Woman in the Dust.
  D. Hillis, 648(WCR):Apr85-59
Lang, B. Ezechiel.
  M. Greenberg, 318(JAOS):Apr-Jun83-
  472
Lang, C.Y. and E.F. Shannon, Jr. - see
  Tennyson, A.
Lang, H-J. George Orwell.
  R. Asselineau, 189(EA):Jul-Sep85-362
Lange, D.L. and R.T. Clifford. Testing in
  Foreign Languages, ESL, and Bilingual
  Education, 1966-1979.
  C. Stansfield, 399(MLJ):Summer84-157
Lange, P. and M. Vannicelli, eds. The Com-
  munist Parties of Italy, France and
  Spain.
  F. Demers, 275(IQ):Winter84-119
Lange, V. The Classical Age of German Lit-
  erature 1740-1815.
  G. Baumgaertel, 564:Nov84-302
  M.K. Flavell, 83:Spring84-141
  C.A.M. Noble, 529(QQ):Winter84-1019
  H. Reiss, 133:Band17Heft1/2-136
  P. Salm, 221(GQ):Fall84-651
Lange, V. - see Hoffmann, E.T.A.
Langedijk, K. The Portraits of the Medici,
  15th-18th Centuries. (Vols 1 and 2)
  R. Hatfield, 551(RenQ):Autumn84-471
Langer, G. Das Märchen in der tschech-
  ischen Literatur von 1790 bis 1860.
  A. Měšťan, 688(ZSP):Band44Heft1-227
Langer, L.L. Versions of Survival.
  B. Foley, 131(CL):Summer84-282
Langer, S.K. Mind. (Vol 1)
  H. Osborne, 289:Spring84-83
Langer, S.K. Mind. (Vol 2)
  H. Osborne, 289:Spring84-89
Langer, U. Rhétorique et intersubjecti-
  vité.
  K. Cameron, 208(FS):Jul84-332
  F. Gray, 207(FR):May85-886
  M. Greenberg, 210(FrF):Sep84-361
Langevin, P-G., ed. Franz Schubert et la
  symphonie.
  J. Reed, 410(M&L):Jan84-104
Langhorne, R., ed. Diplomacy and Intelli-
  gence during the Second World War.
  N. Clive, 617(TLS):25Oct85-1198
Langland, E. Society in the Novel.
  J. Adlard, 617(TLS):4Jan85-8
Langland, W. "Piers Plowman" by William
  Langland: An Edition of the C-Text. (D.
  Pearsall, ed)
  D. Gillam, 179(ES):Feb84-74
Langlois, W.G., ed. André Malraux, 5.
  A. Vandegans, 535(RHL):Nov/Dec84-988

Langness, L.L. and G. Frank. Lives.
  M. Fassiotto, 77:Summer84-264
Langowski, G.J. El surrealismo en la
  ficción hispanoamericana.
  A. Blasi, 238:Mar84-149
  K. McDuffie, 240(HR):Autumn84-556
"Langue et Littérature Orales dans l'Ouest
  de la France."
  J. Pohl, 209(FM):Oct84-241
  G. Roques, 553(RLiR):Jan-Jun84-205
Lanham, R.A. The Motives of Eloquence.
  P. Ramsey, 539:Aug85-223
Lankhorst, O.S. Reinier Leers (1654-1714),
  uitgever en boekverkoper te Rotterdam.
  A.E.C. Simoni, 354:Jun84-189
Lanne, J-C. Velimir Khlebnikov; poète
  futurien.
  R.D.B. Thomson, 104(CASS):Winter84-446
Lanning, J. and J., eds. Texas Cowboys.
  L. Milazzo, 584(SWR):Autumn84-462
Lansbury, C. The Reasonable Man.*
  A. Shelston, 447(N&Q):Aug83-360
  R.C. Terry, 49:Jan84-92
Lanser, S.S. The Narrative Act.*
  J. Culler, 153:Spring84-2
  R.M. Eastman, 405(MP):Nov84-233
  A. Fleishman, 301(JEGP):Apr84-256
  W.G. Regier, 223:Fall82-347
Lansing, R.H. From Image to Idea.
  T.G. Bergin, 275(IQ):Spring84-112
Lanzmann, C. Shoah.
  T.G. Ash, 453(NYRB):19Dec85-26
Lao Tzu. Chinese Classics: Tao Te Ching.
  (D.C. Lau, trans)
  W.G. Boltz, 244(HJAS):Jun84-185
Lapeyre, E. - see Grévin, J.
Lapeyre, P. Le Vertige de Rimbaud.*
  E.R. Peschel, 207(FR):Dec84-295
Lapide, P. The Resurrection of Jesus.
  G. Vermes, 617(TLS):1Feb85-116
Lapidus, G.W., ed. Women, Work, and Fam-
  ily in the Soviet Union.*
  M.P. Sacks, 104(CASS):Fall84-340
La Pierre, A. Toponymie française en
  Ontario.*
  L.R.N. Ashley, 424:Mar84-96
Lapierre, D. The City of Joy.
  R. Godden, 441:3Nov85-11
La Pin, D., with L. Guida and L. Pattillo.
  Hogs in the Bottoms.
  R.O. Joyce, 650(WF):Apr84-152
La Plantz, S. The Mad Weave Book.
  L.S., 614:Winter85-27
Laqueur, W. Germany Today.
  T.G. Ash, 617(TLS):15Mar85-278
  D. Gress, 129:Aug85-70
  J. Joffe, 441:28Jul85-15
  442(NY):2Sep85-87
Laqueur, W. A World of Secrets.
  E.J. Epstein, 441:10Nov85-9
"L'Archéologie de L'Iraq du Début de
  L'Époque Néolithique à 333 Avant Notre
  Ère."
  A. Zagarell, 318(JAOS):Oct-Dec83-817
Lardner, R., Jr. All for Love.
  C. Salzberg, 441:5May85-20
Large, D.C. and W. Weber, eds. Wagnerism
  in European Culture and Politics.
  P. Heyworth, 617(TLS):17May85-538
  J. Joll, 453(NYRB):31Jan85-9
Largeault, J. Critiques et controverses.
  Vers une philosophie de la nature.
  J-L. Gardies, 542:Jan-Mar84-113

Lawson, L.A. and V.A. Kramer, eds. Conversations with Walker Percy.
  R. Kimball, 441:4Aug85-9
Lawson, W. The Western Scar.*
  D. Dorsey, 538(RAL):Fall84-435
Lawton, D.A., ed. Middle English Alliterative Poetry and its Literary Background.
  R.A. Peters, 134(CP):Spring84-103
Lawton, M. Some Survived.
  R. Nalley, 441:3Mar85-23
Laxer, J. Oil and Gas.
  M.L. Cross, 529(QQ):Winter84-867
Layman, R. Shadow Man.*
  W.L. Godshalk, 536:Vol6-251
Layton, A. The Squeakers.
  M.J. Evans, 102(CanL):Autumn84-63
Layton, B. The Prodigal Sun.
  M. Harry, 198:Summer84-117
Layton, D. Interpreters of Science.
  A.R. Hall, 324:Apr85-368
Layton, I. A Wild Peculiar Joy.
  R. Berry, 102(CanL):Autumn84-136
Layton, R. The Anthropology of Art.
  G. Chalmers, 289:Summer84-103
Lazenby, J.F. The Spartan Army.
  P. Cartledge, 617(TLS):15Nov85-1302
Lea, K.M. and T.M. Gang - see Tasso, T.
Leach, E. and D.A. Aycock. Structuralist Interpretations of Biblical Myth.*
  S. Larisch, 478:Oct84-306
Leacroft, R. and H. Theatre and Playhouse.
  A. Goolden, 617(TLS):6Sep85-978
Leader, Z. Reading Blake's "Songs."*
  J. Beer, 402(MLR):Apr84-425
  T.A. Vogler, 88:Summer84-39
Leake, R.E., D.B. and A.E. Concordance des "Essais" de Montaigne.*
  J. Céard, 535(RHL):Nov/Dec84-949
Leakey, M. Disclosing the Past.*
  R.D. Martin, 617(TLS):10May85-512
Leal, L. Juan Rulfo.
  N.E. Álvarez, 238:Mar84-151
Leal, R.B. Drieu la Rochelle.
  P. Cryle, 67:Nov84-252
  S.B. John, 208(FS):Jan84-89
Leale, B.C. The Colours of Ancient Dreams.
  L. Mackinnon, 617(TLS):7Jun85-649
Leaming, B. Orson Welles.
  A. Quindlen, 441:15Sep85-9
  442(NY):11Nov85-157
Leante, C. Capitán de Cimarrones.
  F. Carenas, 701(SinN):Jul-Sep84-151
Leapman, M. Arrogant Aussie.
  D. Shaw, 441:26May85-13
Lear, E. Cretan Journal. (R. Fowler, ed)
  R. Fox, 362:24Jan85-26
Lears, T.J.J. No Place of Grace.
  G. McKenna, 396(ModA):Winter84-85
Leary, L. The Book-Peddling Parson.*
  L. Henigman, 165(EAL):Spring85-79
Lease, B. Anglo-American Encounters.*
  R.E. Streeter, 432(NEQ):Mar84-144
Leaska, M.A. - see Woolf, V.
Leatherdale, C. Dracula: The Novel and the Legend.
  C. Baldick, 617(TLS):27Sep85-1066
Leaton, A. Pearl.
  P. Duguid, 617(TLS):19Apr85-435
  M.S. Kaplan, 441:31Mar85-22
Leavis, F.R. The Critic as Anti-Philosopher.* (G. Singh, ed)
  R. Wellek, 402(MLR):Jan84-174

Leavis, Q.D. Collected Essays.* (Vol 1) (G. Singh, ed)
  W.H. Pritchard, 249(HudR):Winter84/85-639
Leavis, Q.D. Collected Essays. (Vol 2) (G. Singh, ed)
  M. Wood, 362:20Jun85-24
Leavitt, D. Family Dancing.*
  J. Mellors, 362:25Apr85-27
Lebeaux, R. Thoreau's Seasons.
  H. Cohen, 617(TLS):14Jun85-661
Leblanc, B.B. La Butte-aux-Anges.
  J-A. Elder, 102(CanL):Autumn84-61
Leblanc, B.B. Tit-Cul Lavoie.
  E.R. Hopkins, 207(FR):Feb85-494
Leblanc, B.B. Variations sur un Thème Anathème.
  R. Ewing, 102(CanL):Autumn84-160
Le Boeuffle, A. - see Hyginus
Lebra, J.C., ed. Japan's Greater East Asia Co-Prosperity Sphere in World War II.
  C.M. Turnbull, 302:Vol20No2-237
Lebra, T.S. Japanese Women.*
  Inoue Teruko, 285(JapQ):Oct-Dec84-460
Lebredo, L. and J. Fortuny-Amat. Business and Economics Workbook.
  E. Spinelli, 399(MLJ):Summer84-192
Lebsock, S. The Free Women of Petersburg.*
  639(VQR):Summer84-79
Lechner, S. Gelehrte Kritik und Restauration.
  M.A. Vega, 202(FMod):No65/67-306
Lecker, R. On the Line.*
  D. Carpenter, 102(CanL):Summer84-115
Lecker, R. and J. David, eds. The Annotated Bibliography of Canada's Major Authors.* (Vols 1, 3 and 4)
  P. Greig, 470:Vol22-104
Lecker, R. and J. David, eds. The Annotated Bibliography of Canada's Major Authors. (Vol 2)
  J. Ferns, 677(YES):Vol 14-344
  P. Greig, 470:Vol22-104
Lecker, R., J. David and E. Quigley, eds. Canadian Writers and Their Works: Fiction Series.* (Vol 1)
  J. Giltrow, 627(UTQ):Summer84-444
  E-M. Kroller, 102(CanL):Autumn84-181
Lecker, R., J. David and E. Quigley, eds. Canadian Writers and Their Works: Poetry Series. (Vol 2)
  W.J. Keith, 105:Spring/Summer84-88
Leckie, R. A Slow Light.
  H.R. Runte, 102(CanL):Autumn84-124
  D. Tacium, 137:May84-11
Leckie, R.W., Jr. The Passage of Dominion.*
  C.L. Neel, 125:Winter84-178
Le Clair, T. and L. McCaffery, eds. Anything Can Happen.*
  R. Pearce, 587(SAF):Spring84-118
  D. Seed, 189(EA):Jul-Sep85-360
Leclanche, J-L., ed. Le Conte de Floire et Blancheflor.*
  F.C. de Vries, 382(MAE):1984/2-327
Leclercq, J. Monks and Love in Twelfth-Century France.
  P.H. Stäblein, 545(RPh):Feb84-361
Le Clézio, J.M.G. Le Chercheur d'or.
  D. Gascoyne, 617(TLS):4Oct85-1113
Le Clézio, J.M.G. Relation de Michoacan.
  J. Duvignaud, 450(NRF):Oct84-92

Lehmann, P.W. and D. Spittle. Samothrace.
(Vol 5)
  A.S. Benjamin, 124:Sep-Oct84-59
  A. Johnston, 90:Jan84-41
  M. Millett, 161(DUJ):Dec83-109
  R.A. Tomlinson, 303(JoHS):Vol 104-251
Lehmann, W., G. Kutscher and G. Vollmer,
eds and trans. Geschichte der Azteken.
  G. Brotherston, 617(TLS):29Mar85-361
Lehmann, W.P. Language.
  J. Algeo, 300:Vol 17-75
Lehmann, W.P. Linguistische Theorien der
Moderne.
  G.B. Holland, 545(RPh):Nov83-202
  B.J. Koekkoek, 406:Fall84-347
  T.F. Shannon, 221(GQ):Spring84-298
Lehmann, W.P. and Y. Malkiel. Per-
spectives on Historical Linguistics.
  H.H. Hock, 350:Mar85-187
Lehnus, L. L'inno a Pan di Pindaro.
  M.C. Howatson, 123:Vol34No2-175
  S.L. Radt, 394:Vol37fasc1/2-171
Lehrberger, J. - see Gladkij, A.V. and I.A.
Mel'čuk
Lehrdahl, F. and R. Jackendoff. A Genera-
tive Theory of Tonal Music.
  W. Drabkin, 415:May84-273
Lehrman, L. and others. Future 21. (P.
Weyrich, ed)
  G.A. Fossedal, 129:Jan85-27
Lehrman, W.D., D.J. Sarafinski and E.
Savage. The Plays of Ben Jonson.
  S. Pearl, 447(N&Q):Apr83-165
Leibfried, E. Literarische Hermeneutik.
  K.E. Kuhn-Osius, 406:Summer84-202
Leibniz, G.W. Escritos políticos. (J. de
Salas, ed and trans)
  J.L. Sagüés, 202(FMod):No65/67-295
Leibniz, G.W. Generales Inquisitiones de
Analysi Notionum et Veritatum. (F.
Schupp, ed)
  M. Schneider, 489(PJGG):Band91Heft2-
415
Leibniz, G.W. New Essays on Human Under-
standing.
  R.M. Mattern, 482(PhR):Apr84-315
  C.M. Sherover, 543:Sep83-129
Leibniz, G.W. Sämtliche Schriften.
(Ser 1, Vol 11)
  A. Robinet, 192(EP):Jul-Sep84-416
Leibniz, G.W. Sämtliche Schriften und
Briefe. (Ser 6, Vol 3)
  G.H.R. Parkinson, 706:Band16Heft1-113
  A. Robinet, 192(EP):Jan-Mar84-121
Leibniz, G.W. Specimen dynamicum.
  A. Robinet, 192(EP):Jan-Mar84-121
Leibovitz, A. Annie Leibovitz: Photo-
graphs.
  J. Kaufmann, 31(ASch):Autumn84-559
  A. Ross, 364:Jul84-107
Leibowitch, J. A Strange Virus of Unknown
Origin.
  L.K. Altman, 441:29Sep85-47
Leigh, R.A., ed. Rousseau After Two Hun-
dred Years.*
  P. Coleman, 173(ECS):Fall84-96
Leigh, R.A. - see Rousseau, J-J.
Leighton, L.G., ed. Studies in Honor of
Xenia Gasiorowska.
  J.J. Rinkus, 104(CASS):Winter84-429
  E.M. Thompson, 550(RusR):Oct84-424
Leighton, L.G. - see Chukovsky, K.I.

Leiner, J., ed. Soleil éclaté.
  C. Wake, 617(TLS):19Jul85-792
Leiner, W., ed. Melanges pour un anniver-
saire, 1973-1983.
  J-P. Dens, 207(FR):Feb85-448
Leiner, W., ed. Six Conférences sur la
littérature africaine de langue fran-
çaise.
  J. Riesz, 547(RF):Band96Heft3-371
  C. Wake, 208(FS):Jan84-106
Leiner, W., with others, eds. Bibliogra-
phie et index thématique des études sur
Ionesco.
  J. Knowlson, 208(FS):Jul84-368
Leinieks, V. The Plays of Sophokles.
  D. Bain, 303(JoHS):Vol 104-198
  M. Lloyd, 123:Vol34No1-127
  G. Ronnet, 555:Vol58fasc1-115
Leinsdorf, E. The Composer's Advocate.*
  R.S. James, 309:Vol5No1/3-267
Leiris, M. Francis Bacon.
  J. Burr, 39:Jan84-71
Leiris, M. Langage tangage.
  J. Sturrock, 617(TLS):4Oct85-1092
Leistner, B. Johannes Bobrowski.
  J. Glenn, 221(GQ):Winter84-162
Leitch, M. Stamping Ground.
  P. Craig, 617(TLS):5Jul85-757
Leitch, V.B. Deconstructive Criticism.*
  W.E. Cain, 128(CE):Dec84-811
  S.F.R., 131(CL):Summer84-263
  T. Riley, 141:Fall84-399
  S. Scobie, 376:Oct84-107
  R. Wolfs, 204(FdL):Jun84-150
Leiter, S. Akhmatova's Petersburg.*
  B. Heldt, 104(CASS):Winter84-445
  S. Ketchian, 574(SEEJ):Fall84-406
  I. Tlusty, 575(SEER):Jul84-445
Leith, D. A Social History of English.
  E.C. Traugott, 355(LSoc):Dec84-540
Leith-Ross, P. The John Tradescants.*
  B. Boardman, 39:Jun84-465
Leithauser, B. Equal Distance.*
  S. Lardner, 442(NY):11Mar85-135
Lejosne, R. La Raison dans l'oeuvre de
John Milton.
  G. Campbell, 677(YES):Vol 14-315
Leland, J. The Last Sandcastle.
  D. Montrose, 617(TLS):4Jan85-9
Lelchuk, A. Miriam in Her Forties.
  S. Shem, 441:3Nov85-15
Lelchuk, A. and G. Shaked, eds. Eight
Great Hebrew Short Novels.
  N. Aschkenasy, 390:May84-54
Lele, J., ed. Traditions and Modernity in
Bhakti Movements.
  E.B. Findly, 318(JAOS):Apr-Jun83-436
  D.N. Lorenzen, 293(JASt):Nov83-189
Lell, R. Kamikaze Polar Bear Sinks
Nuclear Submarine.
  J. Carter, 219(GaR):Winter84-881
Lelyveld, J. Move Your Shadow.
  N. Gordimer, 453(NYRB):7Nov85-5
  A. Sampson, 441:13Oct85-1
Lem, S. Imaginary Magnitude.*
  S. Clark, 617(TLS):8Feb85-140
Lem, S. Microworlds. (F. Rottensteiner,
ed)
  J. Culler, 441:24Mar85-28
  T.M. Disch, 617(TLS):27Dec85-1478
  442(NY):22Apr85-143
Lemaire, J. Meschinot, Molinet, Villon.
  A. Foulet, 545(RPh):Nov83-256

Lemann, N. Lives of the Saints.
V. Martin, 441:30Jun85-20
J. Wolcott, 453(NYRB):27Jun85-33
Lemann, N. Out of the Forties.*
L. Jasud, 585(SoQ):Summer85-101
L. Milazzo, 584(SWR):Autumn84-462
Lemartinel, J. and C. Minguet - see de
Vega Carpio, L.
Lemay, J.A.L. and P.M. Zall - see Franklin,
B.
Le Men, S. Les abécédaires français illus-
trés du XIXe siècle.
D. Coward, 617(TLS):29Mar85-356
Lemerle, P. and others, eds. Actes de
Lavra. (Pt 4)
D.M. Nicol, 303(JoHS):Vol 104-272
Lemert, C.C. Sociology and the Twilight
of Man.
P. Munz, 488:Sep84-403
Lemert, C.C. and G. Gillan. Michel Fou-
cault.*
K.S. Rothwell, 125:Winter84-171
M. Sprinker, 141:Fall84-383
Lemieux, G. La Vie paysanne 1860-1900.*
E-M. Kroller, 102(CanL):Summer84-148
Len, V., G. Mayer and R. Ziegler - see
"Neue Russische Literatur"
Lencek, R.L. The Structure and History of
the Slovene Language.
W.W. Derbyshire, 574(SEEJ):Spring84-
137
J.F. Kess, 104(CASS):Spring-Summer84-
156
H. Leeming, 575(SEER):Oct84-579
Lencek, R.L. and H.R. Cooper, Jr., eds.
Papers in Slavic Philology, 2.
H. Leeming, 575(SEER):Jul84-431
Lendvai, E. The Workshop of Bartók and
Kodály.
J. Samson, 607:Dec84-39
Lenman, B. The Jacobite Clans of the
Great Glen 1650-1784.
G. Donaldson, 617(TLS):1Feb85-125
Lennon, M. - see Mailer, N.
Lennon, N. Alfred Jarry.
G. Marcus, 62:Dec84-73
Lennon, N. Mark Twain in California.
P.D. Morrow, 649(WAL):May84-74
Lennon, T.M., J.M. Nicholas and J.W. Davis,
eds. Problems of Cartesianism.*
P.D. Cummins, 319:Jan85-104
M. Phillips, 542:Oct-Dec84-471
H.A.S. Schankula, 518:Jul84-140
Lensen, G.A. Balance of Intrigue.
M. Bassin, 550(RusR):Apr84-206
Lensing, L.A. and H-W. Peter, eds. Wil-
helm Raabe.*
M. Swales, 402(MLR):Apr84-500
Lenski, R. Toward a New Science of Man.
D.R. Vining, Jr., 396(ModA):Fall84-389
da Lentini, G. Poesie. (Vol 1) (R. Anton-
elli, ed)
J.H. Levin, 545(RPh):May84-497
Lentricchia, F. After the New Criticism.*
W.W. Holdheim, 52:Band19Heft3-288
J. Robinson, 289:Summer84-116
Lentricchia, F. Criticism and Social
Change.*
D.P. Slattery, 435:Fall/Winter84-89
Lenz, C.R.S., G. Greene and C.T. Neely,
eds. The Woman's Part.*
M. Ferguson, 677(YES):Vol 14-313
J. Simons, 541(RES):Feb84-108

Lenz, H. Ein Fremdling.
S. Dickson, 268(IFR):Summer85-123
Leon, J.M. - see under Messer Leon, J.
Léon, P. Les Voleurs d'étoiles de Saint-
Arbrousse-Poil.
D. Thaler, 102(CanL):Autumn84-168
Léon, P. and J. Yashinsky, eds. Options
Nouvelles en Didactique du Français
Langue Etrangère.
J.B. Goepper, 399(MLJ):Summer84-166
León, V. Diccionario de argot español.
I. Lerner, 552(REH):Jan84-154
León Tello, F.J. La Estetica y la Filos-
ofía del Arte en España en el siglo XX.
(Vol 1)
H. Osborne, 89(BJA):Autumn84-377
Leonard, E. Glitz.
R. Kaplan, 129:May85-64
S. King, 441:10Feb85-7
L. Sante, 453(NYRB):28Mar85-18
442(NY):18Feb85-122
Leonard, E. La Brava.
639(VQR):Spring84-54
Leonard, F.M. Laughter in the Courts of
Love.*
J.H. Anderson, 604:Winter84-1
Leone, A. L'Italiano Regionale di Sicilia.
J. Siracusa, 399(MLJ):Spring84-83
Leopardi, G. Appressamento della morte.
(L. Posfortunato, ed)
M. Marti, 228(GSLI):Vol 161fasc516-615
Leopardi, G. A Leopardi Reader.* (O.M.
Casale, ed and trans)
N.R. Havely, 447(N&Q):Dec83-575
Leopardi, G. Operette Morali. (G.
Cecchetti, ed and trans) Moral Tales.
M. Caesar, 278(IS):Vol39-139
Leopardi, G. Porphyrii De vita Plotini et
ordine librorum eius. (C. Moreschini,
ed)
S. Timpanaro, 228(GSLI):Vol 161fasc516-
609
Leopold, J.H. Gedichten I.
P.F. Schmitz, 204(FdL):Jun84-136
Leozappa, M.E. - see Zola, É.
Lepage, Y.G. - see Richard de Fournival
Le Pan, D. Something Still to Find.
J. Kertzer, 198:Spring84-89
Lepape, C. and T. Deffert. From the
Ballets Russes to Vogue.
P-L. Adams, 61:Jan85-101
Le Patourel, J. Feudal Empires. (M.
Jones, ed)
J.R. Maddicott, 617(TLS):4Jan85-19
Le Pen, J-M. Les Français d'abord.
R.M. Webster, 207(FR):Mar85-613
Le Pichon, Y. The Real World of the
Impressionists.
M.B., 62:May85-4
Lepper, G., J. Steitz and W. Brenn. Ein-
führung in die deutsche Literatur des 18.
Jahrhunderts. (Vol 1)
J. Golz, 654(WB):5/1984-867
Lepschy, A.L. and G. La lingua italiana.
M.D. Barrado, 202(FMod):No74/76-315
Lequin, F. Het personeel van de Verenigde
Oost-Indische Compagnie in Azië in de
achttiende eeuw, meer in het bijzonder
in de vestiging Bengalen.
R. Rocher, 173(ECS):Fall84-118

Lerdahl, F. and R. Jackendoff. A Generative Theory of Tonal Music.
   J.K. Chambers, 320(CJL):Fall84-157
   S. Feld, 355(LSoc):Mar84-133
   J. Peel and W. Slawson, 308:Fall84-271
   J.P. Swain, 317:Spring84-196
   R. Swift, 451:Fall84-164
de Lerma, D-R. Bibliography of Black Music. (Vol 4)
   W. Collins, 187:Spring/Summer85-384
Lermontov, M. Major Poetical Works.* (A. Liberman, ed and trans)
   T.J. Binyon, 617(TLS):25Jan85-87
   J.F. Cotter, 249(HudR):Autumn84-496
   J.L. Laychuk, 104(CASS):Winter84-434
Lermontov, M. Vadim. (H. Goscilo, ed and trans)
   T.J. Binyon, 617(TLS):25Jan85-87
Lerner, L. The Literary Imagination.*
   R. Albanese, Jr., 478:Apr84-135
Lerner, L. My Grandfather's Grandfather.
   J. Mellors, 362:22Aug85-30
   J.K.L. Walker, 617(TLS):21Jun85-702
Lerner, L., ed. Reconstructing Literature.*
   M. Cusin, 189(EA):Jul-Sep85-298
   S.G. Kellman, 395(MFS):Summer84-399
Lerner, L. Selected Poems.*
   H. Lomas, 364:Jun84-84
Leroi-Gourhan, A. Les chasseurs de la Préhistoire. Le fil du temps. Mécanique vivante. Les racines du monde.
   C. Cohen, 98:May84-384
Lerot, J. Abrégé de linguistique générale.
   G. Kleiber, 553(RLiR):Jul-Dec84-462
Le Roux, B. Louis Veuillot, un homme de combat.
   W. De Spens, 450(NRF):Nov84-86
Le Roy Ladurie, E. Love, Death and Money in the Pays d'Oc.* (French title: L'argent, l'amour et la mort en pays d'oc.)
   R.B. Bottigheimer, 196:Band25Heft3/4-354
   P.M.S.D., 148:Autumn84-93
Le Roy Ladurie, E. Parmi les historiens.
   H. Cronel, 450(NRF):Jan84-132
Le Roy Ladurie, E. La Sorcière de Jasmin.*
   P. Burke, 453(NYRB):28Feb85-32
   N. Hampson, 208(FS):Apr84-212
Lerski, H.H. William Jay.
   R. O'Donnell, 90:Apr84-240
Lervik, Å.H. Gjennom kvinneøyne.
   M.K. Norseng, 563(SS):Spring84-176
Lesch, J.E. Science and Medicine in France. [correcting entry in last vol]
   R. Fox, 617(TLS):2Nov84-1264
Leskov, N. Five Tales.
   A. Fitzlyon, 364:Mar85-103
Lesky, A. Greek Tragic Poetry.
   B. Knox, 124:Jan-Feb85-229
   W.C. Scott, 615(TJ):May84-289
Leslau, W. Ethiopians Speak. (Vol 4)
   G. Hudson, 318(JAOS):Oct-Dec83-773
Lesley, C. Winterkill.*
   M. Hollister, 448:Vol22No3-142
Leslie, A. Randolph. (British title: Cousin Randolph.)
   J. Jolliffe, 617(TLS):9Aug85-886
   A. Watkins, 362:9May85-23
   442(NY):26Aug85-88

Leslie, D.D. Islamic Literature in Chinese, Late Ming and Early Ch'ing.
   B.L.K. Pillsbury, 293(JASt):Nov83-136
Lessard, A. Comme parfois respire la pierre.
   K.W. Meadwell, 102(CanL):Autumn84-95
Lesser, M. Clarkey.
   A. Schlee, 617(TLS):1Feb85-117
Lessing, D. The Diaries of Jane Somers.*
   A. Lurie, 453(NYRB):19Dec85-8
Lessing, D. The Good Terrorist.
   D. Donoghue, 441:22Sep85-3
   P. Kemp, 362:17Oct85-34
   S. Lardner, 442(NY):14Oct85-136
   A. Lurie, 453(NYRB):19Dec85-8
   J. Melmoth, 617(TLS):13Sep85-999
Lessing, D. The Sentimental Agents of the Volyen Empire.
   F. Kelly, 376:Feb84-133
"L'estasi di Santa Cecilia di Raffaello da Urbino nella Pinacoteca Nazionale di Bologna."
   C. Gould, 39:Apr84-304
Lester, G.A., ed. Three Late Medieval Morality Plays.
   A.C. Cawley, 447(N&Q):Oct83-450
   S. Carpenter, 541(RES):Aug84-352
Lester, J. Do Lord Remember Me.
   R. Hoffman, 441:17Feb85-9
Lester, J. Harmony in Tonal Music.
   P. Breslauer, 308:Spring84-142
Lester, R.K. "Trivialneger."
   M. Dietz-Lenssen, 343:Heft9/10-143
Lesure, F., ed. La musique à Paris en 1830-31.
   D. Charlton, 415:Jun84-334
Lesure, F. - see "Cahiers Debussy"
Letessier, D. A Breath of Air.
   M. Véron, 441:31Mar85-13
Letessier, D. Loïca.
   L.A. di Benedetto, 207(FR):May85-917
Letiche, J.M. and B. Dmytryshyn. Russian Statecraft.
   J.H. Billington, 441:29Dec85-9
Lett, J., Jr. and others. Reflejos. (2nd ed)
   A. Dias, 399(MLJ):Spring84-97
Letwin, S.R. The Gentleman in Trollope.*
   V. Sanders, 447(N&Q):Dec83-543
   R.C. Terry, 637(VS):Winter84-271
Leuci, B. Doyle's Disciples.
   N. Callendar, 441:6Jan85-29
de Leusse, H. Des "Poemes" aux "Lettres d'hivernage": Senghor.
   A. Songolo, 538(RAL):Spring84-85
Leuthner, S. The Railroaders.*
   639(VQR):Spring84-46
Leuwers, D., ed. Pierre-Jean Jouve I.
   J. Onimus, 535(RHL):Nov/Dec84-987
Levac, R. L'Hiver dans les os.
   M. Benson, 102(CanL):Autumn84-157
Levarie, S. and E. Levy. Musical Morphology.
   W. Drabkin, 410(M&L):Jul84-275
   J. Levinson, 290(JAAC):Winter84-222
   J. Ronsheim, 42(AR):Summer84-377
Levasseur, L. Contes des bêtes et des choses.
   D. Thaler, 102(CanL):Autumn84-168
Levenson, J.C. - see Crane, S.
Levenson, J.C. and others - see Adams, H.
Levenson, L. With Wooden Sword.
   D. Kiberd, 272(IUR):Spring84-142

Lever, C. Naturalized Mammals of the
World.
   M. Coe, 617(TLS):27Dec85-1487
Lever, J. Soccer Madness.
   A. Metcalfe, 529(QQ):Winter84-1051
Lever, J.W. The Tragedy of State.
   L.S. Young, 568(SCN):Winter84-71
Lever, M. Le sceptre et la marotte.
   A-C. Brès, 542:Jan-Mar84-99
Levere, T.H. Poetry Realized in Nature.*
   M.K. Nurmi, 591(SIR):Fall84-420
   I.M. Wylie, 541(RES):Aug84-394
Levernier, J.A. and D.R. Wilmes, eds.
American Writers Before 1800.*
   E. Emerson, 27(AL):Oct84-429
   S. Fender, 617(TLS):11Jan85-33
Levertov, D. Oblique Prayers.
   F. Garber, 29(APR):Sep/Oct85-14
Levertov, D. Poems 1960-1967.
   L. Goldensohn, 491:Apr84-40
Leveson, M. - see Campbell, R.
Lévesque, C. and C.V. McDonald, eds.
L'oreille de l'autre.*
   G. Good, 102(CanL):Summer84-133
Lévesque, S. L'Amour langue morte.
   P. Collet, 102(CanL):Winter83-171
Levey, M. An Affair on the Appian Way.*
   442(NY):2Sep85-87
Levey, S.M. Lace.
   J. Arnold, 90:Jun84-358
   M. Dillon, 39:Aug84-149
   L. von Wilckens, 471:Apr/May/Jun84-211
Levi, I. Decisions and Revisions.
   L.J. Cohen, 617(TLS):1Feb85-112
Levi, I. The Enterprise of Knowledge.*
   H.E. Kyburg, Jr., 449:May84-347
Levi, P. The Echoing Green.*
   A. Stevenson, 493:Jun84-66
Levi, P. The English Bible 1534-1859.
   617(TLS):27Sep85-1072
Levi, P. Grave Witness.
   N. Callendar, 441:6Oct85-35
   R. Hill, 617(TLS):5Apr85-394
   M. Laski, 362:18Apr85-26
Levi, P. A History of Greek Literature.
   W.G. Arnott, 617(TLS):12Apr85-407
Levi, P. If Not Now, When?
   F. Eberstadt, 129:Oct85-41
   H.S. Hughes, 441:21Apr85-7
   442(NY):15Jul85-85
Levi, P. The Periodic Table.*
   N. Ascherson, 453(NYRB):17Jan85-8
   F. Eberstadt, 129:Oct85-41
   H.S. Hughes, 617(TLS):29Mar85-337
Lévi, R. La philosophie égarée.
   R.W., 555:Vol58fasc1-126
Levi D'Ancona, M. Botticelli's "Prima-
vera."
   C. Dempsey, 551(RenQ):Spring84-98
Lévi-Strauss, C. The View From Afar.*
   (French title: Le Regard éloigné.)
   S. Hicks, 614:Spring85-32
   R.A. Shweder, 441:14Apr85-38
Lévi-Strauss, C. The Way of the Masks.*
   E. Brady, 650(WF):Oct84-269
   H. Glassie, 292(JAF):Oct-Dec84-482
Leviant, C. - see Aleichem, S.
Levin, B. Hannibal's Footsteps.
   T. Hinde, 617(TLS):27Dec85-1477
   B. Mooney, 362:21Nov85-35
Levin, G. Edward Hopper.
   G. Marcus, 62:Dec84-71

Levin, H. The Power of Blackness.*
   A. Massa, 447(N&Q):Jun83-277
Levin, H.M. Cost-Effectiveness.
   R.E.G., 185:Jan85-396
Levin, M. Whatever Happened to Lady Chat-
terley's Lover?
   D. Finkle, 441:25Aug85-17
Levin, R. New Readings vs. Old Plays.
   R. Stamm, 179(ES):Apr84-162
Levinas, E. Otherwise than Being or
Beyond Essence.*
   R.A. Cohen, 480(P&R):Vol 17No4-245
Levinas, E. Totality and Infinity.
   L.L. Landen, 543:Jun84-863
Levine, A. Arguing for Socialism.
   M.W.H., 185:Jul85-972
Levine, D. Don't Ask.
   B. Raffel, 363(LitR):Fall84-154
Levine, G. The Realistic Imagination.*
   P. Coustillas, 189(EA):Oct-Dec85-474
   R. O'Kell, 529(QQ):Summer84-444
Levine, H.J. Yeats's Daimonic Renewal.
   T. Parkinson, 177(ELT):Vol27No2-171
Levine, J.S. and J.L. Rotman. Undersea
Life.
   D. Quammen, 441:15Dec85-21
Levine, M. The History and Politics of
Community Mental Health.
   G.R. Lowe, 529(QQ):Spring84-188
Levine, M.G. Contemporary Polish Poetry,
1925-1975.*
   G.T. Kapolka, 497(PolR):Vol29No4-98
   B.W. Mazur, 402(MLR):Jan84-255
Levine, N. Champagne Barn.
   C. Rooke, 376:Oct84-120
Levine, P. A.G. Spalding and the Rise of
Baseball.
   B. Atkinson, 441:15Sep85-25
Levine, R.A., ed. The Victorian Exper-
ience: The Poets.*
   P.M. Ball, 637(VS):Winter84-264
   M.E. Gibson, 405(MP):Nov84-211
   M. Shaw, 541(RES):Nov84-567
Levine, R.A., ed. The Victorian Experi-
ence: The Prose Writers.
   A. Shelston, 637(VS):Spring84-386
Levine, S.J. Guía de Bioy Casares.*
   P. Hulme, 86(BHS):Jan84-60
Levins, R. and R. Lewontin. The Dialec-
tical Biologist.
   P. Thompson, 441:29Sep85-14
Levinsky, S.A. A Bridge of Dreams.
   M. Barrett, 469:Vol 10No3-114
Levinson, A. Ballet Old and New.*
   S.J. Cohen, 151:Nov83-90
Levinson, H.S. The Religious Investiga-
tions of William James.
   R. Giuffrida, Jr., 619:Spring84-194
Levinson, P., ed. In Pursuit of Truth.*
   T.E. Burke, 518:Jul84-167
   D.E. Williams, 529(QQ):Autumn84-679
Levinson, S.C. Pragmatics.*
   G.L. Dillon and others, 350:Jun85-446
   W.P. Lehmann, 215(GL):Vol24No2-123
Le Vot, A. F. Scott Fitzgerald.*
   D. Bradshaw, 617(TLS):2Aug85-857
   R. Coles, 639(VQR):Spring84-337
   S. Donaldson, 534(RALS):Autumn82-239
   G. Garrett, 569(SR):Summer84-495
   V.A. Makowsky, 536:Vol6-139
   D.W. Petrie, 395(MFS):Winter84-814
   T. Quirk, 27(AL):Mar84-120
   295(JML):Nov84-440

Levy, A. Vladimir Nabokov.
295(JML):Nov84-484
Levy, B.S. and P.E. Szarmach, eds. The
Alliterative Tradition in the Fourteenth
Century.*
J.A. Burrow, 541(RES):Nov84-526
T. Turville-Petre, 402(MLR):Oct84-892
Lévy, C. Les Romans de Saul Bellow.
J. Tavernier-Courbin, 395(MFS):
Winter84-810
P. Wagner, 189(EA):Jul-Sep85-359
Levy, D. Realism.
C.O. Schrag, 323:May84-207
Levy, D., L. Sneider and F. Gibney.
Kanban.
H. Cortazzi, 60:Jan-Feb84-118
Levy, D.G. The Ideas and Careers of Simon-
Nicolas-Henri Linguet.
J. Lough, 208(FS):Apr84-208
Levy, D.W. Herbert Croly of The New Repub-
lic.
D. Seideman, 441:14Jul85-13
Levy, E.P. Beckett and the Voice of
Species.*
J. Acheson, 299:Number9-150
Levy, J.M. Beethoven's Compositional
Choices.*
D. Greenfield, 317:Spring84-177
Levy, K.D. Jacques Rivière.
W.C. Carter, 207(FR):Oct84-133
Levy, L.W. Emergence of a Free Press.
F.W. Friendly, 441:24Feb85-10
Lewald, H.E., ed and trans. The Web.
M-I. Lagos-Pope, 268(IFR):Summer85-115
Lewicki, Z. The Bang and the Whimper.
P.B. McElwain, 590:Dec84-56
Lewin, B., ed. Japanische Literaturwissen-
schaft. (C. Fischer, I. Hijiya-Kirschne-
reit and R. Schneider, comps)
R-R. Wuthenow, 490:Band15Heft3/4-369
Lewin, M.Z. Out of Time.
T.J. Binyon, 617(TLS):11Jan85-42
Lewis, B. The Jews of Islam.*
L. Rosen, 617(TLS):7Jun85-648
A. Silvera, 441:21Jul85-20
Lewis, D., ed. Inscriptiones Graecae.*
(Vol 1, fasc 1) (3rd ed)
H.B. Mattingly, 24:Fall84-340
Lewis, G., ed. Michael Tippett.
I. Kemp, 617(TLS):23Aug85-931
Lewis, G.K. Main Currents in Caribbean
Thought.
A. Hennessy, 617(TLS):11Jan85-27
Lewis, H.D. The Elusive Self.*
J.M. Hinton, 483:Jan84-137
E. Matthews, 393(Mind):Jan84-152
G.B. Matthews, 484(PPR):Mar85-461
Lewis, H.R. and C.H. Papadimitriou. Ele-
ments of the Theory of Computation.
J.H. Gallier, 316:Sep84-989
Lewis, J. Poems Old and New, 1918-1978.
J. Green, 134(CP):Spring84-111
Lewis, J. The Pursuit of Happiness.*
J. Fliegelman, 656(WMQ):Jul84-516
Lewis, J. The Twentieth Century Book.
G. Cavaliero, 324:Mar85-306
Lewis, J. Women in England 1870-1950.
B. Harrison, 617(TLS):18Jan85-58
Lewis, J.M. The Ewenny Potteries.
G. Wills, 39:Jan84-69

Lewis, M.A. Afro-Hispanic Poetry, 1940-
1980.
I. Dominguez, 263(RIB):Vol34No2-306
639(VQR):Autumn84-138
Lewis, N. Life in Egypt Under Roman Rule.*
A.R. Schulman, 124:Jan-Feb85-229
Lewis, N. A Suitable Case for Corruption.*
P. Lewis, 364:Jul84-99
Lewis, N. Voices of the Old Sea.*
P-L. Adams, 61:Jul85-100
T. Lambert, 617(TLS):4Jan85-6
B.P. Solomon, 441:14Jul85-17
442(NY):10Jun85-141
Lewis, P. and E. Peoples of the Golden
Triangle.
J. Harding, 60:May-Jun84-115
Lewis, R. Most Cunning Workmen.
N. Callendar, 441:2Jun85-38
Lewis, R. On Reading French Verse.*
G.D. Martin, 402(MLR):Jul84-695
D.L. Rubin, 207(FR):Oct84-115
Lewis, R.E. and A. McIntosh. A Descrip-
tive Guide to the Manuscripts of the
"Prick of Conscience."
R. Beadle, 354:Sep84-286
D. Britton, 382(MAE):1984/2-315
T.J. Heffernan, 589:Jan84-238
Lewis, W. Rude Assignment. (T. Foshay,
ed)
J. Symons, 441:10Feb85-29
Lewis, W. Snooty Baronet.* (B. Lafour-
cade, ed)
J-J. Mayoux, 189(EA):Oct-Dec85-479
Lewis, W. The Vulgar Streak. (P. Edwards,
ed)
J. Symons, 617(TLS):8Nov85-1259
Lewis, W.A. Racial Conflict and Economic
Development.
M. Banton, 617(TLS):6Dec85-1390
Lewis, W.N. Willie, a Girl from a Town
Called Dallas.
L. Clayton, 649(WAL):Feb85-341
Lewis, W.S. - see Godwin, W.
Lewis, W.S. and J. Riely - see Walpole, H.
Lewontin, R.C., S. Rose and L.J. Kamin.
Not in Our Genes.*
B.D. Davis, 129:Jan85-71
D.N. Robinson, 533:Fall84-120
"Lexikon Iconographicum Mythologiae
Classicae."* (Vol 1)
V. Tran Tam Tinh, 487:Spring84-98
Leyda, J. Kino. (3rd ed)
J. Naremore, 651(WHR):Autumn84-279
Leyda, J. and Z. Voynow. Eisenstein at
Work.
G. Millar, 362:11Jul85-30
I. Montagu, 707:Summer84-229
von Leyden, W. Hobbes and Locke.
D.A.L. Thomas, 393(Mind):Jul84-448
Leyendecker, H. Zur Phänomenologie der
Täuschungen.
F. Dunlop, 323:May84-206
Leymarie, J. Balthus.*
90:Feb84-102
Leys, S. The Burning Forest.* (French
title: La Forêt en feu.)
J.K. Fairbank, 441:22Dec85-10
Leys, S. Orwell ou l'horreur de la poli-
tique.
T.G. Ash, 617(TLS):8Feb85-147
Lezhnev, A. Pushkin's Prose.
I.P. Foote, 617(TLS):11Jan85-43

Lhalungpa, L.P. - see "The Life of Mil-
arepa"
Li Guoqi. Zhongguo xiandaihuade quyu
yanjiu.
R.K. Schoppa, 293(JASt):Nov83-137
Liang Heng and J. Shapiro. Son of the
Revolution.
M.S. Duke, 293(JASt):May84-522
42(AR):Fall84-506
Liang Ssu-ch'eng. A Pictorial History of
Chinese Architecture.* (W. Fairbank, ed)
A.C. Soper, 57:Vol45No2/3-230
Liangying, X. and Fan Dainian - see under
Xu Liangying and Fan Dainian
Libby, A. Mythologies of Nothing.
B. Costello, 27(AL):Dec84-621
L. Wagner, 659(ConL):Winter85-482
295(JML):Nov84-345
Libby, L.M. The Uranium People.
J.W. Grove, 529(QQ):Spring84-73
Liben, M. New York Street Games and Other
Stories and Sketches.*
L.S. Feuer, 390:Jun/Jul84-42
E. Leites, 390:Jun/Jul84-51
L. Raditsa, 390:Jun/Jul84-46
de Libera, A., E. Weber and E.Z. Brunn -
see Meister Eckhart
Liberman, A. Germanic Accentology.*
(Vol 1)
J. Weinstock, 301(JEGP):Oct84-591
Liberman, A. - see Lermontov, M.
Libo, K. and I. Howe, eds. We Lived There
Too.
S.M. Halpern, 441:7Apr85-14
Librowicz, O.A. - see under Anahory
Librowicz, O.
Lichtenberk, F. A Grammar of Manam.
B. Comrie, 353:Vol21No6-919
Lichtenwanger, W., ed. Oscar Sonneck and
American Music.
P. Morgan, 415:Oct84-574
Liddell, S.K. American Sign Language Syn-
tax.*
W.C. Stokoe, 567:Vol50No1/2-173
Lider, J. British Military Thought after
World War II.
L. Freedman, 617(TLS):30Aug85-944
Lidoff, J. Christina Stead.
M. Harris, 581:Jun84-233
K.M. Stern, 405(MP):Aug84-113
Lie, H. Om sagakunst og skaldskap. (B.
Fidjestøl and others, eds)
F. Amory, 563(SS):Autumn84-382
R. McTurk, 562(Scan):Nov84-167
Lieb, M. Poetics of the Holy.*
M. Evans, 541(RES):Nov84-538
M. Fixler, 405(MP):Feb85-310
J. Wittreich, 536:Vol5-1
Lieb, N. and W-C. von der Mülbe. Johann
Michael Fischer.
A.D.L., 90:Nov84-714
Lieberg, G. Poeta Creator.
J. Perret, 555:Vol58fasc1-144
Lieberman, E.J. Acts of Will.
M.V. Miller, 441:24Mar85-3
M. Shepherd, 176:Nov85-54
Lieberman, L. Eros at the World Kite
Pageant.*
T. Swiss, 569(SR):Summer84-lxx
Lieberson, S. Language Diversity and Lan-
guage Contact.
J. Williams, 355(LSoc):Sep84-423

Liebert, R.S. Michelangelo.*
L. Partridge, 551(RenQ):Summer84-269
E.H. Ramsden, 39:Oct84-290
Liebertz-Grün, U. Seifried Helbling.*
R. Hahn, 654(WB):3/1984-515
Liebman, C.J. The Old French Psalter
Commentary.
S.C. Ferruolo, 589:Apr84-402
Liebmann, M.J. Die deutsche Plastik 1350-
1550.
E. König, 683:Band47Heft4-535
Liedtke, W.A. Architectural Painting in
Delft.
L. de Vries, 600:Vol 14No2-137
Liersch, W. Hans Fallada.*
J.G. Pankau, 564:Sep84-226
Lietz, S. Das Fenster des Barock.
H-E. Paulus, 683:Band4/Heft2-261
Lieury, A. Les procédés mnémotechniques.
L. Millet, 192(EP):Jul-Sep84-417
Lieven, D.C.B. Russia and the Origins of
the First World War.*
L.L. Farrar, Jr., 550(RusR):Apr84-203
L.L. Farrar, Jr., 550(RusR):Jul84-311
M. Perrins, 575(SEER):Oct84-608
A.E. Senn, 104(CASS):Winter84-474
"The Life of Milarepa." (L.P. Lhalungpa,
trans)
J. van de Wetering, 469:Vol 10No1-128
"György Ligeti in Conversation."*
A. Whittall, 410(M&L):Oct84-381
Light, G. Black to Black.
R. Plant, 102(CanL):Summer84-155
Light, P. Artful Work.
R. Pear, 441:21Apr85-47
Lightfoot, D. The Language Lottery.*
F. D'Agostino, 84:Dec84-408
Lightner, T.M. Introduction to English
Derivational Morphology.
G. Bourcier, 189(EA):Jul-Sep85-311
Ligon, L., ed. A Rug Weaver's Sourcebook.
K. Buffington, 614:Spring85-29
Lilius, H. Villa Lante al Gianicolo.
D.R. Coffin, 54:Dec84-695
Lillard, C. A Costal Range.
S. Scobie, 376:Oct84-124
Lillard, C. - see Collison, W.H.
Lillee, D. Over and Out!
A.L. Le Quesne, 617(TLS):28Jun85-734
Lilliedahl, A. Emily Dickinson in Europe.
W. Branch, 447(N&Q):Aug83-379
Lilly, M. The National Council for Civil
Liberties.*
O.R. McGregor, 617(TLS):24May85-569
Lilly, R. and M. Viel. La Prononciation
de l'Anglais. Initiation raisonnée à
la phonétique de l'Anglais.
C. Gussenhoven, 179(ES):Apr84-190
Limentani, U. - see Buonarroti, M.
Liñán de Riaza, P. Poesías. (J.F. Ran-
dolph, ed)
D.G. Walters, 86(BHS):Oct84-508
Lincoln, K. Native American Renaissance.
H.D. Brumble 3d, 651(WHR):Autumn84-288
J.C. Rice, 649(WAL):Aug84-158
P.G. Zolbrod, 219(GaR):Winter84-874
Lincoln, L., ed. Finished in Beauty.
N.J. Blomberg, 2(AfrA):Feb84-83
Lincoln, W.B. In the Vanguard of Reform.
D.C.B. Lieven, 575(SEER):Apr84-285
D.T. Orlovsky, 550(RusR):Jul84-298
N.G.O. Pereira, 104(CASS):Spring-
Summer84-193

Lind, G.R. Estudos sobre Fernando Pessoa.
G. Güntert, 547(RF):Band96Heft4-506
Lindberg, D.C. - see Bacon, R.
Lindberg, G. The Confidence Man in American Literature.*
J.W. Gargano, 579(SAQ):Summer84-351
D. Seed, 541(RES):Aug84-423
J. Seelye, 445(NCF):Mar85-479
Lindberg-Seyersted, B. - see Pound, E. and F.M. Ford
Lindeman, F.O. The Triple Representation of Schwa in Greek and Some Related Problems of Indo-European Phonology.*
W.F. Wyatt, Jr., 215(GL):Vol24No3-199
Lindemann, A.S. A History of European Socialism.
W.G. Regier, 152(UDQ):Spring84-119
Linden, E. City of Razors and Other Poems.
R. Watson, 588(SSL):Vol 19-194
Lindenberger, H. Opera.*
M. Tanner, 617(TLS):1Mar85-229
Lindenfield, F. and J. Rothschild-Whitt, eds. Workplace Democracy and Social Change.
J.J., 185:Jul85-987
Lindenmayr, H. Totalität und Beschränkung.
L.D. Lindsay, 221(GQ):Summer84-505
Lindfors, B. Early Nigerian Literature.
J.H. Summers, 141:Winter84-95
Lindgren, M. Att lära och att pryda.
S. Christie, 341:Vol53No1-34
Lindheim, N. The Structures of Sidney's "Arcadia."*
J.M. Kennedy, 178:Sep84-366
M. Smart, 539:May85-152
Lindholm, C. Generosity and Jealousy.
M.E. Meeker, 293(JASt):May84-576
Lindley, D., ed. The Court Masque.
S. Orgel, 617(TLS):25Jan85-100
Lindley, M. Lutes, Viols and Temperaments.
I. Woodfield, 617(TLS):31May85-619
Lindner, B. Bertolt Brecht.
G. Michels, 221(GQ):Fall84-675
Lindop, G. The Opium-Eater.*
D.G. Gillham, 506(PSt):May84-74
K.M. Hewitt, 447(N&Q):Jun83-257
Lindsay, D. The Crawford Papers. (J. Vincent, ed)
J. Campbell, 617(TLS):8Mar85-249
J. Grigg, 362:7Mar85-26
Lindsay, F. Brond.
G. Mangan, 617(TLS):15Feb85-179
Lindsay, J. Life Rarely Tells.
A. Croft, 364:Feb85-90
Lindsay, M. A Net to Catch the Winds and Other Poems.
R. Watson, 588(SSL):Vol 19-194
Ling, P. Old Shanghai.
D. Wilson, 617(TLS):5Apr85-375
"Lingua Sistemi Letterari e Comunicazione Sociale."
E. Martínez Garrido, 202(FMod):No68/70-420
Link, P. Mandarin Ducks and Butterflies.
M. Doleželová-Velingerová, 244(HJAS):Dec84-578
Link, P., ed. Stubborn Weeds. Roses and Thorns.
M. Goldman, 441:20Jan85-24
Link, P. - see Liu Binyan
Linklater, E. The Merry Muse.
G. Mangan, 617(TLS):29Nov85-1371

Linklater, M., I. Hilton and N. Ascherson. The Fourth Reich.
H.R. Kedward, 617(TLS):15Nov85-1282
Linklater, M., I. Hilton and N. Ascherson. The Nazi Legacy.
F.D. Gray, 453(NYRB):27Jun85-12
Links, J.G. Canaletto.*
W.L. Barcham, 54:Dec84-703
K. Garlick, 39:Jul84-77
Linley, J. The Georgia Catalog, Historic American Buildings Survey.*
M. Thomason, 9(AlaR):Jul84-236
Linowitz, S.M. The Making of a Public Man.
H. Goodman, 441:17Nov85-31
Linscott, G. Murder Makes Tracks.
T.J.B., 617(TLS):16Aug85-907
"The Jack and Belle Linsky Collection in the Metropolitan Museum of Art, New York."
G. de Bellaigue, 90:Nov84-700
van Lint, G.P.J. Tracing the Irretraceable.
A. van Santen, 204(FdL):Jun84-143
Lintott, A. Violence, Civil Strife and Revolution in the Classical City 750-330 B.C.*
T.E. Gregory, 24:Summer84-226
G.T. Griffith, 303(JoHS):Vol 104-237
Lintvelt, J. Essai de typologie narrative.*
R. Zeller, 602:Band15Heft1-175
"Lion de Bourges."* (W.W. Kibler, J-L.G. Picherit and T.S. Fenster, eds)
T.D. Hemming, 208(FS):Apr84-190
Lipka, L. and H. Günther, eds. Wortbildung.*
H. Sauer, 38:Band102Heft3/4-493
Lipking, L., ed. High Romantic Argument.*
M. Roberts, 541(RES):Nov84-558
Lipking, L. The Life of the Poet.*
A.F. Nagel, 131(CL):Spring84-171
M. Wood, 402(MLR):Apr84-407
Lipow, A. Authoritarian Socialism in America.*
W. Lesser, 405(MP):Nov84-220
K.M. Roemer, 125:Winter84-185
Lippincott, L. Selling Art in Georgian London.*
J. Ingamells, 90:Feb84-93
D. Mannings, 83:Autumn84-278
S.J. Rogal, 566:Spring85-180
D. Sutton, 39:Jun84-396
Lippit, N.M. and K.I. Selden, eds and trans. Stories by Contemporary Japanese Women Writers.*
V.V. Nakagawa, 293(JASt):Nov83-155
Lippmann, C. Lyrical Positivism.
A. Chanady, 107(CRCL):Mar84-104
Lippmann, W. Public Philosopher. (J.M. Blum, ed)
W.F. Kimball, 441:22Dec85-14
D. Seideman, 617(TLS):6Dec85-1381
Lipsett, S. Coming Back Up.
K. Ray, 441:29Dec85-18
Lipski, L.L. Dated English Delftware. (M. Archer, ed)
G. Wills, 39:Dec84-439
Lipstadt, D.E. Beyond Belief.
A. Beichman, 441:22Dec85-12
Lipton, M. Capitalism and Apartheid.
C. Ehrlich, 617(TLS):6Dec85-1390
Liria Montañés, P. - see Mandeville, J.

Liscinsky, R.B. Les Fais et Concquestes du Noble Roy Alexandre.
D.J.A. Ross, 208(FS):Jan84-46
de l'Isle-Adam, P.A.M.D. - see under de Villiers de l'Isle-Adam, P.A.M.
Lisner, C. The Australian Ballet.
K. Lowe-Hendricks, 381:Mar84-105
Lispector, C. Family Ties. The Apple in the Dark.
J. Gledson, 617(TLS):25Jan85-86
K.C. O'Brien, 362:14Mar85-27
Liss, P.K. Atlantic Empires.*
J.C. Bradford, 432(NEQ):Mar84-142
Listerman, M.S. Ángel María de Lera.
L. Hickey, 86(BHS):Oct84-514
"Literatur Bulgariens 1944-1980."
E. Bayer, 654(WB):5/1984-875
Litman, T.A. Les Comédies de Corncille.*
M.J. Muratore, 345(KRQ):Vol31No1-109
"La littérature chinoise au temps de la guerre de résistance contre le Japon (de 1937 à 1945)."
M. Doleželová-Velingerová, 293(JASt): Aug84-745
"Les Littératures de langues européennes au tournamt du siècle: Lectures d'aujourd'hui."
Y. Chevrel, 107(CRCL):Mar84-139
Little, J. Comedy and the Woman Writer.*
K.O. Garrigan, 395(MFS):Summer84-373
295(JML):Nov84-345
Little, R. Rimbaud: "Illuminations."
M.E. Birkett, 446(NCFS):Winter-Spring85-162
Littlefield, D.F., Jr. Africans and Creeks.
B.M. Smith, 106:Summer84-185
Littlefield, M.G., ed. Biblia Romanceada I.I.8.
J.E. Keller, 589:Oct84-983
Littlewood, I. The Writings of Evelyn Waugh.*
R. Craig, 659(ConL):Fall85-358
R.M. Davis, 191(ELN):Dec84-75
W. Sullivan, 569(SR):Summer84-442
Littlewood, J. Baron Philippe.
P-L. Adams, 61:Mar85-124
C. Curtis, 441:24Feb85-14
Liu Binyan. People or Monsters? (P. Link, ed)
M. Goldman, 441:20Jan85-24
Liu, J.J.Y. Essentials of Chinese Literary Art.
I.Y. Lo, 318(JAOS):Oct-Dec83-797
Liu, J.J.Y. The Interlingual Critic.
D.J. Levy, 293(JASt):Feb84-320
Liu Jen-kai. Die boshaften, unbotmässigen und rebellischen Beamten in der Neuen offiziellen Dynastiegeschichte der T'ang.
D. Grafflin, 318(JAOS):Oct-Dec83-799
Liu Zheng and others. China's Population.
T. Frejka, 293(JASt):May84-523
Liuzzi, D. - see Manilius
Lively, P. According to Mark.*
D. Taylor, 364:Oct84-90
Lively, P. Perfect Happiness.*
P. Craig, 617(TLS):5Jul85-757
Livesay, D. The Phases of Love.*
W. Keitner, 137:May84-50
A. Parkin, 102(CanL):Autumn84-117
Livi, G. Da una stanza all'altra.
F. Donini, 617(TLS):2Aug85-840

Livia, A. Accommodation Offered.
L. Marcus, 617(TLS):27Sep85-1070
"Living with Nuclear Weapons."*
J. Donaghy, 142:Winter84-181
Livingston, D.W. Hume's Philosophy of Common Life.
J. Deigh, 185:Jul85-959
R. Malpas, 617(TLS):30Aug85-942
Livingston, J. Arctic Oil.
M.L. Cross, 529(QQ):Winter84-867
Livingston, J. Die Again, Macready.*
T.J. Binyon, 617(TLS):15Feb85-179
Livingston, M.C. The Child as Poet: Myth or Reality?
M.S. Willis, 441:10Mar85-20
Livingston, P. Ingmar Bergman and the Rituals of Art.*
B. Steene, 563(SS):Spring84-170
V.W. Wexman, 405(MP):Feb85-342
Livingstone, A. Lou Andreas Salomé.
A. Fitzlyon, 364:Feb85-96
R. Weinreich, 441:14Jul85-23
Livingstone, A. - see Pasternak, B.
Livingstone, D. Love in Time.
J. Saunders, 565:Spring84-55
Livingstone, D. A Rosary of Bone. (2nd ed)
D. Walder, 617(TLS):10May85-527
Livingstone, M. R.B. Kitaj.
M. Podro, 617(TLS):6Dec85-1384
J. Russell, 441:8Dec85-12
"Le livre dans les sociétés pre-industrielles."
M. Harris, 78(BC):Winter84-528
"Livre et lecture en Espagne et en France sous l'Ancien Régime."
G. Díaz-Migoyo, 240(HR):Winter84-83
Livrea, H. - see Triphiodorus
Livrea, H., with P. Eleuteri - see Musaeus
Livy. Tite-Live, "Histoire Romaine," Tome 27, livre 37. (J-M. Engel, ed)
J. Briscoe, 123:Vol34No2-194
Livy. Tite-Live, "Histoire romaine," tome 28, livre 38.* (R. Adam, ed and trans)
J. André, 555:Vol58fasc1-134
Ljungberg, L. Alltför mänskligt.
C. Lofmark, 562(Scan):Nov84-183
Ljunggren, M. The Dream of Rebirth.
V.E. Alexandrov, 550(RusR):Jan84-74
P. Austin, 104(CASS):Spring-Summer84-163
J.D. Elsworth, 575(SEER):Apr84-265
Llompart, G. La pintura medieval mallorquina.
I.G. Bango Torviso, 48:Apr-Jun84-193
Llorach, E.A. - see under Alarcos Llorach, E.
Llorente, J.A. Noticia biográfica (Autobiografía).
A. Gil Novales, 86(BHS):Jan84-66
Llosa, M.V. - see under Vargas Llosa, M.
Lloyd, A.L. Anatomy of the Verb.
J.B. Voyles, 685(ZDL):3/1984-403
Lloyd, C. Camille Pissarro.
R. Schiff, 54:Dec84-681
Lloyd, C. The Well-Chosen Garden.*
R.I. Ross, 617(TLS):22Feb85-215
Lloyd, G.E.R. Science, Folklore and Ideology.
R. Parker, 520:Vol129No2-174
P. Pellegrin, 542:Oct-Dec84-451

Lloyd, H.A. The State, France and the Six-
teenth Century.
  J.R. Major, 551(RenQ):Spring84-82
Lloyd, R. Baudelaire et Hoffmann.
  G.R. Kaiser, 224(GRM):Band34Heft3-356
Lloyd, R. Baudelaire's Literary Crit-
icism.*
  W.T. Bandy, 131(CL):Spring84-186
Lloyd, S. An Indian Attachment.
  J. Mellors, 364:Jun84-107
Lloyd, T. Dinosaur and Co.
  F. Cairncross, 617(TLS):31May85-613
Lloyd, T.H. Alien Merchants in England in
the High Middle Ages.
  S.G. Uhler, 589:Oct84-923
Llull, R. Selected Works of Ramon Llull.
(A. Bonner, ed and trans)
  D.H. Rosenthal, 441:29Sep85-24
Loar, B. Mind and Meaning.*
  J.A.D., 185:Jul85-975
  W.G. Lycan, 482(PhR):Apr84-282
Lobb, E. T.S. Eliot and the Romantic Crit-
ical Tradition.*
  J. Olney, 569(SR):Summer84-451
Lobrano, G. Il potere dei tribuni della
plebe.
  J-C. Richard, 555:Vol158fasc2-344
Lochhead, L. The Grimm Sisters.
  R. Watson, 588(SSL):Vol 19-194
Lochhead, M. Magic and Witchcraft of the
Borders.
  W.F.H. Nicolaisen, 571(ScLJ):Autumn84-
34
Lochnan, K.A. The Etchings of James
McNeill Whistler.
  A. Staley, 617(TLS):18Oct85-1161
Lochte, D. Sleeping Dog.
  N. Callendar, 441:17Nov85-46
Lock, A. and E. Fisher, eds. Language
Development.
  G. Ewing, 350:Sep85-726
Lock, F.P. The Politics of "Gulliver's
Travels."
  J.A. Downie, 83:Spring84-87
Lock, F.P. Swift's Tory Politics.*
  F. Brady, 566:Spring85-169
  J. Hérou, 189(EA):Jul-Sep85-325
  R. Quintana, 402(MLR):Oct84-906
Locke, J. The Correspondence of John
Locke. (Vol 7) (E.S. de Beer, ed)
  J. Bricke, 543:Dec83-394
  M. Phillips, 192(EP):Jan-Mar84-122
Locke, J.L. Phonological Acquisition and
Change.
  M.R. Smith, 350:Dec85-907
Lockett, R. Samuel Prout 1783-1852.
  G. Reynolds, 617(TLS):25Oct85-1216
Lockhart, J. and S.B. Schwartz. Early
Latin America.
  A. Pagden, 617(TLS):14Jun85-659
Lockhart, R.H.B. Memoirs of a British
Agent.
  617(TLS):10May85-531
Lockley, F. Visionaries, Mountain Men
and Empire Builders.
  G. Topping, 649(WAL):May84-78
Lockwood, L. Music in Renaissance Ferrara
1400-1505.
  D. Stevens, 617(TLS):12Apr85-415
Lockwood, W.B. The Oxford Book of British
Bird Names.
  J. Buxton, 617(TLS):26Apr85-476

Lockyer, R. Buckingham.
  P. Christianson, 529(QQ):Autumn84-635
Lodder, C. Russian Constructivism.*
  S.P. Compton, 90:Feb84-98
  N.D. Lobanov, 39:Mar84-224
  L. Senelick, 615(TJ):Oct84-435
Lodge, D. Language of Fiction.
  S. Monod, 189(EA):Oct-Dec85-490
Lodge, D. The Modes of Modern Writing.
  M. Spencer, 494:Vol5No1-182
Lodge, D. Out of the Shelter.
  C. Hawtree, 617(TLS):31May85-599
Lodge, D. Small World.*
  P-L. Adams, 61:Apr85-140
  P. Craig, 617(TLS):29Nov85-1372
  P. Lewis, 565:Autumn84-55
  J. Mellors, 364:Apr/May84-135
  M. Rosenthal, 441:17Mar85-7
  R. Towers, 453(NYRB):15Aug85-26
  442(NY):3Jun85-124
Lodge, D. Working with Structuralism.*
  N. Bradbury, 541(RES):Aug84-428
  F. McCombie, 447(N&Q):Jun83-271
Lodge, R.A. - see Étienne de Fougères
Loeb, L.E. From Descartes to Hume.*
  R. Norman, 393(Mind):Apr84-301
  N. Jolley, 53(AGP):Band66Heft1-103
Loetscher, H. Noah. Das Hugo Loetscher
Lesebuch.
  M. Butler, 617(TLS):4Jan85-17
Loetscher, L.A. Facing the Enlightenment
and Pietism.
  D.W. Robson, 656(WMQ):Apr84-323
Loevy, S.R. William Carlos Williams's "A
Dream of Love."
  L.M. Steinman, 659(ConL):Winter85-497
Loewe, M. Chinese Ideas of Life and Death.
  R.T. Ames, 293(JASt):Nov83-139
  P.W. Kroll, 116:Jul83-197
Loewe, M. Ways to Paradise.*
  S.E. Cahill, 318(JAOS):Jul-Sep83-642
Loewenberg, P. Decoding the Past.
  D. Henry, 583:Summer85-386
Loewinsohn, R. Magnetic Field(s).*
  M.R. Winchell, 569(SR):Spring84-xliii
Lofmark, C. Hj. Söderberg: "Historietter."
  D.M. Mennie, 562(Scan):Nov84-196
Löfroth, E. A World Made Safe.
  A. Charters, 597(SN):Vol156No1-117
Löfstedt, B., ed. Ars Ambrosiana.
  J.J. Contreni, 589:Apr84-480
Löfstedt, B. - see Saint Boniface
Löfstedt, L. - see de Vignay, J.
Loftus, G.R. and E.F. Mind at Play.
  D.J. Murray, 529(QQ):Autumn84-740
Logan, F.D. The Vikings in History.*
  C. Fell, 575(SEER):Oct84-592
Logan, G.M. The Meaning of More's
"Utopia."*
  P.J.C. Field, 506(PSt):Dec84-261
  E. McCutcheon, 539:Feb85-73
  A.L. Prescott, 551(RenQ):Autumn84-444
  G.F. Waller, 529(QQ):Autumn84-717
"Logos Semantikos."
  G.F. Meier, 682(ZPSK):Band37Heft3-398
Logue, C. War Music.
  D. Devlin, 157:No153-46
Logue, J. Socialism and Abundance.
  P. Vinten-Johansen, 563(SS):Spring84-
185

Lowitt, R. The New Deal and the West.*
  639(VQR):Autumn84-115
Lowry, M. Selected Letters of Malcolm
  Lowry. (H. Breit and M.B. Lowry, eds)
  M. Hofmann, 617(TLS):18Oct85-1159
Loyer, F. Architecture of the Industrial
  Age 1789-1914.
  R. Banham, 576:Oct84-277
Loyn, H.R. The Governance of Anglo-Saxon
  England, 500-1087.*
  639(VQR):Autumn84-117
Loze, P. La Palais de Justice de
  Bruxelles.
  A. Willis, 576:Oct84-270
Lozerec'h, B. The Temp.*
  A. Beevor, 617(TLS):8Mar85-265
Lu Gwei-djen and J. Needham. Celestial
  Lancets.
  G. McRae, 293(JASt):Nov83-142
Luber, S. Die Herkunft von Zaporoger
  Kosaken des 17. Jahrhunderts nach
  Personennamen.
  P. Longworth, 104(CASS):Winter84-485
Lubin, G. - see Sand, G.
Lubin, N. Labour and Nationality in
  Soviet Central Asia.
  N. Eberstadt, 441:22Sep85-28
Lubitz, W., ed. Trotsky Bibliography.
  R.B. Day, 550(RusR):Apr84-227
Lucan - see under Mayer, R.
Lucas, A. Chinese Medical Modernization.
  K-C. Yip, 293(JASt):May84-525
Lucas, A.M. Women in the Middle Ages.*
  J. Tormey, 322(JHI):Oct-Dec84-619
  B.A.E. Yorke, 366:Autumn84-262
Lucas, G.R., Jr. The Genesis of Modern
  Process Thought.
  T. Vitali, 619:Spring84-201
Luce, T.J., ed-in-chief. Ancient Writers:
  Greece and Rome.*
  S.F. Wiltshire, 577(SHR):Fall84-350
"Luces Contemporáneas del Otomí: Gramática
  del Otomí de la Sierra."
  J.H. and K.C. Hill, 269(IJAL):Apr84-
  237
Lucey, K.G. and T.R. Machan, eds. Recent
  Work in Philosophy.
  S.W., 185:Jan85-385
Lüchinger, R. Salomon Gessner in Italien.
  F. Meregali, 107(CRCL):Mar84-127
  U. Schulz-Buschhaus, 224(GRM):Band34
  Heft4-471
Lucian. Vera Historia (Alethes Historia).
  (C.S. Jerram, ed)
  C. Fredericks, 121(CJ):Apr-May85-365
Lucie-Smith, E. Art Today.* (new ed)
  90:Feb84-103
Lucie-Smith, E. A History of Industrial
  Design.
  N. Whiteley, 46:Jul84-68
Lucie-Smith, E. The Thames and Hudson
  Dictionary of Art Terms.
  D. Goddard, 324:Oct85-799
Lucke, C. P. Ovidius Naso, "Remedia
  Amoris."
  A.A.R. Henderson, 123:Vol34No2-188
Luckyj, G. Panteleimon Kulish.
  J.A. Barnstead, 550(RusR):Apr84-222
  D.B. Chopyk, 574(SEEJ):Winter84-563
  O.S. Ilnytzkyj, 104(CASS):Winter84-487
Luckyj, G., ed. Vybrani lysty Pantelei-
  mona Kulisha ukrains'koiu movoiu pysani.
  O.S. Ilnytzkyj, 104(CASS):Winter84-487

Lucow, B. James Shirley.* (A.F. Kinney,
  ed)
  G. Bas, 189(EA):Oct-Dec85-457
  D.S. Lawless, 447(N&Q):Apr83-167
Luczak, J.E. Some Rain.
  T.G. Dunn, 615(TJ):Dec84-551
Lüdi, G. and B. Py. Zweisprachig durch
  Migration.
  M. Haus, 209(FM):Oct84-249
Ludlum, R. The Aquitaine Progression.*
  639(VQR):Summer84-97
Ludmerer, K.M. Learning to Heal.
  J.H. Jones, 441:22Dec85-20
Lüdtke, H., ed. Kommunikationstheore-
  tische Grundlagen des Sprachwandels.
  G. Objartel, 685(ZDL):3/1984-387
Luffman, C.A. and R. Reed. The Strategy
  and Performance of British Industry 1970-
  80.
  F. Cairncross, 617(TLS):31May85-613
Luft, D.S. Robert Musil and the Crisis of
  European Culture 1880-1942.*
  W. Braun, 406:Summer84-226
  F.G. Peters, 301(JEGP):Oct84-616
Lug, S. Poetic Techniques and Conceptual
  Elements in Ibn Zaydūn's Love Poetry.
  P.J. Boehne, 589:Jan84-239
Luhrs, K. - see Burke, D.B.
Luibhéid, C. The Council of Nicaea.
  M.P. McHugh, 589:Apr84-482
Luizzi, V. A Naturalistic Theory of Jus-
  tice.*
  E.F. McClennen, 619:Winter84-81
Luján Muñoz, L. El arquitecto mayor Diego
  de Porres (1677-1741).
  D. Angulo Iñiguez, 48:Jul-Sep83-308
Lukach, J.M. Hilla Rebay.*
  A. Berman, 55:Sep84-27
Lukács, G. Entwicklungsgeschichte des
  modernen Dramas. (F. Benseler, ed)
  B. Wirkus, 687:Jan-Mar84-155
Lukács, G. Philosophie de l'art (1912-
  1914).
  A. Reix, 542:Jan-Mar84-94
Lukács, G. Wie ist die faschistische
  Philosophie in Deutschland entstanden?
  Wie ist Deutschland zum Zentrum der
  reaktionären Ideologie geworden?
  P. Somville, 542:Jan-Mar84-93
Lukács, L., ed. The Vatican and Hungary,
  1846-1878.
  L. Péter, 575(SEER):Apr84-286
Lukan, W. and M.D. Peyfuss. Ost- und
  Südosteuropasammlungen in Österreich.
  R.E. McGrew, 550(RusR):Apr84-224
Lukas, J.A. Common Ground.
  J. Beatty, 61:Sep85-108
  K. Erikson, 441:15Sep85-1
  J. Fallows, 61:Aug85-84
Luke, H.M. The Voice Within.
  L. Caldecott, 469:Vol 10No2-100
Luker, K. Abortion and the Politics of
  Motherhood.*
  J. Glover, 453(NYRB):30May85-19
Lukes, S. Marxism and Morality.
  A.C. Danto, 617(TLS):27Sep85-1052
Lull, R. Raimundus Lullus, Opera Latina.
  (Vol 9 ed by A. Madre, Vol 10 ed by L.
  Sala-Molins)
  J.N. Hillgarth, 589:Oct84-925

Lyon, J. Playing God in the Nursery.
P. Starr, 441:31Mar85-28
Lyon, J.K. Bertolt Brecht in America.*
A. Masters, 157:No151-50
C.R. Mueller, 615(TJ):Mar82-128
P. Thomson, 610:Summer84-152
Lyons, A. Three With a Bullet.
N. Callendar, 441:12May85-17
Lyons, D. Ethics and the Rule of Law.*
C.D.J., 185:Jul85-971
Lyons, J. Language and Linguistics.
B.M.H. Strang, 402(MLR):Apr84-410
Lyons, J.D. The Listening Voice.
J. Bailbé, 475:Vol 11No21-732
R.T. Corum, Jr., 210(FrF):Sep84-367
B. Norman, 207(FR):Oct84-122
Lyons, J.D. and S.G. Nichols, Jr., eds.
Mimesis.
P.H. Stablein, 589:Jul84-673
Lyons, R. Thinner You Grow.
J. Carter, 219(GaR):Winter84-881
Lyons, W.E. Emotion.*
R. De Sousa, 484(PPR):Sep84-142
Lyotard, J-F. Le différend.
A. Badiou, 98:Nov84-851
D. Carroll, 153:Fall84-74
Lyotard, J-F. Discours, Figure.
P. Dews, 153:Fall84-40
Lyotard, J-F. Instructions païennes.
C. Lindsay, 153:Fall84-52
Lyotard, J-F. Le Mur du Pacifique.
G. Van Den Abbeele, 153:Fall84-90
Lyotard, J-F. The Postmodern Condition.
(French title: La condition postmoderne.)
R. Rorty, 98:Mar84-181
J.S., 185:Jul85-976
Lyotard, J-F. and J-L. Thébaud. Au juste.
G. Bennington, 153:Fall84-64
C. Lindsay, 153:Fall84-52
Lytle, G.F. and S. Orgel, eds. Patronage
in the Renaissance.*
J.H. Summers, 569(SR):Spring84-278
Lyttelton, G. and R. Hart-Davis. The
Lyttelton Hart-Davis Letters. (Vol 2)
(R. Hart-Davis, ed)
D. Merkin, 441:23Jun85-6
Lyttelton, G. and R. Hart-Davis. The
Lyttelton Hart-Davis Letters.* (Vol 6)
(R. Hart-Davis, ed)
D. Taylor, 364:Jun84-108
Lyttelton, M. and W. Forman. The Romans,
their Gods and their Beliefs.
R. Higgins, 39:Dec84-438

Maalouf, A. The Crusades Through Arab
Eyes.*
442(NY):25Nov85-163
Maas, E. Literatur und Zensur in der
frühen Aufklärung.
V. Kapp, 535(RHL):Jan/Feb84-103
Maas, J. Holman Hunt and The Light of the
World.
J. Bronkhurst, 90:Jun84-365
Maass, J. Kleist.*
A. Vivis, 157:No153-50
Mabbott, T.O. - see Poe, E.A.
Maber, R.G. The Poetry of Pierre Le Moyne
(1602-1671).
Q.M. Hope, 475:Vol 11No20-255
M.M. McGowan, 208(FS):Jul84-335
Mabey, D. The Guiltless Gourmet.
C. Reid, 617(TLS):20Dec85-1467

Mabey, R. The Frampton Flora.
D. May, 362:4Jul85-29
Mabey, R., ed. Second Nature.
J.R. Banks, 148:Winter84-95
Macafee, C. Glasgow.
C.L. Houck, 350:Jun85-499
McAlister, L. The Development of Franz
Brentano's Ethics.
S.L. Krantz, 484(PPR):Dec84-287
E.H. Schneewind, 319:Jan85-119
McAlpin, M.B. Subject to Famine.
A. Appadurai, 293(JASt):May84-481
Macandrew, H. Italian Drawings in the
Ashmolean Catalogue of the Collection
of Drawings. (Vol 3)
J.A. Gere, 39:Oct84-288
Macandrew, H. Italian Drawings in the
Museum of Fine Art, Boston.
J.B. Shaw, 90:Jul84-445
MacAodha, B.S., ed. Topothesia — Essays
presented to T.S. Ó Máille.
W.F.H. Nicolaisen, 424:Mar84-88
McArthur, B. Actors and American Culture,
1880-1920.
J. Hankey, 617(TLS):15Feb85-174
McArthur, T. A Foundation Course for Lan-
guage Teachers.
B.J. Koekkoek, 350:Sep85-727
Macaulay, R. Dangerous Ages. Crewe Train.
N. Lawson, 617(TLS):22Mar85-326
Macaulay, R. They Went to Portugal.
617(TLS):10May85-531
Macaulay, R.W., P.J. Hay and G. Sherman.
Report to the Honourable Susan Fish, Min-
ister of Citizenship and Culture for the
Province of Ontario, by the Special Com-
mittee for the Arts. (Vol 1)
A. Billings, 108:Fall84-116
McBain, E. Snow White and Rose Red.
M. Laski, 362:14Nov85-35
MacBeth, G. The Lion of Pescara.*
J. Mellors, 364:Nov84-105
MacBeth, G. Poems from Oby.*
P. Breslin, 491:Dec84-165
McBride, M. The Going Under of the Even-
ing Land.*
L. Gregerson, 491:Oct84-44
McBride, M.F. Folklore of Dryden's
England.*
R.D. Hume, 566:Autumn84-64
MacBride, S. Crime and Punishment.
T. Garvin, 272(IUR):Spring84-146
McCabe, B. Spring's Witch.
D. Dunn, 617(TLS):26Apr85-470
MacCabe, C., ed. James Joyce.*
295(JML):Nov84-464
McCabe, R.A. Joseph Hall.*
F.L. Huntley, 481(PQ):Fall84-532
J. Mezciems, 402(MLR):Jul84-665
McCabe, W.H. An Introduction to Jesuit
Theatre. (L.J. Oldani, ed)
R. Engle, 615(TJ):Oct84-431
J. Hilton, 617(TLS):22Feb85-208
McCaffery, L. The Metafictional Muse.*
R. Pearce, 587(SAF):Spring84-118
J.C. Rowe, 659(ConL):Summer85-212
McCaffery, S. Knowledge Never Knew.
J. Riddell, 137:May84-7
McCaig, N. A World of Difference.*
D. McDuff, 565:Spring84-72
McCall, D. Queen of Hearts.
J. Marcus, 441:11Aug85-14
McCallum, B. - see Ferris, W.

McCallum, P. Literature and Method.
P. Parrinder, 366:Autumn84-249
MacCana, P. Celtic Mythology.
J. Simpson, 203:Vol195No2-266
McCandless, A. The Burke Foundation.
M. Laski, 362:18Apr85-26
McCanles, M. The Discourse of "Il Prin-
cipe."
P. Bondanella, 276:Winter84-355
McCann, J.S. The Critical Reputation of
Tennessee Williams.
T.P. Adler, 365:Winter84-26
D.W. Gunn, 40(AEB):Vol8No1-57
McCann, P. and F.A. Young. Samuel Wilder-
spin and the Infant School Movement.
M.G. Cooper, 161(DUJ):Dec83-114
MacCannell, D. and J.F. The Time of the
Sign.
D. Lovekin, 480(P&R):Vol 17No3-184
McCarron, W. and R. Shenk. Lesser Meta-
physical Poets.
T.K. Conley, 568(SCN):Fall84-34
McCarthy, A.J., ed. Book to a Mother.
V. Gillespie, 382(MAE):1984/1-133
McCarthy, C. Blood Meridian.
C. James, 441:28Apr85-31
MacCarthy, D. Desmond McCarthy: The Man
and His Writings. (D. Cecil, ed)
J. Bayley, 364:Jun84-89
MacCarthy, F. - see Pritchard, J.
McCarthy, J.A. Christoph Martin Wieland.
G. Bersier, 406:Spring84-91
McCarthy, M. Occasional Prose.
J. Moynahan, 441:5May85-15
McCarthy, M.S. Balzac and His Reader.*
W. Paulson, 210(FrF):Jan84-122
McCarthy, P. Camus.*
P. Henry, 478:Apr84-104
McCarthy, P.A. The Riddles of "Finnegans
Wake."*
V. Mahon, 677(YES):Vol 14-350
R. Mason, 447(N&Q):Aug83-372
McCarthy, P.A. Olaf Stapledon.*
R.M. Philmus, 561(SFS):Mar84-71
McCarthy, S. The Banned Man.
T. Dooley, 617(TLS):15Mar85-294
McCarty, M. The Transforming Principle.
E. Ziff, 441:4Aug85-17
MacCary, W.T. Childlike Achilles.*
J.P. Holoka, 124:Sep-Oct84-49
MacCary, W.T. Friends and Lovers.
G. Taylor, 617(TLS):16Aug85-905
McCaughey, P. Fred Williams.*
U. Hoff, 39:Mar84-225
McCauley, E.A. A.A.E. Disdéri and the
Carte de Visite Portrait Photograph.
A. Anderson, 441:24Nov85-25
P. Conisbee, 617(TLS):6Dec85-1385
McCawley, J.D. Everything You Always
Have Always Wanted to Know About Logic
(but were ashamed to ask).*
W.K. Wilson, 316:Dec84-1407
McCawley, J.D. Thirty Million Theories of
Grammar.*
R. Salkie, 297(JL):Mar84-202
Macchi, V., general ed. Collins Sansoni
Italian Dictionary.
H.K. Moss, 278(IS):Vol39-148
McClanahan, E. Famous People I Have Known.
A. Barnet, 441:24Nov85-25
McClane, K.A. A Tree Beyond Telling.
A. Fulton, 385(MQR):Summer85-492

McClatchy, J.D. Scenes from Another Life.*
R. Pybus, 565:Summer84-56
McClellan, E. Woman in the Crested
Kimono.
I. Buruma, 441:15Sep85-13
McClellan, J.E. 3d. Science Reorganized.
S. Shapin, 617(TLS):22Nov85-1320
McCloskey, H.J. Ecological Ethics and
Politics.*
S.M. Brown, Jr., 482(PhR):Oct84-620
B. Cohen, 483:Apr84-277
O. O'Neill, 393(Mind):Oct84-627
McClung, W.A. The Architecture of Para-
dise.*
D.M. Friedman, 551(RenQ):Autumn84-485
McClure, J. The Artful Egg.
N. Callendar, 441:9Jun85-37
M. Laski, 362:10Jan85-25
McClure, J. Cop World.*
A. Wilkinson, 441:24Mar85-18
McClure, J.D., ed. Scotland and the Low-
land Tongue.
E. Letley, 571(ScLJ):Winter84-37
McClure, M. Fragments of Perseus.
A.W. Knight, 649(WAL):Nov84-238
McCluskey, J., Jr. Mr. America's Last
Season Blues.*
D. Johnson, 577(SHR):Fall84-368
McClymer, J.F. War and Welfare.
A. Finkel, 106:Winter84-465
McColley, D.K. Milton's Eve.*
C. Duncan, 95(CLAJ):Mar85-357
R. Flannagan, 391:Mar84-32
R.B. Waddington, 551(RenQ):Winter84-
672
639(VQR):Winter84-7
McConnell, J. Battlefield Madonna.
M. Laski, 362:18Apr85-26
McConnell, J. English Public Schools.
J. Rae, 362:26Sep85-27
McConnell, R.B., ed. Art, Science and
Human Progress.
M. Yorke, 324:Apr85-369
McConnell-Ginet, S., R. Borker and N.
Furman, eds. Women and Language in Lit-
erature and Society.
E. Marks, 81:Winter84-99
McCorduck, P. The Universal Machine.
S. Boxer, 441:10Nov85-29
McCormack, M.H. What They Don't Teach You
At Harvard Business School.*
F. Cairncross, 617(TLS):31May85-613
MacCormack, S.G. Art and Ceremony in Late
Antiquity.*
M. McCormick, 24:Winter84-494
K.J. Shelton, 122:Jul84-259
G.M. Woloch, 121(CJ):Apr-May85-366
McCormack, T., ed. Culture, Code, and Con-
tent Analyses.
A.D. Grimshaw, 355(LSoc):Mar84-90
McCormack, W.J. Ascendancy and Tradition
in Anglo-Irish Literary History from
1789 to 1939.
D. Donoghue, 617(TLS):1Nov85-1239
McCormack, W.J. and A. Stead, eds. James
Joyce and Modern Literature.*
W. Huber, 72:Band221Heft1-189
McCormick, E.A., ed. Germans in America.
W.D. Kamphoefner, 658:Winter84-306
MacCormick, N. H.L.A. Hart.
D. Lyons, 482(PhR):Jan84-112

Macey, S.L. Money and the Novel.
 D. Blewett, 627(UTQ):Summer84-424
 D. Cottom, 594:Summer84-256
 J. McVeagh, 566:Spring85-191
McFadden, D. Country of the Open Heart.
 B. Pirie, 102(CanL):Autumn84-121
 B. Whiteman, 137:May84-21
McFadden, D. A Pair of Baby Lambs.
 B. Whiteman, 137:May84-21
McFadden, D. Three Stories and Ten Poems.
 A New Romance.
 B. Pirie, 102(CanL):Autumn84-121
McFadden, G. Discovering the Comic.*
 P.R. Berk, 403(MLS):Fall84-82
 R.B. Henkle, 569(SR):Winter84-121
 D. Wheeler, 577(SHR):Fall84-373
McFadden, R. The Selected Roy McFadden.
 (J. Boyd, ed)
 M. Harmon, 272(IUR):Spring84-126
McFarland, G.W. A Scattered People.
 442(NY):21Oct85-151
McFarland, P. Sea Dangers.
 P-L. Adams, 61:Nov85-143
 H. Carlisle, 441:27Oct85-53
McFarland, P. Seasons of Fear.*
 D. Flower, 249(HudR):Summer84-311
McFarland, T. Originality and Imagination.
 K. Hanley, 617(TLS):19Jul85-802
McFarland, T. Romanticism and the Forms
 of Ruin.*
 L. Newlyn, 541(RES):Aug84-388
McFarlane, I.D. Buchanan.
 A.A. MacDonald, 179(ES):Aug84-312
McFarlane, I.D. - see "The Entry of Henri
 II into Paris, 16 June 1549"
McFarlane, I.D. and I. Maclean, eds.
 Montaigne.*
 C.M. Bauschatz, 551(RenQ):Winter84-643
 C. Demure, 192(EP):Oct-Dec84-551
 M.B. McKinley, 210(FrF):May84-253
McFarlane, J., ed. "Slaves of Love" and
 other Norwegian Short Stories.
 A. Simpson, 562(Scan):May84-75
MacFarlane, L.J. The Theory and Practice
 of Human Rights.
 J. Waldron, 617(TLS):8Nov85-1269
MacFarquhar, R. The Origins of the Cul-
 tural Revolution.* (Vol 2)
 639(VQR):Winter84-18
McFee, M. Plain Air.
 S. Anders, 110:Spring85-119
McFie, H., M.R. Menocal and L. Sera. Prim-
 avera.
 A. Mollica, 399(MLJ):Summer84-181
McGaha, M.D., ed. Approaches to the The-
 ater of Calderón.*
 G. Edwards, 86(BHS):Apr84-197
McGahern, J. High Ground.
 P. Craig, 617(TLS):13Sep85-1001
McGann, J.J. The Beauty of Inflections.
 B. Marie, 400(MLN):Dec84-1188
McGann, J.J. A Critique of Modern Textual
 Criticism.*
 R.F. Cook, 478:Oct84-302
 S. Gottlieb, 365:Winter84-32
 B. Marie, 400(MLN):Dec84-1188
McGann, J.J. The Romantic Ideology.*
 M. Fischer, 88:Winter84/85-152
 B. Marie, 400(MLN):Dec84-1188
 P.L. Thorslev, Jr., 340(KSJ):Vol33-205
McGann, J.J. - see Lord Byron
McGary, J. - see Fredson, J.

McGee, H. On Food and Cooking.
 R. Flaste, 441:13Jan85-23
McGhee, G.M. Envoy to the Middle World.*
 A. Watson, 617(TLS):31May85-611
McGhee, R.D. Henry Kirke White.
 D.A. Low, 447(N&Q):Jun83-253
McGilchrist, I. Against Criticism.*
 R. Wellek, 131(CL):Fall84-354
McGinley, P. Foxprints.
 C. Sigal, 441:20Oct85-24
McGinley, P. The Trick of the Ga Bolga.
 H. Kenner, 441:21Jul85-20
 D. Profumo, 617(TLS):13Sep85-1000
McGinn, C. The Character of Mind.*
 T.G. Arner, 482(PhR):Oct84-630
 B.J. Garrett, 393(Mind):Jul84-461
McGinn, C. The Subjective View.
 J.M. Hinton, 483:Apr84-272
 R.G. Swinburne, 518:Jan84-55
McGinn, C. Wittgenstein on Meaning.
 A. Margalit, 617(TLS):24May85-587
McGlathery, J.M. Mysticism and Sexuality.*
 (Pt 1)
 G. Hoffmeister, 149(CLS):Summer84-232
McGrath, D.F. - see "Bookman's Price Index"
McGrath, S. and J. Olsen. The Artists and
 the Desert.
 U. Hoff, 39:Mar84-225
McGrath, T. Passages Toward the Dark.
 F.C. Stern, 649(WAL):May84-50
McGregor, C. Time of Testing.
 K. Tsokhas, 381:Jun84-266
Macgregor, F. Scots Proverbs and Rhymes.
 L.D. Travis, 529(QQ):Winter84-825
McGregor, J.F. and B. Reay, eds. Radical
 Religion in the English Revolution.
 A. Fletcher, 617(TLS):15Feb85-182
MacGregor, R. The Last Season.
 J. Herlan, 168(ECW):Winter84/85-316
MacGregor-Hastie, R. Never To Be Taken
 Alive.
 D. Judd, 617(TLS):24May85-571
McGuane, T. Something to be Desired.*
 J. Neville, 617(TLS):24May85-573
McGuckian, M. Venus and the Rain.*
 B. O'Donoghue, 493:Jun84-61
 W. Scammell, 364:Mar85-90
McGuinness, B., ed. Wittgenstein and his
 Times.*
 H.L. Finch, 518:Jul84-162
 I. McFetridge, 479(PhQ):Jan84-69
 483:Jan84-140
McGuinness, D. When Children Don't Learn.
 J. Drucker, 441:17Nov85-40
McGuire, B.P. The Cistercians in Denmark.
 C.H. Berman, 589:Jan84-185
McGuire, J.E. and M. Tamny. Certain Philo-
 sophical Questions.
 P.M. Harman, 518:Apr84-105
McGuire, J.P. Hermann Lungkwitz.
 G.E. Lich, 585(SoQ):Summer84-85
 L. Milazzo, 584(SWR):Spring84-211
McGuire, M.C. Milton's Puritan Masque.*
 W.P. Shaw, 391:Oct84-95
 639(VQR):Spring84-44
McGuire, W. Bollingen.*
 M. Goldstein, 569(SR):Winter84-viii
Mácha, K.H. Máj.
 R.B. Pynsent, 575(SEER):Oct84-584
Machado, A. The Legend of Alvargonzalez.
 D. McDuff, 565:Spring84-72
MacHale, D. George Boole.
 W.V. Quine, 617(TLS):12Jul85-767

Machatzke, M. - see Hauptmann, G.
Mache, B. Wandel und Sein.
  B.L. Bradley, 221(GQ):Winter84-159
Machin, A. Cohérence et continuité dans
le théâtre de Sophocle.*
  A. Lebeau, 555:Vol58fasc2-291
Machlis, J. The Career of Magda V.
  W.L. Taitte, 441:18Aug85-33
McHugh, R. Annotations to "Finnegans
Wake."*
  W. Füger, 38:Band102Heft1/2-263
McHugh, R. The "Finnegans Wake" Experi-
ence.
  B. Benstock, 454:Winter85-182
McHugh, R. and M. Harmon. Short History
of Anglo-Irish Literature.*
  J.M. Cahalan, 566:Autumn84-71
MacIlvanney, W. The Big Man.
  J. Campbell, 617(TLS):13Sep85-1000
McIlvanney, W. These Words.
  D. Dunn, 617(TLS):26Apr85-470
McInerney, J. Bright Lights, Big City.*
  R. Kaveney, 617(TLS):24May85-572
McInerney, J. Ransom.
  P-L. Adams, 61:Oct85-106
  R. Loewinsohn, 441:29Sep85-42
McInerny, R. Ethica Thomistica.*
  V.J. Bourke, 589:Jan84-241
McInerny, R. The Noonday Devil.
  A.M. Greeley, 441:31Mar85-19
  442(NY):13May85-148
MacInnes, C. Absolute MacInnes. (T.
Gould, ed)
  617(TLS):25Oct85-1219
McInnes, E. Das deutsche Drama des 19.
Jahrhunderts.
  R.C. Cowen, 680(ZDP):Band103Heft4-619
McInnes, G. The Road to Gundagai.
  617(TLS):22Nov85-1339
MacIntyre, A. After Virtue.*
  C. Evangeliou, 543:Sep83-132
  J.M. Heaton, 323:Jan84-97
  D.Z. Phillips, 393(Mind):Jan84-111
  C. Taylor, 473(PR):?/1984-301
  M.W. Wartofsky, 262:Jul84-235
MacIntyre, A. L'inconscient.
  V. Descombes, 98:Oct84-775
McIver, N.J. Come Back, Alice Smythereene!
  N. Callendar, 441:2Jun85-38
Mack, D.S. - see Hogg, J.
Mack, M. Collected in Himself.*
  B.S. Hammond, 83:Autumn84-241
  P. Rogers, 402(MLR):Apr84-419
Mack, M. Alexander Pope.
  P. Davison, 61:Dec85-112
  I. Donaldson, 617(TLS):13Sep85-997
  D. Nokes, 362:29Aug85-22
Mack, M. - see Pope, A.
Mack, M. and G.D. Lord, eds. Poetic Tradi-
tions of the English Renaissance.*
  S. Davies, 148:Winter84-90
  H. Morris, 569(SR):Spring84-290
  H. Smith, 570(SQ):Summer84-241
Mack Smith, D. Cavour.
  D. Beales, 617(TLS):10May85-514
  H. Brogan, 362:28Mar85-28
  D. Johnson, 453(NYRB):13Jun85-24
  G. Steiner, 442(NY):19Aug85-86
  R. Trevelyan, 441:1Sep85-9
Mack Smith, D. Cavour and Garibaldi 1860.
  D. Beales, 617(TLS):10May85-514
McKay, A. The Making of the Atomic Age.
  J. Calado, 617(TLS):21Jun85-693

MacKay, A. and D.S. Severin, eds. Cosas
sacadas de la Historia del rey Don Juan
el Segundo.*
  J.N.H. Lawrance, 382(MAE):1984/2-332
McKay, D. Birding, or Desire.
  J.W. Foster, 102(CanL):Autumn84-177
  N. Zacharin, 137:Feb85-28
Mackay, D. The Modern House.
  J. Gowan, 46:Oct84-83
McKay, D. and H.M. Scott. The Rise of the
Great Powers: 1648-1815.
  P. Dukes, 83:Spring84-96
  D. Kirby, 575(SEER):Apr84-280
McKay, J. Gone to Grass.
  S. Mills, 526:Summer84-83
  C. Rooke, 376:Oct84-126
  M. Stobie, 102(CanL):Autumn84-175
McKay, J.H. Narration and Discourse in
American Realistic Fiction.*
  H.H. Kolb, Jr., 27(AL):Mar84-111
  D. Pizer, 183(ESQ):Vol30No3-193
McKay, N.Y. Jean Toomer, Artist.
  A. Rampersad, 578:Fall85-110
Mackay, R.F. Balfour.
  J. Turner, 617(TLS):3May85-489
McKean, C. and D. Walker. Dundee.
  J.S. Curl, 324:Aug85-673
McKee, A. Dresden 1945.
  R. Bailey, 441:3Mar85-23
Macken, R., ed. Quodlibet X.
  B.C. Bazán, 154:Dec84-721
McKenna, P. A New Pricing Guide for Mate-
rials Produced by The Roycroft Printing
Shop. (2nd ed)
  87(BB):Sep84-173
McKenzie, B. Flannery O'Connor's Georgia.
  M. Morton, 392:Winter83/84-89
McKenzie, K.E. - see Rodichev, F.I.
MacKenzie, N. and J. Dickens.
  K. Dierks, 38:Band102Heft1/2-259
Mackenzie, N. and J. - see Webb, B.
Mackenzie, N.H. A Reader's Guide to
Gerard Manley Hopkins.*
  L. Adey, 637(VS):Autumn83-97
McKeon, Z.K. Novels and Arguments.*
  S. Bassett, 478:Oct84-311
  R.P. Fitzgerald, 480(P&R):Vol 17No3-
174
  S. Raval, 402(MLR):Oct84-880
McKercher, B.J.C. The Second Baldwin Gov-
ernment and the United States, 1924-1929.
  J. Turner, 617(TLS):19Apr85-430
McKerrow, R.E., ed. Explorations in
Rhetoric.
  W. Brockriede, 480(P&R):Vol 17No2-125
Mackie, J.L. Ethics.*
  T. Modood, 321:Vol 18No3-237
Mackie, J.L. The Miracle of Theism.*
  J.C.A. Gaskin, 518:Jan84-43
  B. Langtry, 63:Jun84-195
  W.L. Rowe, 258:Dec84-439
McKinley, M.B. Words in a Corner.*
  C. Strosetzki, 72:Band221Heft1-205
McKinnon, A., ed. Kierkegaard.
  E.F. Bertoldi, 154:Sep84-517
MacKinnon, B. Fathers and Heroes.
  H.R. Runte, 102(CanL):Autumn84-124
MacKinnon, E.M. Scientific Explanation
and Atomic Physics.
  J.T. Cushing, 167:Mar84-89
Mackintosh, I. and G. Ashton. Royal Opera
House Retrospective 1732-1982.
  J. Reading, 611(TN):Vol38No1-43

McKitterick, D. Four Hundred Years of University Printing and Publishing in Cambridge 1584-1984.
   I. Bain, 617(TLS):13Dec85-1439
McKitterick, D. The Sandars and Lyell Lectures.
   A. Asaf, 517(PBSA):Vol78No1-103
Macklin, R. Man, Mind and Morality.
   S.M. Brown, Jr., 482(PhR):Jan84-104
Mackridge, P. The Modern Greek Language.
   M. Alexiou, 617(TLS):11Oct85-1151
Maclachlan, M.D. Why They Did Not Starve.
   A. Appadurai, 293(JASt):May84-481
McLagan, P. In France.
   E.G. Lombeida, 207(FR):Dec84-337
   R.J. Melpignano, 399(MLJ):Autumn84-287
MacLaine, S. Dancing in the Light.
   J. Eidus, 441:13Oct85-25
McLaren, I.F. Marcus Clarke.*
   L. Hergenhan, 71(ALS):Oct84-562
Maclaren-Ross, J. Memoirs of the Forties.*
   W. Scammell, 364:Mar85-109
McLaughlin, B. Children's Second Language Learning.
   F. Genesee, 399(MLJ):Summer84-158
McLaughlin, J. Old English Syntax.
   B. Mitchell, 541(RES):May84-217
   R.D. Stevick, 301(JEGP):Oct84-551
McLaverty, B. Secrets, and Other Stories.*
   442(NY):25Feb85-102
MacLean, A. Floodgate.*
   639(VQR):Summer84-98
MacLean, A. San Andreas.
   M.S. Kaplan, 441:20Oct85-34
McLean, A.M. - see Barlowe, W.
MacLean, D. and C. Mills, eds. Liberalism Reconsidered.
   C.W. Anderson, 185:Oct84-149
McLean, J. The Secret Life of Railroaders.
   L. Welch, 198:Summer84-112
Maclean, N. A River Runs Through It.
   P. Wild, 649(WAL):Feb85-350
MacLeish, W.H. Oil and Water.
   C.R. Herron, 441:11Aug85-15
McLellan, D.S. Cyrus Vance.
   C.R. Herron, 441:10Nov85-29
McLelland, J.C., ed. Peter Martyr Vermigli and Italian Reform.
   K. Eisenbichler, 539:May85-131
McLendon, W.L. Une ténébreuse carrière sous l'Empire et la Restauration.*
   M-C. Amblard, 535(RHL):Mar/Apr84-287
McLennan, G. Marxism and the Methodologies of History.
   W. Stafford, 366:Spring84-105
MacLennan, M.C. - see Wilson, T.
MacLennan, T. Singing the Stars.
   G.P. Greenwood, 102(CanL):Summer84-135
   R.W. Harvey, 168(ECW):Winter84/85-344
MacLeod, C. The Convivial Codfish.
   T.J. Binyon, 617(TLS):15Mar85-284
Macleod, C.W. - see Homer
McLeod, J. Greendream.
   M. Thorpe, 198:Spring84-114
McLeod, K. The Last Summer.*
   639(VQR):Autumn84-116
MacLeod, M.J. and R. Wasserstrom, eds. Spaniards and Indians in Southeastern Mesoamerica.
   A. Lavrin, 263(RIB):Vol34No1-99
MacLeod, R. - see Owen, D.

MacLeod, S. Lawrence's Men and Women.
   K. Brown, 617(TLS):18Oct85-1171
   P. Kemp, 362:26Sep85-31
McLoughlin, W.G. Cherokees and Missionaries, 1789-1839.
   J.H. Merrell, 656(WMQ):Oct84-672
McLuhan, E. and T. Hill. Norval Morrisseau and the Emergence of the Image Makers.
   G.W., 102(CanL):Autumn84-199
McLuhan, T.C. Dream Tracks.
   W.L. Heat-Moon, 441:8Dec85-16
MacLulich, T.D. Hugh MacLennan.
   E. Cameron, 627(UTQ):Summer84-456
   W.J. Keith, 99:Apr84-32
McLynn, F. The Jacobites.
   H.T. Dickinson, 617(TLS):27Dec85-1489
McLynn, F.J. The Jacobite Army in England, 1745.
   J. Black, 83:Spring84-109
McMahan, E. Critical Approaches to Mark Twain's Short Stories.
   M. Jacobson, 577(SHR):Winter84-86
MacMahon, B. The Sound of Hooves.
   P. Lewis, 364:Mar85-105
McMahon, R.J. Colonialism and Cold War.
   F.P. Bunnell, 293(JASt):Nov83-198
McManners, H. Falklands Commando.
   J. Strawson, 617(TLS):17May85-556
McManus, J. Chin Music.
   B. Staples, 441:8Sep85-24
McManus, P.F. The Grasshopper Trap.
   P-L. Adams, 61:Nov85-143
   I. Frazier, 441:15Dec85-8
McMaster, G. Scott and Society.*
   D. Hewitt, 571(ScLJ):Winter84-46
   J. Millgate, 541(RES):Nov84-562
McMaster, J. and R. The Novel from Sterne to James.*
   T. Braun, 447(N&Q):Jun83-251
McMenamin, M. and J. Goetsch. Panels of Patterns.
   C.C., 614:Winter85-28
McMillan, C. Women, Reason and Nature.*
   G. Lloyd, 63:Mar84-84
Macmillan, H. War Diaries.*
   442(NY):7Jan85-78
McMillan, J.F. Dreyfus to de Gaulle.
   M. Larkin, 617(TLS):28Jun85-731
Macmillan, M. - see Milingo, E.
McMillin, A. - see Bahdanovič, M., A. Harun and Ź. Biadula
McMorris, P. Crazy Quilts.
   K.S.H., 614:Winter85-20
McMullen, J.P. Cry of the Panther.
   J. Dickey, 441:27Jan85-16
MacMullen, R. Christianizing the Roman Empire (A.D. 100-400).*
   H. Chadwick, 617(TLS):5Apr85-379
McMullen, R. Degas.
   J. House, 617(TLS):22Nov85-1316
   V. Raynor, 441:6Jan85-22
   M. Stevens, 61:Jan85-97
MacMullen, R. Paganism in the Roman Empire.*
   G.J.D. Aalders H. Wzn., 394: Vol37fasc1/2-249
McMurrin, S.M., ed. The Tanner Lectures on Human Values. (Vol 4)
   C.W.G., 185:Apr85-768
McMurrin, S.M., ed. Values at War.
   T.N., 185:Apr85-781

Maffesoli, M., ed. La Galaxie de l'imagin-
aire.
    P.C. Malenfant, 193(ELit):Apr84-189
Magalhães Júnior, R. Vida e Obra de
Machado de Assis.
    J. Gledson, 86(BHS):Jan84-64
Magarotto, L., M. Marzaduri and G. Pagani
Cesa, eds. L'Avanguardia a Tiflis.*
    A.C. Wright, 104(CASS):Spring-Summer84-
    176
Magdalen, I.I. Ana P.
    D. Finkle, 441:11Aug85-14
Magee, B. The Philosophy of Schopenhauer.*
    G. Blair, 84:Jun84-179
    D. Collinson, 479(PhQ):Oct84-510
    D.W. Hamlyn, 483:Apr84-269
    K. Harries, 319:Jul85-441
    C. Janaway, 393(Mind):Oct84-608
Magerøy, H., ed. Bandamanna Saga.
    H. O'Donoghue, 541(RES):Nov84-521
    P. Schach, 301(JEGP):Apr84-308
Maginnis, H.B.J. - see Meiss, M.
Magnani, F. - see Braccesi, A.
Magnani, L. L'Idea della "Chartreuse,"
Saggi Stendhaliani.
    C. Dédéyan, 535(RHL):Mar/Apr84-290
Magnes, J.L. Dissenter in Zion. (A.A.
Goren, ed)
    M.I. Urofsky, 390:Oct84-48
Magnússon, S.A. - see "The Postwar Poetry
of Iceland"
Magocsi, P.R. Galicia. The Rusyn-Ukrain-
ians of Czechoslovakia.
    J-P. Himka, 104(CASS):Winter84-495
"Magyar Néprajzi Lexikon." (Vol 5) (G.
Ortutay, ed-in-chief)
    R. Patai, 292(JAF):Apr-Jun84-221
Mahapatra, J. Life Signs.
    J.F. Cotter, 249(HudR):Autumn84-503
Maharidge, D. and M. Williamson. Journey
to Nowhere.
    B. Atkinson, 441:17Mar85-26
Maheux-Forcier, L. Letter by Letter.
    E. Dansereau, 526:Summer84-88
Maheux-Forcier, L. Un Parc en automne.
    J.B. Moss, 102(CanL):Autumn84-98
Mahler, G. and R. Strauss. Gustav Mahler,
Richard Strauss: Correspondence 1888-
1911.* (H. Blaukopf, ed)
    H.C. Schonberg, 441:3Feb85-23
Mahon, D. The Hunt by Night.*
    T. Eagleton, 565:Winter83/84-77
Mahoney, D.F. Die Poetisierung der Natur
bei Novalis.
    H.M.K. Riley, 406:Spring84-98
Mahoney, T. Hollaran's World War.
    M. Bell, 441:10Nov85-28
Mahony, P. Sundry Extras.
    A.L. Le Quesne, 617(TLS):12Apr85-420
Maier, U. Caesars Feldzüge in Gallien (58-
51 v. Chr.) in ihrem Zusammenhang mit
der stadtrömischen Politik.
    R. Seager, 313:Vol74-209
Mailer, N. Pontifications. (M. Lennon,
ed)
    J. Tavernier-Courbin, 395(MFS):
    Winter84-810
Mailer, N. Tough Guys Don't Dance.*
    A. Alvarez, 453(NYRB):11Apr85-15
    N. Berry, 364:Nov84-108
    A. Bloom, 249(HudR):Winter84/85-622

Mailhot, C.H. 2000 expressions françaises
pratiques et utiles.
    M.G. Elton, 207(FR):May85-907
Maillard, J. Adam de la Halle.
    M. Huglo, 537:Vol70No1-134
Maillard, K. Cutting Through.
    C. Rooke, 102(CanL):Autumn84-149
Maillart, E. Turkestan Solo.
    617(TLS):22Nov85-1339
Maillet, A. Les Drôlatiques, horrifiques
et épouvantables aventures de Panurge,
ami de Pantagruel.
    J.B. Moss, 102(CanL):Autumn84-98
    S.R. Schulman, 207(FR):May85-919
Maillet, A. Pélagie.
    J. Lennox, 168(ECW):Spring84-156
Mailloux, S. Interpretive Conventions.*
    D.K. Hedrick, 478:Apr84-141
    A. Fleishman, 301(JEGP):Apr84-256
    R.G. Seamon, 106:Fall84-337
Maimonides, M. Mose ben Maimon, "Acht
Kapitel." (M. Wolff, ed and trans)
    H. Greive, 489(PJGG):Band91Heft1-207
Main, G.L. Tobacco Colony.*
    K.P. Kelly, 656(WMQ):Oct84-653
Mainardi, P. Quilts.
    M. Kilkenny, 614:Summer85-34
Mainer, J.C. - see Vela, F.
Maingueneau, D. Genèses du discours.
    R. Martin, 553(RLiR):Jul-Dec84-464
Mainor, R.E. To Mister or Sarah Jean.
    C.R. Booker, 95(CLAJ):Jun85-480
Maiorano, R. Balanchine's Mozartiana.
    R. Craft, 453(NYRB):7Nov85-42
    S. Sommer, 441:14Apr85-27
Maire, C-L., ed. Les Convulsionnaires de
Saint-Médard.
    J. McManners, 617(TLS):26Jul85-829
Maisel, E. Charles T. Griffes.
    A. Berger, 453(NYRB):13Jun85-26
Maital, S. and S.L. Economic Games People
Play.*
    D.S., 185:Jan85-386
Maitre, D. Literature and Possible Worlds.
    C.R. Gabriel, 478:Oct84-304
    R.A. Sharpe, 89(BJA):Summer84-263
Majorano, M., ed. Il Roman des Eles di
Raoul de Houdenc.
    G. Roques, 553(RLiR):Jan-Jun84-257
Majumdar, B. Joyce Cary.
    295(JML):Nov84-416
Makogonenko, G.P. Tvorčestvo A.S. Puškina
v 1830-e gody: 1833-1836.
    S. Ketchian, 574(SEEJ):Winter84-541
Makowsky, V.A. - see Blackmur, R.P.
Makuck, P. Where We Live.*
    R. Galvin, 502(PrS):Fall84-110
Malamud, B. The Stories of Bernard Mal-
amud.*
    S. Pinsker, 573(SSF):Spring84-155
    M. Shechner, 473(PR):3/1984-451
Malandain, P. Delisle de Sales, philos-
ophe de la nature (1741-1816).
    G. Bremner, 402(MLR):Apr84-456
    D.C. Spinelli, 207(FR):Dec84-291
Malandain, P. La Fable et l'intertexte.*
    H. Lafay, 535(RHL):Jul/Aug84-606
Malantschuk, G. The Controversial Kierke-
gaard.
    G.J. Stack, 543:Dec83-407
Malatesti, M. Rime. (D. Trolli, ed)
    A. Tissoni Benvenuti, 228(GSLI):
    Vol161fasc514-289

239

Mansfield, K. The Stories of Katherine Mansfield. (A. Alpers, ed)
  G. Tindall, 176:Nov85-59
Manso, P. Mailer.
  A. Burgess, 61:Jun85-100
  B. Goldsmith, 441:19May85-9
  E. Hardwick, 453(NYRB):30May85-3
  C. Hitchens, 617(TLS):30Aug85-943
  P. Whitehead, 362:30ct85-26
Mantel, H. Every Day is Mother's Day.
  C. Hawtree, 617(TLS):29Mar85-341
  J. Mellors, 364:Mar85-100
Manteuffel, T. The Formation of the Polish State.*
  R.C. Hoffmann, 104(CASS):Spring-Summer84-208
Manthey, J. Wenn Blicke zeugen könnten.
  M. Schneider, 384:Sep84-698
Manuel, F.E. The Changing of the Gods.
  P.B. Wood, 529(QQ):Autumn84-745
Manyoni, A. Langzeilentradition in Walthers Lyrik.
  I. Glier, 221(GQ):Spring84-300
Manzoni, A. On the Historical Novel.*
  S.B. Chandler, 276:Autumn84-272
Ma'oz, M. Palestinian Leadership on the West Bank.
  A. Margalit, 453(NYRB):26Sep85-23
Map, W. De nugis curialium. (M.R. James, ed and trans; rev by C.N.L. Brooke and R.A.B. Mynors)
  A.V., 379(MedR):Aug84-293
Maples Arce, M. Las semillas del tiempo. (R. Bonifaz Nuño, ed)
  D.J. Forbes, 241:May84-89
Mapplethorpe, R. Certain People.
  A. Grundberg, 441:8Dec85-22
al-Maqrīzī, T.D. A History of the Ayyubid Sultans of Egypt. (R.J.C. Broadhurst, ed and trans)
  R.S. Humphreys, 318(JAOS):Apr-Jun83-449
Maqua, I.U. - see under Uría Maqua, I.
Maravall, J.M. La política de la transición 1975-1980.
  P. Preston, 86(BHS):Apr84-207
Marc, D. Demographic Vistas.*
  G. Copeland, 583:Winter85-184
Marceau, F. Une insolente liberté.
  J. Aeply, 450(NRF):Feb84-105
Marceau, W. Le Stoïcisme et Saint François de Sales.
  M-O. Sweetser, 207(FR):Mar85-580
Marcenaro, G. - see Gadda, C.E.
Marchais, P. Les mouvances psychopathologiques.
  J-M. Gabaude, 542:Apr-Jun84-242
Marchak, P. Green Gold.
  J.D. Martin, 99:Mar85-34
Marchand, A.B. and C. Rochon. Entre l'oeil et l'espace.
  C-L. Rogers, 102(CanL):Autumn84-147
Marchand, L.A. - see Lord Byron
Marchand, R. Advertising the American Dream.
  J. Brooks, 441:20Oct85-57
Marchant, N. and J. Addis. Kilkenny Design.
  P. Gorb, 324:Jun85-499
Marcheschi, D., ed. Ingiurie, improperi, contumelie, ecc.
  G. Holtus, 553(RLiR):Jan-Jun84-222

Marcil-Lacoste, L. Claude Buffier and Thomas Reid.*
  S.A. Grave, 319:Apr85-262
  D.D. Todd, 154:Sep84-509
Marcone, A. Commento storico al libro VI dell'epistolario de Q. Aurelio Simmaco.
  J.P. Callu, 555:Vol58fasc2-334
Marcotty, T. The Way-Music.
  T. Ellingson, 187:Fall85-530
Marcucci, S. Bentham und Linné.
  K. Düsing, 342:Band75Heft3-340
Marcus, G.J. The Conquest of the North Atlantic.*
  H. O'Donoghue, 382(MAE):1984/2-337
Marcus, J., ed. New Feminist Essays on Virginia Woolf.
  D. Hirst, 541(RES):Nov84-579
Marcus, J., ed. Virginia Woolf.*
  A. Pratt, 268(IFR):Winter85-62
  J. Rivkin, 659(ConL):Summer85-232
Marcus, P.L. - see Yeats, W.B.
Marcus, P.L., W. Gould and M.J. Sidnell - see Yeats, W.B.
Marcus, S. Freud and the Culture of Psychoanalysis.*
  G.D.M., 185:Jul85-982
  F.S. Schwarzbach, 598(SoR):Winter85-220
Marcus, S. and others. Contextual Ambiguities in Natural and Artificial Languages.
  M. Semeniuk-Polkowska, 353:Vol22No5-759
Marek, G.R. Schubert.
  P-L. Adams, 61:Feb85-100
Marenbon, J. Early Medieval Philosophy (480-1150).
  A.P. Martinich, 319:Jul85-426
Marenbon, J. From the Circle of Alcuin to the School of Auxerre.*
  D. Luscombe, 382(MAE):1984/1-100
Margeret, J. The Russian Empire and Grand Duchy of Muscovy.
  D. Rowland, 550(RusR):Jul84-308
Margitić, M.R., ed. Corneille comique.*
  J-P. Dens, 356(LR):Feb/May84-128
  G. Gerhardi, 547(RF):Band96Heft1/2-182
Margitić, M.R. - see Corneille, P.
Margolies, D. Novel and Society in Elizabethan England.
  J.C.A. Rathmell, 617(TLS):10May85-518
Margolies, E. Which Way Did He Go?*
  E.H. Zepp, 125:Spring84-309
Margolies, E. and D. Bakish. Afro-American Fiction 1853-1976.
  A. Rampersad, 402(MLR):Jan84-155
Margolis, J. Art and Philosophy.*
  C. Janaway, 393(Mind):Apr84-294
Mariani, J.F. The Dictionary of American Food and Drink.
  W. and C. Cowen, 639(VQR):Spring84-68
Mariani, P. A Usable Past.
  T. Gardner, 659(ConL):Fall85-351
Mariani, P. William Carlos Williams.*
  M.E. Gibson, 534(RALS):Spring82-103
Marías, J. Ortega: Las trayectorias.
  N.R. Orringer, 238:Dec84-674
Marie de France. Die Lais.* (D. Rieger, with R. Kroll, eds and trans)
  W. Rothwell, 208(FS):Jan84-43
Marie de France. Vier altfranzösische Lais. (E. von Richthoten, ed; 4th ed rev by R. Baehr)
  G.S. Burgess, 208(FS):Oct84-443

Mariën, M. La Marche palière.
  A. Thiher, 207(FR):Feb85-497
Marienstras, E. Les mythes fondateurs de
  la nation américaine.
  J. Appleby, 656(WMQ):Jan84-156
Marigold, W.G. - see von Schönborn, J.P.
Marin, B. La vose de la sera. (E. Serra,
  ed and trans)
  P. Hainsworth, 617(TLS):11Oct85-1148
Marín, J.L.M. - see under Morales y Marín,
  J.L.
Marin, L. Le Portrait du Roi.*
  M. Doueihi, 153:Spring84-66
Marinetti, F.T. Die futuristische Küche.
  H. Rüdiger, 52:Band19Heft1-109
Marini, S.A. Radical Sects of Revolution-
  ary New England.*
  G.A. Rawlyk, 529(QQ):Spring84-89
Marino, A. Littérature roumaine, littéra-
  tures occidentales.
  M. Spariosu, 678(YCGL):No33-104
Marino, G.B. La Galeria. (M. Pieri, ed)
  U. Limentani, 402(MLR):Jul84-722
Marion, J-L. Sur la Théologie blanche de
  Descartes.
  C. Larmore, 311(JP):Mar84-156
Marion, R. Born Too Soon.
  C. Colman, 441:10Nov85-28
Maritain, J. and R. Oeuvres Complètes.
  (Vols 4-6)
  F.C. Copleston, 617(TLS):15Mar85-298
Marius, R. Thomas More.
  N. Barker, 617(TLS):12Apr85-404
  G.R. Elton, 453(NYRB):31Jan85-7
  P. Johnson, 441:6Jan85-11
  A. Kenny, 362:28Mar85-27
Mark, J. Aquarius.
  A. Krystal, 441:20Jan85-18
Mark, R. Experiments in Gothic Structure.
  J. James, 589:Jul84-677
Markandaya, K. Shalimar.
  D. Flower, 249(HudR):Summer84-305
Marker, F.J. and L-L., eds. Ingmar Berg-
  man: A Project for the Theatre.
  M.J. Blackwell, 563(SS):Winter84-80
  A-C.H. Harvey, 615(TJ):Dec84-553
  F. Sprinchorn, 610:Summer84-155
Marker, F.J. and L-L. Edward Gordon Craig
  and "The Pretenders."*
  J.E. Gates, 615(TJ):Dec82-554
Marker, L-L. and F.J. Ingmar Bergman:
  Four Decades in the Theatre.*
  D. Thomas, 610:Summer84-157
Markey, T.L. Frisian.*
  J. Salmons, 685(ZDL):1/1984-116
Markham, E.J. Saibara.*
  D.W. Hughes, 410(M&L):Oct84-359
Markham, S. John Loveday of Caversham
  1711-1789.*
  O. Hedley, 324:Mar85-304
Markiewicz, H. Główne problemy wiedzy o
  literaturze.
  P. Hultberg, 402(MLR):Apr84-511
Markov, V. and D. Worth, eds. From Los
  Angeles to Kiev.
  C.A. Moser, 104(CASS):Winter84-423
Marković, M. Democratic Socialism.
  J.W. Murphy, 258:Jun84-212
Markovich, V.M. I.S. Turgenev i russkii
  realisticheskii roman XIX veka.
  D.A. Lowe, 550(RusR):Jul84-288

Markovits, A.S. and F.E. Sysyn, eds. Na-
  tionbuilding and the Politics of Nation-
  alism.*
  G.B. Cohen, 104(CASS):Spring-Summer84-
  213
  M. Hurst, 575(SEER):Jul84-457
Marks, E.R. Coleridge on the Language of
  Verse.*
  D. Degrois, 189(EA):Jan-Mar85-87
  G. Dekker, 405(MP):Aug84-106
  W.J.B. Owen, 541(RES):Aug84-391
Markstein, L. and L. Hirasawa. Expanding
  Reading Skills: Intermediate
  W.R. Slager, 399(MLJ):Summer84-199
Markus, J. Friends Along the Way.
  A. Lee, 441:4Aug85-10
  442(NY):11Nov85-156
Marlatt, D. How Hug a Stone.
  M.T. Lane, 198:Winter84-96
Marlatt, D. Selected Writing. What
  Matters.
  L. Ricou, 102(CanL):Winter83-151
Marlatt, D. and I. Klassen - see Gadd, M.
Marlow, J. Kessie.
  S. Altinel, 617(TLS):19Jul85-800
de Marly, D. Costume on the Stage, 1600-
  1940.*
  M. Murray, 611(TN):Vol38No3-155
de Marly, D. Fashion for Men.
  E. Hoffman, 441:6Summer85-25
Marly, N-N. Traduction et Paraphrase dans
  Willehalm de Wolfram d'Eschenbach.
  D.H. Green, 402(MLR):Oct84-975
Marney, J. Chiang Yen.
  D.R. Knechtges, 116:Jul83-98
Marnham, P. So Far from God.
  C. Henfrey, 617(TLS):5Jul85-759
  J. Keay, 362:18Jul85-28
  A. Riding, 441:25Aug85-8
Marold, E. Kenningkunst.
  H. Schottmann, 684(ZDA):Band113Heft4-
  166
Marosi, E. Die Anfänge der Gotik in
  Ungarn.
  P. Crossley, 90:Dec84-787
Marotta, K. A Piece of Earth.
  R. Elman, 441:28Apr85-24
Marquardt, B. Schmuck.
  G.S., 90:Jun84-369
Marqués, M.M. - see under Mena Marqués, M.
Marquet, J-F. - see Schelling, F.W.J.
Márquez, G.G. - see under García Márquez,
  G.
Marquez-Sterling, M. Fernán González,
  First Count of Castile.
  C.B. Faulhaber, 545(RPh):Feb84-380
Marres, R.F.M. De vertelsituatie en de
  hoofdmotieven in de Anton Wachter cyclus
  van S. Vestdijk.
  R. van der Paardt, 204(FdL):Dec84-318
Marriott, A. The Circular Coast.
  D. Stephens, 102(CanL):Winter83-157
Marriott, A. A Long Way to Oregon.
  B. Dempster, 99:Feb85-39
Marrone, S.P. William of Auvergne and
  Robert Grosseteste.
  R.C. Dales, 589:Jul84-681
  H.S. Lang, 319:Apr85-255
Marrus, M.R. The Unwanted.
  A.J. Sherman, 617(TLS):11Oct85-1134
Marschall, H.K. Friedrich von Thiersch,
  1852-1921.
  M. Scharabi, 43:Band14Heft1-83

Martin, R.E. American Literature and the Universe of Force.*
R. Gray, 447(N&Q):Dec83-562
D. Pizer, 183(ESQ):Vol30No3-193
D. Seed, 541(RES):Aug84-423
Märtin, R-P. Wunschpotentiale.
J. Hienger, 680(ZDP):Band103Heft2-309
Martin, S. California Writers.*
J.R. Millichap, 395(MFS):Winter84-826
W. Randel, 27(AL):Dec84-608
Martin, S. Wagner to "The Waste Land."*
K. Beckson, 403(MLS):Winter84-91
W. Blissett, 221(GQ):Summer84-508
Martín, V.T. - see under Tovar Martín, V.
Martin, W. An American Triptych.*
S. Juhasz, 536:Vol6-35
L. Rice-Sayre, 432(NEQ):Dec84-613
A. Salska, 27(AL):Dec84-601
295(JML):Nov84-366
Martin, W.E., Jr. The Mind of Frederick Douglass.
G.M. Fredrickson, 453(NYRB):27Jun85-3
Martín Aceña, P. and L. Prados de la Escosura, eds. La nueva historia económica en España.
R. Carr, 617(TLS):4Oct85-1105
Martín Gaite, C. El cuento de nunca acabar.
J.L. Brown, 240(HR):Autumn84-552
Martín Rodríguez, F.G. Arquitectura Doméstica en Canarias.
J.J. Junquera y Mato, 48:Jan-Mar84-121
Martín Villa, R. Al servicio del Estado.
P. Preston, 617(TLS):27Dec85-1471
Martineau, H. Harriet Martineau's Letters to Fanny Wedgwood. (E.S. Arbuckle, ed)
B. Richardson, 477(PLL):Fall84-453
Martines, L. Society and History in English Renaissance Verse.
J.C.A. Rathmell, 617(TLS):23Aug85-932
Martinet, A. La prononciation du français contemporaine. (2nd ed)
F.X. Nève de Mévergnies, 209(FM):Oct84-227
Martinet, A. Sprachökonomie und Lautwandel.
J. Klare, 682(ZPSK):Band37Heft6-729
Martinet, A. and J., eds. Grammaire fonctionnelle du français.*
C. Rubattel, 209(FM):Apr84-72
Martinet, M-M. Le Miroir de l'esprit dans le théâtre élisabéthain.*
H. Levin, 551(RenQ):Spring84-136
Martínez, E.B. - see under Bermejo Martínez, E.
Martinez, O.J. Fragments of the Mexican Revolution.
L. Milazzo, 584(SWR):Spring84-211
Martínez Caviró, B. La loza Dorada.
J.J. Junquera y Mato, 48:Jan-Mar83-84
Martinez Gonzalez, M.D., ed. Un marido entre dos Muzeres.
E. Roditi, 390:Jan84-50
Martini, J., ed. Missile and Capsule.
R. Epp, 343:Heft9/10-132
Martino, E. Roma contra Cántabros y Astures.
N. Mackie, 123:Vol34No1-91
de Martinoir, F. Un été à Mazarques.
D. Aury, 450(NRF):Jun84-97
Martins, H., ed. Antologia de poesia brasileira: Neoclassicismo.
G.R. Lind, 547(RF):Band96Heft1/2-226

Martins, M.T.H-S. - see under Hundertmark-Santos Martins, M.T.
Martinson, M. Women and Appletrees.
A. Becker, 441:29Sep85-46
Martlew, M., ed. The Psychology of Written Language.
W. Frawley, 350:Mar85-237
Martone, M. Alive and Dead in Indiana.*
I. Malin, 573(SSF):Fall84-413
Marty, F. La naissance de la métaphysique chez Kant.
J. Ferrari, 342:Band75Heft3-355
Marty, L. Chanter pour survivre.
C. Pinet, 207(FR):Mar85-619
Marty, M.E. Pilgrims in Their Own Land.*
C.L. Albanese, 676(YR):Winter85-290
Martz, E.M., with R.K. McClure and W.T. La Moy - see Walpole, H.
Martz, L.L. - see H.D.
Marucci, F. I fogli della Sibilla.
L. Adey, 637(VS):Autumn83-97
Marwick, A. Britain in our Century.
N. Shrapnel, 617(TLS):11Jan85-35
H. Young, 441:23Jun85-20
Marx, G. Glaube, Werke und Sakramente im Dienste der Rechtfertigung in den Schriften von Berthold Pürstinger, Bishof von Chiemsee.
M.L. Führer, 589:Apr84-406
Marx, H.J. - see Mattheson, J.
"Marxistische Studien." (1982)
R. Wiltner, 654(WB):4/1984-671
Marzocchi, L. - see Malvasia, C.C.
Masefield, J. Letters from the Front 1915-1917.* (P. Vansittart, ed)
P-L. Adams, 61:Jun85-105
A. Boyer, 441:5May85-25
N. Corcoran, 617(TLS):26Apr85-469
P. Dickinson, 364:Dec84/Jan85-137
442(NY):27May85-99
Masefield, J. John Masefield: Letters to Margaret Bridges (1915-1919).* Selected Poems. (D.E. Stanford, ed of both)
N. Corcoran, 617(TLS):26Apr85-469
Masi, M. Boethian Number Theory.
A. Reix, 542:Oct-Dec84-459
S.F. Wiltshire, 124:Sep-Oct84-53
Masiello, T. La donna tutrice, Modelli culturali e prassi giuridica fra gli Antonini e i Severi.
R. Villers, 555:Vol58fasc2-356
Masing-Delic, I., ed. Slavic Symposium 1982.
J. Graffy, 575(SEER):Jul84-435
Maskell, D. Coleridge's Prose.*
J.A. Davies, 506(PSt):Sep84-191
Maslow, J.E. The Owl Papers.
S. Mills, 617(TLS):18Jan85-73
Mason, A. Understanding Academic Lectures.
D.E. Eskey, 399(MLJ):Autumn84-312
Mason, B. Michel Butor.
M. Spencer, 208(FS):Jan84-99
F. Wolfzettel, 547(RF):Band96Heft3-364
Mason, B.A. In Country.
J. Conarroe, 441:15Sep85-7
D. Johnson, 453(NYRB):7Nov85-15
Mason, C. The Poet Robert Browning and his Kinfolk by his Cousin Cyrus Mason. (W.C. Turner, ed)
J. Maynard, 85(SBHC):Spring-Fall84-177

Mason, H. French Writers and their Society 1715-1800.*
R.C. Rosbottom, 210(FrF):Jan84-120
D. Williams, 83:Spring84-145
Mason, H., ed. Studies on Voltaire and the Eighteenth Century. (Vol 199)
C. Rosso, 535(RHL):Jul/Aug84-617
Mason, H., ed. Studies on Voltaire and the Eighteenth Century. (Vol 208)
M.H. Waddicor, 208(FS):Apr84-210
Mason, H. Voltaire.*
J.H. Davis, Jr., 345(KRQ):Vol31No3-349
J. Vercruysse, 535(RHL):Jul/Aug84-619
Mason, P. The English Gentleman.*
S. Rothblatt, 637(VS):Spring84-394
Mason, R. Chickenhawk.
639(VQR):Winter84-12
Mason Rinaldi, S. Palma il Giovane, l'opera completa.
C. Gould, 39:Aug84-149
F.L. Richardson, 90:Jul84-447
Maspétiol, R. Esprit objectif et sociologie hégélienne.
H. Faes, 542:Oct-Dec84-491
L-P. Luc, 154:Mar84-152
Mass, J.P. The Development of Kamakura Rule, 1180-1250.
R.P. Toby, 318(JAOS):Jul-Sep83-644
Massara, G. Americani.
R. Asselineau, 189(EA):Jul-Sep85-354
Masser, A., ed. Hohenemser Studien zum "Nibelungenlied."
E. Stutz, 684(ZDA):Band113Heft1-15
Massie, A. One Night in Winter.*
P. Lewis, 364:Oct84-93
P. Lewis, 565:Autumn84-55
Massignon, G. and B. Horiot. Atlas linguistique et ethnographique de l'Ouest (Poitou, Aunis, Saintonge, Angoumois). (Vol 3)
C. Straka, 553(RLiR):Jul-Dec84-493
Massignon, L. Parole donnée.
A. Reix, 542:Apr-Jun84-257
Masson, J.M. The Assault on Truth.*
F.S. Schwarzbach, 598(SoR):Winter85-220
Masson, J.M. - see Freud, S.
Mast, G., ed. The Movies in Our Midst.
M. Mullin, 615(TJ):Mar84-139
Masters, A. The Man Who Was M.
T.J. Binyon, 617(TLS):22Mar85-330
C.C. Davis, 441:26May85-15
Masters, B. Killing for Company.
P.D. James, 617(TLS):29Mar85-342
R. Twisk, 362:21Feb85-27
Masters, H. Clemmons.
W. Ferguson, 441:24Feb85-22
442(NY):4Mar85-119
Masters, O. Loving Daughters.
J. Motion, 617(TLS):18Oct85-1173
"Masters of Seventeenth-Century Dutch Genre Painting."
E.H. Gombrich, 453(NYRB):13Jun85-20
Mastrobuono, A. Essays on Dante's Philosophy of History.
C. Cioffi, 379(MedR):Dec84-467
Mastromarco, G. - see Aristophanes
Mastronarde, D.J. and J.M. Bremer. The Textual Tradition of Euripides' "Phoinissai."*
D. Sansone, 487:Autumn84-296
A. Tuilier, 555:Vol58fasc2-292

Masuda Tsuna. Kodō Zuroku. (C.S. Smith, ed)
J.R. Bartholomew, 407(MN):Winter84-467
Mat-Hasquin, M. Voltaire et l'antiquité grecque.*
A. Mason, 83:Spring84-148
Matejic, M. and others. A Biobibliographical Handbook of Bulgarian Authors.* (K.L. Black, ed)
G. Moudrova, 402(MLR):Apr84-512
Mateo Gómez, I. Juan Correa de Vivar.
E. Young, 39:Sep84-216
Materer, T. - see Pound, E. and W. Lewis
"Le Matérialisme du XVIIIe siècle et la littérature clandestine."
M-H. Cotoni, 535(RHL):May/Jun84-457
B.E. Schwarzbach, 173(ECS):Winter84/85-285
Materra, P. Off the Books.
A. Seldon, 617(TLS):12Jul85-766
Mates, B. Skeptical Essays.*
H. Robinson, 393(Mind):Apr84-306
Matfre Ermengaud. Le "Breviari d'Amor" de Matfre Ermengaud. (Vol 5) (P.T. Ricketts, ed)
W.D. Paden, Jr., 545(RPh):Aug83-104
Mathes, J., ed. Clemens Brentano.
H.M.K. Riley, 133:Band17Heft1/2-147
Mathesius, V. Jazyk, kultura a slovesnost.
K. Polański, 300:Vol 17-103
Mathews, A.C., ed. Immediate Man.
A. Douglas, 305(JIL):Sep84-100
Mathews, A.C. Minding Ruth.
M. Riordan, 617(TLS):15Mar85-294
Mathias, J., T. Creamer and S. Hixson, comps. Chinese Dictionaries.
T. Light, 399(MLJ):Autumn84-282
Mathiesen, H.E. Ikaros: the Hellenistic Settlements. (Vol 1)
R. Higgins, 303(JoHS):Vol 104-263
Mathiesen, T.J. - see Aristides
Mathieu-Castellani, G. - see de La Roque, S-G.
Matilal, B.K. The Central Philosophy of Jainism (Anekānta-Vāda).
H. Coward, 485(PE&W):Jan84-114
Matisse, H. Jazz.*
P. Schneider, 453(NYRB):11Apr85-28
Matsche, F. Die Kunst im Dienst der Staatsidee Kaiser Karls VI.
H. Boockmann, 683:Band47Heft3-417
A. Laing, 90:Aug84-507
C.F. Otto, 54:Dec84-700
P. Reuterswärd, 341:Vol153No1-38
Matsubara, H. Cranes at Dusk.
P-L. Adams, 61:Mar85-124
J. Burnham, 617(TLS):14Jun85-678
R. O'Meally, 441:24Mar85-24
Matsui, M. and others. Japanese Performing Arts.
D. Waterhouse, 187:Fall85-512
Matsumoto, K. Jodai-Gire.
S. Hicks, 614:Summer85-27
Matte, E.J. Histoire des modes phonétiques du français.*
P. Jolivet, 209(FM):Oct84-260
Matte, J.A. The History of Washington County.
L.R. Atkins, 9(AlaR):Jan84-60
Mattei, A.E.R. - see under Ramírez Mattei, A.E.
Matter, H. - see Mann, T.

Meddemmen, J. - see Grahame, K.
"Mediaeval Scandinavia 11."
    R. McTurk, 562(Scan):Nov84-169
"Medieval Latin Poems." (F. Adcock, trans)
    E. Osers, 364:Oct84-110
Mědílek, B., ed. Bibliografie Jaroslava
  Haška.
    J. Toman, 575(SEER):Jul84-449
Medina, A. Reflection, Time and the Novel.
    I.W. Alexander, 323:Jan84-90
    B. Cowan, 543:Sep83-134
Medina, E. The Duke.
    V. Bogdanor, 362:4Jul85-31
    N. Rankin, 617(TLS):5Jul85-747
Medley, R. Drawn from the Life.*
    G.K. Hunter, 612(ThS):May84-126
Medvedev, R. Khrushchev.
    A. Kemp-Welch, 575(SEER):Jan84-145
Medvedev, Z.A. Andropov.*
    A. Dallin, 550(RusR):Apr84-185
    R.J. Hill, 575(SEER):Jul84-467
Mee, C. Rhodes in the Bronze Age.
    V. Hankey, 303(JoHS):Vol 104-247
    S. Hood, 123:Vol34No1-146
    S.A. Immerwahr, 487:Summer84-177
Meehan-Waters, B. Autocracy and Aristoc-
  racy.*
    S.L. Hoch, 104(CASS):Spring-Summer84-
    189
Meek, M.R.D. Hang the Consequences.
    M. Laski, 362:10Jan85-25
Meeks, W.A. The First Urban Christians.*
    H. Lomas, 249(HudR):Summer84-321
    S.G. Wilson, 529(QQ):Autumn84-750
Megged, A. Asahel.
    S.G. Kellman, 390:Jan84-62
Meggle, G. Grundbegriffe der Kommunika-
  tion.
    A. Bassarak, 682(ZPSK):Band37Heft6-746
Meggs, P.B. A History of Graphic Design.
    S. Heller, 507:Jan/Feb84-109
Megill, A. Prophets of Extremity.
    A.C. Danto, 441:15Sep85-26
Mehl, D. Die Tragödien Shakespeares.
    E. Auberlen, 189(EA):Jul-Sep85-318
Mehlberg, H. Time, Causality, and the
  Quantum Theory.
    M. Heller, 543:Dec83-408
Mehlman, J. Legacies of Anti-Semitism in
  France.
    D. Stephens, 207(FR):Mar85-615
Mehnert, K. The Russians and Their Favor-
  ite Books.
    D. Brown, 104(CASS):Winter84-451
    S.A. Shuiskii, 574(SEEJ):Fall84-414
Mehrotra, A.K. Middle Earth.
    A. Stevenson, 617(TLS):19Apr85-449
Mehta, V. A Family Affair.
    R.L. Hardgrave, Jr., 293(JASt):Nov83-
    191
Meid, W. and K. Heller. Sprachkontakt als
  Ursache von Veränderungen der Sprach-
  und Bewusstseinsstruktur.
    G. Wienold, 260(IF):Band89-324
Meidal, B. Från profet till folktribun.
    M. Mattsson, 563(SS):Winter84-84
    M. Robinson, 562(Scan):May84-67
Meier, C. Caesar. Die Ohnmacht des all-
  mächtigen Dictators Caesar.
    R. Seager, 313:Vol74-209
Meier, G.M. and D. Seers, eds. Pioneers
  in Development.
    W. Elkan, 617(TLS):17May85-559

Meier, R., comp. Richard Meier, Architect
  1964/1984.
    W.H. Jordy, 441:17Mar85-13
Meier, S. Animation and Mechanization in
  the Novels of Charles Dickens.
    L. Hartveit, 179(ES):Feb84-83
Meiggs, R. Trees and Timber in the
  Ancient Mediterranean World.*
    G.E. Rickman, 123:Vol34No1-120
Meijer, B.W. and C. van Tuyll. Disegni
  Italiani del Teylers Museum.
    M. Royalton-Kish, 39:Aug84-147
    J.B. Shaw, 90:Jul84-445
Meiland, J.W. and M. Krausz, eds. Relativ-
  ism.*
    R.B.S., 185:Jan85-384
Meillet, A. Altarmenisches Elementarbuch.
    B.G. Hewitt, 361:Jan/Feb84-149
Mein, M. Thèmes proustiens.
    M. Muller, 546(RR):May84-391
Meinel, C. - see Jungius, J.
Meininger, A-M. - see Stendhal
Meiring, D. A Talk with the Angels.
    T.J.B., 617(TLS):8Nov85-1267
Meisel, M. Realizations.*
    N. Auerbach, 344:Winter85-120
    R.A. Donovan, 290(JAAC):Fall84-93
    J.R. Reed, 400(MLN):Dec84-1264
    G.B. Tennyson, 445(NCF):Jun84-113
Meisel, P. and W. Kendrick - see Strachey,
  J. and A.
Meisler, R. Trying Freedom.
    J. Saari, 42(AR):Fall84-505
Meiss, M. Francesco Traini. (H.B.J.
  Maginnis, ed)
    A. Ladis, 617(TLS):27Dec85-1488
von Meissen, H. - see under Frauenlob
Meissner, G., ed. Allgemeines Künstler-
  Lexikon. (Vol 1)
    N. MacGregor, 90:Dec84-737
Meissner, W.W. Psychoanalysis and Reli-
  gious Experience.
    G.D.M., 185:Jul85-980
Meister, K. Die Ungeschichtlichkeit des
  Kalliasfriedens und deren historische
  Folgen.
    B.S. Strauss, 124:Sep-Oct84-58
Meister, M.W., with M.A. Dhaky, eds. Ency-
  clopaedia of Indian Temple Architecture.
  (Vol 1, Pt 1)
    M. Rabe, 293(JASt):May84-578
    G. Welbon, 318(JAOS):Oct-Dec83-782
Meister, P.W. and H. Reber. European Por-
  celain of the Eighteenth Century.
    G. Wills, 39:Apr84-306
Melada, I. Guns for Sale.
    E. Hollahan, 594:Fall84-352
    J.R. Reed, 395(MFS):Winter84-754
"Mélanges à la mémoire de Franco Simone."*
    J. Marmier, 535(RHL):Jan/Feb84-120
"Mélanges de langue et littérature fran-
  çaises du Moyen Age et de la Renaissance
  offerts à Monsieur Charles Foulon."
    M. Eusebi, 547(RF):Band96Heft3-341
"Mélanges offerts à Georges Couton."
    N. Ferrier-Caverivière, 535(RHL):
    Nov/Dec84-955
Melanson, L. Otto de la Veuve Hortense.
    R.J. Hartwig, 207(FR):Mar85-600
Melchiori, G., ed. Joyce in Rome.
    J. Mays, 272(IUR):Autumn84-304

Melchor, J.R., N.G. Lohr and M.S. Melchor. Eastern Shore, Virginia, Raised-Panel Furniture, 1730-1830.
    E.S. Cooke, Jr., 658:Spring84-89
Mel'čuk, I.A. Towards a Language of Linguistics.
    R. Beard, 574(SEEJ):Fall84-416
Meldau, R. Sinnverwandte Wörter der englischen Sprache.
    F.W. Gester, 72:Band221Heft1-154
Melde, W. Landeskunde und Spracherwerb.
    G. Price, 208(FS):Jan84-113
Meléndez Valdés, J. Obras en verso.* (Vol 1) (J.H.R. Polt and G. Demerson, eds)
    J. Dowling, 240(HR):Autumn84-539
    I.L. McClelland, 86(BHS):Oct84-526
Mclillo, J.V., ed. Market the Arts!
    A. Courtney, 108:Fall84-122
Melis, L. Les circonstants et la phrase.
    P. Swiggers, 350:Mar85-225
Mell, D.C., Jr., ed. English Poetry, 1660-1800.*
    D.L. Vander Meulen, 365:Winter84-29
Mellard, J.M. The Exploded Form.*
    E. Gallafent, 447(N&Q):Apr83-190
Mellenkamp, P. and P. Rosen, eds. Cinema Histories, Cinema Practices.
    M. Hansen, 533:Summer84-95
Mellers, W. Beethoven and the Voice of God.
    L. Pike, 410(M&L):Jan84-78
Mellers, W. A Darker Shade of Pale.*
    R. Gilbert, 362:10Jan85-23
Mellick, J.S.D. The Passing Guest.
    B. Elliott, 71(ALS):May84-419
de Mello Vianna, F., ed. Diccionario Inglés for Spanish Speakers.
    J. Ortega, 399(MLJ):Summer84-191
Mellor, A.K. English Romantic Irony.*
    I. Donaldson, 677(YES):Vol 14-331
Mellor, D.H. Real Time.*
    P. Fitzgerald, 484(PPR):Dec84-281
    D.H. Sanford, 482(PhR):Apr84-289
Mellor, R.E.H. The Soviet Union and its Geographical Problems.
    D.J.B. Shaw, 575(SEER):Jan84-143
Mellow, J.R. Invented Lives.*
    D. Bradshaw, 617(TLS):2Aug85-857
Meltzer, D., ed. Death.
    D.J. Enright, 362:28Feb85-24
Meltzer, J. Metropolis to Metroplex.
    R. Caplan, 441:31Mar85-23
Meltzer, M., P.G. Holland and F. Krasno - see Child, L.M.
Melville, H. Mardi. (R. Celli, trans)
    R. Millet, 450(NRF):Mar84-137
Melville, H. Typee, Omoo, Mardi.* (G.T. Tanselle, ed)
    D.A.N. Jones, 362:4Apr85-26
Melville, J. The Death Ceremony.
    T.J. Binyon, 617(TLS):15Nov85-1294
Membreño, A. Hondureñismos.
    J.M. Lipski, 238:Mar84-156
Mena Marqués, M. Dibujos italianos de los siglos XVII y XVIII en la Biblioteca Nacional.
    N. Turner, 39:Dec84-439
Mena Marqués, M. Dibujos italianos del siglo XVII, Museo del Prado.
    D. Angulo Íñiguez, 48:Jan-Mar84-124

Ménage, G. The History of Women Philosophers.
    J. Tormey, 322(JHI):Oct-Dec84-619
"Le Menagier de Paris."* (G.E. Brereton and J.M. Ferrier, eds)
    M. Boulton, 545(RPh):Feb84-385
Menander. Menander Rhetor. (D.A. Russell and N.G. Wilson, eds and trans)
    D.M. Schenkeveld, 394:Vol137fasc1/2-193
Menander. Samia. (D.M. Bain, ed)
    W.G. Arnott, 123:Vol34No2-310
Ménard, N. Mesure de la richesse lexicale.
    C. Muller, 553(RLiR):Jul-Dec84-469
    P. Thoiron, 209(FM):Oct84-257
Ménard, P. Les fabliaux, contes à rire du moyen âge.*
    T. Hunt, 208(FS):Apr84-191
    C. Lee, 379(McdR):Apr84-129
Ménard, P., ed. Fabliaux français du Moyen Age. (Vol 1)
    S. Kay, 545(RPh):Nov83-247
Menas Patricius. Menae Patricii cum Thoma referendario De scientia politica dialogus quae exstant in codice Vaticano palimpsesto. (C.M. Mazzucchi, ed)
    J. Dunbabin, 313:Vol74-251
Menchú, R. I, Rigoberta Menchú.* (E. Burgos-Debray, ed)
    S. Christian, 441:27Jan85-24
Mencken, H.L. A Carnival of Buncombe. (M. Moos, ed)
    O.D. Edwards, 617(TLS):27Sep85-1076
Mende, U. Die Bronzetüren des Mittelalters 800-1200.
    H. Westermann-Augerhausen, 617(TLS):27Dec85-1488
Mendelsohn, L. Paragoni.*
    M. Howard, 89(BJA):Spring84-175
Mendelssohn, J. The Kinks Kronikles.
    J. Maslin, 441:20Jan85-9
de Mendelssohn, P. - see Mann, T.
Mendès France, P. Oeuvres complètes. (Vols 1 and 2)
    D. Johnson, 617(TLS):16Aug85-898
Meng Han-ch'ing. Die Puppe (Mo-ho-lo) Ein Singspiel der Yüan-Zeit. (H. Höke, ed and trans)
    G.A. Hayden, 318(JAOS):Oct-Dec83-802
Mengham, R. The Idiom of the Time.
    C. Sprague, 395(MFS):Summer84-370
Menhennet, A. The Romantic Movement.
    E.A. Blackall, 680(ZDP):Band103Heft4-611
    G. Finney, 406:Summer84-214
Menikoff, B. Robert Louis Stevenson and The Beach of Falesá.
    J. Sutherland, 617(TLS):21Jun85-705
Menne, K. - see Mitscherlich, A.
Menton, S. Narrativa de la Revolución Cubana.
    L.S. Thompson, 263(RIB):Vol34No1-100
Mentrup, W., ed. Konzepte zur Lexikographie.*
    H. Maxwell, 221(GQ):Summer84-461
Ménudier, H. Das Deutschlandbild der Franzosen in den 70er Jahren.
    K. Heitmann, 72:Band221Heft1-223
Menzel, H-B. Abkürzungen im heutigen Französisch.
    G. Kleiber, 553(RLiR):Jan-Jun84-230
Meo, O. La Malattia mentale nel pensiero di Kant.
    A. Stanguennec, 542:Jan-Mar84-82

Mercader, M. La chuña de los huevos de oro.
 C. Delacre Capestany, 37:May-Jun84-59
Merchi, G. Le guide des écoliers de guitarre; Traité des agrémens de la musique.
 M. Criswick, 415:Mar84-161
Meredith, P. and J.E. Tailby, eds. The Staging of Religious Drama in Europe in the Later Middle Ages.
 R.J. Pentzell, 130:Winter84/85-374
Merino-Morais, J. Différence et répétition dans les "Contes" de La Fontaine.
 M. Vincent, 207(FR):Apr85-729
Meriwether, J.B. - see Faulkner, W.
Merrell, F. Pararealities.
 E. Hollahan, 395(MFS):Summer84-413
Merrell, F. Semiotic Foundations.*
 R.A. Champagne, 399(MLJ):Autumn84-299
Merriam, A.P. African Music in Perspective.
 I.V. Jackson, 91:Spring84-131
 R. Kauffman, 187:Spring/Summer85-374
Merrifeld, D.F. Praktische Anleitung zur Interpretation von Dichtung.
 H. Slessarev, 221(GQ):Summer84-459
Merrifield, R. London: City of the Romans.*
 A.A. Barrett, 124:Jan-Feb85-219
Merrill, E.A. "For the Sake of the Trust."
 E.S. Lauterbach, 395(MFS):Summer84-379
Merrill, J. Late Settings.
 B. Leithauser, 453(NYRB):26Sep85-11
 P. Stitt, 441:1Sep85-11
Merrill, T. In Bare Apple Boughs.
 E. Trethewey, 102(CanL):Summer84-84
Merrill, T.F. The Poetry of Charles Olson.*
 G.F. Butterick, 30:Winter84-87
 S. Paul, 301(JEGP):Oct84-585
Merrill, W.M. and L. Ruchames - see Garrison, W.L.
Merriman, J.M. The Red City.
 E. O'Shaughnessy, 441:22Sep85-23
"The Merry Thought." (Pts 2-4)
 P-G. Boucé, 189(EA):Oct-Dec85-492
Mersereau, J., Jr. Russian Romantic Fiction.*
 P. Debreczeny, 574(SEEJ):Summer84-258
Mertens, W. American Minimal Music.
 W. Mellers, 415:Jun84-328
 M. Paddison, 607:Mar84-49
Merton, T. The Hidden Ground of Love. (W.H. Shannon, ed)
 J.T. Ellis, 441:11Aug85-7
Merwin, W.S. Opening the Hand.*
 P. Breslin, 491:Dec84-167
 F. Garber, 29(APR):Sep/Oct85-14
 D. St. John, 42(AR):Summer84-364
 639(VQR):Spring84-60
Mesnard, J. - see Madame de Lafayette
de Mesquita, B.B. - see under Bueno de Mesquita, B.
Messent, P. and T. Paulin - see James, H.
Messent, P.B., ed. Literature of the Occult.
 A.L. Smith, 183(ESQ):Vol130No4-260
Messer Leon, J. The Book of the Honeycomb's Flow.* (I. Rabinowitz, ed and trans)
 H. Tirosh-Rothschild, 551(RenQ): Summer84-234

Messerer, A. Classes in Classical Ballet. (notated by E. Golubkova)
 M. Horosko, 151:Jan84-98
Messerli, D. Some Distance.
 J. Retallack, 472:Fall/Winter84-213
Messerli, D. - see Barnes, D.
Messina Montelli, M. - see Torni, B.
"Metal Box National Crafts Exhibition."
 J. Povey, 2(AfrA):Nov83-30
Metcalf, J. Kicking Against the Pricks.*
 S. Neuman, 102(CanL):Summer84-153
Metcalf, J., ed. Making It New.
 A. Brennan, 198:Spring84-105
Metcalf, J., ed. Third Impressions.*
 A. Brennan, 198:Spring84-105
Metcalf, J. and L. Rooke, eds. Best Canadian Stories 82.
 A. Brennan, 198:Spring84-105
 R. Hatch, 102(CanL):Summer84-140
Metcalf, P. A Borneo Journey into Death.
 J.M. Atkinson, 292(JAF):Apr-Jun84-233
"Metropol." (V. Aksyonov and others, eds)
 R.E. Peterson, 574(SEEJ):Spring84-128
Metscher, T. Kunst, Kultur, Humanität. (Vol 1)
 J. Marquardt, 654(WB):12/1984-2087
Metz, C. The Imaginary Signifier.
 N. Carroll, 290(JAAC):Winter84-211
 L. Oswald, 567:Vol48No3/4-293
Metz, J. Halley's Comet, 1910.
 442(NY):14Oct85-146
Metzeltin, M. Altspanisches Elementarbuch, I.
 E. Blasco Ferrer, 379(MedR):Aug84-306
Metzger, B.M. Manuscripts of the Greek Bible.*
 N.G. Wilson, 589:Jan84-187
Metzger, E.A. and M.M., eds. Herrn von Hoffmannswaldau und andrer Deutschen bisher noch nie zusammen-gedruckter Gedichte. (Pt 5)
 J.A. Parente, Jr., 221(GQ):Spring84-311
Metzger, M. and K. Mommsen, eds. Fairy Tales as Ways of Knowing.
 T. Schiff, 221(GQ):Spring84-346
Metzger, R. - see Hurd, P.
Metzger, W. Beispielkatechese der Gegenreformation.
 H. Pörnbacher, 196:Band25Heft3/4-355
Mews, S. Carl Zuckmayer.*
 B.L. Spahr, 564:May84-146
Mewshaw, M. Short Circuit.
 D. Macintosh, 529(QQ):Winter84-1053
de Meyer, A. L'Après-midi d'un Faune.
 R. Philp, 151:Dec84-104
Meyer, D. and M. Fernández Olmos, eds. Contemporary Women Authors of Latin America.
 M. Agosin, 238:May84-314
 C. Delacre Capestany, 37:Mar-Apr84-60
 P.B. Dixon, 395(MFS):Summer84-338
Meyer, E.H. Early English Chamber Music from the Middle Ages to Purcell.* (2nd ed rev by E.H. Meyer and D. Poulton)
 M. Tilmouth, 415:Mar84-152
Meyer, H., ed. Bibliographie der Buch- und Bibliotheksgeschichte. (Vol 2)
 354:Jun84-203
Meyer, H. Die Entwicklung der kommunistischen Streitkräfte in China von 1927 bis 1949.
 W. Kirby, 293(JASt):Nov83-144

250

Meyer, J.W. and W.R. Scott, eds. Organiza-
tional Environments.
   M.H. Brown, 583:Spring85-300
Meyer, M. The Met.
   E. Forbes, 415:May84-275
Meyer, M. Strindberg.
   E. Bentley, 441:1Sep85-3
   I-S. Ewbank, 617(TLS):25Oct85-1211
   442(NY):11Nov85-159
Meyer, P.G. Sprachliches Handeln ohne
Sprechsituation.
   C. Schwarz, 682(ZPSK):Band37Heft6-747
Meyer, S.M. The Dynamics of Nuclear Pro-
liferation.
   A. Dowty, 617(TLS):25Jan85-83
Meyer, T.   see Williams, J.
Meyer, W.J. Modalverb und semantische
Funktion.
   G. Kleiber, 553(RLiR):Jan-Jun84-217
Meyer-Wehlack, B. and I. Vrkljan. Die
Sonne des fremden Himmels. (R. Quittek,
ed)
   P.J. Campana, 399(MLJ):Summer84-176
Meyers, D.T. Inalienable Rights.
   J. Waldron, 617(TLS):8Nov85-1269
Meyers, J., ed. The Craft of Literary
Biography.
   J. Campbell, 617(TLS):19Jul85-795
Meyers, J. Disease and the Novel, 1880-
1960.
   I. McGilchrist, 617(TLS):13Dec85-1415
Meyers, J. Hemingway.
   R. Carver, 441:17Nov85-3
Meyers, J., ed. Hemingway: The Critical
Heritage.
   J.M. Cox, 569(SR):Summer84-484
   K. McSweeney, 529(QQ):Winter84-877
Meyers, J. D.H. Lawrence and the Exper-
ience of Italy.*
   É. Delavenay, 189(EA):Jan-Mar85-114
   D. Edwards, 363(LitR):Fall84-165
   C. Tomlinson, 364:Jun84-103
Meyers, J., ed. D.H. Lawrence and Tradi-
tion.
   K. Brown, 617(TLS):18Oct85-1171
Meynell, H. Freud, Marx and Morals.*
   W.L. McBride, 543:Dec83-409
Mezger, W. Hofnarren im Mittelalter.*
   W. Salmen, 680(ZDP):Band103Heft3-450
Mezzanotte, G. L'architettura della Scala
nell'età neoclassica.
   R. Middleton, 90:Dec84-790
Mezzich, J.E. and C.E. Berganza. Culture
and Psychopathology.
   G.M., 185:Apr85-774
Mianney, R. Maurice Rollinat, poète et
musicien du fantastique.
   G. Cesbron, 446(NCFS):Summer-Fall84-
   188
Miard, L. Francisco Bilbao.
   J-R. Derré, 535(RHL):Sep/Oct84-809
Micha, A. Étude sur le "Merlin" de Robert
de Boron, roman du XIIIe siècle.
   M. Schöler-Beinhauer, 547(RF):Band96
   Heft3-336
   C-A. Van Coolput, 356(LR):Aug84-250
Micha, A. - see "Lancelot, roman en prose
du XIIIe siècle"
Micha, A. - see Robert de Boron
Michael, C.V. Choderlos de Laclos.
   M. Alcover, 535(RHL):Sep/Oct84-805
   R.C. Rosbottom, 207(FR):Apr85-731

Michael, J.A., ed. The Lowenfeld Lectures.
   K.M. Lansing, 289:Summer84-122
Michaels, W.B. - see "Glyph 8."
Michaud, J. La Perdriole.
   D. Thaler, 102(CanL):Summer84-161
Michaud, Y. Hume et la fin de la philos-
ophie.*
   P. Carrive, 192(EP):Oct-Dec84-567
Michaux, J-P., ed. George Gissing.*
   M. Collie, 637(VS):Spring84-389
Michel, F-B. Le Souffle coupé (Respirer
et écrire).
   J. Pfeiffer, 450(NRF):Jul/Aug84-179
Michel, J-C. Les Ecrivains noirs et le
surréalisme.
   F. Sellin, 538(RAL):Spring84-97
Michel, M.R. Watteau.
   N. Bryson, 617(TLS):22Mar85-322
Michel, P. Les Barbares, 1789-1848.*
   P. France, 402(MLR):Jan84-195
Michelangelo. Il Carteggio di Michel-
angelo.* (Vols 4 and 5) (G. Poggi, with
P. Barocchi and R. Ristori, eds)
   E.H. Ramsden, 90:Jul84-443
di Michele, M. Necessary Sugar.
   J. Kertzer, 99:Jun/Jul84-41
   S.S., 376:Jun84-148
Michelet, J. Mother Death.* (E.K.
Kaplan, ed and trans)
   O.A. Haac, 446(NCFS):Summer85-302
Michelet, J. and A.A. La Mer.
   J. Gaulmier, 535(RHL):Nov/Dec84-977
Micheli, G. Kant storico della filosofia.
   R. Brandt, 489(PJGG):Band91Heft2-425
Michelini, A.N. Tradition and Dramatic
Form in the "Persians" of Aeschylus.
   A.F. Garvie, 123:Vol34No1-126
Michell, J. Eccentric Lives and Peculiar
Notions.
   R.F. Shepard, 441:20Jan85-19
Michelman, I.S. The Roots of Capitalism
in Western Civilization.
   J.S. Worley, 651(WHR):Spring84-88
Michelson, A. - see Vertov, D.
Michener, J.A. Poland.
   H. Nordon, 390:Mar84-54
   S.L. Sharp, 390:Jun/Jul84-59
   Z. Sierpiński, 497(PolR):Vol29No4-102
Michener, J.A. Texas.
   H. Rudd, 441:13Oct85-9
Michie, D. and R. Johnston. The Knowledge
Machine.
   S. Chace, 441:9Jun85-12
Michiko, I. - see under Ishimure Michiko
Michio, T. - see under Tanigawa Michio
Michon, J. - see Gay, J.
Michon, P. Vies minuscules.
   R. Millet, 450(NRF):May84-107
"The Middle East and North Africa 1984-
1985." (31st ed)
   G. Best, 617(TLS):26Apr85-471
Middlebrook, M. The Schweinfurt-Regens-
burg Mission.
   639(VQR):Spring84-46
Middlekauff, R. The Glorious Cause.*
   A.G. Condon, 106:Fall84-287
Middleton, C. 111 Poems.*
   T. Eagleton, 565:Summer84-76
Middleton, C. - see von Goethe, J.W.
Middleton, R. The Bells of Victory.
   L. Colley, 617(TLS):23Aug85-922
Middleton, R. and D. Horn - see "Popular
Music"

Middleton, S. The Daysman.*
  P. Craig, 617(TLS):5Jul85-757
Middleton, S. Entry into Jerusalem.
  M. Théry, 189(EA):Jul-Sep85-348
Middleton, S. Valley of Decision.
  B. Hardy, 617(TLS):1Mar85-226
  J. Mellors, 362:28Feb85-27
Midgley, M. Animals and Why They Matter.*
  P. Singer, 453(NYRB):17Jan85-46
Midgley, M. Heart and Mind.*
  E.H. Wolgast, 154:Mar84-172
Mieczkowski, B. Social Services for Women
  in Eastern Europe.
  J.L. Porket, 575(SEER):Jul84-465
  T. Yedlin, 104(CASS):Fall84-365
Mieder, W. International Proverb Scholar-
  ship.*
  R.G. Alvey, 70:Mar-Apr84-120
Mignault, G. Bonjour, Monsieur de La Fon-
  taine.
  D. Thaler, 102(CanL):Summer84-161
  J.A. Yeager, 207(FR):Feb85-498
Miguet-Ollagnier, M. La Mythologie de
  Marcel Proust.
  F.C. St. Aubyn, 207(FR):May85-896
Míguez Bonino, J. Toward a Christian
  Political Ethics.
  N.B., 185:Oct84-190
Mikalson, J.D. Athenian Popular Religion.*
  A.C. Brumfield, 124:Jan-Feb85-228
  K.J. Dover, 487:Summer84-197
Mikhail, E.H. Brendan Behan: An Annotated
  Bibliography of Criticism.
  G. O'Brien, 677(YES):Vol 14-358
Mikkola, K., ed. Alvar Aalto vs. the Mod-
  ern Movement.
  W.C. Miller, 576:Dec84-374
Milbank, C.R. Couture.
  A. Shapiro, 441:15Dec85-22
Milde, W. Gesamtverzeichnis der Lessing-
  Handschriften.* (Vol 1)
  S.D. Martinson, 173(ECS):Winter84/85-
  300
Mileck, J. Hermann Hesse.*
  A. Hsia, 268(IFR):Summer85-112
Mileham, J.W. The Conspiracy Novel.*
  J. Dargan, 210(FrF):Sep84-377
  A. Finch, 402(MLR):Apr84-462
Miles, H. The Track of the Wild Otter.
  T. Halliday, 617(TLS):28Jun85-735
Miles, J. Collected Poems: 1930-1983.
  J.F. Cotter, 249(HudR):Autumn84-499
  639(VQR):Spring84-62
Mileur, J-P. Vision and Re-Vision.*
  T. Rajan, 591(SIR):Summer84-262
Milhaud, D. Notes sur la musique, essais
  et chroniques. (J. Drake, ed)
  J-R. Julien, 537:Vol70No1-142
Milhous, J. and R.D. Hume - see Coke, T.
Milingo, E. The World in Between. (M.
  Macmillan, ed)
  A.D. Jones, 617(TLS):28Jun85-729
Mill, J.S. The Collected Works of John
  Stuart Mill.* (Vol 1: Autobiography and
  Literary Essays.) (J.M. Robson and
  J. Stillinger, eds)
  D.J. De Laura, 301(JEGP):Apr84-245
Mill, J.S. The Collected Works of John
  Stuart Mill.* (Vol 6: Essays on England,
  Ireland, and the Empire.) (J.M. Robson,
  ed)
  J.B. Schneewind, 154:Sep84-554

Mill, J.S. Essays on French History and
  Historians. (J.M. Robson, ed)
  S. Collini, 617(TLS):8Nov85-1251
Millard, A. Welcome to Ancient Rome.
  F.C. Mench, 124:Nov-Dec84-139
Miller, A. The Archbishop's Ceiling. Two-
  Way Mirror.
  D. Devlin, 157:No154-49
Miller, A. and I. Morath. "Salesman" in
  Beijing.*
  S.B. Garner, Jr., 385(MQR):Summer85-
  508
Miller, B., ed. Women in Hispanic Litera-
  ture.
  M. Bieder, 395(MFS):Winter84-738
  S. Magnarelli, 238:Mar84-140
  D.F. Urey, 345(KRQ):Vol31No4-458
  639(VQR):Autumn84-126
Miller, B.S. - see Kramrisch, S.
Miller, C. Father and Sons.
  J. Tagg, 106:Winter84-451
Miller, C.H. Auden.*
  D. Bromwich, 569(SR):Summer84-492
Miller, C.H. and others - see More, T.
Miller, D. Anarchism.
  L. Kolakowski, 617(TLS):4Jan85-3
Miller, D. Philosophy and Ideology in
  Hume's Political Thought.*
  N. Capaldi, 543:Jun84-864
  K. Haakonssen, 63:Dec84-410
  T.A. Roberts, 393(Mind):Apr84-303
Miller, D. and L. Siedentop, eds. The
  Nature of Political Theory.*
  R.H., 185:Jan85-381
Miller, D.A. Narrative and Its Discon-
  tents.*
  M. Boulby, 107(CRCL):Mar84-135
  K. Graham, 402(MLR):Apr84-402
  M. Torgovnick, 223:Fall81-415
Miller, D.G. Homer and the Ionian Epic
  Tradition.*
  J.T. Hooker, 303(JoHS):Vol 104-191
Miller, D.L. - see Mead, G.H.
Miller, D.M. Frank Herbert.*
  M.E. Barth, 395(MFS):Summer84-346
Miller, D.W. - see Popper, K.R.
Miller, H. Opus Pistorum.*
  639(VQR):Winter84-25
Miller, H. The World of Lawrence. (E.J.
  Hinz and J.J. Teunissen, eds)
  K. Brown, 617(TLS):18Oct85-1171
Miller, H.B. and W.H. Williams, eds. The
  Limits of Utilitarianism.
  H.A. Bedau, 185:Jan85-333
  L. Holborow, 63:Mar84-90
  J. Skorupski, 479(PhQ):Apr84-165
Miller, I.M. Albert Einstein's Special
  Relativity.
  M. Heller, 543:Mar84-642
Miller, J. The Greater Leisures.
  R. McDowell, 249(HudR):Spring84-127
  639(VQR):Winter84-24
Miller, J. Rousseau.*
  J.H. Mason, 617(TLS):29Mar85-365
Miller, J. and D. Pelham. The Facts of
  Life.*
  E. Korn, 617(TLS):4Jan85-18
Miller, J.C. - see Poe, E.A.
Miller, J.G. Theater and Revolution in
  France since 1968.
  R. Pouilliart, 356(LR):Nov84-336

Miller, J.H. Fiction and Repetition.*
S. Gatrell, 541(RES):Aug84-429
T.C. Moser, 405(MP):Nov84-216
M. Sprinker, 131(CL):Summer84-274
Miller, J.M. French Structuralism.
S. Lawall, 207(FR):Oct84-141
J. Sturrock, 208(FS):Jan84-103
Miller, J.P. Numbers in Presence and
Absence.
R. Cobb-Stevens, 543:Sep83-136
Miller, J.W. The Paradox of Cause and
Other Essays.* The Definition of the
Thing.* The Philosophy of History.*
The Midworld of Symbols and Functioning
Objects.* In Defense of the Psycholog-
ical.*
J.P. Fell, 31(ASch):Winter83/84-123
Miller, K. Doubles.
D. Bromwich, 617(TLS):5Jul85-751
A. Massie, 362:4Jul85-27
Miller, K.A. Emigrants and Exiles.
W.V. Shannon, 441:1Dec85-15
Miller, M. The Ransomed Wait.
B. Brown, 95(CLAJ):Sep84-102
Miller, M.R. Place-Names of the Northern
Neck of Virginia from John Smith's 1606
Map to the Present.
G.L. Cohen, 35(AS):Summer84-178
M.I.M., 300:Vol 17-123
V. Zinkin, 424:Sep84-333
Miller, N. Heavenly Caves.
J.D. Hunt, 576:Mar84-95
Miller, N.K. The Heroine's Text.*
S. Harvey, 208(FS):Apr84-209
Miller, R. Bunny.
C. Brown, 617(TLS):8Mar85-269
M. Lenehan, 441:8Sep85-18
Miller, R.A. Japan's Modern Myth.*
J.J. Chew, Jr., 293(JASt):May84-475
Miller, R.W. Analyzing Marx.
D. Braybrooke, 150(DR):Spring84-190
Miller, S. El mundo de Galdós.
F. Anderson, 238:Sep84-473
Miller, S.C. "Benevolent Assimilation."
B. Jenkins, 106:Winter84-441
N.G. Owen, 293(JASt):Aug84-808
Miller, V. Struggling to Swim on Concrete.
D.E. Richardson, 598(SoR):Spring85-547
Miller, V.R. and R.P. - see Descartes, R.
Miller, W.D. Dorothy Day.
B. Sicherman, 617(TLS):15Mar85-296
Millet, H. Les chanoines du chapitre
cathédral de Laon, 1272-1412.
J.B. Freed, 589:Apr84-408
Millet, R. L'Innocence.
F. de Martinoir, 450(NRF):May84-109
Millett, A.R. and P. Maslowski. For the
Common Defense.
D. Middleton, 441:3Feb85-23
Millett, B., ed. Hali Meidhad.*
J. Bugge, 589:Apr84-410
C. Clark, 179(ES):Oct84-466
Millgate, J. Walter Scott.
E. Anderson, 362:23May85-30
L. Mackinnon, 617(TLS):1Mar85-240
Millgate, M. Thomas Hardy.*
L. Björk, 301(JEGP):Jul84-450
S. Dean, 637(VS):Summer84-530
S. Hunter, 402(MLR):Jan84-162
M. Steig, 178:Jun84-229
M. Williams, 447(N&Q):Dec83-548
Millgate, M. - see Hardy, T.

Milligan, S. Where Have All the Bullets
Gone?
H. Wackett, 362:24Oct85-34
Millikan, R.G. Language, Thought and
Other Biological Categories.
C. Peacocke, 617(TLS):4Jan85-22
Millington, B. Wagner.
G. Abraham, 617(TLS):1Feb85-115
Millot, C. Horsexe.
J. Le Hardi, 450(NRF):Jan84-134
Mills, D. The Fishing Here is Great.
A. Atha, 617(TLS):20Dec85-1466
Mills, H. Mailer.*
G. Garrett, 569(SR):Summer84-495
Mills, R.J., Jr. - see Ignatow, D.
Milne, E. The Folded Leaf.
M. Harmon, 272(IUR):Spring84-126
Milne, L. - see Bulgakov, M.
Milner, A.C. Kerajaan.
C.A. Trocki, 293(JASt):Aug84-809
Milner, G. A Bloody Scandal.
M. Buck, 441:3Nov85-26
Milner, J. Vladimir Tatlin and the Rus-
sian Avant-Garde.*
Å. Fant, 341:Vol53No1-42
Miłosz, C. The History of Polish Litera-
ture. (2nd ed)
G.T. Kapolka, 497(PolR):Vol29No3-99
Miłosz, C. Poeticheskii traktat.
R. Volynska-Bogert, 550(RusR):Apr84-
221
Milosz, C. The Separate Notebooks.*
J.F. Cotter, 249(HudR):Autumn84-498
Miłosz, C. The Witness of Poetry.*
J.M. Baer, 497(PolR):Vol29No3-97
B. Howard, 271:Fall84-171
Milosz, O.V.D. The Noble Traveller. (C.
Bamford, ed)
L. Caldecott, 441:20Oct85-35
S. Caldecott, 469:Vol 10No4-97
Milotte, M. Communism in Modern Ireland.
J. Lee, 617(TLS):5Jul85-743
Milroy, J. Regional Accents of English:
Belfast.*
J.D. McClure, 571(ScLJ):Autumn84-39
Milton, J. Complete Prose Works of John
Milton. (Vol 8) (M. Kelly, ed)
T.N. Corns, 506(PSt):Sep84-179
R. Lejosne, 189(EA):Jul-Sep85-322
J.T. Shawcross, 391:Mar84-27
Milton, J. Milton's "Lycidas." (rev)
(C.A. Patrides, ed)
R. Flannagan, 391:May84-65
Milton, J. Paradise Lost. (R.A. Shepherd,
ed)
P.J. Gallagher, 391:Mar84-34
Milton, J.R. The Novel of the American
West.
K. Carabine, 447(N&Q):Apr83-188
H.N. Smith, 677(YES):Vol 14-355
"Milton Studies." (Vol 14) (J.D. Simmonds,
ed)
D.D.C. Chambers, 541(RES):May84-228
"Milton Studies."* (Vol 15) (J.D. Sim-
monds, ed)
M. Evans, 541(RES):Nov84-538
"Milton Studies."* (Vol 16) (J.D. Sim-
monds, ed)
T. Wheeler, 569(SR):Spring84-304
"Milton Studies." (Vol 17) (J.D. Simmonds,
ed)
T. Wheeler, 569(SR):Spring84-304
639(VQR):Summer84-82

"Milton Studies." (Vol 20) (J.D. Simmonds, ed)
J. Pitcher, 617(TLS):23Aug85-932
Minc, R.S., ed. Literature and Popular Culture in the Hispanic World.
J. Tittler, 238:May84-309
Minc, R.S., ed. Literatures in Transition.
O. de la Suarée, 238:May84-310
Minde, F. Johannes Bobrowskis Lyrik und die Tradition.
J. Glenn, 221(GQ):Spring84-334
Minden, M.R. Arno Schmidt.*
J.J. White, 402(MLR):Oct84-993
Miner, E. Japanese Linked Poetry.
M. Morris, 318(JAOS):Apr-Jun83-467
Miner, M.M. Insatiable Appetites.
W-C. Dimock, 219(GaR):Winter84-869
M. Fee, 376:Jun84-150
Miner, V. Movement.
J-A. Goodwin, 617(TLS):19Jul85-800
Mingelgrün, A. Essai sur l'évolution esthétique de Paul Éluard.
G. Cesbron, 356(LR):Feb/May84-137
Minhinnick, J. At Home in Upper Canada.
W.N., 102(CanL):Summer84-187
Minhinnick, R. Life Sentences.*
R. Pybus, 565:Autumn84-73
Mininni, G. Psicosemiotica.
J. Vizmuller-Zocco, 355(LSoc):Dec84-567
Minis, C. Zur Vergegenwärtigung vergangener philologischer Nächte.
H. Kratz, 221(GQ):Spring84-140
Minissale, F. Curzio Rufo, un romanziere della Storia.
P. Jal, 555:Vol58fasc2-330
Minissi, N., N. Kitanovski and U. Cinque. The Phonetics of Macedonian.
J.R. Baldwin, 575(SEER):Apr84-255
"Des Minnesangs Frühling."* (Pt 3) (H. Moser and H. Tervooren, eds)
W.C. McDonald, 406:Fall84-350
Minnis, A.J. Chaucer and Pagan Antiquity.*
F.N.M. Diekstra, 179(ES):Dec84-559
G. Schmitz, 72:Band221Heft2-369
Miño-Garcés, F. Early Reading Acquisition.
D. Biber, 350:Mar85-239
Minogue, K. Alien Powers.
A. Quinton, 362:14Mar85-24
A. Ryan, 617(TLS):1Mar85-221
Minor, R.N. "Bhagavad-Gītā."
K.W. Bolle, 293(JASt):May84-581
R. Salomon, 318(JAOS):Apr-Jun83-438
Minsky, M., ed. Robotics.
R. Draper, 453(NYRB):24Oct85-46
Minter, D. William Faulkner.
J. Aeply, 450(NRF):Nov84-87
Minton, M.H., with J.L. Block. What Is a Wife Worth?
A. Hacker, 453(NYRB):28Feb85-37
Mintz, A. Ḥurban.
R. Alter, 129:Jan85-39
Mintz, S.I., A. Chandler and C. Mulvey, eds. From Smollett to James.
R. Ashton, 541(RES):May84-269
S. Monod, 402(MLR):Jul84-671
K. Watson, 447(N&Q):Jun83-252
Mintz, S.W. Sweetness and Power.
J.H. Elliott, 453(NYRB):24Oct85-20
J. Goody, 441:28Jul85-16
Minuchin, S. Family Kaleidoscope.
D. Goleman, 441:17Mar85-27

Minus, E. Kite.
D. Guy, 441:15Sep84-21
Miola, R.S. Shakespeare's Rome.*
R. Ornstein, 250(HLQ):Autumn84-312
Miranda, G. Grace Period.
W.H. Pritchard, 249(HudR):Summer84-327
"The Mirroure of the Worlde, MS Bodley 283 (England c. 1470-1480)."*
L.E. Voigts, 589:Apr84-413
Mish, F.C., ed. 9,000 Words.
R.R.B. and C.A., 35(AS):Fall84-254
Mish, F.C. - see "Webster's Ninth New Collegiate Dictionary"
Mishima, Y. Cinq nō modernes.
J-L. Gautier, 450(NRF):May84-136
Mishima, Y. Yukio Mishima on Hagakure.
617(TLS):27Sep85-1072
Misiunas, R.J. and R. Taagepera, eds. The Baltic States.
J. Hiden, 575(SEER):Oct84-619
Miska, J. Canadian Prose Written in English 1833-1980.
T. Craig, 470:Vol122-118
Misler, N. and J.E. Bowlt, eds. Pavel Filonov.
J. Milner, 617(TLS):7Jun85-640
Misra, B.G. - see Koshal, S.
Misra, K.P. and S.C. Gangal, ed. Gandhi and the Contemporary World.
M. Juergensmeyer, 293(JASt):Feb84-293
Mistry, F. Nietzsche and Buddhism.*
I. Jappinen, 406:Winter84-463
V. Rajapakse, 485(PE&W):Jul84-332
Mitcham, A. The Literary Achievement of Gabrielle Roy.*
B. Godard, 627(UTQ):Summer84-479
Mitcham, A. The Northern Imagination.
T. Quigley, 268(IFR):Winter85-66
D.O. Spettigue, 529(QQ):Winter84-1012
Mitchell, B. Old English Syntax.
T.A. Shippey, 617(TLS):28Jun85-716
Mitchell, B. and H. Penrose - see Penrose, J.
Mitchell, B. and F.C. Robinson. A Guide to Old English. (rev)
R.H. Bremmer, Jr., 179(ES):Aug84-366
D.G. Calder, 589:Apr84-416
M.A.L. Locherbie-Cameron, 382(MAE): 1984/1-111
H. Peters, 38:Band102Heft1/2-147
M. Rissanen, 439(NM):1984/4-523
Mitchell, D. Britten and Auden in the Thirties: The Year 1936.*
A. Wasserstein, 72:Band221Heft1-190
Mitchell, D., ed. Indonesian Medical Traditions.
A.P. McCauley, 293(JASt):May84-606
Mitchell, E. Furnished Rooms.*
H. Davies, 617(TLS):1Feb85-128
Mitchell, J. Sometimes You Could Die.
T.J. Binyon, 617(TLS):2Aug85-855
Mitchell, J. and J. Rose, eds. Feminine Sexuality.*
J. Forrester, 208(FS):Oct84-501
Mitchell, K. Sinclair Ross.*
R. Thacker, 649(WAL):May84-41
Mitchell, L. Irish Spinning, Dyeing and Weaving.
M. Wilkins, 614:Summer85-26
Mitchell, L. Staging Premodern Drama.
L. Kiziuk, 615(TJ):May84-278

Mitchell, R.G., Jr. Mountain Experience.
P. Donnelly, 529(QQ):Winter84-1054
639(VQR):Summer84-98
Mitchell, R.H. Censorship in Imperial
Japan.
J.L. Huffman, 407(MN):Spring84-101
Mitchell, R.L. Corbière, Mallarmé,
Valéry.*
F.S. Heck, 546(RR):Jan84-115
Mitchell, R.L., ed. Pre-Text, Text, Con-
text.
A. Tooke, 208(FS):Jan84-82
Mitchell, S. The Water Inside the Water.*
P. Breslin, 491:Dec84-167
Mitchell, S. - see Rilke, R.M.
Mitchell, S. and M. Rosen, eds. The Need
for Interpretation.
T. Pateman, 494:Vol5No1-166
D.J. Shaw, 518:Jan84-36
Mitchell, W.J.T. Blake's Composite Art.
P.M.S.D., 148:Winter84-93
Mitchell, W.J.T., ed. The Language of
Images.*
S.L. Carr, 88:Summer84-35
Mitchell, W.J.T., ed. On Narrative.*
J. Beaty, 678(YCGL):No32-139
Mitchell, W.J.T., ed. The Politics of
Interpretation.
S.G. Kellman, 395(MFS):Summer84-399
Mitchell, W.O. Dramatic W.O. Mitchell.
J. Ditsky, 649(WAL):Aug84-144
R. Wallace, 102(CanL):Winter83-105
Mitchell, W.O. Since Daisy Creek.
P. O'Flaherty, 99:Nov84-96
Mitchiner, J.E. Studies in the Indus
Valley Inscriptions.*
K.R. Norman, 361:Jul-Aug84-313
Mitchison, N. Among You Taking Notes ...
(D. Sheridan, ed)
P. Craig, 617(TLS):5Jul85-746
D.A.N. Jones, 362:22Aug85-28
Mitford, J. Faces of Philip.*
C. Sigal, 441:13Jan85-28
Mitscherlich, A. Gesammelte Schriften.
(Vol 10) (K. Menne, ed) Ein Leben für
die Psychoanalyse.
M. Rutschky, 384:Sep84-709
Mittelmann, H. Die Utopie des weiblichen
Glücks in den Romanen Theodor Fontanes.
W. Paulsen, 133:Band17Heft1/2-149
Mitterand, H. Le discours du roman.*
N. Schor, 494:Vol4No1-138
Mitterer, B. Zur Dichtung Jorge Guillén's.
S. Herpoel, 356(LR):Aug84-259
Mixon, W. Southern Writers and the New
South Movement, 1865-1913.
R. Gray, 677(YES):Vol 14-343
Mo, T. Sour Sweet.*
M. Leapman, 441:31Mar85-35
442(NY):27May85-98
Mockler, A. Haile Selassie's War.*
H. Goodman, 441:18Aug85-21
Mócsy, I.I. The Effects of World War I:
The Uprooted.
L. Congdon, 104(CASS):Winter84-499
"The Modern Encyclopedia of Russian and
Soviet Literatures (Including Non-
Russian and Emigré Literatures)." (Vol
5) (H.B. Weber, ed)
D. Dyrcz-Freeman, 574(SEEJ):Fall84-394
"The Modern Encyclopedia of Russian and
Soviet Literatures (Including Non-
[continued]

[continuing]
Russian and Emigré Literatures)." (Vol
6) (H.B. Weber, ed)
D. Dyrcz-Freeman, 574(SEEJ):Fall84-394
W.J. Leatherbarrow, 402(MLR):Oct84-
1001
Modiano, P. Quartier perdu.
A. Duchêne, 617(TLS):2Aug85-856
Modlin, C.E. - see Anderson, S.
Moeller, J. and others. Blickpunkt
Deutschland. (2nd ed)
D.C. Hausman, 399(MLJ):Autumn84-294
Moeller, J., H. Liedloff and H. Lepke.
Kaleidoskop.
J.L. Cox, 399(MLJ):Spring84-79
Moffat, G. Grizzly Trail.
T.J. Binyon, 617(TLS):11Jan85-42
Moffett, J. Whinny Moor Crossing.*
E. Grosholz, 249(HudR):Winter84/85-658
M. McFee, 110:Fall84-87
Moffitt, I. The Retreat of Radiance.
R. Smith, 441:4Aug85-16
Mogenet, J. and others. Nicéphore Gré-
goras.
I. Bulmer-Thomas, 123:Vol34No2-363
Moggach, D. Porky.*
P. Craig, 617(TLS):25Jan85-102
Mohanti, P. Through Brown Eyes.
H. Kureishi, 617(TLS):20Dec85-1445
Mohanty, J.N. Husserl and Frege.
P. McCormick, 319:Jan85-121
E. Pivčević, 323:Jan84-86
P.M. Simons, 479(PhQ):Jul84-420
Mohanty, J.N. and R.W. Shahan, eds.
Essays on Kant's Critique of Pure Reason.
R. Velkley, 543:Jun84-865
Mohr, J.C., with R.E. Winslow 3d, eds.
The Cormany Diaries.
I. Berlin, 441:24Feb85-24
Mohraz, J.E. - see Crane, L.
Mohrmann, U. Engagierte Freizeitkunst.
W. Jacobeit, 654(WB):9/1984-1557
Moir, A. Caravaggio.*
R.E. Spear, 90:Mar84-162
Moir, J.S. A History of Biblical Studies
in Canada.
D. Fraikin, 529(QQ):Autumn84-748
Moise, E.E. Land Reform in China and
Vietnam.
V. Shue, 293(JASt):May84-508
Mojsisch, B. Die Theorie des Intellekts
bei Dietrich von Freiberg.
J. Jolivet, 542:Jan-Mar84-69
Mojsisch, B. and others - see Dietrich von
Freiberg
Mokwa, M.P., W.M. Dawson and E.A. Prieve,
eds. Marketing the Arts.
A. Courtney, 108:Fall84-122
Molager, J. - see Saint Cyprian
Mole, J. In and Out of the Apple.*
D. Davis, 362:6Jun85-31
Mole, J. Sail or Return.
T. Fitton, 617(TLS):28Jun85-733
Molesworth, C. Donald Barthelme's Fic-
tion.*
S. Fogel, 106:Winter84-487
D. Seed, 447(N&Q):Aug83-381
Molière. Four Comedies. (R. Wilbur,
trans)
R.S. Gwynn, 569(SR):Fall84-644
Moline, J. Plato's Theory of Understand-
ing.*
C.C.W. Taylor, 393(Mind):Jan84-127

255

Molino, J., ed. Le nom propre.
P. Swiggers, 350:Sep85-708
Molino, J. and J. Tamine. Introduction à l'analyse linguistique de la poésie.*
D. Scott, 208(FS):Jul84-371
Molinsky, S.J. and B. Bliss. Side by Side.
L.A. Kupetzky, 399(MLJ):Winter84-426
Moll, J. - see de Paredes, A.V.
Moll, K. Der junge Leibniz.* (Vols 1 and 2)
A. Robinet, 192(EP):Jan-Mar84-123
Mollenhauer, P. Friedrich Nicolais Satiren.
L.E. Kurth-Voigt, 221(GQ):Winter84-150
Mollenkopf, J.H. The Contested City.
S.B. Warner, Jr., 432(NEQ):Sep84-428
Möller, H-M. Adorno, Proust, Beckett.
A. Corbineau-Hoffmann, 72:Band221Heft2-336
C. Koelb, 221(GQ):Spring84-290
Mollier, J-Y. Michel et Calmann Lévy.
P. Fawcett, 617(TLS):12Apr85-412
Mollinger, R.N. Psychoanalysis and Literature.
D. Leverenz, 223:Fall82-341
Molloy, F. No Mate for the Magpie.
P. Craig, 617(TLS):17May85-561
K.C. O'Brien, 362:16May85-28
Molnar, T. Le Dieu immanent.
J.J. Wunenburger, 192(EP):Jul-Sep84-417
Moltmann, J. On Human Dignity.
D.S., 185:Jul85-979
Molyneux, J. Leon Trotsky's Theory of Revolution.
R.B. Day, 550(RusR):Apr84-226
Mombello, G. Le raccolte francesi di favole esopiane dal 1480 alla fine del secolo XVI.*
D. Beyerle, 72:Band221Heft2-434
Momen, M. An Introduction to Shi'i Islam.
N. Calder, 617(TLS):4Oct85-1110
P. Mansfield, 362:18Jul85-27
Mommsen, W.J. Max Weber and German Politics 1890-1920.
G. Roth, 441:11Aug85-12
Mommsen, W.J. and G. Hübinger - see Weber, M.
Monchi-Zadeh, D., ed. Die Geschichte Zarēr's.
D.N. MacKenzie, 259(IIJ):Apr84-155
Mondelli, R.J., P. François and R.M. Terry. Accent. (4th ed)
S. Hecht, 207(FR):Apr85-773
Mondor, H. and L.J. Austin - see Mallarmé, S.
Monegal, E.R. - see under Rodriguez Monegal, E.
Monette, M. Petites Violences.
J-A. Elder, 102(CanL):Autumn84-61
Monetti, F. and F. Ressa. La costruzione del Castello di Torino (oggi Palazzo Madama), inizio secolo XIV.
D.F. Glass, 589:Apr84-484
Money, J. The Destroying Angel.
C. Tavris, 441:16Jun85-25
Money, K. Anna Pavlova.
T. Strini, 151:Feb84-112
Monga, L., ed. Discours viatiques de Paris à Rome et de Rome à Naples et Sicile (1588-1589).
B.L.O. Richter, 207(FR):Mar85-575

Monk, E. Fernsehfilm "Die Geschwister Oppermann."
K. Modick, 384:Mar84-219
Monk, P. The Smaller Infinity.*
M. Peterman, 168(ECW):Spring84-102
F. Radford, 178:Dec84-476
S. Stone-Blackburn, 102(CanL):Winter83-69
Monnerie, A. Intercodes.
M.A. Barnett, 399(MLJ):Summer84-162
Monnier, A. Un publiciste frondeur sous Catherine II.*
M. Colin, 549(RLC):Jan-Mar84-119
Monnier, G. L'Architecte Henri Pacon 1882-1946.
E.G. Grossman, 576:Dec84-373
Monnier, G. Pastels from the 16th to the 20th Century.*
B. Scott, 39:Sep84-217
Monod, S. - see Conrad, J.
Monod-Becquelin, A. La Pratique Linguistique des Indiens Trumai (Haut-Xingu, Mato Grosso, Brésil).
H.E.M. Klein, 269(IJAL):Apr84-243
Monroe, M. The Upper Room.
C. Blaise, 441:3Mar85-31
Monsaingeon, B. Mademoiselle.
E. Zukerman, 441:6Oct85-14
Montagu, J. Alessandro Algardi.
F. Haskell, 617(TLS):12Jul85-763
Montague, J. The Dead Kingdom.*
E. Grosholz, 249(HudR):Winter84/85-649
B. O'Donoghue, 493:Sep84-70
W. Scammell, 364:Mar85-90
de Montaigne, M.E. Journal de voyage. (F. Garavini, ed)
D. Maskell, 208(FS):Oct84-453
Montalbán, M.V. - see under Vázquez Montalbán, M.
Montale, E. Quaderno di quattro anni.
R. Scrimaeri, 202(FMod):No65/67-336
Montañés, P.L. - see under Liria Montañés, P.
Montano, R. and U. Barra, eds. Comprendere Dante.
D. Mancusi-Ungaro, 275(IQ):Winter84-102
de Montclos, J-M.P. L'architecture à la française, XVIe, XVIIe, XVIIIe siècles.
J. Guillaume, 576:Dec84-370
Montefiore, A., ed. Philosophy in France Today.*
J.S., 185:Jul85-981
Montell, W.L. Don't Go Up Kettle Creek.
L.C. Jones, 650(WF):Apr84-151
J.H. Speer, 292(JAF):Oct-Dec84-480
Montelli, M.M. - see under Messina Montelli, M.
Montén, K.C. Fredrika Bremer in Deutschland. Zur Rezeptionsgeschichte Fredrika Bremers in Deutschland.
G. Hird, 562(Scan):May84-61
Montes de Oca, M.A. Twenty-One Poems.
T. Hoeksema, 238:Mar84-152
Montgomery, B. Shenton of Singapore.
H. Toye, 617(TLS):18Jan85-68
Montgomery, F.M. Textiles in America 1650-1870.
B. Nevill, 617(TLS):22Feb85-213
Montgomery, M. Why Flannery O'Connor Stayed Home.*
T.H. Pickett, 577(SHR):Fall84-372

de Montherlant, H.M. Romans II. (M. Raimond, ed)
 A. Blanc, 535(RHL):Nov/Dec84-992
Monti, R.C. The Dido Episode and the "Aeneid."
 M.C.J. Putnam, 122:Jan84-72
Montuori, M. Socrates, Physiology of a Myth.
 G.J. de Vries, 394:Vol37fasc1/2-180
Moody, M.D. The Interior Article in "de"-Compounds in French.
 R. de Gorog, 545(RPh):May84-465
Moody, S. Penny Dreadful.
 T.J. Binyon, 617(TLS):29Mar85-340
 M. Laski, 362:10Jan85-25
Moody, T.W. Davitt and Irish Revolution, 1846-82.
 T.E. Hachey, 637(VS):Autumn83-112
Mooij, J.J.A. Idee en verbeelding.
 C.F.P. Stutterheim, 204(FdL):Mar84-77
Mooney, B. The Anderson Question.
 J. Mellors, 362:21Mar85-25
Moorcock, M. The Laughter of Carthage.*
 T. Rutkowski, 441:10Feb85-24
Moore, B. Black Robe.
 J. Carroll, 441:31Mar85-7
 P. Craig, 617(TLS):7Jun85-627
 442(NY):8Jul85-72
Moore, B. Cold Heaven.*
 M.P. Gallagher, 272(IUR):Spring84-131
 C.R., 376:Feb84-139
Moore, B., Jr. Privacy.
 R. Brown, 617(TLS):16Aug85-896
 B. Williams, 453(NYRB):25Apr85-36
Moore, C. Louisbourg Portraits.*
 J. Axtell, 656(WMQ):Jan84-153
Moore, D., ed. Barry.
 K.O. Morgan, 617(TLS):27Dec85-1490
Moore, D. and M. Pick. The English Room.
 A. Stevens, 441:8Sep85-24
Moore, D.D., ed. Webster: The Critical Heritage.
 J.J. Peereboom, 179(ES):Oct84-468
Moore, E.C. - see Peirce, C.S.
Moore, G. The Unashamed Accompanist.
 442(NY):14Oct85-144
Moore, G. and U. Beier, eds. The Penguin Book of Modern African Poetry. (3rd ed)
 A. Appiah, 441:11Aug85-22
Moore, G.H. Zermelo's Axiom of Choice.*
 J.E. Rubin, 316:Jun84-659
Moore, J.H. Vespers at St. Mark's.
 D. Arnold, 410(M&L):Jul84-291
Moore, J.M. Aristotle and Xenophon on Democracy and Oligarchy.
 D.L. Stockton, 123:Vol34No1-141
Moore, J.N. Edward Elgar.* Spirit of England.*
 R. Anderson, 415:Aug84-442
Moore, K. The Lotus House.
 L. Taylor, 617(TLS):4Jan85-9
Moore, L. Self-Help.
 J. McInerney, 441:24Mar85-32
 D. Montrose, 617(TLS):8Nov85-1267
 R. Towers, 453(NYRB):15Aug85-26
Moore, M. Complete Poems. (rev)
 617(TLS):1Feb85-131
Moore, M.H. and others. Dangerous Offenders.
 N. Morris, 441:3Mar85-8
Moore, R.S. That Cunning Alphabet.*
 J.R. Russo, 594:Spring84-128

Moore, S. A Reader's Guide to William Gaddis's "The Recognitions."*
 R.G. Seamon, 106:Fall84-337
Moore, S.R. The Drama of Discrimination in Henry James.*
 S. Perosa, 395(MFS):Summer84-295
 A.R. Tintner, 594:Fall84-326
 295(JML):Nov84-459
Moore, T. The Journal of Thomas Moore. (Vol 1) (W.S. Dowden, with B. Bartholomew and J.L. Linsley, eds)
 B. Dolan, 305(JIL):Jan-May84-141
 M. Harmon, 272(IUR):Autumn84-275
 L.A. Marchand, 340(KSJ):Vol33-237
 C. Rawson, 617(TLS):6Sep85-963
Moore, T. The Journal of Thomas Moore. (Vol 2) (W.S. Dowden, ed)
 C. Rawson, 617(TLS):6Sep85-963
Moore, T. and C. Carling. Language Understanding.* (British title: Understanding Language.)
 M. Deuchar, 297(JL):Sep84-374
Moore-Ede, M.C., F.M. Sulzman and C.A. Fuller. The Clocks that Time Us.
 M. Obonsawin, 529(QQ):Spring84-200
Moorehead, C. Sidney Bernstein.*
 G. Brown, 707:Spring84-155
Moorehead, C. Freya Stark.
 A. Huth, 362:5Dec85-27
Moorhouse, A.C. The Syntax of Sophocles.*
 A.L. Brown, 303(JoHS):Vol 104-199
Moorhouse, G. To the Frontier.
 P-L. Adams, 61:Jun85-105
 E. Claridge, 364:Oct84-102
 R. Dinnage, 453(NYRB):13Jun85-29
 P. Glazebrook, 441:16Jun85-26
 R. Trevelyan, 362:17Jan85-24
Moorjani, A.S. Abysmal Games in the Novels of Samuel Beckett.
 S.E. Gontarski, 395(MFS):Winter84-777
Moorman, M. George Macaulay Trevelyan.
 J.V. Jensen, 77:Winter84-91
Moos, M. - see Mencken, H.L.
von Moos, S. and C. Smeenk, eds. Avant Garde und Industrie.
 R. Banham, 576:Oct84-277
Mora, P. and L., with P. Philippot. Conservation of Wall Paintings.*
 I.C. Bristow, 324:Nov85-890
Morais, R.J. Social Relations in a Philippine Town.
 M.R. Hollnsteiner, 293(JASt):Nov83-200
Morales Carrión, A. Puerto Rico.
 R. Serrano Geyls, 701(SinN):Oct-Dec83-68
Morales y Marín, J.L. Vicente López.
 N. Glendinning, 90:Jan84-46
Morán, F. and others. Third World Instability. (A.J. Pierre, ed)
 F. Lewis, 441:19May85-13
Moran, I. After London.
 L.M. Munby, 326:Summer84-33
Moran, J.H. The Growth of English Schooling, 1340-1548.
 J. Catto, 617(TLS):9Aug85-884
Moran, M. Politics and Society in Britain.
 F. Cairncross, 617(TLS):4Oct85-1084
Moran, M.H. Margaret Drabble.
 K.O. Garrigan, 395(MFS):Summer84-373
 J. Hannay, 659(ConL):Summer85-239
Morand, P. Venises.
 C. Dis, 450(NRF):Mar84-112

Morante, E. Aracoeli.
   G. Annan, 453(NYRB):14Mar85-27
   M. Fusco, 98:Aug/Sep84-600
   F. de Martinoir, 450(NRF):Nov84-99
   R. Rosenthal, 441:13Jan85-24
Moravánszky, Á. Die Architektur der Jahr-
   hundertwende in Ungarn und ihre Beziehun-
   gen zu der Wiener Architektur der Zeit.
   D. Klein, 43:Band14Heft2-179
Moravcsik, J. and P. Temko, eds. Plato on
   Beauty, Wisdom and the Arts.
   J. Beatty, 258:Mar84-91
   W. Charlton, 393(Mind):Apr84-296
Moravia, A. Erotic Tales.
   A. Mars-Jones, 617(TLS):20Dec85-1464
Moravia, A. 1934.
   G. Carsaniga, 381:Dec84-493
Moravia, S. Filosofia e scienze umane
   nell'età dei lumi.
   A.J. Bingham, 149(CLS):Fall84-353
Mordden, E. Demented.
   G. Walker, 441:9Jun85-13
More, T. The Complete Works of St. Thomas
   More. (Vol 3, Pt 2: Latin Poems.) (C.H.
   Miller and others, eds)
   J. McConica, 617(TLS):12Apr85-404
Moreau, F. Un Aspect de l'imagination cré-
   atrice chez Rabelais.
   F. Rigolot, 207(FR):Feb85-445
Moreau, F. L'Image littéraire.
   K. Anderson, 208(FS):Apr84-246
Moreau, J. Stoïcisme, épicurisme, tradi-
   tion hellénique.
   C. Natali, 53(AGP):Band66Heft1-98
Moreau, J-P. Rome ou Angleterre?
   G. Bernard, 617(TLS):25Oct85-1213
Moreau, P. Clodiana Religio, un procès
   politique en 61 avant J-C.
   P. Jal, 555:Vol58fasc2-331
Moreau, P-F. Le Récit utopique, droit nat-
   urel et roman de l'état.*
   H. Cronel, 450(NRF):Apr84-128
   D. Leduc-Fayette, 542:Jan-Mar84-101
Morelli, G., ed. L'invenzione del gùsto.
   M. Talbot, 410(M&L):Oct84-367
Morello, J. Jean Rotrou.
   H. Phillips, 208(FS):Jan84-54
Morelon, R. - see al-Gazālī
Moreno, J. and P. Peira. Crestomatía
   Románica Medieval.
   J. Cantera, 202(FMod):No68/70-375
Moreno Alcalde, M. Sobre escultera en
   Segovia.
   M. Estella, 48:Apr-Jun83-167
Moreschini, C. - see Leopardi, G.
Moretti, F. Signs Taken for Wonders.
   A.H. Pasco, 478:Oct84-298
Morfi, A. Historia crítica de un siglo de
   teatro puertorriqueño.
   L. de Arrigoitía, 701(SinN):Oct-Dec83-
   74
   L.M. Umpierre, 352(LATR):Fall84-137
Morgan, A.L., ed. Contemporary Designers.
   K.S. Hofweber, 614:Summer85-21
Morgan, B. Lawrence Ferlinghetti.
   T.A. Goldwasser, 517(PBSA):Vol78No2-
   257
Morgan, C. A Touch of the Other.
   S. Hearon, 441:16Jun85-24
Morgan, D.H. Harvesters and Harvesting
   1840-1900.
   N. Philip, 203:Vol195No2-263

Morgan, D.T., ed. The John Gray Blount
   Papers. (Vol 4)
   E.A. Miles, 9(AlaR):Jan84-62
Morgan, E. Sonnets from Scotland.
   D. Dunn, 617(TLS):26Apr85-470
Morgan, F. Northbook.*
   J. Mazzaro, 569(SR):Winter84-xi
Morgan, H.W. Drugs in America.
   J. Tagg, 106:Winter84-451
Morgan, J. Agatha Christie.*
   P-L. Adams, 61:Jul85-100
   A. Fraser, 441:23Jun85-8
Morgan, J. No Gangster More Bold.
   K.O. Morgan, 617(TLS):2Aug85-846
Morgan, K.O., ed. The Oxford Illustrated
   History of Britain.*
   V. Bogdanor, 176:Jan85-44
Morgan, M.R., ed. La continuation de Guil-
   laume de Tyr (1184-1197).*
   J.A. Brundage, 589:Oct84-987
Morgan, N. A Survey of Manuscripts Illumi-
   nated in the British Isles, Early Gothic
   Manuscripts, I.
   W.B. Clark, 589:Oct84-928
   L.M.C. Randall, 39:Jan84-67
Morgan, P. A Winter Visitor.*
   R. Pybus, 565:Autumn84-73
Morgan, P.F. Literary Critics and Review-
   ers in Early 19th-Century Britain.
   P. Flynn, 179(ES):Dec84-581
   R.D. McMaster, 627(UTQ):Summer84-425
Morgan, R., ed. Sisterhood is Global.
   A. Hacker, 441:27Jan85-12
Morgan, R.E. Disabling America.
   L. Winnick, 441:13Jan85-18
Morgan, T. FDR.
   V. Royster, 441:13Oct85-11
Morgan, W. The Almighty Wall.
   A. Saint, 46:May84-86
   B.F. Tolles, Jr., 432(NEQ):Jun84-315
Morgana, S.S. - see under Scotti Morgana,
   S.
Morgenthau, H.J. and K.W. Thompson. Poli-
   tics Among Nations.
   S. Hoffmann, 61:Nov85-131
Morgner, I. Amanda, ein Hexenroman.
   H. Kähler, 601(SuF):Jan-Feb84-177
Moritz, A.F. Between the Root and the
   Flower.
   E. Trethewey, 102(CanL):Summer84-84
Moritz, K.P. Werke. (H. Günther, ed)
   T.P. Saine, 462(OL):Vol139No1-91
Morley, J. The Making of the Royal Pavil-
   ion, Brighton.
   N. Penny, 90:Dec84-792
Morley, J.D. Pictures from the Water
   Trade.
   I. Buruma, 453(NYRB):18Jul85-18
   D.J. Enright, 362:30May85-31
   A. Tyler, 441:2Jun85-13
Morley, S. The Other Side of the Moon.
   442(NY):30Dec85-79
Morley, S. Shooting Stars.
   G. Playfair, 157:No152-52
Morley-Fletcher, H. and R. McIlroy.
   Christie's Pictorial History of Euro-
   pean Pottery.
   G. Wills, 39:Oct84-291
Morón Arroyo, C. Calderón.
   S.L. Fischer, 238:Sep84-472
Morpurgo-Tagliabue, G. Demetrio: dello
   stile.*
   D.M. Schenkeveld, 394:Vol137fasc1/2-192

Morreall, J. Taking Laughter Seriously.*
  H.E. Baber and J. Donnelly, 484(PPR):
    Dec84-290
  F. Berenson, 89(BJA):Winter84-74
  J.H. Kupfer, 289:Spring84-124
  M. Vorobej, 258:Sep84-337
Morrell, D. The Fraternity of the Stone.
  J. Sullivan, 441:3Nov85-26
Morrice, K. For All I Know.
  R. Watson, 588(SSL):Vol 19-194
Morris, A.D. The Origins of the Civil
  Rights Movement.
  P. Giddings, 441:10Mar85-25
Morris, A.J.A. The Scaremongers.*
  K. Robbins, 617(TLS):15Feb85-166
Morris, B. - see Shakespeare, W.
Morris, C. and D.E. Thompson. Huánuco
  Pampa.
  N. Hammond, 617(TLS):27Dec85-1476
Morris, C.B. García Lorca: "Bodas de
  sangre."*
  E. Williamson, 402(MLR):Apr84-478
Morris, D.B. Alexander Pope.
  D. Donoghue, 617(TLS):8Feb85-139
  D. Griffin, 173(ECS):Summer85-558
  J. Sitter, 191(ELN):Jun85-69
Morris, E. and M. Evans. Catalogue of
  Foreign Paintings, Drawings, Miniatures,
  Tapestries, Post-Classical Sculpture and
  Prints (Lady Lever Art Gallery, Port Sun-
  light).
  N. Penny, 90:Nov84-708
Morris, G.L. A World of Order and Light.
  L.C. Butts, 573(SSF):Fall84-417
  R.A. Morace, 363(LitR):Summer85-617
  R.A. Morace, 395(MFS):Winter84-845
  295(JML):Nov84-446
Morris, J. Journeys.*
  R. Fox, 362:24Jan85-27
Morris, J. Last Letters from Hav.
  P-L. Adams, 61:Jul85-101
  T.M. Disch, 441:2Jun85-41
  A. Huth, 362:24Oct85-33
  A. Mars-Jones, 617(TLS):18Oct85-1178
  442(NY):2Sep85-86
Morris, J. The Matter of Wales.
  P-L. Adams, 61:May85-104
  T. Hayden, 441:28Apr85-34
  G.H. Jenkins, 617(TLS):1Mar85-236
  D.A.N. Jones, 362:24Jan85-28
  442(NY):8Apr85-129
Morris, J. The Spectacle of Empire.
  W.N., 102(CanL):Winter83-188
Morris, J.P. and L.H. Warner - see Harper,
  A.S.
Morris, J.W., ed and trans. The Wisdom of
  the Throne.
  T. Dolan, 318(JAOS):Oct-Dec83-767
Morris, M. The Bus of Dreams.
  E. Ottenberg, 441:18Aug85-12
Morris, N. Madness and the Criminal Law.
  M.S. Moore, 185:Jul85-909
Morris, R. The Captain's Lady.
  W. Boyd, 617(TLS):2Aug85-845
  B. Maddox, 362:22Aug85-28
Morris, R. Time's Arrows.
  W. Stockton, 441:21Apr85-38
  442(NY):11Feb85-128
Morris, R.B. Witnesses at the Creation.
  A. Boyer, 441:17Nov85-31
Morris, W. A Book of Verse by William Mor-
  ris.
  G.L. Aho, 536:Vol5-74

Morris, W. A Cloak of Light.
  E. Abbey, 441:17Feb85-9
Morris, W. The Collected Letters of Wil-
  liam Morris.* (Vol 1) (N. Kelvin, ed)
  T. Hilton, 453(NYRB):25Apr85-22
  L. Lambourne, 62:Nov84-92
  R. Watkinson, 326:Summer84-30
  639(VQR):Autumn84-122
Morris, W. The Ideal Book. (W.S. Peter-
  son, ed)
  P. Thompson, 59:Dec84-496
Morris, W. The Juvenilia of William
  Morris. (F.S. Boos, ed)
  P. Thompson, 59:Dec84-496
Morris, W. William Morris: "The Defence
  of Guenevere" and Other Poems. (M.A.
  Lourie, ed)
  G.L. Aho, 536:Vol5-73
Morris, W. William Morris: "News from No-
  where" and Selected Writings and Designs.
  (A. Briggs, ed)
  P. Thompson, 59:Dec84-495
Morris, W. The Novels on Blue Paper by
  William Morris. (P. Fitzgerald, ed)
  G.L. Aho, 536:Vol5-74
Morris, W. The Political Writings of Wil-
  liam Morris.* (A.L. Morton, ed)
  J. Fyrth, 326:Summer84-37
Morris, W. Socialist Diary by William
  Morris. (F. Boos, ed)
  G.L. Aho, 536:Vol5-74
  P. Stansky, 637(VS):Autumn83-132
Morris, W. Solo.*
  M. Ellmann, 569(SR):Fall84-661
  M. Washington, 649(WAL):May84-72
"Morris and Company in Cambridge."
  P. Thompson, 59:Dec84-496
"William Morris and Kelmscott."
  G.L. Aho, 536:Vol5-73
"William Morris Today."
  P. Thompson, 59:Dec84-496
Morris-Suzuki, T. Showa.
  J. McMullen, 617(TLS):11Jan85-32
Morrison, A. Tales of Mean Streets.
  S. Monod, 189(EA):Jan-Mar85-113
Morrison, B. Dark Glasses.*
  C. Boyle, 364:Oct84-76
  J. Mole, 176:Feb85-51
Morrison, G., ed. History of Persian Lit-
  erature from the Beginnings of the
  Islamic Period to the Present Day.
  W.L. Hanaway, Jr., 318(JAOS):Apr-Jun83-
    452
Morrison, J. Stories of the Waterfront.
  B. Roberts, 381:Sep84-408
Morrison, K. Canters and Chronicles.
  E. Brater, 130:Summer84-191
  B.F. Dukore, 397(MD):Mar84-142
  J. Schlueter, 615(TJ):Dec84-552
Morrison, K.F. The Mimetic Tradition of
  Reform in the West.
  L.B. Pascoe, 589:Apr84-419
Morrissey, L.J. Henry Fielding.*
  C.J. Rawson, 402(MLR):Apr84-421
Morrow, L. The Chief.
  S. Cheever, 441:27Jan85-3
Morscher, E., O. Neumaier and G. Zecha,
  eds. Philosophie als Wissenschaft/
  Essays in Scientific Philosophy.
  R. Stranzinger, 679:Band15Heft1-177
Morse, D. Perspectives on Romanticism.*
  J.A. Michie, 447(N&Q):Aug83-382

Morse, R.A. and T. Hooper, eds. The Illus-
trated Encyclopedia of Beekeeping.
  D. Galton, 617(TLS):23Aug85-935
Morse, S.F.B. Lectures on the Affinity of
Painting with the Other Fine Arts by Sam-
uel F.B. Morse. (N. Cikovsky, Jr., ed)
  E. Johns, 658:Summer/Autumn84-215
Morselli, P. and G. Corti. La Chiesa di
Santa Maria delle Carceri in Prato.
  R.A. Goldthwaite, 551(RenQ):Summer84-
  263
  A. Hughes, 59:Sep84-378
Morsiani, J. Da Tutuola a Rotimi.
  M. Fabre, 189(EA):Oct-Dec85-488
Mortensen, K.P. Ironi og utopi.
  K.H. Ober, 563(SS):Summer84-302
Mortier, R. L'originalité.
  F. Baasner, 547(RF):Band96Heft1/2-183
  J.H. Mason, 402(MLR):Apr84-457
  M. Meyer, 540(RIPh):Vol38fasc1/2-196
  A. Nivelle, 52:Band19Heft3-311
Mortimer, E. Faith and Power.*
  G.M. Wickens, 529(QQ):Autumn84-751
Mortimer, E. The Rise of the French
Communist Party 1920-1947.*
  R. Paxton, 441:10Feb85-28
Mortimer, G.L. Faulkner's Rhetoric of
Loss.
  D. Krause, 395(MFS):Winter84-819
  295(JML):Nov84-437
Mortimer, J. Paradise Postponed.
  D.J. Enright, 362:3Oct85-28
  A. Hislop, 617(TLS):15Nov85-1294
Mortimer, M. Mouloud Mammeri.
  A. Lippert, 207(FR):Oct84-117
  L. Tremaine, 538(RAL):Spring84-92
Mortimer, P. The Handyman.
  C. Bancroft, 441:1Dec85-12
  J. Updike, 442(NY):21Oct85-145
Mortley, R. Womanhood.
  N.R.E. Fisher, 123:Vol34No2-343
Morton, A.L. - see Morris, W.
Morton, B.N. Americans in Paris.
  D. Stephens, 207(FR):Feb85-479
Morton, C. Printed Matter.
  C. Tapping, 102(CanL):Summer84-158
Morton, P. The Vital Science.
  G. Beer, 617(TLS):14Jun85-673
Morvan, A., ed. Conformité et déviances.
  R.A. Day, 189(EA):Oct-Dec85-447
Morvan, A. La Tolérance dans le roman
anglais de 1726 à 1771.
  I.C. Ross, 189(EA):Oct-Dec85-463
Moscato, M. and L. Le Blanc, eds. The
United States of America v. One Book
Entitled "Ulysses" by James Joyce.*
  M. Magalaner, 395(MFS):Winter84-760
  A. Rieke, 70:May-Jun84-155
Moser, D-R. Verkündigung durch Volks-
gesang.
  R.W. Brednich, 196:Band25Heft1/2-145
Moser, H. and H. Tervooren - see "Des Min-
nesangs Frühling"
Moser, T.C. The Life in the Fiction of
Ford Madox Ford.*
  D. Hewitt, 541(RES):Aug84-412
  J. Newman, 161(DUJ):Dec83-148
  M. Stannard, 402(MLR):Jul84-684
Moses, C.G. French Feminism in the Nine-
teenth Century.
  J.F. McMillan, 617(TLS):8Feb85-153
Moses, D.D. Delicate Bodies.
  P. Klovan, 102(CanL):Winter83-119

Moses, J. The Novelist as Comedian.*
  R.B. Henkle, 569(SR):Winter84-121
  T.L. Jeffers, 651(WHR):Summer84-181
  D.D. Stone, 445(NCF):Jun84-109
  W.F. Wright, 301(JEGP):Jan84-134
Mosey, D. Boycott.
  A.L. Le Quesne, 617(TLS):15Nov85-1303
Mosher, S.W. Journey to the Forbidden
China.
  B. Johnson, 441:4Aug85-17
Mosimann, A. Cuisine Naturelle.
  C. Reid, 617(TLS):20Dec85-1467
Mosino, F. Le origini del volgare in Cala-
bria. Testi calabresi antichi (Sec. XV).
(A. Piromalli, ed)
  A. Varvaro, 379(MedR):Apr84-138
Mosk, C. Patriarchy and Fertility.
  R. Napier, 293(JASt):Aug84-767
Mosley, D. Loved Ones.
  A. Chisholm, 617(TLS):29Mar85-338
  I. Hislop, 362:28Mar85-29
Mosley, J. British Type Specimens before
1831.
  J. Dreyfus, 617(TLS):16Aug85-911
Moss, A. Ovid in Renaissance France.*
  R.W. Hanning, 551(RenQ):Spring84-56
Moss, A. Poetry and Fable.
  T. Cave, 617(TLS):18Jan85-66
Moss, G. Stitch Guide.
  C. Campbell, 614:Spring85-21
Moss, H. New Selected Poems.
  P. Stitt, 441:1Sep85-11
Moss, H. Rules of Sleep.*
  F. Garber, 29(APR):Sep/Oct85-14
  R. Phillips, 491:Mar85-351
  P. Stitt, 219(GaR):Winter84-857
Moss, J., ed. The Canadian Novel: Modern
Times.
  R. Billings, 102(CanL):Autumn84-109
Moss, R. Moscow Rules.
  L. Gruson, 441:17Feb85-20
Moss, R. and A. de Borchgrave. Monimbó.
  639(VQR):Winter84-27
Mossberg, B.A.C. Emily Dickinson.*
  N. Baym, 301(JEGP):Jan84-148
  S. Juhasz, 536:Vol6-35
  D. Porter, 432(NEQ):Mar84-106
Mosse, G.L. German Jews Beyond Judaism.
  G. Craig, 453(NYRB):13Jun85-3
Most, G.W. and W.W. Stowe, eds. The
Poetics of Murder.
  R. Markley, 223:Fall83-304
Mosti, R., ed. I protocolli di Iohannes
Nicolai Pauli.
  C.L. Stinger, 589:Oct84-988
Mothersill, M. Beauty Restored.
  R. Wollheim, 617(TLS):22Mar85-315
Motion, A. Dangerous Play.
  D. Davis, 362:3Jan85-26
  M. Hofmann, 617(TLS):18Jan85-54
  J. Mole, 176:Feb85-52
Motion, A. Independence.
  S. Regan, 148:Autumn84-89
Motion, A. The Poetry of Edward Thomas.*
  J. Batchelor, 447(N&Q):Aug83-367
  W. Cooke, 565:Winter83/84-57
  R.D. Sell, 541(RES):Feb84-104
Mott, M.C. The Seven Mountains of Thomas
Merton.*
  E. Rice, 469:Vol 10No1-111
  442(NY):18Feb85-121
Mottahedeh, R. The Mantle of the Prophet.
  F. Ajami, 441:25Aug85-5

Mottram, R. Inner Landscapes.
  R. Bryden, 441:10Feb85-18
Motut, R. Maurice Constantin-Weyer.
  V. Harger-Grinling, 102(CanL):Autumn84-75
Mouligneau, G. Mme de La Fayette roman-
  cière?*
  J. Campbell, 208(FS):Apr84-201
  A. Niderst, 535(RHL):Jan/Feb84-99
Moulton, G.E., ed. Atlas of the Lewis and
  Clark Expedition.
  J.P. Ronda, 656(WMQ):Jul84-530
Mounce, H.O. Wittgenstein's "Tractatus."
  I. McFetridge, 479(PhQ):Jan84-69
Mounier, J. La Fortune des écrits de Jean-
  Jacques Rousseau dans les pays de langue
  allemande de 1782 à 1813.
  R. Grimsley, 208(FS):Jan84-64
Mouré, E. Wanted Alive.*
  R. Donovan, 137:May84-30
  H. Kirkwood, 526:Autumn84-82
  P. O'Brien, 168(ECW):Winter84/85-339
  P. Stuewe, 529(QQ):Winter84-1013
Moureau, F. Dufresny, auteur dramatique
  (1657-1724).
  W.D. Howarth, 208(FS):Apr84-203
Moureau, F. Le "Mercure galant" de
  Dufresny (1710-1714) ou le journalisme a
  la mode.
  A.A. Sokalski, 173(ECS):Spring85-451
Mouriaux, R. Les Syndicats dans la
  société française.
  M. Bertrand, 207(FR):Oct84-175
Mousnier, R.E. The Institutions of France
  under the Absolute Monarchy 1598-1789.
  (Vol 2)
  D. Parker, 617(TLS):12Jul85-781
Mowat, C. The Outport People.
  R.G. Moyles, 102(CanL):Autumn84-101
Mowat, F. My Discovery of America.
  T. Schmitz, 441:22Dec85-19
Mowat, F. Sea of Slaughter.
  L. Charlton, 441:7Apr85-15
Mowat, I.R.M. Easter Ross 1750-1850.
  R.A. Dodgshon, 83:Spring84-118
Mowl, T. and B. Earnshaw. Trumpet at a
  Distant Gate.
  C. Aslet, 617(TLS):23Aug85-934
  P. Johnson, 362:13Jun85-24
Moyles, R.G. The Text of "Paradise Lost."
  A.S.G. Edwards, 617(TLS):13Dec85-1436
Mozart, W.A. The Six "Haydn" String
  Quartets.
  G. Abraham, 617(TLS):25Oct85-1205
Mozet, N. La Ville de province dans
  l'oeuvre de Balzac — l'espace roman-
  esque.*
  O. Heathcote, 446(NCFS):Summer-Fall84-182
Mtshali, O. Fireflames.
  D. Walder, 617(TLS):10May85-527
Mu, C. - see under Ch'ien Mu
Mudry, P. - see Celsus
Muecke, D.C. Irony and the Ironic.
  P. Chilton, 307:Aug84-156
  R.J. Dingley, 447(N&Q):Dec83-570
Mueller, D.C., ed. The Political Economy
  of Growth.
  M.W., 185:Jan85-390
Mueller, G.O.W. and F. Adler. Outlaws of
  the Ocean.
  P. Benchley, 441:3Mar85-27
Mueller, I. - see Wyclif, J.

Mueller, J. Astaire Dancing.
  J.L. Mankiewicz, 441:8Dec85-17
Mueller, J.M. The Native Tongue and the
  Word.
  J. Scattergood, 617(TLS):1Mar85-241
Mühl, K. "Verwandlung" im Werk Rilkes.
  I.H. Solbrig, 406:Summer84-223
Mühlberg, D., ed. Arbeiterleben um 1900.
  W. Jacobeit, 654(WB):12/1984-2104
Muhlenfeld, E. Mary Boykin Chesnut.
  L.J. Taylor, 534(RALS):Spring82-87
Muhlethaler, J-C. Poétiques du quinzième
  siècle.
  D.A. Fein, 207(FR):Feb85-444
  J. Fox, 208(FS):Jul84-325
  F. Rigolot, 546(RR):Nov84-506
Muhr, K. Sprachwandel als soziales Phäno-
  men.*
  N.C. Dorian, 355(LSoc):Jun84-262
Muir, E. Edwin Muir: Uncollected Scottish
  Criticism.* (A. Noble, ed)
  T. Crawford, 571(ScLJ):Winter84-54
  E.W. Mellown, 588(SSL):Vol 19-274
  J.R. Watson, 402(MLR):Jul84-686
Muir, E. Scottish Journey.
  617(TLS):25Oct85-1219
Muir, K., ed. Interpretations of Shake-
  speare.
  G. Taylor, 617(TLS):16Aug85-905
Muir, K. - see Shakespeare, W.
Muir, K., J.L. Halio and D.J. Palmer, eds.
  Shakespeare, Man of the Theater.*
  J.R. Brown, 570(SQ):Winter84-485
Mukherjee, P. Le Sāṁkhya.
  M. Adam, 542:Apr-Jun84-258
Mukherjee, S. Translation as Discovery.
  P. Kumar, 314:Winter-Spring84-218
Muldoon, P. Quoof.*
  T. Eagleton, 565:Summer84-76
  A. Frazier, 174(Éire):Spring84-123
  M. Harmon, 272(IUR):Spring84-126
  B. O'Donoghue, 493:Jan84-53
Mulhallen, K., D. Bennett and R. Brown,
  eds. Tasks of Passion.
  T. Middlebro', 168(ECW):Winter84/85-140
Mulisch, H. The Assault.
  H. Beaver, 441:16Jun85-7
  S. Spender, 453(NYRB):5Dec85-65
Mulisch, H. L'Attentat.
  P. Mahillon, 450(NRF):Nov84-103
Mull, M. and A. Rucker. The History of
  White People in America.
  E. Wald, 441:29Sep85-50
Mullen, W. Choreia.*
  A. Burnett, 122:Apr84-154
Muller, A.V. - see Soloviev, S.M.
Müller, A.W. Praktisches Folgern und
  Selbstgestaltung nach Aristoteles.
  A.W. Price, 123:Vol34No1-134
Muller, C.R. and T.D. Rieman. The Shaker
  Chair.
  J. Giovannini, 441:15Sep85-25
Müller, D. "Daniel vom Blühenden Tal" und
  "Garel vom Blühenden Tal."
  F.H. Bäuml, 406:Fall84-353
  O. Ehrismann, 680(ZDP):Band103Heft3-458
Muller, J.P. and W.J. Richardson. Lacan
  and Language.
  J. Forrester, 208(FS):Jan84-101
Muller, M. Leave a Message for Willie.
  N. Callendar, 441:3Feb85-37

Muller, M. There's Nothing to be Afraid Of.
   N. Callendar, 441:6Oct85-35
Müller, P. Emile Zola — der Autor im Spannungsfeld seiner Epoche.
   H. Sanders, 72:Band221Heft2-456
Muller, P.E. Goya's "Black" Paintings.
   N. Glendinning, 617(TLS):31May85-602
Müller-Kotchetkova, T.V. Stendhal, Trieste, Civitavecchia et ... Riga.
   F. Claudon, 605(SC):15Oct84-43
Müller-Michaels, H. Literatur im Alltag und Unterricht.
   B. Bieberle, 682(ZPSK):Band37Heft4-527
Müller-Seidel, W., ed. Kleists Aktualität.
   B. Leistner, 654(WB):5/1984-871
Mullings, L. Therapy, Ideology and Social Change.
   E. Gillies, 617(TLS):7Jun85-633
Mullins, E., ed. The Arts of Britain.
   C. Ashwin, 592:Vol 197No1005-60
Mullins, E. The Painted Witch.
   L. Ellmann, 617(TLS):23Aug85-928
Multhaup, U. James Joyce.
   E. Kreutzer, 72:Band221Heft2-380
Mulvey, C. Anglo-American Landscapes.*
   H.W. Emerson, 366:Spring84-130
   R.E. Streeter, 432(NEQ):Mar84-144
Munari, F. - see Matthew of Vendôme
Munce, H. Graphics Handbook.
   G. Biren, 507:Jan/Feb84-110
Mundkur, B. The Cult of the Serpent.
   J. Simpson, 203:Vol95No1-130
Munemitsu, M. - see under Mutsu Munemitsu
Munley, A. The Hospice Alternative.
   P.W. Simon, 529(QQ):Autumn84-705
Muñoz, B. Sons of the Wind.
   T. Murad, 395(MFS):Summer84-343
Muñoz, L.L. - see under Luján Muñoz, L.
Muñoz Cadima, W.O. Teatro boliviano contemporáneo.
   B.H. Reynolds, 238:May84-314
Munro, A. The Moons of Jupiter.*
   W.B. Stone, 573(SSF):Spring84-160
Munro, A. Something I've Been Meaning to Tell You.
   P. Craig, 617(TLS):29Nov85-1372
Munson, J. - see Clark, A.
Münster, A. Studien zu Beethovens Diabelli-Variationen.
   B. Cooper, 410(M&L):Jan84-71
Munsterberg, H. The Japanese Print.
   S. Markbreiter, Jr., 60:Mar-Apr84-125
Murad, M.A. Intellectual Modernism of Shibli Nu'mani.
   A. Schimmel, 318(JAOS):Oct-Dec83-810
"Murasaki Shikibu: Her Diary and Poetic Memoirs."* (R. Bowring, trans)
   T.H. Rohlich, 293(JASt):May84-539
Murase, M. Iconography of "The Tale of Genji."
   J. Meech-Pekarik, 407(MN):Winter84-476
Muratore, M.J. The Evolution of the Cornelian Heroine.*
   G.J. Mallinson, 402(MLR):Apr84-451
Muray, P. Le 19e siècle à travers les âges.
   A-C. Faitrop, 207(FR):Dec84-323
Murdoch, A. In Her Own Image.
   C. Gaiser, 441:13Oct85-26
   J. Neville, 617(TLS):6Sep85-973

Murdoch, I. The Good Apprentice.
   B. Maddox, 362:26Sep85-30
   S. Medcalf, 617(TLS):27Sep85-1047
Murdoch, I. The Philosopher's Pupil.*
   J.L. Halio, 598(SoR):Winter85-204
   A. Jenkins, 376:Feb84-136
   639(VQR):Spring84-56
Murnane, W.J. The Penguin Guide to Ancient Egypt.*
   H. Goedicke, 124:Nov-Dec84-129
Murphy, A.B. Mikhail Zoshchenko.
   M.A. Nicholson, 402(MLR):Jul84-766
Murphy, C.J. Alienation and Absence in the Novels of Marguerite Duras.*
   J. Baetens, 547(RF):Band96Heft3-370
   N. Bailey, 208(FS):Apr84-238
   D. Coward, 402(MLR):Jul84-719
   P.H. Solomon, 395(MFS):Summer84-393
Murphy, D. Muddling Through in Madagascar.
   D. Sweetman, 617(TLS):1Nov85-1243
Murphy, G.E., Jr. The Editors' Choice. (Vol 1)
   A.S. Grossman, 441:28Apr85-29
Murphy, G.R. Brecht and the Bible.*
   E. Dönt, 52:Band19Heft1-110
Murphy, J.G. Evolution, Morality, and the Meaning of Life.*
   M. Ruse, 154:Sep84-527
   G.A. Schrag, 389(MQ):Summer85-510
Murphy, L. The Sea Within.
   A. Bernays, 441:21Apr85-20
Murphy, O.T. Charles Gravier, Comte de Vergennes.*
   J. Popkin, 173(ECS):Winter84/85-270
Murphy, R. The Price of Stone.
   B. O'Donoghue, 617(TLS):6Dec85-1405
Murphy, R.C. Guestworkers in the German "Reich."
   R. Blanke, 104(CASS):Winter84-489
Murphy, S. The Duchess of Devonshire's Ball.
   442(NY):20May85-127
Murphy, T. Famine. The Gigli Concert. The Sanctuary Lamp.
   C. Murray, 272(IUR):Autumn84-280
Murray, C. Hamewith.
   A. Fraser, 588(SSL):Vol 19-305
Murray, C. Losing Ground.*
   B. Berger, 129:Jan85-66
   C. Jencks, 453(NYRB):9May85-41
Murray, C. - see Robinson, L.
Murray, D.J. A History of Western Psychology.
   R.G. Weyant, 529(QQ):Winter84-1037
Murray, G.E. Repairs.
   M. Carrino, 436(NewL):Fall84-106
Murray, J. Practical Remarks on Modern Paper.
   P.S. Koda, 536:Vol5-183
Murray, J. The Proustian Comedy.*
   295(JML):Nov84-497
Murray, J. Samarkland.
   C. Hawtree, 617(TLS):7Jun85-644
Murray, L. Michelangelo.
   C. Gould, 324:Feb85-234
Murray, L.A. Persistence in Folly. The People's Otherworld.
   B. Morrison, 617(TLS):9Aug85-873
Murray, M. Marcel Dupré.
   R. Nichols, 617(TLS):20Dec85-1459
Murray, N.D. - see Flanner, J.
Murray, P. - see Burckhardt, J.

Murray, W. The Change in the European Balance of Power, 1938-1939.
D.C. Watt, 617(TLS):6Sep85-984
Murray, W. The Hard Knocker's Luck.
H. Gold, 441:10Nov85-15
442(NY):23Dec85-92
Murray-Smith, S., ed. The Dictionary of Australian Quotations.
J. Neville, 617(TLS):25Jan85-88
G.W. Turner, 71(ALS):Oct84-552
Murshid, G. Reluctant Debutante.
J. Walsh, 293(JASt):Aug84-785
Musaeus. Hero et Leander.* (H. Livrea, with P. Eleuteri, eds)
M. Campbell, 303(JoHS):Vol 104-220
Muschamp, H. Man About Town.
T.S. Hines, 505:Dec84-99
G. Williams, 45:May84-117
Muschg, A. The Blue Man.
E. Pawel, 441:19May85-12
G. Steiner, 442(NY):8Jul85-71
Muschg, A. Das Licht und der Schlüssel.
M. Butler, 617(TLS):4Jan85-17
J. Manthey, 384:Dec84-944
Mushabac, J. Melville's Humor.*
H. Raff, 616:Spring/Summer84-51
"Music for London Entertainment, 1660-1800." (Ser A: The Theater of Music.)
M. Sands, 611(TN):Vol38No1-46
Musil, R. Essais.
G. Quinsat, 450(NRF):Jul/Aug84-186
Muske, C. Wyndmere.
C. Kizer, 441:3Nov85-13
Mussell, K. Fantasy and Reconciliation.
N. Pogel, 27(AL):Dec84-622
Muthesius, S. The English Terraced House.*
R. Banham, 576:Mar84-91
S. Meacham, 637(VS):Spring84-382
M.N. Woods, 45:Mar84-73
Muthmann, F. Der Granatapfel.*
L. Burn, 303(JoHS):Vol 104-268
R. Ling, 123:Vol34No1-152
Mutsu Munemitsu. Kenkenroku.* (G.M. Berger, ed and trans)
B.W. Kahn, 293(JASt):May84-548
Muyskens, J. and others. Rendezvous.
M. Donaldson-Evans, 399(MLJ):Summer84-164
Myant, M.R. Socialism and Democracy in Czechoslovakia, 1945-1948.*
J.F. Zacek, 104(CASS):Fall84-357
"Carl Mydans: Photojournalist."
J. Manning, 441:6Oct85-28
Myer, V.G., ed. Laurence Sterne.
D. Profumo, 617(TLS):29Nov85-1352
Myers, D.K. Temple, Household, Horseback.
K.B., 614:Winter85-30
Myers, J.B. Tracking the Marvelous.*
J. Sturman, 55:Apr84-30
639(VQR):Summer84-100
Myers, M., Jr. Liberty Without Anarchy.
L.D. Cress, 656(WMQ):Jan84-174
D.W. Dumas, 432(NEQ):Jun84-285
Myers, N. The Primary Source.*
D.J. Mabberley, 617(TLS):18Jan85-71
Myers, R. and M. Harris, eds. The Sale and Distribution of Books from 1700.
M.J. Crump, 354:Jun84-194
Myers, R.E., ed. The Intersection of Science Fiction and Philosophy.
R.S. Bravard and M.W. Peplow, 590:Dec84-60
J. Fekete, 561(SFS):Nov84-335

Myers, R.H., ed. The Modern Chinese Economy. China During the Interregnum, 1911-1949.
D.D. Buck, 293(JASt):May84-459
Myers, S.L. Ho for California.
K. Carabine, 447(N&Q):Apr83-188
Myerson, J. Ralph Waldo Emerson.*
J. Loving, 534(RALS):Spring82-81
Myerson, J., ed. Studies in the American Renaissance, 1983.
L. Buell, 432(NEQ):Sep84-435
de Mylius, J. H.C. Andersens romaner mellem romantik og realisme.
E. Bredsdorff, 562(Scan):Nov84-171
Mylne, V. Diderot: "La Religieuse."*
I.H. Smith, 67:Nov84-248
J. Whatley, 207(FR):Feb85-453
Mynors, R.A.B. - see Erasmus
Mysse, J.W. The Classics — Fisherman Knits.
K. Buffington, 614:Spring85-19
"Mythes, Images, Représentations."
M. Levy, 549(RLC):Oct-Dec84-479
"La mythologie au XVIIe siècle."
F. Graziani-Giacobbi, 549(RLC):Oct-Dec84-488

van der Naald, A.C. Nuevas tendencias en el teatro español.
B.S. McSorley, 238:Mar84-146
Naar, M. - see Kant, I.
Nabb, M. Death in Autumn.
T.J.B., 617(TLS):26Apr85-457
Nabokov, V. Lectures on Russian Literature. (F. Bowers, ed)
P. Carden, 574(SEEJ):Spring84-124
Nabokov, V. Le Don.
J. Blot, 450(NRF):Feb84-116
Nabokov, V. The Man from the U.S.S.R. and Other Plays.
442(NY):25Feb85-105
Naccarato, F. - see Eiximenis, F.
Nadal, J.M. and M. Prats. Història de la llengua catalona. (Vol 1)
M.W. Wheeler, 86(BHS):Jan84-56
Nadaud, A. L'Archéologie du zéro.
A. Clerval, 450(NRF):May84-114
Nadel, I.B. Biography.
V. Glendinning, 617(TLS):18Jan85-53
Nadelhoffer, H. Cartier, Jewelers Extraordinary.
C. Gere, 617(TLS):22Feb85-213
Naef-Hinderling, A. The Search for the Culprit.
S. Monod, 189(EA):Jan-Mar85-113
Naff, A. Becoming American.
J.D. Yohannan, 441:27Oct85-41
Nagarkar, K. Seven Sixes Are Forty-Three.
P. Lewis, 565:Spring84-64
Nagata, Y. Materials on the Bosnian Notables.
R. Murphey, 318(JAOS):Oct-Dec83-772
Nagatomi, M. and others, eds. Sanskrit and Indian Studies.
J.W. de Jong, 259(IIJ):Jul84-223
Nagel, G. The Structure of Experience.*
S.E., 185:Jan85-394
Nagel, G.L., ed. Critical Essays on Sarah Orne Jewett.
T. Wortham, 445(NCF):Mar85-488

Nagel, J., ed. Ernest Hemingway.*
　　L. Butts, 594:Winter84-448
　　R.P. Weeks, 395(MFS):Winter84-807
Nagel, P.C. Descent from Glory.*
　　P. Marshall, 83:Autumn84-256
　　D.F. Musto, 432(NEQ):Sep84-462
Nagel, T. Questions mortelles.
　　M. Adam, 542:Apr-Jun84-259
　　F. Recanati, 98:May84-362
Nagler, A.M. Shakespeare's Stage.
　　R.J. Steen, 214:Vol 11No41-124
Nagorski, A. Reluctant Farewell.
　　A. Austin, 441:13Oct85-25
Nagy, J.F. The Wisdom of the Outlaw.
　　B. O'Donoghue, 617(TLS):1Nov85-1242
Nahas, G. La Filière du rail.
　　G.P. Ashley, 207(FR):Feb85-500
Nahrebecky, R. Wackenroder, Tieck, E.T.A.
　　Hoffmann, Bettina von Arnim.
　　A. Fehn, 221(GQ):Spring84-339
Naik, M.K. A History of Indian English
　　Literature.
　　R. Juneja, 314:Winter-Spring84-222
Naik, M.K., ed. Perspectives on Indian
　　Prose in English.*
　　J.P. Gemmill, 314:Winter-Spring84-201
Naimark, N.M. Terrorists and Social Demo-
　　crats.*
　　A. Ascher, 550(RusR):Jul84-315
　　639(VQR):Spring84-50
Naipaul, S. Beyond the Dragon's Mouth.*
　　J. Krich, 441:24Mar85-13
Naipaul, V.S. Finding the Centre.*
　　W. Boyd, 364:Apr/May84-128
Naisbitt, J. and P. Aburdene. Re-invent-
　　ing the Corporation.
　　W.H. Donaldson, 441:20Oct85-52
Naismith, R.J. Buildings of the Scottish
　　Countryside.
　　H.G. Slade, 617(TLS):23Aug85-934
Naison, M. Communists in Harlem During
　　the Depression.
　　T. Draper, 453(NYRB):30May85-44
Najder, Z. Joseph Conrad.*
　　D.L. Higdon, 445(NCF):Sep84-231
　　S. Monod, 189(EA):Jul-Sep85-342
　　D.R. Schwarz, 395(MFS):Summer84-355
　　J.M. Szczypień, 497(PolR):Vol29No3-89
　　B.E. Teets, 177(ELT):Vol27No4-333
　　R. Tennant, 136:Vol 17No1-50
　　295(JML):Nov84-421
Najder, Z., ed. Conrad under Familial
　　Eyes.*
　　J.M. Szczypień, 497(PolR):Vol29No3-89
Najemy, J.M. Corporatism and Consensus in
　　Florentine Electoral Politics, 1280-
　　1400.*
　　D. Kent, 589:Oct84-930
　　N. Rubinstein, 278(IS):Vol39-117
Najita, T. and J.V. Koschmann, eds. Con-
　　flict in Modern Japanese History.*
　　A. Gordon, 293(JASt):Nov83-163
Nakadate, N., ed. Robert Penn Warren.*
　　R. Gray, 677(YES):Vol 14-356
　　M.R. Winchell, 106:Summer84-229
Nakam, G. Les "Essais" de Montaigne.
　　R.D. Cottrell, 207(FR):May85-886
Nakam, G. Montaigne et son temps.*
　　B. Lydgate, 210(FrF):Jan84-113
　　I. Maclean, 402(MLR):Jan84-185
　　A. Tournon, 535(RHL):Nov/Dec84-946

Nakamura, T. Economic Growth in Prewar
　　Japan.
　　R. Rice, 293(JASt):Feb84-331
Nakhimovsky, A.D. and A.S., eds. The Semi-
　　otics of Russian Cultural History.
　　S. Monas, 617(TLS):23Aug85-916
Nakhimovsky, A.S. Laughter in the Void.*
　　S. Pratt, 550(RusR):Apr84-193
Nalbantian, S. Seeds of Decadence in the
　　Late Nineteenth-Century Novel.
　　P.S. Nichols, 395(MFS):Winter84-854
Naldini, N. Vita di Giovanni Comisso.
　　U. Varnai, 617(TLS):11Oct85-1147
Naldini, N. - see Comisso, G.
Nalimov, V.V. Realms of the Unconscious;
　　The Enchanted Frontier. (R.G. Colodny,
　　ed)
　　J. Largeault, 542:Jan-Mar84-108
Nally, T.H. The Spancel of Death. (A.
　　Dalsimer, ed)
　　R.G. Yeed, 305(JIL):Jan-May84-146
Naman, A.A. The Jew in the Victorian
　　Novel.*
　　S.M. Smith, 677(YES):Vol 14-339
Namjoshi, S. The Conversations of Cow.
　　A. Haverty, 617(TLS):8Nov85-1266
Nancy, J-L. L'impératif catégorique.*
　　J-M. Gabaude, 540(RIPh):Vol38fasc3-324
Nandy, P., ed. The Vikas Book of Modern
　　Indian Love Poetry.
　　A. Hashmi, 314:Winter-Spring84-219
Nanez Falcon, G. - see Bonner, T., Jr.
Nanjou-Flaux, N. and M-N. Gary-Prieur, eds.
　　Lexique 1.
　　O. Deutschmann, 547(RF):Band96Heft3-
　　305
Napoli, D.J. and E.N. Rando. Syntactic
　　Argumentation.
　　C. Cullen, 297(JL):Mar84-192
Narayan, R.K. Under the Banyan Tree and
　　Other Stories.
　　A. Kazin, 441:21Jul85-1
　　N. Shack, 617(TLS):18Oct85-1168
Nardin, T. Law, Morality, and the Rela-
　　tions of States.
　　J.E. Hare, 518:Oct84-240
　　C.B. Joynt, 185:Apr85-761
Narkiss, B. Hebrew Illuminated Manu-
　　scripts in the British Isles.* (Pt 1)
　　D. Goldstein, 354:Mar84-73
Naroll, R. The Moral Order.
　　K.S., 185:Apr85-772
Narváez, J.R.C. - see under Cirici Narváez,
　　J.R.
Narveson, J., ed. Moral Issues.
　　R.E.G., 185:Jan85-381
Nasaw, D. Children of the City.
　　A. Corman, 441:28Apr85-15
Nash, G.H. The Life of Herbert Hoover:
　　The Engineer, 1884-1914.
　　J. Willson, 396(ModA):Spring/Summer84-
　　248
Nash, J.R. The Mafia Diaries.
　　N. Callendar, 441:3Mar85-35
Nash, R. Settlement in a School of Whales.
　　N. Zacharin, 526:Autumn84-78
Nash, R. and D. Belaval, eds. Readings in
　　Spanish-English Contrastive Linguistics.
　　(Vol 2)
　　D.M. Jeuda, 35(AS):Fall84-240

Nash, R. and D. Belaval, eds. Readings in Spanish-English Contrastive Linguistics. (Vol 3)
S.M. Daniele-Sotillo, 355(LSoc):Dec84-569
Nash, R.H. The Concept of God.
D. Basinger, 258:Jun84-203
Nash, S. Paul Valéry's "Album de vers anciens."*
W.N. Ince, 208(FS):Jan84-87
R. Pickering, 402(MLR):Jul84-714
Nasr, S.H. Islamic Life and Thought.
A. Schimmel, 318(JAOS):Oct-Dec83-809
Nasr, S.H. Knowledge and the Sacred.
T. Dean, 485(PE&W):Apr84-211
H. Smith, 485(PE&W):Jan84-111
Nasta, D-T. Saint-John Perse et la découverte de l'être.
M-N. Little, 207(FR):Feb85-462
Natale, M. Museo Poldi Pezzoli: Dipinti.
J. Pope-Hennessy, 39:Mar84-223
Nathan, A.J. Chinese Democracy.
J.F. Burns, 441:22Sep85-14
Nathan, D. Glenda Jackson.
T. Minter, 157:No154-52
Nathan, M. Le Ciel des Fouriéristes.
F.P. Bowman, 535(RHL):Jul/Aug84-633
Nathan, N.M.L. Evidence and Assurance.
J. Heil, 518:Jan84-60
Nathanail, P., ed. Greek Dictionary.
M. Alexiou, 617(TLS):26Apr85-473
"The National Collection of Watercolours in the Victoria and Albert Museum on Colour Microfiche."
380:Summer84-220
"The National Gazetteer of the United States of America: New Jersey 1982."
E.W. McMullen, 424:Dec84-454
"National Library of Scotland, Catalogue of Manuscripts acquired since 1925." (Vol 4)
M. Nickson, 354:Sep84-290
Nattiez, J-J. Proust musicien.
J.M. Cocking, 617(TLS):8Mar85-255
M. Erman, 98:Oct84-845
"Le naturalisme dans les littératures de langues européennes."
M. Mrozowicki, 343:Heft9/10-156
Naud, A.D. and O. Dazat - see under Dag
Naud, A. and O. Dazat
Naudé, G. Lettres de Gabriel Naudé à Jacques Dupuy (1632-1652). (P. Wolfe, ed)
E. Kearns, 402(MLR):Apr84-453
Naughton, J.T. The Poetics of Yves Bonnefoy.
M. Edwards, 617(TLS):19Jul85-792
de Navacelle, T. Sublime Marlene.*
G. Annan, 453(NYRB):14Feb85-5
Navratilova, M., with G. Vecsey. Martina.
G. Shister, 441:30Jun85-21
Nawata, T. Mazandarani.
B. Comrie, 350:Sep85-720
Nawata, T. Parachi.
B. Comrie, 350:Mar85-226
Naylor, G. Linden Hills.
R. Kaveney, 617(TLS):24May85-572
M. Watkins, 441:3Mar85-11
Ndaw, A. La pensée africaine.
W. MacGaffey, 538(RAL):Winter84-616
Neale-Silva, E. and R.L. Nicholas. Motivos de conversación.
T. Dvorak, 238:Dec84-684

Neary, P. and P. O'Flaherty. Part of the Main.
M. McAlpine, 102(CanL):Autumn84-174
Nebehay, C.M. Vienna 1900.
P.V., 90:Nov84-713
Nebes, N. Funktionsanalyse von "kāna yafᶜalu."
J. Heath, 350:Mar85-228
Neckel, G., ed. Edda. (Vol 1) (5th ed rev by H. Kuhn)
S.A. Mitchell, 563(SS):Autumn84-403
Nedelijkovic, M. L'aube d'une Nation.
C. Roderick, 189(EA):Jul-Sep85-352
V. Smith, 71(ALS):May84-425
Nederlof, A.B. Pyrrhus van Epirus.
J.H. Croon, 394:Vol37fasc3/4-459
Nedjalkov, V.P., ed. Tipologija rezul'tativnyx konstrukcij.
B. Comrie, 350:Sep85-707
Needham, J. "The Completest Mode."*
J. Newman, 83:Spring84-123
P. Parrinder, 366:Autumn84-249
J.S. Ryan, 67:May84-103
Needham, J. Science in Traditional China.*
Ho Peng Yoke, 302:Vol20No2-205
Needham, J. The Shorter Science and Civilisation in China. (Vol 2) (C.A. Ronan, ed)
Ho Peng Yoke, 302:Vol20No2-204
Needham, J. - see Tsien Tsuen-hsuin
Needham, P. Twelve Centuries of Bookbindings, 400-1600.
G. Colin, 517(PBSA):Vol78No2-233
Needham, R. Against the Tranquility of Axioms. Exemplars.
M. Carrithers, 617(TLS):7Jun85-634
Needle, J. and P. Thomson. Brecht.
G. Mason, 406:Summer84-233
C.R. Mueller, 615(TJ):Mar82-128
Needleman, J. The Way of the Physician.
J. Zaleski, 469:Vol 10No4-104
Necsoc, G. Heraklit heute.
M.R. Wright, 123:Vol34No2-332
Negri, A. L'anomalie sauvage.
R. Hébert, 154:Jun84-315
Negulesco, J. Things I Did ... and Things I Think I Did.
J. Houseman, 441:24Feb85-19
Neighbour, O. The Consort and Keyboard Music of William Byrd.
L.L. Perkins, 414(MusQ):Winter84-134
Neighbour, O., ed. Music and Bibliography.
L. Madden, 447(N&Q):Apr83-178
Neighbour, O., P. Griffiths and G. Perle. Second Viennese School.
J. Dunsby, 410(M&L):Oct84-385
M. Rochester, 415:Jun84-331
Neill, W. Galloway Landscape and Other Poems.
R. Watson, 588(SSL):Vol 19-194
Neiskanen, P. - see Tuominen, A.
Neizvestnyj, È. O sinteze v iskusstve/On Synthesis in Art.
A. Leong, 574(SEEJ):Spring84-130
Nelde, P.H. Volkssprache und Kultursprache.
J.B. Berns, 685(ZDL):2/1984-268
Nelkin, D. and M.S. Brown. Workers at Risk.
M.L., 185:Jan85-400
Nelligan, E. The Complete Poems of Emile Nelligan. (F. Cogswell, ed and trans)
G.V. Downes, 102(CanL):Autumn84-153

Neuss, P., ed and trans. The Creacion of
the World.
    T. Coletti, 612(ThS):Nov84-253
    D. Devlin, 157:No151-48
    R.T. Meyer, 130:Spring84-95
Neuss, P. - see Skelton, J.
Neuwirth, A. Studien zur Komposition der
mekkanischen Suren.
    A.T. Welch, 318(JAOS):Oct-Dec83-764
Nevill, B.S. - see under St.-John Nevill,
B.
Nevill, G. Exotic Groves.
    I. Colegate, 617(TLS):3May85-489
Neville, G.H. A Memoir of D.H. Lawrence.*
(C. Baron, ed)
    K.M. Hewitt, 541(RES):May84-261
Neville, J. Last Ferry to Manly.
    P. Lewis, 364:Dec84/Jan85-148
    K.C. O'Brien, 362:14Mar85-27
    L. Taylor, 617(TLS):1Feb85-109
    442(NY):26Aug85-87
Neville, R.C. Reconstruction of Thinking.*
    R.S. Brumbaugh, 480(P&R):Vol 17No3-182
Neville, R.C. The Tao and The Daimon.*
    J. Ching, 322(JHI):Jul-Sep84-476
Nevin, D. Dream West.*
    S. Altinel, 617(TLS):17May85-561
Nevins, F.M., Jr. and M.H. Greenberg - see
Brand, C.
Nevo, R. Comic Transformations in Shake-
speare.
    I. Donaldson, 402(MLR):Jan84-144
New, C. Shanghai.
    R. Goodman, 441:7Jul85-16
"The New England Science Fiction Associa-
tion Index to the Science Fiction Maga-
zines and Original Anthologies 1982."
    R.M. Philmus, 561(SFS):Jul84-204
"The New Grove Italian Baroque Masters."
    D. Stevens, 617(TLS):25Jan85-101
"The New Jerusalem Bible."
    A. Kenny, 362:19/26Dec85-50
"The New Our Bodies, Ourselves."
    F. Randall, 441:13Jan85-16
"The New Testament in Scots." (W.L. Lori-
mer, trans)
    A. Main, 571(ScLJ):Autumn84-36
Newby, E. The Big Red Train Ride.
    617(TLS):8Mar85-271
Newby, E., ed. A Book of Travellers'
Tales.
    J. Campbell, 617(TLS):27Dec85-1477
Newby, E. On the Shores of the Mediterra-
nean.*
    C. Thubron, 617(TLS):4Jan85-6
    442(NY):29Apr85-133
Newby, E. Something Wholesale.
    617(TLS):7Jun85-651
Newell, W.H., ed. Japan in Asia, 1942-
1945.
    A.W. McCoy, 293(JASt):Feb84-370
Newey, V. Cowper's Poetry.*
    P. Faulkner, 161(DUJ):Dec83-141
    M. Golden, 661(WC):Summer84-114
    V. Klinkenborg, 173(ECS):Fall84-89
    K. Williamson, 541(RES):Nov84-553
Newlove, J. The Green Plain.
    P. Klovan, 102(CanL):Winter83-119
Newman, A. - see Sutherland, L.
Newman, C. The Post-Modern Aura.
    B. Bawer, 129:Sep85-77
    E. Gould, 441:16Jun85-42

Newman, J. Saul Bellow and History.*
    K.M. Opdahl, 395(MFS):Winter84-834
Newman, J., ed. Design and Practice in
British Architecture.
    D. Watkin, 617(TLS):5Apr85-372
Newman, J. Foundations of Religious Tol-
erance.
    K.M. Parsons, 529(QQ):Spring84-222
    E.J. Thiessen, 154:Mar84-121
Newman, J., with R. Sproat. Old High
German Reader with Computer-Formatted
Translation, Glossary and Concordance.
    E.M. Wilkinson, 67:May84-115
Newman, L.W. - see Barsov, A.A.
Newman, P.C. Company of Adventurers.
(Vol 1)
    A.H. Malcolm, 441:15Dec85-27
Newman, S.L. Liberalism at Wits' End.
    D.S. King, 617(TLS):14Jun85-657
    C. Morris, 441:20Jan85-19
Newman, S.M., ed. Bonnard.
    J. House, 617(TLS):19Apr85-446
Newmark, L., P. Hubbard and P. Prifti.
Standard Albanian.
    D. Deletant, 575(SEER):Apr84-254
Newmeyer, F.J. Grammatical Theory.
    P. Coopmans, 320(CJL):Fall84-179
    R.P. Ebert, 399(MLJ):Autumn84-298
    J.D. McCawley, 350:Sep85-668
Newmyer, R.K. Supreme Court Justice
Joseph Story.
    M. Kammen, 441:2Jun85-26
Newton, I. The Mathematical Papers of
Isaac Newton. (Vol 8) (D.T. Whiteside,
with A. Prag, eds)
    A.J. Apt, 84:Sep84-303
Newton, K.M. George Eliot, Romantic Human-
ist.*
    D. Carroll, 447(N&Q):Aug83-361
Newton, R. The Crime of Claudius Ptolemy.
    D. Rawlins, 529(QQ):Winter84-969
Newton, R. Eighteenth Century Exeter.
    P. Cornfield, 617(TLS):23Aug85-922
Newton, S.M. Fashion in the Age of the
Black Prince.*
    M.A. Michael, 447(N&Q):Oct84-448
Newton-Smith, W.H. The Rationality of
Science.*
    D. Christensen, 482(PhR):Jul84-471
    M. Tamny, 393(Mind):Jul84-465
Ney, J.W. Semantic Structures for the
Syntax of Complements and Auxiliaries
in English.
    P.C. Collins, 67:May84-110
Ngara, E. Stylistic Criticism and the
African Novel.
    M.B. Cham, 538(RAL):Fall84-441
    C.P. Sarvan, 395(MFS):Winter84-864
"Nicaragua." [World Bibliographical Ser-
ies]
    A.R. Williams, 37:Sep-Oct84-62
Ničev, A. La Catharsis Tragique
d'Aristote.*
    P. Louis, 555:Vol58fasc2-296
    I. Rutherford, 123:Vol34No2-212
Nichol, B.P. Continental Trance.
    J. Orange, 102(CanL):Autumn84-112
Nichol, B.P. The Martyrology, Book 5.
    A. Munton, 102(CanL):Winter83-137
Nicholl, C. The Fruit Palace.
    A. Henman, 617(TLS):13Sep85-993

Nicholls, P. Ezra Pound: Politics, Economics and Writing.
  L. Mackinnon, 617(TLS):11Jan85-33
Nicholls, R. The Wellcome Gems.
  J. Boardman, 123:Vol34No2-351
Nichols, G. The Fat Black Woman's Poems.
  M. Shaw, 493:Sep84-67
Nichols, P., ed. The Science in Science Fiction.
  R. Dwyer, 561(SFS):Jul84-214
Nichols, S.G., Jr. Romanesque Signs.*
  R.H. Bloch, 589:Apr84-421
  R.K. Emmerson, 401(MLQ):Sep83-314
Nicholson, L. India in Luxury.
  P. Chetwode, 617(TLS):2Aug85-863
Nicholson, M. Across the Limpopo.
  S. Uys, 617(TLS):17May85-562
Nicholson, M.G. Catalogue of Pre-1900 Imprints Relating to America in the Royal Library Brussels.
  N. Birk, 87(BB):Dec84-242
Nicholson, N.L. and L.M. Sebert. The Maps of Canada.
  A. Rayburn, 424:Mar84-81
Nickerson, C.C. and J.W. Osborne - see Cobbett, W.
Nickl, T. and H. Schnitzler - see Schnitzler, A.
Nickum, J.E., ed. Water Management Organization in the People's Republic of China.
  C.W. Pannell, 293(JASt):Feb84-322
Nicol, D.M. The Despotate of Epiros 1267-1479.
  M. Angold, 617(TLS):25Jan85-84
Nicolai, R.R. Kafkas Amerika-Roman "Der Verschollene."
  M.L. Caputo-Mayr, 221(GQ):Fall84-677
Nicolet, C., ed. Demokratia et aristokratia.
  M.H. Crawford, 313:Vol74-256
Nicolet, C., ed. Rome et la conquête du monde méditerranéen. (Vol 2)
  M.H. Crawford, 313:Vol74-209
Nicolet, C. - see Dumont, J-C. and others
Nicolson, W. The London Diaries of William Nicolson, Bishop of Carlisle 1702-1718. (C. Jones and G. Holmes, eds)
  J. Kenyon, 617(TLS):30Aug85-941
Nicosia, G. Memory Babe.
  D.W. Petrie, 395(MFS):Winter84-814
  42(AR):Winter84-120
Niebaum, H. Dialektologie.
  B.J. Koekkoek, 221(GQ):Fall84-637
Niederländer, H. Französische Schulgrammatiken und schulgrammatisches Denken in Deutschland von 1850 bis 1950.
  J. Langenbacher-Liebgott, 72:Band221 Heft1-199
Niehues-Pröbsting, H. Der Kynismus des Diogenes und der Begriff des Zynismus.
  G. Striker, 53(AGP):Band66Heft1-95
Nielsen, C. and A.M. Carl-Nielsen. Carl Nielsen: dagbøger og brevveksling med Anne Marie Carl-Nielsen. (T. Schousboe, ed)
  J. Horton, 415:Mar84-154
Nielsen, E., ed. Focus on Vienna 1900.
  W. Nehring, 680(ZDP):Band103Heft2-294
  W.E. Yates, 402(MLR):Jan84-241
Nielsen, K. and S.C. Patten, eds. Marx and Morality.*
  A.W. Wood, 482(PhR):Apr84-306

Nielsen, L.O. Theology and Philosophy in the Twelfth Century.
  J.H. Newell, Jr., 589:Apr84-425
Nielsen, W.A. The Golden Donors.
  A. Hacker, 441:29Dec85-5
Niesewand, P. The Word of a Gentleman.
  J. Lester, 441:12May85-19
Nietzsche, F. Daybreak.* (R.J. Hollingdale, trans)
  F.R. Love, 221(GQ):Summer84-512
  G.J. Stack, 543:Dec83-411
Nietzsche, F. Sämtliche Werke. (G. Colli and M. Montinari, eds) Nietzsche Werke.
  O. Distelmaier, 489(PJGG):Band91Heft1-189
Nietzsche, F. Untimely Meditations.* (R.J. Hollingdale, trans)
  R. Hollinrake, 410(M&L):Oct84-388
  C.S. Taylor, 518:Oct84-214
Nietzsche, V.R. - see under Rodríguez Nietzsche, V.
Nihom-Nijstad, S. Reflets du siècle d'or.
  P. Hecht, 90:Jun84-357
Niklaus, R. Beaumarchais: "Le Mariage de Figaro."
  W.D. Howarth, 208(FS):Oct84-466
"Patriarch Nikon on Church and State." (V.A. Tumins and G. Vernadsky, eds)
  M. Matejic, 574(SEEJ):Spring84-109
Nilsen, D.L.F. and A.P., eds. The Language of Humor: The Humor of Language.
  P. Demers, 616:Spring/Summer84-57
Nin, A. The Early Diary of Anaïs Nin. (Vol 4)
  S. Spencer, 441:16Jun85-20
Nincic, M. and P. Wallenstein, eds. Dilemmas of Economic Coercion.
  D.S., 185:Jan85-402
Nipperdey, T. Deutsche Geschichte 1800-1866.*
  H-U. Wehler, 384:Jul84-570
Nischik, R.M. Einsträngigkeit und Mehrsträngigkeit der Handlungsführung in literarischen Texten.*
  H.J. Schnackertz, 72:Band221Heft1-198
Nishitani, K. Religion and Nothingness.*
  D.A. Dilworth, 407(MN):Summer84-214
Nishitani, K. Was ist Religion?
  H. Rombach, 489(PJGG):Band91Heft2-437
Nissen, H., ed. Scandinavia During the Second World War.
  O. Høidal, 563(SS):Autumn84-378
Nissenson, H. The Tree of Life.
  I. Doig, 441:27Oct85-14
  442(NY):23Dec85-89
Nissim ben Jacob ibn Shāhīn. An Elegant Composition Concerning Relief After Adversity. (W.M. Brinner, ed and trans)
  R.P. Mottahedeh, 318(JAOS):Oct-Dec83-771
Niven, L. and J. Pournelle. Footfall.
  G. Jonas, 441:8Sep85-28
Nixon, E., ed. Thomas of Erceldoune.
  P. Bawcutt, 571(ScLJ):Winter84-39
Nixon, H.M. British Bookbindings Presented by Kenneth H. Oldaker to the Chapter Library of Westminster Abbey.*
  N. Barker, 78(BC):Winter84-531
  A. Hobson, 90:Jun84-358
  R. Nikirk, 517(PBSA):Vol78No4-528

Norris, G. Looking for Bobby.
B. Tritel, 441:14Jul85-22
442(NY):26Aug85-87
Norris, H. The Christmas Wife.
A. Becker, 441:15Dec85-28
Norris, K. Autokinesis.
R. Sommer, 137:Feb85-30
Norris, K. and P. Van Toorn, eds. The
Insecurity of Art.
J.H. Ferres, 168(ECW):Winter84/85-153
Norrman, R. The Insecure World of Henry
James's Fiction.*
S. Perosa, 395(MFS):Summer84-295
J.A. Ward, 597(SN):Vol56No1-115
North, J. Freedom Rising.
N. Ascherson, 453(NYRB):18Jul85-3
J. de St. Jorre, 441:14Jul85-21
442(NY):2Sep85-87
Norton, C.A. Writing "Tom Sawyer."*
R.B. Hauck, 395(MFS):Summer84-299
Norton, D.F. David Hume.*
K. Haakonssen, 63:Dec84-410
J. Immerwahr, 482(PhR):Jul84-444
A. MacIntyre, 449:May84-379
D.R. Raynor, 319:Jan85-113
A. Rosenberg, 529(QQ):Spring84-213
Norton, G.P. The Ideology and Language of
Translation in Renaissance France and
their Humanist Antecedents.
T. Cave, 617(TLS):18Jan85-66
Norton, P., ed. Law and Order and British
Politics.
A.W.B. Simpson, 617(TLS):29Mar85-342
Norton, T.E. and J.E. Patterson. Living
It Up.
D.W. Dunlap, 441:6Jan85-21
Norton-Smith, J. - see James I of Scotland
Norwich, J.J. The Architecture of South-
ern England.
J.M. Richards, 617(TLS):20Sep85-1020
Norwich, J.J., ed. A Taste for Travel.
J. Campbell, 617(TLS):27Dec85-1477
Nothofer, B. Dialektatlas von Zentral-
Java.
J.U. Wolff, 318(JAOS):Oct-Dec83-787
Nouhaud, M. L'utilisation de l'histoire
par les orateurs attiques.
M. Menu, 555:Vol58fasc2-297
N. Robertson, 487:Winter84-381
Nouveau, G. Pages complémentaires. (M.
Pakenham, ed)
A.L. Amprimoz, 446(NCFS):Winter-
Spring85-163
R. Little, 402(MLR):Jul84-711
Nouveau, G. Valentines and Other Poems.
(F. Clitheroe, ed and trans)
A.L. Amprimoz, 446(NCFS):Winter-
Spring85-163
"Le Nouveau Bescherelle 3."
P. Trescases, 207(FR):May85-908
"Il Nouveau Roman, punto e a capo."
D. Coste, 535(RHL):Sep/Oct84-818
"Nouvelles recherches sur 'Bouvard et
Pécuchet" de Flaubert."
C. Bernheimer, 494:Vol4No1-193
Novak, B. Nature and Culture.*
A. Wilton, 90:Feb84-99
Novak, J. Courrier de Varsovie.
H. Cronel, 450(NRF):Oct84-106
Novak, J. The Willys Dream Kit.
P-L. Adams, 61:Sep85-115
A. Codrescu, 441:11Aug85-23

Novak, M. Confession of a Catholic.
A.H. Burleigh, 396(ModA):
Spring/Summer84-255
Novak, M.E. Eighteenth-Century English
Literature.
S. Soupel, 189(EA):Jan-Mar85-82
Novak, M.E. Realism, Myth, and History in
Defoe's Fiction.*
I.A. Bell, 566:Autumn84-61
T.K. Meier, 173(ECS):Spring85-457
I. Rivers, 83:Autumn84-251
M. Schonhorn, 401(MLQ):Dec83-410
W.A. Speck, 366:Autumn84-270
639(VQR):Winter84-8
Novick, M. At Her Age.
A.S. Grossman, 441:13Oct85-24
Nowak, J. Death at the Crossings.
N. Callendar, 441:8Dec85-76
Nowak, L. Property and Power.
K. Sołtan, 185:Oct84-160
Nowlan, A. Will Ye Let the Mummers In?
D. Martens, 99:Feb85-38
Nowlan, K.B. and M.R. O'Connell. Daniel
O'Connell.
T. Garvin, 272(IUR):Autumn84-306
Noyes, R.W. The Sun, Our Star.
E. Argyle, 529(QQ):Summer84-466
Nozick, R. Philosophical Explanations.*
A. Ellis, 393(Mind):Jul84-450
L. Stevenson, 84:Mar84-83
Ntonfo, A. L'homme et l'identité dans le
roman des Antilles et Guyane françaises.
W. Bader, 343:Heft9/10-135
K. Smyley, 538(RAL):Spring84-105
Nuchelmans, G. Judgment and Proposition.
J.W. Yolton, 518:Oct84-200
Nuiten, H., W.T. Bandy and F.G. Henry, eds.
Les Fleurs expliquées.
A.S. Rosenthal, 446(NCFS):Summer85-295
Nunes, M.L. The Craft of An Absolute
Winner.*
N.H. Vieira, 238:May84-316
Núñez, J.A.G. and P. Alcázar López - see
under González Núñez, J.A. and P.
Alcázar López
Núñez, J.P. - see under Paredes Núñez, J.
Nuño, R.B. - see under Bonifaz Nuño, R.
Nussbaum, F.A. The Brink of All We Hate.*
M.J.M. Ezell, 568(SCN):Fall84-42
M. Schonhorn, 566:Spring85-190
S. Soupel, 189(EA):Jul-Sep85-324
Nuttall, A.D. A New Mimesis.*
C.M. Mazer, 615(TJ):Dec84-557
R. Paulson, 570(SQ):Winter84-492
R. Shusterman, 89(BJA):Summer84-264
Nuttall, A.D. Pope's "Essay on Man."*
S. Soupel, 189(EA):Apr-Jun85-234
Nuttall, Z. - see "The Codex Magliabechi-
ano"
Nuttgens, P. and B. The Story of Architec-
ture.
J. van der Wateren, 46:Mar84-56
Nwachukwu, P.A. Towards an Igbo Literary
Standard.
E. Ubahakwe, 355(LSoc):Jun84-283
Nye, J.S., Jr., ed. The Making of Amer-
ica's Soviet Policy.*
639(VQR):Autumn84-135
Nye, R.A. Crime, Madness, and Politics in
Modern France.
M. Ignatieff, 617(TLS):1Mar85-235
Nygren, E.J. James Ward's Gordale Scar.
W. Vaughan, 59:Sep84-368

Nyírö, L., ed. Literature and its Interpretation.
O. Scherer, 549(RLC):Jul-Sep84-353

Oakes, P. From Middle England.
639(VQR):Summer84-88
Oakeshott, M. On History and Other Essays.
W.A. Speck, 402(MLR):Apr84-384
Oakley, A. The Captured Womb.
E. Roberts, 617(TLS):28Jun85-719
Oakley, A. The Making of Marx's Critical
Theory.
D.I., 185:Jul85-984
Oakley, F. The Western Church in the
Later Middle Ages.
617(TLS):25Oct85-1219
Oakley, M. Managing Product Design.
M.W. Taylor, 324:Feb85-236
Oates, J.C. Last Days.*
C. Rumens, 617(TLS):18Oct85-1170
Oates, J.C. Solstice.
A. Duchêne, 617(TLS):22Mar85-327
R. Jones, 362:2May85-27
R.P. Sinkler, 441:20Jan85-4
Oates, S.B. Abraham Lincoln.*
42(AR):Fall84-508
Oats, W.N. A Question of Survival.
B. Godlee, 617(TLS):6Dec85-1409
O'Bell, L. Pushkin's "Egyptian Nights."
I.P. Foote, 617(TLS):11Jan85-43
Ober, W.U., ed. The Story of the Three
Bears.*
J. McMaster, 178:Mar84-120
Oberhammer, G., ed. Transzendenzerfahrung,
Vollzugshorizont des Heils.
H. Alper, 318(JAOS):Oct-Dec83-813
Oberhammer, G. - see Krick, H.
Oberhammer, G. and E. Steinkellner - see
Frauwallner, E.
Oberhuber, K. Raffaello.
D. Ekserdjian, 90:Jul84-440
Oberman, H.A. Luther.
G.O. Forde, 551(RenQ):Winter84-615
"Objects of Adornment."
D. La Plantz, 614:Spring85-26
Obolensky, D. The Byzantine Inheritance
of Eastern Europe.*
W.F. Ryan, 575(SEER):Jan84-153
O'Brian, J. David Milne and the Modern
Tradition of Painting.*
L.S. Carney, 627(UTQ):Summer84-504
O'Brien, D. Theories of Weight in the
Ancient World.* (Vol 1)
I. Mueller, 122:Jul84-240
O'Brien, E. A Fanatic Heart.*
A. Mars-Jones, 453(NYRB):31Jan85-17
O'Brien, F. - see under na Gopaleen, M.
O'Brien, K. Farewell Spain.
617(TLS):10May85-531
O'Brien, K. That Lady.
P. Craig, 617(TLS):5Jul85-757
O'Brien, M., ed. All Clever Men, Who Make
Their Way.*
I.B. Holley, Jr., 579(SAQ):Autumn84-
473
O'Brien, M. The Politics of Reproduction.
D. Réaume, 529(QQ):Summer84-474
O'Brien, T. The Nuclear Age.
G. Paley, 441:17Nov85-7
J. Romano, 61:Oct85-105

Obrist, B. Les débuts de l'imagerie
alchimique (XIV-XV siècles).
L.S. Dixon, 54:Dec84-692
J.M. Massing, 90:Aug84-505
de Oca, M.A.M. - see under Montes de Oca,
M.A.
O'Callaghan, J. Edible Anecdotes and
Other Poems.*
A. Hollinghurst, 493:Jan84-62
O'Casey, S. The Complete Plays of Sean
O'Casey. (Vol 5)
G. O'Connor, 617(TLS):19Apr85-441
Ochs, C. Women and Spirituality.
R.M. McCleary, 185:Oct84-165
Ochs, M. Rock Archives.
J. Maslin, 441:20Jan85-9
Ochshorn, J. The Female Experience and
the Nature of the Divine.
J. Tormey, 322(JHI):Oct-Dec84-619
Ochsner, J.K. H.H. Richardson: Complete
Architectural Works.*
J.V. Turano, 16:Spring84-93
Ockham, William of. Guillemus de Ockham:
Quaestiones in librum secundum Senten-
tiarum (Reportatio). (G. Gal and R.
Wood, eds) Guillemus de Ockham: Quaes-
tiones in librum tertium Sententiarum
(Reportatio). (F.E. Kelley and G.I.
Etzkorn, eds)
T.M. Tomasic, 589:Jul84-708
A.B. Wolter, 543:Mar84-633
Ocko, J.K. Bureaucratic Reform in Provin-
cial China.
J. Porter, 293(JASt):Aug84-747
"Seán Ó Conaill's Book." (S. Ó Duilearga,
ed)
N. Philip, 203:Vol95No2-264
O'Connor, D. The Metaphysics of G.E.
Moore.
P. Butchvarov, 543:Jun84-868
N. Fotion, 319:Jan85-125
T. Govier, 518:Jan84-27
O'Connor, D. Revision Exercises for Stu-
dents of Italian.
L.J. Iandoli, 399(MLJ):Winter84-408
O'Connor, F. The Presence of Grace and
Other Book Reviews by Flannery O'Connor.
(L.J. Zuber, comp; C.W. Martin, ed)
J.F. Desmond, 396(ModA):
Spring/Summer84-296
W.J. Stuckey, 395(MFS):Winter84-832
639(VQR):Winter84-7
O'Connor, G. Darlings of the Gods.*
A.E. Kalson, 615(TJ):Dec84-559
A. Vivis, 157:No154-50
O'Connor, L.F. Religion in the American
Novel.
B.H., 395(MFS):Winter84-794
O'Connor, M. Hebrew Verse Structure.*
G.M. Schramm, 350:Jun85-473
O'Connor, R. Mistress of Evergreen Plan-
tation. (A.B.W. Webb, ed)
T. Bonner, Jr., 392:Spring84-206
O'Connor, T.E. The Politics of Soviet Cul-
ture.
L. McReynolds, 104(CASS):Winter84-483
O'Connor, U. All the Olympians.
D. Rushe, 441:3Mar85-12
D. Shawe-Taylor, 442(NY):13May85-145
O'Connor, U. Celtic Dawn.
272(IUR):Autumn84-309

O'Conor, C. The Letters of Charles
O'Conor of Belanagare, 1731-1790.*
(C.C. and R.E. Ward, eds)
M.J. Durkan, 174(Éire):Spring84-139
Odegard, D. Knowledge and Scepticism.*
W.R. Abbott, 154:Dec84-725
E.H. Wolgast, 483:Jan84-133
Odets, C. Clifford Odets: Six Plays.
D. Devlin, 157:No151-48
Odin, S. Process Metaphysics and Hua-Yen
Buddhism.
D. Applebaum, 485(PE&W):Jan84-107
F.H. Cook, 293(JASt):May84-527
Odmark, J., ed. Language, Literature and
Meaning I.*
J.S. Mostow, 494:Vol4No1-181
Odmark, J. An Understanding of Jane
Austen's Novels.*
P. Honan, 447(N&Q):Jun83-254
J. Simons, 541(RES):Aug84-396
Odoevceva, I.V. Na beregax seny.
V. Krejd, 558(RLJ):Winter-Spring84-311
O'Donnell, L. Ladykiller.
N. Callendar, 441:3Feb85-37
O'Donnell, P. John Hawkes.
J.T. Matthews, 223:Spring83-108
O'Donnol, S.M. American Costume, 1915-
1970.
N. Boretz, 615(TJ):Mar84-129
O'Donoghue, B. The Courtly Love Tradi-
tion.*
G.R. Mermier, 207(FR):Dec84-280
O'Donoghue, B. Razorblades and Pencils.*
A. Stevenson, 493:Jun84-66
O'Donoghue, B. - see Hoccleve, T.
O'Donovan, J. G.B. Shaw.
B. Dolan, 305(JIL):Sep84-100
"Patrick O'Donovan: A Journalist's
Odyssey."
D. Trelford, 362:24Oct85-30
O'Driscoll, G.P. and M.J. Rizzo. The
Economics of Time and Ignorance.
P.C. Roberts, 617(TLS):11Oct85-1129
Ó Duilearga, S. - see "Seán Ó Conaill's
Book"
Oe, K., ed. The Crazy Iris.
F.M. Holloran, 441:8Sep85-14
Oelman, T. - see Pinto Delgado, J., A.
Enríquez Gómez and M. de Barrios
Oesch, M. Das Handlungsproblem.*
A. Renaut, 192(EP):Apr-Jun84-269
Oeste, R. Arno Holz.
R.H. Lawson, 133:Band17Heft1/2-162
Oettinger, N. Die Stammbildung des hethit-
ischen Verbums.
C. Watkins, 318(JAOS):Apr-Jun83-473
"Oeuvres de Jordaens au Musée de Besançon."
380:Summer84-221
O'Faolain, J. The Irish Signorina.*
D. Taylor, 364:Oct84-90
O'Faolain, J. The Obedient Wife.
L. Furman, 441:1Dec85-24
442(NY):16Dec85-168
O'Faolain, J. Women in the Wall.
P. Craig, 617(TLS):5Jul85-757
O'Flaherty, J.C. Johann Georg Hamann.
M.L. Baeumer, 406:Spring84-89
A.J. Niesz, 221(GQ):Winter84-148
O'Flaherty, W.D. Dreams, Illusions, and
Other Realities.*
C. Shackle, 617(TLS):25Oct85-1214
O'Flaherty, W.D., G. Michell and C. Berk-
son - see Berkson, C.

Ogayar, J.H. - see under Hidalgo Ogayar, J.
Ogburn, C. The Mysterious William Shake-
speare.*
E.A.J. Honigmann, 453(NYRB):17Jan85-23
Ogden, J. Jewellery of the Ancient World.
G. Seidmann, 471:Apr/May/Jun84-212
Ogletree, T.W. The Use of the Bible in
Christian Ethics.
R.M.M., 185:Oct84-191
Ogunbadejo, O. The International Politics
of Africa's Strategic Minerals.
D. Carlton, 617(TLS):8Nov85-1257
Ogunbiyi, Y., ed. Drama and Theatre in
Nigeria.
O. Owomoyela, 538(RAL):Fall84-451
Ohala, M. Aspects of Hindi Phonology.
P. Dasgupta, 261:Mar/Dec83-103
R. Singh, 320(CJL):Fall84-225
N.V. Smith, 297(JL):Sep84-417
Ohanessian, G. - see H.D.
O'Hanlon, R. Into the Heart of Borneo.*
R. Dinnage, 453(NYRB):13Jun85-29
J. Keay, 362:31Jan85-25
V. Young, 441:14Apr85-24
442(NY):27May85-99
O'Hara, D.T. Tragic Knowledge.*
S. Neuman, 506(PSt):Sep84-196
O'Hare, D., ed. Psychology and the Arts.*
J.M. Kennedy, 289:Summer84-110
O'Hear, A. Experience, Explanation and
Faith.
S.G.P., 185:Apr85-771
O'Hear, A. Karl Popper.*
J.M. Brown, 84:Mar84-86
D.E. Williams, 529(QQ):Autumn84-679
O'Hear, A. What Philosophy Is.
D.W.D. Owen, 617(TLS):4Oct85-1095
O'Heffernan, P., A.B. Lovins and L.H.
Lovins. The First Nuclear World War.
A. Dowty, 617(TLS):25Jan85-83
O'Hehir, D. I Wish This War Were Over.*
S. Altinel, 617(TLS):3May85-492
J. Mellors, 362:25Apr85-27
O'Higgins, J. Yves de Vallone.
S. O'Cathasaigh, 208(FS):Apr84-204
Ohmae, K. Triad Power.
J. Rostowski, 617(TLS):6Dec85-1391
Ohnheiser, I. Wortbildung und Synonymie.
R. Belentschikow, 682(ZPSK):Band37
Heft6-722
Ohrn, S., ed. Passing Time and Traditions.
P. Bach, 614:Summer85-31
Ohsima, J. A Unified Sensibility.
J.W. Gargano, 284:Fall84-69
O Huigin, S. The Story's Dream.
A. Brooks, 102(CanL):Autumn84-115
B. Whiteman, 526:Summer84-75
Oka, Y. Konoe Fumimaro.*
A.E. Barshay, 293(JASt):May84-550
M.W. Steele, 285(JapQ):Jan-Mar84-90
O'Keefe, B.J. Shooting Ourselves in the
Foot.
O. Schell, 441:15Sep85-14
O'Kelly, S. The Weaver's Grave.
P. Craig, 617(TLS):22Mar85-326
Okimoto, D.I., ed. Japan's Economy.
Mitsuyu Hisao, 285(JapQ):Jan-Mar84-95
I.N. Yoon, 293(JASt):Nov83-167
Okrent, D. Nine Innings.
R. Kahn, 441:5May85-30
Okudžava, B.Š. Svidanie s Bonapartom.
L.A. Krechkova, 558(RLJ):Winter-
Spring84-320

Olafson, F.A. The Dialectic of Action.
    L.J. Goldstein, 488:Sep84-410
del Olaso, E. Escepticismo e Ilustración.
    A. Alberti, 319:Oct85-589
Oldale, B.P. On the Beautiful Trail.
    M. Fee, 102(CanL):Summer84-98
Oldani, L.J. - see McCabe, W.H.
Oldenburg, E. and J. Rohweder. The Excava-
    tions at Tell Darūk (Usnu) and Arab al
    Mulk (Paltos).
    A. Hus, 555:Vol58fasc2-347
Olds, E.F. Women of the Four Winds.
    M. Peters, 441:29Sep85-47
Olds, M.C. Desire Seeking Expression.*
    L.J. Austin, 208(FS):Oct84-479
    U. Franklin, 546(RR):Mar84-266
Olds, S. The Dead and the Living.*
    J.F. Cotter, 249(HudR):Autumn84-503
    L. Gregerson, 491:Oct84-36
    L. McCarriston, 219(GaR):Winter84-899
    639(VQR):Autumn84-138
Oles, C. Quarry.*
    L. Goldensohn, 491:Apr84-40
Olesch, R. Thesaurus Linguae Dravaenopola-
    bicae. (Vol 1)
    G. Stone, 575(SEER):Oct84-571
Olesha, Y. The Complete Plays. (M. Green
    and J. Katsell, eds and trans)
    E.K. Beaujour, 574(SEEJ):Summer84-272
Oleson, J.P. Greek and Roman Mechanical
    Water-Lifting Devices.
    F. Mench, 124:Jan-Feb85-221
Olinto, A. The Water House.
    P-L. Adams, 61:Jul85-100
    442(NY):5Aug85-82
Oliphant, D. On a High Horse.
    A. Struthers, 436(NewL):Fall84-105
Oliphant, D. and T. Zigal, eds. Joyce at
    Texas.
    A.M. Cohn, 329(JJQ):Spring85-332
Oliphant, M.C.S. and T.C.D. Eaves - see
    Simms, W.G.
Oliva, A.B. - see under Bonito Oliva, A.
Olivares, J. The Love Poetry of Francisco
    de Quevedo.*
    J. Iffland, 304(JHP):Winter84-168
    R. Moore, 238:May84-305
Oliver, A. The Elberg Collection.
    442(NY):16Dec85-172
Oliver, C. The Shores of Another Sea.
    D. Barbour, 561(SFS):Jul84-200
Oliver, H.J. - see Shakespeare, W.
Oliver, J.H. The Civic Tradition and
    Roman Athens.
    P. Properzio, 124:Sep-Oct84-56
Oliver, M. American Primitive.
    J. Conway, 236:Fall-Winter84-43
    L. Gregerson, 491:Oct84-38
    A. Turner, 199:Spring85-45
Oliver, P. Songsters and Saints.
    E. Southern, 617(TLS):22Feb85-194
Oliver, R., ed. The Making of an Archi-
    tect, 1881-1981.
    R. Wesley, 576:May84-182
Oliver, R. and G.N. Sanderson, eds. The
    Cambridge History of Africa. (Vol 6)
    R. Harms, 617(TLS):29Nov85-1343
Oliver, V.L. Caodai Spiritism.
    M. Adas, 293(JASt):Nov83-201
Olivová, V. Sports and Games in the
    Ancient World.
    R. Higgins, 39:Dec84-438

Olken, I.T. With Pleated Eye and Garnet
    Wing.
    I. Malin, 651(WHR):Autumn84-301
Olkhovsky, Y. Vladimir Stasov and Russian
    National Culture.
    T. Bullard, 574(SEEJ):Fall84-418
    H. Robinson, 550(RusR):Oct84-440
Ollé, F.G. - see under González Ollé, F.
Oller, J. and P.A. Richard-Amato, eds.
    Methods That Work.
    K.E. Kintz, 207(FR):Feb85-469
del Olmo, J.M.P. - see under Parrado del
    Olmo, J.M.
Olmsted, F.L. The Papers of Frederick Law
    Olmsted.* (Vol 2) (C.E. Beveridge and
    C.C. McLaughlin, with D. Schuyler, eds)
    L.T. McDonnell, 106:Summer84-167
Olney, J., ed. Autobiography.
    P. Tobin, 223:Summer81-288
Olney, J. The Rhizome and the Flower.
    E. Mackenzie, 447(N&Q):Feb83-90
    S. Neuman, 506(PSt):Sep84-196
Olofsson, A. Relative Junctions in Writ-
    ten American English.*
    M. Celce-Murcia, 350:Mar85-220
    U. Oomen, 72:Band221Heft1-158
    E.W. Schneider, 38:Band102Heft1/2-179
Olsen, J.E.W-B. Communication Starters.
    (2nd ed)
    D. Gilliam, 399(MLJ):Summer84-201
Olsen, J.P. Organized Democracy.
    R.B. Kvavik, 563(SS):Winter84-86
Olsen, S. Problems of "seem/scheinen" Con-
    structions and their Implications for
    the Theory of Predicate Sentential Com-
    plementation.*
    F.W. Gester, 72:Band221Heft2-348
Olshan, J. Clara's Heart.
    H.F. Mosher, 441:22Dec85-18
Olson, A.M. and L.S. Rouner, eds. Trans-
    cendence and the Sacred.
    T. Dean, 485(PE&W):Apr84-211
Olson, C. The Maximus Poems. (G.F. But-
    terick, ed)
    639(VQR):Winter84-22
Olson, G. Literature as Recreation in the
    Later Middle Ages.
    M.A. Bossy, 400(MLN):Dec84-1233
    C.S. Brown, 149(CLS):Fall84-348
    R. Hastings, 278(IS):Vol39-119
    A.J. Minnis, 382(MAE):1984/1-109
    M. Thiébaux, 301(JEGP):Jul84-432
    W. Wetherbee, 589:Apr84-429
Olson, R. Science Deified and Science
    Defied.
    M. Ruse, 529(QQ):Summer84-469
Omaggio, A.C. Proficiency-Oriented Class-
    room Testing.
    V. Galloway, 399(MLJ):Winter84-385
Omaggio, A.C. and others. Kaléidoscope.
    J.C. Walz, 207(FR):Mar85-608
Oman, C. English Engraved Silver.
    M.S., 90:Jun84-369
O'Mara, J. An Historical Geography of
    Urban System Development.
    C. Earle, 656(WMQ):Jan84-151
"On Dreaming."
    G.J. Agich, 323:May84-213
O'Nan, M. - see "Folio: Essays on Foreign
    Languages and Literatures"
Ondaatje, M. Secular Love.
    L. Rosenberg, 441:22Dec85-22
    S. Solecki, 99:Jan85-32

273

O'Neil, L.T. Māyā in Śaṅkara.
  M.M. Mehta, 318(JAOS):Jul-Sep83-657
O'Neil, L.T. Towards the Life Divine.*
  J. O'Connor, 293(JASt):May84-582
O'Neill, A. Poesias Completas 1951-1981.
  J. Kleinstück, 384:Jun84-448
O'Neill, E. Eugene O'Neill at Work.* (V.
  Floyd, ed)
  D.S. McDermott, 615(TJ):Dec82-557
  M.L. Ranald, 612(ThS):May84-115
O'Neill, J. Essaying Montaigne.*
  C.M. Bauschatz, 478:Apr84-137
O'Neill, P. German Literature in English
  Translation.*
  J.K. Wikeley, 107(CRCL):Mar84-119
O'Neill, T. The Irish Hand.
  R. McKitterick, 617(TLS):29Mar85-367
O'Neill, T.J. Bakke and the Politics of
  Equality.
  K. Minogue, 617(TLS):16Aug85-899
O'Neill, W.L. A Better World.*
  J. Gardner, 390:Nov84-58
Ong, W.J. Fighting for Life.
  K.H. Jamieson, 480(P&R):Vol 17No3-178
Ong, W.J. Orality and Literacy.*
  J.D. Erickson, 188(ECr):Fall84-86
  E.L. Rivers, 131(CL):Spring84-162
Onians, J. Art and Thought in the Hellen-
  istic Age.
  C.E. Vafopoulou-Richardson, 54:Dec84-
    690
"The Onslaught."
  A. Knopf, 441:19May85-22
Onyeama, D. African Legend.
  M. Crowder, 617(TLS):19Apr85-427
Oomen, U. Die englische Sprache in den
  USA. (Pt 1)
  D. Stark, 350:Mar85-219
Oostens-Wittamer, Y. Victor Horta:
  L'Hôtel Solvay/The Solvay House.
  D.A. Hanser, 576:Mar84-92
"The Open University: Arts; a Third Level
  Course, Modern Art and Modernism."
  S. Watney, 59:Mar84-102
Opfell, O.S. The King James Bible Transla-
  tors.
  R.A. Linenthal, 517(PBSA):Vol78No3-381
Opie, I. and P., eds. The Oxford Book of
  Narrative Verse.*
  M. Jarman, 249(HudR):Autumn84-491
  566:Autumn84-75
  639(VQR):Spring84-60
Opie, I. and P. The Singing Game.
  D.J. Enright, 362:4Jul85-30
  A. Lurie, 453(NYRB):24Oct85-35
  W. Mellers, 617(TLS):29Nov85-1355
Opie, J. Britains Toy Soldiers 1893-1932.
  J. Carswell, 617(TLS):20Dec85-1466
Opiela, S. Le réel dans la logique de
  Hegel.
  H. Faes, 542:Oct-Dec84-485
Opland, J. Anglo-Saxon Oral Poetry.*
  A. Haarder, 677(YES):Vol 14-301
Opolka, U. and others - see Bloch, E.
Oppel, H., ed. Das englische Drama der
  Gegenwart.
  W. Riehle, 224(GRM):Band34Heft1/2-254
Oppenheim, L. Intentionality and Intersub-
  jectivity.
  F. Wolfzettel, 547(RF):Band96Heft3-364
Oppenheimer, H. The Hope of Happiness.
  H. Meynell, 483:Oct84-542

Oppenheimer, R. Robert Oppenheimer: Let-
  ters and Recollections. (A.K. Smith and
  C. Weiner, eds)
  J.W. Grove, 529(QQ):Spring84-73
O'Prey, P. - see Graves, R.
Orbell, M. The Natural World of the Maori.
  G. Palmer, 617(TLS):23Aug85-918
Orcibal, J. - see Benoît de Canfield
Ord-Hume, A.W.J.G. Joseph Haydn and the
  Mechanical Organ.
  D. McCaldin, 415:Jun84-333
"Ordbog over det norrøne i rosasprog."
  M.E. Kalinke, 301(JEGP):Jul84-397
Ordish, G. The Living Garden.
  J. Buxton, 617(TLS):3May85-507
Orduna, G. - see López de Ayala, P.
O'Reilly, T. - see Parker, A.A.
Orel, H., ed. Kipling: Interviews and
  Recollections.*
  H-P. Breuer, 395(MFS):Winter84-752
Orel, V. Mendel.
  R.C. Lewontin, 453(NYRB):10Oct85-18
  J.A. Secord, 617(TLS):18Jan85-70
Oreström, B. Turn-taking in English Con-
  versation.
  J.C.P. Auer, 353:Vol21No5-742
Orgel, J.R. Undying Passion.
  S. Offit, 441:24Feb84-23
Oriard, M.V. Dreaming of Heroes.*
  F. Camoin, 651(WHR):Spring84-78
Origo, I. A Need to Testify.*
  P. Vansittart, 364:Apr/May84-118
Orihuela, A.G. "Las Tres Américas" y el
  modernismo.
  I.M. Zuleta, 263(RIB):Vol34No3/4-432
O'Riordan, J. A Guide to O'Casey's Plays.
  G. O'Connor, 617(TLS):19Apr85-441
Orjuela, H.H. Urupary.
  D. Turner, 238:Mar84-151
Orledge, R. Debussy and the Theatre.*
  J-P. Bracey and J.B. Sanders,
    446(NCFS):Winter-Spring85-181
  M. Cooper, 208(FS):Apr84-220
  R. Howat, 415:Apr84-210
  L.B. Konrad, 210(FrF):Sep84-379
  R. Nichols, 410(M&L):Oct84-379
  R. Swift, 451:Fall84-164
Orlova, A. Musorgsky's Days and Works.
  (R.J. Guenther, ed and trans)
  M. Cooper, 575(SEER):Oct84-601
Orme, N. Early British Swimming 55 B.C.-
  A.D. 1719 With the First Swimming Trea-
  tise in English, 1595.*
  M. West, 551(RenQ):Autumn84-457
Orme, N. From Childhood to Chivalry.
  J. Catto, 617(TLS):9Aug85-884
Ormerod, R. Dead Ringer.
  T.J. Binyon, 617(TLS):5Apr85-394
Ormond, R., with J. Rishel and R. Hamlyn.
  Sir Edwin Landseer.
  S.P. Casteras, 54:Jun84-344
Ormrod, R. Una Troubridge.*
  T. Mallon, 441:8Sep85-3
  J. Neville, 364:Aug/Sep84-148
Ornstein, R. and R.F. Thompson. The Amaz-
  ing Brain.
  I. Rosenfield, 453(NYRB):14Mar85-34
O'Rourke, B. The Conscience of the Race.*
  G. O'Brien, 677(YES):Vol 14-358
O'Rourke, M. Rhetoric and Reform.
  L.V.R., 568(SCN):Fall84-54
Orpen, N. Airlift to Warsaw.
  A. Knopf, 441:3Mar85-23

Pack, R. Faces in a Single Tree.
    R.W. Flint, 441:27Jan85-18
    W.H. Pritchard, 249(HudR):Summer84-332
Packe, M. King Edward III. (L.C.B. Sea-
man, ed)
    R.H. Jones, 589:Oct84-933
Packer, B.L. Emerson's Fall.*
    D. Robinson, 639(VQR):Spring84-353
    R.A. Yoder, 591(SIR):Summer84-268
Packer, W. Henry Moore.
    C. Reid, 617(TLS):15Nov85-1284
Packman, D. Vladimir Nabokov.*
    B.L. Clark, 587(SAF):Spring84-113
Padfield, P. Dönitz.*
    639(VQR):Autumn84-122
Padfield, P. Tide of Empires. (Vol 2)
    L.K.J. Glassey, 566:Spring85-181
Padilla, H. Heroes Are Grazing in My Gar-
den.
    M. Wood, 453(NYRB):18Jul85-33
Padley, G.A. Grammatical Theory in West-
ern Europe 1500-1700.
    V. Salmon, 617(TLS):31May85-612
Padoan, G. La commedia rinascimentale
veneta.
    P. Lagorio, 228(GSLI):Vol 161fasc513-
    143
Padwick, E.W. A Bibliography of Cricket.
(2nd ed)
    T.D. Smith, 617(TLS):12Apr85-419
Paffrath, E., ed. Brecht 1980.
    I. Schuster, 406:Winter84-480
Pagani, I. La teoria linguistica di Dante.
    A. Scaglione, 589:Apr84-432
Pagano, M., ed. Dits des Cornetes.
    G. Roques, 553(RLiR):Jan-Jun84-257
Page, D.H. and V.M.P. Da Rosa. Heritage
of the North American Indian People.
    H. Adams, 529(QQ):Summer84-456
    M. Whitaker, 102(CanL):Winter83-79
Page, D.L., ed. Further Greek Epigrams.*
(rev by R.D. Dawe and J. Diggle)
    O. Masson, 555:Vol158fasc1-97
    H. White, 122:Apr84-163
Page, E. Scent of Death.
    T.J. Binyon, 617(TLS):5Jul85-757
Page, E.C. Political Authority and Bureau-
cratic Power.
    D. Wass, 617(TLS):26Jul85-817
Page, J. Pastorale.
    C. Verderese, 441:19May85-23
Page, M. John Arden.
    H. Rorrison, 157:No153-50
Page, M. Set a Thief.
    T.J. Binyon, 617(TLS):11Jan85-42
Page, N. A Dickens Companion.*
    R.J. Dunn, 594:Winter84-458
    S. Shatto, 155:Summer84-118
Page, N. A.E. Housman.*
    P.B. McElwain, 590:Dec84-58
Page, N., ed. Nabokov: The Critical Her-
itage.*
    J.E. Rivers, 534(RALS):Autumn82-254
    C.T. Williams, 405(MP):May85-445
Page, N. - see "Thomas Hardy Annual"
Page, R. Class. (A.M. Wentink, ed)
    A. Barzel, 151:Jul84-82
Page, S.W. The Geopolitics of Leninism.
    R.H.W. Theen, 104(CASS):Fall84-311
Page, T. - see Gould, G.

Pageaux, D-H., ed. Recherches et Etudes
Comparatistes Ibéro-Françaises de la
Sorbonne nouvelle.
    H-P. Endress, 52:Band19Heft2-223
Pagel, W. Joan Baptista van Helmont.
    T.H. Jobe, 551(RenQ):Autumn84-428
Pagel, W. Paracelsus. (2nd ed)
    A.G. Debus, 111:Fall85-6
Pagels, H.R. Perfect Symmetry.
    M. Gardner, 453(NYRB):13Jun85-31
    J. Polkinghorne, 617(TLS):22Nov85-1320
    D.N. Schramm, 441:22Sep85-15
    442(NY):16Sep85-123
Pagliano, G. Servo e padrone, L'orizzonte
dei testi.
    A. Sempoux, 356(LR):Nov84-327
Pagnini, M. Pragmatica della letteratura.
    A.L. Johnson, 494:Autumn82-169
Paige, C. The Right to Lifers.
    J. Glover, 453(NYRB):30May85-19
Pailin, D.A. Attitudes to Other Religions.
    H. Erskine-Hill, 617(TLS):15Feb85-182
Paillard, D. Voix et Aspect en Russe
contemporain.
    R.D. Brecht, 104(CASS):Spring-Summer84-
    153
Paillet, M. Les Hommes de pouvoir.
    A.D. Ketchum, 207(FR):Feb85-478
Painter, N.I. The Narrative of Hosea
Hudson.
    T. Draper, 453(NYRB):9May85-32
Painter, P. Getting to Know the Weather.
    A. Becker, 441:15Dec85-28
Pais, A. "Subtle is the Lord ... "
    C. Ward, 577(SHR):Spring84-175
Pakenham, M., ed. Portraits littéraires.
    B.C. Swift, 208(FS):Apr84-219
Pakenham, M. - see Nouveau, G.
Pakenham, V. The Noonday Sun.
    E.S. Turner, 617(TLS):24May85-571
Pakula, H. The Last Romantic.
    P-L. Adams, 61:Apr85-141
    R. Lacey, 441:14Apr85-44
    G. Noel, 362:27Jun85-30
    S. Runciman, 617(TLS):4Oct85-1106
Pal, P. Art of Tibet. Tibetan Paintings.
    M. Aris, 617(TLS):29Mar85-360
Pal, P. and L. Fournier. A Buddhist Para-
dise.*
    D. Klimburg-Salter, 293(JASt):Feb84-
    359
de Palacio, J. William Godwin et son
monde intérieur.*
    A.G. Fredman, 340(KSJ):Vol33-229
Palacios, M.A. - see under Asín Palacios,
M.
Palau de Nemes, G. Inicios de Zenobia y
Juan Ramón Jiménez en América.
    R.A. Cardwell, 402(MLR):Apr84-479
    M. Coke-Enguídanos, 400(MLN):Mar84-399
    J.C. Wilcox, 240(HR):Spring84-244
Paley, G. Later the Same Day.
    R.R. Harris, 441:14Apr85-7
    A. Mars-Jones, 617(TLS):22Nov85-1311
    R. Towers, 453(NYRB):15Aug85-26
Paley, M.D. The Continuing City.*
    H. Adams, 191(ELN):Jun85-72
    S.D. Cox, 173(ECS):Spring85-391
    F. Piquet, 189(EA):Apr-Jun85-236
Palla, R. - see Prudentius
Palladas. Poems. (T. Harrison, trans)
    C. Rawson, 617(TLS):4Jan85-10

Pallis, M. A Buddhist Spectrum.
S.H. Nasr, 485(PE&W):Oct84-451
Pallucchini, R. La Pittura Veneziana nel
Seicento.
J. Fletcher, 90:Sep84-581
Pallucchini, R. and A. Mariuz. L'opera
completa di Piazzetta.
K. Garlick, 39:May84-387
Pallucchini, R. and F. Rossi. Giovanni
Cariani.
C. Gould, 39:Aug84-149
G. Robertson, 90:Sep84-574
Pallucchini, R. and P. Rossi. Tintoretto.*
D. Rosand, 90:Jul84-444
Palm, C. Greule, Golch und Geigerich.
F. Freund, 597(SN):Vol56No2-239
Palma-Cayet, P-V. L'Histoire Prodigieuse
du Docteur Fauste.* (Y. Cazaux, ed)
E.S. Ginsberg, 539:May85-150
Palma-Ferreira, J. Do pícaro na litera-
tura portuguesa.
M. Guterres, 86(BHS):Oct84-529
Palmer, A. Movable Feasts.*
S. Soupel, 189(EA):Oct-Dec85-490
Palmer, A. and V. Who's Who in Shake-
speare's England.*
D.M. Zesmer, 570(SQ):Summer84-244
Palmer, A.S., P.J.M. Groot and G.A. Tros-
per, eds. The Construct Validation of
Tests of Communicative Competence.*
D. Biber, 350:Mar85-240
Palmer, B., Jr. The 25-Year War.*
A.H. Bernstein, 129:Mar85-77
E.A. Cohen, 441:21Jul185-6
Palmer, C., ed. The Britten Companion.*
M. Cooper, 415:Oct84-573
M. Hall, 607:Dec84-41
Palmer, F.R. Modality and the English
Modals.
R. Hickey, 38:Band102Heft3/4-494
Palmer, H. - see Kant, I.
Palmer, J.J.N., ed. Froissart, Historian.*
M. Vale, 382(MAE):1984/1-142
Palmer, K. - see Shakespeare, W.
Palmer, M. First Figure.
R. Waldrop, 441:1Dec85-36
Palmer, R.R. The Improvement of Humanity.
R.N. Gildea, 617(TLS):26Apr85-462
Panā, Z., ed. Poezii din închisori.
D. Deletant, 617(TLS):4Jan85-10
Pancake, B.D'J. The Stories of Breece D'J
Pancake.*
R. Nelson, 639(VQR):Winter84-169
Pang-Hsin, T. - see under Ting Pang-Hsin
Pang-Yuan, C. and others - see under Chi
Pang-Yuan and others
Panhuis, D.G.J. The Communicative Perspec-
tive in the Sentence.
P.J. Hopper, 350:Jun85-466
J.G.F. Powell, 123:Vol34No1-75
Paniagua, M.R.P. - see under Prieto Pani-
agua, M.R.
Panichas, G.A. - see Babbitt, I.
Panisse, C.R. - see under Ríos Panisse, C.
Panofsky, E. Idea (Contribution à l'his-
toire du concept de l'ancienne théorie
de l'art).
P. Dubrunquez, 450(NRF):Oct84-94
Panthel, H.W., ed. Materialen zu Rainer
Maria Rilkes Tod.
B.L. Bradley, 133:Band17Heft1/2-167
T. Ritmeester and E. Schwarz, 564:
Sep84-225

Papanek, H. and G. Minault, eds. Sep-
arate Worlds.
P.J. Bertocci, 293(JASt):May84-583
Pape, G. and T. Aspler. The Music Wars.
N. Callendar, 441:13Oct85-29
"Papel de Aleluyas."
S. Herpoel, 356(LR):Feb/May84-136
Papenfuse, E.C. and J.M. Coale 3d, comps.
The Hammond-Harwood House Atlas of His-
torical Maps of Maryland, 1608-1908.
J.H. Long, 656(WMQ):Jan84-146
Paper, L.J. Brandeis.
J.L. Rauh, Jr., 432(NEQ):Sep84-430
Paperno, D. Zapiski moskovskogo pianista.
H. Robinson, 550(RusR):Jul84-294
Papernyj, Z.S. Vopreki vsem pravnilam.
M. Heim, 574(SEEJ):Spring84-117
"Papers on Monetary Economics."* [Mon-
etary Authority of Singapore]
Y.C. Jao, 302:Vol20No2-243
Papineau, D. For Science in the Social
Sciences.
B. Fay, 488:Dec84-529
Papmehl, K.V. - see Soloviev, S.M.
Paradis, M., ed. Readings in Aphasia in
Bilingual Polyglots.
L.M. Stanford, 320(CJL):Spring84-83
Parain-Vial, J. Philosophie des sciences
de la nature.
J. Largeault, 542:Apr-Jun84-227
Pare, R. Photography and Architecture:
1839-1939.*
L. Koltun, 627(UTQ):Summer84-520
Paré, Y. La Mort d'Alexandre.
J.M. Paterson, 102(CanL):Winter83-142
de Paredes, A.V. Institución y origen del
arte de la imprenta. (J. Moll, ed)
D.W. Cruickshank, 304(JHP):Spring84-
239
Paredes Núñez, J. Los cuentos de Emilia
Pardo Bazán.
M. Lentzen, 547(RF):Band96Heft1/2-217
Paredi, A. A History of the Ambrosiana.
382(MAE):1984/2-342
Parekh, B. Contemporary Political Think-
ers.
R. Nelson, 628(UWR):Spring-Summer85-93
Parel, A., ed. Ideology, Philosophy and
Politics.
R.E.G., 185:Jan85-387
Parel, A. and T. Flanagan, eds. Theories
of Property.
A.W.J. Harper, 154:Sep84-559
Parent, M.N. The Roof in Japanese Bud-
dhist Architecture.
W.H. Coaldrake, 407(MN):Autumn84-366
Parent-Lardeur, F. Les Cabinets de lec-
ture.*
B.T. Cooper, 446(NCFS):Summer-Fall84-
231
Paretsky, S. Killing Orders.
N. Callendar, 441:15Sep84-33
442(NY):2Sep85-87
Parfit, D. Reasons and Persons.*
A.C. Baier, 518:Oct84-220
Parfitt, G. English Poetry of the Seven-
teenth Century.
J. Briggs, 617(TLS):13Dec85-1436
Parfitt, T. Operation Moses.
B. Wasserstein, 617(TLS):13Dec85-1420

Parins, J.W., R.J. Dilligan and T.K.
Bender. A Concordance to Conrad's
"Nostromo."
H.H. Kollmeier, 136:Vol 17No1-75
Paris, J. Après une légère indisposition.
M. Fougères, 207(FR):Apr85-759
Paris, R-M. Camille Claudel 1864-1943.*
J. Revol, 450(NRF):Jul/Aug84-190
Parish, H.R. Las Casas as a Bishop/Las
Casas, Obispo.*
A. Pagden, 86(BHS):Jan84-67
Park, J. Learning to Dream.
N. Wapshott, 362:6Jun85-31
Park, K. Doctors and Medicine in Early
Renaissance Florence.
J.N. Stephens, 617(TLS):20Dec85-1465
Park, M. and G.E. Markowitz. Democratic
Vistas.
A. Boyer, 441:18Aug85-20
Parker, A.A. The Philosophy of Love in
Spanish Literature. (T. O'Reilly, ed)
R. Boase, 304(JHP):Fall84-67
A. Fowler, 617(TLS):8Nov85-1260
Parker, G. and others. The Thirty Years'
War.
J. Israel, 617(TLS):17May85-552
Parker, H. Flawed Texts and Verbal Icons.
L. Mackinnon, 617(TLS):15Feb85-177
Parker, R. Miasma.*
J. Herington, 124:Jul-Aug85-615
É. des Places, 555:Vol58fasc2-289
Parker, R.B. A Catskill Eagle.
N. Callendar, 441:30Jun85-29
442(NY):22Jul85-90
Parker, R.B., ed. "The Glass Menagerie."
E.M. Jackson, 397(MD):Jun84-277
Parker, R.B. Inscrutable Earth.
S. Boxer, 441:6Jan85-21
Parker, R.B. - see Jonson, B.
Parker, T. Soldier, Soldier.
L. Taylor, 617(TLS):27Sep85-1050
C. Wain, 362:3Oct85-25
Parker, T.J. Laguna Heat.
N. Callendar, 441:8Dec85-76
Parker, W.E. - see Schwarz, H.
Parkin, D., ed. The Anthropology of Evil.
J.D.M. Derrett, 617(TLS):19Jul85-805
W. Kaminer, 441:6Oct85-29
Parkin, F. Krippendorf's Tribe.
J. Grace, 617(TLS):12Apr85-406
Parkin, F. Marxism and Class Theory.
W. Westergard-Thorpe, 104(CASS):Fall84-
370
Parkinson, G.H.R., ed. Marx and Marxisms.
S. Bann, 483:Jan84-128
Parkinson de Saz, S.M. A University
English Grammar for Spanish Speakers.
J. Bregazzi, 202(FMod):No68/70-404
Parks, R.N., ed. Rhode Island.
N.N. Shipton, 432(NEQ):Sep84-447
517(PBSA):Vol78No3-383
Parks, T. Tongues of Flame.
J. Winterson, 617(TLS):13Sep85-1001
Parmalee, P.L. Brecht's America.*
C.R. Mueller, 615(TJ):Mar82-128
Parmenides. Parménide, "Le Poème." (J.
Beaufret, ed)
M. Haar, 192(EP):Jul-Sep84-404
Parmenter, R. Lawrence in Oaxaca.
D. Cavitch, 441:14Apr85-30
442(NY):13May85-147
Parnell, M. Eric Linklater.*
G. Mangan, 617(TLS):26Apr85-459

Pàroli, T. La morte di Beowulf.
T.H. Leinbaugh, 589:Oct84-935
Parpulova, L. Bǎlgarskite vǎlšebni
prikazki vǎvedenie v poetikata. (P.
Dinekov, ed)
W. Ziel, 196:Band25Heft1/2-150
Parr, J., ed. Childhood and Family in
Canadian History.
L.R., 102(CanL):Winter83-189
Parr, N. James Hogg at Home.*
K. Costain, 588(SSL):Vol 19-277
Parrado del Olmo, J.M. Los escultores
seguidores de Berruguete en Palencia.
M. Estella, 48:Jan-Mar84-122
Parret, H. Contexts of Understanding.
D.H. Whalen, 307:Apr84-91
Parret, H., ed. Le langage en contexte.
P. Swiggers, 567:Vol50No3/4-283
Parrinder, P. James Joyce.
D. Sexton, 617(TLS):5Apr85-390
Parrinder, P. Science Fiction.*
S. Thomason, 161(DUJ):Dec83-150
J.M. Walker, 677(YES):Vol 14-366
Parris, L., ed. Pre-Raphaelite Papers.
D. Cherry and G. Pollock, 59:Dec84-480
M. Pointon, 90:Jun84-365
Parris, L., ed. The Pre-Raphaelites.
D. Cherry and G. Pollock, 59:Dec84-480
Parronchi, A. Un trattato inedito di
architettura militare riferibile a
Baldassare Peruzzi.
F.P. Fiore, 576:Mar84-79
Parrott, B. Politics and Technology in
the Soviet Union.
A. Brown, 617(TLS):27Sep85-1078
A.H. Smith, 575(SEER):Oct84-622
Parrott, J., with V. Ashkenazy. Beyond
Frontiers.
P.G. Davis, 441:28Apr85-12
Parry, G. The Golden Age Restor'd.*
R.R. Rea, 577(SHR):Winter84-82
P. Thomas, 90:May84-300
Parry, G. Seventeenth-Century Poetry.
J. Briggs, 617(TLS):13Dec85-1436
Parry, L. William Morris Textiles.*
P. Thompson, 59:Dec84-496
Parry, M., A. Lord and D. Bynum, eds.
Serbo-Croatian Heroic Songs. (Vols 3, 6
and 14)
I. Markoff, 187:Fall85-522
Parshall, L.B. The Art of Narration in
Wolfram's "Parzival" and Albrecht's
"Jungerer Titurel."*
M.E. Gibbs, 406:Fall84-351
K. Smits, 680(ZDP):Band103Heft3-451
Parsons, A. The Pride and the Fall.*
R.W. Apple, Jr., 441:21Apr85-16
D. Spanier, 176:Apr85-74
442(NY):19Aug85-90
Parsons, C. Mathematics in Philosophy.
W.V. Quine, 311(JP):Dec84-783
Parsons, D.S.J. Roy Campbell.*
R. Smith, 538(RAL):Spring84-140
Parsons, T. Nonexistent Objects.*
G. Bealer, 316:Jun84-652
K. Fine, 519(PhS):Jan84-95
Partee, M.H. Plato's Poetics.*
R.J. Yanal, 449:Mar84-184
Partlow, R.B., Jr. and H.T. Moore, eds.
D.H. Lawrence.
K.M. Hewitt, 541(RES):Aug84-415

Partner, P. The Murdered Magicians.
F.L. Cheyette, 589:Oct84-937
C. Fasolt, 551(RenQ):Spring84-67
Partnow, E., ed. The Quotable Woman.
B. Brophy, 617(TLS):26Jul85-814
Partridge, A.C. Language and Society in
Anglo-Irish Literature.
D. Kiberd, 617(TLS):2Aug85-848
Partridge, C. Minor American Fiction 1920-
1940.
G. Scharnhorst, 395(MFS):Winter84-803
Partridge, E. A Dictionary of Slang and
Unconventional English.* (8th ed) (P.
Beale, ed)
L. Rosten, 176:Feb85-27
Partridge, F. Everything to Lose.
C. Driver, 362:14Nov85-43
M. Forster, 617(TLS):25Oct85-1210
Pascal, B. Les "Pensées" de Pascal. (F.
Kaplan, ed)
C. Meurillon, 475:Vol 11No20-241
Pascal, B. and P. de Fermat. La correspon-
dance de Blaise Pascal et de Pierre de
Fermat. (P-J. About and M. Boy, eds)
D. Merllié, 542:Jul-Sep84-394
Pascal, R. Kafka's Narrators.*
K. von Abrams and J.J. White, 402(MLR):
Jul84-750
J. Lothe, 172(Edda):1984/1-55
Pascall, R., ed. Brahms.*
B. Newbould, 410(M&L):Jan84-73
R. Swift, 451:Fall84-164
Pascoli, G. Selected Poems. (P.R. Horne,
ed)
E. Mahler-Schächter, 278(IS):Vol139-140
Pascual, F.J.B. - see under Blasco Pascual,
F.J.
Paskoff, P.F. and D.J. Wilson, eds. The
Cause of the South.*
F. Hobson, 392:Winter83/84-128
Pasolini, P.P. Actes Impurs [suivi de]
Amado Mio. (C. D'Angeli, ed)
F. Poirié, 450(NRF):Apr84-137
Pasolini, P.P. A Violent Life.
A. Rice, 441:3Nov85-38
Passacaqua, M., ed. Tre Testi Grammat-
icali Bobbiesi (GL V 555-566; 634-654;
IV 207-216 Kiel).
A.C. Dionisotti, 313:Vol74-202
Passeron, R., ed. La création collective.
A. Neuschäfer, 72:Band221Heft2-463
Passuth, K. Moholy-Nagy.
A. Anderson, 441:4Aug85-16
R. Arnheim, 617(TLS):12Jul85-764
Pasternak, A. A Vanished Present.* (A.P.
Slater, ed and trans)
H. Robinson, 441:21Jul85-8
Pasternak, B. I Remember.
R.B. Anderson, 395(MFS):Winter84-734
Pasternak, B. My Sister — Life [and] A
Sublime Malady.*
E. Grosholz, 249(HudR):Spring84-138
S. Pratt, 574(SEEJ):Summer84-271
Pasternak, B. Pasternak on Art and Cre-
ativity. (A. Livingstone, ed)
S. Karlinsky, 617(TLS):22Nov85-1315
Pasternak, B. Selected Poems.
J.F. Cotter, 249(HudR):Autumn84-497
639(VQR):Spring84-61
Pasternak, B., M. Tsvetayeva and R.M.
Rilke. Letters: Summer 1926. (Y.
Pasternak, Y. Pasternak and K.M.
[continued]

[continuing]
Azadovsky, eds)
J. Bayley, 453(NYRB):5Dec85-3
V.S. Pritchett, 442(NY):25Nov85-159
H. Robinson, 441:21Jul85-8
Pastorius, F.D. Deliciae Hortenses or
Garden-Recreations and Voluptates
Apianae. (C.E. Schweitzer, ed)
H. Heinen, 564:May84-132
Paszkiewicz, H. The Rise of Moscow's
Power.
T.S. Noonan, 104(CASS):Winter84-452
Patai, D. Myth and Ideology in Contempor-
ary Brazilian Fiction.
P.B. Dixon, 395(MFS):Summer84-338
R.A. Preto-Rodas, 238:May84-316
Patai, D. The Orwell Mystique.
T.G. Ash, 617(TLS):8Feb85-147
V. Held, 441:3Feb85-12
Patai, R. On Jewish Folklore.
G. Haskell, 650(WF):Oct84-278
M. Slobin, 292(JAF):Oct-Dec84-473
Pater, W. The Renaissance. (D.L. Hill,
ed)
L. Brake, 506(PSt):May84-78
Patera, T. Obzor tvorčestva i analiz mos-
kovskix povestej Jurija Trifonova.
R.N. Porter, 574(SEEJ):Fall84-411
Paterson, A. Herbs in the Garden.
G. Ordish, 617(TLS):26Jul85-835
Patey, D.L. Probability and Literary Form.
A. Morvan, 189(EA):Oct-Dec85-462
Patnaik, N. A Second Paradise.
442(NY):11Nov85-158
Paton, W. Man and Mouse.
P. Singer, 453(NYRB):17Jan85-46
Patricius, M. - see under Menas Patricius
Patrick, J. Architecture in Tennessee,
1768-1897.*
C.W. Bishir, 658:Summer/Autumn84-217
Patrick, V. Family Business.
A. Krystal, 441:3Nov85-30
Patrides, C.A., ed. Approaches to Sir
Thomas Browne.*
J. van Dorsten, 179(ES):Apr84-181
P.E. Forte, 539:Feb85-62
D.B.J. Randall, 579(SAQ):Summer84-359
G.M. Ridden, 506(PSt):Dec84-263
Patrides, C.A. Premises and Motifs in
Renaissance Thought and Literature.*
J. Egan, 568(SCN):Spring-Summer84-3
R. Flannagan, 391:May84-64
M-M. Martinet, 189(EA):Jul-Sep85-316
F.P., 604:Winter84-3
Patrides, C.A. - see Milton, J.
Pattaro, S.T. - see under Tugnoli Pattaro,
S.
Patterson, A. Censorship and Interpreta-
tion.
H.R. Woudhuysen, 617(TLS):25Oct85-1204
Patterson, A., ed. Roman Images.
639(VQR):Summer84-99
Patterson, M. Peter Stein.*
D. Thomas, 610:Summer84-157
Patterson, M.L.P., with W. Alspaugh.
South Asian Civilizations.
R. Young, 318(JAOS):Oct-Dec83-815
Patterson, R. Emily Dickinson's Imagery.
(M.H. Freeman, ed)
C.R. Steele, 106:Spring84-63
Patterson, W.C. The Plutonium Business
and the Spread of the Bomb.
P. Windsor, 617(TLS):17May85-557

280

Patterson, W.T. The Genealogical Struc-
ture of Spanish.*
  T.R. Dvorak, 238:Mar84-156
Patti, A.L.A. Why Vietnam?*
  T.B. Lam, 293(JASt):May84-607
Pattison, D.G. From Legend to Chronicle.
  L. Chalon, 304(JHP):Fall84-75
Pattison, R. On Literacy.*
  C. Kramarae, 301(JEGP):Oct84-549
Patzer, H. Die griechische Knabenliebe.
  D. Bain, 123:Vol34No1-86
  K.J. Dover, 303(JoHS):Vol 104-239
Pau-Llosa, R. Sorting Metaphors.
  D. Trakas, 219(GaR):Summer84-440
Paufošima, R.F. Fonetika slova i frazy v
severnorusskix govorax.
  W. Lehfeldt, 559:Vol18No2-188
Paul, D. Prima Donna at Large.
  N. Callendar, 441:13Oct85-29
Paul, R.A. The Tibetan Symbolic World.*
  G.R. Elder, 485(PE&W):Apr84-230
Pauler, R. Das Regnum Italiae in otton-
ischer Zeit.
  D.H. Miller, 589:Oct84-989
Pauli, L. The Alps.
  S. Piggott, 617(TLS):8Feb85-149
Paulin, T. Ireland and the English Crisis.
  P. Craig, 617(TLS):19Apr85-441
Paulin, T. Liberty Tree.*
  T. Eagleton, 565:Summer84-76
  A. Frazier, 174(Éire):Spring84-123
  M. Harmon, 272(IUR):Spring84-126
Paulin, T. A New Look at the Language
Question.
  M. Harmon, 272(IUR):Spring84-126
Paulin, T. The Riot Act.
  D. Davis, 362:5Dec84-33
Paulis, L. Technique and Design of Cluny
Lace.
  C. Campbell, 614:Spring85-30
Paulsen, W. Deutsche Literatur des Expres-
sionismus.
  G.P. Knapp, 680(ZDP):Band103Heft2-298
Paulsen, W., ed. Österreichische Gegen-
wart.
  J.F. Bodine, 133:Band17Heft1/2-184
  V.W. Hill, 406:Winter84-468
Paulsen, W. and H.G. Hermann, eds. Sinn
und Unsinn.*
  K-H. Schoeps, 301(JEGP):Jul84-416
Paulson, M.G. and T. Álvarez-Detrell - see
de Vega Carpio, L.
Paulson, R. Book and Painting.*
  G. Ashton, 570(SQ):Autumn84-373
  R.M. Frye, 551(RenQ):Autumn84-488
  M.D. Paley, 88:Spring85-223
Paulson, R. Literary Landscape: Turner
and Constable.*
  R.M. Frye, 405(MP):May85-431
  J. Gage, 90:Jun84-362
  P.D. McGlynn, 577(SHR):Spring84-174
  M.D. Paley, 88:Spring85-223
  M. Pointon, 89(BJA):Spring84-177
  M.F. Schulz, 678(YCGL):No32-156
  W. Vaughan, 59:Sep84-368
Paulson, R. Popular and Polite Art in the
Age of Hogarth and Fielding.*
  M. Sokolyansky, 402(MLR):Jan84-154
Paulson, R. Representations of Revolution
(1789-1820).*
  J. Barrell, 59:Mar84-120
  R. Gagnier, 141:Spring84-201
                              [continued]

[continuing]
  J.A.W. Heffernan, 661(WC):Summer84-103
  N. Hilton, 88:Spring85-221
Paulsson, G. and M. Gelfer-Jørgensen, eds.
Konstens världshistoria. (Vol 5)
  K. Ådahl, 341:Vol53No1-30
Paulston, C.B. Swedish Research and
Debate about Bilingualism.
  M. Heller, 350:Jun85-509
Pauly, T.H. An American Odyssey.
  R.M. Goldman, 612(ThS):Nov84-257
  L. Michaels, 651(WHR):Summer84-189
  A. Todras, 397(MD):Jun84-274
  R. Toscan, 615(TJ):May84-285
Pavis, P. Languages of the Stage.*
  D. Kuznicka, 397(MD):Sep84-459
  B.O. States, 612(ThS):May84-101
Pavlović, M. The Slavs beneath Parnassus.
  C. Hawkesworth, 617(TLS):11Oct85-1150
Pavlovskii, A.I. Anna Akhmatova.
  S. Driver, 550(RusR):Apr84-196
Pavlovskis, Z. The Praise of Folly.
  W.A. Rebhorn, 551(RenQ):Winter84-620
  A. Reix, 542:Oct-Dec84-464
Pavone, J. Implicational Scales and
English Dialectology.
  T.E. Murray, 355(LSoc):Sep84-412
Pawel, E. The Nightmare of Reason.*
  42(AR):Fall84-508
Pawlisch, H.S. Sir John Davies and the
Conquest of Ireland.
  B. Bradshaw, 617(TLS):5Jul85-742
Paxton, J. - see "The Statesman's Year-
Book, 1984-1985"
Payen, J-C. and others. Le Roman.
  E.R. Sienaert, 356(LR):Feb/May84-123
Payne, A. Frank Bridge.
  S. Lloyd, 617(TLS):15Mar85-291
Payne, F.A. Chaucer and Menippean Satire.*
  R.T. Davies, 677(YES):Vol 14-304
  C. von Nolcken, 541(RES):Aug84-355
  J. Ziolkowski, 149(CLS):Summer84-235
Payne, L. Black Novelists and the South-
ern Literary Tradition.*
  J.W. Lee, 577(SHR):Winter84-88
Payne, R.M., ed. Language in Tunisia.
  B. Comrie, 350:Sep85-733
Payne, S.G. Spanish Catholicism.
  F. Lannon, 617(TLS):8Feb85-152
Payot, D. Le philosophe et l'architecte.
  P. Somville, 542:Jan-Mar84-139
Paz, E. and G.F. Waldman, eds. Teatro
Contemporáneo. (2nd ed)
  M.S. Finch, 238:May84-315
  J. Ortega, 399(MLJ):Spring84-94
Paz, O. One Earth, Four or Five Worlds.
  N. Bliven, 442(NY):7Oct85-134
  C.W. Maynes, 441:11Aug85-18
  L.D. Nachman, 129:Sep85-70
Paz, O. Sor Juana Inés de la Cruz o Las
trampas de la fe.
  I.M. Zuleta, 263(RIB):Vol34No2-311
Paz, O. Tiempo Nublado.
  P.M. Alfonso, 37:Jul-Aug84-62
Peace, R. Chekhov.*
  M. Ehre, 574(SEEJ):Fall84-402
  C.A. Hubbs, 397(MD):Jun84-272
  L. Senelick, 550(RusR):Jul84-322
  V. Terras, 529(QQ):Autumn84-701
  295(JML):Nov84-419
  639(VQR):Winter84-7

Peach, L. British Influence on the Birth
of American Literature.*
R.W. Harvey, 106:Fall84-301
Peach, W.B. and D.O. Thomas - see Price, R.
Peacock, M. Raw Heaven.*
P. Stitt, 219(GaR):Fall84-628
Peacocke, C. Holistic Explanation.
A. Bilgrami, 311(JP):Feb84-106
Pearce, B. - see Raskolnikov, F.F.
Pearce, D. and H. Schneidau - see Pound, E.
and J. Theobald
Pearce, E. Hummingbirds and Hyenas.
S. Hoggart, 617(TLS):11Oct85-1128
G. Kaufman, 362:19Sep85-26
Pearce, R. The Novel in Motion.*
R.M. Davis, 223:Fall84-330
P. O'Donnell, 27(AL):Oct84-452
J.A. Varsava, 395(MFS):Summer84-409
42(AR):Summer84-383
295(JML):Nov84-388
Pearce, R.H. - see Hawthorne, N.
Pearce, R.L. Russian for Expository Prose.
P.M. Mitchell, 399(MLJ):Winter84-422
I. Thompson and E. Urevich, 558(RLJ):
Winter-Spring84-273
Pearcy, L.T. The Mediated Muse.
A. Elliot, 617(TLS):10May85-518
Pears, D. Motivated Irrationality.*
I. Thalberg, 185:Jul85-943
"Pears Cyclopaedia." (93rd ed) (C. Cook,
ed)
A. Bell, 617(TLS):26Apr85-472
Pearsall, D. - see Langland, W.
Pearsall, D. and N. Zeeman - see Salter, E.
Pearson, H. The Life of Oscar Wilde.
617(TLS):9Aug85-887
Pearson, J. Tragedy and Tragicomedy in
the Plays of John Webster.*
B. Gibbons, 402(MLR):Jan84-147
Pearson, K. American Crafts.
V.S. Lynn, 139:Feb/Mar84-38
Pearson, L. The Art of Demosthenes.
C.W. Wooten, 122:Jan84-64
Pearson, R. National Minorities in East-
ern Europe, 1848-1945.
J. Hiden, 575(SEER):Jul84-459
Pearson, T.R. A Short History of a Small
Place.
F. Schumer, 441:7Jul85-4
Peary, D. Cult Movies 2.
J. Nangle, 200:Jan84-60
Peavy, C.D. Afro-American Literature and
Culture Since World War II.
A. Rampersad, 402(MLR):Jan84-155
Peck, A. Uncovering the Sixties.
A. Gottlieb, 441:7Jul85-12
442(NY):12Aug85-84
Peck, L.L. Northampton.
S.A. Burrell, 551(RenQ):Autumn84-454
B.L. Parker, 568(SCN):Winter84-67
Peck, S. Halls of Jade, Walls of Stone.
J. Shapiro, 441:29Sep85-23
Peczenik, A. The Basis of Legal Justifica-
tion.
K.S., 185:Oct84-179
Peden, M.S., ed. The Latin American Short
Story.
T.J. Di Salvo, 573(SSF):Winter84-80
P.B. Dixon, 395(MFS):Summer84-338
M.I. Lichtblau, 238:Mar84-149

Pedersen, H. A Glance at the History of
Linguistics. (K. Koerner, ed)
D. Bates, 350:Mar85-212
P. Swiggers, 353:Vol122No2-251
Pedicord, H.W. and F.L. Bergmann - see
Garrick, D.
Peebles, P. Sri Lanka.
M. Roberts, 293(JASt):May84-584
Peele, G. Revival and Reaction.*
A. Hartley, 176:Apr85-65
Peereboom, J.J. Fielding Practice.
A. Morvan, 189(EA):Jul-Sep85-336
Pegg, C.H. Evolution of the European Idea,
1914-1932.
639(VQR):Winter84-18
Péguy, C. and P. Marcel. Correspondance
(1905-1914). (J. Sabiani, ed)
N. Wilson, 208(FS):Oct84-485
Peillon, M. Contemporary Irish Society.
T. Garvin, 272(IUR):Spring84-146
Peirce, C.S., ed. Studies in Logic by
Members of the Johns Hopkins University.
R. Dipert, 619:Fall84-469
Peirce, C.S. The Writings of Charles S.
Peirce.* (Vol 1) (M.H. Fisch, general
ed)
A.B. Wolter, 543:Mar84-643
Peirce, C.S. Writings of Charles S.
Peirce. (Vol 2) (E.C. Moore, ed)
L.J. Cohen, 617(TLS):23Aug85-929
P.S., 185:Apr85-777
de Peiresc, N.C.F. Peiresc: Lettres à
Naudé. (P. Wolfe, ed)
T. Allott, 208(FS):Apr84-196
J.L. Pallister, 568(SCN):Winter84-71
Pekarik, A., ed. Ukifune.*
E. Jackson, Jr., 293(JASt):Feb84-333
D. Waterhouse, 627(UTQ):Winter83/84-
209
Pelckmans, P. Le Sacre du père.
A. Goodden, 402(MLR):Oct84-936
R. Runte, 210(FrF):Sep84-375
N. Segal, 208(FS):Oct84-467
Pelczynski, Z.A., ed. The State and Civil
Society.
J. Waldron, 617(TLS):12Apr85-417
"Le Pèlerinage de Charlemagne/La Peregrin-
ación de Carlomagno." (I. de Riquer, ed
and trans)
M. Bonafin, 379(MedR):Aug84-296
Pelikan, J. The Christian Tradition.*
(Vol 4) The Vindication of Tradition.
H.A. Oberman, 617(TLS):23Aug85-930
Pelikan, J. Jesus Through the Centuries.
A. Burgess, 617(TLS):20Dec85-1443
J. Koenig, 441:22Dec85-1
442(NY):18Nov85-174
Pelinski, R. La musique des Inuit du Car-
ibou.*
P. Laki, 537:Vol70No1-125
Pellegrin, P. La classification des ani-
maux chez Aristote.*
P. Louis, 555:Vol58fasc1-120
J.A. Richmond, 303(JoHS):Vol 104-215
Pellegrino, E.D. and D.C. Thomasma. A
Philosophical Basis of Medical Practice.*
W.G. Warren, 63:Jun84-206
Pelletier, A. - see Josephus
Pelletier, A-M. Fonctions Poétiques.
F. Gutiérrez, 202(FMod):No65/67-334
Pelletier, N. The Rearrangement.
M. Simpson, 441:4Aug85-16
Pelletier, Y., with others - see Aristotle

282

Pelliccia, G. and G. Rocca - see "Dizionario degli istituti di perfezione"
Pellman, R. and K. Amish Crib Quilts.
E. Hoffman, 614:Summer85-17
Pellman, R. and K. The World of Amish Quilts.
K.S.H., 614:Winter85-33
Pellman, R.T. Amish Quilt Patterns.
K.S.H., 614:Winter85-33
Pells, R.H. The Liberal Mind in a Conservative Age.
J. Nuechterlein, 129:Jul85-69
D.M. Oshinsky, 441:10Feb85-3
Pelnar, I. Die mehrstimmigen Lieder Oswalds von Wolkenstein.
F. Dangel-Hofmann, 684(ZDA):Band113 Heft3-116
Péloquin-Faré, L. L'Identité culturelle.
J.P. Gilroy, 207(FR):Oct84-174
Pelous, J-M. Amour précieux.*
H.T. Barnwell, 208(FS):Jul84-339
Pelphrey, B. Love Was His Meaning.
R. Bradley, 589:Jul84-682
Peltenburg, E.J. Recent Developments in the Later Prehistory of Cyprus.*
M. Fortin, 487:Autumn84-265
Pelton, R.D. The Trickster in West Africa.
R.A. Georges, 2(AfrA):Nov83-16
Peñalosa, F. Introduction to the Sociology of Language.
E. Finegan, 350:Sep85-728
Pencak, W. America's Burke.
J.E. Ferling, 656(WMQ):Jan84-161
Pencak, W. War, Politics and Revolution in Provincial Massachusetts.
A.G. Condon, 106:Fall84-287
Penfield, J. Communicating With Quotes.
D. Ben-Amos, 355(LSoc):Mar84-135
P'eng Shu-tse. The Chinese Communist Party in Power.
G.A. Hoston, 293(JASt):Nov84-145
Penkower, M.N. The Jews Were Expendable.*
R.S. Levy, 129:Apr85-70
Penman, S.K. Here Be Dragons.
J. Kaufman, 441:1Sep85-15
Penn, I. Worlds in a Small Room.
J. Guimond, 219(GaR):Summer84-424
Penn, J. Mortal Term.
M. Laski, 362:10Jan85-25
Penney, D.W., D.S. Brose and J.A. Brown. Ancient Art of the American Woodland Indians.
P-L. Adams, 61:Jun85-104
Penniman, H., ed. Australia at the Polls.
J.B. Paul, 617(TLS):10May85-516
Penniman, H.R., ed. Canada at the Polls, 1979 and 1980.
G.M. Betts, 529(QQ):Autumn84-726
Penning-Rowsell, E. The Wines of Bordeaux. (5th ed)
617(TLS):10May85-531
Pennock, J.R. and J. Chapman, eds. Marxism.
F.E. Stockholder, 104(CASS):Fall84-374
639(VQR):Summer84-93
Penrose, A. The Lives of Lee Miller.
A. Grundberg, 441:8Dec85-22
Penrose, J. Letters from Bath 1766-1767. (B. Mitchell and H. Penrose, eds)
G. Lamoine, 189(EA):Oct-Dec85-462
"Pensée hispanique et Philosophie française des lumières."*
A. Llinares, 192(EP):Jul-Sep84-418

Pensom, R. Literary Technique in the "Chanson de Roland."*
W.G. van Emden, 208(FS):Jan84-41
T. Hunt, 402(MLR):Jan84-178
F. Lebsanft, 547(RF):Band96Heft3-330
E.R. Sienaert, 356(LR):Feb/May84-125
Pentland, D.H. and H.C. Wolfart. Bibliography of Algonquian Linguistics.
J.M. Banks, 470:Vol22-123
G.F. Meier, 682(ZPSK):Band37Heft6-730
Pentland, H.C. Labour and Capital in Canada 1650-1860. (P. Phillips, ed)
G. Teeple, 529(QQ):Autumn84-730
Penzl, H. Frühneuhochdeutsch.
B.J. Koekkoek, 350:Mar85-195
Pepetela. Mayombe.
A. Maja-Pearce, 364:Dec84/Jan85-100
Pepicello, W.J. and T.A. Green. The Language of Riddles.
B. Johnstone, 350:Dec85-933
Peplow, M.W. George S. Schuyler.
M. Fabre, 402:Apr84-444
Pepper, D.S. Guido Reni.
E. Waterhouse, 617(TLS):22Mar85-310
Pepper, J. - see Chandler, R.
Peppin, B. and L. Micklethwait. Dictionary of British Book Illustrators: The Twentieth Century.*
S. Houfe, 39:Jul84-74
Pepys, S. The Diary of Samuel Pepys. (Vol 10) (R. Latham and W. Matthews, eds)
P. Harth, 173(ECS):Winter84/85-232
Pera, M. Hume, Kant e l'induzione.*
A. Stanguennec, 542:Oct-Dec84-481
Percival, J. Theatre in My Blood.*
P.J. Rosenwald, 151:Dec83-114
Perdue, C., ed. Second Language Acquisition by Adult Immigrants.
M. Clyne, 353:Vol21No4-650
Perdue, T. - see Boudinot, E.
Pereira, N.G.O. Tsar-Liberator.*
R. Wortman, 550(RusR):Apr84-209
Perelli, L. Il movimento popolare nell'ultimo secolo della repubblica.*
F. Hinard, 555:Vol58fasc2-345
Perelman, C. The Realm of Rhetoric.* (German title: Das Reich der Rhetorik.)
R. Hanna, 543:Dec83-412
G.A. Kennedy, 480(P&R):Vol 17No4-240
Perelmuter Pérez, R. Noche intelectual.
G. Sabat-Rivers, 238:Dec84-677
Peress, G. Telex Iran.
G. Marcus, 62:Dec84-75
Perez, A.S. - see under Sanchez Perez, A.
Perez, L.A., Jr. Cuba Between Empires, 1878-1902.
L. Langley, 263(RIB):Vol34No2-312
Pérez, R.P. - see under Perelmuter Pérez, R.
Pérez de Hita, G. Guerras civiles de Granada. (Pt 1) (S.M. Bryant, ed)
A. Mackay, 86(BHS):Oct84-502
Pérez Firmat, G. Idle Fictions.*
B.B. Aponte, 240(HR):Winter84-102
C.L. King, 593:Winter84/85-334
C. Richmond, 238:May84-307
D.R. Southard, 345(KRQ):Vol31No3-350
J.P. Winfield, 268(IFR):Winter85-58
Pérez Galdós, B. Doña Perfecta. (R. Cardona, ed)
P. Bly, 240(HR):Autumn84-547

Pérez Galdós, B. Misericordia. (L. García Lorenzo, ed)
J. Lowe, 86(BHS):Oct84-511
Peri, Y. Between Battles and Ballots.*
G. Nahshon, 390:Dec84-56
Perkins, E. - see Harpur, C.
Perkins, M.L. Diderot and the Time-Space Continuum.
G. Bremner, 83:Autumn84-269
W.F. Edmiston, 207(FR):May85-893
Perkins, M.R. Modal Expressions in English.
H. McCallum-Bayliss, 350:Sep85-712
P. Westney, 257(IRAL):Aug84-229
Perl, J.M. The Tradition of Return.
A.K. Thorlby, 617(TLS):2Aug85-858
Perle, G. The Operas of Alban Berg.*
(Vol 2: Lulu.)
D. Jarman, 617(TLS):16Aug85-904
Perlman, J., E. Folsom and D. Campion, eds. Walt Whitman.
N. Schmitz, 472:Fall/Winter84-4
Perlmutter, A. Israel.
P. Johnson, 441:1Dec85-7
Perlmutter, D.M., ed. Studies in Relational Grammar 1.*
W.D. Davies, 35(AS):Spring84-84
R.C. De Armond, 320(CJL):Spring84-78
Perlmutter, N. and R.A. The Real Anti-Semitism in America.
W. Maslow, 390:Jan84-61
Perloff, M. The Poetics of Indeterminacy.*
R.J. Dingley, 447(N&Q):Dec83-534
Perlot, J-N. Gold Seeker. (H.R. Lamar, ed)
P-L. Adams, 61:Aug85-91
E.S. Connell, 441:28Jul85-13
Pernick, M.S. A Calculus of Suffering.
G.F. Drinka, 441:28Apr85-11
Pernot, L. Les "Discours Siciliens" d'Aelius Aristide (Or. 5-6).
P. Hoffmann, 555:Vol158fasc2-274
Peroni, L. The Language of Flowers.
J.L. Faust, 441:8Dec85-28
Perosa, S. American Theories of the Novel, 1793-1903.
R. Asselineau, 189(EA):Jul-Sep85-353
W.B. Clark, 27(AL):Dec84-594
W.C. Hamlin, 395(MFS):Winter84-787
Perradotto, J. and J.P. Sullivan, eds. Women in the Ancient World.
N.R.E. Fisher, 123:Vol34No2-247
Perrault, M. Le Secret de mon enfance.
S.R. Schulman, 207(FR):Feb85-489
Perrault, P. Caméramages. (G. Gauthier and Y. Lacroix, eds)
D. Clandfield, 627(UTQ):Summer84-515
Perrett, G. America in the Twenties.
F. Russell, 396(ModA):Winter84-81
Perriam, W. The Stillness The Dancing.
M. Seymour, 617(TLS):7Jun85-644
Perrin, J. Menlove.
J.A. Smith, 617(TLS):26Apr85-460
Perrin, M. L'homme antique et chrétien.
J-C. Fredouille, 555:Vol158fasc1-159
Perrins, C.M. and A.L.A. Middleton. The Encyclopaedia of Birds.
J. Buxton, 617(TLS):23Aug85-935
Perrolle, P.M. - see Xu Liangying and Fan Dainian
Perrot, P. Le Travail des Apparences.
P. Thody, 617(TLS):4Jan85-7

Perry, A.J.A., ed. La Passion des Jongleurs.*
U. Jokinen, 439(NM):1984/4-516
Perry, E.J., ed. Chinese Perspectives on the Nien Rebellion.
D.E. Kelley, 293(JASt):May84-529
Perry, E.J. Rebels and Revolutionaries in North China, 1845-1945.
E. Wickberg, 302:Vol20No2-193
Perry, H.S. Psychiatrist of America.
R.E. Fancher, 529(QQ):Spring84-171
Perry, M. Arnold Toynbee and the Crisis of the West.
R. Stromberg, 125:Spring84-311
Perry, R. Women, Letters, and the Novel.*
D. Brooks-Davies, 677(YES):Vol 14-319
Perry, R. - see Ballard, G.
Perry, S. and J. Dawson. Nightmare.
R. Cherry, 441:22Sep85-37
Perry, T. Big Fish.
N. Callendar, 441:23Jun85-33
442(NY):20May85-128
Perryman, J., ed. The King of Tars.
P. Bawcutt, 677(YES):Vol 14-303
W. Obst, 38:Band102Heft1/2-209
K. Taylor, 589:Jan84-242
Perryman, P. and C. Voysey. New Designs in Honiton Lace.
C. Campbell, 614:Spring85-26
Perse, S. Amitié du Prince de Saint-John Perse. (A. Henry, ed)
G. Straka, 553(RLiR):Jan-Jun84-260
Perse, S. "Anabase" de Saint-John Perse. (A. Henry, ed)
R. Little, 208(FS):Apr84-228
G. Straka, 553(RLiR):Jan-Jun84-260
Perushek, D.E., ed. The Griffis Collection of Japanese Books.
E. Beauchamp, 407(MN):Spring84-113
Pescador, J.H. - see under Hierro Pescador, J.
Pesce, D., ed and trans. La Tavola di Cebete.
É. des Places, 555:Vol158fasc1-124
Pessen, E. The Log Cabin Myth.*
A. Barnet, 441:3Feb85-23
Pestelli, G. The Age of Mozart and Beethoven.*
D. Charlton, 415:Oct84-575
J. Rushton, 410(M&L):Oct84-412
W.H. Youngren, 61:Jan85-88
Pestman, P.W. and others. A Guide to the Zenon Archive.
J.D. Thomas, 123:Vol34No1-154
Peter, A.M. The Units of Language Acquisition.
W. Frawley, 350:Mar85-235
J. Vizmuller-Zocco, 320(CJL):Fall184-226
Peter, L. The Great Riding.
639(VQR):Summer84-92
Peterley, D. Peterley Harvest. (M. Holroyd, ed)
V. Glendinning, 617(TLS):5Apr85-374
Peters, C. and P. Kiesling, eds. A New Road for America.
L. Lenkowsky, 129:Mar85-54
Peters, E. William Faulkner.
H.H. McAlexander, 27(AL):May84-291
J.G. Watson, 395(MFS):Summer84-319
Peters, E. The Pilgrim of Hate.
T.J. Binyon, 617(TLS):11Jan85-42

Piccinni, G. "Seminare, fruttare, raccog-
liere."
  D.J. Osheim, 589:Jul84-687
Piccitto, G., with others, eds. Vocabo-
lario siciliano.
  S.C. Sgroi, 545(RPh):Feb84-313
Pichois, C. - see Colette
le Pichon, Y. The World of Henri Rous-
seau.* (French title: Le monde du
douanier Rousseau.)
  90:Feb84-102
Pickar, G.B., ed. Adventures of a
Flounder.
  S. Abbott, 221(GQ):Fall84-682
Pickens, R.T., ed. The Sower and his Seed.
  M.T. Bruckner, 589:Oct84-941
  T. Hunt, 402(MLR):Jul84-697
  H.C.R. Laurie, 547(RF):Band96Heft3-334
  E. Vance, 210(FrF):May84-251
Pickering, M. Village Song and Culture.
  A. Howkins, 637(VS):Spring84-385
Pickering, P. Wild About Harry.
  C. Hawtree, 617(TLS):12Apr85-406
  M. Laski, 362:18Jul85-29
Pickering, R. Paul Valéry poète en prose.
  W.N. Ince, 208(FS):Apr84-227
Pickering, S.F., Jr. John Locke and
Children's Books in Eighteenth-Century
England.*
  M. Booth, 577(SHR):Winter84-77
Pickerodt, G., ed. Georg Forster in
seiner Epoche.
  K. Kändler, 654(WB):1/1984-156
Pickford, C.E. and R. Last, eds. The
Arthurian Bibliography.* (Vol 1)
  F. Alexander, 541(RES):Aug84-362
  P.J.C. Field, 382(MAE):1984/1-138
Pickford, I. Silver Flatware.
  G. Wills, 39:Jan84-69
Pickles, D. Problems of Contemporary
French Politics.
  J. Evans, 208(FS):Apr84-244
Pickvance, R. Van Gogh in Arles.
  P-L. Adams, 61:Jul85-100
Picoche, J. Le vocabulaire psychologique
dans les Chroniques de Froissart.
  G. Roques, 553(RLiR):Jul-Dec84-485
Picon, G. Surrealists and Surrealism.
  90:Feb84-102
Picone, M. "Vita Nuova" e tradizione
romanza.
  T. Barolini, 545(RPh):Feb84-382
"Pieces on the 'Jew Bill' (1753)."
  P-G. Boucé, 189(EA):Oct-Dec85-493
Piel, E. Elias Canetti.
  K. Fliedl, 602:Band15Heft2-345
Pieper, U. Über der Aussagekraft statis-
tischer Methoden für die linguistische
Stilanalyse.
  G. Koller, 685(ZDL):1/1984-124
Pierce, C. Philippe at His Bath.
  J. Carter, 219(GaR):Winter84-881
Pierce, C.E., Jr. The Religious Life of
Samuel Johnson.*
  W. Holtz, 173(ECS):Winter84/85-282
  A. Pailler, 189(EA):Jul-Sep85-330
Pierce, H. Philip K. Dick.
  M.E. Barth, 395(MFS):Summer84-346
  J. Fekete, 561(SFS):Mar84-78
Pierce, H.B. A Literary Symbiosis.
  B. Attebery, 561(SFS):Jul84-214
  M.E. Barth, 395(MFS):Winter84-867
                              [continued]

[continuing]
  R.S. Bravard and M.W. Peplow, 590:
  Dec84-60
Pierce, J.R. The Science of Musical Sound.
  C. Taylor, 415:Sep84-505
Pierce, R.A. - see Shelikhov, G.I.
Piercy, M. Stone, Paper, Knife.*
  P. Clinch, 493:Jan84-70
Pieri, M. - see Marino, G.B.
Pierre, A.J. - see Morán, F. and others
Pierre de Hauteville - see under de Haute-
ville
Piersall, J., with R. Whittingham. The
Truth Hurts.
  R. Nalley, 441:21Apr85-25
Pietra, R. Valéry.
  J. Jallat, 535(RHL):Nov/Dec84-978
Pietschmann, H. Staat und staatliche Ent-
wicklung am Beginn der spanischen Koloni-
sation Amerikas.
  I. Buisson, 547(RF):Band96Heft4-498
Piette, A. Gérard Bessette, "L'Incubation"
et ses figures.
  P. Hébert, 627(UTQ):Summer84-471
Pietzcker, C. Einführung in die Psycho-
analyse des literarischen Kunstwerks am
Beispiel von Jean Pauls "Rede des toten
Christus."
  S.L. Gilman, 222(GR):Fall84-166
Pigeaud, J. La maladie de l'âme.
  C. Gill, 303(JoHS):Vol 104-231
Pigeot, J. and J-L. Tschudin. La Littéra-
ture japonaise.
  J. Bésineau, 407(MN):Summer84-200
Pignatti, T. Master Drawings.
  T. Reese, 507:Nov/Dec84-140
van der Pijl, K. The Making of an Atlan-
tic Ruling Class.
  P.J.D.L. Wiles, 617(TLS):11Oct85-1129
Pike, B. The Image of the City in Modern
Literature.*
  J. Duytschaever, 107(CRCL):Mar84-137
  F. Lach, 133:Band17Heft1/2-191
  R. Lehan, 405(MP):Nov84-230
  K. Probert, 106:Spring84-93
  K. Versluys, 549(RLC):Jul-Sep84-366
  A.J. Weitzman, 131(CL):Fall84-378
Pike, D. German Writers in Soviet Exile,
1933-1945.* (German title: Deutsche
Schriftsteller im sowjetischen Exil,
1933-1945.)
  T.S. Hansen, 406:Winter84-481
Pike, K.L. Linguistic Concepts.
  M.L. Bender, 350:Mar85-214
Pike, K.L. Tagmemics, Discourse, and Ver-
bal Art.* (R.W. Bailey, ed)
  P. Swiggers, 107(CRCL):Jun84-271
Pikoulis, J. The Art of William Faulkner.*
  C.S. Brown, 569(SR):Summer84-474
  J.T. Matthews, 27(AL):Mar84-122
  P. Messent, 541(RES):Nov84-586
  L.W. Wagner, 587(SAF):Autumn84-244
Pikser, J. Junk on the Hill.
  N. Callendar, 441:10Nov85-22
Pilkington, W.T., ed. Critical Essays on
the Western American Novel.
  H.N. Smith, 677(YES):Vol 14-355
Pillat, I. Poezii. (Vol 1) (C. Pillat,
ed)
  V. Nemoianu, 617(TLS):13Dec85-1437
Pillau, H. Die fortgedachte Dissonanz.*
  K. Peter, 221(GQ):Fall84-654
  I. Wachsmuth, 654(WB):1/1984-162

Pilling, J. Autobiography and Imagination.*
  A.F.T. Lurcock, 541(RES):Aug84-426
  I.B. Nadel, 506(PSt):Dec84-273
Pilz, K.D. Phraseologie.
  D. Steffens, 682(ZPSK):Band37Heft6-730
Pimlott, B. Hugh Dalton.
  M. Barnes, 362:4Apr85-24
  K.O. Morgan, 617(TLS):15Mar85-281
  J. Schneer, 441:15Sep85-14
Pimsleur, P., B. Pimsleur and F. Suarez-
Richard. Sol y sombra. (3rd ed)
  G.A. Olivier, 399(MLJ):Autumn84-302
Piñal, F.A. - see under Aguilar Piñal, F.
Pincher, C. Too Secret Too Long.*
  J. Keegan, 453(NYRB):14Mar85-15
  H. Rositzke, 441:17Feb85-28
Pinchon, J. and B. Coute. Le Système
verbal du français.*
  T. Klingler, 207(FR):Dec84-331
Pincus-Witten, R. Eye to Eye.
  S. Morgan, 62:Dec84-75
Pincus-Witten, R. Jedd Garet.
  N. Moufarrege, 62:Dec84-74
Pindar. Selections from Pindar. (G. Kirk-
wood, ed)
  D.A. Campbell, 487:Autumn84-272
  C. Carey, 123:Vol34No1-5
Pineda, C. Face.
  J. Clute, 617(TLS):13Dec85-1434
  C. Colman, 441:28Apr85-24
Pinget, R. Between Fantoine and Agapa.
That Voice.
  D.P. Deneau, 268(IFR):Summer85-114
  R.M. Henkels, 577(SHR):Fall84-361
Pingree, D. - see Katz, J.
Pinion, F.B. A George Eliot Companion.
  J. Herron, 637(VS):Autumn83-102
Pinion, F.B. - see Eliot, G.
Pinker, S. Language Learnability and Lan-
guage Development.
  C. Pye, 350:Dec85-903
Pinkster, H., ed. Latin Linguistics and
Linguistic Theory.*
  A. Bammesberger, 215(GL):Vol24No3-208
  T. Janson, 353:Vol22No1-149
Pinkus, B. The Soviet Government and the
Jews, 1948-1967.*
  M. Gilbert, 453(NYRB):30May85-37
Pinney, R. and M. Schlachter, with A.
Courtenay. Bobby.
  M. Hertzig, 441:3Feb85-23
Pinney, S. - see Warner, S.T.
Pino, G.B. Ragionamento sovra del asino.
(O. Casale, ed)
  N. Ordine, 228(GSLI):Vol 161fasc513-
  116
Pinsker, H. Altenglisches Studienbuch.
  R. Hickey, 72:Band221Heft2-357
Pinsky, R. History of My Heart.*
  J.F. Cotter, 249(HudR):Autumn84-504
  639(VQR):Autumn84-137
Pinto, A.A. Isoléxicas portuguesas.
  A. Gier, 553(RLiR):Jul-Dec84-479
Pinto, E. Edgar Poe et l'art d'inventer.
  A. Reix, 542:Apr-Jun84-238
Pinto Delgado, J., A. Enríquez Gómez and M.
de Barrios. Marrano Poets of the Seven-
teenth Century. (T. Oelman, ed and
trans)
  R.M. Price, 86(BHS):Oct84-509

Pinxten, R., ed. Universalism and Relativ-
ism in Language and Thought.
  Shin-Ja Joo Hwang, 355(LSoc):Sep84-396
Pinxten, R., I. van Dooren and F. Harvey.
The Anthropology of Space.
  D. Bahr, 350:Mar85-198
Piore, M.J. and C.F. Sabel. The Second
Industrial Divide.
  R.L. Heilbroner, 441:6Jan85-7
  L.C. Thurow, 453(NYRB):14Feb85-9
Piper, D. Artists' London.
  90:Mar84-170
Piper, J. and R. Ingrams - see under In-
grams, R. and J. Piper
Piper, L.J. The Spartan Twilight.
  P. Green, 617(TLS):16Aug85-891
Pipes, D. In the Path of God.*
  D. Spanier, 176:Apr85-73
Pipes, D. Slave Soldiers and Islam.
  M.W. Dols, 318(JAOS):Jul-Sep83-633
Pippin, R.B. Kant's Theory of Form.*
  M. Gregor, 543:Sep83-138
  T.K. Seung, 449:May84-382
Piquet, J-F. L'Oeil-de-boeuf.
  F. de Martinoir, 450(NRF):Jan84-124
The Duke of Pirajno. A Cure for Serpents.
  617(TLS):25Oct85-1219
Pirandello, L. Théâtre. (Vols 1 and 9)
Nouvelles pour une année. Un, personne
et cent mille. Les vieux et les jeunes.
Ecrits sur le théâtre et la littérature.
  M-A. Lescourret, 98:Nov84-911
Pirie, D.B. William Wordsworth.*
  D.H. Bialostosky, 401(MLQ):Sep83-305
  T.M. Kelley, 591(SIR):Spring84-128
  W.J.B. Owen, 541(RES):Nov84-560
  E. Proffitt, 577(SHR):Summer84-262
Pirie, M. The Book of the Fallacy.
  M. Warnock, 362:31Oct85-33
Pirog, G. Aleksandr Blok's "Ital'ianskie
Stikhi."
  L. Vogel, 104(CASS):Winter84-440
Piromalli, A. - see Mosino, F.
Piron, A. Alexis Piron épistolier. (G.
von Proschwitz, ed)
  S. Roth, 535(RHL):Jul/Aug84-620
  D. Williams, 402(MLR):Apr84-454
Piroue, G. Pirandello.
  M-A. Lescourret, 98:Nov84-911
Pirrotta, N. Music and Culture in Italy
from the Middle Ages to the Baroque.
  M.R. Maniates, 414(MusQ):Fall84-567
Pirrotta, N. and E. Povoledo. Music and
Theatre from Poliziano to Monteverdi.*
  A. Newcomb, 551(RenQ):Spring84-109
de Pisan, C. - see under Christine de
Pisan
Pissarro, C. Correspondance de Camille
Pissarro.* (Vol 1) (J. Bailly-Herzberg,
ed)
  R. Schiff, 54:Dec84-681
"Camille Pissarro, 1830-1903."
  R. Schiff, 54:Dec84-681
Pistone, D., ed. Sur les traces de Fréd-
éric Chopin.
  J. Methuen-Campbell, 415:Dec84-705
Pitcher, H. The Smiths of Moscow.
  A.G. Cross, 617(TLS):1Mar85-224
Pitcher, J. Samuel Daniel: The Brotherton
Manuscript.
  M.G. Brennan, 541(RES):Aug84-364

Pommier, R. Assez décodé!
 R. de Gorog, 545(RPh):May84-472
Pomminville, L. Pitatou et le bon manger.
 D. Thaler, 102(CanL):Summer84-161
Pompa, L. Vico.
 P.J. Fitz Patrick, 83:Spring84-77
Pompa, L. and W.H. Dray, eds. Substance
 and Form in History.
 P.L. Ward, 125:Fall83-75
Pon, G., ed. Recueil des documents de
 l'abbaye de Fontaine-le-Comte (XIIe-
 XIIIe siècles).
 D.F. Callahan, 589:Jul84-725
Ponchie, J.F. French Periodical Index
 (Repertoriex) 1983.
 R. Merker, 207(FR):Feb85-475
Pond, E. From the Yaroslavsky Station.
 D.K. Danow, 558(RLJ):Winter-Spring84-
 290
Pongweni, A.J.C. Songs That Won the Liber-
 ation War.
 N. Masilela, 538(RAL):Winter84-596
Pontbriand, C., ed. Performance Text(e)s
 and Documents.
 A. Greene, 615(TJ):Oct84-440
Pontbriand, J-N. Ephémérides précédé de
 Débris.
 E.G. Lombeida, 207(FR):Apr85-760
Pontiero, G. - see García Márquez, G.
Ponting, C. The Right to Know.
 F. Cooper, 362:28Mar85-24
 B. Williams, 617(TLS):4Oct85-1083
Ponzio, A. Spostamenti, Percorsi e dis-
 corsi sul segno.
 M.A. Bonfantini, 567:Vol52No1/2-119
Poole, R. Popular Leisure and the Music
 Hall in 19th-Century Bolton.
 R. Foulkes, 611(TN):Vol38No3-149
Poole, R. The Unknown Virginia Woolf.
 H. Richter, 594:Spring84-133
Poole, R. - see Hughes, R.
Poovey, M. The Proper Lady and the Woman
 Writer.*
 N. Armstrong, 400(MLN):Dec84-1251
 R.A. Colby, 445(NCF):Dec84-339
 L.A. Finke, 223:Fall84-337
Pope, A. The Last and Greatest Art. (M.
 Mack, ed)
 D.L. Vander Meulen, 566:Spring85-178
Pope, A. Alexander Pope: Collected Poems.
 (B. Dobrée, ed)
 G. Laprevotte, 189(EA):Apr-Jun85-233
Pope-Hennessy, J. Cellini.
 J. Russell, 441:8Dec85-12
Popelar, I. - see Baldinger, K.
Popescu, D.R. The Royal Hunt.
 R. Rosenthal, 441:3Nov85-34
Popham, P. Tokyo.
 442(NY):30Dec85-80
Popkin, R.H. The History of Scepticism
 from Erasmus to Spinoza.
 E. de Olaso, 449:Mar84-136
Poplavskij, B. Sobranie sočinenij v trex
 tomax. (S. Karlinsky and A. Olcott, eds)
 R.D.B. Thomson, 574(SEEJ):Fall84-408
"Popol Vuh." (D. Tedlock, trans)
 P-L. Adams, 61:Aug85-92
Popovsky, M. The Vavilov Affair.
 J.A. Secord, 617(TLS):12Apr85-405
Popper, K.R. L'univers irrésolu. La
 quête inachevée.
 J-C. Dumoncel, 98:Dec84-984

Popper, K.R. A Pocket Popper. (D.W.
 Miller, ed)
 R. Fellows, 518:Oct84-250
Popper, K.R. Postscript to The Logic of
 Scientific Discovery. (Vols 1 and 2)
 (W.W. Bartley 3d, ed)
 R.J. Ackermann, 518:Jul84-164
 J.R. Brown, 154:Dec84-677
 J-C. Dumoncel, 98:Dec84-984
 M. Tiles, 483:Apr84-262
Popper, K.R. Postscript to The Logic of
 Scientific Discovery. (Vol 3) (W.W.
 Bartley 3d, ed)
 R.J. Ackermann, 518:Jul84-164
 J.R. Brown, 154:Dec84-677
 J-C. Dumoncel, 98:Dec84-984
 R. Puccetti, 150(DR):Fall84-632
 M. Tiles, 483:Apr84-262
Popper, K.R. Realism and the Aid of
 Science.* The Open Universe.* (W.W.
 Bartley 3d, ed of both)
 H. Krips, 84:Sep84-253
"Popular Music 1." "Popular Music 2."*
 (R. Middleton and D. Horn, eds of both)
 P. Dickinson, 410(M&L):Jul84-264
Porch, D. The Conquest of the Sahara.
 P-L. Adams, 61:Jan85-100
 P.A. Iseman, 441:20Jan85-19
Porcher, M-C., ed. Inde et littératures.
 L. Bansat-Boudon, 98:Dec84-1022
Porges, H. Wagner Rehearsing the "Ring."*
 A. Whittall, 410(M&L):Jan84-88
Porphyrios, D. Sources of Modern Eclecti-
 cism.*
 W.C. Miller, 576:Dec84-374
Porqueras-Mayo, A. and others, eds. The
 New Catalan Short Story.
 P.J. Boehne, 238:Mar84-148
 E.C. Knowlton, Jr., 573(SSF):Fall84-
 414
 A. Yates, 86(BHS):Oct84-529
Porreco, R., ed. The Georgetown Symposium
 on Ethics.
 C.W.G., 185:Apr85-769
Porritt, J. Seeing Green.
 J. Edmonds, 441:25Aug85-14
 B. Johnson, 617(TLS):4Jan85-4
Porta, G. - see Romano, A.
Porte, J. - see Emerson, R.W.
Portela Silva, E. Le colonizacion cister-
 ciense en Galicia (1142-1250).
 C.V. Graves, 589:Jan84-243
Porter, A.L. and others. A Guidebook for
 Technology Assessment and Impact
 Analysis.
 F. Rapp, 679:Band15Heft2-369
Porter, B.D. The USSR in Third World
 Conflicts.
 P. Windsor, 617(TLS):17May85-557
Porter, C. Seeing and Being.*
 G.S. Jay, 153:Spring84-36
Porter, D. Dickinson.*
 C.R. Steele, 106:Spring84-63
Porter, D. The Pursuit of Crime.*
 G. Grella, 536:Vol5-211
"Eliot Porter's Southwest."
 A. Grundberg, 441:8Dec85-24
Porter, H. Lies, Damned Lies and Some
 Exclusives.*
 M. Davie, 617(TLS):1Feb85-114
Porter, J., ed. The Ballad Image.
 E. Fowke, 187:Winter85-126

Porter, J.A. The Drama of Speech Acts.*
  R. Stamm, 179(ES):Apr84-162
Porter, L.M. The Literary Dream in French
  Romanticism.
  P.J. Whyte, 208(FS):Jul84-362
Porter, M.G. The Art of Grit.*
  S. Fogel, 106:Winter84-487
Porter, P. Collected Poems.*
  J. Saunders, 565:Autumn84-66
Porter, P. Fast Forward.
  C. Boyle, 364:Mar85-85
  L. Mackinnon, 617(TLS):18Jan85-54
  J. Mole, 176:Feb85-48
Porter, R. English Society in the Eigh-
  teenth Century.*
  L.K.J. Glassey, 566:Spring85-181
Porter, R., ed. Mackeson Book of Averages.
  H. Jacobson, 617(TLS):20Dec85-1453
Porter, R.B. The U.S. — U.S.S.R. Grain
  Agreement.
  G. Frost, 617(TLS):23Aug85-917
Portis, C. Masters of Atlantis.
  J.A. West, 441:27Oct85-32
  442(NY):25Nov85-163
"Portrait of Mr. B."
  R. Craft, 453(NYRB):7Nov85-42
  M. Gurewitsch, 617(TLS):21Jun85-686
  J. Lobenthal, 151:Dec84-104
Porzio, D., with R. and M. Tabanelli, eds.
  Lithography.*
  T. Reese, 507:May/Jun84-114
Poschmann, H. Georg Büchner.
  U. Kaufmann, 654(WB):8/1984-1404
Posfortunato, L. - see Leopardi, G.
Posidonius. Die Fragmente. (W. Theiler,
  ed)
  F.H. Sandbach, 303(JoHS):Vol 104-218
Posner, R. Rational Discourse and Poetic
  Communication.
  E. Vos, 204(FdL):Mar84-65
Posner, R. and J.N. Green, eds. Trends in
  Romance Linguistics and Philology.*
  (Vol 2)
  C. Silva-Corvalán, 545(RPh):Feb84-328
Posner, R. and J.N. Green, eds. Trends in
  Romance Linguistics and Philology.*
  (Vols 3 and 4)
  D. Walker, 320(CJL):Fall84-228
Posner, R.A. The Federal Courts.
  P.J. Mishkin, 441:18Aug85-7
Posnock, R. Henry James and the Problem
  of Robert Browning.
  L. Mackinnon, 617(TLS):13Sep85-1012
Post, J.F.S. Henry Vaughan.*
  M. Elsky, 551(RenQ):Autumn84-501
  B. King, 569(SR):Spring84-284
  K. Lynch, 568(SCN):Spring-Summer84-9
van der Post, L. and J. Taylor. Testament
  to the Bushmen.
  M. Shostak, 441:7Jul85-17
  C. Thubron, 617(TLS):17May85-562
Poster, M. Foucault, Marxism and History.
  A. Sheridan, 617(TLS):5Apr85-389
Postlethwaite, D. Making It Whole.
  J. Adlard, 617(TLS):6Dec85-1408
Postman, N. Amusing Ourselves to Death.
  A. Broyard, 441:24Nov85-9
  D. Denby, 61:Nov85-136
"The Postwar Poetry of Iceland."* (S.A.
  Magnússon, trans)
  P. Firchow, 563(SS):Summer84-282

Potichnyi, P.J. and J.S. Zacek, eds. Pol-
  itics and Participation under Communist
  Rule.
  P.H. Juviler, 550(RusR):Oct84-444
Potok, C. Davita's Harp.
  P. Cowan, 441:31Mar85-12
  442(NY):15Apr85-129
Potter, J. The Liberty We Seek.*
  E.P. McCaughey, 656(WMQ):Apr84-316
Potter, J. The Taking of Agnes.
  J. Pilling, 617(TLS):19Apr85-434
Potter, J.H. Five Frames for the "Decam-
  eron."*
  A. Bonadeo, 400(MLN):Jan84-168
  P. Hainsworth, 382(MAE):1984/2-336
  J.L. Smarr, 276:Autumn84-274
Potter, K.H., ed. Encyclopedia of Indian
  Philosophies: Advaita Vedānta Up to Śam-
  kara and His Pupils.*
  H. Alper, 318(JAOS):Jul-Sep83-663
Pottle, F.A. James Boswell: The Earlier
  Years 1740-1769.
  C. Rawson, 441:13Jan85-37
Potts, L.W. Arthur Lee.
  G. Morgan, 656(WMQ):Oct84-668
Potvin, C. Le Canada français et se lit-
  térature de jeunesse.
  C. Gerson, 102(CanL):Summer84-127
Pou, P.J. - see under Jauralde Pou, P.
Poulenc, F. Journal de mes mélodies.
  J. Sams, 617(TLS):22Nov85-1317
Poulet, G. Exploding Poetry.
  F.G. Henry, 446(NCFS):Summer85-288
Poulin, G. Abel.
  J. Cowan, 102(CanL):Summer84-117
Pound, E. and F.M. Ford. Pound/Ford.* (B.
  Lindberg-Seyersted, ed)
  R. Lewis, 184(EIC):Apr84-169
Pound, E. and W. Lewis. Pound/Lewis.
  (T. Materer, ed)
  G. Lewis, 441:30Jun85-21
  J. Symons, 617(TLS):8Nov85-1259
Pound, E. and D. Shakespear. Ezra Pound
  and Dorothy Shakespear: Their Letters
  1909-1914.* (O. Pound and A.W. Litz,
  eds)
  R. Blythe, 362:31Jan85-21
  M. Korn, 617(TLS):8Nov85-1258
Pound, E. and J. Theobald. Ezra Pound/
  John Theobald: Letters. (D. Pearce
  and H. Schneidau, eds)
  M. Korn, 617(TLS):8Nov85-1258
Poundstone, W. Big Secrets.
  639(VQR):Summer84-99
Poundstone, W. The Recursive Universe.
  R. Penrose, 441:17Mar85-34
Pountain, C.J. Structures and Transforma-
  tions.
  J.A. Brill, 207(FR):Feb85-486
  J.N. Green, 353:Vol21No6-909
  J. Vizmuller-Zocco, 320(CJL):Spring84-
  95
Poupart, J-M. and Y. Lafontaine. Rétrovis-
  eurs.
  A. Moorhead, 207(FR):Oct84-161
  D. Thaler, 102(CanL):Summer84-161
Powell, A. O, How the Wheel Becomes It!*
  D. Flower, 249(HudR):Summer84-301
  J.L. Halio, 598(SoR):Winter85-204
Powell, A. The Strangers All Are Gone.
  R.J. Voorhees, 395(MFS):Summer84-367

Powell, A.G., E. Farrar and D.K. Cohen. The Shopping Mall High School.
G.I. Maeroff, 441:20Oct85-26
Powell, B. Epic and Chronicle.*
I. Corfis, 240(HR):Autumn84-525
R. MacDonald, 589:Oct84-947
Powell, G. Language as Being in the Poetry of Yvor Winters.
D. Bromwich, 402(MLR):Jul84-692
Powell, H. and D. Leatherbarrow, eds. Masterpieces of Architectural Drawing.
R.L. Castro, 529(QQ):Spring84-169
Powell, M. Fabula Docet.
M.P. McDiarmid, 571(ScLJ):Autumn84-11
Powell, N. A Season of Calm Weather.
B. Ruddick, 148:Autumn84-39
Powell, P. Edisto.*
S. Estess, 584(SWR):Autumn84-477
Powell, S., ed. The Advent and Nativity Sermons from a Fifteenth-Century Revision of John Mirk's "Festial."*
N.F. Blake, 72:Band221Heft1-172
A.J. Fletcher, 382(MAE):1984/1-137
Powell, S. Any Act of Leaving.
J. Carter, 219(GaR):Summer84-415
Power, B. The Ford of Heaven.
H.R. Lieberman, 441:27Jan85-23
Power, M.S. The Killing of Yesterday's Children.
J. Mellors, 364:Feb85-102
D. Sexton, 617(TLS):1Feb85-110
Powers, J. Philosophy and the New Physics.
J. Page, 479(PhQ):Jan84-75
Powers, R. Three Farmers on Their Way to a Dance.
M. Portales, 441:1Sep85-14
Powers, T. The Anubis Gates.
C. Greenland, 617(TLS):5Jul85-757
Powers, W.K. Oglala Religion.
B.M. Smith, 106:Summer84-185
Powers, W.K. Yuwipi.*
G.A. Schultz, 106:Winter84-433
Powis, J.K. Aristocracy.
J. Habakkuk, 617(TLS):22Feb85-205
Powys, J.C. Paddock Calls.
G. Cavaliero, 617(TLS):15Feb85-174
Powys, J.C. L'Art du bonheur.
T. Cordellier, 450(NRF):Oct84-108
Powys, J.C. Les Sables de la mer.
C. Jordis, 450(NRF):May84-133
Powys, J.C. Three Fantasies.
J. Melmoth, 617(TLS):14Jun85-677
Powys, J.C. Wolf Solent. Weymouth Sands.
J. Bayley, 453(NYRB):28Mar85-26
Powys, J.C. Une philosophie de la solitude.
T. Cordellier, 450(NRF):Oct84-108
C. Jordis, 450(NRF):Nov84-97
Powys, T.F. M. Bugby fait peur aux oiseaux.
C. Jordis, 450(NRF):Feb84-120
Pozier, B. Lost Angeles.
N.B. Bishop, 207(FR):Mar85-601
Poznanska-Parizeau, A. La Charge des sangliers.
M.E. Kidd, 102(CanL):Autumn84-92
Prache, A. Ile-de-France Romane.
P.W., 90:May84-304
Pradelli, M. and others. La Raccolta Molinari Pradelli Dipinti del Sei e Settecento.
E. Waterhouse, 90:Nov84-702

Pradier, J. Correspondance. (Vols 1 and 2) (D. Siler, ed)
R. Snell, 617(TLS):12Apr85-414
Prado, H. Gardens.
A. Shapiro, 441:17Nov85-30
Prado, M. More Practical Spanish Grammar.
J.S. Bailey, 399(MLJ):Winter84-416
Prado, M. Practical Spanish Grammar.
L.S. Glaze, 399(MLJ):Autumn84-303
Prager, D. and J. Telushkin. Why the Jews?
639(VQR):Winter84-20
Prance, C.A. Companion to Charles Lamb.
J. Aaron, 339(KSMB):No35-90
P. Morgan, 179(ES):Apr84-187
506(PSt):Sep84-203
Prantera, A. The Cabalist.
M. Seymour, 617(TLS):8Nov85-1266
Prantera, A. Strange Loop.*
P. Lewis, 364:Jul84-99
Prasad, M. Anita Desai.
P. Kumar, 314:Winter-Spring84-216
Prasad, M., ed. Indian-English Novelists.
L.A. Flemming, 293(JASt):May84-505
Prassinos, G. Mon coeur les écoute.
M. Cottenet-Hage, 207(FR):Dec84-315
Prater, D. and V. Michels, eds. Stefan Zweig.
J.B. Berlin, 406:Winter84-476
Pratolini, V. Il mannello di Natascia.
F. Donini, 617(TLS):11Oct85-1148
Pratt, B. L'Évangile selon Albert Camus.
B.G. Garnham, 208(FS):Apr84-237
Pratt, C. El anglicismo en el español peninsular contemporáneo.*
R. Santiago Lacuesta, 202(FMod): No68/70-412
Pratt, E.J. E.J. Pratt on His Life and Poetry.* (S. Gingell, ed)
C.M. Pfaff, 102(CanL):Autumn84-183
S.S., 376:Feb84-145
F.W. Watt, 627(UTQ):Summer84-451
Pratt, J.C., ed. Vietnam Voices.*
R. Smith, 617(TLS):15Feb85-168
Pratt, M.L. Towards a Speech Act Theory of Literary Discourse.
J. Culler, 153:Spring84-2
Pratt, N.T. Seneca's Drama.
G.W.M. Harrison, 124:Jan-Feb85-218
Prausnitz, F. Score and Podium.
H. Williams, 415:Jun84-330
Prauss, G. Kant über Freiheit als Autonomie.
K-H. Ilting, 53(AGP):Band66Heft3-335
A. Wood, 311(JP):May84-270
Praz, M. An Illustrated History of Interior Decoration.
A. Betsky, 505:Sep84-223
90:Jan84-50
Praz, M. Lettere a Bruno Migliorini.
F. Donini, 617(TLS):29Mar85-337
Praz, M. Studi e svaghi inglesi.
M. Bacigalupo, 402(MLR):Oct84-954
Prebish, C.S. American Buddhism.
K.P. Pedersen, 485(PE&W):Jan84-95
Prędota, S. Konfrontative Phonologie Polnisch-Niederländisch.
P. Proeme, 204(FdL):Jun84-153
R. Sadziński and J. Jeziorski, 361:Sep84-95
Prelinger, E. Edvard Munch.
R. Cardinal, 617(TLS):22Mar85-320
J.B. Smith, 39:Dec84-437

Prelutsky, J., ed. The Walker Book of
Poetry for Children.
  B. Morrison, 617(TLS):8Feb85-154
"Les Premiers Psychanalystes - Minutes de
la Société psychanalytique de Vienne."
(Vol 4)
  H. Cronel, 450(NRF):Sep84-110
Preminger, E.L. Gypsy and Me.*
  C. Brown, 617(TLS):26Apr85-458
Prenshaw, P.W., ed. Conversations with
Eudora Welty. Eudora Welty.
  D. Trouard, 659(ConL):Winter85-520
Press, G.A. The Development of the Idea
of History in Antiquity.
  J.L. Creed, 518:Apr84-83
  R.A. Markus, 487:Summer84-200
  P. Pellegrin, 542:Jan-Mar84-66
Pressly, W.L. The Life and Art of James
Barry.* James Barry: The Artist as
Hero.
  380:Summer84-220
Preston, D.J. Young Frederick Douglass.
  G.M. Fredrickson, 453(NYRB):27Jun85-3
Preston, P. A Dictionary of Pictorial
Subjects from Classical Literature.
  J.M. Hurwit, 124:Nov-Dec84-135
Preston, P., ed. Revolution and War in
Spain 1931-1939.
  R. Carr, 453(NYRB):17Jan85-39
  S.G. Payne, 617(TLS):17May85-553
Preston, P. and D. Smyth. Spain, the EEC
and NATO.
  N. Harrison, 617(TLS):22Mar85-328
Preston-Mafham, R. and K. Spiders of the
World.
  F. Vollrath, 617(TLS):18Jan85-69
Prete, R.A. and H. Ion, eds. Armies of
Occupation.
  G. Best, 617(TLS):15Feb85-168
Preuss, P. Broken Symmetries.
  G. Jonas, 441:20Jan85-21
"André Previn's Guide to Music."
  P. Standford, 415:Jun84-331
L'Abbé Prévost. Histoire du Chevalier des
Grieux et de Manon Lescaut. (R. Mauzi,
ed)
  R.A. Francis, 208(FS):Jan84-65
Prévot, J. La Première Institutrice de
France.*
  A. Carriat, 535(RHL):Jan/Feb84-101
du Prey, P.D. John Soane.*
  R. Lewis, 31(ASch):Summer84-406
  R.W. Liscombe, 529(QQ):Summer84-425
  T.J. McCormick, 173(ECS):Fall84-143
  J.M. Robinson, 39:Apr84-303
  A. Windsor, 576:Mar84-84
Price, A. Sion Crossing.
  N. Callendar, 441:15Sep85-33
  M. Laski, 362:10Jan85-25
Price, A.W., ed. "A Midsummer Night's
Dream."
  É. Cuvelier, 189(EA):Oct-Dec85-454
Price, D.K. America's Unwritten Constitu-
tion.
  639(VQR):Spring84-57
Price, G. The Languages of Britain.*
  F. Chevillet, 189(EA):Jul-Sep85-308
  M.I.M., 300:Vol 17-124
Price, G. and D.A. Wells - see "The Year's
Work in Modern Language Studies"
Price, J. Everything Must Go.
  D. Davis, 362:6Jun85-31
  B. Morrison, 617(TLS):10May85-527

Price, K., ed. On Criticizing Music.*
  S.D. Miller, 289:Summer84-113
  R.A. Sharpe, 89(BJA):Winter84-78
Price, K.A. The Captain's Paramours.
  T. Fitton, 617(TLS):8Mar85-266
  P. Lewis, 364:Mar85-105
Price, M. Forms of Life.*
  É. Delavenay, 189(EA):Jan-Mar85-76
  J. Gindin, 301(JEGP):Jul84-447
  E. Goodheart, 405(MP):Feb85-339
  T.L. Jeffers, 651(WHR):Autumn84-283
  G. Levine, 191(ELN):Mar85-76
  M. McClintick, 478:Apr84-139
  J. Preston, 402(MLR):Oct84-881
  D.D. Stone, 637(VS):Summer84-524
  295(JML):Nov84-389
Price, R. The Correspondence of Richard
Price.* (Vol 1) (W.B. Peach and D.O.
Thomas, eds)
  J. Dunn, 83:Autumn84-262
  J.W. Osborne, 656(WMQ):Apr84-321
Prickett, S., ed. The Context of English
Literature: The Romantics.
  P. Hamilton, 447(N&Q):Dec83-552
Prickett, S., ed. The Romantics.
  M. Roberts, 541(RES):Aug84-385
Priessnitz, H., ed. Anglo-Amerikanische
Shakespeare-Bearbeitungen des 20. Jahr-
hunderts.*
  C.W. Thomsen, 38:Band102Heft3/4-561
Priest, C. The Glamour.*
  G. Jonas, 441:16Jun85-18
Priest, P. Dante's Incarnation of the
Trinity.
  S. Bemrose, 278(IS):Vol139-115
Priestman, M. Cowper's "Task."
  W.B. Hutchings, 83:Autumn84-248
Prieto Paniagua, M.R. La arquitectura
románico-mudéjar en la provincia de
Salamanca.
  I.G. Bango Torviso, 48:Apr-Jun84-195
Prigogine, I. From Being to Becoming.
  P.A.Y. Gunter, 543:Dec83-414
  C. Hooker, 486:Jun84-355
Primeau, M-A. Maurice Dufault, sous-
directeur.
  R. Ewing, 102(CanL):Autumn84-160
Prince, G. Narratology.*
  M.L. Apte, 350:Mar85-245
  H. Bredin, 89(BJA):Winter84-84
  L.C. Perelman, 355(LSoc):Spr84-377
  M.D. Rapisarda, 395(MFS):Summer84-403
  J.S. Ryan, 67:May84-107
Prince, P. The Good Father.
  K. Ray, 441:7Apr85-15
Pring, J.T. - see under "The Oxford Dic-
tionary of Modern Greek"
Pringle, D. Science Fiction.
  T.M. Disch, 617(TLS):27Dec85-1478
Prins, G., ed. The Choice.
  P. Glynn, 617(TLS):4Jan85-4
Prioleau, E.S. The Circle of Eros.*
  A. Delbanco, 587(SAF):Autumn84-236
  K. Vanderbilt, 445(NCF):Jun84-105
Priollaud, N., ed. 1871: la Commune de
Paris.
  Hi Sook Hwang, 446(NCFS):Winter-
  Spring85-178
Prior, M., ed. Women in English Society,
1500-1800.
  L. Stone, 453(NYRB):11Apr85-21
Prisco, M. Lo specchio cieco.
  I. Quigly, 617(TLS):26Jul85-832

Pritchard, J. View from a Long Chair.*
(F. MacCarthy, ed)
R. Grant, 324:Feb85-239
J. Rutherford, 90:Nov84-711
Pritchard, W.H. Frost.*
R. Blythe, 362:21Mar85-24
R.J. Calhoun, 580(SCR):Spring85-112
W. Harmon, 472:Fall/Winter84-72
R. Poirier, 453(NYRB):25Apr85-26
R. Wells, 617(TLS):2Aug85-857
Pritchet, C.D., ed. Iohannis Alexandrini
commentaria in librum "De Sectis" Galeni.
A. Wasserstein, 123:Vol34No2-315
Pritchett, V.S. Dead Man Leading.
W. Balliett, 442(NY):8Apr85-127
Pritchett, V.S. A Man of Letters.
D.J. Enright, 617(TLS):22Nov85-1309
Pritchett, V.S. More Collected Stories.*
639(VQR):Spring84-54
Pritchett, V.S., ed. The Oxford Book of
Short Stories.
D. Hewitt, 541(RES):May84-275
Pritchett, W.K. The Greek State at War.
(Pt 3)
C. Leach, 447(N&Q):Feb83-92
Pritchett, W.K. Studies in Ancient Greek
Topography.* (Vols 3 and 4)
J. Ober, 487:Autumn84-268
Pritsak, O. The Origin of Rus'.* (Vol 1)
J. Lindow, 563(SS):Summer84-304
P. Sawyer, 550(RusR):Apr84-212
Probonas, I.K. Hē Mykēnaikē epikē poiēsē
me basē ta mykēnaika keimena kai ta
omērika epē.
G.P. Edwards, 123:Vol34No1-125
J.T. Hooker, 303(JoHS):Vol 104-191
Probst, G.F. and J.F. Bodine, eds. Per-
spectives on Max Frisch.*
M.E. Stewart, 402(MLR):Oct84-993
"Proceedings of the Kentucky Foreign Lan-
guage Conference 1983: Slavic Section."
(B. Sorokin, ed)
G. Slobin, 550(RusR):Jul84-320
Procházka, T., Sr. The Second Republic.
H. Hanak, 575(SEER):Apr84-306
J.F. Zacek, 104(CASS):Fall84-357
Proclus. Commentaire sur le Parménide de
Platon.* (Vol 1) (G. de Moerbeke, trans;
C. Steel, ed)
S. Gersh, 589:Jan84-244
Proclus. Théologie platonicienne.* (Bk 4)
(H.D. Saffrey and L.G. Westerink, eds
and trans)
D.A. Bertrand, 555:Vol58fasc2-311
Proclus. Trois études sur la providence.*
(Vol 3) (D. Isaac, ed and trans)
A. Meredith, 123:Vol34No1-137
A. Sheppard, 303(JoHS):Vol 104-223
Proctor, R. Waiting for Surabiel.
P. Lewis, 565:Spring84-64
Proctor, R.M. and J.F. Lew. Surface
Design for Fabric.
K.S.H., 614:Winter85-30
Proffer, E. Bulgakov.*
G. Steiner, 442(NY):16Dec85-160
Z. Zinik, 617(TLS):19Jul85-801
Proffitt, N. Gardens of Stone.*
42(AR):Fall84-509
Profumo, D. and G. Swift, eds. The Magic
Wheel.
A. Atha, 617(TLS):20Dec85-1466
Prokosch, F. The Asiatics.
J-M. Luccioni, 189(EA):Jul-Sep85-363

Prokosch, F. Voices.*
J-M. Luccioni, 189(EA):Jul-Sep85-363
295(JML):Nov84-337
Prokosch, F. Voix dans la nuit.
J. Aeply, 450(NRF):Oct84-115
Pronko, L.C. Eugène Labiche and Georges
Feydeau.*
S.B. John, 402(MLR):Jan84-199
von Proschwitz, G. - see Piron, A.
Prose, F. Hungry Hearts.
G. Davenport, 569(SR):Winter84-128
Pross, W. Arno Schmidt.
M. Silberman, 406:Summer84-237
Prosser, E. Shakespeare's Anonymous
Editors.*
W.C. McAvoy, 377:Mar84-58
M. Spevack, 156(JDSh):Jahrbuch1984-225
Prost, A. Petite histoire de la France au
XXe siècle.
P.A. Ouston, 208(FS):Apr84-243
Proust, M. Correspondance de Marcel
Proust.* (Vol 10) (P. Kolb, ed)
A. Arénilla, 450(NRF):Jan84-115
Proust, M. Correspondance de Marcel
Proust. (Vols 11 and 12) (P. Kolb, ed)
J.M. Cocking, 617(TLS):19Apr85-451
Proust, M. Selected Letters, 1880-1903.*
(P. Kolb, ed)
W. Fowlie, 569(SR):Spring84-xxxv
E. Weber, 31(ASch):Spring84-279
S.L. Wolitz, 395(MFS):Winter84-717
639(VQR):Winter84-10
Provensano, A. and M. Leonardo da Vinci.
E. Korn, 617(TLS):4Jan85-18
Proverbio, G., ed. Le sfida linguistica.
W. Ax, 260(IF):Band89-356
Prpić, G.J. Croatia and the Croatians.
G.M. Terry, 575(SEER):Jan84-149
Prucha, F.P. Indian-White Relations in
the United States.
G.A. Schultz, 106:Winter84-433
Prude, J. The Coming of Industrial Order.
P. Faler, 432(NEQ):Jun84-293
Prudentius. Prudenzio, "Hamartigenia."*
(R. Palla, ed and trans)
J.J. Thierry, 394:Vol37fasc1/2-224
Prunty, W. The Times Between.*
J. Saunders, 565:Spring84-55
Prvulović, Ž.R. Njegoševa teorija saz-
nanja i sistem.
P. Herrity, 575(SEER):Oct84-586
Prynne, J.H. Poems.
J. Rasula, 703:No10-165
Pryse, M. - see Freeman, M.E.W.
Pseudo-Mayne. Über das Bewusstsein.
J. Kulenkampff, 687:Nov-Dec84-683
Ptolemy. Ptolemy's "Almagest."* (G.J.
Toomer, ed)
I. Bulmer-Thomas, 123:Vol34No2-299
É. des Places, 555:Vol58fasc2-312
Ptolemy. Tetrabiblos. (2nd ed) (F. Rob-
bins, trans)
D. Rawlins, 529(QQ):Winter84-969
Pucci, I. The Epic of Life.
J. Boon, 441:15Dec85-22
Pucci, P. The Violence of Pity in Eurip-
ides' "Medea."
M. Griffith, 122:Apr84-160
Pucciani, O.F. and J. Hamel. Langue et
langage. (4th ed)
J.W. Zdenek, 399(MLJ):Summer84-167
"Giacomo Puccini: La bohème."
M. Carner, 415:May84-275

Pugh, P. Educate, Agitate, Organize.
  J. Harris, 617(TLS):11Oct85-1126
Puhvel, J. Hittite Etymological Diction-
  ary.
  J.A.C. Greppin, 617(TLS):31May85-612
  P.H. Salus, 350:Sep85-710
Puhvel, J. - see Dumézil, G.
Pulega, A. I sermoni in verso e
  l'"Arlabecca."
  C. Lee, 379(MedR):Dec84-446
Pullen, J.J. Comic Relief.
  D.E.E. Sloane, 27(AL):Oct84-432
Pulman, S.G. Word Meaning and Belief.*
  H. Holmback, 353:Vol21No5-748
Pulmer, K. Die dementierte Alternative.
  J. de Mylius, 562(Scan):Nov84-175
Pulos, A.J. American Design Ethic.*
  K.L. Ames, 658:Summer/Autumn84-226
  C. Ashwin, 592:Vol 197No1005-60
  N. Whiteley, 46:Jul84-68
Punter, D. Blake, Hegel and Dialectic.*
  D. Dahlstrom, 319:Apr85-267
Punter, D. The Hidden Script.
  A. Storr, 617(TLS):20Sep85-1040
Pupo-Walker, E. Historia, creación y pro-
  fecía en los textos del Inca Garcilaso
  de la Vega.
  W.C. Bryant, 238:Sep84-476
  R. González-Echevarría, 676(YR):
    Winter85-281
  I. Lerner, 240(HR):Autumn84-554
Pupo-Walker, E. La vocación literaria del
  pensamiento histórico en América.*
  P.T. Bradley, 86(BHS):Jan84-58
  R. González-Echevarría, 676(YR):
    Winter85-281
  S. Merrim, 403(MLS):Summer84-93
Puppi, L., G. Romanelli and S. Biadene.
  Longhena.
  D. Howard, 90:Aug84-507
Purcell, V.W.W.S. "How Unpleasant to Meet
  Mr. Eliot!" (S. Sullivan, ed)
  617(TLS):10May85-531
Purdy, A. Morning and It's Summer.
  C.R. Steele, 99:Nov84-38
Purdy, D.H. Joseph Conrad's Bible.
  D. Kramer, 573(SSF):Fall84-425
Purdy, J. On Glory's Course.*
  R. Kaveney, 617(TLS):8Mar85-266
  639(VQR):Autumn84-132
Purdy, R.L. and M. Millgate - see Hardy, T.
Puri, G. Bharatiya Jana Sangh.
  C. Baxter, 293(JASt):Aug84-786
Purishkevich, V.M. The Murder of Rasputin.
  (M.E. Shaw, ed)
  J. Koslow, 441:14Apr85-15
Pursglove, G. Francis Warner and Tradi-
  tion.
  R.J. Steen, 214:Vol 11No41-129
Purtillo, R. and C. Gassel. Ethical Dimen-
  sions in the Health Professions.
  R. Baker, 185:Jan85-370
Purves, A.C. and S. Takala, eds. An Inter-
  national Perspective on the Evaluation
  of Written Composition.
  J.R. Squire, 128(CE):Feb84-137
Püschel, U. Semantisch-syntaktische Rela-
  tionen.
  K. Welke, 682(ZPSK):Band37Heft4-528
Pushkin, A.S. The Bronze Horseman. (D.M.
  Thomas, trans)
  L. O'Bell, 399(MLJ):Summer84-185

Pushkin, A.S. Complete Prose Fiction.*
  (P. Debreczeny and W. Arndt, trans)
  J.D. Clayton, 104(CASS):Winter84-432
  S. Dayvdov, 550(RusR):Oct84-405
  S. Driver, 574(SEEJ):Fall84-397
  I.P. Foote, 617(TLS):11Jan85-43
Pushkin, A.S. The History of Pugachev.*
  (E. Sampson, trans) The Tales of Belkin.
  (G. Aitken and D. Budgen, trans)
  I.P. Foote, 617(TLS):11Jan85-43
Pushkin, A.S. Mozart and Salieri, and The
  Little Tragedies.* (A. Wood, trans)
  M. Shapiro, 574(SEEJ):Winter84-543
Pushkin, A.S. Eugene Onegin. (2nd ed)
  (W. Arndt, ed and trans)
  D.M. Bethea, 574(SEEJ):Spring84-112
Pushkin, A.S. and M. Lermontov. Narrative
  Poems by Alexander Pushkin and by Mik-
  hail Lermontov.* (C. Johnston, trans)
  T.J. Binyon, 617(TLS):25Jan85-87
  J.F. Cotter, 249(HudR):Autumn84-497
  639(VQR):Spring84-61
Putnam, H. Realism and Reason.
  F. Recanati, 98:May84-362
  483:Jul84-420
Putnam, H. Reason, Truth and History.*
  (German title: Vernunft, Wahrheit und
  Geschichte; French title: Raison,
  vérité et histoire.)
  R. Bubner, 384:Jun84-436
  M. Devitt, 482(PhR):Apr84-274
  F. Recanati, 98:May84-362
  R.K. Shope, 484(PPR):Jun85-644
  M. Williams, 311(JP):May84-257
Putnam, L.L. and M.E. Pacanowsky, eds.
  Communication and Organizations.
  M.H. Brown, 583:Spring85-300
Putnam, M.C.J. Virgil's Poem of the
  Earth.*
  V. Schmidt, 394:Vol137fasc1/2-210
Putschögl-Wild, A.M. Untersuchungen zur
  Sprache im Fremdenverkehr.
  R.M. Piñel, 202(FMod):No68/70-410
Putt, S.G. The Golden Age of English
  Drama.*
  R.W. Dent, 405(MP):Nov84-202
  J. Drakakis, 447(N&Q):Oct83-465
  H. Hawkins, 541(RES):May84-221
  J.J. Peereboom, 179(ES):Oct84-468
Pütz, H. Über die Syntax der Pronominal-
  form "es" im modernen Deutsch.
  M.L. Schilling Rodríguez, 202(FMod):
  No68/70-397
Pütz, J. "Verschollener" — ein Bildungs-
  roman?
  J. Jacobs, 680(ZDP):Band103Heft2-300
Pütz, M. - see Emerson, R.W.
Putzel, M. Genius of Place.
  M. Grimwood, 578:Fall85-101
Puzo, M. The Sicilian.*
  E.J. Hobsbawm, 453(NYRB):14Feb85-12
Pym, B. Crampton Hodnet.
  P-L. Adams, 61:Jun85-104
  M. Dorris, 441:1Sep85-14
  P. Kemp, 362:27Jun85-31
  M. Seymour, 617(TLS):28Jun85-720
  442(NY):29Jul85-76
Pym, B. A Few Green Leaves.
  M. Rutschky, 384:Apr84-332
Pym, B. No Fond Return of Love.*
  J.L. Halio, 598(SoR):Winter85-204

Pym, B. A Very Private Eye.* (H. Holt and
H. Pym, eds)
   J. Halperin, 395(MFS):Winter84-780
   K.B. Heberlein, 659(ConL):Fall85-368
   V. Meyers, 395(MFS):Winter84-783
   J. Nardin, 152(UDQ):Spring85-133
   42(AR):Fall84-507
Pym, F. The Politics of Consent.*
   I. Davidson, 176:Apr85-71
Pynchon, T. Slow Learner.
   D. Seed, 189(EA):Oct-Dec85-488
   G. Strawson, 617(TLS):11Jan85-41
Pyritz, H. and I. Bibliographie zur deut-
schen Literaturgeschichte des Barock-
zeitalters.* (Pt 2, fasc 1, 2 and 4)
   K.F. Otto, Jr., 301(JEGP):Apr84-270
Pyritz, H. and I. Bibliographie zur
deutschen Literaturgeschichte des Barock-
zeitalters.* (Pt 2, fasc 3)
   R.J. Alexander, 406:Summer84-209
   K.F. Otto, Jr., 301(JEGP):Apr84-270
Pyron, D.A., ed. Recasting.
   J.B. Wittenberg, 395(MFS):Winter84-796
   42(AR):Summer84-380

Qing, A. - see under Ai Qing
Quade, Q.L., ed. The Pope and Revolution.
   M.M. Brennan, 396(ModA):
      Spring/Summer84-294
Qualls, B.V. The Secular Pilgrims of Vic-
torian Fiction.*
   R.J. Dunn, 637(VS):Spring84-384
   P. Parrinder, 366:Spring84-128
Quammen, D. Natural Acts.
   T. Ferrell, 441:21Apr85-39
Quammen, D. The Zolta Configuration.
   T.J. Binyon, 617(TLS):15Feb85-179
Quantrill, M. Alvar Aalto.*
   W.C. Miller, 576:Dec84-374
Quasimodo, S. Complete Poems of Salvatore
Quasimodo.*
   C. Tomlinson, 364:Jul84-70
Quayle, E. Early Children's Books.*
   B. Alderson, 354:Sep84-305
Quednau, R. Die Sala di Costantino im
Vatikanischen Palast.*
   B. Wollesen-Wisch, 90:Jul84-440
de Quehen, A.H., ed. Editing Poetry From
Spenser to Dryden.
   I. Grundy, 447(N&Q):Feb83-77
Quesada, M.A.L. - see under Ladero Quesada,
M.A.
Questa, C. Il reiziano ritrovato.
   H.D. Jocelyn, 123:Vol34No2-236
   J. Soubiran, 555:Vol58fasc1-128
Quested, R.K.I. "Matey" Imperialists?*
   M. Bassin, 550(RusR):Apr84-206
   R.H.G. Lee, 293(JASt):May84-531
   H. Seton-Watson, 575(SEER):Apr84-288
   J.J. Stephan, 302:Vol20No2-222
Quet, M-H. La mosaïque cosmologique de
Mérida.*
   H. Whitehouse, 313:Vol74-226
Quignard, P. Les tablettes de buis
d'Apronenia Avitia.*
   A. Clerval, 450(NRF):Jun84-100
   J. Piel, 98:Nov84-939
Quijano, J.A.C. - see under Calderón Qui-
jano, J.A.
Quillien, J. G. de Humboldt et la Grèce.
   A. Reix, 542:Oct-Dec84-482

Quilligan, M. Milton's Spenser.
   A.K. Hieatt, 391:Oct84-94
   A.L. Prescott, 604:Fall84-61
"The Quilt Digest 3." (M.M. Kile, ed)
   K.S. Hofweber, 614:Spring85-28
"Quilts from Cincinnati Collection."
   R.L. Shep, 614:Summer85-33
Quine, W.V. Theories and Things.*
   C. Cherniak, 482(PhR):Jan84-128
   J. Van Evra, 154:Sep84-558
Quinlan, D. The Illustrated Guide to Film
Directors.
   J. Nangle, 200:Oct84-503
   639(VQR):Summer84-99
Quinlivan, P. and P. Rose. The Fenians in
England, 1865-1872.
   J.W. O'Neill, 637(VS)·Summer84-522
Quinn, C. Yarn.
   D. Musick, 614:Summer85-38
Quinn, P.F. - see Poe, E.A.
Quinn, T.J. Athens and Samos, Lesbos and
Chios, 478-404 B.C.*
   L. Kallet-Marx, 121(CJ):Dec84/Jan85-
      163
Quinn, W.A. and A.S. Hall. Jongleur.*
   N. Jacobs, 382(MAE):1984/2-311
Quinones, R.J. Mapping Literary Modernism.
   R. Brown, 617(TLS):27Sep85-1075
Quint, D. Origin and Originality in
Renaissance Literature.*
   W.F.M., 604:Spring-Summer84-36
Quintal, C., ed. L'Émigrant québécois
vers les États-Unis: 1850-1920. The
Little Canadas of New England.
   G.R. Montbertrand, 207(FR):Dec84-326
Quintal, C. and A. Vachon, eds. Situation
de la recherche sur la Franco-Américanie.
   G.R. Montbertrand, 207(FR):Dec84-326
Quintero, R.T. - see under Torres Quintero,
R.
Quirk, R. and Others. A Comprehensive
Grammar of the English Language.
   D. Crystal, 362:27Jun85-26
   J.M. Sinclair, 617(TLS):28Jun85-715
Quirk, T. Melville's Confidence Man.*
   J. Bryant, 403(MLS):Fall84-85
   J.R. Russo, 594:Spring84-128
   J. Seelye, 445(NCF):Mar85-479
Quittek, R. - see Meyer-Wehlack, B. and I.
Vrkljan

Raabe, H. Apposition.
   G. Koller, 685(ZDL):1/1984-120
Raabe, W. Novels. (V. Sander, ed)
   D.C. Riechel, 399(MLJ):Winter84-406
Ra'anan, G.D. International Policy Forma-
tion in the USSR.
   W. Hahn, 550(RusR):Jul84-307
Raas, F. Die Wette der drei Frauen.
   H. Heinen, 301(JEGP):Oct84-596
   H-J. Uther, 196:Band25Heft3/4-356
   S.L. Wailes, 133:Band17Heft1/2-129
Raban, J. Foreign Land.
   T.J. Binyon, 617(TLS):28Jun85-721
   T.R. Edwards, 441:3Nov85-9
   D.J. Enright, 453(NYRB):5Dec85-35
   J. Mellors, 362:13Jun85-32
"Rabbits, Crabs, etc." - see under Birn-
baum, P.

Rabelais, F. Le Disciple de Pantagruel
(Les Navigations de Panurge). (G.
Demerson and C. Lauvergnat-Gagnière, eds)
T. Thomson, 402(MLR):Jan84-183
Rabil, A., Jr. Laura Cereta.*
D. Robey, 382(MAE):1984/2-335
Rabinovitz, R. The Development of Samuel
Beckett's Fiction.
M.J. Friedman, 659(ConL):Winter85-516
M. Gee, 617(TLS):21Jun85-698
Rabinow, P. - see Foucault, M.
Rabinowitz, H.N., ed. Southern Black
Leaders of the Reconstruction Era.*
A.W. Trelease, 579(SAQ):Autumn84-472
Rabinowitz, I. - see Messer Leon, J.
Rabkin, E.S. Arthur C. Clarke.
P. Fitting, 561(SFS):Mar84-88
Rabkin, E.S., M.H. Greenberg and J.D. Olan-
der, eds. The End of the World.
D. Watson, 561(SFS):Nov84-329
Rabkin, E.S., M.H. Greenberg and J.D.
Olander, eds. No Place Else.
D.D. Todd, 478:Oct84-309
Rabkin, N. Shakespeare and the Problem of
Meaning.*
E.A.J. Honigmann, 402(MLR):Oct84-895
Rabon, I. The Street.
J. Daynard, 441:18Aug85-20
S.S. Prawer, 617(TLS):30Aug85-946
Raby, P. "Fair Ophelia."*
E. Brody, 446(NCFS):Summer-Fall184-210
C. Thompson, 451:Summer84-69
J. Williamson, 611(TN):Vol38No1-47
Racevskis, K. Michel Foucault and the
Subversion of Intellect.
A. Demaitre, 207(FR):Dec84-303
J. Rajchman, 529(QQ):Autumn84-623
K.S. Rothwell, 125:Winter84-171
M. Seltzer, 153:Spring84-78
M. Sprinker, 141:Fall184-383
42(AR):Winter84-119
Racine, J. Andromache.* (R. Wilbur,
trans)
R.S. Gwynn, 569(SR):Fall184-644
Racine, J. Four Greek Plays.* (R.C.
Knight, trans)
M-O. Sweetser, 475:Vol 11No20-248
Racine, J. Fragments indicatifs.
L.A. di Benedetto, 207(FR):Dec84-316
Racine, J. Théâtre complet. (Vol 1) (J-P.
Collinet, ed)
M-O. Sweetser, 475:Vol 11No20-220
Raddatz, F.J. - see Tucholsky, K.
Rader, B.G. In Its Own Image.
L. Mifflin, 441:24Feb85-23
Rader, D. Tennessee.
F. Rich, 441:21Apr85-3
G. Vidal, 453(NYRB):13Jun85-5
Radford, C.J. and S. Minogue. The Nature
of Criticism.*
S. Trombley, 541(RES):Aug84-430
al-Radi, S.M.S. Phlamoudhi Vounari.
Y. Calvet, 555:Vol58fasc1-106
Radiguet, R. Le Diable au corps. (R.
Griffiths, ed)
J. Cruickshank, 208(FS):Apr84-229
Radnitzky, G. and G. Andersson, eds. The
Structure and Development of Science.
R. Nola, 84:Jun84-184
Radnitzky, G. and G. Andersson, eds. Vor-
aussetzungen und Grenzen der Wissen-
schaft.*
M. Schmid, 679:Band15Heft1-179

Radosh, R. and J. Milton. The Rosenberg
File. (British title: Dossier Rosen-
berg.)
G. Bullert, 396(ModA):Spring/Summer84-
252
J-F. Revel, 176:Dec85-44
J.A. Stein, 31(ASch):Summer84-410
D. Stone, 390:Mar84-64
Radrigán, J. Teatro de Juan Radrigán.
K.F. Nigro, 238:Dec84-679
Radtke, B. Al-Ḥakīm at-Tirmiḏī ein islam-
ischer Theosoph des 3./9. Jahrhunderts.
F.W. Zimmermann, 294:Vol 15-139
Radway, J.A. Reading the Romance.*
A. Calder, 617(TLS):15Feb85-162
Rae, D. and others. Equalities.
A. Sen, 185:Jul185-934
Raeburn, J. Fame Became of Him.*
L. Simon, 385(MQR):Summer85-502
R.P. Weeks, 395(MFS):Winter84-807
Raeff, M. Understanding Imperial Russia.
N. Tolstoy, 441:20Jan85-30
Raeff, M. The Well-Ordered Police State.
R.P. Bartlett, 575(SEER):Oct84-600
C.R. Friedrichs, 104(CASS):Winter84-
455
M. Hughes, 83:Spring84-111
C. Peterson, 550(RusR):Apr84-214
Raether, M. Der "Acte gratuit," Revolte
und Literatur.*
N. Segal, 208(FS):Jan84-105
Raffaelli, R. Ricerche sui versi lunghi
di Plauto e di Terenzio.
H.D. Jocelyn, 123:Vol134No2-239
J. Soubiran, 555:Vol58fasc1-137
Raffel, B. American Victorians.
E. Sagan, 152(UDQ):Winter85-107
Raffel, B. Ezra Pound, Prime Minister of
Poetry.
M. Korn, 617(TLS):8Nov85-1258
Rafferty, E. Discourse Structures of the
Chinese Indonesian of Malang.
S. Cumming, 350:Mar85-230
Raftis, J.A., ed. Pathways to Medieval
Peasants.
P.R. Hyams, 382(MAE):1984/1-147
E. Searle, 589:Jan84-197
Raghunandana Bhaṭṭācārya. The Divyatattva
of Raghunandana Bhaṭṭācārya.* (R.W.
Lariviere, ed and trans) [shown in prev
under ed and trans]
S. Pollock, 293(JASt):Nov83-192
Ragotzky, H. Gattungserneuerung und Laien-
unterweisung in Texten des Strickers.*
O. Ehrismann, 680(ZDP):Band103Heft3-
455
Ragusa, O. Pirandello.*
E. Licastro, 276:Summer84-177
Ragussis, M. The Subterfuge of Art.
B.G. Caraher, 599:Winter84-106
Rahman, F. Major Themes of the Qur'ān.
W.A. Graham, 318(JAOS):Apr-Jun83-445
Rahn, J. Basic Atonal Theory.
D.H. Smyth, 513:Fall-Winter83/Spring-
Summer84-549
Rahn, J. A Theory for All Music.
R.B. Cantrick, 290(JAAC):Spring85-321
T. Rice, 627(UTQ):Summer84-522
Rahner, K. Grundkurs des Glaubens.
F. Marti, 489(PJGG):Band91Heft1-176

Raphael, B. The Anatomy of Bereavement.
  639(VQR):Spring84-64
Raphael, D.D. Moral Philosophy.
  J.M. Day, 393(Mind):Jul84-442
Raphael, F. Byron.
  P.W. Martin, 339(KSMB):No35-97
Raphael, F. Heaven and Earth.
  W. Ferguson, 441:20Oct85-34 .
  J. Mellors, 364:Mar85-100
  G. Strawson, 617(TLS):8Feb85-140
Raphael, F. Oxbridge Blues and Other
  Stories.
  D.R. Slavitt, 385(MQR):Fall85-660
"Raphaël et la seconde main."
  V.D.L., 605(SC):15Jan85-189
Rapin, N. Oeuvres.* (Vol 1) (J. Brunel,
  ed)
  P. Chilton, 208(FS):Jul84-329
Rapin, N. Oeuvres. (Vol 2) (J. Brunel,
  ed)
  P. Chilton, 208(FS):Jul84-329
  R. Zuber, 535(RHL):Nov/Dec84-951
Rapoport, A. Mathematical Models in the
  Social and Behavioral Sciences.
  E. Menefee, 186(ETC.):Spring84-95
Rapp, C. William Carlos Williams and
  Romantic Idealism.
  L.M. Steinman, 659(ConL):Winter85-497
Rapp, F. Analytical Philosophy of Technol-
  ogy.*
  A.C. Michalos, 488:Sep84-427
  J. Van Evra, 154:Dec84-745
Rapp, G., Jr. and J. Gifford, eds. Troy:
  The Archaeological Geology.
  R.W.V. Catling, 123:Vol34No1-144
"Rapporti della Soprintendenza per i Beni
  Artistici e Storici per le provincie di
  Bologna, Ferrara, Forli e Ravenna."
  (No 29)
  R. Gibbs, 90:Jul84-438
Raschella, F.D., ed and trans. The So-
  called Second Grammatical Treatise.
  E. Haugen, 563(SS):Winter84-65
Rashke, R. Stormy Genius.
  C.H. Lavin, 441:29Dec85-19
Rasico, P.D. Estudis sobre la fonologia
  del català preliterari.
  R. de Gorog, 589:Oct84-950
Raskolnikov, F.F. Kronstadt and Petrograd
  in 1917. (B. Pearce, ed and trans)
  L. Schapiro, 575(SEER):Apr84-298
Rasmussen, P. El verbo "hacer" en expres-
  iones temporales.
  R. Penny, 86(BHS):Apr84-189
Rasor, D. The Pentagon Underground.
  M. Kilian, 441:1Dec85-35
Raspa, A. The Emotive Image.
  A. Low, 551(RenQ):Winter84-656
  A. Rudrum, 627(UTQ):Summer84-421
Raspe, R.E. The Adventures of Baron
  Munchausen. (R. Searle, illustrator)
  I. Parry, 617(TLS):29Mar85-355
Ratcliff, C. John Singer Sargent.*
  T.J. Fairbrother, 432(NEQ):Mar84-147
  R. Shone, 90:Nov84-709
Ratcliff, C. Andy Warhol.
  J. Bell, 55:Apr84-29
Ratcliffe, S. Campion: On Song.*
  M. Booth, 577(SHR):Winter84-78
  L. Dunn, 184(EIC):Jul84-244
Rath, R. Kommunikationspraxis.
  G. Koller, 685(ZDL):3/1984-389

Rathbone, J. Lying in State.
  M. Laski, 362:14Nov85-35
Ratner, L. The Musical Experience.
  P. Standford, 415:Sep84-503
Ratushinskaya, I. Poems.
  A. Shaw, 385(MQR):Summer85-514
Ratzinger, J., with V. Messori. The Rat-
  zinger Report.
  J.A. Komonchak, 441:22Dec85-9
Rau, F. Zur Verbreitung und Nachahmung
  des "Tatler" und "Spectator."*
  C. Winton, 536:Vol6-129
Rauch, I. and G.F. Carr, eds. Language
  Change.
  P. Beade, 361:Jul-Aug84-325
  W.G. Moulton, 350:Sep85-680
Raulet, G. Humanisation de la nature,
  naturalisation de l'homme.
  P. Somville, 542:Jan-Mar84-95
Raval, S. Metacriticism.
  R.D. Denham, 405(MP):Nov84-235
Ravel, A. Second Chance.
  J. Wasserman, 102(CanL):Summer84-91
Raven, S. The Face of the Waters.
  T. Fitton, 617(TLS):13Sep85-1000
  D.A.N. Jones, 362:15Aug85-28
van Ravenswaay, C. Drawn from Nature.
  M. Jebb, 617(TLS):29Nov85-1368
Raverty, R.G., ed and trans. Selections
  from the Poetry of the Afghans.
  A. Schimmel, 318(JAOS):Oct-Dec83-810
Ravier, X. Atlas linguistique et ethno-
  graphique du Languedoc Occidental.
  (Vols 1 and 2)
  G. Tuaillon, 553(RLiR):Jan-Jun84-244
Ravin, N. Seven North.
  M. Levin, 441:19May85-22
Ravindra, R. Whispers from the Other
  Shore.
  M. Heyneman, 469:Vol 10No1-136
Ravisé, J.S. Tableaux culturels de la
  France.
  T. Scanlan, 207(FR):Dec84-340
Ravitch, D. The Schools We Deserve.
  B. Berger, 129:Oct85-74
  P.W. Jackson, 441:2Jun85-39
  R. Meisler, 385(MQR):Fall85-650
Ravitch, D. The Troubled Crusade.*
  M. Beloff, 176:Feb85-54
  J. Rury, 42(AR):Spring84-256
  639(VQR):Winter85-21
Rawling, T. The Old Showfield.
  L. Mackinnon, 617(TLS):28Jun85-732
Rawlings, H.R. 3d. The Structure of Thu-
  cydides' History.*
  M. Chambers, 122:Jan84-58
Rawlings, M.K. Selected Letters of Mar-
  jorie Kinnan Rawlings. (G.E. Bigelow
  and L.V. Monti, eds)
  A.E. Rowe, 578:Spring85-133
  R.E. Spiller, 27(AL):Mar84-129
  W.J. Stuckey, 395(MFS):Summer84-316
Rawlinson, J. Cradle Song.
  E. Fisher, 617(TLS):22Feb85-197
Rawson, C., ed. The Character of Swift's
  Satire.
  J. Hérou, 189(EA):Jul-Sep85-326
  C.T. Probyn, 566:Autumn84-53
Rawson, C. Order from Confusion Sprung.
  D. Nokes, 617(TLS):8Nov85-1261
Rawson, H. A Dictionary of Euphemisms and
  Other Doubletalk.*
  J.R. Gaskin, 569(SR):Winter84-114

Rawson, P. The Art of Drawing.
　J. Burr, 39:Dec84-439
Ray, L. Nuages, nuit.
　D. Leuwers, 450(NRF):Jan84-114
Ray, R. Change in Bengal Agrarian Society
　c. 1760-1850.
　J.R. McLane, 293(JASt):Feb84-362
Ray, R.B. A Certain Tendency of the Holly-
　wood Cinema, 1930-1980.
　R. Grenier, 617(TLS):13Dec85-1423
　C. Temerson, 441:28Jul85-19
Ray, W. Literary Meaning.
　S. Scobie, 376:Oct84-107
Raymo, C. The Soul of the Night.
　R. Wright, 441:20Oct85-35
Raymond, D. The Devil's Home on Leave.
　M. Laski, 362:18Apr85-26
Raymond, F., ed. Jules Verne 3.
　H. Codin, 208(FS):Oct84-475
Raymond, M. and G. Poulet. Marcel Raymond
　— Georges Poulet, Correspondance: 1950-
　1977.* (P. Grotzer, ed)
　J. Birkett, 208(FS):Jan84-97
Raymond, M.B. and M.R. Sullivan - see
　Browning, E.B.
Raynaud, J-M. Voltaire, soi-disant.
　J. Renwick, 402(MLR):Jul84-707
Raz, S. Tigre Grammar and Texts.
　M.L. Bender, 350:Jun85-504
Razoumovskaïa, M.V. Stanovlenie novovo
　romama vo Frantsii i zapriot na roman
　1730-kh godov.
　C. Mervaud, 535(RHL):Nov/Dec84-965
Rea, A.M. Once a River.*
　C. Hood, 649(WAL):Feb85-337
Rea, D., ed. Political Cooperation in
　Divided Societies.
　T. Garvin, 272(IUR):Spring84-146
Rea, R.R. - see Ware, J.D.
Read, B. Victorian Sculpture.*
　T.J. Edelstein, 637(VS):Winter84-242
　A. Yarrington, 59:Mar84-110
Read, D., ed. Edwardian England.
　P. Williamson, 161(DUJ):Dec83-126
Read, F. '76: One World and "The Cantos"
　of Ezra Pound.*
　R. Casillo, 536:Vol6-275
Read, J. The Simon and Schuster Pocket
　Guide to Spanish Wines.
　W. and C. Cowen, 639(VQR):Spring84-68
Read, M.K. The Birth and Death of Lan-
　guage.
　M. Johnston, 304(JHP):Winter84-159
　E.L. Rivers, 238:Dec84-666
"A Readable 'Beowulf.'"* (S.B. Greenfield,
　trans)
　D.K. Fry, 131(CL):Spring84-177
Reading, A. Psychological Aspects of Preg-
　nancy.
　D. and A. Muir, 529(QQ):Winter84-1041
Reading, P. C.
　M. Imlah, 617(TLS):4Jan85-10
Reading, P. Diplopic.*
　R. Pybus, 565:Autumn84-73
Reading, P. and D. Butler. 5x5x5x5x5.
　M. Imlah, 617(TLS):4Jan85-10
Ready, W.B. Files on Parade.
　B. Whiteman, 556:Winter84/85-323
"Reallexikon der Assyriologie und vorder-
　asiatischen Archäologie." (Vol 6, Pt 6)
　P. Swiggers, 350:Sep85-719

Reaney, J. The Donnellys.
　T. McNamara, 526:Summer84-84
　T. McNamara, 529(QQ):Winter84-1008
Reasoner, H. Before the Colors Fade.
　A. Chenoweth, 569(SR):Winter84-171
Reay, B. The Quakers and the English
　Revolution.
　B. Coward, 617(TLS):7Jun85-628
Rebhorn, W.A. Courtly Performances.
　F. Graziani, 549(RLC):Jul-Sep84-358
Récanati, F. Les Enoncés Performatifs.
　B. de Cornulier, 209(FM):Apr84-115
　F. Nef, 209(FM):Apr84-121
"Recherches en français parlé."
　F. Maziere, 209(FM):Apr84-88
"Recherches sur le français parlé." (No 5)
　P. Swiggers, 353:Vol22No6-930
Reckert, S. Espírito e letra de Gil
　Vicente.
　T.R. Hart, 400(MLN):Mar84-393
Rector, L. The Sorrow of Architecture.
　F. Garber, 29(APR):Sep/Oct85-14
　R. McDowell, 249(HudR):Spring84-127
　R. McDowell, 364:Feb85-45
　P. Stitt, 219(GaR):Fall84-628
Recuero, P.P., ed. Antología de Cuentos
　Sefardíes.
　E. Roditi, 390:Jan84-50
Réda, J. L'Herbe des talus.*
　F. Trémolières, 450(NRF):Sep84-91
Redding, D. Learning to Weave with Debbie
　Redding.
　D.M., 614:Winter85-27
Redenbarger, W.J. Articulator Features
　and Portuguese Vowel Height.*
　I.S. Shaw, 361:Apr84-167
Redfern, B. Dance, Art and Aesthetics.
　G.M. Burke, 89(BJA):Autumn84-370
Redfern, W. Puns.
　S.D. Smith, 441:17Feb85-21
Redford, D.B. Akhenaten.
　K. Kitchen, 617(TLS):29Mar85-361
Redgrave, M. In My Mind's I.* (British
　title: In My Mind's Eye.)
　J. Nangle, 200:Feb84-113
　G. Playfair, 157:No151-50
Redgrove, P. The Apple-Broadcast and
　Other Poems.
　B. Howard, 344:Winter85-124
Redgrove, P. The Man Named East and Other
　New Poems. The Working of Water.
　J. Mole, 176:Jul/Aug85-52
　N. Roberts, 617(TLS):28Jun85-732
Redlich, S. Propaganda and Nationalism in
　Wartime Russia.
　H.J. Tobias, 104(CASS):Fall84-320
Redmond, D.A. Sherlock Holmes.*
　L. Lane, Jr., 178:Dec84-501
　E.S. Lauterbach, 395(MFS):Summer84-379
　J.B. Shaw, 70:Sep-Oct83-29
Redmond, J., ed. Drama and Symbolism.*
　P. Hollindale, 541(RES):Nov84-590
Redmond, J., ed. Drama and the Actor.
　Drama and Mimesis. Drama and Religion.
　G. Bas, 189(EA):Oct-Dec85-450
Redmond, J., ed. Drama, Dance and Music.
　G. Bas, 189(EA):Oct-Dec85-450
　F. Claudon, 549(RLC):Oct-Dec84-481
Redondo, A., ed. XIXe Colloque Interna-
　tional d'Études Humanistes, Tours, 5-17
　juillet 1976: L'Humanisme dans les let-
　tres espagnoles.*
　D.E. Carpenter, 545(RPh):May84-507

Rée, H., ed. The Henry Morris Collection.
  S. Maclure, 617(TLS):25Jan85-85
Reed, A. Romantic Weather.*
  T.M. Kelley, 661(WC):Summer84-129
Reed, A., ed. Romanticism and Language.
  R. Ashton, 617(TLS):5Jul85-752
Reed, J. By the Fisheries.*
  B. O'Donoghue, 493:Jun84-61
Reed, J. The Schubert Song Companion.
  P. Hamburger, 617(TLS):6Sep85-971
Reed, J. Sir Walter Scott.*
  W. Ruddick, 447(N&Q):Aug83-353
Reed, J.R. The Natural History of H.G.
  Wells.*
  D.Y. Hughes, 561(SFS):Mar84-61
  F. McConnell, 637(VS):Autumn83-116
  P. Parrinder, 125:Winter84-181
Reed, J.S. Southerners.
  639(VQR):Winter84-21
Reed, K. Story First.
  D. Kirby, 128(CE):Mar84-248
Reed, M. The Georgian Triumph, 1700-1830.*
  A. McInnes, 566:Autumn84-73
Reed, W. and R. The Illustrator in Amer-
  ica 1880-1980.
  P-L. Adams, 61:Feb85-100
Reed, W.L. An Exemplary History of the
  Novel.*
  J. Levine, 627(UTQ):Spring84-296
van Reenen, P. Phonetic Feature Defini-
  tions.
  L. Barratt, 350:Sep85-707
  F. Nolan, 361:Oct/Nov84-238
Rees, D. Painted Desert, Green Shade.
  N. Philip, 617(TLS):21Jun85-703
Rees, J. The Poetry of Dante Gabriel
  Rossetti.*
  P.M. Ball, 637(VS):Winter84-264
  E.D. Mackerness, 447(N&Q):Apr83-175
  B. Richards, 541(RES):May84-281
Rees, M. Northern Ireland.
  C. Townshend, 617(TLS):1Nov85-1231
Rees, M.A., ed. Teresa de Jesús and Her
  World.
  C.P. Thompson, 86(BHS):Apr84-195
Rees, N. Sayings of the Century.
  G. Marshall, 617(TLS):1Feb85-114
Reese, S.C. Songs of Freedom.
  B. Brown, 95(CLAJ):Sep84-102
Reeve, M.D. - see Longus
Reeves, G. Real Stories.
  C. Boyle, 364:Mar85-85
  L. Mackinnon, 617(TLS):26Jul85-834
Reeves, H. Atoms of Silence.*
  42(AR):Fall84-507
Reeves, R. Doubting Thomas.
  P-L. Adams, 61:Mar85-125
Reeves, R. The Reagan Detour.
  M. Kramer, 441:10Nov85-18
  442(NY):18Nov85-175
Reff, T. Manet and Modern Paris.
  T.D. Stamm, 446(NCFS):Summer-Fall84-
  200
  R. Thomson, 59:Jun84-259
"Reform of Social Security."
  F. Cairncross, 617(TLS):20Sep85-1025
Regan, D.H. Utilitarianism and Coopera-
  tion.*
  B. Barley, 449:Mar84-152
Regan, M.S. Love Words.*
  P. Bondanella, 131(CL):Spring84-180
  H. Morris, 569(SR):Spring84-290

Regan, T. All That Dwell Therein.*
  P. Singer, 453(NYRB):17Jan85-46
Regan, T. The Case for Animal Rights.
  H. Lehman, 154:Dec84-669
  P. Singer, 453(NYRB):17Jan85-46
Regan, T., ed. Just Business.
  J.W. Dienhart, 185:Jul85-969
Regan, T. and D. Vandeveer, eds. And
  Justice For All.*
  A. Schafer, 154:Jun84-366
Regehr, E. and S. Rosenblum, eds. Canada
  and the Nuclear Arms Race.
  R.W. Reford, 529(QQ):Winter84-1005
Regent, P. Laughing Pig and Other Stories.
  L. Caldecott, 441:2Jun85-37
  D. Montrose, 617(TLS):4Jan85-9
Rehder, R. Wordsworth and the Beginnings
  of Modern Poetry.*
  L. Newlyn, 541(RES):May84-243
  W.J.B. Owen, 402(MLR):Jul84-675
Reibetanz, J.M. A Reading of Eliot's
  "Four Quartets."
  295(JML):Nov84-431
Reich, N.B. Clara Schumann.
  J. Chernaik, 617(TLS):22Nov85-1317
  H.C. Schonberg, 441:11Aug85-15
Reich, R.B. and J.D. Donahue. New Deals.
  J. Flint, 441:7Jul85-5
Reich-Ranicki, M., with U. Weinzierl - see
  Polgar, A.
Reichenberger, K. and R., with T. Berchem
  and H.W. Sullivan. Bibliographisches
  Handbuch der Calderón-Forschung/Manual
  bibliográfico calderoniano. (Vols 1 and
  3)
  J.J. Allen, 345(KRQ):Vol31No3-343
Reichhold, J. From the dipper ... drops.
  404:Winter-Spring84-44
Reichl, K. Categorial Grammar and Word-
  Formation.*
  P. Collins, 67:May84-113
  J. Vizmuller-Zocco, 257(IRAL):May84-
  150
  S. Wolff, 660(Word):Aug84-187
Reid, A. and D. Marr, eds. Perceptions of
  the Past in Southeast Asia.
  R.J. Young, 318(JAOS):Oct-Dec83-815
Reid, C. Katerina Brac.
  D. Davis, 362:5Dec85-33
Reid, D., ed. The Party-Coloured Mind.
  G. Donaldson, 588(SSL):Vol 19-265
Reid, F. Theatre Administration.
  J. Pick, 157:No153-53
Reid, G. Billy.
  D. Devlin, 157:No153-46
Reid, J. Easy Money.
  N. Shack, 617(TLS):6Dec85-1407
Reid, J.P. In Defiance of the Law.*
  L. Kennett, 173(ECS):Spring85-440
Reid, M. The Dream of Snowy Owls.
  C. Matyas, 168(ECW):Winter84/85-352
Reid, P. and M. Michel. Prisoner of War.
  H. Strachan, 617(TLS):22Mar85-330
Reid, P.L.D. Tenth-Century Latinity.
  D.G. Brearley, 589:Jan84-199
  B.R. Reece, 121(CJ):Apr-May85-368
Reid, P.R. Colditz.
  H. Strachan, 617(TLS):22Mar85-330
Reid, T.R. The Chip. (British title:
  Microchip.)
  A. Hodgkin, 617(TLS):6Dec85-1404
  R. Wright, 441:3Mar85-8

Reilly, B.F., ed. Currier and Ives.
  C. Fox, 617(TLS):19Apr85-445
Reilly, B.F. The Kingdom of León-Castilla
  under Queen Urraca, 1109-1126.*
  R.I. Burns, 589:Jul84-690
Reilly, P. Jonathan Swift.*
  L. Speirs, 179(ES):Apr84-183
Reiner, E. Die etymologischen Dubletten
  des Französischen.*
  H. and R. Kahane, 545(RPh):Nov83-188
Reinfeld, B.K. Karel Havlíček (1821-1856).
  R. Weltsch, 104(CASS):Spring-Summer84-
  215
Reinhardt, S.G., ed. The Sun King.
  F. Brooks, 207(FR):Mar85-620
Reinhart, T. Anaphora and Semantic Inter-
  pretation.
  H. Holmback, 353:Vol22No6-865
Reinharz, J. Chaim Weizmann.
  T.S. Harmerow, 129:Nov85-125
  C. Raphael, 441:30Jun85-8
Reinhold, K.L. Korrespondenz 1773-1788.
  (Vol 1) (R. Lauth, E. Heller and K.
  Hiller, eds)
  L.W. Beck, 319:Oct85-596
Reinhold, U. Tendenzen und Autoren.
  W. Hässner and R. Rösler, 654(WB):
  8/1984-1397
Reiser, M.F. Mind, Brain, Body.
  B.A. Farrell, 453(NYRB):18Jul85-36
  R.M. Restak, 441:20Jan85-1
Reisinger, R. Die Rolle des Schweigens in
  der Dichtungstheorie von Rimbaud bis
  Valéry.
  U. Schützenberger, 602:Band15Heft2-347
Reiss, A.H., ed. The Arts Management
  Reader.
  J.G. Green, 108:Fall84-124
Reiss, E. Boethius.*
  G.C. Roti, 589:Jul84-727
Reiss, E. William Dunbar.
  W. Weiss, 38:Band102Heft3/4-538
Reiss, K. and H.J. Vermeer. Grundlegung
  einer allgemeinen Translationstheorie.
  H. Lindquist, 350:Sep85-737
Reiss, T.J. The Discourse of Modernism.*
  J. Birkett, 366:Spring84-110
  C. Gaudiani, 188(ECr):Winter84-92
  F.E.L. Priestley, 561(SFS):Mar84-82
Reiter, T. Starting from Bloodroot.
  F. Allen, 496:Fall84-171
Reitz, C. Die Nekyia in den "Punica" des
  Silius Italicus.
  R. Mayer, 123:Vol34No2-327
Rejhon, A.C. Cân Rolant.
  A.V., 379(MedR):Aug84-295
Rela, W. 15 cuentos para una antología.
  G.J. Fernández, 238:Sep84-482
Relleke, W. Ein Instrument spielen.
  A. Fehn, 221(GQ):Spring84-339
Remacle, L. La différenciation des gémi-
  nées MM, NN en MB, ND.
  G. Merk, 553(RLiR):Jul-Dec84-491
Remini, R.V. Andrew Jackson and the
  Course of American Democracy, 1833-1845.*
  639(VQR):Autumn84-118
Rémond, A. Montand.
  S. Fischer, 207(FR):Oct84-167
"Renaissance Drama." (Vol 13) (L. Barkan,
  ed)
  J.R. Siemon, 130:Spring84-89

"Renaissance Painting in Manuscripts:
  Treasures from the British Library."
  C. De Hamel, 39:Jul84-73
Renan, J.E. Souvenirs d'enfance et de
  jeunesse. (J. Pommier, ed)
  J. Gaulmier, 535(RHL):Nov/Dec84-977
Renaud, B. La Grande Question de Tom-
  atelle.
  D. Thaler, 102(CanL):Autumn84-168
Renaud, P. Les trajets du Phénix de "La
  Chanson du mal-aimé" à l'ensemble
  d'"Alcools."
  T. Mathews, 208(FS):Oct84-487
Rendell, R. The Tree of Hands.
  T.J. Binyon, 617(TLS):15Mar85-284
Rendell, R. An Unkindness of Ravens.
  T.J.B., 617(TLS):13Sep85-999
  N. Callendar, 441:10Nov85-22
  442(NY):21Oct85-152
Renehan, R. Greek Lexicographical Notes.
  P.G.W. Glare, 123:Vol34No1-73
Renfrew, C. and M. Wagstaff, eds. An
  Island Polity.
  R.W.V. Catling, 123:Vol34No1-98
Renner, D. Die Koptischen Textilien in
  den Vatikanischen Museen.
  M.H. Rutschowscaya, 90:Jun84-352
Rennert, J. and A. Weill. Alphonse Mucha.
  J. Yau, 62:Dec84-73
Rennie, N. The Cargo.*
  H. Lomas, 364:Aug/Sep84-141
Renoir, A. and A. Hernández - see Foley,
  J.M. and others
Renwick, J. Voltaire et Morangiés 1772-
  1773, ou les Lumières l'ont échappé
  belle.
  T.E.D. Braun, 207(FR):Feb85-452
  D. Fletcher, 402(MLR):Apr84-455
Renwick, R.D. English Folk Poetry.*
  J.W. Saunders, 541(RES):Aug84-420
Renza, L.A. "A White Heron" and the Ques-
  tion of Minor Literature.
  T. Wortham, 445(NCF):Mar85-488
Renzi, L. Einführung in die romanische
  Sprachwissenschaft.* (G. Ineichen, ed)
  I. Burr, 547(RF):Band96Heft1/2-104
  G.F. Meier, 682(ZPSK):Band37Heft1-116
Rescher, N. Induction.
  M. Heller, 543:Dec83-416
  G.E. Jones, 486:Mar84-176
Rescher, N. Kant's Theory of Knowledge
  and Reality.
  T.E. Wilkerson, 518:Apr84-117
Rescher, N. Leibniz's Metaphysics of
  Nature.*
  G.H.R. Parkinson, 53(AGP):Band66Heft3-
  313
Reschke, K. Verfolgte des Glücks.
  E. Henscheid, 384:Sep84-691
Resina Rodrigues, I., J.A. de Freitas
  Carvalho and A. Navarro. IV Centenario
  do Nascimento de Francisco de Quevedo.
  R.M. Price, 86(BHS):Oct84-523
Resler, M. - see Der Stricker
Resnais, A. La Vie est un roman.
  J. Michalczyk, 207(FR):Feb85-466
Resnick, M.C. Introducción a la historia
  de la lengua española.*
  S.N. Dworkin, 545(RPh):Feb84-371
  S.C. Sgroi, 379(MedR):Apr84-147

Resnik, M.D. Frege and the Philosophy of
Mathematics.*
   M. Hallett, 479(PhQ):Jul84-425
   E-H.W. Kluge, 449:May84-340
Restak, R.M. The Brain.*
   I. Rosenfield, 453(NYRB):14Mar85-34
Restany, P. Botero.
   L. Liebmann, 62:Dec84-73
"Restauro e conservazione delle opere
d'art su carta."
   380:Summer84-220
Restif de la Bretonne. Oeuvres érotiques.
   (D. Baruch and others, eds)
   D. Coward, 617(TLS):25Oct85-1197
Restle, M. Studien zur frühbyzantinischen
Architektur Kappadokiens.
   C. Foss, 589:Jul84-656
Reston, J., Jr. Sherman's March and
Vietnam.
   S.W. Sears, 441:17Feb85-13
Rétat, P., ed. Le Journalisme d'Ancien
Régime.*
   P. Jansen, 535(RHL):Jul/Aug84-612
"Rethinking History."
   M.D. Biddiss, 208(FS):Apr84-248
Reucher, T. Die situative Weltsicht
Homers.
   J.S. Clay, 124:Nov-Dec84-131
Reuchlin, J. On the Art of the Kabbalah.
   D. Ruderman, 551(RenQ):Autumn84-432
   T.W., 111:Fall85-7
Reuckert, W.H. Kenneth Burke and the
Drama of Human Relations. (2nd ed)
   42(AR):Summer84-383
Reudenbach, B. G.B. Piranesi: Architektur
als Bild.
   J.W-E., 90:Sep84-584
Reuter, Y. Archives Albert Camus. (Vol 4)
   T. Keefe, 208(FS):Jul84-369
Reuther, H. Balthasar Neumann.
   A. Laing, 90:Oct84-642
   C.F. Otto, 576:Mar84-85
   H. Thies, 471:Oct/Nov/Dec84-404
Reuther, T. - see Apresjan, J.D.
Revel, J-F. Culture and Cuisine.
   W. and C. Cowen, 639(VQR):Spring84-65
   T. Whittaker, 529(QQ):Autumn84-785
Revel, J-F. Le Rejet en l'état.
   P. McCarthy, 617(TLS):22Feb85-212
Revel, J-F., with B. Lazitch. How Demo-
cracies Perish.*
   J. Casey, 617(TLS):3May85-487
   C.C. O'Brien, 453(NYRB):17Jan85-21
   A. Ryan, 362:21Mar85-23
Revel-Macdonald, N. Kudaman, une épopée
palawan chantée par Usuj.
   Trân Van Khê, 537:Vol7 No1-122
Reveley, E. In Good Faith.*
   K. Kramer, 441:21Jul85-6
Revell, P. Quest in Modern American
Poetry.*
   R. Gray, 447(N&Q):Jun83-287
Reventlow, H.G. The Authority of the
Bible and the Rise of the Modern World.
   J. Drury, 617(TLS):5Apr85-393
Rewald, J. Paul Cézanne: The Watercolours.
   L. Gowing, 617(TLS):22Mar85-321
Rey-Flaud, H. La Névrose courtoise.
   J. le Hardi, 450(NRF):May84-130
Reyes Enriquez, A. Surveyors of the Ligua-
san Marsh.
   P. Lewis, 565:Spring84-64

Reynolds, C.W. and C. Tello, eds. U.S.-
Mexico Relations.
   L. Cardenas, Jr., 263(RIB):Vol34No1-95
Reynolds, G. Constable's England.
   W. Vaughan, 59:Sep84-368
Reynolds, G. The Later Paintings and
Drawings of John Constable.*
   J. Gage, 617(TLS):18Jan85-56
   D. Sutton, 39:Dec84-435
Reynolds, G. - see Constable, J.
Reynolds, J. Aphrodisias and Rome.*
   S. Mitchell, 123:Vol34No2-291
   K.J. Rigsby, 487:Spring84-102
Reynolds, J. William Callow, R.W.S.*
   P. Noon, 380:Spring84-85
Reynolds, J. Birket Foster.
   K. Flint, 617(TLS):8Feb85-141
   T. Russell-Cobb, 324:Oct85-798
Reynolds, J.H. and others. Letters from
Lambeth.* (J. Richardson, ed)
   J.C. Grigely, 339(KSMB):No35-113
Reynolds, M.S., ed. Critical Essays on
Ernest Hemingway's "In Our Time."*
   S. Donaldson, 587(SAF):Spring84-116
   L.W. Wagner, 573(SSF):Winter84-79
Reynolds, M.S. Hemingway's Reading, 1910-
1940.
   K. McSweeney, 529(QQ):Winter84-877
Reynolds, M.T. Joyce and Dante.*
   H. de Almeida, 149(CLS):Summer84-242
   C.D. Lobner, 329(JJQ):Winter85-223
Reynolds, O. Skevington's Daughter.
   D. Davis, 362:5Dec85-33
Reyto, M. The Cloned Mammoth.
   M. Fiamengo, 102(CanL):Summer84-145
Rézeau, P. Dictionnaire des régionalismes
de l'Ouest entre Loire et Gironde.
   G. Straka, 553(RLiR):Jul-Dec84-496
Rézeau, P. Les prières aux saints en fran-
çais à la fin du moyen âge. (Vol 1)
   B. Cazelles, 589:Jul84-692
   A. Gier, 553(RLiR):Jan-Jun84-247
   L. Löfstedt, 439(NM):1984/3-380
von Rezzori, G. The Death of My Brother
Abel.
   G. Annan, 453(NYRB):26Sep85-34
   R. Leiter, 441:29Sep85-18
   442(NY):21Oct85-150
Rheault, R. - see Sand, G.
Rhees, R., ed. Ludwig Wittgenstein:
Personal Recollections.
   I. McFetridge, 479(PhQ):Jan84-69
   483:Jan84-140
Rheims, M. Le Saint Office.
   M. Naudin, 207(FR):Mar85-602
"Rhetorik." (Vol 3)
   R. Mortier, 547(RF):Band96Heft3-328
Rheuban, J. Harry Langdon.
   W.K. Everson, 200:Jan84-58
Rhodes, D.E. A Catalogue of Incunabula in
All the Libraries of Oxford University
Outside the Bodleian.*
   P. Morgan, 447(N&Q):Oct83-453
   M.R. Perkin, 402(MLR):Apr84-400
   J.E. Walsh, 517(PBSA):Vol178No2-238
   70:Sep-Oct83-29
Rhodes, D.E. Incunabula in Greece: A
First Census.*
   J.E. Walsh, 517(PBSA):Vol178No2-238
Rhodes, D.E. Studies in Early Italian
Printing.
   L. Balsamo, 354:Jun84-187
   J. Tedeschi, 517(PBSA):Vol178No4-497

Rhodes, J.W. Keats's Major Odes.
  W.H. Hildebrand, 87(BB):Dec84-238
Rhodes, N. Elizabethan Grotesque.*
  G.R. Hibbard, 677(YES):Vol 14-306
Rhodes, N. - see Cowper, W.
Rhodes, P.J. A Commentary on the Aristo-
  telian "Athenaion Politeia."*
  G.J.D. Aalders H. Wzn., 394:
  Vol37fasc1/2-187
Rhodes, R.E. and D.I. Janik, eds. Studies
  in Ruskin.
  P. Conner, 59:Dec84-499
  B. Richards, 637(VS):Winter84-274
van der Rhoer, E. The Shadow Network.
  639(VQR):Summer84-94
Rhys, J. The Letters of Jean Rhys.*
  (British title: Jean Rhys: Letters 1931-
  1966.) (F. Wyndham and D. Melly, eds)
  P. Craig, 617(TLS):27Sep85-1068
  A. Ross, 364:Jun84-105
Rhys, J. Smile Please.
  J. Marcus, 395(MFS):Winter84-745
de Riaza, P.L. - see under Liñán de Riaza,
  P.
Ribaillier, J. - see William of Auxerre
Ribeiro, A. Dress in Eighteenth Century
  Europe 1715-1789.
  C. Fox, 617(TLS):22Feb85-213
Ribeiro, A. The Dress Worn at Masquerades
  in England, 1630-1790.
  R.L. Shep, 614:Spring85-20
Ribeiro, A. A Visual History of Costume:
  The Eighteenth Century.*
  B. Scott, 39:Aug84-148
Ribeiro, D. Maíra.*
  J. Gledson, 617(TLS):20Dec85-1462
Riberette, P. - see de Chateaubriand, F.R.
Ricapito, J.V. Bibliografía razonada y
  anotada de las obras maestras de la
  picaresca española.*
  P.J. Donnelly, 402(MLR):Jul84-727
Ricard, A. Le Tir à blanc.
  J. Moss, 207(FR):May85-915
  J.B. Moss, 102(CanL):Autumn84-98
Ricatte, R. and others - see Giono, J.
Ricci, D.M. The Tragedy of Political
  Science.
  M. Cranston, 617(TLS):8Mar85-253
Riccioli, G. "Bonheur" e società.
  P. Thompson, 535(RHL):Jul/Aug84-628
Madame Riccoboni. Lettres de Milady
  Juliette Catesby.
  L. Kovacs, 450(NRF):Jan84-118
Rice, A. The Vampire Lestat.
  N. Auerbach, 441:27Oct85-15
Rice, D. and P. Schofer. Rhetorical
  Poetics.
  J.P. Houston, 207(FR):May85-881
  A. Moss, 208(FS):Oct84-497
  B. Stoltzfus, 395(MFS):Winter84-727
Rice, T.J. James Joyce.
  E. Kreutzer, 72:Band221Heft2-380
Rich, A. The Fact of a Doorframe.
  C. Muske, 441:20Jan85-5
Rich, A. A Wild Patience Has Taken Me
  This Far.
  J. Saunders, 565:Spring84-55
Rich, D.C. Degas.
  J. House, 617(TLS):22Nov85-1316
Richard, J-P. Pages, Paysages.*
  G. Cesbron, 356(LR):Nov84-323
  J.A. Moreau, 98:Dec84-1000

Richard de Fournival. L'Oeuvre lyrique
  de Richard de Fournival.* (Y.G. Lepage,
  ed)
  N. Wilkins, 208(FS):Jul84-324
Richard of Campsall. The Works of Richard
  of Campsall. (Vol 2) (E.A. Synan, ed)
  E. Stump, 589:Apr84-437
Richards, A. An Iban-English Dictionary.
  J.U. Wolff, 293(JASt):Nov83-204
Richards, D.B. Goethe's Search for the
  Muses.
  P. Salm, 221(GQ):Winter84-153
Richards, E. A History of the Highland
  Clearances. (Vol 2)
  B. Lenman, 617(TLS):27Dec85-1489
Richards, E.J. Dante and the "Roman de la
  Rose."*
  R. Stillers, 72:Band221Heft2-470
Richards, G. The Philosophy of Gandhi.
  M. Juergensmeyer, 293(JASt):Feb84-293
Richards, J. The Age of the Dream Palace.*
  R. Murphy, 707:Autumn84-304
Richards, J.C. and R.W. Schmidt, eds. Lan-
  guage and Communication.
  B. Oreström, 596(SL):Vol138No2-179
Richardson, A. Participation.
  R.M.M., 185:Jul85-991
Richardson, G., ed. Teaching Modern Lan-
  guages.*
  G. Guntermann, 238:Dec84-683
Richardson, J. Colette.*
  295(JML):Nov84-420
Richardson, J. - see Reynolds, J.H. and
  others
Richardson, J.A., F.W. Coleman and M.J.
  Smith. Basic Design.
  J.A. Hobbs, 289:Fall84-121
Richardson, M. Architects of the Arts and
  Crafts Movement.*
  J.M. Robinson, 39:Apr84-303
Richardson, M., ed. Maddened by Mystery.
  D.R. Bartlett, 102(CanL):Autumn84-134
Richardson, S. Clarissa or The History of
  a Young Lady. (A. Ross, ed)
  J. Mullan, 617(TLS):27Sep85-1066
Richer, J., ed. L'empereur Julien.
  R. Trousson, 549(RLC):Jan-Mar84-117
Richetti, J.J. Philosophical Writing.
  J.M. Hill, 566:Autumn84-55
  R.W.F. Kroll, 319:Jul85-437
Richler, M., ed. The Best of Modern
  Humour.*
  C.R., 376:Jun84-151
Richlin, A. The Garden of Priapus.*
  B. Ellis, 292(JAF):Oct-Dec84-494
  R.W. Minadeo, 121(CJ):Apr-May85-364
  J.P. Sullivan, 124:Jul-Aug85-611
Richman, M.H. Reading Georges Bataille.*
  V. Conley, 207(FR):Oct84-139
  J. Gallop, 131(CL):Winter84-83
Richman, R.J. God, Free Will, and Moral-
  ity.
  R. Bronaugh, 518:Oct84-224
  H.S. Chandler, 185:Apr84-743
Richmond, A. A Long View from the Left.
  T. Draper, 453(NYRB):9May85-32
Richmond, C. Un análisis de la novela
  "Las guerras de nuestros antepasados" de
  Miguel Delibes.
  L. Hickey, 402(MLR):Jul84-735
  R. Jordan, 86(BHS):Oct84-513
  H.R. Romero, 238:Mar84-148
Richmond, C. - see Alas, L.

Richmond, C. - see Gómez de la Serna, R.
Richmond, D.W. Venustiano Carranza's
  Nationalist Struggle, 1893-1920.
  D.G. La France, 263(RIB):Vol34No2-313
Richmond, H.M. Puritans and Libertines.
  R.D. Cottrell, 207(FR):Oct84-121
  J. Daalder, 541(RES):Nov84-529
Richter, E. Der Tod des alten Mannes.
  M. Straub, 654(WB):9/1984-1533
Richter, G. Art and Human Consciousness.
  L. Antonsen, 469:Vol 10No4-116
Richter, G.M.A. The Portraits of the
  Greeks. (rev by R.R.R. Smith)
  R. Higgins, 39:Dec84-438
Richter, H., ed. Das Rolandslied des
  Pfaffen Konrad.*
  J. Ashcroft, 402(MLR):Jul84-740
Richter, P. and I. Ricardo. Voltaire.
  H. Mason, 208(FS):Jan84-62
Richter, R., ed. Die Troubadourzitate im
  "Breviari d'Amor."
  W.D. Paden, Jr., 545(RPh):Aug83-104
von Richthofen, E. - see Marie de France
Ricken, F. Allgemeine Ethik.
  M. Riedinger, 687:Nov-Dec84-677
Ricketts, P.T. - see Matfre Ermengaud
Ricklefs, M.C. A History of Modern Indo-
  nesia, ca. 1300 to the Present.
  J.R.W. Smail, 293(JASt):May84-609
Rickman, G. The Corn Supply of Ancient
  Rome.
  B.S. Spaeth, 24:Fall84-361
Ricks, B., comp. T.S. Eliot.
  A.M. Cohn, 365:Winter84-37
Ricks, C. The Force of Poetry.*
  B. Bergonzi, 176:Feb85-39
  H. Bevington, 441:17Mar85-11
  D. Donoghue, 533:Spring85-97
  J. Lucas, 493:Sep84-64
  W.H. Pritchard, 249(HudR):Winter84/85-
  639
Ricoeur, P. Time and Narrative.* (French
  title: Temps et Récit.) (Vol 1)
  J.S., 185:Jul85-976
Ridderbos, B. Saint and Symbol.
  P. Humfrey, 324:Nov85-886
Ridenour, R. Nationalism, Modernism and
  Personal Rivalry in 19th-Century Russian
  Music.*
  R. Oldani, 309:Vol5No4-380
Rider, P.R. - see Heywood, T.
Ridgway, B.S. Fifth Century Styles in
  Greek Sculpture.*
  F.L. Bastet, 394:Vol37fasc3/4-463
Riding, A. Distant Neighbors.
  R.R. Fagen, 441:6Jan85-5
  S.K. Purcell, 61:Feb85-97
Ridington, J. and R. People of the Long-
  house.
  M. Whitaker, 102(CanL):Winter83-79
Ridley, J. Henry VIII.
  C. Haigh, 617(TLS):22Feb85-204
  M. Quilligan, 441:11Aug85-11
Ridley, M. The Problems of Evolution.
  S.P. Stich, 617(TLS):29Nov85-1367
Ridley, R.T. - see Zosimus
Rieber, A.J. Merchants and Entrepreneurs
  in Imperial Russia.*
  J.H. Bater, 104(CASS):Spring-Summer84-
  191
Rieber, R.W., ed. Dialogues on the Psy-
  chology of Language and Thought.
  W. Washabaugh, 215(GL):Vol24No3-201

Riede, D.G. Dante Gabriel Rossetti and
  the Limits of Victorian Vision.*
  D. Sonstroem, 637(VS):Summer84-519
  M. Warner, 90:Dec84-792
Riedel, E. Strukturwandel in der Lyrik
  Rimbauds.
  M. Cranston, 207(FR):Dec84-295
  H.H. Wetzel, 72:Band221Heft2-453
Riedel, N. Uwe Johnson: Bibliographie
  1959-1980.* (Vol 1) (2nd ed)
  W.G. Cunliffe, 406:Summer84-241
  M. Humble, 402(MLR):Apr84-504
Riedel, W.E. Das literarische Kanadabild.
  W. Pache, 107(CRCL):Mar84-154
Rieder, J. Canarsie.
  P.S. Appelbaum, 129:Aug85-64
  H.J. Gans, 441:31Mar85-26
  D.H. Wrong, 617(TLS):6Sep85-966
Riege, H. - see Klopstock, F.G.
Rieger, D., with R. Kroll - see Marie de
  France
Riehle, W. The Middle English Mystics.*
  S.J. Ogilvie-Thomson, 541(RES):Feb84-
  76
Riemer, J. and N. Stampfer, eds. Ethical
  Wills.
  H. Merker, 390:Nov84-60
Rien, H. Leandro Fernández de Moratín.
  J.H.R. Polt, 86(BHS):Oct84-510
Riera, G.G. - see under García Riera, G.
Riese, U. Zwischen Verinnerlichung und
  Protest.
  H. Wüstenhagen, 654(WB):3/1984-508
Riess, J.B. Political Ideals in Medieval
  Italian Art.
  R. Brentano, 589:Jan84-201
Riesz, J. Beat Ludwig von Muralts "Let-
  tres sur les Anglais et les Français et
  sur les Voyages" und ihre Rezeption.
  E. Mass, 547(RF):Band96Heft4-474
Rietra, M., ed. Jung Österreich.*
  H. Steinecke, 680(ZDP):Band103Heft2-
  284
Rifaat, A. Distant View of Minarete and
  Other Stories.*
  K. Fitzlyon, 364:Apr/May84-137
Riffaterre, M. Text Production.* (French
  title: La Production du texte.)
  T.F. Berg, 107(CRCL):Jun84-275
  G. Cesbron, 356(LR):Feb/May84-142
  M.J. Worton, 208(FS):Oct84-498
Rigaud, N.J. George Etherege.
  J.P. Vander Motten, 179(ES):Aug84-372
Rigaudière, A. Saint-Flour, ville d'Auver-
  gne au bas moyen âge.
  S.F. Roberts, 589:Jul84-694
Rigelhof, T.F. The Education of J.J. Pass.
  K. Garebian, 526:Winter84-84
Riggan, W. Picaros, Madmen, Naifs, and
  Clowns.
  D. Milivojević, 558(RLJ):Winter-
  Spring84-300
Riggio, T.P., J.L.W. West 3d and N.M. West-
  lake - see Dreiser, T.
"The Right to Know."
  A. Protheroe, 362:28Mar85-25
Rigolot, F. Le Texte de la renaissance.
  C.M. Bauschatz, 207(FR):Oct84-119
  J. Sproxton, 402(MLR):Jul84-698
  A. Williams, 208(FS):Jan84-51
Rihoit, C. Soleil.
  R. Buss, 617(TLS):14Jun85-678

Rivera, C., ed. Language Proficiency and
Academic Achievement.
   S.J. Savignon, 399(MLJ):Winter84-385
Rivera Blanco, J.J. Arquitectura de la
segunda mitad del siglo XVI en León.
   A. Bustamante García, 48:Jan-Mar83-84
Rivers, C. Virgins.*
   J. Stephen, 617(TLS):28Jun85-733
Rivers, E.L. Quixotic Scriptures.
   J.J. Allen, 238:Dec84-665
   M.K. Read, 304(JHP):Winter84-157
Rivers, J.W. Proud and on My Feet.*
   J. Elledge, 491:May84-107
   R. Mitchell, 460(OhR):No33-134
Rivet, A. and C. Sarrau. Correspondance
intégrale. (Vol 3) (H. Bots and P.
Leroy, eds)
   R. Zuber, 535(RHL):May/Jun84-452
Rivet, A.L.F. and C. Smith. The Place-
names of Roman Britain.
   E.M. Wightman, 24:Summer84-232
Rivière, M. Selected Poems.
   J. Mole, 176:Feb85-50
Rizvi, S.A.A. Shāh 'Abd al-'Azīz.
   B.B. Lawrence, 293(JASt):May84-586
Rizzi, B. The Bureaucratization of the
World.
   L. Coser, 441:15Sep85-12
Rizzo, G. Tommaso Briganti inedito poeta
romantico.
   A. Mangione, 228(GSLI):Vol 161fasc516-
   617
Rizzo, S. Catalogo dei codici della "Pro
Cluentio" ciceroniana.
   M.D. Reeve, 123:Vol34No1-40
Roach, E. - see Coudrette
Roach, F.A. Cultivated Fruits of Britain.
   J. Grigson, 617(TLS):26Jul85-835
Roach, M. Another Name for Madness.
   M. Clark, 441:18Aug85-10
Roach, P. English Phonetics and Phonology.
   P. Rösel, 257(IRAL):Aug84-233
Roach, W., ed. The Continuations of the
Old French Perceval. (Vol 5)
   G. Roques, 553(RLiR):Jul-Dec84-506
Roaf, C. - see Speroni, S.
Roazen, P. Helene Deutsch.
   S. Turkle, 441:26May85-8
Robbe-Grillet, A. Le Miroir qui revient.
   J. Sturrock, 617(TLS):12Apr85-412
Robbins, C. Absolute Liberty. (B. Taft,
ed)
   H.T. Dickinson, 566:Autumn84-75
Robbins, H. Descent from Xanadu.*
   639(VQR):Autumn84-130
Robbins, J. and G. Thomas. Hands All
Around Making Cooperative Quilts.
   P.B., 614:Winter85-24
Robbins, J.A. - see "American Literary
Scholarship, 1978"
Robbins, K. The First World War.
   P. Parker, 364:Aug/Sep84-156
Robbins, R. - see Browne, T.
Robbins, T. Jitterbug Perfume.*
   442(NY):7Jan85-78
Robbins, W.G., R.J. Frank and R.E. Ross,
eds. Regionalism and the Pacific North-
west.
   H.P. Simonson, 649(WAL):Feb85-315
Roberson, W.H. Louis Simpson.
   W.J. Buckingham, 534(RALS):Spring82-67
Robert, L. The Dipo Flight.
   T.J. Binyon, 617(TLS):20Sep85-1029

Robert, M. Franz Kafka's Loneliness.
   J. Lothe, 172(Edda):1984/1-55
Robert, M. Origins of the Novel.*
   J. Levine, 627(UTQ):Spring84-296
Robert, R. Le Conte de fées littéraire en
France de la fin du XVIIe à la fin du
XVIIIe siècle.
   P. Hourcade, 535(RHL):Nov/Dec84-963
Robert, R., ed. Il était une fois les
fées.
   F. Wybrands, 450(NRF):Dec84-87
Robert de Boron. Merlin, roman du XIIIe
siècle.* (A. Micha, ed)
   F. Bogdanow, 208(FS):Jul84-322
Roberts, B. The Mad Bad Line.
   K. Beckson, 637(VS):Winter84-251
Roberts, C.H. Manuscript, Society and
Belief in Early Christian Egypt.*
   P.J. Parsons, 313:Vol74-254
Roberts, C.H. and T.C. Skeat. The Birth
of the Codex.*
   P.J. Parsons, 313:Vol74-254
Roberts, D. The Holy Land.
   P. van der Merwe, 90:Dec84-791
Roberts, E. A Woman's Place.
   P. Willmott, 617(TLS):18Jan85-58
Roberts, G. - see Pole, D.
Roberts, J., ed. The Guthlac Poems of the
Exeter Book.
   H. Gneuss, 447(N&Q):Jun83-244
Roberts, J.A. - see Wroth, M.
Roberts, J.M. The Triumph of the West.
   D. Hunt, 362:12Sep85-24
Roberts, J.R. John Donne: An Annotated
Bibliography of Modern Criticism, 1968-
1978.*
   E. Miner, 405(MP):Feb85-323
Roberts, J.W. Richard Boleslavsky.*
   J.M. Symons, 612(ThS):May84-121
Roberts, K. Black Apples.
   S. Stone-Blackburn, 102(CanL):Autumn84-
   140
Roberts, K. Flash Harry and the Daughters
of Divine Light.
   J. Acheson, 102(CanL):Autumn84-162
Roberts, K. Kiteworld.
   C. Greenland, 617(TLS):30Aug85-946
Roberts, K. Stonefish and Other Poems.*
   M. Thorpe, 198:Spring84-114
Roberts, L.E.J. Nuclear Power and Public
Responsibility.
   K.E. Jermy, 324:Jul85-514
Roberts, M. The Visitation.
   L. Marcus, 617(TLS):27Sep85-1070
Roberts, M.J. The Spiders of Great Brit-
ain and Ireland. (Vols 1 and 3)
   J.L. Cloudsley-Thompson, 617(TLS):
   28Jun85-735
Roberts, P.C. The Supply-Side Revolution.*
   A. Cairncross, 617(TLS):6Dec85-1389
   639(VQR):Summer84-92
ap Roberts, R. Arnold and God.
   P. Honan, 289:Fall84-124
   G.B. Tennyson, 445(NCF):Jun84-114
   639(VQR):Summer84-81
Roberts, R. No Bells on Sunday.* (A.
Walker, ed)
   B. Weeks, 18:Mar85-56
Roberts, W. A Bibliography of D.H. Law-
rence.* (2nd ed)
   B.C. Bloomfield, 78(BC):Summer84-240
   R.A. Gekoski, 402(MLR):Jan84-170
Robertson, A. - see Lawrence, D.H.

Robinson, W.H. Phillis Wheatley.
  P. Edwards, 538(RAL):Spring84-127
  J.A.L. Lemay, 365:Fall84-85
Robinson, W.H., ed. Phillis Wheatley and
Her Writings.
  W.J. Scheick, 165(EAL):Fall85-173
Robinson-Valéry, J., ed. Fonctions de
l'esprit.
  J. Largeault, 542:Apr-Jun84-229
  R. Pickering, 208(FS):Oct84-484
  F. Trémolières, 450(NRF):May84-125
Robison, J. Rumor.
  R. Hansen, 441:25Aug85-18
Robison, M. An Amateur's Guide to the
Night.
  D. Flower, 249(HudR):Summer84-307
  639(VQR):Summer84-97
Robison, W.L., M.S. Pritchard and J. Ellin,
eds. Profits and Professions.
  D.B., 185:Oct84-193
Robreau, Y. L'Honneur et la honte.*
  J. Pritchard, 382(MAE):1984/2-326
Robson, J.M. - see Mill, J.S.
Robson, J.M. and J. Stillinger - see Mill,
J.S.
Robson, L.S. Ride the Wind.
  D.D. Quantic, 649(WAL):May84-60
Robson, W.W. The Definition of Literature
and Other Essays.*
  J. Birkett, 366:Autumn84-261
  L. Lerner, 89(BJA):Spring84-181
  D. Newton-De Molina, 184(EIC):Jan84-70
Roby, K.E. Joyce Cary.
  295(JML):Nov84-417
Rochberg, G. The Aesthetics of Survival.
  W.H. Youngren, 61:Sep85-112
Roche, D. Le Peuple de Paris.
  R. Darnton, 173(ECS):Fall84-99
Roche, J. North Italian Church Music in
the Age of Monteverdi.
  J. Whenham, 617(TLS):12Apr85-415
Rochefort, C. Le Monde est comme deux
chevaux.
  B. Wright, 617(TLS):15Feb85-160
Lord Rochester. Lyrics and Satires of
John Wilmot, Earl of Rochester. (D.
Brooks, ed)
  P.E. Hewison, 447(N&Q):Oct83-473
  K. Robinson, 677(YES):Vol 14-317
Lord Rochester. The Poems of John Wilmot
Earl of Rochester. (K. Walker, ed)
  C. Rawson, 617(TLS):29Mar85-335
Rochester, M.B. and others. Bonjour, ça
va?
  M. Donaldson-Evans, 399(MLJ):Summer84-
165
  K.E. Kintz, 207(FR):Feb85-472
Rochlin, H. and F. Pioneer Jews.
  H. Mayer, 441:3Feb85-30
Rochlitz, R. Le jeune Lukács (1911-1916).
  A. Reix, 542:Jan-Mar84-94
Rock, I. The Logic of Perception.
  S. Lederman, 529(QQ):Autumn84-742
Rockmore, T. and others. Marxism and
Alternatives.*
  D. Schweickart, 550(RusR):Jan84-95
Rockwell, H. Steal Away, Steal Away Home.
  B. Staples, 441:30Jun85-20
Rockwell, J. All American Music.*
  E. Barkin, 513:Fall-Winter83/Spring-
Summer84-533
  W. Mellers, 415:Apr84-207

Rockwell, J. Evald Tang Kristensen.*
  H.O. Nygard, 292(JAF):Jan-Mar84-74
Rodd, L.R. and M.C. Henkenius - see
"Kokinshū"
Roddick, A. - see Brasch, C.
Roddick, N. A New Deal in Entertainment.*
  P. French, 707:Winter83/84-69
Rodenberger, L.H., ed. Her Work.
  N.O. Nelson, 649(WAL):May84-63
Rodger, I. Radio Drama.
  P. Hollindale, 541(RES):Aug84-424
Rodgers, A.T. The Universal Drum.*
  T.D. Adams, 599:Winter84-109
Rodi, F. - see "Dilthey-Jahrbuch für
Philosophie und Geschichte der Geistes-
wissenschaften"
Rodichev, F.I. Vospominaniia i ocherki o
russkom liberalizme. (K.E. McKenzie, ed)
  G.M. Hamburg, 550(RusR):Apr84-210
Rodin, A. Art: Conversations with Paul
Gsell.*
  A.B. Sandback, 62:Dec84-71
Rodin, K. Räven predikar för Gässen.
  W. Mieder, 196:Band25Heft3/4-358
Rodino, R.H. Swift Studies, 1965-1980.
  J.I. Fischer, 566:Autumn84-52
Roditi, G. L'esprit de perfection.
  C. Rosset, 98:May84-439
Rodman, H., S.H. Lewis and S. Griffith.
The Sexual Rights of Adolescents.
  R.T., 185:Apr85-784
Rodmell, G.E. Marivaux: "Le Jeu de
l'amour et du hasard" and "Les Fausses
Confidences."*
  J. Whatley, 207(FR):Feb85-453
Rodrigues, I.R., J.A. de Freitas Carvalho
and A. Navarro - see under Resina Rodri-
gues, I., J.A. de Freitas Carvalho and A.
Navarro
Rodríguez, A.V. - see under Vespertino
Rodríguez, A.
Rodríguez, F.G.M. - see under Martín Rod-
ríguez, F.G.
Rodriguez, R. Hunger of Memory.*
  M.R. De Long, 35(AS):Fall84-230
Rodríguez Buzón, M. La Colegiata de Osuna.
  D. Angulo Iñiguez, 48:Oct-Dec83-420
Rodriguez Monegal, E. Jorge Luis Borges.
  R. Millet, 450(NRF):Jan84-159
Rodríguez Nietzsche, V. Del dulce pie tu
caminar tranquilo.
  J. González, 701(SinN):Jul-Sep84-146
Rodway, A. The Craft of Criticism.*
  J. Birkett, 366:Autumn84-261
Roe, D. Dynamos and Virgins.
  J. Cummings, 441:7Apr85-15
Roebuck, J. Urban Development in Nine-
teenth Century London.
  R.G. Rodger, 637(VS):Winter84-261
Roegiest, E. Les prépositions A et DE en
espagnol contemporain.
  R. Eberenz, 547(RF):Band96Heft1/2-141
Roesch, P. Études béotiennes.
  R.J. Buck, 487:Winter84-385
  F.W. Walbank, 303(JoHS):Vol 104-243
Roethel, H.K. and J.K. Benjamin. Kandin-
sky: Catalogue Raisonné of the Oil Paint-
ings.* (Vol 1)
  J. Langner, 471:Jan/Feb/Mar84-99
  J.B. Smith, 39:Dec84-437
  P. Weiss, 127:Spring84-91

Rose, M.A. Old Belly Dancing Moon.
G.C. Little, 404:Autumn84-54
Rose, M.A. Parody//Meta-fiction.
A. Jefferson, 494:Summer82-231
Rose, P. Parallel Lives.*
H. Bryant, 580(SCR):Fall84-115
S. Pickering, 569(SR):Fall84-xcv
Rose, P. Writing of Women.
C. Bancroft, 441:23Jun85-21
Rose, W. El pastor de la muerte.
M.L. Miller, 238:Dec84-673
Roseberry, W. Coffee and Capitalism in
the Venezuelan Andes.
J. Ewell, 263(RIB):Vol34No2-314
Rosecrance, B. Forster's Narrative
Vision.*
F.P.W. McDowell, 177(ELT):Vol27No2-163
M. Millar, 529(QQ):Winter84-1031
R.J. Voorhees, 395(MFS):Summer84-367
Rosecrance, R. The Rise of the Trading
State.
C. Johnson, 61:Dec85-106
Rösel, H. Wörterbuch zu den tschechischen
Schriften des J.A. Comenius.
D. Short, 575(SEER):Jul84-430
Roseliep, R. Rabbit in the Moon.
R. Spiess, 404:Winter-Spring84-35
Rosen, C. Plays of Impasse.
W. Fulks, 529(QQ):Autumn84-702
M. Hinden, 397(MD):Sep84-449
Rosen, C. and H. Zerner. Romanticism and
Realism.*
L. Eitner, 617(TLS):31May85-601
J. Hunter, 249(HudR):Winter84/85-660
S.Z. Levine, 533:Winter85-133
A. Solomon-Godeau, 55:Oct84-32
B. Weller, 344:Winter85-114
Rosen, D. and A. Porter, eds. Verdi's
"Macbeth."
G. Steiner, 617(TLS):29Mar85-339
Rosen, F. Jeremy Bentham and Representa-
tive Democracy.
L.J. Hume, 319:Jul85-444
Rosen, G. Growing Up Bronx.
M.B. Tack, 441:13Jan85-22
Rosen, M. Hegel's Dialectic and its Criti-
cism.*
P.A. Gorner, 518:Apr84-122
J. Lampert, 543:Mar84-648
W.A. de Vries, 482(PhR):Jul84-450
Rosen, M.J. A Drink at the Mirage.
L.M. Rosenberg, 441:7Apr85-12
Rosen, S. The Limits of Analysis.*
R. Brague, 192(EP):Oct-Dec84-544
K. Dorter, 154:Sep84-556
Rosen, S. Plato's "Sophist."*
R.J. Cavalier, 124:Jan-Feb85-221
N. White, 319:Jul85-419
Rosenau, H. The Ideal City.* (3rd ed)
90:Sep84-584
Rosenbaum, B. and P. White, comps. Index
of English Literary Manuscripts.* (Vol
4, Pt 1)
I. Jack, 541(RES):May84-278
Rosenbaum, H. Formen der Familie.
A. Neef, 654(WB):3/1984-494
Rosenberg, A. Nicolas Gueudeville and His
Work (1652-172?).
P.H. Meyer, 207(FR):Dec84-289
Rosenberg, D.K. - see Hermann von Sachsen-
heim

Rosenberg, H. Art and Other Serious Mat-
ters.
C.B. McGee, 441:24Mar85-25
Rosenberg, H. The Tradition of the New.
The Anxious Object. Artworks and Pack-
ages.
J.A. Richardson, 289:Spring84-93
Rosenberg, J.F. One World and Our Knowl-
edge of It.*
H. Pilot, 53(AGP):Band66Heft3-339
Rosenberg, J.F. Thinking Clearly About
Death.*
H.S. Silverstein, 482(PhR):Jul84-492
Rosenberg, L. The Angel Poems.
J. Carter, 219(GaR):Winter84-881
Rosenberg, L. The Errand Runner.
M. Stobie, 102(CanL):Winter83-159
Rosenberg, M.J. The Cybernetics of Art.
J. Reichardt, 89(BJA):Autumn84-374
Rosenberg, R. Zehn Kapitel zur Geschichte
der Germanistik.
G. Müller, 654(WB):7/1984-1223
H. Müller, 221(GQ):Spring84-287
H. Müller, 221(GQ):Fall84-287
Rosenberg, S., ed. Sentence Production.
G.F. Meier, 682(ZPSK):Band37Heft4-523
Rosenberg, S.N. and others. Harper's
Grammar of French.*
M.C. Jacobs, 399(MLJ):Spring84-74
Rosenblatt, J. Brides of the Stream.
J. Fitzgerald, 102(CanL):Autumn84-154
S.S., 376:Feb84-140
Rosenblatt, R. Witness.
R. Shaplen, 441:4Aug85-3
Rosenblum, R. and H.W. Janson. 19th-Cen-
tury Art.* (British title: Art of the
Nineteenth Century.)
J. Flam, 62:Dec84-76
D. Sutton, 39:Aug84-84
Rosenfeld, A.H. Imagining Hitler.
F. Stern, 441:12May85-7
Rosenfeld, M.N. Largillière and the
Eighteenth-Century Portrait.
R. Wrigley, 59:Mar84-126
380:Autumn84-330
Rosenfeld, S. The Georgian Theatre of
Richmond Yorkshire.
T.R. Griffiths, 617(TLS):20Sep85-1034
Rosenfeldt, N.E. and C. Pape. Politikens
Ruslandshistorie. (Vol 3)
D. Kirby, 575(SEER):Oct84-594
Rosenfield, D.L. Politique et liberté.
A. Reix, 542:Oct-Dec84-494
Rosenkranz, H. and others, comps. Thür-
ingisches Wörterbuch. (Vols 4 and 5)
H. Friebertshäuser and K.P. Andriessen,
685(ZDL):2/1984-247
Rosenmeyer, T.G. The Art of Aeschylus.*
A.F. Garvie, 303(JoHS):Vol 104-195
D. Konstan, 130:Fall84-276
A.J. Podlecki, 487:Autumn84-275
Rosenstiel, A. Red and White.
D.F. Littlefield, Jr., 649(WAL):Nov84-
255
Rosenthal, J.T. Anglo-Saxon History.
R. McKitterick, 617(TLS):15Nov85-1303
Rosenthal, M. Constable.*
M. Cormack, 90:Jun84-361
G. Reynolds, 39:May84-387
W. Vaughan, 59:Sep84-368
B. Weller, 344:Winter85-114

313

Rosenthal, M.L. and S.M. Gall. The Modern
Poetic Sequence.*
    S. Birkerts, 472:Fall/Winter84-78
    J. Duemer, 134(CP):Spring84-96
    W. Harmon, 219(GaR):Spring84-182
    J. Olney, 569(SR):Summer84-451
    D. Porter, 432(NEQ):Mar84-106
    L. Ricou, 102(CanL):Autumn84-192
Rosenthal, P. Words and Values.
    639(VQR):Autumn84-126
Roseveare, N.T. Mercury's Perihelion from
Le Verrier to Einstein.
    D. Raine, 84:Jun84-188
Rosier, I. La grammaire spéculative des
Modistes.
    M.A. Covington, 350:Mar85-212
Roskies, D.G. Against the Apocalypse.*
    R. Alter, 129:Jan85-39
    L. Field, 395(MFS):Winter84-837
    A.J. Sherman, 617(TLS):24May85-586
Roskill, M. and D. Carrier. Truth and
Falsehood in Visual Images.
    J. Cauvel, 290(JAAC):Fall84-107
Ross, A. Colours of War.
    M. Evans, 39:Feb84-148
    R. Shone, 90:Oct84-646
Ross, A. - see Richardson, S.
Ross, B.D. Iwo Jima.
    D. Ghitelman, 441:21Apr85-25
Ross, C. Richard III.*
    C.T. Wood, 589:Jan84-202
Ross, D.H. and T.F. Garrard, eds. Akan
Transformations.
    M. Posnansky, 2(AfrA):Feb84-23
Ross, I.C. - see Sterne, L.
Ross, J. Allez France!
    A.G. Suozzo, Jr., 207(FR):Oct84-149
Ross, J.F. Portraying Analogy.
    D.A. Cruse, 297(JL):Sep84-351
    E.S., 185:Oct84-180
Ross, N. Vrangel' v Krymu.
    P. Kenez, 550(RusR):Jan84-78
Ross, S.D. Perspective in Whitehead's
Metaphysics.*
    R. Hanna, 543:Mar84-650
Ross, S.D. A Theory of Art.*
    F. Schier, 393(Mind):Jan84-136
Ross, T.W. - see Chaucer, G.
Ross, V. Dark Secrets.
    A. Brennan, 198:Autumn84-90
Ross, W. Der ängstliche Adler.*
    J. Kjaer, 462(OL):Vol139No2-179
Rossant, C. Colette's Slim Cuisine.
    W. and C. Cowen, 639(VQR):Spring84-66
Rossebastiano Bart, A., ed. Vocabolari
Veneto-Tedeschi del secolo XV.
    M. Pozzi, 228(GSLI):Vol 161fasc513-137
Rosseel, E., ed. La langue française dans
les pays du Bénélux.
    J-M. Klinkenberg, 209(FM):Oct84-239
Rosselli, J. The Opera Industry in Italy
from Cimarosa to Verdi.*
    J. Budden, 415:Aug84-446
Rosset, C. La Force majeure.
    M. Jarrety, 450(NRF):Feb84-109
Rosshandler, F. Passing Through Havana.*
    639(VQR):Summer84-96
Rossi, A. A Scientific Autobiography.*
Il libro azzuro . I miei progetti.
    P. Lombardo, 98:Aug/Sep84-681

Rossi, D. Concordanza delle "Stanze" di
Angelo Poliziano.
    S. Orlando, 228(GSLI):Vol 161fasc513-
    139
Rossi, P. The Dark Abyss of Time.
    R. Porter, 617(TLS):27Sep85-1077
Rossi, P., ed. La nuove ragione.
    W. Büttemeyer, 679:Band15Heft1-184
Rossi-Landi, F. Language as Work and
Trade.
    K. O'Donnell, 355(LSoc):Dec84-558
Rossi-Manaresi, R. and O. Nonfarmale.
Rapporti della Soprintendenza per i Beni
Artistici e Storici per le provincie di
Bologna, Ferrara, Forlì e Ravenna. (No
26)
    R. Gibbs, 90:Jul84-438
Rössler, H. Karl Kraus und Nestroy.*
    W.E. Yates, 402(MLR):Jul84-754
Rosso, C. Mythe de l'Egalité et rayonne-
ment des Lumières.
    A. Vartanian, 546(RR):Jan84-110
Rosso, C. Pagine al vento.*
    L. van Delft, 475:Vol 11No20-259
van Rossum-Guyon, F. and M. van Brederode,
eds. Balzac et "Les Parents Pauvres."*
    M. Tilby, 208(FS):Apr84-211
Rosta, H.J. In the Blood.
    I. Huggan, 526:Winter84-82
Roston, M. Milton and the Baroque.
    W. McQueen, 577(SHR):Winter84-83
Rostow, W.W. The Barbaric Counter-
Revolution.*
    S. Brittan, 176:Apr85-56
Rosumek, P. Index des Périodiques
dépouillés dans la Collection de
Bibliographie classique et Index de
leurs Sigles.
    W.M. Calder 3d, 121(CJ):Dec84/Jan85-
    162
Roszak, T. Dreamwatcher.
    J. Kaufman, 441:24Feb85-22
Rotella, A. After an Affair.
    J. Winke, 404:Autumn84-55
Rotella, A. Harvesting Stars.
    E.S. Lamb, 404:Summer84-39
Rotella, A. On a White Bud.
    404:Autumn84-60
Rotermund, E. Zwischen Exildichtung und
Innerer Emigration.*
    H.G. Nerjes, 221(GQ):Winter84-161
Roth, F. Das Buch des Lebens.
    F.P. Ingold, 384:Jun84-443
Roth, J. Berliner Saisonbericht.
    F. Dieckmann, 384:Oct84-815
    G. Eisler, 617(TLS):8Mar85-254
Roth, J. Confession of a Murderer.
    J.A. Snead, 441:14Jul85-22
Roth, J. La Crypte des Capucins.
    R. Millet, 450(NRF):Feb84-118
Roth, L.M. McKim, Mead and White, Archi-
tects.*
    P.R. Baker, 432(NEQ):Dec84-573
    W.B. Rhoads, 576:May84-175
Roth, M-L. Robert Musil.
    W. Braun, 406:Summer84-226
Roth, O. Die Gesellschaft der "Honnêtes
Gens."
    G. Damblemont, 475:Vol 11No20-262
Roth, P. The Anatomy Lesson.*
    A. Alvarez, 453(NYRB):11Apr85-15
    M. Gorra, 249(HudR):Spring84-152
    J.L. Halio, 598(SoR):Winter85-204

Roth, P. The Prague Orgy.
P. Kemp, 362:31Oct85-34
C. Sinclair, 617(TLS):18Oct85-1167
Roth, P. Zuckerman Bound.
H. Bloom, 441:19May85-1
442(NY):10Jun85-139
Roth, P.A. Bram Stoker.*
B.G. Caraher, 637(VS):Summer84-527
Róth, R. and L. Prijs. Hebräische Hand-
schriften. (Pt 1A)
D. Goldstein, 354:Jun84-180
Roth, S. Aventure et Aventuriers au dix-
huitième siècle. Les Aventuriers au
XVIIIe siècle.
V. Kapp, 72:Band221Heft2-445
Rothblatt, S. The Revolution of the Dons.
A.H. Halsey, 447(N&Q):Jun83-258
Rothchild, J. Up for Crabs.
N. Miller, 441:19May85-23
Rothenberg, G.E., B.K. Király and P.F.
Sugar, eds. East Central European Soci-
ety and War in the Pre-Revolutionary
Eighteenth Century.*
H.L. Agnew, 104(CASS):Spring-Summer84-
228
Rothenberg, J. and D., eds. Symposium of
the Whole.*
L. Bartlett, 649(WAL):Nov84-252
Rothenberg, R. The Neoliberals.*
L. Lenkowsky, 129:Mar85-54
Rothenstein, J. John Nash.
C. Hartley, 39:Jun84-466
A. Ross, 364:Jul84-107
Rothgeb, J. - see Jonas, O.
Rothman, S. and S.R. Lichter. Roots of
Radicalism.*
A.S. Kraditor, 396(ModA):Winter84-74
de Rothschild, G. The Whims of Fortune.
T. Zeldin, 441:5May85-22
Rothschild, J. Ethnopolitics.
S.R. Burant, 104(CASS):Fall84-372
Rothstein, E. Restoration and Eighteenth-
Century Poetry, 1660-1780.*
G. Midgley, 541(RES):May84-234
V. Newey, 83:Spring84-132
Rotroff, S.I. The Athenian Agora. (Vol
22)
D.M. Bailey, 123:Vol34No2-351
P.J. Callaghan, 303(JoHS):Vol 104-261
Rotrou, J. Cosroès. (D.A. Watts, ed)
H.T. Barnwell, 208(FS):Oct84-458
Rottensteiner, F. - see Lem, S.
Rotter, G., ed. Löwe und Schakal.
U. Marzolph, 196:Band25Heft3/4-362
Röttges, H. Dialektik als Grund der
Kritik.
G. Wohlfart, 342:Band75Heft1-104
Rötzer, H.G. Märchen. Sage.
E. Moser-Rath, 196:Band25Heft1/2-153
Rouault, G. and A. Suarès. Georges
Rouault — André Suarès: Correspondance
1911-1939. (A.B. Low-Beer, ed and trans)
90:Feb84-102
Roubaud, A-C. Journal 1979-1983.
J. Bens, 450(NRF):Apr84-103
Roubaud, J. La Belle Hortense.
M. Hutchinson, 617(TLS):11Oct85-1155
Rouberol, J. L'esprit de Sud dans
l'oeuvre de Faulkner.*
N. Polk, 395(MFS):Summer84-324
Roud, R. A Passion for Films.
J. Nangle, 200:Feb84-112

Rouget, G. La musique et la transe.
G. Béhague, 187:Fall85-495
Rouner, L.S., ed. Foundations of Ethics.
S.S., 185:Apr85-771
Rouse, C. William Schumann: Documentary.
P. Dickinson, 415:Jan84-28
Rousseau, A. and L. Doutreleau - see Saint
Irenaeus
Rousseau, G. L'Image des États-Unis dans
la littérature québécoise (1775-1930).*
D.M. Hayne, 107(CRCL):Jun84-330
Rousseau, G.S. Tobias Smollett.*
J.C. Beasley, 579(SAQ):Autumn84-482
M. Irwin, 541(RES):Nov84-552
D.K. Jeffrey, 577(SHR):Fall84-354
Rousseau, J-J. Correspondance complète.*
(Vols 37-40) (R.A. Leigh, ed)
J.S. Spink, 208(FS):Jan84-62
Roussel, R. Impressions of Africa. Locus
Solus. How I Wrote Certain of My Books.
L. Sante, 453(NYRB):31Jan85-14
Rousselet, J. - see Faret, N.
Rousset, J. Leurs yeux se rencontrèrent.*
D. Lesko, 188(ECr):Summer84-103
Roustang, F. Dire Mastery.
P. Roazen, 529(QQ):Autumn84-736
Roux, J., ed. A l'Abrò de Z-Alaièr.
J-P. Chambon, 553(RLiR):Jul-Dec84-447
Roux, L. - see de Sorbière, S.
Rouzeaud, P., ed. Le Roman historique
(XVIIe-XXe Siècles).
P.J. Yarrow, 208(FS):Oct84-494
Rovan, J. and W. Weidenfeld, eds.
Elemente eines deutsch-französischen
Dialogs.
K. Heitmann, 72:Band221Heft1-223
Rovin, J. The Encyclopedia of Superheroes.
L. Falk, 441:15Dec85-20
Rowan, A. Designs for Castles and Country
Villas by Robert and James Adam.
K. Downes, 617(TLS):13Dec85-1424
Rowan, A.N. Of Mice, Models, and Men.*
P. Singer, 453(NYRB):17Jan85-46
Rowe, C.J. Philosophers in Context: Plato.
A. Price, 617(TLS):19Apr85-432
Rowe, J.C. The Theoretical Dimensions of
Henry James.
P. Rawlings, 617(TLS):13Sep85-1012
Rowe, J.C. Through the Custom-House.*
R.W. Harvey, 106:Fall84-301
J. Limon, 405(MP):Feb85-335
J.E. Miller, Jr., 27(AL):May84-271
P. O'Donnell, 223:Spring83-99
L.A. Renza, 495(PoeS):Jun84-24
Rowe, M. Chicago Blues.
A. Prévos, 91:Fall84-270
Rowe, W. Clapp's Rock.
R.G. Moyles, 102(CanL):Autumn84-101
Rowell, G. Mountains of the Middle
Kingdom.
J. Guimond, 219(GaR):Summer84-424
T.J. Lyon, 649(WAL):May84-67
C. Thubron, 617(TLS):5Jul85-759
Rowell, G. - see Gilbert, W.S.
Rowland, B., ed and trans. Medieval
Woman's Guide to Health.
E.M. Fulton, 178:Mar84-94
Rowland, J. The Ultimate Violation.
W. Kaminer, 441:17Mar85-27
Rowland, R. Filigree in Blood.
G. Burns, 381:Sep84-460
Rowley, A.R. Fersentaler Wörterbuch.
M. Hornung, 684(ZDA):Band113Heft1-47

Rowley, T. The Origins of Open-Field
Agriculture.
F.L. Cheyette, 589:Oct84-956
Rowse, A.L. Eminent Elizabethans.
R.J. Schoeck, 570(SQ):Winter84-498
Rowse, A.L. Glimpses of the Great.
I. Hislop, 362:28Mar85-29
J.H.C. Leach, 617(TLS):31May85-600
Rowse, A.L. Prefaces to Shakespeare's
Plays.
G. Taylor, 617(TLS):16Aug85-905
Rowse, A.L. Shakespeare's Characters.
T. Hawkes, 617(TLS):11Jan85-29
Rowse, A.L. - see Shakespeare, W.
Roxan, M.M. - see Mann, J.C.
Roy, C. Permis de séjour 1977-1982.
C. Dis, 450(NRF):Feb84-93
Roy, C.D. The Dogon of Mali and Upper
Volta.
L. Aronson, 2(AfrA):May84-26
Roy, J. and J.J. Staczek. Lecturas de
prensa.
J.J. Deveny, Jr., 399(MLJ):Autumn84-
304
Royce, A.P. Movement and Meaning.
J. Hankey, 617(TLS):25Jan85-100
Royce, K. The Mosley Receipt.
M. Stasio, 441:16Jun85-25
Royer, J. Ecrivains contemporains.
(Vol 1)
L. Monkman, 102(CanL):Winter83-100
Royle, E. and J. Walvin. British Radicals
and Reformers 1760-1848.
J. Epstein, 579(SAQ):Autumn84-476
D. Nicholls, 637(VS):Spring84-397
J. Stevenson, 83:Spring84-97
Royle, T. Companion to Scottish Litera-
ture.*
E. Hulse, 470:Vol122-128
G.R.R., 588(SSL):Vol 19-299
Royle, T. The Kitchener Enigma.
K. Jeffery, 617(TLS):13Dec85-1417
Royster, C. Light Horse Harry Lee and the
Legacy of the American Revolution.*
A.G. Condon, 106:Fall84-287
Royster, V. The Essential Royster. (E.
Fuller, ed)
C.R. Herron, 441:15Sep85-25
Royster, V. My Own, My Country's Time.
639(VQR):Winter84-15
Rozanova, N.N. Moskovskaya knizhnaya
ksilografiya 1920/30-kh godov.
354:Mar84-104
Rozenblit, M. The Jews of Vienna 1867-
1914.
R.S. Wistrich, 617(TLS):28Jun85-730
Rozett, M.T. The Doctrine of Election and
the Emergence of Elizabethan Tragedy.
G. Taylor, 617(TLS):16Aug85-905
Ruark, G. Keeping Company.*
B. Bawer, 491:Sep84-349
D. St. John, 42(AR):Summer84-369
P. Stitt, 219(GaR):Spring84-166
639(VQR):Autumn84-139
Ruas, C. Conversations with American
Writers.
J. Cott, 441:13Jan85-14
Rubens, B. Mr. Wakefield's Crusade.
T.M. Disch, 441:17Nov85-20
J. Mellors, 362:30May85-32
G. Strawson, 617(TLS):31May85-599
"Peter Paul Rubens: Werk und Nachruhm."
J.M. Muller, 54:Mar84-163

Rubenstein, C. The Honey Tree Song.
P. Metcalf, 617(TLS):13Dec85-1432
Rubin, B. Secrets of State.
C.A. Kojm, 441:26May85-15
Rubin, C.E., ed. Southern Folk Art.
K.S. Hofweber, 614:Spring85-30
Rubin, D.J. The Knot of Artifice.*
K. Meyer-Minnemann, 547(RF):
Band96Heft1/2-176
Rubin, J. Injurious to Public Morals.
J.L. Huffman, 407(MN):Autumn84-355
Irie Takanori, 285(JapQ):Oct-Dec84-459
Rubin, J.H. Realism and Social Vision in
Courbet and Proudhon.*
K. Herding, 54:Sep84-533
Rubin, L.B. Just Friends.
M.S. Kennedy, 441:15Sep85-35
Rubin, L.D., Jr., with others, eds. The
History of Southern Literature.
R.W.B. Lewis, 441:1Dec85-18
Rubin, W., ed. "Primitivism" in 20th
Century Arts.
E. Cowling, 617(TLS):6Sep85-969
Rubinger, R. Private Academies of
Tokugawa Japan.*
G.K. Goodman, 293(JASt):Nov83-168
Rubino, C.A. and C.W. Shelmerdine, eds.
Approaches to Homer.*
P.V. Jones, 123:Vol34No2-303
Rubinstein, D. Marx and Wittgenstein.
A.W. McHoul, 488:Dec84-567
Rubinstein, W.D. The Left, the Right, and
the Jews.
N. Weyl, 390:Jun/Jul84-55
Rubio, C.G. - see under Gonzalo Rubio, C.
Rubio, E. - see de Larra, M.J.
Rubio, H.E. Der Manierismus in der Vokal-
polyphonie des 16. Jahrhunderts.
C. Meyer, 537:Vol70No1-136
Rubio, M. - see Grove, F.P.
Rubottom, R.R. and J.C. Murphy. Spain and
the United States.
P. Preston, 617(TLS):27Dec85-1471
Rücker, G. Dame vor Spiegel.
W. Jähnichen, 654(WB):6/1984-1019
Rucker, R. Master of Space and Time.
G. Jonas, 441:10Mar85-31
Ruckhäberle, H-J., ed. Bildung und Organ-
isation in den deutschen Handwerksgesel-
len- und Arbeitervereinen in der Schweiz.
G. Kolde, 685(ZDL):3/1984-400
Rudisill, M., with J.C. Simmons. Truman
Capote.
G. Garrett, 569(SR):Summer84-495
Rudman, M. In the Neighboring Cell.
639(VQR):Winter84-22
Rudman, M. Robert Lowell.*
W. Sharpe, 189(EA):Jul-Sep85-356
Rudnick, L.P. Mabel Dodge Luhan.
J. Moynahan, 441:6Jan85-8
Rudnik-Smalbraak, M. Samuel Richardson.
L. Speirs, 179(ES):Aug84-376
Rudolf von Ems. Weltchronik [together
with] Der Stricker. Karl der Grosse.
N.H. Ott, 684(ZDA):Band113Heft3-110
Rudolph, K. Gnosis.*
H. Chadwick, 617(TLS):23Aug85-930
Rudrum, A. - see Vaughan, H.
Rudrum, A., with J. Drake-Brockman - see
Vaughan, T.
Rudwick, M.J.S. The Great Devonian Contro-
versy.
P.J. Bowler, 441:7Jul85-10

Ruether, R.R. Womanguides.
  E.H. Pagels, 441:7Apr85-3
Ruether, R.R. and R.S. Keller, eds. Women
  and Religion in America.
  42(AR):Summer84-379
Ruffié, J. Traité du vivant.
  P. Pellegrin, 542:Jan-Mar84-115
Ruffle, J. and others, eds. Glimpses of
  Ancient Egypt.
  V. Condon, 318(JAOS):Jul-Sep83-667
Ruffo-Fiore, S. Niccolò Machiavelli.
  O.Z. Pugliese, 276:Autumn84-276
Ruggiero, G. The Boundaries of Eros.
  O.M.T. Logan, 617(TLS):23Aug85-921
Ruh, K., with others, eds. Die deutsche
  Literatur des Mittelalters: Verfasser-
  lexikon.* (Vols 1 and 2) (2nd ed)
  G. Vollmann-Profc and B.K. Vollmann,
  224(GRM):Band34Heft4-465
Ruh, K., with others, eds. Die deutsche
  Literatur des Mittelalters: Verfasser-
  lexikon.* (Vol 3) (2nd ed)
  N.F. Palmer, 402(MLR):Apr84-482
Ruhe, E. - see Lamy, B.
Ruiz, P.G., C. Nachón González and M. Díaz
  Cuétara - see under Giménez Ruiz, P., C.
  Nachón González and M. Díaz Cuétara
Ruiz, U.E. - see under Espinosa Ruiz, U.
Rukschcio, B. and R. Schachel. Adolf Loos.
  C.C. Collins, 576:Mar84-86
Rule, J.B. Insight and Social Betterment.
  P. Shaw, 488:Jun84-273
Rumens, C. Direct Dialling.
  D. Davis, 362:6Jun85-31
  M. Hofmann, 617(TLS):29Nov85-1370
Rumens, C., ed. Making for the Open.
  D. Davis, 362:6Jun85-31
  M. Hofmann, 617(TLS):29Nov85-1370
Rumens, C. Scenes from the Gingerbread
  House.*
  J. Saunders, 565:Spring84-55
Rumens, C. Star Whisper.*
  R. Pybus, 565:Autumn84-73
Rumold, R. Gottfried Benn und der Expres-
  sionismus.
  W. Paulsen, 564:Sep84-220
Rumphius, G.E. The Poison Tree. (E.M.
  Beekman, ed and trans)
  J.J. Fox, 293(JASt):Feb84-365
Rumsey, T. Pictures from a Trip.
  J. Kaufmann, 441:28Apr85-18
Runciman, W.G. A Treatise on Social
  Theory.* (Vol 1)
  J. Gray, 483:Jul84-406
Runte, H.R., H. Niedzielski and W.L. Hen-
  drickson, eds. Jean Misrahi Memorial
  Volume.
  A. Iker-Gittleman, 545(RPh):Aug83-100
Ruppersburg, H.M. Voice and Eye in Faulk-
  ner's Fiction.*
  C.S. Brown, 569(SR):Summer84-474
  T.L. McHaney, 585(SoQ):Summer84-88
  K.J. Phillips, 268(IFR):Winter85-56
  E.L. Volpe, 587(SAF):Autumn84-240
  J.G. Watson, 395(MFS):Summer84-319
Rupprecht, B. and W-C. von der Mülbe. Die
  Brüder Asam.
  B. Heisner, 576:May84-180
Rush, C. A Twelvemonth and a Day.
  G. Mangan, 617(TLS):16Aug85-909
Rush, J. Earth Dreams.
  B. Pirie, 102(CanL):Winter83-146

Rushdie, S. Shame.*
  M. Gorra, 249(HudR):Spring84-162
  J.L. Halio, 598(SoR):Winter85-204
  M. Hollington, 381:Sep84-403
Rushton, J. W.A. Mozart: "Don Giovanni."*
  F.W. Sternfeld, 410(M&L):Oct84-377
Rusich, L.G. Un carbonaro molisano nei
  due mondi.*
  A. Blasi, 263(RIB):Vol34No1-103
Rusinko, S. Terence Rattigan.
  J. Daubenas, 397(MD):Jun84-263
Ruskin, J. John Ruskin: Letters from the
  Continent 1858.* (J. Hayman, ed)
  P. Conner, 59:Dec84-499
  P. Morgan, 178:Dec84-495
Russ, J. The Female Man.
  L. Marcus, 617(TLS):27Sep85-1070
Russ, J. How to Suppress Women's Writing.
  K.O. Garrigan, 395(MFS):Summer84-373
Russ, J. Magic Mommas, Trembling Sisters,
  Puritans and Perverts.
  B. Ehrenreich, 441:29Sep85-50
Russ, L. Cellar.
  639(VQR):Summer84-89
Russell, A. I'm Not Making This Up, You
  Know. (J. Vickers, ed)
  J. McCourt, 441:15Dec85-9
Russell, B. The Collected Papers of Ber-
  trand Russell.* (Vol 1: Cambridge
  Essays 1888-1899.) (K. Blackwell and
  others, eds)
  C.H. Kabelis and R.H. Bell, 31(ASch):
  Summer84-418
  C.W. Kilmister, 84:Dec84-403
Russell, D. The Tamarisk Tree. (Vol 3)
  J. Harris, 617(TLS):11Oct85-1126
  M. Jones, 362:12Sep85-28
Russell, D.A. Costume History and Style.
  H.L. Camburn, 615(TJ):Mar84-128
Russell, D.A. Criticism in Antiquity.*
  W.R. Johnson, 122:Jul84-250
  B.R. Rees, 303(JoHS):Vol 104-225
Russell, D.A. and N.G. Wilson - see Menan-
  der
Russell, E.F. Men, Martians and Machines.
  D. Barbour, 561(SFS):Jul84-200
Russell, J. The Meanings of Modern Art.
  S. Watney, 59:Mar84-102
Russell, J. Paris.* (rev)
  S.S., 376:Feb84-145
Russell, J.B. Lucifer.
  D.J.R. Bruckner, 441:28Apr85-25
  N. Cohn, 453(NYRB):25Apr85-13
  D.J. Enright, 617(TLS):22Mar85-304
Russell, K.S. Das Problem der Identität
  in Gottfried Kellers Prosawerk.
  K.L. Komar, 221(GQ):Winter84-157
Russell, M. Visions of the Sea.*
  D. Cordingly, 90:Nov84-703
"Russkaja literatura i fol'klor." (A.A.
  Gorelov, ed)
  J.L. Conrad, 574(SEEJ):Winter84-558
Russo, R. La metodologia del sapere nel
  sermone di S. Bonaventura "Unus est
  magister vester Christus."
  R.J. Long, 589:Apr84-441
Rust, R.D. - see Cooper, J.F.
Rustin, M. For a Pluralist Socialism.
  J. Campbell, 617(TLS):15Nov85-1285
Rutherford, P. A Victorian Authority.
  R. Cook, 102(CanL):Winter83-78
Rutland, E.D. - see Ringwood, G.P.

Rutman, D.B. and A.H. A Place in Time.
  E.S. Morgan, 453(NYRB):17Jan85-44
Rutschky, M. Wartzeit.
  H-J. Ortheil, 384:Jan84-89
Ruttencutter, H.D. Previn.
  A. Zito, 441:15Sep85-25
Rutter, C.C., ed. Documents of the Rose
  Playhouse.
  A. Gurr, 617(TLS):15Feb85-174
van Ruusbroec, J. Opera Omnia. (Vols 1
  and 2) (G. de Baere, ed)
  L.V.R., 568(SCN):Fall84-51
Ruuth-Bäcker, K. En litterär resa genom
  det svarta Afrika.
  R. Granqvist, 538(RAL):Spring84-130
Ruwet, N. Grammaire des insultes et
  autres études.
  K.E.M. George, 208(FS):Jul84-374
Ryan, A. Cast a Cold Eye.
  P. Craig, 617(TLS):19Apr85-434
Ryan, A. Property and Political Theory.*
  J. Christman, 185:Jul85-941
  H. Perkin, 617(TLS):18Jan85-59
Ryan, D.P. Beyond the Ballot Box.
  S. Thernstrom, 432(NEQ):Jun84-298
Ryan, E.B. and H. Giles, eds. Attitudes
  Towards Language Variation.*
  T.C. Frazer, 215(GL):Vol24No1-73
Ryan, J. The Uncompleted Past.
  M.S. Fries, 454:Winter85-179
Ryan, M. Marxism and Deconstruction.*
  J.A. Flieger, 223:Fall83-297
  J.J. Stuhr, 478:Oct84-291
Ryan, N.J. A History of Malaysia and
  Singapore.
  C.M. Turnbull, 302:Vol20No2-236
Ryan, W.F. and C.B. Schmitt, eds. Pseudo-
  Aristotle, "The Secret of Secrets."
  F.W. Zimmermann, 123:Vol134No1-139
Ryba, M. Pig Art.
  639(VQR):Winter84-29
Rycroft, C. Psychoanalysis and Beyond.
  R. Dinnage, 617(TLS):13Sep85-1006
Rydell, R.W. All the World's a Fair.
  W.S. McFeely, 441:26May85-11
Ryder, F.G. - see Keller, G.
Ryder, R.D. Victims of Science. (rev ed)
  P. Singer, 453(NYRB):17Jan85-46
Rydland, K. Vowel Systems and Lexical-
  Phonemic Patterns in South-East Cumbria.
  B. Cottle, 541(RES):Aug84-433
  J.D. McClure, 571(ScLJ):Autumn84-39
  W. Viereck, 685(ZDL):1/1984-105
du Ryer, P. Esther. (P. Gethner and E.J.
  Campion, eds)
  J.A. Schmidt, 207(FR):Mar85-578
Ryga, G. Two Plays.
  S. Stone-Blackburn, 102(CanL):Autumn84-
  140
Rykwert, J. and A. The Brothers Adam.
  K. Downes, 617(TLS):13Dec85-1424
Rystad, G., ed. Europe and Scandinavia.
  J. Larson, 563(SS):Autumn84-370
Rywkin, M. Moscow's Muslim Challenge.*
  D.S. Carlisle, 550(RusR):Jan84-101
Rzhevsky, N. Russian Literature and Ideol-
  ogy.*
  R. Freeborn, 575(SEER):Oct84-587

Saagpakk, P.F., comp. Eesti-Inglise
  Sõnaraamat.*
  J.E. Cathey, 563(SS):Winter84-77

Saagpakk, P.F., comp. Estonian-English
  Dictionary.
  J. Kõvamees-Kitching, 574(SEEJ):
  Winter84-567
Saavedra, M.D. - see under de Cervantes
  Saavedra, M.
Sabarsky, S., ed. Gustav Klimt: Drawings.
  P. Vergo, 617(TLS):22Mar85-320
Sabban, A. Gälisch-englischer Sprachkon-
  takt.*
  S.M. Embleton, 350:Sep85-719
  D. Nehls, 257(IRAL):May84-154
  E.W. Schneider, 300:Vol 17-109
Saberhagen, F. The Berserker Throne.
  G. Jonas, 441:4Aug85-20
Sabiani, J. - see Péguy, C. and P. Marcel
el Sabio, A. - see under Alfonso el Sabio
Sabor, P. - see Cleland, J.
Sabrafin, G. Leyendas, Tradiciones,
  Cuentos Fabulosos, y otros relatos fan-
  tasticos de las islas Cabrera, Formen-
  tera, Eivissa, Menorca y Mallorca.
  L. Grinsell, 203:Vol195No1-134
Sachar, A.L. The Redemption of the
  Unwanted.
  M. Syrkin, 390:Feb84-56
Sachar, H.M. Diaspora.
  E. Alexander, 129:Dec85-68
  R. Sanders, 441:21Apr85-17
Sachedina, A.A. Islamic Messianism.
  P.E. Walker, 318(JAOS):Jul-Sep83-631
Sachs, J. - see Hummel, J.N.
von Sachsenheim, H. - see under Hermann
  von Sachsenheim
Sackett, R.E. Popular Entertainment,
  Class, and Politics in Munich, 1900-1923.
  N.M. Decker, 221(GQ):Fall84-690
Sacks, M.P. Work and Equality in Soviet
  Society.
  D. Herr, 550(RusR):Jan84-97
Sacks, O. The Man Who Mistook His Wife
  for a Hat.
  A. Clare, 362:5Dec85-35
Sacks, O. Migraine.
  I. Rosenfield, 441:7Jul85-8
Sackville-West, V. The Letters of Vita
  Sackville-West to Virginia Woolf.* (L.
  De Salvo and M.A. Leaska, eds)
  C.G. Heilbrun, 344:Spring85-127
  M. Meyer, 364:Nov84-100
von Sacrobosco, J. Die deutsche Sphaera.
  (K. von Megenberg, trans, F.B. Brévart,
  ed)
  R. Hildebrandt, 685(ZDL):3/1984-399
von Sacrobosco, J. Konrad Heinfogel:
  "Sphaera Materialis." (K. Heinfogel,
  trans, F.B. Brévart, ed)
  R.F.M. Byrn, 402(MLR):Jan84-226
  B.D. Haage, 680(ZDP):Band103Heft3-470
von Sacrobosco, J. Johannes von Sacro-
  bosco, "Das Puechlein von der Spera."
  (F.B. Brévart, ed)
  B.D. Haage, 680(ZDP):Band103Heft3-470
de Sacy, S.S. - see de Balzac, H.
el-Sadat, A. Those I Have Known.*
  W.V. O'Brien, 617(TLS):19Apr85-428
Saddlemyer, A. - see Synge, J.M.
Sadek, A.I. The Amethyst Mining Inscrip-
  tions of Wadi el Hudi. (Pt 1)
  V.L. Davis, 318(JAOS):Oct-Dec83-791

Saint-Pierre, A. La Fille bègue.
I. Joubert, 298:Fall84-164
J.R. Waelti-Walters, 102(CanL):
Summer84-90
de Saint Pierre, I. Richard Dadd — His
Journals.
A. Brownjohn, 617(TLS):12Jul85-776
St. Pierre, P. Smith and Other Events.*
E. Nicol, 102(CanL):Autumn84-102
Duc de Saint-Simon. Mémoires (1691-1701).
(Y. Coirault, ed)
J. von Stackelberg, 475:Vol 11No20-218
de Ste. Croix, G.E.M. The Class Struggle
in the Ancient Greek World.*
W. Eder, 122:Oct84-341
J.A.S. Evans, 529(QQ):Summer84-324
Saisselin, R.G. The Bourgeois and the
Bibelot.
P-L. Adams, 61:Mar85-124
Saisselin, R.G. Bricabracomania.
M. Jordan, 617(TLS):2Aug85-843
Saito, S., ed. Philippine-American Rela-
tions.
B. Jenkins, 106:Winter84-441
Sakharov, A.N. Diplomatiia drevnei Rusi.
E.S. Hurwitz, 550(RusR):Apr84-211
Sala, M. and others. El español de Amér-
ica. (Vol 1)
D. Gifford, 86(BHS):Oct84-500
Sala-Molins, L. - see Lull, R.
Salam-Liebich, H. The Architecture of the
Mamluk City of Tripoli.
H. Crane, 576:May84-173
Salaman, W. Living School Music.
P. Standford, 415:Sep84-503
de Salas, J. - see Leibniz, G.W.
de Salas Ortueta, J. El Conocimiento del
Mundo Externo y el problema crítico en
Leibniz y en Hume.
J.L. Sagüés, 202(FMod):No65/67-295
Salazar Rincón, J. Fray Luis de León y
Cervantes.
P.J. Donnelly, 86(BHS):Oct84-521
Sale, K. Dwellers in the Land.
R. Williams, 441:6Oct85-15
Salemme, C. Strutture semiologiche nel
"De rerum natura" di Lucrezio.
J-M. André, 555:Vol58fasc1-139
Salenius, E.W. Harley Granville Barker.
R. Berry, 570(SQ):Autumn84-374
C.M. Mazer, 130:Summer84-190
Sales, H. Einstein, o Minigênio.
M. Silverman, 238:Mar84-155
Sales, R. English Literature in History,
1780-1830.
M. Myers, 340(KSJ):Vol33-231
Salisbury, H. A Journey for Our Times.
M. Ellmann, 569(SR):Fall84-661
Salisbury, H.E. The Long March.
M. Oksenberg, 441:29Sep85-7
Sallenave, D. Un printemps froid.
C. Coustou, 450(NRF):Feb84-99
Saller, R.P. Personal Patronage Under the
Early Empire.*
K.R. Bradley, 121(CJ):Apr-May85-357
Salmen, W., general ed. The Social Status
of the Professional Musician from the
Middle Ages to the 19th Century. (H.
Kaufman and B. Reisner, eds and trans)
A.M. Hanson, 410(M&L):Oct84-402
Salmieri, S. and O. Edwards. Cadillac.
B. Staples, 441:15Dec85-21

Salmon, E. Granville Barker.*
R. Berry, 570(SQ):Autumn84-374
J.P. Wearing, 177(ELT):Vol27No3-258
Salmon, N.U. Reference and Essence.*
P. Coppock, 311(JP):May84-261
G. Forbes, 393(Mind):Apr84-305
D.E. Over, 518:Jan84-1
J. Tienson, 316:Dec84-1417
Salom, P. The Projectionist.*
M. Macleod, 381:Sep84-457
Saloman, H.P., with J. de Lange. Portrait
of a New Christian, Fernão Álvares Melo
(1569-1632).
P.E.H. Hair, 86(BHS):Oct84-516
Salt, B. Film Style and Technology.
R. Dungnat, 707:Summer84-227
Salter, C.H. Good Little Thomas Hardy.*
R. Mason, 447(N&Q):Jun83-261
Salter, E. Fourteenth-Century English
Poetry.* (D. Pearsall and N. Zeeman,
eds)
N.F. Blake, 179(ES):Aug84-368
T. Outakoski, 439(NM):1984/3-376
Salter, M.J. Henry Purcell in Japan.
M. Kinzie, 29(APR):Nov/Dec85-7
L.M. Rosenberg, 441:7Apr85-12
Saltman, R.B. The Social and Political
Thought of Michael Bakunin.
D. Hardy, 550(RusR):Oct84-428
Salu, M., ed. Essays on "Troilus and
Criseyde."
F.N.M. Diekstra, 179(ES):Dec84-555
Salvaggio, R. Dryden's Dualities.
E. Duthie, 566:Autumn84-58
Salwak, D. A.J. Cronin.
I. Murray, 571(ScLJ):Autumn84-23
Salwak, D. John Wain.
P. Miles, 447(N&Q):Jun83-269
Samaltanos, K. Apollinaire.
S. Morgan, 62:Dec84-72
Samatar, S.S. Oral Poetry and Somali
Nationalism.
J.W. Johnson, 538(RAL):Winter84-598
Sambrook, J. - see Thomson, J.
Sammons, J.L. Heinrich Heine — A Modern
Biography.* Heinrich Heine — A Selected
Critical Bibliography of Secondary Lit-
erature, 1956-1980.
R. von Tiedemann, 52:Band19Heft1-68
Samples, G. Lust for Fame.*
D.J. Watermeier, 615(TJ):Mar84-127
Sampson, A. Empires of the Sky.*
M. Bender, 441:10Feb85-9
Sampson, A. and S., eds. The Oxford Book
of Ages.
A. Watkins, 362:8Aug85-28
442(NY):11Nov85-158
Sampson, E.E. Justice and the Critique of
Pure Psychology.
J.L.H., 185:Jan85-382
Sampson, G. An End to Allegiance.*
S. Brittan, 176:Apr85-55
Sampson, G. Liberty and Language.
F. D'Agostino, 488:Jun84-251
Sampson, G. Schools of Linguistics.*
F.P. Dinneen, 215(GL):Vol24No2-131
F.J. Sullivan, 355(LSoc):Sep84-375
Sams, E. The Songs of Hugo Wolf. (2nd ed)
P. Branscombe, 415:Apr84-210
R. Swift, 451:Fall84-164
Samuel, C. The Chilkat Dancing Blanket.
B. King, 614:Spring85-18

Samuel, H.E. The Cantata in Nuremberg
during the Seventeenth Century.
   L. Hübsch-Pfleger, 410(M&L):Jan84-95
Samuel, R.H. and H.M. Brown. Kleist's
Lost Year and the Quest for "Robert Guis-
kard."*
   D. Grathoff, 406:Summer84-219
   E. Stopp, 402(MLR):Jan84-235
Samuels, A. Jung and the Post-Jungians.
   A. Storr, 617(TLS):22Feb85-190
Samuels, M.S. Contest for the South China
Sea.
   F.W. Houn, 293(JASt):Nov83-147
Samuelson, A. With Hemingway.
   P-L. Adams, 61:Jan85-100
   F. Raphael, 617(TLS):16Aug85-894
Sánchez, R. Chicano Discourse.
   V. Arizpe, 399(MLJ):Winter84-419
Sánchez-Albornoz, C. Dípticos de Historia
de España.
   C. De Paepe, 356(LR):Aug84-260
Sanchez-Albornoz, N., ed. La moderniza-
ción económica de España 1830-1930.
   R. Carr, 617(TLS):4Oct85-1105
Sanchez Perez, A. Blake's Graphic Work
and the Emblematic Tradition.
   J.S. Salemi, 88:Summer84-50
Sánchez Romeralo, A., S.G. Armistead and
S.H. Petersen. Bibliografía del roman-
cero oral, 1.
   A. González, 457(NRFH):Tomo32núm1-234
Sand, G. Lucrezia Floriani. (J. Eker,
trans)
   D. Bair, 441:11Aug85-9
Sand, G. Mademoiselle Merquem.* (R.
Rheault, ed) Correspondance. (Vol 17)
(G. Lubin, ed)
   L.J. Austin, 208(FS):Oct84-472
Sandberg, K.C. and G. Zask. Le Français
à propos.
   T.M. Scanlan, 399(MLJ):Autumn84-289
Sandel, M.J. Liberalism and the Limits of
Justice.*
   R. Amdur, 473(PR):2/1984-306
   C. Larmore, 311(JP):Jun84-336
Sander, A. Photographs of an Epoch (1904-
1959).
   D. Barnouw, 221(GQ):Winter84-119
Sander, V. - see Dürrenmatt, F.
Sander, V. - see Raabe, W.
Sanders, C.R. and K.J. Fielding - see
Carlyle, T. and J.W.
Sanders, E.P. Jesus and Judaism.
   J.L. Houlden, 617(TLS):5Apr85-391
   J. Koenig, 441:22Dec85-1
Sanders, L. The Fourth Deadly Sin.
   L. Gruson, 441:28Jul85-18
Sanders, L. The Loves of Harry Dancer.
   D. Fitzpatrick, 441:29Dec85-18
Sanders, S.R. Wilderness Plots.
   S.W.L., 219(GaR):Summer84-442
   42(AR):Spring84-259
Sanderson, M. From Irving to Olivier.
   I. Wardle, 617(TLS):15Feb85-174
Sanderson, M., ed. International Handbook
of Contemporary Developments in Architec-
ture.
   R.H. Bletter, 576:Mar84-76
Sandford, G.W. From Hitler to Ulbricht.*
   M. McCauley, 575(SEER):Apr84-308

Sandler, L.F. The Psalter of Robert de
Lisle.
   F. Chevillet, 189(EA):Jul-Sep85-277
   C. De Hamel, 39:Jul84-73
Sandoz, M. Gabriel Briard (1725-1777).
   R. Wrigley, 59:Mar84-126
Sandqvist, S., ed. Trois contes français
du XIVe siècle tirés du recueil
intitulé "Le Tombel de Chartrose."
   P.E. Bennett, 402(MLR):Jan84-180
   M.E. Winters, 589:Apr84-443
Sandred, K.I. Good or Bad Scots.
   P. Morere, 189(EA):Jul-Sep85-311
Sands, M. Robson of the Olympic.
   J. Donohue, 637(VS):Autumn83-91
Sandwith, H. and S. Stainton. The Na-
tional Trust Manual of Housekeeping.
   B. Scott, 324:Mar85-302
Sandy, G.N. Heliodorus.*
   K. Dowden, 123:Vol34No1-25
Sandy, S. Riding to Greylock.*
   B. Bawer, 491:Sep84-351
Saner, R. Essay on Air.
   R.W. Flint, 441:27Jan85-18
   P. Stitt, 219(GaR):Spring84-166
Sanfilippo, C.M., ed. Carteggio Rajna-
Salvioni.
   G. Costa, 545(RPh):Nov83-243
Sanford, A.J. Cognition and Cognitive
Psychology.
   N.S. Sutherland, 617(TLS):13Sep85-1006
Sanford, G. Polish Communism in Crisis.*
   G. Schöpflin, 575(SEER)Jul84-469
Sanford, J. The Color of the Air.
   R.G. Davis, 441:10Nov85-57
Sanguineti, E. Segnalibri.
   J. Risset, 98:Aug/Sep84-617
Sankoff, G. The Social Life of Language.
   D. Laycock, 567:Vol48No3/4-367
   C.R. Whitehead, 320(CJL):Spring84-97
Sanon, J.B. Images socio-politiques dans
le roman négro-africain.
   C.L. Dehon, 207(FR):May85-882
Sansom, B. The Camp at Wallaby Cross.
   F. Myers, 355(LSoc):Jun84-254
Sansone, D. - see Euripides
Santamaría Conde, A. and L.G. García-Saúco
Beléndez. La iglesia de Santa María del
Salvador de Chinchilla.
   A. Bustamante, 48:Oct-Dec83-419
Santangelo, G.S. and C. Vinti. Le Tradu-
zioni italiane del teatro comico fran-
cese dei secoli XVII e XVIII.
   H.G. Hall, 208(FS):Apr84-205
   A. Tissier, 549(RLC):Jul-Sep84-358
van Santen, A. De morfologie van het
Nederlands.
   G.E. Booij, 204(FdL):Jun84-137
Santí, E.M. Pablo Neruda.*
   S. Karsen, 593:Winter84/85-331
   C. Perriam, 86(BHS):Oct84-519
Santiago, D. Famous All Over Town.*
   C.L. Crow, 649(WAL):Feb85-347
Santmyer, H.H. "...And Ladies of the
Club."*
   S. Altinel, 617(TLS):13Dec85-1434
Santmyer, H.H. Herbs and Apples.
   A. Hulbert, 441:10Nov85-28
Santoli, A. To Bear Any Burden.
   C. Trueheart, 441:9Jun85-23
Santos, J.F. - see under Fernandez Santos,
J.

321

Santos, S. Accidental Weather.*
　　P. Stitt, 344:Summer85-123
Santschi, M. Voyage avec Michel Butor.
　　D. Coste, 207(FR):May85-900
Sanzio, A. and P-L. Thirard. Luchino Vis-
conti cinéaste.
　　C. Thomas, 98:Aug/Sep84-662
Sao Saimöng Mangrāi. The Pāḍaeng Chron-
icle and the Jengtung State Chronicle
Translated.
　　F.K. Lehman, 293(JASt):Aug84-811
Sappenfield, J.A. and E.N. Feltskog - see
Cooper, J.F.
Sarde, M. Regard sur les Françaises: Xème
siècle — XXème siècle.
　　N. Aronson, 207(FR):Oct84-173
Sargent, C. Luftwaffe Snowshoes.
　　M. Galvin, 496:Fall84-177
Sargent-Baur, B.N. and R.F. Cook. "Aucas-
sin et Nicolete."*
　　M. Bonafin, 379(MedR):Aug84-297
　　K. Busby, 547(RF):Band96Heft3-333
　　J. Tattersall, 208(FS):Oct84-448
Sargeson, F. Conversation in a Train and
Other Critical Writing. (K. Cunningham,
ed)
　　C.K. Stead, 617(TLS):12Apr85-403
Sarkissian, A., ed. Children's Authors
and Illustrators.
　　E. Pilon, 470:Vol22-127
Sarkissian, J. Catullus 68.
　　H. Dettmer, 124:Sep-Oct84-63
Sarles, H. After Metaphysics.
　　W. Stokoe, 355(LSoc):Mar84-123
Sarlós, R.K. Jig Cook and the Province-
town Players.*
　　G. Anthony, 106:Fall84-361
　　J.E. Barlow, 612(ThS):May84-113
　　L. Ben-Zvi, 397(MD):Sep84-451
Saroyan, A. William Saroyan.*
　　G. Haslam, 649(WAL):Nov84-248
Saroyan, W. My Name is Saroyan. (J.H.
Tashjian, comp)
　　G. Haslam, 649(WAL):Nov84-248
Sarraute, N. Childhood.* (French title:
Enfance.)
　　G.R. Besser, 207(FR):May85-921
Sarton, M. The Magnificent Spinster.
　　J. Humphreys, 441:27Oct85-26
Sartorius, R., ed. Paternalism.
　　J. Woodward, 185:Jan85-353
　　R. Young, 63:Dec84-434
Sartre, J-P. Les Carnets de la drôle de
guerre.* Lettres au Castor et à quel-
ques autres.* (Vols 1 and 2) (S. de
Beauvoir, ed)
　　A. van den Hoven, 628(UWR):Spring-
　　Summer85-98
Sartre, J-P. The Family Idiot.* (Vol 1)
　　T.H. Adamowski, 627(UTQ):Fall83-107
　　G. Falconer, 529(QQ):Summer84-415
　　W.L. McBride, 543:Dec83-417
Sartre, J-P. The War Diaries of Jean-Paul
Sartre: November 1939/March 1940.
　　A.C. Danto, 441:31Mar85-12
Sartre, M. Trois études sur l'Arabie
romaine et byzantine.
　　J. Desanges, 555:Vol58fasc1-165
Sass, H.M. Martin Heidegger.
　　W. Franzen, 687:Nov-Dec84-690
　　C. Spadoni, 40(AEB):Vol8No1-60

Sassoon, S. Diaries 1915-1918. (R. Hart-
Davis, ed)
　　B. Bergonzi, 506(PSt):Dec84-267
　　C. Lloyd, 541(RES):May84-263
　　295(JML):Nov84-503
Sassoon, S. Diaries 1920-1922. (R. Hart-
Davis, ed)
　　M. Thorpe, 179(ES):Apr84-188
　　295(JML):Nov84-503
Sassoon, S. Diaries 1923-1925. (R. Hart-
Davis, ed)
　　I. Colegate, 617(TLS):8Mar85-249
　　R. Ingrams, 362:25Apr85-23
　　P. Parker, 364:Feb85-87
Sassoon, S. Siegfried Sassoon's Long
Journey. (P. Fussell, ed)
　　M. Moran, 556:Winter84/85-326
Sassoon, S. The War Poems. (R. Hart-
Davis, ed)
　　C. Lloyd, 541(RES):May84-263
　　J. Saunders, 565:Autumn84-66
Satijn, N. Le labyrinthe de la cité
radieuse.*
　　A. Callen, 402(MLR):Jan84-205
　　H. Klüppelholz, 356(LR):Feb/May84-141
Sato, E.M.T., M. Sakihara and L.I. Shish-
ido. Japanese Now. (Vol 2)
　　T.M. Critchfield, 399(MLJ):Winter84-
　　408
Sato, E.M.T., L.I. Shishido and M. Saki-
hara. Japanese Now. (Vol 1)
　　T.M. Critchfield, 399(MLJ):Spring84-84
Satō, M. Chinese Ceramics.
　　B. Parr, 60:Mar-Apr84-128
Sattelmeyer, R. - see Thoreau, H.D.
Sattler, D.E. Friedrich Hölderlin.
　　R. Reschke, 654(WB):9/1984-1560
Sauer, L. Marionetten, Maschinen, Auto-
maten.
　　H.M.K. Riley, 133:Band17Heft1/2-146
Sauer, T.G. A.W. Schlegel's Shakespearean
Criticism in England, 1811-1846.
　　E. Behler, 107(CRCL):Jun84-310
Sauerländer, W. From Stilus to Style.
　　M. Warnke, 384:Jul84-566
Sauermost, H.J. and W-C. von der Mülbe.
Istanbuler Moscheen.
　　M. Restle, 471:Jan/Feb/Mar84-100
Saunders, A. The Art and Architecture of
London.
　　C. Fox, 324:May85-427
　　J.M. Robinson, 39:Jul84-78
Saunders, G. Bilingual Children.
　　G.G. Gilbert, 355(LSoc):Dec84-544
Saunders, J.W. A Biographical Dictionary
of Renaissance Poets and Dramatists,
1520-1650.*
　　J. Egan, 568(SCN):Fall84-43
Saunders, T.J. - see Aristotle
Saurín de la Iglesia, M.R. Apuntes y docu-
mentos para una historia de Galicia en
el siglo XIX.
　　D. Mackenzie, 86(BHS):Jan84-66
de Saussure, F. Saggio sul vocalismo ind-
europeo. (G.C. Vincenzi, ed)
　　A.L. Prosdocimi, 260(IF):Band89-329
Sauter, J-H. Interviews mit Schriftstel-
lern.
　　L. Volke, 654(WB):4/1984-697
Sauvel, K.S. and P. Munro. Chem'ivillu'.
　　J. Heath, 350:Jun85-505

de Sauvigny, C.D. and D.H. Pinkney - see under de Bertier de Sauvigny, G. and D.H. Pinkney

Savage, T. For Mary, with Love.
P. Wolfe, 502(PrS):Winter84-108

Savalle, J. Travestis, métamorphoses, dédoublements.
H.P. Lund, 535(RHL):Jul/Aug84-637
P.J. Whyte, 208(FS):Apr84-211

Savard, P., ed. Aspects de la civilisation canadienne-française.
D.M. Hayne, 627(UTQ):Summer84-475

Savater, F. Childhood Regained.
G. Avery, 447(N&Q):Dec83-554

Savel'eva, E.A. Olaus Magnus i ego "Istoriia severnykh narodov."
H.F. Graham, 550(RusR):Oct84-442

Saviane, G. Getsèmani.
C. Di Biase, 275(IQ):Spring84-121

Savignon, S.J. Communicative Competence.
C.B. Christensen, 399(MLJ):Autumn84-276

Savile, A. The Test of Time.*
D. Carrier, 311(JP):Apr84-226
R. Hanna, 543:Dec83-418
P. Lewis, 479(PhQ):Jan84-73
R.A. Sharpe, 393(Mind):Jul84-467
P. Somville, 542:Apr-Jun84-239
C. Welch, 154:Sep84-544

Savile-Troike, M. The Ethnography of Communication.*
G. Håkansson, 596(SL):Vol38No2-185

Savitch, J. Anchorwoman.
A. Chenoweth, 569(SR):Winter84-171

Savoie, P. Acrobats.*
I. Sowton, 102(CanL):Winter83-154

Savona, P. and G. Sutija, eds. Eurodollars and International Banking.
D. Delamaide, 617(TLS):6Sep85-968

Saward, S. The Golden Age of Marie de' Medici.
A. Hughes, 59:Sep84-378

Sawey, O. Charles A. Siringo.
T.F. Averill, 649(WAL):May84-76

Sawislak, A. Dwarf Rapes Nun; Flees in UFO.
P. Hamill, 441:1Sep85-10

Sawyer, P.H. Kings and Vikings.
B.E. Gelsinger, 589:Apr84-485

Saxena, S.K. Aesthetical Essays.*
J.A. Martin, Jr., 485(PE&W):Jan84-105

Saxon, A.H. - see Barnum, P.T.

Saxton, J. The Power of Time.
C. Greenland, 617(TLS):18Oct85-1167

Sayce, O. The Medieval German Lyric 1150-1300.*
A. Groos, 680(ZDP):Band103Heft3-449
C. Locher, 131(CL):Summer84-268
A. Robertshaw, 402(MLR):Oct84-973
E. Simon, 589:Jan84-204

Sayce, R.A. and D. Maskell. A Descriptive Bibliography of Montaigne's "Essais," 1580-1700.*
R.D. Cottrell, 207(FR):Apr85-724
M.M. McGowan, 208(FS):Oct84-451

Sayen, J. Einstein in America.
M. Peters, 441:18Aug85-21
442(NY):5Aug85-83

Sayer, C. Costumes of Mexico.
E. Hoffman, 614:Summer85-21

Sayer, I. and D. Botting. Nazi Gold.
D. Goddard, 441:5May85-18

Sayre, H.M. The Visual Text of William Carlos Williams.
S. Paul, 301(JEGP):Oct84-580
D. Pope, 27(AL):Dec84-617
L.M. Steinman, 659(ConL):Winter85-497
639(VQR):Spring84-45

Sayre, K.M. Plato's Late Ontology.*
D.H. Frank, 319:Oct85-579
J.C.B. Gosling, 518:Apr84-79
E. Halper, 124:Jul-Aug85-609

Sayres, S. and others, eds. The Sixties, Without Apology.
G. Marcus, 62:Dec84-77
D.T. O'Hara, 659(ConL):Fall85-335

de Saz, S.M.P. - see under Parkinson de Saz, S.M.

Scaffai, M. - see "Baebii Italici, 'Ilias Latina.'"

Scaglione, A., ed. The Emergence of National Languages.
S.M. Embleton, 350:Sep85-732

Scaglione, A. The Theory of German Word Order from the Renaissance to the Present.*
R.J.E. d'Alquen, 406:Fall84-345
L.H. Hathaway, 301(JEGP):Jul84-403
W.J. Jones, 402(MLR):Jul84-739
A. Mešťan, 549(RLC):Jan-Mar84-109

Scalamandrè, R. F. Vielé-Griffin e il platonismo.*
M. Tilby, 208(FS):Jan84-80

Scammell, M. Solzhenitsyn.*
J. Bayley, 362:28Feb85-23
G. Hosking, 617(TLS):1Mar85-223
V.S. Pritchett, 442(NY):18Mar85-125

Scammell, W. A Second Life.*
T. Eagleton, 565:Winter83/84-77

Scammell, W., ed. Between Comets.
J. Mackinnon, 617(TLS):19Apr85-449

Scammell, W. Jouissance.
S. Rae, 617(TLS):23Aug85-933

Scannell, V. Winterlude.
R. Pybus, 565:Winter83/84-68

Scaramuzzi, F. Per dilettatione grande et per utilità incredibile.
D. Butchart, 410(M&L):Jan84-98

Scarisbrick, D. Jewellry.
R.L. Shep, 614:Spring85-19

von Scarpatetti, B.M. Die Handschriften der Stiftsbibliothek St. Gallen.
R. McKitterick, 354:Dec84-404

von Scarpatetti, B.M. and others, eds. Katalog der datierten Handschriften in der Schweiz in lateinischer Schrift vom Anfang des Mittelalters bis 1550.
L.V.R., 568(SCN):Fall84-52

Scarpellini, P. Perugino: L'opera completa.
N. Penny, 617(TLS):30Aug85-952

Scarre, C., ed. Ancient France, 6000-2000 B.C.*
C. Thomas, 176:Jan85-48

Scattergood, V.J. and J.W. Sherborne, eds. English Court Culture in the Later Middle Ages.
J. Backhouse, 354:Dec84-406
V. Gillespie, 184(EIC):Apr84-155

Schaar, C. "The Full Voic'd Quire Below."*
A-L. Scoufos, 179(ES):Feb84-76

Schacht, R. Nietzsche.*
P.F., 185:Oct84-186
A. Nehamas, 482(PhR):Oct84-641
C.S. Taylor, 518:Oct84-212

Schachter, A. Cults of Boiotia.
L. Darmezin, 487:Winter84-388
Schaefer, D. and L. Salvato. Masters of
Light.
T. McDonough, 18:Sep85-68
Schaeffer, J-M. and T. Todorov - see von
Goethe, J.W.
Schaeffer, S.F. The Madness of a Seduced
Woman.*
G. Johnson, 584(SWR):Winter84-93
Schaeffer, S.F. Mainland.
S.A. Toth, 441:7Jul85-6
Schäfer, H.D. Das gespaltene Bewusstsein.
H. Siefken, 220(GL&L):Jan85-180
Schäfer, J., ed. Commonwealth-Literatur.
G. Düsterhaus, 72:Band22lHeft2-391
Schafer, R. The Analytic Attitude.
C. Gildiner, 529(QQ):Autumn84-737
Schäfer, W.E. Johann Michael Moscherosch.
K. Kiesant, 654(WB):10/1984-1755
Schain, M.A. French Communism and Local
Power.
J.E.S. Hayward, 617(TLS):10May85-516
Schaller, G.B. and others. The Giant
Pandas of Wolong.
S.J. Gould, 453(NYRB):15Aug85-12
Schaller, M. The American Occupation of
Japan.
D.S. Zagoria, 441:27Oct85-9
Schamber, E.N. The Artist as Politician.
R.R. Denommé, 207(FR):May85-926
Schank, R.C., with P.G. Childers. The
Cognitive Computer.
S. Chace, 441:9Jun85-12
Schanze, F. Meisterliche Liedkunst
zwischen Heinrich von Mügeln und Hans
Sachs. (Vol 1)
C. Petzsch, 72:Band22lHeft2-339
Schaper, E., ed. Pleasure, Preference and
Value.
T.J. Diffey, 290(JAAC):Fall84-96
C. Lyas, 89(BJA):Summer84-256
G. McFee, 483:Oct84-535
Schapiro, B.A. The Romantic Mother.
T.R. Frosch, 340(KSJ):Vol33-208
F. Kirchoff, 661(WC):Summer84-132
Schapiro, L. The Russian Revolutions of
1917.*
639(VQR):Autumn84-117
Schapiro, M. The Romanesque Sculpture of
Moissac.
C.B. McGee, 441:13Oct85-25
Schärer, K. Pour une poétique des "Chim-
ères" de Nerval.*
R.T. Denommé, 207(FR):Oct84-130
Scharfstein, B-A. The Philosophers.*
W.I. Matson, 262:Jul84-330
Scharnhorst, G. and J. Bales. Horatio
Alger, Jr. (British title: The Lost
Life of Horatio Alger, Jr.)
A. Gribben, 26(ALR):Spring84-144
P. Renshaw, 617(TLS):18Oct85-1160
Scharnhorst, J. and E. Ising, eds. Grund-
lagen der Sprachkultur. (Pt 2)
G. Frohne, 682(ZPSK):Band37Heft6-740
Schaub, M. Müntzer contre Luther.
M. de Gandillac, 98:Dec84-1025
de Schauensee, R.M. The Birds of China.
C. Perrins, 617(TLS):18Jan85-72
Schauer, F.F. Free Speech.*
M. Glass, 529(QQ):Spring84-210
F.S. Haiman, 480(P&R):Vol 17No3-176
D. Tucker, 63:Mar84-82

Schechner, R. Between Theater and Anthro-
pology.
C.M. Turnbull, 441:22Sep85-21
Schechner, R. The End of Humanism.
T.J. Taylor, 397(MD):Sep84-455
Scheer, R., with N. Zacchino and C. Mat-
thiessen. With Enough Shovels.*
T.N., 185:Apr85-781
Scheffer, C.F. Lettres particulières à
Carl Gustaf Tessin 1744-1752. (J.
Heidner, ed)
G. Engwall, 597(SN):Vol56No1-124
Å. Grafström, 553(RLiR):Jul-Dec84-517
G. Walton, 54:Dec84-701
Scheffers, H. Höfische Konventionen und
die Aufklärung.
P. Riesz-Musumeci, 343:Heft9/10-159
Scheffler, S. The Rejection of Consequen-
tialism.*
S. Conly, 482(PhR):Jul84-489
S.L. Darwall, 311(JP):Apr84-220
T. Hurka, 154:Mar84-165
J. Loughran, 258:Jun84-208
D. Lyons, 185:Jul85-936
Scheffler, W. Goldschmiede Ostpreussens.
G. Schiedlausky, 471:Jul/Aug/Sep84-306
Schefold, K. Die Bedeutung der griech-
ischen Kunst für das Verständnis des
Evangeliums.
M. Robertson, 123:Vol34No2-352
Scheidegger, J. Arbitraire et motivation
en français et en allemand.*
M. Harris, 208(FS):Oct84-504
Scheier, L. The Larger Life.*
J. Carson, 526:Autumn84-80
S.S., 376:Feb84-140
Scheler, L. La Grande Espérance des
poètes, 1940-1945.
S. Michaud, 535(RHL):Jul/Aug84-649
Scheler, M. Politisch-pädagogische Schrif-
ten. (M.S. Frings, ed)
W. Henckmann, 489(PJGG):Band91Heft2-
405
Scheler, M. Problems of a Sociology of
Knowledge.
K. Dixon, 488:Jun84-263
Schell, E. Strangers and Pilgrims.
P.W. Travis, 551(RenQ):Autumn84-490
639(VQR):Winter84-9
Schell, O. Modern Meat.*
P. Singer, 453(NYRB):17Jan85-46
Schell, O. To Get Rich Is Glorious.
K. Lieberthal, 441:17Feb85-8
Schelling, F.W.J. Contribution à l'his-
toire de la philosophie moderne, Leçons
de Munich.* (J-F. Marquet, ed and trans)
J-F. Courtine, 192(EP):Jul-Sep84-421
Schelling, F.W.J. Historisch-Kritische
Ausgabe.* (1st Ser, Vol 2) (H. Buchner
and J. Jantzen, with others, eds)
H. Brockard, 687:Apr-Jun84-334
Schelling, F.W.J. Historisch-Kritische
Ausgabe.* (1st Ser, Vol 3) (H. Buchner,
W.G. Jacobs and A. Pieper, eds)
H. Brockard, 687:Apr-Jun84-334
A. White, 319:Oct85-597
Schelling, F.W.J. Texte zur Philosophie
der Kunst. (W. Beierwaltes, ed)
J-F. Courtine, 192(EP):Jan-Mar84-124
Schemann, H. Das idiomatische Sprach-
zeichen.
K. Böckle, 72:Band22lHeft2-331

Schenkein, J., ed. Studies in the Organi-
zation of Conversational Interaction.
  M. Coulthard, 355(LSoc):Sep84-363
Schepelern, H.D. - see Borch, O.
Schepens, G. L'"autopsie" dans la méthode
des historiens grecs du Ve siècle avant
J.-C.
  B.M. Mitchell, 303(JoHS):Vol 104-240
Scherer, C. Comédie et société sous Louis
XIII.
  C. Carlin, 207(FR):Apr85-727
Scherer, F. and M. Poley. The Soho Char-
cuterie Cookbook.
  W. and C. Cowen, 639(VQR):Spring84-67
Scherer, J. Racine et/ou la Cérémonie.
  J-L. Backès, 535(RHL):Jul/Aug84-606
  J. Morel, 475:Vol 11No20-270
  R.W. Tobin, 210(FrF):Jan84-115
Scherer, J.L. Handbook on Soviet Military
Deficiencies.
  D.R. Jones, 104(CASS):Fall84-354
Scherer, J.L. - see "China: Facts and
Figures Annual, Vol 4"
Scherer, K.R. and P. Ekman, eds. Hand-
book of Methods in Nonverbal Behavior
Research.
  J. Skupien, 567:Vol50No3/4-359
Scherer, W. and E. von Steinmeyer. Brief-
wechsel 1872-1886. (H. Brunner and J.
Helbig, eds)
  L. Denecke, 684(ZDA):Band113Heft1-44
  H. Schmidt, 682(ZPSK):Band37Heft6-731
Schermbrucker, B. Chameleon and Other
Stories.
  J.W. Lennox, 102(CanL):Autumn84-187
Scherwinsky, F. Die Neologismen in der
modernen französischen Science-Fiction.
  K.E.M. George, 208(FS):Jul84-374
Scheuer, N. - see de Saint-Aubin, C.G.
Schevill, J. The American Fantasies.
  A. Fulton, 385(MQR):Summer85-492
Schiavo, L. Historia y novela en Valle-
Inclán.*
  A. Sinclair, 402(MLR):Apr84-476
Schick, F. Having Reasons.
  D. Braybrooke, 150(DR):Fall84-626
Schickel, R. Cary Grant.
  J. Nangle, 200:May84-310
Schickel, R. D.W. Griffith.*
  R. Giroux, 200:Aug/Sep84-440
  J. Rosenbaum, 707:Autumn84-302
Schickel, R. Intimate Strangers.
  C. Brightman, 441:17Mar85-15
  442(NY):27May85-99
Schieb, G. and others, eds. Beiträge zur
Erforschung der deutschen Sprache.
(Vol 1)
  J. Schildt, 682(ZPSK):Band37Heft1-107
Schieder, T. Friedrich der Grosse.*
  J. Kunisch, 384:Jul84-574
Schier, K., ed. Märchen aus Island.
  H. Engster and K. Pulmer, 196:Band25
  Heft3/4-366
Schifano, J-N. Chroniques napolitaines.
  V.D.L., 605(SC):15Apr85-296
  R. Millet, 450(NRF):Oct84-90
Schiff, D. La Ligne de Sceaux.
  F.C. St. Aubyn, 207(FR):Mar85-603
Schiff, D. The Music of Elliott Carter.*
  A. Whittall, 410(M&L):Jul84-276
Schiff, E. From Stereotype to Metaphor.
  N. Sandrow, 397(MD):Sep84-462

Schiff, Z. and E. Ya'ari. Israel's Leba-
non War.*
  W.V. O'Brien, 617(TLS):17May85-556
Schiffer, E. Zwischen den Zeilen.
  M. Dierks, 680(ZDP):Band103Heft2-305
Schiffman, H.F. A Reference Grammar of
Spoken Kannada.
  S.B. Steever, 350:Mar85-196
Schillebeeckx, E. The Church with a Human
Face.
  N. Lash, 617(TLS):6Sep85-986
Schiller, F. On the Naive and Sentimental
in Literature. (H. Watanabe-O'Kelly,
trans)
  M.E. Schubert, 221(GQ):Winter84-152
Schimmel, H.D. and P.D. Cate - see de
Toulouse-Lautrec, H. and W.H.B. Sands
Schings, H-J. Der mitleidigste Mensch ist
der beste Mensch.*
  C.J. Wickham, 406:Spring84-93
Schinz, M. and S. Littlefield. Visions of
Paradise.
  J.L. Faust, 441:8Dec85-28
Schipper, M., ed. Het Zwarte Paradijs.
  L.K. Altes, 538(RAL):Summer84-290
Schipper, M., ed. Unheard Words.
  S. Nasta, 617(TLS):29Nov85-1374
Schirmer, G.A. The Poetry of Austin
Clarke.*
  B. Dolan, 305(JIL):Jan-May84-145
  272(IUR):Spring84-152
Schirmer, K-H., ed. Das Märe.
  S. Krause, 196:Band25Heft3/4-369
Schirmer, W.F. Geschichte der englischen
und amerikanischen Literatur.
  R. Asselineau, 189(EA):Jan-Mar85-109
Schiroli, M.G.C. - see under Cavalca
Schiroli, M.G.
Schlaefer, M. Kommentierte Bibliographie
zur deutschen Orthographietheorie und
Orthographiegeschichte im 19. Jahrhun-
dert.
  A. Lötscher, 685(ZDL):3/1984-394
Schlaffer, H. Faust Zweiter Teil.*
  H.E. Seelig, 406:Winter84-460
Schlee, A. The Proprietor.*
  D. Flower, 249(HudR):Summer84-309
Schlee, A. Wandlungen musikalischer Struk-
turen im Werke Thomas Mann.
  A. Fehn, 221(GQ):Spring84-339
Schlegel, F. Vom Wiener Kongress zum
Frankfurter Bundestag. (J-J. Anstett,
with U. Behler, eds) Die Epoche der
Zeitschrift Concordia. (E. Susini, ed)
  M. Csáky, 602:Band15Heft1-153
Schleicher, A. Die Sprachen Europas in
systematischer Übersicht. (new ed)
  T.F. Shannon, 350:Dec85-920
  P. Swiggers, 353:Vol22No3-427
Schleicher, A., E. Haeckel and W. Bleek.
Linguistics and Evolutionary Theory.
  F. Chevillet, 189(EA):Jul-Sep85-304
  D.H., 355(LSoc):Jun84-285
  P. Swiggers, 353:Vol22No3-427
Schleifer, R. and R. Markley, eds. Kierke-
gaard and Literature.
  M. Kipperman, 400(MLN):Dec84-1269
Schlereth, T.J. Artifacts and the Amer-
ican Past.*
  D.J. Russo, 106:Winter84-397

Schlereth, T.J., ed. Material Culture
Studies in America.
M.M. Lovell, 658:Winter84-287
D.J. Russo, 106:Winter84-397
Schlesinger, G.N. Metaphysics.
P. Helm, 518:Jan84-58
T.V. Morris, 258:Jun84-205
Schlobin, R.C., ed. The Aesthetics of
Fantasy Literature and Art.*
D. Collinson, 89(BJA):Winter84-79
M. Tatar, 221(GQ):Fall84-691
Schlobin, R.C. Urania's Daughters.
S.L. Nickerson, 561(SFS):Nov84-340
Schloss, C.S. Travel, Trade and Tempta-
tion.*
H-J. Raupp, 600:Vol 14No2-140
Schlossstein, S. Trade War.*
M. Sayle, 453(NYRB):28Mar85-33
Schlueter, J. The Plays and Novels of
Peter Handke.*
K-H. Schoeps, 301(JEGP):Jan84-97
Schlundt, R., ed. Sagen aus Rheinland-
Pfalz.
G. Petschel, 196:Band25Heft3/4-370
Schmalfeldt, J. Berg's "Wozzeck."*
D. Hush, 317:Summer84-424
D. Jarman, 410(M&L):Jul84-294
Schmalstieg, W.R. Indo-European Linguis-
tics.
J.H. Jasanoff, 350:Dec85-922
Schmalstieg, W.R. An Old Prussian Grammar.
Studies in Old Prussian.
P. Swiggers, 353:Vol21No4-647
Schmaltz, B. Griechische Grabreliefs.
C.M. Havelock, 124:Jan-Feb85-223
Schmeling, M. - see Kaiser, G.R.
Schmidgall, G. Shakespeare and the
Courtly Aesthetic.
J.C. Perryman, 570(SQ):Spring84-118
Schmidgall-Tellings, A.E. and A.M. Stevens.
Contemporary Indonesian-English Diction-
ary.
J. Dreyfuss, 293(JASt):Nov83-205
Schmidlechner, K.M. Die steirischen Ar-
beiter im 19. Jahrhundert.
F.L. Carsten, 575(SEER):Oct84-634
Schmidlin, Y. and others - see Bürgin, H.
and H-O. Mayer
Schmidt, A. History and Structure.
J. Hoffman, 125:Summer84-426
Schmidt, B. and others. Frankreich-
Lexikon. (Vol 1)
H. Sonneville, 356(LR):Feb/May84-122
R.J. Steiner, 207(FR):Feb85-487
Schmidt, B. and others. Frankreich-
Lexikon. (Vol 2)
H. Sonneville, 356(LR):Aug84-248
Schmidt, E. Geschichte der Karyatide.
R.A. Tomlinson, 303(JoHS):Vol 104-254
Schmidt, H. A Grand Strategy for the West.
D.P. Calleo, 441:1Dec85-14
Schmidt, H.J. - see Büchner, G.
Schmidt, K. Mandlighedens positioner.*
A. Born, 562(Scan):May84-72
Schmidt, M. Choosing a Guest.*
B. O'Donoghue, 493:Sep84-70
Schmidt, M., ed. Some Contemporary Poets
of Britain and Ireland.*
B. Morrison, 493:Jan84-55
Schmidt, M. Albert Speer.
H.A. Turner, Jr., 441:3Mar85-9

Schmidt, S.J. Foundations for the Empiri-
cal Study of Literature.* (German title:
Grundriss der Empirischen Literaturwis-
senschaft.) (Pt 1) (R. de Beaugrande, ed
and trans of English edition)
H. Hauptmeier and R. Viehoff, 494:
Vol4No1-153
J. Wirrer, 567:Vol52No1/2-131
N. Würzbach, 490:Band15Heft3/4-342
Schmidt, S.J. Grundriss der empirischen
Literaturwissenschaft. (Pt 2)
H. Hauptmeier and R. Viehoff, 494:
Vol4No1-153
N. Würzbach, 490:Band15Heft3/4-342
Schmidt, W. Geschichte der deutschen
Sprache. (2nd ed)
M.S. Notario Bueno, 202(FMod):No68/70-
381
von Schmidt, W.A. and H. Hinrichs. Blick
und Einsicht. (2nd ed)
R.H. Buchheit, 399(MLJ):Summer84-179
Schmidt-Biggemann, W. Topica universalis.
C.B. Schmitt, 319:Apr85-257
Schmidt-Knaebel, S. Schizophrene Sprache
in Monolog und Dialog.
R. Wodak, 353:Vol22No2-255
Schmidt-Radefeldt, J., ed. Paul Valéry.
B. Münzer, 224(GRM):Band34Heft3-363
Schmidt-Wiegand, R., ed. Wörter und
Sachen im Lichte der Bezeichnungsfors-
chung.
H. Beck, 260(IF):Band89-365
Schmidtke, D. Studien zur dingalle-
gorischen Erbauungsliteratur des Spät-
mittelalters am Beispiel der Garten-
allegorie.*
S.L. Wailes, 301(JEGP):Jan84-86
Schmiedt, H. Karl May.
K. Hasselbach, 406:Spring84-104
Schmitt, A., ed. Ein kurtzweilig lesen
von Dil Ulenspiegel.
W. Virmond, 684(ZDA):Band113Heft3-130
Schmitt, C.B. Aristotle and the Renais-
sance.*
L.V.R., 568(SCN):Winter84-78
Schmitt, C.B. John Case and Aristotelian-
ism in Renaissance England.
E.J. Ashworth, 154:Sep84-534
L.V.R., 568(SCN):Fall84-53
Schmitt, C.B. - see Cranz, F.E.
Schmitt, J-C. The Holy Greyhound.
S. Dickman, 589:Jul84-699
Schmitt, R. Grammatik des Klassisch-Armen-
ischen mit sprachvergleichenden Erläuter-
ungen.
R. Bielmeier, 260(IF):Band89-338
Schmitt-Sasse, J. Das Opfer der Tugend.
P.M. Lützeler, 133:Band17Heft1/2-140
Schmitz, A. Une Poignée de jours.
M-N. Little, 207(FR):Dec84-318
Schmitz, D. Singing.
A. Williamson, 441:23Jun85-26
Schmitz, H.R. Progrès social et révolu-
tion, l'illusion dialectique.
A. Reix, 542:Apr-Jun84-260
Schmitz, N. Of Huck and Alice.
H. Hill, 27(AL):May84-275
S.S., 376:Feb84-144
Schmitz, W., ed. Der Teufelsprozess vor
dem Weltgericht nach Ulrich Tennglers
"Neuer Layenspiegel" von 1511.
R.E. Schade, 221(GQ):Spring84-305

Schorr, N.G. En Revue.
J. Van Eerde, 399(MLJ):Spring84-74
Schorske, C.E. Fin-de-siècle Vienna.
(French title: Vienne fin de siècle.)
A. Clerval, 450(NRF):Jun84-115
M-A. Lescourret, 98:Apr84-313
H. Uhr, 222(GR):Spring84-75
Schott, R.L. and D.S. Hamilton. People,
Positions, and Power.
639(VQR):Autumn84-135
Schouls, P.A. The Imposition of Method.*
M.B. Bolton, 449:Mar84-120
Schousboe, T. - see Nielsen, C. and A.M.
Carl-Nielsen
Schrag, C.O. Radical Reflection and the
Origin of the Human Sciences.
M.J. Hyde, 488:Jun84-270
Schrameier, W. Te-ling Chiao-chou-wan
(Ts'ing-tao) chih ti-cheng tzu-liao.
R. Myers, 293(JASt):Nov83-149
Schreiber, J. Jerzy Andrzejewskis Roman
"Ciemności kryją ziemię" und die Dar-
stellung der Spanischen Inquisition in
Werken der fiktionalen Literatur.
N. Taylor, 575(SEER):Apr84-274
Schricker, G.C. A New Species of Man.*
D. Kiberd, 272(IUR):Autumn84-301
Schrimpf, G. Das Werk des Johannes Scot-
tus Eriugena im Rahmen des Wissenschafts-
verständnisses seiner Zeit.
P.E. Dutton, 319:Apr85-253
A. Zimmermann, 53(AGP):Band66Heft1-101
Schröder, S. Komparatistik und Ideen-
geschichte.
U. Weisstein, 52:Band19Heft2-198
Schröder, W., ed. Eine alemannische Bear-
beitung der "Arabel" Ulrichs von dem
Türlin.
A. Schnyder, 680(ZDP):Band103Heft3-464
Schröder, W. Die Namen im "Parzival" und
im "Titurel" Wolframs von Eschenbach.
D.H. Green, 402(MLR):Apr84-484
Schröder, W. - see Wolfram von Eschenbach
Schrodt, R. System und Norm in der Dia-
chronie des deutschen Konjunktivs.
T.A. Lovik, 350:Mar85-221
Schroedel, J.E. Alone in a Crowd.
A. Kessler-Harris, 441:4Aug85-12
Schroeder, J. Pierre Reverdy.*
I. Higgins, 208(FS):Jul84-365
Schroll-Fleischer, N.O. Der Gottesge-
danke in der Philosophie Kants.
W. Steinbeck, 342:Band75Heft1-120
Schubert, D. Works and Days. (T. and R.
Weiss, eds)
R. Hadas, 472:Fall/Winter84-133
R. Phillips, 491:Mar85-351
Schubert, W. and R. Woderich. Wissen-
schaftlich-technischer Fortschritt und
Arbeitskultur.
M. Hofmann and G.K. Lehmann, 654(WB):
7/1984-1206
Schuer, F. Free Speech.
L. Reinhardt, 483:Jan84-130
Schuhmacher, G., ed. Felix Mendelssohn
Bartholdy.
R.L. Todd, 410(M&L):Jan84-99
Schuhmann, K. and J. Möller. Jonathan
Swift.
H-J. Müllenbrock, 677(YES):Vol 14-321
Schulberg, B. The Four Seasons of Success.
A. Arthur, 649(WAL):Feb85-333

Schulman, G. Hemispheres.
L.M. Rosenberg, 441:7Apr85-12
Schulman, I.A. - see Martí, J.
Schulman, M. and E. Mekler. Bringing Up a
Moral Child.
S. Scarr, 441:29Sep85-44
Schulte, B. Die Goldprägung der gall-
ischen Kaiser von Postumus bis Tetricus.
C.E. King, 123:Vol34No2-358
Schulte, E. William Morris, I Pellegrini
della Speranza.
H. Brill, 326:Winter84/85-26
Schulte, G. Hegel oder das Bedürfnis nach
Philosophie.
W. Maker, 543:Dec83-420
Schulte-Wülwer, U. Das Nibelungenlied in
der deutschen Kunst des 19. und 20.
Jahrhunderts.
J. Kühnel, 224(GRM):Band34Heft1/2-199
Schulthess, P. Relation und Funktion.
E. Fries, 53(AGP):Band66Heft3-327
Schultz, J.A. The Shape of the Round
Table.
M.E. Kalinke, 301(JEGP):Oct84-593
Schultz, P. Deep Within the Ravine.
R. Tillinghast, 441:31Mar85-14
Schulz, A.M. Antonio Rizzo.
B. Boucher, 39:Oct84-287
R. Munman, 551(RenQ):Autumn84-466
J. Pope-Hennessy, 90:Sep84-573
Schulz, D. Suche und Abenteuer.
R.P. Lessenich, 72:Band221Heft1-184
Schulz, M.F. Black Humor Fiction of the
Sixties.
M. Leaf, 447(N&Q):Jun83-276
Schulz-Hoffmann, C. and J. Weiss, eds.
Max Beckmann.
F. Whitford, 617(TLS):22Mar85-312
Schulze, F. Mies van der Rohe.
A.L. Huxtable, 441:1Dec85-1
Schumacher, J.N. Revolutionary Clergy.
D.R. Sturtevant, 293(JASt):Nov83-207
Schumann, E. Memoirs. (M. Busch, ed)
A. Fitz Lyon, 617(TLS):22Nov85-1317
Schumann, O. - see "Lateinisches Hexameter-
Lexikon"
Schumann, R. Tagebücher.* (Vol 3) (G.
Neuhaus, ed)
P.F. Ostwald, 451:Fall84-176
Schumann, W. - see Grimm, J. and W.
Schunck, F. Joseph Conrad.
W. Klooss, 38:Band102Heft1/2-260
Schupp, F. - see Leibniz, G.W.
Schürmann, R. Le principe d'anarchie.*
B. Flynn, 543:Sep83-143
J. Pestieau, 154:Sep84-520
Schüssler, I. Philosophie und Wissen-
schaftspositivismus.*
R. Stuhlmann-Laeisz, 53(AGP):Band66
Heft3-323
Schütrumpf, E. Die Analyse der Polis
durch Aristoteles.
G.J.D. Aalders H. Wzn., 394:
Vol37fasc1/2-183
Schutte, O. Beyond Nihilism.
P. Franco, 185:Jul85-953
Schutte, W.M. Index of Recurrent Elements
in James Joyce's "Ulysses."*
A. Goldman, 447(N&Q):Aug83-371
Schütz, E.H. Alfred Andersch.
M. Silberman, 406:Summer84-237

Schützeichel, R. Codex Pal.lat.52: Stud-
ien zur Heidelberger Otfridhandschrift,
zum Kicila-Vers und zum Georgslied.
M.W. Wierschin, 221(GQ):Summer84-465
Schvey, H.I. Oskar Kokoschka.*
W. Paulsen, 133:Band17Heft1/2-159
Schwab, J.C. Acht Briefe über einige
Widersprüche und Inconsequenzen in
Herrn Professor Kants neuesten Schriften.
R. Malter, 342:Band75Heft1-127
Schwantes, C.A. Coxey's Army.
K. Caplan, 441:29Dec85-19
Schwarberg, G. The Murders at Bullenhuser
Damm.*
L.L. Langer, 385(MQR):Winter85-125
M.A. Meyer, 390:Dec84-57
639(VQR):Autumn84-133
Schwartz, B. Super Chief.
639(VQR):Winter84-10
Schwartz, B. The Unpublished Opinions of
the Warren Court.
A. Lewis, 441:29Dec85-20
Schwartz, B.I. The World of Thought in
Ancient China.
W.J. Peterson, 441:1Dec85-20
Schwartz, D. Letters of Delmore Schwartz.*
(R. Phillips, ed)
H. Vendler, 453(NYRB):11Apr85-7
A. Wald, 385(MQR):Summer85-511
Schwartz, J. Caught.
A.M. Martin, 441:1Dec85-43
Schwartz, J. The Sexual Politics of Jean-
Jacques Rousseau.
S.H., 185:Apr85-778
J.H. Mason, 617(TLS):29Mar85-365
Schwartz, K. Studies on Twentieth-Century
Spanish and Spanish American Literature.
P.B. Dixon, 395(MFS):Summer84-338
R.A. Parsons, 238:May84-309
Schwartz, L. Diderot and the Jews.*
R.H. Popkin, 173(ECS):Fall84-115
Schwartz, L.S. Disturbances in the Field.
M. Gorra, 249(HudR):Spring84-159
Schwartz, L.S. We Are Talking About Homes.
S. Raab, 441:24Nov85-18
Schwarz, B. Music and Musical Life in
Soviet Russia 1957-1981. (rev)
H. Robinson, 550(RusR):Jul84-292
Schwarz, D.R. Conrad: The Later Fiction.*
T.K. Bender, 577(SHR):Summer84-269
W. Bonney, 268(IFR):Winter85-52
A. Hunter, 447(N&Q):Aug83-366
Schwarz, E., ed. Hermann Hesses "Steppen-
wolf."
R. Koester, 406:Spring84-109
Schwarz, H. Art and Photography. (W.E.
Parker, ed)
C.H., 62:Summer85-97
Schwarz, H. - see Trier, J.
Schwarz, W. - see Kant, I.
Schwarzbaum, H. Biblical and Extra-Bibli-
cal Legends in Islamic Folk-Literature.*
J. Rosenhouse, 294:Vol 15-141
Schwarze, C., ed. Analyse des préposi-
tions.*
S. Norwood, 545(RPh):Aug83-114
Schweitzer, C.E. - see Pastorius, F.D.
Schwemmer, O. Philosophie der Praxis.
W. Steinbeck, 342:Band75Heft2-252
Schwendowius, B. and W. Dömling, eds. J.S.
Bach.
442(NY):11Mar85-137

Schwerin, D. Rainbow Walkers.
D. Cole, 441:31Mar85-22
Schwob, M. Chroniques. (J.A. Green, ed)
P. Berthier, 535(RHL):Mar/Apr84-297
A. Gier, 72:Band221Heft1-213
Schwob, M. The King in the Golden Mask
and Other Writings.
A. Szogyi, 441:21Apr85-24
Sciascia, L. Pirandello e la Sicilia.
M-A. Lescourret, 98:Nov84-911
Sciascia, L. Stendhal e la Sicilia.
(French title: Stendhal et la Sicile.)
V.D.L., 605(SC):15Jul85-376
Sciascia, L. Le théâtre de la mémoire.
C. Ambroise, 98:Aug/Sep84-606
Sciascia, L. The Wine-Dark Sea. (French
title: La Mer couleur de vin.)
F. Ferrucci, 441:24Nov85-27
G. Josipovici, 617(TLS):20Dec85-1464
J. Serradifalco, 450(NRF):Mar84-143
Sclauzero, M. Narcissism and Death.
D. Kuspit, 62:Dec84-73
Scliar, M. The Centaur in the Garden.
J. Franco, 441:30Jun85-12
Scodel, R. The Trojan Trilogy of Eurip-
ides.
T.J. Sienkewicz, 24:Winter84-482
Scohy, A. Salomé.
P.S. Rogers, 207(FR):Oct84-162
Scollon, R. and S.B.K. Narrative, Liter-
acy, and Face in Interethnic Communica-
tion.*
J. Verschueren, 355(LSoc):Dec84-489
Scott, A.C. Actors are Madmen.
J.L. Faurot, 293(JASt):Nov83-151
B. Prophet, 615(TJ):May84-282
Scott, B.K. Joyce and Feminism.
B. Benstock, 454:Winter85-182
B. Brothers, 329(JJQ):Winter85-236
R. Brown, 617(TLS):11Jan85-40
M. Magalaner, 395(MFS):Winter84-760
J. Mays, 272(IUR):Autumn84-304
J.C. Voelker, 573(SSF):Fall84-426
295(JML):Nov84-465
639(VQR):Autumn84-128
Scott, C. Antichthon.*
L.K. MacKendrick, 198:Spring84-110
Scott, D. Chains.
R. Elman, 441:6Jan85-20
Scott, D. A Quiet Gathering.
J. Mole, 176:Jul/Aug85-55
Scott, G.W. An Illustrated Guide to Mak-
ing Oriental Rugs.
K.B., 614:Winter85-25
Scott, H. No Exit.
N. Callendar, 441:22Dec85-30
Scott, H. Working Your Way to the Bottom.
I.V. Sawhill, 441:19May85-18
Scott, J. A Little Darling, Dead.
T.J.B., 617(TLS):19Apr85-434
Scott, J. TACTICS: face à face.
S. Keane, 399(MLJ):Winter84-400
Scott, J. and C. Griff. Directors of
Industry.
L. Hannah, 617(TLS):26Jul85-828
Scott, J.S. A Death in Irish Town.
N. Callendar, 441:8Dec85-76
Scott, J.W. Madame de Lafayette.
J. Campbell, 208(FS):Oct84-461
Scott, P. Travel Diaries of a Naturalist.
(Vol 2)
J. Buxton, 617(TLS):27Dec85-1486

Sebold, R.P. Trayectoria del romanticismo español.
  S. García Castañeda, 240(HR):Autumn84-541
  R.B. Klein, 238:May84-306
von Seckendorff, K. Hermann Hesses propagandistische Prosa.
  R. Koester, 133:Band17Heft1/2-173
Secor, R. John Ruskin and Alfred Hunt.*
  P. Conner, 59:Dec84-499
  C.N., 90:Dec84-796
Secor, R. and M. - see Hunt, V.
Secrest, M. Kenneth Clark.*
  J. Darracott, 364:Oct84-100
  J. Meyers, 441:3Feb85-17
  W. Mostyn-Owen, 617(TLS):17May85-537
  D. Sutton, 39:Nov84-296
Sedelow, W.A. and S.Y., eds. Computers in Language Research, 2.
  M.A. Covington, 350:Mar85-248
von See, K. Edda, Saga, Skaldendichtung.
  M. Ciklamini, 563(SS):Summer84-300
Seebold, E. Etymologie.
  K.H. Schmidt, 685(ZDL):1/1984-87
von Seefranz-Montag, A. Syntaktische Funktionen und Wortstellungsveränderung.
  W.P. Ahrens, 350:Jun85-498
Seel, G. Die Aristotelische Modaltheorie.
  I. Boh, 319:Apr85-250
Seel, P.C. Erkenntniskritik als Ökonomiekritik.
  G-W. Küsters, 342:Band75Heft4-501
Seelig, S.C. The Shadow of Eternity.*
  F. Dinshaw, 541(RES):Nov84-536
  A. Green, 161(DUJ):Dec83-134
  B. King, 569(SR):Spring84-284
Seelow, H., ed. Hálfs saga ok Hálfsrekka.*
  F.W. Blaisdell, 301(JEGP):Jul84-422
  S.A. Mitchell, 563(SS):Summer84-307
Seelye, H.N. Teaching Culture.
  R.C. Lafayette, 399(MLJ):Winter84-387
  A.G. Suozzo, Jr., 207(FR):Mar85-609
Seeman, K.D., ed. Russische Lyrik.
  A. McMillin, 575(SEER):Jan84-151
Segal, C. Dionysiac Poetics and Euripides' "Bacchae."*
  E.M. Jenkinson, 161(DUJ):Dec83-112
  C.A. Rubino, 487:Autumn84-279
  R. Seaford, 303(JoHS):Vol 104-203
Segal, C. Tragedy and Civilization.*
  M.C. Hoppin, 24:Spring84-108
Segal, E. The Class.
  S. Isaacs, 441:21Apr85-9
Segal, L. Her First American.
  C. Kizer, 441:19May85-7
Segalen, M. Love and Power in the Peasant Family.*
  J.S. Allen, 446(NCFS):Summer-Fall84-225
Segalen, V. The Great Statuary of China.
  P. Berger, 318(JAOS):Apr-Jun83-465
Segerberg, K. Classical Propositional Operators.
  R. Fleming, 316:Sep84-993
Segers, R.T., ed. Lezen en laten lezen.
  H. Dyserinck, 678(YCGL):No32-146
Segev, T. 1949 — The First Israelis.
  A. Margalit, 453(NYRB):26Sep85-23
Segre, C. Semiotica filologica.* Semiotica, storia e cultura.
  P. Pugliatti, 494:Vol5No1-196

"II Simposio sobre el padre Feijoo y su siglo."
  E.V. Coughlin, 240(HR):Winter84-89
Seibel, H.D. and U.G. Damachi. Self-Management in Yugoslavia and the Developing World.
  D. McGlue, 575(SEER):Jan84-141
Seidel, F. Men and Woman.
  C. Boyle, 364:Oct84-76
  P. Hainsworth, 617(TLS):24May85-574
Seidenfaden, E. Guide to Bangkok, 1928.
  617(TLS):22Nov85-1339
Seidensticker, B. Palintonos Harmonia.
  C. Collard, 123:Vol34No2-199
Seidensticker, E. Low City, High City.
  H. Smith, 407(MN):Summer84-206
  639(VQR):Winter84-15
Seidl, H.A. Medizinische Sprichwörter im Englischen und Deutschen.
  W. Mieder, 196:Band25Heft1/2-155
Seidler, H. Österreichischer Vormärz und Goethezeit.*
  D.G. Daviau, 301(JEGP):Oct84-606
Seidlin, O. Von erwachendem Bewusstsein und vom Sündenfall.
  J.F. Hyde, Jr., 406:Spring84-93
Seidman, S. Liberalism and the Origins of European Social Theory.
  C.W. Anderson, 185:Oct84-149
Seifert, A. Untersuchungen zu Hölderlins Pindar-Rezeption.*
  M. Fink, 52:Band19Heft1-90
Seifert, J. An Umbrella From Piccadilly.*
  M.H. Heim, 441:30Jun85-33
Seifert, W. Theorie und Didaktik der Erzählprosa.
  W. Höppner, 654(WB):7/1984-1215
Seigel, J.E. Comeuppance.
  639(VQR):Winter84-22
Seiler, B.W. Die leidigen Tatsachen.
  W. Hoffmeister, 680(ZDP):Band103Heft4-604
Seiler, H. Possession as an Operational Dimension of Language.
  G. Bossong, 361:Oct/Nov84-229
Seiler, H. and C. Lehmann, eds. Apprehension. (Pt 1)
  P. Ramat, 361:Apr84-357
Seiler, H. and F.J. Stachowiak, eds. Apprehension. (Pt 2)
  P. Ramat, 361:Apr84-357
Seip, T.L. The South Returns to Congress.
  W.C. Harris, 9(AlaR):Oct84-306
Seitz, G. Die Brüder Grimm.
  R.B. Bottigheimer, 617(TLS):29Mar85-355
Seitz, W.C. Abstract Expressionist Painting in America.*
  M. Amaya, 39:Jul84-76
  L. Cooke, 90:Aug84-509
Sekora, J. and D.T. Turner, eds. The Art of Slave Narrative.
  B. Paige-Pointer, 579(SAQ):Summer84-353
Selbmann, R. Theater im Roman.
  S.L. Cocalis, 133:Band17Heft1/2-144
Selbourne, D. The Making of "A Midsummer Night's Dream."*
  G. Playfair, 157:No152-52
Seldes, G., comp. The Great Thoughts.
  A. Burgess, 61:Apr85-134
Seldon, M. Poppies and Roses.
  D. Thomas, 362:16May85-27

Selfe, L. Normal and Anomalous Representational Drawing Ability in Children.
P. Meeson, 89(BJA):Spring84-186
Selig, R.L. George Gissing.
M. Collie, 637(VS):Spring84-389
P. Coustillas, 177(ELT):Vol27No1-71
P. Coustillas, 189(EA):Jan-Mar85-93
Seliger, H.W. and M.H. Long, eds. Classroom Oriented Research in Second Language Acquisition.
L.A.W. van Lier, 608:Jun85-356
Seling, H. Die Kunst der Augsburger Goldschmiede, 1529-1868.
R.W. Lightbown, 90:Jun84-356
Selkirk, E.O. The Syntax of Words.
A. Carstairs, 297(JL):Sep84-361
Sell, R.D. Robert Frost.*
R. Belflower, 541(RES):Feb84-106
Sell, R.D., ed. Three Lectures on Literature in English.
S. Monod, 189(EA):Jan-Mar85-110
Seller, M.S., ed. Ethnic Theatre in the United States.
M.K. Fielder, 615(TJ):May84-276
Sellery, J.M. and W.O. Harris. Elizabeth Bowen.*
J.H. Winterkorn, 517(PBSA):Vol78No3-379
Sellin, P.R. John Donne and "Calvinist" Views of Grace.
T.G. Sherwood, 539:Aug85-231
Seltzer, M. Henry James and the Art of Power.
N. Bradbury, 617(TLS):8Mar85-264
de Selve, L. Les Oeuvres spirituelles sur les évangiles des jours de caresme et sur les festes de l'année. (L.K. Donaldson-Evans, ed)
W.J. Beck, 207(FR):May85-887
Selzer, R. Letters to a Young Doctor.
J. Meyers, 569(SR):Summer84-lxii
"Semantics from Different Points of View."
G.F. Meier, 682(ZPSK):Band37Heft3-403
Semmel, B. John Stuart Mill and the Pursuit of Virtue.
R.J. Arneson, 185:Apr85-757
Semprun, J. What a Beautiful Sunday!
L.D. Nachman, 560:Spring-Summer84-286
Sen, A. Poverty and Famines.*
A. Appadurai, 293(JASt):May84-481
R.M. Solow, 473(PR):2/1984-312
Sen, A. Resources, Values and Development.
M. Lipton, 617(TLS):26Jul85-827
Sen, A., P. Chatterjee and S. Mukherji. Perspectives in Social Sciences 2.
J.R. McLane, 293(JASt):Feb84-362
Sen, A. and B. Williams, eds. Utilitarianism and Beyond.*
H.A. Bedau, 185:Jan85-333
R.G. Frey, 393(Mind):Jul84-444
L. Holborow, 63:Mar84-90
J. Skorupski, 479(PhQ):Apr84-165
Sen, R. - see under Rāmprasād Sen
Seneca. Oedipus. (B.W. Häuptli, ed)
C.D.N. Costa, 123:Vol34No2-326
Seneca. Lucio Anneo Seneca "De Tranquillitate Animi."* (M.G. Cavalca Schiroli, ed)
H.M. Hine, 123:Vol34No1-132
Senelick, L. Gordon Craig's Moscow "Hamlet."*
V. Emeljanow, 611(TN):Vol38No1-45
[continued]

[continuing]
M. Heim, 615(TJ):Mar84-142
G. Janecek, 550(RusR):Apr84-192
Senelick, L., ed and trans. Russian Satiric Comedy.
M.L. Hoover, 574(SEEJ):Winter84-545
Senelick, L. Serf Actor.
P. Storfer, 157:No153-51
Sengle, F. Literaturgeschichtsschreibung ohne Schulungsauftrag.
A.T. Alt, 406:Summer84-201
Seniff, D.P. - see Alfonso XI
Senior, E.K. British Regulars in Montreal.
S.E. Read, 102(CanL):Winter83-83
Senkoro, F.E.M.K. The Prostitute in African Literature.
F. Ojo-Ade, 538(RAL):Fall84-438
Senn, A.E. Assassination in Switzerland.
R.B. Day, 104(CASS):Fall84-316
Senn, F. Nichts gegen Joyce.
E. Henscheid, 384:Sep84-688
C. Koelb, 395(MFS):Winter84-764
Senn, H.A. Were-Wolf and Vampire in Romania.*
D.E. Bynum, 104(CASS):Spring-Summer84-180
Sennett, R. Verfall und Ende des öffentlichen Lebens.
G. Mattenklott, 384:Jan84-77
Sensibar, J.L. The Origins of Faulkner's Art.*
M. Grimwood, 578:Fall85-101
Sepúlveda, A., ed. Esta urticante pasión de la pimienta.
L.M. Villar, 701(SinN):Oct-Dec83-78
Serafin, J.M. Faulkner's Uses of the Classics.
N. Polk, 395(MFS):Summer84-326
295(JML):Nov84-437
Serbat, G. Cas et fonctions.*
P. Swiggers, 350:Sep85-705
Sereny, G. The Invisible Children.
P-L. Adams, 61:Apr85-141
A. Campbell, 441:19May85-32
Serguine, J. Les Barbares.
M. Herz, 207(FR):Oct84-163
de la Serna, R.G. - see under Gómez de la Serna, R.
Serra, E. - see Marin, B.
Serrano, C.S. - see under Sotos Serrano, C.
Serrano, E. Historia de la fotografía en Colombia.
W.P. Carty, 37:May-Jun84-62
Serrera Contreras, J.M. Hernando de Esturmio.
I. Mateo Gómez, 48:Apr-Jun84-191
Serres, M. Détachement.
T. Cordellier, 450(NRF):Mar84-130
Serres, M. Genèse. Rome, le livre des fondations.
J. Largeault, 542:Jan-Mar84-121
Serroy, J. Roman et Réalité.
J. Descrains, 535(RHL):Jul/Aug84-594
U. Döring, 475:Vol 11No20-273
Servan-Schreiber, J.J. The World Challenge.
E. Friedler, 390:Jan84-58
Servies, J.A., ed. The Log of H.M.S. Mentor, 1780-1781.
R.E. Johnson, 9(AlaR):Jan84-61
Servodidio, M. and M.L. Welles, eds. From Fiction to Metafiction.
P.B. Dixon, 395(MFS):Summer84-338

Sesboué, B., G-M. de Durand and L. Doutre-
leau - see Basile de Césarée
Sestary, C.J. Needlework.
   P. Bach, 614:Spring85-25
Sesterhenn, R. Das Bogostroitel' stvo bei
Gor'kij und Lunačarskij bis 1909.
   A.L. Tait, 575(SEER):Jul84-447
Seth, V. The Humble Administrator's Gar-
den.
   D. Davis, 362:5Dec85-33
Setton, K.M. The Papacy and the Levant
(1204-1571), (Vols 3 and 4)
   M. Mallett, 617(TLS):18Oct85-1190
Seung, T.K. Semiotics and Thematics in
Hermeneutics.*
   W.W. Holdheim, 149(CLS):Summer84-217
   G.J. Stack, 543:Sep83-146
Seung, T.K. Structuralism and Hermene-
utics.
   R. Sokolowski, 543:Dec83-422
Sevčenko, I. and F.E. Sysyn, eds. Eucha-
risterion.
   I. Boba, 104(CASS):Fall84-355
"Seven Poets."
   R. Watson, 588(SSL):Vol 19-194
Severo, R. Lisa H.
   E.W. Schrier, 441:10Feb85-11
Seward, J. Japanese in Action.* (2nd ed)
   J. Hinds, 215(GL):Vol24No3-187
Sewell, B. In the Dorian Mode.
   G.A. Cevasco, 177(ELT):Vol27No3-262
Sewell, W.H., Jr. Structure and Mobility.
   W. Scott, 617(TLS):1Nov85-1226
Sexauer, W.D. Frühneuhochdeutsche Schrif-
ten in Kartäuserbibliotheken.
   H. Wolf, 685(ZDL):1/1984-96
Sexton, A. No Evil Star. (S.E. Colburn,
ed)
   J. Daynard, 441:29Sep85-47
Seybert, G. Die unmögliche Emanzipation
der Gefühle.
   K.J. Crecelius, 446(NCFS):Summer85-285
Seyffert, P. Soviet Literary Structural-
ism.
   S. Monas, 617(TLS):23Aug85-916
Seymour, G. Field of Blood.
   R. Cohen, 441:6Oct85-28
   442(NY):16Sep85-124
Seymour, M.C. - see Hoccleve, T.
Seymour, W. British Special Forces.
   K. Jeffery, 617(TLS):17May85-555
Seymour-Smith, M. Robert Graves.*
   W. Harmon, 577(SHR):Summer84-277
   J. McKinley, 536:Vol6-263
   J. Wexler, 77:Fall84-363
   295(JML):Nov84-448
Seymour-Smith, M. Macmillan Guide to Mod-
ern World Literature.
   S.S. Prawer, 617(TLS):2Aug85-840
Sfendoni-Mentzou, D. Probability and
Chance in the Philosophy of C.S. Peirce.
[in Greek]
   P.D. Nicolacopoulos, 619:Summer84-346
Shabtai, Y. Past Continuous.
   I. Howe, 453(NYRB):10Oct85-32
   A. Lelchuk, 441:21Apr85-23
Shachtman, T. Decade of Shocks.
   639(VQR):Spring84-46
Shacochis, B. Easy in the Islands.
   C. Fein, 441:17Feb85-13
Shackleford, G.T.M. Degas: The Dancers.
   J. House, 617(TLS):22Nov85-1316

Shackleton Bailey, D.R. Profile of Hor-
ace.*
   K. Quinn, 487:Summer84-189
Shaeffer, C. Price It Right.
   E. Hoffman, 614:Summer85-32
Shaeffer, C.B. Sew Successful.
   P. Bach, 614:Summer85-35
Shaffer, E. Canada's Oil and the American
Empire.
   M.L. Cross, 529(QQ):Winter84-867
Shaffer, L. Mao and the Workers.
   G. Benton, 293(JASt):May84-533
Shafir, M. Romania.
   D. Deletant, 617(TLS):7Jun85-630
Shaham, N. The Other Side of the Wall.*
   M. Haltrecht, 617(TLS):4Jan85-9
Shahan, R.W. and J.N. Mohanty, eds. Think-
ing about Being.
   M.A.G., 185:Jul85-981
Shahîd, I. Rome and the Arabs. Byzantium
and the Arabs in the Fourth Century.
   F. Millar, 617(TLS):15Nov85-1301
ibn Shāhīn, N.B. - see under Nissim ben
Jacob ibn Shāhīn
Shaiken, H. Work Transformed.
   R. Draper, 453(NYRB):24Oct85-46
   A.H. Raskin, 441:21Apr85-40
Shakespeare, W. As You Like It/Wie es
euch gefällt. (H. Geisen and D. Wessels,
eds) The Tempest/Der Sturm. (G. Strat-
mann, ed)
   H.F. Plett, 156(JDSh):Jahrbuch1984-246
Shakespeare, W. Hamlet.* (H. Jenkins, ed)
   R. Jacobs, 175:Spring84-55
   D. Mehl, 156(JDSh):Jahrbuch1984-236
Shakespeare, W. Henry V.* (G. Taylor, ed)
   R.A. Cave, 610:Summer84-141
Shakespeare, W. King Richard II/König
Richard II. (W. Braun, ed) The Mer-
chant of Venice/Der Kaufmann von Venedig.
(I. Heine-Harabasz, ed) The Comedy of
Errors/Die Komödie der Irrungen. (K.
Tetzeli von Rosador, ed)
   H.F. Plett, 156(JDSh):Jahrbuch1984-245
Shakespeare, W. King Richard III.* (A.
Hammond, ed)
   D. Mehl, 156(JDSh):Jahrbuch1984-236
   G. Taylor, 541(RES):Nov84-533
Shakespeare, W. Measure for Measure.*
(M. Eccles, ed)
   G. Taylor, 541(RES):Aug84-369
Shakespeare, W. Much Ado About Nothing.*
(A.R. Humphreys, ed)
   D. Mehl, 156(JDSh):Jahrbuch1984-236
   J. Pearson, 447(N&Q):Oct83-462
Shakespeare, W. Romeo and Juliet.* (B.
Gibbons, ed)
   K. Bartenschlager, 38:Band102Heft1/2-
233
Shakespeare, W. Romeo and Juliet. Hamlet.
Julius Caesar. The Merchant of Venice.
A Midsummer Night's Dream. The Tempest.
(A.L. Rowse, ed of all)
   T. Hawkes, 617(TLS):11Jan85-29
Shakespeare W. Shakespeare's Plays in
Quarto.* (M.J.B. Allen and K. Muir, eds)
   D. Bevington, 405(MP):Feb85-317
   B. Thorne, 529(QQ):Winter84-1033
Shakespeare, W. The Sonnets/La Sonetj.
(W. Auld, trans)
   M. Boulton, 447(N&Q):Oct83-461

333

Shakespeare, W. The Taming of the Shrew.*
(B. Morris, ed)
  D. Mehl, 156(JDSh):Jahrbuch1984-236
Shakespeare, W. The Taming of the Shrew.*
(H.J. Oliver, ed)
  R.A. Cave, 610:Summer84-141
  G.B. Evans, 570(SQ):Winter84-495
  A. Thompson, 402(MLR):Oct84-897
Shakespeare, W. Troilus and Cressida.*
(K. Muir, ed)
  R.A. Cave, 610:Summer84-141
  G.B. Evans, 402(MLR):Oct84-898
Shakespeare, W. Troilus and Cressida.*
(K. Palmer, ed)
  G.B. Evans, 402(MLR):Oct84-898
  D. Mehl, 156(JDSh):Jahrbuch1984-236
"Shakespeare-Jahrbuch, 119."
  E. Auberlen, 189(EA):Jul-Sep85-318
"Shakespeare Survey."* (Vol 34) (S. Wells,
ed)
  D.J. Palmer, 541(RES):Nov84-531
  R.S. White, 447(N&Q):Oct83-465
"Shakespeare Survey."* (Vol 36) (S. Wells,
ed)
  M. Grivelet, 189(EA):Oct-Dec85-455
"Shakespeare Survey." (Vol 37) (S. Wells,
ed)
  G. Taylor, 617(TLS):16Aug85-905
Shallis, M. On Time.
  639(VQR):Spring84-63
Shange, N. Betsey Brown.
  P. Wheatley, 617(TLS):6Dec85-1406
  N. Willard, 441:12May85-12
Shange, N. A Daughter's Geography.
  M. Honey, 502(PrS):Winter84-111
Shank, T. American Alternative Theatre.*
  T. Dunn, 214:Vol 11No41-125
Shankman, S. Pope's "Iliad."*
  J. Engell, 301(JEGP):Apr84-239
  J. King, 173(ECS):Summer85-574
  H. Weber, 83:Autumn84-242
Shanks, B. This Land Is Your Land.
  P. Shabecoff, 441:5May85-25
Shannon, R. Gladstone.* (Vol 1)
  P. Stansky, 637(VS):Spring84-377
Shannon, W.H. - see Merton, T.
Shannon, W.V. A Quiet Broker?
  C. Townshend, 617(TLS):1Nov85-1231
Shanor, D.R. Behind the Lines.
  J. Laber, 441:24Mar85-14
  P. Reddaway, 453(NYRB):10Oct85-5
Shao, P. The Origin of Ancient American
Cultures.
  A. McBain, 60:Sep-Oct84-123
Shapcott, T. The Birthday Gift.*
  P. Lewis, 565:Spring84-64
Shapcott, T. White Stag of Exile.
  J. Davidson, 381:Jun84-231
Shapira, A. Berl.
  B. Wasserstein, 617(TLS):28Jun85-730
Shapiro, A. The Courtesy.
  E. Grosholz, 249(HudR):Winter84/85-650
Shapiro, A-L. Housing the Poor of Paris,
1850-1902.
  J.F. McMillan, 617(TLS):9Aug85-883
Shapiro, A.L. Istoriografiia s drev-
neishikh vremen po XVIII vek.
  D. Das, 550(RusR):Jul84-304
Shapiro, B.J. Probability and Certainty
in Seventeenth-Century England.
  C. Hill, 366:Spring84-121
  J.W. Yolton, 551(RenQ):Summer84-280

Shapiro, D. John Ashbery.
  R. White, 106:Spring84-109
Shapiro, D. Jasper Johns: Drawings 1954-
1984.
  D. Rosand, 617(TLS):6Sep85-970
Shapiro, G. and A. Sica, eds. Hermeneu-
tics.
  R. Shusterman, 290(JAAC):Winter84-216
  J. Weinsheimer, 478:Oct84-308
Shapiro, K. Love and War/Art and God.
  R. Tillinghast, 441:31Mar85-14
Shapiro, M. Hieroglyph of Time.*
  R. Griffin, 545(RPh):May84-516
Shapiro, M. The Sense of Grammar.
  E. Walther, 567:Vol52No1/2-111
Shapiro, M.C. and H.F. Schiffman. Lan-
guage and Society in South Asia.
  P. Dasgupta, K.S. Nagaraja and S.R.
  Sharma, 261:Sep/Dec82-49
  C.P. Masica, 293(JASt):Nov83-193
Shapiro, M.J. Language and Political
Understanding.*
  K. Masugi, 543:Mar84-652
Shapiro, N.L. and R. Padgett, eds. The
Point.
  D. Kirby, 128(CE):Mar84-248
Shapiro, N.R. - see "Fables from Old
French"
Shapiro, S., ed and trans. Jews in Old
China.
  R.F. Shepard, 441:10Mar85-25
Sharaf, M. Fury on Earth.
  P. Roazen, 99:Jun/Jul84-39
Sharma, M.M. Inscriptions of Ancient
Assam.*
  R. Salomon, 318(JAOS):Apr-Jun83-439
Sharma, R.K. Isolation and Protest.
  295(JML):Nov84-427
Sharma, T.R.S. Robert Frost's Poetic
Style.
  J.R. Bennett, 599:Winter84-114
Sharp, A. A Green Tree in Gedde.
  G. Mangan, 617(TLS):29Nov85-1371
Sharp, F.M. The Poet's Madness.*
  T.J. Casey, 402(MLR):Jan84-245
  J. De Vos, 602:Band15Heft1-158
Sharp, M., ed. Accounts of the Constables
of Bristol Castle in the Thirteenth and
Early Fourteenth Centuries.
  A.Z. Freeman, 589:Apr84-486
Sharpe, J.A. Crime in Seventeenth-Century
England.
  É. Cuvelier, 189(EA):Oct-Dec85-459
  C. Hill, 366:Autumn84-268
Sharpe, L. Schiller and the Historical
Character.*
  S.L. Cocalis, 222(GR):Spring84-79
  W. Koepke, 301(JEGP):Apr84-282
  W. Wittkowski, 221(GQ):Summer84-477
Sharpe, R.A. Contemporary Aesthetics.
  G.R. Holmes, 89(BJA):Autumn84-367
  C. Lyas, 479(PhQ):Oct84-511
  D. Shaw, 518:Oct84-247
Sharpe, T. Wilt on High.*
  C. Hawtree, 364:Oct84-85
  J. Kaufman, 441:12May85-18
Sharratt, B. The Literary Labyrinth.
  C. Baldick, 617(TLS):17May85-560
Sharratt, P. and P.G. Walsh - see Buchanan,
G.

Sharrer, H.L. and F.G. Williams, eds.
Studies on Jorge de Sena by his Col-
leagues and Friends.
H. Macedo, 86(BHS):Apr84-210
Sharrock, R.   Saints, Sinners and Comedi-
ans.
S. Monod, 189(EA):Oct-Dec85-481
A. Young, 617(TLS):22Feb85-199
Sharrock, R. and J.F. Forrest - see Bunyan,
J.
Shatto, S. and M. Shaw - see Tennyson, A.
Shattock, J. and M. Wolff, eds.   The Vic-
torian Periodical Press.*
A. Blake, 366:Spring84-129
S. Elwell, 637(VS):Winter84-253
Shattuck, R.   The Innocent Eye.
G. Bree, 441:3Feb85-14
S. Hampshire, 453(NYRB):9May85-18
F. Tuten, 62:Mar85-87
Shaw, E. and J. Darling.   Female Strate-
gies.
R. Cherry, 441:17Mar85-31
Shaw, F., ed.   Karl der Grosse und die
schottischen Heiligen.*
N.F. Palmer, 402(MLR):Apr84-486
M.W. Wierschin, 221(GQ):Summer84-465
Shaw, G.B.   Collected Letters.   (Vol 3)
(D.H. Laurence, ed)
N. Annan, 453(NYRB):15Aug85-3
M. Holroyd, 617(TLS):31May85-595
H. Kenner, 441:30Jun85-1
G. Millar, 362:19Sep85-24
D. Shawe-Taylor, 442(NY):23Dec85-88
Shaw, G.B.   Bernard Shaw, "Arms and the
Man": A Facsimile of the Holograph Manu-
script.   Bernard Shaw: "Candida" and
"How He Lied to Her Husband": Facsimiles
of the Holograph Manuscripts.   Bernard
Shaw: "The Devil's Disciple": A Fac-
simile of the Holograph Manuscript.
Bernard Shaw: "Major Barbara": A Fac-
simile of the Holograph Manuscript.
C.A. Berst, 615(TJ):Dec82-550
Shaw, G.B. and A. Douglas.   Bernard Shaw
and Alfred Douglas: a Correspondence.*
(M. Hyde, ed)
A.P. Barr, 637(VS):Winter84-279
D. Leary, 70:Nov-Dec83-54
Shaw, G.B. and F. Harris.   The Playwright
and the Pirate, Bernard Shaw and Frank
Harris.*   (S. Weintraub, ed)
A.P. Barr, 637(VS):Winter84-279
C. Day, 272(IUR):Spring84-150
Shaw, H.B.   Gwendolyn Brooks.
M. Fabre, 402(MLR):Apr84-444
Shaw, H.E.   The Forms of Historical Fic-
tion.*
A. Brown, 155:Autumn84-169
G. Dekker, 445(NCF):Dec84-348
F. Jordan, 661(WC):Summer84-119
J. Wilt, 594:Summer84-254
Shaw, J.B.   The Italian Drawings of the
Frits Lugt Collection.*
N. Turner, 380:Summer84-206
Shaw, J.S.   The Management of Scottish
Society 1707-1764.
R.L. Emerson, 173(ECS):Summer85-580
A. Murdoch, 83:Spring84-110
Shaw, M.E. - see Purishkevich, V.M.
Shaw, V.   The Short Story.*
J.G. Roberts, 571(ScLJ):Autumn84-26

"Shaw: The Annual of Bernard Shaw
Studies."*   (Vol 1) (C.A. Berst, ed)
V.G. Myer, 447(N&Q):Dec83-557
Shawcross, J.T.   Milton: A Bibliography
for the Years 1624-1700.
617(TLS):22Mar85-316
Shawcross, J.T.   With Mortal Voice.*
R.T. Fallon, 70:May-Jun84-154
M. Fixler, 405(MP):Feb85-310
D.L. Russell, 568(SCN):Spring-Summer84-
6
J. Wittreich, 536:Vol5-1
Shawcross, W.   The Quality of Mercy.*
J. Fenton, 617(TLS):18Jan85-51
Shea, W.L.   The Virginia Militia in the
Seventeenth Century.
639(VQR):Spring84-48
Shearman, J.   The Pictures in the Collec-
tion of Her Majesty the Queen: The Early
Italian Pictures.*
C. Gould, 39:Mar84-224
Sheed, W.   Frank and Maisie.
R. Towers, 441:10Nov85-12
442(NY):9Dec85-162
Sheehan, S.   Kate Quinton's Days.*
A. Hacker, 453(NYRB):28Feb85-37
Sheehan, T.   Heidegger.
T.J. Harrison, 543:Sep83-146
Shefter, M.   Political Crisis/Fiscal
Crisis.
S. Roberts, 441:27Oct85-34
Sheidley, W.E.   Barnabe Googe.*
D.S. Lawless, 447(N&Q):Oct83-456
El-Sheikh, I.A., C.A. van de Koppel and R.
Peters, eds.   The Challenge of the
Middle East.
M.M. Badawi, 294:Vol 15-146
Sheldon, D.   The Dreams of an Average Man.
R. Kaveney, 617(TLS):24May85-572
J. Mellors, 362:22Aug85-30
Sheldon, S.   If Tomorrow Comes.
M. Watkins, 441:10Mar85-24
Sheldon-Williams, I.P., with L. Bieler -
see Scotus, J.D.
Shelikhov, G.I.   A Voyage to America, 1783-
1786.   (R.A. Pierce, ed)
J.A. Miller, 550(RusR):Jul84-317
Shell, M.   The Economy of Literature.*
Language and Thought.
J. Vernon, 81:Fall83-243
Shell, M.   Money, Language, and Thought.
M. Doueihi, 153:Spring84-66
Shelley, M.W.   The Letters of Mary Woll-
stonecraft Shelley.*   (Vol 1) (B.T. Ben-
nett, ed)
P.M.S. Dawson, 677(YES):Vol 14-334
Shelley, M.W.   The Letters of Mary Woll-
stonecraft Shelley.   (Vol 2) (B.T.
Bennett, ed)
J. Clubbe, 661(WC):Summer84-118
J. Stillinger, 340(KSJ):Vol33-225
Shelnutt, E.   Air and Salt.
R. Mitchell, 460(OhR):No33-134
Shelton, R.   Selected Poems 1969-1981.*
H.J.F. de Aguilar, 472:Fall/Winter84-
245
R. Mitchell, 460(OhR):No33-134
Shelton, W.G.   Dean Tucker and Eighteenth-
Century Economic and Political Thought.
M. Jack, 173(ECS):Fall84-132
Shem, S.   Fine.
N. Ramsey, 441:17Mar85-12

Shenker, I. Coat of Many Colors.
H. Nissenson, 441:17Mar85-12
442(NY):12Aug85-84
Shenker, I. Harmless Drudges.
T.E. Murray, 35(AS):Fall84-246
Shepard, S. Motel Chronicles and Hawk
Moon.
M. Hofmann, 617(TLS):1Mar85-227
R. Mazzocco, 453(NYRB):9May85-21
Shepherd, N. A Refuge from Darkness.
R.S. Levy, 129:Apr85-70
Shepherd, R.A. - see Milton, J.
Shepherd, S. Amazons and Warrior Women.*
J. Halden, 568(SCN):Fall84-41
Shepherd, S., ed. The Women's Sharp
Revenge.
B. Brophy, 617(TLS):26Jul85-814
Sheppard, F.H.W., ed. Survey of London.*
(Vol 41)
J. Harris, 90:Apr84-241
Shergold, N.D. and J.E. Varey. Representa-
ciones palaciegas: 1603-1699.
T.A. O'Connor, 240(HR):Summer84-406
Sheridan, A. Michel Foucault.
J. Rajchman, 529(QQ):Autumn84-623
Sheridan, D. - see Mitchison, N.
Sheridan, R.B. Doctors and Slaves.
J. Ward, 617(TLS):21Jun85-699
Sherman, C.R., with A.M. Holcomb, eds.
Women as Interpreters of the Visual Arts,
1820-1979.*
F. Spalding, 90:Jan84-48
"Cindy Sherman."*
L. Liebmann, 62:Dec84-74
J. Sturman, 55:Nov84-35
Sherman, J. Lords of Shouting.*
B. Pirie, 102(CanL):Autumn84-121
Sherman, K. Words for Elephant Man.*
M.S. Madoff, 628(UWR):Spring-Summer85-
84
R. Stevenson, 137:Feb85-20
Sherman, L.B. Fire on the Mountain.
M. Pundeff, 104(CASS):Spring-Summer84-
227
Sherman, M., ed. Productivity.
S.W., 185:Apr85-791
Sherred, T.L. and L. Biggle, Jr. Alien
Main.
G. Jonas, 441:8Sep85-28
Sherry, C. Wordsworth's Poetry of the
Imagination.*
P. Drew, 677(YES):Vol 14-332
Sherry, J. Converses.
J. Retallack, 472:Fall/Winter84-213
Sherwood, J. A Botanist at Bay.
T.J. Binyon, 617(TLS):2Aug85-855
Sherzer, J. Kuna Ways of Speaking.
A. Wiget, 292(JAF):Oct-Dec84-468
Shesgreen, S. Hogarth and the Times-of-
the-Day Tradition.
J. Blair, 566:Autumn84-66
D. Mannings, 89(BJA):Autumn84-378
S. Soupel, 189(EA):Jul-Sep85-328
Shevchenko, A.N. Breaking with Moscow.
L.H. Gelb, 441:17Feb85-3
I. Levkov, 129:May85-78
C.C. O'Brien, 453(NYRB):11Apr85-3
P. Reddaway, 617(TLS):30Aug85-945
J. Simpson, 362:6Jun85-27
Shevchenko, T. Selected Works.
T. Prokopov, 399(MLJ):Spring84-89
Shewey, D. Sam Shepard.
G. Johnson, 441:22Dec85-18

Shi, D.E. Matthew Josephson.
R.F. Bogardus, 577(SHR):Spring84-189
Shi, D.E. The Simple Life.
I. Rosenfield, 441:20Jan85-14
Shideler, J. A Medieval Catalan Noble
Family.
R.A. Fletcher, 617(TLS):19Jul85-807
Shields, C. A Fairly Conventional Woman.
W. Keitner, 102(CanL):Winter83-116
Shields, D. Heroes.
A. Krystal, 441:3Feb85-22
Shiff, R. Cézanne and the End of Impres-
sionism.
J. Flam, 62:Dec84-77
L. Gowing, 617(TLS):22Mar85-321
Shigeru, H. - see under Honjō Shigeru
Shikes, R.E. and P. Harper. Pissarro.
R. Schiff, 54:Dec84-681
Shikes, R.E. and S. Heller. The Art of
Satire.
C.B. McGee, 441:20Jan85-18
Shikibu, M. see under Murasaki Shikibu
Shimao, T. The Sting of Death and Other
Stories.
J. Mellen, 441:1Dec85-24
Shimizu, K. A Bibliography of Saljuq
Studies.
R. Murphey, 318(JAOS):Oct-Dec83-811
Shingleton, R.G. John Taylor Wood.
F.C. Drake, 106:Winter84-407
Shinran. Passages on the Pure Land Way.
The True Teaching, Practice and Realiza-
tion of the Pure Land Way.
T.P. Kasulis, 407(MN):Winter84-481
Shipler, D.K. Russia.
A. Friendly, Jr., 550(RusR):Oct84-413
Shipley, J.T. The Origins of English
Words.*
P.H. Salus, 350:Sep85-710
Shipps, J. Mormonism.
D.B. Davis, 453(NYRB):15Aug85-15
R.L. Moore, 441:21Jul85-11
Shire, H.M. - see Fraser, O.
Shires, L.M. British Poetry of the Second
World War.
N. Corcoran, 617(TLS):4Oct85-1090
Shirt, D.J. The Old French "Tristan"
Poems.
B. Schmolke-Hasselmann, 547(RF):
Band96Heft1/2-169
I. Short, 208(FS):Oct84-445
Shiv Das Lakhnawi - see under Lakhnawi,
S.D.
Shivers, A.S. The Life of Maxwell Ander-
son.
295(JML):Nov84-402
Shizuo, K. - see under Katsumata Shizuo
Shkilnyk, A.M. A Poison Stronger than
Love.
M. Abley, 617(TLS):23Aug85-918
Shklar, J.N. Ordinary Vices.*
M. Warnock, 441:7Feb85-25
Shklovsky, V. A Sentimental Journey.
617(TLS):27Sep85-1071
Shloss, C. Flannery O'Connor's Dark
Comedies.*
M. Morton, 392:Winter83/84-89
Shlyapnikov, A. On the Eve of 1917.
L. Schapiro, 575(SEER):Apr84-298
Shoemaker, I.H. and E. Broun. The Engrav-
ings of Marcantonio Raimondi.
J.T. Spike, 90:Jul84-441

Shoemaker, S. Identity, Cause and Mind.
J. Cottingham, 617(TLS):3May85-506
Shoemaker, S. and R. Swinburne. Personal Identity.*
D. Smith, 617(TLS):15Feb85-180
Shoemaker, W.H. The Novelistic Art of Galdós.*
L.J. Hoar, Jr., 593:Spring84-81
Shope, R.K. The Analysis of Knowing.*
A.R. White, 518:Jan84-56
Shore, B. Sala'ilua.
J. Clifford, 384:Mar84-208
Shore, J. The Sachertorte Algorithm.
J. Gleick, 441:21Apr85-30
Shore, M.M.J. O Canada, Canada.
J.W. Lennox, 102(CanL):Autumn84-187
Short, J.P. Racine: "Phèdre."
J. Campbell, 208(FS):Oct84-462
J.J. Supple, 402(MLR):Oct84-934
Shostak, A.B. and G. McLough, with L. Seng. Men and Abortion.
W. Kaminer, 441:3Feb85-23
Shostakovich, D. Dmitri Schostakowitsch: Erfahrungen: Aufsätze, Erinnerungen, Reden, Diskussionsbeiträge, Interviews, Briefe. (C. Hellmundt and K. Meyer, eds)
M. Barry, 410(M&L):Jul84-284
Shostakovich, D. Testimony.
H. Ticktin, 390:Feb84-48
Shoumatoff, A. The Mountain of Names.
J. Pfeiffer, 441:28Jul85-11
Shoup, P.S. The East European and Soviet Data Handbook.
A.H. Smith, 575(SEER):Jan84-156
Showalter, E., Jr. Exiles and Strangers.
D.B. Parsell, 207(FR):Mar85-587
Showalter, E., ed. The New Feminist Criticism.
H. Moglen, 441:16Jun85-16
Shreve, L.G. Tench Tilghman.
P.D. Chase, 656(WMQ):Jan84-163
Shrive, F.J. The Diary of a P.B.O.
S.E. Read, 102(CanL):Winter83-83
Shroff, H.J. The Eighteenth-Century Novel.
A. Morvan, 189(EA):Jul-Sep85-335
Shu-tse, P. - see under P'eng Shu-tse
Shudakov, G. Pioneers of Soviet Photography.
J. Sturman, 55:Oct84-29
Shukman, A. - see under Lotman, J.M. and B.A. Uspenskij
Shukshin, V. Roubles in Words, Kopeks in Figures.
D. Cole, 441:9Jun85-22
Shuldham-Shaw, P. and E.B. Lyle, eds. The Greig-Duncan Folk Song Collection. (Vol 2)
I.A. Olson, 571(ScLJ):Winter84-35
Shulman, D.D. Tamil Temple Myths.*
E. Leach, 567:Vol49No1/2-161
Shulman, N. Social Security.
J. Neville, 617(TLS):21Jun85-701
Shumaker, W. Renaissance Curiosa.*
F.L. Borchardt, 551(RenQ):Spring84-61
H. Ormsby-Lennon, 405(MP):May85-417
Shuoyun, Y., ed. Palaces of the Forbidden City.
M. Sullivan, 617(TLS):3May85-505
Shurin, A. The Graces.
D.L. Strauss, 703:No11-188

Shurr, W.H. The Marriage of Emily Dickinson.*
N. Baym, 301(JEGP):Oct84-576
W.J. Buckingham, 27(AL):Dec84-598
S.C., 219(GaR):Summer84-439
D. Porter, 432(NEQ):Mar84-106
295(JML):Nov84-426
Shurr, W.H. Rappaccini's Children.*
L. Gordon, 541(RES):May84-271
R.W. Harvey, 106:Fall84-301
Shusterman, R. The Object of Literary Criticism.
A. Bony, 189(EA):Jul-Sep85-299
L. Stern, 290(JAAC):Spring85-327
Shutt, H. The Myth of Free Trade.
J. Rostowski, 617(TLS):6Dec85-1391
Shuttle, P. The Child-Stealer.
M. O'Neill, 493:Jan84-65
R. Pybus, 565:Autumn84-73
Shuttleworth, S. George Eliot and Nineteenth-Century Science.*
J.L. Bradley, 184(EIC):Oct84-356
G. Levine, 445(NCF):Dec84-354
Shweder, R.A. and R.A. Le Vine, eds. Culture Theory.
A.F.C. Wallace, 441:10Mar85-36
Siblewski, K. Ritterlicher Patriotismus und romantischer Nationalismus in der deutschen Literatur 1770-1830.
G.F. Peters, 406:Fall84-365
Sibley, M.M. Lone Stars and State Gazettes.
L. Milazzo, 584(SWR):Winter84-88
Sibley, W.F. The Shiga Hero.
W.E. Naff, 302:Vol20No2-229
Sibony, D. L'Amour inconscient.
H. Raczymow, 450(NRF):Feb84-115
Sibum, N. Among Other Howls In The Storm.
A. Brooks, 102(CanL):Autumn84-115
Sicherman, B. Alice Hamilton: A Life in Letters.*
A.S. Grossman, 617(TLS):18Jan85-68
E. Janeway, 441:6Jan85-14
J. Strouse, 453(NYRB):9May85-38
Sick, G. All Fall Down.
S. Hoffmann, 441:16Jun85-1
442(NY):19Aug85-90
Sidel, R. and V.W. The Health of China.
K-C. Yip, 293(JASt):May84-525
Sider, D. - see Anaxagoras
Sider, S., ed. Cebes "Tablet."
P.J. Donnelly, 86(BHS):Oct84-521
Sidnell, M.J. Dances of Death.
H. Carpenter, 617(TLS):11Jan85-29
Sidney, R. The Poems of Robert Sidney.* (P.J. Croft, ed)
C. MacDonald, 362:14Mar85-26
J.C.A. Rathmell, 184(EIC):Oct84-344
Siebers, T. The Mirror of Medusa.
T.M. Butler, 400(MLN):Dec84-1206
Siebers, T. The Romantic Fantastic.*
G.L. Green, 223:Fall84-322
639(VQR):Autumn84-127
Siedentopf, H.B. Corpus vasorum Antiquorum. (Deutschland, Vol 49)
B.A. Sparkes, 303(JoHS):Vol 104-257
Siedentopf, M. Die britischen Pläne zur Besetzung der spanischen und portugiesischen Atlantikinseln während des zweiten Weltkrieges.
M.R.D. Foot, 86(BHS):Oct84-528

Siefken, H. Thomas Mann.
   R. Dumont, 549(RLC):Jul–Sep84–373
   S.R. Pukhat, 406:Summer84–230
Siegchrist, M. "Rough in Brutal Print."
   J. Woolford, 447(N&Q):Aug83–362
Siegel, L. and J. Markoff. The High Cost
of High Tech.
   D.E. Sanger, 441:20Oct85–51
Sieghart, P. The Lawful Rights of Mankind.
   D. Pannick, 617(TLS):19Jul85–790
Siegler, R.W. The Standing Commissions of
the Supreme Soviet.
   A.J. Matejko, 104(CASS):Fall84–332
von Siegroth-Nellesen, G. Versuch einer
exakten Stiluntersuchung für Meister
Eckhart, Johannes Tauler und Heinrich
Seuse.
   P. Michel, 684(ZDA):Band113Heft2–75
Siemek, A. La Recherche morale et esthé-
tique dans le roman de Crébillon fils.*
   G.E. Rodmell, 83:Spring84–146
Siepe, H.T. Der Leser des Surrealismus.
   R. Cardinal, 208(FS):Jan84–95
Siess, J. – see "Vermittler"
Sievers, S.L. Flowers in Salt.
   C. Broderick, 285(JapQ):Jul–Sep84–333
   P.G. Steinhoff, 407(MN):Summer84–219
Signorini, R. La "Fabella" di Psiche e
altra mitologia secondo l'interpreta-
zione pittorica di Giulio Romano nel
Palazzo del Te a Mantova.
   E. McGrath, 90:Aug84–505
Sigouin, G. Théâtre en lutte.*
   R. Usmiani, 102(CanL):Winter83–72
Siikala, J. Cult and Conflict in Tropical
Polynesia.
   R. Mitchell, 292(JAF):Apr–Jun84–235
Silagi, G., ed. Paläographie 1981.
   K. Schneider, 684(ZDA):Band113Heft3–
101
Silberman, C.E. A Certain People.
   N. Glazer, 441:1Sep85–1
   A. Hertzberg, 453(NYRB):21Nov85–18
   R.R. Wisse, 129:Nov85–108
Silberman, M. Heiner Müller.
   M. Gerber, 406:Winter84–479
Silburn, L. Śivasūtra et Vimarśinī de
Kṣemarāja.*
   J.W. de Jong, 259(IIJ):Jan84–70
Siler, D. – see Pradier, J.
Silk, M.S. and J.P. Stern. Nietzsche on
Tragedy.*
   D.L. Levine, 543:Dec83–423
   M. Tanner, 483:Jul84–403
Silkin, J. Autobiographical Stanzas.*
   A. Stevenson, 493:Jun84–66
Silko, L.M. Storyteller.* (Italian title:
Raccontare.) (L. Coltelli, ed and trans
of Italian edition)
   R. Asselineau, 189(EA):Jul–Sep85–364
Sill, G.M. Defoe and the Idea of Fiction.
   D. Cottom, 594:Summer84–256
   F.H. Ellis, 651(WHR):Summer84–183
Sillitoe, A. Life Goes On.
   P. Smelt, 617(TLS):6Dec85–1407
Sillitoe, A. Sun Before Departure.
   L. Mackinnon, 617(TLS):7Jun85–649
Silone, I. Severina. (D. Silone, ed)
   F. Zangrilli, 275(IQ):Winter84–109
Silva, E.P. – see under Portela Silva, E.
Silva, J.D. – see under de Alta Silva, J.
Silva, M.O. – see under Otero Silva, M.

Silva, V.M.D. – see under de Aguiar e
Silva, V.M.
da Silva Dias, J.S. Camões no Portugal de
Quinhentos.
   M. Guterres, 86(BHS):Oct84–528
Silve, E. Paul Léautaud et le Mercure de
France.
   J. Ducruet, 605(SC):15Jul85–378
Silver, A. Thimblerig.
   I. Gaskell, 198:Spring84–97
   J. Wasserman, 102(CanL):Summer84–91
Silver, B.R. Virginia Woolf's Reading
Notebook.*
   E. Heine, 395(MFS):Winter84–756
Silver, C. Twentieth-Century Richmond.
   639(VQR):Autumn84–116
Silver, C.G., ed. The Golden Chain.
   G.L. Aho, 536:Vol5–73
   E.D. Le Mire, 637(VS):Spring84–399
   P. Thompson, 59:Dec84–496
Silver, C.G. The Romance of William
Morris.
   E.D. Le Mire, 637(VS):Spring84–399
Silver, E. Begin.*
   E. Alexander, 129:May85–68
Silver, L. The Paintings of Quinten
Massys with Catalogue Raisonné.
   L. Campbell, 90:Dec84–787
Silver-Lillywhite, E. All That Autumn.
   639(VQR):Autumn84–138
Silverberg, R. Gilgamesh the King.*
   S. Altinel, 617(TLS):13Dec85–1434
Silverberg, R., ed. Great Adventures in
Archaeology from Belzoni to Woolley.
   617(TLS):27Sep85–1071
Silverberg, R. Tom O'Bedlam.
   G. Jonas, 441:4Aug85–20
Silverlight, J. Words.
   D.J. Enright, 362:20Jun85–27
Silverman, K. The Life and Times of
Cotton Mather.*
   A. Axelrod, 658:Winter84–299
   R. Middlekauff, 432(NEQ):Dec84–592
   M.K. Spears, 249(HudR):Winter84/85–631
   B. Tucker, 173(ECS):Summer85–590
   42(AR):Summer84–382
Silverman, K. The Subject of Semiotics.*
   M. Bal, 494:Vol5No4–857
   P. Brunette, 18:Apr85–58
Silverstone, R. Framing Science.
   A. Singer, 362:6Jun85–29
Sim, K. David Roberts R.A. (1796–1864).*
   P. van der Merwe, 90:Dec84–791
Simek, R., ed. Zwei Ritter Sagas.
   I. Marquardt, 196:Band25Heft1/2–159
Simenon, G. Intimate Memoirs.*
   639(VQR):Autumn84–120
Simenon, G. Maigret Bides His Time.
   442(NY):1Jul85–98
Simenon, G. Maigret's Memoirs.
   442(NY):23Dec85–92
Simenon, G. The Survivors.
   442(NY):13May85–146
Simic, C. Austerities.*
   R. Pybus, 565:Summer84–56
Simic, C. Weather Forecast for Utopia and
Vicinity.
   W.H. Pritchard, 249(HudR):Summer84–335
Simic, C. White: A New Version.
   F. Muratori, 448:Vol22No3–121
Siminovitch, E. There Are No Dragons.
   R. Plant, 102(CanL):Summer84–155

Simmerman, J. Home.*
P. Stitt, 219(GaR):Spring84-166
Simmler, F. Graphematisch-phonematische
Studien zum althochdeutschen Konsonant-
ismus insbesondere zur zweiten Lautver-
schiebung.
J.B. Voyles, 361:Jul-Aug84-350
Simmonds, J.D. - see "Milton Studies"
Simmons, P. Turning Wool into a Cottage
Industry.
M. Wilkins, 614:Spring85-31
Simmons, R.C. and P.D.G. Thomas, eds. Pro-
ceedings and Debates of the British
Parliaments Respecting North America,
1754-1783. (Vol 1)
J. Gwyn, 656(WMQ):Jul84-510
B.S. Schlenther, 83:Spring84-106
Simms, W.G. The Letters of William Gil-
more Simms. (Vol 6) (M.C.S. Oliphant
and T.C.D. Eaves, eds)
C.S. Watson, 392:Winter83/84-120
Simon, B. Mind and Madness in Ancient
Greece.
C. Gill, 303(JoHS):Vol 104-231
Simon, D., ed. Erkundungen.
R. Links, 654(WB):6/1984-1007
Simon, J. Sprachphilosophie.
W. Hogrebe, 687:Nov-Dec84-672
Simon, J.L. and H. Kahn, eds. The Re-
sourceful Earth.
D.J. Mabberley, 617(TLS):18Jan85-71
Simon, M.A. Understanding Human Action.*
D. Dutton, 518:Jan84-38
Simon, P. and others. World Dictionaries
in Print 1983.
E.A. Ebbinghaus, 215(GL):Vol24No3-192
Simon, R. and A. Smart. The Art of
Cricket.*
T. Crombie, 39:Jan84-71
Simon, R.L. California Roll.
N. Callendar, 441:21Jul85-18
Simon Díaz, J. Manual de bibliografía de
la literatura española. (3rd ed)
H. Sonneville, 356(LR):Feb/May84-119
Simonin, M. - see Boaistuau, P.
Simons, J.D. Friedrich Schiller.
B. Kieffer, 221(GQ):Spring84-320
L. Sharpe, 402(MLR):Jan84-235
Simons, M.A. Sémiotisme de Stendhal.*
J.F. MacCannell, 567:Vol148No1/2-143
Simonson, H.P. Radical Discontinuities.
W.H. Shurr, 649(WAL):Aug84-169
"Simpliciana." (Vols 1-3)
G. Hoffmeister, 221(GQ):Spring84-308
Simpson, A.C. Simpson's Sherlockian
Studies.
E.S. Lauterbach, 395(MFS):Summer84-379
Simpson, A.W.B. Cannibalism and the Com-
mon Law.*
D. Braybrooke and J. Fingard, 185:
Apr85-745
Simpson, C.M. A Good Southerner.
K. Ray, 441:20Oct85-35
Simpson, D. Fetishism and Imagination.*
J. McClure, 405(MP):May85-439
D.D. Stone, 637(VS):Summer84-524
Simpson, D. German Aesthetic and Literary
Criticism.
549(RLC):Oct-Dec84-471
Simpson, D. Last Seen Alive.
T.J. Binyon, 617(TLS):5Apr85-394

Simpson, D. Wordsworth and the Figurings
of the Real.*
D.H. Bialostosky, 401(MLQ):Sep83-305
Simpson, E. Poets in Their Youth.*
H. Beaver, 472:Fall/Winter84-123
G. Garrett, 569(SR):Summer84-495
G. Hill, 184(EIC):Jul84-262
F. Kermode, 473(PR):1/1984-138
M. Wood, 402(MLR):Apr84-407
Simpson, E. Reason Over Passion.
J.D. Wallace, 449:May84-337
Simpson, H. D.H. Lawrence and Feminism.*
J.B. Humma, 594:Spring84-111
Simpson, J. and J. Bennett. The Disap-
peared.
P. Whitehead, 362:15Aug85-26
Simpson, J. and A.G. McCrew, eds. The
International Nuclear Non-Proliferation
System.
P. Windsor, 617(TLS):17May85-557
Simpson, J.A. - see "The Concise Oxford
Dictionary of Proverbs"
Simpson, L. The Best Hour of the Night.*
P. Breslin, 491:Dec84-161
R.S. Gwynn, 502(PrS):Fall84-103
H. Lazer, 639(VQR):Autumn84-739
R. McDowell, 249(HudR):Spring84-120
B. Ramke, 460(OhR):No33-124
Simpson, L. People Live Here.*
J. Elledge, 491:May84-107
H. Lazer, 639(VQR):Autumn84-739
R. McDowell, 249(HudR):Spring84-119
B. Ramke, 460(OhR):No33-124
Simpson, L.E. and M. Weir. The Weaver's
Craft. (13th ed)
D. Musick, 614:Spring85-32
Simpson, M. Making Arrangements.
T. Eagleton, 565:Winter83/84-77
Simpson, M.S. The Illustration of an Epic.
B.W. Robinson, 39:Jul84-32
Simpson, N. Across Water.
J. Carter, 219(GaR):Summer84-415
Sims, J.H. and L. Ryken, eds. Milton and
Scriptural Tradition.
J. Pitcher, 617(TLS):23Aug85-932
J.M. Steadman, 250(HLQ):Autumn84-314
Sims, R.L. The Evolution of Myth in Gab-
riel García Márquez from "La hojarasca"
to "Cien años de soledad."
W.L. Siemens, 238:May84-311
von Simson, G., comp. Sanskrit-Wörterbuch
der buddhistischen Texte aus den Turfan-
Funden. (Pt 3)
W. Thomas, 260(IF):Band89-310
Sinclair, A. Beau Bumbo. The Breaking of
Bumbo. My Friend Judas.
T. Fitton, 617(TLS):12Jul85-777
Sinclair, C. Blood Libels.
L. Taylor, 617(TLS):13Sep85-999
Sinden, D. Laughter in the Second Act.
H.M. Hyde, 362:28Mar85-29
M. Sanderson, 617(TLS):19Apr85-440
Sinfield, A. Literature in Protestant
England, 1560-1660.*
W.B. Patterson, 569(SR):Spring84-xxiv
Sinfield, A., ed. Society and Literature
1945-1970.*
L.L. Doan, 395(MFS):Winter84-859
295(JML):Nov84-338
Singal, D.J. The War Within.*
R. Allen, 579(SAQ):Spring84-233

Smith, B.G. Ladies of the Leisure Class.
L. Gellott, 125:Fall83-98
Smith, C. Canaan.
C. Verderese, 441:21Apr85-24
Smith, C. Snow Blind.
C. Hawtree, 617(TLS):16Aug85-907
Smith, C. and G. Litton. Musical Comedy
in America.
M. Knapp, 615(TJ):Mar82-133
Smith, C.S. Chicago and the American Lit-
erary Imagination, 1880-1920.
S.E. Marovitz, 26(ALR):Autumn84-280
D. Stouck, 395(MFS):Winter84-800
295(JML):Nov84-338
Smith, C.S. - see Masuda Tsuna
Smith, D. Dream Flights.* Homage to
Edgar Allan Poe.* Onliness.*
P. Christensen, 472:Fall/Winter84-154
Smith, D. In the House of the Judge.*
S. Burris, 502(PrS):Summer84-100
P. Christensen, 472:Fall/Winter84-154
Smith, D. Local Assays.
H. Vendler, 453(NYRB):7Nov85-53
Smith, D. - see Helvétius, C-A.
Smith, D.M. - see under Mack Smith, D.
Smith, D.R. Masks of Wedlock.*
S.D. Kuretsky, 551(RenQ):Summer84-274
Smith, D.W. and R. McIntyre. Husserl and
Intentionality.*
W. Mays, 518:Jan84-25
Smith, E. Photographs 1935-1971.
T. Papageorge, 617(TLS):15Feb85-169
Smith, F.B. Florence Nightingale.
M.J. Peterson, 637(VS):Spring84-381
Smith, G. The Novel and Society.*
E.D. Engel, 155:Autumn84-171
Smith, G.C., ed. The Boole-De Morgan Cor-
respondence 1842-1864.
T. Hailperin, 316:Jun84-657
Smith, H. The Tension of the Lyre.*
R. Jacobs, 541(RES):Aug84-372
A.M. McLean, 539:Aug85-228
H.M. Richmond, 131(CL):Spring84-181
Smith, H.L. Reason's Disciples.*
W. Mitchinson, 529(QQ):Summer84-478
D.W. Pearson, 568(SCN):Spring-Summer84-
16
J. Tormey, 322(JHI):Oct-Dec84-619
Smith, I. Shakespeare's First Playhouse.*
(D. George, ed)
S.P. Cerasano, 570(SQ):Autumn84-380
W. Habicht, 72:Band221Heft1-177
Smith, I.C. The Exiles.*
B. O'Donoghue, 493:Sep84-70
W. Scammell, 364:Mar85-90
Smith, I.C. Selected Poems 1955-1980.*
(R. Fulton, ed)
R. Watson, 588(SSL):Vol 19-194
Smith, I.C. The Tenement.
J. Campbell, 617(TLS):9Aug85-874
Smith, J. Shakespearian and Other Essays.
R. Stamm, 179(ES):Apr84-162
Smith, J.A. John Buchan.
617(TLS):5Apr85-395
Smith, J.B. Frederick Delius and Edvard
Munch.
R. Anderson, 415:Jun84-329
Smith, J.C. Nuremberg.*
S. Ozment, 551(RenQ):Winter84-609
Smith, J.H. and W. Kerrigan, eds. Taking
Chances.
W.B. Warner, 400(MLN):Dec84-1195

Smith, J.I. and Y.Y. Haddad. The Islamic
Understanding of Death and Resurrection.*
M.M. Ayoub, 318(JAOS):Apr-Jun83-447
Smith, J.P. The Man from Marseille.
T. Fitton, 617(TLS):29Mar85-341
Smith, J.S. Elsie de Wolfe.
C. Brandimarte, 658:Winter84-314
Smith, J.Z. Imagining Religion.
B. Elson, 529(QQ):Autumn84-747
S.L. Ross, 185:Oct84-169
Smith, K. The Poet Reclining.*
J. Matthias, 598(SoR):Winter85-183
R. Pybus, 565:Winter83/84-68
Smith, L. Family Linen.
J. Ehle, 441:6Oct85-15
442(NY):9Dec85-160
Smith, L. Lawrence Ferlinghetti.*
J.S. Robinson, 27(AL):Mar84-119
295(JML):Nov84-440
Smith, L.E., ed. English for Cross-
Cultural Communication.
J. Verschueren, 355(LSoc):Dec84-489
Smith, L.P. A Chime of Words.* (E.
Tribble, ed) All Trivia.*
L. Auchincloss, 534(RALS):Autumn82-234
Smith, L.W. Jane Austen and the Drama of
Woman.
R.A. Colby, 445(NCF):Dec84-339
P.M. Spacks, 219(GaR):Fall84-621
Smith, M. Rābi'a the Mystic and her
Fellow-Saints in Islam.
J. Baldick, 617(TLS):19Jul85-789
Smith, M.A. Gustav Stickley.
W.S. Ayres, 658:Spring84-95
Smith, M-A.T. The Book of Phoebe.
P-L. Adams, 61:Aug85-91
R. Goldstein, 441:14Jul85-11
Smith, M.I. José Asunción Silva.*
J. Wilson, 402(MLR):Jul84-737
Smith, N.S. George.
B. Hepburn, 617(TLS):11Jan85-44
Smith, N.V., ed. Mutual Knowledge.*
T.J. Taylor and A. Reed, 307:Apr84-87
Smith, O. The Politics of Language 1791-
1819.
P. Hamilton, 617(TLS):20Sep85-1037
Smith, O.L. Scholia Graeca in Aeschylum
quae extant omnia. (Pt 2, fasc 2)
G.O. Hutchinson, 123:Vol34No1-3
Smith, P. America Enters the World.
J.M. Elukin, 441:16Jun85-25
Smith, P. The Book of Nasty Legends.
J. Simpson, 203:Vol195No2-265
Smith, P. A Land Remembered.
M. Jones, 441:6Jan85-31
Smith, P. Pound Revised.
R. Machin, 89(BJA):Summer84-266
C.F. Terrell, 30:Fall83-81
Smith, P. Public and Private Value.
S. Connor, 155:Autumn84-170
Smith, P. Realism and the Progress of
Science.
K.S., 185:Oct84-184
C. Wright, 393(Mind):Jul84-463
Smith, P.C.F. The Empress of China.
H.A.C. Forbes, 432(NEQ):Dec84-602
Smith, P.M. On the Hymn to Zeus in
Aeschylus' "Agamemnon."*
N.S. Rabinowitz, 122:Jan84-57
Smith, R. Toward an Authentic Interpreta-
tion of the Organ Works of César Franck.
J. Dalton, 415:Nov84-669

Smith, R. and S. Guppy, eds. Rainshadow.
  R.H. Ramsey, 102(CanL):Winter83-149
Smith, R.A. The Carving of Mount Rushmore.
  J.S., 62:Summer85-97
Smith, R.A. Late Georgian and Regency
  England 1760-1837.
  A. Morvan, 189(EA):Oct-Dec85-467
Smith, R.B. An International History of
  the Vietnam War. (Vol 2)
  C. Thorne, 617(TLS):27Dec85-1472
Smith, R.D. - see Wickham, A.
Smith, R.J. Japanese Society.*
  D.W. Plath, 407(MN):Winter84-471
Smith, R.J. Kurusu.
  D. Faure, 302:Vol20No2-228
Smith, R.J. and E.L. Wiswell. The Women
  of Suye Mura.
  D.W. Plath, 293(JASt):Feb84-339
Smith, R.M., ed. Land, Kinship and Life-
  Cycle.
  B. Dobson, 617(TLS):12Jul85-779
Smith, R.R.R. - see Richter, G.M.A.
Smith, R.T. Finding the Path.
  J. Carter, 219(GaR):Winter84-881
Smith, S. Ideas of the Great Psychol-
  ogists.
  D.J. Murray, 529(QQ):Winter84-1035
Smith, S. Inviolable Voice.*
  T. Eagleton, 565:Spring84-47
Smith, S. Me Again. (J. Barbera and W.
  McBrien, eds)
  A.N. Jeffares, 651(WHR):Summer84-170
Smith, S.A. Red Petrograd.
  R.C. Elwood, 104(CASS):Winter84-476
  639(VQR):Winter84-16
Smith, S.B. The Great Mental Calculators.*
  L.K. Obler, 350:Jun85-510
Smith, W.C. Towards a World Theology.
  P.B. Riley, 485(PE&W):Jan84-108
Smith, W.E. Charles Dickens in the Origi-
  nal Cloth. (Pt 2)
  R.L. Patten, 517(PBSA):Vol78No4-521
Smith, W.F. Noticiario: Primer Nivel.
  A. Labarca, 399(MLJ):Spring84-98
Smith, W.H., with others. The Yale
  Edition of Horace Walpole's Correspon-
  dence. (Vols 44-48: Index)
  J.W. Reed, 517(PBSA):Vol78No4-461
Smith, W.L. The One-Eyed Goddess.*
  R.P. Das, 259(IIJ):Oct84-319
Smith, W.S. Bishop of Everywhere.*
  C. Day, 272(IUR):Spring84-150
Smith-Rosenberg, C. Disorderly Conduct.
  E. Janeway, 441:25Aug85-11
Smither, E. Shakespeare Virgins.
  B. O'Donoghue, 617(TLS):5Jul85-753
Smithies, E. The Black Economy in England
  since 1914.
  A. Seldon, 617(TLS):12Jul85-766
Smithson, A. As in DS.
  J. Glancey, 46:Feb84-78
Smits, K., W. Besch and V. Lange, eds.
  Interpretation und Edition deutscher
  Texte des Mittelalters.*
  R.M. Kully, 564:May84-127
Smitten, J.R. and A. Daghistany, eds.
  Spatial Form in Narrative.*
  M. Spencer, 494:Vol5No1-182
Smollett, T. The Adventures of Peregrine
  Pickle. (J.L. Clifford, ed; rev by P-G.
  Boucé) The Expedition of Humphry Clink-
  er. (L.M. Knapp, ed; rev by P-G. Boucé)
  S. Soupel, 189(EA):Jan-Mar85-111

Smollett, T. Humphry Clinker. (J.L. Thor-
  son, ed)
  S. Soupel, 189(EA):Jul-Sep85-337
Smoodin, R. Inventing Ivanov.
  C. Sternhell, 441:19May85-26
Smulders, W.H.M. De literaire misleiding
  in De Donkere kamer van Damokles.
  P.F. Schmitz, 204(FdL):Sep84-231
Smullyan, R. Alice in Puzzle-Land.*
  H. Mellar, 617(TLS):8Mar85-268
Smuszkiewicz, A. Zaczarowana gra.
  E. Stachniak, 561(SFS):Mar84-96
Smyers, V.L. and M. Winship - see Blanck,
  J.
Smyser, W.R. The Independent Vietnamese.
  W.J. Duiker, 293(JASt):Feb84-371
Smyth, D. Quilt.
  B. Godard, 198:Autumn84-83
Snelgrove, D. Paul Mellon Collection Cata-
  logue. (Vol 3)
  L. Lambourne, 90:Sep84-582
Snell, A.M. Hacia el verbo.
  B.W. Ife, 402(MLR):Jan84-214
  R.M. Price, 86(BHS):Apr84-198
Snell, K.D.M. Annals of the Labouring
  Poor.
  G.E. Mingay, 617(TLS):6Sep84-983
Snell, R. Théophile Gautier.*
  R. Lethbridge, 208(FS):Jul84-356
  A.B. Smith, 207(FR):Dec84-292
  T.D. Stamm, 446(NCFS):Summer-Fall84-
  202
Snell-Hornby, M. Verb Descriptivity in
  German and English.
  G. Bourcier, 189(EA):Jul-Sep85-312
  B.J. Koekkoek, 350:Mar85-222
Snider, W.D. Helms and Hunt.
  J. Brinkley, 441:23Jun85-21
Snipes, K. Robert Penn Warren.
  J.L. Idol, Jr., 573(SSF):Fall84-422
Snitow, A.B. Ford Madox Ford and the
  Voice of Uncertainty.
  H. Carpenter, 617(TLS):14Jun85-673
  R.A. Cassell, 395(MFS):Winter84-750
  295(JML):Nov84-441
  639(VQR):Summer84-86
Snorri Sturluson. Edda.* (A. Faulkes, ed)
  L. Holm-Olsen, 562(Scan):May84-59
Snow, H.F. My China Years.*
  D.J. Enright, 362:10Jan85-22
Snow, J.T. - see de Valdivielso, J.
Snow, P., comp. The United States: a
  Guide to Library Holdings in the UK.
  B. Lawson-Peebles, 541(RES):Nov84-595
Snow, R. and K. Kanai. Coney Island.*
  442(NY):8Apr85-129
Snowman, D. The World of Plácido Domingo.
  R. Christiansen, 617(TLS):3May85-490
Snukal, S. Talking Dirty.
  N. Carson, 102(CanL):Autumn84-189
Snyder, E.E. Portland Names and Neighbor-
  hoods.
  W.G. Loy, 424:Mar84-82
Snyder, G. Axe Handles.*
  B. Bawer, 491:Sep84-346
  P. Fortunato, 181:Vol34No2-150
  G.H. Holthaus, 649(WAL):Feb85-311
  J. Matthias, 598(SoR):Winter85-183
  R. Peters, 703:No10-179
Snyder, J. and A. Peckolick. Herb Lubalin.
  R. McLean, 617(TLS):20Sep85-1043
Snyder, G.S. Maps of the Heavens.
  A.B. Sandback, 62:Dec84-77

343

Sŏ Chŏngju. Sŏ Chŏngju: Winter Sky.
S-K. Kim, 293(JASt):Feb84-348
Soames, S. and D.M. Perlmutter. Syntactic
Argumentation and the Structure of
English.
C. Cullen, 297(JL):Mar84-192
Soares, J. Loaded Dice.
G. Johnson, 441:22Sep85-23
Sobejano, G. - see Alas, L.
Sobejano, G. - see Delibes, M.
Sober, E. The Nature of Selection.
S.P. Stich, 617(TLS):29Nov85-1367
Sobin, G. The Earth as Air.
A. Mobilio, 703:No12-156
Sobrero, A.A. and M.T. Romanello. L'ital-
iano come si parla in Salento.
E. Radtke, 72:Band221Heft2-421
Sobti, K. Blossoms in Darkness.
A.L. Weir, 314:Winter-Spring84-209
Soellner, R. "Timon of Athens."*
L. Walker, 570(SQ):Spring84-120
Soga, M. Tense and Aspect in Modern Collo-
quial Japanese.
W.M. Jacobsen, 293(JASt):Aug84-771
Kyoko Inoue, 353:Vol22No1-141
G.D. Prideaux, 320(CJL):Spring84-92
Sogliuzzo, A.R. Luigi Pirandello, Direc-
tor.*
M. Carlson, 612(ThS):May84-120
Sohm, P.L. The Scuola Grande di San Marco
1437-1550.
D. Howard, 576:May84-179
Sohrweide, H. Türkische Handschriften.
(Pt 3)
E. Birnbaum, 318(JAOS):Apr-Jun83-413
Sokolow, J.A. Eros and Modernization.
S. Stage, 432(NEQ):Dec84-620
Solan, L. Pronominal Reference.
R.J. Bogue, 350:Mar85-235
W. O'Grady, 320(CJL):Fal184-211
de Solano, F., ed. Estudios sobre la
Ciudad Iberoamericana. (2nd ed)
J.J. Junquera y Mato, 48:Jul-Sep84-329
Solberg, C. Hubert Humphrey.*
H. Brogan, 617(TLS):1Mar85-238
Solé, C.A. and Y.R. Español.*
I. Wherritt, 399(MLJ):Spring84-98
Solensten, J. Good Thunder.
L.M. Hasselstrom, 649(WAL):Nov84-235
Solimena, A. Repertorio dello Stil novo.
S. Lazard, 553(RLiR):Jul-Dec84-480
Solkin, D.H. Richard Wilson.
W. Vaughan, 59:Sep84-368
Sollers, P. Femmes.*
M-N. Little, 207(FR):Apr85-761
Sollers, P. Portrait du Joueur.
J.H. Mole, 617(TLS):8Mar85-265
Solmsen, F., R. Merkelbach and M.L. West -
see Hesiod
Sologub, F. The Petty Demon.
O. Markof-Belaeff, 550(RusR):Jan84-91
J.M. Mills, 574(SEEJ):Spring84-119
Solomon, B.M. In the Company of Educated
Women.
A. Simmons, 441:6Oct85-34
Solomon, D.A. In My Father's House.
M.C. Bateson, 441:24Feb85-37
Solomon, R.C. The Passions.
O. Letwin, 483:Jul84-410
Soloviev, S.M. History of Russia. (Vol
24 ed and trans by A.V. Muller, Vol 29
ed and trans by K.A. Papmehl, Vol 35 ed
[continued]

[continuing]
and trans by R. Hantula)
M. Okenfuss, 104(CASS):Spring-Summer84-
185
Solta, G.R. Einführung in die Balkanlin-
guistik mit besonderer Berücksichtigung
des Substrats und des Balkanlateinischen.
W.P. Schmid, 260(IF):Band89-359
de Somaize, A.B. Le Procez des Pretieuses
en vers burlesques. (E. Biancardi, ed)
R. Zuber, 535(RHL):Nov/Dec84-953
Sommella, P.P. La Mode au XVIIe siècle
d'après la "Correspondance" de Mme de
Sévigné.
P. Weed, 208(FS):Oct84-461
Sommella, P.P. Marcel Proust e i movi-
menti pittorici d'avanguardia.
M. Tilby, 208(FS):Oct84-482
Sommer, S. Hazzard's Head.
S. Tanenhaus, 441:27Oct85-9
Sommerhage, C. Eros und Poesis.
D.W. Adolphs and E. Schwarz, 133:
Band17Heft1/2-176
S.R. Cerf, 221(GQ):Spring84-326
H.T. Tewarson, 222(GR):Summer84-126
Sommers, F. The Logic of Natural Lan-
guage.*
G.B. Keene, 479(PhQ):Apr84-174
Somoza, O.U., ed. Nueva narrativa chicana.
C. Tatum, 238:Dec84-681
Somville, P. Art et Symbole à la Renais-
sance.
M. Adam, 542:Apr-Jun84-240
H. Osborne, 89(BJA):Summer84-270
Sonderegger, S. Schatzkammer deutscher
Sprachdenkmäler.
L. Denecke, 684(ZDA):Band113Heft1-6
"Sonderforschungsbericht 100 'Elektron-
ische Sprachforschung.'"
G. Koller, 685(ZDL):2/1984-270
Sondheimer, J. Castle Adamant in Hamp-
stead.
A.C. Percival, 324:Dec84-72
Song, C. Picture Bride.
L. Goldensohn, 491:Apr84-40
Sonnenfeld, A. Crossroads.*
R.D. Reck, 546(RR):Nov84-509
H.H. Watts, 395(MFS):Summer84-420
295(JML):Nov84-390
Sonnevi, G. The Economy Spinning Faster
and Faster.
D. McDuff, 565:Summer84-68
Sontag, S. A Susan Sontag Reader.* (E.
Hardwick, ed)
S. Brown, 569(SR):Fal184-649
I. Thomson, 364:Jul84-103
Soons, A. Juan de Mariana.*
R.M. Price, 402(MLR):Apr84-474
R.A. Stradling, 86(BHS):Oct84-505
Sophocles. Oedipus Rex. (R.D. Dawe, ed)
P.T. Stevens, 303(JoHS):Vol 104-197
Sophocles. The Oedipus Trilogy. (S.
Spender, trans)
I. Hamilton, 617(TLS):22Nov85-1307
D.A.N. Jones, 362:21Nov85-28
Sophocles. Sophocles I: Three Tragedies.
(D. Grene, R. Fitzgerald and E. Wyckoff,
trans) The Oedipus Cycle of Sophocles.
(D. Fitts and R. Fitzgerald, trans)
Three Tragedies of Sophocles. (H.D.
Kitto, trans) Oedipus the King. (S.
Berg and D. Clay, trans) Sophocles:
[continued]

Sparshott, F.E. The Theory of the Arts.*
  M. Beardsley, 290(MAL):Spring85-317
  A. Berleant, 478:Oct84-279
  D. Novitz, 63:Jun84-199
  H. Osborne, 89(BJA):Winter84-68
  M.M. van de Pitte, 529(QQ):Spring84-214
  F. Schier, 483:Oct84-549
  B.R. Tilghman, 289:Winter84-95
Spater, G. William Cobbett.*
  J. Clive, 656(WMQ):Jan84-171
  P.M.S. Dawson, 339(KSMB):No35-84
  V. Nemoianu, 400(MLN):Dec84-1257
  W. Thomas, 541(RES):Nov84-557
  D.A. Wilson, 529(QQ):Spring84-174
Spear, J.L. Dreams of an English Eden.
  H.W., 636(VP):Winter84-457
Spear, R.E. Domenichino.*
  J.B., 380:Summer84-216
  J. Connors, 576:Mar84-80
  A.S. Harris, 90:Mar84-166
Spear, T. Traditions of Origin and Their
  Interpretation.
  J. Lamphear, 538(RAL):Summer84-301
Spearing, A.C. Medieval to Renaissance in
  English Poetry.
  H. Cooper, 617(TLS):27Dec85-1483
Specht, H. Chaucer's Franklin in "The
  Canterbury Tales."*
  G.C. Britton, 447(N&Q):Feb83-72
  P. Hardman, 541(RES):Nov84-528
  A.A. MacDonald, 179(ES):Apr84-110
  J.T. Reakes, 38:Band102Heft1/2-218
Specht, R. Recherches sur Nicolas de
  Vérone.
  L. Formisano, 379(MedR):Aug84-299
  A. Limentani, 554:Vol 104No2-261
Spector, R.D. The English Gothic.
  G.L. Green, 223:Fall84-322
Spector, R.D. Tobias Smollett.*
  P-G. Boucé, 402(MLR):Apr84-423
Spee, F. Trutznachtigall.* (G.R. Dimler,
  ed)
  J. Leighton, 402(MLR):Oct84-979
Speirs, R. Brecht's Early Plays.
  B. Bennett, 397(MD):Jun84-273
  R.H. Paslick, 221(GQ):Summer84-501
  J. Rouse, 130:Summer84-187
Speiser, S.M. How to End the Nuclear
  Nightmare.
  S. Brittan, 176:Apr85-60
Spellman, C.C. An Excess of Love.
  L. Prinz, 441:23Jun85-21
Spence, J.D. The Memory Palace of Matteo
  Ricci.*
  J. Gernet, 617(TLS):27Sep85-1059
  R. Scott, 362:23May85-31
  H.R. Trevor-Roper, 453(NYRB):13Jun85-12
  J. Updike, 442(NY):17Jun85-121
Spencer, H. The Man Versus the State.
  A.M. Diamond, Jr., 396(ModA):
    Spring/Summer84-286
Spencer, T.J.B. - see Ford, J.
Spencer, W.F. The Confederate Navy in
  Europe.
  W.N. Still, Jr., 9(AlaR):Jan84-65
Spencer-Noël, G. Zénon ou le thème de
  l'alchimie dans "L'Oeuvre au noir" de
  Marguerite Yourcenar.*
  C. Rigolot, 207(FR):Dec84-304
Spender, D. Man Made Language.*
  S. Lawson, 35(AS):Winter84-369

Spender, D. There's Always Been a Women's
  Movement this Century.
  J. Tormey, 322(JHI):Oct-Dec84-619
Spender, D. Women of Ideas.*
  T. McCormack, 529(QQ):Summer84-471
Spender, L. Intruders on the Rights of
  Men.*
  L. Bland, 89(BJA):Summer84-267
  S. Lavabre, 189(EA):Jan-Mar85-109
Spender, S. Journals 1939-1983. (J. Gold-
  smith, ed) Collected Poems 1928-1985.
  I. Hamilton, 617(TLS):22Nov85-1307
  D.A.N. Jones, 362:21Nov85-28
Spender, S. and D. Hockney. China Diary.
  J. Hunter, 249(HudR):Autumn84-516
  90:Feb84-102
Spengemann, W.C. The Forms of Autobiog-
  raphy.*
  P. Tobin, 223:Summer81-288
"Spenser Studies."* (Vol 3) (P. Cullen
  and T.P. Roche, Jr., eds)
  L.E. Orange, 568(SCN):Spring-Summer84-5
Spero, S. Worcester Porcelain.
  T. Hughes, 324:Aug85-672
Speroni, S. Canace e Scritti in sua
  difesa [together with] Giraldi Cinzio, G.
  Scritti contro la Canace.* (C. Roaf, ed)
  C. Fahy, 402(MLR):Oct84-952
Sperry, R. Science and Moral Priority.*
  R. Kearney, 63:Dec84-430
Spevack, M. and J.W. Binns, general eds.
  Renaissance Latin Drama in England.*
  (1st Ser, Vols 1-4)
  C. Davies, 123:Vol34No2-362
  H. Kelliher, 354:Jun84-183
  G. Schmitz, 72:Band221Heft2-372
Spevack, M. and J.W. Binns, general eds.
  Renaissance Latin Drama in England.
  (1st Ser, Vols 9 and 12)
  H. Kelliher, 354:Jun84-183
Spicehandler, D. The Serpent and the
  Eagle.
  M. Skakun, 287:Jan84-26
Spiegel, M. Your True Marcus. (F.L.
  Byrne and J.P. Soman, eds)
  P-L. Adams, 61:Jun85-104
Spiegel, R. Doris Lessing.
  M.M. Rowe, 395(MFS):Summer84-377
Spiegel, S.L. The Other Arab-Israeli Con-
  flict.
  D. Pipes, 129:Oct85-66
  N. Safran, 441:5May85-13
Spiegelberg, H. The Context of the Phenom-
  enological Movement.*
  A.G. Pleydell-Pearce, 323:Oct84-312
  C.O. Schrag, 543:Sep83-148
  R.N. Smid, 687:Apr-Jun84-338
Spiegelberg, H. The Phenomenological
  Movement.
  A.G. Pleydell-Pearce, 323:Oct84-312
Spiegelberg, H. and E. Ave-Lallemant, eds.
  Pfänder-Studien.
  F. Dunlop, 323:Jan84-101
Spielberg, P. Crash-Landing.
  R.P. Mills, 441:31Mar85-22
Spiller, R.F. and others - see Cooper, J.F.
Spiller, S. Stories of Men and of Rats.
  E. Johnston, 102(CanL):Winter83-114
Spindler, M. American Literature and
  Social Change.
  L.L. Doan, 395(MFS):Winter84-859
    [continued]

Starr, C.G. The Roman Empire 27 B.C.-A.D.
476.
  D.L. Stockton, 123:Vol34No1-143
Starr, K. Inventing the Dream.
  N. Bliven, 442(NY):12Aug85-82
  W. Stegner, 441:24Feb85-1
Starr, P. The Social Transformation of
American Medicine.*
  S. Bernstein, 42(AR):Winter84-118
  S.E.D. Shortt, 529(QQ):Summer84-452
Starr, R. The Rise and Fall of New York
City.
  A. Hacker, 441:5May85-11
  L. Lenkowsky, 129:Jul85-66
Starr, S.F. Red and Hot.*
  P. Schwendener, 31(ASch):Summer84-429
Stashower, D. The Adventure of the Ecto-
plasmic Man.
  M. Berkley, 441:28Apr85-24
"The State of India's Environment, 1982."
  R.G. Varady, 293(JASt):May84-563
"The Statesman's Year-Book, 1984-1985."
  (J. Paxton, ed)
  G. Best, 617(TLS):26Apr85-471
Stathatos, C.G. A Gil Vicente Bibliogra-
phy (1940-1975).
  D. Mackenzie, 86(BHS):Jan84-64
Statler, O. Japanese Pilgrimage.*
  J.H. Foard, 293(JASt):May84-557
Stavinohova, Z. Les temps passés de
l'indicatif dans le français contemp-
orain.
  C. Perlick, 682(ZPSK):Band37Heft6-724
Stavrou, T.G., ed. Art and Culture in
Nineteenth-Century Russia.
  T.T. Rice, 90:Apr84-240
  A.C. Wright, 104(CASS):Winter84-463
Stead, C.K. All Visitors Ashore.*
  J. Mellors, 364:Jul84-106
Stead, C.K. In the Glass Case.
  D. Davin, 541(RES):Feb84-109
Stead, C.K. Poems of a Decade. Paris.
  B. O'Donoghue, 617(TLS):5Jul85-753
Stead, P.J. The Police of France.
  M. Ignatieff, 617(TLS):1Mar85-235
Steadman, J.M. The Hill and the Labyrinth.
Milton's Biblical and Classical Imagery.
  J. Pitcher, 617(TLS):23Aug85-932
Steadman, R. I, Michelangelo.* (French
title: Moi, Léonard de Vinci.)
  A. Suied, 98:Nov84-941
Stearns, P.N. Arbeiterleben.
  I. Dietrich, 654(WB):1/1984-170
Stebbins, S. Maxima in minimis.
  D. Bell, 402(MLR):Jul84-741
Stebbins, T.E., Jr., C. Troyen and T.J.
Fairbrother. A New World.
  N. Harris, 432(NEQ):Jun84-271
Steblin-Kamenskij, M.I. Myth.
  L. Thompson, 133:Band17Heft1/2-131
Stedman, R.W. Shadows of the Indian.
  T. King, 649(WAL):Aug84-156
Steegmüller, B. Das von der Schrift-
sprache abweichende Vokabular in Célines
"Mort à crédit [sic]."
  G. Holtus, 72:Band221Heft2-462
Steel, C. - see Proclus
Steel, D. Family Album.
  J. Austin, 441:3Mar85-22
Steel, D. Partners in One Nation.
  S. Jenkins, 617(TLS):20Sep85-1024
Steel, D. Secrets.
  D. Bianculli, 441:17Nov85-30

Steel, G.H. Chronology and Time in "A la
recherche du temps perdu."
  R. Gibson, 208(FS):Jan84-86
Steele, B. - see Lawrence, D.H.
Steele, C., ed. Taking Stock.
  T. Goldie, 102(CanL):Winter83-93
Steele, H.T. The Hawaiian Shirt.*
  K.S.H., 614:Winter85-25
Steele, J. and E. Abraham. Andropov in
Power.*
  R.J. Hill, 575(SEER):Jul84-467
Steele, R. The Guardian. (J.C. Stephens,
ed)
  J.J. Gold, 301(JEGP):Jan84-129
  C. Winton, 536:Vol6-129
Steele, T. The Prudent Heart. [correc-
tion of mistiled entry in last vol]
  D. Gioia, 461:Fall/Winter83/84-99
Steele, V. Fashion and Eroticism.
  M. Douglas, 617(TLS):8Nov85-1254
  E. Hoffman, 614:Summer85-24
Steen, S.J. - see Brome, R.
Steene, B. August Strindberg.
  H.G. Carlson, 397(MD):Jun84-269
Steensma, R.C. Dr. John Arbuthnot.
  W.J. Burling, 568(SCN):Fall84-44
Steer, G. Hugo Ripelin von Strassburg.*
  H. Hildebrandt, 685(ZDL):3/1984-396
Steer, J. Alvise Vivarini.*
  D. Howard, 54:Sep84-528
Stéfan, J. Laures.
  T. Cordellier, 450(NRF):Sep84-93
Stefenelli, A. Geschichte des franzö-
sischen Kernwortschatzes.*
  K. Brademann, 72:Band221Heft2-409
Stegner, W. One Way to Spell Man.*
  D.S. Miller, 569(SR):Winter84-160
Stegner, W. Wolf Willow.
  K. Carabine, 447(N&Q):Apr83-188
Stegner, W. and R.W. Etulain. Conversa-
tions with Wallace Stegner on Western
History and Literature.
  K. Ahearn, 651(WHR):Winter84-383
  F.G. Robinson, 649(WAL):Nov84-245
Steiger, R. Die syntaktisch-semantische
Textanalyse und automatisierte Indexi-
erung.
  K. Albrecht, 682(ZPSK):Band37Heft6-725
Steimberg, A. Como todas las mañanas.
  C. Delacre Capestany, 37:May-Jun84-59
Stein, A. Seeds of the Seventies.
  R. Caplan, 441:1Sep85-15
Stein, A.F. After the Vows Were Spoken.
  E. Letley, 617(TLS):13Sep85-1012
Stein, B. Peasant State and Society in
Medieval South India.*
  P. Kolenda, 318(JAOS):Jul-Sep83-665
Stein, D. Ada.
  T. Kidder, 441:29Dec85-6
Stein, G. The Yale Gertrude Stein. (R.
Kostelanetz, ed)
  R. Bridgman, 402(MLR):Oct84-920
Stein, K.W. The Land Question in Pales-
tine, 1917-1939.*
  M.E. Yapp, 617(TLS):15Feb85-167
Stein, L. - see Schoenberg, A.
Stein, P. Connaissance et emploi des lan-
gues à l'Île Maurice.*
  P. Baker, 355(LSoc):Sep84-390
Stein, P.K. and others, eds. Sprache —
Text — Geschichte.*
  I. Glier, 221(GQ):Spring84-301

Stein, S. The Touch of Treason.
  H. Jackson, 441:26May85-15
Steinberg, A. Word and Music in the
  Novels of Andrey Bely.*
  V.E. Alexandrov, 550(RusR):Jan84-75
  J.D. Elsworth, 402(MLR):Apr84-509
  S.J. Rabinowitz, 104(CASS):Spring-
    Summer84-164
Steinberg, D.D. Psycholinguistics.*
  J. Bahns, 38:Band102Heft3/4-468
Steinberg, D.J. The Philippines.
  D. Wurfel, 293(JASt):Aug84-814
Steinberg, L. The Sexuality of Christ in
  Renaissance Art and in Modern Oblivion.*
  A. Chastel, 98:Dec84-945
  N. Moufarrege, 62:Dec84-76
Steinberg, M.P. - see Broch, H.
Steinberg, M.W. - see Klein, A.M.
Steinberg, M.W. and U. Caplan - see Klein,
  A.M.
Steinbrink, B. Abenteuerliteratur des 19.
  Jahrhunderts in Deutschland.
  J. Hienger, 680(ZDP):Band103Heft2-309
Steinbuch, K. Kommunikationstechnik.
  G.F. Meier, 682(ZPSK):Band37Heft1-120
Steinecke, H. Literaturkritik des Jungen
  Deutschland.*
  J.L. Sammons, 52:Band19Heft1-94
Steinem, G. Outrageous Acts and Everyday
  Rebellions.*
  S. Brown, 569(SR):Fall84-649
  J. Neville, 364:Apr/May84-122
Steiner, C. and R. Jacobson. Opera People.
  C.J. Gianakaris, 615(TJ):May84-286
Steiner, G. After Babel.
  K. Reichl, 38:Band102Heft3/4-458
Steiner, G. A Reader.
  K. Fitzlyon, 364:Nov84-102
Steiner, J. - see Storm, T. and T. Fontane
Steiner, P., ed. The Prague School.*
  C.E. Reeves, 494:Vol4No1-177
  D. Short, 575(SEER):Jan84-151
  J. Vizmuller-Zocco, 355(LSoc):Dec84-
    571
Steiner, P. Russian Formalism.
  C.R. Pike, 617(TLS):15Mar85-295
Steiner, W. The Colors of Rhetoric.*
  D. Davis, 89(BJA):Winter84-81
  K. Kroeber, 403(MLS):Winter84-94
  J.A. Richardson, 289:Spring84-93
  M. Torgovnick, 454:Fall84-81
  E. Vos, 204(FdL):Dec84-310
Steiner, W., ed. Image and Code.
  C. Hasenmueller, 567:Vol50No3/4-335
Steinhardt, N.S. and others. Chinese Tra-
  ditional Architecture.
  A.C. Soper, 57:Vol45No2/3-233
Steinhauer, K. Hegel-Bibliography-Bibliog-
  raphie.*
  H-M. Sass, 125:Summer84-424
Steinmeyer, G. Historische Aspekte des
  "Français Avancé."*
  R. de Gorog, 545(RPh):May84-462
Steinmüller, A. and K. Andymon.
  O.R. Spittel, 654(WB):10/1984-1715
Steinsaltz, A. Biblical Images.
  A. Kurzweil, 469:Vol 10No2-108
Steitz, L. Grammatik der Saarbrücker Mun-
  dart.
  H. Fix, 685(ZDL):2/1984-243
Stellmacher, D. Niederdeutsch.
  E. Seebold, 685(ZDL):2/1984-261

Stellmacher, D. Niedersächsische (Dialekt/
  Hochsprache — kontrastiv).
  D. Rosenthal, 260(IF):Band89-380
Steltzer, U. A Haida Potlatch.
  P-L. Adams, 61:May85-104
  B. Hall, 441:10Mar85-24
Stelzer, H. Narzissmusproblematik und
  Spiegeltechnik in Joseph Conrads Romanen.
  W. Senn, 136:Vol 17No3-251
Stemmer, N. The Roots of Knowledge.
  G. Stahl, 542:Apr-Jun84-232
Stemshaug, O., ed. Norsk Personnamnlek-
  sikon.
  W.F.H. Nicolaisen, 424:Sep84-325
Stendhal. Lucien Leuwen.* (A-M. Meinin-
  ger, ed)
  K. Ringger, 535(RHL):Mar/Apr84-288
Stendhal. Souvenirs d'égotisme. (B.
  Didier, ed)
  J-J. Hamm, 446(NCFS):Summer-Fall84-180
Stenson, P. Lights.
  S. Mills, 617(TLS):26Apr85-460
Stent, A. From Embargo to Ostpolitik.
  A.H. Smith, 575(SEER):Jan84-139
Stenzel, J. - see von Canitz, F.R.L.
Stepelevich, L.S. and D. Lamb, eds.
  Hegel's Philosophy of Action.
  M.A.G., 185:Apr85-778
Stephan, J.J. Hawaii Under the Rising
  Sun.*
  J.H. Buck, 407(MN):Summer84-210
  Maeda Hisao, 285(JapQ):Jul-Sep84-323
Stephanopoulos, T.K. Umgestaltung des
  Mythos durch Euripides.*
  E.M. Craik, 303(JoHS):Vol 104-202
Stephens, J.C. - see Steele, R.
Stephens, J.N. The Fall of the Florentine
  Republic, 1512-1530.
  J. Hook, 278(IS):Vol39-128
Stephens, J.R. The Censorship of English
  Drama 1824-1901.*
  D. Barrett, 615(TJ):Dec82-548
Stephenson, A.M.G. The Rise and Decline
  of English Modernism.
  T. Baker, 617(TLS):5Apr85-392
Stephenson, D. The Governance of Gwynedd.
  G.H. Jenkins, 617(TLS):1Mar85-236
Stephenson, R.H. Goethe's Wisdom Litera-
  ture.
  M. Sprinker, 400(MLN):Dec84-1246
Steppat, M. The Critical Reception of
  Shakespeare's "Antony and Cleopatra"
  from 1607 to 1905.*
  T.R. Griffiths, 677(YES):Vol 14-312
Sterba, J.P., ed. The Ethics of War and
  Nuclear Deterrence.
  R. Hardin, 185:Apr85-763
Sterchi, B. Blösch.*
  M. Rutschky, 384:Apr84-329
Sterling, C. The Time of the Assassins.*
  K. Kellen, 390:May84-59
Stern, F.C. F.O. Matthiessen.*
  J. Kronick, 284:Fall84-66
Stern, G. Paradise Poems.*
  A. Turner, 199:Spring85-45
Stern, G. Rejoicings.
  E. Grosholz, 249(HudR):Winter84/85-653
Stern, H.H. Fundamental Concepts of Lan-
  guage Teaching.
  J.P.B. Allen, 257(IRAL):May84-146
  R. Sussex, 67:Nov84-258
Stern, I. The Greater Medieval Historians.
  J. Ruud, 125:Spring84-309

Stern, M., ed. Expressionismus in der
Schweiz.*
    R. Kieser, 406:Spring84-110
Stern, R.A.M., G. Gilmartin and J.M. Mas-
sengale. New York 1900.*
    P.R. Baker, 432(NEQ):Dec84-573
Stern, S. The Moon and Ruben Shein.
    M. Buck, 441:10Feb85-24
Sterne, L. The Life and Opinions of Tris-
tram Shandy, Gentleman.* (I.C. Ross, ed)
    H. Anderson, 594:Summer84-259
    C.H. Flynn, 402(MLR):Oct84-909
    B.S.H., 83:Autumn84-282
    I. Simon, 179(ES):Dec84-579
Sterne, L. A Sentimental Journey. (I.
Jack, ed)
    P-G. Boucé, 189(EA):Oct-Dec85-493
Sternhell, Z. Ni droite ni gauche.
    J-F. Fourny, 207(FR):Dec84-321
Sternlicht, S. - see Colum, P.
Stevens, C.C. and S. Whittington. 18th
Century English Furniture — The Norman
Adams Collection.
    G. Wills, 39:Jun84-466
Stevens, D. English Renaissance Theatre
History.
    D.M. Bergeron, 570(SQ):Summer84-253
Stevens, J.M., C.M. Woodhouse and D.J.
Wallace. British Reports on Greece 1943-
1944. (L. Baerentzen, ed)
    S. Wichert, 575(SEER):Jan84-138
Stevens, K. and E. Dally. Surrogate
Mother.
    P. Toynbee, 617(TLS):11Oct85-1131
Stevens, M. The Accounting Wars.
    K.W. Arenson, 441:30Jun85-21
Stevens, R.P. Kant on Moral Practice.
    A. Broadie, 342:Band75Heft3-357
Stevenson, C.B. Victorian Women Travel
Writers in Africa.
    C.F. Behrman, 637(VS):Summer84-521
Stevenson, I. Unlearned Language.
    W. Frawley, 350:Sep85-739
Stevenson, L.C. Praise and Paradox.
    H.R. Woudhuysen, 617(TLS):10May85-518
Stevenson, L.F. The Metaphysics of Exper-
ience.
    G.H. Bird, 518:Jul84-169
    A. Stanguennec, 542:Oct-Dec84-483
    T.E. Wilkerson, 479(PhQ):Oct84-511
Stevenson, R.L. "An Old Song" and Edify-
ing Letters of the Rutherford Family.
(R.G. Swearingen, ed)
    E.M. Eigner, 445(NCF):Dec84-351
Stevenson, S. Gold Earrings.
    S. Scobie, 376:Oct84-124
Stevick, E.W. Teaching and Learning Lan-
guages.
    R.J. Alexander, 257(IRAL):Aug84-231
    R.F. Comeau, 399(MLJ):Spring84-65
Stewart, A. Attika.
    C.E. Vafopoulou-Richardson, 54:Dec84-
    690
Stewart, A. Skopas in Malibu.
    O. Palagia, 123:Vol34No2-277
Stewart, E. Ariana.
    W.J. Harding, 441:26May85-14
Stewart, F.M. The Titan.
    J. Daynard, 441:7Apr85-14
Stewart, G. Death Sentences.
    J. Bayley, 617(TLS):21Jun85-697
Stewart, G. The Tenth Virgin.
    D.W. Madden, 649(WAL):Feb85-338

Stewart, J. - see Jones, B.
Stewart, J.D. Sir Godfrey Kneller and the
English Baroque Portrait.*
    K. Garlick, 39:Jun84-465
Stewart, J.H. Colette.
    R.D. Cottrell, 207(FR):Mar85-585
    E. Marks, 188(ECr):Fall84-83
Stewart, J.I.M. The Naylors.
    L. Duguid, 617(TLS):25Jan85-86
    E. Toynton, 441:15Sep85-30
Stewart, M.A., ed. Law, Morality and
Rights.
    R.H., 185:Oct84-180
Stewart, R., ed. A Dictionary of Politi-
cal Quotations.
    G. Marshall, 617(TLS):1Feb85-114
Stewart, S. On Longing.
    G.G. Harpham, 533:Spring85-107
Stewart-Gordon, F. and N. Hazelton. The
Russian Tearoom Cookbook.
    K.L. Nalibow, 574(SEEJ):Spring84-140
Stickland, G. Structuralism or Criticism?
    D. Knight, 494:Vol4No1-186
Stierlin, H. Encyclopedia of World Archi-
tecture.
    J.M. Robinson, 39:Apr84-303
Stiewe, K. and N. Holzberg, eds. Poly-
bios.*
    M-R. Guelfucci, 555:Vol58fasc1-121
Stijnen, S. and T. Vallen. Dialect als
Onderwijsprobleem.
    D. de Haan, 355(LSoc):Mar84-104
Stillers, R. Maurice Blanchot: "Thomas
l'obscur."*
    J. Baetens, 547(RF):Band96Heft1/2-199
Stillman, L. Alfred Jarry.
    J. Kestner, 446(NCFS):Winter-Spring85-
    183
Stillman, N.A. The Jews of Arab Lands.*
    R.G. Lewis, 390:Apr84-59
Stillwell, M.B. Essays on the Heritage of
the Renaissance from Homer to Gutenberg.
    E.L. Eisenstein, 517(PBSA):Vol78No4-
    504
Stimm, H., ed. Zur Geschichte des gespro-
chenen Französisch und zur Sprachlenkung
im Gegenwartsfranzösischen.*
    J. Stéfanini, 209(FM):Apr84-91
Stimpson, B. Paul Valéry and Music.
    J.M. Cocking, 617(TLS):8Mar85-255
Stinger, C.L. The Renaissance in Rome.
    P. Partner, 617(TLS):25Oct85-1213
Stobbe, P. Utopisches Denken bei V. Chleb-
nikov.
    A. Pyman, 575(SEER):Jan84-112
Stock, I. Fiction as Wisdom.*
    F. McCombie, 447(N&Q):Apr83-179
Stock, J. Disegni veneti di collezioni
inglesi.
    380:Summer84-219
Stock, N. The Life of Ezra Pound.
    617(TLS):27Sep85-1071
Stock, R.D. The Holy and the Daemonic
from Sir Thomas Browne to William Blake.*
    J.M. Armistead, 161(DUJ):Dec83-131
    L.M. Dorsey, 396(ModA):Fall84-386
    C. Fox, 88:Winter84/85-144
    P. Rogers, 541(RES):Aug84-377
    P.M. Spacks, 405(MP):Nov84-206
Stockdale, J. and S. In Love and War.
    H. Bering-Jensen, 129:Jan85-75
    K. Buckley, 441:28Apr85-25

Stott, M.   Before I Go ...
   M. Jones, 362:21Mar85-24
   P. Willmott, 617(TLS):12Apr85-400
Stoumen, L.   Times Square.
   D.W. Dunlap, 441:16Jun85-24
   442(NY):12Aug85-85
Stout, J.P.   The Journey Narrative in Amer-
   ican Literature.
   G.R. Griffin, 432(NEQ):Dec84-605
   W.C. Hamlin, 395(MFS):Winter84-787
Stove, D.C.   Popper and After.*
   R. Fellows, 518:Oct84-250
   J.F. Fox, 63·Mar84-99
   J.M.B. Moss, 84:Sep84-307
Stow, R.   The Suburbs of Hell.*
   P. Lewis, 565:Autumn84-55
   J. Mellors, 364:Apr/May84-135
Stow, R.   To the Islands.
   B. King, 569(SR):Winter84-136
Stow, R.   Tourmaline.*
   B. King, 569(SR):Winter84-136
   P. Wolfe, 502(PrS):Summer84-105
Stow, R.   Visitants.
   P. Lewis, 565:Spring84-64
Stowe, H.B.   Uncle Tom's Cabin, The Minis-
   ter's Wooing, Oldtown Folks.*   (K.K.
   Sklar, ed)
   D.A.N. Jones, 362:4Apr85-26
Stowe, W.W.   Balzac, James, and the Realis-
   tic Novel.*
   M. Danahy, 446(NCFS):Summer-Fall184-214
   M.J. Friedman, 454:Fall184-92
   S. Perosa, 395(MFS):Summer84-295
   J.C. Rowe, 445(NCF):Fall184-223
   A.R. Tintner, 594:Fall184-326
Strachan, W.J.   Henry Moore: Animals.*
   R. Berthoud, 39:Feb84-144
Strachey, B.   Remarkable Relations.
   S. Rudikoff, 31(ASch):Spring84-274
Strachey, B.   The Strachey Line.
   N. Annan, 362:21Nov85-26
Strachey, B. and J. Samuels - see Berenson,
   M.
Strachey, J. and A.   Bloomsbury/Freud.
   (P. Meisel and W. Kendrick, eds)
   P. Stansky, 441:29Dec85-14
Strack, F.   Im Schatten der Neugier.
   D.P. Haase, 221(GQ):Fall184-659
   R. Immerwahr, 564:Nov84-304
Strahan, L.   Just City and the Mirrors.
   J. Brett, 381:Sep84-423
   N. McLachlan, 617(TLS):25Jan85-88
Straight, M.   After Long Silence.*
   P. Hollander, 473(PR):1/1984-146
Strand, M.   Art of the Real.
   J. Sturman, 55:Mar84-40
Strand, M.   Mr. and Mrs. Baby.
   W. Lesser, 441:17Mar85-16
Strangeup, H.   The Road to Lagoa Santa.
   G. Kearns, 249(HudR):Winter84/85-616
Strasser, S.   Jenseits des Bürgerlichen.
   R. Maurer, 489(PJGG):Band91Heft1-212
Strathern, G.M., comp.   Alberta, 1954-1979.
   D.W. McLeod, 470:Vol22-122
Stratton, A.   Nurse Jane Goes to Hawaii.
   R. Plant, 102(CanL):Summer84-155
Stratmann, K. - see Shakespeare, W.
Straub, P.   Wild Animals.
   J. Eidus, 441:24Mar85-15
Strauss, B.   Tumult.*   Der junge Mann.
   R. Ockenden, 617(TLS):22Feb85-210

Strauss, D.   Die erotische Dichtung von
   Robert Burns.
   T. Crawford, 571(ScLJ):Autumn84-1
Strauss, L.   Studies in Platonic Political
   Philosophy.
   M.F. Burnyeat, 453(NYRB):30May85-30
   R.M., 185:Apr85-779
Stravinsky, I.   Stravinsky: Selected Cor-
   respondence.*   (Vol 1) (R. Craft, ed)
   R. Holloway, 607:Mar84-40
Stravinsky, I.   Stravinsky: Selected Cor-
   respondence.*   (Vol 2) (R. Craft, ed)
   A. Fitzlyon, 364:Dec84/Jan85-143
   S. Karlinsky, 617(TLS):5Jul85-740
Stravinsky, I.   Stravinsky: Selected Cor-
   respondence.   (Vol 3) (R. Craft, ed)
   L. Botstein, 441:22Sep85-18
Strawson, J.   A History of the SAS Regiment.
   T. Geraghty, 617(TLS):29Mar85-363
Strawson, P.F.   Skepticism and Naturalism.
   W.V. Quine, 453(NYRB):14Feb85-32
   B. Stroud, 617(TLS):14Jun85-664
Streatfield, D.C. and A.M. Duckworth.
   Landscape in the Gardens and the Litera-
   ture of Eighteenth-Century England.
   J.D. Hunt, 402(MLR):Jul84-669
   A. London, 541(RES):Feb84-89
Street, J.S.   French Sacred Drama from
   Bèze to Corneille.
   G. Jondorf, 208(FS):Jul84-334
Strehler, G.   Un théâtre pour la vie.   (S.
   Kessler, ed)
   G. Banu, 98:Aug/Sep84-671
Strelka, J.   Stefan Zweig.*
   D.G. Daviau, 564:May84-148
Strelka, J.P.   Exilliteratur.
   R. Koester, 680(ZDP):Band103Heft4-630
Stribling, T.S.   Laughing Stock.   (R.K.
   Cross and J.T. McMillan, eds)
   E.J. Piacentino, 585(SoQ):Fall184-87
   J.B. Wittenberg, 395(MFS):Winter84-796
Strick, P.   Great Movie Actresses.
   J.L. Mankiewicz, 441:8Dec85-17
Der Stricker.   Daniel von dem Blühenden
   Tal.   (M. Resler, ed)
   T.E. Hart, 133:Band17Heft1/2-124
   S.L. Wailes, 301(JEGP):Jul84-406
Der Stricker - see under Rudolf von Ems
Stricker, R.   Robert Schumann.
   J. Chissell, 617(TLS):6Sep85-971
Strickland, G.   Structuralism or Criticism?
   R.L. Bogue, 478:Oct84-301
Strickler, S., ed.   John Frederick Kensett.
   B.J. Wolf, 617(TLS):22Nov85-1316
Strieder, P.   Dürer.*
   J.M. Massing, 90:Dec84-788
Strindberg, A.   By the Open Sea.*   (M.
   Sandbach, trans)
   A.M. Davidon, 441:17Nov85-30
Strindberg, A.   Plays from the Cynical
   Life.   (W. Johnson, trans)
   C.S. McKnight, 563(SS):Spring84-195
Strindberg, A.   Strindberg: Five Plays.*
   (H.G. Carlson, trans)
   A-C.H. Harvey, 615(TJ):Dec84-553
Stringer, K., ed.   Essays on the Nobility
   of Medieval Scotland.
   A.A.M. Duncan, 617(TLS):27Dec85-1489
Strittmatter, E.   Der Laden.
   H. Kaufmann, 601(SuF):Mar-Apr84-411
Strobl, A.   Gustav Klimt: Die Zeichnungen.
   (Vols 1 and 2)
   P. Vergo, 90:Nov84-710

Strobl, A. Gustav Klimt: Die Zeichnungen. (Vol 3)
P. Vergo, 617(TLS):22Mar85-320
Strohm, R. Essays on Handel and Italian Opera.
W. Dean, 453(NYRB):19Dec85-44
Ströker, E., ed. Lebenswelt und Wissenschaft in der Philosophie Edmund Husserls.
E. Agazzi, 687:Apr-Jun84-341
Strong, J. Elsewhere.
A. Hoffman, 441:29Sep85-46
Strong, R. Art and Power.
D. Norbrook, 617(TLS):19Apr85-425
Strong, R. Pre-Requiem for a Clown.
M. Harmon, 272(IUR):Spring84-126
Strong, R. Strong Points.
B. Mooney, 362:21Nov85-35
Strong, S.R. History of American Ceramics.
E.P. Denker, 658:Winter84-289
Stroop, J. Nederlands dialectonderzoek.
C. Hamans, 204(FdL):Sep84-238
Stroud, B. The Significance of Philosophical Scepticism.
C. McGinn, 617(TLS):22Feb85-192
Stroud, D. Sir John Soane, Architect.*
D. Linstrum, 324:Mar85-305
D. Watkin, 39:Jul84-78
Stroup, T. Westermarck's Ethics.
C. Wellman, 319:Apr85-269
Strouse, J. Alice James.
R. Thorberg, 396(ModA):Spring/Summer84-280
Strum, P. Louis D. Brandeis.
S.R. Letwin, 617(TLS):5Apr85-373
P.L. Merkel, 639(VQR):Autumn84-734
Struve, N. Ossip Mandelstam.*
L. Fleishman, 550(RusR):Jul84-289
D. Myers, 575(SEER):Apr84-267
Stryk, L., ed. World of the Buddha.
J.P. McDermott, 318(JAOS):Oct-Dec83-812
Strzeminski, W. and K. Kobro. L'espace uniste.
Y-A. Bois, 98:Jan-Feb84-70
Stubblebine, J.H. Dugento Paintings.
F. Russell, 39:May84-389
Stubbs, J. Tobacco on the Periphery.
V. Bulmer-Thomas, 617(TLS):2Aug85-847
Stubbs, M. Discourse Analysis.
R. Wodak, 350:Jun85-493
Stüben, P.E. Die Struktur und Funktion transzendentaler Argumentationsfiguren.
N. Hruby, 489(PJGG):Band91Heft1-206
Stüdel, D.H. Arno Schmidt "Zettels Traum."
T.S. Hansen, 221(GQ):Spring84-336
"Studi di cultura francese ed europea in onore di Lorenza Maranini."
H. Peyre, 207(FR):Feb85-442
"Studi di lessicografia italiana." (Vol 1)
E. Radtke, 553(RLiR):Jan-Jun84-201
"Studi di Letteratura Francese." (Vol 6)
M.R. Ansalone, 475:Vol 11No20-288
"Studies in Athenian Architecture, Sculpture, and Topography Presented to Homer A. Thompson."
H. Fracchia, 487:Winter84-392
Stueck, W.W. The Road to Confrontation.
R. Bothwell, 106:Spring84-99
Stuip, R.E.V., ed. Langue et littérature françaises du moyen-âge.
M.C. Ducey, 545(RPh):Aug83-119

de Stúñiga, L. Lope de Stúñiga: Poesías.* (J. Battesti-Pelegrin, ed)
M. Ciceri, 547(RF):Band96Heft1/2-207
Sturges, R. and others. Jules Breton and the French Rural Tradition.*
G. Pollock, 59:Sep84-359
Sturgess, R.W., ed. The Great Age of Industry in the North East.
A.J. Heesom, 161(DUJ):Dec83-122
Sturluson, S. - see under Snorri Sturluson
Sturm, J. Morpho-syntaktische Untersuchungen zur "phrase négative" im gesprochenen Französische.
F.J. Hausmann, 547(RF):Band96Heft3-302
Stürmer, M., ed. Die Weimarer Republik.
D. Barnouw, 221(GQ):Winter84-119
Sturrock, J., ed. Structuralism and Since.*
J. Rutherford, 447(N&Q):Apr83-182
Stussi, A. Studi e documenti di storia della lingua e dei dialetti italiani.
C. Marazzini, 228(GSLI):Vol 161fasc515-466
Stutman, S. - see Wolfe, T. and A. Bernstein
Styan, J.L. Modern Drama in Theory and Practice.* (Vols 1-3)
N. Grene, 447(N&Q):Oct83-477
A.P. Hinchliffe, 148:Winter84-85
S.F. Parham, 152(UDQ):Spring85-154
Styan, J.L. Max Reinhardt.*
R. Berry, 570(SQ):Autumn84-374
A. Vivis, 157:No153-50
Stylianou, A. and J.A. The Painted Churches of Cyprus.
C. Mango, 617(TLS):4Oct85-1108
Suarez, F. De legibus, IV. (A. García y García and others, eds and trans)
J-L. Gardies, 542:Jan-Mar84-76
Suarez, F. Suarez on Individuation.*
(J.J.E. Gracia, ed and trans)
A. Kenny, 382(MAE):1984/2-341
Suárez, J.A. The Mesoamerican Indian Languages.*
W.F. Hanks, 353:Vol21No5-741
Suárez Galbán, E. Balada de la guerra hermosa.
M.A. Robatto, 701(SinN):Jul-Sep84-144
Suarez-Richard, F. Un Encuentro con Latinoamerica.
J.F. Ford, 399(MLJ):Summer84-195
Suchting, W.A. Marx.
639(VQR):Spring84-52
Suckiel, E.K. The Pragmatic Philosophy of William James.*
B. Kuklick, 53(AGP):Band66Heft3-334
Sugano, K. Das Rombild des Hieronymus.
E.D. Hunt, 123:Vol34No2-323
Sugiyama, J. Classic Buddhist Sculpture: The Tempyō Period.
D.F. McCallum, 407(MN):Summer84-183
Sukenick, R. In Form.
T. Tanner, 441:22Sep85-26
Suknaski, A. The Land They Gave Away.
A. Amprimoz, 526:Winter84-92
Suknaski, A. Montage for an Interstellar Cry.
M.T. Lane, 198:Winter84-96
J. Orange, 102(CanL):Autumn84-112
S.S., 376:Feb84-140
Sulaiman, K.A. Palestine and Modern Arab Poetry.
M. Booth, 617(TLS):12Jul85-771

Suleiman, E.N., ed. Bureaucrats and
Policy Making.
D. Wass, 617(TLS):26Jul85-817
Suleiman, S.R. Authoritarian Fictions.*
E. van Alphen, 204(FdL):Jun84-158
D.S. Goodrich, 454:Winter85-173
A.W. Halsall, 494:Vol5No4-874
J.O. Lowrie, 207(FR):Apr85-719
T.E. Morgan, 223:Fall84-318
L. Waldeland, 599:Spring84-225
H.H. Watts, 395(MFS):Summer84-420
Sullivan, A., ed. British Literary Maga-
zines: The Augustan Age and the Age of
Johnson, 1698-1788.
B. Katz, 87(BB):Jun84-108
566:Autumn84-66
Sullivan, A., ed. British Literary Maga-
zines: The Romantic Age, 1789-1836.
B. Katz, 87(BB):Jun84-108
D.E. Latané, Jr., 577(SHR):Fall84-355
Sullivan, A.T. Thomas-Robert Bugeaud,
France and Algeria, 1784-1849.*
L.H. Gann, 396(ModA):Spring/Summer84-
282
Sullivan, E.D.S., ed. The Utopian Vision.
G.F. Waller, 529(QQ):Autumn84-717
Sullivan, E.W. 2d - see Donne, J.
Sullivan, F. Mrs. Demming and the Myth-
ical Beast.
N. Ramsey, 441:17Nov85-30
Sullivan, H.W. Calderón in the German
Lands and the Low Countries.*
F. Meregalli, 52:Band19Heft3-298
H.T. Oostendorp, 610:Autumn84-261
Sullivan, J.P. Literature and Politics in
the Age of Nero.
T.P. Wiseman, 617(TLS):5Jul85-755
Sullivan, M. Chinese Landscape Painting
in the Sui and T'ang Dynasties.
P.W. Kroll, 318(JAOS):Oct-Dec83-798
Sullivan, R., ed. Stories by Canadian
Women.
S. Erlichman, 99:Mar85-38
Sullivan, R.E. John Toland and the Deist
Controversy.
C.J. Betts, 83:Spring84-138
Sullivan, S. - see Purcell, V.W.W.S.
Sullivan, S.A. The Dutch Camepiece.
M. Russell, 617(TLS):19Apr85-446
Sullivan, W. Landprints.
T. Vale, 441:6Jan85-22
Sullivan, W.H. Obbligato 1939-1979.*
A. Watson, 617(TLS):31May85-611
Sultana, D., ed. New Approaches to Cole-
ridge.
L.M. Findlay, 447(N&Q):Feb83-87
G. Little, 541(RES):Feb84-95
Sulzberger, C.L. Such a Peace.
A.A. Offner, 550(RusR):Jul84-300
Sumerkin, A. and V. Schweitzer - see
Tsvetaeva, M.
Summerfield, G. Fantasy and Reason.
P. Rogers, 617(TLS):8Mar85-270
Summers, A. Gamble for Power.
K. Tsokhas, 381:Jun84-266
Summers, A. Goddess.
L. Duguid, 617(TLS):22Nov85-1338
Summers, C.J. E.M. Forster.
J.S. Herz, 177(ELT):Vol27No3-246
K.C. Odom, 594:Winter84-467
R.J. Voorhees, 395(MFS):Summer84-367

Summers, C.J. and T-L. Pebworth, eds.
Classic and Cavalier.
D.L. Peterson, 551(RenQ):Summer84-313
Summers, C.J. and T-L. Pebworth, eds.
"Too Rich to Clothe the Sunne."
S. Gottlieb, 541(RES):May84-227
Summers, M. Calling Home.*
H. Barratt, 198:Spring84-116
Summers, M.W. Railroads, Reconstruction,
and the Gospel of Prosperity.
639(VQR):Autumn84-115
Summers, R.S. Lon L. Fuller.
K.I. Winston, 185:Apr85-751
Summerscale, P. The East European Predica-
ment.
H. Hanak, 575(SEER):Apr84-312
Summerson, J., D. Watkin and G-T. Molling-
hoff. John Soane.*
P.D. du Prey, 576:May84-181
Summerson, R. Dishonourable Intentions.
S. Altinel, 617(TLS):12Jul85-776
Sumner, L.W. Abortion and Moral Theory.*
R. Wertheimer, 482(PhR):Jan84-97
Sun Chang, K-I. The Evolution of Chinese
Tz'u Poetry.
J.R. Allen, 318(JAOS):Oct-Dec83-801
J.M. Hargett, 116:Jul83-114
Sund, R. Ish River.*
J.W. Clark, 649(WAL):Nov84-240
Sundberg, B. Sanningen, myterna och
intressenas spel.*
T. Geddes, 562(Scan):Nov84-185
Sundquist, E.J., ed. American Realism.*
S.K. Culver, 284:Fall84-63
A. Kaplan, 676(YR):Autumn84-126
H.H. Kolb, Jr., 27(AL):Mar84-111
P. O'Donnell, 223:Spring83-99
D. Pizer, 183(ESQ):Vol30No3-193
Sundquist, E.J. Faulkner.*
C.S. Brown, 569(SR):Summer84-474
J.T. Matthews, 27(AL):Mar84-122
D. Minter, 301(JEGP):Jul84-464
N. Schwartz, 141:Summer84-285
J.G. Watson, 395(MFS):Summer84-319
Suñer, M. Syntax and Semantics of Spanish
Presentational Sentence-Types.
F. Van Putte, 603:Vol8No3-439
Suomela-Härmä, E. Les Structures narra-
tives dans le "Roman de Renart."*
K. Busby, 547(RF):Band96Heft1/2-166
A. Lodge, 382(MAE):1984/1-141
Suozzo, A.G., Jr. The Comic Novels of
Charles Sorel.*
G. Verdier, 207(FR):Oct84-124
Super, R.H. Trollope in the Post Office.*
K. Gamerschlag, 72:Band221Heft1-187
A. Shelston, 447(N&Q):Aug83-360
Supple, J.J. Arms Versus Letters.
C. Clark, 617(TLS):2Aug85-860
"A Supplement to the Oxford English Dic-
tionary."* (Vol 3) (R.W. Burchfield, ed)
B. Cottle, 541(RES):Nov84-517
J.R. Gaskin, 569(SR):Winter84-114
K. Sørensen, 179(ES):Feb84-86
Surtees, V. - see Brown, F.M.
Surtz, R.E. and N. Weinerth, eds. Cre-
ation and Re-creation.
E.J. Neugaard, 238:May84-303
Susiluoto, I. The Origins and Develop-
ments of Systems Thinking in the Soviet
Union.
L. Graham, 550(RusR):Oct84-431
Susini, E. - see Schlegel, F.

355

Tacitus. P. Cornelivs Tacitvs, "Annales."
(Vol 1 and Vol 2, fasc 1-4) (H. Heubner,
ed)
   P. Flobert, 555:Vol58fasc2-326
Tadié, J-Y. Le Roman d'aventures.*
   P. Coustillas, 189(EA):Jul-Sep85-301
   J. Delabroy, 535(RHL):May/Jun84-474
   P.J. Whyte, 208(FS):Jan84-83
Taeschner, T. The Sun is Feminine.
   S. Gal, 350:Mar85-244
Taft, B. - see Robbins, C.
Taft, M. Blues Lyric Poetry.
   D. Evans, 292(JAF):Oct-Dec84-491
   D.D. Harrison, 91:Spring84-135
Taggart, J.M. Nahuat Myth and Social
Structure.
   J. Bierhorst, 292(JAF):Oct-Dec84-470
Tagliabue, J. The Great Day.
   J.F. Cotter, 249(HudR):Autumn84-501
Tagliacozzo, G., ed. Vico.
   M. Goretti, 276:Autumn84-253
Tagliacozzo, G., ed. Vico and Marx.
   M. Goretti, 276:Autumn84-254
   D.I., 185:Jul85-984
Taliacozzo, G. and D.P. Verene, eds. New
Vico Studies. (Vol 1)
   M. Goretti, 276:Autumn84-258
   S.R. Luft, 319:Jul85-429
Tagore, R. Selected Poems.
   M. Lago, 617(TLS):27Sep85-1054
   A. Robinson, 362:29Aug85-26
"The Tain." (T. Kinsella, trans)
   B. O'Donoghue, 617(TLS):1Nov85-1242
Takada, S. Fresh Green.
   404:Winter-Spring84-44
Takamiya, T. and D. Brewer, eds. Aspects
of Malory.*
   P. Gradon, 382(MAE):1984/2-322
   O.D. Macrae-Gibson, 541(RES):Aug84-359
   J. Ruud, 125:Fall83-93
Takayoshi, K. - see under Kido Takayoshi
Talashoma, H. Hopitutuwutsi/Hopi Tales.
(E. Malotki, ed)
   L. Simms, 649(WAL):Feb85-320
Talbert, R.J.A. The Senate of Imperial
Rome.
   F. Millar, 617(TLS):15Feb85-175
Talbot, A-M.M. Faith Healing in Late
Byzantium.
   B. Baldwin, 589:Jul84-702
Talbott, S. Deadly Gambit.*
   D. Blair, 129:Feb85-62
   M. Jay, 362:31Jan85-23
   P. Windsor, 617(TLS):17May85-557
Tallent, E. Museum Pieces.
   L. Erdrich, 441:7Apr85-10
   442(NY):8Apr85-128
Talmor, S. Glanvill.
   J.W. Yolton, 518:Apr84-103
Tálos, E. and W. Neugebauer, eds. "Austro-
faschismus."
   F.L. Carsten, 575(SEER):Oct84-616
Tamarkin, B. The New Gatsbys.
   N. Kristof, 441:28Jul85-19
Tambiah, S.J. The Buddhist Saints of the
Forest and the Cult of Amulets.
   R. Gombrich, 617(TLS):29Mar85-359
Tamer, Z. Tigers on the Tenth Day and
Other Stories.
   M. Beard, 441:22Sep85-22
Taminiaux, J. Naissance de la philosophie
hégélienne de l'Etat.
   H. Faes, 542:Oct-Dec84-485

Tammany, J.E. Henrick Ibsen's Theatre Aes-
thetic and Dramatic Art.
   J.E. Gates, 615(TJ):Dec82-554
Tanaka, R. The Shino Suite.
   A. Saijo, 649(WAL):Aug84-138
Tanaka, Y. and E. Hanson, eds and trans.
This Kind of Woman.
   V.V. Nakagawa, 293(JASt):Nov83-155
Tanase, V. L'Amour, l'amour, roman senti-
mental.
   P.L. Horn, 207(FR):Apr85-762
Tang, T.N., with D. Chanoff and D.V. Toai.
A Vietcong Memoir.
   R. Manning, 441:26May85-12
   A. Puddington, 129:Aug85-60
   R. Steel, 453(NYRB):30May85-11
Tanguy Baum, M. Der historische Roman im
Frankreich der Julimonarchie.
   T.M. Scheerer, 72:Band221Heft2-447
Tani, S. The Doomed Detective.
   J.A. Cannon, 395(MFS):Winter84-740
   D.I. Grossvogel, 276:Winter84-359
   295(JML):Nov84-390
Tanigawa Michio. Chūgoku shitaifu kaikyū
to chiiki shakai to no kankei ni tsuite
no sōgōteki kenkyu.
   J.A. Fogel, 244(HJAS):Jun84-225
Tanizaki, J. In Praise of Shadows.
   J. Kirkup, 617(TLS):29Mar85-360
Tanizaki, J. Naomi.
   B. Leithauser, 453(NYRB):21Nov85-23
   M. Miyoshi, 441:200ct85-12
   J. Updike, 442(NY):18Nov85-171
Tannen, D. Conversational Style.
   E. Chaika, 350:Dec85-912
Tannenbaum, L. Biblical Tradition in
Blake's Early Prophesies.
   S.C. Behrendt, 661(WC):Summer84-106
   G.P. Landow, 536:Vol6-21
   J.J. McGann, 88:Fall84-120
Tanner, C.L. Indian Baskets of the South-
west.
   L. Milazzo, 584(SWR):Winter84-88
Tanner, T. Thomas Pynchon.
   D. Seed, 447(N&Q):Aug83-381
Tanselle, G.T. - see Melville, H.
Taper, B. Balanchine. (3rd ed)
   J. Anderson, 441:14Apr85-27
   R. Craft, 453(NYRB):7Nov85-42
Tapping, G.C. Austin Clarke.
   P. Diskin, 447(N&Q):Dec83-559
   A.E. McGuinness, 677(YES):Vol 14-352
Tapply, W.G. The Dutch Blue Error.
   N. Callendar, 441:14Apr85-16
Tapply, W.G. Follow the Sharks.
   N. Callendar, 441:8Dec85-76
Tapscott, S. American Beauty.
   E.P. Bollier, 646:Winter84-30
   N. Schmitz, 472:Fall/Winter84-4
   L.M. Steinman, 659(ConL):Winter85-497
Tarán, L. Speusippus of Athens.*
   J.D.G. Evans, 303(JoHS):Vol 104-208
Taras, R. Ideology in a Socialist State.
   A. Nove, 617(TLS):18Jan85-60
Tarbuck, J. Tarbuck on Showbiz.
   H. Jacobson, 617(TLS):20Dec85-1453
Tarde, G. Les lois de l'imitation. (R.
Boudon, ed) Fragment d'histoire future.
(R. Trousson, ed)
   I. Joseph, 98:Jun/Jul84-548
Tardieu, J. Les Tours de Trébizonde.
   C. Dis, 450(NRF):Jun84-88

Taruskin, R. Opera and Drama in Russia as
Preached and Practiced in the 1860s.*
  R. Oldani, 309:Vol5No4-380
  R. Swift, 451:Fall84-164
Tashjian, T.H. - see Saroyan, W.
Tasso, T. Godfrey of Bulloigne.* (E.
Fairfax, trans; K.M. Lea and T.M. Gang,
eds)
  I. Rivers, 447(N&Q):Oct83-459
Tasso, T. Tasso's Dialogues. (C. Lord
and D.A. Trafton, eds and trans)
  J.H. Bryce, 278(IS):Vol39-136
Tatchell, P. Democratic Defence.
  P. Windsor, 617(TLS):17May85-557
Tate, G., ed. Black Women Writers at
Work.
  M. Fabre, 189(EA):Jul-Sep85-366
  R.B. Jones, Jr., 27(AL):May84-298
  L. Waldeland, 395(MFS):Summer84-301
Tate, D. The East German Novel.
  J.J. White, 617(TLS):22Feb85-210
Tate, J. Constant Defender.
  W. Logan, 491:Nov84-99
  W.H. Pritchard, 249(HudR):Summer84-334
  D. Revell, 219(GaR):Spring84-186
Tate, R.B., ed. Essays on Narrative Fic-
tion in the Iberian Peninsula in Honour
of Frank Pierce.
  B.W. Ife, 402(MLR):Jan84-211
Tatham, D. Abraham Tuthill.
  J.H. Braunlein, 440:Winter-Spring84-
119
Tatian. "Oratio ad Graecos" and Frag-
ments.* (M. Whittaker, ed and trans)
  N.G. Wilson, 123:Vol34No1-130
Tatlow, A. and T-W. Wong, eds. Brecht and
East Asian Theatre.
  G.W. Brandt, 610:Summer84-153
Tátrai, V. Mittelitalienische Cinque-
centogemälde.
  R. Kultzen, 471:Jan/Feb/Mar84-102
Tatschmurat, C. Arbeit und Identität.
  I. Dölling, 654(WB):3/1984-501
Tatum, C.M. Chicano Literature.
  D. Gerdes, 238:Mar84-154
Tauber, W. Der Wortschatz des Hans Sachs.
(Vol 2)
  F. Hartweg, 680(ZDP):Band103Heft3-473
Taubken, H. Niederdeutsch, Niederländisch,
Hochdeutsch.*
  G. Cornelissen, 680(ZDP):Band103Heft1-
151
Taubman, M. Gwen John.
  P. Greenham, 617(TLS):11Oct85-1141
Taubman, W. Stalin's American Policy.
  W.O. McCagg, Jr., 104(CASS):Fall84-321
Tauli, V. Standard Estonian Grammar.
(Pt 2)
  B. Comrie, 353:Vol22No2-246
Tavernier, J. Naïma fille des dieux.
  M. Naudin, 207(FR):Apr85-763
Taviani, F. and M. Schino. Il segretto
della commedia dell'arte.
  G. Banu, 98:Aug/Sep84-671
Tawa, N. A Sound of Strangers.
  P. Dickinson, 415:Jan84-28
Taylor, A. Laurence Oliphant, 1829-1888.
  R. Adelson, 637(VS):Spring84-392
Taylor, A. Our Fathers' Lies.
  T.J. Binyon, 617(TLS):29Nov85-1353
  M. Laski, 362:18Jul85-29
Taylor, A.J.P. How Wars End.
  J. Erickson, 617(TLS):19Jul85-803

Taylor, A.J.P. An Old Man's Diary.*
  R.J. Margolis, 441:30Jun85-21
Taylor, A.J.P. A Personal History.*
  639(VQR):Winter84-10
Taylor, A.J.P. The Trouble Makers.
  617(TLS):7Jun85-651
Taylor, A.R. Male Novelists and Their
Female Voices.
  P. Boumelha, 541(RES):Aug84-422
  J. Harris, 402(MLR):Jul84-670
Taylor, B. Eve and the New Jerusalem.
  J. Parr, 99:Aug/Sep84-43
Taylor, C. Philosophical Papers.
  R. Rorty, 617(TLS):6Dec85-1379
Taylor, C. Radical Tories.*
  W. Cragg, 154:Dec84-704
Taylor, C. Village and Farmstead.
  F.L. Cheyette, 589:Oct84-956
Taylor, E. The Devastating Boys. Palla-
dian. The Wedding Group.
  P. Craig, 617(TLS):29Nov85-1372
Taylor, F. Walking Shadows.
  R. Smith, 441:3Mar85-22
  442(NY):1Apr85-112
Taylor, G. Le parler quechua d'Olto, Ama-
zonas (Pérou). Diccionario normalizado
y comparativo quechua: Chachapoyas-Lamas.
  G.D. Bills, 269(IJAL):Jan84-118
Taylor, G., ed. Plays by Samuel Foote and
Arthur Murphy.
  J. Hérou, 189(EA):Jul-Sep85-334
Taylor, G. - see Shakespeare, W.
Taylor, G. - see under Wells, S.
Taylor, G.D. The New Deal and American
Indian Tribalism.
  B.M. Smith, 106:Summer84-185
Taylor, G.O. Chapters of Experience.
  L. Simon, 219(GaR):Spring84-184
Taylor, I. Tarantara! Tarantara!
  T.G. Dunn, 615(TJ):Dec84-551
Taylor, I. - see Gilbert, W.S. and A.S.
Sullivan
Taylor, J., ed. Notebooks/Memoirs/
Archives.*
  M.M. Rowe, 395(MFS):Summer84-377
  R. Rubenstein, 538(RAL):Fall84-478
Taylor, J. Shadows of the Rising Sun.
  Fujiwara Sakuya, 285(JapQ):Oct-Dec84-
457
  M. Sayle, 453(NYRB):28Mar85-33
Taylor, J. Themes in Biogeography.
  W. George, 617(TLS):1Mar85-242
Taylor, J.R. Alec Guinness.*
  G. Playfair, 157:No153-49
Taylor, J.R. Strangers in Paradise.
  S.J. Whitfield, 385(MQR):Fall85-634
  295(JML):Nov84-339
Taylor, L. and I. Maar. The American Cow-
boy.
  J.W. Clark, 649(WAL):Aug84-154
  L. Milazzo, 584(SWR):Winter84-88
Taylor, M.C. Erring.
  J.M. Perl, 617(TLS):25Oct85-1214
Taylor, M.C. Journeys to Selfhood.
  G.J. Stack, 543:Sep83-150
  M. Westphal, 125:Summer84-415
Taylor, P. The Old Forest.
  A. Mars-Jones, 617(TLS):23Aug85-923
  J. Rae, 362:1Aug85-29
  R. Towers, 441:17Feb85-1
Taylor, P. Popular Music Since 1955.
  G. Brown, 617(TLS):26Apr85-476

Taylor, R. Beyond Art.
E. Wright, 494:Vol4No1-141
Taylor, R., Jr. Fiddle and Bow.
L. Walburn, 441:22Sep85-22
Taylor, R. Having Love Affairs.
J.F.M. Hunter, 154:Jun84-370
Taylor, R. Understanding the Elements of
Literature.
A. Rodway, 447(N&Q):Oct83-480
Taylor, R.H. The Neglected Hardy.*
S. Gatrell, 541(RES):Nov84-572
D. Kramer, 637(VS):Spring84-393
Taylor, R.J., G.J. Lint and C. Walker -
see Adams, J.
Taylor, T.J. Linguistic Theory and Struc-
tural Stylistics.*
J. Thorne, 541(RES):May84-215
Taylor, W. Faulkner's Search for a South.*
C.S. Brown, 569(SR):Summer84-474
H.H. McAlexander, 27(AL):May84-291
N. Polk, 536:Vol6-1
T. Schaub, 301(JEGP):Apr84-253
J.G. Watson, 395(MFS):Summer84-319
Taylor-Gooby, P. Public Opinion, Ideology
and State Welfare.
R. Klein, 617(TLS):16Aug85-899
Taylour, W.D., E.B. French and K.A. Wardle.
Well Built Mycenae.
O.T.P.K. Dickinson, 303(JoHS):Vol 104-
249
S. Hood, 123:Vol134No1-145
Tchaikovsky, P.I. Guide to Practical Har-
mony.
P. Standford, 415:Sep84-503
Tebbel, J. and S.M. Watts. The Press and
the Presidency.
H. Brogan, 441:13Oct85-27
Tec, N. When Light Pierced the Darkness.
T.G. Ash, 453(NYRB):19Dec85-26
Tedeschi, R. - see Gide, A. and D. Bussy
Tedlock, D. - see "Popol Vuh"
Teed, C.A., H.C. Raley and J.B. Barber.
Conversational Spanish for the Medical
and Health Professions.*
R. Hoff, 238:May84-317
Tegethoff, W. Mies van der Rohe: The
Villas and Country Houses.* (German
title: Mies van der Rohe: Die Villen
und Landhausprojekte.)
A.L. Huxtable, 441:1Dec85-1
R. Pommer, 576:Mar84-88
Tehan, A.B. Henry Adams in Love.
R.F. Sommer, 27(AL):Dec84-605
Teitelbaum, M.S. and J.M. Winter. The
Fear of Population Decline.
P. Gupte, 441:8Dec85-50
Teleky, R., ed. The Oxford Book of French-
Canadian Short Stories.*
F. Cogswell, 529(QQ):Winter84-1010
Tellegen-Couperus, O.E. Testamentary
Succession in the Constitutions of
Diocletian.
B.W. Frier, 123:Vol34No2-234
Tellgren, C. På barnens bokmarknad.
I. Broch, 172(Edda):1984/1-53
Tello, F.J.L. - see under León Tello, F.J.
Teloh, H. The Development of Plato's Meta-
physics.*
G. Fine, 482(PhR):Jan84-143
J.W. Forrester, 449:Sep84-521
P.M. Huby, 393(Mind):Jan84-129

Temperley, N., ed. The Athlone History of
Music in Britain.* (Vol 5)
P. Dickinson, 607:Mar84-42
R. Swift, 451:Fall84-164
W. Weber, 637(VS):Autumn83-133
Temperley, N. and C.G. Manns. Fuging
Tunes in the Eighteenth Century.
R.M. Wilson, 415:Oct84-599
Tempesti, A.F. - see under Forlani Tem-
pesti, A.
Temporini, H. and W. Haase. Aufstieg und
Niedergang der römischen Welt. (Pt 2,
Vol 30, fasc 1)
D.P. Fowler, 123:Vol34No1-45
Ten, C.L. Mill on Liberty.*
P. Carrive, 192(EP):Jan-Mar84-124
"Les Tendances Nouvelles." (J. Fineberg,
ed)
J. Lloyd, 90:Apr84-242
Tennant, E. Black Marina.
P. Kemp, 617(TLS):21Jun85-689
K.C. O'Brien, 362:11Jul85-32
Tennant, E. The Half-Mother.
R. Billington, 441:12May85-14
442(NY):20May85-126
Tennant, E. Woman Beware Woman.*
P. Craig, 617(TLS):25Jan85-102
Tennyson, A. Idylls of the King.* (J.M.
Gray, ed)
W.D. Shaw, 627(UTQ):Summer84-431
Tennyson, A. In Memoriam. (S. Shatto and
M. Shaw, eds)
W.E. Fredeman, 354:Sep84-306
J. Korg, 536:Vol6-75
E.D. Mackerness, 447(N&Q):Dec83-547
E.F. Shannon, Jr., 405(MP):Nov84-214
Tennyson, A. The Letters of Alfred Lord
Tennyson.* (Vol 1) (C.Y. Lang and E.F.
Shannon, Jr., eds)
E. Block, Jr., 577(SHR):Winter84-80
S. Shatto, 447(N&Q):Dec83-545
Tennyson, G.B. - see Carlyle, T.
Tennyson, H. The Haunted Mind.*
J.R.B., 148:Winter84-94
P. Dickinson, 364:Apr/May84-143
Teodorsson, S-T. Anaxagoras' Theory of
Matter.*
D. Babut, 542:Jul-Sep84-386
P. Louis, 555:Vol58fasc1-112
M. Schofield, 123:Vol34No1-52
D. Sider, 121(CJ):Oct-Nov84-71
Teodorsson, S-T. The Phonology of Attic
in the Hellenistic Period.
H. Schmoll, 260(IF):Band89-354
von Tepl, J. Der Ackermann aus Böhmen.
(M.O. Walshe, ed)
W. Schröder, 684(ZDA):Band113Heft4-174
de Terán, L.S. The Tiger.*
L. Graeber, 441:13Oct85-24
P. Lewis, 364:Oct84-93
Terhune, A.M. and A.B. - see Fitz Gerald,
E.
Terkel, S. The Good War.*
M. Hastings, 617(TLS):29Mar85-363
Terracini, B. Linguistica al bivio.
(G.L. Beccaria and M.L. Porzio Gernia,
eds)
P. Beninca, 545(RPh):Feb84-337
Terraine, J. The Right of the Line.
M. Carver, 617(TLS):17May85-555
J. Grigg, 362:16May85-25
Terras, V. F.M. Dostoevsky.
P. Debreczeny, 268(IFR):Winter85-61

Thesing, W.B. The London Muse.*
 E. Auerbach, 651(WHR):Spring84-82
 J. Beaty, 579(SAQ):Winter84-120
 J-P. Hulin, 189(EA):Jan-Mar85-89
 L. Poston, 637(VS):Autumn83-114
 M. Timko, 588(SSL):Vol 19-281
Thesleff, H. Studies in Platonic Chronol-
 ogy.*
 P. Louis, 555:Vol58fasc1-119
Theunissen, M. Sein und Schein.
 M. Greene, 543:Dec83-426
Thevet, A. Les Singularités de la France
 antarctique.*
 R. Zuber, 535(RHL):Jul/Aug84-590
Thibaudeau, C. The Martha Landscapes.
 J. Seim, 99:Feb85-40
Thieberger, R. Gedanken über Dichter und
 Dichtungen. (A. Faure, Y. Flesch and A.
 Nivelle, eds)
 A. Drijard, 564:Feb84-69
van Thiel, H. Iliaden und Ilias.*
 M.M. Willcock, 303(JoHS):Vol 104-188
van Thiel, P.J.J. and C.J. de Bruyn Kops.
 The Dutch Picture Frame in the Seven-
 teenth Century.
 E. Schrijver, 39:Sep84-218
Thiel, U. Lockes Theorie der personalen
 Identität.
 N. Jolley, 518:Oct84-203
Thiele, J. Wortbildung der französischen
 Gegenwartssprache.
 M. Perl, 682(ZPSK):Band37Heft1-121
Thiem, C. Disegni di Artisti Bolognesi
 dal Seicento all'Ottocento.
 J.B. Shaw, 90:Jul84-445
Thierry, A. - see d'Aubigné, A.
Thiher, A. Words in Reflection.
 D. Hayman, 454:Spring85-270
Thinès, G. Les Vacances de Rocroi.
 M. Malone, 207(FR):Oct84-164
wa Thiong'o, N. Devil on the Cross.
 C. Nwankwo, 459:Vol8No2/3-190
Thirlwall, J. - see Williams, W.C.
Thirsk, J., ed. The Agrarian History of
 England and Wales. (Vol 5, Pts 1 and 2)
 M. Havinden, 617(TLS):27Dec85-1490
Thody, P. Roland Barthes.
 295(JML):Nov84-405
Thody, P. and H. Evans, with G. Rees.
 Faux Amis and Key Words.
 G. Craig, 617(TLS):26Apr85-475
 H. Wackett, 362:28Mar85-26
Thom, G.B. The Human Nature of Social Dis-
 content.
 R.S.D., 185:Jul85-973
Thom, R. Paraboles et catastrophes, Entre-
 tiens sur les mathématiques, la science
 et la philosophie.
 J. Largeault, 542:Jan-Mar84-122
Thomas, A.G. and J.A. Brigham. Lawrence
 Durrell.
 A. Rota, 78(BC):Autumn84-379
Thomas, B. Astaire.*
 D. Powell, 617(TLS):21Jun85-686
Thomas, B. James Joyce's "Ulysses."*
 B. Benstock, 454:Winter85-182
 W. Harmon, 569(SR):Summer84-466
 R.D. Newman, 577(SHR):Summer84-280
Thomas, B.P. and H.M. Hyman. Stanton.
 O.D. Edwards, 176:Jan85-34
Thomas, C. and J. Lennox. William Arthur
 Deacon.*
 C. MacMillan, 178:Dec84-498

Thomas, D. The Day the Sun Rose Twice.
 M. Laski, 362:18Jul85-29
Thomas, D. The Experience of Handicap.
 J.E. Burton, 529(QQ):Spring84-189
Thomas, D. Naturalism and Social Science.*
 M. Martin, 488:Jun84-265
Thomas, D. Dylan Thomas: The Collected
 Letters. (P. Ferris, ed)
 P. Kemp, 362:5Dec85-28
Thomas, D.A. Dickens and the Short Story.*
 M. Cotsell, 155:Summer84-117
 J. Kucich, 577(SHR):Summer84-266
Thomas, D.M. Swallow.*
 P-L. Adams, 61:Jan85-100
Thomas, E. Edward Thomas on the Country-
 side. (R. Gant, ed) A Language Not to
 be Betrayed. (E. Longley, ed) Edward
 Thomas: Selected Poems and Prose. (D.
 Wright, ed)
 W. Cooke, 565:Winter83/84-57
Thomas, G. Mr. Speaker.
 H. Wilson, 362:28Feb85-22
Thomas, H. Le Migrateur.*
 M. Alhau, 450(NRF):Feb84-90
Thomas, J.D. The Epistrategos in Ptole-
 maic and Roman Egypt. (Pt 2)
 R. Coles, 123:Vol34No1-93
Thomas, J.L. Alternative America.*
 J. Higham, 639(VQR):Summer84-507
Thomas, J.R., comp. Biographical Diction-
 ary of Latin American Historians and His-
 toriography.
 A. Macias, 263(RIB):Vol34No3/4-433
Thomas, J.W. The Best Novellas of Medie-
 val Germany.
 J. Schultz, 222(GR):Summer84-116
Thomas, K. Man and the Natural World.*
 R.C. Richardson, 366:Autumn84-267
 J.P. Sisk, 31(ASch):Summer84-416
Thomas, L. Late Night Thoughts on Listen-
 ing to Mahler's Ninth Symphony.*
 J. Parini, 249(HudR):Spring84-173
 42(AR):Summer84-384
 639(VQR):Spring84-63
Thomas, L., ed. 200 Years of Australian
 Painting.
 U. Hoff, 39:Nov84-361
Thomas, L. - see Kozloff, M.
Thomas, M. One of These Fine Days.
 W. Cooke, 565:Winter83/84-57
Thomas, M.M. Hard Money.
 P. Erdman, 441:7Jul85-9
Thomas, N. The Narrative Works of Günter
 Grass.
 S. Abbott, 221(GQ):Fall84-683
 M.S. Fries, 395(MFS):Summer84-387
Thomas, R. Athletenstatuetten der Spätar-
 chaik und des strengen Stils.
 A-M. Adam, 555:Vol58fasc2-347
Thomas, R. Briarpatch.*
 N. Callendar, 441:3Mar85-35
 R. Kaplan, 129:May85-64
 M. Laski, 362:18Jul85-29
Thomas, R.F. Lands and Peoples in Roman
 Poetry.
 H.B. Evans, 121(CJ):Feb-Mar85-265
 N. Horsfall, 123:Vol34No1-133
 J. Perret, 555:Vol58fasc1-143
Thomas, R.G. Edward Thomas.
 R. Wells, 617(TLS):4Oct85-1090
Thomas, R.H. Nietzsche in German Politics
 and Society, 1890-1918.*
 D.F. Krell, 323:Oct84-321

Thomas, S., comp. Indexes to Fiction in "Time" (1879-91), "Murray's Magazine" (1887-91) and "The Quarto" (1896-98).
J. Shattock, 402(MLR):Jul84-682
Thomas Aquinas - see under Aquinas, T.
Thompson, B. Franz Grillparzer.*
R.C. Cowen, 406:Winter84-462
I.F. Roe, 402(MLR):Jan84-236
Thompson, B. and C.A. Viggiani, eds. Witnessing André Malraux.
E.S. Apter, 546(RR):Mar84-268
Thompson, C.W. Le Jeu de l'ordre et de la liberté dans "La Chartreuse de Parme."
G.C. Jones, 67:Nov84-249
F. Landry, 535(RHL):Mar/Apr84-291
G. May, 207(FR):Feb85-455
P. Park, 446(NCFS):Winter85-155
G. Strickland, 208(FS):Jul84-350
Thompson, D. Creachhadh na Clàrsaich (Plundering the Harp).
R. Pybus, 565:Winter83/84-68
Thompson, D. Cesare Pavese.*
M. Caesar, 402(MLR):Jan84-208
Thompson, D. Poems 1950-1974.
J. Mole, 176:Feb85-50
Thompson, D. Raphael.*
P. Joannides, 278(IS):Vol39-109
T. Puttfarken, 59:Dec84-504
Thompson, D.W., ed. Performance of Literature in Historical Perspectives.
V.C. Brann, 615(TJ):Mar84-130
Thompson, E.A. Saint Germanus of Auxerre and the End of Roman Britain.
C. Thomas, 617(TLS):25Jan85-97
Thompson, E.P. The Heavy Dancers.
R.W. Johnson, 617(TLS):29Mar85-364
Thompson, F.H., ed. Studies in Medieval Sculpture.
P. Williamson, 90:Jan84-42
I. Wood, 59:Jun84-253
Thompson, G.A., Jr. Key Sources in Comparative and World Literature.
W.P. Friederich, 678(YCGL):No33-98
Thompson, G.J. Verbal Judo.
S.H. Elgin, 350:Jun85-507
Thompson, G.R. - see Poe, E.A.
Thompson, H. Only So Far.
A. Brooks, 102(CanL):Autumn84-115
Thompson, I.E. Being and Meaning.
C.O. Schrag, 323:Jan84-98
Thompson, J. No Picnic.
J. Strawson, 617(TLS):17May85-556
Thompson, J. Orwell's London.
T.G. Ash, 617(TLS):8Feb85-147
Thompson, J. Pop. 1280. The Getaway. A Hell of a Woman. The Killer Inside Me.
L. Sante, 453(NYRB):28Mar85-18
Thompson, J. The Woman Driver.
L. Grierson, 441:7Jul85-17
Thompson, J.B. and D. Held - see Habermas, J.
Thompson, L. Stig Dagerman: "Nattens lekar." (2nd ed)
D.M. Mennie, 562(Scan):Nov84-196
Thompson, L. The Political Mythology of Apartheid.
V. Crapanzano, 441:15Dec85-7
A. Ryan, 617(TLS):13Dec85-1419
D. Tutu, 453(NYRB):26Sep85-3
Thompson, M. Alexander's Drachm Mints. (Vol 1)
J.H. Oakley, 124:Nov-Dec84-138

Thompson, N.W. The People's Science.
G. Himmelfarb, 617(TLS):28Jun85-726
Thompson, P.M. The Shen Tzu Fragments.
W.A. Rickett, 318(JAOS):Apr-Jun83-460
Thompson, P.V. and D.J. - see Swift, J.
Thompson, R.F. Flash of the Spirit.*
D.J. Crowley, 2(AfrA):May84-17
Thompson, R.F. Painting from a Single Heart.
M. Adams, 2(AfrA):Feb84-80
Thompson, R.H. Gordon R. Dickson.
G.K. Wolfe, 561(SFS):Mar84-95
Thompson, S. Close-Ups.*
C. Brookhouse, 110:Fall84-85
W. Koon, 573(SSF):Fall84-405
639(VQR):Summer84-97
Thompson, T. - see Lower, L.
Thomsen, M-L. The Sumerian Language.
J. Hayes, 350:Dec85-925
Thomson, D. Renaissance Paris.
J. Frew, 324:Oct85-797
H. Zerner, 441:26May85-17
Thomson, D. Suspects.
P. Lopate, 441:30Jun85-11
A. Sarris, 18:Jul/Aug85-52
N. Shack, 617(TLS):7Jun85-644
Thomson, D.C. Jean Lesage and the Quiet Revolution.
E. Dumas, 99:Dec84-31
Thomson, J. The Seasons.* (J. Sambrook, ed)
D. Fairer, 447(N&Q):Feb83-83
M. Smith, 541(RES):May84-239
Thomson, P. Shakespeare's Theatre.*
W. Habicht, 156(JDSh):Jahrbuch1984-254
R. Proudfoot, 611(TN):Vol38No3-149
A. Vivis, 157:No154-50
Thomson, R. Seurat.
J. Russell, 441:8Dec85-12
Thomson, R.M. Manuscripts from St. Albans Abbey, 1066-1235.*
R.W. Pfaff, 589:Apr84-445
Thomson, V. A Virgil Thomson Reader.
R. French, 451:Summer84-64
Thông, H.S. - see under Huỳnh Sanh Thông
Thonis, E. The English-Spanish Connection.
J.V. Tinajero, 399(MLJ):Autumn84-280
Thoreau, H.D. Cape Cod. (photos by W.F. Robinson)
W.L. Heat-Moon, 441:8Dec85-16
Thoreau, H.D. Journal.* (Vol 1) (J.C. Broderick and others, eds)
R. Du Pree, 577(SHR):Winter84-93
Thoreau, H.D. The Writings of Henry D. Thoreau. (Vol 1: Journal, 1837-1844.) (E.H. Witherell and others, eds)
Q. Anderson, 536:Vol5-17
Thoreau, H.D. The Writings of Henry D. Thoreau. (Vol 2: Journal, 1842-1848) (R. Sattelmeyer, ed)
H. Cohen, 617(TLS):14Jun85-661
Thornbrough, G. - see Fletcher, C.
Thorne, B., C. Kramarae and N. Henley, eds. Language, Gender, and Society.
R. King, 320(CJL):Spring84-81
Thorne, C. The Issue of War.
P. Kennedy, 617(TLS):9Aug85-870
Thornhill, R. and J. Alcock. The Evolution of Insect Mating Systems.
T. Halliday, 617(TLS):18Jan85-69
Thorniey, R. Attempts to Join Society.
J. Mellors, 364:Mar85-100
G. Strawson, 617(TLS):29Mar85-340

Thornton, P. Authentic Decor.*
J.M. Crook, 617(TLS):10May85-519
Thornton, R.K.R. The Decadent Dilemma.
K. Beckson, 177(ELT):Vol27No2-161
Thornton, R.K.R. - see Clare, J.
Thorold, A., comp. A Catalogue of the Oil
Paintings of Lucien Pissarro.
F. Fitzgerald, 39:Feb84-148
Thorp, J. Free Will.*
A. Flew, 488:Dec84-585
Thorpe, J.D. John Milton.
R. Flannagan, 391:Mar84-32
T. Wheeler, 569(SR):Spring84-304
639(VQR):Autumn84-120
Thorslev, P., Jr. Romantic Contraries.
V. Nemoianu, 400(MLN):Dec84-1230
Thorson, J.L. - see Smollett, T.
Thráinsson, H. On Complementation in
Icelandic.
J.T. Faarlund, 452(NJL):Vol7No1-63
Thrale, H. Dr. Johnson by Mrs. Thrale.
(R. Ingrams, ed)
442(NY):30Dec85-80
Threatte, L. The Grammar of Attic Inscrip-
tions. (Vol 1)
J.H.W. Penney, 123:Vol34No1-71
Thrower, N.J.W., ed. Sir Francis Drake
and the Famous Voyage, 1577-1580.
N. Canny, 617(TLS):8Mar85-251
Thubron, C. A Cruel Madness.*
J. Wheatcroft, 441:10Nov85-16
442(NY):7Oct85-140
Thubron, C. Where Nights Are Longest.*
R. Dinnage, 453(NYRB):13Jun85-29
Thulstrup, N. Commentary on Kierkegaard's
"Concluding Unscientific Postscript."
P. Gardiner, 617(TLS):12Apr85-417
Thulstrup, N. Kierkegaard's Relation to
Hegel.*
M. Westphal, 125:Summer84-415
Thum, B. Aufbruch und Verweigerung.*
V. Schupp, 224(GRM):Band34Heft1/2-223
Thun, H. Probleme der Phraseologie.
K.E.M. George, 208(FS):Jul84-374
Thurin, E.I. Emerson as Priest of Pan.
R.A. Yoder, 591(SIR):Summer84-268
Thurley, G. The Turbulent Dream.
295(JML):Nov84-529
Thurley, J. The Burning Lake.
M. Couto, 617(TLS):12Jul85-777
Thurm, M. Floating.*
639(VQR):Summer84-98
Thurman, J. Isak Dinesen.*
G. Garrett, 569(SR):Summer84-495
Thurow, L.C., ed. The Management Chal-
lenge.
M. Sayle, 453(NYRB):28Mar85-33
Thurow, L.C. The Zero-Sum Solution.
C. Johnson, 61:Dec85-106
L. Silk, 441:20Oct85-44
Thurston, E.T. The Flower of Gloster.
H. Carpenter, 617(TLS):16Aug85-909
Thwaite, A. Edmund Gosse.*
J. Malcolm, 453(NYRB):14Mar85-7
N. Miller, 42(AR):Fall84-503
F. Wood, 364:Aug/Sep84-159
Thwaite, A. Poems 1953-1983.*
N. Corcoran, 493:Jun84-64
H. Lomas, 364:Jun84-84
Tibble, A. - see Clare, J.
Tibble, A. and R.K.R. Thornton - see
Clare, J.

Tibble, J.W. and A. John Clare. (rev)
G. Crossan, 591(SIR):Winter84-581
Tibiletti, G. Le lettere private nei
papiri greci del III e IV secolo d.C.
A. Cameron, 303(JoHS):Vol 104-244
Tichane, R. Ching-te-chen.
N.V. Robinson, 60:Nov-Dec84-125
Tichy, S. The Hands in Exile.*
L. Gregerson, 491:Oct84-43
639(VQR):Winter84-24
Tick, E. On Sacred Mountain.
404:Autumn84-59
Tidcombe, M. The Bookbindings of T.J.
Cobden-Sanderson.*
G. Warr, 250(HLQ):Autumn84-317
Tidholm, H. The Dialect of Egton in North
Yorkshire.*
W. Viereck, 38:Band102Heft1/2-169
Tiedemann, R. - see Benjamin, W.
Tiefenbrun, S.W. Signs of the Hidden.
H.G. Hall, 208(FS):Jul84-340
A. Jefferson, 447(N&Q):Apr83-181
Tien, H.Y., ed. Population Theory in
China.
Wong Siu Lun, 302:Vol20No2-221
Tierney, B. Religion, Law, and the Growth
of Constitutional Thought, 1150-1650.*
C.J. Nederman, 539:May85-147
Tierney, N. William Walton.
M. Kennedy, 617(TLS):15Mar85-291
Tiersky, R. Ordinary Stalinism.
M. McAuley, 617(TLS):4Oct85-1104
Tigerstedt, E.N. Interpreting Plato.
C. Griswold, 543:Sep83-151
Tigg, E.R. The Dutch "Elckerlijc" is
Prior to the English "Everyman."
A.C. Cawley, 541(RES):Aug84-434
Tilby, M. Gide: "Les Faux-monnayeurs."*
A. Goulet, 535(RHL):May/Jun84-468
A.E. Pilkington, 208(FS):Jul84-364
Tiles, J.E. Things that Happen.*
E. Hirsch, 482(PhR):Jan84-126
C. MacDonald, 393(Mind):Apr84-308
Tilghman, B.R. But is it Art?
D. Carrier, 617(TLS):11Jan85-30
Till, N. Rossini.
J. Methuen-Campbell, 415:Apr84-211
Tillis, M., with W. Wager. Stutterin' Boy.
M. Kirby, 441:19May85-31
Tillotson, K. - see Dickens, C.
Timko, M., F. Kaplan and E. Guiliano - see
"Dickens Studies Annual"
Timm, U. Der Mann auf dem Hochrad.
J. Neves, 617(TLS):22Feb85-210
Timmermann, W. Studien zur allegorischen
Bildlichkeit in den Parobolae Bernhards
von Clairvaux.
D.A. Wells, 402(MLR):Apr84-396
von Timroth, W. Russische und sowjetische
Soziolinguistik und tabuisierte Varietä-
ten des Russischen (Argot, Jargons,
Slang, Mat).
F.E. Knowles, 575(SEER):Oct84-577
Tindall, G. Rosamond Lehmann.
P. Craig, 617(TLS):15Feb85-162
M. Walters, 176:Jul/Aug85-44
Ting Pang-Hsin. Chinese Phonology of the
Wei-Chin Period.
G.W. Roy, 318(JAOS):Apr-Jun83-463
Tinniswood, P. You Should See Us Now.
D. Devlin, 157:No153-46
Tinsley, J.B. He Was Singin this Song.
J. Rosenberg, 187:Fall85-509

Tipton, D. Wars of the Roses.
   L. Mackinnon, 617(TLS):23Aug85-933
Tiptree, J., Jr. Brightness Falls From
   the Air.
   G. Jonas, 441:16Jun85-18
Tirman, J., ed. The Fallacy of Star Wars.
   S. Zuckerman, 441:20Jan85-6
Tischler, H. The Earliest Motets (to
   circa 1270).*
   S. Fuller, 414(MusQ)Summer84-404
   D. Hiley, 415:Jan84-49
Tischler, J. Hethitisch-deutsches Wörter-
   verzeichnis.
   E. Neu, 260(IF):Band89-301
Tischler, J. Das hethitische Gebet der
   Gassulijawija.
   H. Otten, 260(IF):Band89-298
Tischler, S. Footballers and Businessmen.
   B.D. Culverwell, 637(VS):Autumn83-129
Tismar, J. Das deutsche Kunstmärchen des
   zwanzigsten Jahrhunderts.*
   J.M. McGlathery, 301(JEGP):Jan84-98
Tison-Braun, M. L'introuvable origine.*
   H. Merkl, 72:Band221Heft1-215
   A.E. Pilkington, 208(FS):Apr84-240
Tissier, A., ed. La Farce en France de
   1450 à 1550. (2nd Ser, Vol 1)
   C. Mazouer, 535(RHL):Jan/Feb84-96
Tissoni Benvenuti, A. and M.P. Mussini
   Sacchi, eds. Teatro del Quattrocento.
   B. Guthmüller, 547(RF):Band96Heft4-486
Titley, E.B. Church, State and the Con-
   trol of Schooling in Ireland 1900-1944.
   J. Coolahan, 272(IUR):Autumn84-299
Titley, N.M. Persian Miniature Painting.*
   J.W. Allan, 90:Dec84-791
   B. Gray, 39:Apr84-302
Toba, S. Khaling. (2nd ed)
   B. Comrie, 350:Sep85-722
Tobin, D.N. The Presence of the Past.
   J.S., 636(VP):Winter84-458
Tobin, J.J.M. Shakespeare's Favourite
   Novel.
   G. Taylor, 617(TLS):16Aug85-905
Tobin, P.D. Time and the Novel.
   M. Spencer, 494:Vol5No1-182
Tobler, S.J. The Grammar of Karipúna
   Creole.
   C. Corne, 350:Mar85-233
Tobriner, S. The Genesis of Noto, an
   Eighteenth-Century Sicilian City.
   M.L. Berkvam, 173(ECS):Spring85-444
   K. Downes, 90:Jun84-360
Toby, R.P. State and Diplomacy in Early
   Modern Japan.
   J.W. Hall, 407(MN):Winter84-459
de Tocqueville, A. Alexis de Tocqueville:
   Selected Letters on Politics and Society.
   (R. Boesche, ed)
   A. Boyer, 441:9Jun85-23
   F. Furet, 453(NYRB):27Jun85-23
Todd, C. Voltaire: "Dictionnaire philoso-
   phique."*
   J.H. Brumfitt, 208(FS):Jul84-342
Todd, E. L'enfance du monde.
   J-F.R., 176:Feb85-31
Todd, J., ed. Jane Austen.
   J.L. Epstein, 141:Fall84-387
   P.M. Spacks, 219(GaR):Fall84-621
Todd, J., ed. A Dictionary of British and
   American Women Writers 1660-1800.
   B. Brophy, 617(TLS):26Jul85-814

Todd, J., ed. Women Writers Talking.
   C. Wright, 219(GaR):Fall84-639
Todd, J.M. Women's Friendship in Litera-
   ture.*
   V. Mylne, 208(FS):Jan84-68
   R.C. Rosbottom, 131(CL):Spring84-183
Todd, L. Modern Englishes.
   R.B. Le Page, 617(TLS):8Feb85-155
Todd, R.L. Mendelssohn's Musical Educa-
   tion.
   W. Drabkin, 415:Mar84-153
   J. Hollander, 410(M&L):Jul84-288
Todd, S., ed. Women and Theatre.
   C. Ludlow, 364:Apr/May84-142
da Todi, J. - see under Jacopone da Todi
Todorov, T. Mikhail Bakhtin.
   G.S. Morson, 441:10Feb85-32
   D.B. Polan, 494:Vol4No1-145
Todorov, T. The Conquest of America.*
   (French title: La Conquête de l'Amér-
   ique.)
   R. González-Echevarría, 676(YR):
   Winter85-281
Todorov, T. Critique de la critique.
   J. Sturrock, 617(TLS):4Jan85-16
Todorov, T. The Fantastic.
   A.L. Smith, 183(ESQ):Vol30No4-260
Todorov, T. Introduction to Poetics.*
   M. Robertson, 462(OL):Vol139No3-284
Todorov, T. Theories of the Symbol.*
   (French title: Théories du symbole.)
   J. Fletcher, 366:Spring84-112
   R.E. Innis, 543:Dec83-429
Toellner, R., ed. Aufklärung und Humanis-
   mus.
   H.B. Nisbet, 83:Spring84-144
Toësca, G. Itinéraires et lieux communs.
   J.B. Davis, 207(FR):Feb85-474
Toft, G. Die bäuerliche Struktur der
   deutschen Volksgruppe in Nordschleswig.
   L.H. Eriksen, 684(ZDA):Band113Heft4-
   183
Togawa, M. The Master Key.
   T.J. Binyon, 617(TLS):11Jan85-42
Tokmakoff, G. P.A. Stolypin and the Third
   Duma.
   R.T. Fisher, Jr., 550(RusR):Oct84-429
Tokson, E.H. The Popular Image of the
   Black Man in English Drama, 1550-1688.*
   L.A. Johnson, 538(RAL):Fall84-455
Toland, J. Gods of War.
   W. Schott, 441:21Apr85-22
Toland, J. Infamy.*
   A.H. Ion, 529(QQ):Summer84-442
Toliver, H. The Past That Poets Make.*
   J. Chandler, 405(MP):Aug84-117
Tolkien, J.R.R. The Book of Lost Tales.*
   (Pts 1 and 2) (C. Tolkien, ed)
   S. Medcalf, 617(TLS):19Jul85-802
Tolkien, J.R.R. The Old English "Exodus."*
   (J. Turville-Petre, ed)
   P.J. Lucas, 447(N&Q):Jun83-243
Toll, R.C. The Entertainment Machine.
   B. McArthur, 615(TJ):Oct84-437
Tolles, B.F., Jr., with C.K. Tolles.
   Architecture in Salem.
   R. Urquhart, 432(NEQ):Sep84-444
Tolstoy, N. The Quest for Merlin.
   J. Bayley, 362:2May85-23
   C. Thomas, 617(TLS):5Apr85-387
   442(NY):29Jul85-78
Tolstoy, N. The Tolstoys.
   639(VQR):Spring84-50

Tolstoy, S.   The Diaries of Sofia Tolstoy.
P. Beer, 362:26Sep85-28
Tomalin, M.   The Fortunes of the Warrior
Heroine in Italian Literature.*
A. Caesar, 402(MLR):Oct84-950
Tomasson, R.F.   Iceland.
J. Logue, 563(SS):Winter84-70
Tomberlin, J., ed.   Agent, Language, and
the Structure of the World.
F.F., 185:Jul85-980
Tomiak, J.J., ed.   Soviet Education in the
1980s.
V. Mallinson, 575(SEER):Oct84-626
Tomizza, F.   Il male viene dal nord.
G. Reid, 617(TLS):29Nov85-1373
Tomlinson, C.   Notes from New York and
Other Poems.*
H. Lomas, 364:Aug/Sep84-141
W.H. Pritchard, 249(HudR):Summer84-339
Tomlinson, C., ed.   The Oxford Book of
Verse in English Translation.
D.S. Carne-Ross, 473(PR):1/1984-151
Tomlinson, C.   Translations.*
D. McDuff, 565:Summer84-68
W.H. Pritchard, 249(HudR):Summer84-339
Tomlinson, P.   Jean Mairet et ses protec-
teurs.
J-P. Dens, 210(FrF):Sep84-369
Tomlinson, R.   La Fête galante — Watteau
et Marivaux.*
C. Miething, 72:Band221Heft1-206
Tomlonson, J.S.   Mennonite Quilts and
Pieces.
M. Kilkenny, 614:Summer85-29
Tomory, W.M.   Frank O'Connor.
C. Kearney, 447(N&Q):Apr83-177
G. O'Brien, 677(YES):Vol 14-358
Tompkins, J.   Sensational Designs.
J. Fryer, 357:Fall85-77
Tonelli, F.   Sophocles' Oedipus and the
Tale of the Theatre.
J.M. Walton, 610:Autumn84-264
Tong, X. - see under Xiao Tong
Toohey, R.E.   Liberty and Empire.
D.O. Thomas, 83:Spring84-93
Tooley, M.   Abortion and Infanticide.
P.E. Devine, 483:Oct84-545
E.J., 185:Jan85-382
Toomer, G.J. - see Ptolemy
Toop, D.   The Rap Attack.
G.M., 62:May85-4
van den Toorn, P.C.   The Music of Igor
Stravinsky.*
E. Antokoletz, 317:Summer84-428
A. Pople, 410(M&L):Jan84-56
J. Straus, 308:Spring84-129
R. Swift, 451:Fall84-164
639(VQR):Winter84-28
Topolski, D.   Boat Race.
I. Thomson, 617(TLS):15Nov85-1303
Topor, T.   Coda.
N. Callendar, 441:17Mar85-39
Toporov, V.N.   Akhmatova i Blok.
J. Graffy, 575(SEER):Apr84-266
Topp, C.   Philosophie als Wissenschaft.
J.W. Burbidge, 543:Dec83-431
Tordoff, W.   Government and Politics in
Africa.
R. Robinson, 617(TLS):16Aug85-895
Torelli, M. and others.   Le délit relig-
ieux dans la cité antique.
J. Linderski, 122:Apr84-174

Torgovnick, M.   Closure in the Novel.*
D.A. Miller, 223:Winter81-527
Torkar, R.   Eine altenglische Übersetzung
von Alcuins "De Virtutibus et Vitiis,"
Kap. 20 (Liebermanns Judex).
E.G. Stanley, 38:Band102Heft1/2-199
Torni, B.   Opuscoli filosofici e medici.
(M. Messina Montelli, ed)
N.G. Siraisi, 551(RenQ):Spring84-59
Törnqvist, N.   Das niederdeutsche und
niederländische Lehngut im schwedischen
Wortschatz.
D. Stellmacher, 685(ZDL):2/1984-266
de Torquemada, A.   Jardín de flores curi-
osas.   (G. Allegra, ed)
M.L. Cozad, 304(JHP):Spring84-243
B.M. Damiani, 240(HR):Summer84-399
della Torre, P.F.   Viva Britannia.
P. Cairncross, 617(TLS):40ct85-1083
Torres, J.L.R. - see under Romero Torres,
J.L.
Torres Quintero, R., ed.   Bello en Colom-
bia, estudio y selección.   (2nd ed)
O.T. Myers, 545(RPh):May84-528
Torretti, R.   Relativity and Geometry.
M. Friedman, 449:Nov84-653
Torrey, E.F.   The Roots of Treason.*
T.C.D. Eaves, 27(AL):Oct84-447
L. Menand, 676(YR):Autumn84-119
M. Palmer, 703:No10-159
C.F. Terrell, 468:Spring84-149
295(JML):Nov84-494
Torrey, E.F.   Surviving Schizophrenia.
M.V. Seeman, 529(QQ):Winter84-1039
Tortelier, P. and D. Blum.   Paul Tortelier:
Self Portrait.
R. Anderson, 415:Aug84-446
Tosches, N.   Unsung Heroes of Rock 'n'
Roll.
G. Marcus, 62:Dec84-75
Tosh, J.   The Pursuit of History.
A. Briggs, 176:Jan85-51
Tostevin, L.L.   Color of Her Speech.
M. Fee, 102(CanL):Summer84-98
Tostevin, L.L.   Gyno-Text.
J. Fitzgerald, 102(CanL):Autumn84-154
Toth, K.   Der Lehnwortschatz der althoch-
deutschen Tatian-Übersetzung.
J. Splett, 680(ZDP):Band103Heft1-128
Toth, S.A.   Blooming.
P.M. Paton, 271:Fall84-191
Tougas, G.   Destin Littéraire du Québec.*
E.F. Nardocchio, 102(CanL):Autumn84-94
Toulouse, G.   Le Mercenaire.
M. Naudin, 207(FR):Apr85-763
de Toulouse-Lautrec, H. and W.H.B. Sands.
The Henri de Toulouse-Lautrec — W.H.B.
Sands Correspondence.   (H.D. Schimmel
and P.D. Cate, eds)
639(VQR):Spring84-54
Touraine, A. and others.   Solidarity.
J. Woodall, 575(SEER):Oct84-630
Tournon, A.   Montaigne.
A. Compagnon, 208(FS):Oct84-452
F. Gray, 551(RenQ):Summer84-294
Toussaint, H.   La Liberté guidant le
peuple de Delacroix.
P.J., 90:Apr84-243
Tout, K.   Tank!
K. Jeffery, 617(TLS):17May85-555
Tovar Martín, V.   El Real Pósito de la
Villa de Madrid.
A. Bustamante García, 48:Jul-Sep84-332

Trenton, P. and P.H. Hassrick. The Rocky Mountains.*
R. Tyler, 658:Winter84-307
"Tres dramaturgos rioplatenses."
C. Kaiser-Lenoir, 352(LATR):Fall84-138
Trescases, P. Le Franglais vingt ans après.
P. Pupier, 320(CJL):Fall84-216
Tresmontant, C. Le Christ hébreu.
B. Dubourg, 98:Mar84-248
"Trésor de la langue française." (Vols 9 and 10) (B. Quemada, ed)
V. Väänänen, 439(NM):1984/2-254
Treue, W. Wirtschafts- und Technikgeschichte Preussens.
H-U. Wehler, 384:Jul84-572
Trevelyan, R. A Hermit Disclosed.
617(TLS):27Sep85-1071
Treverton, G.F. Making the Alliance Work.
J. Luxmoore, 617(TLS):29Nov85-1345
Trevor, M. Japan's Reluctant Multinationals.
Angegawa Tomofumi, 285(JapQ):Jan-Mar84-93
Trevor, W. Fools of Fortune.*
M. Gorra, 249(HudR):Spring84-158
639(VQR):Spring84-55
Trevor, W. The Stories of William Trevor.
M. Gorra, 249(HudR):Spring84-158
639(VQR):Spring84-56
Trevor-Roper, H. Renaissance Essays.
R. Briggs, 617(TLS):22Nov85-1321
J. Grigg, 362:22Aug85-27
Trévou, C. Les Dames de la poste.
B.T. Cooper, 207(FR):May85-929
Triadú, J. La novel·la catalana de postguerra.
A. Yates, 86(BHS):Apr84-210
Tribble, E. - see Smith, L.P.
Tribe, L.H. Constitutional Choices.
P.J. Mishkin, 441:18Aug85-7
Tribe, L.H. God Save This Honorable Court.
D. Margolick, 441:10Nov85-29
Tributsch, H. How Life Learned to Live.
J.R. Nursall, 529(QQ):Summer84-437
Trier, J. Wege der Etymologie. (H. Schwarz, ed)
E.S. Dick, 133:Band17Heft1/2-112
Trifonov, Y. The House on the Embankment.* Another Life.*
F. Eberstadt, 129:Jul85-37
G. Hosking, 617(TLS):6Dec85-1386
J. Updike, 442(NY):15Apr85-110
Trifonov, Y. The Long Goodbye.
F. Eberstadt, 129:Jul85-37
Trifonov, Y. The Old Man.
F. Eberstadt, 129:Jul85-38
H. Robinson, 441:3Feb85-18
Trigano, S. La République et les juifs.
A.D. Ketchum, 207(FR):Oct84-172
Trillin, C. With All Disrespect.
A. Buchwald, 441:14Apr85-10
442(NY):15Jul85-86
Tripathi, D. The Dynamics of a Tradition.
H. Spodek, 293(JASt):Aug84-791
Triphiodorus. La prise d'Ilion.* (B. Gerlaud, ed and trans) Ilii excidium.* (H. Livrea, ed)
M. Campbell, 303(JoHS):Vol 104-220
Tristan, F. La Cendre et la foudre.
C. Le Goff, 207(FR):Apr85-764
"Tristán e Iseo." (A. Yllera, trans)
J. Cantera, 202(FMod):No68/70-371

Tritton, P. John Montagu of Beaulieu.
T.C. Barker, 617(TLS):20Dec85-1452
Trocard, C. Aspects de l'allégorie dans les arts et la poésie.
P. Wagner, 189(EA):Jan-Mar85-83
Trocki, C.A. Prince of Pirates.
C. Wake, 302:Vol20No2-241
Trocmé, H. Les Américains et leur architecture.
R.A. Benson, 576:May84-177
Trofimenkoff, S.M. Stanley Knowles.
G. Woodcock, 102(CanL):Winter83-81
"Troisième supplément au répertoire toponymique du Québec."
A. Lapierre, 424:Sep84-329
Trolli, D. - see Malatesti, M.
Trollope, A. The Complete Short Stories.* (Vol 5) (B.J. Breyer, ed)
C.D.C., 636(VP):Spring84-92
Trollope, A. The Letters of Anthony Trollope.* (N.J. Hall, ed)
J.R. Kincaid, 445(NCF):Sep84-217
N. Miller, 42(AR):Summer84-379
Trollope, F. Domestic Manners of the Americans.
G.J. Forgue, 189(EA):Jul-Sep85-365
Trombley, S. "All That Summer She Was Mad."*
D. Hirst, 541(RES):Nov84-579
H. Richter, 594:Spring84-133
E. Slater, 447(N&Q):Aug83-373
Tromly, A. The Cover of the Mask.*
G. Kelly, 178:Dec84-488
Trommelen, M.T.G. The Syllable in Dutch.
H. van der Hulst, 204(FdL):Sep84-233
Tromp, H., ed. Nueva narrativa neerlandesa.
E. Bernárdez, 202(FMod):No68/70-400
Tronchetti, C. Ceramica attica a figure nere.
N.H. Ramage, 124:Jul-Aug85-612
Trotter, D. The Making of the Reader.*
295(JML):Nov84-394
Trouillard, J. La Mystagogie de Proclos.*
C. Guérard, 542:Jul-Sep84-389
Trousdale, M. Shakespeare and the Rhetoricians.*
E.S. Donno, 551(RenQ):Summer84-304
C. Hoy, 569(SR):Spring84-256
Trousson, R. Balzac disciple et juge de Jean-Jacques Rousseau.
G. Jacques, 356(LR):Aug84-257
Trousson, R. Thèmes et mythes.*
M. Beller, 678(YCGL):No32-140
Trousson, R. - see Tarde, G.
Trow, G.W.S. The City in the Mist.*
J.L. Halio, 598(SoR):Winter85-204
Trow, M.J. The Supreme Adventure of Inspector Lestrade.
P-L. Adams, 61:Dec85-119
Troxell, H.A. The Coinage of the Lycian League.
B. Burrell, 124:Jan-Feb85-226
Troy, N.J. The de Stijl Environment.
S. Frank, 505:Feb84-162
G. van Hensbergen, 90:Jun84-367
Troyat, H. Ivan the Terrible.
639(VQR):Autumn84-124
Troyat, H. Tchekhov.
V.L. Smith, 617(TLS):11Jan85-43
de Troyes, C. - see under Chrétien de Troyes

Trudgill, P., ed. Language in the British Isles.
    F. Chevillet, 189(EA):Jul-Sep85-309
Trudgill, P. On Dialect.
    P. Gingiss, 351(LL):Dec84-115
    K.I. Sandred, 596(SL):Vol38No2-165
    B. Weltens, 179(ES):Dec84-582
    H.B. Woods, 320(CJL):Spring84-99
Trudgill, P. Sociolinguistics.
    P. Gingiss, 351(LL):Dec84-115
    S. Romaine, 353:Vol21No6-915
Trudgill, P. and J.K. Chambers. Dialectology.
    K.I. Sandred, 596(SL):Vol38No2-165
Trudgill, P. and J. Hannah. International English.*
    A. Dada, 355(JSoc):Jun84-270
    D. Nehls, 257(IRAL):Nov84-325
Trueblood, P.G., ed. Byron's Political and Cultural Influence in Nineteenth-Century Europe.*
    P.W. Martin, 339(KSMB):No35-97
Truhlar, R. Parisian Novels.
    J. Riddell, 137:Feb85-14
Tsagarakis, O. Form and Content in Homer.
    J.B. Hainsworth, 487:Spring84-89
    W.G. Thalmann, 124:Sep-Oct84-52
Tsaloumas, D. The Observatory. (P. Grundy, ed) The Book of Epigrams.
    P. Levi, 617(TLS):4Oct85-1117
Tschinkel, W. Wörterbuch der Gottscheer Mundart. (Vol 2)
    K. Rein, 685(ZDL):2/1984-259
Tschudi-Madsen, S. Henrik Bull.
    E. Sundler, 341:Vol53No1-41
Tschuppik, K. Von Franz Joseph zu Adolf Hitler.
    A. Obermayer, 564:Nov84-306
Tse, K.K. Marks and Spencer.
    F. Cairncross, 617(TLS):31May85-613
Tseng, H. - see under Hsiao Tseng
Tsereteli, K. Grammatik der modernen assyrischen Sprache (Neuostaramäisch).*
    P. Swiggers, 353:Vol21No4-645
Tsien Tsuen-hsuin. Science and Civilisation in China. (Vol 5, Pt 1) (J. Needham, ed)
    D. Helliwell, 617(TLS):1Nov85-1247
    A. Singer, 362:10Oct85-27
Tsitsishvili, D. and others. Rugs and Carpets from the Caucasus.
    J. Thompson, 617(TLS):17May85-563
Tsongas, P. Heading Home.
    B. Greene, 441:6Jan85-11
Tsuen-hsuin, T. - see under Tsien Tsuenhsuin
Tsuna, M. - see under Masuda Tsuna
Tsvetaeva, M. Stikhotvoreniya i poemy v pyati tomakh. (A. Sumerkin and V. Schweitzer, eds)
    H. Gifford, 617(TLS):11Oct85-1135
Tuan, Y-F. Dominance and Affection.
    P. Robinson, 441:10Feb85-35
Tucci, G. The Religions of Tibet.
    J.P. McDermott, 318(JAOS):Apr-Jun83-443
Tuccille, J. Trump.
    M. Sterne, 441:4Aug85-17
Tuchman, P. George Segal.
    J. Bell, 55:Apr84-29
Tucholsky, K. Briefe: Auswahl 1913-1955.
    F. Dieckmann, 384:Oct84-816

Tucholsky, K. Castle Gripsholm.
    D.J. Enright, 617(TLS):13Dec85-1433
Tucholsky, K. Kurt Tucholsky: Unser ungelebtes Leben. (F.J. Raddatz, ed)
    W.J. King, 402(MLR):Jul84-756
Tucker, F.H. The Frontier Spirit and Progress.
    B.H. Meldrum, 649(WAL):Nov84-251
Tucker, G.H. A Goodly Heritage.*
    J. Bayley, 453(NYRB):9May85-3
Tucker, H.F., Jr. Browning's Beginnings.
    C.D. Ryals, 402(MLR):Jan84-157
    A. Wordsworth, 541(RES):May84-254
Tucker, L. Stephen and Bloom at Life's Feast.
    R. Brown, 617(TLS):11Jan85-40
    R.M. Kain, 329(JJQ):Spring85-330
Tucker, P.H. Monet at Argenteuil.*
    H. Clayson, 54:Jun84-346
Tucker, R.W. The Nuclear Debate.
    F. Sauzey, 441:22Dec85-19
Tuckey, J.S. - see Twain, M.
Tuczay, C. Der Unhold ohne Seele.
    U. Ströbel-Dettmer, 196:Band25Heft1/2-160
Tudor, D. Popular Music.
    E. Southern, 91:Spring84-137
Tudor, D., N. Tudor and B. Struthers - see "Canadian Book Review Annual 1980"
Tufte, E.R. The Visual Display of Quantitative Information.
    T. Goss, 507:May/Jun84-110
Tugendhat, E. Traditional and Analytical Philosophy.*
    S. Crowell, 258:Mar84-95
    J. Llewelyn, 262:Mar84-149
Tugnoli Pattaro, S. Metodo e sistema delle scienze nel pensiero di Ulisse Aldrovandi.
    P.R. Blum, 687:Jan-Mar84-161
Tugwell, S. Ways of Imperfection.
    D. Crane, 617(TLS):8Mar85-267
Tulard, J. Napoleon.
    442(NY):28Jan85-99
Tully, J. A Discourse on Property.
    J. Barnouw, 543:Sep83-153
Tully, M. and S. Jacob. Amritsar.
    J. Grigg, 362:12Dec85-31
Tumarkin, N. Lenin Lives!*
    A. Kemp-Welch, 575(SEER):Oct84-635
    S.F. Starr, 550(RusR):Jul84-285
Tumins, V.A. and G. Vernadsky - see "Patriarch Nikon on Church and State"
Tung, F.H. - see under Fei Hsiao Tung
Tunstall, W.B. Disconnecting Parties.
    E. Berg, 441:24Feb85-23
Tuohy, F. The Collected Stories.*
    J. Cantor, 441:6Jan85-20
    P. Lewis, 364:Feb85-105
    J. Mellors, 362:24Jan85-29
Tuomela, R. Human Action and Its Explanation.
    D. Gustafson, 449:Mar84-112
Tuominen, A. The Bells of the Kremlin. (P. Neiskanen, ed)
    J.H. Hodgson, 550(RusR):Jan84-88
Turbayne, C.M., ed. Berkeley.*
    D. Berlioz-Letellier, 542:Oct-Dec84-483
    F.E. Tait, 518:Jan84-21
Turbett, P. Cut and Sew.
    S. Sherrer, 614:Summer85-22

Turcan, R-A. Mithra et le mithriacisme.
P.W. van der Horst, 394:Vol37fasc3/4-
460

Turcotte, D. La politique linguistique en
Afrique francophone.
A. Lipou, 355(LSoc):Sep84-426

Turcotte, E. Dans le delta de la nuit.
S. Lawall, 207(FR):Feb85-501

Turgenev, I.S. Letters.* (A.V. Knowles,
ed and trans)
R. Freeborn, 575(SEER):Oct84-633
C.A. Moser, 574(SEEJ):Summer84-260
639(VQR):Spring84-53

Turgenev, I.S. Letters. (D. Lowe, ed and
trans)
C.A. Moser, 574(SEEJ):Summer84-260

Turgeon, P. The First Person.
E. Dansereau, 526:Summer84-88

Turing, P. Hans Hotter.*
E. Forbes, 415:Sep84-503

Türk, D.G. School of Clavier Playing.*
H. Krebs, 308:Spring84-154

Turkle, S. The Second Self.*
J. Marsh, 129:Feb85-66

Turley, G.H. The Easter Offensive.
R. Caplan, 441:21Jul85-23

Turner, A. To Make a Poem.
D. Kirby, 128(CE):Mar84-248

Turner, B.I. Doderer and the Politics of
Marriage.
M. Bachem, 221(GQ):Fall84-678

Turner, B.S. The Body and Society.
R. Littlewood, 617(TLS):4Jan85-7

Turner, D.H. The Hastings Hours.
M. Camille, 59:Dec84-508
J.F. Cotter, 249(HudR):Summer84-297

Turner, F. The New World.
W. Logan, 441:27Oct85-14

Turner, F. Rediscovering America.
J. Tallmadge, 441:3Nov85-27

Turner, F.M. The Greek Heritage in Victor-
ian Britain.*
R.L. Brett, 541(RES):Aug84-398
P. Fontaney, 189(EA):Oct-Dec85-472
S. Monod, 549(RLC):Jul-Sep84-363

Turner, H.A., Jr. German Big Business and
the Rise of Hitler.
G.G. Field, 441:27Jan85-1
J. Joll, 453(NYRB):26Sep85-5
A. Milward, 617(TLS):5Jul85-744

Turner, H.A., Jr., ed. Hitler — Memoirs
of a Confidant.
A. Bullock, 453(NYRB):7Nov85-23
G.A. Craig, 441:25Aug85-10

Turner, J. Without God, Without Creed.
R. Nisbet, 441:28Apr85-16

Turner, K.J. Lyndon Johnson's Dual War.
J. Midgley, 441:30Jun85-10
C. Seymour-Ure, 617(TLS):13Dec85-1418

Turner, L.W. The Ninth State.
D.B. Cole, 656(WMQ):Apr84-325
F.C. Mevers, 432(NEQ):Jun84-290

Turner, M. and M. Geare. Gluttony, Pride
and Lust, and Other Sins from the World
of Books.
617(TLS):1Feb85-131

Turner, P., ed. American Images.
S.M. Halpern, 441:1Dec85-25

Turner, S. Secrecy and Democracy.
E.J. Epstein, 129:Oct85-53
T. Powers, 441:16Jun85-1
442(NY):29Jul85-77

Turner, S. and B. Skiöld. Handmade Paper
Today.
L.B. Schlosser, 517(PBSA):Vol78No3-371

Turner, S.P. Sociological Explanation as
Translation.
D. Dutton, 488:Dec84-581

Turner, T. The Diary of Thomas Turner
1754-1765.* (D. Vaisey, ed)
J. Barrell, 617(TLS):8Feb85-138

Turner, V., ed. Celebration.
E.A. Early, 650(WF):Oct84-265

Turner, W.C. - see Mason, C.

Turnock, D. The Historical Geography of
Scotland Since 1707.
C.W.J. Withers, 595(ScS):Vol27-71

Turville-Petre, J. - see Tolkien, J.R.R.

Tusell, J. Oligarquía y caciquismo en
Andalucía (1890-1923).
R. Carr, 617(TLS):4Oct85-1105

Tuska, J., ed. The American West in Fiction.
J.D. Nesbitt, 649(WAL):May84-59

Tuska, J. Dark Cinema.
M. Sidone, 590:Jun85-49

Tuska, J. and V. Piekarski, eds-in-chief.
Encyclopedia of Frontier and Western
Fiction.*
R.W. Etulain, 649(WAL):May84-54

Tuveson, E.L. The Avatars of Thrice Great
Hermes.*
M. Fixler, 591(SIR):Spring84-132
G. Gillespie, 345(KRQ):Vol31No4-451
J. Neubauer, 221(GQ):Summer84-479
G.S. Rousseau, 173(ECS):Winter84/85-
263

Tuwim, J. Ball at the Opera. (Polish
title: Bal w Operze.)
S. Barańczak, 574(SEEJ):Summer84-234

Twain, M. The Adventures of Huckleberry
Finn (Tom Sawyer's Companion): A
Facsimile of the Manuscript.* (L.J.
Budd, ed)
H. Beaver, 402(MLR):Oct84-915
H.N. Smith, 594:Summer84-241
70:Mar-Apr84-122

Twain, M. The Adventures of Tom Sawyer/A
Facsimile of the Author's Holograph Manu-
script.* (P. Baender, ed)
M.J. Fertig, 26(ALR):Spring84-133
H. Hill, 534(RALS):Autumn82-223

Twain, M. The Devil's Race-Track. (J.S.
Tuckey, ed)
S. Fender, 541(RES):May84-256

Twain, M. The Science Fiction of Mark
Twain. (D. Ketterer, ed)
T.A. Shippey, 617(TLS):1Feb85-111
T. Wortham, 445(NCF):Mar85-487

Twardowski, K. Zur Lehre vom Inhalt und
Gegenstand der Vorstellungen, Eine
psychologische Untersuchung.
J-L. Gardies, 542:Jan-Mar84-98

Tweedie, J. Jewels.
R. Robinson, 441:14Apr85-26

Twichell, C. Northern Spy.
R. McDowell, 364:Feb85-44

Twitchell, J.B. Dreadful Pleasures.
L. Rose, 441:1Dec85-16

Twitchell, J.B. The Living Dead.*
A.V.C. Schmidt, 447(N&Q):Jun83-274

Twitchell, J.B. Romantic Horizons.
W. Walling, 661(WC):Summer84-108

Twitchett, D. Printing and Publishing in Medieval China.*
  F. Wood, 354:Dec84-400
Twohig, D. - see Washington, G.
Twomey, A.C. Needles to the North.* (W.C. James, ed)
  B. Greenfield, 198:Spring84-101
Ty-Casper, L. Awaiting Trespass (A Pasión).
  C. Fein, 441:27Oct85-40
Tydeman, W., ed. Four Tudor Comedies.
  617(TLS):5Apr85-395
Tydeman, W. - see Robertson, T.
Tyler, A. The Accidental Tourist.
  P-L. Adams, 61:Oct85-106
  D. Johnson, 453(NYRB):7Nov85-15
  L. McMurtry, 441:8Sep85-1
  A. Mars-Jones, 617(TLS):4Oct85-1096
  J. Mellors, 362:7Nov85-28
  J. Updike, 442(NY):28Oct85-106
Tyler, R., ed. Alfred Jacob Miller.
  L. Milazzo, 584(SWR):Winter84-88
Tyler, R. Visions of America.*
  L. Milazzo, 584(SWR):Winter84-88
Tyler, R. and S.D. Elizondo. The Characters, Plots and Settings of Calderon's Comedias.
  J.M. Duarte, 552(REH):Jan84-159
Tyler, W.T. The Shadow Cabinet.*
  639(VQR):Summer84-96
Tymieniecka, A-T., ed. The Phenomenology of Man and the Human Condition.
  D. Moran, 323:Oct84-314
Tymieniecka, A-T., ed. The Philosophical Reflection of Man in Literature.*
  J.A. Varsava, 478:Apr84-131
Tymieniecka, A-T. - see Wojtyla, K.
Tyrrell, J., comp. Leoš Janáček: "Kát'a Kabanová."*
  M. Beckerman, 414(MusQ):Spring84-283
  J. Smaczny, 410(M&L):Jan84-68
Tyrrell, R.E., Jr. The Liberal Crack-Up.
  J.W. Bishop, Jr., 129:Feb85-69
  A. Weinstein, 441:3Feb85-27
Tyrrell, W.B. Amazons.*
  639(VQR):Autumn84-128
Tysdahl, B.J. William Godwin as Novelist.*
  N.H. Roe, 541(RES):May84-242
Tyson, B. The Story of Shaw's "Saint Joan."*
  C. Day, 272(IUR):Spring84-150
  M. Levin, 174(Éire):Summer84-154
  A. Saddlemyer, 178:Sep84-377
Tytler, G. Physiognomy in the European Novel.*
  D.K. Danow, 567:Vol50No1/2-157
  N. McWilliam, 59:Mar84-115
  E.J. Talbot, 149(CLS):Summer84-239
  M. Tatar, 131(CL):Fall84-366
Tzareva, E. Rugs and Carpets from Central Asia.
  J. Thompson, 617(TLS):17May85-563
Tzitsikas, H. La supervivencia existencial de la mujer en las obras de Benavente.
  G.M. Scanlon, 86(BHS):Oct84-527
Tzu, L. - see under Lao Tzu
Tzvetan, T. Symbolisme et interprétation.
  J.A. Millán, 202(FMod):No65/67-324

Uamanobe, T., ed. Opulence.
  R.L.S., 614:Winter85-29

de Ubeda, F.L. - see under López de Ubeda, F.
Ubersfeld, A. Claudel, autobiographie et histoire, "Partage de Midi."
  M. Malicet, 535(RHL):Jul/Aug84-648
Udovitch, A.L. and L. Valensi. The Last Arab Jews.
  C. Geertz, 453(NYRB):28Feb85-14
  L. Rosen, 617(TLS):7Jun85-648
Ueberroth, P., with R. Levin and A. Quinn. Made in America.
  M. Gallagher, 441:1Dec85-24
Ueberweg, F. Grundriss der Geschichte der Philosophie. (Vol 3) (H. Flashar, ed)
  J. Barnes, 520:Vol129No2-188
Ueda, M. Modern Japanese Poets and the Nature of Literature.
  J. Beichman, 285(JapQ):Apr-Jun84-218
  J.T. Rimer, 407(MN):Summer84-198
  R. Spiess, 404:Autumn84-50
Ugah, A. Naked Hearts.
  I.I. Elimimian, 538(RAL):Winter84-609
Ugarte, F. España y su civilización. (3rd ed rev by M. Ugarte)
  R.L. Sheehan, 399(MLJ):Autumn84-305
Uhlig, C. Theorie der Literarhistorie.
  R. Wellek, 52:Band19Heft1-59
  W. Zacharasiewicz, 602:Band15Heft1-181
Uhse, B. Gesammelten Werken. (Vols 5 and 6) (G. Caspar, ed)
  U. Dietzel, 601(SuF):Mar-Apr84-417
Ulam, A.B. Dangerous Relations.
  A. Brown, 617(TLS):4Oct85-1104
  639(VQR):Winter84-19
Ulf, C. Das römische Lupercalienfest.
  P. Flobert, 555:Vol58fasc2-343
  E.N. Lane, 124:Nov-Dec84-126
Ulibarrí, S.R. Primeros Encuentros/First Encounters.
  D. Maceri, 399(MLJ):Spring84-99
Ullendorff, E. and C.F. Beckingham, eds and trans. The Hebrew Letters of Prester John.
  K.R. Stow, 589:Apr84-447
Ullmann, L. Choices.
  M. Dowd, 441:17Feb85-21
  442(NY):4Mar85-119
"Doris Ulmann, American Portraits."
  S.M. Halpern, 441:9Jun84-22
Ulmer, G. Applied Grammatology.
  C. Norris, 617(TLS):15Mar85-295
Ulrich, A. Anton Ulrich Herzog zu Braunschweig und Lüneburg: "Bühnendichtungen." (Vol 1, Pts 1 and 2) (B.L. Spahr, ed)
  K.F. Otto, Jr., 301(JEGP):Apr84-274
Ulset, T. Det genetiske forholdet mellom Ágrip.
  T.M. Andersson, 563(SS):Autumn84-372
Ultan, L. and G. Hermalyn. The Bronx in the Innocent Years, 1890-1925.
  A. Corman, 441:8Dec85-40
de Unamuno, M. Niebla. (M.J. Valdés, ed)
  P.R. Olson, 400(MLN):Mar84-396
"The Unborn." (N. Waddell, trans)
  T. Buckley, 469:Vol10No2-90
Underwood, G.N. The Dialect of the Mesabi Range.
  M.D. Linn, 35(AS):Winter84-359
Underwood, T.L. and R. Sharrock - see Bunyan, J.

Ungar, S. Roland Barthes.*
    R. Sarkonak, 188(ECr):Winter84-91
    S. Scobie, 376:Oct84-107
    M.B. Wiseman, 290(JAAC):Summer85-415
Ungar, S.J. Africa.
    X. Smiley, 441:1Sep85-4
Ungar, S.J., ed. Estrangement.
    D. Watt, 441:22Dec85-21
Unger, L. Eliot's Compound Ghost.*
    P.M.S. Dawson, 541(RES):Nov84-584
    W. Harmon and S.W. Smock, 577(SHR):
        Summer84-270
    J. Olney, 569(SR):Summer84-451
Unger, P. Philosophical Relativity.
    A. Morton, 617(TLS):15Feb85-180
von Ungern-Sternberg, J. - see Gelzer, M.
"Unlawful Sex."
    A.W.B. Simpson, 617(TLS):6Dec85-1382
Unrau, J. Ruskin and St. Mark's.
    P. Conner, 59:Dec84-499
    J.G. Links, 324:Jan85-157
    M.W., 90:Dec84-796
Unschuld, P.U. Medical Ethics in Imperial
China.
    M.L. Chiu, 318(JAOS):Apr-Jun83-466
Unsworth, B. Stone Virgin.
    S. Altinel, 617(TLS):30Aug85-946
    K.C. O'Brien, 362:19Sep85-28
Unwin, T.A. - see Flaubert, G.
Updike, J. Facing Nature.
    G. Ewart, 441:28Apr85-18
Updike, J. Hugging the Shore.*
    J. Parini, 249(HudR):Spring84-170
    295(JML):Nov84-381
Updike, J. Rabbit est riche.
    P-Y. Petillon, 98:Mar84-214
Updike, J. The Witches of Eastwick.*
    N. Baym, 271:Fall84-165
    A. Bloom, 249(HudR):Winter84/85-622
    G. Johnson, 584(SWR):Summer84-342
    D.R. Slavitt, 385(MQR):Winter85-134
Uphaus, R.W. Beyond Tragedy.*
    T. Hawkes, 541(RES):Aug84-367
    C. Hoy, 569(SR):Spring84-256
Upton, D. Mental Health Care and National
Health Insurance.
    S.S., 185:Apr85-787
Upward, E. Pastoral Madness.
    J. Rodriguez, 102(CanL):Autumn84-145
Urang, S. Kindled in the Flame.
    L.D. Clark, 177(ELT):Vol27No2-173
Urbańczyk, S., with R. Olesch, eds. Die
altpolnischen Orthographien des 16. Jahr-
hunderts.
    H. Leeming, 575(SEER):Oct84-574
Urbański, E.S. Hispanic America and Its
Civilizations.
    J. Sarnacki, 497(PolR):Vol29No1/2-168
Urdang, C. Only the World.*
    L. Goldensohn, 491:Apr84-40
Urdang, L. and F.R. Abate, eds. Fine and
Applied Arts Terms Index.
    K. Stanley, 35(AS):Winter84-356
Urdang, L. and F.G. Ruffner, Jr. Allu-
sions — Cultural, Literary, Biblical,
and Historical.*
    H. Schnelling, 568(SCN):Spring-
        Summer84-19
Urel, H., ed. Kipling: Interviews and
Recollections.*
    N. Page, 177(ELT):Vol27No4-323

Ureland, P.S., ed. Die Leistung der Stra-
taforschung und der Kreolistik.*
    R. Werner, 547(RF):Band96Heft3-313
Urey, D.F. Galdós and the Irony of
Language.*
    A.M. Gullón, 240(HR):Winter84-94
    M.Z. Hafter, 240(HR):Winter84-96
    C.E. Klein, 552(REH):Oct84-458
    E. Rodgers, 86(BHS):Jan84-53
    J. Whiston, 131(CL):Fall84-370
Uría Maqua, I. - see de Berceo, S.
Urioste, G.L., ed and trans. Hijos de
Pariya Qaqa.
    R. Harrison, 238:Dec84-682
Urkowitz, S. Shakespeare's Revision of
"King Lear."*
    M. Spevack, 156(JDSh):Jahrbuch1984-225
Urquhart, J. The Little Flowers of Madame
de Montespan.
    J. Carson, 526:Autumn84-80
    S.S., 376:Jun84-149
Urquhart, T. The Jewel.* (R.D.S. Jack
and R.J. Lyall, eds)
    M.R.G. Spiller, 571(ScLJ):Winter84-44
Ursell, G. The Running of the Deer.
    R. Plant, 102(CanL):Summer84-155
Ursell, G., ed. Saskatchewan Gold.
    R.H. Ramsey, 102(CanL):Winter83-149
Ursell, G. Trap Lines.
    A. Amprimoz, 526:Winter84-92
    M.T. Lane, 198:Winter84-96
    S.S., 376:Feb84-142
Ursu, L., ed. 15 Young Romanian Poets.
    T. Eagleton, 565:Summer84-76
Urwin, K., ed. The Life of Saint John the
Almsgiver.*
    A.J. Holden, 402(MLR):Jul84-696
    B. Merrilees, 382(MAE):1984/2-324
    C. Rebuffi, 379(MedR):Apr84-125
Ušakov, V.E. Akcentologičeskij slovar'
drevnerusskogo jazyka XIV veka.
    W. Lehfeldt, 559:Vol8No2-167
Usborne, R. - see Wodehouse, P.G.
"Usborne Picture Dictionary." "Usborne
Children's Wordfinder."
    C. Fox, 617(TLS):8Mar85-270
Usher, D. The Economic Prerequisite to
Democracy.* (German title: Die ökono-
mischen Grundlagen der Demokratie.)
    P.G. Kielmansegg, 384:Mar84-202
Usher, S. The Historians of Greece and
Rome.
    617(TLS):12Jul85-783
Ushiba, A. L'Image de l'eau dans "A la
recherche du Temps perdu."
    E. Nakamura, 535(RHL):Nov/Dec84-983
Usiskin, M. Uncle Mike's Edenbridge.
    E. Orenstein, 627(UTQ):Summer84-496
Usmiani, R. Second Stage.
    D. Bessai, 108:Winter84-151
Usmiani, R. Michel Tremblay.*
    L.E. Doucette, 627(UTQ):Summer84-483
Uspenskij, B.A. Jazykovaja situacija
Kievskoj Rusi i ee značenie dlja istorii
russkogo literaturnogo jazyka.
    D. Freydank, 559:Vol8No3-313
Uspensky, B. A Poetics of Composition.
    A. Nakhimovsky, 574(SEEJ):Winter84-554
Uspenskogo, B.A., ed. Rossijskaja gram-
matika Antona Alekseeviča Barsova.
    G. Freidhof, 559:Vol8No3-326
"Utopie et socialisme au Portugal."
    J. Voisine, 549(RLC):Jan-Mar84-124

Uzzle, B. All American.
    R. Ranck, 441:7Jul85-16

"The V and A Album 3." (A.S. Cocks, ed)
    C. Buxton, 324:Jul85-579
Väänänen-Jensen, I., ed. Finnish Short
    Stories.
    K.O. Dana, 563(SS):Autumn84-403
Vachek, J., ed. Praguiana.
    F. Chevillet, 189(EA):Oct-Dec85-451
Vadim, R. The Hungry Angel.*
    639(VQR):Spring84-55
Vaget, H.R. Goethe: Der Mann von 60
    Jahren.*
    W.P. Hanson, 402(MLR):Apr84-491
    M.W. Jennings, 221(GQ):Summer84-476
Vagluov, K. Sobranie stikhotvorenii. (J.
    Chertkov, ed)
    A.A. Anemone, Jr., 550(RusR):Jul84-291
Vago, R.M., ed. Issues in Vowel Harmony.
    B. Comrie, 297(JL):Mar84-188
Vaisey, D. - see Turner, T.
Vajda, G.M., ed. Le Tournant du siècle
    des lumières 1760-1820.
    A.O. Aldridge, 52:Band19Heft2-183
    F. Jost, 149(CLS):Spring84-52
Vajl', P. and A. Genis. Sovremennaja russ-
    kaja proza.
    E. Chances, 574(SEEJ):Summer84-267
    V. Golovskoj, 558(RLJ):Winter-Spring84-
    306
Valas, P. Oedipe reviens, tu es pardonné!
    J. le Hardi, 450(NRF):Sep84-112
Valderrama Andrade, C. - see Caro, M.A.
Valdés, G., T.P. Hannum and R.V. Teschner.
    Cómo se escribe.*
    R. Hogan, 238:Mar84-159
Valdés, J.M. - see under Meléndez Valdés,
    J.
Valdés, M.J. Shadows in the Cave.*
    P. Bly, 268(IFR):Winter85-55
Valdés, M.J. - see de Unamuno, M.
Valdinoci, S. Les Fondements de la Phe-
    nomenologie Husserlienne.
    R. Kearney, 323:May84-205
de Valdivielso, J. Auto famoso de la des-
    censión de Nuestra Señora en la Santa
    Yglesia de Toledo, quando trujo la cas-
    ulla al gloriossíssimo San Ilefonso su
    santo arçobispo y patrón nuestro (BN
    Madrid, MS. Res. 80). (J.T. Snow, ed)
    D.W. Cruickshank, 402(MLR):Oct84-959
Vale, J. Edward III and Chivalry.
    R.H. Jones, 589:Oct84-933
Vale, V. The American Peril.
    T.C. Barker, 617(TLS):24May85-585
Valencia, P. and S.C. Bacon. En Marcha.
    M.S. Finch, 399(MLJ):Autumn84-306
Valency, M. The Cart and the Trumpet.
    R. Simard, 615(TJ):Dec84-548
Valenzuela, L. Other Weapons.
    M. Resnick, 441:6Oct85-38
Valéry, P. Les Principes d'an-archie pure
    et appliquée [suivi de] Valéry, F.
    Paul Valéry et la politique.
    M. Jarrety, 450(NRF):Sep84-106
Valesio, P. Novantiqua.*
    B. van Heusden, 204(FdL):Jun84-141
Valgard, J. and E. Wessel, eds. Frauen
    und Frauenbilder.
    H.M.K. Riley, 133:Band17Heft1/2-122

Valin, R. Perspectives psychomécaniques
    sur la syntaxe.*
    C. Wimmer, 553(RLiR):Jan-Jun84-213
    P. Wunderli, 547(RF):Band96Heft1/2-108
Valis, N.M. The Decadent Vision in Leo-
    poldo Alas.*
    N.G. Round, 402(MLR):Jan84-217
Valiska, J. Nemecké nárečie Dobšinej.
    P. Trost, 685(ZDL):1/1984-101
Valkenier, E.K. The Soviet Union and the
    Third World.*
    C.R. Saivetz, 550(RusR):Jul84-302
del Valle, A.B.F. - see under Basave Fer-
    nández del Valle, A.
Valleau, M.A. The Spanish Civil War in
    American and European Films.*
    L. Schwartz, 125:Spring84-308
Vallet, G., ed. Les "dévaluations" à Rome.
    (Vol 2)
    C.E. King, 313:Vol74-222
"Il valore dei dipinti dell'ottocento."
    (2nd ed)
    N. Powell, 39:Dec84-440
Van Antwerp, M.A. and S. Johns, eds.
    Dictionary of Literary Biography Docu-
    mentary Series. (Vol 4: Tennessee Wil-
    liams)
    T.P. Adler, 365:Winter84-26
Vance, C. Hard Choices.*
    W.S. Burke, 396(ModA):Spring/Summer84-
    264
Vance, C.S., ed. Pleasure and Danger.
    D. Spender, 441:14Apr85-32
Vance, J.A. Samuel Johnson and the Sense
    of History.
    D. Nokes, 617(TLS):29Nov85-1351
Vance, N. The Sinews of the Spirit.
    S.R. Letwin, 362:14Nov85-32
Vancouver, G. A Voyage of Discovery to
    the North Pacific Ocean and Round the
    World 1791-1795. (W.K. Lamb, ed)
    B.M. Gough, 617(TLS):20Sep85-1041
Vandalkovskaia, M.G. Istoriia izucheniia
    russkogo revoliutsionnogo dvizheniia
    serediny XIX veka: 1890-1917.
    W.F. Woehrlin, 550(RusR):Oct84-426
Vandenbroucke, R. Athol Fugard.
    T. Vincent, 538(RAL):Fall84-458
Van Den Hengel, J.W. The Home of Meaning.
    M. Adam, 542:Jan-Mar84-96
Vanderbilt, G. Once Upon a Time.
    B.G. Harrison, 441:14Apr85-9
    442(NY):13May85-147
Vanderford, K.H. - see Alfonso el Sabio
Vandergriff, J. - see under Bartelt, G.,
    S.P. Jasper and B. Hoffer
Vanderhaeghe, G. Man Descending.*
    D. Carpenter, 102(CanL):Summer84-115
    A. Gray, 441:13Oct85-28
    442(NY):14Oct85-140
Vanderhaeghe, G. My Present Age.
    P-L. Adams, 61:Dec85-118
    M. Thorpe, 99:Nov84-35
    442(NY):14Oct85-140
Van der Kiste, J. and B. Jordaan. Dearest
    Affie ...
    B. Fothergill, 617(TLS):1Feb85-117
Vander Meer, P. Farm-Plot Dispersal.
    S-M. Huang, 293(JASt):Aug84-750
Vander Motten, J.P. Sir William Killigrew
    (1606-1695).
    S.J. Steen, 568(SCN):Spring-
    Summer84-12

Vandier, J. Manuel d'archéologie égyp-
tienne. (Vol 6)
  A. Badawy, 318(JAOS):Jul-Sep83-668
Van Dijk, C. Rebellion Under the Banner
of Islam.
  H.H. Roe, 293(JASt):Aug84-815
Vane-Wright, R.I. and P.R. Ackery, eds.
The Biology of Butterflies.
  M. Ridley, 617(TLS):23Aug85-935
Van Ghent, D. Keats.* (J.C. Robinson, ed)
  S.J. Wolfson, 340(KSJ):Vol33-221
Van Kirk, S. Many Tender Ties.
  B. Wahlstrom, 649(WAL):Feb85-346
Van Laan, T.F. Role-Playing in Shake-
speare.
  L. Salingar, 570(SQ):Autumn84-361
Van Leeuwen, T.M. The Surplus of Meaning.
  M. Adam, 542:Jan-Mar84-96
Van Lustbader, E. Jian.
  N. Ramsey, 441:11Aug85-15
Vann, J.A. The Making of a State.
  639(VQR):Autumn84-115
Vanneste, H.M.C. Northern Review, 1945-
1956.*
  W. Francis, 105:Fall/Winter84-84
  B. Whiteman, 168(ECW):Winter84/85-124
Vañó-Cerdá, A. "Ser" y "Estar" +
Adjetivos.
  F. Rainer, 547(RF):Band96Heft3-315
  H. Ruiz M., 238:Mar84-158
Van Roey-Roux, F. La Littérature intime
du Québec.
  G. Frémont, 193(ELit):Autumn84-420
  P. Hébert, 627(UTQ):Summer84-477
Van Rutten, P-M. Le Langage poétique de
Saint-John Perse.
  A. Purdy, 107(CRCL):Jun84-324
Vanry, F. Der Zaungast.
  F.L. Carsten, 575(SEER):Jul84-475
Vansittart, P. Paths from a White Horse.
  M. Jones, 362:29Aug85-25
  P. Oakes, 617(TLS):2Aug85-844
Vansittart, P. Voices 1870-1914.
  D. Taylor, 364:Apr/May84-140
Vansittart, P. - see Masefield, J.
Van Steenberghen, F. Le thomisme.*
  B.C. Bazán, 154:Dec84-729
Van Toorn, P. and K. Norris, eds.
Cross/cut.*
  J. Bayly, 137:Feb85-34
  K. Sherman, 102(CanL):Winter83-148
Van Uchelen, A.R.A.C. - see under Croiset
Van Uchelen, A.R.A.
Varacalli, J.A. Toward the Establishment
of Liberal Catholicism in America.
  J. Hitchcock, 31(ASch):Spring84-263
Vardy, S.B. and A.H., eds. Society in
Change.
  T. Spira, 104(CASS):Winter84-500
Varela, J.L. Larra y España.
  J. Escobar, 240(HR):Autumn84-544
  P.L. Ullman, 238:Sep84-473
Varela, J.L. - see de Larra, M.J.
Varey, S. - see "Lord Bolingbroke: Contri-
butions to the 'Craftsman'"
Vargas Llosa, M. Historia de Mayta.
  M. Deas, 617(TLS):8Mar85-256
Vargas Llosa, M. The War of the End of
the World.* (Spanish title: La Guerra
del Fin del Mundo.)
  V. Bogdanor, 362:4Jul85-31
  G. Brotherston, 617(TLS):17May85-540
  M. Wood, 453(NYRB):28Feb85-7

Varnedoe, K. Duane Hanson.
  S. Laschever, 441:24Mar85-24
Varnhagen, R. Gesammelte Werke. (K.
Feilchenfeldt, U. Schweikert and R.E.
Steiner, eds)
  R. Paulin, 617(TLS):2Aug85-859
Varro. Varron, "Satires Ménippées."
(fasc 6) (J-P. Cèbe, ed and trans)
  R. Astbury, 123:Vol34No2-317
Várvaro, A. Lingua e storia in Sicilia.
(Vol 1)
  J. Siracusa, 399(MLJ):Summer84-182
Vasari, G. Leben der ausgezeichnetsten
Maler, Bildhauer und Baumeister von
Cimabue bis zum Jahre 1567. (J. Klie-
mann, ed)
  M. Warnke, 384:Jul84-564
Vasey, L. - see Lawrence, D.H.
Vasilenko, E., A. Yegorova and E. Lamm.
Russian Verb Aspects.
  M.K. Frank, 399(MLJ):Spring84-90
Vassberg, D.E. La venta de tierras bal-
días.
  H. Nader, 551(RenQ):Autumn84-453
Vatai, F.L. Intellectuals in Politics in
the Greek World, from Early Times to the
Hellenistic Age.
  T.J. Saunders, 617(TLS):8Feb85-150
Vattier, G. La vie, fragments, éclats.
  M. Adam, 542:Apr-Jun84-259
de Vaucher Gravili, A. Loi et transgres-
sion.
  E. Boggio Quallio, 475:Vol 11No20-235
Vaughan, D. Controlling Unlawful Organiza-
tional Behavior.
  T.J.D., 185:Oct84-196
Vaughan, D. Portrait of an Invisible Man.
  R. Brown, 707:Spring84-156
Vaughan, H. The Complete Poems.* (A.
Rudrum, ed)
  T.W., 111:Fall85-6
Vaughan, M., M. Kolinsky and P. Sheriff.
Social Change in France.
  B. Rigby, 208(FS):Apr84-244
Vaughan, T. The Works of Thomas Vaughan.*
(A. Rudrum, with J. Drake-Brockman, eds)
  K.J. Knoespel, 111:Fall85-5
Vaughan-Thomas, W. Wales.
  M. Hurst, 617(TLS):1Mar85-236
  D.A.N. Jones, 362:24Jan85-28
Vaughn, J.A. Early American Dramatists.
  M. Reilingh, 615(TJ):Mar82-134
Vaughn, W.P. The Anti-Masonic Party in
the United States, 1826-1843.
  P.H. Bergeron, 9(AlaR):Jan84-63
Vaught, C.G. The Quest for Wholeness.
  W. Desan, 480(P&R):Vol 17No2-121
  E. von der Luft, 543:Sep83-154
Vaut, E.D. ESL/Coping Skills for Adult
Learners.
  M.R. Webb, 399(MLJ):Summer84-200
Vax, L. Lexique de logique.
  A. Reix, 542:Jan-Mar84-124
Vázquez, L.C. - see under Cortés Vázquez,
L.
Vázquez Montalbán, M. Murder in the
Central Committee.*
  W. Herrick, 441:30Jun85-20
Vedung, E. Political Reasoning.
  J.L.H., 185:Jan85-389
Vega, A.L. and C. Lugo Filippi. Vírgenes
y Mártires.
  J.L. Méndez, 701(SinN):Oct-Dec83-61

de la Vega, G. - see under Garcilaso de la
Vega
de la Vega, J.S.L. - see under Lasso de la
Vega, J.S.
de Vega Carpio, L. "La Corona Trágica" de
Lope de Vega.* (M.G. Paulson and T.
Álvarez-Detrell, eds)
F. Pierce, 402(MLR):Jan84-215
de Vega Carpio, L. El nuevo mundo descu-
bierto por Cristóbal Colón. (J. Lemar-
tinel and C. Minguet, eds)
V. Dixon, 86(BHS):Oct84-523
Vegh, C. I Didn't Say Goodbye.
W. Kaminer, 441:23Jun85-11
Veilleux, A. - see "Pachomian Koinonia"
Vejsälov, F. Alman dilinin fonetikasy.
C.F. Meier, 682(ZPSK):Band37Heft1-124
Vela, F. Inventario de la modernidad.
(J.C. Mainer, ed)
N.R. Orringer, 240(HR):Summer84-415
Veldman, H. La Tentation de l'inaccess-
ible.*
C. Gothot-Mersch, 535(RHL):Jul/Aug84-
653
Velie, A.R. Four American Indian Literary
Masters.*
D. Mogen, 223:Winter84-417
Vellacott, J. Bertrand Russell and the
Pacifists in the First World War.
L. Pineau, 529(QQ):Summer84-464
Velleius Paterculus. Histoire Romaine.*
(Vols 1 and 2) (J. Hellegouarc'h, ed and
trans)
F.R.D. Goodyear, 123:Vol34No2-196
Veloudis, G. Germanograecia.
D. Theodoridis, 343:Heft9/10-165
Veltman, C. Language Shift in the United
States.
T.C. Frazer, 350:Mar85-243
Vendler, H., ed. The Harvard Book of Con-
temporary American Poetry.
447(NY):23Dec85-90
Vendler, H. The Odes of John Keats.*
M. Butler, 249(HudR):Spring84-143
H.J. Levine, 223:Winter84-419
A. Ward, 661(WC):Summer84-92
529(QQ):Summer84-490
Vendler, H. Wallace Stevens.
L. Beckett, 617(TLS):24May85-575
Vendler, Z. The Matter of Minds.
J. Hornsby, 617(TLS):4Oct85-1095
Vennemann, T., ed. Silben, Segmente,
Akzente.
B.J. Koekkoek, 221(GQ):Fall84-637
Ventimiglia, C. Società, Politica,
Diritto.
M. Adam, 542:Oct-Dec84-474
Ventura, M. Shadow Dancing in the U.S.A.
H. Sheehan, 441:27Oct85-54
Vera, D. Commento Storico alle "Rela-
tiones" di Quinto Aurelio Simmaco.
J-P. Callu, 555:Vol58fasc1-147
Vera, L.C. - see under Cervera Vera, L.
Verbeke, G. The Presence of Stoicism in
Medieval Thought.
M.L. Colish, 589:Apr84-449
G.M. Ross, 123:Vol34No2-224
Vercier, B. and J. Lecarme, with J.
Bersani. La littérature en France
depuis 1968.*
G. Brée, 208(FS):Jan84-100

Vercors, J. Les Occasions perdues ou
l'étrange déclin.
J. Kolbert, 207(FR):Dec84-325
Verdi, G. Don Carlos. (U. Günther, with
L. Petazzoni and F. Degrada, eds)
D. Lawton, 414(MusQ):Winter84-107
Verdi, G. Rigoletto. (M. Chusid, ed)
J. Budden, 414(MusQ):Spring84-266
Verdi, R. Klee and Nature.
J. Gage, 617(TLS):23Aug85-928
Verdonk, R.A. La lengua española en
Flandes en el siglo XVII.
K-H. Körner, 72:Band221Heft2-415
W. Mettmann, 547(RF):Band96Heft1/2-139
P. Quijas Corzo, 457(NRFH):Tomo32núm1-
233
Verey, R. Classic Garden Design.
C. Jellicoe, 46:Dec84-81
Vergara, F., V.A. Serpa and J.R. Curry.
Aquí, allá y accullá.
D.R. McKay, 399(MLJ):Winter84-412
E.J. Mullen, 238:Dec84-687
Vergara, L. Rubens and the Poetics of
Landscape.*
C. Brown, 90:Nov84-703
J. Ferguson, 324:Dec84-68
J.M. Muller, 551(RenQ):Summer84-271
M. Pointon, 89(BJA):Spring84-177
Verger, C. Intempéries.
N.S. Hellerstein, 207(FR):May85-910
Verger, J. and J. Jolivet. Bernard —
Abélard, ou le cloître et l'école.
S.C. Ferruolo, 589:Jul84-728
A. Reix, 542:Oct-Dec84-465
Vergil. The Aeneid.* (R. Fitzgerald,
trans)
E.A. Havelock, 249(HudR):Autumn84-483
W.R. Johnson, 31(ASch):Autumn84-562
G. Williams, 569(SR):Fall84-630
639(VQR):Spring84-60
Vergil. Virgil: Selections from "Aeneid"
VI. (A. Haward, ed)
F. Mench, 124:Jul-Aug85-610
Vergil. Virgil: The "Eclogues" and
"Georgics."* (R.D. Williams, ed)
W.W. Briggs, Jr., 121(CJ):Dec84/Jan85-
171
R. Coleman, 123:Vol34No1-28
Verharen, C. Rationality in Philosophy
and Science.
S.H. Lee, 543:Jun84-872
Verlaine, P. Poésies (1866-1880). (M.
Décaudin, ed)
D. Hillery, 208(FS):Jan84-78
Verlet, P. Les Meubles Français du XVIIIe
siècle.* (2nd ed)
M. Stürmer, 683:Band47Heft4-573
Verlet, P. The Savonnerie.*
A. Völker, 683:Band47Heft3-410
Verma, S.K. and R.N. Sahai. The Oxford
Progressive English-Hindi Dictionary.
M.C. Shapiro, 318(JAOS):Oct-Dec83-749
Vermaseren, M.J. Die orientalischen
Religionen im Römerreich.
P.W. van der Horst, 394:
Vol37fasc1/2-252
Vermazen, B. and M.B. Hintikka. Essays on
Davidson.
P. Snowdon, 617(TLS):27Dec85-1485
"Vermittler." (Vol 1) (J. Siess, ed)
W. Patt, 52:Band19Heft1-104

Vernant, J-P. Myth and Thought among the Greeks.
  D.F., 185:Oct84-189
Vernant, J-P. The Origins of Greek Thought.*
  J. Percival, 529(QQ):Summer84-432
Vernant, J-P. and others. Entretiens sur l'antiquité classique. (Vol 27)
  N.J. Richardson, 303(JoHS):Vol 104-234
Vernay, H. Syntaxe et sémantique.
  W.A. Bennett, 208(FS):Jan84-114
Verne, J. Family without a Name.
  G.W., 102(CanL):Winter83-188
Vernon, J. Money and Fiction.
  D. Walder, 617(TLS):6Dec85-1408
Véronique, D.G. Analyse contrastive, analyse d'erreurs.
  G. Mounin, 320(CJL):Fall84-207
Verran, R., ed. The Land of Six Seasons.
  R. Spiess, 404:Autumn84-57
Versényi, L. Holiness and Justice.*
  R. Burger, 543:Sep83-156
  J.L. Creed, 303(JoHS):Vol 104-205
Versnel, H.S., ed. Faith, Hope and Worship.*
  J. Linderski, 24:Spring84-111
Versteeg, M., S. Thomas and J. Huddleston, comps. Index to Fiction in "The Lady's Realm."
  J. Shattock, 402(MLR):Jul84-682
Versteeg, M., S. Thomas and J. Huddleston, comps. The Lady's Realm.
  L. Madden, 447(N&Q):Apr83-172
Vertov, D. Kino-Eye. (A. Michelson, ed)
  R. Durgnat, 18:Oct84-78
Vervliet, R. De literaire manifesten van het Fin de Siècle in de Zuidnederlandse periodieken 1878-1914.
  J. Goedegebuure, 204(FdL):Dec84-314
Vesey, G., ed. Idealism Past and Present.*
  W. Matson, 483:Jan84-126
Vespertino Rodríguez, A., ed. Leyendas aljamiadas y moriscas sobre personajes bíblicos.
  O. Hegyi, 304(JHP):Spring84-246
  A.V., 379(MedR):Apr84-156
Vester, E. Instrument and Manner Expressions in Latin.
  P. Flobert, 555:Vol58fasc2-317
Vetta, M. - see Theognis
"Vetus Latina." (Vol 11, Pt 1) (E. Beuron, ed)
  M-J. Rondeau, 555:Vol58fasc1-151
Veyne, P. L'Élégie érotique romaine.*
  F. Cairns, 617(TLS):4Oct85-1118
Veyrenc, J. Etudes sur le Verbe russe.
  R.D. Brecht, 104(CASS):Spring-Summer84-153
Viala, A. Naissance de l'écrivain.
  P. France, 617(TLS):4Oct85-1094
Vialatte, A. Badonce et les créatures.
  M. Chefdor, 207(FR):Mar85-604
Vialla, J. Les Pickersgill-Arundale.
  T. Crombie, 39:Mar84-226
Viallaneix, P. - see de Vigny, A.
Viani, M.C.B. - see under Bandera Viani, M.C.
Vianna, F.D. - see under de Mello Vianna, F.
Viatte, A. Histoire comparée des littératures francophones.
  R. Jones, 208(FS):Jan84-105

Viazzi, A. Cucina e Nostalgia.
  W. and C. Cowen, 639(VQR):Spring84-66
Vicarelli, F., ed. Keynes's Relevance Today.
  D. O'Keeffe, 617(TLS):6Sep85-968
Vicent, V.D. - see under de Cedenas y Vicent, V.
Vicinus, M. Independent Women.
  J.B. Ciulla, 441:11Aug85-13
  R. Delmar, 617(TLS):6Dec85-1409
Vickers, B., ed. Occult and Scientific Mentalities in the Renaissance.*
  S.J. Linden, 111:Spring85-4
Vickers, B., ed. Shakespeare: The Critical Heritage. (Vol 5)
  S. Monod, 549(RLC):Jul-Sep84-357
Vickers, B., ed. Shakespeare: The Critical Heritage. (Vol 6)
  R.J.A. Weis, 179(ES):Dec84-574
Vickers, H. Cecil Beaton.
  C. Fox, 617(TLS):26Jul85-820
Vickers, J. - see Russell, A.
Vickery, J.B. Myths and Texts.
  W. Fowlie, 569(SR):Summer84-lvi
  G.L. Lucente, 651(WHR):Winter84-388
  P. Stevick, 395(MFS):Winter84-857
Vico, G. Origine de la poésie et du droit. (C. Henri and A. Henry, eds and trans)
  J. Prieur, 450(NRF):Mar84-122
Queen Victoria. Queen Victoria in Her Letters and Journals. (C. Hibbert, ed)
  H. Benedict, 441:26May85-15
  A. Burgess, 61:May85-97
  I. Vinogradoff, 617(TLS):11Jan85-44
Victorio, J., ed. Mocedades de Rodrigo.
  C. de Paepe, 356(LR):Feb/May84-125
Vidal, G. Lincoln.*
  O.D. Edwards, 176:Jan85-33
  M. Howard, 676(YR):Winter85-xvi
Vidal-Naquet, P. - see under Arrian
"The Vidas of the Troubadours." (M. Egan, trans)
  A.V., 379(MedR):Dec84-449
Vieillard-Baron, J-L. L'illusion historique et l'espérance céleste.
  A. Reix, 192(EP):Jan-Mar84-125
Vielwahr, A. Sous le signe des contradictions.
  M. Sheringham, 208(FS):Jul84-367
Vieth, D.M. Rochester Studies, 1925-1982.
  C. Rawson, 617(TLS):29Mar85-335
Vietta, S., ed. Die literarische Frühromantik.
  C. Zelle, 72:Band221Heft2-343
Vigato, J.C. Le Jeu des modèles — Les Modèles en jeu.
  E.G. Grossman, 576:Dec84-373
Vigeveno, G. The Bomb and European Security.
  639(VQR):Spring84-58
de Vignay, J. Li livres Flave Vegece de la chose de chevalerie. (L. Löfstedt, ed)
  G. Roques, 553(RLiR):Jan-Jun84-249
de la Vigne, A. Le voyage de Naples.*
  (A. Slerca, ed)
  E. Chevallier, 549(RLC):Oct-Dec84-485
Vigneaux, J. Branque-Iliade.
  J. Decock, 207(FR):Dec84-312
de Vigny, A. Les Destinées, Poèmes philosophiques. (P. Viallaneix, ed)
  J.C. Ireson, 402(MLR):Oct84-943

Viguerie, R. The Establishment vs. the People.
   G.A. Fossedal, 129:Jan85-27
Vijayalakshmy, R. A Study of Cīvakacintā-maṇi.
   I.V. Peterson, 318(JAOS):Oct-Dec83-779
Vijn, J.P. Carlyle and Jean Paul.
   I. Campbell, 571(ScLJ):Autumn84-21
Villa, R.M. - see under Martín Villa, R.
Villa, S.H. and M.K. Matossian. Armenian Village Life Before 1914.
   J. Cicala, 292(JAF):Jan-Mar84-91
Villadsen, P. The Underground Man and Raskolnikov.
   E. Egeberg, 172(Edda):1984/2-121
Villanueva, D., ed. La novela lírica.
   K.M. Glenn, 240(HR):Autumn84-549
Villar, F. Ergatividad, acusatividad y género en la familia lingüística indo-europea.*
   G. Bossong, 361:Mar84-239
Villard, L., ed. Corpus Vasorum Anti-quorum. (France, fasc 32)
   B.A. Sparkes, 303(JoHS):Vol 104-257
Villares, R. La propiedad de la tierra en Galicia, 1500-1936.
   J. Harrison, 86(BHS):Apr84-201
Ville, G. La gladiature en occident des origines à la mort de Domitien.*
   H.M. Lee, 24:Fall84-363
Mme. de Villedieu. Les désordres de l'amour. (A. Flannigan, ed)
   F. Assaf, 475:Vol 11No21-727
   J. Chupeau, 535(RHL):Jul/Aug84-608
   D. Kuizenga, 207(FR):Feb85-450
Villemaire, Y. Ange Amazone.*
   J. Viswanathan, 102(CanL):Autumn84-128
Villey, M. Le droit et les droits de l'homme.*
   J-L. Gardies, 542:Jan-Mar84-102
de Villiers de l'Isle-Adam, P.A.M. Eve of the Future Eden.* (M.G. Rose, trans)
   J. Anzalone, 207(FR):Apr85-735
de Villiers de l'Isle-Adam, P.A.M. Tomor-row's Eve.* (R.M. Adams, trans)
   J. Anzalone 207(FR):Apr85-735
   D. Gerould, 561(SFS):Nov84-318
Villordo, O.H. Genio y figura de Adolfo Bioy Casares.
   W.H. Katra, 238:May84-310
Vincent, A. and R. Plant. Philosophy, Pol-itics and Citizenship.
   P. Clarke, 617(TLS):15Feb85-164
Vincent, G. D'Ambition à zizanie.
   J-F. Brière, 207(FR):Feb85-477
Vincent, J. - see Lindsay, D.
Vincent, K.S. Pierre-Joseph Proudhon and the Rise of French Republican Socialism.
   D.G. Charlton, 617(TLS):26Jul85-831
Vincent, R. Klassieke Ballettechniek.
   M. Horosko, 151:Jan84-99
Vincent, T.B., comp. Joseph Howe.
   E. Pilon, 470:Vol22-119
Vincenzi, G.C. - see de Saussure, F.
Vines, L. A Guide to Language Camps in the U.S.: 2.
   M.W. Conner, 399(MLJ):Spring84-67
Vinge, J.D. Phoenix in the Ashes.
   G. Jonas, 441:28Apr85-20
Vinson, J., with D.L. Kirkpatrick, eds. Twentieth-Century Western Writers.*
   S.E. Marovitz, 87(BB):Mar84-42

Virga, P.H. The American Opera in 1790.
   R. Fiske, 410(M&L):Jul84-301
Virgil - see under Vergil
Virgo, S. Through the Eyes of a Cat.
   J.W. Lennox, 102(CanL):Autumn84-187
Virilio, P. Guerre et Cinéma. (Vol 1) L'Espace critique.
   F. de Mèredieu, 450(NRF):Sep84-113
Virmond, W., ed. Aerdig Leven Thyl Ulen-spiegel.
   W. Braungart, 196:Band25Heft1/2-163
Virshup, B. Coping in Medical School.
   P. Klass, 441:20Oct85-35
Visage, B. Tous les soleils.
   A. Clerval, 450(NRF):Nov84-82
"Les visages de l'Amour au XVIIe siècle."
   G. Cesbron, 356(LR):Nov84-325
Viscusi, W.K. Risk by Choice.
   M.L., 185:Jan85-400
Vishnevskaya, G. Galina.*
   A. Fitz Lyon, 617(TLS):3May85-490
   J. Drummond, 362:7Mar85-25
de Visser, J. City Light.
   W.N., 102(CanL):Summer84-186
Visson, L. The Complete Russian Cookbook.
   K.L. Nalibow, 574(SEEJ):Spring84-140
Vitale-Brovarone, A., ed. Recueil de galanteries (Torino, Archivio di Stato, J.b.IX.10).
   J.W. Hassell 3d, 589:Oct84-963
Vitoux, F. Fin de saison au Palazzo Pedrotti.
   M.B. Kline, 207(FR):Apr85-765
Vittinghoff, F., ed. Stadt und Herrschaft.
   J.B. Freed, 589:Jan84-209
Vitz, P.C. and A.B. Glimcher. Modern Art and Modern Science.
   M.H. Bornstein, 290(JAAC):Spring85-330
Vivante, P. The Epithets in Homer.
   J.B. Hainsworth, 487:Spring84-89
   P.V. Jones, 123:Vol134No2-304
Vizinczey, S. An Innocent Millionaire.
   S. Tanenhaus, 441:16Jun85-14
Vlach, J.M. Charleston Blacksmith.*
   L.G. Kozma and T. Kozma, 650(WF):Oct84-270
Vlahos, O. Doing Business.
   W. Smith, 441:17Nov85-31
Vlasopolos, A. The Symbolic Method of Coleridge, Baudelaire, and Yeats.
   L. Metzger, 661(WC):Summer84-127
Vliet, R.G. Scorpio Rising.
   T. Rutkowski, 441:5May85-9
"Vocabulaire québécois parlé de l'Estrie (Fréquence, dispersion, usage)."
   G. Dulong, 320(CJL):Spring84-80
Voge, W.M. The Pronunciation of German in the 18th Century.
   M.T. Zurdo, 202(FMod):No68/70-384
Vogel, E.F. Comeback.
   C.M. Aho, 441:15Sep85-32
Vogel, H., ed. Die sowjetische Interven-tion in Afghanistan.
   S. Kirschbaum, 104(CASS):Fall84-329
Vogeler, M.S. Frederic Harrison.
   J.W. Burrow, 617(TLS):1Feb85-117
Vogelsang, A. A Planet.*
   D. St. John, 42(AR):Summer84-370
Vogt, E., ed. Neues Handbuch der Litera-turwissenschaft.* (Vol 2)
   J. Laborderie, 555:Vol58fasc1-109
Voisin, M. Le Soleil et la nuit.^
   M. Eigeldinger, 535(RHL):Jul/Aug84-636

Voit, P. Franz Anton Pilgram (1699-1761).*
 H. Lorenz, 683:Band47Heft4-560
Voitle, R. The Third Earl of Shaftesbury,
 1671-1713.
 K.H.D. Haley, 617(TLS):18Jan85-57
Volkan, V.D. and N. Itzkowitz. The Immor-
 tal Atatürk.
 A. Mango, 617(TLS):4Oct85-1107
Volkoff, V. The Set-Up.
 R. Gadney, 364:Dec84/Jan85-152
Volkov, S. Balanchine's Tchaikovsky.
 J. Anderson, 441:26May85-17
 R. Craft, 453(NYRB):7Nov85-42
Vollertsen, P. Die Rekonstruktion unver-
 zerrter Kommunikation und Interaktion.
 H.A. Pausch, 107(CRCL):Mar84-99
Völlger, W. Das Windhahnsyndrom.
 C. Berger, 601(SuF):Jul-Aug84-870
Vološin, M. Stixotvorenija.* (Vol 1)
 (B. Filippova and È. Rajsa, eds)
 M. Reese-Antsaklis, 574(SEEJ):Spring84-
 121
Volotsky, I. The Monastic Rule of Iosif
 Volotsky. (D.M. Goldfrank, ed and trans)
 A. Kazhdan, 589:Jul84-729
de Voltaire, F.M.A. Candide ou l'opti-
 misme. (R. Pomeau, ed)
 J.H. Brumfitt, 208(FS):Apr84-206
 C. Mervaud, 535(RHL):Jan/Feb84-112
de Voltaire, F.M.A. Romans et contes. (F.
 Deloffre and J. Van den Heuvel, eds)
 C. Mervaud, 535(RHL):Jan/Feb84-110
"Voltaire et Rousseau en France et en
 Pologne."
 M. de Rougemont and J. Voisine,
 549(RLC):Oct-Dec84-490
Volynska-Bogert, R. and W. Zalewski.
 Czesław Miłosz.
 N. Taylor, 575(SEER):Jul84-451
Volz, R. Strindbergs Wanderungsdramen.
 O. Oberholzer, 562(Scan):Nov84-181
"Von Reinicken Fuchs."
 W.G. Ganser, 680(ZDP):Band103Heft1-146
Vondel, J.V.D. Gebroeders.
 E. Kraggerud, 172(Edda):1984/4-253
Vonnegut, K. Galápagos.
 T.M. Disch, 617(TLS):8Nov85-1267
 L. Moore, 441:6Oct85-7
 R. Towers, 453(NYRB):19Dec85-23
Vopěnka, P. Mathematics in the Alterna-
 tive Set Theory.
 A. Levy, 316:Dec84-1423
Vopěnka, P. and P. Hájek. The Theory of
 Semisets.
 A. Levy, 316:Dec84-1422
Vorlat, E. The Development of English
 Grammatical Theory 1586-1737.
 K. Reich, 38:Band102Heft1/2-158
Vormweg, H. Peter Weiss.*
 C. Poore, 406:Winter84-477
Voslensky, M. Nomenklatura.*
 442(NY):14Jan85-119
Voss, R. Die Artusepik Hartmanns von Aue.
 U. Schulze, 684(ZDA):Band113Heft3-105
Vosskamp, W., ed. Utopieforschung.
 H. Weinrich, 384:Jun84-454
Vovelle, M. Théodore Desorgues ou La
 Désorganisation.
 N. Hampson, 617(TLS):26Jul85-831
Vovelle, M. La Mort et l'Occident de 1300
 à nos jours.*
 J-P. Guinle, 450(NRF):Apr84-129

Voyat, G. Cognitive Development among
 Sioux Children.
 A. Garnham, 353:Vol22No2-253
Voyat, R. Les Etangs de Niigata.
 J. Kirkup, 617(TLS):8Mar85-265
Voyles, J.B. Gothic, Germanic, and North-
 west Germanic.*
 W.G. Moulton, 685(ZDL):1/1984-81
Vranich, S.B. Ensayos sevillanos del
 Siglo de Oro.*
 C. Iranzo, 241:May84-87
Vreeland, D. D.V.* (G. Plimpton and C.
 Hemphill, eds)
 F. Tuten, 62:Dec84-74
de Vries, J. European Urbanization 1500-
 1800.
 P. Slack, 617(TLS):15Mar85-297
de Vries, M.G. The International Monetary
 Fund 1972-78.
 T. Congdon, 617(TLS):6Dec85-1400
Vromans, J. and others. Woordenboek van
 de Brabantse dialecten. (7th ed)
 D. Stellmacher, 685(ZDL):2/1984-260
Vroom, W.H. De financiering van de kathe-
 draalbouw in de middeleeuwen, in het
 bijzonder van de dom van Utrecht.
 H. van der Wee, 576:Oct84-267
Vroon, R. Velimir Khlebnikov's Shorter
 Poems.
 R.D.B. Thomson, 104(CASS):Winter84-446
Vucinich, W.S., ed. At the Brink of War
 and Peace.*
 S. Blank, 104(CASS):Fall84-361
Vucinich, W.S., ed. The First Serbian Up-
 rising, 1804-1913.*
 M. Wheeler, 575(SEER):Jan84-126
Vuletić, A. Quand je serai grand comme la
 fourmi.
 L. Kovacs, 450(NRF):Jun84-128

"W kręgu 'Chimery,' Sztuka i literatura
 polskiego modernizmu."
 J.T. Baer, 497(PolR):Vol29No1/2-159
"The WPA Guide to New Orleans."
 P.W.P., 585(SoQ):Summer84-91
Wachtel, C. Joe the Engineer.*
 J. Clute, 617(TLS):6Dec85-1406
Waddell, N. - see "The Unborn"
Waddicor, M.H. - see Desfontaines, P.F.G.
Waddington, I. The Medical Profession in
 the Industrial Revolution.
 I. McGilchrist, 617(TLS):22Mar85-308
Waddington, M. Summer at Lonely Beach and
 Other Stories.*
 H. Barratt, 198:Spring84-116
Wade, E.L., C. Haralson and R. Strickland.
 As in a Vision.
 C. Taylor, 2(AfrA):May84-87
Wade-Gayles, G. No Crystal Stair.
 M. De Costa-Willis, 95(CLAJ):Jun85-464
Wadsworth, M., ed. Ways of Reading the
 Bible.
 E.S. Shaffer, 402(MLR):Apr84-391
Waegner, C. Recollection and Discovery.
 D. Krause, 395(MFS):Winter84-819
Waelti-Walters, J. Fairy Tales and the
 Female Imagination.
 B.J. Bucknall, 107(CRCL):Jun84-332
 L. Weir, 102(CanL):Winter83-68
Wagar, W.W. Terminal Visions.*
 D. Watson, 561(SFS):Nov84-329

Wagenbach, K. Franz Kafka.
442(NY):11Feb85-128
Wagenknecht, C. Deutsche Metrik.*
I. Glier, 684(ZDA):Band13Heft4-161
Wagenknecht, E. American Profile, 1900-1909.
B. Maine, 577(SHR):Fall84-364
Wagenknecht, E. Daughters of the Covenant.
A.R. Tintner, 390:Aug/Sep84-58
Wagenknecht, E. The Novels of Henry James.
M. Deakin, 395(MFS):Winter84-791
A.R. Tintner, 594:Fall84-326
Wagenknecht, E. The Tales of Henry James.
M. Seymour, 617(TLS):13Dec85-1438
Waggoner, H.H. American Visionary Poetry.
P. Balakian, 30:Winter85-83
C. Bedient, 569(SR):Fall84-1xxx
E. Folsom, 646:Summer04-44
C. Sanders, 289:Summer84-123
Waggoner, H.H. The Presence of Hawthorne.
A. Easson, 447(N&Q):Feb83-88
Wagner, A., ed. Canada's Lost Plays: Colonial Quebec.
J. Ripley, 102(CanL):Autumn84-142
Wagner, E. and others. The Transylvanian Saxons.
D. Deletant, 575(SEER):Jan84-123
Wagner, I.J.R. Manuel Godoy.
J.J. Junquera y Mato, 48:Apr-Jun84-191
van Wagner, J.K.C. Women Shaping Art.
J.S., 62:Summer85-97
Wagner, L.W. Ellen Glasgow.*
E. Ammons, 587(SAF):Spring84-115
F.P.W. McDowell, 191(ELN):Sep84-73
Wagner, N. Terre étrangère.
M-A. Lescourret, 98:Apr84-313
Wagner, P. - see Cleland, J.
Wagner, R. Wagner: My Life. (M. Whittall, ed)
R. Anderson, 415:Jul84-389
R. Taylor, 410(M&L):Jul84-296
Wagoner, D. First Light.*
J. Askins, 472:Fall/Winter84-331
R. Pickett, 649(WAL):Nov84-241
Wagoner, D. Landfall.
J. Askins, 472:Fall/Winter84-331
Wah, F. Breathin' My Name with a Sigh.
A. Mandel, 102(CanL):Summer84-149
Wailes, S.L. Studien zur Kleindichtung des Stricker.*
F.H. Bäuml, 406:Fall84-352
O. Ehrismann, 680(ZDP):Band103Heft1-143
Wain, J. - see Johnson, S.
Wainwright, W.J. Mysticism.
J.Y. Fenton, 485(PE&W):Jul84-337
Wais, K. Europäische Literatur im Vergleich. (J. Hösle, D. Janik and W. Theile, eds)
F. Meregalli, 52:Band19Heft2-200
Wakefield, D. French Eighteenth-Century Painting.
D. Posner, 617(TLS):22Mar85-322
Wakefield, D. Selling Out.
D. Fitzpatrick, 441:12May85-33
Wakefield, D. Stendhal.
V.D.L., 605(SC):15Apr85-295
Wakefield, T. Drifters.
J. Melmoth, 617(TLS):11Jan85-42
Walbank, F.W. A Historical Commentary on Polybius.* (Vol 3)
P.S. Derow, 313:Vol74-231

Walbank, F.W. and others, eds. The Cambridge Ancient History. (2nd ed) (Vol 7, Pt 1)
P. Green, 617(TLS):16Aug85-891
Walcott, D. Midsummer.*
P. Breslin, 491:Dec84-171
J. Figueroa, 364:Dec84/Jan85-128
J. Hollander, 676(YR):Autumn84-xi
W.H. Pritchard, 249(HudR):Summer84-331
P. Stitt, 219(GaR):Summer84-402
639(VQR):Summer84-90
Wald, A.M. The Revolutionary Imagination.*
J. Salzman, 432(NEQ):Mar84-118
E. Sproat, 42(AR):Winter84-117
Waldbaum, J.C. Metalwork from Sardis.
K.J. Shelton, 589:Jul84-707
Walden, D. The Ravished Image.
C. Gould, 324:Oct85-797
S.E. Lee, 441:22Sep85-16
Waldenfels, H. Absolute Nothingness.*
D.A. Dilworth, 407(MN):Summer84-214
Walder, D. Dickens and Religion.*
R.B., 148:Winter84-94
T.J. Cribb, 541(RES):Aug84-403
N.K. Hill, 152(UDQ):Winter85-111
S.M., 549(RLC):Jul-Sep84-362
N. Pope, 637(VS):Autumn83-130
T.R. Wright, 161(DUJ):Dec83-146
Waldmeir, J.J., ed. Critical Essays on John Barth.
E.B. Safer, 677(YES):Vol 14-360
Waldmeir, J.J. and K. Marek, eds. Up in Michigan.
S. Pinsker, 395(MFS):Summer84-310
Waldschmidt, E. Kleinere Sanskrit-Texte III.
D.S. Ruegg, 318(JAOS):Jul-Sep83-651
Wales, R. Harry.
S. Altinel, 617(TLS):12Jul85-776
Walhout, D. Send My Roots Rain.
R.K.R. Thornton, 541(RES):Aug84-409
Walicki, A. Philosophy and Romantic Nationalism.
L. Kolakowski, 575(SEER):Jan84-129
Walker, A. An Account of a Voyage to the North West Coast of America in 1785 and 1786.* (R. Fisher and J.M. Bumsted, eds)
R.L. Buckland, 649(WAL):Aug84-163
J. Giltrow, 102(CanL):Winter83-75
Walker, A. The Color Purple.
J.L. Halio, 598(SoR):Winter85-204
L. Marcus, 617(TLS):27Sep85-1070
Walker, A. Dietrich.*
G. Annan, 453(NYRB):14Feb85-5
Walker, A. Horses Make a Landscape Look More Beautiful.
L.M. Rosenberg, 441:7Apr85-12
Walker, A. In Love and Trouble.
L. Marcus, 617(TLS):27Sep85-1070
J. Mellors, 362:10Jan85-24
Walker, A. In Search of Our Mothers' Gardens.*
B.L. Clark, 395(MFS):Summer84-334
Walker, A. Franz Liszt.* (Vol 1)
A. Keiler, 414(MusQ):Summer84-374
A. Main, 410(M&L):Oct84-402
R.C. Mueller, 317:Spring84-185
Walker, A. The Third Life of Grange Copeland.
L. Marcus, 617(TLS):27Sep85-1070
Walker, A. - see Roberts, R.

379

Walker, C.B.F. Cuneiform Brick Inscrip-
tions in the British Museum, the Ash-
molean Museum, Oxford, the City of
Birmingham Museum and Art Gallery, the
City of Bristol Museum and Art Gallery.
  H. Neumann, 318(JAOS):Oct-Dec83-788
Walker, D. Louis le Brocquy.
  R. Tracy, 174(Éire):Fall84-157
Walker, D. Lean, Wind, Lean.
  P. Warner, 617(TLS):22Mar85-330
Walker, D. Jack London and Conan Doyle.
  E.S. Lauterbach, 395(MFS):Summer84-379
Walker, D.C. Dictionnaire inverse de
l'ancien français.*
  D.A. Kibbee, 207(FR):Apr85-769
  P. Swiggers, 353:Vol22No4-557
Walker, D.C. An Introduction to Old
French Morphophonology.*
  J. Felixberger, 547(RF):Band96Heft1/2-
121
  J. Klare, 682(ZPSK):Band37Heft6-732
Walker, D.H. - see Genet, J.
Walker, G. The Works of Carl P. Rollins.
  A. Lerner, 517(PBSA):Vol78No1-105
Walker, J. The Making of a Modernist.
  L. Simon, 454:Fall84-89
Walker, J. Metaphysics and Aesthetics in
the Works of Eduardo Barrios.
  D.W. Foster, 263(RIB):Vol34No3/4-434
Walker, J. The Once and Future Film.
  N. Wapshott, 362:6Jun85-31
Walker, J. Portraits: 5000 Years.
  T. Goss, 507:May/Jun84-111
Walker, J. - see Cunninghame Graham, R.B.
Walker, J.B. and J. The Light on Her Face.
  T. McDonough, 18:Sep85-68
  A. Shapiro, 441:24Feb85-22
Walker, J.R. and R.J. De Mallie, eds.
Lakota Society.
  G.A. Schultz, 106:Winter84-433
Walker, K. - see Lord Rochester
Walker, L. American Shelter.
  R. Banham, 617(TLS):26Apr85-476
Walker, M. The Literature of the United
States of America.
  A. Bleikasten, 189(EA):Jul-Sep85-353
Walker, S., ed. The Graywolf Annual.
  A.S. Grossman, 441:28Apr85-29
Walker, S., ed. Who Is She?
  S. Sheridan, 71(ALS):Oct84-546
Walker, T. You've Never Heard Me Sing.
  T. Dooley, 617(TLS):15Nov85-1296
Walker, W. The Two Dude Defense.
  N. Callendar, 441:9Jun85-37
  442(NY):8Jul85-75
Walkley, C. The Ghost in the Looking
Glass.
  P.E. Malcolmson, 637(VS):Autumn83-124
Wall, J.F. Skibo.
  A. Bell, 617(TLS):15Mar85-299
Wall, K. L'Inversion dans la subordonnée
en français contemporain.
  G. Price, 208(FS):Jan84-116
Wallace, B. Signs of the Former Tenant.
  J. Bayly, 526:Winter84-88
  S.S., 376:Feb84-142
Wallace, C.M. The Design of "Biographia
Literaria."
  J.A. Davies, 506(PSt):Sep84-191
  P.C. Rule, 661(WC):Summer84-101
Wallace, D.R. The Klamath Knot.
  P.T. Bryant, 649(WAL):May84-68

Wallace, D.R. The Turquoise Dragon.
  J. Berry, 441:7Apr85-14
Wallace, M. and G.P. Gates. Close Encoun-
ters.*
  T. Gitlin, 18:Jan/Feb85-57
Wallace, R. Writing Poems.
  D. Kirby, 128(CE):Mar84-248
Wallace, R. and C. Zimmerman, eds. The
Work.*
  U. Kareda, 397(MD):Mar84-151
  A. Messenger, 102(CanL):Winter83-135
Wallace, R.K. Jane Austen and Mozart.*
  P. Goubert, 189(EA):Jan-Mar85-112
  C.L. Johnson, 445(NCF):Dec84-336
  L. Kramer, 451:Spring85-277
  P.M. Spacks, 219(GaR):Fall84-621
Wallace, T.G. - see Burney, F.
Wallace, W.A. Galileo and His Sources.
  A.C. Crombie, 617(TLS):22Nov85-1319
Wallace, W.A. Prelude to Galileo.*
  E.D. Sylla, 482(PhR):Jan84-157
Wallace-Hadrill, A. Suetonius.*
  A.R. Birley, 313:Vol74-245
  E.T. Salmon, 124:Jul-Aug85-616
Wallach, M. and L. Psychology's Sanction
for Selfishness.
  N.M., 185:Apr85-774
Waller, M. - see Channer, C.C.
Wallinder, A. Författaren, förlaget och
barnboken.
  C.S. McKnight, 563(SS):Spring84-196
Walpole, H. Memoirs of King George II.
(J. Brooke, ed)
  L. Colley, 617(TLS):20Sep85-1035
Walpole, H. The Yale Edition of Horace
Walpole's Correspondence. (Vols 40-42)
(W.S. Lewis and J. Riely, eds)
  M. Kallich, 173(ECS):Spring85-426
Walpole, H. The Yale Edition of Horace
Walpole's Correspondence.* (Vol 43)
(E.M. Martz, with R.K. McClure and
W.T. La Moy, eds)
  J.W. Reed, 517(PBSA):Vol78No4-461
Walsdorf, J.J. William Morris in Private
Press and Limited Editions.*
  W.S. Peterson, 517(PBSA):Vol78No2-248
Walsdorf, J.J., ed. Printers on Morris.
  G.L. Aho, 536:Vol5-74
Walser, H. Die illegale NSDAP in Tirol
and Vorarlberg, 1933-1938.
  F.L. Carsten, 575(SEER):Oct84-636
Walser, M. Briefe an Lord Liszt.
  J. Grambow, 601(SuF):Mar-Apr84-432
Walser, M. The Inner Man.
  D.J. Enright, 453(NYRB):28Mar85-31
  J. Simon, 441:24Feb85-11
Walser, M. Letter to Lord Liszt.
  J. Banville, 441:15Sep85-11
Walser, M. Liebeserklärungen.
  R. Voris, 221(GQ):Summer84-450
Walser, M. Messmers Gedanken. Brandung.
  J. Neves, 617(TLS):15Nov85-1298
Walser, R. Selected Stories.*
  M. Harman, 221(GQ):Summer84-492
Walsh, J. American War Literature — 1914
to Vietnam.
  T. Dunn, 366:Spring84-132
  T. Myers, 395(MFS):Spring84-165
Walsh, K. A Fourteenth-Century Scholar
and Primate.*
  A. Hudson, 382(MAE):1984/2-317
Walsh, P.G. - see Capellanus, A.

Walsh, V. and H. Gram. Classical and Neo-
Classical Theories of General Equilib-
rium.
   D.L. Hammes and L.A. Boland, 488:Mar84-
   107
Walsh, W. Introduction to Keats.*
   M. Allott, 447(N&Q):Aug83-354
   V. Newey, 541(RES):May84-250
Walsh, W. R.K. Narayan.*
   B. King, 569(SR):Winter84-136
Walshe, M.O. - see von Tepl, J.
Walshe, R. Wales' Work.
   N. Shack, 617(TLS):16Aug85-907
Walter, C. Art and Ritual of the Byzan-
tine Church.
   H. Maguire, 589:Jan84-210
   T.F. Mathews, 54:Mar84-155
Walter, H. Enquête phonologique et vari-
étés régionales du français.*
   N. Gueunier, 209(FM):Oct84-230
Walter, H., ed. Phonologie des usages du
français.
   P. Swiggers, 350:Sep85-717
Walter, J.A. Fair Shares?
   F. Cairncross, 617(TLS):20Sep85-1025
Walter, T. Hope on the Dole.
   F. Cairncross, 617(TLS):20Sep85-1025
Walter-Karydi, E., W. Felten and R.
Smetana-Scherrer. Alt-Ägina. (Pt 2,
Vol 1)
   J. Boardman, 123:Vol34No1-148
Walter-Schneider, M. Denken als Verdacht.
   J. Ryan, 454:Spring85-262
Walther, J. Bewerbung bei Hofe.
   G. Müller-Waldeck, 654(WB):2/1984-319
Walton, D. Evening Out.
   K. Cushman, 573(SSF):Winter84-75
Walton, D.N. Topical Relevance in Argumen-
tation.
   A. Bremerich-Vos, 353:Vol22No6-927
Walton, I. The Compleat Angler.* (J.
Bevan, ed)
   J.R. Mulder, 551(RenQ):Winter84-665
Walton, J.M. - see Craig, E.G.
Walvin, J. English Urban Life 1776-1851.
   J. Stevenson, 617(TLS):27Dec85-1490
Walz, J.C. Error Correction Techniques
for the FL Classroom.
   F.W. Medley, Jr., 399(MLJ):Autumn84-
   273
Walz, T. Trade between Egypt and Bilād As-
Sūdān, 1700-1820.
   N. Hanna, 318(JAOS):Jul-Sep83-632
Walzer, M. Exodus and Revolution.
   R.M. Brown, 441:20Jan85-8
Walzer, M. Spheres of Justice.*
   T.D. Campbell, 518:Oct84-236
   B. Paskins, 483:Jul84-413
Wambaugh, J. The Secrets of Harry Bright.
   J. Lardner, 441:6Oct85-11
   442(NY):18Nov85-177
Wandersee, W.D. Women's Work and Family
Values, 1920-1940.
   F.H. Early, 106:Summer84-199
Wandor, M., ed. On Gender and Writing.
   S. Oldfield, 89(BJA):Autumn84-376
Wandor, M. Understudies.
   E. Diamond, 397(MD):Mar84-145
Wandruszka, U. Studien zur italienischen
Wortstellung.
   H. Stammerjohann, 72:Band221Heft2-416
Wands, J.M. - see Hall, J.

Wandschneider, D. Raum, Zeit, Relativität.
   L.S. Stepelevich, 543:Sep83-157
Wang Fai-hsi. Chinese Revolutionary.
   J. Ch'en, 302:Vol20No2-187
Wang, G.C., ed and trans. Economic Reform
in the PRC.
   R.M. Field, 293(JASt):May84-535
Wangerin, W., Jr. The Book of Sorrows.
   M. Malone, 441:11Aug85-11
Wanner, E. and L.R. Gleitman, eds. Lan-
guage Acquisition.
   A. Elliot, 297(JL):Mar84-201
Wapnewski, P. Richard Wagner. (2nd ed)
   R. Hollinrake, 410(M&L):Jan84-87
Ward, A. The Blood Seed.
   S.S. Klass, 441:22Dec85-18
Ward, B. Miracles and the Medieval Mind.
   J.C. Poulin, 589:Apr84-450
   C.L. Scarborough, 345(KRQ):Vol31No4-
   453
   N. Tanner, 382(MAE):1984/1-148
Ward, C.A., P. Shashko and D.E. Pienkos,
eds. Studies in Ethnicity.
   I.P. Winner, 104(CASS):Spring-Summer84-
   235
Ward, C.C. and R.E. - see O'Conor, C.
Ward, D. - see Grimm, J. and W.
Ward, G.C. Before the Trumpet.
   S. Ware, 441:14Jul85-27
   442(NY):10Jun85-140
Ward, J. A Late Harvest.
   T. Eagleton, 565:Winter83/84-77
Ward, J.P. Poetry and the Sociological
Idea.
   T. Eagleton, 541(RES):Aug84-427
Ward, J.P. Wordsworth's Language of Men.
   P. Hamilton, 617(TLS):20Sep85-1037
Ward, R. Red Baker.
   P. Barker, 441:19May85-14
Ward, S., ed. DHSS in Crisis.
   F. Cairncross, 617(TLS):20Sep85-1025
Ward, W.A. Studies in Scarab Seals.
   (Vol 1)
   N. Scott, 318(JAOS):Apr-Jun83-483
Warden, J., ed. Orpheus.*
   J.B. Friedman, 589:Jan84-213
   R.H. Terpening, 276:Autumn84-278
Warden, M.R. The Illinois Suite.
   W. Geyer, 649(WAL):Feb85-327
Wardhaugh, R. How Conversation Works.
   L. Hudson, 617(TLS):22Mar85-307
Wardhaugh, R. Language and Nationhood.
   T.C. Frazer, 350:Mar85-243
   L.G. Kelly, 320(CJL):Fall84-199
Wardman, A. Religion and Statecraft among
the Romans.
   S.R.F. Price, 123:Vol34No1-139
Ware, G. William Hastie.
   J.W. Ward, 441:10Mar85-37
   442(NY):11Mar85-137
Ware, J.D. George Gauld. (rev by R.R.
Rea)
   D.C. Weaver, 9(AlaR):Jul84-233
Warga, W. Hardcover.
   N. Callendar, 441:17Nov85-46
Warlop, E. The Flemish Nobility Before
1300.
   N. Tolstoy, 617(TLS):22Feb85-206
Warner, A. Complementation in Middle
English and the Methodology of Histori-
cal Syntax.*
   B.G. Hewitt, 361:Jan/Feb84-157

Warner, E., ed. Virginia Woolf.
V. Glendinning, 176:Mar85-62
Warner, E. and G. Hough, eds. Strangeness
and Beauty.
L. Brake, 506(PSt):Dec84-265
I. Small, 89(BJA):Summer84-276
Warner, K.P. Thomas Otway.
W.J. Burling, 568(SCN):Spring-
Summer84-13
Warner, M. Monuments and Maidens.
P. Beer, 362:21Nov85-30
S. Brownmiller, 441:1Dec85-13
M. Lefkowitz, 617(TLS):20Dec85-1446
Warner, P. Kitchener.
K. Jeffery, 617(TLS):13Dec85-1417
Warner, S.T. Letters.* (W. Maxwell, ed)
Scenes of Childhood.* The True Heart.
Lolly Willowes, or the Loving Huntsman.
E. Perényi, 453(NYRB):18Jul85-27
Warner, S.T. One Thing Leading to
Another.* (S. Pinney, ed)
J. Mellors, 364:Jul84-96
E. Perényi, 453(NYRB):18Jul85-27
Warner, W.B. Reading "Clarissa."*
F. Rau, 38:Band102Heft1/2-245
Warnicke, R.M. Women of the English Ren-
aissance and Reformation.
L. Martines, 551(RenQ):Autumn84-447
Warnock, G.J. Morality and Language.*
M.F. Murchison, 83:Spring84-140
Warren, D., with J. Cagney. James Cagney.
M. Buckley, 200:Jan84-60
Warren, G.H. Fountain of Discontent.
F.C. Drake, 106:Winter84-407
Warren, J., ed. Orpheus.
V. Worthy, 391:Oct84-102
Warren, L. Répertoire des ressources en
littérature de jeunesse.
C. Gerson, 102(CanL):Summer84-127
Warren, R. Each Leaf Shines Separate.
T. Sleigh, 441:21Jul85-24
Warren, R.P. Chief Joseph of the Nez
Percé.*
P. Balla, 472:Fall/Winter84-267
A. Shelley, 364:Apr/May84-97
639(VQR):Winter84-22
Warren, R.P. Jefferson Davis Gets his
Citizenship Back.*
R. Gray, 677(YES):Vol 14-356
Warren, R.P. New and Selected Poems.
H. Bloom, 453(NYRB):30May85-40
J. Gardner, 129:Nov85-122
W.H. Pritchard, 441:12May85-8
Warren, R.P. Rumor Verified.*
P. Balla, 472:Fall/Winter84-267
R. Pybus, 565:Winter83/84-68
Warrender, H. - see Hobbes, T.
von Wartburg, W. Französisches etymolo-
gisches Wörterbuch. (fasc 135-141)
P. Swiggers, 464:Vol30fasc1/2-269
von Wartburg, W. Französisches Etymolo-
gisches Wörterbuch.* (fasc 143) (C.T.
Gossen, ed)
R. Arveiller, 209(FM):Apr84-100
von Wartburg, W. Französisches Etymol-
ogisches Wörterbuch. (fasc 144) (C.T.
Gossen, ed)
R. Arveiller, 209(FM):Oct84-264
G. Roques, 553(RLiR):Jan-Jun84-226
Warwick, P.S. and M.H. Greenberg - see
Dick, P.K.
Washburn, M. Distant Encounters.
E. Argyle, 529(QQ):Winter84-1047

Washburn, Y. Juan José Arreola.
S. Menton, 238:May84-313
Washington, B.T. The Booker T. Washington
Papers. (Vol 12) (L.R. Harlan and R.W.
Smock, eds)
C.H. Johnson, 9(AlaR):Oct84-297
Washington, G. The Papers of George Wash-
ington. (Vols 1 and 2) (W.W. Abbot and
others, eds)
D.H. Kent, 656(WMQ):Jan84-137
Washington, G. The Papers of George Wash-
ington: The Journal of the Proceedings
of the President, 1793-1797. (D. Twohig,
ed)
L.K. Herber, 656(WMQ):Jan84-169
Wass, D. Government and the Governed.*
I. Davidson, 176:Apr85-71
Wasserman, G.R. Roland Barthes.*
P. Collier, 402(MLR):Apr84-467
Wasserman, J.N., J.L. Linsley and J.A.
Kramer, eds. Edward Albee.
A. Paolucci, 397(MD):Sep84-453
Wasserstein, A. - see Galen
Wasserstein, D. The Rise and Fall of the
Party-Kings.
R. Fletcher, 617(TLS):18Oct85-1190
Wasson, B. Count No 'Count.
C.S. Brown, 569(SR):Summer84-474
J.V. Creighton, 395(MFS):Summer84-327
M. Grimwood, 578:Fall85-101
A.F. Kinney, 587(SAF):Autumn84-237
295(JML):Nov84-437
"Waterbury Clocks."
G. Wills, 39:Jan84-69
Waterhouse, K. Waterhouse at Large.
B. Mooney, 362:21Nov85-35
Waterhouse, R. A Heidegger Critique.
S.L. Bartky, 482(PhR):Jan84-135
Waterlow, S.J. Nature, Change and Agency
in Aristotle's "Physics."*
J.D.G. Evans, 479(PhQ):Jan84-78
C.A. Freeland, 482(PhR):Jul84-439
M. Schofield, 483:Jul84-392
C.J.F. Williams, 393(Mind):Apr84-297
Waterlow, S.J. Passage and Possibility.*
J.M. Day, 518:Apr84-81
J.D.G. Evans, 479(PhQ):Jan84-78
C.A. Freeland, 482(PhR):Jul84-439
M. Schofield, 483:Jul84-392
M.J. White, 303(JoHS):Vol 104-212
C.J.F. Williams, 393(Mind):Apr84-297
Waters, K.H. Herodotos the Historian.
S. Hornblower, 617(TLS):1Mar85-222
Waters, M. The Comic Irishman.*
272(IUR):Autumn84-309
Waters, M. The Stories in the Light.
J. Carter, 219(GaR):Summer84-415
Waterson, M., ed. The Country House Remem-
bered.
A. Bell, 617(TLS):20Dec85-1452
P. Johnson, 362:13Jun85-24
Watkin, D. Morality and Architecture.
617(TLS):5Apr85-395
Watkin, D. The Royal Interiors of Regency
England.
J.M. Crook, 617(TLS):10May85-519
J.S. Curl, 324:Jun85-500
Watkin, D. Athenian Stuart.*
J.M. Robinson, 39:Apr84-303
Watkin, D. and P. Campbell, eds. A House
in Town.
C.G. Gilbert, 90:Nov84-705

Watkins, F.C. Then and Now.*
A. Ball, 585(SoQ):Winter84-95
L. Casper, 651(WHR):Spring84-87
N. Nakadate, 392:Winter83/84-115
V. Strandberg, 579(SAQ):Summer84-358
295(JML):Nov84-514
Watkins, L. Dark with Stars.
404:Autumn84-59
Watkins, S.M. Clothing.
E.H., 614:Winter85-19
Watrous, J. A Century of American Print-
making 1880-1980.
K. Baker, 617(TLS):8Feb85-141
Watson, A.G. Catalogue of Dated and Dat-
able Manuscripts c. 435-1600 in Oxford
Libraries.
A.J. Piper, 617(TLS):25Jan85-103
Watson, C.N., Jr. The Novels of Jack
London.*
S.C. Brennan, 594:Fall84-355
J. Tavernier-Courbin, 651(WHR):
Autumn84-286
Watson, D. Caledonia Australis.
N. Ascherson, 617(TLS):12Apr85-402
Watson, G., ed. Free Will.
M.B., 185:Jan85-383
Watson, G.R. The Roman Soldier.
617(TLS):27Sep85-1071
Watson, H.L. Jacksonian Politics and Com-
munity Conflict.
J.R. Sharp, 106:Spring84-49
Watson, J.R. Wordsworth's Vital Soul.*
J.A. Hodgson, 591(SIR):Spring84-121
Watson, L. Heaven's Breath.
P.T. O'Conner, 441:15Sep85-25
Watson, M. York Bowen.*
S.R. Craggs, 415:Nov84-647
Watson, R. The Literature of Scotland.
G. Mangan, 617(TLS):19Apr85-450
Watson, R. The Playfair Hours.
C. de Hamel, 617(TLS):29Mar85-367
Watson, R.N. Shakespeare and the Hazards
of Ambition.
G. Taylor, 617(TLS):16Aug85-905
Watson, W. Gramsci x 3.
A. Wilson, 526:Autumn84-88
Watson, W. Tang and Liao Ceramics.
N. Wood, 617(TLS):3May85-505
Watson-Williams, H. The Novels of Natha-
lie Sarraute.
J. Baetens, 547(RF):Band96Heft1/2-203
G.R. Besser, 207(FR):Dec84-303
Watt, G. The Fallen Woman in the Nine-
teenth Century English Novel.*
V. Colby, 445(NCF):Dec84-344
J. Marcus, 395(MFS):Winter84-745
R.T. Vanarsdel, 594:Winter84-469
Watt, J.G., with D. Wead. The Courage of
a Conservative.
F. Barnes, 441:20Oct85-28
Watt, W.S. - see Cicero
Wattenberg, B.J. The Good News Is the Bad
News Is Wrong.*
S. McCracken, 129:Mar85-68
Watters, D.H. "With Bodilie Eyes."*
P. Lindholdt, 568(SCN):Spring-Summer84-
18
Watters, J. and Horst. Return Engagement.*
G.M., 62:May85-5
Watts, C. R.B. Cunninghame Graham.
J. Walker, 177(ELT):Vol27No3-260
Watts, C. A Preface to Conrad.
295(JML):Nov84-422

Watts, D.A. - see Rotrou, J.
Watts, E.S. The Businessman in American
Literature.*
B. Maine, 577(SHR):Fall84-363
L.N. Neufeldt, 301(JEGP):Jan84-150
W.W. Westbrook, 536:Vol6-191
Watts, G.S. The Revolution of Ideas.*
B. Langtry, 63:Sep84-315
Watts, P.M. Nicolaus Cusanus.
D.F. Duclow, 589:Apr84-453
Watts, S.J. A Social History of Western
Europe 1450-1720.
G. Parker, 617(TLS):19Apr85-444
Watzlauer, A., ed. Dictionary of Geo-
sciences (English-German/German-English).
(2nd ed)
R.R.B. Von Frese, 399(MLJ):Spring84-80
Waugh, A. The Diaries of Auberon Waugh.
(A. Galli-Pahlari, ed)
D. Trelford, 362:12Sep85-25
Waugh, A. The Foxglove Saga. Path of
Dalliance. Who are the Violets Now?
Consider the Lilies. A Bed of Flowers.
J.K.L. Walker, 617(TLS):26Apr85-479
Waugh, E. The Essays, Articles and
Reviews of Evelyn Waugh.* (D. Gallagher,
ed)
C. Hawtree, 364:Apr/May84-130
Waugh, E. Labels. Remote People.
617(TLS):1Feb85-131
Waugh, L.R. and M. Halle - see Jakobson, R.
Waugh, P. Metafiction.
C. Baldick, 617(TLS):15Mar85-295
Wayman, T. Counting the Hours.
M. Bowering, 102(CanL):Autumn84-138
B. Whiteman, 526:Summer84-75
Wayman, T. Inside Job.*
M. Bowering, 102(CanL):Autumn84-138
J. Daniels, 526:Summer84-78
Weales, G. Canned Goods as Caviar.
P. Brunette, 441:8Sep85-25
"Wealth of the Ancient World."
J. Boardman, 123:Vol34No2-350
Wearing, J.P. The London Stage, 1910-
1919.*
T.R. Griffiths, 611(TN):Vol38No3-152
Weatherford, R. Philosophical Foundations
of Probability Theory.*
P. Milne, 84:Mar84-95
Weaver, G., ed. The American Short Story
1945-1980.
R.L. Johnson, 651(WHR):Autumn84-298
C. Moran, 573(SSF):Winter84-81
M. Rohrberger, 395(MFS):Summer84-335
Weaver, M. Julia Margaret Cameron, 1815-
1879.
C. Gere, 39:Sep84-218
Webb, A.B.W. - see O'Connor, R.
Webb, B. The Diary of Beatrice Webb.*
(Vol 1) (N. and J. Mackenzie, eds)
B. Caine, 637(VS):Autumn83-81
Webb, B. The Diary of Beatrice Webb.
(Vol 3) (N. and J. Mackenzie, eds)
J. Harris, 617(TLS):11Oct85-1126
Webb, B. The Diary of Beatrice Webb.
(Vol 4) (N. and J. Mackenzie, eds)
J. Harris, 617(TLS):11Oct85-1126
M. Warnock, 362:24Oct85-28
Webb, C.C. and M. Chapian. Forgive Me.
A. Grimes, 441:15Dec85-17
Webb, J.C. Mechanism, Mentalism, and Meta-
mathematics.*
H.T. Hodes, 311(JP):Aug84-456

Webb, K., ed. Lilliput Goes to War.
  E.S. Turner, 617(TLS):29Nov85-1346
Webb, P. The Vision Tree. (S. Thesen, ed)
  J.F. Hulcoop, 168(ECW):Winter84/85-359
  B. Pell, 628(UWR):Spring-Summer85-108
Webb, P. and R. Short. Hans Bellmer.
  R. Cardinal, 617(TLS):23Aug85-928
Webb, R.C., with S.A. Webb. Jean Genet
  and his Critics.*
  D.H. Walker, 402(MLR):Jan84-204
Webb, S.S. 1676.*
  617(TLS):27Dec85-1491
Webb, T., ed. English Romantic Hellenism,
  1700-1824.*
  P.J. Manning, 591(SIR):Fall84-401
Webb, T. Georgia O'Keeffe.
  L. Liebmann, 62:Dec84-75
Weber, B. - see Crane, H.
Weber, B.N. and H. Heinen, eds. Bertolt
  Brecht.*
  C.R. Mueller, 615(TJ):Mar82-128
Weber, H.B. - see "The Modern Encyclopedia
  of Russian and Soviet Literatures ... "
Weber, J. Gestalt Bewegung Farbe.
  R. Arnheim, 290(JAAC):Spring85-319
Weber, M. Gesamtausgabe. (Section 1,
  Vol 15) (W.J. Mommsen and G. Hübinger,
  eds)
  T. Bottomore, 617(TLS):19Apr85-429
Weber, N. Das gesellschaftlich Ver-
  mittelte der Romane österreichischer
  Schriftsteller seit 1970.
  J. Koppensteiner, 406:Winter84-469
  K. Müller, 602:Band15Heft1-159
Weber, R.W. Der moderne Roman.
  U. Riese, 654(WB):3/1984-505
Weber, S. Unwrapping Balzac.
  F. Jameson, 81:Fall83-227
Webster, B.S. Blake's Prophetic Psychol-
  ogy.*
  S.D. Cox, 173(ECS):Spring85-391
  F. Piquet, 189(EA):Oct-Dec85-466
  639(VQR):Summer84-84
Webster, C. From Paracelsus to Newton.
  S. Schaffer, 84:Jun84-191
Webster, D. The Papers of Daniel Webster:
  Legal Papers. (Vols 1 and 2) (A.S.
  Konefsky and A.J. King, eds)
  G.W. Gawalt, 656(WMQ):Apr84-329
  H.A. Johnson, 432(NEQ):Sep84-453
Webster, J. The Selected Plays of John
  Webster. (J. Dollimore and A. Sinfield,
  eds)
  D. Mehl, 72:Band221Heft2-479
"Webster's Ninth New Collegiate Diction-
  ary." (F.C. Mish, ed-in-chief)
  T.L. Clark, 35(AS):Spring84-70
  H. Käsmann, 38:Band102Heft3/4-499
Wechsler, J. A Human Comedy.*
  A. McCauley, 54:Jun84-342
  N. McWilliam, 59:Mar84-115
Weck, H. Die "Rechtssumme" Bruder Bert-
  holds, eine deutsche abecedarische Bear-
  beitung der "Summa confessorum" des
  Johannes von Freiburg.
  F.W. von Kries, 589:Apr84-455
Wedberg, A. A History of Philosophy.
  (Vol 2)
  J. Collins, 319:Apr85-273
Wedderburn, R. The Complaynt of Scotland
  (c. 1550).
  M.P. McDiarmid, 588(SSL):Vol 19-292

Wedgwood, C.V. The Spoils of Time.
  P-L. Adams, 61:Apr85-140
  A. Briggs, 176:Jan85-52
  P. Johnson, 441:7Apr85-7
Weeber, K-W. Funde in Etrurien.
  P. Flobert, 555:Vol58fasc1-168
Weedman, J.B. Samuel Delany.
  P. Fitting, 561(SFS):Mar84-88
Weeks, A. The Paradox of the Employee.*
  L.R. Shaw, 221(GQ):Spring84-330
Wegman, W. Everyday Problems.
  J. Yau, 62:Dec84-76
Wegman, W. $19.84.
  M. Wilson, 62:Dec84-2
Wehdeking, V. Alfred Andersch.
  R.W. Williams, 402(MLR):Jul84-757
Wehle, W. Novellenerzählen.*
  E. Schulze-Witzenrath, 490:Band15
  Heft1/2-185
  H. Wentzlaff-Eggebert, 72:Band221Heft2-
  428
Wehrli, M. Geschichte der deutschen Liter-
  atur von den Anfängen bis zur Gegenwart.*
  (Vol 1: Geschichte der deutschen Litera-
  tur vom frühen Mittelalter bis zum Ende
  des 16. Jahrhunderts.)
  F.G. Gentry, 406:Fall84-356
Wehse, R., ed. Märchenerzähler — Erzählge-
  meinschaft.
  L. Dégh, 196:Band25Heft1/2-164
Wehse, R., ed. Warum sind die Ostfriesen
  gelb im Gesicht?
  B.J. Warneken, 196:Band25Heft3/4-378
Wei Chuang. The Song-Poetry of Wei Chuang
  (836-910 A.D.). (J.T. Wixted, ed and
  trans)
  S.E. Cahill, 318(JAOS):Apr-Jun83-458
Wei, K. and T. Quinn. Second Daughter.
  D. Davin, 617(TLS):5Apr85-375
Weiand, C. Die Gerade und der Kreis.
  F. Claudon, 605(SC):15Apr85-291
Weible, R., ed. Essays from the Lowell
  Conference on Industrial History 1982
  and 1983.
  B. King, 614:Spring85-21
Weidert, A. Componential Analysis of
  Lushai Phonology.
  D.L. Goyvaerts, 464:Vol30fasc1/2-281
Weidner, R.I., comp. American Ceramics
  before 1930.
  E.P. Denker, 658:Winter84-289
Weigel, S. "Und selbst im Kerker
  frei. ... "
  C. Poore, 221(GQ):Summer84-507
Weigl, B. and T.R. Hummer, eds. The Imag-
  ination as Glory.
  R.J. Calhoun, 578:Fall85-116
Weigle, M. Spiders and Spinsters.
  C.L. Edwards, 650(WF):Apr84-146
  B. Stoeltje, 649(WAL):May84-69
Weijnen, A.A. The Value of the Map Config-
  uration.
  C.V.J. Russ, 685(ZDL):1/1984-125
Weiler, I. Der Sport bei den Völkern der
  Alten Welt.*
  J-P. Thuillier, 555:Vol58fasc1-167
Weimann, R. Kunstensemble und Öffentlich-
  keit.
  H-G. Werner, 601(SuF):Jan-Feb84-195
de Weinberg, M.B.F. - see under Fontanella
  de Weinberg, M.B.

Weinblatt, A. T.S. Eliot and the Myth of
Adequation.
  295(JML):Nov84-432
Weinbrot, H.D. Alexander Pope and the
Traditions of Formal Verse Satire.*
  V. Carretta, 405(MP):May85-427
  J.V. Guerinot, 568(SCN):Spring-
  Summer84-10
  W. Kupersmith, 191(ELN):Mar85-74
  D.C. Mell, 173(ECS):Fall84-137
  P.J. Schakel, 125:Spring84-288
  J. Sitter, 301(JEGP):Jan84-127
  H.M. Solomon, 577(SHR):Summer84-260
  T. Woodman, 677(YES):Vol 14-326
Weiner, E.S.C., comp. The Oxford Guide to
English Usage.*
  R.W. Zandvoort, 179(ES):Jun84-286
Weiner, H. Sixteen. Spoke.
  J. Retallack, 472:Fall/Winter84-213
Weiner, M. and M.F. Katzenstein, with
K.V.N. Rao. India's Preferential
Policies.
  P. Wallace, 293(JASt):Aug84-792
Weiner, R. Das Amerikabild von Karl Marx.
  W. Hoffmeister, 133:Band17Heft1/2-188
Weinglass, D.H. - see Fuseli, H.
Weinig, M.A. Verbal Pattern in "Four
Quartets."
  295(JML):Nov84-433
Weinmayer, B. Studien zur Gebrauchssitua-
tion frühen deutscher Druckprosa.
  E. Kleinschmidt, 684(ZDA):Band113Heft3-
  127
Weinreb, B. and C. Hibbert, eds. The
London Encyclopaedia.*
  I. Grant, 592:Vol 196No1004-54
Weinreb, R.P. Premiers poèmes, avec
exercices de vocabulaire, de grammaire
et de prononciation.
  M.A. Barnett, 399(MLJ):Spring84-75
Weinreb, R.P. Visions et révisions.
  M.G. Shockey, 207(FR):Dec84-342
Weinreich-Haste, H. and D. Locke, eds.
Morality in the Making.
  J. Darling, 518:Oct84-230
Weinstein, A. Fictions of the Self: 1550-
1800.*
  J. Kolbert, 207(FR):Oct84-120
Weinstein, B. and A. Segal. Haiti.
  A. Valdman, 207(FR):Dec84-327
Weinstein, D. and R.M. Bell. Saints and
Society.*
  C.W. Bynum, 589:Apr84-457
  P. Partner, 551(RenQ):Summer84-228
Weinstein, F.S. A Hidden Childhood.
  J. Burnley, 441:8Sep85-30
Weinstein, M.A. The Wilderness and the
City.*
  P.H. Hare, 319:Oct85-601
  A.J. Reck, 543:Jun84-874
Weinstein, P.M. The Semantics of Desire.
  S. Cohan, 454:Spring85-267
  T. Docherty, 617(TLS):1Mar85-240
Weintraub, S., ed. British Dramatists
since World War II.
  T.P. Adler, 615(TJ):Mar84-137
Weintraub, S. The Unexpected Shaw.*
  A.P. Barr, 637(VS):Winter84-279
  F.P.W. McDowell, 130:Winter84/85-378
  M. Meisel, 177(ELT):Vol27No1-64
Weintraub, S. - see Shaw, G.B. and F.
Harris

Weintraub, W. Poeta i prorok. Profecja i
profesura.
  D.A. Frick, 497(PolR):Vol29No1/2-135
Weinzierl, E. and K. Skalnik. Österreich
1918-1938.
  R. Schneider, 384:Jul84-578
Weir, R.F. Selective Nontreatment of Hand-
icapped Newborns.*
  A. Hacker, 453(NYRB):28Feb85-37
  K.K., 185:Apr85-787
Weir, R.M. Colonial South Carolina.
  R.N. Klein, 656(WMQ):Jul84-503
Weisberg, G.P., ed. The European Realist
Tradition.*
  M.S. Kinsey, 446(NCFS):Winter-Spring85-
  173
  R. Pickvance, 90:Feb84-95
  C. Pollock, 59:Sep84-359
  A. Solomon-Godeau, 55:Oct84-32
Weisberg, R.H. The Failure of the Word.
  A.W.B. Simpson, 617(TLS):29Mar85-342
  B. Thomas, 454:Spring85-274
Weisman, R. Witchcraft, Magic, and
Religion in Seventeenth-Century Mass-
achusetts.*
  B. Rosenthal, 432(NEQ):Dec84-598
  K. Silverman, 165(EAL):Winter84/85-300
Weiss, B. and L.C. Pérez. Juan de la
Cueva's "Los inventores de las cosas."
  A. Porqueras-Mayo, 552(REH):May84-319
Weiss, P. Privacy.*
  E. Pols, 543:Jun84-875
Weiss, T. Recoveries.* The Man from Por-
lock.*
  W. Spiegelman, 472:Fall/Winter84-315
Weiss, T. A Slow Fuse.
  R. Tillinghast, 441:31Mar85-14
Weiss, T. and R. - see Schubert, D.
Weiss, U. Das philosophische System von
Thomas Hobbes.
  J. Barnouw, 543:Sep83-159
Weissberg, M.P. Dangerous Secrets.
  P. Lomas, 617(TLS):22Feb85-190
Weissbort, D., ed. Modern Poetry in Trans-
lation, 1983.
  639(VQR):Winter84-23
Weissenborn, J. and W. Klein, eds. Here
and There.
  G.F. Meier, 682(ZPSK):Band37Heft3-405
Weissman, J. - see Carruth, H.
Weissmann, G. The Woods Hole Cantata.
  A. Fels, 441:29Sep85-19
  442(NY):18Nov85-176
Weisstein, U. Vergleichende Literaturwis-
senschaft.
  M. Schmeling, 678(YCGL):No32-155
Weitz, H-J. - see Boisserée, S.
Weitzman, L.J. The Divorce Revolution.
  B.F. Williamson, 441:13Oct85-39
Weitzman, M.L. The Share Economy.
  S. Brittan, 176:Apr85-58
  W. Diebold, 441:14Apr85-10
  L.C. Thurow, 453(NYRB):14Feb85-9
Weixlmann, J. American Short-Fiction Crit-
icism and Scholarship, 1959-1977.*
  J.M. Flora, 534(RALS):Spring82-116
von Weizsäcker, C.F. The Unity of Nature.
  M.L.G. Redhead, 84:Sep84-274
von Weizsäcker, R. Die Deutsche Ge-
schichte geht Weiter.*
  T.G. Ash, 453(NYRB):31Jan85-33
Welch, A.T. and P. Cachia, eds. Islam.*
  M. Swartz, 318(JAOS):Apr-Jun83-444

Welch, C.B. Liberty and Utility.*
  E. Kennedy, 173(ECS):Summer85-561
Welch, D. I Left My Grandfather's House.*
  P. Parker, 364:Nov84-96
Welch, D. The Journals of Denton Welch.*
  (M. De-la-Noy, ed)
  J. Baumel, 441:10Mar85-25
  P. Parker, 364:Nov84-96
Welch, H. and A. Seidel, eds. Facets of
Taoism.*
  J.S. Major, 318(JAOS):Apr-Jun83-462
Welch, J. Out Walking.
  L. Mackinnon, 617(TLS):23Aug85-933
Welch, L. and C. Address: Rimbaud, Mal-
larmé, Butor.
  J.M. Cocking, 208(FS):Jul84-359
  F. Wolfzettel, 547(RF):Band96Heft3-364
Welch, R.E., Jr. Response to Revolution.
  J.I. Dominguez, 441:8Dec85-77
Welcome, J. The Sporting World of R.S.
Surtees.
  L. Schachterle, 637(VS):Winter84-276
Weldon, F. Letters to Alice.*
  H. Wolitzer, 441:30Jun85-9
Weldon, F. Polaris and Other Stories.
  A.S. Byatt, 617(TLS):9Aug85-875
Weldon, F. Rebecca West.
  A. Huth, 362:5Dec85-27
Weldon, M. The Psychotronic Encyclopedia
of Film.
  J. Nangle, 200:Mar84-183
  T. Wiener, 18:Mar85-57
Wellbery, D.E. Lessing's "Laocoon."
  J.P. Stern, 617(TLS):25Jan85-99
Wellek, R. The Attack on Literature and
Other Essays.*
  D.G. Marshall, 678(YCGL):No32-151
  G.A. Panichas, 149(CLS):Spring84-103
  P. Parrinder, 366:Autumn84-249
Wellek, R. Four Critics.*
  E.L. Corredor, 478:Apr84-134
  J.P. Strelka, 149(CLS):Summer84-249
Wellesbourne, P. Bomb New York!
  S. Altinel, 617(TLS):13Dec85-1434
Wellikoff, A. The American Historical
Supply Catalogue.
  W. Smith, 441:3Feb85-22
Wellington, J.S., comp. Dictionary of
Bibliographic Abbreviations Found in
the Scholarship of Classical Studies
and Related Disciplines.
  W.M. Calder 3d, 121(CJ):Dec84/Jan85-
162
Wells, D.A. - see "The Year's Work in Mod-
ern Language Studies"
Wells, G.A. Goethe and the Development of
Science 1750-1900.
  N. Reeves, 447(N&Q):Dec83-574
Wells, H.G. Experiment in Autobiography.*
  S. Hynes, 441:3Mar85-14
Wells, H.G. The New Machiavelli. Chris-
tina Alberta's Father. Mr. Britling
Sees it Through.
  P. Kemp, 617(TLS):27Dec85-1479
Wells, H.G. H.G. Wells in Love.* (G.P.
Wells, ed)
  S. Hynes, 441:3Mar85-14
  D. Taylor, 364:Aug/Sep84-146
Wells, H.G. The Wheels of Chance. Kipps.
  P. Reading, 617(TLS):25Jan85-102
Wells, J.C. Accents of English.*
  M. Görlach, 38:Band102Heft1/2-176
  W. Viereck, 257(IRAL):May84-149

Wells, P.S. Farms, Villages, and Cities.
  A. Sherratt, 617(TLS):25Oct85-1215
Wells, R. Insurrection.
  M. Fitzpatrick, 83:Spring84-115
Wells, R.H. Spenser's "Faerie Queene" and
the Cult of Elizabeth.
  C.A.H., 604:Winter84-6
  J.H. King, 250(HLQ):Spring84-139
Wells, S. Modernizing Shakespeare's Spell-
ing [together with] Taylor, G. Three
Studies in the Text of "Henry V."*
  M. Spevack, 156(JDSh):Jahrbuch1984-225
Wells, S. - see "Shakespeare Survey"
Welsch, R. Shingling the Fog and Other
Plains Lies.
  K. Carabine, 447(N&Q):Apr83-188
Welsh, A. Reflections on the Hero as
Quixote.*
  R. Wilson, 405(MP):Aug84-120
Welskopf, E.C., ed. Soziale Typenbegriffe
im alten Griechenland und ihr Fortleben
in den Sprachen der Welt. (Vols 3-5)
  F. Gschnitzer, 260(IF):Band89-345
  É. Will, 555:Vol58fasc1-113
Welskopf, E.C., ed. Soziale Typenbegriffe
im alten Griechenland und ihr Fortleben
in den Sprachen der Welt. (Vols 6 and 7)
  F. Gschnitzer, 260(IF):Band89-345
"Weltliteratur: Die Lust am Übersetzen im
Jahrhundert Goethes."
  J. Voisine, 549(RLC):Jan-Mar84-121
Welty, E. One Writer's Beginnings.*
  S.C., 219(GaR):Winter84-902
  R. Drake, 396(ModA):Spring/Summer84-
  276
  H. Kirkwood, 99:Nov84-36
  L. Smith, 578:Spring85-120
Welzig, W., ed. Predigt und soziale Wirk-
lichkeit.
  P.V. Brady, 402(MLR):Jan84-230
  R.E. Schade, 133:Band17Heft1/2-134
Welzig, W. and others - see Schnitzler, A.
Wendelius, L. Bilden av Amerika i svensk
prosafiktion 1890-1914.
  R. McKnight, 563(SS):Summer84-308
Wendorf, R. William Collins and Eigh-
teenth-Century English Poetry.
  D. Fairer, 541(RES):Nov84-550
  A.T. McKenzie, 405(MP):Aug84-104
Wendorf, R. and C. Ryskamp - see Collins,
W.
Wendt, A. Shaman of Visions.
  B. O'Donoghue, 617(TLS):5Jul85-753
Wenk, A. Claude Debussy and Twentieth-
Century Music.
  M. Rolf, 451:Spring85-280
Wennberg, R.N. Life in the Balance.
  B. Harvey, 441:17Nov85-31
Wentink, A.M. - see Page, R.
Wentworth, M. James Tissot.
  M. Levey, 90:Oct84-644
  D. Sutton, 39:Jun84-398
  M. Warner, 324:Dec84-70
de Werd, G. Jan de Beijer.
  A-M.L., 380:Summer84-218
Werenskiold, M. The Concept of Expression-
ism, Origin and Metamorphoses.*
  M.R. Lagerlöf, 341:Vol53No3-133
van der Werf, H. The Emergence of Gregor-
ian Chant. (Vol 1)
  F.J. Guentner, 377:Mar84-56

Werner, C.H. Paradoxical Resolutions.*
    R.G. Seamon, 106:Fall84-337
    P. Stevick, 301(JEGP):Jul84-463
    S. Trachtenberg, 587(SAF):Autumn84-243
Werner, J.S. Peasant Politics and Reli-
  gious Sectarianism.
    M. Adas, 293(JASt):Nov83-201
Werth, N. Être communiste en U.R.S.S.
  sous Staline.
    H. Cronel, 450(NRF):Mar84-135
Werth, P. Focus, Coherence, and Emphasis.
    P. Bosch, 353:Vol22No5-755
Wescott, R.W. Sound and Sense.
    D. Justice, 545(RPh):Nov83-237
Wesenberg, B. Beiträge zur Rekonstruktion
  griechischer Architektur nach literaris-
  chen Quellen.
    W. Hoepfner, 43:Band14Heft2-172
Wesker, A. Distinctions.
    D.A.N. Jones, 362:9May85-27
    J.K.L. Walker, 617(TLS):6Sep85-978
Wesley, M. Harnessing Peacocks.
    R. Kaveney, 617(TLS):28Jun85-721
Wesling, D. The Chances of Rhyme.
    M. McKie, 184(EIC):Apr84-160
Wessling, B.W. Furtwängler.
    M. Tanner, 617(TLS):4Oct85-1089
West, A. Heritage.*
    D. Taylor, 364:Aug/Sep84-146
West, A. H.G. Wells.*
    B. Bergonzi, 176:Jul/Aug85-34
    M. Harris, 648(WCR):Jun84-52
    D. Taylor, 364:Aug/Sep84-146
West, A.M. The National Education Associa-
  tion.
    R.G. Sherer, Jr., 9(AlaR):Jan84-66
West, B. Epic, Folk, and Christian Tradi-
  tions in the "Poema de Fernán González."
    C.L. Scarborough, 238:Sep84-470
West, C.K. The Social and Psychological
  Distortion of Information.
    M. Hickson 3d, 583:Winter85-185
West, D. Trenchmist.
    S. Morrissey, 137:Feb85-42
West, D.C. and S. Zimdars-Swartz. Joachim
  of Fiore.
    R.K. Emmerson, 589:Oct84-964
West, J. The State of Stony Lonesome.
    J. Austin, 441:6Jan85-20
West, J. Town Records.
    M.W. Greenslade, 617(TLS):4Jan85-20
West, J.A. The Traveler's Key to Ancient
  Egypt.
    M. Lev, 469:Vol 10No3-110
West, J.L.W. 3d, ed. Conversations with
  William Styron.
    J. Daynard, 441:1Dec85-25
West, J.L.W. 3d. The Making of "This Side
  of Paradise."
    S. Pinsker, 395(MFS):Summer84-310
West, M.L. Greek Metre.*
    J. Diggle, 123:Vol34No1-66
    C.W. Willink, 303(JoHS):Vol 104-226
West, M.L. The Hesiodic Catalogue of
  Women.
    M.C. Stokes, 617(TLS):7Jun85-643
West, M.L. The Orphic Poems.*
    F. Vian, 555:Vol58fasc2-287
West, N. MI6.
    H. Rositzke, 441:17Feb85-28
West, N. A Thread of Deceit.
    C.C. Davis, 441:14Apr85-27

West, R. Cousin Rosamund.
    P. Craig, 617(TLS):18Oct85-1168
West, R. This Real Night.*
    A. Burgess, 61:Mar85-116
    L. Sage, 441:18Aug85-28
    442(NY):8Apr85-128
West, S. - see Homer
West, T.G., ed. Symbolism.
    R.J. Dingley, 447(N&Q):Apr83-180
West, W.J. - see Orwell, G.
Westbrook, M. Confrontations.
    W. Geyer, 649(WAL):Feb85-327
Westerberg, K. Cypriote Ships from the
  Bronze Age to c. 500 B.C.
    M. Fortin, 487:Autumn84-266
    H. Frost, 303(JoHS):Vol 104-246
Westergaard, K-E. Skrifttegn og symboler.
    E.H. Antonsen, 301(JEGP):Jan84-100
    J.E. Knirk, 563(SS):Autumn84-397
Westfall, R.S. Never at Rest.
    C. Ward, 577(SHR):Spring84-175
Westlake, D.E. High Adventure.
    M. Kaylan, 441:1Sep85-14
Westlund, J. Shakespeare's Reparative Com-
  edies.
    G. Taylor, 617(TLS):16Aug85-905
Weston, J. The Real American Cowboy.
    A. Sinclair, 617(TLS):20Sep85-1022
Westphall, V. Mercedes Reales.
    L. Milazzo, 584(SWR):Winter84-88
Weststeijn, W.G. Velimir Chlebnikov and
  the Development of Poetical Language in
  Russian Symbolism and Futurism.
    R.D.B. Thomson, 104(CASS):Winter84-449
Westwood, J.N. Endurance and Endeavour.*
  (2nd ed)
    D.C.B. Lieven, 575(SEER):Jan84-153
Westwood, J.N. Soviet Locomotive Technol-
  ogy during Industrialization 1928-1952.
    S.R. Thompstone, 575(SEER):Apr84-303
Wetherbee, W. Chaucer and the Poets.
    B. O'Donoghue, 617(TLS):12Apr85-416
Wetmore, A., R.F. Pasquier and S.L. Olson.
  The Birds of the Republic of Panama.
  (Pt 4)
    C. Perrins, 617(TLS):27Dec85-1486
Wetsel, D. L'Ecriture et le reste.*
    E. Moles, 208(FS):Jul84-337
    E. Morot-Sir, 207(FR):Dec84-286
Wetterer, A. Publikumsbezug und Wahr-
  heitsanspruch.*
    D. Koester, 221(GQ):Spring84-313
Wetzel, C. Joseph von Eichendorff.
    O. Seidlin, 221(GQ):Fall84-660
Weyrich, P. - see Lehrman, L. and others
"The Whale and Other Uncollected Transla-
  tions." (R. Wilbur, trans)
    R.S. Gwynn, 569(SR):Fall84-644
Whalen, P. Heavy Breathing.
    A.W. Knight, 649(WAL):Nov84-238
Whaley, J., ed. Mirrors of Mortality.*
    617(TLS):12Jul85-783
Whaley, J. Religious Toleration and
  Social Change in Hamburg 1529-1819.
    A. Hamilton, 617(TLS):8Nov85-1272
Whalley, G. - see Coleridge, S.T.
Whallon, W. Inconsistencies.
    A. Crépin, 189(EA):Jan-Mar85-73
Wharton, E. Ethan Frome.
    C. Jordis, 450(NRF):Jun84-123
Wharton, W. Pride.
    R.P. Sinkler, 441:24Nov85-11

Whatley, R. "Du Chicot."
   B.A. Byers, 207(FR):Apr85-770
Wheatcroft, G. The Randlords.
   P. Johnson, 362:25Jul85-30
   D. Welsh, 617(TLS):25Oct85-1200
Wheatley, P. and T. See. From Court to
   Capital.
   F. Kakubayashi, 302:Vol20No2-231
Wheaton, B.K. Savoring the Past.
   R.W. Tobin, 207(FR):Feb85-476
Wheeler, K., ed. German Aesthetic and Lit-
   erary Criticism.
   D. Kuspit, 62:Dec84-3
Wheeler, K.M. The Creative Mind in Cole-
   ridge's Poetry.*
   J.O. Hayden, 223:Winter84-435
   W.J.B. Owen, 541(RES):Aug84-391
Wheeler, K.M. Sources, Processes and
   Methods in Coleridge's "Biographia
   Literaria."*
   M.G. Cooke, 506(PSt):Sep84-188
Wheeler, K.V., P. Arnell and T. Bickford,
   eds. Michael Graves: Buildings and
   Projects 1966-1981.
   A. Betsky, 505:Mar84-100
Wheeler, M. English Fiction of the Victor-
   ian Period 1830-1890.
   D. Walder, 617(TLS):6Dec85-1408
Wheeler, P. Bodyline.*
   R. Nalley, 441:27Jan85-22
Wheeler, R.P. Shakespeare's Development
   and the Problem Comedies.*
   J. Schiffer, 405(MP):Feb85-320
Wheen, F. The Battle for London.
   G. Stamp, 617(TLS):13Sep85-1009
Whelan, H.W. Alexander III and the State
   Council.*
   D.C.B. Lieven, 575(SEER):Jan84-131
   T. Taranovski, 550(RusR):Jan84-87
Whelan, R. Robert Capa.
   H. Simons, 441:22Sep85-13
Whicker, A. Whicker's New World.
   A. Holden, 617(TLS):20Sep85-1023
Whiffen, M. and F. Koeper. American Archi-
   tecture, 1607-1976.*
   C.V. Brown, 658:Winter84-292
Whistler, L. The Laughter and the Urn.
   I. Anscombe, 617(TLS):1Nov85-1244
   J. Drummond, 362:7Nov85-27
Whiston, J. The Early Stages of Composi-
   tion of Galdós' "Lo prohibido."
   G. Gullón, 345(KRQ):Vol31No2-239
Whitaker, B., ed. Minorities.
   A. Ryan, 362:7Mar85-27
Whitaker, M., ed. The Princess, the Hoc-
   key Player, Magic and Ghosts.
   M.J. Evans, 102(CanL):Summer84-124
"Whitaker's Almanack." (117th ed)
   A. Bell, 617(TLS):26Apr85-472
White, A. Schelling.
   E. Beach, 518:Jul84-157
White, A. The Uses of Obscurity.
   R. Docherty, 541(RES):May84-264
White, A.R. The Nature of Knowledge.*
   A. Palmer, 518:Jul84-174
White, A.R. Rights.
   P. Pettit, 617(TLS):8Feb85-143
White, B.E. Renoir.
   P-L. Adams, 61:Feb85-100
   M. Brenson, 441:27Jan85-27
   T. Hilton, 617(TLS):22Mar85-319

White, C. The Life and Times of Little
   Richard.*
   G. Marcus, 62:Dec84-74
   J. Stokes, 617(TLS):24May85-583
White, C. Rembrandt.*
   C. Brown, 617(TLS):19Apr85-446
White, D.A. The Grand Continuum.*
   295(JML):Nov84-465
White, D.G. Ar'n't I a Woman?
   E. Kolbert, 441:1Dec85-25
White, E. Caracole.
   D.R. Slavitt, 441:15Sep85-15
White, E., ed. Fashion 85.
   P.B., 614:Winter85-22
White, E.W. Benjamin Britten. (2nd ed)
   (J. Evans, ed)
   P. Evans, 410(M&L):Jul84-279
White, E.W. A History of English Opera.*
   L. Foreman, 607:Mar84-44
   R.D. Hume, 612(ThS):Nov84-255
   C.A. Price, 317:Fall84-603
White, E.W. A Register of First Perform-
   ances of English Operas and Semi-Operas
   from the 16th Century to 1980.
   R.D. Hume, 612(ThS):Nov84-255
White, F.C. Knowledge and Relativism.
   483:Jul84-420
White, G. and J. Maze. Harold Ickes of
   the New Deal.
   K.S. Davis, 441:12May85-13
   K.O. Morgan, 617(TLS):14Jun85-658
White, G.T. The United States and the
   Problem of Recovery after 1893.*
   A. Finkel, 106:Winter84-465
White, H. and M. Brose, eds. Representing
   Kenneth Burke.*
   C.A. Carter, 223:Fall84-344
White, J.F. - see Mann, T.
White, J.P. The Aims of Education
   Restated.
   R. Barrett, 154:Dec84-742
White, K. Blue North.
   V. Young, 441:27Jan85-13
White, K.S. Einstein and Modern French
   Drama.
   R.E. Hiedemann, 397(MD):Sep84-464
White, L.H. Free Banking in Britain.
   S.G. Checkland, 617(TLS):3May85-486
White, M.L. The Birmingham District.
   W. Flynt, 9(AlaR):Jul84-228
White, P. Beyond Domination.*
   R.A.H., 185:Apr85-788
White, P. Flaws in the Glass.
   W. Walsh, 569(SR):Winter84-140
White, P. Seventeen Odes.
   G.P. Greenwood, 102(CanL):Summer84-135
   P. Stuewe, 529(QQ):Spring84-206
White, R. Two on the Isle.
   L. Irvine, 441:2Jun85-30
White, R.L. Gertrude Stein and Alice B.
   Toklas.
   L.W. Wagner, 573(SSF):Fall84-425
White, R.S. Shakespeare and the Romance
   Ending.*
   T. Hawkes, 541(RES):Aug84-367
White, T. Catch a Fire.
   T. Doherty, 77:Fall84-370
White, T. Rock Stars.
   J. Maslin, 441:20Jan85-9
White, T.H. A Joy Proposed.*
   F. Gallix, 189(EA):Jan-Mar85-97

Williams, R.C. and P.L. Cantelon, eds.
The American Atom.
R. Nalley, 441:30Jun85-21
Williams, R.D. - see Vergil
Williams, R.L. Gabriel García Márquez.
G.H. Bell-Villada, 454:Spring85-281
Williams, R.W. Carl Sternheim.
J.M. Ritchie, 402(MLR):Jul84-753
Williams, S. Diocletian and the Roman Re-
covery.
T.D. Barnes, 617(TLS):5Jul85-755
Williams, S. A Job to Live.
A. Hodgkin, 617(TLS):6Dec85-1404
Williams, S.A. Segunda vista.
R.W. Hatton, 238:Dec84-685
Williams, S.H. The Lewis Carroll Handbook.
(D. Crutch, ed)
W. Keutsch, 38:Band102Heft1/2-273
Williams, T. Collected Stories.
R. Price, 441:1Dec85-11
Williams, T.H. The Selected Essays of T.
Harry Williams.*
M. Kreyling, 392:Winter83/84-97
Williams, T.I. Howard Florey.
W.F. Bynum, 617(TLS):12Apr85-405
Williams, U. and W. Williams-Krapp, eds.
Die "Elsässische Legenda aurea." (Vol 1)
M. Görlach, 67:Nov84-253
R. Hildebrandt, 685(ZDL):3/1984-396
Williams, W. The Tragic Art of Ernest
Hemingway.*
H. Claridge, 447(N&Q):Dec83-564
J.M. Cox, 569(SR):Summer84-484
K. McSweeney, 529(QQ):Winter84-877
Williams, W.C. The Selected Letters of
William Carlos Williams. (J. Thirlwall,
ed)
S. Friebert, 199:Spring85-52
Williams, W.D., ed. Southeastern Indians.
B.M. Smith, 106:Summer84-185
Williamsen, V.G. The Minor Dramatists of
Seventeenth-Century Spain.*
M. Wilson, 402(MLR):Apr84-475
Williamson, A. Introspection and Contempo-
rary Poetry.*
D. Davis, 617(TLS):15Mar85-293
R. Kern, 659(ConL):Summer85-221
Williamson, C., ed and trans. A Feast of
Creatures.*
C.L. Edwards, 650(WF):Apr84-144
W.J. Pepicello, 292(JAF):Jan-Mar84-73
Williamson, D. Fireside Tales of the
Traveller Children.
N. Montgomerie, 571(ScLJ):Winter84-58
Williamson, E. The Half-Way House of Fic-
tion.
R. Ruiz, 454:Winter85-189
M. Vargas Llosa, 617(TLS):26Jul85-815
Williamson, H. Methods of Book Design.
(3rd ed)
J. Commander, 78(BC):Autumn84-382
Williamson, J. The Crucible of Race.*
D.B. Davis, 617(TLS):30Aug85-939
Williamson, P. Romanesque Sculpture.
G. Zarnecki, 90:Apr84-238
Williamson, S.R., Jr. and P. Pastor, eds.
Essays on World War I: Origins and
Prisoners of War.
R. Frucht, 104(CASS):Spring-Summer84-
230
Willig, R.F. - see "The Changelings"
Willis, C. Fire Watch.
G. Jonas, 441:10Mar85-31

Willis, J.R. Pleasures Forevermore.
B. Murray, 395(MFS):Summer84-364
Willis, M.S. Only Great Changes.
A. Gelb, 441:10Feb85-24
Willis, R. - see de Heusch, L.
Willner, A.R. The Spellbinders.*
C.N.S., 185:Jul85-987
Willoughby, L. Texas Rhythm, Texas Rhyme.
L. Milazzo, 584(SWR):Autumn84-462
Wills, G. George Washington and the En-
lightenment.
M. Cranston, 617(TLS):24May85-584
Willson, A.L., ed. Dimension.
W. Blomster, 399(MLJ):Spring84-81
Willson, A.L., ed. German Romantic Crit-
icism.
T.C. Hanlin, 399(MLJ):Summer84-168
Wilmer, C. Devotions.
T. Eagleton, 565:Winter83/84-77
B. Ruddick, 148:Autumn84-39
Wilmeth, D.B. The Language of American
Popular Entertainment.
A.H. Saxon, 615(TJ):Dec82-558
Wilmut, R. Tony Hancock "Artiste."
617(TLS):27Dec85-1491
Wilner, E. Shekhinah.
M. Kinzie, 29(APR):Nov/Dec85-7
von Wilpert, G., ed. Lexikon der Weltlit-
eratur.
J.K. Wikeley, 107(CRCL):Mar84-117
Wilshere, A.D. - see Saint Edmund of Abing-
don
Wilshire, B. Role Playing and Identity.*
R. Danner, 478:Apr84-145
D. Reeves, 323:May84-197
R.L. Smith, 130:Summer84-185
Wilson, A. Diversity and Depth in Fic-
tion.* (K. McSweeney, ed)
J.H. Stape, 627(UTQ):Summer84-435
42(AR):Summer84-385
Wilson, A. Magical Thought in Creative
Writing.
C. Gauvin, 189(EA):Oct-Dec85-449
R. McGillis, 49:Jan84-86
Wilson, A.N. Hilaire Belloc.*
P. Lewis, 364:Apr/May84-125
B. McCabe, 453(NYRB):7Nov85-38
F.D. Wilhelmsen, 396(ModA):Fall84-381
442(NY):14Jan85-118
Wilson, A.N. Gentlemen in England.
D.A.N. Jones, 362:19Sep85-26
J. Sutherland, 617(TLS):6Sep85-972
Wilson, A.N. How Can We Know?
H. Lomas, 364:Feb85-111
C.H. Sisson, 617(TLS):1Feb85-116
Wilson, A.N. The Life of John Milton.*
D.A. Loewenstein, 191(ELN):Dec84-70
J.T. Shawcross, 551(RenQ):Spring84-148
T. Wheeler, 569(SR):Spring84-304
639(VQR):Winter84-12
Wilson, A.N. Scandal.*
W. Balliett, 442(NY):14Jan85-116
M. Wood, 441:17Feb85-27
Wilson, A.N. Wise Virgin.*
639(VQR):Summer84-96
Wilson, B. Murder in the Collective.
M. Laski, 362:10Jan85-25
Wilson, B.E. Ambitious Women.
L. Marcus, 617(TLS):27Sep85-1070
Wilson, B.K. Antipodes Jane.* (British
title: Jane Austen in Australia.)
P. Beer, 441:21Jul85-12
D.J. Taylor, 176:Sep-Oct85-53

Wilson, D.M. Anglo-Saxon Art.*
  C.A. Ralegh Radford, 324:Sep85-734
Wilson, D.M. The Bayeux Tapestry.
  P-L. Adams, 61:Nov85-144
Wilson, E. The Forties. (L. Edel, ed)
  J. Groth, 31(ASch):Summer84-422
  C.C. Nash, 219(GaR):Spring84-199
Wilson, E. The Mental as Physical.
  S.C. Wheeler 3d, 449:Mar84-145
Wilson, E.O. Biophilia.*
  H. Caton, 617(TLS):18Jan85-71
Wilson, G. Selections from the Decorative
  Arts in the J. Paul Getty Museum.
  P. Hughes, 39:Nov84-359
Wilson, G.M. The Intentionality of Human
  Action.
  J.M. Fischer, 482(PhR):Jul84-483
Wilson, G.M. Alexander McDonald, Leader
  of the Miners.
  S. Meacham, 637(VS):Autumn83-100
Wilson, H.E. Social Engineering in Singa-
  pore.
  C.M. Turnbull, 302:Vol20No2-246
Wilson, J. and L. Udall. Folk Festivals.
  S.D. Celsor, 650(WF):Oct84-268
Wilson, J.D. The Romantic Heroic Ideal.*
  L. Buell, 587(SAF):Spring84-110
  F.W. Shilstone, 577(SHR):Summer84-263
Wilson, J.O. The Power Economy.
  Y-A. Istel, 441:18Aug85-11
Wilson, J.Q., ed. Crime and Public Policy.
  J.L.H., 185:Jan85-402
Wilson, J.Q. and R.J. Herrnstein. Crime
  and Human Nature.
  J. Kaplan, 441:8Sep85-7
Wilson, K.M. The Policy of the Entente.
  Z. Steiner, 617(TLS):5Apr85-388
Wilson, L.A. From the Bottom Up.*
  G. Morris, 502(PrS):Fall84-113
Wilson, M.I. William Kent.*
  C.C. Gilbert, 90:Nov84-705
Wilson, N.G. Scholars of Byzantium.
  D.J. Constantelos, 124:Sep-Oct84-47
Wilson, P. Guide to French Noun Gender.
  R. de Gorog, 545(RPh):May84-468
Wilson, R. Ohiyesa.
  W. Churchill, 649(WAL):Aug84-152
Wilson, R., Jr. Dancing for Men.
  W.P. Keen, 573(SSF):Fall84-408
Wilson, R. and E. Crouch. Risk/Benefit
  Analysis.
  T.P., 185:Oct84-193
Wilson, R.G. McKim, Mead and White, Archi-
  tects.*
  P.R. Baker, 432(NEQ):Dec84-573
  W.B. Rhoads, 576:May84-175
Wilson, R.J.A. Piazza Armerina.*
  N.B. Rankov, 123:Vol34No2-354
Wilson, R.W.J. Henry James's Ultimate Nar-
  rative.
  W.R. Macnaughton, 106:Fall84-323
Wilson, S. Ideology and Experience.
  N. Wilson, 208(FS):Apr84-222
Wilson, S.T. and D.F. Kennedy. Of Cover-
  lets.
  J.T. Federico, 139:Jun/Jul84-37
Wilson, T. Inflation, Unemployment, and
  the Market. (M.C. MacLennan, ed)
  P. Minford, 617(TLS):12Jul85-766
Wilson-Kastner, P., ed. A Lost Tradition.
  H. Mayo, 589:Jan84-217
Wilton, A. Turner Abroad.*
  90:Dec84-796

Wiltse, D. The Fifth Angel.
  M. Laski, 362:14Nov85-35
  E. Zuckerman, 441:14Apr85-12
Wimmer, R. Jesuitentheater, Didaktik und
  Fest.
  J. Schmidt, 221(GQ):Summer84-468
  P. Skrine and N. Griffin, 402(MLR):
  Oct84-978
Wimsatt, J.I. Chaucer and the Poems of
  "Ch" in University of Pennsylvania MS
  French 15.*
  A. Crépin, 189(EA):Jan-Mar85-79
  F.N.M. Diekstra, 179(ES):Dec84-562
Winans, R.B. A Descriptive Checklist of
  Book Catalogues Separately Printed in
  America 1693-1800.
  E. Wolf 2d, 78(BC):Spring84-103
Winchester, S. Outposts.
  A. Sykes, 617(TLS):27Dec85-1477
"The Winchester Anthology."
  H. Cooper, 541(RES):Aug84-354
  N. Jacobs, 382(MAE):1984/1-135
  H. Käsmann, 38:Band102Heft1/2-222
  D. Pearsall, 447(N&Q):Apr83-161
  A.G. Rigg, 589:Jan84-218
Wind, E. The Eloquence of Symbols. (J.
  Anderson, ed)
  A. Whittick, 324:Apr85-373
Wind, H.W. Following Through.
  R.R. Harris, 441:10Nov85-28
Windeatt, B.A., ed and trans. Chaucer's
  Dream Poetry.*
  F.N.M. Diekstra, 179(ES):Dec84-558
  D. Pearsall, 447(N&Q):Jun83-248
Windeatt, B.A. - see Chaucer, G.
Windfuhr, M. - see Heine, H.
"Windsor Yearbook of Access to Justice."
  (Vols 1 and 2) (W.E. Conklin and others,
  eds)
  B.M. Baker, 154:Dec84-734
Winitz, H., ed. Native Language and
  Foreign Language Acquisition.*
  W. Wolfram, 35(AS):Summer84-184
Winkelmann, O. Artikelwahl, Referenz und
  Textkonstitution in der französischen
  Sprache.
  M. Harris, 208(FS):Jan84-113
Winkler, C. Untersuchungen zur Kadenzbil-
  dung in deutscher Rede.
  E. Beneš, 685(ZDL):3/1984-383
Winks, R.W. Modus Operandi.*
  G. Grella, 536:Vol5-211
Winling, R. La théologie contemporaine
  (1945-1980).
  A. Reix, 542:Jan-Mar84-109
Winn, C. Legal Daisy Spacing.
  R.B. Swain, 441:6Oct85-29
Winn, J.A. Unsuspected Eloquence.*
  N.C. Carpenter, 131(CL):Winter84-75
  M.H. Frank, 301(JEGP):Oct84-547
  C. Price, 566:Spring85-188
  S. Weiner, 481(PQ):Spring84-273
Winn, M.B., ed. La Chasse d'Amours.
  G. Roques, 553(RLiR):Jul-Dec84-514
Winnifrith, T. - see Brontë, C.
Winnifrith, T. - see Brontë, P.B.
Winnifrith, T., P. Murray and K.W. Grans-
  den, eds. Aspects of the Epic.*
  S. Murnaghan, 124:Jan-Feb85-224
Winson, J. Brain and Psyche.
  B.A. Farrell, 453(NYRB):18Jul85-36
  R.M. Restak, 441:20Jan85-1

Winston, C.M. Workers and the Right in
Spain 1900-1936.
  M. Blinkhorn, 617(TLS):7Jun85-629
Winston, K. V ... — Mail. (S. Winston, ed)
  J.M. Elukin, 441:6Oct85-29
Winston, K.I. - see Fuller, L.L.
Winter, D.E., ed. Shadowings.
  M.E. Barth, 395(MFS):Winter84-867
Winter, K.H. Marietta Holley.
  M. Graulich, 357:Fall85-76
Winternitz, E. Leonardo da Vinci as a
Musician.*
  E.J. Olszewski, 551(RenQ):Summer84-267
Winters, C-A. Mao or Muhammad.
  J.N. Lipman, 293(JASt):Nov83-152
Winterson, J. Boating for Beginners.
  E. Fisher, 617(TLS):1Nov85-1228
Winterson, J. Oranges Are Not the Only
Fruit.
  R. Kaveney, 617(TLS):22Mar85-326
Wintle, J. Mortadella.
  C. Hawtree, 617(TLS):22Feb85-197
Winton, T. An Open Swimmer.
  P. Lewis, 565:Spring84-64
Winward, W. Rainbow Soldiers.
  K. Jeffery, 617(TLS):23Aug85-920
Wippel, J.F. The Metaphysical Thought of
Godfrey of Fontaines.
  A.S. McGrade, 589:Oct84-967
Wise, D. The Children's Game.
  639(VQR):Spring84-57
Wise, G. Willis R. Whitney, General Elec-
tric, and the Origins of U.S. Industrial
Research.
  D. Diamond, 441:20Oct85-51
Wise, M.R. and H. Boonstra, eds. Conjun-
ciones y otros nexos en tres idiomas
amazónicos.
  W. Frawley, 350:Mar85-232
Wiseman, C. An Ocean of Whispers.
  E. Trethewey, 102(CanL):Summer84-84
Wiseman, T.P. Catullus and His World.
  F. Cairns, 617(TLS):1Nov85-1245
Wiser, W. The Crazy Years.*
  42(AR):Winter84-120
  295(JML):Nov84-340
Wismeijer, H. Diversity in Harmony.
  J.R. Williams, 293(JASt):Nov83-194
Wistrand, M. Cicero Imperator.
  J.J. Barlow, 121(CJ):Oct-Nov84-68
Wistrich, R.S., ed. The Left Against Zion.
  J.N. Porter, 390:May84-61
Wistrich, R.S. Socialism and the Jews.
  A. Ascher, 575(SEER):Apr84-291
de Wit, W., ed. The Amsterdam School.*
  S. Williams, 45:May84-117
Witherell, E.H. and others - see Thoreau,
H.D.
Withers, C.W.J. Gaelic in Scotland 1698-
1981.*
  S.M. Embleton, 350:Sep85-718
Witherspoon, P. The Drink-Spotty Book.
  H. Jacobson, 617(TLS):20Dec85-1453
Withey, L. Dearest Friend.*
  A.F. Scott, 579(SAQ):Summer84-356
Witt, G. Ästhetik des Sports.
  R. Hartke, 654(WB):12/1984-2094
Witt, R.G. Hercules at the Crossroads.
  C. Kalendorf, 568(SCN):Fall84-52
Witte, S.P. and L. Faigley. Evaluating
College Writing Programs.
  B.J. Wagner, 128(CE):Feb84-133

Wittgenstein, L. Remarks on the Philoso-
phy of Psychology. (Vol 1) (G.E.M.
Anscombe and G.H. von Wright, eds)
  C. Diamond, 482(PhR):Jul84-458
Wittgenstein, L. Remarks on the Philoso-
phy of Psychology. (Vol 2) (G.H. von
Wright and H. Nyman, eds)
  C. Diamond, 482(PhR):Jul84-458
  P. Engel, 542:Jan-Mar84-131
Wittgenstein, L. Remarques sur les fonde-
ments des Mathématiques. (M-A. Lescour-
ret, trans)
  T. Cordellier, 450(NRF):Feb84-102
  P. Engel, 542:Jan-Mar84-128
Wittkowski, W., ed. Friedrich Schiller.*
  L. Sharpe, 402(MLR):Apr84-493
Wittmann, R. Buchmarkt und Lektüre im 18.
und 19. Jahrhundert.
  H. Heckmann-French, 301(JEGP):Apr84-
  276
  A. Ward, 402(MLR):Jul84-742
Wittmann, R. and B. Hack, eds. Buchhandel
und Literatur.
  J.L. Flood, 354:Jun84-191
Wittreich, J. "Image of that Horror."
  G. Taylor, 617(TLS):16Aug85-905
Wittrock, W., comp. 25 Jahre Universal
Limited Art Editions.
  M.S. Young, 39:Jan84-70
Wixman, R. The Peoples of the USSR.
  J.A.C. Greppin, 617(TLS):7Jun85-624
Wixted, J.T. - see Wei Chuang
Wode, H., ed. Papers on Language Acquisi-
tion, Language Learning and Language
Teaching.
  M.A.S. Smith, 353:Vol22No1-144
Wodehouse, L. Ada Louise Huxtable.
  M. Filler, 453(NYRB):5Dec85-11
Wodehouse, P.G. Four Plays.
  D. Devlin, 157:No151-48
Wodehouse, P.G. Wodehouse Nuggets. (R.
Usborne, ed)
  D.J. Dooley, 616:Spring/Summer84-52
Wohlfart, G. Der Augenblick.*
  H. Graubner, 342:Band75Heft4-506
Wohmann, G. Der Irrgast.
  M. Kane, 617(TLS):11Oct85-1153
Woisetschläger, K. and others, comps.
Dehio-Handbuch Steiermark (ohne Graz).
  G. Biedermann, 471:Jul/Aug/Sep84-302
Wojahn, D. Icehouse Lights.*
  P. Stitt, 344:Summer85-123
Wojtyla, K. [Pope John Paul II] Personne
et acte. The Acting Person. (A-T.
Tymieniecka, ed of both)
  A. Reix, 542:Apr-Jun84-261
Wolandt, B. - see Alphéus, K.
Wolf, A. Variation und Integration.
  J.H. Marshall, 208(FS):Oct84-447
Wolf, B.J. Romantic Re-Vision.*
  F. Garber, 678(YCGL):No32-148
  U. Janssens-Knorsch, 179(ES):Aug84-327
  E. Johns, 54:Dec84-705
  R.B. Stein, 445(NCF):Mar85-459
  E.J. Sundquist, 141:Summer84-277
Wolf, C. Cassandra.* (German title:
Kassandra.)
  T.G. Ash, 453(NYRB):31Jan85-33
  J. Crick, 617(TLS):15Nov85-1298
  M. Hulse, 364:Feb85-99
  H. Kaufmann, 601(SuF):May-Jun84-653
Wolf, C. No Place on Earth.
  M. Hulse, 364:Feb85-99

Woodward, B. Wired.*
S. Booth, 617(TLS):8Mar85-269
G. Marcus, 62:Dec84-2
J. Simpson, 362:21Feb85-26
Woodward, C.V. - see Chesnut, M.
Woodward, C.V. and E. Muhlenfeld - see
Chesnut, M.
Woodward, J.B. The Symbolic Art of Gogol.*
A. McMillin, 575(SEER):Apr84-260
A. Stokes, 402(MLR):Jan84-251
J. Zeldin, 104(CASS):Spring-Summer84-
159
Woodward, K., ed. The Myths of Informa-
tion.
M. Silberman, 406:Fall84-344
Woolf, V. The Complete Shorter Fiction of
Virginia Woolf. (S. Dick, ed)
L. Gordon, 617(TLS):27Dec85-1479
A. Huth, 362:19Sep85-27
Woolf, V. The Diary of Virginia Woolf.*
(Vol 5) (A.O. Bell, with A. McNeillie,
eds)
C.G. Heilbrun, 344:Spring85-127
W. Maxwell, 442(NY):25Feb85-99
Woolf, V. To the Lighthouse: The Critical
Holograph Draft.* (S. Dick, ed) Pointz
Hall: The Earlier and Later Typescript
of "Between the Acts." (M.A. Leaska, ed)
E. Heine, 395(MFS):Winter84-756
Woolford, E. and W. Washabaugh, eds. The
Social Context of Creolization.*
S. Romaine, 353:Vol22No1-137
Woolford, E.B. Aspects of Tok Pisin Gram-
mar.
J. Aitchison, 541(RES):Feb84-75
Woolfson, C. The Labour Theory of Culture.
G.W. Hewes, 355(LSoc):Dec84-572
Woolhouse, R.S. Locke.
P.A. Schouls, 518:Apr84-97
Woollatt, R. Eastbound from Alberta.*
L. Welch, 198:Summer84-112
Woolmer, J.H. Malcolm Lowry.*
D.H. Keller, 87(BB):Dec84-240
P.M. St. Pierre, 102(CanL):Autumn84-
186
Wooten, C.W. Cicero's "Philippics" and
their Demosthenic Model.
B.P. Newbound, 313:Vol74-237
Wootton, D. Paolo Sarpi.*
E.G. Gleason, 551(RenQ):Winter84-622
Wordsworth, D. Letters of Dorothy Words-
worth. (A.G. Hill, ed)
N. Fruman, 617(TLS):28Jun85-711
Wordsworth, J. William Wordsworth.
M. Baron, 175:Spring84-71
J.A. Butler, 661(WC):Summer84-85
S. Logan, 184(EIC):Jul84-254
Wordsworth, W. Benjamin the Waggoner.
(P.F. Betz, ed)
S. Gill, 541(RES):Aug84-390
Wordsworth, W. Poems, in Two Volumes, and
Other Poems, 1800-1807.* (J. Curtis, ed)
Descriptive Sketches. (E. Birdsall and
P.M. Zall, eds) An Evening Walk. (J.
Averill, ed) The Manuscript of William
Wordsworth's "Poems, in Two Volumes"
(1807). (W.H. Kelliher, ed)
G. Lindop, 617(TLS):19Apr85-447
Wordsworth, W. and D. The Letters of Wil-
liam and Dorothy Wordsworth.* (Vol 6,
Pt 3) (2nd ed) (A.G. Hill, ed)
M. Isnard, 189(EA):Jul-Sep85-338

Wordsworth, W. and M. The Love Letters of
William and Mary Wordsworth.* (B. Dar-
lington, ed)
J.R. Nabholtz, 405(MP):Nov84-209
Worm, H. Studien über den jungen Ōsugi
Sakae und die Meiji-Sozialisten zwischen
Sozialdemokratie und Anarchismus unter
besonderer Berücksichtigung der Anarchis-
musrezeption.
F.G. Notehelfer, 407(MN):Spring84-103
Wormald, F. and P.M. Giles. A Descriptive
Catalogue of the Additional Illuminated
Manuscripts in the Fitzwilliam Museum.*
D. Byrne, 90:May84-292
J. Tarrant, 589:Jul84-730
Wormald, J. Court, Kirk, and Community.
B.C. Weber, 539:Aug85-227
Wormell, D. Sir John Seeley and the Uses
of History.
D.R. Woolf, 529(QQ):Autumn84-524
Wörner, F.J. Architektur des Frühklas-
sizismus in Süddeutschland.*
A. Laing, 90:Jan84-46
Woronoff, J. Japan's Wasted Workers.
W.H. Newell, 293(JASt):Feb84-344
Woronzoff, A. Andrej Belyj's "Petersburg,"
James Joyce's "Ulysses," and the Symbol-
ist Movement.
T.R. Beyer, Jr., 550(RusR):Jan84-73
Worp, K.A. Das Aurelia Charite Archiv (P.
Charite).
H. Maehler, 123:Vol134No1-116
Worpole, K. Dockers and Detectives.*
P. Gillen, 381:Dec84-525
Worpole, K. Reading by Numbers.
A. Calder, 617(TLS):15Feb85-162
Worrall, N. - see Galsworthy, J.
Worth, D.S. The Origins of Russian Gram-
mar.
D. Birnbaum, 550(RusR):Jul84-321
Worth, K. Oscar Wilde.*
272(IUR):Autumn84-308
Worthen, J. D.H. Lawrence and the Idea
of the Novel.
P. Preston, 447(N&Q):Aug83-368
Worthen, J. - see Lawrence, D.H.
Wouk, H. Inside, Outside.
J. Michener, 441:10Mar85-1
Wouters, A. The Grammatical Papyri from
Graeco-Roman Egypt.*
D. Holwerda, 394:Vol37fasc1/2-199
Woytek, E. T. Maccius Plautus: "Persa."*
S.M. Goldberg, 122:Jul84-247
Wray, H. and H. Conroy, eds. Japan Exam-
ined.*
Kanō Masanao, 285(JapQ):Jul-Sep84-325
Wreen, M.J. and D.M. Callen - see Beards-
ley, M.C.
Wren, K. Hugo: "Hernani" and "Ruy Blas."
T. Raser, 446(NCFS):Winter-Spring85-
179
J.J. Supple, 402(MLR):Oct84-944
Wren, R.M. Achebe's World.
R. Mane, 189(EA):Jan-Mar85-108
Wright, A. Anthony Trollope.*
R. ap Roberts, 445(NCF):Mar85-474
Wright, A.D. The Counter-Reformation.
T.H. Clancy, 377:Mar84-60
Wright, A.M. The Formal Principle in the
Novel.*
A. Fleishman, 301(JEGP):Apr84-256
W.L. Reed, 405(MP):Feb85-351

Wright, C. Country Music.*
   J. Parini, 617(TLS):1Mar85-239
Wright, C. Frege's Conception of Numbers
   as Objects.
   J.P. Burgess, 482(PhR):Oct84-638
   D. Gillies, 393(Mind):Oct84-613
   I. Hacking, 479(PhQ):Jul84-415
   M.D. Resnik, 311(JP):Dec84-778
   J.E. Tiles, 518:Jul84-159
Wright, C. The Other Side of the River.*
   P. Stitt, 219(GaR):Summer84-402
   A. Turner, 199:Spring85-45
Wright, C. Wittgenstein on the Founda-
   tions of Mathematics.*
   M. Steiner, 316:Dec84-1415
Wright, C.D. Translations of the Gospel
   Back into Tongues.
   L. Goldensohn, 491:Apr84-40
Wright, D. The Persians Amongst the
   English.
   P. Mansfield, 362:7Feb85-22
Wright, D. - see Thomas, E.
Wright, D.G. Characters in Joyce.
   C.D. Lobner, 329(JJQ):Fall84-87
   M. Magalaner, 395(MFS):Winter84-760
Wright, E. Death in the Old Country.
   P-L. Adams, 61:Sep85-114
   T.J. Binyon, 617(TLS):30Aug85-946
   N. Callendar, 441:6Oct85-35
Wright, E. Psychoanalytic Criticism.
   C. Gordon, 617(TLS):19Jul85-788
Wright, E.P. Thomas Deloney.
   D.S. Lawless, 447(N&Q):Oct83-456
Wright, G. Between The Guillotine and
   Liberty.
   M. Ignatieff, 617(TLS):1Mar85-235
   639(VQR):Winter84-17
Wright, G. Building the Dream.*
   R. Gutman, 576:Mar84-91
von Wright, G.H. Philosophical Papers.
   (Vols 1 and 2)
   J-L. Gardies, 542:Apr-Jun84-233
von Wright, G.H. Wittgenstein.
   P. Engel, 542:Jan-Mar84-132
   H.L. Finch, 518:Jul84-162
   I. McFetridge, 479(PhQ):Jan84-69
von Wright, G.H. and H. Nyman - see Witt-
   genstein, L.
Wright, J. Explications/Interpretations.
   J. Hollander, 676(YR):Autumn84-xvii
Wright, J.P. The Sceptical Realism of
   David Hume.
   L.W. Beck, 173(ECS):Winter84/85-254
   A. Flew, 393(Mind):Jul84-446
   B. Gower, 83:Autumn84-263
   K. Haakonssen, 63:Dec84-410
   D.F. Norton, 518:Jul84-144
Wright, K. Bump-Starting the Hearse.*
   R. Pybus, 565:Autumn84-73
Wright, K., ed. Poems for Over 10-Year-
   Olds.
   A. Hollinghurst, 617(TLS):8Feb85-154
Wright, M.R. - see Empedocles
Wright, P. On Living in an Old Country.
   D.A.N. Jones, 362:31Oct85-31
Wright, R. Cut Stones and Crossroads.*
   P. Bennett, 37:Nov-Dec84-62
   J. Keay, 362:31Jan85-25
Wright, R. Late Latin and Early Romance
   in Spain and Carolingian France.*
   S. Fleischman, 589:Jan84-222
   P.M. Lloyd, 240(HR):Summer84-367
                              [continued]

[continuing]
   S. Levin, 215(GL):Vol124No3-194
   R. Penny, 86(BHS):Jan84-43
Wright, R. Sacred Rage.
   L. Robinson, 441:27Oct85-12
Wright, R.B. The Teacher's Daughter.
   M.F. Dixon, 102(CanL):Winter83-168
Wright, R.K., Jr. The Continental Army.
   C.H. Lesser, 656(WMQ):Apr84-314
Wright, S. James Dickey.
   J.E. Kibler, Jr., 517(PBSA):Vol78No3-
   369
Wright, S. Andrew Nelson Lytle.
   E. Sarcone, 392:Spring84-201
Wright, S. Meditations in Green.*
   639(VQR):Summer84-95
Wright, W. The Social Logic of Health.
   A.W., 185:Oct84-194
Wrigley, C., ed. A History of British
   Industrial Relations, 1875-1914.
   J.R. Hay, 637(VS):Winter84-258
"WRIT 14." (R. Greenwald, ed)
   C. Leland, 627(UTQ):Summer84-493
"Written in the Book of Life." (M. Skryp-
   nik, trans)
   V.A. Woodbury, 399(MLJ):Summer84-186
Wroth, M. The Poems of Lady Mary Wroth.
   (J.A. Roberts, ed)
   S. Woods, 551(RenQ):Winter84-653
   639(VQR):Winter84-24
Wroth, W. Christian Images in Hispanic
   New Mexico.
   K.F. Turner, 292(JAF):Jul-Sep84-361
Wu, A.K. Turkistan Tumult.
   617(TLS):22Nov85-1339
Wu, D.Y.H. The Chinese in Papua New
   Guinea, 1880-1980.
   J.T. Omohundro, 293(JASt):May84-612
Wu, K-M. Chuang Tzu.
   J. Ching, 322(JHI):Jul-Sep84-476
Wu, S.H.L. Passage to Power.
   A.Y.C. Lui, 302:Vol20No2-197
Wu, T-W. The Kiangsi Soviet Republic,
   1931-1934.
   Shum Kwi-Kwong, 302:Vol20No2-192
Wühr, P. Das falsche Buch.
   F.P. Ingold, 384:Jun84-445
Wulz, W. Der spätstaufische Geschichts-
   schreiber Burchard von Ursberg.
   H.A. Myers, 589:Oct84-991
Wunberg, G., ed. Die Wiener Moderne.
   J.F. Bodine, 133:Band17Heft1/2-182
Wunderli, R.M. London Church Courts and
   Society on the Eve of the Reformation.
   J.R. Wright, 589:Jan84-245
Wunderlich, W., ed. Dyl Vlenspiegel.
   W. Virmond, 684(ZDA):Band113Heft3-130
Wunderlich, W., ed. Das Lalebuch.
   H. Trümpy, 196:Band25Heft1/2-144
Wuorinen, C. Simple Composition.
   M.A. Joyce, 309:Vol5No1/3-265
Wurlitzer, R. Slow Fade.*
   N. Shack, 617(TLS):1Feb85-110
Würzbach, N. Anfänge und gattungstypische
   Ausformung der englischen Strassen-
   ballade 1550-1650.
   H. Shields, 292(JAF):Jan-Mar84-94
Wüscher, H.J. Liberty, Equality and Fra-
   ternity in Wordsworth 1791-1800.*
   N. Roe, 447(N&Q):Feb83-86
Wuthenow, R-R. Im Buch die Bücher oder
   der Held als Leser.*
   W.H. McClain, 221(GQ):Winter84-134

Wuthenow, R.R. - see Forster, G.
Wyatt, D.K. and A. Woodside, eds. Moral
  Order and the Question of Change.
    C.J. Reynolds, 293(JASt):Feb84-374
Wyatt, R. Foreign Bodies.
    C. McLay, 102(CanL):Autumn84-87
Wyatt, W. Confessions of an Optimist.
    J. Aitken, 362:6Jun85-28
    J. Turner, 617(TLS):9Aug85-881
Wyatt-Brown, B. Southern Honor.*
    A. Rowe, 392:Winter83/84-109
Wycherley, W. The Plays of William Wycher-
  ley.* (A. Friedman, ed)
    W.J. Burling, 568(SCN):Winter84-70
Wycherley, W. The Plays of William Wycher-
  ley.* (P. Holland, ed)
    E. Burns, 541(RES):Aug84-435
Wyclif, J. Tractatus de Universalibus.
  (I. Mueller, ed) On Universals (Tracta-
  tus de Universalibus). (A. Kenny, trans)
    G. Leff, 617(TLS):9Aug85-885
Wyman, D.S. The Abandonment of the Jews.*
    R.S. Levy, 129:Apr85-70
Wynand, D. Pointwise.
    I. Sowton, 102(CanL):Autumn84-125
Wynand, D. Second Person. Fetishistic.
    S. Scobie, 376:Oct84-125
Wynder, E.L., ed. The Book of Health.
    529(QQ):Summer84-486
Wyndham, F. Mrs. Henderson and Other
  Stories.
    A. Hollinghurst, 617(TLS):26Apr85-457
Wyndham, F. and D. Melly - see Rhys, J.
Wyndham, J. Love Lessons.
    L. Hopkinson, 617(TLS):26Apr85-458
Wynette, T. Stand By Your Man.
    J.L. Tharpe, 585(SoQ):Spring84-145
Wynot, E.D., Jr. Warsaw Between the World
  Wars.*
    J.H. Bater, 104(CASS):Winter84-490
Wyrwa, T. La résistance polonaise et la
  politique en Europe.
    A.J. Matejko, 497(PolR):Vol29No4-96
Wyse, P. Canadian Foreign Aid in the
  1970s.
    D. Powell, 298:Winter84/85-130
Wysling, H. Narzissmus und illusionäre
  Existenzform.
    D.W. Adolphs and E. Schwarz, 133:
      Band17Heft1/2-178
    S.R. Cerf, 221(GQ):Spring84-326
    M. Dierks, 680(ZDP):Band103Heft2-302
    M. Swales, 402(MLR):Oct84-990
Wyss, U. Die wilde Philologie.
    N.R. Wolf, 685(ZDL):1/1984-89
Cardinal Wyszynski, S. A Freedom Within.
    Z. Pelczynski, 617(TLS):18Jan85-61
Wytrzens, G. Bibliographie der literar-
  wissenschaftlichen Slavistik, 1970-1980.
    G. Donchin, 575(SEER):Jul84-477

Xanthakis-Karamanos, G. Studies in Fourth-
  Century Tragedy.*
    R.D. Dawe, 122:Jan84-61
Xiao Tong. Wen xuan or Selections of
  Refined Literature. (Vol 1) (D.R.
  Knechtges, ed and trans)
    D. Bryant, 244(HJAS):Jun84-249
    C.S. Goodrich, 116:Jul83-95

Xu Liangying and Fan Dainian. Science and
  Socialist Construction in China. (P.M.
  Perrolle, ed)
    L.A. Schneider, 293(JASt):May84-536

Yadin, Y. The Temple Scroll.
    G. Vermes, 617(TLS):3May85-501
Yadin, Y., ed. The Temple Scroll.
    G. Vermes, 617(TLS):3May85-501
Yaguello, M. Alice au pays du langage.*
    A. Valdman, 207(FR):Mar85-590
Yajun, Z. and Mao Cheng-dong - see under
  Zhang Yajun and Mao Cheng-dong
Yalden, J. The Communicative Syllabus.
    B.A. Lafford, 399(MLJ):Spring84-68
Yamamura, K., ed. Policy and Trade Issues
  of the Japanese Economy.*
    S.B. Levine, 293(JASt):May84-558
Yaney, G. The Urge to Mobilize.*
    W.E. Mosse, 575(SEER):Apr84-290
    J.Y. Simms, Jr., 104(CASS):Spring-
      Summer84-194
Yang Hsüan-chih. Memories of Loyang.
  (W.J.F. Jenner, trans)
    P.W. Kroll, 116:Jul83-106
"Ralph Webster Yarborough at 80."
    L. Milazzo, 584(SWR):Autumn84-462
Yashpal. Yashpal Looks Back. (C. Friend,
  ed and trans)
    S. Wolpert, 318(JAOS):Oct-Dec83-786
Yates, J.M. Fugue Brancusi.*
    J. Orange, 102(CanL):Autumn84-112
Yates, J.M. Insel.
    S. Scobie, 376:Oct84-124
Yates, R. Liars in Love.* Revolutionary
  Road. Eleven Kinds of Loneliness. The
  Easter Parade. Disturbing the Peace. A
  Good School.
    G. Cuomo, 152(UDQ):Spring85-127
Yates, R. Young Hearts Crying.*
    W. Balliett, 442(NY):14Jan85-116
    G. Cuomo, 152(UDQ):Spring85-127
Yau, J. Corpse and Mirror.
    R. McDowell, 249(HudR):Spring84-126
    639(VQR):Winter84-23
Yavetz, Z. Julius Caesar and his Public
  Image.
    E. Rawson, 123:Vol134No1-142
Yeager, C. and L. Janos. Yeager.
    D. Henahan, 441:7Jul85-3
"The Yearbook of English Studies." (Vol
  11) (G.K. Hunter and C.J. Rawson, eds)
    J.R. Watson, 161(DUJ):Dec83-149
"The Year's Work in Modern Language
  Studies." (Vol 43, 1981) (D.A. Wells,
  ed)
    A.H. Diverres, 208(FS):Jan84-112
    O. Klapp, 547(RF):Band96Heft1/2-101
"The Year's Work in Modern Language
  Studies." (Vol 44, 1982) (G. Price and
  D.A. Wells, eds)
    A.H. Diverres, 208(FS):Oct84-503
Yeats, W.B. La Rose secrète.
    R. Fréchet, 189(EA):Oct-Dec85-486
Yeats, W.B. The Secret Rose.* (P.L.
  Marcus, W. Gould and M.J. Sidnell, eds)
  The Death of Cuchulain. (P.L. Marcus,
  ed)
    J. Olney, 569(SR):Summer84-451

Yeats, W.B. W.B. Yeats: The Poems.* (R.J. Finneran, ed)
  D. Albright, 453(NYRB):31Jan85-29
  B. Dolan, 305(JIL):Jan-May84-142
  J. Mays, 272(IUR):Autumn84-303
Yeazell, R.B. Language and Knowledge in the Late Novels of Henry James.
  W.R. Macnaughton, 106:Fall84-323
Yebra, V.G. - see under García Yebra, V.
Yehoshua, A.B. A Late Divorce.*
  R. Alter, 617(TLS):3May85-498
  I. Kalka, 362:3Jan85-27
  639(VQR):Autumn84-132
Yenal, E. Christine de Pisan.*
  J.B. Beston, 589:Apr84-462
Yerkes, D. Syntax and Style in Old English.*
  D.G. Calder, 589:Jan84-246
Yerushalmi, Y.H. Zakhor.*
  J. Shatzmiller, 287:May84-24
Yevtushenko, Y. Ardabiola.*
  R. Hingley, 441:23Jun85-13
  442(NY):29Jul85-77
Yevtushenko, Y. Wild Berries.*
  F. Eberstadt, 129:Jul85-41
  P. Lewis, 364:Oct84-93
  J. Updike, 442(NY):15Apr85-115
Ying, H. and J.M. Brown. Speaking Chinese in China.
  V. Hsu, 293(JASt):May84-537
Yllera, A. - see "Tristán e Iseo"
Yoder, J.H. When War is Unjust.
  R. Hardin, 185:Apr85-763
Yolton, J. John Locke.
  J.G. Cottingham, 617(TLS):13Dec85-1430
Yolton, J.W. Perceptual Acquaintance from Descartes to Reid.
  J.A.D., 185:Jul85-985
  R.A. Watson, 319:Jul85-433
  M.D. Wilson, 617(TLS):16Aug85-908
  639(VQR):Autumn84-128
Yolton, J.W. Thinking Matter.*
  A.J.D., 185:Jan85-395
  R.A. Watson, 319:Jul85-433
  R.S. Woolhouse, 483:Oct84-554
Yon, M., ed. Dictionnaire illustré multilingue de la céramique du Proche Orient ancien.
  R.M. Cook, 303(JoHS):Vol 104-257
Yoshikawa Kōjirō. Jinsai, Sorai, Norinaga.
  T. Najita, 407(MN):Spring84-98
Young, A. Dada and After.*
  F. Berry, 541(RES):May84-267
  P. Brown, 323:May84-211
  R. Fisher, 565:Winter83/84-51
Young, A.R., comp. Thomas Head Raddall.
  E. Waterston, 627(UTQ):Summer84-455
  B. Whiteman, 470:Vol22-120
Young, B.M. Ueda Akinari.*
  L. Rogers, 293(JASt):Feb84-346
Young, D. and J. Lang. Incognito.*
  C. Blaise, 102(CanL):Summer84-106
  S. Fogel, 168(ECW):Spring84-150
Young, G. Slow Boats Home.
  J. Keay, 362:18Jul85-28
  N. Rankin, 617(TLS):30Aug85-947
Young, G.D. Ugarit in Retrospect.
  S. Rummel, 318(JAOS):Apr-Jun83-474
Young, G.M., Jr. Nikolai F. Fedorov.
  M. Hagemeister, 688(ZSP):Band44Heft2-440
  E. Koutaissoff, 575(SEER):Jan84-98

Young, H.T. The Line in the Margin.*
  D. Fernández-Morera, 107(CRCL):Jun84-317
Young, K. and P.L. Garside. Metropolitan London.
  R.G. Rodger, 637(VS):Winter84-261
Young, P. Crystal Clear.
  D. Devlin, 157:No154-49
Young, P. Hawthorne's Secret.*
  S.W.L., 219(GaR):Fall84-664
  L. Marx, 453(NYRB):14Feb85-29
Young, R. Canadian Development Assistance to Tanzania.
  D. Glover, 298:Winter84/85-133
Young, R. Fables de La Fontaine traduites en créole seychellois. (A. Bollée and G. Lionnet, eds)
  A. Hull, 207(FR):Dec84-332
Young, R., ed. Untying the Text.*
  T.J. Taylor, 541(RES):Aug84-342
  E. Wright, 494:Vol4No1-173
Young, R.F. Resistant Hinduism.*
  J.W. de Jong, 259(IIJ):Jul84-213
Young, R.V. Richard Crashaw and the Spanish Golden Age.*
  G.F. Dille, 568(SCN):Spring-Summer84-8
  J.V. Mirollo, 301(JEGP):Jul84-438
  A. Raspa, 539:May85-142
Young, R.W. and W. Morgan. The Navajo Language.
  J. Kari and J. Leer, 269(IJAL):Jan84-124
Young, T.D. Tennessee Writers.* The Past in the Present.*
  R.L. Phillips, 569(SR):Spring84-xxxviii
Young, T.D. Waking Their Neighbors Up.*
  R.L. Phillips, 569(SR):Spring84-xxxviii
  M.R. Winchell, 106:Summer84-229
Young, T.D. and G. Core - see Ransom, J.C.
Young, T.D. and J. Hindle - see Ransom, J.C.
Young, T.D. and J.J. Hindle - see Bishop, J.P. and A. Tate
Young, V.B. Dark Tides.
  404:Summer84-40
Young, W. and D.E. Kaiser. Postmortem.
  H. Brogan, 617(TLS):27Dec85-1474
Young-Bruehl, E. Hannah Arendt.*
  D. Barnouw, 221(GQ):Winter84-119
Youngson, A.J. Hong Kong.
  F. Herschede, 293(JASt):Aug84-754
Youngson, A.J. The Prince and the Pretender.
  J. Robertson, 617(TLS):26Jul85-830
Yourcenar, M. The Dark Brain of Piranesi.*
  H. Lloyd-Jones, 441:24Feb85-16
  442(NY):11Feb85-126
Yourcenar, M. Mishima ou la vision du vide.
  I. Buruma, 453(NYRB):10Oct85-15
Yourcenar, M. Oriental Tales.
  J. Burnham, 617(TLS):8Nov85-1266
  S. Koch, 441:22Sep85-42
  442(NY):21Oct85-149
Yourcenar, M. Le Temps, ce grand sculpteur.*
  J. Blot, 450(NRF):Mar84-115
Yourcenar, M. With Open Eyes.
  442(NY):11Feb85-127

Youssef, Z. La Poésie de l'eau dans les "Fables" de La Fontaine.
  P. Malandain, 535(RHL):Jul/Aug84-604
Yovel, Y. Kant and the Philosophy of History.*
  W. Bartuschat, 53(AGP):Band66Heft3-315
  R. Brandt, 489(PJGG):Band91Heft2-422
Yu, A.C., ed and trans. The Journey to the West.
  D.J. Levy, 249(HudR):Autumn84-507
Yu, B. The Great Circle.
  E.N. Harbert, 432(NEQ):Dec84-624
Yü, C-F. The Renewal of Buddhism in China.
  M-W. Liu, 302:Vol20No2-198
Yü-fa, C. - see under Chang Yü-fa
Yue Daiyun and C. Wakeman. To the Storm.
  B.P. Solomon, 441:29Dec85-15
Yuill, W.E. and P. Howe, eds. Hugo von Hofmannsthal: Commemorative Essays.
  I.F. Roe, 402(MLR):Jan84-243
Yuyama, A. Vinaya-Texte.
  D.S. Ruegg, 318(JAOS):Jul-Sep83-650

Zac, S. La philosophie religieuse de Hermann Cohen.
  P. Constantineau, 154:Sep84-532
Zachariadou, E.A. Trade and Crusade.
  A.E. Laiou, 589:Jul84-712
Zachau, R.K. Stefan Heym.
  G. Opie, 402(MLR):Jul84-759
Zaganelli, G. Aimer, sofrir, joïr.
  P.T. Ricketts, 589:Jul84-731
Zagoria, D.S., ed. Soviet Policy in East Asia.
  H. Warshawsky, 293(JASt):Feb84-302
Zagorin, P. Rebels and Rulers, 1500-1660.*
  C. Hill, 366:Spring84-120
  D.W. Pearson, 568(SCN):Spring-Summer84-14
  D. Underdown, 551(RenQ):Summer84-254
Zakhara, I.S. Bor'ba idei v filosofskoi mysli na Ukraine na rubezhe XVII-XVIII vv. (Stefan Iavorskii).
  T.D. Zakydalsky, 550(RusR):Jan84-104
Zalavsky, R. Platonic Myth and Platonic Writing.
  J. Longeway, 125:Fall83-95
Zaller, R. The Cliffs of Solitude.
  D. Davis, 617(TLS):15Mar85-293
  T. Hunt, 30:Winter85-90
  P. Lagayette, 189(EA):Jul-Sep85-355
  W.H. Nolte, 27(AL):Dec84-614
Zancani, D., ed. Il Manganello.
  M. Chiesa, 228(GSLI):Vol 161fasc515-453
  C. Fahy, 278(IS):Vol39-103
Zander, H. Shakespeare "bearbeitet."
  H. Priessnitz, 490:Band16Heft3/4-364
Zangrilli, F. L'arte novellistica di Pirandello.
  G.W. Anderson, 275(IQ):Spring84-117
Zanier, G. Medicina e filosofia tra '500 e '600.
  J.M. Riddle, 551(RenQ):Winter84-605
Zanni, R. Heliand, Genesis und das Altenglische.*
  C.M. Barrack, 406:Fall84-350
  H. Beck, 680(ZDP):Band103Heft1-126
Zanzotto, A. Il Galateo in bosco. Fosfeni.
  P. Di Meo, 98:Aug/Sep84-648

Zapantis, A.L. Greek-Soviet Relations, 1917-1941.
  S. Wichert, 575(SEER):Oct84-618
Zarubina, N.D. and N.S. Ozhegova. Puteshestvie po Sovetskoi strane.
  M.K. Frank, 399(MLJ):Spring84-91
Zaslavsky, V. The Neo-Stalinist State.
  D. Chirot, 104(CASS):Fall84-342
Zatlin, L.G. The Nineteenth-Century Anglo-Jewish Novel.
  T.M. Endelman, 637(VS):Autumn83-94
Zavos, S. Faith of Our Fathers.*
  P. Lewis, 565:Spring84-64
Zawawi, S.M. Loan Words and Their Effect on the Classification of Swahili Nominals.
  K. Legère, 682(ZPSK).Band37Heft4-529
Zayas-Bazán, E. and G.J. Fernández. Así somos.
  J.E. McKinney, 399(MLJ):Autumn84-307
Zazoff, P. and H. Gemmensammler und Gemmenforscher.
  G. Seidmann, 90:Feb84-93
Zeami. On the Art of Nō Drama.* (J.T. Rimer and Yamazaki Masakazu, trans)
  P.G. O'Neill, 407(MN):Winter84-474
Zebrowski, M. Deccani Painting.*
  D.J. Ehnbom, 293(JASt):May84-590
van der Zee, J. Bound Over.
  P-L. Adams, 61:Sep85-116
Zeh, J. Die deutsche Sprachgemeinschaft in Nordschleswig.
  L.H. Eriksen, 684(ZDA):Band113Heft4-186
Zeitler, W.M. Entscheidungsfreiheit bei Platon.
  C.C.W. Taylor, 123:Vol34No2-333
Zeitlin, S.J., A.J. Kotkin and H.C. Baker. A Celebration of American Family Folklore.
  J. Ice, 292(JAF):Apr-Jun84-244
  R.O. Joyce, 650(WF):Apr84-152
Zeldin, T. The French.*
  A.J. Bingham, 577(SHR):Fall84-358
  E. Weber, 31(ASch):Winter83/84-130
Zelinsky, B., ed. Die russische Novelle.
  V. Terras, 574(SEEJ):Fall84-396
Zell, H.M., C. Bundy and V. Coulon, eds. A New Reader's Guide to African Literature.* (2nd ed)
  J. Povey, 2(AfrA):May84-89
Zeller, M., ed. Aufbrüche: Abschiede.
  K. Peter, 221(GQ):Winter84-165
Zeman, H., ed. Die österreichische Literatur.*
  W.E. Yates, 402(MLR):Jul84-749
Zeman, J. Untersuchungen zur Satzgliedstellung im Nebensatz in der deutschen Sprache der Gegenwart.
  A. Lötscher, 685(ZDL):3/1984-384
Zemtsov, I. Andropov.
  A. Dallin, 550(RusR):Apr84-185
Zend, R. Beyond Labels.
  C. Tapping, 102(CanL):Summer84-158
Zepeda, O., ed. Mat Hekid O Ju.
  D.H., 355(LSoc):Jun84-286
Zepeda, O. A Papago Grammar.
  D.L. Shaul, 269(IJAL):Oct84-462
Zernov, H.M. Zakatnye Gody.
  M. Bayuk, 558(RLJ):Winter-Spring84-331
Zerubavel, E. The Seven Day Circle.
  A.P. Lightman, 441:23Jun85-12

Zettersten, A., ed. East African Litera-
ture.
    R. Mane, 189(EA):Jul-Sep85-352
Zetzner, L. and others, eds. Theatrum
Chemicum.
    T.W., 111:Fall85-7
Zhang Yajun and Mao Cheng-dong, eds. Chi-
nese 300.
    L. Yang, 399(MLJ):Winter84-390
Zheleznova, I., ed. Russian 19th-Century
Verse.
    V.A. Babenko-Woodbury, 399(MLJ):
    Winter84-423
Zheng, L. and others - see under Liu
Zheng and others
Zholkovsky, A. Themes and Texts.
    D. Polan, 494:Vol5No4-870
    D. Rancour-Laferriere, 494:Vol5No4-872
"Zhongguo Da Baike Quanshu: Waiguo Wenxue."
    W.J.F. Jenner, 617(TLS):21Jun85-692
Ziegler, E. Julius Campe.
    M.A. Vega, 202(FMod):No65/67-310
Ziegler, H. and C. Bigsby, eds. The
Radical Imagination and the Liberal
Tradition.*
    N. Roe, 447(N&Q):Dec83-560
    T. Steele, 395(MFS):Summer84-423
Ziegler, P. Mountbatten.
    D. Cannadine, 453(NYRB):9May85-6
    A. Cooke, 442(NY):9Sep85-101
    M. Gilbert, 441:26May85-18
    B. Gutteridge, 364:Mar85-93
    M. Howard, 617(TLS):12Apr85-401
    D. Hunt, 362:14Mar85-22
    E. Kedourie, 129:Dec85-45
Zielinski, S. Veit Harlan.
    M. Silberman, 221(GQ):Fall84-693
Ziem, J. Uprising in East Germany.
    M. Tucker, 441:15Sep85-24
Ziemke, H-J. Frankfurter Malerei zur Zeit
des jungen Goethe.
    J. Gage, 90:Apr84-241
Ziermann, K. Vom Bildschirm bis zum Gros-
chenheft.
    G. Wüstenhagen, 654(WB):9/1984-1553
Zietlow, E.R. A Country For Old Men and
Other Stories.
    A. Cuelho, 649(WAL):Nov84-239
Zilbergeld, B. The Shrinking of America.
    G.R. Lowe, 529(QQ):Winter84-1038
Zil'bershtein, I.S. and V.A. Samokov,
comps. Sergei Diagilev i russkoe
iskusstvo.
    J.E. Bowlt, 104(CASS):Spring-Summer84-
    174
Zima, P.V. Der gleichgültige Held.
    B. Winklehner, 602:Band15Heft2-349
Zima, P.V. L'Indifférence romanesque.
    R. Jones, 402(MLR):Jul84-717
Zimmer, G. Römische Berufsdarstellungen.
    D.C. Bellingham, 313:Vol74-227
Zimmer, H. Artistic Form and Yoga in the
Sacred Images of India.
    J. Leoshko, 469:Vol 10No2-115
Zimmer, P. Family Reunion.
    P. Stitt, 491:Jul84-231
    V. Young, 472:Fall/Winter84-307
Zimmer, R. Dramatischer Dialog und ausser-
sprachlicher Kontext.
    E.H. Rockwell, 221(GQ):Summer84-500
Zimmer, R. Probleme der Übersetzung form-
betonter Sprache.
    K. Henschelmann, 72:Band221Heft2-328

Zimmer, R.K. James Shirley.*
    G. Bas, 189(EA):Oct-Dec85-456
Zimmer, S.K. The Beginning of Cyrillic
Printing, Cracow, 1491. (L. Krzyzanow
and I. Nayerski, eds)
    H. Świderska, 354:Dec84-408
    H. Świderska, 575(SEER):Oct84-595
    J.L. Wieczynski, 104(CASS):Winter84-
    488
Zimmer, S.K. Thoreau i jego otoczenie.
    B.T. Lupack, 497(PolR):Vol29No1/2-162
Zimmerman, E. Swift's Narrative Satires.
    F.M. Keener, 566:Spring85-173
Zimmerman, F.B. Henry Purcell, 1659-1695.*
(2nd ed)
    N. Fortune, 415:Jul84-388
    C.A. Price, 410(M&L):Oct84-357
Zimmermann, A., with G. Vuillemin-Diem,
eds. Miscellanea Mediaevalia. (Vol 14)
    J. Jolivet, 542:Jan-Mar84-71
    J.F. Wippel, 543:Jun84-878
Zimmermann, A. and G. Vuillemin-Diem, eds.
Miscellanea Mediaevalia. (Vol 15)
    J. Jolivet, 542:Jan-Mar84-73
Zimmermann, E.M. La liberté et le destin
dans le théâtre de Jean Racine.*
    E.J. Campion, 405(MP):Feb85-325
    J. Morel, 475:Vol 11No20-292
    M-O. Sweetser, 207(FR):Dec84-287
    A. Viala, 535(RHL):Mar/Apr84-285
Zimmermann, F. La Jungle et le fumet des
viandes.
    A. Reix, 542:Jan-Mar84-104
    R. Tucker, 293(JASt):Aug84-795
Zimmermann, F.W. - see al-Fārābī
Zimmermann, H.D. Trivialliteratur?
    J. Schönert, 224(GRM):Band34Heft1/2-
    241
Zink, M. Roman rose et rose rouge.
    A.J. Holden, 554:Vol 104No2-265
Zinoviev, A. Homo Sovieticus.
    J.B. Dunlop, 617(TLS):11Oct85-1136
Zinsser, H. Rats, Lice and History.
    617(TLS):22Nov85-1339
Zinsser, W. Writing With a Word Processor.
    F.A. Hubbard, 128(CE):Feb84-128
Ziolkowski, T. Varieties of Literary
Thematics.*
    M. Beller, 52:Band19Heft3-294
    M. Swales, 564:Sep84-231
Zipes, J. Breaking the Magic Spell.*
    E. Schwarz, 222(GR):Summer84-123
Zipes, J. Rotkäppchens Lust und Leid.
    D. Blamires, 402(MLR):Apr84-401
    R.B. Bottigheimer, 196:Band25Heft1/2-
    168
Zipes, J. The Trials and Tribulations of
Little Red Riding Hood.*
    H.S. Madland, 399(MJL):Autumn84-278
Zipper, Y. and C. Spilberg, eds. Canadian
Jewish Anthology/Anthologie juive du
Canada.
    E. Orenstein, 627(UTQ):Summer84-496
Zirngibl, M.A. Rare African Short Weapons.
    J. Abbink, 2(AfrA):May84-88
Zlotnick, J. Portrait of an American City.
    H. Wirth-Nesher, 395(MFS):Summer84-337
Żmigrodzki, J. Towarzystwo Demokratyczne
Polskie (1832-1862). (Vols 1A and 1B)
    P. Brock, 497(PolR):Vol29No4-89
Zoeppritz, M. Syntax for German in the
User Speciality Language.
    W. Hoeppner, 353:Vol22No4-564

Zoete, A., ed. Handelingen van de Leden
en van de Staten van Vlaanderen (1405–
1419).
   B. Lyon, 589:Jan84-247
Zohn, H. - see Kraus, K.
Zola, É. The Attack on the Mill and Other
Stories. (D. Parmée, trans)
   D. Coward, 617(TLS):25Jan85-102
Zola, É. Correspondance.* (Vol 3) (B.H.
Bakker, with C. Becker, eds)
   R. Lethbridge, 208(FS):Oct84-476
   J. Newton, 188(ECr):Winter84-90
Zola, É. Correspondance.* (Vol 4) (B.H.
Bakker, ed)
   D. Baguley, 446(NCFS):Summer85-300
   M.G. Lerner, 356(LR):Nov84-329
Zola, É. Lettres de Paris — Notes parisi-
ennes, Le Sémaphore de Marseille, 1871–
1877. (M.E. Leozappa, ed)
   C. Becker, 535(RHL):Jul/Aug84-640
Zolbrod, L.M. Haiku Painting.
   S. Matisoff, 293(JASt):Nov83-171
Zolbrod, P.G. Diné bahané.
   C.R. Farrer, 469:Vol 10No3-121
   J. Highwater, 441:3Feb85-11
Zolotova, G.A. Kommunikativnye aspekty
russkogo sintaksisa.
   M. Guiraud-Weber, 559:Vol8No2-184
   J.M. Kirkwood, 575(SEER):Oct84-580
Zonabend, F. The Enduring Memory.
   J.F. McMillan, 617(TLS):20Sep85-1036
Zonailo, C. A Portrait of Paradise.
   S. Morrissey, 137:Feb85-42
   S.S., 376:Feb84-140
Zosimus. New History. (R.T. Ridley, ed
and trans)
   A. Cameron, 123:Vol134No1-27
Zotter, H. Antike Medizin.
   R. Grambo, 64(Arv):Vol138-176
Zuber, L.J. - see O'Connor, F.
Zucconi, G. La smortina.
   J. Gatt-Rutter, 617(TLS):26Jul85-832
Zuckerman, M., ed. Friends and Neighbors.
   J.W. Frost, 656(WMQ):Apr84-307
Zuckmayer, C. Der Seelenbräu.
   M. Lynch, 399(MLJ):Winter84-403
Zuelzer, W. The Nicolai Case.
   D. Barnouw, 221(GQ):Winter84-119
Zufferey, F. Bibliographie des poètes pro-
vençaux des XIVe et XVe siècles.
   G. Brunel-Lobrichon, 554:Vol 104No2-
   281
Zuk, G. Zuk.
   R.W. Harvey, 168(ECW):Winter84/85-344
Zukowsky, J., P. Saliga and R. Rubin.
 Chicago Architects Design.
   J.W. Stamper, 576:May84-184
Zunder, W. The Poetry of John Donne.
   H. Dubrow, 551(RenQ):Summer84-311
   B. King, 569(SR):Spring84-284
Zunz, O. The Changing Face of Inequality.
   H.P. Chudacoff, 639(VQR):Winter84-154
Zunz, O., ed. Reliving the Past.
   J. Merriman, 441:20Oct85-14
Žuravlev, V.K. Vnešnie i vnutrennie fak-
tory jazykovoj èvolucii.
   H. Birnbaum, 350:Mar85-242
Zürcher, E.J. The Unionist Factor.
   A. Mango, 617(TLS):4Oct85-1107
Zurier, R. The American Firehouse.*
   A.S. Lee, 658:Spring84-100

Zuriff, G.E. Behaviorism.
   P.N. Johnson-Laird, 617(TLS):19Jul85-
   787
Zutshi, M.E. Literary Theory in Germany.
   M. Totten, 221(GQ):Spring84-290
Zuurdeeg, A.D. Narrative Techniques and
Their Effects in "La Mort le Roi Artu."
   D.D.R. Owen, 208(FS):Oct84-450
Zwaal-Lint, T. Bobbin Lace Patterns.
   C. Campbell, 614:Spring85-17
Zwanenburg, W. Productivité morphologique
et emprunt.
   D.C. Walker, 361:Dec84-377
Zweig, P. Eternity's Woods.
   E. Hirsch, 441:16Jun85-19
Zweig, P. Walt Whitman.*
   R. Asselineau, 189(EA):Jul-Sep85-286
   M.J. Killingsworth, 27(AL):Dec84-598
   J. Loving, 646:Summer84-42
   R. Nelson, 639(VQR):Autumn84-723
   N. Schmitz, 472:Fall/Winter84-4
   42(AR):Fall84-508
Zweig, P.L. Belly Up.
   S.C. Gwynne, 441:20Oct85-48
Zweig, S. Tagebücher.
   E. Timms, 617(TLS):24May85-570
Zweite, A., ed. Kandinsky in München.
   H. Watts, 221(GQ):Spring84-343
Zweite, A. Marten de Vos als Maler.
   L. Silver, 683:Band47Heft2-269
Zwicker, S.N. Politics and Language in
Dryden's Poetry.
   J. Barnard, 617(TLS):29Mar85-336
   J.A. Winn, 385(MQR):Fall85-665
Zwinger, A. A Desert Country Near the Sea.
   C.S. Long, 649(WAL):Feb85-334
Zwirner, E. and K. Grundfragen der phono-
metrischen Linguistik. (3rd ed)
   B.J. Koekkoek, 350:Mar85-214
Žygas, E.V. and P. Voorheis, eds. Folk-
lorica.
   L. Kürti, 292(JAF):Oct-Dec84-489
Zytaruk, G.J. and J.T. Boulton - see Law-
rence, D.H.

WITHDRAWAL